Nineteenth-Century
Literature Criticism

Guide to Gale Literary Criticism Series

For criticism on	Consult these Gale series
Authors now living or who died after December 31, 1959	*CONTEMPORARY LITERARY CRITICISM (CLC)*
Authors who died between 1900 and 1959	*TWENTIETH-CENTURY LITERARY CRITICISM (TCLC)*
Authors who died between 1800 and 1899	*NINETEENTH-CENTURY LITERATURE CRITICISM (NCLC)*
Authors who died between 1400 and 1799	*LITERATURE CRITICISM FROM 1400 TO 1800 (LC)* *SHAKESPEAREAN CRITICISM (SC)*
Authors who died before 1400	*CLASSICAL AND MEDIEVAL LITERATURE CRITICISM (CMLC)*
Black writers of the past two hundred years	*BLACK LITERATURE CRITICISM (BLC)*
Authors of books for children and young adults	*CHILDREN'S LITERATURE REVIEW (CLR)*
Dramatists	*DRAMA CRITICISM (DC)*
Hispanic writers of the late nineteenth and twentieth centuries	*HISPANIC LITERATURE CRITICISM (HLC)*
Native North American writers and orators of the eighteenth, nineteenth, and twentieth centuries	*NATIVE NORTH AMERICAN LITERATURE (NNAL)*
Poets	*POETRY CRITICISM (PC)*
Short story writers	*SHORT STORY CRITICISM (SSC)*
Major authors from the Renaissance to the present	*WORLD LITERATURE CRITICISM, 1500 TO THE PRESENT (WLC)*

ISSN 0732-1864

Volume 51

Nineteenth-Century Literature Criticism

Criticism of the Works of
Novelists, Poets, Playwrights,
Short Story Writers, Philosophers, and
Other Creative Writers Who Died between
1800 and 1899, from the First Published
Critical Appraisals to Current Evaluations

Marie Lazzari
Editor

An ITP Information/Reference Group Company

Changing the Way the World Learns

NEW YORK • LONDON • BONN • BOSTON • DETROIT
MADRID • MELBOURNE • MEXICO CITY • PARIS
SINGAPORE • TOKYO • TORONTO • WASHINGTON
ALBANY NY • BELMONT CA • CINCINNATI OH

STAFF

Marie Lazzari, *Editor*

Denise Kasinec and Jelena O. Krstović, *Contributing Editors*

Catherine C. Dominic and Mary L. Onorato, *Associate Editors*

Matthew C. Altman, Gerald R. Barterian, and Ondine Le Blanc, *Assistant Editors*

Susan M. Trosky, *Managing Editor*

Marlene Hurst, *Permissions Manager*
Margaret A. Chamberlain and Maria L. Franklin, *Permissions Specialists*
Susan Brohman, Diane Cooper, Michele Lonoconus, Maureen Puhl, Shalice Shah,
Kimberly F. Smilay, and Barbara A. Wallace, *Permissions Associates*
Sarah Chesney, Edna Hedblad, Margaret McAvoy-Amato, Tyra A. Phillips,
Lori Schoenenberger, and Rita C. Velázquez, *Permissions Assistants*

Victoria B. Cariappa, *Research Manager*
Barbara McNeil, *Research Specialist*
Maria E. Bryson, Mary Beth McElmeel, Donna Melnychenko, Tamara C. Nott, Michele P. Pica,
Tracie A. Richardson, Norma Sawaya, and Amy Terese Steel, *Research Associates*
Alicia Noel Biggers and Julia C. Daniel, *Research Assistants*

Mary Beth Trimper, *Production Director*
Deborah L. Milliken, *Production Assistant*

Barbara J. Yarrow, *Graphic Services Manager*
Erin Martin, *Desktop Publisher*
Randy Bassett, *Image Database Supervisor*
Pamela A. Hayes, *Photography Coordinator*

∞™ This book is printed on acid-free paper that meets the minimum requirements of American National Standard for Information Sciences—Permanence Paper for Printed Library Materials, ANSI Z39.48-1984.

Library of Congress Catalog Card Number 84-643008
ISBN 0-8103-9297-6
ISSN 0732-1864
Printed in the United States of America

I(T)P™   Gale Research, an International Thomson Publishing Company.
ITP logo is a trademark under license.

10 9 8 7 6 5 4 3 2 1

Contents

Preface   vii

Acknowledgments   xi

Preface

Since its inception in 1981, *Nineteenth-Century Literature Criticism* has been a valuable resource for students and librarians seeking critical commentary on writers of this transitional period in world history. Designated an "Outstanding Reference Source" by the American Library Association with the publication of its first volume, *NCLC* has since been purchased by over 6,000 school, public, and university libraries. The series has covered more than 300 authors representing 26 nationalities and over 15,000 titles. No other reference source has surveyed the critical reaction to nineteenth-century authors and literature as thoroughly as *NCLC*.

Scope of the Series

NCLC is designed to introduce students and advanced readers to the authors of the nineteenth century, and to the most significant interpretations of these authors' works. The great poets, novelists, short story writers, playwrights, and philosophers of this period are frequently studied in high school and college literature courses. By organizing and reprinting commentary written on these authors, *NCLC* helps students develop valuable insight into literary history, promotes a better understanding of the texts, and sparks ideas for papers and assignments. Each entry in *NCLC* presents a comprehensive survey of an author's career or an individual work of literature and provides the user with a multiplicity of interpretations and assessments. Such variety allows students to pursue their own interests; furthermore, it fosters an awareness that literature is dynamic and responsive to many different opinions.

Every fourth volume of *NCLC* is devoted to literary topics that cannot be covered under the author approach used in the rest of the series. Such topics include literary movements, prominent themes in nineteenth-century literature, literary reaction to political and historical events, significant eras in literary history, prominent literary anniversaries, and the literatures of cultures that are often overlooked by English-speaking readers.

NCLC continues the survey of criticism of world literature begun by Gale's *Contemporary Literary Criticism (CLC)* and *Twentieth-Century Literary Criticism (TCLC),* both of which excerpt and reprint commentary on authors of the twentieth century. For additional information about *TCLC, CLC,* and Gale's other criticism series, users should consult the Guide to Gale Literary Criticism Series preceding the title page in this volume.

Coverage

Each volume of *NCLC* is carefully compiled to present:

- criticism of authors, or literary topics, representing a variety of genres and nationalities
- both major and lesser-known writers and literary works of the period
- 6-10 authors or 4-6 topics per volume
- individual entries that survey critical response to an author's work or a topic in literary history, including early criticism to reflect initial reactions, later criticism to represent any rise or decline in reputation, and current retrospective analyses.

Organization

An author entry consists of the following elements: author heading, biographical and critical introduction, list of principal works, excerpts of criticism (each preceded by a bibliographic citation and an annotation), and a bibliography of further reading.

- The **Author Heading** consists of the name under which the author most commonly wrote, followed by birth and death dates. If an author wrote consistently under a pseudonym, the pseudonym will be listed in the author heading and the real name given in parentheses on the first line of the biographical and critical introduction. Also located at the beginning of the introduction to the author entry are any name variations under which an author wrote, including transliterated forms for an author whose language uses a nonroman alphabet.

- The **Biographical and Critical Introduction** outlines the author's life and career, as well as the critical issues surrounding his or her work. References are provided to past volumes of *NCLC* in which further information about the author may be found.

- Most *NCLC* entries include a **Portrait** of the author. Many entries also contain reproductions of materials pertinent to an author's career, including manuscript pages, title pages, dust jackets, letters, and drawings, as well as photographs of important people, places, and events in an author's life.

- The list of **Principal Works** is chronological by date of first publication and identifies the genre of each work. In the case of foreign authors with both foreign-language publications and English translations, the English-language version is given in brackets. Unless otherwise indicated, dramas are dated by first performance, not first publication.

- **Criticism** in each author entry is arranged chronologically to provide a perspective on changes in critical evaluation over the years. All titles of works by the author featured in the entry are printed in boldface type to enable the user to easily locate discussion of particular works. Also for purposes of easier identification, the critic's name and the publication date of the essay are given at the beginning of each piece of criticism. Unsigned criticism is preceded by the title of the journal in which it appeared. Publication information (such as publisher names and book prices) and parenthetical numerical references (such as footnotes or page and line references to specific editions of works) have been deleted at the editors' discretion to provide smoother reading of the text.

- A complete **Bibliographic Citation** designed to facilitate location of the original essay or book precedes each piece of criticism.

- Critical excerpts are prefaced by **Annotations** providing the reader with information about both the critic and the criticism that follows. Included are the critic's reputation, individual approach to literary criticism, and particular expertise in an author's works. Also noted are the relative importance of a work of criticism, the scope of the excerpt, and the growth of critical controversy or changes in critical trends regarding an author. In some cases, these annotations cross-reference excerpts by critics who discuss each other's commentary.

- An annotated list of **Further Reading** appearing at the end of each entry suggests secondary sources on the author. In some cases it includes essays for which the editors could not obtain reprint rights.

Cumulative Indexes

- Each volume of *NCLC* contains a cumulative **Author Index** listing all authors who have appeared in Gale's Literary Criticism Series, along with cross-references to such biographical series as *Contemporary Authors* and *Dictionary of Literary Biography.* Useful for locating authors within the various series, this index is particularly valuable for those authors who are identified with a certain period but who, because of their death dates, are placed in another, or for those authors whose careers span two periods. For example, Fyodor Dostoevsky is found in *NCLC,* yet Leo Tolstoy, another major nineteenth-century Russian novelist, is found in *TCLC* because he died after 1899.

- Each *NCLC* volume includes a cumulative **Nationality Index** which lists all authors who have appeared in *NCLC,* arranged alphabetically under their respective nationalities, as well as Topics volume entries devoted to particular national literatures.

- Each new volume in Gale's Literary Criticism Series includes a cumulative **Topic Index**, which lists all literary topics treated in *NCLC, TCLC, LC 1400-1800,* and the *CLC* Yearbook.

- Each new volume of *NCLC,* with the exception of the Topics volumes, contains a **Title Index** listing the titles of all literary works discussed in the volume. In response to numerous suggestions from librarians, Gale has also produced a **Special Paperbound Edition** of the *NCLC* title index. This annual cumulation lists all titles discussed in the series since its inception and is issued with the first volume of *NCLC* published each year. Additional copies of the index are available on request. Librarians and patrons have welcomed this separate index: it saves shelf space, is easy to use, and is recyclable upon receipt of the following year's cumulation. Titles discussed in the Topics volume entries are not included in the *NCLC* cumulative index.

Citing *Nineteenth-Century Literature Criticism*

When writing papers, students who quote directly from any volume in Gale's Literary Criticism Series may use the following general forms to footnote reprinted criticism. The first example pertains to material drawn from periodicals, the second to material reprinted from books:

[1]T.S. Eliot, "John Donne," *The Nation and Athenaeum*, 33 (9 June 1923), 321-32; excerpted and reprinted in *Literature Criticism from 1400-1800,* Vol. 10, ed. James E. Person, Jr. (Detroit: Gale Research, 1989), pp. 28-9.

[2]Clara G. Stillman, *Samuel Butler: A Mid-Victorian Modern* (Viking Press, 1932); excerpted and reprinted in *Twentieth-Century Literary Criticism,* Vol. 33, ed. Paula Kepos (Detroit: Gale Research, 1989), pp. 43-5.

Suggestions Are Welcome

In response to suggestions, several features have been added to *NCLC* since the series began, including annotations to excerpted criticism, a cumulative index to authors in all Gale literary criticism series, entries devoted to criticism on a single work by a major author, more illustrations, and a title index listing all literary works discussed in the series.

Readers who wish to suggest authors or topics to appear in future volumes, or who have other suggestions, are cordially invited to write: The Editors, *Nineteenth-Century Literature Criticism,* 835 Penobscot Bldg., 645 Griswold St., Detroit, MI 48226-4094; call toll-free at 1-800-347-GALE; or fax to 1-313-961-6599.

Acknowledgments

The editors wish to thank the copyright holders of the excerpted criticism included in this volume and the permissions managers of many book and magazine publishing companies for assisting us in securing reprint rights. We are also grateful to the staffs of the Detroit Public Library, the Library of Congress, the University of Detroit Mercy Library, Wayne State University Purdy/Kresge Library Complex, and the University of Michigan Libraries for making their resources available to us. Following is a list of the copyright holders who have granted us permission to reprint material in this volume of *NCLC*. Every effort has been made to trace copyright, but if omissions have been made, please let us know.

COPYRIGHTED EXCERPTS IN *NCLC*, VOLUME 51, WERE REPRINTED FROM THE FOLLOWING PERIODICALS:

Critical Inquiry, v. 16, Autumn, 1989 for "Representation, Conversion, and Literary Form: Harrington and the Novel of Jewish Identity" by Michael Ragussis. Copyright © 1989 by The University of Chicago. Reprinted by permission of the publisher and the author.—*ELH,* v. 32, December, 1965. Copyright © 1965, renewed 1993 by The Johns Hopkins University Press. All rights reserved. Reprinted by permission of Johns Hopkins University Press.—*Journal of the History of Ideas,* v. XXXVI, April-June, 1975; v. XLIII, January-March, 1982. Copyright 1975, 1982, Journal of the History of Ideas, Inc. Both reprinted by permission of Johns Hopkins University Press.—*Modern Language Quarterly,* v. XXX, 1969. © 1971 University of Washington. Reprinted with permission of Duke University Press.—*Nineteenth-Century Literature,* v. 48, March, 1994 for "Lady Delacour's Library: Maria Edgeworth's Belinda and Fashionable Reading" by Heather MacFadyen; v. 49, June, 1994 for "Commerce and Character in Maria Edgeworth" by Teresa Michals. © 1994 by the Regents of the University of California. Both reprinted by permission of the publisher and the respective authors.—*Papers of the Michigan Academy of Science, Arts, and Letters,* v. LI, 1966. Copyright 1966 by the University of Michigan. Reprinted by permission of the publisher.—*Studies in English Literature, 1500-1900,* v. XVII, Autumn, 1977 for "The Didacticism of Edgeworth's 'Castle Rackrent'" by Gerry H. Brookes. © William Marsh Rice University. Reprinted by permission of the publisher and the author.—*Studies in Romanticism,* v. 28, Summer, 1989. Copyright 1989 by the Trustees of Boston University. Reprinted by permission of the publisher.—*Texas Studies in Literature and Language,* v. 33, Spring, 1991 for "Enclosed in Openness: Northanger Abbey and the Domestic Carceral" by Paul Morrison. Copyright © 1991 by the University of Texas Press. Reprinted by permission of the publisher and the author.—*The South Atlantic Quarterly,* v. 71, Winter, 1972. Copyright © 1972 by Duke University Press, Durham, NC. Reprinted with permission of the publisher.—*University of Toronto Quarterly,* v. XLIV, Fall, 1974. © University of Toronto Press 1974. Reprinted by permission of University of Toronto Press Incorporated.

COPYRIGHTED EXCERPTS IN *NCLC*, VOLUME 51, WERE REPRINTED FROM THE FOLLOWING BOOKS:

Baker, Ernest. From "Maria Edgeworth and the English Novel" in *Family Chronicles: Maria Edgeworth's "Castle Rackrent."* Edited by Cóilín Owens. Wolfhound Press, 1987. © 1987 Wolfhound Press. Introduction, Selection and Editing © 1987 Cóilín Owens. Essays © individual contributors. All rights reserved. Reprinted by permission of the publisher.—Barbour, Judith. From "Dr. John William Polidori, Author of 'The Vampyre'" in *Imagining Romanticism: Essays on English and Australian Romanticisms.* Edited by Deirdre Coleman and Peter Otto. Locust Hill Press, 1992. © 1992 Deirdre Coleman and Peter Otto. All rights reserved. Reprinted by permission of the publisher.—Beecher, Jonathan. From *Charles Fourier: The Visionary and His World.* University of California Press, 1986. © 1987 by The Regents of the University of California. Reprinted by permission of the publisher and the author.—Burlin, Katrin Ristkok. From *Jane Austen: Bicentenary Essays.* Edited by John Halperin. Cambridge University Press, 1975. © Cambridge University Press 1975. Reprinted with the permission of the publisher.—Butler, Marilyn. From *Maria Edgeworth: A Literary Biography.* Oxford at the Clarendon Press, 1972. © Oxford University Press 1972. Reprinted by permission of the author.—Bryon, Lord George Gordon. From a letter in *"So Late Into*

Northanger Abbey

Jane Austen

The following entry presents criticism of Austen's novel *Northanger Abbey* (1818). For further information on Austen's complete career, see *NCLC,* Volume 1; for discussion of the novel *Pride and Prejudice,* see *NCLC,* Volume 13; for discussion of the novel *Emma,* see *NCLC,* Volume 19; and for discussion of the novel *Persuasion,* see *NCLC,* Volume 33.

INTRODUCTION

Originally written between 1798 and 1799, but not published until 1818, *Northanger Abbey* is considered Jane Austen's first significant work of fiction. The novel is in part a burlesque of the Gothic and sentimental fiction that was popular in the late eighteenth and early nineteenth centuries, particularly of Ann Radcliffe's novels, such as *The Mysteries of Udolfo.* In addition to its parodic elements, *Northanger Abbey* also follows the maturation of Catherine Morland, a naive eighteen-year-old, ignorant of the workings of English society and prone to self-deception. Influenced by her reading of novels rife with the overblown qualities of horror fiction, Catherine concocts a skewed version of reality by infusing real people, things, and events with terrible significance. However, Catherine's mistaken impressions, though clouded by Gothic sentiment, often hint at an insightful, if unconscious, judgment of character that cuts through the social pretensions of those around her. In this respect Austen's novel carries on an ironic discourse which makes it not only a satire, but also a sophisticated novel of social education.

Plot and Major Characters

Catherine's introduction into society begins when Mr. and Mrs. Allen, her neighbors in Fullerton, invite her to spend some time with them while vacationing in the English town of Bath. There she meets the somewhat pedantic clergyman Henry Tilney and the histrionic Isabella Thorpe, who encourages Catherine in her reading of Gothic fiction. Her circle of acquaintances widens with the arrival of James Morland, Catherine's brother and a love interest for Isabella, and John Thorpe, Isabella's rude, conniving brother. The setting shifts from Bath to Northanger Abbey, the ancestral home of the Tilneys, when John deceives General Tilney, Henry's father, into believing that Catherine is an heiress. Austen's satire of Gothic horror novel conventions begins as Henry and Catherine drive up to the Abbey and the former plays on the heroine's romantic expectations of the place. When Catherine reaches her destination she is disappointed to find a thoroughly modern building, completely lacking in hidden passageways, concealed dungeons, and the like. Later, Austen allows Catherine's imagination to run amok,

only to reveal the objects of her fears as ordinary and mundane. At the climax of the novel, General Tilney—whom Catherine suspects of having murdered or shut up his wife somewhere in the abbey—turns the heroine out after learning that she does not come from a wealthy family. At the close of the novel, the outraged Henry proposes marriage to Catherine, now divested of her delusions by Henry and his sister Eleanor. General Tilney, who proves to be not a murderer, but rather an individual of questionable moral and social character, eventually gives his consent to the marriage after learning that his daughter Eleanor is also engaged—to a wealthy Viscount.

Major Themes

While ostensibly a burlesque of the conventional modes of Gothic horror fiction, *Northanger Abbey* is also a novel of education that focuses on the theme of self-deception. Austen portrays Catherine as an inversion of the typical Gothic heroine, making her neither beautiful, talented, nor particularly intelligent, but rather ordinary in most respects. In contrast, several other characters in the novel are presented as pastiches of stock Gothic characters—Isabella and

General Tilney, for example, are parodies of the damsel and the domestic tyrant. These individuals seem to fit into Catherine's deluded perspective of the world which, in the tradition of Miguel de Cervantes's *Don Quixote*, leaves her unable to distinguish between reality and the romanticized version of life she finds in popular novels. Other characters in the novel serve to balance the work. Henry Tilney is often regarded by critics as Austen's mouthpiece—though he, too, is occasionally an object of irony and ridicule. For example, he fails to realize that Catherine's delusions, though excessive, hint at the true nature of people and events. Thus, Catherine is the first to understand that General Tilney, although not a murderer, is cruel and mercenary. This ironic aspect of the novel alludes to a larger theme in the work, that of the moral significance of social conventions and conduct—a subject that Austen explored in greater detail in later novels.

Critical Reception

Critics have generally regarded *Northanger Abbey* to be of lesser literary quality than the remainder of Austen's mature works. Some scholars have observed occasional lapses in her narrative technique of a sort that do not appear in later novels. By far the greatest debate surrounding *Northanger Abbey,* however, is the question of its aesthetic unity. Critics have traditionally seen the work as part novel of society, part satire of popular Gothic fiction, and therefore not a coherent whole. Detractors, focusing on the work as a parody, have found its plot weak, its characters unimaginative and superficial, and its comedy anticlimactic due to its reliance on an outmoded style of fiction. Others, while conceding the lack of an easily discernable organizing principle, argue that the work is i unified on the thematic level as not merely a satire of popular fiction, but also an ironic presentation of a self-deceived imagination that is quixotically wrong about reality but right about human morality. In addition, critics have considered Northanger Abbey a transitional work, one that moves away from the burlesque mode of the *Juvenilia* and toward the stylistic control of such masterpieces as *Mansfield Park* and *Emma*.

CRITICISM

Dorothy Scarborough (essay date 1917)

SOURCE: "The Gothic Romance," in *The Supernatural in Modern English Fiction*, 1917. Reprint by Octagon Books, 1967, pp. 6-53.

[*In the following excerpt, Scarborough describes* Northanger Abbey *as a clever burlesque of the Gothic novel.*]

Perhaps the most valuable contribution that the Gothic school made to English literature is Jane Austen's inimitable satire of it, *Northanger Abbey*. Though written as her first novel and sold in 1797, it did not appear till after her death, in 1818. Its purpose is to ridicule the Romanticists and the book in itself would justify the terroristic school, but she was ahead of her times, so the editor feared to publish it. In the meantime she wrote her other satires on society and won immortality for her work which might never have been begun save for her satiety of medieval romances. The title of the story itself is imitative, and the well-known materials are all present, yet how differently employed! The setting is a Gothic abbey tempered to modern comfort; the interfering father is not vicious, merely ill-natured; the pursuing, repulsive lover is not a villain, only a silly bore. The heroine has no beauty, nor does she topple into sonnets nor snatch a pencil to sketch the scene, for we are told that she has no accomplishments. Yet she goes through palpitating adventures mostly modelled on Mrs. Radcliffe's incidents. She is hampered in not being supplied with a lover who is the unrecognized heir to vast estates, since all the young men in the county are properly provided with parents.

The delicious persiflage in which Jane Austen hits off the fiction of the day may be illustrated by a bit of conversation between two young girls.

> "My dearest Catherine, what have you been doing with yourself all the morning? Have you gone on with *Udolpho?*"
>
> "Yes; I have been reading it ever since I woke, and I have got to the black veil."
>
> "Are you, indeed? How delightful! Oh, I would not tell you what is behind that black veil for the world! Are you not wild to know?"
>
> "Oh, yes, quite! What can it be? But do not tell me— I would not be told on any account. I know it must be a skeleton; I am sure it is Laurentina's skeleton. Oh, I am delighted with the book! I should like to spend my whole life reading it, I assure you. If it had not been to meet you, I would not have come away from it for the world."
>
> "Dear creature! How much obliged I am to you; and when you have finished *Udolpho,* we will read *The Italian* together; and I have made out a list of ten or twelve more of the same kind for you."
>
> "Have you, indeed? How glad I am! What are they all?"
>
> "I will read you their names directly; here they are, in my pocket-book: *Castle of Wolfenbach, Clermont, Mysterious Warnings, Necromancer of the Black Forest, Midnight Bell, Orphan of the Rhine,* and *Horrid Mysteries*. These will last us some time."
>
> "Yes, pretty well; but are they all horrid? Are you sure they are all horrid?"
>
> "Yes, quite sure; for a particular friend of mine,

a Miss Andrews—a sweet girl, one of the sweetest creatures in the world—has read every one of them!" . . .

Jane Austen's stupid bore, John Thorpe, and Mr. Tilney, the impeccable, pedantic hero, add their comment to Gothic fiction, one saying with a yawn that there hasn't been a decent novel since *Tom Jones,* except *The Monk,* and the other that he read *Udolpho* in two days with his hair standing on end all the time.

But the real cleverness of the work consists in the burlesque of Gothic experiences that Catherine, because of the excited condition of her mind induced by excess of romantic fiction, goes through with on her visit to Northanger Abbey. She explores secret wings in a search for horrors, only to find sunny rooms, with no imprisoned wife, not a single maniac, and never skeleton of tortured nun. Mr. Tilney's ironic jests satirize all the elements of Gothic romance. Opening a black chest at midnight, she finds a yellowed manuscript, but just as she is about to read it her candle flickers out. In the morning sunshine she finds that it is an old laundry list. The only result of her suspicious explorings is that she is caught in such prowlings by the young man whose esteem she wishes to win. He sarcastically assures her that his father is not a wife-murderer, that his mother is not immured in a dungeon, but died of a bilious attack. These delicately tipped shafts of ridicule riddle the armor of medievalism and give it at the same time a permanency of interest because of Jane Austen's treatment of it. The Gothic novel will be remembered, if for nothing else, for her parody of it. . . .

Andrew H. Wright (essay date 1953)

SOURCE: "Heroines, Heroes, and Villains," in *Jane Austen's Novels: A Study in Structure,* Chatto & Windus, 1953, pp. 83-172.

[*Below, Wright investigates Catherine Morland's character, especially as it is highlighted by the words and actions of Henry Tilney and John Thorpe.*]

Catherine Morland

As a satire of the Gothic horror tale, **Northanger Abbey** contains all the ingredients of this *genre* except the hero and heroine, who are deliberately normalized, partly for the purpose of heightening the ridicule. Like all parodies the book exhibits two sets of values: one is satirized, the other (by implication) is shown to be 'truer'. Here, the illusions of Gothic sentimentality are contrasted to the less flashy but more durable values of good sense; the Gothic world is one of fancy, the world as apprehended by good sense is 'real'. But the book goes somewhat beyond these limits—it goes beyond to explore the limitations of good sense itself. And Jane Austen shows us that though we must reject the Gothic world as inadequate and false, we cannot altogether apprehend the real world by good sense alone. Good

sense, ironically, is limited too.

In sketching Catherine Morland's background, appearance, and disposition, her author manages to suggest both the typical Gothic heroine and, in Catherine herself, the inverse:

> [Catherine] had a thin awkward figure, a sallow skin without colour, dark lank hair, and strong features;—so much for her person;—and not less unpropitious for heroism seemed her mind. She was fond of all boys' plays, and greatly preferred cricket not merely to dolls, but to the more heroic enjoyments of infancy, nursing a dormouse, feeding a canary-bird, or watering a rosebush. . . . Such were her propensities—her abilities were quite as extraordinary. She never could learn or understand any thing before she was taught; and sometimes not even then, for she was often inattentive, and occasionally stupid. . . . What a strange, unaccountable character!

So she was at the age of ten, but when we find her, on the brink of a six weeks' visit to Bath, she has grown:

> . . . her heart was affectionate, her disposition cheerful and open, without conceit or affectation of any kind—her manners just removed from the awkwardness and shyness of a girl; her person pleasing, and, when in good looks, pretty—and her mind about as ignorant and uninformed as the female mind at seventeen usually is.

Her experiences, on first arriving at Bath, are a combination of what might be expected from the Gothic heroine, and the very reverse. The Allens, whose guest she is, are an ordinary, unexciting Wiltshire couple; her first visit to the Upper Rooms produces ennui rather than rapture; the young man she meets is no silent, olive-faced seducer from Southern Europe, but a talkative, sardonic clergyman from Gloucestershire named Henry Tilney, whose father is a general, and who lectures Catherine on the inadequacies of young ladies as letter-writers and other things. On the other hand, she meets Isabella Thorpe, who begins as a regular Gothic confidante (though she ends as an Austenian villain), who induces Catherine to read *The Mysteries of Udolpho* and will give her a list of 'horrid' books to read; she encounters the flashy and dishonest John Thorpe who endeavours to take her to Blaize Castle.

But far more important than her Gothic indoctrination at Bath is her own emergence as a human being—though she is not to be cured of the Gothic infection until her experience at Northanger Abbey, in the second volume. At once she is drawn to Isabella Thorpe, whose conversation is expert on such subjects as:

> . . . dress, balls, flirtations, and quizzes. . . . These powers received due admiration from Catherine, to whom they were entirely new; and the respect which they naturally inspired might have been too great for familiarity, had not the easy gaiety of Miss Thorpe's manners, and her frequent expressions of delight on this acquaintance with her, softened down every feeling

of awe, and left nothing but tender affection.

Youth and a natural credulousness have led her to make this unquestioning friendship with Isabella; but John Thorpe affects her differently even at the beginning of their acquaintance. He is stout, loud, impudent, boastful, insensitive, and dishonest—and:

> Little as Catherine was in the habit of judging for herself, and unfixed as were her general notions of what men ought to be, she could not entirely repress a doubt, while she bore with the effusions of his endless conceit, of his being altogether agreeable.

Indeed she is soon forced to make a conscious and quite firm judgment against him, when he lies to her in order to persuade her to ride to Blaize Castle with him. Made to think for herself on this occasion, and increasingly allied with the sensible Tilney family, she is gradually able to see Isabella with greater objectivity. When the latter claims that Miss Tilney has supplanted her in Catherine's heart:

> Catherine thought this reproach equally strange and unkind. Was it the part of a friend thus to expose her feelings to the notice of others? Isabella appeared to her ungenerous and selfish, regardless of every thing but her own gratification.

But Catherine is forced to suspend, or soften, her judgment of Isabella when the latter becomes engaged to Catherine's brother James. Meanwhile, Catherine's increased intimacy with the Tilneys (and a mistaken impression on the general's part as to her wealth) evokes an invitation to Northanger Abbey, the setting of the major part of the second volume.

Here, with beautifully comic anti-climax, Jane Austen traces Catherine's Gothic adventures. Having expected 'long damp passages . . . narrow cells and [a] ruined chapel . . . some awful memorials of an injured and ill-fated nun', she finds 'lodges of a modern appearance . . . a smooth, level road of fine gravel, without obstacle, alarm or solemnity of any kind. . . . ' In her bedroom, which is far from horrifying in most respects, she finds a mysterious chest—it contains a cotton counterpane; she later spies another chest which frightens her out of a full night's sleep—this contains an inventory of linen. She steals to the room where Mrs. Tilney died, expecting to see evidence that the lady is still alive and cruelly imprisoned—but finds instead a neat, well-lighted, empty bedroom. Henry Tilney finally convinces her that his mother died quite normally, of a ' "bilious fever" '. And so at last Catherine is purged of her Gothic illusions.

> Charming as were all Mrs. Radcliffe's works, and charming even as were the works of all her imitators, it was not in them perhaps that human nature, at least in the midland counties of England, was to be looked for. Of the Alps and Pyrenees, with their pine forests and their vices, they might give a faithful delineation. . . . But in the central part of England there was surely some security for the existence even of a wife not beloved, in the laws of the land, and the manners

of the age. Murder was not tolerated, servants were not slaves, and neither poison nor sleeping potions to be procured, like rhubarb, from every druggist.

But, side by side with her awakening from the Gothic dream, is her much more important emergence as a human being of good sense—and the gradual realization of the limitations of even that quality. It is chiefly through her relationship with Isabella and with John Thorpe that she is thus educated.

We have already seen that at first Catherine is disposed to like Isabella, to accept her unquestioningly as a friend, largely because of the older girl's high spirits. This acceptance is questioned briefly when Isabella expresses some jealousy about the relationship of Catherine to Miss Tilney—but modified when James Morland and Isabella become engaged. Catherine is shocked when Captain Tilney (Henry's older brother) and Isabella commence a flirtation; but she is too good-heartedly naïve to be suspicious:

> It seemed to her that Captain Tilney was falling in love with Isabella, and Isabella unconsciously encouraging him; unconsciously it must be, for Isabella's attachment to James was as certain and well acknowledged as her engagement. To doubt her truth or good intentions was impossible; and yet, during the whole of their conversation her manner had been odd.

Catherine grows resentful, however, of Isabella's insensitivity, but is rather surprised, when she hears that Captain Tilney and Isabella have become engaged (James having been thrown off), that she does not much regret the loss of Isabell's friendship.

> To say the truth, though I am hurt and grieved, that I cannot still love her, that I am never to hear from her, perhaps never to see her again, I do not feel so very, very much afflicted as one would have thought.

But this is not the end of her relationship to Isabella, who coolly writes that she loves James after all, and urges Catherine to intervene with her brother on their behalf.

> Such a strain of shallow artifice could not impose even upon Catherine. Its inconsistencies, contradictions, and falsehood, struck her from the very first. She was ashamed of Isabella, and ashamed of having ever loved her. Her professions of attachment were now as disgusting as her excuses were empty, and her demands impudent. 'Write to James on her behalf!—No, James should never hear Isabella's name mentioned by her again.

If the relationship to the Thorpes shows Catherine the value of common sense in evaluating life's difficulties, the relationship to the Tilneys (except the Gothic trimmings) discloses the limits of this virtue. She meets and is attracted to, though she is rather baffled by, Henry Tilney; she becomes the friend of Eleanor; she is treated with affectionate kindness by the rather terrifying General Tilney—and then suddenly she is dismissed without explanation, on the general's return from a short journey to London. She is stunned, almost overcome with grief, and returns home to Wiltshire in deep humiliation; there she meets with the unfailing kindness and sympathy of her family, and is induced to walk to the Allens', who live near by.

> As they walked home again, Mrs. Morland endeavoured to impress on her daughter's mind the happiness of having such steady well-wishers as Mr. and Mrs. Allen, and the very little consideration which the neglect or unkindness of slight acquaintance like the Tilneys ought to have with her, while she could preserve the good opinion and affection of her earliest friends. There was a great deal of good sense in all this; but there are some situations of the human mind in which good sense has very little power; and Catherine's feelings contradicted almost every position her mother advanced.

And so, momentarily, Catherine sees the unresolvable irony between the strong heart and the clear mind: she has been educated by her experiences at Bath and at the Tilney's to the superior value of common sense. Now, almost before she has been able to absorb the lesson, she learns that good sense cannot deal with the crisis that has forced her sudden expulsion. But the happy *dénouement* is less than ten pages away, the heroine in the arms of her beloved Henry; and Jane Austen writes, sardonically: 'I leave it to be settled by whomever it may concern: whether the tendency of this work be altogether to recommend parental tyranny, or reward filial disobedience.

Compared to Jane Austen's later heroines Catherine Moreland is somewhat thin. Professor Mudrick remarks: [in *Jane Austen: Irony as Defense and Discovery*, 1952]: 'She is too simple and too slight, too narrowly a symbol of the author's rejection of romantic nonsense, to assert the claim of personal feeling and value beyond mere function.' Howells writes of her [in *Heroines of Fiction*, 1901]:

> Catherine Morland is a goose, but a very engaging goose, and a goose you must respect for her sincerity, her high principles, her generous trust of others, and her patience under trials that would be too great for much stronger heads . . . and in spite of her romantic folly she has so much good heart that it serves her in place of good sense.

It seems to me that both these critics rather miss the point about Catherine: her inadequacies as a heroine, such as they are, exist because Jane Austen tries to do too much with her—to establish her both as a gooselike parody of the sentimental-Gothic heroine, and to advance claims for her as a human being who would learn good sense, and learn even to go beyond it. To be sure, irony is not central to the story; *Northanger Abbey*'s delight lies principally in the amusing parody which it presents. But the indication that there is more on earth than mere common sense gives the book an ironic dimension of enduring value.

Henry Tilney and John Thorpe

Henry Tilney is the only one of Jane Austen's heroes who shares her ironic viewpoint, the only one who ever threatens the primacy of a heroine. But this must be, for in *Northanger Abbey* Jane Austen chooses a heroine who is marvellously credulous and naïve—but who, miraculously, wins our affection and even admiration, as Harriet Smith (for instance) does not. John Thorpe contrasts sharply with Henry Tilney in being gross where the latter is refined, stupid rather than brilliant, boorish rather than elegant; Thorpe appears very little, is dismissed early, and is, altogether, the least interesting of his author's villains—partly, perhaps, because the real villain of the piece (though a rather nice one) consists of Catherine's Gothic illusions.

Henry Tilney first appears—as is appropriate to a burlesque of the novel of terror—on a *decrescendo*. Instead of encountering the heroine mysteriously or in a situation of great danger, he is introduced to her by the Master of Ceremonies of the Lower Rooms at Bath. After playfully inquiring as to her activities in Bath, he engages her on the subject of female letter-writing. He observes:

> 'As far as I have had the opportunity of judging, it appears to me that the usual style of letter-writing among women is faultless, except in three particulars.'
>
> 'And what are they?'
>
> 'A general deficiency of subject, a total inattention to stops, and a very frequent ignorance of grammar.'

His function throughout the novel is not only to provide by his cleverness, his wit, and his *savoir-vivre,* a sharp contrast to the 'goosish' heroine, but to take over as leading proponent of Jane Austen's viewpoint, whenever circumstances require.

Naturally, the relationship between Henry and Catherine deepens, the latter usually bewildered by his bursts of cleverness. When, finally, she is invited to visit Northanger Abbey, he engagingly readies her for the terrors of the place. ' ". . . are you prepared to encounter all the horrors that a building such as 'what one reads about' may produce?—Have you a stout heart?—Nerves fit for sliding pannels and tapestry?" ' But of course it does not live up to her Gothic expectations. All in all, he adds up to a thoroughly attractive young man, quite exceeding his functional responsibilities. R. W. Chapman, discussing the heroes of Jane Austen's novels [in *Jane Austen Facts and Problems*], says: '. . . I retain a sneaking preference for Henry Tilney: for no better reason, perhaps, than that I find in him a resemblance to my youthful priggishness. But he has more wit than any of her young men except Henry Crawford.'

John Thorpe is not much worse than rude, vain, selfish, stupid, boastful and dishonest. He does not seduce anyone, like John Willoughby; defame anyone, like George Wickham; coolly run off with a married woman, like Henry

Crawford; deceive anyone (except General Tilney), like Frank Churchill; or insolently ignore the claims of an indigent widow, like Mr. Elliot. John Thorpe is simply:

> . . . a stout young man of middling height, who, with a plain face and ungraceful form, seemed fearful of being too handsome unless he wore the dress of a groom, and too much like a gentleman unless he were easy where he ought to be civil, and impudent where he might be allowed to be easy.

He does not even deceive Catherine Morland very long; before he lies to her about the Tilneys, she is put off by his endless chatter of the famous parties in his Oxford rooms, races, shooting-parties, fox-hunting—in all of which he claims to have played a leading and heroic role.

But his worst defection lies in his behaviour when he desires that Catherine accompany him to Bristol, where (with Isabella Thorpe and James Morland) they will visit Blaize Castle. She tells him that she is already engaged to go walking with the Tilneys; he replies that the latter have already set out in a carriage and therefore will not go walking that day. So Catherine acquiesces; but, *en route,* catches sight of the Tilneys on foot. Thorpe has lied—but will not stop, despite Catherine's strong entreaties. Catherine is furious; her eyes are now thoroughly opened to his character—and henceforth he fades out of the picture very fast, leaving the heroine to battle only her own illusions. The reader is left with the feeling that John Thorpe is the least necessary of Jane Austen's villains, and is perhaps the least interesting both to his author and to his audience.

As in Jane Austen's other novels, hero and villain in *Northanger Abbey* function principally to sharpen and define the position, the personality, and the development of the heroine. John Thorpe is a crude Lovelace, whose defects Catherine sees almost at once—despite the overlay of Gothic fantasy in her mind; Henry Tilney is the agent of Catherine's gradual unillusionment, but as an attractive young man to whom she responds ardently, he unknowingly leads her to the edge of common sense— and beyond.

Frank J. Kearful (essay date 1965)

SOURCE: "Satire and the Form of the Novel: The Problem of Aesthetic Unity in *Northanger Abbey,*" in *ELH,* Vol. 32, No. 4, December, 1965, pp. 511-27.

[*In the following essay, Kearful argues that* Northanger Abbey *achieves a complex unity of fiction, satire, parody, burlesque, comedy, and tragedy.*]

I

The most important—and most interesting—critical problem concerning *Northanger Abbey* is the question of its aesthetic unity. Generally critics are forced to conclude that while brilliant in many of its parts, the book as a whole lacks a sufficiently consistent technique or unified form to make it a coherent work of art. Some would point to Henry Tilney's ambivalent position as surrogate ironic commentator for the author *and* object of her irony; some to the structural "detachability" of the "Gothic" chapters; some to the shallowness of Catherine's characterization as measured against her ostensibly central role; some to an uneasy coexistence within the same narrative of several narrative modes, ranging from apparently outright literary burlesque and parody to assumedly straightforward naturalistic reportage. Furthermore, a few characters, notably John Thorpe, never really participate in the Gothic world of *Northanger Abbey,* while others, notably General Tilney, in straddling its Gothic and its daylight worlds, may fail to inhabit either. Indeed, Catherine's own role as ironic Gothic-sentimental heroine is at best intermittently sustained.

Occasionally efforts have been made to reduce the book's apparent disunity to at least a partial order. While few if any recent critics would have us read *Northanger Abbey* as a consistent burlesque of specific literary works, some would impose upon it more general but hardly more convincing parodic patterns. So, for example, [in *Jane Austen: Irony as Defense and Discovery,* 1952] Marvin Mudrick would make of John Thorpe an anti-type of the Gothic unwelcome suitor and Mrs. Allen, presumably because "she is neither wicked nor vigilant," an anti-type of the Gothic chaperone. Indeed Mudrick is able to convince himself that with the partial and artistically unfortunate exception of Henry Tilney "the most interesting novelistic fact about all these characters is that—whatever else they may be—they are consistently, even rigidly functional" as anti-types of figures recurring in Gothic novels. Undoubtedly we can make ourselves see the characters of *Northanger Abbey* primarily as ironic avatars of Gothic archetypes, but to do so as systematically as Mudrick does is to rob them of much of their vitality and to distort perversely the genuine complexity of Jane Austen's creative achievement.

A somewhat more convincing method of creating if not quite finding unity within the book is to view it in terms of a single organizing theme. So, for example, [in *Jane Austen's Novels: The Fabric of Dialogue,* 1962] Howard Babb by concentrating on one fictional component—dialogue—so as to demonstrate its function as a dramatization of the process of Catherine's education, would have us be content that Catherine's "making a morally secure discovery of herself at the Abbey, arriving at a fuller understanding of her enemies, whether the Thorpes or General Tilney, and finally winning Henry, the champion of reason," are all aspects of a single main action expressed through the means of a consistent technique. Babb's individual critical observations are often illuminating, but his special concern with dialogue and what it reveals about Jane Austen's art should not—any more than Mudrick's special pleading for his conception of Jane Austen's "defensive" irony—force us to reduce the aesthetic complexity of the book itself to the simplicity of the critic's *a priori* framework.

Critics like Mudrick and Babb have not sufficiently taken into account that the way one attempts to resolve the vexing problem of the unity of *Northanger Abbey* depends directly on one's theoretical assumptions about the relationships of prose fiction and satire. The novel as a literary type is, in fact, significantly different from satire as a literary type, both in intrinsic structure and in the illusion its fiction creates. Whereas a novel typically creates an imaginatively self-contained world, the imagined world of satire exists only through its implied or indirect reference to a world outside its own. The novel is a mimetic representation wherein there should be no apparent discrepancy between the action represented and the representation itself; satire, conversely, is based on our recognition of the exaggerated, distorted nature of its representation. The illusion *it* creates is, therefore, fundamentally different from that of the novel: no one complains that it is not "true-to-life" in the same way we expect a novel generally to be.

Satire, of course, is protean. It may be incidental, momentary, merely a linguistic device within a larger structure. But some works are *structurally* satiric, all their materials being so organized and expressed as to support a consistently satiric action. So in reading *Gulliver's Travels,* for example, we are always aware that what we are reading is *a satire,* not simply a novel with satiric moments or overtones, like *Tom Jones.* Of course some prose fictional works which we call satiric are neither structurally integral satires nor novels but more or less ambivalent compounds. Waugh's *Decline and Fall* and *Vile Bodies* are modern instances of such hybridization; by contrast, such later Waugh prose fictions as *Brideshead Revisted* and the Crouchback trilogy are consistently novelistic in structure although they incorporate incidental satire. Indeed the special genius of Waugh, now apparently lost, was in his earlier books to seem to be writing something like a novel which was wildly unlike a novel.

In *Northanger Abbey* Jane Austen was in her own way experimenting with an artistic form compounded of radically different elements. But whereas a Waugh succeeds in fusing two disparate modes into one tonality, Austen allows them to exist side by side in seeming contradiction. Accordingly, at times the fiction presented seems purely (*i.e.,* structurally) satiric and at other times purely novelistic, with the result that our expectations are made to work at cross-purposes. That, however, is the key point of the book as a whole and its organizing principle.

II

The first two chapters of *Northanger Abbey* are usually regarded as literary burlesque or parody and as essentially satiric in design. They are, however, neither burlesque nor parody in any usual simple sense of those terms, for in them we are always keenly aware of a critical narrator who, far from exaggeratedly or incongruously imitating literary conventions or formulae, cynically denies their relevance to *her* story. She is aware of popular literary-sentimentalist conventions, but repeatedly points out how miserably her characters fail to live up to them. In the first chapter, for example, we are informed that Catherine had "a thin awkward figure, a sallow skin without colour, dark lank hair, and strong features;—so much for her person;—and not less unpropitious for heroism seemed her mind." Thus Catherine in her chrysalis at age ten. The chapter then traces her maturation from tomboy to young lady: she becomes no longer the gawky child she was but still reaches "the age of seventeen, without having inspired one real passion, and without having excited even any admiration but what was very moderate and transient." Furthermore, the books Catherine is reading (however superficially or naively) by this time are not sentimental, romantic, or Gothic novels, but rather Pope, Gray, Thompson (*sic*), and Shakespeare.

Not only the felt presence of a critical narrator but also the fact that the characters themselves are not living out a delusion prevents the first two chapters from becoming an orthodox burlesque or parody. This is well illustrated by the two paragraphs in which we are told of the Morlands' preparations for Catherine's trip to Bath. The narrator begins by inviting the reader to speculate on the "thousand alarming presentiments of evil" which "will be naturally supposed" to afflict Mrs. Morland at this "terrific separation." Certainly she will have to "relieve the fulness of her heart" by offering "advice of the most important and applicable nature," such as "cautions against the violence of such nobleman and baronets as delight in forcing young ladies away to some remote farm-house." After concluding her suppositions with a "Who would not think so?" the narrator then reveals not what any novel-reader might suppose would be going on inside Mrs. Morland's mind but what in fact was: "But Mrs. Morland knew so little of lords and baronets, that she entertained no notion of their general mischievousness, and was wholly unsuspicious of danger to her daughter from their machinations. Her cautions were confined to the following points. 'I beg Catherine, you will always wrap yourself up very warm about the throat, when you come from the Rooms at night; and I wish you would try to keep some account of the money you spend;—I will give you this little book on purpose.'" The paragraph following dispels whatever sentimental notions we might have had about Catherine's own emotions or those of her sister and father. "Every thing relative to this important journey was done, on the part of the Morlands, with a degree of moderation and composure, which seemed rather consistent with the common feelings of common life, than with the refined susceptibilities, the tender emotions which the first separation of a heroine from her family ought always to excite."

What Jane Austen accomplishes through this strategy is altogether different from what she did in *Love and Friendship,* wherein the characters were freely allowed to pursue exaggerated versions of sentimental-romantic literary conventions. There the satiric device employed was to expose absurdity by seeming naively to embrace it in magnified form, the reader through his laughter at the resultant caricature of human life being relied on to assert his own common sense. The fiction presented was, accordingly, entirely satiric: it did not create a self-contained imaginative world of its own but instead a point of critical reference to a literary reality outside itself, the world of late eighteenth-century novelistic fiction. However, in Chapters I and II of *Northanger Abbey* the delusions being satirically examined are not those of the ostensible narrator nor of the characters themselves. Furthermore, the fiction presented has, we are warned, nothing to do with any conventional novelistic world with which we might be tempted to associate it, satirically or otherwise. In point of fact, Austen's satiric victim is the reader's own stock expectations, whose responses she disallows, as they are shown to be preposterous when superimposed on the fiction actually presented.

But while we are still in Chapter II we can detect a significant alteration in fictional technique, which coincides with Catherine's arrival in Bath. No longer does the narrator teasingly play off the fictional "facts" against the reader's expectations (a strategy which after all delivers progressively diminishing returns), to establish the reality of the illusion presented simply by showing the absence of unreality. Early in the chapter the narrator had seemingly offhandedly let fall the information that Catherine's "heart was affectionate, her disposition cheerful and open, without conceit or affectation of any kind—her manners just removed from the awkwardness and shyness of a girl; her person pleasing, and, when in good looks, pretty—and her mind about as ignorant and uninformed as the female mind at seventeen usually is." In the latter part of Chapter II, wherein occur her first encounters with Bath life, this "real" Catherine is allowed to act out that character sketched briefly before. The quality of the narration changes correspondingly, for as the "real" illusion of the novel is initiated, Austin's prose style becomes more smoothly modulated, her eye for minute but suggestive sociological detail sharpens, and dialogue becomes more plentiful. This change in tone and technique really begins with the initial description of Mrs. Allen: here we have speaking the voice of "the novelist" rather than "the satirist," although this novelist obviously has a penchant for making incidental incisive satirical remarks.

In Chapter III, when Catherine meets Henry Tilney, *Northanger Abbey* begins to be transformed into a novel of education, as for the next several chapters Catherine will be encountering new people, new situations, and new problems, each providing a different opportunity for her to become a mature person. She will follow, then, a general pattern repeated in all Austen's later novels with the possible exception of *Mansfield Park*: a young girl in some important respects immature undergoes a series of experiences leading to major self-discoveries and discoveries about others, which, cumulatively, bring about a new orientation of the heroine toward herself and her environment. Catherine's "progress" differs from the typical pattern, however, in that she must acquire illusions she was wholly free of at the beginning of the book before she can begin the process of self-discovery and adjustment.

Initially the fiction embodying this process of education is presented novelistically. The narrator does make incidental satiric observations on the action, but the action

itself is realized as structurally independent of the narrator's view of it. This makes *Northanger Abbey* again quite different from a throughgoing satire like *Gulliver's Travels,* wherein there is no fiction with an existence independent of the narrator's conception of it. In *Gulliver's Travels* everything that "happens" we are told of only through Gulliver's account, and nothing related within the narrative has a definable objective existence outside that account. Swift's fiction is, in effect, a series of variously distorting mirrors erected by the central character-narrator, whom Swift regulates by remote control. We are not provided with a self-contained world *in which* the main character exists, but an imaginative construct which is a projection of his own (unbalanced) mind. We never take it, therefore, with the same variety of seriousness we do a novelistic fiction, of which we demand an objectified consistency and coherence independent of any one character's view of it. Even a first-person narrated novel (insofar as it is not structurally satiric nor a psychological study of pure hallucination, like perhaps Beckett's *Malone Dies*) gives us a sense of a fictional world *about which* the narrator is reporting. Our understanding and/or evaluation of it may differ sharply from his, but we are aware of a world of which he is a part, not simply the maker. Even Faulkner's Benjy conveys a real sense of a fictional world outside himself. By contrast, Gulliver's world has no illusionary substance independent of Gulliver. We are not imaginatively drawn into his world as if it were subsisting in any fashion outside his report, for we remain critical observers of an action functional as satire, wherein the fictional world exists as a means of vision rather than an object of contemplation. This is no less true of satiric fictions narrated in the third person, such as those narrated in *MacFlecknoe* and the *Dunciad.* They are satiric distortions of the nonfictional world; but they are not fictional worlds of their own apart from their function as satiric distortions. We are not meant to feel that the "events" of the *Dunciad* happened in a "real" fictional world and that the narrator is merely making satiric comments *about* them.

Apart from the specific stylistic traits and fictional tactics already noted as coming into play by the end of Chapter II of *Northanger Abbey,* in the Bath chapters two general strategies support the essentially novelistic illusion being presented. First, the narrator's satiric statements are for the most part momentary observations on the action rather than the action itself. Henry Tilney, of course, is himself something of a satiric commentator: but he remains a character within the action, whom we see mainly through his relationship with Catherine, and, furthermore, as Austen keeps him offstage much of the time, he never has the opportunity of becoming a fully controlling commentator. His is but one point of view among many, even if the most nearly "right" one.

The fact that Austen while primarily interested in Catherine's progress and closely akin intellectually to Henry is able to introduce a diversity of characters with a variety of viewpoints further assists her in producing a novelistic illusion. Satire, typically, selects only one angle of vision. It is Gulliver's viewpoint in *Gulliver's Travels* just as it is the narrator's viewpoint in *MacFlecknoe* and in the *Dunciad* that constitute the satiric prism. Willingness to present the same "facts" as they appear to several different characters usually implies that those facts have an objective existence outside any one character. That is to say, an illusion becomes more autonomously real the more subjective viewpoints we have of it, even if only because we see that no one character's experience can entirely account for it. Accordingly, in *Northanger Abbey* the diversity of characters, each with his own outlook on the fictional "facts," serves to create not so much a satiric *exposé* of the sentimental and/or Gothic novel, as a positive, novelistic alternative to both.

We may conclude that Austen's strategy as it has thus far revealed itself is much more like Fielding's in *Joseph Andrews* than Swift's or Dryden's or Pope's in their satires. Both Fielding and Austen, having earlier written parodies of books they were impelled to expose through unmitigated satire, sought in their first attempts to produce an independently real prose fiction to provide a substitute for rather than merely an attack upon their favorite victims. So, while *Joseph Andrews* and *Northanger Abbey* begin as satiric parasites on the literature they are "answering," after their introductory quasi-parodic chapters they abruptly drop any strong suggestion of specific literary burlesque. Thus they criticize the falsity of the conventions they are reacting against not by exaggerating those conventions to the point of ridiculous absurdity, but by placing them in a more ample context. This essentially novelistic method is the reverse of that of satire: the former dissolves absurdity, the latter magnifies it. But, interestingly enough, both *Joseph Andrews* and *Northanger Abbey* after having apparently dropped the structurally satiric strategy of the early chapters reactivate that strategy at later points in the narrative—in *Joseph Andrews* in the late chapters wherein Pamela and her Squire are brought on stage, and in *Northanger Abbey* both in the Abbey section and at the very end of the novel. In both books, the writer attempts to incorporate within the world of the novel the world of satire as well. And, most interestingly, both Fielding and Austen in the way they manage the endings of their novels imply that even a "novel" which dissolves delusion is, after all, itself only an illusion.

III

All readers of *Northanger Abbey* sense in the chapters set at the Abbey a radical shift in fictional strategy. By critics they are usually taken with the first two chapters as relatively autonomous interludes of satiric burlesque or parody. So Austen's latest book-length critic, A. Walton Litz, regards them [in *Jane Austen: A Study of Her Artistic Development*, 1965] as "detachable units" which are "mainly devoted to literary burlesque and parody." He suspects that they "may not have been a part of Jane Austen's original plan," but suggests that as a "subplot" they nevertheless do illuminate "Catherine's general action and behavior." In short, they are non-essential and at best tangential to the "real" action but not wholly useless as an indirect comment upon it.

Without denying their manifest differences in technique, one can still make a case for the structural coherence of the Abbey chapters (in the standard Chapman edition, V to X of Volume II). It is not too much to say that they along with the first two chapters and the final chapter form an integral part of the complex design which is the entire book. Indeed it would be strange (and probably disastrous) if the structural beginning, virtual middle, and ending of a narrative were irrelevant to the main action or merely a subplot.

Northanger Abbey is an illusion about illusion and delusion, a book about life not being a book about life. Its alternation of fictional strategies is an appropriate manner of presenting its action, for that action is itself a paradox. Chapters I and II are primarily a satiric attack upon the expectations of many late-eighteenth-century novel-readers—the sort who might be expected eagerly to pick up a book titled *Northanger Abbey*. They serve to disillusion the reader about the "real" nature of the characters introduced, especially Catherine. They do not so much, therefore, create an independent (or novelistic) illusion as destroy a delusion. In the Bath chapters which follow, an independent (i.e., novelistic or "real") illusion is initiated—which is concerned with Catherine's "real" but false illusions (i.e., delusions). After the disillusioning satire of the first chapters, the reader can easily recognize many of Catherine's controlling illusions as delusions: as Catherine becomes deluded (by becoming an avid Gothic novel reader and a victim of Isabella's meretricious sentimentalism), the reader himself becomes more confirmed in his powers of understanding and classifying illusion and delusion. The Abbey section is functionally important because it turns the tables on the too-secure reader. Thus it is not so much a satiric attack on the sentimentalist or the Gothic novel or even on Catherine's acuity (which have *already* been discredited), as a means of challenging the reader's overly facile distinctions between illusions and delusions.

Catherine departs from Bath, with the Tilney family, in Chapter V of Volume II. During the trip to Northanger Abbey, Henry takes the opportunity to tease Catherine about what terrifying experiences her reading must lead her to expect. His lengthy parodic account of all that Catherine can only too easily imagine ("Oh! Mr. Tilney, how frightful!—This is just like a book!"), analogous to his ironic quizzing of Catherine's sentiments during their first conversation at Bath, allows the reader to laugh with Henry at Catherine's credulity. Although Henry's conversation with Catherine takes up most of Chapter V, we are also kept aware of General Tilney, who Henry himself never talks of. Significantly, early in the chapter we are told that "General Tilney, though so charming a man, seemed always a check upon his children's spirits, and scarcely any thing was said but by himself; the observation of which, with his discontent at whatever the inn afforded, and his angry impatience at the waiters, made Catherine grow every moment more in awe of him. . . ." For some unexplained reason, he never does come within range of Henry's parodic predictions.

While Catherine is at the Abbey her two main adventures are discovering a laundry list and finding out the facts of Mrs. Tilney's death. The first is pure comedy, again operating at the expense of Catherine's credulity. Prepared by the two opening satiric chapters of Volume I and by Henry's patently ironic forecast, we are not ourselves drawn closely into Catherine's subjective emotions but rather await the comic explanation which we sense must somehow follow. And it does. What Austen effects in her handling of Catherine's first adventure, then, is not so much a satiric attack upon Gothic novels as much as a good-natured comic *exposé* of the overly sympathetic imagination which *makes* such novels a substitute for actual life.

For several reasons Catherine's second adventure is considerably different. To begin with, its main stimulant, General Tilney, has been throughout the book thus far an enigmatic and rather foreboding figure. The fact that in following Catherine's first adventure we could depend on Henry's ironic anticipatory account to put everything in a comic light now works against us, for Henry has never made his father either the subject or object of his irony. The General's peremptory manner and genuinely unpleasant behavior remain quite outside the range of burlesque diminution. Also, the main concern of this adventure, Mrs. Tilney's death, is unquestionably real: here our starting-point is not merely the projection of an obviously over-active imagination. A real death from unexplained causes is naturally more a subject for our concern than imaginary trap-doors. Furthermore, Austen never quite dissolves this second adventure in a comic or satiric solution. The suspense is maintained over several chapters, the reader waiting less assuredly than in the preceding adventure for some development to remove what is less certainly subjective delusion. Finally when an explanation is forthcoming, from Henry, it is not entirely satisfying to us although it seems to be to Catherine. Since our reaction to Henry's revelation of the "facts" is subtly controlled by the tone Austen employs, we must read very carefully the last paragraphs of Chapter IX.

After being told the medical causes of his mother's death, Catherine asks: "But your father . . . was *he* afflicted?" Henry, who had spoken at length of his own and his sister's reactions but had neglected any reference to his father's, responds:

> "*For a time,* greatly so. You have erred in supposing him not attached to her. He loved her, *I am persuaded, as well as it was possible for him to*—We have *not all,* you know, the same tenderness of disposition—and *I will not pretend* to say that while she lived, *she might not often have had much to bear,* but though his temper *injured her,* his judgment never did. His value of her was sincere; and, *if not permanently,* he was truly afflicted by her death." (Italics added.)

While apparently endeavoring to vindicate his father, Henry through his careful qualifications and deviously negative and double negative circumlocutions actually raises more questions than he answers. The net result of Henry's ambivalent protestations is to make the General perhaps even more sinister than before.

After Catherine interjects "I am very glad of it . . . it would have been very shocking!", Henry replies:

> "If I understand you rightly, you had formed a surmise of such horror as I have hardly words to—Dear Miss Morland, consider the dreadful nature of the suspicions you have entertained. What have you been judging from? Remember the country and the age in which we live. Remember that we are English, that we are Christians. Consult your understanding, your own sense of the probable, your own observation of what is passing around you—Does our education prepare us for such atrocities? Do our laws connive at them? Could they be perpetuated without being known, in a country like this, where social and literary intercourse is on such a footing; where every man is surrounded by a neighborhood of voluntary spies, and where roads and newspapers lay everything open? Dearest Miss Morland, what ideas have you been admitting?"

> They had reached the end of the gallery; and with tears of shame she ran off to her own room.

There is in this speech by Henry a disquieting ironic note. The initial artificially, open-mouthed histrionic sentence; the uncomfortably emphatic and complacent assertion "Remember that we are English, that we are Christians"; the somehow too bland to be innocent phrasing of the rhetorical questions; the sudden intrusion of "where every man is surrounded by a neighbourhood of voluntary spies" at the end of an implied general accolade of English society, which of course would never countenance the least unpleasant deed; the fact that Henry himself does not directly answer all our questions about General Tilney but instead falls back on a calculated rhetorical performance to shame "Dear Miss Morland" (who was already probably blushing at the possible attribution of "voluntary spies" to herself)—all these things leave us uncertain in our response. Catherine has been satisfied, but are we not impelled to respond to each of Henry's unanswered questions, "Yes, it *can* happen here."?

Our unsettled reaction at the end of Chapter IX is reinforced by the fact that the first and second Abbey adventures seem to have operated at cross-purposes. The first was essentially comic, and for its duration we remained amused spectators. The second has taken advantage of our false psychological security, as Henry's irony as it were turns against us, making us feel that the "delusion" he makes Catherine reject may not have been so clearly and completely explained away after all. Whereas the first adventure confirmed our presuppositions, the second has unexpectedly subverted them.

IV

Chapter X begins: "The visions of romance were over. Catherine was completely awakened." Now, presumably, we will leave the twilight Gothic world of the last several chapters to resume existence in the daylight of a more familiar novelistic world. As for Catherine, "her thoughts being still chiefly fixed on what she had with such causeless terror felt and done, nothing could be clearer, than that it had all been a voluntary, self-created delusion, each trifling circumstance receiving importance from an imagination resolved on alarm, and every thing forced to bend to one purpose by a mind which, before he entered the Abbey, had been craving to be frightened." With respect to General Tilney she did not now "fear to acknowledge some actual specks" in his character, and, indeed, was forced to conclude him "to be not perfectly amiable." However, all the "grossly injurious suspicions" she once entertained were now revealed as completely preposterous. Catherine's sense of enlightenment is ironically undercut by the amused detachment of the narrator: "Her mind made up on these several points, and her resolution formed, of always judging and acting in the future with the greatest good sense, she had nothing to do but to forgive herself and be happier than ever. . . . "

Unbeknownst to Catherine, her real disillusionment has not yet begun, for there is to occur shortly the discovery of Isabella's true nature, the expulsion from the Tilney family circle, and the apparently senseless persecution by the motivelessly malignant General Tilney. In short, Catherine must learn that there is more to life than being able to tell the difference between it and books. Consquently, during Catherine's last night at the Abbey "her anxiety had foundation in fact, her fears in probability; and with a mind so occupied in the contemplation of actual and natural evil, the solitude of her situation, the darkness of her chamber, the antiquity of the building were felt and considered without the smallest emotion; and though the wind was high, and often produced strange and sudden noises throughout the house, she heard it all as she lay awake, hour after hour, without curiosity or terror."

With the narrative on the verge of becoming now a psychological novel, the narrator, in Chapter XIV, once again surprises us with a radical alteration in technique. Entering the narration quite self-consciously in the first-person as "the author," she manages to strike a delicate balance between empathy with and humorous detachment from her heroine. So, in a manner which must remind us of Fielding, she describes Catherine's return home:

> A heroine returning, at the close of her career, to her native village, in all the triumph of recovered reputation, and all the dignity of a countess, with a long train of noble relations in their several phaetons, and three waiting-maids in a travelling chaise-and-four, behind her, is an event on which the pen of the contriver may well delight to dwell; it gives credit to every conclusion, and the author must share in the glory she so liberally bestows.—But my affair is widely different; I bring my heroine to her home in solitude and disgrace; and no sweet elation of spirits can lead me into minuteness. A heroine in a hack post-chaise, is such a blow upon sentiment, as no attempt at grandeur or pathos can withstand. Swiftly therefore shall her post-boy drive through the village, amid the gaze of Sunday groups, and speedy shall be her descent from it.

But, whatever might be the distress of Catherine's mind,

as thus she advanced towards the Parsonage, and whatever the humiliation of her biographer in relating it, she was preparing enjoyment of no every-day nature for those to whom she went; first, in the appearance of her carriage—and secondly, in herself. . . .

By this combination of pathos and comedy the reader is prevented, on the one hand, from entering too closely into the experience as it might have been felt internally by Catherine, and, on the other hand, from regarding Catherine merely as a comic victim. We are placed, then, neither in the usual world of the novel nor in the usual world of satire, but rather in an ambivalent world compounded of both.

In the last chapter, XV, the narrator as first-person author ever more and more openly asserts not only her presence in but her absolute control of the action. The book becomes *her* creation, its entire illusion dependent on her will. General Tilney as if by magic (the "novelistic" explanation offered is hardly convincing) reverses himself, and with all obstacles blocking their happiness providentially removed (the narrator acknowledges matters must be handled with dispatch, for she is running out of pages), the lovers can look forward to interminable bliss. But the narrator herself is not so uncritically empathetic:

> To begin perfect happiness at the respective ages of twenty-six and eighteen, is to do pretty well; and professing myself moreover convinced, that the General's unjust interference, so far from being injurious to their felicity, was perhaps rather conducive to it, by improving their knowledge of each other, and adding strength to their attachment, I leave it to be settled by whomsoever it may concern, whether the tendency of this work be altogether to recommend parental tyranny, or reward filial disobedience.

The book thus ends by denying the autonomy of the illusion it has presented, as in a Prospero-like closing gesture the narrator disperses the creatures of her imagination and the world they inhabit.

Those who object to the inconsistency of technique and structure in ***Northanger Abbey*** as well as those who reduce it to a univocal form have missed the main point of what they have read. Austen is writing what is not simply a novel or a satire, a burlesque or a parody, a comedy or a tragedy, a romance or an anti-romance. She is, rather, combining elements of all these in such a fashion as to make us aware of the paradoxical nature of all illusion— even those illusions by which we master illusion.

A. Walton Litz (essay date 1965)

SOURCE: "The Sympathetic Imagination: *Northanger Abbey* and *Sense and Sensibility*," in *Jane Austen: A Study of Her Artistic Development*, Oxford University Press, 1965, pp. 58-83.

[*In the following excerpt, Litz examines complexity of*

theme and unevenness of narrative technique in Northanger Abbey.]

Viewed as a whole, **Northanger Abbey** is certainly the earliest of Jane Austen's major works. Although it was begun in 1798 after the first drafts of **Sense and Sensibility** and **Pride and Prejudice** had been written, both of these novels underwent radical revision shortly before their publication in 1811 and 1813, while Jane Austen's *Advertisement* to **Northanger Abbey** states that it was "finished in the year 1803." There is some possibility that the novel was touched up after 1803, but these revisions could not have been extensive; and we are justified in taking **Northanger Abbey** as the only major work that was completely a product of the first half of Jane Austen's career. Certainly all the evidence of style and narrative method points toward an early date: many of the characters are two-dimensional, and Jane Austen never seems quite sure of her relationship to Henry Tilney. She frequently allows him to usurp her authority, to voice her judgments and wield her irony, and the result is considerable ambiguity concerning her attitude toward the novel's "hero." But if **Northanger Abbey** lacks the narrative sophistication of the later works it does not lack their complexity of theme, and it would be a mistake to think that Jane Austen is manipulating a straightforward contrast between Gothic nonsense and "the common feelings of common life." If she started out to expose the absurdities of Gothic fiction she ended by exposing much more, and any analysis of **Northanger Abbey** must begin with an examination of the relation between the subplot (Catherine's reading of Gothic novels and its impact on her behavior) and the work's main action. For in learning to handle the fictions of the Gothic world Catherine comes to recognize the other fictions which haunt her life.

A close reading of the subplot in **Northanger Abbey** suggests that it may not have been a part of Jane Austen's original plan. The chapters devoted mainly to literary burlesque and parody (I-II, XX-XXV) form detachable units, and the other references to Gothic fiction and Catherine's role as a "heroine" could easily have been inserted into the original story of Catherine's entrance into the world. But whether the subplot developed as part of the author's original intention, or whether it was added later to reinforce the main action, the artistic impact is the same; and the Gothic elements are a brilliant commentary on Catherine's general character and behavior.

The era of the Gothic novel's greatest popularity was amazingly brief: it began in the early 1790's, reached its peak with the publication of *The Mysteries of Udolpho* (1794) and *The Monk* (1796), and started to decline shortly after the publication of Mrs. Radcliffe's *The Italian* in 1797. One of the first signs of this decline in popularity was the appearance of a series of burlesques and satires, ranging from *The Rovers* (a four-act burlesque in the *Anti-Jacobin* for 1798) through Maria Edgeworth's *Angelina* (1801) to E. S. Barrett's *The Heroine* (1813). Although **Northanger Abbey** was not published until six months after its author's death in 1817, and Jane Austen had felt compelled in 1816 to apologize for "those parts of the

work which thirteen years have made comparatively obsolete," at the time of the first draft **Northanger Abbey** was a pioneer criticism of the Gothic form, once more demonstrating Jane Austen's extraordinary grasp of current literary trends and opinions. She was always among the first to recognize the decay of a literary form, and to see in the lifeless conventions a field for irony. In **Northanger Abbey** she could write a recipe for the conventional "heroine," and then invert this formula to produce her Catherine, simply because the average Gothic fiction had become a standard mixture of familiar ingredients. The *Magasin encyclopédique* for 1797 printed the following *"Recipe"* for "a good mixture of shudders and fright, in three volumes":

> An old castle, half of it crumbling down,
> A long corridor, with numerous doors many of
>   which must be hidden,
> Three corpses still weltering in their blood,
> Three skeletons carefully wrapped up,
> An old woman hanged, stabbed several times in
>   her throat,
> Robbers and ruffians galore,
> A sufficient dose of whispers, stifled moans and
>   frightful din.

> All those ingredients well mixed and divided into three parts or volumes give an excellent mixture which all those who have no black blood may take just before going to bed while having their baths. They will feel all the better for it. Probatum est.

The impossibility of locating a single "source" for the Gothic elements in **Northanger Abbey** testifies to this standardization of the form: Mary Lascelles finds in Catherine's behavior a point-by-point inversion of the career of Charlotte Smith's Emmeline, while C. L. Thomson believes that Jane Austen's model was the heroine of *Udolpho.* Actually Catherine Morland is a mirror-image of the "standard" heroine, and the burlesque of **Northanger Abbey** depends in large measure on the virtual identity of all the Gothic heroines. Jane Austen's target was the form in general, not any particular thriller. We should remember that the Gothic novel was not a completely separate genre but rather an extension of the novel of sensibility, and that in the midst of the Black Forest or on the mountains of Sicily the stale conventions of sensibility still held true. In fact the terrors of the Gothic world were evoked in response to a need for situations that would work on the heroine's sensibility with greater violence than any to be met in the life of the Home Counties. German horror, anti-clericalism, and the native English graveyard tradition were all welded upon the novel of sensibility to produce the Gothic fiction of the 1790's. In his fine essay on "The Northanger Novels," Michael Sadleir has shown [in *The Northanger Novels,* 1927] that Jane Austen was well read in this fiction, and keenly aware of the two divergent "schools": that of Monk Lewis, violent, revolutionary, shocking; and that of Mrs. Radcliffe, where the titillation of the audience depends not so much on the quality of the horrors as on the contrast between the secure world of the reader and the perilous world of the fiction. As we shall see later, Jane Austen is primarily interested in the Gothicism of Mrs. Radcliffe, although she fairly divides Isabella's list of horrid fiction between the two schools.

It is important to place *Northanger Abbey* as part of a general reaction against Gothic conventions, but it is more important to note the differences between Jane Austen's method and that of the other anti-Gothic satires. Typical of these is Barrett's *The Heroine,* which Jane Austen thought "a delightful burlesque, particularly on the Radcliffe style." In *The Heroine* the formula of the "Quixotic" novel is applied to the Gothic world; Barrett's heroine, her head stuffed with fictions, tries to impose her imaginary world on reality, and is continually rebuffed. But Jane Austen was too subtle to use this formula, which usually produced passages of broad burlesque alternating with obvious moralizing. Instead of creating a deluded young woman who considers herself a Gothic heroine forced to live in an alien environment, Jane Austen fashioned in Catherine Morland an "anti-heroine," whose early life is at every point the reverse of the classic heroine's; when Catherine is exposed to the influence of Gothic fiction she is not deluded into thinking herself a heroine, but rather into imagining that the world around her is inhabited by Gothic horrors. Thus she is never exposed to the charge of vanity or selfishness, and Jane Austen is able to use the Gothic subplot as a means of commenting on Catherine's education into reality. Of course there is a good deal of broad burlesque in *Northanger Abbey,* and some purely literary satire (especially in the Conclusion, where the gratuitous explanation for the origin of the laundry bills is a spoof on Mrs. Radcliffe's habit of relating every improbable event to "actuality"). But the "literary" interest in *Northanger Abbey* is much less than in the *Juvenilia,* and the Gothic motif is merely one movement—although an important one—in a complex drama of illusion and recognition.

I have said that although Jane Austen demonstrates a familiarity with both "schools" of Gothic fiction, her main concern is with that of Mrs. Radcliffe. This is because she plainly saw the complacency which underlay the form. Whereas Monk Lewis was dealing, however sensationally, with Byronic materials, and using Gothic devices to figure forth certain psychological truths, Mrs. Radcliffe deliberately fostered a sense of remoteness in her Gothic fictions. "She has uniformly selected the south of Europe for her place of action," said Scott, a locale where "passions, like the weeds of the climate, are supposed to attain portentous growth." When Catherine Morland compares Bath's Beechen Cliff with the "south of France"—much to the surprise of Henry Tilney—she is speaking from broad fictional knowledge. The appeal of the Radcliffean novel was founded on the contrast between the dangers of the heroine's life and the security of the reader's, between the violence of Sicily and the tranquillity of Twickenham. Jane Austen understood this appeal to vicarious emotion, and was determined to expose both its basic sentimentality and fundamental unreality. Not only does the reader of Radcliffean fiction get her emotions at second hand, she indulges in the comforting illusion that

violent passions are confined to alien landscapes. As Lionel Trilling has suggested [in *The Opposing Self,* 1955], Catherine's belief in a violent and uncertain life lurking beneath the surface of English society is nearer the truth than the complacent conviction, shared by the readers of Mrs. Radcliffe, that life in the Home Counties is always sane and orderly. General Tilney's actual abuse of Catherine is as bad in its way as anything she had imagined, and her flight from Northanger Abbey, alone and outcast, is an event straight from the Gothic repertory. Jane Austen's irony is not directed at Catherine's sympathetic imagination, but at her misuse of it; and the novel's deepest criticism is reserved for the average reader's complacent reaction to the exposure of Catherine's "folly." Those who read *Northanger Abbey* as a straightforward drama in which Sense conquers Sensibility, and the disordered Imagination is put to flight by Reason, are neglecting the novel's ultimate irony.

A good example of Jane Austen's subtle handling of illusion and reality may be found in the scene where Henry Tilney exploits Catherine's innocent remark that "something very shocking indeed, will soon come out in London." Eleanor Tilney has misunderstood Catherine's reference to the publication of a new "horrid" novel, and fears that some social "riot" is threatened. At this point Henry adjudicates:

> "My dear Eleanor, the riot is only in your own brain. The confusion there is scandalous. Miss Morland has been talking of nothing more dreadful than a new publication which is shortly to come out, in three duodecimo volumes, two hundred and seventy-six pages in each, with a frontispiece to the first, of two tombstones and a lantern—do you understand?—And you, Miss Morland—my stupid sister has mistaken all your clearest expressions. You talked of expected horrors in London—and instead of instantly conceiving, as any rational creature would have done, that such words could relate only to a circulating library, she immediately pictured to herself a mob of three thousand men assembling in St. George's Fields; the Bank attacked, the Tower threatened, the streets of London flowing with blood, a detachment of the 12th Light Dragoons, (the hopes of the nation,) called up from Northampton to quell the insurgents, and the gallant Capt. Frederick Tilney, in the moment of charging at the head of his troop, knocked off his horse by a brickbat from an upper window. Forgive her stupidity. The fears of the sister have added to the weakness of the woman; but she is by no means a simpleton in general."

On the surface this appears to be a lively and reasonable rebuke of Eleanor's borrowed terrors; the riot which Henry describes so graphically seems absurd and unreal against the quiet background of Bath society. But in fact Henry is constructing his imaginary disaster out of the actual details of the 1780 Gordon Riots, and the burden of the passage is not the comforting assurance that "it can't happen here." The ironies of this misunderstanding are directed at complacent sense as well as exaggerated sensibility, and the entire scene prefigures the time when Catherine's imaginary horrors at Northanger Abbey will yield to the real terrors of life.

When Henry Tilney discovers Catherine outside his mother's room, and learns of her suspicion that General Tilney murdered her, his first words are those of triumphant common-sense:

> "Dear Miss Morland, consider the dreadful nature of the suspicions you have entertained. What have you been judging from? Remember the country and the age in which we live. Remember that we are English, that we are Christians. Consult your own understanding, your own sense of the probable, your own observation of what is passing around you—Does our education prepare us for such atrocities? Do our laws connive at them?"

So far Henry's rebuke reflects the assumptions of the average reader, an easy assurance that Gothic horror is alien to eighteenth-century England. But, as D. W. Harding has shrewdly observed [in *Scrutiny* VIII (March, 1940)], Henry's remarks gradually take on a more intricate meaning.

> "Could they [such atrocities] be perpetrated without being known, in a country like this, where social and literary intercourse is on such a footing; where every man is surrounded by a neighbourhood of voluntary spies, and where roads and newspapers lay every thing open? Dearest Miss Morland, what ideas have you been admitting?"

Gothic violence is not impossible in English society, only repressed and rigidly controlled, and "a neighborhood of spies" is hardly the description of an idyllic society. Jane Austen might have said, with Henry James, "I have the imagination of disaster—and see life as ferocious and sinister." Her criticism of Catherine's imagination is not that it is ridiculous or dangerous *per se,* but that it is uncontrolled by judgment. When the "alarms of romance" give way to the "anxieties of common life" at Northanger, these anxieties are not less intense because of their foundation in probability; indeed, they are "mournfully superior in reality and substance." And when Catherine learns the true motives for General Tilney's outrageous behavior, she feels "that in suspecting General Tilney of either murdering or shutting up his wife, she had scarcely sinned against his character, or magnified his cruelty." Jane Austen records this emotion with an irony which does not entirely invalidate it.

In the *"Recipe"* for a Gothic novel quoted earlier in this chapter the *Magasin encyclopédique* describes the formula as an excellent tonic for readers to take "just before going to bed while having their baths," and this is a perceptive observation on the sentimental bracketing of remote horrors and immediate comforts which characterized the Gothic craze. Like Byron and Monk Lewis, Jane Austen knew that the reader's feeling of cozy security was an illusion, and that the ridiculousness of the average Gothic fiction lay in its sentimentality and improbability, not in the emotions which it presented in debased form.

Kenneth Clark has said [in *The Gothic Revival,* 1950] that "every Romantic style reflects the daydream of its creators," a daydream which is, "in some measure, complementary to the real world."

> When life is fierce and uncertain the imagination craves for classical repose. But as society becomes tranquil, the imagination is starved of action, and the immensely secure society of the eighteenth century indulged in daydreams of incredible violence.

Clark's generalization can easily be applied to the artificially restricted life of Catherine Morland, a life which fosters illusion. It was Jane Austen's purpose to destroy the daydream, but she refused to replace it with the greater illusion that all of life is probable and orderly. If she had intended to launch a full-scale ironic attack on the dangers of imagination, as some critics have claimed, she would have turned Catherine into the standard "heroine" of a Quixotic novel, self-confident, rebellious, an exaggerated figure of of burlesque. But by making Catherine's self-delusion completely probable, by emphasizing her lack of pretension, and by integrating the literary satire into a classic tale of "education," Jane Austen acknowledged a larger aim. At its deepest level *Northanger Abbey* probes the virtues and limitations of what the eighteenth century would have called the sympathetic imagination, that faculty which promotes benevolence and generosity. Henry Tilney, who is never far from the author, is quick to discern this quality in Catherine's personality.

> "With you, it is not, How is such a one likely to be influenced? What is the inducement most likely to act upon such a person's feelings, age, situation, and probable habits of life considered?—but, how should *I* be influenced, what would be *my* inducement in acting so and so?"

Now it seems clear that Jane Austen, in her life and in her art, was an admirer of the sympathetic imagination. It is the faculty which sweetens Catherine's character, the main source of Henry's affection. But Jane Austen also knew how easily such sympathy can be duped or deluded, and in *Northanger Abbey* she dramatized the dangers of uncontrolled sympathy. When untempered by judgment and reason the sympathetic imagination leads Catherine to her naïve mistakes in assessing both situation and character. Her projection of Gothic motives into the life at Northanger, and her misunderstanding of Isabella's nature, result from uncritical acceptance of fictions: in the one case the fictions of art are taken as reality, in the other the fictions of outward appearance are mistaken for the substance of character. The sympathetic imagination must be regulated; this is the sum of Catherine's education. She is cured of her illusions by being initiated into the real world, which is neither more nor less fierce than the fictional world, only different. In *Northanger Abbey* Jane Austen explored a problem to which she would return again and again, the problem of accommodating reason and feeling, of regulating sympathy without destroying it.

Stated in the abstract, the leading themes of *Northanger*

Abbey sound as rich and subtle as those of Jane Austen's later works; but when we encounter them in the novel we find that their expression is hampered by lapses in tone and curious shifts in narrative method. We can isolate in *Northanger Abbey* most of the techniques that mark Jane Austen's greatest fiction, but they never coalesce into a satisfactory whole. What we miss is that sense of a controlling attitude which is part of the "atmosphere" in *Pride and Prejudice* or *Emma*. It is not that Jane Austen has difficulty in keeping herself out of the novel in *Northanger Abbey*—to say that would be to judge the work by the standards of a different kind of fiction. The real problem is inconsistency: some passages point forward to the dramatic ironies of the mature works, while others revert to the cruder methods of the *Juvenilia*. Typical of the latter is the famous "defence" of novel-reading in Chapter V:

> . . . I will not adopt that ungenerous and impolitic custom so common with novel writers, of degrading by their contemptuous censure the very performances, to the number of which they are themselves adding—joining with their greatest enemies in bestowing the harshest epithets on such works, and scarcely ever permitting them to be read by their own heroine, who, if she accidentally take up a novel, is sure to turn over its insipid pages with disgust. Alas! if the heroine of one novel be not patronized by the heroine of another, from whom can she expect protection and regard? I cannot approve of it. . . . "And what are you reading, Miss———?" "Oh! it is only a novel!" replies the young lady; while she lays down her book with affected indifference, or momentary shame.—"It is only Cecilia, or Camilla, or Belinda;" or, in short, only some work in which the greatest powers of the mind are displayed, in which the most thorough knowledge of human nature, the happiest delineation of its varieties, the liveliest effusions of wit and humour are conveyed to the world in the best chosen language. Now, had the same young lady been engaged with a volume of the Spectator, instead of such a work, how proudly would she have produced the book, and told its name; though the chances must be against her being occupied by any part of that voluminous publication, of which either the matter or manner would not disgust a young person of taste: the substance of its papers so often consisting in the statement of improbable circumstances, unnatural characters, and topics of conversation, which no longer concern any one living; and their language, too, frequently so coarse as to give no very favourable idea of the age that could endure it.

This is not a simple passage; although Jane Austen is obviously serious in attacking the craven attitudes of contemporary novelists and their readers, she cannot resist the protective irony of overstatement. What is jarring about the passage is the intrusion of the author after we have come to accept Henry Tilney as her spokesman. Henry's attitudes merge with those of his creator on so many occasions that we are disturbed when she speaks to us directly, or when Henry is suddenly subjected to her irony. All this is but to say that Jane Austen was experimenting in *Northanger Abbey* with several narrative methods she had not fully mastered, and the result is a lack of consistency in viewpoint. From time to time she confines our knowledge to Catherine's horizons, using

her heroine as a "center of consciousness," but Catherine's lack of introspection prevents any consistent use of this technique. The most sophisticated sections of the novel, and those that remind us most strongly of the later novels, are the dramatic exchanges where Jane Austen allows a character to expose his own nature through word and gesture.

Chapter XVIII provides a superb example of Jane Austen's command of dramatic action. Here she confines herself to dialogue between Catherine and Isabella, to simple description, and to recording Catherine's naïve reactions; the author scarcely intrudes upon the scene, and our awareness of Isabella's changing opinions is derived entirely from her conversation. The opening sequence of action and dialogue—Isabella's choice of an "out of the way" bench which commands the whole room, her anxious glances, her indifference to James's possible appearance—is a clear indication to the reader of her changing attitudes. Her familiar reference to "Tilney" (in contrast with Catherine's "Mr. Tilney") confirms her new interest in him. And when Catherine, after disclaiming any special affection for John Thorpe, comforts Isabella with the reminder: "And, you know, we shall still be sisters," Isabella replies in a manner which makes her ambition obvious to the reader, if not to Catherine: "Yes, yes," (with a blush) "there are more ways than one of our being sisters.—But where am I wandering to?" Isabella's conversation then dwells on the fickleness of young opinion, culminating in a quotation from Captain Tilney on the subject: "Tilney says, there is nothing people are so often deceived in, as the state of their own affections . . . " At this point Captain Tilney enters the room, and his whispered exchange with Isabella makes the situation clear to all but Catherine, who evolves the naïve theory that Isabella is "unconsciously" encouraging Captain Tilney. The chapter ends with a fine passage in which Jane Austen records Catherine's troubled reactions to the scene she has just witnessed.

> It seemed to her that Captain Tilney was falling in love with Isabella, and Isabella unconsciously encouraging him; unconsciously it must be, for Isabella's attachment to James was as certain and well acknowledged as her engagement. To doubt her truth or good intentions was impossible; and yet, during the whole of their conversation her manner had been odd. She wished Isabella had talked more like her usual self, and not so much about money; and had not looked so well pleased at the sight of Captain Tilney. How strange that she should not perceive his admiration! Catherine longed to give her a hint of it, to put her on her guard, and prevent all the pain which her too lively behaviour might otherwise create both for him and her brother.

> The compliment of John Thorpe's affection did not make amends for this thoughtlessness in his sister. . . . Isabella talked of his attentions; *she* had never been sensible of any; but Isabella had said many things which she hoped had been spoken in haste, and would never be said again; and upon this she was glad

to rest altogether for present ease and comfort.

In this chapter we see Jane Austen moving toward that easy balance of dramatic action and psychological exposition—Henry James's "scene" and "picture"—which was to become the hallmark of her greatest fiction. Long before the reader comes to the *sotto voce* exchange between Isabella and Captain Tilney he is aware of the relationship which has developed between the two since their meeting at the dance, but Jane Austen has been careful to communicate this knowledge only through action and dialogue. Her own voice has been reserved for the recording of Catherine's naïve opinions, leaving the reader free to interpret the scene's dramatic irony. We are hardly conscious of Jane Austen's presence, yet she has retained control over our developing awareness. Such a complex method combines the effects of dramatic irony with the privilege of psychological interpretation, and allows us to regard the action both from Catherine's limited point-of-view and the author's omniscient perspective. But before this method could be confidently pursued on a large scale Jane Austen had to solve the structural problems that confronted her in *Northanger Abbey* and, more acutely, in *Sense and Sensibility*. . . .

Sheridan Baker (essay date 1965)

SOURCE: "The Comedy of Illusion in *Northanger Abbey*," in *Papers of the Michigan Academy of Science, Arts, and Letters*, Vol. LI, 1966, pp. 547-58.

[*In the following essay, Baker describes Austen's ironic use of self-delusion in* Northanger Abbey.]

Northanger Abbey, the third written but least revised and hence most pristine of Jane Austen's early novels, has not lacked admirers. Indeed, Andrew Wright, John K. Mathison, Alan D. McKillop, and Henrietta Ten Harmsel have led us progressively to see the dimensions of realism and validity within the novel's burlesque of Gothic romance. But there is still room, I believe, to emphasize the extent to which Jane Austen uses romance itself not merely as a comic delusion from which a young girl grows awake, but as a central symbol of one of the most persistent realities of life: the inescapable comic and ironic propensity of the human mind to delude itself.

All of us have tended to think of Jane Austen's Gothic burlesque as having a certain youthful exuberance that would have evaporated into the broader comic landscape had Miss Austen revised *Northanger Abbey* as thoroughly as she did *Sense and Sensibility*. [In *From Jane Austen to Joseph Conrad,* edited by Robert C. Rathburn and Martin Steinmann, Jr., 1958] McKillop considers the Gothic business a "breach [in] imaginative continuity," and even Miss Ten Harmsel, who [in her dissertation, *Jane Austen's Use of Literary Conventions,* 1962] sees the Gothic burlesque as "chiefly redeemed from its apparent extraneousness" by its central educating of Catherine, finds the final Gothic step of education "perhaps an indefensibly emphatic one," and feels that the burlesque "at times endangers the artistic unity," although Miss Austen demonstrates her mastery by achieving a real novel after all. Jane Austen's own brief prefatory paragraph, of course, apologizes for "Those parts of the work which thirteen years have made comparatively obsolete." But my enthusiasm for *Northanger Abbey* urges me to believe that the mature Jane Austen, even ill and depressed, valued the Gothic portions for their power to burlesque not only superficial fiction but man himself, because of those continual fictions that are part of his mental reality. Mary Lascelles points out [in *Jane Austen and Her Art,* 1939] that Jane Austen's interest in burlesque had revived in her last years with her satirical "plan of a novel," her niece's impromptu oral burlesquing of novels for her amusement, and her enjoyment of E. S. Barrett's burlesque novel, *The Heroine* (read in 1814). I believe that she kept the Gothic portions, for the modification of which she had had ample opportunity both on the manuscript retrieved from her unpublishing publisher and on the copy she had kept in her possession, precisely because of their centrality to her whole comedy of illusion, the comedy she saw within the very process of fiction, in man as an essentially romancing and fiction-making creature.

The line I wish to strengthen is that indicated by Wright (though he sees the parody as something slightly apart, and oddly believes that "irony is not central to the story") when he says [in *Jane Austen's Novels: A Study in Structure,* 1953] that *Northanger Abbey* moves beyond "good sense" to the deeper illustration of its inadequacies. This line is extended by Miss Ten Harmsel when she sees Austen's "ironic reversal of the apparent burlesque" that "touches upon essential relationships between life and literature and provides a lasting insight into life itself"; and by Lionel Trilling and Mathison, whom Miss Ten Harmsel quotes. Trilling makes the essential point:

> Catherine Moreland, having become addicted to novels of terror, has accepted their inadmissible premise, she believes that life is violent and unpredictable. And that is exactly what life is shown to be by the events of the story: it is we who must be disabused of our belief that life is sane and orderly.

Mathison underlines it; the Gothic novels are precisely what have educated Catherine to the possibilities of evil in the world beyond her country village and innocent years: "The forms of cruelty and violence in the Gothic novels were unreal, but cruelty and violence do exist in the well-ordered society of the English midlands." The Gothic burlesque, then, is the very means whereby the reader is drawn into the comedy of human illusions that runs throughout the book.

In having Catherine read a romance and then misjudge life from her reading, Jane Austen is following a line of 18th-century comedy, both in the novel and in the theater, that goes directly back to Cervantes and *Don Quixote*. Fielding's *Joseph Andrews* had popularized the idea in England—the idea of having a person comically misjudge reality from the reading of too many books. Jane Austen, too, is writing what Fielding called a "comic romance." But even before Fielding, the girl who reads romances and misjudges life from her romantic ideas had appeared on the English stage and was to become a stock comic figure. Catherine Morland comes from a long line of romance-reading girls with their comic mistakes about reality, and perhaps the most important point here is that Jane Austen's readers would recognize the type, and that Jane Austen was working with a general expectation, almost a general literary convention: introduce a young girl who reads romances, in other words, and everyone is alert for comic mistakes about the way life really is.

But what Jane Austen does with Catherine's comic mistakes about reality is a new, surprising, and refreshing step beyond the convention, beyond the usual expectation. The conventional romance-reading heroine is simply comically wrong about reality. Catherine Morland is also comically right about romance. Jane Austen, by whatever instinct or genius, reaches the same comic depth that Cervantes had reached in his own burlesque of romance, showing that reality and romance are both wrong, because each is only part of the whole truth, and, similarly, that reality and romance are both right.

Northanger Abbey becomes a comedy of human illusions, demonstrating in effect that not only Catherine, but most people, misjudge the world by their own illusions. It is the comedy of general human imperception, and the final joke is on the reader's own imperceptions themselves, since we and Jane Austen's audience of the time expect that Catherine's romantic illusions will simply prove wrong. The final joke is in their proving essentially right: her reading of romances has led her to think that General Tilney is a villain; and he indeed proves to be one, not in the way in which she had imagined, of course, but his character is just about as violent and selfish as her romantic imaginings have led her to believe.

Jane Austen has been playing with the reader, in other words, first fulfilling our expectations that Catherine's romancing will prove comically wrong and then tricking us at last, and humbling our pride in thinking that we can outguess the story and that we know what is *really* going on, by showing that we too have our illusions. This is an example of Jane Austen's constant irony, what Miss Ten Harmsel has also called her central irony—this comic teasing and outmaneuvering of our expectations. It is a feminine refinement of Cervantes, really; it shows us that our ideas of reality and practicality are partly right and partly wrong, and that our romantic illusions have a certain validity, even within their practical falseness. We all have our illusions and our myopias, she seems to say, and perhaps the youthful daydreams of romance are the least harmful after all.

Perhaps the most delicious illustration of the persistence of romance within the knowledge of reality is Catherine's awakening from her romantic fears that General Tilney had either murdered his wife or kept her immured somewhere in the Abbey, sustained only by "a nightly supply of coarse food." She does learn from romances her most important lesson, as Mathison [in *English Literary Histo-*

ry XXIV, 1957] and Miss Ten Harmsel point out—that good and evil are mixed in human beings. But Miss Austen has outmaneuvered even these two astute scholars—and even Mary Lascelles, who also quotes some of the crucial passage below as evidence of Catherine's cure—for even this truth is sustained in comic irony. Catherine cannot give up all of her illusions. And Jane Austen is partly ironic as she opens her chapter with "The visions of romance were over. Catherine was completely awakened." These are indeed Catherine's opinions of herself, as summarized by the author, for we see immediately that Catherine's awakening is by no means complete. The irony, indeed, is threefold, first in having Catherine persist in some of her illusions about romantic places, then in having the truth about good and bad seem amusingly youthful and pat, hence still slightly comic in its confident imperception, and finally in tinging even her accurate and romantically induced estimate of General Tilney with defensive rationalization. In the following paragraph, I underline some of Catherine's rationalized concessions and affirmations, which show her thoughts still comically surrounded with romance as she faces reality—the more amusing for her little English chauvinisms, and for the fact that she is repeating the substance of Henry's scolding as if it were her own original thinking.

> Charming as were all Mrs. Radcliffe's works, and charming even as were the works of all her imitators, it was not in them *perhaps* that human nature, *at least in the midland counties of England,* was to be looked for. Of the Alps and Pyrenees, with their pine forests and their vices, they might give a faithful delineation; and Italy, Switzerland, and the South of France, might be as fruitful in horrors as they were there represented. Catherine dared not doubt beyond her own country, and of even that, if hard pressed, would have yielded the northern and western extremities. *But in the central part of England. . . .* Among the Alps and Pyrenees, perhaps, there were no mixed characters. There, such as were not as spotless as an angel, might have the dispositions of a fiend. *But in England it was not so; among the English,* she believed, in their hearts and habits, there was a general though unequal mixture of good and bad. Upon this conviction, she *would not be surprised if even* in Henry and Eleanor Tilney, *some slight* imperfection might hereafter appear; and upon this conviction she need not fear to acknowledge some actual *specks* in the character of their father, who, though cleared from the grossly injurious suspicions which she must ever blush to have entertained, she *did believe, upon serious consideration, to be not perfectly amiable.*

Here is Jane Austen's central comedy of the mind's subtle self-deceptions. It is central to Elizabeth Bennet's partly true and partly false "first impressions," and to Emma's romance-induced fantasy about Harriet's noble parentage. The center of Jane Austen's ironic art is precisely this subtle exhibit of the play between illusion and reality as she paraphrases her heroines' thoughts in such a way as to set even their true perceptions comically within a context of partial illusion. The *paraphrase* of thought is the secret of Jane Austen's best irony—no one, not even Wayne Booth in his superb *Rhetoric of Fiction,* seems yet to have seen that her secret is in her paraphrasing, although Wright is considering the phenomenon in what he calls "interior disclosures"—for she can insert a guiding irony of her own, as with "fruitful in horrors," as she tells us in her own voice what her heroine is saying to herself, now giving us her heroine's inner words directly, now rising to a swift, ironic summary, which deftly illuminates the imperceptions and the dramatic ironies. She can thus turn even true knowledge comic (Catherine's discovery that good and bad are mixed in people), making it another comic illustration of what perpetual and endearing fools these mortals be, by having it remain too youthful and simple, and having the discoverer's pride in her new knowledge blind her to its over-simplicity. The mind itself is an essentially amusing irony, Jane Austen shows, because even its truest perceptions are limited within the broader context of all knowledge, while the perceiver takes them for infinite wisdom itself. This broad context of some implied totality of wisdom is what gives Jane Austen's irony its power, as each particular truth becomes a gently comic part of the perpetual romance each ego plays to its own illusionary audience.

Thus the cohesion of romance and reality in *Northanger Abbey* and hence the unity of the book itself comes not only through Catherine's comic mental synthesis of the two. It comes from all of the characters, so realistically portrayed, as they exhibit this favorite of Jane Austen's ironies: that illusions, what we might call "romancing," are one of the realities of life. First, there is Mrs. Allen, who lives in a constant daydream of clothes, who cannot see the reality of Catherine's unhappiness in their first days at Bath, who merely wishes that some friends will turn up, who cannot advise her about the Thorpes, because of her constant illusion of silks and cambrics and gloves and hats. Then her friend Mrs. Thorpe, apparently a slightly more devious personality, but doing no more than any parent in her circumstances, that is, trying to marry off her children well. Her illusion is the excellence and goodness of her children. Between Mrs. Allen and Mrs. Thorpe, Jane Austen develops a glimpse of the comedy of illusion worthy of Laurence Sterne (whom Jane Austen mentions early in the book): Mrs. Allen is " . . . never satisfied with the day unless she spent the chief of it by the side of Mrs. Thorpe, in what they called conversation, but in which there was scarcely ever any exchange of opinion, and not often any resemblance of subject, for Mrs. Thorpe talked chiefly of her children, and Mrs. Allen of her gowns." Or again, Mr. Allen is objecting to the idea of young men and women driving around the country in open carriages, objecting on the grounds of custom and propriety, and thinking about his responsibility to Catherine's parents to guard her conduct. He ends by saying this: "Mrs. Allen, are not you of my way of thinking? Do not you think these kind of projects objectionable?"

"Yes, very much so indeed [Mrs. Allen replies]. Open carriages are nasty things. A clean gown is not five minutes wear in them. You are splashed getting in and out; and the wind takes your hair and your bonnet in every direction. I hate an open carriage myself." Mrs. Allen is trapped within her illusion—her daydream, her romance of clothing, in which all existence is reduced to seeing herself moving before admiring eyes in perpetually new frocks.

Isabella Thorpe is a more complex example of the private romance that each of us plays, with himself or herself as perpetual hero or heroine. Clothing, again, is one of the indications of superficiality. She is telling Catherine of how much she loves James Morland, Catherine's brother: "The very first day that Morland came to us last Christmas—the very first moment I beheld him—my heart was irrecoverably gone. I remember I wore my yellow gown, with my hair done up in braids. . . . " But Jane Austen also pins Isabella's superficiality and her self-deception in the very cliché's of romance, of which she, too, is a reader: "Had I command of millions, were I mistress of the whole world, your brother would be my only choice"— "A cottage in some retired village would be ecstasy." Isabella constantly trims herself, in her mind's eye, to the romantic pattern, deluding not only Catherine but herself: "There is nothing I would not do for those who are really my friends. I have no notion of loving people by halves, it is not my nature. My attachments are always excessively strong." The evidence, of course, is all to the contrary. And although the evidence is before us, and indeed before Catherine, we do not see very soon that Isabella's motive in cultivating Catherine's friendship is to win marriage with Catherine's brother, whom Isabella, on her own brother's inflated estimate, thinks is very rich. Catherine never sees the full extent of the reality, and Isabella, in her final letter, cannot, herself, see herself or understand Catherine's personality, since Isabella assumes that she can still patch up her engagement with James in her old fluttery way. Isabella remains deluded and limited by her own interests, her own romance of herself, in which she plays all-conquering heroine in her daydreams. Jane Austen gives us only the outer evidence; but Isabella's remarks are constant reports from the continuous inner daydream.

John Thorpe is perhaps the book's best inner romancer. Again Jane Austen gives us only the outer evidence, in what he says and does. We get no transcription of his inner thoughts. But there can be no doubt that Thorpe plays for himself a constant little drama, with himself as the dashing young hero, the superb horseman, the superb man-about-town, the superb drinker, the superb ladykiller. Yet we see the reality with wonderfully comic clarity. He is stout, of middle height, ungraceful, with a plain face. And his horsemanship is well displayed when, after much warning of a wild and spirited horse, he tells the groom, with great importance, to let the horse's head go—and the horse starts off with the "quietest manner imaginable." Perhaps the most skillful and pleasantest touch of Jane Austen's plotting in this book is to use John Thorpe's unbookish romancing as the mover of the innocent Catherine's fortunes. Thorpe, playing his own private drama in his head for himself, boasts to General Tilney of how rich Catherine is because her supposed richness fits his private daydream. Furthermore, his picture of himself as a dashing young man, irresistible to women, prohibits him from seeing that he has not the remotest chance of winning Catherine's hand. His private romance makes her rich and him the conquering hero all at a stroke.

This, in turn, feeds General Tilney's own private daydream. He wants to marry his second son to a rich young woman. His son seems interested—so immediately, without further inquiry or thought, General Tilney cultivates Catherine's friendship and whisks the prize out of Thorpe's reach by inviting her to Northanger Abbey. And then when both Isabella's and John Thorpe's daydreams prove false, Thorpe, the habitual exaggerator and romancer, now disappointed and angry, tells General Tilney that Catherine's family is very poor and mere fortune hunters, denouncing them now in terms that, with fine comic irony, exactly describe himself and his own family: the Morlands, he says, are a family not respected in their own neighborhood, "aiming at a style of life which their fortune could not warrant; seeking to better themselves by wealthy connexions; a forward, bragging, scheming race." So the General in a fury sends Catherine away, and so also, when the reality of Catherine's wealth becomes known as not so bad as Thorpe had pictured it, the General can easily adjust his very limited and selfish views of life to accepting Catherine after all.

James Morland, Catherine's brother, has his own delusions—that Thorpe is a great fellow, and that Isabella is a wonderful woman. "Poor Thorpe," he says in his letter to Catherine, thinking that Thorpe will be disappointed in his sister's frivolity: "his honest heart would feel so much," he writes. And he ends with a pleasant despair in his being the tragically wounded lover, in the full innocence of dramatic irony, saying of Isabella, who has demonstrated her worthlessness for all to see: "I can never expect to know such another woman!" Similarly, Mrs. Morland, Catherine's mother, at the end of the book, cannot see that Catherine is sick at heart from her disappointed love of Henry Tilney; so she recommends to Catherine a good moral essay from a magazine on how young girls should not acquire frivolous tastes.

The whole comedy of reality versus romance centers, of course, on Catherine; and the literary romances of Ann Radcliffe serve as the means of demonstration. *Reality,* of course, is essentially "seeing things as they really are"; and *romance* is "seeing things as we wish them to be." Catherine's romancing is most healthily unselfish. She hardly thinks about herself at all. Consequently, though very naïve, she can learn to see things as they are. She is wrapped in fictitious adventures in haunted castles and abbeys; for a few moments at Northanger Abbey she imagines herself the adventurous heroine of a Gothic romance. But her character is absolutely honest and open and selfless and naïve. She has a saving common sense, and she swears in humility that she will never again pry into other people's affairs on the promptings of making some romantic discovery. Catherine, who seems to be the most romantically deluded person in the book, is really the most honest and undeluded. She has no illusions about herself; she hardly has thoughts about herself at all. Her open interest and pleasure in Henry Tilney's company is

what attracts him to her. Her pleasure makes her eyes sparkle. She is really the soul of pleasant unillusioned young womanhood. She is far less "romantic" than Isabella and John Thorpe, whom we had taken as realists.

But Henry Tilney is the most realistic and the most unromantic person in the book. He has an amused penetration into human blindness and illusion that very nearly equals Jane Austen's own. As Wright says, he is "the only one of Jane Austen's heroes who shares her ironic viewpoint, the only one who ever threatens the primacy of a heroine," although Frank Churchill eventually reveals a very similar Austen-like propensity to play along ironically with the more limited assumptions of other people. Henry enters puckishly into Mrs. Allen's daydream of clothing, seeing it exactly for what it is, amusing himself amiably and harmlessly at her expense: Mrs. Allen has mentioned the price she paid for the cloth of her dress. "That is exactly what I should have guessed it, madam," says Tilney, and then proceeds to play along in a conversation with Mrs. Allen about different cloths and prices until Catherine "feared . . . that he indulged himself a little too much with the foibles of others."

Tilney does enjoy human foibles, just as Jane Austen does, and one of the delights of the book is in the little romance he makes up for Catherine as they drive to Northanger. This is pieced together from the commonplaces of romances, and demonstrates that he had certainly read romances, as both he and his sister have said he has. It also shows that he can enjoy imaginative daydreams without being taken in by them, that romance is fine and pleasant so long as we do not succumb to its illusions. And one of Jane Austen's finest touches here is in having Henry tell us a romance that we almost begin to believe, that we actually want to go on, so that we can find out what happens, and then playfully break it off to show that it was only play, as it should have been. Henry teases Catherine, and Jane Austen teases us.

The whole teasing uncertainty of human perceptions in the face of reality and romance is nicely demonstrated as Henry puts into his story the ebony-and-yellow lacquered cabinet. He knows that it is in the room Catherine is to inhabit at Northanger. He uses the improbable commonplace of romance that the heroine should somehow not have seen such a huge piece of furniture when she first examined the room. We smile. And then Jane Austen turns the tables on us. For Catherine later does really, in fact, see the cabinet that she had really somehow missed when she first looked around the room. Real life does sometimes imitate romances in its strangeness; human perceptions are just as fallible in fact as they are in fiction.

The whole novel, indeed, is a teasing of the reader's perceptions and expectations as it comically displays the limitations of human perceptions, because we start with an emphatically unromantic heroine. She does not start life tragically as an orphan. No boy in the neighborhood had been found on a doorstep; there is not one young man in the neighborhood whose origin is unknown. She is a simple naïve but normal young girl. But then, after her unromantic experiences at Northanger Abbey, we have the pleasant and playful surprise of learning that she will fill out our romantic hopes after all. She will marry a young man considerably higher up the social ladder than she is, and we discover after all that the story has been a pleasant fictive excursion.

Jane Austen's final irony is exactly here. This has not been reality, real as it has seemed. This has been only a story, an illusion, a romance. Life may be very like this; but this is not life itself, nor is it like all of life. As Henry Tilney has suggested through his little interrupted romance: romance is fine and pleasant so long as we do not succumb completely and forever to its illusions. Jane Austen, through her final irony, implies that she knows and we know that perfect felicity is unobtainable in this life, that love will change and youth grow old—but that we all enjoy the illusion of romance; we like to think of "living happily ever after." And yet she ends playfully, with an acknowledgment that in the fictions of romance one can also learn some good lessons about life: she adds a playful moral to her tale, and she means the moral almost seriously. Romance is useful. We can laugh at its illusions; we can even learn something valid about life, if we do not take it too seriously. And this is why Jane Austen is great: beyond the illusion and the lesson and the comedy, ironically, we can sense something in Jane Austen of the full, sweet, sad impermanence of life, even of life's own slightly illusory quality.

Everett Zimmerman (essay date 1969)

SOURCE: "The Function of Parody in *Northanger Abbey*," in *Modern Language Quarterly,* Vol. XXX, 1969, pp. 53-63.

[*Here, Zimmerman maintains that* Northanger Abbey *both parodies and employs conventional elements of sentimental fiction.*]

Most studies of *Northanger Abbey* have noted that the central problem it poses for the critic is one of unity. In addition to dealing with Catherine Morland's adventures, the book parodies other novels and thus raises the question of the relationship of the parody to the total structure. The attempted solutions of this critical problem, many of them quite cogently argued, are almost exclusively attempts to show thematic relationships between the two elements—Catherine's adventures and the references to novels. But there is another dimension to the problem. Although thematic coherence is an element in unity, the parts of an individual work, or indeed of several quite different works, may cohere thematically without necessarily convincing the reader of their aesthetic unity. Despite the inevitable danger that discussion will lapse into the mere cataloguing of subjective reactions, the reader's response is relevant and must be examined.

Wayne Booth's concept of the implied reader [in *The Rhetoric of Fiction,* 1960] is a most useful attempt to direct the discussion toward the text, rather than exclu-

sively toward the reader's psyche: "The author creates, in short, an image of himself and another image of his reader; he makes his reader, as he makes his second self, and the most successful reading is one in which the created selves, author and reader, can find complete agreement." A reader, who may be far different from the person who is reading, is defined by the work. To comprehend the work, the person reading must, at least tentatively, accept the role offered him. To apprehend the work as an aesthetic unity, the person reading must be able and willing to become the reader implied by the work. If this created reader is muddled or inappropriate, the work, no matter how demonstrable its thematic coherence, will not have a unified effect.

In a discussion of the parody in *Northanger Abbey,* we are then obliged to ask the following questions: (1) Does the parody within the novel create a response consonant with the nonparodic elements and integral to a unified effect? (2) Is the reader implied by the parody consistent with the reader implied elsewhere? The mere fact that so much of the criticism recognizes a problem suggests that in the realm of response, outside the arguments of formal criticism, *Northanger Abbey* has not achieved a unified effect. In one of the more interesting discussions, Frank J. Kearful contends that the disunity is deliberate, that the book is a layering of satire and novel designed to discomfit the reader and reveal the unreality of all novels—including its own unreality. But this solution finds the unity in a critical argument, rather than in the book. If the work is part satire and part novel, and one is not subsumed in the other, then it must be conceded that the work will appear incoherent to the reader.

Failure to sense unity may, however, be the result of something extraneous to the work—some irrelevant attitude that prevents one from becoming the "implied reader" defined in the work. This problem arises most frequently with literature that requires one to recover historical information or attitudes before one can become an appropriate reader. In *Northanger Abbey* the parody implies an interest in the sentimental novel, which, though natural enough in a late eighteenth- or early nineteenth-century reader, the modern reader rarely has. Consequently, there is a tendency to interpret the parody as a sharper attack on sentimental fiction than is consonant with the entire structure of the book. Too often the modern assumption is that all parody, like burlesque, must ridicule its object. But Samuel Johnson's definition of parody in his *Dictionary*—"a kind of writing, in which the words of an author or his thoughts are taken, and by a slight change adapted to some new purpose"—does not imply that the effect must be derogatory to the work parodied. Although parody is usually assumed to be literary satire, it does not always function as satire. Sometimes it is a tribute, e.g., Fielding's parody of Cervantes in *Joseph Andrews.* And when parody criticizes aspects of literature, its thrust is not necessarily toward denying or destroying the appeal of the parodied literature. *Don Quixote,* for example, unmercifully exposes the excesses of some romances, but the narrative reworks romance patterns and, especially in the subplots, appeals to the same tastes as do the romances.

Although the central character is a buffoon, in the course of his ludicrous adventures he exemplifies the genuine values of chivalry. In short, the reader who responds most fully to *Don Quixote* is likely to be the lover of romances. The parody in Cervantes' novel allows the reader to enjoy what his critical faculties tell him to reject.

The parody in *Northanger Abbey* functions in a similar manner. It sometimes mocks conventional elements of sentimental fiction, but at the same time it creates and satisfies an interest in those conventions. The reader who consistently interprets the function of the parody as satiric will find the parody conflicting with, rather than elucidating, Catherine's adventures. For example, when Catherine and Mrs. Allen travel to Bath, "Neither robbers nor tempests befriended them, nor one lucky overturn to introduce them to the hero." After they arrive at Bath, Catherine has no acquaintance even in the midst of crowds (as Mrs. Allen repeatedly notes), and no young man "started with rapturous wonder on beholding her . . ." The references to the hackneyed devices of the sentimental novel are amusing, to be sure, but this is not to say that the reader of *Northanger Abbey* is to gain satisfaction from the heroine's *not* meeting the hero. Quietly and unobtrusively the narrator explains that shortly *after* the ball, Henry Tilney was introduced to Catherine by the master of ceremonies in the Lower Rooms. The parody arouses a conventional interest that is then satisfied in an unexpected way.

The early chapters of *Northanger Abbey* make clear that we are being given the etiology of a sentimental heroine. Although most of the information given about Catherine obscures her heroic qualities, the rhetorical function of this material is to make more prominent those few hints of her grander capabilities. In general, these chapters are a catalogue of how Catherine differs from the heroine, but buried in the opening chapter is the understated comment: "with all these symptoms of profligacy at ten years old, she had neither a bad heart nor a bad temper. . . ." The good heart is, of course, the essential and central quality of the true sentimental heroine, and, in case the reader misses the clue, the narrator addresses him directly at the beginning of Chapter II:

> In addition to what has been already said of Catherine Morland's personal and mental endowments, when about to be launched into all the difficulties and dangers of a six weeks' residence in Bath, it may be stated, for the reader's more certain information, lest the following pages should otherwise fail of giving any idea of what her character is meant to be; that her heart was affectionate, her disposition cheerful and open, without conceit or affectation of any kind—her manners just removed from the awkwardness and shyness of a girl; her person pleasing, and, when in good looks, pretty— and her mind about as ignorant and uninformed as the female mind at seventeen usually is.

Apart from the limitations of Catherine's beauty, this would be an accurate description of a heroine like Fanny Burney's *Evelina*. The narrator has made it difficult for Catherine not to be recognized as a potential heroine, but

because the language is understated and Catherine's ignorance is emphasized, the reader may continue to feel that he himself has ferreted out Catherine's heroic potentialities.

At the very beginning of the book, the reader is involved in the narrative. That Catherine is to be a heroine is asserted obliquely, but nevertheless clearly, in the first sentence: "No one who had ever seen Catherine Morland in her infancy, would have supposed her born to be an heroine." "No one . . . would have supposed" challenges the reader to sort out the hidden heroic qualities, and at the same time implies that Catherine's heroic stature will be confirmed later. The rhetorical function of the following list of conventions that she does not fulfill is to engage the reader in the attempt to comprehend those qualities that will eventually fit her to be a heroine. Thus the comedy lies in the juxtaposition of the mundane Catherine of childhood with the sentimental heroine, not in a catalogue of sentimental absurdities.

The reader's engagement in the narrative reaches such proportions that he becomes, in effect, the author's accomplice. After a one-paragraph description of the Thorpe family, the narrator comments:

> This brief account of the family is intended to supersede the necessity of a long and minute detail from Mrs. Thorpe herself, of her past adventures and sufferings, which might otherwise be expected to occupy the three or four following chapters; in which the worthlessness of lords and attornies might be set forth, and conversations, which had passed twenty years before, be minutely repeated.

It is assumed that the reader realizes the folly of pretending that conversations of twenty years ago can be repeated verbatim, recognizes that a long account from Mrs. Thorpe would be tedious, and participates in the author's decision to let the short account stand without amplification.

The involving aspects of the parody prepare the reader to deal with Catherine's later adventures. He is alerted to those conventions that will appear in revised form. Consider the introduction of Mrs. Allen:

> It is now expedient to give some description of Mrs. Allen, that the reader may be able to judge, in what manner her actions will hereafter tend to promote the general distress of the work, and how she will, probably, contribute to reduce poor Catherine to all the desperate wretchedness of which a last volume is capable—whether by her imprudence, vulgarity, or jealousy—whether by intercepting her letters, ruining her character, or turning her out of doors.

This description is "expedient" only if the reader understands the probabilities of a chaperon's behavior in a novel, but, if he does not, the information necessary to enable him to assume the role of an experienced reader is given. When applied to the dull Mrs. Allen, the conventional characteristics of the chaperon are comic; yet variations of the events alluded to reduce Catherine to wretchedness in the last volume. General Tilney, for a salient example, turns Catherine out of Northanger Abbey while she is under his protection.

The reader created in the early chapters will see Catherine as an ambiguous heroine—in some ways similar, in some ways superior, and in some ways inferior to the conventional heroine. She is frequently contrasted with the sentimental heroine so that the rationality of her responses may be set against the excesses of the heroine's behavior. When Henry Tilney returns to Bath, and Catherine first sees him with a young woman on his arm, the narrator suggests the possibilities of extravagant assumption and conduct open to the heroine of the sentimental novel— possibilities that do not even occur to Catherine. But the parody also suggests that Catherine is a drastically scaled down version of the heroine. When Henry Tilney visits Catherine's box at the theater, "it was agreed that the projected walk should be taken as soon as possible; and, setting aside the misery of his quitting their box, she was, upon the whole, left one of the happiest creatures in the world." Catherine's feelings are here described in the extravagant terms appropriate to a heroine like Evelina, who, when deserted in the theater by Lord Orville, is left to face the contempt of her relatives and the schemes of her would-be seducers. In the context of *Northanger Abbey,* however, the narrator's use of these extreme terms to describe Catherine's commonplace feelings emphasizes her ordinariness.

This later parody is less extensive than that at the opening of the book, but in its varying patterns it performs a similar function. Because Catherine and her adventures must be judged within the heroic context, it becomes increasingly apparent that the entire book is to be seen as a variation on sentimental patterns, different from, but also similar to, them. Everything must be evaluated in the context of the parody. But if the reader makes the simple assumption that the parody is a rejection of sentimental novels, he will be led to notice in Catherine's adventures only the contrasts with other fiction and will miss the significant similarities. To control the reader's responses to novels, to make him discriminate finely, Jane Austen includes direct comment on novels by both narrator and characters.

The defense of novels at the end of Chapter V and the conversation in Chapter VI are an excellent example of how comment by the narrator meshes with succeeding event to aid the reader in evaluating both character and novels. The defense of novels is an attack on the convention of attacking novels. Selected for praise are Fanny Burney and Maria Edgeworth, who wrote novels "in which the greatest powers of the mind are displayed, in which the most thorough knowledge of human nature, the happiest delineation of its varieties, the liveliest effusions of wit and humour are conveyed to the world in the best chosen language." Both women wrote novels of character in the Richardsonian tradition, but not novels primarily emphasizing external event in the manner of some of the

"horrid" Gothic novelists. The opening paragraph of Chapter VI links it to the preceding commentary on novels:

> The following conversation, which took place between the two friends in the Pump-room one morning, after an acquaintance of eight or nine days, is given as a specimen of their very warm attachment, and of the delicacy, discretion, originality of thought, and literary taste which marked the reasonableness of that attachment.

Isabella's use of novelistic clichés immediately betrays her shallowness. The novels she recommends to Catherine—beginning with *The Castle of Wolfenbach* and ending with *Horrid Mysteries*—show that her interest is primarily in the Gothic novel of event having little relation to a "thorough knowledge of human nature." Some of these novels combine the sentimental with the Gothic and deal extensively with the heroine's inner world as she undergoes her horrid experiences. Catherine and Isabella share an interest in *The Mysteries of Udolpho,* one of these sentimental-Gothic novels, but the fact that Catherine also enjoys *Sir Charles Grandison* shows that, unlike Isabella, she is interested in the kinds of novels recommended by the narrator. The values that the narrator shares with Catherine but not with Isabella are underlined when Isabella assumes, in her convention-bound manner, that Catherine's mother must object to novels. Catherine points out, however, that Mrs. Morland "very often reads *Sir Charles Grandison* herself."

What the reader is led to value in novels is a preparation for his evaluation of the events of *Northanger Abbey.* He must learn to look for significance not just in external event but in human nature, in the feelings underlying the event rather than in the event itself. Although the Northanger segment of the novel is often regarded as ineffective, it exemplifies these necessary discriminations between event and feeling.

To begin, one must concede a deficiency in the episode. Catherine's delusions about General Tilney are an inconsistency in characterization. The earlier Catherine is never seriously misled by her reading of fiction, and there is no adequate preparation for her believing, in sunlight as well as in storm, that General Tilney murdered his wife. But much of the episode is consistent and relevant in characterization, theme, and rhetoric.

Earlier, the convention of the quixotic heroine is parodied:

> The time of the two parties uniting in the Octagon Room being correctly adjusted, Catherine was then left to the luxury of a raised, restless, and frightened imagination over the pages of Udolpho, lost from all worldly concerns of dressing and dinner, incapable of soothing Mrs. Allen's fears on the delay of an expected dressmaker, and having only one minute in sixty to bestow even on the reflection of her own felicity, in being already engaged for the evening.

Mrs. Allen's interest in dress has already been ridiculed, and John Thorpe, Catherine's partner for the evening, has already been shown to be a boor. It is consistent with the structure of the book that after this parody Catherine should go through a version of the quixotic experience. And on her first night at the Abbey, she sees some of the stock Gothic props in her room, is frightened by a storm, and imagines Gothic horrors.

But also consistent with the structure of the book is the Gothic reality of her Northanger experience. Eleanor's coming to announce to Catherine that General Tilney has ordered her out of the house is described in full-blown Gothic:

> At that moment Catherine thought she heard her step in the gallery, and listened for its continuance; but all was silent. Scarcely, however, had she convicted her fancy of error, when the noise of something moving close to her door made her start; it seemed as if some one was touching the very doorway—and in another moment a slight motion of the lock proved that some hand must be on it. She trembled a little at the idea of any one's approaching so cautiously; but resolving not to be again overcome by trivial appearances of alarm, or misled by a raised imagination, she stepped quietly forward, and opened the door. Eleanor, and only Eleanor, stood there. Catherine's spirits however were tranquillized but for an instant, for Eleanor's cheeks were pale, and her manner greatly agitated.

The early part of the Northanger episode is a trivial, although amusing, reworking of the quixotic pattern because it touches Catherine's emotions in only a superficial way. But the subsequent reworking of the Gothic pattern is "mournfully superior in reality and substance." The wind, creaking floors, and moving locks are conventions taking on significance from the human emotions they touch. The reader is trained by Jane Austen's rhetoric to penetrate to what is important in Gothic and sentimental patterns—the human nature that is represented in them.

Like Catherine, the reader must learn to discriminate between surface and feeling. He must recognize that Catherine differs from a heroine only in superficial matters. Because she does assume the inappropriate conduct derived from romances, because she does not disguise her motivations in conventional language, she affirms the strength and validity of her own feelings. In this respect she contrasts with Isabella Thorpe, who, by foolishly adapting the language and conventions of the sentimental novel to inappropriate situations, rejects the personal feelings that provide the basic guide for the conduct of heroines of sensibility. By not assuming the heroic alternatives to her behavior, Catherine more nearly approximates the heroine than Isabella does by seizing these alternatives. The reader is not thwarted in his desire for a heroine; he is merely compelled to make careful discriminations in order to find her.

The novel does not attack Catherine's imagination; rather it attacks the selfishly circumscribed imagination represented by the Thorpes and General Tilney. Catherine's problem is not that of limiting her imagination, but rather of using it to discern what aspects of human nature lie beyond convention. The characters who are most understanding of human nature and who teach Catherine most—Henry and Eleanor Tilney—are associated with an imaginative world that the Thorpes do not comprehend. John Thorpe is early identified as entirely ignorant of novels, but Henry reads them avidly. Isabella likes Gothic novels, but, without attempting to read *Sir Charles Grandison,* decides that it is unreadable; Eleanor's tastes, far from being limited to Gothic novels, are so broad that they include even history. And in compensation for Catherine's aborted trip to Blaize Castle with the Thorpes, Henry initiates her into one of the pleasures of the sentimental heroine—the picturesque.

The parodic context for the narrative in *Northanger Abbey* determines the manner in which we can interpret the novel. Far from being extraneous, the parody interlocks with the narrative and creates the precise involvement that leads to an understanding of the characters and of the relevant novelistic traditions. The reader implied is appropriate and consistent. He will recognize Catherine as the heroine in an unheroic society, the heroine of sensibility in the midland counties of England. She is both a static heroine who steadfastly maintains the integrity of her own feelings and a developing character who is enlightened about the ways in which others use conventional outward expressions of feeling for unfeeling purposes. If we see the parody as part of Jane Austen's rhetoric and if we try to understand the reader implied by that rhetoric, we are likely to read the book from a perspective less distorted by twentieth-century assumptions.

When Jane Austen wrote *Northanger Abbey,* the sentimental novel had both proliferated and degenerated. Situations, characters, and language had hardened into stereotypes, and to escape the banal, novelists overinflated what was already inflated. In her *juvenilia* Jane Austen burlesqued these failings of popular fiction; in *Northanger Abbey* she attempts to resuscitate the fiction and certain values on which it is based. Sentimental ethics, as developed through Shaftesbury and others, were based on the assumption that impulses in the individual led not only to self-gratification, but also to the preservation of society: the "private affections" and "public affections" of which Shaftesbury wrote. But as the language of sentiment became widespread, it provided a convenient screen for even the most unfeeling and egocentric behavior. In *Northanger Abbey* Jane Austen disentangles true from false sensibility, and in doing so she both appeals to the interest in sentimental fiction and expresses contempt for the perversions of sentimental values in life and literature. The heroines of her later novels are also versions of the heroine of sensibility, but they have survived the age of sensibility. They struggle to exemplify values that their societies no longer wholeheartedly endorse, and they must fight a rearguard action to preserve these values. Jane Austen undertakes just such an action in *Northanger Abbey.*

A. N. Kaul (essay date 1970)

SOURCE: "Jane Austen," in *The Action of English Comedy: Studies in the Encounter of Abstraction and Experience from Shakespeare to Shaw,* Yale University Press, 1970, pp. 193-249.

[*In the following excerpt, Kaul characterizes* Northanger Abbey *as a novel of education with a somewhat formulaic comic quality.*]

Northanger Abbey is the story of a young girl's education, or rather her double education: first through a selective and highly self-conscious course of literary readings, and then through various experiences that teach her to differentiate the real from the bookish world and thus cause her to readjust the attitudes and expectations derived from literature. In the first chapter, which offers the early history of the heroine and which seems in many ways a simple piece of burlesque writing, Jane Austen is already working toward this double comic purpose. On the one hand we are given in Catherine Morland an ordinary girl, rather plain and tomboyish in childhood, with a commonplace family background which as little as her personal appearance can be said to mark her out as a future heroine of romance. Showing above all no aptitude for drawing or music or any of the other required accomplishments, her mind seems definitely "unpropitious for heroism"—up to the age of fifteen. But at fifteen appearances suddenly start mending, and Catherine, despite her disqualifications, considers herself from this point on as avowedly "in training for a heroine." She undertakes a preliminary study of the appropriate literature and is soon determined, not unlike the heroine of *Love and Freindship,* to have the world live up to the romance she has developed out of her reading. She knows that the neighborhood contains neither lords nor baronets and that not even young men of mysterious origin or ordinary foundlings are to be found anywhere within reach. "But when a young lady is to be a heroine, the perverseness of forty surrounding families cannot prevent her. Something must and will happen to throw a hero in her way."

The emphasis here, as elsewhere in the novel, falls on the mind—on its vulnerability to illusion even in the most unlikely external circumstances. Catherine Morland's mind is a tabula rasa, a fact Jane Austen underlines before embarking on the story proper in the following chapter. Summing up her heroine's "personal and mental endowments, when about to be launched into all the difficulties and dangers of a six weeks' residence in Bath," she observes that although Catherine's "heart was affectionate, her disposition cheerful and open, without conceit or affectation of any kind," her mind was "about as ignorant and uninformed as the female mind at seventeen usually is." What the generalized comment about the female mind at seventeen makes clear is that Catherine Morland is to be regarded not as a subject for burlesque or satire, but essentially as a representative comic heroine—someone who is neither freakish nor abnormal, but rather typical. She is, however, also typical in a less universal and more important sense: she embodies the dangers of a cultural

situation in which the youthful mind is apt to be seduced by a peculiarly perverse variety of romantic delusion. This is in fact what happens to Catherine as soon as she steps into the fashionable world of Bath. But if a basically good-natured and unaffected girl like Catherine can so easily fall prey to well-cultivated illusions, her sound temperament also contains the promise of eventual awakening and the possibility of a second and more sound education. This is why Jane Austen gives us a stage-by-stage history of her heroine's early years in the preparatory first chapter. And herein we see, too, the advantage of an omniscient point of view for a comic novel, a point of view that can surround the consciousness of a character with a larger consciousness, aware from the beginning of more than is the character himself. Thus unlike *Love and Freindship,* which is told in letters by the heroine throughout, *Northanger Abbey* is not locked within the mind of a deluded character. We are rather shown Catherine Morland in the process of deluding herself, being made witness at the same time to her normalcy in other ways, so that for us her self-deception carries at each stage its own seeds of final undeception.

Thus we are not surprised when, much later in the novel—at the height of the Bath adventure—the author assures us that Catherine, for all her submission to romance, still possessed feelings "rather natural than heroic." By this time, however, there is little need to direct our attention through authorial comment. For with Catherine's arrival at Bath and her entering into relationships with the novel's two other principal characters, the conflict between nature and heroism becomes a dramatic issue. Mrs. Allen, under whose protection the girl has come to Bath, is herself characterized by total "vacancy of mind, and incapacity for thinking." The charge of educating Catherine's mind falls accordingly to her two new acquaintances: Isabella Thorpe, the "friend," who becomes the abettor of romantic illusion; and Henry Tilney, the potential lover, who assumes early the office of mildly but constantly ridiculing the visions of romance. The friend and the lover thus pull their weight in opposed directions.

To a large extent the plot turns on romance of the Gothic variety. Under Isabella's tutorship Catherine comes readily to believe that she could happily spend her whole life reading *Udolpho,* and very soon she learns to look upon the world as a scene expressly arranged for the purpose of corroborating the truth of Mrs. Radcliffe's imagination. She welcomes an excursion to Blaize Castle as an opportunity for "exploring an edifice like Udolpho," but this is only a preparatory touch for her later visit to Northanger Abbey, the family-seat of the Tilneys—a visit during which she develops around the old house a complete history of Gothic deeds involving her host, General Tilney, as the villain and his dead wife as the victim. This leads her to a series of blunders followed by humiliating discoveries, such as the well-known midnight perusal of a manuscript which Catherine takes for a record of secret crimes committed and suffered in the Abbey but which on examination turns out to be an inventory of linen: if "the evidence of sight might be trusted," actually a "washing-bill." And, of course, there is Henry Tilney's equally well-known final admonition of Catherine which brings this line of adventure to an end:

> Consult your own understanding, your own sense of the probable, your own observation of what is passing around you. Does our education prepare us for such atrocities? Do our laws connive at them? Could they be perpetrated without being known in a country like this, where social and literary intercourse is on such a footing? . . . Dearest Miss Morland, what ideas have you been admitting?

Among the many ironies of this passage, the one that has escaped attention is the most obvious and telling one: namely, Catherine's "education" and "social and literary intercourse" are precisely the factors that have paved the way to the trap into which she has fallen. Her disillusionment, however, is now complete: "The visions of romance were over. Catherine was completely awakened."

Yet the Gothic self-deceptions are not nearly so important as the deceptions of another variety—the deceptions of sensibility—with which they are connected in the novel. This aspect of romance cuts more vitally into Catherine's story, and while Isabella Thorpe and Henry Tilney remain the two other principal actors, this part of the story involves in one way or another the entire cast of characters. In it, furthermore, the roles of Isabella and Henry are not only opposed to each other but also doubled and at the same time reversed. As a sentimental tutor, Isabella is the Laura of *Love and Friendship* transferred from the world of burlesque to that of comedy. Her overt function is the same: to educate Catherine "in the finesse of love" and "the duties of friendship." Of course, in this respect Catherine is never quite as taken in as she is in the matter of *Udolpho*. The very fact that she can enter into a relationship with Henry Tilney assures us of her natural resistance to the attitudes of a sentimental heroine. The remark already cited about her being "rather natural than heroic" is made in relation to her feelings for Henry. Considering that, as Jane Austen tells us a little later, even her "passion for ancient edifices was next in degree to her passion for Henry Tilney," it is not surprising that given his presence on the scene, the passion for sensibility never takes firm root. As a matter of fact, Henry precedes Isabella in Catherine's acquaintance and has already burlesqued the fashionable sentimental attitudes in his first meeting with her, a short time before Isabella can start advocating them. Nevertheless in the end it is Isabella who first opens Catherine's eyes to that which "the finesse of love" and "the duties of friendship" are really meant to conceal: money and the matrimonial maneuver. For, profuse as have been her professions of friendship for Catherine and love for Catherine's brother, Isabella calmly throws both overboard the moment she fancies herself within reach of a better prospect—Captain Tilney. Although earlier she had held up the ideal of love with as little cash to interfere as possible—the "ecstasy" of living in a "cottage in some retired village"—she now concedes with a facility that astonishes poor Catherine that "after all that romancers may say, there is no doing without money."

This is Catherine's first lesson in the realities of bourgeois life, and it is offered to her by the "romantic" Isabella Thorpe. Of course she learns how timely and plausible a lesson it has been when General Tilney—hitherto a model of courtly grace and hospitality—unceremoniously throws her out of the Abbey. This is the climax of the story—the true surprise of its surprise ending. Catherine's fate now seems identical with that of her brother, and for the same reason. The General, it turns out, had sought and entertained her as a suitable match for his son; but happening to discover his mistake in her, finding out that in fact she was "guilty . . . of being less rich than he had supposed," he now sends her packing with brutal abruptness. Her brother's situation had already caused the "anxieties of common life" to supersede "the alarms of romance" in Catherine's mind; her own present case drives the point home—"Yet how different now the source of her inquietude . . . how mournfully superior in reality and substance! Her anxiety had foundation in fact, her fears in probability."

By thus translating Gothic terror into real-life terms, Jane Austen removes its comforting quality of vicarious indulgence. "Oh! Mr. Tilney, how frightful! This is just like a book! But it cannot really happen to me," Catherine exclaims to Henry's playful description of Northanger Abbey and "the horrors that a building such as 'what one reads about' may produce." But in a surprising and to her unexpected—and therefore more terrifying—way, it does happen to her. She had always wondered about General Tilney, knowing that something "was certainly to be concealed," only to dissipate in Gothic fantasy rather than try to understand this persistent feeling caused by the General. The monster of avarice, when she finally recognizes him, turns out to be as cruel and ruthless as any monster she had imagined, and not half so remote. In the end she realizes that there was nothing absurd about her early conjunction of "Tilneys and trap-doors" except the notion she then had of traps. Otherwise, "in suspecting General Tilney of either murdering or shutting up his wife, she had scarcely sinned against his character or magnified his cruelty."

Yet this is not the last word of Catherine's story. While the sentimental Isabella and the chivalric General educate her liberally in the realities of life, it remains for the antiheroic Henry to offer himself as a figure of romance—true-life romance as opposed to the make-believe finesse of love. For though money and prudence rule the world, they do not rule it to the total exclusion of more disinterested feelings. A Henry Tilney may prove himself a hero after all by standing up to his father, by refusing to accompany him to Herefordshire in pursuit of prudential matrimony, and by quietly presenting himself instead at the Morland parsonage. Certainly in the novel Henry's reality is as indubitable as that of the General, and on the whole so is the reality of the relationship that Jane Austen develops between him and Catherine. In this respect "the tell-tale compression" (according to Jane Austen herself) of the last pages, the "hastening together to perfect felicity," can create a false impression. The final chapter of *Northanger Abbey*, like the final chapter of *Mansfield*

Park, is a quick winding-up. Its jauntiness is directed not so much at what is being wound up as at the custom and necessity of literary windings-up in general. It certainly should not be allowed to wipe out at one stroke all that has been shown as happening between Henry and Catherine. What has developed between them is not a great love—suspect as all great loves would be in the context—but a quiet and convincing affection appropriate to the general purpose of the novel.

The real weakness of the novel lies in this very general purpose. It is not an absolute but only a relative weakness. The novel would have sufficed to make the literary fortune of a lesser comic writer, if a lesser comic writer could possibly have written it. It is weak only as a Jane Austen comedy, being too directly and heavily involved with books, too closely and crudely dependent upon the presence of the source of its inspiration—sent into the world powerless, as it were, to dispense with its umbilical cord. Or, to change the metaphor, it may be regarded as the chrysalis of Jane Austen's comedy: an enormous step forward from burlesque-parody, but still a work whose full effect demands a visible correspondence to a literary formula and whose comic quality is therefore itself a little too formulaic. . . .

Robert Kiely (essay date 1972)

SOURCE: *"Northanger Abbey:* Jane Austen," in *The Romantic Novel in England,* Harvard University Press, 1972, pp. 118-35.

[*In the excerpt below, Kiely focuses on the thematic importance of language in* Northanger Abbey.]

Jane Austen thought the capabilities of language, correctly used, considerable, and early in *Northanger Abbey* she opens her gentle assault on romantic fiction with a defense of the novel:

> I will not adopt that ungenerous and impolitic custom so common with novel writers, of degrading by their contemptuous censure the very performances, to the number of which they are themselves adding—joining with their greatest enemies in bestowing the harshest epithets on such works, and scarcely ever permitting them to be read by their own heroine, who, if she accidentally take up a novel, is sure to turn over its insipid pages with disgust. [A novel at its best can be a] work in which the greatest powers of the mind are displayed, in which the most thorough knowledge of human nature, the happiest delineation of its varieties, the liveliest effusions of wit and humor are conveyed to the world in the best chosen language.

That is what a novel *might* be. But it is clear from the start that Catherine Morland, the heroine of *Northanger Abbey,* while an enthusiastic reader of novels, admires that class of fiction in which human nature, wit, and choice language are secondary considerations. Catherine Morland is an admirer of Ann Radcliffe. She reads, not to be instructed or entertained, but to be frightened.

Northanger Abbey embraces two worlds—the world of Catherine's subjective fancy and that of social convention as it is interpreted primarily by Henry Tilney. As nearly all critics of the novel have recognized, the book is, because of this juxtaposition of worlds, part parody romance and part realistic novel. But what may appear as a division of purpose—an early and therefore forgivable lapse on Austen's part—is really a precise comic analogue to a genre which was itself divided. By contrasting Bath to the Abbey, Austen is not doing anything that Radcliffe, Godwin, and Lewis had not done before her in placing rational, social, daylight worlds against dark, subjective prisons. If Catherine's "prison" is of her own making, so, to a large extent, were those of Emily St. Aubert, Caleb Williams, and Ambrosio.

There *is* parody in *Northanger Abbey,* and though it is broader in the romance sections, it pervades both worlds, romantic and realistic, without totally rejecting either. The book is entertaining, and it was obviously Austen's purpose to ridicule the excesses of an untutored imagination. But though she shows us that Catherine's Gothic dreams are derived from false suspicions and inadequate information, Austen does not pretend that the collision of a susceptible mind with the world of hard reality is a false situation or even a wholly ludicrous one. *Northanger Abbey* is split in a way familiar to a close reader of romantic novels and it shows, despite its surface frivolity, that Austen understood the source and nature of that division very well.

Young, impressionable, good-hearted and a little simple-minded, Catherine imagines herself a romantic heroine in a world fraught with Gothic possibilities. Unlike Ann Radcliffe, however, Jane Austen does not allow her heroine's emotions to dominate the vision of reality presented to the reader. On the contrary, through the speeches of other characters and through the steady narrative voice of the author, the reader is constantly shown a world which corresponds in almost no way to the apprehensions of the heroine. Having set down her copy of *The Mysteries of Udolpho* to attend a ball during her visit to Bath, Catherine finds sufficient cause for romantic musings when momentarily "abandoned" by her dancing partner:

> To be disgraced in the eye of the world, to wear the appearance of infamy while her heart is all purity, her actions all innocence, and the misconduct of another the true source of her debasement, is one of those circumstances which peculiarly belong to the heroine's life.

That the language is far in excess of what the situation justifies is obvious, but Jane Austen also shows that it is not even an apt indication of the girl's own feelings. For within ten minutes she is roused out of her "humiliation" by the approach of another and preferable partner. The episode is trivial and amusing, but through it Jane Austen demonstrates how language can exceed as well as fall short of human experience. There are words to describe balls at Bath and the disappointment of young ladies who have not been asked to dance, but Catherine's reading habits have not helped her to find them.

But if Catherine's misuse of language is the innocent result of inexperience and undiscriminating susceptibility to romantic fiction, there are other examples of exaggerated language which are of less innocent origin. The first acquaintance Catherine makes at Bath is Isabella Thorpe, an attractive and comparatively sophisticated girl, who overwhelms her new friend with repeated professions of undying devotion and sisterly affection. It soon becomes clear to the reader, if not to Catherine, that Isabella overestimates the Morlands' wealth and hopes to marry Catherine's brother James. The more convinced she becomes of the family's wealth, the more extravagant become her praises of the beauty and brilliance of the relatively plain and intellectually unexceptional Catherine. At first, Catherine takes her friend's exaggerations as signs of her romantic nature and high spirits. For Isabella, the most ordinary things, when associated in any way with the Morland family, become "inconceivable, incredible, impossible"; to be separated from her friend for an afternoon seems "ages"; to wish to question her about her brother is to have "thousands of things to say to her"; to take leave of her until the next morning is to part in "utter despondency."

Even Catherine eventually becomes aware that Isabella's language, far from being the spontaneous overflow of a brimming heart, is a consciously manipulated instrument with which she attempts to satisfy herself while seeming to think of others. One day when Isabella has her mind set on taking a ride with Catherine and her brother, she is irritated to learn that Catherine has already promised to spend the day with other friends. She urges her to do what "would be so easy," that is, tell them that she had "just been reminded of a prior engagement." "No, it would not be easy," answers Catherine. "I could not do it. There has been no prior engagement." Carelessness about the correspondence between words and events can be, as Catherine realizes, a form of dishonesty. Truth, as understood by Jane Austen, is not determined merely by the urges of the ego, but by the discernible events of a world outside the self. If some of those events are beyond mortal powers of articulation, others are perfectly capable of being named. One danger of romantic scorn for the reliability of words is that it introduces confusion where there is none, creates a muddle for the innocent and a camouflage for the disingenuous.

Two other examples of the mismanagement of words—without benefit of Radcliffean aura—are provided by Catherine's companion and hostess at Bath, Mrs. Allen, and Isabella's braggart brother John. Both are vain and dull-witted characters who demonstrate the folly, selfishness, and tedium of using words as adornments of the self rather than as means of communication. Mrs. Allen has one subject, fashion, and nearly all of her talk, wherever it begins, comes around eventually to the tilt of her bonnet or the state of her muslin. While she is a relatively harmless and comic character, she is also incapable of doing good. She cannot comfort Catherine nor serve as a moral guide, because she cannot think of her except as the wearer of so many yards

of material. When Catherine asks her opinion about the correctness of riding in an open carriage with a man to whom one is not engaged, Mrs. Allen displays the limit of her understanding and sympathy: "Open carriages are nasty things. A clean gown is not five minutes wear in them. You are splashed getting in and getting out; and the wind takes your hair and your bonnet in every direction. I hate an open carriage myself."

John Thorpe is a vulgarized, stupider version of his sister. Also thinking the Morlands are wealthy, he continually attempts to impress and flatter Catherine. He boasts about his horses, his carriage, his drinking parties at Oxford, repeats and contradicts himself, and punctuates every other sentence with an oath. Words fail him only when he tries to enumerate Catherine's qualities:

> "You have more good-nature and all that, than anybody living I believe. A monstrous deal of good-nature, and it is not only good-nature, but you have so much, so much of everything; and then you have such—upon my soul I do not know any body like you."

The humor of the scene stems from the fact that the missing word for which Thorpe seems to be groping is all too plain. It is not language which fails the man, but the man who fails language, and in doing so reveals his want of honesty, affection, and wit along with his want of words. Catherine, too, at this relatively early point in the novel may be said to fail language—she does not use words precisely and does not easily see through the muddled jargon of the Thorpes. But her failure is not of a moral sort. She is merely ignorant. By learning the ways of words, she will gradually come to know more of the world and of herself.

Her teachers are Eleanor Tilney and, more particularly, Eleanor's brother Henry, two conventional, yet sincere, charming, and even noble persons. Through them—and especially through the way they speak—Jane Austen makes an impressive defense of social convention and shows the egotism and futility of ignoring or scorning it. When Catherine and Eleanor first meet, they exchange the usual pleasantries, but after the absurd exclamations of Isabella Thorpe, polite commonplaces seem almost rich with meaning. At least, they convey the idea that two young ladies are happy to have met and are content in one another's company, though neither may find the other, after five minutes, dearer than her own life, the sweetest creature she ever saw, "amazingly" clever, ravishing, clairvoyant, in short, a combination of virtues altogether "inconceivable, incredible, impossible." In the company of Eleanor Tilney, Catherine does not reach for superlatives nor is she showered with them. Jane Austen merely tells us that they met with "civility" and "good will":

> And though in all probability not an observation was made, nor an expression used by either which had not been made and used some thousands of times before, under that roof, in every Bath season, yet the merit of their being spoken with simplicity and truth, and without personal conceit, might be something uncommon.

Catherine's most instructive teacher is Eleanor's brother Henry, the hero of the novel. He is, in nearly all respects, the reverse of the male protagonist of a romantic novel. He is at home in society, a minister and country gentleman, cheerful-natured, an obedient son and courteous brother, well-educated, slightly pedantic, presentable but not striking, intelligent but not a genius. His courtship of Catherine takes the form of a series of lessons in semantics, through which he reveals his own affection for her and teaches her to judge and discriminate among words as an aid in judging and discriminating among people and circumstances.

Henry's first lesson stresses the importance of language as a conventional approximation of reality, an artificial convenience which can express much so long as it is not confused with the reality itself. He draws a comparison between a dance and a marriage which demonstrates the metaphorical nature of language while defining the necessarily conventional basis of all social intercourse:

> "We have entered into a contract of mutual agreeableness for the space of an evening, and all our agreeableness belongs solely to each other for that time. Nobody can fasten themselves on the notice of one, without injuring the rights of the other. I consider a country-dance as an emblem of marriage. Fidelity and complaisance are the principal duties of both; and those men who do not choose to dance or marry themselves, have no business with the partners or wives of their neighbors."

> "But they are such very different things!—"

> "That you think they cannot be compared together."

> "To be sure not. People that marry can never part, but must go and keep house together. People that dance, only stand opposite each other in a long room for half an hour."

For the moment, Catherine has missed the point of the lesson as well as the bantering tone of the teacher. But Jane Austen's hero, thinking it unnecessary to speak up for order, speaks up instead for the importance of recognizing its essential components. For Catherine, marriage is marriage and dancing is dancing. Like most other things in her mind, they have no connection. Different names for different things with no apparent basis for comparison. Yet Tilney has begun to show that the most trivial as well as some of the most important social actions involve, in one way or another, making contracts which involve rights, duties, and most un-Godwinian of all, voluntary mutual conformity. The characters in *Northanger Abbey,* as in all of Jane Austen's novels, are constantly "engaging" themselves to others, to walk, to dine, to visit, to marry. And the worst thing a person can do is to enter into an engagement dishonestly—like Isabella with James Morland—or to break it without sufficient cause—again like Isabella, or like General Tilney when he expels Catherine from his house after having invited her to stay as long as she pleased.

In the next lesson, Henry attempts to show that language too is a kind of "contract of mutual agreeableness" with principles and rules which ought to govern those who "engage" to use it in the presence of others. Though he is a minister, it is not the meditational but the conversational precision of Catherine which he seeks to improve. Like Isabella, though without her ulterior motives, Catherine tends to use words like "amazing," "horrid," and "tremendous" to describe matters of little consequence. One day, while walking with Henry Eleanor Tilney, she asks Henry if he does not think *The Mysteries of Udolpho* "the nicest book in the world."

> "The nicest;—by which I suppose you mean the neatest. That must depend upon the binding."

> "Henry," said Miss Tilney, "you are very impertinent. Miss Morland, he is treating you exactly as he does his sister. He is forever finding fault with me, for some incorrectness of language, and now he is taking the same liberty with you. The word 'nicest,' as you used it, did not suit him; and you had better change it as soon as you can, or we shall be overpowered with Johnson and Blair all the rest of the way."

> "I am sure," cried Catherine; "I did not mean to say anything wrong; but it *is* a nice book, and why should not I call it so?"

> "Very true," said Henry, "and this is a very nice day, and we are taking a very nice walk, and you are two very nice young ladies. Oh! it is a very nice word indeed! It does for everything."

In a world of Catherine Morlands—to say nothing of Isabella and John Thorpes—Henry's schoolmarmish manner seems forgivable if not heroic. Having demonstrated something of the analogical nature of language in his first lesson, Tilney proceeds to argue that a verbal representation of reality—even if it cannot reproduce that reality to perfection—need not miss it by a mile. Human experience is rich and varied, but Jane Austen and her hero, both admirers of Dr. Johnson, could not agree that the English language was without resources to describe a considerable portion of it. One remedy for speechlessness or, what amounts to the same thing, the indiscriminate use of a few words, is a larger vocabulary—a mind in touch with other minds through the conventional but many-faceted medium of language.

Of course, a good heart is essential, for, without it, language, however precise, can become a fashion like any other, vain, inconsequential, and inert, a piece of mental apparel to be put on and off without feeling or taste. Right feelings we know Catherine possesses: Jane Austen explains that though she often "knew not what to say and her eloquence was only in her eyes . . . the eight parts of speech shone out most expressively, and [one] could combine them with ease." But taste, or the ability to see connections and to make distinctions, Catherine lacks from want of instruction and practice. When Isabella Thorpe decides, for example, to wear exactly the same dress as

Catherine at a ball so that the men will take notice of them both, Catherine does not see it as a tasteless and unfeeling maneuver to flatter and outshine her at the same time. Isabella borrows styles in dresses, as in words, without regard to elegance or sensitivity to the feelings of others, but to gratify a momentary vanity. She lives from whim to whim and from day to day, changing her manners and moods as the wind blows, and following no governing principle beyond that of "improving her situation." She is without taste for the same reason that, on another level, she is without morality: she does not make coherent connections between herself and other people; between her words and her actions, or even among her own utterances, which Catherine eventually recognizes as a tissue of "inconsistencies" and "contradictions."

Unlike Isabella's, most of Catherine's mistakes originate from an excessively high opinion of nearly everyone. Still, there is a narrowness, a kind of selfishness, even in this, for it stems from judging the world only in terms of the self rather than in relation to a larger social context. Catherine always means what she says, even when her words are not well chosen, and she assumes therefore that everyone else is the same. Tilney's third lesson, then, is an attempt to urge Catherine to weigh words against the habits and actions of the speaker rather than simply against her own feelings. When she attributes Henry's brother's flirtatious interest in Isabella to his "good-nature," Henry tries to show her the basis of the error:

> "With you, it is not: How is such a one likely to be influenced? What is the inducement most likely to act upon such a person's feelings, age, situation, and probable habits of life considered?—but how should *I* be influenced, what would be *my* inducement in acting so and so?"
>
> "I do not understand you."
>
> "Then we are on very unequal terms, for I understand you perfectly well."
>
> "Me?—yes; I cannot speak well enough to be unintelligible."
>
> "Bravo!—an excellent satire on modern language."

Catherine has unwittingly put her finger on one of the most important points that Henry has been trying to make: that language is worthless if not intelligible. But she has not yet seen that the "intelligibility" of words depends upon several things, including their emblematic relationship to external reality, their logical relationship to one another, their personal relationship to the speaker, and their circumstantial relationship to the one being addressed. Until she can see the importance of these relationships she will continue to misuse words and misjudge people.

Jane Austen realizes that, though Henry Tilney is an excellent teacher, his lessons are too abstract and subtle to have immediate effect on his pupil. Catherine needs a concrete confrontation with the errors of her ways and the

applicability of his theories. Her opportunity comes when General Tilney, the widowed father of Eleanor and Henry, invites Catherine to visit their country house, Northanger Abbey. Already fond of the brother and sister, and intrigued by the thought of living in a reconstructed Gothic ruin, Catherine accepts. Actually, the house is bright, cheerful, and Gothic only in a few minor details, but Catherine is hardly in it before she begins imagining herself in the role of a Radcliffean heroine. She digs for ancient parchments in chests and cabinets, lies awake trembling on windy nights, and deduces, from the strict and domineering manner of the General, that he must have persecuted his wife and sealed her up in some hidden chamber of the house until she went mad or died.

Determined to get to the bottom of the "mystery" and expose the General to justice, Catherine resolves to visit the bedroom where Mrs. Tilney is said to have died of a fever nine years earlier. All the more suspicious because the General does not show her this room when giving a tour of the house, Catherine ventures to it alone one afternoon before tea, expecting she hardly knows what "gloomy objects," what "proofs" of the General's cruelty. She finds, instead, a "well-proportioned apartment, an handsome dimity bed, arranged as unoccupied with an housemaid's care, a bright Bath stove, mahogany wardrobes and neatly painted chairs on which the warm beams of a western sun gaily poured through two sash windows!" Disappointed and ashamed, she dashes out into the hall where she meets Henry and confesses her suspicion, which he greets with mild dismay and a rational explanation.

The point, of course, is that Mrs. Tilney's death is a subject about which Catherine really has nothing to say. It is both amusing and rather touching that she should crave so frantically to "explain"—even in absurd terms—the death of her friends' mother. It is the only subject in the novel which Jane Austen seems to admit is "beyond words." The image of death—one of the rare examples in all of Austen's works—is not a blood-stained dagger or a murky chamber, but "unoccupied" bed in a perfectly neat, ordinary, though empty room. Mrs. Tilney dead is Mrs. Tilney "not present," a vacancy except in the memory of her family. Neither Catherine Morland nor the reader has cause or capacity to say anything more about her. And in the world of Jane Austen, the best thing to do when one has nothing to say—that is, nothing which can add to the instruction or comfort of others—is not to lament the impotence of words, but to turn to subjects where they can be of some use.

If, for example, Catherine had devoted the time spent wondering about the late Mrs. Tilney in speaking to and, above all, listening to General Tilney, she might have deduced, not that he was an English Montoni, but a prosperous parent with military fondness for order and obedience, and a tendency to petulance when his dinner was not served on time. She might further have deduced, from his comments about his house, his son, and her family (which he has never met), that he thinks her a good match for Henry and, for some reason, imagines her wealthier than she is. General Tilney is a quick-tempered snob, not a murderer, but Catherine learns that these unsensational vices are quite enough to cause her a kind of pain which has nothing to do with old parchments or phantom footsteps. When the General conveys through his daughter that Catherine must terminate her visit and return unaccompanied to her parents' home, she suffers genuine anguish for the first time in the novel. In comparing the distress of her first and last nights at Northanger Abbey, Catherine finally perceives distinctions of the sort Henry Tilney had tried to show her from the beginning:

> That room, in which her disturbed imagination had tormented her on her first arrival, was again the scene of agitated spirits and unquiet slumbers. Yet how different now the source of her inquietude . . . Her anxiety had foundation in fact, her fears in probability; and with a mind so occupied in the contemplation of actual and natural evil, the solitude of her situation, the darkness of her chamber, the antiquity of the building were felt and considered without the smallest emotion.

Though Catherine is not altogether sure why the General is angry with her, she realizes that his rude termination of her visit is an "evil" more immediate than the sort by Mrs. Radcliffe. His sudden breaking of a social engagement is both cause and symbol of serious ruptures in the life of Catherine, of her friendship with Eleanor and her love for Henry. Catherine learns from the General's treatment, that a human being need not be a murderer or rapist to do harm. Later, it turns out that John Thorpe, who had originally exaggerated Catherine's wealth to the General, had also informed him, upon seeing his own suit discouraged, that she was an opportunist from a family of scheming paupers. Henry finally clears away the confusion, apologizes to Catherine and her family, secures his father's grudging consent, and marries his well-instructed pupil.

It may be argued that, in dismissing physical violence and emotional extremes from her novels, Jane Austen too artificially limits, not only the size of her own canvas, but, by implication, the range of describable reality; that in a novel like *Northanger Abbey,* she seems to be saying, not simply, "I choose to write about 'this' because it is what I know," but "I do not choose to write about 'that' because it is silly, unimportant, or unreal."

Though by no means her richest or greatest work, *Northanger Abbey* is perhaps the most useful of her novels to consider in a discussion of this problem. It is more than a joke at the expense of Ann Radcliffe. Aside from the epistolary parody, *Love and Friendship,* it is the one sustained and explicit example we have of Jane Austen's reaction to the subject matter and technical devices common to much romantic fiction. As for subject matter, our insight into Jane Austen's attitude comes, as usual, from a speech of Henry Tilney's. When Catherine blurts out her suspicion that his father is a murderer, Henry reacts with characteristic logic:

> "Dear Miss Morland, consider the dreadful nature of the suspicions you have entertained. What have you been judging from? Remember the country and the age in which we live. Remember that we are English, that we are Christians . . . Does our education prepare us for such atrocities? Do our laws connive at them? Could they be perpetrated without being known in a country like this, where social and literary intercourse is on such a footing?"

. . . [If] we take Tilney's dismay at face value, we have neither followed the advice he gave Catherine to judge a person's words in relation to his "feelings, age, situation, and probable habits of life," nor have we understood the extent to which Austen's irony enlarges possibilities even at the expense of her own heroes and heroines. Tilney himself is not too perfect to fall into priggish overstatement which reveals the limitation of his otherwise "nice" perceptions. That Catherine's particular suspicions are without substantial cause or probability is evident, but that a concealed murder is unthinkable in Christian England is by no means so.

If Catherine's behavior has often shown ignorance of the value of social and verbal convention, Henry—like his father, though with less rigidity—shows in this speech the absurdity of overreliance on conventional assumptions. True, Catherine is shown to be foolish to have mistaken the world for a Gothic romance, but then Jane Austen does not quite let her hero get away with endowing his countrymen and era with all the virtues of reason and self-control. In fact, she emphasizes the silliness of Henry's speech by making Catherine believe it wholeheartedly, just as she had believed what was contrary to it three minutes before. Later, in the privacy of her room, she meditates and elaborates upon her new-found wisdom: "Among the Alps and Pyrenees, perhaps, there were no mixed characters. There, such as were not as spotless as an angel, might have the dispositions of a fiend. But in England it was not so; among the English, she believed, in their hearts and habits, there was a general though unequal mixture of good and bad."

By viewing her hero's complacency ironically, Austen reveals that her own had its bounds. Her circumvention of the dark and "large" themes characteristic of romantic fiction, represents, not a failure to see all painful realities, but one way of acknowledging their force. Like her favorite, Dr. Johnson, her representations of rational order often derive their vigor from a vivid sense of the alternatives. True, those alternatives were not madness or violent death, but isolation, sterility, the sense of a life without security, affection, or use. Yet they were no less desperate for being unsensational.

What Johnson achieved through constant inquiry and argument, Jane Austen achieved in her own way through irony: elasticity within a convention. "Freedom" is not a word she uses very often, whereas "grace" is everywhere in her fiction. As she demonstrates in *Northanger Abbey* and all of her other novels, an ironical vision is cynical only when the conventional forms employed are thought to be without value and are manipulated for purposes contrary to mutual "convenience." As Henry Tilney sees, at least most of the time, where more than one person is involved, conventional forms are necessary stays against intellectual confusion and moral riot. They are, in the literal sense, guardians of sanity. He also sees that any convention—verbal or social—insofar as it is a sign of a "coming together," must involve compromise and never can, under any conceivable circumstance, suit all the peculiarities and complexities of a single human being. Austen's—and to some degree, Tilney's—recognition of the importance of the individual sensibility and its inevitably imperfect adjustment to established form is one source of the ironic tone of the novel.

Henry Tilney, when not lapsing into priggishness, speaks with a witty lightness which shows that he can appreciate a convention and express himself through it without letting it manipulate, rigidify, and annihilate his human nature. His realm is not a prison cell but a ballroom, and

---

Duckworth on Catherine's moral growth:

Northanger Abbey, while it does not reflect the same persistent awareness of an economically debased society, takes its own close look at the conditions of social existence. As well as being a response to the Gothic novel, it is, to borrow Malcolm Bradbury's phrase describing E. M. Forster's fiction, a "sociomoral" novel, and in her description of Catherine, Jane Austen, provides an early attempt at defining proper moral behavior in the face of a largely immoral world. In describing Catherine's journey from Fullerton to Bath, to Northanger, and then back to Fullerton, Jane Austen follows the pattern of the English novel of education in which, from Defoe and Fielding onward, movement through space has accompanied a moral enlightenment on the part of the protagonist. In Catherine's case, there is little psychological development, and while this is not a *sine qua non* of the novel of education—Tom Jones undergoes little psychological change—it becomes in *Northanger Abbey* a matter of dissatisfaction both for the reader and, I think, for the author. . . .

But if Jane Austen fails structurally and thematically to combine a novel of manners and a literary response to the Gothic novel, we should nevertheless be aware of her positive moral intentions in *Northanger Abbey*. An examination of the heroine's experience in Bath with the Thorpes and at Northanger with Henry Tilney reveals Jane Austen's direction, even if the moral journey is not completed satisfactorily.

Alistair M. Duckworth, The Improvement of the Estate: A Study of Jane Austen's Novels, *The John Hopkins Press, 1971.*

---

his wish is not to escape it but to master the rules and share their benefits with others. Convinced that some form is necessary and that no form suits all temperaments, he is not interested—as so many romantic heroes are—in changing the laws of society or nature. He maintains enough distance to show that he sees the inadequacy even of those conventions he finds necessary and pleasing.

Though he is forever talking about precision, his primary lesson is one of balance. Just because people, like words, are imperfect, there is no reason for them, through carelessness, to permit themselves to be irrational and immoral as well.

Jane Austen's answer in the same period of challenge which produced so much radical and passionate literature, is reached not by rebellion and flight, but through education. When Catherine tells Henry that she has "learned" from Eleanor to love a hyacinth, he congratulates her, saying, in his briefest but perhaps most effective lesson, "It is well to have as many holds upon happiness as possible." Jane Austen nowhere denies the splendor of Mont Blanc; she merely speaks up for hyacinths. *Northanger Abbey* is a modest, even slight book, about one quarter the length of *The Mysteries of Udolpho*. But as a display of the disciplined mind and the well-chosen word it does more than all the hysterical criticism of the periodicals to deflate some of the poses and excesses of Romanticism. When Catherine suggests to Henry that "to torment" is a good synonym for "to instruct," he agrees that discipline is often painful:

> But . . . even you yourself, who do not seem altogether particularly friendly to very severe, very intense application, may perhaps be brought to acknowledge that it is very well worth while to be tormented for two or three years of one's life, for the sake of being able to read all the rest of it. Consider—if reading had not been taught, Mrs. Radcliffe would have written in vain—or perhaps might not have written at all.

Once again, Catherine has used a word imprecisely and Henry has corrected her. And once again his lesson appears to be after Jane Austen's own heart. Yet the impression lingers after reading this book that if one character makes too much of words like "torment," the other makes too little of them. A reasonable and socially conventional man can educate a young woman out of her unfounded fears, but he is not, therefore, St. George. There are dragons he cannot touch. Through a crack in the door of an empty bedroom and the petulance of a narrow-minded father, Austen gives a glimpse of the demons which prevent Henry Tilney from looming with perfect invulnerability over the fretful Catherine Morland. Austen's mode is ironic and her range modest, but she has explored the same division of mind which is at the core of romantic fiction.

Jane Nardin (essay date 1973)

SOURCE: "Propriety and the Education of Catherine Morland: *Northanger Abbey*," in *Those Elegant Decorums: The Concept of Propriety in Jane Austen's Novels*, State University of New York Press, 1973, pp. 62-81.

[*In the following essay, Nardin discusses Catherine's education in the moral significance of social propriety.*]

Northanger Abbey is, in part, a spoof of gothic and sentimental novels. But its main action—the realistically drawn picture of an unformed young girl's education in the complexities of real life—can be fairly easily detached from the elements of literary burlesque with which it is surrounded and discussed on its own terms. By tracing the development of Catherine Morland's character we can discover that her misconceptions about the true nature and value of proper manners play a role in her most serious errors of judgment. Since the nature and significance of the literary allusions Jane Austen makes in *Northanger Abbey* have been intelligently and, in my opinion, exhaustively discussed by other critics, I intend to mention them here only insofar as they are relevant to the real adventures of that believable human being, Catherine Morland, whose growing up is one of the main subjects of *Northanger Abbey*. Literature plays a part in Catherine's education, as it does in that of so many other Jane Austen heroines, but to approach the novel as primarily a literary satire tends to force the reader to overestimate the importance of burlesque elements in Catherine's characterization. I hope to demonstrate here that literature does not, in fact, play the central role in the learning process which the ignorant Catherine must undergo if she is to cope effectively with the rigors of adult life.

At the beginning of *Northanger Abbey,* Catherine is unformed, but it would be a mistake to consider her as a mere tabula rasa. In the course of the novel, a number of scattered references are made to the nature of Catherine's family and to the sort of upbringing she has been given. If we combine the bits of evidence with which we are provided in these references, we can form a fairly adequate idea of the sort of sheltered world Catherine has known before her introduction into the wider and more perilous society of Bath. It is, of course, from the world of her childhood that Catherine has drawn the opinions concerning manners, morals, and human nature with which she will evaluate the new society she is entering.

Perhaps the most significant thing which we learn about Catherine at the opening of the novel is that she is "as free from the apprehension of evil as from the knowledge of it." The neighborhood of Catherine's home at Fullerton parsonage apparently has provided her with only a very small circle of intimate acquaintances and those mostly of the best moral character. Her own parents are sensible, unpretentious, modest, generous, and well-bred. They are, in fact, "plain, matter-of-fact people, who seldom aimed at wit of any kind; her father, at the utmost, being contented with a pun, and her mother with a proverb; they were not in the habit therefore of telling lies to increase their importance." Outside of her own immediate family, Catherine's only close friends are the Allens. When in search of amusement in the country, Catherine tells Henry Tilney, "I can only go and call on Mrs. Allen." "'What a picture of intellectual poverty,'" Henry replies, and he is certainly right. For Mrs. Allen, as Jane Austen takes pains to point out, is a veritable cipher of a woman, "one of that numerous class of females whose society can raise no other emotion than surprise at their being any men in the world who could like them well enough to marry them." And Mr. Allen is just such another plain

and unpretentious man as Catherine's own father. We can conclude Catherine's other acquaintances to be neither numerous, nor intimate. Unlike Isabella Thorpe, Catherine mentions no old friends by name. And we learn that not one family in the neighborhood of Fullerton has a son of anything like the proper age for becoming Catherine's lover. All this suggests a very restricted society.

It seems safe to conclude, then, that Catherine's limited circle of acquaintances has provided her with several examples of unpretending merit, but has given her virtually no first-hand knowledge of evil in any of its human forms. One of the most important things that is going to happen to Catherine in the course of *Northanger Abbey* is her encounter with evil. She must discover for herself the characteristic ways in which human evil manifests itself in polite English society. In this task the experiences of her early life can help Catherine in only two possible ways. First, she can hope to recognize evil by its contrast with the sort of goodness she has previously known. Second, she can trust to the experiences of a wider world than that of Fullerton, which her reading has vicariously given her, as a guide in understanding the new types of people she will encounter at Bath. For Catherine is a reader. We learn that before going to Bath, Catherine has read some history, which she dislikes, some Pope, some Gray, some Thompson, and some Shakespeare, plus Richardson's *Sir Charles Grandison,* entire. This list is rather impressive and there can be no doubt that the quality of Catherine's literary fare drops sharply when Isabella Thorpe begins recommending her own favorite novels. On Isabella's advice, Catherine switches from Richardson to the genteel gothic fiction of Mrs. Radcliffe. She is, apparently, also planning to read several books by imitators of the sensational gothic novelist, "Monk" Lewis. We might hope that Catherine's earlier reading of respectable authors has provided her with ideas that will prove useful in evaluating the varied society of Bath, but Jane Austen makes it clear that Catherine's reading has been of a desultory and light-hearted nature and cannot be expected to supply anything "serviceable" in dealing with the "vissisitudes" of her new life. It is, as we shall see later, only the reading in gothic novels which Catherine does *after* she reaches Bath, that remains fresh enough in the young heroine's mind to be drawn upon for aid in understanding and interpreting her unprecedented experiences of evil. The didactic literature of which Mrs. Morland is fond (*Grandison* is her favorite, and she is impressed by *The Mirror's* instructive essays) has made little or no lasting impression on her daughter. And this probably represents Jane Austen's considered opinion of the educational value of didactic fiction for the average young mind.

Catherine's experiences before she goes to Bath, then, have not taught her how to deal with people who are selfish, vain, pretentious, and improper in their social behavior. Her first acquaintance with such people is in Bath. Her first reaction to such people is characterized by her failure to realize that they are different from people whom she has previously known. Catherine's own family are completely without pretensions to being anything other than ordinary people; they do not affect to rise above "the common feelings of common life." Their manners are conventionally proper, their understanding of reality quite adequate to the demands of everyday life. There is no need for Catherine to take her parents at anything other than their face value and for a long time she fails to realize that the world is full of pretentious and affected people who cannot be accepted at their own estimates of themselves. Indeed, an excessive willingness to believe what people say of themselves remains a part of Catherine's character throughout the novel, and this trait is moderated, rather than completely cured, by her experiences.

Catherine first encounters human evil, which in *Northanger Abbey* typically takes the form of selfishness, vanity, pretension, and impropriety, in the persons of Isabella and John Thorpe. It immediately becomes clear to the reader that both John and Isabella have absolutely no feeling for others and no commitment to truth of any sort. They are also greedy and financially ambitious. In *Northanger Abbey,* as in *Pride and Prejudice,* a man's manners are seen as the social manifestations of his moral condition. Manners here reveal, rather than conceal (as is partially the case in *Persuasion,* for example), the reality of character. And the manners of the Thorpes mirror their characters perfectly. They are both pretentious, but too shallow and foolish to ground their pretensions on any solid understanding of reality, and John and Isabella betray both their dishonesty and their inability to understand the real world in their manners. Neither has much understanding of even the minor rules of propriety governing ordinary social interaction. Both create their own idiosyncratic codes of propriety designed to meet the needs of their overweening egos. Thus John Thorpe "seemed fearful of being . . . too much like a gentleman unless he were easy where he ought to be civil, and impudent where he might be allowed to be easy." In other words, John disregards all the ordinary, minor rules of civility in order to prove to himself and to others that he is in command of any social situation. John's disregard of conventional decorum when it conflicts with his own ends extends to the major, as well as the minor, rules of propriety. He is quite prepared to lie about both trivial and very important matters at any time and doesn't even have the sense to be disturbed when he is found out. The rule of propriety which prohibits lying (whether in everyday social relations or where something crucially important is concerned) is a very basic and significant one, resting virtually on the line where conventional propriety and pure morality merge. Yet John ignores it openly and repeatedly, telling lies which are sure to be found out about even the most significant aspects of social relations. And this is the outward evidence that he has absolutely no idea of what is important in social behavior, either from the point of view of mere social acceptability or from that of morality. He is beyond the pale.

Isabella's social behavior is a bit less divorced from social and moral reality than her brother's—but not much. Like John, Isabella invents her own rules of propriety (both major and minor) to suit the needs of the moment. When James Morland, for example, asks her to dance twice at the same ball, Isabella comments to Catherine: "'Only conceive, my dear Catherine, what your brother wants me to do. He wants me to dance with him again, though I tell him that it is a most improper thing, and entirely against the rules. It would make us the talk of the place.'" To this James replies, somewhat perplexed, "'Upon my honour . . . in these public assemblies it is as often done as not,'" and the reader can entertain no doubt that he is quite correct. Not only does Isabella invent her own rules as she goes along, but in addition, she interprets the significance of other people's social behavior—which is, of course, the outward manifestation of their inward feelings and judgments—in a totally idiosyncratic fashion. The significance which Isabella reads into other people's manners bears virtually no resemblance to the significance those manners would have if interpreted according to the clues contained in the conventional code of propriety. Thus, when Isabella sees a young man, with whom she and Catherine are unacquainted, looking at Catherine, her immediate conclusion is, "'I am sure he is in love with you.'" And when she is informed that the Tilneys seemed out of spirits the day Catherine dined with them, Isabella reads their behavior as symptomatic of "pride, pride, insufferable haughtiness and pride."

To some extent, Isabella's idiosyncratic code of propriety is of an ad hoc nature. She is willing to make up a rule to suit a particular occasion, use it once, and drop it forever. Nonetheless, her code of propriety at all times displays certain characteristic qualities. Isabella's own rules of propriety and mode of interpreting the social behavior of others are drawn from sentimental fiction and disregard, as we have said, the conventional propriety of real life. Like the heroine of a sentimental novel who finds herself drawn by an irresistible affinity towards a mind of similar excellence, Isabella forms friendships which "passed so rapidly through every gradation of increasing tenderness, that there was shortly no fresh proof of it to be given." This "literary" mode of forming friendships ignores the cautious rules of conventional propriety, the purpose of which is, in part, to make it impossible for two people to achieve a high degree of intimacy before they have had time to gain real knowledge of each other's characters. Similarly, in seeing evidences of romantic passion in a passing glance, Isabella is judging manners by the significance they would have in a sentimental novel and disregarding the fact that manners have a very different sort of significance in common life.

Isabella's motives for attempting to import the manners of literature into real life are not difficult to discover. She is a beautiful, but undowered, young woman whose every hope of achieving status, comfort, and respect in life depends on her ability to make a good marriage. Marriage and the flirtation and romance which lead up to it are the only things that have any real significance or interest for Isabella. And the conventions of behavior characterizing the sentimental novel, conventions which attribute extraordinary emotional importance to the most ordinary social behavior, permit Isabella to find the romance she is searching for, virtually everywhere she looks. If she operated according to the minor conventions of everyday propriety, it would be much more difficult for Isabella to think of romance all the time.

The pursuit of a husband for a young lady of Jane Austen's era was necessarily a passive one, mostly a question of waiting to be chosen. Isabella, it is true, makes this pursuit as active as she can, physically chasing good-looking young men through the streets of Bath. Yet it is clear that even though Isabella is willing to violate the major rules of propriety which forbid her to seek a husband actively, the scope for action that will not obviously defeat its own ends is very narrow in this area. Isabella is therefore terribly bored and part of her attempt to live according to the conventions of literature is motivated by her desire to give some interest and significance to her own trammelled existence. By describing her own life as if she were the heroine of a sentimental novel, Isabella can convince herself that she is a fascinating woman experiencing exciting adventures. Thus, she discusses her extremely placid and commonplace romance with James Morland in completely inappropriate terms: "'The very first moment I beheld him—my heart was irrecoverably gone. . . . Oh! Catherine, the many sleepless nights I have had on your brother's account— . . . I am grown wretchedly thin I know . . . ' " etc., etc.

All this reflects not only Isabella's boredom and her anxiety about her own fate, but also her vanity and her over-weaning desire for attention and consequence. She wishes to seem fascinating not only in her own eyes, but also in the eyes of others. Jane Austen does not overlook any of the pressures which make Isabella's behavior what it is, yet she has no sympathy with her. One of the most fundamental points made in *Northanger Abbey* is simply that decent and intelligent people must come to terms with the fact that real life is usually dull, that it provides only restricted opportunities for action, and that most people (even if they are well above average in every way) can hope neither to be exciting in themselves, nor born to exciting fates. Early in the novel, Jane Austen describes a conversation between Catherine and Miss Tilney in which "not an observation was made, nor an expression used by either which had not been made and used some thousands of times before . . . in every Bath season." But Jane Austen does not censure Catherine and Miss Tilney for the fact that their remarks are totally unoriginal in content. Instead, she congratulates them on the manner in which they have spoken: "with simplicity and truth and without personal conceit." For this is, indeed, "something uncommon." Catherine and Miss Tilney are to be congratulated because boredom and conceit are not strong enough forces in their natures—as they are in Isabella's—to make them wish to escape from the restrictions of dull reality. They have come to terms with their own essential ordinariness. It is, of course, ironic that true adventure will come to both of them—as it never will to Isabella—yet they would not be rational if they were to expect it, and they would be less rational still if they were to expect it as a part of every day's program. The minor rules of propriety receive Jane Austen's approval in *Northanger Abbey* because she believes them to be based upon an understanding and an acceptance of the restrictive reali-

ties of everyday life. The proprieties of the sentimental novel, according to which Isabella attempts to live, however, are based upon an attempt to transcend the restrictions of everyday reality and to achieve a freer and more exciting state of being. Such an attempt Jane Austen believes to be doomed from the start, simply because most human beings, and therefore their everyday lives, are extremely limited.

And Isabella's is not the only example of an attempt to import the conventions of literature into real life which can be found in *Northanger Abbey*. Indeed the novel is full of attacks on a variety of false and unrealistic conventions of taste, emotion, language, and manners, ultimately drawn from the world of the sentimental novel, which have become acceptable in polite society. The convention of taste which dictates that everyone must get tired of Bath after six weeks, for example, is derived from the common assumption of sentimental fiction that truly exalted minds are peculiarly susceptible to the charms of nature. Yet the very people who profess a disgust with Bath and a passion for the country, as Henry Tilney points out, "'lengthen their six weeks into ten or twelve, and go away at last because they can afford to stay no longer.'" Similarly, the manners of the fop, which Henry parodies, derive from fiction their basic assumption that the most trivial relationships between a man and a woman must be charged with emotion. Thus, when Catherine tells Henry that she has been in Bath about a week, he replies:

"Really!" with affected astonishment.

"Why should you be surprized, sir?"

"Why, indeed!" said he, in his natural tone—"but some emotion must appear to be raised by your reply."

All these basically literary conventions of taste and proprieties of behavior have gained currency because people wish to give to their own daily lives some of the excitement characteristic of the lives of fictional heroes. But Jane Austen points out that no set of proprieties can make sense unless it accepts, as its starting point, the fact that real life—not invariably, as Catherine will discover, but basically nonetheless—does not share the excitement of fiction. Real life can be exciting, but it is certainly not exciting all day and every day, and the minor rules of propriety are meant to apply to everyday conduct. When excitement does come into real life, it comes, as we shall see, in its own characteristic manner, which is not the manner of sentimental or gothic fiction.

Since before meeting the Thorpes, Catherine has had virtually no experience with the sort of person who pretends to be something that he is not and who therefore cannot be taken at face value, for a long time it simply does not occur to her to doubt that the Thorpes are exactly the sort of people they pretend to be. John, of course, does not take Catherine in nearly as long as Isabella does. This is partly because his lies and distortions of fact are so blatant and frequent that even the credulous Catherine cannot help noticing them. But Catherine comes to dislike

John Thorpe less because she sees through his pretentions than because she dislikes the sort of person he is pretending to be. The role John chooses to play is that of the hard-drinking, free-spending, yet financially shrewd, man-of-the-world, who despises sentiment, ceremony, and literature, who can dominate any social situation, and who never denies himself a pleasure. Catherine never even realizes consciously that John is any thing but the shrewd, skilled, and dominating manipulator of others he believes himself to be—she dislikes him because the sort of man he pretends to be is totally offensive to her both from a moral and from an aesthetic point of view.

With Isabella the case is far different. Isabella presents herself as the heroine of a sentimental novel: full of warm, generous, uncontrollable feelings, loyal to her friends, uninterested in money. Catherine wholeheartedly approves of such a heroine. When Isabella professes a sentiment like, "'were I mistress of the whole world, your brother would be my only choice,'" Catherine finds it a "grand idea." Since Catherine approves of the sort of heroine Isabella is pretending to be, she cannot reject Isabella until she sees through the falseness of Isabella's pretentions. This sort of looking below the surface is something Catherine finds very difficult to do—consciously at least—yet Catherine begins to suspect Isabella before she leaves Bath to visit Northanger Abbey.

While she remains at Bath, Catherine begins to understand Isabella's essential dishonesty only because Isabella's selfishness and vanity often cause her behavior to be radically at variance with the dictates of conventional propriety. And to the rules of conventional propriety, it soon becomes clear, Catherine has a deep and fairly well-considered commitment. When, for example, Mr. Allen hints to Catherine that there may be some impropriety in the unchaperoned drives she has been taking with John Thorpe, Catherine immediately reproaches Mrs. Allen, "'Dear Madam . . . then why did not you tell me so before? I am sure if I had known it to be improper, I would not have gone with Mr. Thorpe at all.'" Considerations of propriety always come before considerations of mere pleasure with Catherine, and not merely because Catherine is afraid to judge and act for herself. Fairly early in the novel, John and Isabella try to convince Catherine to break an engagement she has made to take a country walk with the Tilneys, on the false excuse that she has just been reminded of a prior engagement to drive with them. Catherine's reactions to this incident prove that she has a basically sound, though not a consciously worked-out or really theoretical, understanding of the functions fulfilled by the conventional rules of propriety in an ordered society. In refusing to violate the minor rule of propriety which forbids one to break an engagement merely because one has received a second invitation, Catherine tells the Thorpes, "'Indeed I cannot go. If I am wrong, I am doing what I believe to be right.'" Thinking the incident over later, she reflects that "she had not been withstanding them on selfish principles alone [she does, of course, prefer to go with the Tilneys], she had not consulted merely her own gratification; . . . no, she had attended to what was due to others, and to her own char-acter in their opinion." Catherine understands the basic moral function of the minor rules of propriety: that they provide a fairly sensible guide to the consideration and attention we owe to other people in society. And she also understands that since these rules are commonly accepted and commonly believed to be sensible and moral, we can violate them only at the risk of losing the good opinion of others. Therefore, when Catherine sees Isabella disregarding some of the most significant and moral minor rules of propriety, she begins, though tentatively, to suspect that her friend is not quite the generous and sensitive person she pretends to be. When Isabella urges Catherine to lie to the Tilneys, Catherine is even capable of suspecting that Isabella may in fact be "ungenerous and selfish, regardless of everything but her own gratification." When Isabella's literary pretensions conflict even with the everyday minor rules of propriety, there is never any question that Catherine's approval and allegiance remain with the rules.

Catherine's commitment to both the major and minor rules of conventional propriety is deep. Yet for such an unreflective and unsophisticated young lady, she seems to have a very reliable instinct concerning which minor rules of propriety are important because they have moral significance and which may be safely disregarded, on occasion, because they are matters of custom and ceremony only. A distinction virtually identical to the one made in *Pride and Prejudice* is at issue here. The rules of propriety are divided into those with a basic moral justification (this class includes all the major and many minor rules) and those which are matters of fashion and convenience alone (only minor rules fall into this class). But Catherine's understanding of the distinction, unlike Elizabeth Bennet's, seems to be instinctual, rather than conscious. Catherine is adamant in her refusal to break her engagement with the Tilneys (which would be inconsiderate and hurtful, hence immoral). But after she discovers that John Thorpe has broken the engagement behind her back, she chases the Tilneys home to their lodgings "and the servant still remaining at the open door [which they have just entered], she used only the ceremony of saying that she must speak with Miss Tilney that moment and hurrying by him proceeded upstairs" to set matters right. That her mode of entry is highly improper (the general finds it very odd) does not bother Catherine. She seems to sense that on this one occasion she has a rational and moral reason for breaking the minor rule which says that a visitor must wait to be shown in by a servant—and she is quite right in her assumption that the Tilneys will understand and approve her motives. Catherine believes that when an essentially moral or justifiable intention conflicts with a minor rule of propriety, the rule must go. However, her deep commitment to all the rules of conventional propriety simply because they are rules indicates that she does not consider this likely to happen very frequently.

It is difficult, then, for Catherine to appreciate the value of Henry Tilney's somewhat unorthodox manners. His disregard of ceremony, particularly in the interests of a joke, is often striking. Compared to Catherine herself,

Henry plays fast and loose with the minor rules of decorum. Catherine sees that Henry's "manner might sometimes surprize" a person deeply committed to the conventional rules of propriety. When she first meets him, this leads her to suspect that "he indulged himself a little too much with the foibles of others," in other words, that his unorthodox manners indicated a want of respect for and kindness towards other people. But when she gets to know him better (and, incidentally, falls in love with him) she is able to see, and quite correctly so, that in spite of his frequent disregard of ceremony "his meaning must always be just." The fact that the narrator pokes fun at Catherine's infatuated willingness to admire even "what she did not understand" in Henry's social behavior, does not in any way invalidate Catherine's essentially sound estimate of Henry's manners. After Henry reproaches Catherine for the liberties she has been taking with his father's character, she is overwhelmed with guilt and self-reproach and fears she has lost his good opinion forever. But when the two next meet, Henry alters his manners and pays Catherine "rather more attention than usual." This "soothing politeness" gradually raises her spirits "to a modest tranquility." It also proves that Henry understands that the essence of good manners is a generous, moral consideration for others, rather than a lifeless adherence to all the conventional rules of propriety. At the end of the novel, Henry refuses to break, at his Father's command, his tacit engagement to marry Catherine—an incident which parallels Catherine's earlier refusal to break her engagement to walk with Henry and his sister. Like Catherine, Henry will not break the important, moral rules of propriety, but he sets considerably less store than she does on the minor rules which regulate only custom and ceremony. The main difference between Catherine and Henry's views of propriety is that Henry is quite conscious that he violates the conventional minor rules when he feels himself justified in doing so, while Catherine, though she occasionally acts upon this principle, never consciously realizes that technical impropriety is frequently justified.

Catherine's encounters with the Thorpes and with Henry Tilney have demonstrated that though her judgment of others may not be shrewd or penetrating, her instinctive understanding of the nature and function of good manners is basically sound. It is Catherine's encounter with General Tilney—by far the most evil person she meets in the course of the novel—that will reveal the inadequacies of her ideas concerning propriety as tools for understanding others. General Tilney, to an even greater degree than John and Isabella Thorpe, is selfish, vain, pretentious, and ambitious. His manners express his character just as clearly as their manners express theirs. But, unlike John and Isabella, the general is intensely aware of the rules of conventional propriety and though his every action violates the spirit of those rules, their letter is sacred to him. The general's particular pretension is that of good breeding. He describes and considers himself as the most courteous man in the world. When Catherine is first introduced to General Tilney, he receives her with "ready . . . solicitous politeness. . . . To such anxious attention was the General's civility carried that, not aware of her ex-

traordinary swiftness in entering the house [as described above, Catherine has pushed her way past the servant] he was quite angry with the servant whose neglect had reduced her to open the door of the apartment herself . . . it seemed likely that William would lose the favor of his master forever, if not his place, by her rapidity." Thus, on General Tilney's first appearance in the story, the character of his manners is clearly revealed. All the ceremonies of civility are offered to Catherine, whom the general wishes to please for purely selfish reasons. All the content of truly proper social behavior is ignored in the general's suspicious and resentful conduct to his blameless, but also helpless, servant.

Catherine, as we have seen, has a deep commitment to the conventional rules of propriety, though she is also willing to dispense with some of their purely ceremonious manifestations. And she is unusually slow in seeing through the pretensions of others. The general's pretension to good breeding, supported as it is by a consistent, if superficial, adherence to the conventional propriety Catherine values, takes Catherine in completely. Insofar as Catherine is able to see through Isabella's pretensions, it is because Isabella's behavior repeatedly and fairly openly violates rules which Catherine understands and approves. But the general pretentiously parades his allegiance to those very rules and for a long time this confuses Catherine deeply. When she dines with the Tilneys, Catherine is puzzled that "in spite of [General Tilney's] great civilities to her—in spite of his thanks, invitations, and compliments—it had been a release to get away from him." When Catherine sees that the forms of conventional propriety are absent from Isabella's behavior, she is capable, though dimly, of suspecting that the moral and emotional content of true propriety is absent too. But with the general, Catherine mistakes the form for the content and fails to realize that the presence of the former is no guarantee of the latter. Catherine's own behavior demonstrates that, tacitly at least, she is able to discriminate between the important or moral and the trivial or merely ceremonial rules of propriety. But that virtually all the major and minor rules can be divorced from their moral content, manipulated in a manner directly contrary to their basic intention, and yet not quite openly violated, simply does not occur to her. Yet this is precisely what General Tilney characteristically does.

> "Well, Eleanor, may I congratulate you on being successful in your application to your fair friend [to visit Northanger]?" [he asks his daughter.]
>
> "I was just beginning to make the request, sir, as you came in."
>
> "Well, proceed by all means. I knew how much your heart is in it. My daughter, Miss Morland," he continued, without leaving his daughter time to speak, "has been forming a very bold wish."

Passages such as this one demonstrate that General Tilney's commitment to the proprieties is extremely superficial. Though he pays lip service to the rule of decorum which says he must allow his daughter time to finish the private conversation which he has unwittingly interrupted, in actuality he doesn't let her say another word. The hypocrisy with which he manipulates the forms of politeness is so transparent that Catherine's persistence in viewing him as a model of decorum becomes striking evidence of an almost pathological inability to look below the surface of social pretence. Before her visit to Northanger Abbey, Catherine senses something odd about the general, but is quite unable to define what is wrong. Although one purpose of good manners is to put others at their ease, the general's behavior makes Catherine intensely uncomfortable. However, she attributes this discomfort solely to "her own stupidity" and not to something lacking in his manners.

When she is thrown into intimate contact with General Tilney, as a guest in his house, prolonged and close observation of his character forces Catherine to consider the question of why "so charming a man seemed always a check upon his children's spirits," why everyone is afraid of him in spite of his ostentatious politeness. It is in attempting to solve this mystery—and for her it really is a mystery—that Catherine first tries to apply the notions she has recently derived from gothic fiction to real life. It is not unnatural that General Tilney should remind Catherine of a gothic villain. The unmitigated evil that she senses in him is, as we shall see, really there. What gothic fiction has taught Catherine is that evil men, such as she suspects the general of being, express their wickedness in violent ways, but shroud their crimes in the deepest mystery. Two ways of solving the puzzle of the general are open to Catherine. The correct way is to conclude that General Tilney's superficially civil manners are not good manners, because they actually express his selfishness and egotism in a disguised, but perfectly recognisable, form. The incorrect, "gothic" way—which Catherine, characteristically, adopts—is to accept his conventionally proper manners at face value (as good manners, that is) and to conclude that those manners are an elaborate blind which conceals his real, horrible character. Thus, Catherine's first conclusion about the general is that there is a radical disparity between his good manners and his bad morals, and that those bad morals have expressed themselves *only* in secret crime. Such a conclusion is supported both by the view of human nature Catherine has found in the gothic novels she read at Bath and by her own unquestioned value for the forms of conventional propriety as good in themselves.

Henry and Eleanor Tilney, it might be added, are not in the least confused about their father's character or manner, and both attempt to enlighten Catherine on these points by discreet hints. But the rules of propriety demanding filial respect prohibit Henry and Eleanor from speaking openly about General Tilney's faults and Catherine, for a long while, consistently misinterprets their hints in accordance with her gothic preconceptions. Eleanor's decorous attempts to enlighten Catherine about the general invariably misfire. On Catherine's first morning at Northanger, for example, the general wishes to take an early walk at the precise moment when Catherine fervently wants to be shown around the Abbey. Characteristically, he masks his selfishness beneath the forms of propriety. "'Which would she [Catherine] prefer? He was equally at her service.—Which did his daughter think would most accord with her fair friend's wishes?—But . . . Yes, he certainly read in Miss Morland's eyes a judicious desire of making use of the present smiling weather.— . . . He yielded implicitly and would fetch his hat.'" No less characteristically, Catherine accepts his speech at face value and laments to Eleanor "that he should be taking them out of doors against his own inclination, under a mistaken idea of pleasing her." Eleanor, who is well aware of her father's motives and meaning, is confused by the fact that propriety forbids her to speak openly and says only, "'Do not be uneasy on my father's account, he always walks out at this time of day.'" This hint seems plain enough, but Catherine "did not exactly know how [it] was to be understood. Why was Miss Tilney embarrassed? Could there be any unwillingness on the General's side to show her over the Abbey?" And it is at this moment that the idea of a dark crime which General Tilney has committed within the Abbey's walls begins to take form in Catherine's mind. If Catherine had been able to understand the general's manners on her own or from Eleanor and Henry's hints, her gothic delusions would have had no mystery to give them their start.

Henry's hints about his father—never as guarded as Eleanor's—grow gradually more open as he comes to know Catherine better. It is mostly as a result of Henry's instruction that Catherine finally comes to a valid understanding of the general's character and manners—and we must next examine the process by which she reaches this understanding. To a large degree, Henry's own manners can be seen as a reaction against his father's social behavior. The general respects the forms of propriety while disregarding their spirit. Henry, on the other hand, tends to be rather careless about the minor forms, but is at all times considerate of others and faithful in discharging his moral obligations. Henry can refer to Eleanor in public, most improperly, as "my stupid sister," yet his company and kindness are clearly her greatest comforts. General Tilney, on the other hand, is scrupulously polite to his daughter, yet tries her patience continually and severely. Henry's own manners provide a running commentary on those of his father and it is her observation of Henry, as we have noted, that first suggests to Catherine that "meaning" may sometimes be more significant than "manner." Thus Henry's manners have provided Catherine, from the beginning, with the key to General Tilney's mystery. But Henry's explicit instructions are also needed if Catherine is to learn how to use that key.

Puzzled by the disparity she finds between the general's "good" manners and the evil which she senses is a part of his character, Catherine, as we have seen, invents a gothic solution. The general is a criminal, probably a wife-murderer, who carefully hides his true character under a mask of propriety. Luckily for Catherine, Henry discovers her suspicions (which are not very well concealed) and reads her a long lecture on their injustice.

Dear Miss Morland, consider the dreadful nature of the suspicions you have entertained. What have you been judging from? Remember the country and the age in which we live. . . . Consult your own understanding, your own sense of the probable, your own observation of what is passing around you.—Does our education prepare us for such atrocities? Do our laws connive at them? Could they be perpetrated without being known, in a country like this, where social and literary intercourse is on such a footing; where every man is surrounded by a neighborhood of voluntary spies, and where roads and newspapers lay everything open?

This is an interesting speech. In the first place, Henry makes no real attempt to defend his father's character; he does not claim that his father is a good man who would not wish to commit a murder under any circumstances. No, Henry's defense of his father from Catherine's charges rests on quite other premises. The basic assumption here is that even criminals are rational and are not likely to commit crimes that are going to be discovered and punished. And the age is such a public and suspicious one that a prominent man like the general could not hope to murder his wife and escape exposure and ruin. Therefore, the general probably did not murder his wife. This, it seems to me, is the logical structure of the argument Henry is making here. Evil exists, as Catherine now suspects, but evil people are not going to act in ways that will get them into trouble. For they can easily find ways of expressing their true natures without openly violating the accepted "laws of the land, and the manners of the age." This, of course, is what General Tilney does.

Henry's lecture makes a deep impression on Catherine, but she does not really understand it. In the first place, she is somewhat confused by Henry's assertion that his father loved his mother as well as such a cold man can love anyone. In making this claim, Henry is not trying to prove to Catherine that his father is basically a good man. On the contrary, he refers explicitly to his father's bad temper and lack of tenderness and says nothing that indicates a belief that the general might not have had criminal impulses of various sorts toward people other than his wife. But this distinction is lost upon Catherine. She now sees that "the manners of the age" must be "some security for the existence even of a wife not beloved," but she again makes her characteristic error of confounding "manner" and "meaning," or "habit" and "heart." If the manners of the age do not permit murder, if the general has not, in fact, murdered his wife, then Catherine concludes that the impulse to commit murder or other sorts of crime must also be absent from the general's psychological makeup. Yet this is precisely the assertion that Henry cleverly avoids making. "Among the Alps and Pyrenees [where the extreme manners of gothic fiction hold sway]," Catherine muses, "perhaps there were no mixed characters. There, such as were not spotless as an angel, might have the dispositions of a fiend. But . . . among the English, she believed, in their *hearts and habits,* there was a general, though unequal, mixture of good and bad" (my italics). Because English laws and manners forbid murder

or other extreme forms of violence, Catherine concludes that there are no English fiends. And since the general has been cleared from her "grossly injurious suspicions," the most Catherine is willing to say against him is that he is "not perfectly amiable." Though the narrator presents Catherine's conclusions without apparent irony of tone, it soon becomes clear that Catherine is mistaken in her belief that General Tilney's is a mixed character containing more good than bad.

Henry soon becomes aware that in spite of his instructions, the removal of her gothic delusion has left Catherine with the almost equally erroneous belief that the general's superficially civil manners are evidence of a basically sound, if not perfectly amiable, character. When the general civilly remarks that Henry need pay no special attention to the dinner he is to give for his family at Woodston, Catherine as usual accepts the statement at face value. Henry is forced to tell her quite openly that the general is being insincere and, in fact, expects a superb dinner to be prepared for him. This is a revelation to Catherine. "The inexplicability of the General's conduct dwelt much on her thoughts . . . why he should say one thing so positively, and mean another all the while, was most unaccountable! How were people, at that rate, to be understood?" Catherine has finally asked herself the appropriate question. How can people be understood if the forms of good manners are no guarantee that the content is present? The answer is breathtakingly simple: people's pretensions to good manners must be consciously and continually questioned, not only when, as with Isabella and John Thorpe, the forms are often absent, but also, as with General Tilney, when the forms appear to be present.

The revelation of Isabella's two-faced conduct toward Catherine's brother James provides a catalyst which arranges all Catherine's earlier vague suspicions of her friend in a clear and ordered pattern. She realizes at last that Isabella "'is a vain coquette . . . she never had any regard either for James or for me.'" Similarly, General Tilney's character must be revealed in a dramatic and unmistakeable form if Catherine is to understand it—and fortunately for Catherine, such a revelation is made. General Tilney has been courting Catherine as a wife for Henry under the mistaken impression that she is an heiress on a spectacular scale. Learning his mistake, he turns her from his house in the rudest possible manner and orders his son to think of her no more. Henry, however, is delightfully loyal to Catherine and when he tells her the whole story of his father's motives, Catherine concludes "that in suspecting General Tilney of either murdering or shutting up his wife, she had scarcely sinned against his character or magnified his cruelty." This is Catherine's final judgment of the general and I believe it to be essentially valid, in spite of the fact that it sounds less balanced than her earlier conclusion that the general had a mixed character.

Jane Austen seems to have in mind here a simple estimate of the moral significance of murder which she considers relevant to General Tilney's behavior. Murder may be conceived as a totally egotistical act. For in practical terms, even if he is not aware of it, a murderer necessarily values his own desires or needs at an infinitely higher rate than those of his victim. Even the victim's right to live cannot influence the murderer, who must think only of himself. Now this sort of unbounded selfishness, which I think Jane Austen has in mind here as part of the very definition of a murderer, is the general's most prominent character trait. And when General Tilney expells Catherine from his house, Jane Austen means us to see his action as a domestic parody of a killing. Catherine's continued existence in the general's vicinity has become highly disagreeable to him and in this respect Catherine resembles the typical murder victim. The general, like a real murderer, wants his victim eliminated as completely and quickly as possible from his world. In turning Catherine out of his house without the slightest consideration for the rights which the code of propriety gives her at his hands, the general parodies the actions of the murderer whose own interests necessarily are more important to him than any of his victim's rights. As Catherine now realizes, the general really is something of a fiend.

The difference between General Tilney and the average gothic villain, then, is not to be found in the quantity or quality of evil in their hearts. Rather it resides, as Henry has known all along, in the manner in which that evil is expressed. Murder is quite decorous in gothic fiction, but in England it is likely to be punished, for it violates the laws and manners of the age. Villians like General Tilney will therefore tend to express their evil impulses without defying law and custom openly enough to get themselves into trouble. General Tilney, of course, represents an extreme manifestation of this tendency. His manners invariably express the evil in his heart, but General Tilney is able to preserve all the forms of conventional propriety intact, except on the one occasion when he expells Catherine from Northanger. Here, his wrath and resentment are so great that they simply cannot be expressed within even the purely formal constraints of his usual code of propriety. However, it is significant that even in his most extreme wrath, the general violates only the minor rules of propriety and not the laws of the realm. At the worst, he has exposed himself to such halfhearted censure as Mrs. Allen's, "'I really have not patience with the General'"—but he is certainly safe from any serious form of punishment. And this, it seems to me, is what Catherine must learn about the difference between life and gothic fiction: the same evil and potential for violence are present in both, but in real life evil tends to be expressed in ways which are customary and socially acceptable and which therefore expose the evil doer to little risk of punishment. And the rules of propriety, though basically moral in intention, in practice are quite flexible enough to permit bad people to express the evil in their hearts without getting themselves into serious trouble. Life and fiction differ in "manner" more than in "meaning." It is only by realizing how completely a conventionally proper manner can be divorced from the basic moral meaning it ought to have, that Catherine can come to understand the relationship between General Tilney and the typical gothic villain.

Catherine's original gothic fantasies about General Tilney represent a garbling of the truth, rather than a complete delusion. And when she reacts to Henry's remonstrance by concluding that there is no resemblance between life and gothic fiction and that the general is a mixed character whose professions of civility and generosity have at least some value, Catherine is as far from the truth as ever. It is only at the end of the novel (and with the help of a very complete revelation), that Catherine begins to gain some real understanding of General Tilney. The narrator describes General Tilney's letter consenting to Henry and Catherine's marriage as a document "very courteously worded in a page full of empty professions." I think we can assume that the narrator's viewpoint here is now shared by Catherine. Catherine has finally realized that courteous professions can be empty, that the forms of good manners are ultimately quite separable from the inward virtues they are supposed to represent. Catherine has never, as we have seen, made this mistake in her conduct—her manners have always been based on good morals and a realistic, if tacit, understanding of what is important in social behavior. But she has been only too willing to accept other people's unsupported pretensions to good manners or good taste at their own valuations. Catherine's rejection of Isabella Thorpe and General Tilney shows that she finally realizes that in her own era a more or less well-supported pretension to virtue and propriety is the characteristic manner of evil.

Eric Rothstein (essay date 1974)

SOURCE: "The Lessons of *Northanger Abbey*," in *University of Toronto Quarterly,* Vol. XLIV, No. 1, Fall, 1974, pp. 14-30.

[*Here, Rothstein explores Austen's narrative technique in* Northanger Abbey, *claiming that the central theme of the novel emerges from the interplay between the respective educations of Catherine and the reader.*]

In *Northanger Abbey,* as in a number of works of eighteenth-century fiction (say, *Tom Jones*), the protagonist and the reader undergo parallel, but in almost no way identical, educations. The reader, as Austen's irony announces in the first paragraph, is to be led toward something better than the conventional novels to which she alludes again and again in the course of the book. As to the protagonist, the first chapter offers a dry account of Catherine's progress in music and drawing; these early lessons are extended by Mrs Allen and Henry Tilney, who teach her how to choose muslins and compose picturesque scenes, and are also extended by Catherine herself, who learns first from books and then by testing experience through trial and error. All this is obvious enough. The connections between Catherine's education and ours, however, are less obvious: so are those between two modes in Catherine's own development, the social (Bath) and the literary (Northanger Abbey). Here, to some critics, the coherence of the novel seems to break down, an event to be explained from Austen's biography. She did, after all, move from literary satire in her earliest works toward psychological and moral issues in her mature fiction: *Northanger Abbey,* in between the two, seems to look both ways, and Janus Austen fails where young Jane or mature Jane succeeded. I do not think that this is a necessary hypothesis, and I should like to devote the rest of this article to proposing a more flattering one, in which the tables are turned. That is, I propose that the strength of *Northanger Abbey,* and its theme, emerge from the connections between Catherine's education and ours, and between the social and literary modes in her experience.

The connections are made peculiarly complex by Austen's granting Catherine an autonomy from the novel, of the sort that we readers naturally maintain. A look at the first chapter will suggest what I mean. There, a volley of innuendos about her future heroism makes one include under 'education' all Catherine's movements toward 'heroic' status, the freshening of her adolescent complexion as well as her growth in memorizing moral sentences. Much of Austen's irony at this point comes from her pretence that in real life, the life that *her* novel imitates, Catherine can 'learn to be a heroine,' a category not proper to real life at all, but only to the repertoire of fiction. Superficially, such irony looks like a special irony of Fielding's, the 'transformation of a spontaneous and impromptu action into one performed to accord with a formal pattern . . . [which] imposes on the unthinking or spontaneous actions and deductions of the characters a strong suggestion of deliberations and definite intention; the instinctive and intuitional become conscious and purposeful.' But in Fielding, such a transformation is a means of enlarging the scope of expectations within which we see the character. As his diction grows more formal, trivia try on epic armour for size and so are given their proper measure within the limits of action. No matter how trivial Catherine may or may not be, however, she cannot be given proper measure by trying on a heroine's furbelows, because the formal patterns that stand behind her spontaneous actions have no set value. Dignity, in Fielding, is at least a provisional norm; novelistic heroism in the first chapter of *Northanger Abbey* is not. As we see Catherine passing from infancy to mid-adolescence, we see the firm fact of her normality measuring the truth to nature of the sort of fiction which trades in heroines. The method of Fielding has been stood on its head so decisively that Catherine, in her nondescript childhood, becomes the main witness of Austen's own imitative truth to nature. In *Northanger Abbey,* then, the characters are declared to be logically prior to the fiction, and therefore ideally autonomous of it. Fielding establishes the world for Tom Jones; Catherine, as an index of normality, establishes the world for Austen, and thus exceeds the fiction in which she appears. At the same time, obviously, the novel contains Catherine and offers us a way of dealing with her experience—according to the laws of fiction—which she cannot know.

We can see this play between control and independence still more openly in Austen's treatment of Eleanor's marriage, 'an event,' the narrator says, 'which I expect to give general satisfaction among all her acquaintance. My own joy on the occasion is very sincere.' Here the moc-biographer's pose amuses us, especially because the mar-

riage seems to have been brewed up all of a sudden to get the plot together, and the narrator to be rejoicing not for Eleanor but for her own last-minute ingenuity. As the passage goes on, however, she checks our amusement by continuing the pose to say something for which we no longer feel irony appropriate: 'I know no one more entitled, by unpretending merit, or better prepared by habitual suffering, to receive and enjoy felicity.' This is not funny. The narrator seems to be taking the independence of Eleanor seriously, rather in the manner of a biographer, who knows that for him character and form are independent as well as interdependent. Is the 'tell-tale compression of the pages' by which the reader forsees a quick and happy dénouement, for example, the comment of a biographer or of a contriver of fiction? For both kinds of author, after all, the compression of pages is telltale, although the source of control over length differs.

Similarly, when Catherine comes back to her home in Fullerton, Austen repeats the tone of heavy irony about heroines and heroism with which Catherine was introduced to us at the beginning of the book, also in Fullerton: 'A heroine in a hack post-chaise, is such a blow upon sentiment, as no attempt at grandeur or pathos can withstand.' Nothing, at first glance, seems less appropriate than this tone. The irony does not, as in the first chapter, preclude tragedy or sympathy: twenty-eight chapters of *Northanger Abbey* have cured us of looking for tragedy and left us incurable as to sympathy for Catherine. Nor does she now fancy herself a prospective heroine; for the first time, she does not. Yet it is no accident that this renewal of irony comes just after the point that corresponds to the anagnorisis and peripeteia of an Aristotelian plot, when her expulsion from the Abbey has informed her what the spirit of Gothic violence might really mean, and has set in motion for her a redefinition of the Abbey, of Bath society (as typified by John and Isabella Thorpe, whose casual slander and golddigging glamour respectively refer straight to the General's motives), and eventually of Fullerton itself, whose adequacy Catherine is to find she has outgrown. It is at this point in the book that she can be least scathed by Austen's irony, and therefore when Austen finds it safest to reassert her authorial context of order, correlative with Catherine's. I will turn to Austen's context, which is connected with our education, and Catherine's, which is concerned with her own, quite shortly.

First, however, I might note that the autonomy of the characters is not merely a logical inference. It is intended and purposive. It sets this novel apart from the formulaic novels being satirized, novels that pretend to let one look directly at the lives of the characters without an author's intrusions, but which in fact impose a crude and familiar pattern on those lives. Austen lays claim to more frankness and less imposing of patterns. Another purpose of the autonomy enjoyed by the characters is to make quite clear a parallel between Catherine and us. She, with her free and unconstrained will, is trying to 'read' events, using inferences from her experience (including that from novels); we are doing the same thing, except that the events we are 'reading' are those within a novel. Finally, the autonomy of the characters, and therefore their free-dom, is important in a novel which puts stress on educa-tion, a matter of choice within a context of established possibilities. The co-ordinates of values and prediction that operate here refer directly to a freedom of assessment and to an ability to erect at least provisory laws, in short to a balance between the claims of 'liberty' and 'necessi-ty' (as Hume called them). The *Mysteries of Udolpho,* with its formulae, concentrates on necessity, the imposi-tions of the unchosen on individuals; the narrator's voice in *Northanger Abbey* supplies that dimension, but Austen must, and does, balance it with the other dimension, that of liberty, to enable education to go on. She makes the form of the book, unlike that of *Emma* or *Persuasion,* independent of the heroine's mind or perceptiveness, and the heroine ingenuous and unfledged enough, unlike Emma Woodhouse or Anne Elliot, not to cloud with her own personality the world she must interpret. This reduction of personality makes it possible for Austen to keep our attention on Catherine's freedom and also to bring pro-tagonist and reader into line with each other. To Austen, after all, her 'reader' is also a creature of reduced person-ality, a mere common denominator of real people, marked by a good heart, a moderate knowledge of the world, and a certain alertness.

As to Catherine's 'context of order,' as I have called it, it is designed to be, and is in fact, simply the sum of her experience as recorded in *Northanger Abbey.* Austen's, which is also made ours, has an additional depth, from literary convention. I can illustrate the effect of this dif-ference most easily with an example. Near the end of chapter 1 comes a list of choice phrases from 'works [that] heroines must read to supply their memories with those quotations which are so serviceable and so soothing in the vicissitudes of their eventual lives.' At first, Austen seems only to be making fun of sententiousness, or per-haps of pulling such moral blossoms from their proper gardens in Pope, Gray, Thomson, and Shakespeare. A closer look suggests that she has a positive point: so as to make the blossoms grow in new soil, they have to be part of a new garden. Catherine's literary snippets do respond in some degree to the forthcoming vicissitudes of her 'heroism.' The subjects of the six quotations are every one of them to be a major theme in Catherine's life, for they include (in order) social unkindness, obscured merit, education, passionate deductions from trifles, equality of suffering regardless of rank, and the pain of thwarted love. If the quotations do not soothe Catherine, they at least serve her. They offer her a matrix for her experience, and incidentally, they rebuke by anticipation the sort of liter-al-mindedness that Catherine is later to exhibit in apply-ing literature—Gothic formulas—to life. None of the quotations, as stated, actually works out in her adven-tures. She does not bear about the mockery of woe, suffer jealousy, sit like Patience on a monument, get trodden on like a beetle, or waste her sweetness on the air of Fuller-ton; nor does she meet anyone who does any of these. 'The young idea' is taught 'how to shoot,' but not (as in Catherine's source, Thomson's *Spring*) by parents, all of whom—the Morlands, the Allens by proxy, Mrs. Thorpe, and General Tilney—make pedagogues at best mediocre.

What the quotations do, then, is to point to modes of experience cognate or complementary to Catherine's. She must translate these modes into her own idiom and make them existentially viable, if only by rejecting them for alternative responses in dealing with her public, personal, and inner lives.

She cannot, of course, do this. Once she loses the con-text—her destiny as a heroine—which is her principle of economy and selection for these quotations, the quota-tions themselves seem pointless for her. For us, however, the novel itself provides the principle of selection. Whereas for Catherine heroism and her real life are disjunct, we see them as parts of a single continuous mode of experi-ence, a novel, within which whatever the novelist selects maintains a purpose. In addition, we can transfer the meaning of the quotations because Austen has shown us how to do it. This same first chapter, after identifying Catherine with the natural, has already converted the child of nature into something very much like a child of the novelist's art. The thin sallow tomboy, that is, has grown steadily prettier. The little girl has traded her insensibility for the shallow sensitivity of the adolescent, which for a heroine is the right direction. This process hints to us that Austen's irony will not turn out to be so exclusive as one might have thought at the start of the chapter. The seem-ingly excluded elements, without their conventional plum-age, can reappear in the perspective her irony creates, to do their jobs under new working conditions. Without this hint to improve upon, and without the fact and form of the novel to offer pattern to her, Catherine's reality re-mains only the immediate linear sequence of her young life. She cannot be, like us the readers, objective and systematic. When her sense of her heroism ebbs, her collection of literary snippets has no meaning *qua* collec-tion for her, but for us it is an artistic grouping contrived by Jane Austen, and thus has a meaning beyond any that the most profound and alert heroine, living within the novel, could find in it.

Another, more important, intermeshing of the social and literary themes in *Northanger Abbey,* as seen through the independent perspectives of Catherine and the reader, comes in chapter 14. Here Henry Tilney confesses quite honestly that he enjoys the tear-stained maidens and sat-urnine Italians of Mrs Radcliffe. From such a paragon of ironists, a confession like this is not to be taken lightly, and we are appropriately grateful for plain evidence of Henry's humanity. None the less, we must look at his commendation in context. The discussion about Mrs Rad-cliffe is parenthetized by Catherine's being twitted for misuse of words ('amazingly,' 'nice'). There follows an exchange about history, which Eleanor says she likes both for its truth and for its fiction (its dramatic embellish-ments of the attested facts); then an exchange about ed-ucation, promptly illustrated by Catherine's being taught informally about the picturesque; and lastly a contretemps in which Eleanor takes Catherine's intimation about 'some-thing dreadful' to come out in London as prophetic of a riot instead of a Gothic thriller.

Ignoring the separate benefits of all these discussions for

Catherine, one can see that the subjects discussed are really an analysis of the Gothic novel into components: words, pleasure for readers, history, didacticism, picturesque scenery, and the violence of life which it professes to imitate. Austen makes clear that these are in fact Gothic elements. The words that Catherine abuses appear in her discussion of *Udolpho,* and the 'something dreadful' turns out to be a novel. Picturesque scenery comes up because the 'beautiful verdure and hanging coppice' of Beechen Cliff remind Catherine of the French scenery in *Udolpho.* Historians are compared with novelists here, and elsewhere the age of Blaize Castle ('The oldest in the kingdom,' John Thorpe assures her) and Northanger Abbey clearly connects the past and the Gothic novel. As to novelistic didacticism, or what one can and cannot learn from novels, that is so obvious a theme in this book, and so obvious a concern of writers like Mrs Radcliffe, that I need not press the point.

In chapter 14, then, Austen fans out these components of the Gothic novel, so that each is exposed against a norm of some sort. The discussion moves in steady sequence from the more abstract to the more immediate, from the proper use of affective words to the proper horror at the mobs of Gordon or Robespierre, or, as I think more historically likely, of the United Irish Society. In between, on either side of the talk about education, lie the use of fictional art to dress raw annals, and, as its more substantial counterpart, the use of picturesque art to organize one's view of raw nature. We seem to have the full range of novelistic pretensions tested against norms, and to discover that on every ground but that of giving pleasure, the novels fail at doing what they should. Their indiscriminate emotionalism leads to a collapse of verbal and moral precision. Their historical and scenic folderol teaches one neither to understand nor to see. Henry's commendations are given the limits that he himself only half bothers to voice: the context asserts the *dulce,* but hardly the *utile* of fiction. The only crucial element in novels which chapter 14 does not mention, and thereby spares, is the least 'literary' of all; I mean the mimetic. Austen has suggested earlier, in chapter 5, that this is the genuinely useful part of fiction, which clarifies the dispositions of character and social intelligence in actual life. She has exemplified her point through the whole of her original volume 1 (chapters 1-15) during which the overtly 'literary'—the source of Catherine's illusions and Isabella Thorpe's poses—has been opposed to the real world, plain language, and calm analysis.

The second half of the novel, however, is to reintegrate the real world and that of literary convention through the central symbol (and titular 'character') of the novel, Northanger Abbey itself. Therefore, just as Catherine's group of literary clichés in chapter 1 turns out to provide a sort of thematic index for her later adventures, so the grouping of chapter 14 provides an index to the Abbey, in which her novelistic and social interests coincide. Words and violence, history and scenery, and education come together in two levels at Northanger Abbey. We have appearances: rhetorical gallantry from a military man, taking place in a building that blends medieval grandeur

with modern comfort, set among 'knolls of old trees, or luxuriant plantations, and . . . steep woody hills rising behind to give it shelter.' Appearances have their seamy side in the duplicity of the General's words and the brutality of his conduct, and in the subjugation of history and scenery alike to his greed for mercenary succession in the family and for show. These two treatments of the grouping in chapter 14, each modifying but not denying the other, are Austen's complex alternative to the stock components of the novel. In our—and Catherine's—movement between these two complementary treatments is the education in 'reading' that stands at the midpoint of the grouping in chapter 14, where 'to torment' and 'to instruct' may become synonyms. The process of learning through pain makes Catherine's and Henry's exercise in subjective lexicography end up a good bit truer than either could realize.

Another kind of revision that we can perform, and Catherine cannot, carries predictive weight within the story. I am thinking of the translation of the Radcliffean dramatis personae into the idiom of *Northanger Abbey*. If we consider the sequence of Mrs Allen, the younger Thorpes, and General Tilney, we find that we have pastiches of the Gothic novel's watchful chaperone, confidante, unwelcome suitor, and titled villain. But they are not pastiches of the same sort. Mrs Allen is the null version of the chaperone. Isabella is a genuine but corrupt confidante, and her brother a shrunken but certainly genuine unwelcome suitor. The General, finally, is a reasonable facsimile, within a social world, of a Montoni or Schedoni. The sequence moves from burlesque to imitation (in the eighteenth-century sense) of the Gothic, setting up complementary ways of using Gothic fiction within the new idiom of *Northanger Abbey*. By the time Catherine spends her last wakeful night in the darkness of the Abbey, the Gothic mode has been emptied through the transfer of its energies into her experience and ours. For Catherine, this is psychologically and finally true. For us, as we are sympathetic with her, it is aesthetically true: we at once see the General as the point of convergence where the evil of a Radcliffe villain can meet everyday life, and also as the point of divergence where everyday life fades off into the silliness of dark keeps and darker plots. If we define the General's power of villainy by his character as a Montoni, we cannot forget that sensible people find Montoni a cardboard barbarian. The General may also be more menacing because he is less absurdly parodic, 'realer,' than the other Gothic pastiches; but he shares with Mrs Allen and the Thorpes a literary allusiveness that is predictive. His acts are limited by our knowledge of their Gothic ancestry, and his villainy lives within a world whose claim to be final and tragic has been disputed by the smiling irony of the narrator from the first paragraph on.

Austen reinforces our sense of sequence among these characters—Mrs Allen, the young Thorpes, General Tilney—by making them progressive examples of a single theme, that of egoism, which is particularly appropriate to the self-aggrandizement and self-indulgence that Gothic novels nourish. She starts with Mrs Allen's costume, an external embellishment for a woman barren of both mind and children, a woman for whom dressing takes the place of beauty and social graces. Here the tone is light, the vice fixed on transiency (fashion, individual appearances at discrete events) and therefore without effect. The Thorpes advance this one notch. The egoism of John Thorpe has as its concrete symbol a horse and carriage, which suggests a mobility and continuity denied Mrs Allen. His main interest, in getting someplace, shows itself through gossip and anecdote and fantasy, all shoddy forms of historical sequence. And like his sister, he dispossesses objective time for the profit of personal time, connected with the speed of his horses, as Isabella's is connected with duration and punctuality in romantic or social engagements. Isabella is her brother's counterpart too in her claim of permanence, through fictions of Mrs Radcliffe's or her own, for her flux of actions. For her and John fiction and autobiography are identical. Her concrete symbol, the Gothic novel, and John's, his equipage, join in the abortive trip to Blaize Castle, that sham of the 1760s which John declares the oldest castle in the kingdom. When we pass to the General, and Gothic interest shifts from Blaize Castle to Northanger Abbey, we shift from the false history that the Thorpes represent to the real history of the General. His material version of the Thorpes' fantasy life, centring upon familial past and succession, has a real expression in property. The temporal and spatial extension of General Tilney, his ownership of the world, is greater than the Thorpes', and the Thorpes' than Mrs Allen's, just as is true of the share of reality granted each as a Gothic pastiche. The General's zeal for punctual attendance to his wishes follows from the Thorpes' use of personal time, completing the series of progressive analogies.

Austen dwells upon these thematic analogies to the extent that her characters share traits they need not have, like imprudence (would a real General Tilney be taken in by an obvious upstart like John Thorpe?), inability to put themselves in the place of others, and a disregard for truth. These characteristics are plausible enough, but one can think of unpleasant egoists—Blifil, for instance, or Mr Murdstone—who do not fit this mould. In *Northanger Abbey,* we get a continuity of temperament from one to the other so as to keep the analogies on the surface. We also get a continuity in the narrative. Mrs Allen introduces Catherine to the Thorpes, in a scene that not only broaches the theme of false history, in Mrs Thorpe's interminable reports of her familial past and present, but also implies some equivalence between Mrs Allen's and Mrs Thorpe's obsessions. The young Thorpes, whose mother imparts to them her garrulous self-centredness and her abilities as a historian, take over the middle of the novel, counterposed by their antitheses, Henry and Eleanor Tilney. From this opposition emerge the last two characters we meet, General and Captain Tilney, who are at least half Thorpean, certainly more than half in their sense of ethics. Therefore, one of our first glimpses of each of these men is in connection with a Thorpe—John and General appear, for a task of pretence, at a play; the Captain and Isabella in the superficial concord of a dance—

and the two liaisons thus formed determine the action of the rest of the novel through Catherine's leaving the Abbey.

Such continuity in the thematic action lends strength to our predictions. We can, for instance, limit our fears of what each malefactor may do, simply because each acts under the largely discredited aegis of his predecessor. In Bath, a lie from John Thorpe succeeds in snatching Catherine from the amiable Tilneys, in a parody of the stock abduction scene: she cries out for him to stop while he laughs, smacks his whip, encourages his horse, makes odd noises, and drives on. When the same man's lie leads to her being snatched from the same amiable company at Northanger Abbey, the pattern reaffirms itself to the discredit of the General, who has been its agent. We do not know at the time of Catherine's exodus why she is being cast out, so that our scorn is largely retrospective; but in between the two events, the narrator mockingly remarks of the General's eldest son, Captain Tilney, that his admiration of Catherine 'was not of a very dangerous kind. . . . *He* cannot be the instigator of the three villains in horsemen's great coats, by whom she will hereafter be forced into a travelling-chaise and four, which will drive off with incredible speed.' Thorpe's parodic action, followed some chapters later by the narrator's irony about the same kind of action, can hardly help bringing our sense of pattern and our literary consciousness to bear upon the General's brutality, cutting it down to size. Similarly, pattern limits one interpretation of the General's puzzling courtliness to Catherine, that he himself has amorous designs on the heroine after the fashion of Manfred in *The Castle of Otranto* or the Marquis of Montalt in Radcliffe's *The Romance of the Forest.* John Thorpe has been such an idiotic suitor that his example keeps the potential menace of General Tilney leashed; and Austen reinforces the pattern by showing us the triviality, and benefits, of Captain Tilney's faithlessness to Isabella, which Catherine learns of in the chapter before the General displays his faithlessness to her.

If one asks why Austen had to supply such close narrative continuity to get this sort of analogical effect, the answer may lie in her equivocal treatment of the genre 'novel.' In *Northanger Abbey,* the normative schemes of the genre meet with such irony that they must be lent a provisional validity by the procedure of the plot, which is our immediate reading experience. Austen lends them validity too by making us feel the degree to which she, as author, is in conscious control. For example, in the first half of the book, she offers us a symmetry of characters. Three girls visit Bath, one a false friend of Catherine's, one a true. Each has a brother who courts Catherine, and Catherine and Eleanor have a brother who courts Isabella. Both Catherine's friends have widowed parents, an indulgent mother for Isabella and a tyrannic father for Eleanor. Each Morland child is the companion of one, and the victim of the other, Thorpe child. When this sort of symmetry has been exploited, and Catherine leaves Bath for Northanger, Austen turns to a different sort of patterning, a balance of chapters. The novel as a whole has one chapter each of introduction and conclusion which bracket fifteen chapters in Bath and fourteen after Bath, the breaking point here being Eleanor's invitation to Northanger Abbey. Three chapters (17-19) pass between that invitation and the actual departure from Bath, three between Eleanor's declaration that Catherine must leave the Abbey (28) and the chapter of conclusion. The intervening period of visit has as its midpoint the imbroglio about the General's treatment of his wife (23-4); which, with its Gothic and social elements, acts as a transition between the three chapters (20-2) in which historical reality chastizes Catherine's conventional Gothicism, and those three (25-7) in which reality chastizes her romantic friendship with Isabella. The reader can hardly muster up surprise when he learns that Austen has placed the Abbey on so direct a line with Fullerton and Bath that Catherine's journey home is almost a physical repetition of her journey to the Tilneys.

In what she does for us, Austen is partially reminiscent, once again, of Fielding, the Fielding of *Tom Jones*. He too helps the reader with thematic analogies, uses formal pattern to assure one of his control, and flaunts a well-developed self-awareness of his own job as novelist, so that we in turn become aware of ours as readers. She differs from him, though—and I mention him largely as the greatest and most obviously congenial predecessor of *Northanger Abbey*—in two important ways, her use of allusion (the Gothic pastiches) to offer valid a priori predictive patterns to us, and her refusal ever to deceive us as our fairweather friend, the narrator of *Tom Jones*, so often does. A strong measure of a priorism is not surprising from someone writing when Austen did, nor is the fact that with the Gothic pastiches, as with Catherine's quotations and the conventions of the formulaic novel, we are dealing with the redemption of groups or structures by transplanting them, not simply with categorizing or assimilating individual phenomena. Austen's method thus is quite different from the burlesque of her juvenilia or the typical use of allusion for praise or blame. Her refusal to deceive us as Fielding does, makes our job easier but forfeits a measure of sympathetic understanding between her reader and her heroine; never forced to realize that we share Catherine's incapacities, we can remain rather olympian. As a result, one is inclined to see the book as a rational exploration of a certain kind of problem, the way in which reading a work of fiction differs from 'reading' real life, with the formulaic novel of Mrs Radcliffe and the redemptive novel of Jane Austen as two cases in point.

If in fact that is the problem set by *Northanger Abbey,* let us turn to Catherine, unprotected and naïve, to see what her methods of 'reading' are. She has no narrative continuity or balance of chapters to help her, but conceivably her novelistic reading might lead her to see analogies and Gothic pastiches, and thus to be offered clues of some necessarily vague sort. Catherine, however, only reads *in sensu litterali*. When her Gothic fears about the cabinet and the General prove false, she gives up on them, instead of trying to see how they might apply to the perceivable realities of life at the Abbey. In that idiom the General is, as we have said, Austen's Montoni—an avaricious warrior with an eye for a young lady's inherit-

ance—and the laundry list in the cabinet, as we learn by the end of the novel, is the social memoirs of a wretched captive. Here is the cue for the conscious tear: the mute voice of a young lover who stayed in the same room as Catherine, suffered from the same relative poverty as Catherine, and met with a contempt that anticipates her fate, just as his being freed for money and marriage anticipates (and effects) her fate. The narrator pretends to introduce this last point only as a means of doing her own laundry, tidying her novel, but as we have seen, that pose of hers does not deny the autonomy of her characters.

Catherine simply underreads, not overreads, in the Abbey. Once 'the visions of romance were over,' she still lacks common sense, which in this novel has no limits except those inextricable from human frailty: common sense knows that if fiction exists, and if people eagerly read it, there must be something to what it says. A kind of clue to this is offered Catherine by that model of common sense, Henry Tilney. He remonstrates with her, for her suspicions of his father, in one of those periods that make even amateur Jane-ites gasp: 'Does our education prepare us for such atrocities? Do our laws connive at them? Could they be perpetrated without being known, in a country like this, where social and literary intercourse is on such a footing; where every man is surrounded by a neighbourhood of voluntary spies, and where roads and newspapers lay every thing open?' These spies and this sinister 'laying open' are inversions of Gothic secrecy which are quite equivalent to it in restrictiveness. The power of inversion is to be shown in the General's anti-Gothic crime, that of posting the heroine to the bosom of her family on a Sabbath in spring—admittedly under conditions that make the General almost criminal indeed. But understandably, a Catherine lost in her shame cannot pick up Henry's nuance of tone. If she were a subtle enough reader to have done so at any time, she would not have had to be lectured in the first place.

Social forms, then, are the only a priori patterns which Catherine can use as a guide. To some extent, within the social classes among which she moves, they are a passable guide, but more for us than for her. We know that the economy of a novel tends to exclude the unique discontinuities of behaviour that mark our own lives, the results of a morning's dyspepsia or an afternoon's look at the state of the stock market. Novelistic acts are likely to be emblematic acts, expressions of a character's ethos within social norms. In real life, where such economy is rarer, one must test the degree to which acts are emblematic. The tool is empathy, intuiting someone else's dispositions and loci of action. Although a debased form of empathy is the art that the Gothic novel most demands, Catherine has never learned it. As Henry Tilney tells her: 'With you, it is not, How is such a one likely to be influenced? What is the inducement most likely to act upon such a person's feelings, age, situation, and probable habits of life considered?—but, how should *I* be influenced, what would be *my* inducement in acting so and so?' We have talked about a lack of empathy in our sequence of egoists, about Mrs Allen's assuming universal concern with her pelisse, or Thorpe's bragging about his bibulous nights to a shocked country girl. In terms of values, Catherine's egoism is far more benign than theirs, since it rides on the crupper of her guilelessness and good nature. In terms of prediction, however, it is deadly. Even if it were not, Austen's problems of prediction are such as can baffle the exemplary Tilneys, who misconstrue Catherine's riding off with Thorpe when she was to walk with them. They take her association with the Thorpes as a token of one thing, we of another; and this *is* a matter of empathy. But even we are as badly fooled as is Catherine when Eleanor asks her to visit the Abbey 'in an embarrassed manner.' What we put down to modesty really comes from the moral humiliation of having to perform a friendly act to a friend hypocritically, at parental command. Both motives, within the same set of social norms, would fit Eleanor's character; we work by probabilities and are wrong. In this 'novel of manners,' manners express character and ethical values, but completely so only in retrospect, only in the shape of history or art, not life.

All Catherine's education can do for her, then, is to lead her to realize how various situations might turn out, to see the alternatives to her own way of putting things together. Such a realization about ambiguities and the need for at once thinking like oneself and like others is the groundwork for irony. I do not mean an irony for the sake of detachment, except insofar as judgment needs disinterest, but for the sake of keeping open the complementary perspectives on the judgments one has made. That sort of irony is the goal, within the story as related, of Catherine's education. Her marriage to its finest exponent, Henry Tilney, marks not so much her leap to reason and wisdom—no one in a sensible book is wise at eighteen, if indeed at all—as her being united to a source of ironic vision, and thus becoming genuinely educable. Catherine's *Bildung,* we may suppose, shifts into high gear only after **Northanger Abbey** ends.

Jane Austen circa 1802; from a watercolor sketch drawn by her sister, Cassandra.

What the narrator's voice does in the form of the novel, then, Henry Tilney does in the narrative. Their irony sets forth the middle road between personal freedom and constraint. Personal freedom as an absolute ideal marks the wilful hypocrisy of the General and the Thorpes, whose worlds are fictions of their own contriving. Constraint marks the Gothic novel, in which fate and chance make all acts of will tentative. Henry and the narrator treat personal power or impotence, learning and fallibility, as part of a universal plan involving those Humean categories, liberty and necessity. Both can accept the valid shaping function, and also the limits, of personal fictions. The sign of their acceptance is their flexibility. Henry's first meeting with Catherine is an exercise in ironic pretence that echoes the narrator's pretence, he in terms of social form as she of novelistic form. Henry starts with the role of the Dutiful Partner, shaping 'his features into a set smile, and affectedly softening his voice . . . with a simpering air.' He next thrusts upon Catherine the role of the Dutifully Journalizing Ingenue. And then, with a straight face, he communes with Mrs Allen about muslins, entering into an impromptu reduction of reality, with improvised rules, instead of the stock reductions of a moment before. Henry's behaviour roughly approximates the narrator's taking the role of the Authoress in chapter 1, thrust-

ing upon Catherine that of the Heroine, and then entering into the characters' own versions of reality with an irony suddenly more covert. One of the crucial functions of the first three chapters is to use a transference of what the philosophers call 'dispositional' values, from the novelistic to the social idiom, so as to make Henry the narrator's viceroy. With this level of control now established within the narrative, Austen can introduce Catherine to its parodies, the Thorpes and the Gothic, in chapters 4 through 7. Henry's pliability and comprehensiveness are norms by which one tests their rigidity of disposition.

The narrator's viceregal use of Henry does not keep her from intervening too. It is easy to see why. Henry's irony tries to place within his world the characters and events that emerge within his field of experience. The narrator's irony tries to place within her world, the novel, the characters and events that she has endowed with their own life. To a large extent, these worlds and their populations coincide so that Henry can be a kind of spokesman for the narrator, and share in directing the energies of good sense. None the less, one of the themes of **Northanger Abbey** is precisely that the described world is different from the description of that world, in that the one is free and the other is fixed. Henry is to Catherine as the narrator is to us. To have a character take over the narrator's voice, therefore, would destroy a major interest of the book, by conflating its analogous but competing idioms. For this reason the narrator must continue to intervene. Perhaps one might add as a principle that the narrator ought to use a range of tones and techniques as great as she can, just so long as she does not distract the reader. The greater her formal virtuosity, the more energy she pumps into the organization of her novel, the more the aesthetic perspectives of *Northanger Abbey* can compete for our attention with the story being told. One of the virtues of this book is its controlled restlessness of narrative modes. Conversely, once Henry Tilney has proved his flexibility of response, he need show no range of ironic (or narrative) techniques. He must give validity to his irony by showing its relative adequacy to the situations around him; and so the situations around him grow increasingly complex and demanding, to test Henry's attitudes in this way. The narrative voice, then, is capable of change but not development; Austen's characters, including Henry, are quite capable of development but only rarely and surprisingly of change.

As I disagree with those critics who charge inconsistencies in tone between the 'Gothic' and sociological parts of the novel, I disagree with those who charge inconsistencies in viewpoint. Austen chose in *Northanger Abbey,* for elaborate and well-defined aesthetic reasons, to adopt a mode common in her predecessors. 'Inconsistencies' mark *Tom Jones* and *Tristram Shandy* too, if one takes the speaking voice behind the novel as that of a character rather than that of a rhetor. Unlike Henry Tilney, the narrator is not viewing events but relating them. Hence her concern about her function as novelist. The points of view that she may adopt, moment by moment, in helping the reader grasp the subject matter may very well be continuous with the points of view represented by the different characters. Her decision to say what one of her characters might have said, given his ethos, may be captious or uneconomical—though in *Northanger Abbey,* when the rhetorical demands of specific cases are considered, it almost never is—but such a decision cannot create inconsistency in method with her letting the characters speak for themselves on other occasions. Similarly, Henry Tilney may, without being inconsistent, imitate a stock character on one occasion, and, on another, speak in his own ironic voice. In short, shifting rhetorical techniques do not entail shifts in character because they do not entail character at all. At this level of abstraction, the narrator and Henry are interchangeable. But only the narrator remains at this level of abstraction.

Henry has a character of his own, then, which Austen must keep distinct from her narrator's personality. He is fallible, so as to show us the profits and pitfalls of someone's doing in real life what we keep doing as readers, solving difficulties and making predictions by using a priori structures. Although his intelligence makes us believe in his independence, he is deeply bound up in the action of the novel. At each step in the second half of the novel, someone hedges him into embarrassment: first his brother, then his father, and finally his fiancée-elect. Our

sight of him at Fullerton, numb, dumb, and blushing, sets him as far apart from the narrator as does the act of moral courage that has brought him there, for blushes and bravery (unlike shifting rhetoric) do refer to character. Weakness and strength both proceed from commitment, which representationally frees Henry from the narrator and grants him the sort of autonomy that Catherine and Eleanor enjoy by the end of the book. Once he stands firmly and solely within the depicted world of the novel, he can go on with his nuptial duties long after the final paradox on the final page of the book. What Catherine has not learned along with us, from the form of the novel, she will learn from the narrator's kindred spirit, who has now moved to her side. Henry, a clergyman like her father, can carry her off to Woodston, which is a kind of Fullerton plus civilization, and can improve the stock moralizing of her mother's *Mirror* (or of the narrator's final, tongue-in-cheek sententiousness) into a moral perceptiveness answerable to experience.

Our education is so parallel with Catherine's that we might be expected to have a formal equivalent, within the process of reading our novel, to the irony of complementary perspectives which she must learn to apply to 'reading' real life. That formal equivalent is, of course, the necessary ambiguity of the narrative in terms of its freedom from and dependence upon the hackneyed devices of fiction, and in terms of its priority to and dependence upon the characters whose lives it describes. The ambiguity can not be resolved, but just held in equilibrium like the figure and ground relationship in an optical illusion: are the ascending white stairs 'really,' when the drawing is turned about, black stairs going down? We conceive the illusion only by maintaining both possibilities at once. Austen's way of keeping this equilibrium is, as far as I know, original enough, although her self-consciousness about the powers of the novel points back to her legacy from Fielding and Sterne, who also knew that the epistemological patterns of novelistic form create a gulf between reader and character. The more the character approaches the freedom of the reader, the further apart grow their respective ways of dealing with reality, except perhaps in those books where form becomes a function of a protagonist's psychology. That is the kind of novel to which Austen turned after *Northanger Abbey,* with a subtlety and force of moral analysis not to be found here. Those virtues, fortunately for her reputation and for our pleasure, can compensate to us for her having abandoned the novel of ideas, and deserted the eighteenth-century—and modern—theme of the interplay between writer, reader, and character.

Katrin Ristkok Burlin (essay date 1975)

SOURCE: "'The Pen of the Contriver': The Four Fictions of *Northanger Abbey*," in *Jane Austen: Bicentenary Essays,* edited by John Halperin, Cambridge University Press, 1975, pp. 89-111.

[*In the following essay, Ristkok Burlin interprets* Northanger Abbey *as a "single, complex treatment of the theme of fiction."*]

In *Northanger Abbey,* Jane Austen came to terms with her art in a single, complex treatment of the theme of fiction. Every character in this novel is implicated in the fictive process. Its heroine is a novel-reader, its hero an inveterate inventor of fictions, its villains liars, contrivers of fictions. The complicated plot is based totally on fictions, each of its major crises being precipitated by a fiction. The first crisis is obviously Catherine's discovery of the delusive nature of Gothic romances, the second crisis, her discovery of the delusive fictions of Bath. The third, and most important crisis, Catherine's sudden and violent expulsion from the Abbey, is curiously precipitated by a mysterious, self-contradictory double-fiction, told at Bath but revealed only retrospectively. The secret working out of this double-fiction is the real plot of *Northanger Abbey,* responsible for its principal action, but kept deliberately a secret from heroine, hero, and reader alike. From the distressing perplexities of this mystery her favorite characters can be extricated only by the timely 'intrusion' of the author, who, with her superior knowledge as the supreme fiction-maker, demonstrates the necessity for the professional novelist in a world thoroughly permeated by delusive fictions. From her astonishingly aggressive authorial 'intrusion' near the opening pages of *Northanger Abbey* to defend the novel, to her noisy re-entrance at its end, Jane Austen's motive is to fight for her craft, to prove that it is the responsible novelist who protects us by teaching us through his art to recognize and discriminate among the fictions of life and art alike.

The traditional reading of *Northanger Abbey* sees it as falling unhappily into two disparate halves: a satisfying 'Bath' volume of realistic fiction, exploring social and moral values, and a disappointing 'Northanger' volume of rather flat burlesque of the Gothic, sentimental novel. But A. Walton Litz [in *Jane Austen: A Study of Her Artistic Development,* 1965] offers the key to unlock the door between these volumes by suggesting that 'in learning to handle the fictions of the Gothic world Catherine comes to recognize the other fictions which haunt her life.' Those 'other fictions' are, in fact, the principal concern of *Northanger Abbey*. Jane Austen's method is to expose the reader to four kinds of fiction: (1) the absurd extravagance of sentimental Gothic fictions; (2) the satiric, educative fictions of Henry Tilney; (3) the manipulative, egotistical fictions of the Thorpes; and (4) the satiric and realistic fiction of *Northanger Abbey* itself. Volume I (Bath) is dedicated to the creation of fictions; Volume II (Northanger Abbey), to their realization. The elegant thematic and structural transition between the volumes is effected by Henry Tilney's creation of a burlesque fiction, as he drives Catherine in his curricle from the one locale to the other.

Since the basic structural unit of all these fictions is language, the relationship between fiction and the chosen word is a major theme in *Northanger Abbey*. How Jane Austen's characters use language serves as an index to the kinds of fiction they create, as Joseph Wiesenfarth has elegantly demonstrated in *The Errand of Form*. There are four different kinds of language: (1) the 'best-chosen language,' the tool of the responsible novelist; (2) 'novel slang,' the vocabulary of the sentimental, Gothic novelist; (3) 'common cant,' the basis for social fictions; and (4) 'nice' diction, the instrument of corrective fiction. The battle for the heroine's understanding as well as her person, waged among these fictions with their distinctive linguistic weapons, creates the strategy of *Northanger Abbey*'s action and structure.

Because it begins as a burlesque, the novel initially invites laughter at its heroine's expense. But some important suggestions lurk beneath that burlesque. In the exploration of Catherine's early response to fiction the emphasis, however comic, falls on the unthinking nature of her enjoyment, 'for provided that nothing like useful knowledge could be gained from them, provided they were all story and no reflection,' she liked fictional narratives very much. Unheroically normal, Catherine's 'mental development' fits neatly into Dr Johnson's outline of 'The Climacterics of the Mind':

> If we consider the exercises of the mind, it will be found that in each part of life some particular faculty is more eminently employed. When the treasures of knowledge are first opened before us, while novelty blooms alike on either hand, and every thing equally unknown and unexamined seems of equal value, the power of the soul is principally exerted in a vivacious and desultory curiosity. She applies by turns to every object, enjoys it for a short time, and flies with equal ardour to another. She delights to catch up loose and unconnected ideas, but starts away from systems and complications which would obstruct the rapidity of her transitions, and detain her long in the same pursuit. (*Rambler* No. 151)

Catherine's 'slovenly' attitude to 'complications' leads characteristically to the adolescent's problem of discriminating among fictions.

If *Northanger Abbey* is Catherine's 'introduction into life' through fiction, Henry Tilney is the master of ceremonies. He is to enrich her understanding by making her acquainted with a complex world of fictions, to guide her to the point of his own cool judgment of literary fictions and keen sense of social fictions. But why should this experienced critic of both society and fiction, this wit and champion of the integrity of language, take interest in an inexperienced, literal-minded, uncritical young girl with a small stock of ideas and utter ignorance of the implications of language? If *Northanger Abbey* is to be more than a burlesque, if it is to meet the standards set by the new realistic novel, we must be made to believe in Henry Tilney's attraction to Catherine. One realizes through Jane Austen's success in achieving this in *Northanger Abbey* how much less schematic and more subtle it is as a novel than *Sense and Sensibility,* where Jane Austen 'flattened' her characters for the sake of its argument. Surely *Northanger Abbey* bears the marks of a mature re-working. Catherine never loses her youthful 'roundness.'

The relationship between Henry and Catherine is believable for many reasons: he is an eager teacher, she, an ardent pupil; she is found of him, he is found of admiration. But what makes the relationship most persuasive is that Catherine is unaffectedly good, and Henry, like Jane Austen herself, admires goodness more than cleverness. Jane Austen thinks this an important point, and indicates so by qualifying the disparaging remarks on Catherine's 'mental endowments' with which she had opened the novel with the more flattering remarks on the excellence of Catherine's disposition, with which she opens the chapter immediately following. It is *she* who tips the scale from 'mind' (ignorant) to heart ('affectionate').

Catherine's simplicity, her tendency to express honestly what she thinks and feels, and her puzzlement when confronted with deliberate ambiguity are exploited by Jane Austen to expose the fictions of the society to which she is now introduced. As Hugh Blair indicated [in *Lectures on Rhetoric and the Belles Lettres*, 1965], however, 'The great advantage of simplicity of style, like simplicity of manners, [is] that it shows us a man's sentiments and turn of mind, laid open without disguise.' To effect her exposure of social fictions, the novelist endows her heroine with what Blair terms, for want of a better English adjective, 'the naive style':

> It always expresses a discovery of character . . . that sort of amiable ingenuity or undisguised openness which seems to give us some degree of superiority over the person who shows it; a certain infantine simplicity, which we love in our hearts, but which displays some features of the character that we think we could have art enough to hide; and which, therefore, always leads us to smile at the person who discovers this character.

For those who want to hide sordid motives behind the cloak of ambiguity, Catherine's simple requests for clarification and explanation prove a source of perpetual embarrassment. This aspect of her naïveté delights Henry. He uses it both to teach her to understand the meanings to which she may give unconscious expression and to give her innocent satires a sophisticated thrust. In a typical scene, the interplay of dialogue between Catherine's naïve and Henry's sophisticated styles satirizes common social fictions and abuses of language, while suggesting the novel's fundamental theme.

The task, then, of teaching Catherine falls to Henry, whom most critics have perceived as her mentor, or guide, or even as Jane Austen's surrogate. She is rescued from the tedium of a conventional Bath ballroom by the witty fictions of Henry Tilney precisely at the moment she is most conscious of 'intellectual poverty.' It is Henry's ability to bewilder her through those fictions that charms Catherine immediately; there is a mystery in his manner, and she finds mystery intriguing. As Stuart M. Tave points out [in *Some Words of Jane Austen*, 1973], 'Henry knows how to use art.' Like his author, he has a multiplicity of poses, and in this scene he adopts that of a conventional Bath beau, satirizing ballroom dialogue while testing the quality of Catherine's responses. He is able to create such a fictional character of himself because Bath beaux have, in fact, begun to model themselves after the pattern estab-

lished by heroes of sentimental novels. As Howard S. Babb points out [in *Jane Austen's Novels: The Fabric of Dialogue*, 1961], Henry's satire is designed to prick the bubble of false emotionality, and his artificial manner ought to warn Catherine that she is entering a world of 'assumed' poses and affected responses.

When he perceives that his first fiction has puzzled Catherine, for she has 'turned away her head,' Henry reshapes the situation with yet another fiction: Catherine must keep a journal. Each entry in this fictive journal is cleverly 'contrived' as an explicit expression of Catherine's interest in Henry; implicit in each is Henry's interest in Catherine. The verbal artifact of the fictive journal permits him to indulge himself in the novelist's delight in exploring points of view. He shows Catherine how different he might appear from two possible views: he is the subject of both fictive entries, but each presents him as an utterly different character. And through the medium of this fiction he also immediately shapes her point of view: the 'heroine' in the 'sprigged muslin robe with blue trimmings—plain black shoes' is delighted with her author and eager to review his future 'novels.' And indeed, Henry has invented this fictive journal precisely to win her critical esteem.

But if the fiction of Catherine's journal was invented largely to foster intimacy between author and reader, Henry must abandon it if he is to generalize about 'journalizing'; her journal had to be flattering, and Henry's real opinion of the habit directly contrasts with his ironically expressed praise. When he enlarges his attack to incorporate journal-keeping in general, it becomes difficult, if not impossible, to separate as objects of Jane Austen's irony the language and conventions of the popular novel from those of Bath society. The shift from creator of verbal artifacts to critic, however, clearly points to the novel's theme; while Norman Page has said that all of Jane Austen's early novels are '*about* language,' I would prefer to say of **Northanger Abbey** that it is about language as it is shaped into pseudo-fictions, imitations of novels.

Henry's satire of the trivial and narcissistic journals kept by young ladies at Bath alludes also to the tiresome convention by which popular novelists expediently advance a narrative: the journal kept for 'absent cousins' that enables a heroine to detail her adventures at length. Henry's distaste is provoked by the carelessness of style all journal-keeping fosters. Preserved as a journal must be from rigorous critical scrutiny, it makes no demands on its author, and only reinforces bad habits of language and insipidity of thought. Dr Johnson's contemptuous description of the familiar letter as 'pages of inanity' (*Rambler* No. 152) would perhaps best express Henry's real opinion of ladies' journals. His extravagant praise of 'journalizing' as leading 'to the easy style of writing for which ladies are so generally celebrated' is Catherine's introduction to irony. For the first time she perceives that words may be used to convey the opposite of their literal meaning. Henry does *not* admire an 'easy style of writing,' which he sees as compounded of 'a general deficiency of subject, a total inattention to stops, and a very frequent ignorance of grammar.' To call such a style 'easy' is to cover careless and hasty execution with a flattering cliché. It is a misplacement of value on 'quickness' or on 'ease' above precision and care that Henry isolates as pernicious to good writing and rational communication.

Henry's notorious concern for precision in language, first commented upon by his sister, has been too frequently rehearsed to require elaboration here. His lectures on correct usage are scattered throughout the novel, his own tutors having been, as Eleanor points out, Johnson and Blair. The words whose misuse offends Henry, such as 'nice' and 'amazingly,' had in some part been collected by Blair in a list of synonyms 'to show the necessity of attending to the exact import of words.' His definition of 'amazement' ('I am amazed, with what is incomprehensible') indicates the direction in which Henry works to disabuse Catherine. Henry, the inveterate fiction-maker, possesses in his artful language those qualifications Dr Johnson set for modern fiction: 'It requires, together with that learning which is to be gained from books, that experience which can never be gained by solitary diligence, but must arise from general converse, and accurate observation of the living world.' Learned, sociable, articulate and critical, Henry creates fictions 'to initiate youth by mock encounters in the art of necessary defense, and to increase prudence without impairing virtue' (*Rambler* No. 4).

His fictions are thus very much like Jane Austen's: delicious inventions with a moral core. Satiric by nature, he too believes that fiction ought 'to give the power of counteracting fraud' (*Rambler* No. 4). His expressed opinions are nearly always consistent with his author's; he teaches in the same way and with nearly equal success. But his own fictions, those made up quite independently of his author, ought not to be accepted uncritically, as if they were hers. Henry is but the creature of Jane Austen's imagination, with a properly subordinate place in her work.

Ardent, eager, and empty, Catherine's mind is stimulated by Henry's fictions and prepared to encounter the world of the novel itself, experience heightened by fiction. But when removed from his direct influence, she is shown to have been rendered vulnerable to the world of real fictions, the novels of the circulating library. Again Jane Austen, in drawing a realistic picture of her heroine's intellectual development, seems to follow the guidance of Dr Johnson's analysis of the growing mind in *Rambler* No. 151.

> While the judgment is yet unformed and unable to compare the draughts of fiction with their originals, we are delighted with improbable adventures, impracticable virtues, and inimitable characters.

With one important qualification, her solid integrity, Catherine's mind is the prototype of the typical novel-reader's, described by Dr Johnson in *Rambler* No. 4. As such, it would seem vulnerable to the dangers Johnson finds in 'The Comedy of Romance.' This is his term for the new novel, dangerous in providing

> the entertainments of minds unfurnished with ideas,

and therefore easily susceptible of impressions; not fixed by principles, and therefore easily following the current of fancy; not informed by experience, and consequently open to every false suggestion and partial account.

Perhaps one of the happiest uses of fiction is its capacity to teach those who, like Catherine, are 'not altogether . . . particularly friendly to very severe, very intense application.' It would be foolish to patronize Catherine because she prefers fiction to history. Her choice of fiction and her infatuation with it are silly. But the tendency of her mind, its bent towards fiction, is not. What it manifests is a craving—in the midst of a trivial little world—'for a more splendid order of things.' Blair discovers a satisfying explanation for man's urge for fiction in Lord Bacon:

> Lord Bacon takes notice of our taste for fictitious history, as a proof of the greatness and dignity of the human mind. He observes very ingeniously, that the objects of this world, and the common train of affairs which we behold going on in it, do not fill the mind, nor give it entire satisfaction. We seek for something that shall expand the mind in a greater degree: we seek for more heroic and illustrious deeds, for more diversified and surprising events, for a more splendid order of things, a more regular and just distribution of rewards and punishments than what we find here: *because we meet not with these in true history, we have resource to [the] fictitious. We create worlds according to our fancy, in order to gratify our capacious desires.* (italics mine)

The Thorpes, too, have a 'taste for fictitious history,' but it is a corrupt taste, 'satisfying' a corrupt palate. They do not crave 'a more splendid order of things,' but the 'things' themselves. They do not have the novelist's passion for an 'ordered' world. The issue they take with 'the common train of affairs' is not that it does not 'fill the mind' but that it fails to fill the pocket. They seek, through their fictions, not to celebrate heroic deeds or the triumph of justice—as do even the 'romancers' *Northanger Abbey* often mocks. Their fictions are a mockery of poetic justice, for the Thorpes want to pervert justice to reward only themselves. Neither Thorpe as 'novelist' is interested in the possibilities of the imagination for 'expanding' the mind; imagination is not something they value except as a means to an end. Their fictions, therefore, are not a 'proof of the greatness and dignity of the human mind,' but of its meanness and egotism. They do, indeed, 'create worlds according to their fancy, in order to gratify their capacious desires,' but those desires are 'capacious' only in the sense of the largeness of their greed.

Isabella's quick intimacy with Catherine is itself a borrowing from the novel of sensibility, but Catherine is too naive to perceive that her new friend is herself a fiction, her character, vocabulary, and sentiments all emanating from the circulating library to which she now introduces Catherine. The further introduction to John Thorpe merely precipitates the heroine deeper into the 'land of fiction,' a world of factitious novelists. Under the influence of a self-created delusion that Catherine is rich, Thorpe affects not only admiration for her, but, through the 'cant terms of men of fashion,' a fictional presence that he thinks will win her. His steady stream of aggressively masculine fabrications rather offends than pleases Catherine. Despite his vigorous assertion that he has 'something else to do' than read novels, 'the stupidest things in creation,' that 'something else' proves to be the business of creating fictions and plots of his own to entrap the presumed heiress.

To alert the reader to the complexity and subtlety of social fictions, Jane Austen makes the Thorpes not only the fiction-makers we are accustomed to meet in society, but ironically turns them into 'novelists.' They structure their fictions according to the novel's conventional form, incorporating plots (often unfolded by consequent action), detailed description, the creation of character and dialogue, and the establishment of setting. All these novelistic devices are intended to create the illusion of verisimilitude.

Though the reader has been prepared for John's first major 'novel' by his history of petty fictions, its extravagant inventiveness and richness of detail still astonish—extravagance and richness directed, however, to 'exalt' neither the mind nor the morals. He simply wishes to alter circumstances to suit his present ambitions. Starting with a simple though false eye-witness account, claiming four times to have seen the fictive Tilneys abandoning Catherine, he proceeds rapidly from false journalism to the creation of a 'novel' of betrayed friendship, always adapting his technique to the ideals of 'the Familiar Novelists' whose complex constructs attempt to create the illusion of truth.

When one realistic possibility still holds Catherine back from crossing the threshold of Thorpe's fictive world, he brings together all the elements of his fiction to dramatize its fable. It is a final extension that comes closest to a piece of literary fiction, incorporating the creation of character and circumstance, illustrated with a piece of action, again characteristic of Thorpe's horseflesh-fancy ('a man who was just passing by on horseback').

Catherine's hesitation ends with the ending of the fiction. For not having recognized Thorpe's story as a fiction, she is forced to pay the consequences, which, ironically, take the form of the romantic heroine's most conventional dilemma—being kidnapped by the villain and misunderstood by the hero. A moment later Thorpe falls through the trap-door of his own staged fiction when he unwittingly tests it by reality. Catherine's reflections at the moment of revelation are a mixture of Thorpe's fiction and Mrs Radcliffe's, unconsciously battling with Henry Tilney's truth. Each of her discoveries about fiction is made in a context richly confected with layer upon layer of fictions, each serving as an ironic commentary on the other. Thus Catherine submits to Thorpe's novel because she had already so extravagantly tasted of Mrs Radcliffe's.

The Thorpes' second major fiction lies at the heart of the novel and is co-authored; its intent is to reshape the existing situation. Isabella provides the conventional social fiction of the 'previous engagement'; John invents the detail, embroidering the dull social fiction with a novelist's delight in particularity and fitness. While Catherine energetically strives for the truth, Thorpe has put Isabella's social fiction into action, playing author to a fictive Catherine, making her his creature, writing her dialogue, endowing her with his own motives and morals, determining her actions, and deciding her fate. Clearly, had Catherine not denied Thorpe the right 'to *invent* any such message,' it would have altered relationships, changed attitudes, and settled an impenetrable mist of indistinctness upon the heroine's language, style, and judgment.

Henry, on the other hand, uses his witty fictions to introduce Catherine to the complexities of the real world and the abuses of the Thorpes. Because Babb has offered so excellent an analysis of the materials of Henry's most elegantly witty fiction, the marriage/country-dance emblem, I will not discuss it here. I will point, however, to its being clearly a fiction, and not the product of a technique Babb terms 'metaphoric indirection.' Henry is not only making a fiction, but acting the part of the novelist. Having no space to prove the point at large, I introduce two excellent witnesses to the character of my argument: Dr Johnson and Jane Austen herself. Henry's invention of the emblem is 'an effusion of wit,' a product of the same qualities we saw mapped out by Dr Johnson as necessary for the novelist in *Rambler* No. 4; in *Rambler* No. 194, he identifies the same qualities as necessary for such an 'effusion':

> Wit, you know, is the unexpected copulation of ideas, the discovery of some occult relation between images in appearance remote from each other; *an effusion of wit* therefore presupposes an accumulation of knowledge: a memory stored with notions, which the imagination may cull out to compose new assemblages.

Jane Austen, in her own 'Defense' of fiction, cites the requisite qualities for the novel, or for the kind of mind necessary to produce it:

> some work, in which the greatest powers of the mind are displayed, in which the most thorough knowledge of human nature, the happiest delineation of its varieties, the liveliest *effusions of wit* and humour are conveyed to the world in the best chosen language (my italics).

Henry's third attempt at fiction-making occurs in the context of one of the most significant chapters in *Northanger Abbey*. Chapter xiv, almost entirely taken up with the walk 'round Beechen Cliff,' forms the nexus of the central themes of this novel: it explores at many levels the consequences of the abuse of language and is rich in implications about the use and abuse of fiction. During the walk, Henry is to discover how lost in fiction Catherine has become, and how her originally simple point of view and small vocabulary have been limited by the narrow scope of her reading and acquaintance—the novels of Mrs Radcliffe and of the Thorpes.

The walk begins with a significant discussion of fiction. Catherine discovers the error of one of her commonplace assumptions, that 'young men despised novels amazingly,' for in his witty defense of *Udolpho,* Henry allows that once he had begun that romance, 'I could not lay it down again—my hair standing on end the whole time.' He defends romances, though satirically, and attacks facile generalizations instead. Continuing in the parodic mode, he further encourages Catherine in her naïve acceptance of the Gothic as real, referring to the 'Julias and Louisas' of that world as if he assumed them to be as intimate with her as 'your friend Emily.'

When Eleanor turns the subject to history, we learn something crucial; what Catherine 'cannot be interested in' is 'history, real solemn history'; her preference again is for the ideal over the real. But Jane Austen also uses Catherine's candor to score a few points for her own craft. Catherine finds history to be more sensational than fiction—'the quarrels of popes and kings, with and pestilences, in every page.' It is 'tiresome' in that it has no mixed characters, less relevance to everyday experience than novels, and, though 'a great deal of it must be invention,' that invention is 'dull.' By pointing to the strong element of fiction in any history, Jane Austen indirectly argues for the role fiction plays in revealing truth. As the recorder of more commonplace events, the novel has a respectability of its own and need not descend to that common dodge of beleaguered novelists and masquerade as 'history.'

In the ensuing discussion of picturesque beauty, Jane Austen unites the three themes of point of view, language, and fiction. The Tilneys, in their knowledge of the picturesque, have a better vantage point and richer vocabulary than Catherine's. Henry attempts to teach these to Catherine: 'He talked of fore-grounds, distances, and second distances—side-screens and perspectives—lights and shades.' Correcting Catherine's conventional and limited point of view, he again attempts to teach her to see imaginatively, and critically. But while Jane Austen allows Henry thus to jostle Catherine's mind into action, she also uses his lessons to satirize a fashionable cult with its own slang and advances her theme of fiction. For Catherine is 'so hopeful a scholar' of the picturesque that she dismisses what her common sense tells her, even of present realities, so 'that when they gained the top of Beechen Cliff, she voluntarily rejected the whole city of Bath.' Adopting Gilpin's point of view, she populates the land with romantic figures.

The discussion of the picturesque forms 'an easy transition' from the regions of rhetoric back to the 'fields of fiction.' Jane Austen is forcing us to realize that the real world *does* serve as a source of fiction if looked at from the imaginative point of view, with a mind alive to the possibilities of the scene presented. In his 'Observations on the Mountains and Lakes of Cumberland and Westmorland,' Gilpin himself suggests the relation of the picturesque—as it comprehends the sublime—to the imagination and its creation of fiction:

> It is impossible to view such scenes as these without feeling the imagination take fire . . . Every object here is sublime, and wonderful: not only the eye is pleased; but the imagination is filled. We are carried at once into the *'fields of fiction,'* and romance. Enthusiastic ideas take possession of us; and we suppose ourselves among the inhabitants of fabled times. The transition, indeed, is easy and natural, from romantic scenes to romantic inhabitants.

The more sensible Henry, viewing the land, ponders instead 'inclosures' and 'the state of the nation.'

In the context of Henry's 'short disquisition' on politics, Catherine's report of having heard 'that something very shocking indeed, will soon come out in London,' is not recognized by Eleanor as 'novel slang,' but to mean the coming of a dreadful riot. By repeatedly stressing that the words Catherine uses are a friend's (probably Isabella's), Jane Austen deliberately transfers the responsibility from Catherine's intimacy with the wrong kind of fiction to one with the wrong kind of person. Eleanor's fears are a fiction based on a fiction, which Henry clarifies by turning Catherine's repetition of novel slang into the thing itself: 'Three duodecimo volumes, two hundred and seventy-six pages in each, with a frontispiece to the first, of two tombstones and a lantern.' But the danger of a careless use of violent words is expressed in Henry's fabrication of his own vivid but realistic horror-story. He is not content to relegate the 'horrors' Catherine had inadvertently raised to the world of the circulating library; these dangers have to be expressed through a novel different in quality from *Udolpho.* His novel is a vivid but realistic horror-story. He even makes his fiction personal, bringing truth home, by exercising the authorial prerogative to dispense with his characters, and knocking down his brother Frederick with a brickbat for the sake of his theme. His exploitation of extravagant cliché—'the streets of London flowing with blood' and 'the hopes of the nation'—suggests that such language is not limited to novels where it titillates the private sensibility, but may be exploited by the unscrupulous to work up the emotions of a mob into acts of violence. Henry is remembering the Gordon Riots as he reminds Catherine of the consequences of inflammatory language in the real world. [Norman Page, in *The Language of Jane Austen,* 1972] comments perceptively on this passage: 'an illustration, very pertinent to the central theme of the novel, of the confusions arising when the make-believe of fiction is mistaken for reality.'

The first volume seems to end with a stalemate in the battle of fictions for Catherine's mind. Isabella has successfully carried off her fiction of love and friendship, for she is engaged to James. But, through the power of his story-telling, Henry has strong hold of Catherine's mind. We do not yet know that Catherine is being carried to Northanger Abbey because of a fiction. During the journey, however, when Henry tries through his last fiction to laugh Catherine out of her romantic expectations of the Abbey, he succeeds instead in inadvertently persuading her of their truth. What makes this fiction of Henry's different from his others is that he yields to the temptation to go beyond his parodic intent. Catherine's flattering comparison of his fiction with those she has read, and his own delight in his skill of invention, is so gratifying that he is unable to resist taking advantage of the novelist's power to control—even to infatuate—his audience. For the first time Henry takes conscious advantage of Catherine's naïveté, and does so to her disadvantage. Because he forms his parody from the materials of her reading at Bath, it releases the effects of 'that sort of reading' in which she had there 'indulged' and seizes such power over her imagination as to determine the major portion of her actions at Northanger.

Unthinkingly, or perhaps because he is a 'novelist' of the commonplace by nature after all, Henry furnishes his fictional abbey with the chests and cabinets of the real Abbey. Unfortunately, he has transformed them through the medium of his fancy into enchanted objects. When Catherine finds herself surrounded by the apparatus of Henry's fiction at the Abbey itself, she believes quite naturally that she is indeed in a world ruled by the laws of fiction. Henry's 'novel' eases her over the threshold of the fictional world by making her feel familiar with its interior. But what is most significant about *this* fiction is that at the crisis of his narrative Henry abdicates his authorship, telling his heroine 'to use her own fancy' to complete it. If Catherine is indeed preoccupied with her 'fancy' during the first portion of her stay at Northanger Abbey, she has been given leave to do so. This is the first fiction Henry has not finished, and the first he has not wholly shaped to fit satiric or pedagogic purposes. With the interruption of the story, a temporal dimension is for the first time introduced into Henry's fictions. All his other fictions were carefully separated from reality, established as verbal artifacts, a 'journal,' an 'emblem,' the circulating library 'history' of the 'riot.' When Henry fails to enclose *this* fiction, it breaks loose and invades the rest of the novel.

Her Gothic adventures at Northanger are frequently referred explicitly to the influence of Henry's fiction by Catherine herself. Ultimately she blames him for some of her 'folly.' The 'darkness impenetrable' of Catherine's mind symbolizes the point of greatest submission to fancy; the illusions of fiction do not stand the test of daylight. But each time experience reveals to Catherine the absurdity of a romantic expectation she repents heartily—only to fall again the next moment a victim to further temptation. Her unconscious persistence in imaginings is indicated to us by the way in which she assigns malignant motives to inanimate objects, blaming a chest or cabinet for misleading her instead of herself for being misled.

Jane Austen deflects the responsibility for her heroine's delusions from Mrs Radcliffe's professional fiction to Henry's arrogantly amateurish interpretation of it. Whatever the cause, the effect is to call into question Henry's wisdom as satirist and maker of fictions. In this last fiction Henry is 'dangerously' close to usurping the author's place. 'Dangerously,' because without the author's prov-

idential powers he involves his heroine in perplexities he has not foreseen, while even the popular novelist is responsibly capable of seeing the heroine through to the resolution of her troubles. And there are perplexities he cannot foresee, such as those brought about by his own father's involving Catherine in fictions. General Tilney is as interested as the Thorpes in seducing Catherine for his own 'interest' through the creation and manipulation of fictions; like the Thorpes, the General maintains a fiction about himself. To realize his ambitions he uses language much as the Thorpes do.

But General Tilney is himself to prove more naïvely and dramatically susceptible to the most extravagant of fictions than Catherine. It is *his* belief in fictions, not hers, that is to change the course of her life. Though we cannot know that the sudden and excessive fiction of his friendship for Catherine has originated in his belief in John Thorpe's tales about her, we ought as alert readers to have suspected it, for even Catherine notes the change in the General's attitude to her after he has been talking to Thorpe. To dramatize the dangerously secret pervasiveness of fiction, Jane Austen keeps deliberately silent about *this* fiction while keeping the reader distracted at the forestage of her fable—trying to keep him, that is, abreast of the fictions in which Catherine is steadily entangled despite her own efforts to understand her experience.

As Catherine attempts to act out Henry's fiction, experience helps dissipate its effects. She comes to perceive its absurdity, to discover that it is impossible to sustain a fiction of this kind in the real world. But the more powerful and therefore more pernicious influence of Gothic fiction cannot be cured by experience alone. Jane Austen is careful to deflect responsibility away from Henry to Mrs Radcliffe for Catherine's most horrid delusion about the Abbey: her impertinent suspicions about his father's involvement in his mother's death. These distasteful speculations are clearly related to her reading of *Udolpho*—she thinks General Tilney a Montoni—and free Henry to scold her for her delusions.

Henry has to summon all his energy to address to Catherine that passionately forthright lecture. He may never engage in fiction-making again. His appeal to her that she use judgment must bring forcefully home to her that she has never once judged her reading by any critical standards. Henry's 'address' and Catherine's response to it have been so fully discussed by critics that I will only point to what may need further attention. Henry's catalogue of the rational bases of judgment 'Consult your own understanding, your own sense of the probable, your own observation of what is passing around you'—is really a thinly disguised statement of the laws of probability Jane Austen feels ought to govern the world of the novel as they do the real world. Catherine's 'disenchantment' is used similarly. It states more or less explicitly some of Jane Austen's own convictions about the limitations of 'romance' (while acknowledging its charms), and suggests some of the values of the new realistic fiction, such as the admission of 'mixed characters' into the 'literary corporation.' Other than this, it is important for the thematic cohesiveness of *Northanger Abbey* that Jane Austen should in both passages nominate language as a means by which evil is dissipated.

Catherine's new anxieties are realistic, for they originate in her acquaintance with the illusory realities of the Thorpes, 'mournfully superior in reality and substance' to those caused by Mrs Radcliffe—not because their fictions are more real or substantial than hers, but because their *consequences* are more painful and lasting in reality and substance. She is the innocent victim of their deceptions; she has played no conscious part in their illusions.

Isabella's letter is important but again so commonly discussed that I will only note its salient features for this argument. Isabella writes obviously in hopes of salvaging a fiction of feeling for James, and tries to invoke Catherine's help to remake the illusion. Her letter is, therefore, a testament to the Thorpes' faith that false words can 'set all to rights,' that they can talk into and out of existence whatever they wish. This letter is replete with fictions besides those of love and friendship: the language of fiction ('He is the only man I ever did or could love'), the fiction of the 'cold, or something,' the fiction of not understanding the quarrel, perhaps even the fiction of having 'mislaid' James's 'direction.' Isabella's shoddy reconstruction of the fiction of sentiment no longer deludes a Catherine made sensitive to fictions. Catherine acknowledges that she has never known the real Isabella at all: 'So much for Isabella,' she cried, 'and for all our intimacy!' When Catherine wishes she had never known an Isabella, Henry assures her, 'It will soon be as if you never had.'

But the Thorpes' fictions are not as easily dissipated as Henry's assurance to Catherine would suggest. The atmosphere created by delusions is so thick that it confuses even the deceivers. The Thorpes' lies actually change reality. We now see Catherine become the 'involuntary, unconscious object of a deception' over which she has no control. When the General discovers the futility of his fiction of friendship for Catherine, he dismisses her from the Abbey in a rage that postpones explanations. Catherine is violently forced into acting out the violence the Thorpes have done to language. Henry's retrospective narrative at Fullerton of John Thorpe's double-lie reveals that when Thorpe boasted to Henry's father about Catherine to enrich his own image, the wily General had planned to plunder him of his spoils. But to believe either of Thorpe's extravagant fictions (Catherine as the 'heiress of Fullerton,' possessing a 'rich aunt,' and 'sinking' siblings, etc.) the General must indeed have read pamphlets to the exclusion of novels, or he would have recognized in Thorpe's stories the sentimental clichés John has so obviously borrowed from the circulating-library novel.

The General's easy acceptance of Thorpe's double-fiction as real explains that violent act of his in expelling Catherine from the Abbey, an act for which Jane Austen has been so roundly criticized. Maria Edgeworth protested that 'the behaviour of the General in *Northanger Abbey,* packing off the young lady without a servant or the common civilities which any bear of a man, not to say gentleman, would have shown, is quite outrageously out of drawing and out of nature.' But the General's act is psychologically consistent and 'artful' as well.

Subject to his fictions about himself and what is truly valuable, the General has ceased to be real and thus becomes susceptible to behaving like a figure in a novel rather than a real man. He *is* a villain, just as Catherine thought, but in a fiction of John Thorpe's making rather than Ann Radcliffe's—or even Jane Austen's. If the General cannot judge Thorpe's fictions rationally, how can he be expected to behave rationally? If he somehow does believe in romantic nonsense, why should he not follow its codes?

When Thorpe discovers the reality that negates his original fiction, he contradicts it with another of equal but negative extravagance. This double-lie about Catherine to the General is therefore clearly prefigured in the earlier double-lie to Catherine about James's gig. We are thus shown that the trouble with a personal, impulsive motive behind the creation of fictions is the subjectivity that leads the creator to destroy as impulsively as he creates. Life imitates art, and by exposing Thorpe's double-lie Jane Austen reverses the formula by demonstrating how easily she can manipulate such conventional plots as Thorpe's, how casually create and destroy at will. The damage done by Thorpe's lies is too extensive for her own characters to cope with successfully. Jane Austen must step in to reorder the world of *Northanger Abbey*—not, indeed, to its original order, for that is permanently changed, but into happier terms than the manipulations of the Thorpes have effected.

For Jane Austen, language is not the appropriate medium for the expression of strong emotion. She *distrusts* the language of emotion: in making the expression of feeling too facile, it dissipates its strength and encourages insincerity and hypocrisy. Language is a corrupt mirror for feeling: it distorts emotion by reflecting it as either grotesquely overblown or excessively shallow. Because Catherine's feelings are fresh and strong, she has neither the need nor the vocabulary to parade them; her emotion is expressed in the 'language of nature,' though she 'knew not what to say':

> her eloquence was only in her eyes. From them, however, the eight parts of speech shone out most expressively, and James could combine them with ease.

The superiority of this silent grammar of emotion is confirmed in Blair's *Lectures:*

> Now the tone of our voice, our looks, and gestures, interpret our ideas and emotions no less than words do; nay, the impression they make on others, is frequently much stronger than any that words can make. . . . The signification of our sentiments, made by tones and gestures, has this advantage above that made by words, that it is the language of nature. It is that

method of interpreting our mind, which nature has dictated to all, and which is understood by all; whereas, words are only arbitrary conventional symbols of our ideas; and, by consequence, must make a more feeble impression.

Jane Austen exploits the irony that mute gesture is actually more eloquent than the most extravagant and elevated language of emotion to point up the absurdity of the Thorpes' parade of sentiment: all their excesses of sentimental language communicate less feeling than one look or gesture or movement or silence of Catherine's. In one sense, the 'silence' into which the 'good' characters fall as the novel reaches its conclusion is a mute protest against the corruptions of language that have brought their affairs to a crisis.

Even eloquent, witty, language-conscious Henry, the eager follower of Blair and Johnson, is reduced to silence under the influence of strong emotion. When, anxious and embarrassed, he arrives at Fullerton, his powers of speech desert him. At the Allens, Henry 'talked at random, without sense or connection'; to Mrs Morland, who has difficulty 'finding conversation for her guest,' he can say 'nothing to the purpose.' Henry has come close to usurping his author's role of teaching the importance of precise language. Now he becomes the victim of her benign irony. For just before the chapter that introduces Henry to the Morlands, Jane Austen has noisily re-entered her novel to claim authorship, and to take possession of its characters and materials. The assertion of herself as the 'contriver' of this fiction is dramatized by reducing her creations to silence as she raises *her* voice.

Her tone toward her own fiction at the beginning of the novel (always excepting the 'Defense') is quite different from that of the voice in the 'intrusions.' Unassuming, unassertive, she affects to be bemused by the strangeness of the fiction it has devolved upon her to relate: it is so strangely like life and so unlike romance that she does not know quite what to make of it. Most of the burlesque of the Gothic/sentimental fiction in the Bath episodes is characterized by this ironic tone. In reserving till later most of her intrusions as acknowledged author, while drawing her reader's attention to the faults and follies of another fiction, she quietly allows her own fiction-makers to set their contrivances in motion; as Darrel Mansell says in another context [in *The Novels of Jane Austen,* 1975] 'this puckish withholding on the narrator's part . . . creates a faint comedy between Jane Austen and her own characters that runs through the novels.'

In fact she does not raise her voice until her heroine finds herself in perplexities based on fictions from which she is unable to extricate herself without her author's help. It is Catherine's violent and unexplained dismissal from the Abbey and ignominious return to Fullerton which prompt Jane Austen to make her second major 'intrusion' into *Northanger Abbey:*

> A heroine returning at the close of her career, to her native village, in all the triumph of recovered reputation . . . is an event on which the pen of the contriver may well delight to dwell; it gives credit to every conclusion, and the author must share in the glory she so liberally bestows. But my affair is widely different.

Assuming an ironic sympathy with the shallow artistic fulfillment, the 'sweet elation of spirits' for what are essentially fairy-tale devices, Jane Austen implies that not only do such contrived and fantastic 'happy endings' suspend the judgment of the reader by making him too happy to be critical, but they seem to have the same effect on the author.

From such fictions Jane Austen carefully distinguishes her 'affair.' The thrust of *Northanger Abbey,* whose hero falls in love with the heroine from gratitude for her esteem, is a 'blow upon sentiment.' Its attempt is at neither 'grandeur' nor 'pathos' but at the 'midland counties' and 'central parts' of emotion. Appropriately, Jane Austen concludes the passage with a realistic touch, apt to the quality of her fiction different from popular novels—the brief reference to the Sunday loiterers of this small town for whom a passing hack postchaise is an occasion for the exercise of 'fancy.'

By reminding the reader at the crisis of the novel's affairs that it *is* a novel, the artist's delighted assertion of controlling power points explicitly to fiction as the central theme of *Northanger Abbey*. Jane Austen's rescue of her favorite characters from the consequences of irresponsible fiction-making calls attention to her own supremacy as fiction-maker. In each 'intrusion' she strengthens the novelist's position by speaking out boldly as the contriver of fictions of which she is not ashamed, but proud to shape and control. Making overt her own novel's parody of bad fiction, she explicitly distinguishes what she is doing from the efforts of others. [In *Nineteenth Century Fiction* 25 (1970)] Donald D. Stone cites Frank Kermode's idea that the novel is 'a history of anti-novels,' adding his own observation that 'it is by attacking the conventions of "fiction" that the novel maintains its position as a transcriber of reality.' Frankly acknowledging her craft, Jane Austen draws the reader into the process of fiction-making—even, in one 'intrusion,' soliciting his help for the best, i.e., the most probable, disposition of her materials. The reader is obliged to read fictions less passively, and, by taking a creative attitude to the novel, to appreciate it as an intellectual exercise, not as a sentimental escape. Encouraging his consciousness of *Northanger Abbey* as fiction, she opens its materials to him and endows him with some of her own awareness of its possibilities. Emulating Henry's advice to Catherine, she can even appeal to her reader's imagination for help in concluding her fiction satisfactorily: 'Consult your own understanding, your own sense of what is probable, your own observation of what is around you.'

In sharing with her reader the true fictional process, after having shown him the nature and consequence of 'false' fiction, lies Jane Austen's strongest, most telling defense of the novel. But perhaps its most charming revelation is Jane Austen's notion that the real motive for authorship should be the creation of joy in the assembling of materials to express truth. That is the explanation for the cheer with which she breaks into the novel to share directly with her readers her confidence in their mutual happiness at her ingenious invention of a reward for all of Eleanor Tilney's sufferings. The sketchy portrait of Eleanor's lover is, of course, exquisitely appropriate to the merry tone of the passage, while the particular detail with which Jane Austen condescends to 'finish' her depiction of Eleanor's lover mocks the superficial neatness of the Gothic novel. She has constructed her own novel, so surely to expose its 'tendency'—the exploration and resolution of fiction—that she impertinently invites us at the end of *Northanger Abbey* to misinterpret its materials.

She can permit herself the fun of making her heroines patronize the source of their being, the circulating library, itself a world of fictions, and form their friendships through the reading and discussion of fictions, without ever compromising their reality. She even interrupts them in their reading by suddenly exhorting other novelists to defend the fiction her own heroines so richly enjoy. This infamous defense of fiction is strategically placed early in her novel. What it achieves in this position is to force the reader to scrutinize the fictive process. With its apparent contradiction of the burlesque opening, the 'Defense' makes it plain that the parodic passages of *Northanger Abbey* are not intended to reject fiction, but to refine and redefine it.

Another such strategically placed defense occurs in her two critical 'asides'—to society, and to 'the capital pen of a sister author'—where Jane Austen yokes fiction with society, making clear at an important stage of the novel that the value of fiction (if it is responsibly handled) lies in the power to tell truth about life. For the source of this kind of fiction, unlike that of an *Udolpho,* is society; the novel pays back its debt through offering society a corrective fiction.

As Catherine increasingly submits her understanding to fiction, before we judge her we ought to remember that we have been warned. The world in which Catherine exists is itself an illusion; we can therefore only judge her foolishness as long as we ourselves foolishly believe in the reality of the fiction that gave *her* being, the 'reality' by which we determine what is 'illusion.' That Henry Tilney believes in the superior power of fiction over 'naked instruction' is demonstrated each time he engages to teach Catherine. For Jane Austen believes as firmly as Blair that it is not the novel but 'the faulty manner of its execution, that can expose it to any contempt.'

It is in her 'dear Dr Johnson' that we find a practical justification for the novel. For if Dr Johnson intended in *Rambler* No. 4 to warn readers and writers of the 'new' novel's dangerous possibilities, he also saw its use as a safeguard for innocence. In depicting society realistically, the 'modern' novel taught innocence what to fear, and ignorance what to detest:

> These familiar histories may perhaps be made of greater use than the solemnities of professed morality, and convey the knowledge of vice and virtue with more efficacy than axioms and definitions. . . .

> The purpose of these writings is surely not only to show mankind, but to provide that they may be seen hereafter with less hazard; to teach the means of avoiding the snares which are laid by Treachery for Innocence, without infusing any wish for that superiority with which the betrayer flatters his vanity; to give the power of counter-acting fraud, without the temptation to practice it; to initiate youth by mock encounters in the art of necessary defence, and to increase prudence without impairing virtue.

Northanger Abbey is, of course, a novel of this nature. It offers through the depiction of its innocent heroine in the hands of a manipulative, greedy society—her head the more easily turned because of the irresponsible fiction in which she indulges—a moral lesson for young readers. But it offers also a far more sophisticated lesson, for more sophisticated readers, about the nature of fiction and the art of the novel.

Michael Williams (essay date 1986)

SOURCE: "*Northanger Abbey:* Some Problems of Engagement," in *Jane Austen: Six Novels and Their Methods,* The Macmillan Press Ltd., 1986, 10-30.

[*Below, Williams analyzes style in* Northanger Abbey, *arguing that the novel exhibits a complex unity that eludes simple classification.*]

> *'Oh! I am delighted with the book! I should like to spend my whole life in reading it. I assure you, if it had not been to meet you, I would not have come away from it for all the world.'*

(Catherine Morland on *The Mysteries of Udolpho*)
Everybody knows that *Northanger Abbey* is a parody of the Gothic novel. Everyone sees that it is also, to borrow the sub-title of Fanny Burney's *Evelina,* the 'history of a young lady's entrance into the world'. And a well-established tradition insists that these two aspects of the novel are incompatible, even that the existence of each one is an active threat to the functioning of the other. Of course, the novel is also about reading and pleasure, reading and instruction. Does this help to heal the fracture?

The novel was probably first drafted after the earliest versions of what were to become *Sense and Sensibility* and *Pride and Prejudice.* In 1803 the manuscript was sold to a publisher, but never published by him, and Austen repurchased it thirteen years later. After 1803, she probably revised it at least once, but the nature of the revisions can only be guessed at, and in the last months of her life she wrote of having laid it aside in an apparently unsatisfactory condition: it was published posthumously. All of this seems to suggest that the novel is both 'early' and 'unfinished'; that it is a not-quite-successful experiment by a novelist who was yet to achieve the coherence of maturity; and that it is not much more than a bridge between the vigorous and percipient parodies of the juvenilia, and the substantial achievements of the later novels.

The novel has, of course, never lacked defenders: but if their attempts are regarded successively, then they can still seem in fact to be revealing an incoherence in the novel. Unifying patterns are perceived, but only by including some and not all of the novel's facets. What is omitted is then often criticised as being crude or irrelevant. A sophisticated account of the problem has been given by A. Walton Litz [in *Jane Austen: A Study of Her Artistic Development,* 1965]. He suggests that the chapters primarily concerned with parody—the first two, and the five concerned with Catherine's Gothic fantasies at the Abbey—'from detachable units.' He concedes that 'the Gothic elements are a brilliant commentary on Catherine's general character and behaviour', and he argues that Catherine is at once the anti-heroine, created in reaction to the Gothic conventions, and a heroine being educated 'into reality'. Yet he also insists that the expression of the novel's main themes is 'hampered by lapses in tone and curious shifts in narrative method', and he concludes that 'Jane Austen was experimenting in *Northanger Abbey* with several narrative methods she had not fully mastered, and the result is a lack in consistency of viewpoint'. In other words, the reader is prevented from engaging fully with the text.

Others have tried to perceive a unity in just this diversity of method. Katrin Ristkok Burlin [in *Jane Austen: Bicentenary Essays,* edited by John Halperin, 1975] insists that the novel is a 'single, complex treatment of the theme of fiction', in which the reader is exposed to four different kinds of fiction. These are 'the absurd extravagance of sentimental Gothic fictions', 'the satiric, educative fictions of Henry Tilney', 'the manipulative, egotistical fictions of the Thorpes', and 'the satiric and realistic fiction of *Northanger Abbey* itself'. But surely the novel is not only about reading and fictionalising, in the way that this categorising suggests? Jan Fergus concedes that 'the novel is about writing novels', but her interest is largely confined to the elements of burlesque; and, though she also claims that the processes of education are important in the novel, this is only as far as they affect the reader, since for Fergus the heroine is deliberately excluded from such processes. Eric Rothstein [in *University of Toronto Quarterly* XLIV (Fall 1974)] takes a significantly larger view of the question of education, in developing his argument about how 'the strength of *Northanger Abbey,* and its theme, emerge from the connections between Catherine's education and ours, and between the social and literary modes of her experience'. But, since his is a sophisticated extension of the contrast between high-flown Gothic improbabilities, and the ordinariness of the everyday, he is silent on the important non-Gothic literary links with the novel. Frank J. Kearful [in *ELH* 32 (December 1965)] claims that the unity of the novel resides in a complicated interplay of satire and serious novel: but he has to redefine the parody in the first two chapters to make it into satire and thus a part of his formulation.

Kearful also exemplifies the danger of making too much of the novel as a many-faceted thing. For him, Austen

> is writing what is not simply a novel or a satire, a burlesque or a parody, a comedy or a tragedy, a romance or an antiromance. She is, rather, combining elements of all these in such a fashion as to make us aware of the paradoxical nature of all illusion—even those illusions by which we master illusion.

But that begins to read like Polonius's recommendation of the Players; certainly it is more than Kearful's argument actually supports. Then, too, he assumes that the differing 'methods' exist as large and sequential blocks of chapters, but this leaves him insufficient scope for dealing with the way that there can be a shift of 'method' from sentence to sentence, or even within one sentence.

It begins therefore to seem that the novel is indeed attempting to pose important and difficult questions about the links between fictional and actual worlds. But, if we are not to conclude that the questions are muddled, we must find a form in which the different elements of parody, satire and education novel can each take their due part. This means in turn that we must establish a way in which the reader is able to respond simultaneously in different ways to the different elements, when they combine. Perhaps we need to think in terms of a continuum, one that will enable us to perceive a diversity of positions, and the complex interchange between the different positions that are reflected in the novel. At one end, there are accounts of Gothic, some so broad as to be pastiche, or even simple imitation, rather than parody; there are the occasions of genuine and cutting parody of the Gothic, and there are the significant echoes, often parodic, of non-Gothic literature; there is the standing of parody of novels into satire on the reading of novels, and that satire into a different but related satire on the social life of Bath, where art is the stylised representation of life, and life can seem to be an imitation of the imitation; there is the more straightforward reading of books for entertainment and education, and there are other means of acquiring education to be tried out, as a means of preparing for and coping with the exigencies and the commonplaces of everyday life. If the novelist touches frequently on different points along this continuum, singly and in combination, then it will be possible for the reader to see the Gothic and the anti-Gothic elements mingling, but also in contrast. Catherine Morland is a heroine in everyday ordinary unheroineliness; she avidly follows the careers of 'genuine' heroines in the books she reads: but she can also—on occasion—quite naturally become a comic approximation to the specifications of the high Gothic. None of these possibilities is complete in itself; each exists and functions in combination with the others.

That begins to hint at the complexities of the dialectic relationship between the reader and *this* text. But it is not merely that *Northanger Abbey* presents a complex combination of elements with which the reader can engage in a correspondingly complex dialectic relationship. The artful playing with possibilities and combinations that constitutes the text suggests that Austen is in some special sense aware of the potential that exists in the resulting dialectic. One could say that she is inviting the reader to share a joke with her about the nature of that dialectic. One could say that she is playing a 'game' with the reader in which she seeks to outwit him (and the reader who does not fully perceive the 'game' will still help to create a dialectic but will do so with what is significantly less than the text). Either way, this implies a large, conscious, ironic awareness on the part of both author and reader of the relationship between text and reader.

This is not to turn Austen into a daringly experimental twentieth-century novelist. Fielding and Sterne had already variously demonstrated how far a novelist could go in not dealing directly with his readers, but in teasing and mystifying, in digressing and explaining, and in arguing with his readers about the way the novel should develop. If *Northanger Abbey* is a direct descendant of these novels then we should expect it to declare its ancestry nowhere more clearly than in the opening pages, because, when a novel is self-consciously concerned with its existence as a novel, and its relations with its readers, the opening will of course be the ground for the first skirmishings with the reader. The obvious example of this must be the first pages of *Tristram Shandy*; but, for the purposes of *Northanger Abbey*, *Tom Jones* is probably more instructive. Fielding's interest in opening chapters turns out to be an elaborate joke at the expense of the reader. Authors, his narrator argues, should provide a 'bill of fare' before inviting readers to partake. The irony behind the seemingly reasonable suggestion becomes obvious when he tells us that his own bill of fare is 'no other than HUMAN NATURE', since this, he admits, is 'the subject of all the romances, novels, plays and poems, with which the stalls abound'. But what counts, he says, is 'the author's skill in well dressing it up'. And in extending his metaphor he is soon parodying the use of metaphor, so that we can smile with him while knowing that he is laughing at us. All he offers is the broadest of declarations—that at first his will be the 'more plain and simple manner' and that he will later add 'all the high French and Italian seasoning'. But then, in not answering the questions he sets himself, Fielding's narrator has actually demonstrated something significant about the way he intends to handle his material, and the kind of relationship he is seeking with his reader.

At the opening of *Northanger Abbey* Austen, like Fielding, sets out to play on her reader's expectations, and to reveal something of her narrator's functioning. But we are left less sure of what that functioning is, and of how her narrator stands, exactly, in relation to the material of the novel. If Fielding's narrator is ambiguous, he is at least a recognisable force, constantly and insistently drawing attention to his actuality and his opinions. Austen's is puzzlingly demure.

> No one who had ever seen Catherine Morland in her infancy, would have supposed her born to be an heroine. Her situation in life, the character of her father and mother, her own person and disposition, were all

equally against her. Her father was a clergyman, without being neglected, or poor, and a very respectable man, though his name was Richard—and he had never been handsome. He had a considerable independence, besides two good livings—and he was not in the least addicted to locking up his daughters. Her mother was a woman of useful plain sense, with a good temper, and, what is more remarkable, with a good constitution. She had three sons before Catherine was born; and instead of dying in bringing the latter into the world, as any body might expect, she still lived on—lived to have six children more—to see them growing up around her, and to enjoy excellent health herself. A family of ten children will be always called a fine family, where there are heads and arms and legs enough for the number; but the Morlands had little other right to the word, for they were in general very plain, and Catherine, for many years of her life, as plain as any.

And so we move on through the list of all the ways in which Catherine Morland is not a heroine. The effect, though, is to threaten any attempt by the reader to find a secure basis for his understanding. The opening sentence appears to have behind it the authority of the axiom, yet it carries no actual endorsement from the narrator, and is no more than an appeal to the consensus that is yet to be established. The ambiguity centres on the word 'heroine', and if we glance down the page then it seems at first as if there is just a simple irony at work: Catherine is a straightforward inversion of some of the more hackneyed conventions of the popular novel. But such a formulation soon fails to contain the problem, because, if Catherine is not a typical heroine, then what *is* she?

We are faced with the engaging puzzle of finding a way of being interested in a heroine who is 'ordinary' and thus 'realistic', but also not 'real'; is necessarily a heroine, even if a dull one, whose dimensions and functions can only be communicated to us by way of the dangerous and confusing and ridiculed literary conventions. Nor is it only that the realistic account of the education of an ordinary girl is beset by complicated jokes and questions about the way novels are written and the way they are read. The biographical details of this seemingly unsuccessful heroine are themselves a tangled string of paradoxes and ironies, each requiring a slightly different kind of unravelling from the one that precedes it, each weakening a little our grasp of what has already been revealed. A 'family of ten children' is 'fine', at least in the everyday conversational sense, but then this loose usage is criticised by the application of serious and good sense; serious, that is, until we realise that it is heads, as well as arms and legs that must be counted. Then we are told that the Morlands are 'in general very plain', so the word 'fine' is entirely inappropriate except in the already discredited conversational sense.

Later, it is revealed that Catherine's abilities are 'extraordinary', and the narrator seems to be operating with fairly simple reversals, since it is clear that Catherine is 'extraordinary' only because she is ordinary. It is natural therefore that she 'never could learn or understand anything before she was taught', since this places her in direct opposition to the absurd literary convention by which heroines acquire extraordinary knowledge and abilities unaided. But then we are told that Catherine is also 'often inattentive, and occasionally stupid', and here no simple reversal seems possible: 'ordinary' may mean 'life-like' but it is also rather dull. Yet of course it is a well established (though not quite universal) convention that a heroine be beautiful: and it *is* a universal convention that a heroine be interesting in some way. It is only at the very end of the long first paragraph, when we are told of her love of 'rolling down the green slope at the back of the house', that we can properly disentangle the ambiguities. It is the vividness, the particularity of this small detail, given ostensibly in Catherine's favour but apparently operating against her, that has on reinterpretation to be seen to work for her, that fixes some secure basis for our interest in Catherine. If she is ordinary, then she is also refreshingly natural, and she possesses the natural vitality of a ten-year-old child.

This security, though, is also momentary. The second paragraph informs us, with a telling irony, that Catherine becomes 'almost pretty'; the third that she has lost her tomboyish ways and is 'in training for a heroine'. So she stocks her memory with quotations that will comfort and sustain her through the 'vicissitudes' of heroineship. The quotations themselves are not surprising, given that this is a family in which *Sir Charles Grandison* is read (a favourite, incidentally, of Austen herself), but 'new books' are not easily obtained. Yet they present us with a very complex irony. Catherine, the vital 'person' who once enjoyed rolling down banks, and who even now has only a vague apprehension of what it is to be a heroine, is nevertheless *the* heroine of this novel, one who attempts to study the habits and functions of other heroines. Her eager response to *Twelfth Night,* which the narrator argues is proof that she is a promising apprentice heroine, is also evidence of the naïve literalness with which Catherine sometimes approaches literature. And this is a quality that will actively determine her career as the heroine of *this* novel. To Catherine, 'a young woman in love always looks—"like Patience on a monument / Smiling at Grief"'.

In many ways, the opening chapters of *Northanger Abbey* are the most challenging and disconcerting for the reader. Elsewhere the separate workings of the parody, the satire and the education novel, and the different ways in which they combine, can be as complicated and surprising (can even surprise because we have lapsed into a false security): but the later chapters tend to be a more thorough exploring of possibilities that have already been sketched. In this respect, the range of literary reference in the opening pages is interesting. It is usually assumed that this is confined to the Gothic, but, as the questions about beautiful and interesting heroines suggest, the range is actually much wider. And in this breadth there is an important clue of the functioning of the literary allusions and the parody in the rest of the novel, and to the connections between this and other elements in the novel.

The Mysteries of Udolpho (1794), much discussed in the novel, is obviously one source, but it is not the only Gothic

source. Further, Mary Lascelles has shown that the signally unaccomplished Catherine Morland of the first chapters is much more like the opposite of Charlotte Smith's *Emmeline* (1788) than anything in the Radcliffe novels: she adds the wise proviso that there is 'great similarity among the heroines of that age'. This takes us away from the purely Gothic, since *Emmeline,* though it has distinct Gothic touches, is also a quite respectable daughter of a Fanny Burney novel. The range of reference extends even beyond this point: being locked up by one's father is an almost indispensable part of a Gothic heroine's career, yet it is also a practice common to the fathers of Sophia Western and Clarissa Harlowe. And, when we are told that Catherine is so unheroinely as to prefer cricket 'not merely to dolls, but to the more heroic enjoyments of infancy, nursing a dormouse, feeding a canary-bird, or watering a rose-bush', we have moved to the area of the then current children's literature, and the pages of Thomas Day's *Sandford and Merton* (1783-9), or—even more likely—Sarah Trimmer's *Fabulous Histories* (1786): teaching children to be kind to animals was a part of Day's function and it was central to Trimmer's; both were also eager to offer practical instruction in natural history.

This widening of the range of reference operates as yet another means of undermining our attempts to find a simple and coherent pattern. There is, though, another significant consequence: Austen is not merely warning us that a too-literal application of fictional conventions can be dangerous; she is also deliberately invoking and examining the literary tradition within which such warnings were given. In eighteenth-century writing, the omnivorous tradition that charts an excessive preoccupation with reading, and demonstrates its consequences for characters whose expectations of reality are too much governed by the conventions of literature, became, itself, a stock part of the literary landscape, so that it could be established by a few hints. In *The Rivals* (1775) Sheridan's Lydia Languish illustrates the point exactly: we know precisely what to make of her as soon as we know of her voracious delight in novels; it becomes natural that she should have 'very singular taste'. We can anticipate that she would hugely enjoy an elopement; we can even guess the terms in which she would understand the experience: '—so becoming a disguise!—so amiable a ladder of Ropes!— Conscious Moon—horses—Scotch parson.'

Northanger Abbey has been connected by the critics with a particular strand within the tradition. This is made up of the many rigid imitators of *Don Quixote,* for whom the delusions generated by popular literature are *the* theme, rather than merely *a* theme, and who borrow Cervantes's shape to suit their own narrowly didactic purposes. Thus Charlotte Lennox's *The Female Quixote* (1752) looks to the heroic French romance of the previous century; Richard Graves treats Methodism and John Wesley in *The Spiritual Quixote* (1773); Maria Edgeworth's tale *Angelina: or, L'Amie Inconnue* (1801) is aimed at the excesses of the sentimental novel. And Eaton Stannard Barrett's *The Heroine* (1813) is directed at the Gothic novel, but also includes references to works as diverse as *Sir Charles Grandison,* Johnson's *Lives of the Poets,* and Madame de

Staël's *Corinne.* Austen herself responded with 'very high' pleasure to *The Female Quixote,* and she thought *The Heroine* a 'delightful burlesque' (**Letters**). Something of this can be glimpsed if we consider a passage from *The Heroine.* Cherry Wilkinson is convinced that she is a 'Heroine', and that her real name must be Cherubina de Willoughby; so her father, a mere farmer, cannot be her father.

> 'What!' cried I, 'can nothing move thee to confess thy crimes? Then hear me. Ere Aurora with rosy fingers shall unbar the eastern gate—'
>
> 'My child, my child, my dear darling daughter!' exclaimed this accomplished crocodile, bursting into tears, and snatching me to his bosom, 'what have they done to you? What phantom, what horrid disorder is distracting my treasure?'
>
> 'Unhand me, guileful adulator,' cried I, 'and try thy powers of tragedy elsewhere, for—*I know thee*!' I spoke, and extricated myself from his embrace.
>
> 'Dreadful, dreadful!' muttered he. 'Her sweet senses are lost.' . . .
>
> I relate the several conversations, in a dramatic manner, and word for word, as well as I can recollect them, since I remark that all heroines do the same. Indeed I cannot enough admire the fortitude of these charming creatures, who, while they are in momentary expectation of losing their lives, or their honours, or both, sit down with the utmost unconcern, and indite the wittiest letters in the world.

Barrett's version is of particular interest in relation to *Northanger Abbey,* because of the way it does not confine its attention to a single kind of literature. But it must also be clear that this kind of parody can only work in superficial and crude ways, and in this respect Barrett is typical of this strand of the tradition. There is a certain lack of skill and confidence, an uneasy interaction between 'fancy' and 'reality': in the passage from *The Heroine,* for instance, the joke about heroines writing elegant accounts of horrible experiences is apt, but only if we are not made—as we are—to think too closely of Cherubina actually sitting down to write this account. So, in general, the frequent and earnest reminders of the realism of the setting are self-defeating, and require as frequent explanations of the elaborate mechanisms at work in sustaining the illusions of the central character. That means, inevitably, that the sustained illusion will become progressively less likely, less interesting, less entertaining. Similarly, there is an over-eagerness in emphasising the moral: usually there is a solemn invocation of Cervantes, and the moral lesson he can teach; usually too there appears a worthy and wordy doctor of divinity, at the end of the novel, to lecture the character into a proper understanding of himself, and to ensure that the reader also gets the point.

It is worth noting, by contrast, that Cervantes himself never allows these problems to obtrude in *Don Quixote.* He relies, rather, on the degree to which he can control our sympathetic laughter, and he trusts to the workings of the burlesque. There is none of the muddling preoccupation with the problems of realism: the Don sees giants, we *know* they are windmills. Consequently, also, Cervantes shows no felt need to preach illusions out of the reader, can afford even to suggest that religious discourse is an ineffectual means of curing the Don: it is turned into the joke about a 'great and pleasant Inquisition' of the Don's books; quickly becomes parody, in the pedantic debate of the merits of each book; then becomes a satire on the careless zeal of such Inquisitions, when the priest loses interest and the books are indiscriminately burned.

While it would be perfectly correct to argue that Austen has a share in this tradition, it is surely wrong to suggest that *Northanger Abbey* is a significant reflection of that share. It is in the juvenilia, in works such as **Love and Friendship,** that there is the single-minded burlesquing of the Lennox or Barrett kind. Even here Austen shows herself, unlike them, to be free from the distracting preoccupation with the need to ensure that the picture is 'real' and the character 'deluded', and like Cervantes she turns the moralising into a target for more burlesque. When Sophia dies—she is 'carried . . . off' by 'a galloping Consumption', the result of fainting on damp ground—it is as one *heroine* speaking to another, not as someone cured by her desperate plight of the fanciful illusions generated by novels, that she utters her last words to her friend: 'Beware of swoons Dear Laura. . . . A frenzy fit is not one quarter so pernicious; it is an exercise to the Body & if not too violent, is I dare say conducive to Health in its consequences—Run mad as often as you chuse; but do not faint—' (**Minor Works**).

But there is another strand of the tradition that links Cervantes with Austen, one that will occasionally borrow something from the more simple burlesquers, but is much more broadly interested in the relationship between fiction and truth. Fielding acknowledged his debt to Cervantes on the title page of *Joseph Andrews,* and in that novel he made what he had borrowed into something that is very much his own. Smollett and Sterne are both under the influence of the same tradition, and Scott connects interestingly with it when, at the start of *Waverley,* he explains how Edward Waverley's reading has coloured his mind: Scott deliberately repudiates any link between his novel and the simple burlesques in imitation of *Don Quixote,* and the contrast he draws with Cervantes is put in terms which could be applied, almost exactly, to Catherine Morland. His subject, he says, is not

> such total perversion of intellect as misconstrues the objects actually presented to the senses, but that more common aberration from sound judgement, which apprehends occurrences indeed in their reality, but communicates to them a tincture of its own romantic tone and colouring.

It is after all the mere sight of the furnishings of Mrs Tilney's room that destroys Catherine's most fervid Gothic imaginings. Henry's subsequent lecture merely helps to fix that lesson. So, in making its own distinctive contribution to this more elevated strand of the tradition, *Northanger Abbey* is also showing how it fulfils the promise of its opening chapters. Catherine is the 'heroine' deluded by reading who must be brought to her senses, and yet she is also, more broadly and subtly, the young girl who has been somewhat confused by the difference between appropriate and inappropriate ways of understanding the world. She is put right by the pedagogically inclined 'hero': but Henry, while he can be pedantic, can also at times be possessed of a narrator-like irony, and he can be a young man who is rather too partial to his own wit. Further, he can teach her so well, and she be so effectively taught, not only for the sound literary reason that he is the wise hero and she the erring heroine, but because they are, albeit unequally, in love. There is also a final twist: we can see the way parody shades into satire, and the way both are intimately bound up with the education novel, but the parody is also a parody of parody, and Henry, the exhorting clergyman who has just come back from attending to affairs in his parish when he finds Catherine outside his mother's room, is also Austen's mocking echo of the wordy divine who so often dogs the closing pages of the lesser burlesques.

That should alert us to the way that the relation between *Northanger Abbey* and its sources and targets is constantly varying. Eric Rothstein argues that there is a pattern in the variation of treatment from character to character: 'Mrs Allen is the null version of the chaperone. Isabella is a genuine but corrupt confidante, and her brother a shrunken but certainly genuine unwelcome suitor. The General, finally, is a reasonable facsimile, within a social world, of a Montoni or Schedoni.' But this only partially holds. Isabella is a 'confidante', but she also sees herself as a 'heroine', and is a much closer and more consistent approximation to the Gothic model than Catherine herself. John Thorpe is the 'unwanted suitor' but he also comes close, on occasion, to displacing the General as 'villain'; and the General's 'villainy' is modified by the fact that he is the dupe of John Thorpe. Even Mrs Allen is not always merely the 'null version of the chaperone': it is clear that she in no way fits the Gothic requirements of her role, and it is as clear that she cannot properly fulfil ordinary everyday expectations about chaperones, since she is incapable of giving Catherine almost any useful guidance. But there are occasions when she much more actively inverts her role. Catherine's entrance to Bath's Upper Rooms is delayed until Mrs Allen, herself, is provided with 'a dress of the newest fashion'; they enter late because it is Mrs Allen who is 'so long in dressing'; and then Mrs Allen does so with 'more care for the safety of her new gown than for the comfort of her protegée'.

The range of variation in the use of literary devices is most obvious with Catherine herself. After her first meeting with Henry, for example, she is puzzled by his apparent disappearance from Bath: 'This sort of mysteriousness, which is always so becoming in a hero, threw a fresh grace in Catherine's imagination around his person and manners . . .'. A perfectly understandable response, but one which does not allow for the actual and perfectly ordinary explanation, yet also begins to suggest the excitement that a genuine Gothic heroine could have wrung from the situation. Conversely, when John Thorpe carries her off in a carriage, away from the interesting Tilneys, and towards the delightful horrors of Blaize Castle, the parody seems obvious enough, especially when we realise that, though Catherine thinks it genuine, Blaize is sham Gothic; especially when John Thorpe's bluster ('But Mr Thorpe only laughed, smacked his whip, encouraged his horse, made odd noises, and drove on') is the caricature of a typical Gothic villain. In fact the moment brings together a rich diversity of literary and social patterns. The business of the heroine being abducted in a carriage is a familiar enough Gothic cliché, but a famous non-Gothic literary abduction (one that Catherine herself would have known of) occurs in the exemplary pages of *Sir Charles Grandison*. And in *Northanger Abbey* part of the force and part of the comedy derives from the fact that Catherine is, on this occasion at least, entirely unresponsive to literary parallels, whether Richardsonian or Gothic, and sensibly and volubly insists on regarding John Thorpe's behaviour as being no more than rude and deceitful.

The practice of writing and reading novels is of course also openly debated by the narrator. The most obvious instance, outside the opening and closing chapters, is the 'defence of the novel' and, here as elsewhere, what might appear plain and simple turns out to be difficult and divergent. As the appeal for sisterly support from other heroines suggests, a criticism of silly improbable novels and dull over-literal readers is not a rejection of the novel as a form—a point that none of the simpler burlesques make with any conviction. It is also an energetic assertion of the 'genius, wit and taste' that can be found in novels. But the narrator becomes increasingly enthusiastic in defending novels, and begins to take up the role of a too-consciously partisan novelist, defending her art a little too vehemently: the polemic seems at once to be serious and a self-parody. The novel is, we are told, 'only some work in which the greatest powers of the mind are displayed, in which the most thorough knowledge of human nature, the happiest delineation of its varieties, the liveliest effusions of wit and humour are conveyed to the world in the best chosen language'. The real ground for the defence of the novel must lie a little lower than the heights of these superlatives. Then, too, there is the implied need for some means of discriminating between novels: *Cecilia* can perhaps be more enlightening and more substantially entertaining than, say, *The Castle of Wolfenbach*. But on what basis, exactly, do we judge this? How, more particularly, does the naïve reader learn to make the judgement?

For there is Catherine, herself a 'heroine', and one known to 'take up a novel'. Though the 'defence' has all the appearance of a digression into generalities, it is sandwiched between the first mention of the fact that Catherine and Isabella read novels, and an account of their pleasure in reading *The Mysteries of Udolpho*, and it is fair to ask how far the 'defence' connects with Catherine. In fact, she is something of an embarrassment to it: true, she does not scorn novels, true she does derive a great deal of the promised pleasure from reading them; but what of the high claims about 'the most thorough knowledge of human nature'? All Catherine herself claims, even for *Sir Charles Grandison,* is that it is 'very entertaining', and it is doubtful that the novels of Burney and Edgeworth, so eagerly praised by the narrator, would necessarily elicit a wider response from Catherine. Yet of course Catherine does take instruction from *some* novels: as with her means of finding entertainment in novels, though, she does it rather indiscriminately. Thus she rather credulously acquires a 'great store of information' about the ways of love, and the contours of French and Italian landscape, and the behaviour to be found in abbeys. But there is another complication, because, though she sometimes assumes that life is like literature, she has a firm-enough grasp, if not fully consciously, of the idea that literature is not like life. Her intense delight in 'Laurentina's skeleton', her insistence that she should not be told what is 'behind the black veil', both show that she clearly considers them to belong to the province of fiction and not reality. Similarly, when Henry offers for her terror and delight a pastiche Gothic novel it is clear that she at least half understands what he is about. And, when Isabella declares that, 'were I mistress of the whole world, your brother would be my only choice', we are told that Catherine is as much struck by the 'novelty' of this utterance, as she is by the way it reminds her of 'all the heroines of her acquaintance'. What this seems most cogently to suggest is a need to consider the ways in which these complex half-perceptions can be made whole, and Catherine can become more fully aware of the confusing border between fiction and life—a border that has been teasing and perplexing the reader since the start of the novel.

So we return to **Northanger Abbey** as an education novel. This too is an incomplete form, and we have to take it in conjunction with the other forms. We are told that Catherine 'never could learn or understand anything before she was taught' and this has already been noted as the pillorying of a popular fictional convention. But it is also a statement of the empiricist contention that experience is the prime source of all knowledge, summed up in John Locke's famous notion of the *tabula rasa.* This notion underlies much of the novel. It is obvious that Catherine is handicapped by a lack of experience, and that, as her experience, direct and indirect, widens, so she begins to build, sometimes usefully and sometimes not, on her understanding. Isabella introduces her to the pleasure of *Udolpho,* a pleasure which she at first assumes to be universal. John Thorpe's brash and muddled assertions about novels persuade her to revise this assumption, and so she hesitates to mention this favourite topic to Henry because 'gentlemen read better books'. Henry's response, though she does not fully understand it, persuades her to make yet another assessment.

But, then, the empiricist pattern, like all the others, does not hold completely, and Catherine is often moving, not always unprofitably, beyond the realms of her experience. Were she no more than the application of Lockean principles then there might be more justification than actually

exists for those critics who find her 'dull', or who claim that her mind is a 'somewhat implausible blank', because then the development of her understanding could be a steady and mechanical progression, as experience widens and knowledge grows. But no such orderly structure exists. Catherine's relationship with Isabella is illuminating, here, because Isabella is four years older than Catherine, and 'at least four years better informed'—at least in the matter of balls, fashions, flirtations and quizzes. It is hardly necessary to warn the reader of the selfishness, the false intensification, the constant reliance on trick and deception, that make up Isabella's behaviour; but it is interesting to notice how the 'naïve' Catherine responds. We might expect that she would tend to accept Isabella's version of the world, at least until experience proved it false, but in fact what happens is more complicated and less predictable. In their first long conversation in the Pump Room, she sometimes does respond unquestioningly, but at other times she is more critical, even if the criticism is not always quite consciously made. At some points, she rejects what Isabella says for reasons that are firmly based on her own experience, as when she questions Isabella's opinion of *Sir Charles Grandison* because she has herself read it. At others, though her criticisms are no less appropriate, they are much less the result of anything that she has experienced. This is most apparent when the talk turns to the interesting subject of young men. Henry Tilney's name is mentioned and Isabella offers some sisterly support but Catherine is able to reach something rather more profound than Isabella's gushing.

> 'Where the heart is really attached, I know very well how little one can be pleased with the attention of any body else. Every thing is so insipid, so uninteresting, that does not relate to the beloved object! I can perfectly comprehend your feelings.'

> 'But you should not persuade me that I think so very much about Mr Tilney, for perhaps I may never see him again.'

We know already that Catherine has been toying fancifully with the fact of Henry's absence, and this indicates the quite precise limits that she actually sets herself. And, though her only experience, in this area, comes from novels, she is not using that experience or she would more readily assume the inevitability of a happy ending. Even Harriet Byron, despite her much-prolonged doubts, does finally become Lady Grandison.

The arrival of John Thorpe brings another combinaton of possibilities and difficulties. It is easy not to like him, but it is worth noting how far Catherine moves towards an active dislike of him, since, as the narrator observes, she does not 'understand the propensities of a rattle'. Then, and it is another reminder of her vulnerability, her dislike is bought off by the fact that he is James's friend and Isabella's brother, and that he has offered himself as a partner for the evening, so there is a complex interaction of 'friendship' and 'flattery', of 'diffidence' and 'youth'.

With Henry, the links and the contrasts are most various.

For Catherine, he is the desirable suitor, who is also a useful instructor, as well as being a habitual and sometimes puzzling wit. His delight in his own wit is frequently at odds with his functioning as a teacher, and both are sometimes complicated and compromised as he becomes increasingly a lover: there are also times when, though he seems to be reaching the heights of a narrator-like detachment, he is himself firmly under the ironic scrutiny of the narrator. Inevitably, critics have tended to see this either as further evidence of the incoherence of the novel, or else have tried to regularise and simplify his functioning. But he is actually an integral part of the process by which different patterns are made to exist simultaneously.

Catherine herself is not merely the ingenuous admirer of Henry. After their first dance, she finds him 'as agreeable as she had already given him credit for being. He talked with fluency and spirit—and there was an archness and pleasantry in his manner which interested, though it was hardly understood by her'. This is entirely predictable from an open, good-natured and ignorant girl of seventeen: we need, it seems, only pause to note how similarly Catherine is quickly delighted with Isabella's friendship, and so to record how vulnerable this tendency makes her. Yet there is more. The distance between Henry and Catherine is never greater than when he gently but pointedly satirises the ways of Bath, which she is just beginning tentatively to understand, and uses a way of thinking and talking that is quite beyond the reaches of her experience. But she still perceives a good deal of his meaning, and, though she is uncertain, her impulse is to laugh with him. When he exercises his wit on a subject so well known to her as Mrs Allen, she can even wonder whether 'he indulged himself a little too much with the foibles of others', a view that is not entirely without justification, but is also probably coloured by the fear (not, perhaps, fully thought out) that, just as the quite unwitting Mrs Allen is being teased, so might she herself have been unwittingly amusing him. It is only later, when she is completely enthralled by him, that she more confidently, if a little confusedly, assumes that 'Henry Tilney could never be wrong. His manner might sometimes surprize, but his meaning must always be just:—and what she did not understand, she was almost as ready to admire, as what she did'. And, having thus discovered the beauty of his perfection, it is by an ironic reversal of the conventional love story that she is able, later still, to admit to herself the possibility, at least in theory, that he may have some minor flaws.

In himself, Henry stands for a succession of differing possibilities. In the early encounters with Catherine, he is obviously charmed by her frankness and innocence, but he is also highly amused by her, and will laugh secretly at her, for example, when he talks of the country dance as an emblem for marriage, and she insistently refuses to see an emblem as an emblem. But later at least some of the laughs are against him: on the walk round Beechen Cliff, for instance, the narrator dwells pointedly on the advantages to a young woman, at least if she is 'good-looking', of being ignorant, and then goes on to describe one of Henry's more serious attempts to lessen that ignorance by

way of a lecture on the picturesque, 'in which his instructions were so clear that she soon began to see beauty in every thing admired by him, and her attention was so earnest, that he became perfectly satisfied of her having a great deal of natural taste'. Clearly each is, to a degree, unwittingly duping the other and the self. Yet it is also uncertain, at least for Henry, whether this is more than a momentary lapse, since he soon appears to be complete master of the conversation again, and he presides with a narrator-like amusement over the confusion generated by Catherine's vision of the unreal Gothic horror, and Eleanor's knowledge of the real violence of the Gordon riots or the Reign of Terror. Later still, just at the point when he begins to find her 'irresistible', the ironist in him is muted and may even be silent: when Captain Tilney asks Isabella to dance, and Catherine assumes that he is motivated only by kindness, Henry tells her that she is 'superior in good nature . . . to all the rest of the world', and it is not certain whether this is a very gentle reminder of his satirising powers, or whether these are the words of a young man who is beginning to be decidedly in love.

All of which suggests that the events at the Abbey, far from being a tiresome interruption, are a natural, indeed crucial, part of a complex whole, as the novel works to its conclusion. It is entirely appropriate to his diverse functions that Henry, who on the way to the Abbey delightedly fuels Catherine's Gothic expectations, should also be the one to ask her, insistently, what 'ideas' she has 'been admitting' when she subsequently takes things ludicrously too far. Catherine enters the Abbey in ignorance, but with high literary expectations, and at first assumes an easy access to the superficial trappings of the Gothic— bloody daggers and lost manuscripts. When that proves illusory, she makes the second but much more interesting mistake of actually trying to apply the psychology of the Gothic to the person of the General. She treats the Abbey as if it *were* something in a novel; her excited 'terrors' are much more like those induced by 'Laurentina's skeleton' than anything she would actually feel if Northanger really were the place she imagines it to be. So, when the 'visions of romance' are over, when she is 'awakened', she has at last a firm hold on much that has previously been close to her understanding, but has never before been properly in perspective, about life and about novels. In this way she takes the decisive step into adulthood.

Or so it would seem. Certainly there is a lesson clearly learned, but how exactly is Catherine transformed? The novel does not, in point of fact, resolve its complexities quite so easily. Catherine sees through Isabella's letter and this might suggest an advance in her understanding, but it is one that is all but forced upon her by the fact that she already knows James's side of the story. And there is the moment when Catherine, having resisted all the Gothic blandishments of a stormy night, a late, noisy and unexpected arrival at the Abbey, and mysterious noises outside her bedroom door, finds that Eleanor has come to tell her that she must precipitously leave the Abbey, in what looks like the best Gothic tradition. Is this an intrusion of the Gothic as it might actually be found in real social life? We could then say that, though Catherine was wrong to think that the General had murdered his wife, she had actually fastened on to something ugly in his nature. But this will not quite do, since her ideas about him are based only subliminally on what could have been the useful evidence of the discomfort she feels in his presence, a discomfort which seems also to be felt by his children. Her thoughts derive much more from nonsensical pseudo-literary speculations about the General's relationship with his wife ('He did not love her walk:—could he therefore have loved her?'). Equally, it is possible to argue that the General exhibits no more than the social vice—about which there is nothing especially Gothic—of rudeness. If we believe that he is the dupe of John Thorpe, then the General will regard Catherine, such is the irony, as a kind of Isabella; and, given that he is irascible and forceful, his treatment of Catherine could *almost* be said to be reasonable. And there is Catherine's solitary journey home, which, since she survives unscathed, could be said to point to her newly acquired maturity, except that she seems too stunned by the suddenness of her departure to worry about its consequences, and the thing seems to point as much to the ordinariness of the everyday, or even to be an opportunity for the narrator, while seeming to apologise for the unnovelistic nature of the event, to make jokes about a 'heroine in a hack post-chaise'.

And so the matter of the exact change in Catherine finally evades us and comes to be something that we can merely speculate about, something that is still to be negotiated with a future that is outside the pages of this novel. The novel has examined ways of understanding the world, and the links between these ways as they exist in fiction and in reality, but it will not resolve itself into a too-easy aphorism about moral or psychological or social development that Catherine's progress could be said to demonstrate, and the reader who needs such a thing must devise his own. So, too, this novel about an ordinary unheroinely heroine ends, fully in the spirit of the opening pages, with the narrator deliberately reminding us that this is, itself, a novel shaped by art; it is not 'life'. The resolution of the difficulties of heroine and hero is so contrived as to be a joke about the clumsy unreality and the necessity of endings in fiction. Likewise there is a claim, for the 'perfect' future happiness of the hero and heroine, that can only belong to the fictional world. As a final joke at the expense of the reader, in the closing words of the novel's last sentence a spurious debate is initiated about what this novel can be said to 'recommend'.

Paul Morrison (essay date 1991)

SOURCE: "Enclosed in Openness: *Northanger Abbey* and the Domestic Carceral," in *Texas Studies in Literature and Language,* Vol. 33, No. 1, Spring, 1991, pp. 1-23.

[*In the following essay, Morrison undertakes a feminist, post-structural analysis of gender-specific spaces and sensibilities in* Northanger Abbey.]

Notre avis est . . . que si les aventures rapportées dans cet ouvrage ont un fonds de vérité, elles n'ont pu arriver que dans d'autres lieux ou d'autres temps; et nous blâmons beaucoup l'auteur, qui, séduit apparemment par l'espoir d'intéresser davantage en se rapprochant plus de son siècle et de son pays, a osé faire paraître sous notre costume et avec nos usages, des moeurs qui nous sont si étrangères.

—Laclos, *Les liaisons dangereuses*

Wir nennen das unheimlich, Sie nennen's heimlich.
quoted by Freud, "Das Unheimliche"

Catherine Morland, the protagonist of *Northanger Abbey,* Jane Austen's gothic parody, is ultimately disabused of her gothic illusions:

"If I understand you rightly, you had formed a surmise of such horror as I have hardly words to—Dear Miss Morland, consider the dreadful nature of the suspicions you have entertained. What have you been judging from? Remember the country and the age in which we live. Remember that we are English, that we are Christians. Consult your own understanding, your own sense of the probable, your own observation of what is passing around you—Does our education prepare us for such atrocities? Do our laws connive at them? Could they be perpetrated without being known, in a country like this, where social and literary intercourse is on such a footing; where every man is surrounded by a neighbourhood of voluntary spies, and where roads and newspapers lay every thing open? Dearest Miss Morland, what ideas have you been admitting?"

The outrageous ideas that Miss Morland has admitted are clearly literary in origin: she has been reading of the exploits of another young woman, Emily St. Aubert, the protagonist of Ann Radcliffe's *The Mysteries of Udolpho.* Catherine's release from these ideas, moreover, is also implicitly literary (or socioliterary, as Henry quite properly argues for the imbrication of the literary and the social): the exhortation to remember the country and age in which she lives reminds us that gothic atrocities conventionally occur in another country and time; the exhortation to remember that she is Christian (read: Protestant) reminds us that the gothic is conventionally associated with a deviant Catholicism. The man who disabuses Catherine of her illusions no doubt shares her taste for *le genre noir.* "Gentlemen" may "read better books," genre may be gender specific as Catherine herself maintains, yet Henry openly admits to having read *Udolpho,* and he is too fully conversant with the conventions of the gothic to plead immunity to its charms.

I begin with Henry's scene of instruction because I accept his contention that an economy of visibility or light ("a country like this, where roads and newspapers lay everything open"), what I shall characterize as an ideology of the *heimlich,* is everywhere operable in *Northanger Abbey.* I do not share in his assumption, however, his ideologically comforting assumption, that the *heimlich,* the dispensation of light or enlightenment that is now and is England, is the symmetrical opposite of the carceral economies, the gothic spaces, of the other country and time.

Henry ultimately posits—his celebrated wit and charm, his thoroughly ironic relation to the discourse of others notwithstanding—a Manichaean world of stable oppositions, a victory of the domestic forces of light over the alien and archaic forces of darkness. Against Henry, however, or against his tendency to circumscribe interpretive possibilities, I shall argue for the presence of an "unheimlich" movement, both within *Northanger Abbey* and between *Northanger Abbey* and *The Mysteries of Udolpho,* subversive of the oppositions here/there, now/then, light/dark, open/closed, the various binarisms that structure his celebration of "a country like this."

Before proceeding, however, a word or two about my use of the word "subversive," which is now something of a staple in the critical lexicon: I in no way mean to suggest that the subversion of a binary opposition, which is currently the most routine of critical gestures, is necessarily subversive in any broader ideological or political sense. In Freud's "Das Unheimliche," for example, which will figure prominently in what follows, the uncanny is both "a word the meaning of which develops in the direction of ambivalence, until it finally coincides with its opposite," and a return of the repressed, something that occurs "either when infantile experiences which have been repressed are once more revived by some impression, or when primitive beliefs which have been surmounted seem once more to be confirmed." And an uncanny effacement of the binary, or an uncanny return of the repressed, does indeed render unstable the opposition between the primitive and the civilized that is everywhere operable in Henry's ethnocentric ideology of the *heimlich.* Yet if the instability of the opposition subverts Henry's ethnocentrism, it nevertheless remains the basis of the sexual politics of "a country like this," of the power Henry wields over Catherine and Eleanor, for *Northanger Abbey* is everywhere given to a gender specific version of the modality of power that Foucault, who will also figure prominently in what follows, terms "panoptic" or "disciplinary." And panoptic power, like the Freudian "uncanny," also involves the "return" of the "repressed," the recovery of "primitive" technologies of the carceral, the gothic dungeon, in the civilized or enlightened mode of "compulsory visibility." *Northanger Abbey,* I shall argue, reinscribes the gothic carceral as the carceral positioning of the reading subject, a fully gendered subject, in relation to the literature of the carceral. "I cannot speak well enough to be unintelligible," Catherine tells Henry, and therein lies the principle of her claustration: in the panoptic hold of a gender-specific intelligibility or legibility from which there is no escape. But this is to anticipate much of what follows, and I want only to warn against too easy an identification of the subversion of the binary with subversion in a broadly political or ideological sense.

The oppositions that govern Henry's celebration of "a country like this" are perfectly explicit in his rebuke to his "Dearest Miss Morland": Catherine lives here, not there, now, not then; she is therefore disqualified from true participation in (as opposed to the mere literary perusal of) gothic surmises, gothic horrors. But what Henry does not realize, although it is implicit in the fact that he

is the source of the rebuke, is that Catherine's surmises do conform to at least one of the requirements of the legitimately gothic, which is the temporary absence of an authorized male presence or aesthetic principle. For Catherine indulges in wild speculation at a time when she is effectively outside parental or paternal control, when she is in essence nobody's daughter, and when she is not yet effectively under Henry's control, when she is in fact nobody's wife. And as her speculations are in error, gothic surmises, Catherine's "dreadful" ideas, are associated with but a negative order of freedom, a respite from male standards of probability and propriety to which she will yet revert. "What have you been judging from?" asks Henry, the answer to which is not only *The Mysteries of Udolpho* or *The Romance of the Forest,* those narratives of other times and places, but from a female sensibility that is itself apparently incapable of judging properly. Yet it is precisely these other narratives, or these narratives of other times and places, that identify the gothic as an excess of female sensibility and that are therefore implicit in the very rebuke that seeks to argue their irrelevance.

Emily St. Aubert, for example, indulges in wild speculation (which, at least as it touches upon supernatural phenomena and certain aspects of her parents' marriage, is no less erroneous than Catherine's) at a time when she too is effectively outside parental or paternal control, when she can no longer be defined as anybody's daughter, and when she is not yet effectively under Valancourt's control, when she is not yet anybody's wife. Catherine is rebuked retroactively for her dreadful surmises, and Emily is warned proleptically of the dangers of sensibility. Both, however, simply deviate from a norm; both are placed, put in their place, in relation to male standards of propriety and proper representation:

> "Above all, my dear Emily," said he, "do not indulge in the pride of fine feeling, the romantic error of amiable minds. Those, who really possess sensibility, ought early to be taught, that it is a dangerous quality, which is continually extracting the excess of misery, or delight, from every surrounding circumstance. . . . We become the victim of our feelings, unless we can in some degree command them. . . . I know you will say, that you are contented sometimes to suffer, rather than to give up your refined sense of happiness, at others; but, when your mind has been long harassed by vicissitude, you will be content to rest, and you will then recover from your delusion."

These words of paternal advice possess both the authority of the deathbed and the power to reverberate throughout the entirety of Radcliffe's narrative: "When your mind has been long harassed by vicissitude, you will be content to rest, and you will then recover from your delusion" reads very much as an economical summary of the adventures Emily has yet to experience and, hence, as an implicit warning against the danger that is *The Mysteries of Udolpho* itself. Emily is explicitly enjoined by her dying father not to read certain documents: "These papers you must burn—and, solemnly I command you, *without examining them.*" She is also implicitly instructed, as it were, how not to read the novel in which she figures.

Emily, however, "unremembers" the paternal injunction ("forgets" seems too active a word for this, the most passive of all possible heroines) and proceeds to extricate every possibility for emotional identification from every situation:

> As she gazed, the light died away on its [the fortress of Udolpho's] walls, leaving a melancholy purple tint, which spread deeper and deeper, as the thin vapour crept up the mountain, while the battlements above were still tipped by splendour. . . . As the twilight deepened, its features became more awful in obscurity, and Emily continued to gaze, till its clustering towers were alone seen, rising over the tops of the woods, beneath whose thick shade the carriages soon after began to ascend.

Emily weaves dreamscape and landscape in an absorption that unites them psychologically, not a mimesis that divorces them aesthetically: her "poetic" might be rather broadly characterized as "Longinian." Her father, however, had implicitly advocated something resembling Aristotelian standards of probability and objectivity, and *Udolpho,* in finally rationalizing its supernatural phenomena, capitulates to the paternal preference. It is significant, of course, that the preference is paternal and, hence, socially authorized. The implicit connection between social and aesthetic propriety works negatively as well as positively, and Radcliffe is eager to exploit the former once the latter has been established. Emily is first found in polite if rather limited society, comfortably at home in her parlor; she is then transported to the "other country," isolated from the familiar social conventions that would both temper misjudgment and allow her to distinguish the projections of excessive sensibility from the legitimately threatening. It is not accidental that Emily constructs her Longinian reverie or nightmare at a time when she is effectively neither daughter nor wife, when she is exiled from the domestic parlor of her father and when she has not yet recovered that parlor with Valancourt. Social and aesthetic indeterminacy are here one and the same: both are analogous to the theological explanation of evil as *defectus* or deficiency, evil as the simple absence of the good. The absence is that of an authorized male presence or aesthetic principle.

The very existence of *The Mysteries of Udolpho* seems, then, predicated on a determinate distance that separates the world of Emily and her father from the world of Emily and Montoni. The very existence of **Northanger Abbey,** moreover, seems predicated on a determinate distance that separates the world of Catherine and Henry from the world of Emily and Montoni. Henry can release Catherine from her gothic illusions, however, only by invoking the ideological standards that are themselves the staple of the gothic, which suggests that the distance between texts will not hold. And it may be that the distances within the text of the gothic proper are equally unstable, for it is precisely the distance that separates the world of Emily and her father from Emily and Montoni—which is also the epistemological space that separates "male" discourses of the objective and probable from "female" discourses of the subjective and psychological—that *Udolpho* cannot maintain.

La Vallée, for example, Emily's paternal home, is initially characterized in terms of its seclusion, concealment in its benign form. St. Aubert retires to "this remote corner of the earth," as Madame Quensel contemptuously calls it, out of a principled weariness with the world. Indeed, the intrusion of the Quensels into this world, with their talk of court intrigues and secret treaties, only confirms the view that the world has been well lost to the Auberts. Here the *heimlich* or "homely" participates only in what Freud characterizes as "two sets of ideas, which, without being contradictory, are yet very different: on the one hand it means what is familiar and agreeable, and on the other, what is concealed and kept out of sight." Yet what is first presented as difference without contradiction soon dissolves into nonfunctional differences, the *heimlich* as the *unheimlich,* the "homely" as the other country, the other country as home.

Emily in Montoni's clutches, for example, in the gothic portion of *Udolpho* proper, is both literally concealed and the victim of concealed motives and machinations. Emily herself, however, conceals her presentiments of her father's impending death in the opening scenes of the novel, and knowledge of her aunt's fate is concealed from her, the meaning of which it will take her much of the novel to discover. Geography distances the pastoral retreat of La Vallée from the political intrigues of Paris, as it distances Emily's domestic parlor from Montoni's gothic fortress. Yet what geography divides, an economy of secrecy and concealment unites. The world of Montoni is posited as foreign, deviant, as half the product of a female sensibility in want of properly male standards of objectivity and probability (Radcliffe shows us Udolpho through the eyes of her protagonist, which means that the precise nature of the danger that confronts Emily is never fully specified). The ostensibly deviant, however, proves to be little more than a gothic fortress in which women characteristically retire to the chambers above, while below port-drinking men decide the fate of the world. It is a fully recognizable picture of eighteenth-century domestic life. It is also an implicit suggestion that the unspecified danger that confronts Emily is the world of her domestic parlor. Emily does experience the *unheimlich* as what Freud calls the "gloomy," the "dismal," the "ghastly." But as Freud's study of the uncanny is at pains to show, and as Radcliffe's narrative perhaps unwittingly suggests, the *unheimlich* does not function as the symmetrical opposite of the familiar or the congenial.

Emily's retreat into the world of Longinian reverie, her "unremembering" of the paternal injunction, cannot, in other words, be fully distinguished from all things objective, the realities of patriarchal culture. The gothic can thus be seen as the literalization of subjective experience, the actualization in the object world of dreams, fears, and desires, or the deliteralization of objective experience, the projection of contemporary social experience as dreams, fears, and desires. It cannot be seen, however, as the symmetrical opposite of the domestic. Emily "writes" the text of her life at a time when she is effectively neither daughter nor wife, she writes it as distinctly gothic. There is a sense, however, in which her own "writing" only serves to expose the fact that the world has already been written for her, by fathers and husbands, as gothic. The opposition between discourse as objective representation and subjective projection, a fully gendered opposition, will not hold. And from the collapse of this opposition is born the gothic *unheimlich*: "An uncanny effect," as Freud argues, "is often and easily produced when the distinction between imagination and reality is effaced, as when something we have hitherto regarded as imaginary appears before us in reality, or when a symbol takes over the full functions of the thing it symbolizes."

Now all this is not implicit in Henry Tilney's rebuke to Catherine Morland, although much of it is to be found in Austen's implicit rebuke to Henry, who in fact is not permitted the last world on the gothic. For if Henry enjoins Catherine to consult her sense of the probable, Austen implicitly enjoins the reader to do the same:

> To begin perfect happiness at the respective ages of twenty-six and eighteen, is to do pretty well; and professing myself moreover convinced, that the General's unjust interference, so far from being really injurious to their felicity, was perhaps rather conducive to it, by improving their knowledge of each other, and adding strength to their attachment, I leave it to be settled by whomsoever it may concern, whether the tendency of this work be altogether to recommend parental tyranny, or reward filial disobedience.

General Tilney is manifestly innocent of Catherine's happiness: the tendency of the work is altogether to reward filial disobedience, not to recommend parental tyranny. But if the general is innocent, Austen is not, and it is with good grace that she admits culpability in the affair: for a woman of no significant fortune to begin perfect happiness at the age of eighteeen is not only to do "pretty well," it is to do improbably well. Austen is fully aware that her novel is in no meaningful sense a parody of romance—she manages only to distinguish her own "white" romance from *le genre noir*—and that even this is accomplished not by disabusing her protagonist of gothic illusions but by releasing her novel from the standards of novelistic probability.

It is a release that is most blatantly engineered for the sake of Eleanor Tilney, who is the beneficiary of the eleventh-hour introduction into the narrative of "the most charming young man in the world." And the part unwittingly played by "this most charming young man" in Catherine's most alarming adventures, in her wildly improbable gothic fantasies—"this was the very gentleman whose negligent servant left behind him that collection of washing-bills"—cannot be distinguished, at least on the crucial basis of probability, from the part he plays in Austen's allegedly realistic discourse, in her wildly im-

probable every-Jill-shall-have-her-Jack conclusion. In one sense, realistic discourse frames Catherine's delusions. In another sense, however, it is indistinguishable from them. And it is this conflation of alleged opposites that recalls Radcliffe, the world in which reverie cannot ultimately be distinguished from socially mimetic discourse. Indeed, had Austen remained in the mode of novelistic probability, the very real evils of her father's home would have claimed Eleanor, and *Northanger Abbey,* at least from the perspective of one of its characters, would have been rather more dark than white romance. Austen advises the reader early in her work that she will not "adopt that ungenerous and impolitic custom so common with novel writers, of degrading by their contemptuous censure the very performances, to the number of which they are themselves adding." She might have warned the reader late in her work that she will not adopt an unequally ungenerous and impolitic custom, that of degrading romance writers while she herself is adding to their numbers.

Austen's early promise of solidarity or sorority with her precursors needs to be emphasized, for we are indeed given an "ungenerous" and "impolitic" assessment of Radcliffe: "Charming as were all Mrs. Radcliffe's works, and charming even as were the works of all her imitators, it was not in them perhaps that human nature, at least in the midland counties of England, was to be looked for." The dismissive attitude toward Radcliffe is almost universally read as an index of Catherine's new-found maturity and, hence, as a reflection of Austen's own "impolitic" (from the perspective of any feminist attempt to rethink the dynamics of literary history) reading of her precursor. Certainly the new contempt represents a radical change from the Catherine who, under the influence of Isabella, read *Udolpho* with pleasure. But it may be that the "mature" Catherine has learned little more than to ape the opinions of Henry, who is something of a self-appointed arbiter of literary good taste within *Northanger Abbey,* but hardly an adequate spokesperson for Austen herself. It is difficult to know, for example, how that oft-quoted statement—"It was not in them [Mrs. Radcliffe's 'charming' works] . . . that human nature, at least in the midland counties of England, was to be looked for"—can constitute a critique of Radcliffe, as Radcliffe is herself at pains to posit as foreign or Other the evil she represents. (Emily St. Aubert lives in the south of France, not the midlands of England, but even for her, evil is allegedly always elsewhere.) Indeed, the critique may be directed not against Radcliffe but against Catherine's new acceptance of Henry's reading of Radcliffe, the paradoxical critical enterprise that seeks to discredit the gothic by adopting an ethics of the positional (here, not there; now, not then) that is itself an ideological staple of the gothic.

Stuart M. Tave argues [in *Some Words of Jane Austen,* 1973] that it is Catherine's refusal to generalize beyond her own limited experience that is the index of her new-found maturity. She lives in the "midland counties of England" (a specification that seems at once geographical and ethical), and she quite properly substitutes her observation of what is passing around her for the extravagant improbabilities of Radcliffe's gothic. Certainly Catherine has learned to adopt the "middle position" that is said to be the characteristic English genius, and she carefully and quite comically eschews "extremities" ("Catherine dared not doubt beyond her own country, and even of that, if hard pressed, would have yielded the northern and western extremities") of all varieties:

> . . . in the central part of England there was surely some security for the existence even of a wife not beloved, in the laws of the land, and the manners of the age. Murder was not tolerated, servants were not slaves, and neither poison nor sleeping potions to be procured, like rhubarb, from every druggist. Among the Alps and Pyrenees, perhaps, there were not mixed characters. There, such as were not as spotless as an angel, might have the dispositions of a fiend. But in England it was not so; among the English, she believed, in their hearts and habits, there was a general though unequal mixture of good and bad.

There can be no doubt that this sounds judicious—the original owner of my edition, obviously a student of E. M. Forster, has written in the margins: "round characters, not flat, Catherine has grown"—but is it in fact an accurate reading of "a country like this"? It may be comforting to learn that Catherine will not be "surprised" should some "slight imperfection" eventually manifest itself in Henry and that her life will no longer be subject to the criteria of heroine and villain that dominate her sojourn at Northanger. But even as she utters this commitment to the admixture of good and evil that is now and England, she defeats herself both by her assumption of absolute guilt and by her refusal to assign guilt absolutely.

For Catherine's dismissal of Radcliffe is prefaced by the inaccurate remark that her gothic "reading" of Northanger "had been all a voluntary, self-created delusion," when in fact she has little more than "literalized" the plot provided for her by Henry, the association of women with the literal or literalization being the most familiar of cultural constructs. And Catherine's dismissal of Radcliffe concludes with the tepid observation that General Tilney is "not perfectly amiable," a characterization that both contradicts our own observations of what has passed around Catherine and that is superseded by her own later and better judgment: "Catherine, at any rate, heard enough to feel, that in suspecting General Tilney of either murdering or shutting up his wife, she had scarcely sinned against his character, or magnified his cruelty." There is nothing judicious about this—the margins of my edition now read: "flat characters, not round, Catherine has indeed grown"—but it is strictly and disturbingly accurate. Here, in the midlands of England, there is an indigenous Montoni, a character as evil in his own way as anything to be found in Radcliffe's novel. And Catherine comes to this conclusion not by piously aping the opinions of Henry Tilney but by accepting the gothic as a legitimate, if highly circuitous, mode of comprehending contemporary sociopolitical reality. "Grossly injurious suspicions," gothic surmises Catherine "must ever blush to have entertained," now scarcely sin against the person in question: this in no way validates the opinion that, "charming as were all Mrs. Radcliffe's works," they

are irrelevant to "a country like this."

Neither does it validate Henry's reprimand to Catherine nor the critical readings of *Northanger Abbey* derived from that reprimand, here represented by Tave's spirited defense of Henry:

> Henry's admonition to Catherine, which may seem terribly parochial, or even blindly self-satisfied, as though a happy exemption from serious moral problems were granted God's Englishmen, is, rather, an active direction that she rouse herself to the reality of moral problems. It is she who has been blind, not seeing what is before her, unable to make judgments; she has imposed a single mode of explanation upon her experience, deriving it not from the complexities of life around her but from a much simpler fiction, outside of time and space, requiring no effort.

Because Tave's defense of Henry rehearses rather than reads Henry's own vocabulary of blindness and insight, darkness and light, it necessarily participates in the blindness of Henry's insight. Insight, because Catherine does function within an economy of visibility, in which even the most mundane mechanisms of culture and power (the "roads and newspapers that lay every thing open") serve the interests of a generalized visibility. Gothic atrocities, which characteristically involve the withdrawal of a female subject from visibility, cannot be perpetrated "in a country like this." But also blindness, for Tave's celebration of this economy remains blind to the gendered nature of its operations, to the sexual politics of an economy that reinscribes the gothic claustration of women in the mode of visibility. The point here is not simply that General Tilney recovers romance villainy in the realm of manners; rather, the realm of manners, the domestic parlor, reinscribes gothic incarceration in and as a generalized economy of surveillance.

Certainly Henry's celebration of "a country in which every man is surrounded by a neighbourhood of voluntary spies," in which social interaction is one with the possibility of surveillance, suggests the modality of power that Foucault terms "panoptic":

> The panoptic mechanism arranges spatial unities that make it possible to see constantly and to recognize immediately. In short, it reverses the principle of the dungeon; or rather of its three functions—to enclose, to deprive of light and to hide—it preserves only the first and eliminates the other two. Full lighting and the eye of a supervisor capture better than darkness, which ultimately protected. Visibility is a trap.

This is Foucault on Jeremy Bentham's plan for the Panopticon, a circular prison disposed about a central watchtower in which fully visible prisoners are supervised by unseen guards. In this through-the-looking-glass reversal of the principle of the dungeon, incarceration assumes the form of a "compulsory visibility," a reversal that is neatly symbolized by Bentham's architectural innovation but that is in no way restricted to it. This is because disciplinary power is characterized precisely by its diffusion beyond obviously disciplinary institutions, by its capacity to infiltrate the minutiae of social life. Roads and newspapers are very much the instruments of panoptic power, a power that regulates by laying open, controls by making visible, a power that by virtue of the very banality of its operations seeks to disguise its identity as power. Henry assures Catherine that the parlor is to the dungeon as light is to dark, that the country in which she lives is itself proof against gothic atrocities. And Henry entirely misses the point: far from being opposed to the dungeon as darkness is to light, the parlor reinscribes gothic claustration in the mode of light or visibility, all the more effectively for eschewing the obvious mechanisms and paraphernalia of gothic enclosure. "I use the verb 'to torment,'" Henry tells Catherine in the context of a discussion of *Udolpho,* "as I observed to be your own method, instead of 'to instruct,' supposing them to be now admitted as synonimous." Henry concedes the synonymy or continuity between the practices of the gothic and the domestic only ironically. The novel in which he figures, however, does so in earnest.

Catherine, of course, conceives of the carceral only in the most highly "gothicized" sense: she is thus mortified when her search for evidence of the fate of Mrs. Tilney culminates in the discovery of the famous "inventory of linen," the most mundane and domestic of all possible "texts." Gilbert and Gubar, in a reading that is now largely canonical [in The *Madwoman in the Attick,* 1979], suggest that Austen is pointing to the "real threat" to women's happiness when she describes her heroine finding this list. And doubtless this is so. Yet there is a sense in which the "real threat" is more extensive, more diffuse, than Gilbert and Gubar allow. For as with the figure of General Tilney, the point is not simply that a specific dimension of domestic life reconstitutes the gothic in the realm of manners; rather, the realm of manners is already and always structured as a through-the-looking-glass form of the gothic. Thus, if the specific content of the inventory suggests the recuperation of the gothic carceral in terms of the workaday world of a domestic female lot, the inventory itself, the principle of an inventory, suggests a generalized economy of surveillance, an economy that encloses precisely by its ability to note, to render visible or legible, each and every of its operations. Catherine's greatest fear is that Henry will discover the nature of her suspicions and the mortifying nature of her discovery. There is a sense, however, in which the latter virtually guarantees the former: to discover a hitherto lost or hidden inventory of dirty linen is necessarily to suggest that all dirty linen will be aired in public. Catherine assumes that the chest that contains the inventory is locked. She learns in her attempt to return the inventory, however, that it always was open. And therein lies the principle of her claustration: not in an economy of gothic secrecy, but in a domestic sphere, at once social and psychological, in which there are no secret spaces, in which there is no escape from an openness that encloses.

An openness that encloses, a visibility that incarcerates: the oxymorons of panoptic power find architectural expression in the building from which Austen's text derives its name, in the "enlightened" or "panoptic" renovations "suffered" (Catherine herself might have chosen the word) by the once "venerable" abbey:

> With the walls of the kitchen ended all the antiquity of the Abbey. . . . All that was venerable ceased here. The new building was not only new, but declared itself to be so; intended only for offices, and enclosed behind by stable-yards, no uniformity of architecture had been thought necessary. Catherine could have raved at the hand which had swept away what must have been beyond the value of all the rest, for the purposes of mere domestic economy.

"No uniformity of architecture had been thought necessary": the renovated portion of the abbey is built not to be seen (Catherine would "willingly have been spared the mortification of a walk through scenes so fallen," of an architecture so unresponsive to the demands of ostentation), but to render visible those it shelters. The general insists on the "mortifying" tour with the alleged motive that "to a mind like Miss Morland's, a view of the accommodations and comforts, by which the labours of her inferiors were softened, must always be gratifying," and Catherine, despite her contempt for the "purposes of mere domestic economy," finds herself "impressed, beyond her expectation." Beyond her expectation, however, might better read beyond her comprehension, for General Tilney again proves himself innocent of concern for the comfort or happiness of others. The purpose of the "mortifying" tour is not to "view the apartments" (again: the renovated abbey is unresponsive to the demands of visual consumption) but to view how the apartments place those they shelter on view: "The number of servants continually appearing, did not strike her [Catherine] less than the number of their offices." The labor of domestics is not "softened" in or by these accommodations; rather, it is subjected to a coercive visibility. Concern for the comfort of inferiors provides the alibi of a benign or enlightened intentionality, which is thoroughly characteristic of a power that would pass unnoticed or be known by another name. Yet the purpose of the tour, the source of the general's delight in the tour, belongs to an altogether different order: it is in fact less a tour than a "slight survey," less an exercise in enlightened concern than in panoptic power. Catherine's suspicions that there are "many chambers secreted" survives her chaperoned tour; when the opportunity arises, she sets out alone to view the apartments of Mrs. Tilney, to discover the dark secret of the abbey. The unauthorized tour, however, only succeeds in putting Catherine's own secret suspicions, her "dirty linen," on view. As edifice, Northanger Abbey is an amalgamation of gothic foundations and modern renovations. As text, *Northanger Abbey* thematizes the reinscription of the gothic carceral in the mode of panoptic discipline.

Thus, in the climactic scene of instruction, Catherine is enjoined to consult her own observation of what has passed around her only after she has been observed by Henry: in attempting to read a story of gothic incarceration, of violence directed against a woman, Catherine finds that she is herself read by a man, "incarcerated" in the panoptic hold of visibility. The journey to Northanger begins with a threat to Catherine's "new writing desk," to her status as an autonomous writing subject; and long before she arrives at the abbey, she is effectively "shut up" in Henry's prose, reduced to a character in a story not of her own devising. Catherine implicitly protests against this narrative form of the carceral by augmenting Henry's "plot": she "writes," with the help of Radcliffe's *The Romance of the Forest,* the story of the incarcerated or murdered Mrs. Tilney, the signs of which she then attempts to read. Even this highly attentuated protest, however, proves ineffectual, as the unexpected encounter with Henry effectively repositions Catherine as an object of male scrutiny, as a character to be read and not as a subject who reads. In her chaperoned tour of the abbey, Catherine catches a "transient glimpse" of a staircase that she suspects "might well have favored the barbarous proceedings" of the general. The staircase down which she suspects Mrs. Tilney has been conveyed, however, is the staircase up which Henry ascends: the search for a woman withdrawn from visibility by a man only serves to reveal Catherine's secret suspicions to a man. The principle of gothic incarceration is reversed, but its essential function is reinscribed. Visibility or, better, legibility is a gender specific trap.

This reversal is nothing if not symmetrical, and the effective repositioning of the female reading subject as an object of male scrutiny is clearly one of the ambitions of a gender specific economy of surveillance. Yet as an instance of the operation of a power that is best characterized by its fluidity, by its refusal of any obvious or singular agency, the reversal is altogether too symmetrical, too overt. Panoptic power desires to see without itself being seen, and Henry, in the very act of adumbrating the mechanisms of surveillance, risks subjecting surveillance to surveillance. Yet if it requires an uncharacteristically frank exercise and explanation of panoptic power for Catherine to realize her radical accessibility, her openness before the male gaze, it requires but one. Henry maintains that "teachableness of disposition in a young lady is a great blessing," and by his own standards he is indeed blessed in the woman who is to be his wife. For not only does Catherine learn her lesson, she assumes, in the aftermath of Henry's instruction, responsibility for the principle of her own subjection.

It is this assumption of responsibility that finally structures Catherine's relation both to Eleanor, who is the recipient of a letter from Catherine after the latter's unceremonious dismissal from Northanger, and Isabella, who gains access to Northanger only in the form of her letter to Catherine:

> I have not been to the Rooms this age, nor to the Play, except going in last night with the Hodges's, for a frolic, at half-price: they teased me into it; and I was determined they should not say I shut myself up because Tilney was gone. We happened to sit by the Mitchells, and they pretended to be quite surprized to see me out. . . . Anne Mitchell had tried to put on a turban like mine, as I wore it the week before at the Concert, but made wretched work of it—it happened

to become my odd face I believe, at least Tilney told me so at the time, and said every eye was upon me; but he is the last man whose word I would take. I wear nothing but purple now: I know I look hideous in it, but no matter—it is your dear brother's favourite colour.

I quote from Isabella's letter at such length because it is in the essence of Isabella to go on at length, or at least to occupy as many positions as are available to her in a given space. This is not to suggest that she enjoys an opportunity for self-definition that is denied Catherine, for she too occupies a space already structured by the male gaze. The letter from which I quote, for example, is only nominally addressed to Catherine, as Isabella intends her letter to reach the eyes of James, albeit through the mediation of Catherine. Yet Isabella is not simply defined by the male gaze; she herself actively solicits it, as Catherine does not; she is willing to occupy virtually any position vis-à-vis that gaze on the single condition that she appear either reluctantly visible or visibly reluctant. Thus, she positions herself in the Pump Room at Bath in a seat that commands "a tolerable view of every body" for the professed reason that "it is so out of the way"; she withdraws from the gaze of "two odious young men" only to pursue them through the streets of Bath ("One was . . . very good-looking") under the pretext of showing Catherine a new hat. Isabella clearly wishes to be seen, indeed needs to be seen (the marriage market at Bath is a highly competitive economy of gendered visibility), but only as someone who wishes not to be seen. In brief, the male gaze seeks to fix the female subject in knowledge, and Isabella resists fixity. She thus constitutes a threat to the very gaze that she solicits, although perhaps only Catherine and James are sufficiently naive to be taken in. (The threat to Catherine is, of course, in the order of a bad example, not a romantic entanglement, although the break with Isabella is the implicit precondition of her marriage to Henry.) In any case, the threat Isabella poses in the public spaces of Bath is effectively exorcised in the private spaces of Northanger.

For in her letter to Catherine (or to James via Catherine) that is her only means of access to the abbey, Isabella's attempt to stage the conditions under which she is seen is for the first time seen through: Catherine realizes that it is not because her brother prefers purple that purple it is, that it is not only fear lest her withdrawal from visibility be misinterpreted ("I was determined they should not say I shut myself up because Tilney was gone") that motivates the evening at the theater. Isabella continues to attempt to "stage" the conditions under which she is seen, but as a subject now "shut up" in textuality, her "inconsistencies, contradictions, and falsehood" become apparent "even" to Catherine, although apparently even this is not sufficient. That is, Catherine must not only see through her erstwhile friend, she must be seen to see through; she must not only know Isabella for what she is, it must be known that she now knows. Thus, Catherine functions as an amanuensis not to James, as Isabella intends, but to Henry, to whom she reads the "most material passages" of Isabella's letter. The earlier reluctance "to expose a friend," to share with Henry and Eleanor the knowledge of Isabella gained from James's letter, has disappeared. But perhaps here Catherine is but conceding the inevitable, for even the initial desire to protect Isabella, to deny Henry access to private communication, proves futile. Even as Catherine reads James's letter, Henry's eyes are "earnestly watching her"—her distress is clearly "visible"—and there is again no space in which the female reading subject is free from surveillance. For "privacy" Catherine retreats into the drawing room to reflect on James's letter (her own room is occupied by servants), only to find that "Henry and Eleanor had likewise retreated thither." And although the room is temporarily conceded to her (it is at this point that she resolves not to expose Isabella), Henry already begins "to suspect the truth" when he again meets Catherine in the breakfast room, and he in fact guesses the content of the letter before it is surrendered to him. Private communication is here an oxymoron, as the private is itself structured as the already read or the generally legible, a point Catherine doubly concedes: Not only does she abandon the futile attempt to keep private communication private, she herself composes a letter to Eleanor when in exile from Northanger, informed by the possibility of Henry's perusal, "a letter which Eleanor might not be pained by the perusal of—and, above all, which she might not blush herself, if Henry should chance to see." Henry's access to the letter is merely a "chance" possibility, but his power over Catherine is not thereby diminished. This is because in a panoptic economy the efficacy of power, its constraining force, passes over to what Foucault calls "the other side—to the side of its surface of application," in this case, to Catherine herself. "Shall I tell you what you ought to say?", Henry asks Catherine when they first meet. By the time of her letter to Eleanor, however, what Catherine "ought to say," what she thinks Henry thinks she "ought to say," has become a thoroughly internalized knowledge and compulsion. Indeed, the letter represents the final triumph of panopticism, for in merely assuming the possibility of Henry's perusal, Catherine accepts responsibility for the principle of her own subjection. Even as she writes to a woman, she defines herself as already read by a man: clearly she no longer poses any threat to an economy of gendered legibility.

But if not Catherine, what of the novel in which she figures? Is it too complicit in a coercive economy of openness? Here it is not a question of the novel merely reflecting a panoptic order as an aspect of the "real" but of itself producing, creating in the very process and conditions of its consumption, reading subjects subjected to a coercive legibility.

Now readings of **Northanger Abbey** that merely rehearse Henry's scene of instruction, that merely celebrate his celebration of "a country like this," do participate in the paradox of an openness that encloses: like the roads and newspapers he invokes as proof against Catherine's "dreadful" suspicions, Henry himself serves to foreclose "dreadful" or deviant interpretive possibilities. And if Henry can be said to read or interpret **Northanger Abbey** for the reader, it is in the most literal sense that he reads *Udolpho* to his sister: "Yes," added Miss Tilney, "and I remember

that you undertook to read it [*Udolpho*] aloud to me, and that when I was called away for only five minutes to answer a note, instead of waiting for me, you took the volume . . . and I was obliged to stay till you had finished it." The conditions under which Eleanor is read *Udolpho* effectively replicate the content of the novel she is read: by abducting the text, "by running away with the volume, which, you are to observe, was her own, particularly her own," Henry rehearses the act of abduction thematized by *Udolpho*. True, *Udolpho* is concerned with the abduction of a woman by a man and Henry only abducts a text by a woman from a woman. The difference, however, is for the sake of similarity: the atrocity about which Eleanor reads is repeated, albeit in a different modality, in her experience of reading. Here, however, Henry's "reading" of *Udolpho,* his relation to the text of *Udolpho,* must itself be read, not merely rehearsed.

Henry apparently shares Eleanor's enthusiasm for Radcliffe, yet his own experience of *Udolpho* differs significantly from hers. It is at once uninterrupted (he claims to have read the novel in two days, without pause or break), thoroughly private or privatized (unlike Eleanor, he has a "room" or establishment of his own), and unmediated (he reads the novel to himself; it is not read to him). Henry thus constitutes himself as a reading subject by taking a temporary leave from the world, by a voluntary withdrawal into textual space. It is when Eleanor is called away to answer a note, however, when the obligations of her domestic existence literally impinge on her reading experience, that Henry abducts the text that is "particularly her own." For the "liberal" reading subject as he is conventionally constituted, the gothic may not speak to a "country like this." Certainly Henry fails to find in its thematics of the carceral an image of the freedom that he enjoys as a reading subject (although there is something circular in his position: he voluntarily withdraws from the world in order to read *Udolpho,* yet complains that *Udolpho* fails to address the world from which he is withdrawn). The point, however, is that the liberal reading subject is a "he," that his privileges are gender specific. Neither Eleanor nor Catherine enjoy these privileges. Neither, therefore, can be expected to share Henry's reading of the gothic.

Yet this is precisely Henry's expectation, or the expectation implicit in his tendency to "triangulate" or mediate relationships, be they between women or between women and texts. Catherine, for example, remarks that she has heard that "something very shocking indeed, will soon come out in London," which Eleanor, to whom the remark "was chiefly addressed," takes to mean impending political violence. Henry intervenes with the "correct" reading—"Shall I make you understand each other?" he asks, a question that in itself associates understanding with compulsion—and Catherine's unspecified "something" is revealed to be "nothing more dreadful than a new publication which is shortly to come out, in three duodecimo volumes, two hundred and seventy-six pages in each, with a frontispiece to the first, of two tombstones and a lantern—do you understand?" In the most obvious sense—and for all his irony, Henry is invested in an ideology of the obvious—he construes the meaning of Catherine's words accurately: her unspecified "something" does refer to a new gothic thriller not to impending political violence in the streets of London. Yet in specifying Catherine's meaning correctly, Henry paradoxically "opens" the text to multiple and contradictory meanings, to "dreadful" or deviant interpretive possibilities. He intends, of course, only to correct Eleanor's misreading of Catherine's words, which he does by mocking her fears: the vision of political violence he conjures up, the unlikely scenario in which the "Bank [is] attacked, the Tower threatened," is intended to suggest the absurdity of his sister's misgivings. The vision, however, alludes to the very real violence of the Gordon Riots of 1780, which hardly substantiates the absurdity of Eleanor's fears, and it is everywhere informed by the generalized political turmoil of the 1790s. The Henry who would "make" or compel understanding between Catherine and Eleanor succeeds only in confirming the wisdom of Eleanor's initial (mis)understanding, a (mis)understanding born of an unmediated or untriangulated reading of a woman by a woman. "Something dreadful" has indeed come out in London, and Eleanor is thoroughly justified, if only by virtue of Henry's attempt to prove her in error, in construing this something as domestic political violence. In the very act of specifying or "laying open" meaning, Henry opens *Northanger Abbey* to the interpretive possibilities that he seeks to guard against.

Henry is to *Northanger Abbey* as the roads and newspapers he invokes are to "a country like this": the analogy is significant if only because it is precisely the analogy that Henry himself implicitly seeks to deny. I mean by this that he invokes the circumstances of "a country like this," the circumstances that inhere in Austen's novelistic world, as purely external phenomena, as the rather mundane realities of life in the midlands of England. And in one sense, so they are. In another sense, however, the roads and newspapers to which he alludes, the technologies of surveillance and regulation that he invokes, are indistinguishable from the power he enjoys both in narrative and as narrative. In narrative, because even as he enjoins Catherine to contemplate the regulatory mechanisms of the society in which she lives, he himself performs a regulatory function, precisely in rendering visible or legible the "dreadful" nature of her suspicions. But also as narrative, for the regulatory function he performs is inseparable from the narrative he authors, the gothic plot in which he places Catherine, the better to reduce her to the condition of legibility. The world Henry invokes as fact is thus inseparable from the world he produces as a discursive or textual effect. He frankly (manfully?) acknowledges the former but strategically disavows the latter. The facts thus appear simply as the facts, ideologically innocent, gender neutral, ostensibly untouched by the discursive strategies that constitute them as such.

For Austen, however, or at least the Austen of the concluding moments of *Northanger Abbey,* the "facts" are rather more problematic than Henry allows. If, for example, the part played by the "most charming young man in the world" in Austen's allegedly realistic discourse, in

her patently improbable distribution of husbands, fortunes, and titles, cannot be distinguished, at least on the crucial basis of probability, from the part he plays in Catherine's most alarming adventures, this same young man does serve to distinguish Austen's thoroughly ironic relation to the standards of realism from Henry's unproblematic recourse to the same. Certainly the eleventh-hour introduction into the narrative of the viscount necessarily suggests that he has no prediscursive reality "in the world," no existence innocent of the narrative strategy that requires and constitutes him. The point may seem obvious enough, but the point is not simply that *Northanger Abbey* is fiction rather than fact, for if Austen is only ironically committed to the convention that the facts exist independently of the omniscience that notes and records them, her irony reminds the reader that it is a convention, and one replete with its own ideological significance.

Now there is a sense in which omniscience is nothing more than panopticism by another name, or the formal analogue of a panoptic economy. The operations of an omniscience that seeks to divorce its power to know and see from its power to construct, however, seeks to deny this analogy precisely by mystifying the relation between the "facts" and the discursive strategies that constitute them as such. Thus, D. A. Miller argues in *The Novel and the Police,* the tendency of nineteenth-century omniscient narrators to lament the unhappy fate of their characters is credible only in the context of an arrangement that keeps the function of narration separate from the causalities operating within the narrative: "The *knowledge* commanded in omniscient narration is thus opposed to the *power* that inheres in the circumstances of the novelistic world." In *Northanger Abbey,* Henry, who functions as something of an omniscient narrator within an omniscient narrative, tends to mock rather than lament, and Catherine's fate, as long as she remains committed to a "gothicized" reading of her world, is rather more embarrassing than unhappy. But like the conventional laments of the nineteenth-century narrator, Henry's mockery is credible only in the context of an arrangement in which knowledge is divorced from power, and *Northanger Abbey* refuses to distinguish between the knowledge commanded by Henry's omniscience and the power that inheres in the world he invokes. He enjoins Catherine to consult her own observation, for example, yet fails to note that his own powers of observation collude with the technologies of surveillance that he invites Catherine to survey. Austen, however, brings the most charming young man in the world "instantly before the imagination of us all" as a frankly discursive requirement or construction—his introduction into the narrative, as Austen is at pains to note, conforms to "the rules of composition"—as the product of her power over and within narrative.

And in conspicuously defining the "facts" in relation to standards of probability and propriety that belong exclusively to the order of discourse—or at least the singular and unexpected "fact" that is the discovery of a husband for Eleanor—Austen necessarily broaches an issue that Gerard Genette argues is characteristically encoded in silence: "The relationship between a plausible narrative [*le récit vraisemblable*] and the system of plausibility [*le système de vraisemblance*] to which it subjects itself is . . . essentially mute: the conventions of genre function as a system of natural forces and constraints that the narrative obeys as if without noticing them, and *a fortiori* without naming them." Because the system of plausibility to which the narrative is subjected is little more than a historically determined structure of *bienséance* or "propriety" (a word that tends to figure prominently in studies of Jane Austen), the strategic silence of the plausible narrative can only be an attempt to render "natural" or ahistorical its own historical determinants. To speak the word "plausibility" would be to acknowledge the possibility that mimesis, the representation of the real, is little more than the reinscripscription and reproduction of received ideas about the real. And the "plausible" narrative is characteristically unwilling to entertain any possibility that refuses to distinguish between its knowledge of the world and the operations of power within that world. Yet in **Northanger Abbey,** the strategic silence that governs the inscription and perception of plausibility is broken: in the climactic scene of instruction, Henry invokes the standard of plausibility or probability in its explicitly historical context ("Remember the country and the age in which we live. . . . Consult your own understanding, your own sense of the probable"). In the "tell-tale compression" of the concluding moments of her novel turned romance, moreover, Austen explicitly invokes the "rules of composition," the purely narrative structure of *bienséance,* to which she subjects her "fable." Clearly the relationship between *le récit vraisemblable* and *le système de vraisemblance* does not remain "mute." It is in fact susceptible to various, but ultimately limited, formulations.

For example, it might be argued that as disturbing as are all the works of Mrs. Radcliffe, as disturbing as are all the works of her imitators, it is nevertheless in them that a country like this, even in it midland portions, is to be seen through a gothic glass darkly. Or it might be argued that as charming as is the conclusion of **Northanger Abbey,** as charming as is every flight from standards of mimetic probability, it is nevertheless not in it that a country like this, even in its midland portions, is to be looked for. To argue, however, as Henry Tilney argues, to maintain that the "real" is the simple antidote to "dark romance," is but to rehearse the most ethno- and androcentric ideology of the real. Again, Henry is quite right in arguing the imbrication of the literary and the social and exactly wrong in formulating their relationship. In enjoining Catherine to observe the world around her, he unwittingly provides an argument not for the irrelevance of the gothic carceral but for its reinscription in the mode of panoptic visibility or legibility: horror, like charity, begins at home.

FURTHER READING

Bibliography

Gilson, David. *A Bibliography of Jane Austen.* Oxford: Clarendon Press, 1982, 877 p.

Comprehensive bibliography of primary and secondary materials published through 1975.

Biography

Jenkins, Elizabeth. *Jane Austen.* New York: Grosset & Dunlap, 1948, 410 p.

Exhaustive biographical and critical work noted for its detailed treatment of Austen's life and works.

Criticism

Doubleday, Neal Frank. "Henry & Catherine." In *Variety of Attempt: British and American Fiction in the Early Nineteenth Century,* pp. 19-35. Lincoln: University of Nebraska Press, 1976.

Advances *Northanger Abbey* as an example of Austen's belief in the "inherent absurdity of the novel" as a genre.

Duckworth, Alistair M. "Aspects of *Northanger Abbey* and *Sense and Sensibility.*" In *The Improvement of the Estate: A Study of Jane Austen's Novels,* pp. 81-114. Baltimore: Johns Hopkins Press, 1971.

Analyzes *Northanger Abbey* as a "socio-moral" novel, one that attempts to define "proper moral behavior in the face of a largely immoral world."

Emden, Cecil S. "The Composition of *Northanger Abbey.*" *The Review of English Studies: A Quarterly Journal of English Literature and the English Language* XIX (1968): 279-87.

Suggests that the parodic sections of *Northanger Abbey* were added four years after the composition of the rest of the novel.

Gallon, D. N. "Comedy in *Northanger Abbey.*" *The Modern Language Quarterly* 63, No. 4 (October 1968): 802-09.

Argues that *Northanger Abbey* is a comedy of thematic significance rather than simply a literary burlesque.

Harris, Jocelyn. *"Northanger Abbey."* In *Jane Austen's Art of Memory,* pp. 1-33. Cambridge: Cambridge University Press, 1989.

Explores connections between Catherine Morland's maturation in *Northanger Abbey* and John Locke's theory of knowledge as stated in *An Essay Concerning Human Understanding.*

Levine, George. "Translating the Monstrous: *Northanger Abbey.*" *Nineteenth Century Fiction* 30, No. 3 (December 1975): 335-50.

Describes the way in which the light-hearted parody of *Northanger Abbey* hints at more serious social themes.

Loveridge, Mark. *"Northanger Abbey;* or, Nature and Probability." *Nineteenth Century Literature* 46, No. 1 (June 1991): 1-29.

Regards *Northanger Abbey* as structurally unified and historically significant.

MacDonagh, Oliver. "Girlhood: *Catherine, or The Bower, Northanger Abbey* and *Pride and Prejudice.*" In *Jane Austen: Real and Imagined Worlds,* pp. 66-96. New Haven: Yale University Press, 1991.

Features a comparative analysis of Catherine Morland and Jane Austen, while maintaining that Catherine "embodied Jane Austen's values."

Mathison, John K. *"Northanger Abbey and Jane Austen's Conception of the Value of Fiction." ELH—Journal of English Literary History* 24, No. 2 (June 1957): 138-52.

Claims that *Northanger Abbey* demonstrates Austen's belief in the power of the novel to educate.

McKillop, Alan D. "Critical Realism in *Northanger Abbey.*" In *From Jane Austen to Joseph Conrad: Essays Collected in Memory of James T. Hillhouse.* Edited by Robert C. Rathburn and Martin Steinmann, Jr., pp. 35-45. Minneapolis: University of Minnesota Press, 1958.

Considers *Northanger Abbey* as a satire of eighteenth- and nineteenth-century novelistic conventions.

Page, Norman. "'The Best Chosen Language': Stylistic Modes in Jane Austen." *Ariel* 2, No. 4 (October 1971): 45-51.

Examines Austen's handling of style in *Northanger Abbey* to suggest "the power of minor incidents to suggest major issues."

Scott, P. J. M. "The Question of a Divided Intention (I): 'Lady Susan,' *Sanditon, Northanger Abbey.*" In *Jane Austen: A Reassessment,* pp. 9-53. London: Vision Press, 1982.

Argues that *Northanger Abbey* lacks significant depth of theme.

Sørensen, Knud. "Johnsonese in *Northanger Abbey:* A Note on Jane Austen's Style." *English Studies* L, No. 4 (August 1969): 390-97.

Discusses the influence of Samuel Johnson's style on that of *Northanger Abbey.*

Additional coverage of Austen's life and career is contained in the following sources published by Gale Research: *Concise Dictionary of Literary Biography, Vol. 116; Dictionary of Literary Biography 1789-1832; DISCovering Authors; Nineteenth-Century Literature Criticism, Vols. 1, 13, 19,* and *33;* and *World Literature Criticism.*

Maria Edgeworth

1768-1849

Anglo-Irish novelist, short story writer, dramatist, and educational essayist.

INTRODUCTION

Edgeworth contributed notably to the development of the English novel of manners. Her vivid fiction advanced a tradition that began with Fanny Burney and reached its finest expression in Jane Austen. Although her reputation has suffered from inevitable comparisons to her younger contemporary Austen, literary historians recognize Edgeworth as an important innovator in this genre. Additionally, she is known as the author of popular children's fiction and a well-regarded volume addressing childrearing and educational theory.

Biographical Information

Edgeworth was born to the educator, inventor, and politician Richard Lovell Edgeworth and his first wife. Richard Edgeworth eventually married four times and fathered twenty-two children. As the eldest daughter, Edgeworth left school at the age of fifteen to oversee the care and education of her many siblings; her first children's stories were written to entertain them. She served as her father's secretary as well, and collaborated with him on several nonfiction works, most notably the essays on childrearing collected in *Practical Education* (1798). This volume was followed by children's stories, novels of manners, and satirical short stories of society life. Edgeworth herself lived quietly, residing quietly on her family's estate until her death at age eighty-one.

Major Works

Edgeworth's first novel is her acknowledged masterpiece. *Castle Rackrent: An Hibernian Tale* (1800) is notable for its introduction of several literary innovations. The narrator is not merely an observer, but is integrally involved in the action of the novel. *Castle Rackrent* is also recognized as the first regional novel, depicting the speech, mannerisms, and activities of a specific Irish region and social class. This technique influenced subsequent novelists, including William Thackeray, James Fenimore Cooper, and Sir Walter Scott, who commended "the rich humor, pathetic tenderness, and admirable tact" of Edgeworth's novel and expressed the hope that his own novels would accomplish for Scotland "something . . . of the same kind with that which Miss Edgeworth so fortunately achieved for Ireland." *Castle Rackrent* is also one of the first novels to depict the lives of working-class characters, to chronicle the history of a family through several generations, and to offer logical and psychologically sound character development. In subsequent novels, including *Belinda* (1801) and *Leonora* (1806), Edgeworth

developed the conventions of the novel of manners, realistically depicting and often satirizing the conventions of upper-class Irish society. Her short stories, collected in *Popular Tales* (1804) and *Tales of Fashionable Life* (1812), were more markedly satirical. Edgeworth's stories for children feature accounts of dire fates befalling disobedient children and fortune favoring the well-behaved. This didactic tendency is thought to have been instilled by her father, who urged her always to write with an instructive puprose. Nevertheless, in an era known for joyless, prescriptive children's fiction, several of Edgeworth's stories are notable for lively, fresh characterizations of children who are recognizably human beings rather than character traits personified.

Critical Reception

An early critic pronounced Edgeworth 's fiction worthy of enthusiasm but rued her cheerless utilitarianism. The didacticism that permeates Edgeworth's fiction and nonfiction alike has been attributed to the influence of her father; commentators note that her least didactic novel, *Castle Rackrent,* was written while her father was away from home and thus not able to impose his views. Some critics discern an interplay in many of Edgeworth's longer texts between the didacticism attributed to Richard Edgeworth and an underlying Romantic sensibility attributed to his daughter. Mark Hawthorne, for example, maintains that Edgeworth advanced her own viewpoint "through structure and symbolism" and "did not accept her father's basic premise until she incorporated the demands of the passions." Other commentators have suggested that Edgeworth herself was the source of much of the didacticisim present in her fiction, although there is consensus that her father edited and most likely altered much of her literary work. While *Castle Rackrent* remains her most acclaimed achievement, Edgeworth's entire career has undergone reassessment since the 1980s, with especial focus on her contributions to the development of the novel of manners.

PRINCIPAL WORKS

Letters for Literary Ladies (essays) 1795
The Parent's Assistant (short stories) 1796-1800
Practical Education [with Richard Lovell Edgeworth] (essays) 1798; also published as *Essays on Practical Education*, 1815
Castle Rackrent: An Hibernian Tale (novel) 1800
Belinda (novel) 1801
Moral Tales for Young People (short stories) 1801
Essay on Irish Bulls [with Richard Lovell Edgeworth] (essay) 1802
Popular Tales (short stories) 1804
Leonora (novel) 1806
Tales of Fashionable Life (short stories) 1809-12
Patronage (novel) 1814
Comic Dramas (dramas) 1817
Harrington, a Tale, and Ormond, a Tale (novels) 1817
Helen (novel) 1834

CRITICISM

Ernest Baker (essay date 1941)

SOURCE: "Maria Edgeworth and the English Novel," in *Family Chronicles: Maria Edgeworth's "Castle Rackrent,"* edited by Cóilín Owens, Wolfhound Press, 1987, pp. 29-35.

[*In the following essay, Baker considers Edgeworth as an important transitional novelist whose works link eighteenth-century literary conventions with those of the next century.*]

Thanks to a happy chronological accident, a bridge was provided from the eighteenth century to the nineteenth in the work of two novelists, Maria Edgeworth and Jane Austen, who belonged to both the old and the new age. Without any shock of surprise or startling change of scenery, we gradually find that the past has been left behind and we are entering upon the present. There are still many features in the scenes brought before the eye which are now obsolete or quaint and old-fashioned. But compare any of their novels with *Pamela* and *Joseph Andrews,* the second centenary of which will be celebrated a few years hence—the Victorians hardly noticed the first. There the world depicted is not our world; all is remote and unfamiliar, except the general traits that are of our own race and kindred or simply human and of all ages. It is a world seemingly more than four times as far removed as that of Miss Edgeworth and Miss Austen, whose early novels, nevertheless, including their finest, were written only half a century later. In **Castle Rackrent** perhaps, but certainly not in **Tales of Fashionable Life,** *Sense and Sensibility,* or *Pride and Prejudice,* do the manners seem strange or antiquated; still less is there in the bearing and workmanship of the novelist that requires the reader to make allowances.

For the differences between the two groups of novels are in the social physiognomy rather than in the mode of portrayal. The fashion of the world had changed much more than the fashion of novel-writing. In these fifty years, there had been an unexampled advance in order and civilization. England had never been so quiet for so long a space, never more prosperous. The middle classes were merging with the upper classes, in spite of the deference and even obsequiousness paid as much as ever to rank and title; they were in possession of wealth, comfort, and leisure, and were now the most stable element in the community, the portion that was coming more and more to represent the intelligence, the morality and refinement of the nation. Incidentally, they formed the reading public, which was now large enough to make the fortune of a successful novelist. Even the minor novels show clearly the amelioration of manners, the new interests shaping life, the steady transformation of society from centre to circumference, and the gradual suppression of the differences between town and country so far as the more cultivated classes were concerned. In both Miss Edgeworth's and Miss Austen's novels, the stage is oftener a manor-house or a vicarage than the fashionable end of the metropolis, and changes of scene from London or Bath to the country are a very small change of environment. The process of rapid evolution with its reactions upon literature which can be followed in the history of fiction better than anywhere else had completed a definite stage. Actually, it was to go on at an accelerated pace throughout the nineteenth century, till now, when a state of transition seems to be the normal state of mankind. But in essentials the society that we meet in the novels of these two ladies is that of our own contemporaries.

It would be misleading, however, not to make large allowances for the point of view and the different radius of vision of the older and the younger novelists. Simply to contrast Fielding's and Richardson's view of the world with that of Miss Edgeworth and Miss Austen would be to exaggerate the real disparity between the two epochs. Novelists latterly had shown a tendency to confine themselves to those educated classes who read their books. These two ladies kept almost exclusively to their own class; they rarely went outside a limited sphere in which manners and morals were more refined than in any other section of society. Fielding, on the other hand, had been catholic in his range, and never afraid to tell the truth however ugly; he drew his characters from low as well as from high life, as he often stops to point out, and rivalled Hogarth in his insistence on the barbarism of the mob. Even Richardson left in his two chief novels a distorted impression of a lawless state of society by choosing transgressions of the established code for his dramatic material. Fanny Burney, whose novels and letters are on the whole good evidence for the progress of manners at a half-way stage, had for the sake of sensation given some slight glimpses of the vice and brutality of the lower classes, though her chief object was to make fun of the absurdities of those who aped their betters or of the crazes and affectations rampant in a more elevated sphere. But she could have known very little at first hand about the lower classes; she was a woman, like her two successors, with a woman's narrow experience. Maria Edgeworth did not by any means overlook the poorer classes in her Irish stories, as will be seen; but she saw them as one of their superiors, at the best as a charitable observer, not as one who could even in imagination make herself one of them. All three, in short, gave the feminine view of life; they were not qualified to do more, and their delicacy would have shrunk from a candid treatment of many things that could not escape their notice. It needed a man, a Walter Scott, with an eye like Fielding's for all sorts and conditions, to restore the balance, as he did in the novels of his own day or of his yesterday which are the nearest approach to the broad survey of his predecessor. And even Scott is to be read as an historian of society only if some correction is applied for the romantic bias even in his semi-contemporary pictures. He was determined to entertain and enthral, no matter if the exact truth of his version of reality suffered. Thus a great many disturbing factors have to be taken into account if a register of the changes of the last fifty years is sought in the novels.

Miss Edgeworth and Miss Austen found their right medium in the domestic novel, that form of the novel of manners the general scheme of which had evolved and come into chief favour during the last half-century. Fielding's vivid rendering of life as it goes quietly or impetuously on was here applied to a narrower expanse, and was blended as occasion served with Richardson's closer scrutiny of the heart and with his systematic moralism. Both were clear-headed enough to avoid the uncertainty of aim and halting craftsmanship which had rendered the majority of recent novels so glaringly inferior to the pattern set by the illustrious four. They recovered the lost ground. For there was no affectation of any kind in either of them. They wrote simply and sincerely, with a definite and consistent attitude of mind that kept them to the point. Both were writers because they had to be, and were not, as too many of the literary tribe, mercenaries, gushing amateurs, propagandists in disguise, or mere charlatans. Jane Austen wrote to amuse herself; Maria Edgeworth as a practical teacher, whose strong sense of responsibility impelled her to correct and advise the rash and erring. To her, fiction was one of the useful arts; only once did she yield to the

joy of unfettered creation, when she bent the inner ear to listen to old Thady "dictating" the history of Castle Rackrent.

Both were writing in the period of the Romantic movement; but they were both untouched by it, and no doubt were unaware that any such thing as an important literary revolution was going on. Both were well read in English literature, but their culture was that of the eighteenth century. They knew there was a poet named Wordsworth; he visited the Edgeworths in Ireland; but their acquaintance with his poetry was evidently very slight, and neither had an inkling of his inner meaning. Coleridge they had hardly heard of, and Keats and Shelley never appeared on the horizon even to Maria Edgeworth, who outlived these younger poets. Crabbe was much more to their taste, as to that of most readers in what we now call the age of romance. Miss Edgeworth was more interested in people than in books, and among the writers whom she loved not many were poets. She read Scott's lays and novels with enthusiasm, very different from Jane Austen's lukewarm appreciation of the first Waverley novels, the only ones she lived to read. But Scott was romantic without participating in the new romanticism; and it was his rich humanity, the truth and splendour of his dramatization of both present and past, and his discovery "that facts are better than fiction, that there is no romance like the romance of real life," that fascinated Maria Edgeworth. She herself had a weakness for romance of the old stamp, in spite of her ridicule of sentimentalism and of Gothic and other extravagances. The truth is that the deeper romanticism, the romanticism of Wordsworth and his fellows, did not enter fully into English fiction until the time of the Brontë sisters, with their deep-rooted sense of a material world transfused with spirit. Those novelists who were the contemporaries of Wordsworth and Coleridge, Shelley and Keats, reveal not the slightest consciousness of that awakening of the soul and imagination which was of its very essence.

Maria Edgeworth (1767-1849) has some affinity with the school of Bage, Holcroft, and Godwin, in that she embodied a social philosophy in a series of novels and tales; she might almost be considered as the last and best of that group. But she was not, like them, speculative and polemical; and she was not in the habit of talking at large about the abstract principles which she applied to the daily predicaments of practical life. As to political questions, she left them to other people. Her own mind was made up. In truth, she was not a profound thinker: but she was an intelligent woman, the daughter of an able man, Richard Lovell Edgeworth, and the friend of Ricardo and of Étienne Dumont, colleague and expositor of Jeremy Bentham. On the whole, she had a clearer and more consistent view of the social order than was attained by the revolutionary school in all their exposures of injustice, their sentimental contrasts of selfishness and virtue, and their incessant discussions of ethical and political problems in the light of soaring but ill-defined ideals. Whilst they harped upon the rights of man, she and her father were content to point out his duties. Bentham, it will be remembered, likewise denied that the individual had inherent rights, even the right to equality. In effect, their insistence on what every man owes to the community, his obligation to make himself useful to his fellows, is nothing else than Bentham's utilitarianism, the doctrine of the greatest good of the greatest number, of the subservence of each to all, the identification of doing right with social service.

For it would be illusory to suppose that Maria Edgeworth had already grasped the modern conception of the individual as a member of the human family, a function in a living organism, the idea that was soon to displace the mechanical notion which had dominated the minds and circumscribed the imagination both of novelists and of politicians and social reformers. If she ever caught glimpses of this deeper view, its full significance had not dawned upon her. The eighteenth century beheld society merely as a vast aggregation of similar individuals, the arithmetical sum of many equal units, whose position in the social scheme was settled for them, not by personal differences, but by the external accidents of rank, property, privilege, or the inferior lot inherited by the majority. This basic assumption had become instinctive; this was how men thought, how they looked at the world, until the end of the eighteenth century. Defoe and Richardson would have the individual accept resignedly his subjection to the appointed order; the revolutionary novelists would have him rebel and assert his claim to freedom and happiness. Both parties, nevertheless, acquiesced in the same fundamental axiom of the relation of the one to the many.

It is impossible to say at what precise date novelists and others began to think in different terms, though it can be safely asserted that the new view did not become general in fiction until romanticism came in with the Brontës. Then it is that characters are overheard demanding: "What was I created for? What is my place in the world?" It is the view which has prevailed until the event of the present day, when it is being challenged as an inadequate scheme for the realization of a complete personal life, and its corollary, progress, for every progress, is seen to be meaningless. Today personality is felt to be a higher object than any social organization, and it is being recognised that all institutions, including the State itself, exist for the service of personality. Yet Burke's prescient vision of the nation as a living structure, ever developing, and not a mere mechanical sum of identical units, was fruitful in giving a deeper significance to history, as well as a warning to such rash reformers as thought it an easy task to overthrow the fabric and rebuild it from the foundations up. The full conception of the social system as an organism, and of the individual members as each exercising a vital function in the general service, was animating to the sociologist, the moral philosopher, and the novelist. Virtue, integrity, and happiness were thus seen to correspond to the fulfilment of that for which each was fitted; vice was failure and disobedience. Towards some such answer to the social engima Bage, Holcroft, and Godwin had striven according to their lights; but they were more troubled by the breakdown of the old philosophy than ready with a comprehensive and satisfactory one to put in its place, in spite of the genial optimism of the first two and the perfectibilian theories of the last. They complacently

responded to the revolutionary cry of liberty, equality, fraternity, though it was only a sentimental expression of the old individualism.

If Maria Edgeworth was too conservative to be prepared to see men and women all as organs of the body politic, with functions to perform for the common good, she had at any rate a healthy conviction of their duties and responsibilities. She herself belonged to the ruling classes, the classes which up to the time of her entry upon middle age were, in Ireland, unmistakably rulers. She never divested herself of some prejudices in regard to rank and station, and often in her edifying tales for children seems to be simply bidding them do that which is proper to the state of life to which Providence has called them. But her utilitarianism was an adequate working plan. She was not an unenlightened person, and had a right apprehension of the good of society as a whole. The general happiness, social service, the call of duty rather than the assertion of rights, are the ideas implicit in all her stories, whether nursery fables inculcating the social virtues or full-length novels, "tales of fashionable life," for the admonishment and education of the adult.

Her own duty was evident; her function, if she had so regarded it, had been marked out for her by her upbringing and special abilities. As clearly as her father, she saw that the principal need of all classes was education, with a view to the cheerful and efficient performance of their duties in the world. Her mission was to be a teacher, and she carried out her task with zeal and conscientiousness. Now and then she did still better. Moved unawares by the impulse to express herself, to realize her personality, a thing for which there was really no place in her philosophy, for it was the dictate of genius which is ruled by no philosophy, she wonderingly obeyed. She wrote **Castle Rackrent** without even knowing how she did it. And, again, in many parts of **The Absentee** and **Ormond** she built better than she knew. Partly, no doubt, it was the Irish inspiration that seized her; she always wrote best and most easily when the theme was Irish. And thus she was the first writer to render the racial peculiarities of the Irish with the charm of perfect comprehension, although, like Swift, Goldsmith, and Henry Brooke, she was only an adopted child of the country. Her first distinction is, then, to stand foremost among didactic novelists, her second to be the author of the finest Irish story ever written, her third to have given new shape and importance to the short story. This had been the immemorial pattern for fiction with a lesson to propound, and she had a recent model in the *Contes moraux* of Marmontel, whose general level of accomplishment was indeed higher than hers. But a comparison must not be pressed; her aims were so different that comparison loses its point. Among her tales for the young are many small masterpieces of neat workmanship and sympathetic imagination. The more expansive stories of the world in which men and women live out their destinies are not intrinsically superior, but they too helped to re-establish and renovate a form of fiction in which the moderns have excelled.

Katharine West (essay date 1949)

SOURCE: "Maria Edgeworth," in *The Spectator*, Vol. 182, No. 6308, May 20, 1949, pp. 672-73.

[*In the following overview of Edgeworth's career, West discusses Richard Edgeworth's influence on his daughter's literary work.*]

On May 22nd, 1849, Maria Edgeworth died at the age of eighty-two in the arms of her third stepmother, who was a year younger and lived to write her life. Not that Miss Edgeworth's life was especially eventful. It is true that she travelled and met many of her distinguished contemporaries. But the greater part of her life was spent immersed in a family, and filled with work in the house and at her desk. Though she had no children of her own, her father, Richard Lovell Edgeworth, married four times and had twenty children. Maria, as the eldest, had to act as mother during the brief marital interregnums, and provide continuity and cohesion for the several families. Above all, she had to educate them according to her father's theories.

Richard Lovell Edgeworth (1744-1814) was a remarkable man—an inventor whose mind teemed with telegraphs and one-wheeled chaises, the disciple of Rousseau, the friend of Josiah Wedgwood, Erasmus Darwin and Thomas Day, the benevolent despot of his Irish estate at Edgeworthstown, a tyrannical yet lively *paterfamilias*. From Rousseau and Day (the author of *Sandford and Merton*) he imbibed educational doctrines which he ruthlessly carried out on his children. And if some of these children went to the bad or died, the supply was kept up by his marriages with four beautiful, intelligent and submissive young women. His earliest attempts were not successful. The eldest son, who was actually introduced to Rousseau in Switzerland, afterwards ran away to sea. Maria herself suffered more from physical than psychological experiments. She was sent as a child to a London school, where they tried to increase her diminutive stature by hanging her by her neck from a beam; and when she had trouble with her eyes she was dosed at dawn with nauseous tar-water by the great Thomas Day in person.

By the time the children of Mr. Edgeworth's second and third wives (Honora and Elizabeth Sneyd) were growing up, Maria was a young woman. Fortunately, she was a child-lover, who would lie on the floor and let babies crawl all over her. In the constantly replenished nursery she inculcated right principles (i.e., her father's) by means of stories, which were first written on a slate, and ran the gauntlet of schoolroom criticism. Only when they had passed this test were they set down on paper (amid the hubbub of the living-room) and published for the benefit of other children. Thus *Frank, Rosamond, The Parent's Assistant* and the rest came into the world. These stories gave delight in nurseries and schoolrooms throughout the nineteenth century, and are still eminently readable today.

One cannot help wondering, however, if they might not have been even better but for the influence of Mr. Edgeworth. For he was a Utilitarian and a Rationalist, who believed that reason is the master of the universe, usefulness the sole criterion of value, and man (exemplified in Richard Lovell Edgeworth) the measure of all things.

Had he confined these theories to the admirable and curiously modern treatise on *Practical Education* (1798) which he wrote in collaboration with Maria, all would have been well. Unhappily he regarded the stories, too, as propaganda pamphlets. Thanks to his influence they are uncompromisingly practical. Only social virtues are extolled; the moral is always secular, and rewards are earned in *this* world, not the next. Indeed, the unfailing regularity with which such rewards were forthcoming must have caused disillusionment in many young readers when they found them less to be counted on in real life.

Like Mr. Gradgrind in Dickens' *Hard Times*, Edgeworth idolised facts and deplored the faculty of wonder. He therefore naturally disapproved of fairy stories. Yet the fairy-story element was not entirely eliminated by his daughter. Her tales typically contrasted a good boy with a bad. The good one, by working hard or by inventing such pretty novelties as heather mats, excites the interest of a fairy-godmother in the shape of some benevolent spinster or rich old gentleman. His fortune is made, and he lives happily ever after. Whereas the bad boy idles, cheats or gambles his way to a disagreeable end. It must be understood, however, that the children were not *born* good or bad; they had merely been brought up well or foolishly. For it was an axiom with the Edgeworths that nature counted for little, while nurture was all-important.

Although Miss Edgeworth's contrasts of sense and sensibility may have bred complacency and starved the imagination, her children's stories compare favourably with those of her contemporaries in many ways. Her secular view of life, for instance, saved her from the cloying morass of piety. She was, moreover, cheerful. Deathbeds are rare in her stories; and when parents had to die to provide a full complement of self-reliant orphans, they died briskly and astringently. She was also an early exponent of kindness to animals—a creed which she shared with Thomas Day and the Misses Anne and Jane Taylor.

Towards children, too, Maria Edgeworth was unusually merciful. In the stories of that time small nursery faults were normally followed by appalling retribution. Little girls who lighted matches were burned to death, and the theft of a penny led inevitably to the gallows. Every children's tale was a cautionary tale. It may be claimed, of course, that such horrors gave the average child exactly what he wanted, and there is some truth in this. But even so is it moral to pander to childish lust for blood? Moreover, many children, even the most bloodthirsty, must have been shaken by the bland assumption that these disasters might any day befall themselves. After so many dreadful warnings it must have been reassuring to learn from kind Mrs. Edgeworth that disobedience was sometimes punished only by a thorn in the finger or a drop of sealing-wax on the hand.

The Parent's Assistant (1800) contained, despite its forbidding title, the mellowest of Miss Edgeworth's children's stories. Poetry is forever peeping out between the precepts. In ***Simple Susan,*** for instance, the gathering of children to weave their May Day garlands has the idyllic quality of Blake's *Echoing Green.* Sir Walter Scott confessed that he could not put the story down without a tear. But Miss Edgeworth did not only write for children, nor were tears the only tribute paid her by Scott. He stated that his own stories were influenced by ***Castle Rackrent*** and her other tales of Irish life, and he was not the only author to admit as much. It is strange to think that we owe *Fathers and Children* and *A House of Gentlefolk* to the inspiration of Maria Edgeworth. Yet Ivan Turgenieff heard them read aloud as a boy, and wrote years later: "It is possible, nay probable, that if Maria Edgeworth had not written about the poor Irish and the squire and squiress, it would not have occurred to me to give a literary form to my impressions about the classes parallel to them in Russia."

She also wrote some novels of high society, of which ***Belinda*** (1801) is at once the best and the best known. Jane Austen thought highly of this exuberant, witty, absurd conglomeration of fashionable life and rational principles. Yet Maria Edgeworth and her father no doubt saw it as just a moral tale for adults—a post-graduate course in ***Practical Education.*** Thus Maria Edgeworth found an outlet for her affections in a crowded home, and for her intellectual energy in three separate streams of writing. She exercised a steady, lively influence during her life and for years afterwards. Even today she can teach us much about letting children bring themselves up sensibly. It is fitting, therefore, that we should remember her this year, a century after her life and vigour simultaneously ended.

V. S. Pritchett, Jr. (essay date 1953)

SOURCE: "Books in General," in *The New Statesman and Nation,* Vol. XLV, No. 1163, June 20, 1953, pp. 749-50.

[*Pritchett, a modern British novelist, short story writer, and critic, is respected for his mastery of the short story and for what critics describe as his judicious, reliable, and insightful literary criticism. In the following essay, Pritchett praises Edgeworth for her sharp eye for social detail and her gift for dialogue, singling out* Castle Rackrent *as her single enduring masterpiece.*]

> He was greatly mourned at the Curragh where his cattle were well-known; and all who had taken up his bets were particularly inconsolable for his loss to society.

The quotation does not come from *The Irish R.M.,* but from the mother, or should one say the aunt, of the Anglo-Irish novel—Maria Edgeworth. The eighteenth-century note is unmistakable but so, even without the word Curragh, is the Irishness. One will never quite get to the bottom of that sentence out of ***Castle Rackrent.*** On the surface it is felt and goodnatured. "Poor" Sir Kit, after hitting a toothpick out of his adversary's finger in a duel, received a ball in a vital part, and "was brought home in little better than an hour after the affair, speechless on a hand-barrow to my lady." A sad business; but landlords come and go; we know them by their debts; only cattle are eternal. Irish irony has been sharpened to a finer edge; it is more drastic than the corresponding irony of the English writers of the time. Sententious, secure in the collective, educated view of their class, the English ironists regard folly from the strong point of cultivated applause and moral platitude, whereas an Irishwoman, like Maria Edgeworth, has uncertainty under foot. The folly of the death of Sir Kit is only equalled by the absurdity of the mourning; beyond both lies the hopeless disaster of the state of "the unfortunate country."

Behind an ironist like Fielding is assurance, courage and complacency; behind Maria Edgeworth, and Irish irony, lie indignation, despair, the political conscience. The rights and wrongs of Irish politics come into her works by implication. We see the absentees, the rackrenters, the bought politicians, the English, Jewish, Scottish heiresses brought in to save colonial insolvency. We see the buffoon priests and the double-minded retainers. We do not see the rebellion, the boys hiding in the potato fields, but we do catch the tension. The clever, wise daughter of an enlightened father, a woman always ready to moralise about cause and effect in the neat eighteenth-century way, Maria Edgeworth was Irish enough to enjoy without shame the unreasonable climate of human temper and self-will, Irish enough to be generous about the genius for self-destruction. She was a good woman, ardent but—as Sir Walter Scott said—formidably observant, probably cool, perhaps not strong in sensibility; but she was not sentimental. Her irony—and surely this is Irish from Swift to Shaw—is the exploitation of folly by a reckless gaiety.

Castle Rackrent is the only novel of Maria Edgeworth's which can be read with sustained pleasure by the reader of today. Its verve and vivacity are as sharp as a fiddle. It catches on like a jig; if it belongs to the artless time of the English novel, it is not clogged up by old-fashioned usage. I have never read ***The Absentee,*** which is often praised, but I have tried ***Belinda,*** a picture of the London smart set, and ***Ormond.*** They, too, are vivacious, but there is not much point in finding time for them. They have a minor place in the history of the novel. One can only say that she has an original observation of men and women, an unspoiled eye for types; her moralisings are at any rate free from Victorian sentimentality, but are not in themselves interesting. Is it better for affection to follow esteem, or for esteem to follow affection? How are we to keep the peace between sensitiveness and sensibility, between the natural and the frivolous heart? How do we distinguish the line where generosity becomes self-indulgence? All this is good training, no doubt; but Maria Edgeworth was at her best when she was not being explicit about it. Character for its own sake, as the work of so many women novelists has shown, was the strong subject of this kind, clear-headed, irreverent woman, who never disturbs but also rarely comes to the foregone conclusion.

Belinda is a sharp-eyed tour of the London marriage market. No woman is less deceived by other women than this unsoured spinster who adored her father, wrote handbooks on education with him, managed his estate, "got on" with his four wives and looked after his 21 children. The Edgeworths were a nation in themselves. She could draw an old rip like Lady Delacour, a matchmaker like Mrs. Stanhope pushing her débutantes, and a dangerous "metaphysical" woman like Lady Millicent in *Ormond* with "the sweet persuasive voice and eloquent eyes—hers was a kind of exalted sentimental morality, referring everything to feeling, and to the notion of *sacrifice . . .* but to describe her notions she was very nearly unintelligible." Maria Edgeworth was the Major's daughter; the unintelligible was the unforgiveable. It was very plain to her that the Lady Millicents of this world are so exalted that they do not know right from wrong. The men are as firmly drawn as the women. *Ormond* contains a rich portrait of one of those hospitable, sociable, gallant, warm-hearted Irishmen, the souls of courtesy, whose imagination leads them into difficulties and ends by corrupting them, until the warm heart goes stone cold and they become the familiar Irish politician who will sell himself and anybody. Such a portrait might be done flat in bitterness and satire; Miss Edgeworth works in depth, engages our sympathy for the man, makes him captivate us—as he would in life—and gradually undeceives us without melodrama or ill-nature. None of these are great characters, but they are faithful observations of character. They are a truthful gallery, as capricious as life, of the figures of a class and an age. Such—we can be certain—was the life she knew.

Her other gift as a novelist is for writing spirited dialogue. The talk of *Belinda* or *Ormond* is always light, engaging and natural. It is that "modern" talk which goes on from generation to generation—one meets it in Jane Austen; then, after the Regency, it died out, until the modern novel revived it—and which has not been written in, like sub-headings, into the story. Maria Edgeworth owed her gift to her indifference to plot, that great torture-rack of talk in the English novel. Plot was forced on her by her father, the brilliant Major, who suffered from a rather delightful excess of confidence in his own powers; but, like Scott at the beginning of his career, Miss Edgeworth was interested only in sketching the people around her, and that is how the true gift for dialogue arises. Yet she owed something even of this to the Major, for it was he who, determined to out-Rousseau Rousseau, made his daughter write down the dialogue of his 21 children in order that it could be examined afterwards in his moral and linguistic laboratory.

Of course, she had the Irish ear for Irish expressiveness. In *Ormond,* King Corny cries out with the gout:

"Pray now," said he to Harry who stood beside his bed—"now that I've a moment's ease—did you ever hear of the stoics that the bookmen talk of, and can you tell me what good anyone of them got by making it a point to make no noise when they'd be punished and racked with pains of body or mind? Why I tell you all they got—all they got was no pity—who would give them pity, that did not require it? I could bleed to death in a bath, as well as the best of them, if I chose it; or chew a bullet, if I set my teeth to it, with any man in a regiment—but where's the use? Nature knows best, and she says *roar!*"

In a subtler way, she is as good in her plain passages, notably in her scenes between men and women. She hardly can be said to try a love affair, indeed one might say that she has noticed men and women pursue one another but is not sure why they do so. What she likes best is caprice, misunderstanding, the off-days of married life, flirtation: that side of love which, in short, supplies repartee and comedy, sociability or its opposite. Her people are always being interrupted and though this shows some incompetence on the novelist's part, it also allows that crisp animation or restlessness which gives her stories their unaffected drift.

There are no interruptions in *Castle Rackrent*. Thady the steward tells the tale in his plain words and with his devious mind, and he rattles off the decline and fall of the riotous Rackrents over three generations, in a 100 pages. Drink, company, debt and recalcitrant foreign wives ruined these roisterers and Thady's own son, turned lawyer, quietly collected the remnant and indirectly made it his own. At the funeral of one Rackrent, the body was nearly seized for debt:

> But the heir who attended the funeral was against that, for fear of consequences, seeing that those villains who came to serve acted under the disguise of the law; so, to be sure, the law must take its course and little gain had the creditors for their pains. First and foremost, they had the curses of the country and Sir Murtagh Rackrent, the new heir, in the next place, on account of this affront to the body refused to pay a shilling of the debts, in which he was countenanced by all best gentlemen of property and others of his acquaintance, Sir Murtagh alleging in all companies that he all along meant to pay his father's debts of honour, but the moment the law was taken from him, there was the end of the honour to be sure. It was whispered (but none but the enemies of the family believe it) that this was all a sham seizure to get quit of the debts, which he had bound himself to pay in honour. It's a long time ago, there's no saying how it was . . .

That is Defoe, but with whiskey added.

Major Edgeworth did not touch *Castle Rackrent*. He is known to have had a didactic hand in the other works and some have thought he stiffened them. Possibly. Yet his daughter owed her subsequent inspiration to the excitable, inventive, genial mind of the masterful eccentric and amateur. *Castle Rackrent* was the first attempt to present the history of a family over several generations as a subject in itself. It marks a small step in the expansion of the novel.

Where the Major's influence is most felt is in the remarkable range of his daughter's work. Ireland is only one of her scenes. English society, Parisian society, are done with the same natural touch. Her work was a triumph for the Major's revolutionary system of free education. Not a patch on Fanny Burney or Jane Austen, no doubt; the minds of father and daughter were too much dispersed by practical and inventive attention to the good, rational life. Scott thought Edgeworthstown a domestic paradise and possibly noted it was an Abbotsford 150 years old without the worry and the expense. Abbotsford meant absurdity, obsession, and imagination; Edgeworthstown meant enlightenment. In the last count, the good life does not produce the great novelists.

Mark D. Hawthorne (essay date 1967)

SOURCE: "Chapter Two," in *Doubt and Dogma in Maria Edgeworth,* University of Florida Press, 1967, pp. 23-38.

[In the following essay, Hawthorne distinguishes between the didacticism imposed on Edgeworth's fiction by her father and the plot and character development that reflect her own authorial tendency.]

Between 1798 and 1801, Maria Edgeworth earned her reputation as a creative writer. Her father had begun cultivating her talents along this line as early as May, 1780, when he asked her to "send [him] a little tale, about the length of a *Spectator,* upon the subject of Generosity." As a result of his encouragement, her earliest stories are all didactic or, as she would have said, moral. In Ireland surrounded by her little brothers and sisters, she discovered the dearth of children's stories, there being little written expressly for children except Thomas Day's *Sandford and Merton* and a handful of tales by Mrs. Barbauld. So she became interested in didactic stories for children. The result was a series of children's books that occupied her from about 1791 till 1827. She usually wrote the first draft of a story on a slate, then read it to her brothers and sisters. If they approved, she copied it; if they didn't, she rewrote it and tried again. Her apprenticeship was truly a family affair.

This flood of children's fiction was enough to give her a lasting place in literature. *The Parent's Assistant* grew to six volumes by 1800 and was followed by *Early Lessons* (1801), *Moral Tales for Young People* (1801), *Popular Tales* (1804), *Continuation of Early Tales* (1814), *Rosamund, A Sequel to Early Lessons* (1821), *Frank, A Sequel to Frank in Early Lessons* (1822), *Harry and Lucy Continued, Being the Last Part of Early Lessons* (1825), and *Little Plays for Children* (1827). These stories and plays have a delicate brilliance that makes them classics of children's literature. Miss Edgeworth gave an unexpected life to her characters, causing the little children to emerge from her pages with a freshness seldom found in the children's literature of the last hundred years. The only flaw—if it is indeed a flaw—is the moralizing. But even moralizing does not lack charm when it is skillfully done, and Miss Edgeworth always had skill. The appeal of her stories was such that they were reprinted, both in England and America, as late as the 1890's, a remarkable longevity for this type of fiction.

Her work on this level was not an end in itself. When she first turned to adult fiction with *Castle Rackrent* (1800), her talents and her awareness of the art of the novel were already mature, and she immediately revealed herself as an artist and technician. With its rich treatment of Thady and its whimsical humor of situation, *Castle Rackrent* was Maria Edgeworth's only major work to be reprinted thus far in the 1960's, and many call it her masterpiece. But she showed her greatest talents in those books that are seldom read today, in *Belinda* and *Patronage. Castle Rackrent,* like her children's literature, was a step toward her more mature novels.

In her three publications of 1801, we can trace Miss Edgeworth's developing thought and art. For her youngest readers, who had advanced beyond *The Parent's Assistant,* she wrote *Early Lessons,* a primer in four sections. In one section, *Frank, A Tale,* she carefully illustrated Mr. Edgeworth's theories. This little volume is clearly didactic. There is no subtlety, no depth of character portrayal. She was attempting no more than a simple moral tale for six-year-olds. But in *Moral Tales for Young People,* a collection of stories written for teenagers, she was not interested in simple moral tales, regardless of the title. Here she debated against rationalism as she questioned motivation and narrowly limited the definition of reason. She began in this collection to develop her skill in writing on two levels, the surface of dogmatizing and the structure of doubting. The alterations of her father's thought made in *Moral Tales* were fundamental to her third 1801 publication, *Belinda.* In this novel, her first adult fiction since *Castle Rackrent,* she made one of her most subtle, and most devastating, studies of rational utilitarianism while at the same time she appeared to accept all its ramifications.

One of the most remarkable things about Miss Edgeworth's fiction is that the moral tags (whether they be chapter-headings or editorial comments) tend to agree with Mr. Edgeworth's assumptions, but the plots and characters are based on opinions which—to say the least—differ from the more outspoken tags. On this account, we are brought to the same possibilities that we discussed with reference to *Letters for Literary Ladies:* either the fiction was carelessly written, or the inconsistencies are functional.

She never openly admitted her divergence from Mr. Edgeworth's control and continued, even in the *Memoirs of Richard Lovell Edgeworth* (1820), to pay lip service to his doctrine. But she analyzed the rational premises and, when they failed to satisfy her, supplied the premises of emotionalism. The premises she introduced in lieu of the rational ones are fundamental to the symmetry of plot and to the portrayal of character. Mr. Edgeworth carefully supervised her work and was the major force that kept her writing, but she incorporated her disagreements with his philosophy so intricately into her structures that even his red pencil and scissors did not alter her meaning, however much her thought might be obscured by his desire to teach moral lessons. Thus she slowly molded the didactic novel into a radically new form. Her father's ideas everywhere struck the unsuspecting reader, but her plots, her imagery, her characterization were at odds with this surface. The resulting tension gives her mature fiction a depth that is not at all like the usual didactic novel. Had she continued to write in the vein of *Castle Rackrent,* she might have greater posthumous fame. As it was, she captivated the public and taught it to accept the Romantic premises. Thus Grace Oliver called her "emphatically a representative of the utilitarian ideas which Bentham recognized as the great movement" of the eighteenth century and, at the same time, quoted Miss Edgeworth's remarks on the doctrine of association: "Upon its revival, this principle seems to have been over-valued, and, as Sir Walter Scott humorously observed, to have been used as 'a sort of metaphysical pick-lock.' It seems to have been forgotten, in the zeal for the power of association, that there must be something to associate with, some original capacity of feeling or pleasure, probably different in different minds." In a sense, she was a master propagandist—she said what was expected from a demure young lady, but, as she said it, she swayed her readers toward the very ideas that made them afraid of the Romantic giants.

Frank is a classic example of the simple didactic story in the tradition of *Sandford and Merton.* Its sole purpose is to teach the child how to judge the proper way to act and how to avoid rash or imprudent behavior. In short, it is a narrative illustration of *Practical Education,* written for six-year-olds. A simple didactic work, it exemplifies Mr. Edgeworth's demand that "a book exhibiting instances of vice should never be given to a child who thinks and acts correctly" (*Practical Education*). From an adult viewpoint (an adult would probably read it with the child), *Frank* also showed how Mr. Edgeworth's educational system can be put into effect.

Frank is trained by his reflective and emotionless mother who teaches him to reason and not to imagine. But his imagination is not completely atrophied; his mother merely channels it entirely into scientific inquiry, the practice of judgment. In this sense, imagination is the basis of curiosity and of the use of judgment; this is a slight addition to the earlier consideration of this faculty. But overall the story is little more than a representation of the stereotyped mother and son that will show up again and again in Miss Edgeworth's more serious fiction. Because education should be practical, Frank learns such things as the production of linen from flax, the ways to mend broken china, the process of brewing beer, and the method of thatching a roof. Frank's imagination is directed away from the fanciful and to the utilitarian; hence he is obedient and prudent and happy. He is an ideal pupil of rational utilitarianism.

Frank represents the assumption that the well-educated child (the one whose education most closely resembles the doctrines of *Practical Education*) will be obedient, prudent, and useful to his society because he is a rational

being, not a creature of passion. Miss Edgeworth later ridiculed this assumption.

Two of the stories in *Moral Tales* were written in the same style as *Frank,* though addressed to a slightly older audience. In "**The Good French Governess**" and in "**The Good Aunt**," the principal characters are teachers who are rational utilitarians like Frank's mother, and their pupils, like Frank, are the ideal products of rational education. But these stories are more subtle than *Frank,* for they also demonstrate the notion that to follow the rational system will result in the best possible education *with the least trouble to the educator.* Miss Edgeworth examined the implications of this notion in "**The Contrast**," a story in *Popular Tales;* here it merely helped her to take emphasis from the ideal pupil. In addition, Miss Edgeworth inserted premises that ultimately weakened the rational basis of her father's system. As she began to question rationalism, she contrasted the merits of the rational child and the merits of the child whose sole motivation was passion. More and more, the passionate child overshadows the rational one, and the rational child begins to show bad traits.

In his prefatory remarks to "**The Good French Governess**," Mr. Edgeworth called it "a lesson to teach the art of giving lessons" (*Moral Tales).* Miss Edgeworth suggested this superficial reading by centering the story around Madame de Rosier, an *émigrée* and ideal governess. Before her rational influence, Isabella Harcourt, her oldest ward, could recite historical dates but lacked the understanding to make them meaningful; Matilda had come to believe that she had no genius because she lacked Isabella's memory; Favoretta was thoroughly spoiled; and Herbert, the youngest, was unmanageable. In short, the Harcourt nursery was a hotbed of passion and unhappiness, but the rational governess courageously tackles this challenge. She speaks to each child as though he were a rational being. Also she praises only rational and useful actions in order to form and establish pleasurable associations. When these associations become habits, the children are no longer passionate or unhappy. Isabella learns to reason; Matilda discovers that she has mathematical genius; Favoretta turns into a well-behaved little girl; and Herbert becomes manageable. On the surface, "**The Good French Governess**" is a simple story of reason rewarded.

Simple as it might be when compared to her later fiction, the story is complicated. Whereas *Frank* was one-sided, "**The Good French Governess**" contrasts the Harcourts with Miss Fanshaw, who attended a fashionable public school. Through this contrast, Miss Edgeworth emphasized the value of the private, rational education far more than she had been able to in *Frank,* where there was no background against which to judge its merits. Furthermore, she turns Miss Fanshaw's inability to comprehend the delight that Isabella and Matilda have in acquiring new knowledge into a satire on the public school. Public education teaches only one lesson well—the art of duplicity. Miss Fanshaw was proper, reserved, and quiet in public, but "*out of company,* the silent figure became talkative. The charm seemed to be broken, or rather reversed, and she began to chatter with pert incessant rapidity" (*Moral Tales*). Such duplicity is far worse than the uncurbed passions Madame de Rosier found in the Harcourt nursery—it is reason preverted to base ends.

Maria Edgeworth also represents the bad teacher through her portrayal of Mrs. Grace, the mother's waiting-maid. Mrs. Grace creates dissension in the nursery by showing obvious partiality to Favoretta and by irrationally treating Herbert with scorn. Like the Calvinistic God, she showers her "grace" with no apparent logic. Even after Madame de Rosier brings concord, she tries to poison her mistress' mind against the rational procedure. Only when Mrs. Grace openly shows her antagonism and cruelty to Herbert, does Mrs. Harcourt take the boy out of her power. The passionate mother, like Julia in *Letters for Literary Ladies,* immediately recognizes harsh actions. Thereafter, Miss Edgeworth spared no pain in degrading Mrs. Grace: she is abruptly discharged with no character reference after she is found eavesdropping, a vice that the writer strangely classified with gambling and drunkenness.

In addition, Miss Edgeworth showed that the rationality of the nursery eventually touches Mrs. Harcourt, the mother. At first, the mother "lived in a constant round of dissipation" and "had not time to cultivate her understanding, or to attend the education of her family" (*Moral Tales*). But influenced by Madame de Rosier and by her own children, she radically changes: "The plan of education which had been traced out remained yet unfinished, and she feared, she said, that Isabella and Matilda might feel the want of their accomplished preceptress. But these fears were the best omen for her future success: a sensible mother, in whom the desire to educate her family has once been excited, and who turns the energy of her mind to this interesting subject, seizes upon every useful idea, every practical principle, with avidity, and she may trust securely to her own persevering cares. . . . The rapid improvement of Mrs. Harcourt's understanding since she had applied herself to literature, was her reward, and her excitement to fresh application. Isabella and Matilda were now of an age to be her companions, and her taste for domestic life was confirmed every day by the sweet experience of its pleasure" (*Moral Tales*). The redemption of the dissipated lady of quality, a theme fully developed in *Belinda,* illustrates the far-reaching effects of rationalism. Any person, Miss Edgeworth affirmed, will be influenced by reason, if his understanding is once awakened, because no rational being will knowingly choose misery. At this point, the writer, true to her father's assumptions, gave no leeway for honest error.

In **"The Good French Governess,"** Miss Edgeworth showed that, if someone is not rational, he will be imprudent and that imprudence is punished by ridicule or social disgrace. Mrs. Grace was turned out with no character reference; Miss Fanshaw made a fool of herself by her imprudent behavior in the presence of Lady N—, whom she was trying to impress. On the other hand, reason leads to prudence, which, according to rationalism, is its own reward. The Harcourt children were happier because they were rational beings; Mrs. Harcourt learned the pleasures of domestic life.

Obviously Miss Edgeworth wanted to give a greater reward to the educator than to the educated: Madame de Rosier is reunited with her son whom she believed had been guillotined during the Reign of Terror. But this reunion and the later repossession of their French estates presumes a material reward that cannot be reconciled to the rational reward. The rationalist, like Frank's mother, holds that prudence needs no reward other than the happiness it brings, yet from this story on, Miss Edgeworth added a material reward (usually in the form of unexpected money) when the prudent character has successfully withstood temptation and privation. Apparently she could not conceive of a man who was both prudent and poor.

In one respect, her addition of a material reward marked one of the earliest weaknesses that she detected in rationalism: most people need a greater incentive than an abstract love of reason. Few men and no children will be virtuous for the sake of virtue, but add a few pounds or a stick of candy and virtue comes easily. In another respect, the material reward is a fitting opposite of social disgrace (especially like Mrs. Grace's) because it is social prosperity. Seldom referring to religion or to any other-worldliness, Miss Edgeworth maintained the earthliness of all punishment and reward. Thus she translated religious salvation into material prosperity. This was, of course, a comfortable pill for the rising industrial class to swallow, yet material prosperity as the ultimate reward for prudence stands diametrically opposed to the premise that prudence is its own reward. But Miss Edgeworth did not let this obscure her surface moral. At the end of the story she cleverly shifted the interest from Madame de Rosier to Mrs. Harcourt, whose reward is in line with the rational creed. This rejection of a part of that creed passed almost unnoticed. Later she so sacrificed realism and common sense that she invited Croker's charge that "we cannot reconcile ourselves to extreme improbabilities, and events barely within the verge of nature, which excite wonder instead of interest, and disgust rather than surprise." But she moved very cautiously and very slowly in these early tales.

If the adoption of a material reward in **"The Good French Governess"** was in part symptomatic of Miss Edgeworth's dissatisfaction with rationalism, her emphasis on the disobedient child in **"The Good Aunt"** suggests the theme of her later fiction. Insofar as a material reward supports prudence, the role of reason is weakened. Miss Edgeworth realized that people will not cultivate their understandings unless they are promised a tangible gain, but this raised further questions. What happens if someone knows the merits of prudence but still acts imprudently? In other words, is reason really strong enough to alter established habits? If not, the assumption that reason is the sole guide to conduct must be wrong. Miss Edgeworth began to analyze this problem in **"The Good Aunt."**

Here her chief character is young Charles Howard, who lives with his aunt, the rational utilitarian. From the start, the story is a further development of the theme of *Frank* and **"The Good French Governess."** The child, however, no longer lives with his parents; Charles is an orphan.

Moreover, the child's background is much more passionate; Charles' father had been killed in a duel over gambling debts. The boy's education must thus overcome the influence of his earliest childhood, the time when he was the most impressionable. This gives the rational educator a greater challenge than Madame de Rosier's; however, Mrs. Howard, like Mrs. Harcourt, is willing to accept the challenge. She "had the courage to apply herself seriously to the cultivation of her understanding: she educated herself, that she might be able to fulfill the important duty of educating a child." For help she turns to Mr. Russell, a good tutor based in large part on Thomas Day's Mr. Barlow (and also on Mr. Edgeworth's own tutor), and together they mold Charles into a paragon of learning, rationality, and virtue. Again Miss Edgeworth seems to have written a simple didactic story.

But again she questioned the simple morality of the surface. She emphasized the passionate child, Augustus Holloway, by developing him into a fully rounded character. In fact, she developed him so well that he overshadows Charles Howard. Charles prudently cultivates his understanding; Augustus is blindly led into false friendships, gambling, and deceit. Charles receives a "judicious early education" from his aunt and is a brilliant pupil, but only his teachers and Oliver, his single disciple, recognize his merits. The other boys flock around Augustus, buy lottery tickets from him, and lament his losses. Charles is unpopular because he attempts to win admiration only by reason and industry. Augustus wins admiration as a "man of the world" by deceiving the boys' emotions. In short, Charles stands opposed to fashion and to the social world, although he hopes that ultimately his industry will be rewarded. But Augustus stands at the top of the social ladder, the Beau Brummell of the boys' world. While Charles sinks into obscurity, Augustus commands attention. In addition, Miss Edgeworth cast doubt on the assumption that social acceptance is part of the happiness gained by the rational being. She very clearly said that popularity is a false standard of merit. She removed Charles from his peers by making him unpopular, but once he is aligned with the rational adults, he loses what interest he had. Because he is rational and always prudent, he has neither change and development nor conflict. Consequently, the entire plot centers around Augustus' mental and moral struggles. Miss Edgeworth, in other words, continually pointed at the example of the rational child, but her attention was absorbed by the passionate one. The tension and interest of the story are rooted in the troubles of Augustus, not in the felicity of Charles.

At the end of the story, Miss Edgeworth dismissed Augustus with a single sentence: "Mr. Russell was engaged to superintend the education of Holloway" (*Moral Tales*). She had reason for such abruptness. A child, her rational father believed, should not be punished if he confesses his fault because recognition of error is tantamount to its removal *(Practical Education)*. Augustus sees his fault (indeed, he is trapped by circumstance and can do nothing else); therefore, he cannot be punished. Miss Edgeworth, then, was faithful to a rational premise. But this is not her only reason. In terms of the contrast between

Howard and Augustus, this rigid adherence to a rational doctrine weakens the entire moral surface. If she wished to draw a simple contrast, she would have punished Augustus more seriously than Miss Fanshaw. After all, his imprudence brought pain and disgrace to his fellow-pupils, but Miss Fanshaw merely brought ridicule upon herself. Instead, Miss Edgeworth complicated the story by introducing a reversal in the character who ostensibly served only as a contrast to the good child. Even Augustus realizes that Mr. Russell's tutorship promises greater future rewards and that he is not really punished at all. A rigid adherence to rationalism has turned the theory against itself.

According to Mr. Edgeworth, a personality that is neither wholly reasonable nor wholly passionate does not and cannot exist. Passion or imagination, he claimed, results in imprudence and misery while reason alone can result in prudence and happiness; hence no one can be passionate and happy. But Miss Edgeworth portrayed a character who is passionate, happy, and prudent by using the device of making him a foreigner, a device that she often resorted to when openly contradicting rationalism. Little Oliver is "a Creole, lively, intelligent, openhearted, and affectionate in the extreme, but rather passionate in his temper, and averse to application" (*Moral Tales*). Supposedly, he is believable because he is a foreigner and all foreigners are a little unbelievable. When he first appears in **"The Good Aunt,"** he is Augustus' fag and is thereby linked to his master's irrationality. For example, he tolerates harsh treatment because he believes that he is stupid. Only after Charles defends his rights in a fist fight with Augustus (passion can only understand action so reason must stoop to passionate means to achieve rational ends), does he shift to the side of reason, symbolized by Charles. He becomes Charles' friend and learns from him the teachings of the good aunt and tutor. Miss Edgeworth, however, carefully emphasized that Oliver never becomes as rational as his friend. Oliver retains his passionate nature while, at the same time, he becomes prudent. Also, Miss Edgeworth made his development more credible than she had the conversions of Mrs. Harcourt and Augustus. The change is gradual and scarcely perceptible. She supported the premise that reason will win over passion if the understanding is awakened, but she gave a striking illustration of her belief that the awakening of the understanding does not mean the death of the imagination.

After **"The Good Aunt,"** Miss Edgeworth laid aside the clear-cut surface moral of her children's literature and turned toward a greater penetration into character. She had discovered that the didactic form could be molded into a vehicle that dogmatized and doubted at the same time, and she would continue to develop her skill at speaking, as it were, out of the corner of her mouth. But now her attention was drawn to another problem, one that offered ample room for developing her own opinions and for perfecting her art of ironic understatement. Hitherto, she concentrated on the teacher and on the obedient pupil, but her treatments of Augustus and Oliver posed another question: what causes a good teacher to have a disobedient pupil? In **"Forester"** and **"Angelina"** she confronted this question, and through answering it, she reached the premises that she turned to brilliant use in *Belinda*.

In his preface to *Moral Tales,* Mr. Edgeworth announced that the purpose of the volume was "to provide for young people, of a more advanced age [than the audience of *Early Lessons*], a few Tales, that shall neither dissipate the attention, nor inflame the imagination." Later in the same preface he added, "The Tales have been written to illustrate the opinions delivered in 'Practical Education.'" At least in his mind, *Moral Tales* was consistent with his theory. He read only the surface moralizing and overlooked his daughter's delicately balanced plots and the probing undertones of her own opinions. Thus he missed the point of **"Forester"** altogether. In his heavy-handed way he told the public that it was "the picture of an eccentric character—a young man who scorns the common forms and dependencies of civilized society; and who, full of visionary schemes of benevolence and happiness (no doubt like Thomas Day, the prototype of Forester), might, by improper management, or unlucky circumstance, have become a fanatic and a criminal" (*Moral Tales*). Miss Edgeworth did create an eccentric character who is an avid nonconformist, but through an ironic understatement of situation, she twisted the story into a scorching critique of pure reason. Mr. Edgeworth was too literal-minded to understand her irony; after all, he took even Swift literally.

Forester is an imaginative and sensitive young man, a "volatile genius," who possesses such an amiable personality that his peccadillos are no more than misdirected benevolence. In fact, his misanthropy stems from a misdirected contempt for human weakness: "Young Forester was frank, brave, and generous, but he had been taught to dislike politeness so much that the common forms of society appeared to him either odious or ridiculous; his sincerity was seldom restrained by any attention to the feelings of others. . . . His attention had been early fixed upon the follies and vices of the higher classes of people; and his contempt for selfish indolence was so strongly associated with the name of gentleman, that he was disposed to choose his friends and companions from amongst his inferiors: the inequality between the rich and the poor shocked him; his temper was enthusiastic as well as benevolent; and he ardently wished to be a man, and to be at liberty to act for himself, that he might reform society, or at least his own neighbourhood" (*Moral Tales*). In short, he embodies the Romantic humanitarianism that will become essential to such men as Wordsworth, Shelley, and Hunt. Like them and like Rousseau, he wants to level social distinctions to better society. And unlike Charles Howard, who silently accepted social hypocrisy, Forester blatantly rejects any and all falsehood. "Those who do not respect truth in trifles," he firmly believes, "will never respect it in matters of consequence" (*Moral Tales*). The result of such honesty is inevitable—he is a social outcast.

On the one hand, Miss Edgeworth contrasted Forester and Archibald Mackenzie. Through her skillful balancing of character traits, this contrast becomes the struggle between untrammeled but ignorant innocence and tainted but sophisticated cunning. Forester is imprudent because of lofty ideals; Mackenzie is imprudent because he is selfish, cowardly, and hypocritical. In a word, Mackenzie is an out-and-out villain. On the other hand, Miss Edgeworth contrasted Forester and Henry Campbell, the well-educated child. Henry has the benevolence and courage of Forester as well as genuine politeness and social cultivation. He is practical, never carried away by imagination or enthusiasm, and completely controlled by judgment. Forester is, then, poised between opposing forces; he can move in either direction. Mr. Edgeworth or any strict rationalist would have claimed that it was a simple either-or choice, that Forester can either be entirely passionate and bad or be entirely rational and good. But Maria Edgeworth did not think that life is so simple. She showed how Forester learns rational self-control and becomes a worthy member of society without acquiring the corruption of Mackenzie and without losing his enthusiasm.

If she were merely preaching on a rational text, Miss Edgeworth would have made the rational Dr. Campbell play the decisive role in Forester's education. But Forester learns only from his own experience. The rational influence of the Campbell household is not strong enough to alter his deeply rooted habits; like Julia, he must discover for himself whatever he learns, for precepts do him no good. The difference between Mrs. Harcourt and Forester is significant. In Mrs. Harcourt's case, Miss Edgeworth still accepted the notion that vice is the result of error; now her thinking had matured. Forester does not acquire prudence until enthusiasm fails to produce its desired ends, but he does not lose his enthusiasm. Miss Edgeworth here suggested that perhaps there is such a thing as honest error. She no longer held that virtue is a simple matter of judgment, and she doubted that reason is truly as influential as she had thought in **"The Good French Governess."** Thus she pushed Dr. Campbell to the background. When experience, not reason, becomes the determining factor in guiding a young man to prudence, the teacher is superfluous. The rational way to prudence becomes little more than a dream, a tea party that does not exist in the world of hard facts.

Although she showed that reason alone does not influence behavior, she did relate Dr. Campbell to Forester and Mackenzie. She contrasted the lessons that Forester learns away from the doctor and the vices pursued by Mackenzie while living under the doctor's roof. Mackenzie conceals pettiness behind an attack on an innocent woman, deceives Henry's goodness, and proves a coward when challenged to a duel. He remains in the doctor's house but learns nothing. On the other hand, Forester, separated from the doctor, reaches his conclusions without accepting his premises. Yet Miss Edgeworth's emphasis on experience is hardly complimentary. It reduces the need of an educator to mere expediency; the student will learn his lesson equally well, though with greater difficulty, from experience.

When she made material prosperity the reward for prudence, Miss Edgeworth prepared for a still further curtailment of reason. If social well-being is a reward for proper conduct, it follows that a given social order must be good. Miss Edgeworth was a member of the Irish ruling class and sympathized with the defeated French Royalists. She accepted without qualification the social order of the last half of the eighteenth century. In the narrowness of her political bias, she refused to listen to the demands for social equality that were coming from France and even from England. In **"Ennui,"** for example, she even ridiculed men who attempted to raise their social position. Quite the contrary, she staunchly defended the status quo. She believed that the French Revolution was caused by madmen, and she never realized that her own moral philosophy was based on the same premises as the men's whose politics she so abhorred. She calmly affirmed that her society was the norm to which all prudent men must adjust, and the material prosperity she gave to her characters was firmly placed in this norm. In her ideal world, *émigrés* returned to their ancestral estates, the claims of the Irish patriots were brushed aside with scorn, and wealth joined to a middle-class conscience formed the ideal citizen.

A rebel, like Forester, was a threat to such a society and must bend to its demands if it was to prosper; therefore, Miss Edgeworth had little patience with her character's politics. He cannot be a useful member of society until he learns that politeness is necessary, even if it means praising a young lady for talents that she does not have. Reason must adapt to society. And since reason is to further the aims of a certain society, it must, Miss Edgeworth believed, be tempered by experience lest the love of abstract theory, however rational, justify a revolution. Of course, all of this limits reason. Forester, for example, accepts society only when he finds that he cannot change it, not when reason tells him that it must remain unchanged. He first learns from experience that "Jack on his alehouse bench has as many lies as a Czar," then he abandons his hatred for gentlemen. Vice, the result of human imprudence, exists on all levels of society; hence the class which conceals it in order to live in harmony is preferable to a classless society in which all men sink to vulgarity.

In **"Forester"** the rational educator was pushed to the background; nevertheless, he represented certain standards of conduct that were reached through experience. Actually, the framework of the story is similar to that of **"Letters of Julia and Caroline."** But in **"Angelina"** the rational educator does not appear until *after* the main character has significantly changed. Here the author showed that experience alone can lead to prudence.

On the surface, **"Angelina,"** like *Northanger Abbey,* is a satire of the cult of sensibility. Angelina is a young lady who "had passed her childhood with a father and mother, who cultivated her literary taste, but who neglected to cultivate her judgment" (*Moral Tales*). Consequently, Angelina is so impressionable that, like Don Quixote, she creates a dream world of romance based on reading, then sets out into the real world to find it. Hard fact, however, slaps her back to reality every time she thinks she has found the ideal. Miss Edgeworth eked from this discrepancy between the real and the ideal one of her most de-

lightful tales. **"Angelina"** is often as vibrant with rich humor as those sections of *Don Juan* in which the ideal is shattered against the hard world of facts. But Miss Edgeworth had an avowed purpose that Byron lacked. When Angelina finally can hold no longer to her tattered dreams, she turns from them with disgust, and the rational educator, Lady Frances, rushes onto the scene to "save" the unfortunate damsel. Miss Edgeworth cleverly made the story look like another illustration of *Practical Education,* but this too is merely another illusion.

Forester lived in the home of a good teacher; Angelina's guardian is a dogmatic "lady who placed her whole happiness in living in a certain circle of high company in London" (*Moral Tales*). Like Forester, she flees from her guardian and finds herself in serious trouble before the teacher intervenes, but her flight is with different motivation. Forester foolishly thought, "I should be happy if I were a useful member of society; a gardener is a useful member of society, and I will be a gardener, and live with gardeners" (*Moral Tales*). Angelina's imagination, completely neglected by her education, leads her to glorify the authoress of a sentimental novel. The boy wants to escape *into* the world; the girl, *from* the world. Both learn the same lesson: an unattainable sentiment is worthless. And both learn from their progressive disillusionment. But all that Angelina learns comes from her own experience; no Dr. Campbell lurks in the background.

Lady Frances, the counterpart of Dr. Campbell, meets Angelina only after she has begun to rise from her lowest ebb. But Lady Frances lacks the legal and rational powers of Dr. Campbell, who was both guardian and teacher; she is unable to reconcile Lady Diana and her ward. In this case, the first of many in the fiction of Maria Edgeworth, reason has no influence. Miss Edgeworth carefully moralized that under "the friendly and judicious care of Lady Frances" Angelina "acquired that which is more useful to the possessor than genius—common sense" (*Moral Tales*). But she was even more careful to show that Angelina developed "good sense" before Lady Frances entered the story. It is through the frustration of having illusion thwarted by reality that Angelina discovers the disgrace to which sentimentality must inevitably lead: "Longer, much longer, Miss Hodges spoke in the most peremptory voice; but whilst she was declaiming on her favourite topic, her Angelina was 'revolving in her altered mind' the strange things which she had seen and heard in the course of the last half-hour; every thing appeared to her in a new light; when she compared the conversation and conduct of Miss Hodges with the sentimental letters of her Araminta [Miss Hodges' pen name]; when she compared Orlando in description to Orlando in reality, she could scarcely believe her senses: accustomed as she had been to elegance of manners, the vulgarity and awkwardness of Miss Hodges shocked and disgusted her beyond measure. . . . The idea of spending her life in a cottage with Mrs. Hodges Gazabo and Nat overwhelmed our heroine with the double fear of wretchedness and ridicule" (*Moral Tales*). Angelina is willing to choose any escape from this disgrace. Thus Lady Frances' entrance becomes merely expedient, necessary only for the surface moral.

By reducing the educator to a *dea ex machina,* Miss Edgeworth showed both that the result of experience, however passionate, is the same as the result of reason and that experience is a more valid guide to conduct. The passionate person—and all people, it must be remembered, are passionate by nature—will acquire through action what he cannot learn through words. Action, not words, is the basis of the experiences of Forester and Angelina, and such experience teaches the same conclusions as reason. Miss Edgeworth explored the implications of her **"Letters of Julia and Caroline"** and, as a result, limited the role of reason to the point that her premises completely undermine the entire school of rationalism. She showed that a person can learn to be prudent without cultivating his understanding. And even more significant, she asserted that reason was not the sole guide to prudence. Like Oliver, Forester and Angelina are neither wholly passionate nor wholly rational. They become prudent enough to be accepted by the rational educators, but they learn from actions. Miss Edgeworth proved that her own personality can—and does—exist, but in so doing, she discarded the premises of rationalism.

In the process of writing **Moral Tales,** she so perfected her art that she taught what her father wanted her to and at the same time was honest with herself. An inferior artist would have balked at the challenge; he would have done either the one or the other. Miss Edgeworth not only rose to the challenge, she turned the didactic novel into a delicate balance of dogma and doubt. She developed from the simple didactic form a technique that she would use with increasing artistry through the remainder of her career. When she turned to adult fiction with the talents that she had polished in her children's literature, the result was an astonishing array of beautifully constructed, but easily misunderstood, stories and novels.

O. Elizabeth McWhorter Harden (essay date 1971)

SOURCE: "A Final Estimate," in *Maria Edgeworth's Art of Prose Fiction,* Mouton, 1971, pp. 227-38.

[*In the following essay, Harden assesses Edgeworth's strengths and weaknesses as a creative writer.*

Throughout her long literary career, Miss Edgeworth never allowed herself to forget that the great end and aim of her writing was to make her readers substantially happier and better; to correct errors of opinion; and to remove those prejudices which endanger happiness. Sir Walter Scott described her writings as a "sort of essence of common sense", and the description is appropriate. Throughout her works, Miss Edgeworth sought to make wisdom and goodness attractive; she attempted to raise the humbler virtues to their proper importance by illustrating their effectiveness in everyday life, and she hoped to make the loftiest principles and intellectual attainments appealing and agreeable by uniting them with amiable manners and lively temperaments. No writer could propose a nobler or more worthy cause, and yet it is to the unrelaxed intensity of this pursuit that most of Miss Edgeworth's weaknesses

may be attributed. It too frequently gave her a limited conception of the novelist's art and a partial insight into human nature which left small space in her system for imagination, passion, or enthusiasm. A review of the comparative strengths and weaknesses of her artistry will help to explain that although she was a gifted writer, she was not a "great" writer and that her artistic failures, over a period of time, became her didactic failures.

In the stories of **The Parent's Assistant,** Miss Edgeworth sought to teach children the virtues of honesty, sobriety, charity, frugality, and industry. The world of **The Parent's Assistant** is a clearly intelligible world, appealing to a child's mind, for it leaves no questions unanswered. Rewards and punishments are administered with definitive precision, for a child is either "good" or "bad", and he is rewarded accordingly. The stories illustrate a technique which became a misconception of character composition in the works designed for adults. Belinda Portman (**Belinda**), Sophia Mansfield (**"The Prussian Vase"**), Madame de Rosier (**"The Good French Governess"**), Leonora (**Leonora**), the Duchess (**Leonora**), Madame De Fleury (**"Madame De Fleury"**), Ellen (**"The Lottery"**), and Caroline and Rosamond Percy (**Patronage**) are examples of overly-correct, overly-virtuous females who tire because of their excessive goodness. The works are likewise filled with an equal number of prudish, coldly-calculating, and obstinately-correct males: Clarence Hervey (**Belinda**), Henry Campbell (**"Forester"**), Charles Howard (**"The Good Aunt"**), Jervas (**"Lame Jervas"**), Brian O'Neill (**"The Limerick Gloves"**), Farmer Gray (**"Rosanna"**), William Darford (**"The Manufacturers"**), and Alfred, Erasmus, and Godfrey Percy (**Patronage**). These overly-righteous specimens of humanity are pitted against their respective counterparts who, like the antagonists of **The Parent's Assistant,** are "bad" and receive their just rewards. So eager is Miss Edgeworth to punish injustice that she quickly disposes of them by having them killed in duels, shipped off to other continents, or in some way preventing their future happiness. Thus the characters in the mature works are too often reduced to painfully simple terms, for Miss Edgeworth failed to realize that the adult world is more than a duplication of the child's reality. Her major shortcoming in the composition of character centers in these unrelieved contrasts of black and white; the characters too often become the elaboration of some trait (very much like a humor), selected and regarded almost as an idea. Just as the concepts of thrift and thriftlessness compete for attention in **"Waste Not, Want Not",** so also does the idea of self-reliance oppose the idea of dependence in **Patronage.** Likewise, Lady Anne Percival (**Belinda**) represents the qualities of the ideal domestic wife; Vincent (**Belinda**) is the personification of the vice of gambling; Leonora (**Leonora**) personifies the excellence of duty and long-suffering; the earl of Glenthorn (**Ennui**) illustrates the sin of ennui, while Charles Vivian (**Vivian**) is the incarnation of the evils of a weak will and infirm purpose.

Since the characters were conceived primarily as illustrations of didactic purpose, they infrequently experience growth or development in a prescribed course of events.

Initial emphasis is predominantly placed on a given thesis, and the characters' actions are often warped out of their natural course so that the lesson may be taught or the thesis preached. Such a method at once precludes the rendering of psychological complexity in a character, a necessary requisite to his reality as a dynamic character. This shortcoming is especially obvious in the major characters who have the crucial responsibility of developing the serious side of the action. Such examples include Belinda Portman, Clarence Hervey, and Vincent (**Belinda**); Archibald Mackenzie and Henry Campbell ("**Forester**"); Murad and Saladin ("**Murad the Unlucky**"); Farmer Frankland and Farmer Bettesworth ("**The Contrast**"); Basil Lowe ("**Tomorrow**"); Leonora, Mr. L—, and the Duchess (**Leonora**); the earl of Glenthorn (**Ennui**); Vivian (**Vivian**); Harrington (**Harrington**); Lord Oldborough and the Percy and Falconer families (**Patronage**). The weakness is especially devastating in such works as **Harrington** and **Vivian** where the entire significance of the events is attached to a single character.

We have seen that Miss Edgeworth often refuses to confront her characters openly with moral and ethical issues on which the ultimate value and meaning of the works depend. Lady Delacour is rewarded—not punished—for her life of dissipation by being cured of her malady. The earl of Glenthorn is restored to his estate largely as a result of Christy's mismanagement of it rather than as a result of his own exertions. Mr. L—returns to his wife, not because of her duty and long suffering, but because he discovers, through an interception of letters, that his mistress has been false. The Percy family defy patronage, yet they partake of it.

Throughout her writings, Miss Edgeworth taught that man's obedience to duty was his primary responsibility; yet theory again hampered her art, for there is little place in her fiction for erring humanity. Colambre (**The Absentee**) cannot marry Grace Nugent until the stigma of her birth is cleared away; and Harrington (**Harrington**) is much more willing to marry Berenice Montenero when he discovers that she is not Jewish. These characters lack tenderness because they are too closely tethered to their creator. In other instances, Miss Edgeworth damns a character because of a single flaw. Olivia's sin of adultery (**Leonora**) makes her an irreclaimable fallen woman, while Buckhurst Falconer's seduction (**Patronage**) brands him as a ruthless villain. Vincent's fondness for gambling (**Belinda**), Basil Lowe's tendency toward procrastination ("**Tomorrow**"), and Charles Vivian's infirmity of purpose (**Vivian**) likewise receive the author's severest censure. To the cause of illustrating a thesis and teaching a moral, Miss Edgeworth was obliged to sacrifice. And the sacrifice was great, for it adversely affected the majority of her major characters. Yet, Thady Quirk, the faithful old retainer in **Castle Rackrent,** stands as a special tribute and reminder of Miss Edgeworth's potential skill in developing character. Thady's unusual distinction is that he is incomparable, which is all the praise that his creator might seek.

There remains the voluminous gallery of "midway" characters who are free from the responsibility of furthering a thesis or moral purpose. These characters are drawn with a precision and manipulated with a skillful accuracy of detail of which any author might be proud. We have seen Miss Edgeworth's ingenuity in depicting such character types as waiting men and postilions; fashionable snobs and hypocrites; silly, affected, and vulgar women; women of power and authority; and especially, the large variety of Irish natives who compose a distinct classification of their own. A list of such memorable personages would include the following: Mrs. Luttridge and Harriot Freke (**Belinda**); Betty Williams, Miss Burrage, and Nat Gazabo ("**Angelina**"); the innkeeper, Ellinor, M'Leod, Lady Geraldine (**Ennui**); Lady Sarah Lidhurst and Lord Glistonbury (**Vivian**); Lady Clonbrony, Nicholas Garraghty, Sir Terence O'Fay, Lady Dareville, Mr. Soho, Mrs. Petito, Larry Brady, Widow O'Neil, and Mrs. Raffarty (**The Absentee**); Sir Ulick O'Shane, Cornelius O'Shane, Lady O'Shane, Miss O'Faley, Black Conal, and Father Jos (**Ormond**); and Lady Davenant (**Helen**).

Such a list is adequate evidence of Miss Edgeworth's talent in character portrayal. Throughout her works, she displays unusual skill in delineating the foibles and follies of mankind. Yet because her purpose so frequently distorted her vision of human nature, her most pleasing and memorable characters are comic. Like Dickens, she caricatures in order to instruct. At her best, she is a pleasant, amiable satirist who, like Jane Austen, displays ingenuous finesse in making sanity smile. For this reason, her Irish characters are indisputably her best: they are the most striking and interesting, the most individualized, and the most consistently developed of her characters. They are enlivened by the local color of their environment, and they are appealing because of their skillful blending of humor, wit, and pathos. Because Miss Edgeworth knew Ireland intimately, she depicted the customs, manners, and habits of the Irish people and the striking peculiarities of the Irish temperament with unflinching realism. Consequently, it is unlikely that a reader of Miss Edgeworth's novels will fail to feel a special fondness for many of her Irish characters: Thady Quirk (**Castle Rackrent**); Ellinor, M'Leod, Christy O'Donoghoe and the innkeeper (**Ennui**); Lady Clonbrony, Nicholas Garraghty, Sir Terence O'Fay, Lady Dareville, Larry Brady, Widow O'Neil, and Mrs. Raffarty (**The Absentee**); Sir Ulick O'Shane, Cornelius O'Shane, Miss O'Faley, Black Conal, and Father Jos (**Ormond**).

Miss Edgeworth achieves variety in her characters not only by varying the character types but also by varying her methods of character presentation. The characters are frequently introduced through direct summary descriptions which establish their roles in the action. They may be presented in the manner of the playwright, through cross-sections in points of view. The epistolary form dictates this method in **Leonora**. The method is used with special effectiveness in **The Absentee** and **Helen,** where the characters are unfolded with a graceful freedom and ease because the author views them with objective detachment. Miss Edgeworth also uses the method of the dramatist by presenting her characters, at times, almost wholly through action and dialogue; some of the most vivid, memorable scenes in her works consist of character clashes — the heated, defiant opposition of one personality and mind to another. The comic characters are frequently used as a means of attacking hypocrisy and affectation; in a single speech, a character may reveal himself completely according to his rank and philosophy of life. Only rarely is a character revealed through the method of the unfolding of his inner consciousness (Lady Delacour is the most notable example of this method).

It may be re-emphasized that when Miss Edgeworth's characters are not restricted by a moral purpose or thesis, they are spirited and lively creations who are ultimately successful in their assigned roles. At their best, they illustrate their creator's gift for refined observation, for steadiness of dissection, and for diversified delineation. The major characters deserved more freedom, for they were as capable as Miss Austen's characters of pointing their own moral.

Miss Edgeworth's lack of capacity for framing a plot is her greatest failure as a creative writer. Since a literal transcription of life is impossible, the laws of art apply to fiction, and fiction is better for observing them. Such laws include being well-designed and well-proportioned. *Castle Rackrent* alone is completely free from the numerous and often grave deficiencies in plot structure. Miss Edgeworth's failures with plot development are only another example of her misconception of her duty as a writer; her works too often degenerate into a statement of theory, which becomes the more ineffective because it is cast in an imaginative framework. Since distinct weaknesses of individual plots have been dissected, it will be helpful to review the general nature of these weaknesses.

Because of her missionary zeal in reforming her characters and her obsession to punish vice and reward virtue, Miss Edgeworth frequently warped the action of the plot away from its natural outcome and thus destroyed the illusion of reality (see *Belinda*, "The Will", "The Lottery", "The Manufacturers", "The Contrast", "Manoeuvring", and *Harrington*). Rather than choosing a series of events and arranging them for a specific purpose within an imaginative framework, Miss Edgeworth emphasized the explication of a thesis or moral to the exclusion of every other consideration. Consequently, the plots are weighted with extraneous details such as unnecessary digressions, moral commentaries, elementary explanations, and prosy preaching which thwart the flow of the narratives (see *Belinda*, "Forester", "Out of Debt, Out of Danger", "The Manufacturers", "The Contrast", "The Grateful Negro", *Leonora*, "The Dun", "Almeria", *Patronage,* and *Harrington*).

The general interest of the works often lags because the entire significance of the events may hinge on an impossible motif. Consequently, the plots often have little interest because the events which compose them have no parallel in reality (see *Belinda*, "The Prussian Vase", "The Good French Governess", "The Limerick Gloves", "The Lottery", "Murad the Unlucky", "The Contrast", "Tomorrow", *Ennui, Vivian*, "Emilie De Coulanges", *Pa-*

tronage, and *Harrington*). Because Miss Edgeworth endeavored to teach the virtues of duty and common sense through the medium of fiction, her themes are often trivial and childish. Most importantly, they are self-evident and are not in themselves sufficiently complex to hold a reader's interest for very long. They fail to supply motivation to the plot development, they do not leave the characters with anything of importance to do, and they are not adequate sources for mystery and suspense, necessary requisites to any successful plot organization. No reader will deny that a teacher should be capable and efficient (the purpose and consequent theme of **"The Good French Governess"**), or that it is better to be debt-free than in debt (the purpose of **"Out of Debt, Out of Danger"**), or that one should avoid consistent procrastination (the purpose of **"Tomorrow"**). Such simple, elementary themes constitute the whole of *Moral Tales, Popular Tales,* many of the *Tales of Fashionable Life* (*Ennui, Vivian,* **"The Dun"**, **"Manoeuvring"**, **"Madame De Fleury"**, and **"Emilie De Coulanges"**), *Patronage,* and *Harrington*.

Yet the works are filled with examples of very fine writing. We have seen excerpts of Miss Edgeworth's best and worst attainments; at their best, they are of highest excellence. But it is the author's unfortunate choice of themes, her selection of events without parallel in reality, and her deliberate molding of these events toward a given outcome which constitute her serious shortcomings. Since the plot is the novelist's format, a failure to manipulate it with some skill breaks and distorts the imaginary mirror which is held up to life; the initial illusion, however effective, is dispelled and the purpose is rendered worthless. It is useless now to question what might have constituted Miss Edgeworth's plots, had she not been so strongly influenced by her father's theories. It can only be said that the purposes, which gave them cause for existence, were devastating to them as works of art.

The stories in *The Parent's Assistant* are early evidence of Miss Edgeworth's strengths and weaknesses in the use of narrative techniques. They contain examples of her effective manipulation and blending of summary and scene, her ability for handling point of view, her narrative skill, and her development of dialogue. They also contain illustrations of weaknesses which were to loom large in the mature works: frequent unskillful handling of point of view (because of biassed author intrusions), of time (because of hasty reformations and punishments), and of narrative skill (because of awkward transitions). The *Early Lessons* illustrate the use of stilted, artificial dialogue, unsuited to the personalities of the children.

The supreme example of Miss Edgeworth's skill in handling point of view may be seen in *Castle Rackrent*. Never again did the author so skillfully harmonize a character with the style of his narration. The novel's effectiveness undoubtedly results from the presentation of the events from the point of view of a minor character; since the major interest of the story attaches itself to the personality of Thady Quirk and to his particular interpretation of the events, the fabric and texture of the work are richly blended and consistently unified. Presenting the events through his point of view heightens credibility and gives a feeling of informality and intimacy. It imposes unity and order on the plot by depicting the whole as viewed through his consciousness. It makes possible great compression since the events are limited to his observations. The nature of his personality makes possible rich comic and ironic effects, and his simple transparency offers a powerful appeal to the reader's sympathies. Briskness of movement and liveliness of interest combine to achieve both force and brevity; *Castle Rackrent* stands alone as the supreme example of Miss Edgeworth's creative ability. In **"Lame Jervas"** and in *Ennui* the author utilizes the point of view of a personal narrator who is a major character in the story. The versimilitude of the method in **"Lame Jervas"** is questionable, since the narrator unfolds his lengthy life history to his audience during a single sitting. In *Ennui,* the author's purpose interfered with her method, and it is primarily the narrator's malady of ennui which is emphasized rather than the events of his story or his personality.

Throughout her works Miss Edgeworth used predominantly the points of view of the omniscient author and the author-observer, and achieved variety through combinations and variations of the two. For example, the two are combined in *Leonora,* an epistolary novel in which the author primarily assumes an attitude of objective detachment, and the characters have the responsibility of the action. Likewise, in *The Absentee* and in *Helen,* Miss Edgeworth employs the dramatist's technique of introducing her characters from various points of view within the stories, which heightens credibility by placing the characters in the center of the action. The point of view of the omniscient author is vital in *Belinda* and *Helen* where Miss Edgeworth is especially concerned with the analysis of feeling and emotion. No other point of view could present the psychological complexities of Lady Delacour's mind or the emotional intensity of Helen or Cecilia with such effectiveness. It should be remembered that the author's greatest failure in executing the details of *Belinda* is that she failed to provide a unifying focus for the events.

The point has been made that the omniscient author may remain completely anonymous or that he may address the reader personally in the manner of Fielding or Thackeray. Miss Edgeworth's works are filled with such addresses which become burdensomely repetitive and not only clog the flow of the narratives but thwart the natural outcomes of the action. Such addresses constitute her greatest shortcoming in the handling of point of view, for they destroy the value of the imaginative illusion within the stories. Indeed, so determined is the author to influence the reader to the side of her protagonist that she frequently applauds her protagonist or openly condemns her antagonist (see the second half of *Belinda,* **"Forester"**, **"Angelina"**, **"The Good French Governess"**, **"The Will"**, **"The Manufacturers"**, **"The Dun"**, **"Manoeuvring"**, **"Almeria"**, and *Patronage*). The author injects moral commentaries which drive home the meaning of a given scene or which tell the reader that the antagonists should have pursued some other course of action. Such a method is a "false key" to the bulk of Miss Edgeworth's works; the omniscient author or author-observer condescends to the position of moral teacher and a work too often degenerates into a handbook of instruction.

Miss Edgeworth's greatest deficiencies in the handling of time result from her failure to proportion the events of her narratives in such a way that there is adequate time for the working out of the threads of the action in a logical time sequence. The plots of *Belinda, Vivian, Patronage,* and *Harrington* are weighted with excessive and extraneous details which necessitate the author's personal intervention in winding up the events. Miss Edgeworth is especially impatient with profligates and has a tendency to dispose of them in greatest haste. She often leads a reader to expect an outcome from a given complication of events, only to ignore it or dispose of it in a footnote (see especially *Belinda, Ennui, Patronage,* and *Harrington*). *Castle Rackrent, The Absentee, Ormond,* and *Helen* are the best examples of an adequate proportioning of time to the given complication of details (*The Absentee* and *Ormond* are not completely free from this fault because of the hasty alliances between the lovers).

Considerable emphasis has been placed on Miss Edgeworth's narrative skill — her ability to push a narrative forward through summary and scene and her talent for blending the two into a smooth, firm texture. While the works are filled with many admirable examples of this aspect of her art, they are greatly marred by her failure to be consistent, a failure which results from her purpose and philosophy as a writer. Miss Edgeworth frequently exercises judicious judgment in the choice and placement of scenes. In *Castle Rackrent* and *The Absentee,* which are treatments of serious themes, the juxtaposition of comic and serious scenes makes possible an invaluable comic and ironic effect and lends a needed tone of lightness to the plots. At times the author uses the scene for dramatic emphasis, for building a complication of details to their highest intensity (see *Belinda,* **"Angelina"**, **"The Modern Griselda"**, *Ennui, The Absentee, Ormond,* and *Helen*). One of her finest achievements is the use of compact, economical summary which is a result of her artist's view for details, her precise, colorful diction, her balanced sentence structure, and her blending of exposition, description, and narration (examples abound in *Castle Rackrent, Belinda, Ennui, The Absentee, Ormond,* and *Helen*). Such summaries may exist independently of the scenes or they may be scattered throughout as unifying elements which help to push the narrative forward. Scenes are sometimes used indiscreetly in the works (cf. the scenes of Harrington's oration and the picture auction in *Harrington* or the political dinner in *Helen*), for they contribute nothing toward advancing the cause of the theme or action. It may be re-emphasized that Miss Edgeworth fails at times to utilize the scene when a preceding complication of details requires it, a failure especially devastating in the episodes which relate to romantic love (see *Belinda, The Absentee, Patronage, Harrington,* and *Ormond*).

One of Miss Edgeworth's best achievements is her skillful use of dialogue which advances the action and reveals character in a direct and immediate manner. The reader feels that he has been personally acquainted with Thady Quirk (***Castle Rackrent***), Lady Delacour (***Belinda***), Lady Clonbrony, Mrs. Petito, and Mr. Soho (***The Absentee***), King Corny (***Ormond***), and Helen Stanley and Cecilia Davenant (***Helen***) because of the variations in tone and expression among their various occupations, social levels, and nationalities. The dialogue in the novels is nearly always natural and spontaneous; Miss Edgeworth uses it as a valuable tool for conveying personality conflicts and differentiations of character (see especially ***Belinda, The Absentee,*** and ***Helen***). The dialogue of the lower and middling classes is homey, precise, and colloquial. Miss Edgeworth especially succeeds in reproducing all of the striking peculiarities of the Irish dialect, including the quaint diction and idiom and the unusual turns of phrase and sentence structure which make her Irish characters memorable and lovable and blend them with the local color of their environment.

Throughout her life, Maria Edgeworth considered fiction as one of the useful arts. Only in ***Castle Rackrent*** did she yield to the pleasure of unfettered creation, and ***Castle Rackrent,*** her first and best novel, was only a holiday excursion in the course of her serious work. She was early drilled in her father's strong views on education and shared his concern for social and moral improvement. Experiment was the basic principle of Richard Lovell's system of education; obedience to duty rather than the assertion of rights formed the core of his philosophy. And his daughter, who conceived it her mission to be a teacher, propagated her father's views through her writings with conscientiousness and zeal.

After such a rigorous apprenticeship in the workshop of her paternal theorist and reformer, it is remarkable that Miss Edgeworth's works are as spirited and lively as they are; and it now seems almost a miracle that she wrote ***Castle Rackrent.*** Apparently, Richard Lovell Edgeworth never thought that a didactic purpose and creative spontaneity were incompatible; Maria, at any rate, did not seem to think so. Yet the reader today has a way of looking at a novel that is different from the past; he seeks first to be entertained, and he prefers to make up his own mind about the here and the hereafter. He consequently objects to a work in which all the actions, motives, and incidents, which are grouped into a plot, are so fashioned that the story as a whole tends toward the accomplishment of some definite result, such as the reformation of morals.

Miss Edgeworth's greatest failure as a writer is that she used fiction for the propagation of theories of any kind on any subject. The "novel of purpose" is a contradiction of artistic aims, for the novel, as an art form, seeks to present the tendencies which may be either thwarted or stimulated by circumstances in the development of life. The majority of Miss Edgeworth's works have not endured because they contain courses of prescribed action which make their message seem special instead of universal. The artist no longer deals with specified forms of cure for the ills of society; his message is found in every word that he writes.

Duane Edwards (essay date 1972)

SOURCE: "The Narrator of *Castle Rackrent,*" in *The South Atlantic Quarterly,* Vol. 71, No. 1, Winter, 1972, pp. 124-29.

[*In the following essay, Edwards examines the role of the first-person narrator of* Castle Rackrent.

Since ***Castle Rackrent*** was published in 1800, nearly all the critics have agreed that Thady Quirk, the narrator, is aptly described as "faithful Thady," an unintelligent or naïve servant with a "misplaced sense of family honour." Consistent with this is Ernest A. Baker's reference to Thady's "muddleheadedness and repugnance" and George Watson's assertion that "this absurdly loyal family retainer" has a simplicity which makes him a butt. Many other critics have reinforced this view.

Thus James Newcomer's "The Disingenuous Thady Quirk" comes as a surprise. In his article Mr. Newcomer contends that Thady is "artful rather than artless," that he is always the realist, that he has a calculating mind which "shows itself in relation to his niece Judy and Jason." In effect, Newcomer asserts that Thady exploits rather than aids the Rackrents; that Thady's major concern is not loyalty but profit. Defending this position, he seeks to demonstrate that Thady and his dishonest son Jason are allies pitted against the Rackrents. Newcomer contends that the nature of this alliance is subtly conveyed to the reader when Thady calls Jason "my son" or "my son Jason" at least thirty times; when Thady admits he has been privy to Sir Condy's *private* correspondence with Jason; and when Thady himself gives "out in the country that nobody need bid against *us*" (italics mine)—meaning Jason and Thady—for a valuable piece of the Rackrent estate put on sale. Arguing that Thady actively seeks to destroy Sir Condy, Newcomer points out that the old retainer not only gives the stranger in the bar information that destroys the Rackrents, but also fills the drinking horn with the whisky that finally kills Condy.

Newcomer's argument is impressive, but cannot be accepted without extensive qualifications, since ***Castle Rackrent*** contains evidence that Thady (i) is not always shrewd, (ii) exhibits great loyalty on occasion, and (iii) is not allied with Jason at the end of the book. For example, if Thady were shrewd, he would not have revealed his bigotry, his intolerance of Jews and Scots; he would not have revealed his cruelty in letting the "Jewish" die; he would not have admitted that Lady Murtaugh induced him stupidly to repeat the word "Allyballycarricko 'shaughlin" twelve times. If he were disloyal throughout the novel, he would not have wept when Castle Rackrent was signed over to Jason; he would not have tried to borrow money for the ruined Sir Condy, who is in no position to reward him; he would not have engaged in a six-day bedside vigil alongside his dying master. If he had been in league with his son, he would have told Jason about the £500 settlement Condy made on his wife; he would have shared his son's knowledge that Lady Rackrent will not live through the night; he would not have aroused the people against Jason so that Jason is forced to give Condy the Lodge.

What these points suggest is that **Castle Rackrent** contains evidence which conflicts with Newcomer's interpretation of Thady without confirming the traditional view. Thady is neither completely disingenuous nor completely calculating; he is neither completely loyal nor completely disloyal. Instead, he is a sentimental, generally unreflective old man whose love of money causes him to ally himself with Jason, who for some unexplained reason abandons him. Consequently, the father develops an antipathy for the son while remaining sentimentally attached to him long after such an attachment is no longer warranted. Signaling the inception of this antipathy, Thady says: "Now I cannot bear to hear Jason giving out after this manner against the family, and twenty people standing by in the street. Ever since he had lived at the lodge of his own, he looked down, howsomever, upon poor Thady." In the pages that follow this passage, Thady—out of habit, perhaps—calls Jason "my son" six consecutive times, but then calls him simply "Jason" twenty-four consecutive times and so signals the decline of their relationship.

What accounts for the alienation which develops between Jason and Thady? This question cannot be answered fully since the reader knows nothing about Jason other than that he is avaricious and cunning. Much more is known about Thady, however. For example, the assertion is made in the preceding paragraph that Thady is a sentimentalist who lacks self-awareness. This assertion might be modified to read that Thady's sentimentality and unawareness are inextricably bound up in one another. Thady does not know himself partly because he is sentimental. That this is true can be ascertained if we follow the advice which Miss Edgeworth gives us in the Preface, where we read:

> We cannot judge either of the feelings or the characters of men with perfect accuracy from their actions or their appearances in public; it is from their careless conversations, their half-finished sentences, that we may hope with the greatest probability of success to discover their real characters.

Following this procedure, the reader learns that Thady—as sentimental as he is—does not like many people. Referring early in the novel to Lady Murtaugh, Thady says: "But I made the best of a bad case, and laid it all at my lady's door, for I did not like *her* anyhow, nor any body else. . . ." In at least two other passages this point is reinforced. In the first, Thady records that nothing more than a pipe and tobacco is needed to keep his heart from breaking "for poor Sir Murtaugh." In the second, Thady, revealing his predisposition to dislike his master, says: "'Tis an ill wind that blows nobody no good; the same wind that took the Jew Lady Rackrent over to England brought over the new heir to Castle Rackrent." Since he did not like Sir Kit and Sir Murtaugh, Thady prejudicially decides he will not like Condy, his new master.

Strangely, it is because he is sentimental and has no *conscious* dislike of his masters that Thady eventually comes to like Sir Condy. When Newcomer states that Thady has

traditionally been viewed as having "an unthinking and prejudiced loyalty," he reveals how Thady can be attached to men he doesn't like—at least initially. Acting out the role of the "loyal retainer" without respecting his masters, Thady speaks in glowing general terms about the Rackrent family and thus gives himself the opportunity of coming to like Sir Condy. Once he discovers that Condy, like Sir Pat, is well-liked, his fondness for his last master deepens until it culminates in the bedside vigil which ends the book.

The bedside vigil contrasts so strikingly with Thady's reference to the ill wind which brought Sir Condy to Castle Rackrent that one feels compelled to look for other inconsistencies in the old retainer. Such inconsistencies abound. For example, Thady dislikes lawyers, but likes his lawyer son in the first half of the book. He dislikes his mistresses, but respectfully calls them "my lady." He dislikes individual Rackrents, but speaks proudly of the Rackrent family. These inconsistencies are understandable if one keeps in mind that Thady is prejudiced, loyal, and unthinking. This is simply another way of saying that impressionable Thady has those qualities which cause him both to like and to dislike what convention dictates, even when a like and a dislike conflict. Since convention dictates that a servant like a popular master and dislike a stingy one, Thady likes Pat and Condy and dislikes Kit and Murtaugh. Since convention dictates that a man like his blood relatives, Thady sides with his son and niece during most of the book.

Emphasis should be placed on the fact that it is not only convention that causes Thady to like Sir Pat, Sir Condy, Jason, and Judy. Thady's other characteristics contribute also, as the scene involving the stranger illustrates. In this scene, one is struck, first of all, by Thady's willingness to talk to a stranger in a crowd and, secondly, by his eagerness to sound the exploits of his master while drinking with the stranger in a bar. Aided by liquor and a sense of companionship, Thady becomes "a little merry" and so unwittingly delivers to an enemy of the Rackrents evidence which finally destroys Condy.

This scene, placed strategically in the book, bridges the gap between the naive Thady who consciously sought to aid Jason and the disillusioned Thady who withholds information from his son. (Six pages later old Thady voices his disapproval of Jason's "giving out . . . against the family.") In the last third of the novel it is not Thady, but other servants, who provide Jason with the information needed to destroy the Rackrents. Miss Edgeworth does not comment on this directly. Instead, she allows us to see the servants either revealing what they know or actually acquiring information to be used later. Naturally, Thady has access to some of this information as he suggests in saying: "All this the butler told me, who was going backwards and forwards *unnoticed* with the jug, and hot water, and sugar, and all he thought wanting. Since he is privy to what the other servants know, he is able to repeat the end of this conversation which Mrs. Jane has reported to him and to record that the butler wrote down information concerning Sir Condy and sent it

to Jason. Elsewhere we are shown how the servants acquire information to be used against Condy. For example,
it is recorded that "the servant who waited that day behind my master's chair was the first who knew" that Isabella and Condy were to be married and that Mrs. Jane
very conveniently decides to fix Isabella's hair while Isabella is reading a latter.

It must be obvious at this point that Thady is not the only
one who has access to the information which destroys the
Rackrents. It is other servants, rather than Thady, who aid
Jason in the latter part of the novel, although Newcomer's
assertion that Thady "has been privy to the correspondence of Sir Condy" is true. That Thady doesn't tell Jason all he knows about Sir Condy has already been shown.
The reason for this is very simple: Thady likes Condy. It
is not without significance that the pipe which sufficed to
comfort Thady for the death of Sir Murtaugh fails to
provide comfort for the mere absence of Sir Condy. When
Thady fills Sir Condy's drinking horn, he does so not "to
help him to his dying," as Newcomer contends, but because he wants to please his master. When Judy fails to
aid the stricken Sir Condy, Thady, genuinely in anguish,
cries, "'Judy! Judy! have ye no touch of feeling? won't
you stay to help us nurse him?'" Then follows the six-day
bedside vigil. Sentimental, money-loving Thady is also
faithful Thady, but he is not faithful entirely without discrimination. He has learned to reject his son. He has viewed
Sir Murtaugh and Sir Kit with suspicion, although the
latter has given him guineas. He sees, finally, that Judy is
corrupt. Blinded by emotion and a love of money, hindered by cliché-ridden thinking, he is slow to learn, but
he does learn, or at least has learning thrust upon him.

Marilyn Butler (essay date 1972)

SOURCE: "Epilogue: A Literary Perspective," in *Maria
Edgeworth: A Literary Biography,* Oxford at the Clarendon Press, 1972, pp. 481-88.

[*In the following essay, Butler discusses Edgeworth as an
innovator in the development of the novel of everyday life
for a middle-class readership.*]

Whereas Jane Austen was so much the better novelist Maria
Edgeworth may be the more important" P. H. Newby, *Maria
Edgeworth,* 1950]. The critics who agree that this must be
so have tended to focus their discussion on the merits and
demerits of *Castle Rackrent,* parts of *The Absentee,* and
even *Belinda.* If only Maria had asserted her independence
of her father, she could have written about Lady Delacour
without giving her a happy ending, or, better still, have
continued in the native Irish idiom of *Castle Rackrent.*
[These] traditional lamentations are, [dubious] and illogical. For if Maria had gone on in her earliest vein, or written
according to her natural disposition, she would have been
unlikely to have had any real significant influence on the
course of literary history.

Posterity's guess that Maria depended too much on other
people is fair enough, although the story is more complex

than nineteenth-century biographers supposed. It was her
family and not merely her father which was the central
influence in her work throughout her life. Paris in 1802
and London in 1813 made some impression on her, and
the effect of general social experience shows itself towards the end of her life in *Helen.* But from first to last
the family audience was at the forefront of her consciousness. The early works which have been praised because
they have been regarded as free, or in part free, of Edgeworth, do not escape the imprint of the family. Far from
it. The most direct influence on the entire first half of
Maria's career was her literary, lady-like, and humour-
loving aunt Mrs. Ruxton, who liked fiction that was polished and entertaining.

But it is the middle stage of her career, when Maria consciously tried to express her father's ideas, which matters
historically. By getting her to do the spade-work on *Professional Education,* Edgeworth obliged her to make up
her mind on general masculine subjects which she had
previously refused to have opinions on. The interest Dumont expressed in these ideas, coupled with the questions
in his letters about Ireland, were more factors which encouraged her to aim her tales at men of more intellectual
weight than the received idea of the novel-reader. Not
everyone has thought the change an improvement. The
desire to inform someone like Dumont rather than amuse
someone like Mrs. Ruxton accounts for the heavier texture of tales of this group, which at their worst (for example in parts of *Patronage*) can be positively leaden. All
the same, it was on account of these intellectually ambitious tales, not for her sketchier entertainments, that Maria
was praised by her contemporaries for raising the status
and enlarging the scope of the novel. The modern reader
who cares about her historical importance had therefore
better read *Ennui,* from the well-received and influential
Tales of Fashionable Life, rather than the earlier, less
responsible *Castle Rackrent,* which the *Edinburgh* and
Quarterly reviewers were happy to think she had left
behind her.

Just how important an innovation was Maria's? Describing someone as historically more important than Jane
Austen may have sounded impressive when the phrase
was coined, but since Jane Austen lacked disciples it is
really not saying much. A comparison with a novelist of
another period who did wield influence may be more illuminating. With Defoe the novel first began to emerge
as an independent genre, a fictional narrative in prose for
a middle-class readership which dealt recognizably with
daily life. Defoe's adventurers and adventuresses are expressive symbols of the tradesman and entrepreneur on
his way up in the world. Their religious protestations, and
their unconscious egotism, express the ethos of the Dis-
senter trading classes, and Defoe's matter-of-fact style
perfectly conveys the businessman's untheoretical, anti-
aesthetic temper. Defoe identified himself too completely
with the middle classes to make an effective judge of
them; instead he was their spokesman, and he reproduced
them with a historical accuracy that would seem astounding as a piece of analysis, if only we could feel that it was
fully understood by Defoe himself. Richardson and Field-

ing, each in their way greater artists, had more to say about the middle classes; but because they *were* artists, who selected and moulded, they did not give so literal a report of what the middle classes in life were really like. Nor perhaps would the achievements of the great novelists of the seventeen-forties have been possible but for Defoe's feat of mirroring the manners and morals of "the middle station" in the near-documentary form which proved appropriate for that subject and that readership.

Some writers on the novel treat its history as one of evolution; others believe that it has no history at all. If it has an intelligible development between the eighteenth and the nineteenth century, for sociological and historical as well as literary reasons this was interrupted towards the end of the eighteenth century. The great eighteenth-century novelists were all men, and their concerns were not just love and marriage but also money and land. Clarissa's relations with her family are as important as her relations with Lovelace, and morally Tom Jones's reconciliation with Squire Allworthy counts for more than his reunion with Sophia. Both these novels focus on the central character's moral nature in terms of his dealings with society; although society in the eighteenth-century novel is depicted impressionistically, through a number of typical individuals like James Harlowe, Mrs. Sinclair, Allworthy, and Lady Bellaston, rather than painstakingly established as it is in the nineteenth century.

An elaborate combination of factors, felt not only in the novel but also in poetry and drama, drastically reduced the scope of fiction in the last decades of the century. Brilliant though it is, Sterne's *Tristram Shandy* has many of the early signs of a period of decadence: its strong theoretical preoccupation, and its interest in states of feeling, combine to weaken the all-important interaction between the characters and their social environment. It is true that Sterne is often precise about time and place. But his attitude to external reality is equivocal: as a sentimentalist, he implicitly exalts states of feeling, and denies real importance to external factors (except, significantly, chance) in the lives of his characters. Lesser talents in this period were more wholehearted about the social world. But in the hands of Fanny Burney and Elizabeth Inchbald, who as women had the disadvantages of limited education and experience of life, the novel is intellectually far more trivial than under their great male predecessors. The cult of sensibility was even less concerned with the circumstances of social life in the real world; and the tale of terror, though interesting at its best in its handling of the psychology of individual characters, was remotest of all from daily reality. The philosophical novelists of the 1790s had the considerable virtue of taking up public themes again, but they did so in a theoretical spirit, and the sheer intellectual interest of their subject-matter does not outweigh the thinness of their rendering of real life. Without its original foundation in the world of affairs, the three-volume novel had become insubstantial.

Encouraged by her two domestic circles, Maria began her career as a novelist in typical feminine style, in the not despicable but minor tradition of Fanny Burney. She sketched a number of people amusingly, observed upper-class conversation very well, and conveyed impeccable sentiments. Apart from the aberration *Castle Rackrent,* she wrote in this way during the period to about 1808, as long as she was thinking of her audience as primarily made up of women. When after this she began to direct her fiction towards a more serious general public, she began for the first time to tap her own and her father's intellectual milieu. Her really important innovation was to report Ireland as accurately as she could, in the same literal spirit and with the same disregard for aesthetic considerations as Defoe had shown in reporting his world. The result was a fresh lease of life for the novel, and a new fashion for social documentation, although by now, in the early nineteenth century, the science of political economy had taught the educated novelist a great deal about society. Maria wrote about the lives of the peasants and about the relations between the classes in Ireland. She also took up general topics like a man's obligations to society and his need on his own moral account to find a role in the social structure. She "invented nothing", but reported the facts, which was in keeping with the intellectual training her father had got within the Lunar group.

By taking up worldly topics and dealing with them in a prosaic, documentary fashion, Maria came near to repeating Defoe's prescription for the novel. Like him, she was a faithful spokesman for the middle classes at a time when they were strongly in the ascendant. The historical importance of Defoe and Maria Edgeworth does not rest on their artistry; on the contrary, it has a great deal to do with their evident lack of interest in art as such. They achieved success and were widely imitated because they dealt in impersonal and hence in apparently objective terms with real life as their readers knew it. It was not only in contrast with romance writers that they struck their public as admirably serious. It was also in contrast with greater artists, who perhaps preferred the ideal to the actual, or the pattern to the fact.

The reason for Maria Edgeworth's literary importance lies in her development of the techniques of documentation, and in her intelligent understanding of the social scene. The social novel became the dominant form of the first half of the nineteenth century, both in England and Europe, not because of individual writers but because it studied middle-class life and reflected middle-class attitudes. Its explicit reference to real life and fascination with detail was the literary counterpart of the empiricism of the industrial innovators, and so it naturally appealed to the educated but not aesthetic prosperous classes, and to the rapidly expanding proletarian readership. Not only for Maria Edgeworth and Scott, but for Dickens, Thackeray, Mrs. Gaskell, and George Eliot, society itself often becomes the central character: the sub-title "a novel without a hero" could be applied far more widely than to *Vanity Fair,* and Hardy's description of one of his works as a novel "of character and environment" excellently defines the most distinctive quality of the best English fiction of the nineteenth century. For Maria Edgeworth's genre, so often nowadays called in a derogatory way "the provincial novel", does not exist as a separate entity, as the study of its first critics has shown. Her successors may have had a different (and often much more critical) attitude to society, but their concern was, like hers, a detailed and accurate re-creation of the organism as a whole, and not of individuals extrapolated from it. There is the same unbroken line of development as between Defoe and the great novelists of the 1740s.

How much is an innovator worth? In the late 1820s, the 1830s, and 1840s sociological insights would have made their way into the English novel from France, or, more probably, would have been felt spontaneously by the English themselves. How much did it matter to Dickens, Thackeray, and the rest that a flourishing social novel came into being in England two decades earlier than in France, in the form of the provincial or national novel?

There has never been a thorough-going analysis of Scott's influence on the English novelists of the next generation. We know, of course, that they read him. What is equally apparent is that they did not share his attitude to society; the images that came to Thackeray and Dickens when they depicted the contemporary world were Vanity Fair and the Marshalsea Prison, comparisons which conveyed their sense of a corrupt, self-perpetuating structure that dominated and destroyed individual lives. It would never have occurred to Scott or to Maria Edgeworth to use such images. They shared with Ferguson and Burke a sincere respect for society as the natural product of an evolutionary growth; the process to which they regularly subject the heroes of their most typical novels, of learning to know their own nation, is an enriching, not a disillusioning, experience. An individual grows from irresponsibility to a sense of himself as Civil Man, just as a community has advanced from barbarous disunity to its modern ordered complexity.

In order to express their conception of the relation of the individual to the social framework, it was appropriate for Maria Edgeworth and Scott to employ a colourless hero who underwent a series of adventures and met a succession of carefully differentiated people. The purpose of this technique was to bring "the background" into the foreground, which was where they wanted it. Dickens and Thackeray also have a habit of using uninteresting, often immature central figures, who pale in interest compared with the rich panorama for which the consciousness of the hero merely provides a medium. Granted that these later writers belonged to far bitterer times, and tended to see the individual as the passive victim of the social machine, they might usefully have invested their central figures with rather more human potential (if only to have it destroyed); alternatively, in so far as social satire was their object, they might have been expected to employ more critical or reflective observers. But they do not do either of these things.

The English novelists of the first half of the nineteenth century constitute a school with very distinct characteristics, for which they have not in recent years received enough credit. In breadth of scope, attention to detail, and sociological accuracy the mid-nineteenth-century figures

far exceed anything attempted in the eighteenth century. *Tom Jones* and *Vanity Fair* may resemble one another in some of their narrative devices, but they are a world apart in their grasp of the social framework and especially the implications of class. It may be, therefore, that criticizing Dickens or Thackeray or Scott for failing to pay more attention to their heroes and heroines is like so much neo-classical criticism of tragedy; it is the malpractice of deriving from observations of one type of novel the retro-active rules for all novels. The fact is that most English novels between Maria Edgeworth and Thomas Hardy are not primarily about the central characters but about environment, or, at the most, about characters seen specifically within an environment. French and Russian novelists do more to isolate the innerness of their heroes and heroines than any English novelist of the period, even George Eliot. On the other hand, the English novel, relatively weak at this kind of analysis, is scarcely excelled in its powers of recreating the external world, whether it is Dickens's London, George Eliot's Midlands, or Hardy's Wessex. And this is an achievement which would certainly have met with the approval of its pioneers, who had no higher ambition than as artists to realize, as moralists to preach acceptance of, the thing as it is.

Maria Edgeworth's is an ironic career. From first to last her personal preference was for a domestic setting and the company of a few intimates. The one novel which really expresses her tastes, **Helen,** succeeds when in the latter half it becomes intensely feminine. She was thus the last person in the world who would have wished on her own to pioneer the "loose baggy monsters" of nineteenth-century fiction. This was a tradition which in many ways would have been distasteful to her. In its liveliness, vulgarity, and intermittent radicalism it not only describes but expresses the ethos of a commercial world in which, in her lady-like heart of hearts, Maria did not feel at home. But then she did love her father, and he supplied many of the qualities that were needed; he was intellectually more detached than she from the gentry, and he was spontaneous, energetic, and empirical. Through her devotion to Edgeworth, and despite herself, Maria brought Lunar practicality and the Lunar social ethos into the novel, and in doing so helped to set it on a course which it held for over half a century.

Gerry H. Brookes (essay date 1977)

SOURCE: "The Didacticism of Edgeworth's *Castle Rackrent*," in *Studies in English Literature, 1500-1900,* Vol. XVII, No. 4, Autumn, 1977, 593-605.

[In the following essay, Brookes commends the harmony of intent, subject matter, and form of the essentially didactic Castle Rackrent.

Castle Rackrent is often preferred among Maria Edgeworth's works because it seems a creation free of her usual didacticism, a slice of Irish life presented without comment. "In *Castle Rackrent,*" says O. Elizabeth McWhorter Harden, "Miss Edgeworth drew directly from nature;

only in *Castle Rackrent* was she a poet. In her recent major biography, *Maria Edgeworth: A Literary Biography,* Marilyn Butler argues that the story "evolved from a fairly elaborate verbal imitation of a real man" and that the details of the story are arranged, in contrast with her usual practice, around "the character sketch of Thady rather than a didactic theme." Yet there is another view of *Castle Rackrent,* that the book is a powerful condemnation of Irish landlords. Thomas Flanagan, for example, calls the story, "as final and damning a judgment as English fiction has ever passed on the abuse of power and the failure of responsibility."

Flanagan seems closer to the truth here. The story is not a spontaneous imitation of natural events; its subject matter is plainly shaped and carefully evaluated. While the story lacks the explicit moralizing of many of Edgeworth's works, *Castle Rackrent* is implicitly and forcefully didactic, and its success lies in the unique harmony Edgeworth achieved among intention, subject matter, and form.

Castle Rackrent is an act of exemplifying. It is a kind of apologue or moral fable, designed to demonstrate by means of fictional examples that through "quickness, simplicity, cunning, carelessness, dissipation, disinterestedness, shrewdness, and blunder" the Rackrent family has succeeded in destroying its members, its estate, and its dependents, and in disrupting the social order on which its position has depended. *Castle Rackrent* is didactic in form in that it takes its shape from a thesis about or attitudes toward the Irish predicament, not from, say, a plot. Its form is coherent, and the story is plainly a made thing that does not simply reflect the shapelessness of life. For example, the episodic nature of the narrative, which has seemed to some a sign of lack of coherence, is essential to the form. The whole disaster, Edgeworth shows, is brought about by men with certain traits of character operating in a degenerate social order. And an episodic narrative is essential to exemplifying different men with analogous traits causing decline in the family's fortune through time.

The understanding and attitudes that Edgeworth shapes toward these fictional examples are by no means simple. The reader is led to think that the character of the Irish past and the remains of that past in the present render Irish landlords and their tenants particularly unfit to cope with the present, especially in the form of the self-aggrandizing cunning of a Jason Quirk, the middleman. On the other hand, Edgeworth shows that the Irish, self-destructive as they have been, are more colorful, eccentric, and interesting than those who take advantage of them and than the "British manufacturers" who may come after the Union to offer Ireland at least decent management. Furthermore, the vestiges of feudal virtues, resident in the social order, which the Rackrents travesty by their conduct, will also be lost entirely. While these virtues, especially loyalty, honor, bravery, a sense of family and place, and generosity, are present largely as values that the Rackrents have no longer or have only in a debased form, the reader may regret their passing. Edgeworth is less sentimental about them than Scott or Burke, more firmly on the side of industry and a pedestrian order, but she

does use them to help measure the fall of the Rackrents and to help locate the condition of the Irish she represents.

The reader's understanding of the situation of these characters is qualified by the attitudes created by Edgeworth's examples. The characters are consistently foolish, but the destruction they work on themselves, and on those around them, is more than even they deserve. The effect of *Castle Rackrent* is to provoke a peculiar combination of laughter at and pity for the predicament of these Irish landlords and their tenants and, at the same time, to make the reader see the causes of that predicament in the mental and moral confusion of the Irish, which is in turn caused by their own traits of character and encouraged by the degenerate social system they have inherited.

These ideas and attitudes are exemplified by an episodic history of the decline of the Rackrent family, beginning with the assumption of the name by Sir Patrick and ending with its demise at the death of Sir Condy. Each generation has its particular vices. Sir Patrick is a genial entertainer and powerful drinker. He dies in a fit after a drinking bout, belying the song he sang earlier in the evening about the relative virtue of going to bed drunk. He is imprudent in his liquor and in his management of the estate, and at the last his corpse is seized for his debts.

His successor, Sir Murtagh, is a hard, penurious man, who refuses to ransom his father's body, on the dubious ground that he would pay debts of honor, but since the law was involved, it was no longer a question of honor. Sir Murtagh further distinguishes himself by making the first of the family's succession of bad marriages. He weds a Puritanical Miss Skinflint, who turns out to be more penny-pinching than he. Though they disagree about Sir Murtagh's proclivity for good food, they cooperate to make life miserable for the tenantry, taking advantage of them in every available way. He hastens his own ruin, however, through numerous foolish law suits, and dies of a broken blood vessel, provoked by an argument with his wife about an abatement. She and the money for which he married her survive him, and the healthy jointure she takes with her debilitates the estate further.

Sir Kit, Sir Murtagh's younger brother, and heir to Castle Rackrent, displays different vices. He is a young rake and milks the tenants through an agent to support his prodigal ways. He, too, marries badly for money, and his abused Jewish wife survives him. His way with women leads directly to his death at the hands of a representative of the third woman who claimed he had made false promises to her.

Sir Condy, the last Rackrent, is a throwback to Sir Patrick, whom he honors with a new tombstone. He chooses to marry for money, rather than for love, by flipping a coin. This wife is wasteful and extravagant, and she brings him to the brink of ruin. Showing some cunning, he saves himself briefly by getting elected to Parliament, free of his debtors' claims. The progressive financial ruin of the estate falls full upon him, and he dies abandoned by all.

Each character has his own weaknesses, and they all share the inability to manage their lives and their property. Regardless of their attitude toward the estate and its tenants, generous in Sir Patrick's and Sir Condy's cases, careless in Sir Kit's, and predatory in Sir Murtagh's, each manages Castle Rackrent badly, creating a legacy of waste and debt. Their attempts to compensate for their stupidity and incompetence by marrying wealth are in each case frustrated and self-destructive. Especially in marriage the family makes itself susceptible to fortune or "luck," represented most graphically in Sir Condy's act of flipping a coin to decide whom he will marry.

The family also makes itself susceptible to Jason Quirk, who rises with a vengeance from the side of his father, the faithful family retainer, to near control of the estate. Jason is not a paragon of business virtues set against the wastefulness of his former masters, but he has a kind of managerial cunning which they lack and to which they render themselves victims. He is selfish and self-aggrandizing, a wholly unattractive figure. He is, however, important in Edgeworth's scheme to show both how the Rackrent family destroys itself and what agencies will hasten that destruction. She uses Jason as an agent of the family's ruin and also to control the reader's attitudes toward the Rackrent family. As suggested above, the family represents vestiges of a social order that is degenerate and obsolete. This older order, however, even in its degenerate state, is colorful, eccentric, occasionally generous and honorable. Its perpetuation, on the other hand, is dangerous, because it causes suffering among the tenantry, because it is wasteful and self-destructive, and because it creates and encourages aggressive, selfish men like Jason. The passing of the old order with its scant virtues and astonishing eccentricity would be less mourned if one had any assurance that a better order than Jason's would succeed it. Edgeworth holds out some hope in the end: "It is a problem of difficult solution to determine, whether an Union will hasten or retard the amelioration of this country. The few gentlemen of education, who now reside in this country, will resort to England: they are few but they are in nothing inferior to men of the same rank in Great Britain. The best that can happen will be the introduction of British manufacturers in their places." But it seems a meager hope.

The effect of *Castle Rackrent* is intellectual and ethical. The story presents examples which provoke understanding and judgment. The effect is also emotional. Edgeworth constructs her narrative in such a way that the reader is made to laugh at and also to pity the Irish characters from a felt position of superiority. This response is shaped by the facts of the narrative, the action and speech of the characters and the rewards and punishments accorded them. It is also evoked by the artful manipulation of the voice of Thady Quirk, the loyal servant who narrates the tale.

Thady has always been recognized as Edgeworth's finest achievement, and he is crucial to the effects of her apologue. First of all, he is used as an example of the ways in which the wastefulness of the Rackrent family affects those who depend on them. As he tells us, he has descended from "Honest Thady" through "Old Thady" to "Poor Thady" as a result of the family's decline. He is also useful to Edgeworth in bringing to bear loyalty and a sense of family as ideals that the Rackrents fail to abide by.

More importantly, Thady represents an affecting kind of mental and moral confusion that is at the heart of the predicament of the Irish characters in this story. The confusion manifests itself in several ways, in the ironic, implicit judgments that Edgeworth makes of characters through Thady, in the kinds of errors in judgment and sense that Thady makes that reflect solely on him, and in his uncomprehending narration of the stupidity of others. In *Essay on Irish Bulls,* prepared with her father's help, Edgeworth defines a bull as *"a laughable confusion of ideas."* This description captures the state of the Irish mind in *Castle Rackrent,* except that our response to it is not simply laughter, but laughter mixed with pity. Thady himself commits a number of bulls. His remark that the Rackrents' old family name was "O'Shaughlin, related to the kings of Ireland—but that was before my time" is an example. Here Thady's naïve confusion about the past is innocent and laughable enough, but his kind of confusion is continuous with more serious sorts that are both laughable and pitiable.

Sir Tallyhoo Rackrent's situation, for example, is more serious. He "had a fine estate of his own, only never a gate upon it, it being his maxim that a car was the best gate. Poor gentleman! he lost a fine hunter and his life, at last, by it, all in one day's hunt." The confusion manifests itself here in a form like wit. The shift in sense of the verb "lost" between its first object, "hunter," and the second, "life," and, more importantly, the violation of the reader's expectations by the second object, is a kind of zeugma. The casual tidiness with which his carelessness is avenged is likewise surprising, unsettling, and amusing, though one glimpses uneasily through the laughter a world in which hunters and lives are lost with nearly equal regret, "all in one day's hunt." The world the characters inhabit is like this, a vengeful world. The consequences of carelessness, of improvidence, are severe. And these consequences, the reader sees, attend mental and moral confusion of the sort that Edgeworth represents in Thady's speech and in what he reports. Being led to judgment, through laughter and pity, makes the reader aware of an intelligence arranging the fictions before him, makes him aware of what Wayne Booth has called the "implied author," that is, the author implicit in the style and form of the story. And Thady is one of the main devices by which judgments of characters and events are caused. The wit involved in Thady's witless narration makes the reader feel superior to its perpetrator, makes him share with the author the sense of superiority of a mind ordered sufficiently to see the mistake that is being made. The reader is made to think that, in such circumstances, he would know better.

In *Irish Bulls* the Edgeworths show that bulls are closely related to rhetorical figures and that the susceptibility of the Irish to bulls is related directly to their habitual use of colorful language. In *Castle Rackrent* the characters are victimized by their figurative language to some extent, and at the same time they are made more interesting and attractive by it. The bulls in *Castle Rackrent* place the reader in the position of the critic of rhetoric who knows the figures and where they have gone awry. When Thady remarks that Jason sticks to Sir Condy, as Thady "could not have done at the time, if you'd have given both the Indies and Cork to boot," he creates an example of bathos. Yet the humor of his remark is assimilated, as is true throughout, to the particular thesis of *Castle Rackrent*. Thady's bathetic bull is rooted in his parochialism, which is one cause of the Irish predicament.

In a footnote Edgeworth informs us of another "mode of rhetoric common in Ireland." Thady has remarked of Sir Murtagh, "Out of forty-nine suits which he had, he never lost one but seventeen." Edgeworth notes that in such cases, "an astonishing assertion is made in the beginning of a sentence, which ceases to be in the least surprising, when you hear the qualifying explanation that follows." The remarkable achievement of Sir Murtagh turns out, as usual, not to be remarkable at all. Some of the humor of *Castle Rackrent* depends on figurative language, of the sort that concerns the Edgeworths in *Irish Bulls,* but much of it is syntactical humor, of the sort just quoted. Words and phrases are arranged in order to create expectations of one sort that are then undercut by implications of a different sort. Some examples of this kind of wit are periodic sentences. Thady says of Sir Condy, "Born to little or no fortune of his own, he was bred to the bar; at which, having many friends to push him, and no mean natural abilities of his own, he doubtless would, in process of time, if he could have borne the drudgery of that study, have been rapidly made king's counsel, at the least; but things were disposed of otherwise, and he never went the circuit but twice, and then made no figure for want of a fee, and being unable to speak in public." The accumulating qualifications here are devastating. Pretentious expectations for Sir Condy are set up and then destroyed by the pathetic and laughable actualities of his abilities and situation.

The wit of figures and syntax is consistently heightened by the larger context of the reader's increasingly more comprehensive vision of the mental and moral confusion of the Irish. Edgeworth presents to the reader a series of examples of men making both errors in judgment, which reveal themselves as verbal foolishness, and errors in action, based on mistaken judgment. In *Irish Bulls* Edgeworth's phrase for the latter is "practical bulls." The practical bulls committed by the Rackrents are the most likely acts of confusion to create pity as well as laughter in the reader, because they have effects on persons and because they bring severe punishment on their perpetrators. Sir Kit's fate is probably the worst, and Edgeworth catches his misery in a phrase. In good spirits, he lets an opponent off in a duel, knocking a tooth-pick out of his fingers. But, "unluckily," he is hit himself "in a vital part, and was brought home, in a little better than an hour after the affair, speechless on a hand-barrow, to my lady." He

has done what his family constantly does, exposed himself to luck. Sir Condy gambles in choosing a wife and later gambles on his wife's death. Sir Murtagh goes to law, and, as a footnote tells us, that is a kind of lottery. Relying on luck in the providential world of an Edgeworth tale is tempting the rational god of industry in the worst possible way. Salvation in her stories comes through all of the qualities missing in the Irish of *Castle Rackrent,* through honesty, patience, industry, practical knowledge, humility. No one is rewarded much in *Castle Rackrent* because no one has the requisite virtues, but we are meant to feel their absence. We are meant to think Ireland needed those "few gentlemen of education who now reside in this country," needed, Edgeworth must have thought, practical people like herself and her father.

Castle Rackrent is, then, an act of exemplifying, and its parts are shaped to demonstrate the truth of Edgeworth's view of the situation of the Irish and to create an ethical and emotional attitude toward them and their predicament. The story does not simply represent but evaluates through a variety of rhetorical means.

This description of the form of the work has several uses. First of all, describing the story as an apologue, as something different from most of the works we call novels, can preserve us from seeing certain qualities of the book, such as inconsistencies in the representation of Thady and the episodic nature of the narrative, as weaknesses in it. It can also prevent us from looking for qualities of plot normally found in novels. In *Maria Edgeworth the Novelist, 1767-1849: A Bicentennial Study,* James Newcomer, in order to explain Thady's incredible combination of naïveté at times and his remarkable shrewdness at others, argues that, in fact, Thady is shrewd and deceitful throughout, that he plots in collusion with his son to overthrow the Rackrent family. This view plainly misuses evidence, but it is the sort of explanation encouraged by a misperception of the form of the tale and by a misunderstanding of the principles operating within it. If one looks for qualities ordinarily found in novels, consistent development of character, suspense about the fates of characters, then one will be led to extravagant theses like Newcomer's, or one will conclude that this is a badly managed novel.

This description of *Castle Rackrent* as an apologue clarifies both why the work is not objective and historical and why it is taken to be so. The story may represent a view of a particular historical situation that is accurate and can be tested empirically, but our appreciation of its having done so is external to our apprehension of the form of the story. Edgeworth presents fictional examples and not history. Her intention is to shape our attitudes and beliefs toward what we perceive as fictional men in fictional situations and to urge us to make the same judgment of actual men in actual situations. This distinction is crucial for understanding the form of the book and the working of that form. As mentioned above, most of those who argue that the book is a direct portrait of Irish life acknowledge that the picture that comes full blown through the neutral medium of the artist is, somehow, not a flattering one. Ernest A. Baker, for example, in *The History of the Novel,* says that Edgeworth "gave imagination full fling, and did not let any idea of a purpose interfere, although the favorite moral theme is implicit, the nemesis of self-indulgence, extravagance, and folly, as it must needs be in such a register of tragedy." But the work is purposeful, and our understanding and pleasure are dependent on our perception of that didactic, exemplificative purpose. We are stirred by what we perceive as examples of mental and moral confusion. The "moral theme" is not simply "implicit"; it is the cause of our pleasure in reading.

Castle Rackrent is not history, not a psychological case study, not a work which by its form demands empirical verification. If we say, even hypothetically, that it is an apologue, then we can deduce that the characters, including the narrator, will serve the attitudes being shaped. They will seem life-like or take on the kinds of expectations we have for characters in most novels only up to the point at which those features interfere with exemplification of the central attitudes. We can deduce, for example, that what Thady says will be determined by a desire to represent character but that representation of his character will be subordinated to a need to exemplify certain ideas and to shape attitudes. In reading history or a psychological case history, we would perceive this shaping as a flaw. In the case of *Castle Rackrent* the perception that the author is creating and shaping fictional examples is inescapable, and it allows the form to work.

Writing history would make demands on Edgeworth that she does not have to fulfill. She has greater ease in inventing and arranging examples than a historian has. She can create a narrator with some qualities of regional speech and ignorance, but she can manipulate his voice to serve her purpose. In fact, the manipulation of his voice is one of the clues, necessary to her form, that we are reading fiction and not history. The attitudes embedded by the story may be treated subsequently against the actual, and if they hold up, then we will say that she has provided us with a proper historical view. The power of this form is that it can provide us with complex attitudes that we seem to have induced from particular examples, so that when we turn to the actual, we know what sorts of evidence will confirm our now deductive model.

Edgeworth's ability to make us induce from fictional examples ideas that seem plausible when tested against the actual is one cause of the view that she has written history. Another cause is her ability to create life-likeness within the confines of her form. She cannot allow Thady to become as absorbing or as boring as an actual Irishman might be, but she can and does make him vivid and engaging, while he serves the exemplificative and evaluative functions essential to the form. There are two other apparent reasons for thinking she might be representing the actual. The first is the constant reference of her notes and glossary to the actual. They insist that the fictions are not implausible since real events like them have occurred. They tend to generalize her examples, and they encourage testing the hypothetical view of the Irish situation

created by the story against historical occurrences. The second reason is Edgeworth's own insistence that the story came to her spontaneously, that she heard the voice of an old steward speaking to her and simply recorded it. This external evidence is usually linked with two other observations to create an explanation of the genesis of the story that makes it seem simply a slice of life. *Castle Rackrent* was written without the aid or interference, depending on your point of view, of her father, and it lacks the explicit moralizing of her other works, virtually all of which she wrote under his guidance. Free of her father's restraining hand, this romantic argument goes, she could see life clearly and record it without comment. To the contrary she seems to have been free to create a more successful didactic form which embedded judgments and attitudes in examples and did not grind to a halt, as many of her other stories do, to make explicit what is (or ought to be) implicit in her fictions.

Behind the traditional uneasiness about the relation of *Castle Rackrent* to Edgeworth's other works may also be a notion that it is not didactic because it does not display virtue. The story shows, as Dr. Johnson thought narratives should, "that vice is the natural consequence of narrow thoughts, that it begins in mistake, and ends in ignominy," but it does not, as the Doctor would have it, exemplify virtue, except by its absence. To some extent the demands of what Dr. Johnson calls "historical veracity" militated against the display of virtue. Still, the lack of neoclassical moral balance may be a source of continued uneasiness about the work. In 1803 Richard Lovell Edgeworth remarked somewhat defensively, "What we have already published has always tended to improve the education of our country: even *Castle Rackrent* has that object remotely in mind." The emphasis on vice and not on virtue in the tale is enough to explain his hesitation about the story. He does recognize its didactic nature, and there seems to be no evidence to support Marilyn Butler's claim that *Castle Rackrent* is fundamentally different from Maria Edgeworth's other books, that the story is not coherent because Thady's character takes precedence over the author's progressive point of view, and that the Edgeworths rejected the tale, at least for a time, because it did not say what Maria Edgeworth wished. Instead the Edgeworths seem to have recognized its nature and power quite clearly and to have been visibly relieved, as they say in *Irish Bulls,* that the "generosity" of the Irish had let *Castle Rackrent* among them be "generally taken merely as good-humoured raillery, not as insulting satire." The risk that the Irish might take the book more seriously is, of course, implicit in the intention it embodies.

Castle Rackrent stands out from Edgeworth's other stories, not, as some have claimed, by being non-didactic, but by the particular harmony in it of intention, subject matter, and form. The importance of her subject matter should not be overlooked. As Joanne Altieri has shown, Edgeworth's subjects here permit her greater verbal play and more complex stylistic effects than do the more rational subjects of her other stories. Of course, our pleasure in the vernacular is complicated further by the evaluations of it and its speakers that are implicit in every level of the form, especially in syntax and situation.

Many of her stories go awry because they fail to embody a coherent intention and are perceived as mixed or flawed forms. Her apologues are marred by their tendency to break out into plotted novels, into imitations of actions, and her plotted novels are marred by her persistent desire to reduce the complexity of human interactions to aphoristic examples. *The Absentee,* to take an obvious case, is flawed formally because Edgeworth's desire to exemplify the need for absentee Irish landlords to return to their land interferes with her efforts to create hopes and fears for the fate of that paragon, Lord Colambre. There is little doubt that he will succeed in everything he desires, and the plot focuses instead on how he will achieve it. The signals, however, are so clear that happiness resides on the land in Ireland, that one knows all he has to do is to lure his family home. Then, of course, some fortuitous circumstance will reveal Grace Nugent's legitimacy, and all will be well. Edgeworth's faith in the power of virtuous conduct to regulate human affairs and to create happiness is so strong that she has difficulty in making her reader feel satisfaction in seeing a foregone conclusion work itself out. Her beliefs work against subtle plots and encourage a tendency to exemplify. When, for example, Colambre asks a friend whether he should join the army, he cannot ask about his own situation: "Would you advise me—I won't speak of myself, because we judge better by general views than by particular cases—would you advise a young man at present to go into the army?" Her consistent interest is in general views.

Vice, however, seems not to be bound by such rigid rules, and it constantly enlivens her stories, even the moral fables intended to instruct the young. There her evil characters, since they are motivated by probability rather than moral necessity, create suspense that distracts, happily, from the ideas she is trying to exemplify. Hazlitt remarked that except for *Castle Rackrent* her stories "are a kind of pedantic, pragmatical common sense, tinctured with the pertness and pretensions of the paradoxes to which they are so self-complacently opposed." In *Castle Rackrent* she manages harmony between her evaluation of the Irish situation and the fictions she creates to exemplify it. Her examples correspond to the complexity of her view and give us complex pleasure.

Anthony Cronin (essay date 1982)

SOURCE: "Maria Edgeworth: The Unlikely Precursor," in *Heritage Now: Irish Literature in the English Language,* St. Martin's Press, 1982, pp. 17-29.

[*In the following essay, Cronin singles out the specifically Irish characteristics of Edgeworth's* Castle Rackrent, *including a "devouring interest in speech" and the "absence of plot."*]

If Irish literature in English begins anywhere, it begins with Maria Edgeworth's *Castle Rackrent;* and the key

dates in Maria's life as far as the composition of the novel is concerned have a melancholy aptness. Born in England, she had been given a brief, tantalising glimpse of Ireland as a child of six; and then whisked back to become, at the age of eight, a boarder at Mrs. Lataffier's academy for the daughters of gentlefolk at Derby; and—at thirteen— a pupil at Mrs. Davis's seminary in Upper Wimpole Street. When she was fifteen her admired father had decided to settle in the land which his ancestors had called home for upwards of two hundred years; and the family had come back to Edgeworthstown, to an inclement Irish summer when snow fell in June and was cupped for a while in the roses. But the year was 1782; and in April Henry Grattan, still pale and weak from a recent illness, had told the House of Commons in College Green: "Having given a Parliament to the people, the Volunteers will, I doubt not, leave the people to Parliament, and thus close specifically and majestically a great work. . . . Ireland is now a Nation."

Since *Castle Rackrent* has twice in recent years been described by eminent critics as a "regional novel", it is as well to emphasise straightaway that Maria believed in that nationhood: believed in it in 1782; and believed in it seventeen years or so later when she wrote her little masterpiece; for the title page of that work echoes something of the pride with which the claim to nationhood had been made and, up to then, sustained:

CASTLE RACKRENT
AN
HIBERNIAN TALE
Taken From Facts,
And From
The Manners of the Irish Squires,
Before The Year 1782

The phrase, "An Hibernian Tale" may, it is true, give us a little pause. It is hard to savour now because the word Hibernian went from bad to worse; or perhaps from good to worse; and so probably did the word tale, at least in association with Hibernian. She is addressing an English audience, if only by virtue of the fact that her book was first published in London (it was published in Dublin in the same year). But if it is difficult for us now to recapture the exact nuance of what she meant by describing her short novel on its title page as "An Hibernian Tale", it is even more difficult for us to hear again the faint but unmistakeable note of sennet and triumph contained in the phrase, "before 1782".

For, if not after Parnell, then certainly after Arthur Griffith, Ireland began to scorn the nationhood presided over by the Protestant assemblage in College Green. In doing this, it would doubt the evidence of its own senses, for everywhere in Ireland the remains of the extraordinary upsurge of energy and confidence which Grattan's Parliament inspired are visible: in the Georgian streets and squares of the capital; in the great buildings of its centre; in the canals enclosing them and stretching Westward as engineering miracles across the bogs; in many of the big houses with their attendant demesnes; in the great mills and still-standing granaries of the South-East. It was a time of almost unexampled and unbelievable prosperity, affecting many more sections of the population than those at the very top. Tradesmen, artisans and day-labourers benefited in their thousands; and if it did not all begin like a clockwork mechanism released by the Declaration of 1782, the commercial independence gradually extended and finally secured by the Irish Parliament was at the root of it. Even the poorest in their wretched cabins on the worst-managed estates could sniff something, however distant, of the air of prosperity; and around Edgeworthstown, in spite of the snow on the roses, it was a balmy and health-giving breeze.

For Richard Lovell Edgeworth threw himself immediately into the management and improvement of his estate with the energy and optimism which often amused or dismayed the more languid among his contemporaries. He built good slated stone houses. He sacked bailiffs and dispossessed middlemen. He reclaimed bog and mountainside. He chose tenants for their willingness to work and share in the general scheme of improvement rather than for their initial ability—or fancied ability—to pay. He even built a little railway to carry limestone from one place and marl from another. The husband of four wives and father of many children in amorous fact, he was paternalist landlordism personified; though as a saving grace he had serious doubts about the quality of the governing classes in general. The upper and middle classes in Ireland, he said, were poor stuff; the peasants, for all their ignorance, superstition and cruelty had great qualities. Government could bring out the best in them and make Ireland a great country. And at the centre of all this whirl of optimism and activity was his eldest daughter, for it was no part of Richard Lovell Edgeworth's philosophy to exclude women from the government of anything. "Not only his wife but his children knew all his affairs", Maria was to remember. "Whatever business he had to do was done in the midst of the family, usually in the common sitting-room, so that we were intimately acquainted not only with the general principles of conduct, but with the most minute details of their everyday application. I further enjoyed some peculiar advantages; he wished to give me habits of business and allowed me during many years to assist him in copying his letters of business and receiving his rents."

1782, the year of the return to Edgeworthstown, was a memorable year in Maria's life. But more than that, it was a memorable year in the history of her country. In adding the phrase "Before the Year 1782" to her title page, she was hoping to make one thing about her novel abundantly clear. She was writing about "the bad old days".

But she was also, as a matter of probable if not absolutely established fact, writing in 1798: the year of the French landing, the Wexford rebellion and the first serious mootings of a Union with England. Her book was published in 1800 and by that time the failure of nerve and the inner corruption of the aristocracy of which her father had such a low opinion were apparent to all. She was constrained

to add two notes; one by way of preface, the other in the form of an afterword. The prefatory reference to the Union is the more ambiguous of the two:

> The Editor hopes his readers will observe, that these are "tales of other times"; that the manners depicted in the following pages are not those of the present age: the race of the Rackrents has long since been extinct in Ireland, and the drunken Sir Patrick, the litigious Sir Murtagh, the fighting Sir Kit, and the slovenly Sir Condy, are characters which could no more be met with at present in Ireland, than Squire Western or Parson Trulliber in England. There is a time when individuals can bear to be rallied for their past follies and absurdities, after they have acquired new habits and a new consciousness. Nations as well as individuals gradually lose attachment to their identity, and the present generation is amused rather than offended by the ridicule that is thrown upon their ancestors.

> Probably we shall soon have it in our power, in a hundred instances, to verify the truth of these observations.

> When Ireland loses her identity by an union with Great Britain, she will look back with a smile of good-humoured complacency on the Sir Kits and Sir Condys of her former existence.

If this is doubtful, the afterword is bleak:

> It is a problem of difficult solution to determine, whether an Union will hasten or retard the amelioration of this country. The few gentlemen of education who now reside in this country will resort to England: they are few, but they are in nothing inferior to the men of the same rank in Great Britain. The best thing that can happen will be the introduction of British manufacturers in their places.

She was clear-headed enough to see the decline of Irish industry and the abandonment of a wretched country by a wretched aristocracy. She was short-sighted enough to believe that the Union would work; and that the collapse of the "Protestant nation" would be the end of the Irish nation. But perhaps the main thing to note is her conviction that there was, or had been, a separate identity; and if she is Protestant and aristocratic enough to confuse that identity with the character of her own class, she believes that the exploration of it is proper employment for a writer.

In this she is at one with most of her successors, even the less nationally-minded, such as Joyce with his "uncreated conscience", or Kavanagh with the specifically Irish types of his satires. The exploration of the Irish identity is at least a subtheme with most of them, its glorification a major theme with Yeats. Often it gets in the way of criticism, as with J. M. Synge, so that their real theme is obscured. Often it gets in their own way, conflicting with the claims of an art which, they feel, should be more clearly universal, or achieve universality by some other route. Frequently, in the case of lesser writers, it is the exploitation rather than the exploration of identity which provides what can only be called a stock-in-trade. The differences (usually from the English character or identity) are what are important: the mode is, however "realist" it may claim to be, the picturesque, with all that the word implies in the way of charm, oddity, weakness.

In Maria's case the exploration, in *Castle Rackrent* anyway, superseded the claims of the sort of educative guidance and provision of moral examples which she believed to be the main business of an author. The strange thing in her case, though, is not that it merely superseded these or anything else, but that it seems to have brought something along with it as a sort of bonus, or revealed something in her the presence of which could scarcely have been suspected, even by the most enthusiastic among her friends and well-wishers. For all the things that might have been said about or wished upon Byron's "nice little, unassuming 'Jeanie Deans-looking body'. . . . if not handsome certainly not ill-looking", about whom "one would never have guessed that she could write her name", though her father "talked, not, as if he could write nothing else, but as if nothing else was worth writing", the last the most effervescent admirer would have claimed for her was that she was an artist of the greatest subtlety.

She is said to have believed that Macbeth's speech "Tomorrow and to-morrow and to-morrow . . . " was a warning on the evils of procrastination. Her only book before *Castle Rackrent* was *The Parent's Assistant,* written to exemplify the principles contained in her father's treatise, *Practical Education.* She was all her life under the influence of that worthy, inventive, energetic, supremely high-minded man—Byron's "supreme bore"—and his corrective hand lies heavy on all her other work. She followed *Castle Rackrent* with *Early Lessons* and *Moral Tales.* The eighteenth-century illusion that all could be improved—that all *would* be improved—by dint of example and precept, precept and example, an illusion soon to vanish and give way to Dickens' rather more plausible (and for artists marginally more fitting) belief that you could haunt, or terrify or move people into bringing change about has dated her almost beyond redemption. Most of her other work is, whatever thesis writers or variously commissioned literary gents may say, ruined in varying degree and extent by pedagogic and moral purpose. Only *Castle Rackrent* escapes into the realm of non-assertion. It is as delicate, as deliberate and as duplicious as is Henry James.

Now to attribute all this to the fact that in *Castle Rackrent* she was exploring aspects of what she saw as the Irish identity—more especially the quarrelsome, intemperate and extravagant aspects of that identity—may be to oversimplify. But the fact remains that here, and only here, the preacher in Maria, to whom the mere writer, let alone the great artist latent in her was too often made subservient, is kept firmly in its place. Here are none of the sermons, the digressions, the warnings to young ladies, the reproofs to society in general, which mar her other work. Creative excitement, that least definable but most recognisable of any writer's possible qualities, possesses her from the beginning. Though what she has to tell about varies from the merely melancholy to the grotesque to the tragic; though incompetence, waste, callousness and lost possibilities are her themes, the miracle of an art which is its own annealment is accomplished on

every page. Something within this material is giving its manipulator something akin to joy. The wonder with which we may be sure the fifteen-year-old had opened her eyes to Ireland's contradictions and her ears to its speech is not lost in the woman of thirty-three. Indeed it is the discovery of a technique which will allow her to use that speech, with its evasions and ambiguities bewilderingly intertwined with stabs of perception and ruthless honesty, which, more than any other single factor, makes her first and freshest book her greatest.

The story is told—it would probably be more accurate to say that the events are chronicled—by an old family retainer, Thady Quirk. By the standards of an improving eighteenth-century landlord, or a progressive eighteenth-century reformer of any description, he is an obtuse old idiot. In his eyes, no Rackrent, however proud, spendthrift, callous or downright cruel (and most of them are these things in good measure) can do any wrong. His virtue is loyalty: to the head of the house, the chief, if you like of the clan. In the century and upwards that had elapsed since the not quite complete dispossession of the native Irish aristocracy, the Cromwellian and Williamite intruders had come to see themselves as, more or less, the inheritors of ancient Irish ways and customs. Maria's successors, Charles Lever and Lady Morgan, nearly always conferred a Gaelic lineage on their aristocratic principal figures; but this was post-Walter Scott; and, for an author with an eye on the public, a way of cashing in on the romanticism about the clan system that prevailed after *Waverly* and *Rob Roy.* That Maria was aware of the difference that existed in the two, admittedly contiguous and somewhat intertwined aristocracies, the one barely surviving amid the other, is proved by the attitude of his fellow-landowners to the eccentric Count O'Halloran, with his Continental title, his gold-laced coat and his Irish wolfhounds in *The Absentee.* She must also have been aware that the commonly advanced claim to Gaelic lineage was in part an alibi: a way of saying "I can't help it" about your faults of character; and in part snobbism: an admission that the old barbarians were in truth more aristocratic in lineage than their dispossessors. It was also a simple matter of fact that there had been a good deal of inter-marriage; and a rather more complicated matter of fact, related to the conditions and psychology of subservience, that there had been a transference of the old sort of loyalty to the new sort of chieftain, at least by poets, house servants and the like. Maria anticipates Scott and anticipates much in popular romanticism by giving the Rackrents a Gaelic lineage and their servant an essentially Gaelic loyalty. Their real name is O'Shaughlin, changed for inheritance purposes. His attitude is that of a retainer rather than a servant. Thus she solves an early problem of moral stance. The Rackrents have a sort of entitlement to be going downhill, not up. Thady Quirk's loyalty is not servility: it has something of the nobility of Yeats's "My fathers served their fathers before Christ was crucified" in it. We are on somewhat appealing romantic ground to begin with; and she has also performed for herself a distancing trick. If Thady has a totally different way of seeing things from that of his creator, it is one which we can not only understand but with which we are subtly compelled to sympathise. It is a romantic sympathy, not yet exhausted, the appeal of which is proved by the fact that it was soon to sweep Europe. In using Thady to recruit it for the unfeeling Rackrents, Maria is playing a double game.

Of course, this sort of ambiguity was not new. The obtuse narrator—obtuse by the standards of the author's intelligence and moral values—was already a type in eighteenth-century literature. Defoe's woman criminals, Moll Flanders and Roxana, see the world with different eyes from those with which their creator might have been presumed to regard it; and in allowing these inveterate liars, self-deceivers and tricksters to present themselves, Defoe builds up sympathy by presenting also their defenceless situation in a cruel, predatory and exclusivist male world.

What was new was Thady's perfectly modulated, colloquial manner: his loose but pellucid syntax with its sustained natural flow, ideally fitted not only to narration but to a rich and complex mixture of self-deception, self-revelation and devastating realism. And this was not only new, but was to prove Irish. Maria is truly delighted and absorbed by the flow of natural speech, as no major English novelist has been at such length, brief as it is, even yet; as no major American novelist was to be until Mark Twain; and she has given us a central character's thought-process and speech process combined in a way that had to wait until *Ulysses* for its culmination.

The speech-process is integral to the ambiguity. We think in syntax of some sort. We deceive ourselves in syntax of some sort. We justify and assert ourselves in syntax of some sort. We judge and condemn in syntax of some sort. In the matter of Sir Kit's brutal treatment of his Jewish wife, of which the breakfast sausages are a part, Thady is seen at his best:

> Her honey-moon, at least her Irish honey-moon, was scarcely well over, when his honour said one morning to me—"Thady, buy me a pig!"—and then the sausages were ordered, and here was the first open breaking out of my lady's troubles — my lady came down herself into the kitchen to speak to the cook about the sausages, and desired never to see them more at her table.— Now my master had ordered them, and my lady knew that—the cook took my lady's part because she never came down into the kitchen, and was young and innocent in house-keeping, which raised her pity; besides, said she, at her own table, surely, my lady should order and disorder what she pleases—but the cook soon changed her note, for my master made it a principle to have the sausages, and swore at her for a Jew herself, till he drove her fairly out of the kitchen—then for fear of her place, and because he threatened that my lady should give her no discharge without the sausages, she gave up, and from that day forward always sausages or bacon or pig-meat, in some shape or other, went up to table; upon which my lady shut herself up in her own room, and my master said she might stay there, with an oath; and to make sure of her, he turned the key in the door, and kept it ever after in his pocket— We none of us ever saw or heard her speak for seven years after that—he carried her dinner himself—then

> his honour had a great deal of company to dine with him, and balls in the house, and was as gay and gallant, and as much himself as before he was married—and at dinner he always drank my lady Rackrent's good health, and so did the company, and he sent out always a servant, with his compliments to my lady Rackrent, and the company was drinking her ladyship's health, and begged to know if there was anything at table he might send her; and the man came back, after the sham errand, with my lady Rackrent's compliments, and she was very much obliged to Sir Kit—she did not wish for any thing, but drank the company's health.—The country, to be sure, talked and wondered at my lady's being shut up, but nobody chose to interfere or ask any impertinent questions, for they knew my master was a man very apt to give a short answer himself, and likely to call a man out for it afterwards—he was a famous shot—had killed his man before he came of age, and nobody scare dare look at him whilst at Bath. . . .

In this astonishingly punctuated passage, the real emotion, the pity aroused by the friendless young woman's situation is barely allowed through and one shudders to think what Maria in her preacher-moralist role would have made of it. As it is, there are the sly insights about the cook's happiness in having a house-wife she can cheat, the degree of her pity and affection being measured by her swift turnabout. Above all, there is the fact that, at the end, Sir Kit's credentials as a gentleman have been emphasised rather than diminished. It could not have been managed in other than the vivid, colloquial mode in which it is, in which the interest of the situation is shared with the interest of the thought-process and the speech-pattern, and it was not to be managed again until *The Master of Ballantrae,* in which the narrator's syntax is, to a degree, archaic and unStevensonian, but neither so colloquial nor so capable of ambiguity as this.

And so Maria stands at the beginning of that devouring interest in speech, which was to run right through to the twentieth century. Beckett's four or five major prose works have in common with Maria's solitary masterpiece the fact that they are speech-novels, monologues. So, in effect, has *Ulysses,* even if the monologues are interior ones. Less obviously, they all share an interest in syntactical lapses, bathos, irony and a curious sort of ironic eloquence, common to Thady, Leopold Bloom and Malone, but difficult to match elsewhere in the world's literature: and if Flann O'Brien never employed a colloquial narrator to produce these effects, he would be nowwhere without the intrusion of the colloquial into the formal, the bathetic into the eloquent, the ironic under-cut as well as the ironic enrichment that nearly all his dramatis personae employ. One does not suggest, of course, that Maria's influence was so great as to confer on Irish prose literature in English that pervasive talking quality which was to have such magnificent results. It was simply that confronted with an artistic necessity she found a natural mode. The appalling Rackrents could not have been presented directly, least of all by an insensate educator and moralist like herself. If they were to be the subject of a work of art, the presentation had to be suitably oblique. That the mode she found was not only a natural but a national one is proved by its continuance. And it could also be said that she provides the first example of the curious stanceless-ness of the Irish novel at its best. Since the Rackrents are indefensible morally, since Thady can neither explain nor justify but only present and praise them, we are free from the omniscient narrator, with his clearly defined moral certitudes, who was to weigh down Dickens, Thackeray and so many others, spoiling even, to an extent, the novels of D. H. Lawrence. When Thady speaks we are almost, already, in the territory of *Ulysses*. She was, of course, a Protestant. But she lived in a Catholic country where habits of evasion and mendacity had, within five generations, overtaken the straight-backed puritan soldiery of Oliver Cromwell. It was a long way still to Flann O'Brien's "Conclusion of the book, ultimate: Evil is even, truth is an odd number and death is a full stop". Because of Maria's all too well-developed and well-known moral attitudes; because her work is embellished with artistically unfitting footnotes and afterwords, we are aware of her; we know what she feels herself. Indeed on occasion, in the text itself even, Thady falters a bit and she sometimes shows through, but all the same, the suspension of judgment, moral and philosophical, perhaps the product of a reaction from dogma and religious certitude, and the equivocal, enigmatic and even oracular qualities of many of her successors are, in retrospect at least, and however peculiarly, present in Thady's way of telling his story.

And another dominant feature of the Irish novel which she foreshadowed was to be its absence of plot. It may be that certain great Irish writers have been simply incapable of constructing an ordinary machinery of dramatic causation. It may be that some of them, like Joyce, were uninterested in doing so. The line is hard to draw because novelists, like everybody else, turn their failings and weaknesses to advantage. In a later chapter of this book I shall suggest that *The Real Charlotte* is the only major work of prose fiction by an Irish writer which follows the pattern of implanted and pre-arranged dramatic causation which we call plot. The native genius is for the discursive, the anecdotal, the pseudo-historical, in other words chronicle; or else for construction of quite a different and often more complex kind than mere plot constructions. In her own later work Maria Edgeworth was to show herself quite capable of rather wearisome plot devices—the prolonging of Lord Colambre's misunderstandings about Miss Nugent in *The Absentee* for example. But *Castle Rackrent* is a chronicle novel. It, or rather Thady, simply unfolds. He throws away, incidentally, about a hundred possible plot situations while he does so: indeed for a dreadful moment towards the end when it seems as if Sir Condy might, after all, marry Judy McQuirk and somehow procure himself a happy ending, we fear to fear that the author was about to develop one. But happily, she doesn't. Life, she seems to say, is not like that. There is a beginning: Sir Patrick, Sir Kit, Sir Condy come into their inheritance. There is a life-path: in Sir Patrick's case of drunkenness, with the house over-flowing with fellow debauchees and even the chicken-house fitted up for the accommodation of intoxicated guests; in Sir Murtagh's case of all-consuming litigation; in Sir Kit's of gambling

and quarrelling, marriage and philandering; in Sir Condy's of elation and despair as funds are raised and squandered. There are even choices of a sort, as when Sir Condy flips the coin to decide between Judy and Miss Isabella. There is an end: often, considering the characters involved, one of a curious pathos and tattered grandeur. But there are no carefully devised causative mechanisms, no concealed circumstances with a trumpery of possibility and coincidence leading to sudden *bouleversements* and revelations. Maria is a superb story-teller, in *Castle Rackrent* at least: but she does not keep us in suspense; and in this she anticipates, strange though it may seem, both Joyce and Beckett.

She lived to be eighty-two, a life of apparent composure, of more than average fulfilment and, certainly, of fame. She wrote several more novels of which *The Absentee, Ormond, Patronage* and *Ennui* are the most praised. Yet she never repeated the oracle; and there is no use saying she did, though people will say it, for there is a little Maria Edgeworth industry; and of the making of books and articles there is no end. *Castle Rackrent* is the reason why we are interested in Maria; and if it were not for *Castle Rackrent* she would be very nearly forgotten: certainly if it were not for this one little book we would say that she was a worthy, likeable, extremely intelligent person who turned to fiction as a means of doing good; displayed observation, intelligence and even flashes of artistry in the writing of it; but was, in the end, no artist.

But whether or not for the reason that when she wrote it her interest in and excitement about her native land was at its keenest; or whether, even, the brutish but curiously stylish Rackrents released something in her deepest sexual nature which a stick like Lord Colambre could not, *Castle Rackrent* is a great work of art. In nothing is this shown more clearly than in our simultaneous knowledge of the Rackrents' worthlessness and their pathos: indeed, in the case of Sir Condy, squandering the golden guineas even on his deathbed, and dying with a terrible aloneness, she rises above pathos into tragedy:

> The fever came and went, and came and went, and lasted five days, and the sixth he was sensible for a few minutes, and said to me, knowing me very well— "I'm in burning pain all within side of me, Thady,"— I could not speak, but my shister asked him, would he have this thing or t'other to do him good?—"No, (says he) nothing will do me good no more"—and he gave a terrible screech with the torture he was in—then again a minute's ease—"brought to this by drink (says he)—where are all the friends?—where's Judy?—Gone, hey?—Aye, Sir Condy has been a fool all his days"— said he, and there was the last word he spoke, and died. He had but a very poor funeral, after all.

Where are all the friends? It was a question any of them might have asked, including the grasping, litigious Sir Murtagh. The Rackrents may be extreme in their behaviour, but they are in no real sense "Irish eccentrics"; and in death, if not in life, with wives, mistresses, boon companions, fled or gloating in their downfall, their aloneness gives them a share in the human condition which they perhaps do not deserve. Amidst noise and riot and even gaiety, they are truly as alone as Crusoe. They put their faith in marriages of convenience, in boon companions, in political associates; and they have neither intimates, nor, in any true sense, and within any true definition of feudalism, dependants. The land passes into the hands of avaricious middlemen, the wives greet their deaths as an escape from bondage; the boon companions have already deserted them. And Sir Condy dies with his lips framing a terrible question.

Maria went on to write of worthier people; to intelligent discussions of the state of Ireland after the Union in *The Absentee,* from which Ruskin said there was more to be learned about Irish problems than from a thousand blue books; to the creation of some real Irish eccentricity in *Ormond.* But as P. H. Newby shrewdly points out:

> Quite apart from the natural tendency of didactic fiction to deal in types and humours, there was, tucked away at the back of her mind, a deference to the audience for which she was writing, the aristocracy and landed gentry of England. . . . Even so, her readers would probably have accepted much more of the joyous extravagance of the original material than she allowed herself to use. The reception given to *Castle Rackrent* should have shown her that.

After 1817, though she was to live for thirty odd years, and to spend her strength and money on the relief of her tenants during the Famine, she deserted Ireland altogether as a subject. But she had already thrown away the speech weapon, amounting, as her footnotes and glossary suggest she believed, almost to a foreign language to her English readers, which had stood her in such splendid stead. For as long as she wrote about it Ireland brought out the best in her; but reading even *The Absentee* and *Ormond,* which have something of the excitement Ireland always gave her, the reader must agree with Mme. de Staël that, *"Vraiment, Miss Edgeworth est digne de l'enthousiasme mais elle se perd dans votre triste utilité".* Thady had provided her not only with what the years to come were to prove was a characteristically Irish verbal mode, but, because he was a mask, with a mode of perception as well. She wrote some good passages afterwards and created, in Grace Nugent and Dora O'Shane, women characters who had something of the cool attractiveness that she herself may have possessed. But the ambiguities of *Castle Rackrent* she never found again.

Dáithí Ó hÓgáin (essay date 1987)

SOURCE: "'Said an Elderly Man. . . .' : Maria Edgeworth's Use of Folklore in *Castle Rackrent,*" in *Family Chronicles: Maria Edgeworth's "Castle Rackrent,"* edited by Cóilín Owens, Wolfhound Press, 1987, pp. 62-70.

[*In the following essay, Ó hÓgáin commends Edgeworth's faithful depiction of Irish folkways in* Castle Rackrent.]

In approaching *Castle Rackrent* as a folklorist, one is impressed by the authenticity, accuracy, and originality of Maria Edgeworth's observations of the life of the common people of Ireland at the end of the eighteenth century. In these respects, since the interest in folk customs and beliefs had not yet developed as a discipline, the author of *Castle Rackrent* is ahead of her time. Moreover, as an accomplished maker of fiction, she invests these cultural circumstances with persuasive character and social elements to render a powerful portrayal of Irish country life before the Union.

Maria Edgeworth made a courageous decision in choosing to tell the history of the Rackrent family through the mouth of the faithful old retainer, Thady Quirk, as a specimen of a social class other than her own. In eighteenth-century Ireland, this meant creating a credible representative of the Gaelic culture of the ordinary Irish man and woman. There can be little doubt that in Thady we find many characteristics of a person in his position in the Ireland of the Big House. It may have been easy for readers of the novel to regard all those not of the landlord or merchant class in rural Ireland as types, and thus to see Thady as a representative of the faceless mass of peasants. For Maria Edgeworth's artistic purpose, therefore, it is enough that Thady should represent only the servant of the Big House in close contact with its occupiers; but he is also a subtly portrayed character revealing the keen psychological insight of his creator.

Although Thady Quirk has an individual fascination, he also has a distinctively native Irish cultural background. His chronicle contains a good deal of folklore—especially folk-beliefs and folk-customs—and Maria Edgeworth is anxious that her readers should not miss the significance of these elements. She frequently takes care to comment on them in the Glossary. The Glossary also includes much social detail and explanations of linguistic and other data, all of which she saw as further necessary information for the reader and are developments on her skilled attempts at providing the narrative with a particular, observed cultural setting. In view of all this, *Castle Rackrent* well deserves to be taken seriously, not only by the literary scholar, but by the social historian and the folklorist.

"The family of the Rackrents," says Thady, "is, I am proud to say, one of the most ancient in the kingdom—Everybody knows this is not the old family name, which was O'Shaughlin, related to the Kings of Ireland." The reference here seems to be to the name of the famous High King of Ireland at the turn of the eleventh century, Maoilsheachlainn, and we doubtless have an instance of the folk tendency to assume proof from facile etymological evidence. What is much more basic to Thady's attitude, however, is that the Rackrents are seen to derive their moral authority from their Gaelic ancestry. There is ample evidence to show that the tests applied by the native Irish in determining the moral right of landlords were those of nobility of descent, particularly if it were Gaelic. The objections voiced by seventeenth-century Gaelic poets to the Cromwellians, for example, was that these settlers were not of noble ancestry even in England. An extension of this logic was that highest respect was due to those nobility who were Gaelic, or had at least some Gaelic blood, a point which is clear from the works of eighteenth-century Gaelic poets who objected to the Williamite settlers on these criteria. Apart from the social reality of oppression, these attitudes find their basis in the very great importance attributed to genealogy by the Irish from time immemorial. It is also striking that Thady shows that his own ancestors have been servants to the Rackrent family for generations, thus again underlining genealogy as a factor which qualifies social relationships. Because of this, one notices running throughout Thady's narrative, not the servile attitude which the Big House might have expected from a servant, but a feeling of identity and pride which springs from a mutually respected tradition. The strains which the irresponsibility of various members of the Rackrent family put on the relationship account for much of the dramatic tension of the novel, and the eventual destruction of this relationship is heralded by the emergence of the upstart Jason Quirk. Thady's reluctant acceptance of his son's conduct can be explained by his awareness that traditional standards of behaviour no longer hold for either family.

In support of his testimony to the former social distinction of the Rackrents, Thady draws on one famous Irish belief. Before Sir Murtagh Rackrent's death, Thady remarks: "I warned him that I heard the very Banshee that my grandfather heard, before I was born long, under Sir Patrick's window a few days before his death." Maria Edgeworth footnotes this in the following way: "The Banshee is a species of aristocratic fairy, who in the shape of a little hideous old woman has been known to appear, and heard to sing in a mournful supernatural voice under the windows of great houses, to warn the family that some of them are soon to die." She then refers to the belief that in the preceding century, "every great family in Ireland had a Banshee." Very few folk beliefs have survived in Ireland with the same tenacity as has that of the banshee. The belief appears to be a purely Gaelic development: the banshee is a female preternatural being whose lamentation is heard announcing the approaching death of a native Irish person, the image being based on that of the ordinary women of this world who keen the dead through the usual "mirror" transmissions of the natural into the extranatural. The intense psychological concentration involved in the communal mind at the crisis time of death provides the functional context for the belief. The banshee is generally not described very minutely—in fact Maria Edgeworth's account is probably touched up to some extent; but the important point here is that the banshee's lamentation is believed to presage the death of native Irish people only, thus firmly situating the Rackrents both genealogically and communally among the native Irish.

The last sentence of this footnote on the banshee is particularly interesting because the seventeenth century was indeed a milestone in the development of much of the traditional folklore surviving into the Ireland of today. There can be little doubt also that it was in that century that the banshee tradition as we have it today reached its final development. The Cromwellian plantation not only shook Irish tradition to its roots, but it also created a new

departure by placing a merchant class in the position of aristocracy. It is interesting that seventeenth-century references to the banshee place her in direct opposition to the Cromwellian planters. Dáibhí O Bruadair, the most famous of the century's poets, mocks the Cromwellians for the cacophony of their names by comparing them to the—to him—melodious names of famous otherworld women such as Aoibheall. The nobleman-poet Piaras Feiritéar, in a lament for a Norman-Gaelic nobleman about the year 1640, writes this (I translate): "In Dingle the melodious crying was not spared, so that the merchants of the coastland got frightened. They need not fear for themselves, since banshees do not lament their sort." Thady Quirk would not be a true Irish countryman unless he believed in the fairies. Although there is but one reference to them in the main body of the text of the novel (concerning Sir Murtagh who "dug up a fairy-mount against my advice, and had no luck afterwards," Maria Edgeworth adds a lengthy footnote here, and appends a long description of the fairy faith in her Glossary. The belief that misfortune or even death will befall a person who digs up or defaces a mound or rath believed to be a fairy abode is familiar all over Ireland, and examples can still be found today of public authority employees who refuse to interfere with such objects even when instructed to do so.

It was commonly believed that the fairies travelled in a whirlwind, an idea probably born of a folk etymology of the Irish term for the phenomenon *"sí gaoithe"*. The word *sí* here means "thrust" and has a different derivation from the *sí* designating mound or mound-dwellers. The folk made such a connection, however, and thus *sí gaoithe* (meaning "thrust-wind") was taken to be *sí gaoithe* ("wind-fairy") or perhaps more appropriately *sí-ghaoith* ("fairy wind"). Maria Edgeworth refers in her Glossary quite accurately to the custom of saying "God speed ye," or words to that effect, when such a whirlwind rose. The purpose of this was to protect people from the dangers of being struck by the fairies, and such a belief is still quite strong in Ireland. Similarly (as Maria Edgeworth rightly states), the fairies are called *the good people* not out of respect or affection; rather is attention deflected from the feelings of fear. *The good people* is simply one of the most common of many euphemistic or flattering terms for the fairies, including "the gentry," "the people of the hills," "the mysterious people" (i.e. *an slua aerach*), "the wee folk," and "the little people."

The Glossary refers to a couple of popular legends about the fairies. Here Maria Edgeworth claims to have heard of these from "an elderly man." It is obvious that she had made an effort to reproduce faithfully the style and words of her informant. Thus she uses, and glosses, dialect words and expressions such as *air and easy* (quietly), *beast* (horse), *lit* (alighted), *mind* (recollect or know), and *mote* (barrow). The first legend concerns a man who was coming back from a fair late at night. He met a man in the dark who invited him to his house, a fine place, where he received food and drink. He fell asleep, but in the morning he found himself lying not in bed but in the angle of the road where he had first met the strange man. "And I asked him what he thought of it, and from first to last he could think of nothing but for certain sure it must have been the fairies that entertained him so well. For there was no house to see any where nigh hand, or any building, or barn, or place at all, but only the church and the *mote* (barrow)." There is no doubt here that what we are dealing with is a migratory legend which can be traced quite far back. It is well known, for instance, in Scandinavia and Germany, and is found in Scandinavian medieval literary sources. Saxo Grammaticus records it in his *Gesta Danorum* (c. 1200). Versions of it have been collected in Irish folklore in the last two centuries, notably that published by Patrick Kennedy in his *Legendary Fictions of the Irish Celts* (1866). Similar legends of people brought into the other-world dwellings were very popular in Ireland and can be traced to late mediaeval tradition on the Continent. It is to Maria Edgeworth's credit that this is the earliest known recorded version of this particular legend in Ireland. And an accurate piece of collecting it seems to be.

In the same note Maria Edgeworth recounts another story associated with the fairies. She tells of how corpses that "had not a right to be buried in (a certain) church-yard" could not be interred there, because as the funeral procession would try to enter, everybody's feet would seem to be going backwards instead of forwards. It is evident from Irish folklore generally that people attached tremendous importance to their communal graveyard. Since it is so important for people to rest in their own graveyard, it is understandable that a hostility to the burial of strangers there should arise. One story from County Louth, for example, tells of a man who fell asleep and dreamt that he met three men with a coffin. They made him help them carry it to a graveyard, but they were not allowed to go in because nobody with the same family name as the corpse was resting there. This is repeated in the case of other graveyards, until eventually they come to one where the dead man's family is resting. The three coffin-bearers then release the man from his duties, and he wakes up in the same place as he had fallen asleep. Therefore, though we have as yet found no exact parallel from oral tradition to the story of Maria Edgeworth's informant, there is hardly any doubt but that what she has put before us is a piece of genuine folklore.

Maria Edgeworth also describes one custom of lamenting the dead, which is known in many other civilizations, but was especially strong in Irish tradition up to the last century. Thady's description of Sir Patrick's funeral includes the observation: "Then such a fine whillaluh! You might have heard it to the farthest end of the county, and happy the man who could get but a sight of the hearse!" In her Glossary note on this passage, Maria Edgeworth indicates that the source of her information on the custom of keening the dead lies in the *Transcriptions of the Royal Irish Academy*, but from the details she supplies to Thady's account, it is clear that she also witnessed the custom herself. Three types of lamentation of the dead would have been current in eighteenth-century Gaelic Ireland. First, the spontaneous lamenting of the immediate family and close associates of the dead person.

Second, a conventional type of verse-lament, with improvisation, to suit the context, voiced by semi-professional women keeners. Thirdly, a poetic lament composed in strict metre by a literary man for the dead if such were a person of note. The first two types match Maria Edgeworth's description. In the second half of the eighteenth century, a large proportion of the inhabitants of County Longford were still Irish-speaking, and the custom of keening in all its types was closely associated with the use of the native language and did not survive long in English.

Maria Edgeworth has a good deal to say about death-customs apart from keening, and the details she gives here are accurate. Indeed, her notes comprise a valuable contribution to a study of the custom of waking the dead. Wakes as gay social functions, with merriment and games, consumption of tobacco and drink, were until recently, very much part of the Irish way of life. The only suspensions of the rule of liberty would be in the case of the death of a young person, a death in tragic circumstances, or some other public loss, with an exceptional degree of shock or sorrow. The Irish wake tradition may have its roots in ritual placating the dead person and assuring him/her that the living still rejoiced in his/her company. The grotesque account of how Sir Condy pretended to be dead so that he could witness his own funeral can be paralleled by many joke-stories and pranks associated with wakes, such as the tricksters taking the place of the corpse and propping it up so as to make it move. Another parallel is offered by the popular legend of the man who pretended to be dead so as to test his faithless wife (the basis of John Millington Synge's *The Shadow of the Glen*).

In this connection, Sir Condy's trick to secure voting rights for his supporters is of some interest: "Some of our friends were dumb-founded, by the lawyers asking them—had they ever been upon the ground where their freeholds lay?—Now Sir Condy being tender of the consciences of them that had not been on the ground, and so could not swear to a freehold when cross-examined by them lawyers, sent out for a couple of cleaves-full of the sods of his farm of Gulteeshinnagh: and as soon as the sods came into town he set each man upon his sod, and so then ever after, you know, they could fairly swear they had been upon the ground—We gained the day by his piece of honesty." This anecdote is a version of an international folktale, listed as Type No. 1590 in the Aarne-Thompson index, where it is thus summarized: "With earth from his own property in his shoes, the man swears when he is on his neighbour's land, that he is on his own." The footnote report that "This was actually done at an election in Ireland," shows that Maria Edgeworth had heard it herself. The folktale is known throughout much of Europe, but this is one of the earliest examples of it recorded in Ireland, a fact which puts Irish folklorists in debt to the author of ***Castle Rackrent***. In her second edition of the Glossary in 1810, she quotes two other stories of like type from Ireland concerning trick-swearing. Both seem to be offshoots from the Irish version of the same international folktale. By thus quoting parallels to her material, Maria Edgeworth shows herself to be following procedures of which a modern folklorist would approve. It is clear that she approaches these materials with honesty and a fair amount of objectivity.

Besides these, the novel exhibits a miscellany of folk-ways. The author's first Glossary note informs us that it is not by chance that Thady starts his memoirs on a Monday. We are referred to the belief that "no great undertaking can be auspiciously commenced in Ireland on any morning but *Monday morning*," and a number of sayings are quoted in support of the point. The selection of Monday is open to various interpretations. But most simply, as the first workday in the week, the folk mind endows it with special superstitious moment. Since these superstitions have ambivalent implications, we find that side by side with the belief in Monday as a lucky day to undertake some occupation, the belief that Monday is ill-fated. It is not considered lucky, for instance, to shave, to slaughter animals, or to dig a grave on a Monday. It is clear, however, that the positive attitude to Monday prevailed among Maria Edgeworth's sources.

In conclusion, a word about Maria Edgeworth's claim that the culture of *Castle Rackrent* is a thing of the past, a claim which is documented by many explicit details. For instance, the usage "childer" receives the note: "this is the manner in which many of "Thady's rank, and others in Ireland, *formerly* pronounced the word *children*." Again, a subsequent note states that "It *was* the custom in Ireland for those who could not write, to make a cross to stand for their signature." Regarding field forts, her Glossary reports that "*Some years ago,* the common people believed that these Barrows were inhabited by fairies"; and further, that "The country people in Ireland certainly *had* great admiration mixed with reverence, if not dread of fairies." Again, referring to banshees, she notes that "latterly their visits and songs have been discontinued." We know very well from modern Irish folk tradition that all these statements are false, and that each of these phenomena is very much alive in Ireland today. Why, then does she mislead her readers? We can essay an explanation of this if we consider how she makes the same claim in the more politically sensitive areas of the conduct of the gentry. Colonel M'Guire's mistreatment of his wife and the various misdeeds of the Rackrents, we are assured, are "no more to be met with at present in Ireland, than Squire Western or Parson Trulliber in England." This claim that "the manners depicted . . . are not those of the present age" is advanced as an illustration of the social and political observation that "Nations as well as individuals gradually lose attachment to their identity." When we consider that during the writing of *Castle Rackrent,* the great political event of the times, the passage of the Act of Union, constitutionally dissolved Ireland's identity, and that Richard Lovell Edgeworth, M.P. favoured the Act, we can perhaps understand something of his daughter's motives. Was it the emotional conflict engendered by such issues that caused her to shift the action of *Castle Rackrent* to times past? It is clear that *Castle Rackrent* is written "for the information of the *ignorant* English reader," and the distancing of the action seems to have come from a conflict between her affection for the "other times,"

despite their shortcomings, and the new—and promising—world opening up with the Union. Maria Edgeworth wishes to be loyal to both the former "Irish Nation," and the newly defined United Kingdom of Great Britain and Ireland. The folklorist can rejoice, however, that she kept her colonial sentiments in abeyance and did not allow them to disfigure the oral material she so skilfully presents in *Castle Rackrent.*

Mitzi Myers (essay date 1988)

SOURCE: "The Dilemmas of Gender as Double-Voiced Narrative; or, Maria Edgeworth Mothers the *Bildungsroman*," in *The Idea of the Novel in the Eighteenth Century,* edited by Robert W. Uphaus, Colleagues Press, 1988, pp. 67-96.

[*In the following essay, Myers examines relationships between women in Edgeworth's Rosamond stories.*]

> "The proper education of a female, whether
> for use or for happiness, is still to seek,
> still a problem beyond human solution."
> Fanny Burney, *Camilla; or, A Picture of
> Youth* (1796)

> "Oh teach her, while your lessons last,
> To judge the present by the past!
> The mind to strengthen and anneal,
> While on the stithy glows the steel."
> ***Rosamond: A Sequel to Early
> Lessons*** (1821)

> "Open-hearted and open-mouthed as I am, I
> can keep a secret WONDERFUL well."
> ***A Memoir of Maria Edgeworth***

Critics can no longer assume that important narratives deal with war or whales and that, as Virginia Woolf critiqued their consensus in 1929, "This is an insignificant book because it deals with the feelings of women in a drawing room." The schoolroom remains another matter. If the adult woman's novel has moved uptown, early juvenile fictions of female development still reside in the low rent district, excluded from the canon and relegated to skimpy chapters in histories of children's literature. Yet the gendered themes and narrative strategies and the cultural and psychosexual uses of women's juvenile literature offer rich materials for reconceptualizing the Georgian woman writer and the nature of her achievement. As a complex *Bildungsroman* which enacts its author's as well as its protagonist's coming of age—mothering writer, heroine, and reader alike—Maria Edgeworth's Rosamond stories (1796-1821) illuminate an important and neglected writer, normally praised for her manly public scope and sociological realism when she is read at all. Their dialogic interplay of child and adult, daughter and mother, constitutes a double-voiced narrative of some subtlety and considerable literary moment. The issues that the stories address and the relational literary modes in which their themes are inscribed epitomize a disregarded tradition of women's writing that is neither culturally marginal nor aesthetically uninviting. As mothered texts, the tales imply a revisionary approach toward defining the specificities of women's writing and the strategies by which women evade the "anxiety of authorship" endemic to their sex. These claims for the significance of the miniature emerge clearly when contextualized by the kind of adult fiction such stories typically rewrite.

At the heart of most late-eighteenth-century women's fiction is, in Fanny Burney's classic and much borrowed subtitle, "the history of a young lady's entrance into the world." Even though Burney herself gave high marks to the "new walk" in juvenile literature pioneered by authors like Anna Laetitia Barbauld, Sarah Trimmer, and Maria Edgeworth, we still tend to identify women writers' entry into significant literary production with their sentimental or Gothic elaborations and variants. Burney's *Evelina* made *the* woman's plot—the passage from orphanage or isolation to sensibility rewarded that translates women's cultural marginalization and limited options into a satisfying romantic mythology, love canceling victimization, and marriage concluding the *Bildungsroman*.

In a provocative exploration of gender and genre, for example, G. A. Starr argues that such fictions of female development are conventional and unproblematic, that for women the gap between the sentimental novel and the *Bildungsroman* that he finds characteristic of male texts does not exist. The eighteenth-century girl need never grow up. No "shedding of puerility" is requisite, for "the virtues demanded of her as a woman remain those prized in her as a child"—cultural equations of femininity with susceptible feelings, passivity, innocence, and vulnerability insure a "fundamental continuity . . . between girl and woman." For Starr, then, the late-eighteenth-century feminine *Bildungsroman* can simultaneously remain a sentimental novel as a young man's entrance into the world cannot. A maturing hero would have to leave behind the childishness, stasis, and intense though rather impotent feeling that characterize sentimental fiction; a heroine need not, for her culture (like Lord Chesterfield) defines women as merely "children of a larger growth." "Only A Boy" can be a sentimental hero, but even a grownup heroine can relate her life in the gush of seventeen-year-old sensibility. Though more discreetly phrased, Starr's equation of female *Bildung* with arrested development differs little from Hazlitt's dismissal of Burney's plots as "too much 'Female Difficulties'; they are difficulties created out of nothing" or from Walter Allen's assessment of her artlessness: "a mouse's view of the world of cats" delivered via a "camera eye" and "microphone ear."

Despite perceptive feminist analyses of canonical male assumptions like these, the classic heterosexual romance plot remains problematic as the formal inscription of female *Bildung*. Even when rewritten by Cinderella as subject, other feminist critics suggest, romance emplotment intrinsically denies female option and power. *Evelina* dances in fetters, for romance and *Bildung,* love and mature self-definition, cannot coexist. Finding a husband, discovering a father, Evelina cannot elude patriarchal pos-

session or masculine desire, but remains an object passed from one male hand to another. What Nancy K. Miller terms the eighteenth-century "heroine's text" insistently eroticizes the textual socialization of the female self. Whether "euphoric," like *Evelina's* social integration, or "dysphoric," like *Clarissa's* exclusion and death, denouements derive from seductions evaded or embraced: "*Bildung* tends to get stuck in the bedroom." Limited to female developmental plots where maturation ceases at the altar or is realized but in the coffin, we can only "stop reading novels." Or totally rescript romance: Rachel Blau DuPlessis suggests that not until modernists began to write "beyond the ending" could women evade the "scripts of heterosexual romance, romantic thralldom, and a telos in marriage" that muffle female character and repress fully feminocentric narrative. Evelina, then, has been taken as the paradigmatic eighteenth-century female *Bildungsroman:* its maturational pattern and its art somehow puerile when measured by male norms, and whether viewed from a generous or a less sympathetic feminist perspective, its plot and power structures conditioned by men. *Evelina* and *Camilla,* Burney's prototypical novels of female development, are novels of nondevelopment. Their youthful protagonists, however capable of moral insight and growth, are trapped in narrative structures so realistically reiterating feminine powerlessness that their happy courtship resolutions fail to satisfy. The vibrant child cannot be the mother of a woman; she grows down, not up.

Nor do heroines undergoing their crucial initiation into society get help from strong, supportive mothers. Indeed, it is a critical commonplace that "the women novelists of the period from Fanny Burney to Mrs. Gaskell and George Eliot create very few positive images of motherhood"; mothers in the period are "usually bad and living, or good and dead." But if at first glance *Evelina* seems dominated by omnipresent and omnipotent father-tutors, the novel's conclusion is haunted by the missing mother and by obscure intimations of the mature maternal power from which the heroine's entitlement derives. She can be recognized publicly as daddy's girl because she is so visibly her mother's daughter. Like the fairy tale plot it recreates, the Cinderella romance of *Evelina* fosters adolescent initiation through its quasi-magical maternal subtext. Burney's authorial self-imaging suggests the same displacement. Submerging her authority as moral spokeswoman, she aligns herself with the diffidence of her romantic heroines. Should *Evelina* be censured as a "rather bold attempt," it is, after all, just recapitulating a youthful consciousness: "I have not pretended to show the world what it actually *is,* but what it *appears* to a girl of seventeen: and so far as that, surely any girl who is past seventeen may safely do?" Mature wisdom and worldly satire are more safely attributed to male mentors or to the witty older women who may be enjoyed, but must ultimately be disavowed, for Burney "would a thousand times rather forfeit my character as a writer, than risk ridicule or censure as a female." Burney thus doubly embodies the central late-eighteenth-century "tradition of expressing the heroine's sensibilities."

Penetrating the haze of puerility that Starr finds hanging over sentimental fiction, Margaret Anne Doody sees in late-eighteenth-century women writers' work a struggle toward both a new female protagonist and a new narrative strategy that would eventuate in the double-voiced mode of an Austen or an Eliot, the *style indirect libre* which melds grown-up omniscience with the fallible character's perspective via indirect quotation: the inadequacy of a faulty heroine's view of self and world ruthlessly yet sympathetically judged, the inner life preserved yet objectively situated. Though Doody is little interested in girls' fiction, the same maturational efforts toward an educated, enlightened heroine and a knowledgeable narrative presence characterize juvenile authors. Indeed, it can be argued that the attempt to establish in alternating perspective a judicious female voice and the affective truths of feminine experience is revealed most clearly in those works which aspire, like the Rosamond tales, to demonstrate how the child *can* become the mother of the woman. In its choice of authoritative persona, thematic issues, and narrative mode, Edgeworth's Rosamond sequence reads like an answer to the female dilemmas that Burney's achievement poses, albeit (like most answers) one raising further questions. Though written at wide intervals and originally published in separate collections, the interlinked short stories about Rosamond from ***The Parent's Assistant*** (1796), ***Early Lessons*** (1801), ***Continuation of Early Lessons*** (1814), and ***Rosamond: A Sequel*** (1821) add up to a coherent reconceptualization of the female developmental plot.

These tales tracing the growth of an autobiographical heroine from early childhood to adolescence constitute a narrative of development as quintessentially feminine as Burney's *Evelina* and *Camilla*—but rewritten as an overtly mothered text, a prenuptial rather than a patriarchal love plot. Exploring this difference helps illuminate the larger issue of sexual "difference" in writing. Edgeworth's recasting of the heroine's entrance into the world and search for her identity motif is not just the juvenilization of a familiar format, though Rosamond is much involved with the problematics of gendered identity in Georgian society. (She has, for example, a loving but condescending brother whose masculinist pretensions Edgeworth delights in gently mocking.) Foregrounding Evelina's subtext of a powerful maternal presence, the Rosamond series can be read as an alternative kind of early feminocentric fiction. Edgeworth replaces the usual heterosexual romance script fusing female self-definition with relations between the sexes by a mother-daughter educational narrative thematizing domestic realism and enlightened choice, dramatizing through its rationally mothered heroine's tutorial adventures how young readers can learn to cope with their culture. Episode after heuristic episode demonstrates that girls need not fall prey to culturally conditioned sensibility and romantic fantasy; that they can indeed think, judge, and act for themselves—phrases that form the leitmotiv of the tales; that sensibility is not of itself a virtue to be rewarded, but must be assimilated to sense within a revised configuration of female possibility.

Take, for example, the earliest and most famous of the stories, the one inevitably cited in histories of children's literature. Called **"The Purple Jar,"** it might just as aptly be styled "the history of a *very* young lady's entrance into the world." Or "First Impressions," for the working name of *Pride and Prejudice* would fit as many of Edgeworth's tales as Austen's novels. With a surety, economy, and sly humor that entitle her to be termed the Jane Austen of the nursery, Edgeworth brings a similar rationality and realism to bear on similar conflicts: the need to distinguish between true and false vision, sentimental illusion and the solid facts of ordinary life. For Burney's social panoramas, melodramatic actions, and beautiful heroines fulfilling exciting fates, Edgeworth's narrower compass, smaller even than Austen's famous two inches of ivory, follows Rosamond from seven to about thirteen; outings, visits, and friends are in plentiful enough supply, but this is a child's world, its settings and dialogues familial—especially in the earliest tales, where the whole of the story is the interchange between mother and daughter. (Rosamond's father, like Richard Lovell Edgeworth, is involved in his children's education, but the mother is the initiatory teacher). Literally a youngster's entrance into the bustling world of London, **"The Purple Jar"** is a parable of female socialization demonstrating for child and adult audience alike how maternal enlightenment fosters rational girlhood. As Rosamond and her mother journey through the crowded streets, Edgeworth takes a reformer's stance toward Georgian consumerism and fashionable display, exemplifies a progressive, experientially based educational method, and compliments junior misses by imagining them capable of reasoned thought. Paradigmatic of all the tales, **"The Purple Jar"** offers a coherent blueprint for forming a Georgian girl's mind so she can read her culture aright and counter her period's feminine stereotypes.

Rosamond enters the narrative series (as she will conclude it) exclaiming, while her mother as characteristically questions: "Oh! mother, how happy I should be," said she, as she passed a toy-shop, "if I had all these pretty things?" "What, all! Do you wish for them all, Rosamond?" "Yes, mamma, all." Amid the busy streets and crammed shop windows, the plethora of sights and sounds, of playthings, ribbons, lace, blossoms, baubles, jars, Rosamond's bewildered imagination goes window-shopping—"Look, look! blue, green, red, yellow, and purple! Oh, mamma, what beautiful things! . . . if I had money, I would buy roses, and boxes, and buckles, and purple flower-pots, and every thing." Rosamond's immersion graphically depicts the undiscriminating openness to stimuli and inability to make sense of its culture which any small child must resign to become a maturely functioning human being, but her greedy spontaneity also takes a specifically feminine turn. If Rosamond is (as we shall see) Maria Edgeworth, she is also Everygirl, blessed and cursed with those qualities usually attributed to females in her society: expressivity, imagination, a volatile mental set that hops from one thing to another and never stays to connect consequences. Typically, this story centers on a test, a choice that entails a reading of reality: a radiant purple jar in a chemist's window that fancy converts to a flowerpot versus much needed new shoes. Modern critics universally fault the mother, the story, and the author for not simply telling the child that the jar's beautiful color comes

Edgeworth (seated, facing her father) with her father's third wife and some of her siblings.

only from the liquid it contains, rather than letting her find out for herself. Had Rosamond been fully informed, they suggest, she would have chosen the new shoes and not have had to go slipshod for a month. Besides, even if she did choose amiss, it was downright mean to deny her the shoes for so long.

Yet to reason thus is to miss the point of Edgeworth's delicate social comedy. Rosamond's progress from confused passivity to rational agency must originate in her own observations and attempts to think. She asks no questions despite her mother's promptings that she cannot be "quite sure that you should like the purple vase *exceedingly,* till you have examined it more attentively . . . I want you to think for yourself . . . when you are to judge for yourself, you should choose what will make you the happiest." But like a stereotypical girl, seduced by beauty, glamour, and fashion, use or no use, Rosamond mistakes surface for reality, never focuses her attention, never corrects her first impressions, even though she must remove stones from her worn-out shoe all the way back to the shop to purchase the jar of her fantasy: "often was she obliged to hop with pain; but still the thoughts of the purple flower-pot prevailed, and she persisted in her

choice." And so she must take responsibility for it, even if it means waiting a month for new shoes. Edgeworth's woman-centered pedagogic tale insists that a little girl too "must abide by your own choice" if she is to become a self-aware, self-dependent, and responsible woman.

Like the whole sequence tracing Rosamond's maturation, and all are ultimately success stories except this first, **"The Purple Jar"** rewrites cultural stereotypes of females as passive victims at the mercy of external circumstances and their own undisciplined emotions by granting girls potential self-command and rational agency. In one way or another, each tale acts to remedy culturally determined female deficiency in independent thinking and affirms that girls can achieve control of their wits and hence in some measure of their lives. Burney's double register locates feminine potentiality in a world that insists on feminine powerlessness. Scaling the difficulties of female socialization down to a child's level, Edgeworth's stories of progressive education for girls read like a quasi-Wollstonecraftian critique of contemporary women's education and gender definition. They do not deny the difficulties Burney insists on; rather, they make them manageable by miniaturizing them, by offering a repertoire of coping strategies and, more important, a different sense of female selfhood—the rational capabilities underlined by the *Sequel's* epigraph and the tales' insistence that the irrepressibly imaginative and impulsive Rosamond acquire "a taste for truth and realities." Conjoining a vividly imagined domestic realism rich in details of everyday life with the theme of domestic heroism for girls, the stories show how small choices and "seeming trifles" engender "greater virtues." Suave as Wollstonecraft's polemic is not, Edgeworth's tales nonetheless discreetly echo the *Rights of Woman's* demand that women achieve "power . . . over themselves": girls who acquire "self-command" and "power over their own minds" may "be left securely to their own guidance."

More can be claimed for Edgeworth's fictional imagination than this appealing surface reading, however. Less limited than the private expressiveness of Evelina's letters, Edgeworth's double-voiced narrative juxtaposes the child's subjective point of view with the mother's instructive commentary and frames both within an enabling myth of the female author as maternal educator. Yet the interplay among the mother who teaches, the infinitely educable daughter whose apprenticeship to reason is denied closure, and the writer who mothers the story generates its own subtext. The abuse that chroniclers of children's literature heap on Rosamond's powerful, "logically minded mother" attests to the problematics of pedagogy: "you hate the mother. . . . You know she is right, and you loathe rectitude accordingly." Rosamond "is irresistible. It is her Mother who represents Theory"; Rosamond "is an engagingly real child, impetuous, eager, and generous, well-meaning, and quick to repent. But . . . Rosamond's mother chills. She is in fact the prototype of many rational mothers" in early-nineteenth-century juvenile fiction. "Of course she always wins." "Breathes there a child with soul so dead, that would not to itself have said—'I hate, I simply *detest* that mother of Rosamond!' That this was not the impression intended to be conveyed is, however, perfectly certain"; the story was meant to celebrate the "triumph of the Perfect Parent; but every child knows it is Rosamond who triumphs." Resistant to eighteenth-century moral purposiveness and residually fearful of maternal power, these modern readers ignore the author's gendered identity as the product of her historical period and her specific relational matrix. Nor do they notice Edgeworth's own textual ambivalances ironizing the manifest rationality of the maternal discourse she sponsors. More attentive to nuance, a recent reviewer who testifies to the tale's continuing appeal for girl readers terms it "wonderfully written and marvellously ambiguous."

Elucidating this ambiguity requires a closer look at the story's double voices, for a complex mother-daughter dynamics is central to its meaning. When mother tongue meets daughter tongue—and Edgeworth's characters always spring to life through their dialogue, two ways of construing the world intersect: foresighted adult and spontaneous child; cognitive and affective styles of knowing; factual observation and felt experience. The mother's very articulation, clipped and attentive to consequences, demonstrates that if life is a series of tests, it is also amenable to control. Severely referential and given to checking free-flowing juvenile chatter with a "What do you mean by . . . ," the maternal language appropriates the rationalities of the dominant male discourse to insure the Marianne-like child an education in a new style of heroism: "Don't consult my eyes, Rosamond," and her mother turned away her head. "Use your own understanding, because you will not always have my eyes to see with"; "Moderate your transports, my dear Rosamond." The daughter's talk, richly responsive to experience—"I am sorry I can't have every thing I wish," "I don't *know,* mamma, but I *fancy*"—reaches as eagerly for approval and connection: " . . . that is, if you won't think me very silly, mamma"; "Rosamond was very sorry that her mother wanted nothing." Like Austen's sisters, Edgeworth's fictional pairing of mother-daughter in terms of sense-sensibility explores female self-definition through Georgian cultural preoccupations. But the Rosamond tales' implied narrative—of maternal sovereignty and seduction, of an initial daughterly submission and a finally achieved relational individualism—connects importantly with key issues in modern feminist thought as well, particularly the work of psychoanalytical revisionists who argue for the primacy and the ambivalence of the mother-daughter bond in woman's emotional life and her developmental journey from symbiotic mirroring toward differentiation.

Widely influential, the work of Nancy Chodorow and Carol Gilligan epitomizes a school of thinking about women which rewrites traditional oedipal narratives of female development to relocate power and conflict from the father to the preoedipal mother, the figure with whom all infants feel themselves symbiotically connected. Attempting to explain "the reproduction of mothering," Chodorow argues that girls do not undergo differentiation from the mother in the same way that boys do, nor does the father achieve full parity with her as girls mature. Rather, even adult women retain more flexible and fluid ego boundaries than do men, experience a lifelong sense of identification and connection with the female parent, and tend to construe reality itself in relational terms: "The basic feminine sense of self is connected to the world, the basic masculine sense of self is separate." Extending Chodorow's schema to moral development theory, Gilligan finds that the sense of empathy built into the primary definition of female selfhood accounts for different ethical as well as psychic narratives, an "overriding concern with relationships and responsibilities" rather than rights. "Women's sense of self," Jean Baker Miller similarly concludes, "becomes very much organized around being able to make and then to maintain affiliations and relationships." Such studies have obvious implications for assessing fictions of female development. Generic definitions of the *Bildungsroman* embody male maturational norms and linear plots directed toward separation and autonomy, though women's more interdependent sense of self has historically been organized around the weaving and maintenance of intimate relationships, especially those of childhood; female individualism tends toward the connected and the contextual.

Paradoxically, then, infantilizing her story of feminine *Bildung* affords Edgeworth perhaps more freedom than

Burney enjoyed to explore central female issues of power and dependency, individuation and relatedness, of the need to be loved and the need to act as a moral agent: what might be summed up as the "conflict between nurturance and autonomy" that so many recent feminist theorists have found central not only to mother-daughter dynamics, but also to women's whole sense of themselves. Despite its seeming narrative clarity and obvious moral lesson about growing up rational, the Rosamond series' biographical context and emotional subtext generate dualities of voice and message at once more ambiguous and less pessimistic about the possibilities mature female self-definition than Burney's beleaguered self in a man's world. The Georgian rational mother is a cultural symbol of female agency and autonomy, but also alterity and psychic distance. Overwriting the daughter's relational needs and expressive "feminine" voice with the sterner language that offers access to culture and power, she is both a figure to emulate and a figure to fear—a historically necessary if not altogether satisfying double for the original mother incorporated within, the unconditionally responsive nurturer whose affection does not have to be earned by achievement. Edgeworth's autobiographical heroine may be the author's daughter and the narrative environment a way to mother herself more satisfyingly than real life has, but the dialogic voices of mother herself more satisfyingly than real life has, but the dialogic voices of mother and daughter which, as we shall see, recuperate one family situation carry beyond personal self-definition to illuminate larger questions about gender definition and its literary representation as well. Maria Edgeworth's discourse of the daughter who writes qua mother (and via maternal mediation qua father too) engages lively contemporary issues of women's linguistic practice as well as psychic structure.

Thinking of Edgeworth as a woman writer whose narrative structures textualize the nurturing energies of the mother, developing her own selfhood while educating others, is not simply to feminize the reigning explanatory paradigm of paternal influence—for even more than Fanny Burney, Maria Edgeworth signs herself daddy's girl, soliciting what Richard Lovell calls the "paternal *imprimatur*," his encouragement, his criticism, his prefaces, above all, his love. Rather, it is to situate her work within a more complex family dynamics and to argue for the familial situation as at once instigator and central theme in her educational prose and her fiction, whether for child or adult. All her life, whatever she produced—letter, tract, and tale alike, Edgeworth used the very act of writing itself to weave and maintain familial relationships, which (characteristic of her period and especially of her family) she likes to imagine in pedagogic terms. Pledges of love, her tales were "pen-and-ink children" circulated among a widening family network seeking connection and instruction: she "should be *extremely* obliged to the whole Committee of Education and Criticism at Edgeworthstown, if they would send corrections to me from their own brains" goes a typical comment. Someone is always learning (or failing to learn) something in these stories, "the slight figure of a young person" which opens her last (and best) adult novel, *Helen* (1834), threads through all her work,

and her themes invariably foreground the impact of childhood instruction on characters' later lives.

Yet the rather atypical *Castle Rackrent* (1800)—itself an ironized family situation—has towered over any other achievement, just like Maria's flamboyant, much-married father. Whether viewed as enfeebling or enlarging (as her definitive biographer Marilyn Butler and some of Butler's nineteenth-century predecessors have argued), paternal influence has usurped even more space in studies of her work than in her life—no easy feat. Clearly, as she repeatedly testifies, he was a potent inspiriting force. She needed a relational motive to write, whether her father or another of her family: "Without . . . affection I should no more work than a steam engine without fire. . . . *If you take away my motive I cannot move.*" But he was not a literary dictator who forced Maria willynilly to embrace the didactic image typically associated with her work. He was the sole determinant of neither her literary nor her private identity, but a commanding presence within a larger relational field that changed over time, as did his daughter's personality. Appropriately, one late Victorian critic located her as a transitional figure between eighteenth- and nineteenth-century fiction who newly stresses the "gradual development of character in and through action." Just as Edgeworth's adult works partake of the moral tale and structure their themes through family relationships, the best of her children's tales assume this *Bildungsroman* format, informed, like her shrewd and lively letters, with all the "attraction of unconscious autobiography." Paternal and maternal elements, didacticism and self-discovery fuse in her work and in her own evolving life.

To understand Edgeworth's Rosamond tales as a mothered text, a miniaturized psychic autobiography that is at once didactic and autodidactic, we need to review the relational matrix conditioning their authorial stance and narrative shape. Recognizing that minds can think back through fathers or mothers, Virginia Woolf nevertheless maintains that women writers especially "think back through our mothers." Certainly, if Edgeworth anticipates Scott and the nineteenth-century regional novel—the large-scale sociological recreation of a culture—in many of her tales for mature audiences, she also inherits and mothers a rich female tradition more given to what Gaston Bachelard terms the "miniaturizing imagination." She began her writing career with translating Madame de Genlis on education and inventing children's stories for her father's ever increasing household (twenty-two children by four wives), and her last publication in extreme old age was another juvenile moral tale. Though Louisa May Alcott (also a product of parental educational innovators) is often credited with founding the Arcadian family novel, Edgeworth and her sister teachers earlier evolved the genre. The relationally ordered domestic space and the educative purpose centering such stories afford the female author both private gratification and public permission to write.

Late-eighteenth-century women writers legitimated their vocation by what Richard Lovell Edgeworth succinctly terms "that moral tendency, that alone can justify a female for appearing as an author," but the pleasures of "becoming a heroine"—of winning the handsome prince like Evelina or Elizabeth Bennet—have been better explored than those subtler compensations that inhere in imagining oneself as simultaneously child and adult. Children's fiction, a recent critic provocatively suggests, "has the remarkable characteristic of being about something which it hardly ever talks of": "the impossible relation between child and adult." No less than *Peter Pan,* naturalistic moral tales like the Rosamond series play a double game, the author as enlightened mother-teacher improbably coexistent with the author's fallible child self. Personally rewarding, they sustain fantasies of caring and being cared for as they rework and rewrite the story of the unhappily mothered child within, now more satisfyingly nurtured by the narrative environment that the grownup author shapes. They also enlist mothering fantasies inherent in pedagogy for more public purposes, enabling their authors to speak with cultural authority. It is not hard to see why the poet Samuel Rogers joked about his period's literary women: "How strange it is that while we men are modestly content to amuse by our writings, women must be didactic. . . . Miss Edgeworth is a schoolmistress in her tales."

If the choice is limiting in some ways, the maternal educator's voice, less diffident than Burney's, is empowering in others. Edgeworth enjoys describing her books as "*minnikin* attempts," "wee-wee stories," the literal equivalent of the diminutive self whom she always depicts in family correspondence, even in old age, as the perennial child Rosamond: "I beg, dear Sophy," she writes her cousin, "you will not call my little stories by the sublime title of 'my works,' I shall else be ashamed when the little mouse comes forth." But this self defined in terms of juvenile imagination and sensibility plays within a more potent public image; for some years Edgeworth maintained an extraordinary reputation as the voice of "practical good sense," an enlightened cultural benefactor having, as Francis Jeffrey put it in the *Edinburgh Review,* "done more good than any other writer male or female of her generation." Her tales ambitiously aimed to instruct not just children and adolescents, but the whole of adult popular and polite culture as well: "to promote . . . the progress of education, from the cradle to the grave."

The rather bleak record of Maria Edgeworth's earliest years and the teenage letters that explore her coming to writing elucidate why she chose the didactic educator's voice and how her choice expresses and helps her manage a personal dilemma that replicates this period's gender dilemmas and aesthetic dilemmas as well, conflicts that might be subsumed under the familiar rubric of sense versus sensibility (or named more newly, rational discourse versus relational need). Born in England in 1768, Edgeworth spent her first fourteen years there except for a two-year sojourn in Ireland during her father's second marriage, to Honora Sneyd; she remembered nothing of Ireland, but a great deal about the attractive, accomplished, and rather icily perfect Honora, who is the prototype for Rosamond's mother in the tales. Self-controlled, rational, interested in scientific and literary matters, Honora man-

aged to inspire boundless devotion and yet epitomize sense. Anna Seward (who never wearied of celebrating her in verse) and several men fell deeply in love with her, including Richard Lovell while he was still unhappily married to Maria's mother, the first and least loved of his wives. Realizing his danger, he fled to France and only returned when he learned of his wife's death in March 1773; he and Honora were married in July, and Maria found herself with a new mother who reserved her warmth of affection for a much loved husband. The **Memoir** records that Maria's "father and Mrs. Honora Edgeworth were, even in her earliest years, perceived to be far, far above every one else," that the child "felt great awe of her at the time. . . . at her first acquaintance with her: she remembered standing by her dressing table and looking up at her with a sudden feeling of 'How beautiful!'" A mix of maternal laxity and paternal disregard, Maria's first years had been very different from the attentive domestic education and the almost obsessive child nurture that would characterize the environment of the later Edgeworth youngsters and her own juvenile protagonists. In contrast to Maria's own indulgent and decidedly unintellectual mother, Honora embodied a progressive maternal ideal. She did not pamper, set high standards, and was invincibly just; Maria initially sought attention with destructive acts, the rebellions of a shy child, but she was soon painfully eager to please, to play "your dutiful Daughter" as her first extant letter is signed.

Honora personified everything that Maria was not, everything that the cool ideal of female perfection threading through so much of her stepdaughter's fiction is and that Maria clearly internalized, making high-minded self-command her official public persona, however oddly at variance with her voluble, volatile plain little self. Energetic, "remarkable for strong powers of reasoning," much interested in education, Honora began the records of authentic childhood experience that figure so largely as both method and ideology in Maria and Richard Lovell's treatise on **Practical Education** (1798), and it was she who originated the first tiny book in the long family series of educational texts, although her husband usually receives the credit. Indeed, Honora is the foremother of the whole educational project finished only in 1825 when Maria published the last of the **Early Lessons** begun almost half a century before. Far more significant than its size suggests, this initial tale served as manifesto and pilot work for the family educational achievement that Maria always valued more highly than her own fictions composed outside the enterprise. Building on the pioneering work of Mrs. Barbauld, the narrative of Honora's *Practical Education: or, The History of Harry and Lucy* (1780) adroitly links a fresh educational psychology to a fresh domestic realism through "pictures of real life" and real children that juvenile readers are invited to identify with (iv). Almost twenty years later, the expository **Practical Education** credited Honora with the central principle of the family program: "that the art of education should be considered as an experimental science," *Practical* merely signifying "brought to the test of experience," not programmatic Benthamite utilitarianism, as commentators who read only the title seem to suppose. And, affectively as well as intellectually exemplary, Honora was very deeply beloved by the father who must surely—Joanna Baillie joked to Scott decades later—have fed his daughter "love powders," so passionate was Maria's partiality for that "first object and motive of my mind," the initially inattentive parent whom her writing eventually transformed to "critic, partner, father, friend" united.

Honora's health was poor; Maria was sent away to boarding school at seven. Her stiff, anxious letters and the restrained, even-handed replies occasion thought, as does the long letter to his eldest daughter that the grieving Richard Lovell wrote from beside his wife's corpse in 1780. Already, he had advised his "Plain enough" child that "real good sense," "a benevolent heart, complying Temper, & obliging manners" were requisite: "by your mother's assistance you might become a very excellent, & an highly improved woman." Now, excusing "your excellent mother" for perhaps too scrupulous a justice toward her stepdaughter, the death-bed message simultaneously insists that the girl be grateful for this "timely restraint" which "yielded fondness towards you only by the exact measure of your conduct," that she enshrine Honora and "fix her excellent image in your mind." The child's extraordinary sensibility and her "inordinate desire to be beloved" are the core—defined for much of her life as the defect—of her character, but with these Rosamond qualities, she also has Rosamond's "ardent, active desire to improve," which, so the stories wishfully say, "made her the darling of her own family." Since Maria wants to become "amiable, prudent, and of USE," what better way than to emulate "the most exalted character of your incomparable mother" so that the daughter too can earn the praise which Honora's steady rectitude "forces from the virtuous and the wise." No wonder the **Memoir** records that the letter made the intended impression, that Maria "recollected all her life the minutest advice which Mrs. Honora Edgeworth gave to her," or that the wish to enact her father's counsel "became the exciting and controlling power over the whole of her future life." R. L. Edgeworth would marry happily twice more, and though a year younger than Maria, Frances Beaufort, his last wife, became her best friend and "Dearest Mother" for over forty years, delightfully given to the petting Honora withheld; but to the father Honora seems always to have remained the one woman who "equalled the picture of perfection, which existed in my imagination."

Advised by Honora before her death to marry her younger sister (oblique testimony to the woman's strength of mind), Richard Lovell did so before 1780 was over. By mid-1782, Maria's boarding school exile from home, always one of the most resonant words in her vocabulary, was over, and the whole family permanently settled in Ireland. In the early eighties, Maria probably received proportionately more of her father's attention than she ever got again as Richard Lovell supplemented her formal education, trained her in the business of the estate, and set her writing tasks. Busy with childbirth and child care, Elizabeth Sneyd was not the intellectual companion that her sister had been, and the full scale educational project with an eye to publication lapsed until Maria's

work revived it in the nineties. This period's unpublished correspondence of Fanny Robinson, Maria's school friend who "defended me" "where no one liked me," captures the psychic dynamics underlying Maria's self-invention as an educational author and suggests the rich uses of children's literature for the woman writer. Indeed, it can be argued that Edgeworth's letter-writing (she wrote over 2,000 to her family alone) initiates, frames, and ultimately completes the personal *Bildungsroman* that she never permits full closure in the Rosamond tales themselves. Only after her father's death—and perhaps most richly in the vibrant letters where she lets her life round out her art—does she fully integrate the voices of impulsive daughter and knowing mother, sensibility and sense, whose dialogue is the basic structural unit of her fictional autobiography. (It is noteworthy that Edgeworth's most considered appraisal typically images her novelistic art as dialogue, talk, and that the letter and the moral tale similarly encode in their form a relational motive and a dyadic interaction.) Edgeworth's late letters evoke the matriarch, the head of the clan, who is simultaneously her stepmother's beloved daughter, the "old petted nursling" of her "Dearest Mother," and the passionately loving surrogate mother of that stepmother's eldest daughter, the symbolically named Frances Maria; these epistolary texts wholeheartedly enact the loving maternal discourse that eluded the unempathetically mothered child Maria and that the grown-up author's autobiographic mother-daughter fictions more equivocally realize.

If Edgeworth's maturest letters heal the linguistic and emotional disjunction between child and adult that her narrative renderings contingently bridge, her early letters adumbrate the dyadic voices whose interaction weaves the story of her juvenile *Bildungsroman*: the exuberant child Rosamond, hungry for love and anxiously improving herself to earn it, and the all wise, antisentimental mother, appropriating (like Honora) the rational language of the dominant male discourse, the former characterized by her ready emotional and imaginative responsiveness, the latter by her carefully considered process of judgment. Through the letters' stilted seriousness or forced sprightliness (both distinct from Edgeworth's mature epistolary voice), the girl struggles to define herself—"Proteus-like I assume different shapes"—and to discover a vocation that will satisfy her needs for relation and achievement. She has a powerful homegrown model of selfhood, for what better way to consolidate her position with her father than to incorporate the missing mother, to become in some sense Honora?

But the letters also consider more public—and in some sense opposed—models of female authorship: Madame de Genlis, the prototypical rational mother-educator, whose *Adèle et Théodore; ou, Lettres sur L'Éducation* she is excitedly translating ("I am writing a book.—A BOOK!"), and Fanny Burney, whose Lord Orville delights her and whose acquaintance and correspondence the teenager daydreams of acquiring, even though she fears novels act on the mind "as Drams do . . . on the body." Letter after letter, Burney "still runs in my head," but these letters also underscore the dilemma of the plain, small girl painfully aware that she lacks Evelina's graces and beauty's power: "with every *personal* disadvantage . . . I know their value, for I know the want of them." *Evelina's* Cinderella closure deceives girl readers, Maria concludes, defining herself not as romantic heroine, but as *philosophe* in phrases that thread through the mother's language in the Rosamond tales: "surely there is nothing ridiculous in a girl of fifteen's attending to the feelings of her own mind and endeavoring to find out what tends to make her more or less happy & what does a philosopher do more." Edgeworth's assumption of the educator's persona conjoins reasoned language and girlish need; to teach is to acquire a father and a mother for oneself. Reviving and completing the family educational project, she connected herself with Richard Lovell, achieved Honora-like status within the family, and found an authoritative public voice. The didactic "plain, practical sense" dispensed by the "Franklin of novelists" was, paradoxically, relationally generated.

Yet though the woman writer can solve the problem of authority by appropriating reason as a mother tongue, the juvenile writer who is a good mother to her character and herself must also find a place for expressivity and the affective truths of female experience within that dominant discourse. Speaking in the rational mother's voice may censor the woman within, but Edgeworth's juvenilia textualize subversive energies as well as moral lessons. Radically opposing critical assessments suggest the complexity of the Rosamond sequence. For P. H. Newby, the heroine is the sole "rebel in this world of common sense," forever resolving to be more foresighted, forever failing to tame her uncalculating love of life; for Marilyn Butler, who tries to draw a sharp contrast between Maria's self-renderings in her last adult novel, *Helen,* and her earlier juvenile representations, Rosamond must be hopelessly inept, a study in "humility, almost self-abasement," recurrently saved from the disastrous consequences of her imprudence by the "watchful despotism of a parent." Neither is correct—nor wholly incorrect, for Edgeworth's complex mothering of her child's text allows her to have her maturation and elude it too. Philippe Ariès and his fellow researchers in family history have been confirming for some years now that adults invented children, that childhood, like gender, is a cultural construct; looking sympathetically and usually very clear-sightedly at actual children, reformist educators like Honora and Richard Lovell fashioned the child to insure progress, reinventing the future adult as well. But if educators invent children, children turned educators invent juvenile selves that simultaneously support and subvert parental premises.

It is every way significant that Maria chose to encode her own personal narrative of female *Bildung* within the family series of educational tales and to make her alter ego a child character, the very epitome of those juvenile and feminine qualities that her culture (and ours) would range against the *philosophe's* reason. Valorizing the literary miniature in the shape of a child's story, her tales about the problems of judgment and conduct that would face any young girl in everyday family life merge the symbolic dimensions of the small: its capacity to act as "meta-

phor for the interior space and time of the bourgeois subject," to function self-referentially, and its status as a "dominated" world, a model wherein larger-scale problems can be safely manipulated. Once we set aside preconceptions about the juvenile moral tale's transparency as genre, Edgeworth's dual reconceptualizations of the female developmental plot emerge as fantasies of power indulged within domesticated boundaries—the satisfaction of rational achievement, the fulfillment of relational need. Exploiting the powers of the weak, she at once maintains parental love and attention and sustains selfhood. The storyteller's simultaneously aligning herself with sense *and* sensibility realizes a richer model of female selfhood than the tales' direct statement; the implications of her fictional practice round out the standards she endorses. The maternal writer teases and teaches her juvenile self in the interest of more rational girl readers, but writing as a daughter she celebrates that self's imaginative energy and affective needs; better than her mothers real or represented inside the text, the author as mother understands and nurtures the author as daughter.

The story's polemic message valorizes reason and prudent womanhood; that public moral is problematized by its emotional subtext and its exuberant narrative rendering of the errant heroine's perspective, thought processes, and talk, her characteristic volubility and tics of language ("Hey, mamma?")—all the qualities that have won Rosamond renown as the first real living and breathing child in English juvenile literature. Embodying dependence, her need for approval and her very language in its insistent search for connection enacting the relational thinking said to characterize women, Maria's Rosamond nevertheless unmistakably dominates the texts in which she figures. Patterning reality, eliminating the aleatory, the rational narrative logic runs one way, but Rosamond's vivid portrait and ebullient voice tug the reader's attention and heart another direction. Like all the young readers who have seen in her "ever fluctuating mind, an image of their own," we too identify with "her infinite variety of faults, follies, and foibles." The mother earns our respect; Rosamond wins our love.

Writing as at once the daughter of mothers and the mother of daughters, Edgeworth enjoys the opposed gratifications that children's literature paradoxically, perhaps uniquely, permits: wise maturity and positive regression, the fantasies of imaginative self-expression and the rewards of self-restraint. Insistently underlining the mother's power and rationality, the daughter's educability and maturation, the Rosamond series thoughtfully qualifies each as well. It weighs more precisely and more equably than it ever explicitly acknowledges the benefits and the costs of rational womanhood. However much Rosamond learns and improves within the sequence, she also remains irreducibly, unchangeably herself. With its wonderfully realistic final words, a conclusion that denies closure, **"The Purple Jar"** foreshadows the way the whole series will stop: "Oh, mamma . . . how I wish that I had chosen the shoes . . . however, I am sure—no, not quite sure—but, I hope, I shall be wiser another time." The juvenile tales' prenupital plot writes finis when Rosamond answers nosy old

Lady Worral's anticipated question, *"Ma'am, when will Miss Rosamond's education be finished?"* with "Never while she lives!"

Ironically, the more literally the heroine fulfills the Edgeworthian parent's injunctions to improve continually, to embrace the real, to restrain sensibility, the more she subverts the premises to which she defers. To represent the real is to represent the true inner juvenile, "feminine" self that is Rosamond; forever to improve is not to become the grown-up rational mother, but eventually to progress beyond her toward a self-definition that unites sense and sensibility, daughter and mother, in a Maria Edgeworth grown up at last—on her own terms, in the domestic life that mattered most to her. Well aware of the gap between her public face and private self, Maria once confessed to Elizabeth Inchbald, "Would you ever have guessed that the character of Rosamond is like ME? All who know me intimately, say that it is as like as it is possible; those who do not know me intimately, would never guess it," and her letters abound in amused references to her own Rosamond qualities, impatience, impulsiveness, enthusiasm, expressiveness, impressionability, a fondness for "being loved," nonsense, laughing, and building castles in the air that lasted past "Rosamond at sixty" into her eighties: "Love me and laugh at me as you have done many is the year." Fittingly, the *Memoir's* final assessment memorializes Maria's personal *Bildungsroman:* "The most remarkable trait in her character was the prudence with which she acted; the command which she had acquired over her naturally impetuous nature and boundless generosity of spirit"; "She had amazing power of control over her feelings when occasion demanded, but in general her tears or her smiles were called forth by every turn of joy and sorrow among those she lived with." Edgeworth's fictional and actual maturational patterns imply that woman's access to rational discourse may be bought with a price, but her achievement also testifies that relational needs must be met too. Well might she assert, "Reasonable or unreasonable I know my little self." Exploring the latent and manifest content of her juvenile narrative richly expands our sense of women's contribution to the eighteenth-century idea of the novel.

Michael Ragussis (essay date 1989)

SOURCE: "Representation, Conversion, and Literary Form: *Harrington* and the Novel of Jewish Identity," *Critical Inquiry,* Vol. 16, No. 1, Autumn, 1989, pp. 113-43.

[*In the following essay, Ragussis examines* Harrington *in the course of an inquiry into the origin and role of Jewish stereotypes in English literature.*]

In 1817 Maria Edgeworth published *Harrington* as an act of personal "atonement" and "reparation." The year before she had received a letter from Rachel Mordecai, an American Jew who wrote to complain of an anti-Semitic portrait in *The Absentee* (1812). In this local and personal incident between a Christian author and a Jewish reader, the shape of an important tradition of English literature was radically altered. Edgeworth was not the first to give us Jewish portraits in the novel (Daniel Defore and Samuel Richardson had already done that), nor was she the first to give us sympathetic Jewish portraits (Richard Cumberland had already done that for the drama, Tobias Smollett for the novel). *Harrington* was the first work in English to inquire into the nature of the representation of Jewish identity, the first not only to record how and why the English literary tradition was especially susceptible to Jewish stereotypes, but also the first to invent the forms by which such stereotypes could be inspected and perhaps overturned. With such claims, I mean to challenge a critical position accepted for several decades now, namely that the tradition of Jewish portraiture in English literature is consistently naive and unself-conscious in its production of stereotypes.

It was Edgeworth's deeply personal motive in writing *Harrington* that made possible the special self-reflexive quality that informs her novel. In the act of reviewing her role as a reader and a writer of anti-Semitic portraits, she was able to recognize a tradition of discourse she had at once inherited and perpetuated. And only by recognizing such a tradition was she able both to subvert it in *Harrington* and to articulate for future writers the way to move beyond it. In short, she boldly turned her personal self-examination into a cultural critique: she diagnosed a disorder in "the imaginations of the good people of England," and in so doing she issued a challenge and founded a new tradition. In *Harrington* Edgeworth inquires into the trials that the English imagination must undergo if it is to exorcise the powerful figure of Shylock, and thereby issues a challenge taken up in subsequent novels (including *Ivanhoe, Our Mutual Friend, Daniel Deronda,* and *Ulysses*): the tradition I am designating "the novel of Jewish identity" attempts to articulate, investigate, and subvert *The Merchant of Venice"*s function as the English master text for representing "the Jew."

But this novelistic tradition also investigates what I will claim is the oldest and most persistent means of representing the Jew, both inside and outside of England, in ancient as well as modern times: the Jew as a figure of conversion. The novel of Jewish identity explores and exposes the ideology of conversion, both as a literary strategy and as a cultural institution. Comic theory, reducing conversion to a literary trope, has tried to aestheticize the idea of conversion, to depoliticize it, to mask its history as a cultural institution. But, as I will show, the figure of the Jew as convert radicalizes and ironizes the trope of conversion by exposing the ideological juncture at which comic form and Christian culture meet.

"Patronizing Shylock": Representing Jewish Identity

In *Harrington* anti-Semitism is seen as a disease passed down from generation to generation through the medium of the printed word. By acknowledging "the indisputable authority of *printed books*," Edgeworth formulates the question of Jewish identity as a question of the *representation* of the Jew and thereby recognizes the immense power of representation in shaping the English response to Jews. Edgeworth's power to found a tradition from this formulation depends at least in part on her claim, taken up by subsequent novelists from Sir Walter Scott to James Joyce, that *The Merchant of Venice* occupies a critical position in the English imagination and in the English national character in general. The simplest evidence for such a claim is the way in which Shakespeare's text invades the novel from *Harrington* to *Ulysses* as a sign of the play's indisputable authority: no portrait of a Jew can exist in English without reference to it, and the English imagination seems unable to free itself of Shakespeare's text. At the same time, the extraordinarily varied means by which Shakespeare's text invades the novel may suggest the capaciousness and subtlety not only of the invading, parasitic text, but also of the host text; each invasion may in fact signal a deliberate introduction of the disorder in order to trap it, to master it, or, to use the parlance of contemporary theory, to deconstruct it. In other words, each trace of the play in the novel of Jewish identity is an ambiguous sign of a battle of the books, part of a battle of mastery over the figure of the Jew. The history of this novelistic tradition needs to chart the strategies that succeeding novelists use in their attempt at once to recognize and to supersede Shakespeare's master text, that is, to chart the development of a cure for the disorder from which the English imagination suffers.

Edgeworth sets the scene for the kind of textual invasion I am describing by having *Harrington* take place at a special moment in history. While numerous historical markers in the novel (such as the Gordon Riots and the Jewish Naturalization Bill) illuminate the nature of "the Jewish question" in the latter half of the eighteenth century, an event in *literary* history characterizes the national consciousness most powerfully for Edgeworth: Charles Macklin's brilliant revival of the role of Shylock, and his restoration of Shakespeare's text to the English stage. When Harrington has difficulty locating a celebrated Jewish scholar he wishes to meet, Harrington's friend Lord Mowbray offers to "console me for the loss of my chance of seeing my Spanish Jew, by introducing me to the most celebrated Jew that ever appeared in England." Mowbray takes Harrington to encounter Macklin's Shylock, so that the most celebrated Jew that ever appeared in England— nay, "'in all Christendom, in the whole civilized world'"— is presented to Harrington as a substitute and replacement for the Jew Harrington sought. "The real, original Jew of Venice," who of course is only the figurative Jew, the Jew as representation, displaces the real Jew, Mr. Montenero: "I returned home full of the Jew of Venice."

Shylock invades the text here by literally interrupting the plot, as if he walks out of the historical past, a digression whose powerful allusiveness derails the main plot line at least temporarily. Here allusion is clothed in flesh and blood: Edgeworth's text gives us not simply a verbal cue to Shylock but the character embodied in the actor who brings him alive on stage every night. Shylock's power to invade the plot of *Harrington* is matched by the power he seems to exert on the actor who plays him. Macklin, for example, is dissolved in the fictional character he plays, as if Shylock's power (according to the conventional anti-

Semitic slur that claims the Jew is contaminating) parasitically invades the actor: Macklin becomes "'Macklin, the honest Jew of Venice'" and "Macklin the Jew." At the same time, Jewish identity itself disappears, or is mysteriously relocated, as if it exists only behind a mask, only in a performance, only through a Christian mediation that confounds and absorbs it: Jewish identity exists somewhere in Macklin's performance of Shylock. The rebirth of Shylock on the stage at the time in this way functions as a historical marker of Edgeworth's point: Shylock perennially holds the English imagination in thrall, perennially mediates, regulates, and displaces Jewish identity for the English mind.

Harrington's use of Shylock as a fictitious master invention that preempts the "real" Jewish characters the author wants to introduce is duplicated in George Eliot's *Daniel Deronda,* when Daniel introduces Mirah to Mrs. Meyrick and her daughters. Not knowing how to introduce a Jew to these unworldly women, he can count on their having read *Ivanhoe* and consoles himself that they "would at once associate a lovely Jewess with Rebecca in 'Ivanhoe.'" Mirah, then, has a secondary life, a belated existence, in relation to Scott's Rebecca, just as all Jews have a belated existence in relation to "the real, original Jew of Venice." Both in *Harrington* and *Daniel Deronda,* we meet examples of representation to the second power. A fictitious representation (Shylock and Rebecca) takes priority over another fictitious representation that is supposed to be real (Montenero and Mirah) in the world of the novel; and the prior fictitious representation assumes the power of the "original" and the "real." Priority in such a case signals both temporal priority (Shylock predates Montenero) and "signifying" priority (Shylock is the paradigm by which we understand and measure all other Jews). This technique of representation to the second power manages to call into question, in a particularly sophisticated way in the hands of such novelists as Edgeworth and Eliot, the very nature of representation, especially the representation of the racial Other. When Daniel Deronda, for example, reflects on "'whether one oftener learns to love real objects through their representations or the representations through the real objects,'" his comment functions as a gloss on Eliot's self-conscious handling of her role as a (belated) novelist of Jewish identity: in England, where the Jew is primarily a figure of the imagination and where Shylock holds the place of priority, do we learn to *hate* real Jews through their representations? And what would it mean to learn to *love* a real Jewish woman through Rebecca? With such questions this novelistic tradition explores, and ultimately seeks to control, the authority by which "printed books" construct paradigms that nurture racial hatred and perhaps even racial desire.

For this reason the central rhetorical strategy of the novel of Jewish identity is allusion: each "new" novel that comes on the scene is embedded with references to its predecessors, because each "new" novel inspects the representations of Jewish identity that precede it. I include in the category of allusion the revisionary practice of recalling and reinventing the entire shape of earlier works: the way in which, for example, in *Our Mutual Friend* and *Daniel Deronda,* the education of the characters is staged as a conflict between love and money, where characters undergo their moral trials, or receive their rewards, in casket scenes that reinvent the famous casket scene in *The Merchant of Venice;* or the way in which, in the final chapter of *Daniel Deronda,* Eliot meticulously reworks the final chapter of *Ivanhoe,* so that Scott's love triangle (Rowena, Rebecca, Ivanhoe) is replaced by Eliot's (Mirah, Gwendolen, Daniel), while in both novels the rejected woman (the Jew in Scott's version, the Christian in Eliot's) offers a final parting memento to the married couple as the Jewish characters depart from England.

In *Harrington* allusion takes an especially complicated form because Edgeworth alludes both to her own former work and to a much larger tradition of Jewish portraiture. In this way Edgeworth is able to acknowledge that she is already a contributor to a tradition she now wishes to forswear and repudiate. It must be the central irony of Edgeworth's literary life—and perhaps an irony that became a central motive behind the writing of *Harrington*—that those texts that were praised for their sympathetic understanding of an oppressed race (in the case of the Irish) are precisely the texts that caused her to be justly accused of intolerance (in the case of the Jews). This sense of painful irony lies unusually close to the surface of *Harrington* in a remarkable passage in which Edgeworth takes responsibility for writing the kind of book that nurtures prejudice in the young child's mind. She admits this at the very moment when she is almost universally known, in England, America, and on the Continent, not only for her tolerant pictures of the Irish but also for her immensely influential pedagogical works (co-authored with her father) and the celebrated *Moral Tales for Young People* (1801). Harrington recognizes that "in almost every work of fiction, I found them [Jews] represented as hateful beings; nay, even in modern tales of very late years, since I have come to man's estate, I have met with books by authors professing candour and toleration—books written expressly for the rising generation, called, if I mistake not, Moral Tales for Young People." In *Harrington,* then, the strategy of allusion does not eschew self-allusion, even self-punishment. Late in the novel Edgeworth reveals covertly, in a dramatic scene between Harrington and his father, the proper punishment and penitence for her own earlier mistakes. Harrington forces his father to acknowledge that "'your words were a libel upon Jews and Jewesses; and the most appropriate and approved punishment invented for the libeller is—to eat his own words.'" Edgeworth conceives of *Harrington* as an act of reparation precisely insofar as she uses the novel to eat her own former words.

The more typical form that allusion takes in the novel of Jewish identity suggests a similar kind of self-conscious irony, as if in acknowledgment of the fact that writing about Jewish identity as a Christian means occupying a position outside the culture one attempts to represent. The point of departure for such a project is always the same: one must master those prior texts that have presumed to represent Jewish identity. An ironic version of this kind of mastery is explicitly dramatized in *Harrington* when, in order to impress the Monteneros,

> Lord Mowbray appeared to be deeply interested and deeply read in every thing that had been written in their [the Jews'] favour.

> He rummaged over Tovey and Ockley; and "Priestley's Letters to the Jews," and "The Letters of certain Jews to M. de Voltaire," were books which he now continually quoted in conversation. . . . nor could he ever adequately extol Cumberland's benevolent "Jew," or Lessing's "Nathan the Wise." Quotations from one or the other were continually in readiness. . . . This I could also perceive to be an imitation of what he had seen *succeed* with me.

In this passage Harrington condones his own mastery of such works but mocks Lord Mowbray's. As a reflection on Edgeworth's own project in *Harrington,* this passage is at once serious and self-mocking. Edgeworth seems to present her own credentials as a writer about Jewish identity at the same time that she is embarrassed at doing so. This is an anxiety that dominates perhaps the fullest representation of Jews by a non-Jewish writer in English literature, Eliot's *Daniel Deronda,* and in part accounts for the massive learning that buttresses that novel. In any case, the pattern is founded here in *Harrington:* each new novel in this tradition acknowledges the prior texts in the tradition, so that each new novel becomes a kind of storehouse of the materials necessary to write a Jewish story. By the time we get to *Daniel Deronda* and *Ulysses,* this particular practice of allusion becomes encyclopedic; at the same time, in the case of *Ulysses,* we realize that Joyce is not a radical innovator in the matter of (Judaic) allusion but in fact represents only a late stage in the recycling of Jewish materials already alluded to by novelists such as Edgeworth and Eliot.

Harrington provides us with a special theoretical framework within which to explore the system of intertextual allusions by which Jewish identity is inscribed, transmitted, and recirculated. After meeting Macklin, Harrington's appetite to see the actor's celebrated Shylock is satisfied only when Mrs. Harrington promises to take her son "to patronize Shylock." The phrase has the kind of resonance I am suggesting is the hallmark of *Harrington,* managing at once to represent, literally and locally, for Edgeworth's protagonist, the purchase of a theater ticket, but figuratively, for the entire tradition of texts that reinvents Shylock, a specific but nonetheless suggestive intertextual transaction. To patronize Shylock—to protect, support, and favor him, whether in the act of patronage generally or in the specific business transaction that makes us his customer—is what we do when we purchase a ticket to see him, or write a novel in which we uphold him (as Edgeworth did in *The Absentee,* where Mordicai follows in Shylock's footsteps by requiring "'the bond or the body'"). The specific economic meaning of the term "patronize" manages to place the entire history of allusions to Shylock within the context of the most patent stereotype the novel of Jewish identity has to confront: the Jew as peddler, usurer, banker, and so on. And from one angle, the idea of "patronizing Shylock" manages to maintain this stereotype: part of Shylock's power over us is made manifest by our continuing to patronize him, by the interest—economic and emotional—we reinvest periodically in his character. The bond from which Shylock refused to release Antonio has become the bond from which Shylock refuses to release the English imagination and the English pocketbook.

But the subversive uses to which Edgeworth puts this idea of "patronizing Shylock" reveal the Jew not as the originator and controller of such transactions but as the figure of value that Christian authors manipulate and exploit. Mr. Montenero explains, during his first meeting with Harrington, how "'in the *true* story, from which Shakespeare took the plot of the Merchant of Venice, it was a Christian who acted the part of the Jew, and the Jew that of the Christian; it was a Christian who insisted upon having the pound of flesh from next the Jew's heart. But . . . Shakespeare was right, as a dramatic poet, in reversing the characters.'" Instead of being the ur-text, *The Merchant of Venice* is already part of a tradition of intertexts, so that what we have inherited as the truth about Jew and Christian is exposed as merely a textual representation, and a textual "misrepresentation" at that. The purely textual quality of these figures, Jew and Christian, is made apparent by Montenero's sophisticated intertextual argument that Shakespeare did not draw his characters or plot from life but from another text, and what is more, that he drew falsely from the prior text; it was his "business" to exploit the prejudices of his time, an exploitation that has "cost" the Jews dearly: "'it was his business, I acknowledge, to take advantage of the popular prejudice as a *power*.'" In this view, Shakespeare is caught engaging in a business transaction in which the writer uses the Jew to his own advantage. In a crucial role reversal, Shakespeare becomes the extortionist Shylock—not only here, in Montenero's analysis, but also in Stephen Dedalus's analysis a century later in *Ulysses:* "He [Shakespeare] drew Shylock out of his own long pocket. . . . He sued a fellowplayer for the price of a few bags of malt and exacted his pound of flesh in interest for every money lent." Edgeworth and Joyce, then, embed their novels not simply with allusions to Shakespeare's play but with critics of that play who call into question the motives behind the representation of Jewish identity. And virtually anyone who profits from Shylock is seen as exploiting the role of the Jew (while masking his or her own economic motives behind the persona of Shylock), including the actor who plays the role of Shylock. Mowbray tells Harrington, "'Macklin, the honest Jew of Venice, has got the pound, or whatever number of pounds he wanted to get from the manager's heart.'"

Finally, the idea of patronizing Shylock calls to mind the history of the institution of patronage. The patron plays the role of "a defender before a court of justice," almost as if he or she were called on to play the role of Portia as the final arbiter of the conflict between Christian and Jew. But in the position of advocacy, the patron is designated as a guardian of a foreign and displaced Other whose dependence on the patron is demeaning: a patron is "a citizen under whose protection a resident alien placed himself, and who transacted legal business for him and was responsible to the state for his conduct." Patronage itself is a complicated transaction: patrons give their protection "in return for certain services," and those writers who set out to authorize their own version of "the Jew" are always in danger of serving themselves, whether inadvertently or not, by patronizing Jewish identity.

The Primal Scene

Harrington at first appears to be no more than the record of a single, and singularly odd, case history—the story of a child who suffers through several stages of anti-Semitism. But Edgeworth's bold experiment uses a complicated psychological portrait of this deeply troubled child—that is, an investigation into the origins and development of a childhood neurosis—to attempt a cultural critique that questions religious and national values. Edgeworth manages this critique by implicating the national consciousness, and especially the writer's role in this consciousness, in her title character's disorder, which she calls "Jewish insanity." The term "Jewish insanity" ambiguously identifies both the virulent form of the child's anti-Semitism and, after his "cure," what one might call his philo-Semitism, or what his family and friends view as his obsession with Jews, "the constancy" of his "Israelitish taste"; Harrington seems always, in the words of a longtime acquaintance, to be "'intent upon a Jew.'" The exaggerated poles of Harrington's feelings suggest that in either case the Jew functions purely as a figure of the imagination, even as a fetish, and that both of Harrington's responses, whether of dread or desire, are forms of "Jewish insanity."

In the powerful opening pages of *Harrington,* the first-person narrator delineates the means by which he became, at the age of six years, the "slave, and . . . victim" of his nursery maid. With its emphasis on the "history of the mental and corporeal ills of my childhood," and specifically on the pathogenic effect of a critical scene of childhood, this opening is an early romantic harbinger of Freud. In the narrator's declaration of the importance of the conjunction of "the science of morals and of medicine," and in his apologetic and defensive encouragement that we will see "some connexion between these apparently puerile details and subjects of higher importance," he justifies the mainstay of his entire project with the same tone that Freud used when he argued for the importance of early childhood impressions, their power to create a childhood neurosis, and their enduring effects later in life: "We must be content to begin at the beginning, if we would learn the history of our own minds; we must condescend to be even as little children, if we would discover or recollect those small causes which early influence the imagination, and afterwards become strong habits, prejudices, and passions." What is especially remarkable in Edgeworth's enterprise is the attempt to record and to publish the origins of racial prejudice in a child, and to use this case history at once as a self-indictment and an indictment of her culture. In using the psychology of the individual to articulate the psychology of an entire nation or culture, Edgeworth anticipates the kind of study that Freud attempted first in *Totem and Taboo* (1913), when he applied the methods of psychoanalysis to a problem in *Völkerpsychologie,* and for the last time in *Moses and Monotheism* (1939), when the enterprise of *Völkerpsychologie* took as its subject the Jewish people, in a work whose initial generic description (*The man Moses, an historical novel*) makes its kinship with Edgeworth's novel all the more palpable.

In Edgeworth's hands, the principles of late eighteenth-century psychology, and especially the vocabulary of associationism, become the tools by which she records the primal scene in a case history of a child's (erotic) enslavement. Not surprisingly, then, the event around which Edgeworth chooses to construct the primal scene bears a remarkable similarity to Wordsworth's description, in book 7 of *The Prelude,* of the wonderful but shocking experience of arriving in London—only for Harrington this occurs at age six. The opening paragraph of the novel relates the arrival in London through the narrator's explanation, in the language Edgeworth had learned from late eighteenth-century psychology and poetry, of how "my senses had been excited, and almost exhausted, by the vast variety of objects that were new to me." And as in the most memorable spot of time in Wordsworth's London, the poet's encounter with the blind beggar, Harrington's imagination is seized by "the face and figure of an old man." But unlike the blind beggar, this old man would have had little, if any, effect on the protagonist's mind were it not for a mediating figure, the boy's nursery maid, Fowler. In fact, the boy's fleeting initial impression of the old man suggests "a good-natured countenance." But the nursery maid, unable to get the boy to bed, issues a threat that seizes the boy's "fancy" with "terror": "'If you don't come quietly this minute, Master Harrington,' said she, 'I'll call to Simon the Jew there,' pointing to him, 'and he shall come up and carry you away in his great bag.'" Fowler's action is chilling because we recognize in it a simple pedagogical act, grotesquely distorted. By pointing to the man, and designating him with a name, especially with a class name, and finally attaching this name to a rapacious act, the nursery maid produces on the boy's imagination an association of ideas (to use the terminology of David Hartley that so influenced Edgeworth and her father) that miseducates the child and misrepresents the old man in particular and Jews in general. This act of naming, specifically of classifying and libeling, is the first of a variety of forms of anti-Semitism that the narrative will explore. Nonetheless, the special status of this scene is clear: it is the narrative's point of departure, and the fixing moment of Harrington's early life, the primal scene with which his mature life will be burdened.

Much of the power of the opening scenes of *Harrington* depends on the fact that Harrington, in the present telling of his tale, is actually breaking a prohibition against telling, a kind of taboo that emerges from the primal scene. Fowler manages, after successfully embroidering the image of the rapacious Jew over a period of hours and days, to make the boy "promise that I would never tell any body the secret she had communicated"—namely, the secret acts by which Jews "steal poor children for the purpose of killing, crucifying, and sacrificing them." But what she really hides, by sealing the child's lips, are the secret means by which she has nurtured racial terror in the child. Fowler, whose power is sounded in her own name—to foul, to perform the act of libelous naming—is at the same time the force of repression: she requires the oath of silence that hides her power and allows that power to grow in the unconscious and unspoken mind of the child. The ban of silence under which the boy lies is the place within which neurotic terror multiplies. At the same time, the narrative that we read becomes the most patent sign of his eventual recuperation and liberation.

As an etiology of the disease of racial terror, the narrative makes clear its own power to expose the processes by which such terror is born, nurtured, and eventually cured. The single moment that precedes the boy's seeing of the old-clothes man becomes, in this sense, an allegory by which the remainder of the narrative may be read. The first sense impression that the boy records on his London trip is the inexplicable appearance of stars of light in a quick succession not far from his balcony. The eventual discovery of the lamplighter as the cause of this wonder leads the boy to experience "as much delight as philosopher ever enjoyed in discovering the cause of a new and grand phenomenon." The second wonder the child experiences, and the one that shapes his later life—the figure of the Jew (that is, Fowler's use of this figure)—is subjected to the same scrutiny of cause and effect over the course of the entire narrative. It is in this sense that the entire narrative is meant to be a demystification of the origins of prejudice and racial terror, whose secrets will be exposed (as in the example of the lamplighter) once we see the human cause behind an apparently inexplicable phenomenon. To discover its human cause is to put to rout one of the leading ideas about racial hatred at the time, represented by Harrington's mother—namely, that racial hatred may be no more than a "natural antipathy" behind which lies no social or cultural cause.

The boy's promise never to tell is represented in a special terminology that deepens, from the start, the Jewish theme in this novel: the promise is "extorted" from the boy. In other words, the promise is not simply *about* Jews but is secured through an act that takes the form of a conventional anti-Semitic stereotype, only here it is Fowler, the anti-Semite, who is the extortionist, the Shylock who exacts an excessive price for his bond. Moreover, Edgeworth moves the trademark of anti-Semitic literature—namely, the scene of business transaction and exchange—to the beginning of the novel, placing the Jew outside this scene, in precisely the manner Eliot will some decades later, in the famous opening scene of Gwendolen's gambling in *Daniel Deronda.* In other words, while the initial social experience of *Harrington* is centered on a transaction—the enslavement and extortion of a child—Edgeworth shows the way in which the Jew is used, purely as a figure, in such a transaction. In fact, the picture that Fowler gives of the Jew in order to terrorize the child—she tells him "stories of Jews who had been known to steal poor children"—suggests her own enslavement and extortion of Harrington, and her profound alienation of the child from his parents and the rest of the household. The "Jew," in this sense, is quite literally no more than an extension of her own acts and motives.

Once the child's terror (but not its cause) becomes known to his parents, different forms of anti-Semitism are carefully articulated within the domain of the family along the lines of gender. The child's life is shuttled between his mother's and his father's radically different "cures" for his disorder. Both parents are unable to account for their child's sudden change in temper, his sleeplessness, his fits of terror, his tantrums, all of which seize the household with the same inexplicable suddenness they exert in that paradigm of case histories, the case of the Wolf Man—only in *Harrington* no one suspects the nursery maid as the culprit. Harrington's mother, eventually getting a half-confession out of her son (only the reader of *Harrington* knows the entire story), discovers Jews (and not Fowler) as the source of her son's disorder. She and her physician take his terror of Jews as "'the genuine temperament of genius,'" and the boy, who becomes a replica of his mother—"a woman of weak health, delicate nerves, and a kind of morbid sensibility"—is made to "exhibit" his fears to family friends and the fashionable world of London generally.

The father enters the narrative suddenly in order to restore his son's manhood. Absent from the scene of enslavement and the opening chapters of the narrative, the ghostly father ("My father—for all this time, though I have never mentioned him, I had a father living") enters the narrative with the decree that the boy "should be taken out of the hands of the women." Scorning what he calls "the whole *female* doctrine . . . of sympathies and antipathies," and accusing the women of "making . . . a Miss Molly of his boy," the father repossesses the child at the same time that he takes charge of his gender: it is the father's job "to make a man of me." This takes the form of changing the boy's (feminine) terror of Jews to his (masculine) violence against them. In other words, Edgeworth shows us two radically different forms of behavior toward Jews but nonetheless indicts both as forms of anti-Semitism. Now under the influence of his father, Harrington reports that "the Jews were represented to me as the lowest, meanest, vilest of mankind, and a conversion of fear into contempt was partially effected in my mind," until finally "fear and contempt" became "hatred"—in short, until the acquisition of "manly ideas" was complete. Needless to say, the father succeeds not in curing his child's disorder but in advancing it to a different, even more noxious, stage.

For the fullest understanding of the relation between the different stages of Harrington's anti-Semitism and his sexual identity, we must look forward to the way in which *Harrington* recalls and revises *The Merchant of Venice*. At this point it is sufficient to recall that Shylock's celebrated knife-whetting and his threat of the pound of flesh (both mentioned in *Harrington*) represent the Jew as a threat to Christian male identity and as an obstacle to the

happy Christian nuptials in Shakespeare's play. In *Harrington,* in the primal scene of the child's victimization, the nursery maid uses the figure of the Jew to reduce the boy to a "Miss Molly" who can barely leave his bed because of the nervous disorder that is marked specifically as feminine. It remains to be seen how the question of Harrington's manhood succeeds in linking the primal scene at the beginning of the narrative to the marriage plot at the end—and thereby succeeds in linking the plot of *Harrington* with the plot of *The Merchant of Venice.*

The Return of the Repressed

Both Shakespeare and Edgeworth employ the traditional marriage plot of comedy, in which the suitor undergoes a series of trials before winning the woman's (or heiress's) hand. But *Harrington* takes the Christian love plot at the center of Shakespeare's play and gives it to the Jewish characters: Portia and her father become, in Edgeworth's revision, Berenice and Mr. Montenero. In both cases the father protects his rich daughter from fortune hunters at the same time that he finds her a husband who values her properly. But now the Jew, not the Christian, is the teacher of value, testing which suitor will choose lead over gold, will take his daughter "'at all hazards,'" in a reprise of the lead casket's message, "'Who chooseth me must give and hazard all he hath.'"

The obvious obstacle to the hero's success, both in *The Merchant of Venice* and *Harrington,* has hidden behind it other obstacles, some of which the hero can hardly understand himself. In short, the obstacle to the marriage plot in both works is overdetermined and finally suggests a subtle critique of the hero. In this way the obstacle is seen not simply as an external circumstance but also as an element of the hero's character, even as another side of his character. In Shakespeare's play, for example, the money to go courting, and even the solution to the paternal riddle of the caskets, are easily found, only to make Portia realize, when the news of Antonio's impending death interrupts the marriage plans of the young couple, that no marriage (or at least no consummation) with her new husband will be possible until the deep bond he has with Antonio is resolved (and sublimated); and this of course leads to another obstacle, the ring plot, which Portia initiates to set her own trial of her husband, and which Bassanio fails miserably.

The obstacle to the hero's success in *Harrington* appears, even to Harrington's own understanding, as if it will be the difference in religion between himself and Berenice Montenero, but as we will see at the end of the novel, this proves not to be the case. Without knowing it, Harrington has become the victim of a plot to discredit his character. An exaggerated and damning account of his early childhood disorder is made known to the Monteneros and thereby plays on Berenice's horror of insanity, especially of marrying an insane man (as one of her friends has done). This is the unknown obstacle that stands in Harrington's way. But even behind this obstacle stands another: the anti-Semitism that Harrington thinks he has entirely conquered.

The source of the damaging account that has been lodged against Harrington is Fowler: the nursery maid reenters the narrative twenty years later to repeat her earlier crime. The libel against Simon now becomes the libel against Harrington. In other words, Harrington is required to suffer a repetition—now in the role of the Jew—of the initiating moment of his own narrative. The novel has established, in numerous earlier incidents, that the primary crime the Jew suffers is libel, and Harrington knows this firsthand, because he is the vindicator of the Jew in every case (except in the original case of Simon). Harrington passes his earlier trials with ease by being "the champion of the Jews" and proving their innocence against false accusations (while proving his own tolerance)—more than once for Jacob, and at least once for Mr. Montenero. These trials, we now realize, have hidden behind them a deeper trial: to play the role of the Jew, and not merely to save him from a position of strength, but to suffer what he suffers. In this way the suitor's obstacle, the libel lodged against him, leads to a profound psychological trial, making Harrington suffer the role of the Jew, as if this trial were in fact his preparation for marrying a Jew. Moreover, if Harrington's anti-Semitism originated in his belief in the libel against Simon, then the compensatory justice of this tale requires that Harrington suffer from the same crime, initiated by the same woman. We should not forget that this strategy of compensation appears in a text offered as "atonement" and "reparation" for its author's own acts of libel.

Once he discovers it, Harrington portrays the libel against himself as though it constituted merely an external circumstance, but I am suggesting that it represents his most important trial, one whose psychological grounds are at once relevant and profound. The text makes this clear by underscoring the genuine power that Fowler still has over Harrington—her power is not merely accidental, coincidental, but psychological. Her libel of him represents the power she still maintains over him through the primal scene. In short, I am arguing that Fowler's return in the narrative, twenty years later, represents the return of the repressed: as Harrington puts it, "I was carried back so far, so forcibly." While Harrington periodically declares to us that his early trauma and his early prejudice have long been outgrown, Fowler reenters the text to prove otherwise. She corroborates what Mr. Montenero half suspects—that Harrington "had conquered what is so difficult, scarcely possible, completely to conquer—an early prepossession." Harrington correctly reads this remark as a concealed fear that he might "relapse."

Fowler's reappearance is only one return in a plot characterized by many. Along with Fowler's return after twenty years, Mowbray, Jacob, and a number of other characters make dramatic returns to the plot after long absences. And Edgeworth's representation of Macklin's revival of *The Merchant of Venice* is a way of marking the return of "the Jew / That Shakespeare drew." Moreover, the entire narrative impetus of Harrington can be seen as an impulse to return: Harrington, as narrator, returns to the critical scene of childhood, while Edgeworth, in a reinvention of the plot of *The Merchant of Venice,* returns to the English pre-text of the novel of Jewish identity. In both cases, there is a return to the scene of a crime. In this way the return of the repressed is located in **Harrington** in both of the ways Freud began to define it in *Moses and Monotheism:* in the individual case history and, more important, in the national case history. Freud's tentative approach to redefining the return of the repressed from the point of view of *Völkerpsychologie* takes the following form: "What is in question is something in a people's life which is past, lost to view, superseded and which we venture to compare with what is repressed in the mental life of an individual." English anti-Semitism, according to Edgeworth, takes precisely this form:

> In our enlightened days, and in the present improved state of education, it may appear incredible that any nursery-maid could be so wicked as to relate, or any child of six years old so foolish as to credit, such tales; but I am speaking of what happened many years ago: nursery-maids and children, I believe, are very different now from what they were then; and in further proof of the progress of human knowledge and reason, we may recollect that many of these very stories of the Jews, which we now hold too preposterous for the infant and the nursery-maid to credit, were some centuries ago universally believed by the English nation.

Within the context of this half-hearted, and at best ironic, characterization of the history of English attitudes toward the Jews, Edgeworth is bent on showing the way in which, in the words of Freud, "the psychical precipitates of the primaeval period [in a people's life] became inherited property which, in each fresh generation, called not for acquisition but only for awakening," and the way in which *The Merchant of Venice* functions at once as the cause and the symptom of this national awakening, this national relapse. It is in this light that the trial of Harrington as a suitable husband for Berenice may be read as the trial of England: "'Do you think we have not an Englishman good enough for her?,'" Mr. Montenero is asked, as he threatens to take Berenice back to America, where she has grown up in an environment of tolerance.

Fowler quite literally represents the power of repression from the moment she extorts from the boy his oath of silence: it is at this early point that she becomes the secret enemy of the entire narrative enterprise of **Harrington**. And now she reenters the tale to prevent its traditional climax, the marriage of hero and heroine. She reenters the narrative at the decisive moment of Harrington's suit of Berenice because, as the return of the repressed, she represents those symptoms that might make his marriage impossible—not simply because the Monteneros might believe the libel against him, but because he may be genuinely unfit to marry Berenice. Fowler represents, in other words, the potential power to return Harrington to his childhood terror, to make him a child forever, and therefore she reenters the narrative to prevent him from proving his manhood by winning the prize of the beautiful heiress. As the unknown libeler of Harrington's character, Fowler is the power of the unconscious, making us see that the exaggerated charge against Harrington—the bald accusation that he is insane—contains a significant germ of truth, and thereby returning us to the rather specialized meaning such a disorder has in Lord Mowbray's mock diagnosis of Harrington's "Jewish insanity."

In *Harrington,* then, the conventional proof of the hero's manhood—his winning of the maiden's hand—is overlaid with the question of the hero's "Jewish insanity," the debilitating disorder that not only would make "a Jewess" an impossible mate for this hero, but would make the hero himself more woman than man, a "Miss Molly" unable to win a woman's hand. In this way Edgeworth radically revises *The Merchant of Venice.* The anti-Semitism of Shakespeare's play requires that the Jew function as a central obstacle to the marriage plot: Shylock holds Antonio's bond, and thereby holds Bassanio's love in stalemate, so that the Jew's knife threatens the castration of Bassanio as well as Antonio. The Jew, in *The Merchant of Venice,* quite literally stands in the way of the consummation of Bassanio's marriage to Portia, so that the pound of flesh the Jew requires is empowered to prevent that Christian regeneration which is the climax of Shakespeare's comedy. In *Harrington,* on the other hand, it is anti-Semitism itself that functions as a critical obstacle: is Harrington sufficiently recovered from his "Jewish insanity" to love Berenice, to court her, to make her a successful husband, and will he be subject to relapses—to the return of the repressed? The hero's manhood, then, is equated with his overcoming his racial terror, not converting it to racial violence (as his father teaches him to do). In this way the entirety of *The Merchant of Venice* is recast: not only is the Jew no longer on trial (literally in act 4 and figuratively throughout the course of Shakespeare's play), in *Harrington* the Christian is on trial, vis-à-vis the Jew. The test of value the hero of *Harrington* must pass, for himself and for his nation, is the test of anti-Semitism.

The most profound aspect of Harrington's trial, therefore, is conducted as a drama of the unconscious. For Edgeworth as for Freud, the repressed material of the primal scene erupts through the medium of dreams. Puzzled by the mysterious obstacle that Mr. Montenero tells him stands in his way, Harrington, after presenting his suit to his intended father-in-law, has a dream: "I saw beside my bed the old figure of Simon the Jew; but he spoke to me with the voice and in the words of Mr. Montenero." The dream gives Harrington the clue he seeks, but in a language he cannot understand: Simon, not the bride's father, is the obstacle to Harrington's suit. In other words, the child's primitive terror of Jews, generated through Fowler's manipulation of the figure of Simon, stands in the young lover's way twenty years later. A similar dream occurs earlier, just after Harrington meets and falls in love with Berenice: "During the whole of the night, sleeping or waking, the images of the fair Jewess [and] of Shylock . . . were continually recurring, and turning into one another." Simon, the individual Jew, is cancelled in the conventional sign of racial terror and prejudice, just

as earlier, when the street beggars try to impersonate Simon, they mimic "the traditionary representations and vulgar notions of a malicious, revengeful, ominous looking Shylock as ever whetted his knife." In this dream, Shylock stands in the way of Harrington's suit by possessing the power to cancel Berenice's beauty and grace; he does so by realizing a specific side of Harrington's anti-Semitic fear, namely that every Jew (even Berenice) turns into Shylock in the long run. In Harrington's unacknowledged anti-Semitism, then, Shylock returns from *The Merchant of Venice* to prevent another marriage.

Fowler demonstrates the power of the return of the repressed when she reactivates the primal scene not simply by reinventing the scandalous tale in hints she drops in the presence of the Monteneros, but by restaging it and thereby reproducing in Harrington his childish terror. During his visit to a synagogue, for instance, where he hopes to catch a glimpse of Berenice (and to demonstrate his credentials of Jewish tolerance), Harrington suffers a relapse: "Just as I had taken out my purse, I was struck by the sight of a face and figure that had terrible power over my associations—a figure exactly resembling one of the most horrible of the Jewish figures which used to haunt me when I was a child. . . . I was so much surprised and startled by this apparition, that a nervous tremor seized me in every limb. I let the purse, which I had in my hand, fall upon the ground." The dropped purse signals the failure of compensation, both economic and psychological; it signals the failure of another version of the attempt to "patronize Shylock." While his mother tried to cure his childish terror by bribing Simon (and his impersonators, dressed as Shylock), Harrington is about to reproduce the same strategy in his patronage of the Jewish community at the synagogue, but he is interrupted by the apparition from his past. I am suggesting that we see Harrington's intended contribution at the synagogue as a special form of the psychological mechanism Freud called "overcompensation": Harrington's childhood terror of Jews is "repudiated, and even overcompensated, but in the end establishes itself once more." The power that prevents this compensation—that is, the power that comes to light in the end as the return of the repressed—is Fowler. Harrington eventually learns that it was she who returned him to his childish terror in the synagogue: "Fowler had dressed up the figure for the purpose."

But *Harrington* does not refuse the idea of compensation outright. Instead, the novel chooses to specify the form that compensation should take. Instead of paying in coin, Harrington must pay in feeling, specifically in pain. This recalls Shylock's rejection of Bassanio and Portia's offers to pay him three times the sum Antonio owes him; Shylock chooses another form of compensation, namely to make the Christian learn what it is to be in the Jew's power, since the Jew always experiences what it is to be in the Christian's power. Antonio and Bassanio both compensate Shylock in the pain they suffer when unable to meet Shylock's demands. In *Harrington* the entire trial of the hero (including his defense of himself against libel) is characterized by Mr. Montenero as just this sort of compensation: he justifies the pain it has "cost" Harrington by asking rhetorically, "'do you think that the trial cost *me,* cost *us* no pain?'"

Mr. Montenero, as the prospective father-in-law, sets Harrington one final trial, one final cost he must pay: "'it will cost you present pain,'" he warns Harrington, as he asks him to see Fowler one final time in order to forgive her. This forgiveness functions as the final step in the casting out of Fowler, that is, in conquering Harrington's phobia, in mastering the primal scene. Fowler makes a full confession of her plot to libel Harrington, and in so doing makes public the power that until now has remained secret, repressed. Once forgiven, Fowler is given the fate that the Jews themselves typically suffer: exile. While Daniel and Mirah's exile at the end of *Daniel Deronda* is voluntary, and Rebecca and Isaac's at the end of *Ivanhoe* is more or less voluntary, Fowler's exile is involuntary. In **Harrington,** Fowler's exile quite literally takes the place of the exile that the Jews were about to impose on themselves: due to the impending failure to find an English husband for Berenice, Mr. Montenero and his daughter were about to return to America, but now Fowler "'sails tomorrow in the vessel which was to have taken us to America.'"

The Figurative Conversion of Jewish Identity

The sudden departure of the Jewish characters (or Fowler in their place) is not solely, or even primarily, a solution to the formal problem of closure in these novels. These departures are important political markers: they locate the position the Jewish minority occupies in relation to the hegemonic or Christian community. In the tradition of comedy, in which the regeneration of the community is represented through a festive wedding at the end, the departure of the Jew signals that he or she has no place in the reconstituted community. In *The Merchant of Venice,* for example, Shylock's sudden and painfully urgent exit, while not represented as a literal exile, works perhaps even more powerfully through understatement and anticlimax. As he leaves the stage for the last time and disappears from the world of the play, Shylock implores, "I pray you give me leave to go from hence. / I am not well." Having been assigned the role of blocking the regeneration of the Christian community by blocking the act of consummation itself, the Jew in Shakespeare's comedy has no place in the festive reunion and incipient conjugals of the young couples in act 5. But in **Harrington,** where the reconstitution of the community suggests that the racial prejudices of the past (and especially of the hero's parents) are superseded in the young married couple, the exile of the anti-Semite (in place of the Jewish characters) appears to signal a radical turning point in the position of the Jew at the comic climax. Here the Jew is located within the community instead of outside it.

But when we are told at the end of **Harrington** that Berenice is no Jew but a Christian, we come upon a covert form—at once literary and cultural—by which Jewish identity is once again exiled: Berenice's suddenly disclosed Christianity is a way of converting her. I must acknowledge immediately that comedy, like the Christian community it reflects and upholds, offers the conversion of Jewish identity as an alternative to the Jew's exile. Conversion is, after all, the culturally established means by which the Jew is allowed to enter the community. Nonetheless I will argue that the two alternatives that face the Jew, exile or conversion, are in fact the same. But first I wish to identify conversion as a critical trope in comedy and to explain the way in which the Jew exposes the ideological structure of comedy precisely insofar as he or she functions as a figure of conversion.

The sudden unveiling of Berenice's true identity—what I am calling her conversion—is in fact precisely the kind of event that is identified and designated as "conversion" in standard comic terminology, only without the political implications I will give it. Northrop Frye, for example, locates "conversion" at the heart of comic form: "Unlikely conversions, miraculous transformations, and providential assistance are inseparable from comedy." One could read the sudden disclosure of Berenice's Christianity, then, entirely from within the position that views comedy as a purely formal or mythic system. But such a reading is possible only because theorists of comedy understand conversion in a purely figurative sense, as a formal trope, a sudden "twist in the plot," with no cultural or historical signification. Comic theory neglects or erases the meaning the Jew brings to the idea of conversion because the theory of comedy itself is written from within a Christian perspective: "The action of comedy, like the action of the Christian Bible, moves from law to liberty"; even "the crudest of Plautine comedy-formulas has much the same *structure* as the central Christian myth itself"; and Dante's *Commedia,* as the title makes clear, is the central paradigm of the form.

But in a text where Jewish identity is being represented, the reduction of conversion to a purely formal or aesthetic category is no longer possible: the Jewish characters in the text will not allow it, politicizing at once the concept of conversion and the entire shape of comedy. Unable to escape the historic shadow of conversion as a cultural institution, carrying with them the memory of when "'our people were slaughtered wholesale if they wouldn't be baptised wholesale,'" the Jewish characters require us to investigate the variety of ways in which conversion functions ideologically in comic form. It is in this light that I pose the following question: what are the consequences of recognizing that conversion is at once the master trope of a powerful genre (comedy) and the master institution of a powerful culture (Christianity)?

I wish to examine first the way in which the Jew as a figure of conversion functions to test the idea of comic transformation. As a potential convert, the Jew functions as a harbinger of personal transformation, even of radical change. This means that the success or failure with which the Christian community converts the Jew can be used to uphold or undermine the other personal transformations that work at the heart of comedy. In *The Merchant of Venice* we find the locus classicus of this idea when the religious conversions of Jessica (voluntary) and Shylock (involuntary) become a means of interrogating those conversions that we take for granted as the backbone of comic plotting, such as the conversion of property and identity signaled in Portia's relinquishment of herself to Bassanio: "Myself, and what is mine, to you and yours / Is now *converted*" (my emphasis). Does woman occupy the same position as the Jew in an institution that legitimates and facilitates the transfer of her property and her personal identity? Is marriage a kind of conversion?

With such questions we see the way in which the Jew functions to expose the conventions of comic transformation that he or she is meant to serve. In *The Merchant of Venice,* for example, the glaring absence of Shylock after he is ordered to convert tests the limits of personal transformation and of comic resolution: the new or transformed community can claim Shylock in name only. The ideology of conversion, and by extension the ideology of comic form, becomes a brutal erasure of one identity (Jew) in the name of another (Christian). What other kinds, how many other kinds, of conversion does the ideology of the "regenerate," or hegemonic, community require?

It is in this way that Shylock's sudden exit, on receiving the order that "he presently become a Christian," exposes conversion and exile as the single, the sole, alternative that the Christian community offers the Jew. Shylock's failure to reappear, his manifest absence from the stage during act 5, makes of the converted Jew something between a ghost and a pure hypothesis: after conversion the Jew has neither eyes, hands, organs, dimensions, senses; no longer can he bleed or laugh. He is the dark absence that quietly, invisibly, haunts the last act of the comedy: the community can rename him, but it cannot bring him before our eyes, cannot prove to us that he is now a member of the community. Shylock's conversion remains a miracle unproved, and the audience in the theater must take his "renewed" existence on faith.

In light of such a reading we can bring to the surface the political meanings that lie repressed in Frye's purely formal or mythic account of comedy. Comedy locates the relative power of different social (including racial and religious) groups and measures the lengths to which one group is willing to go in order to absorb another (the Other). Comedy makes such measurements by articulating the transformations of identity that are required before an individual of one group may cross over into the community whose power is renewed and celebrated at the end. Conversion, the master trope of this literary form, represents the institutionalization—that is, the legitimization—of one group's mastery and absorption of another group. The triumph of one group over another is marked by a festival of incipient conjugals in which propagation and propaganda become one. In other words, the end of the struggle between the groups is made complete when the audience is persuaded that the life sources of one group have been transferred to another. In a comedy like *The Merchant of Venice,* this pattern takes the form of converting both the property and the identity of the marginal group—depleting its wealth, transferring its goods "legally" to members of the hegemonic group, and finally erasing its religious and legal identity through a set of

procedures that the culture regulates under the aegis of the institution known as conversion.

While I have been demonstrating the ways in which *Harrington* seeks to expose and subvert the comic formula of *The Merchant of Venice* and the conventional stereotyping of Jewish identity, I am now suggesting that Berenice's "conversion" may be a sign of Edgeworth's submission to the ruling ideology. The literal banishment of the anti-Semite (the exiled Fowler) cannot entirely obscure from our view the figurative banishment of the Jew (the converted Berenice). This is especially so because, as I have claimed for this tradition generally, the Jew is always haunted both by the historic shadow of conversion (when death was often the only alternative) and by the contemporary pressure to convert (fueled by the Evangelical revival in the early nineteenth century). In *Harrington* this pressure exists as a constant reminder of what the Christian community desires and requires. For this reason the disclosure of Berenice's Christianity must be seen as no less than a realization, at a figurative level, of what is expressed at a literal level numerous times in the course of the text. Woman's conversion, in this kind of case, is in fact tantamount to a rule and therefore becomes expressed as an apothegm: in the words of Voltaire, "'qu'une femme est toujours de la religion de son amant'." The English version of this rule taunts Berenice by requiring that she in some way repeat Jessica's conversion: "'your Jessica was ready, according to the custom of Jews' daughters, to jump out of a two-pair of stairs window into her lover's arms'." A veritable Christian chorus makes its desire known: "as to her being a Jewess—who knows what changes love might produce?"; perhaps Harrington can "'contrive to convert her'"; even Mr. Harrington may be able to "bring about her conversion." Mr. Harrington's declaration, "'I would give one of my fingers this instant, that she was not a Jewess!'" makes us realize that the pound of flesh is once again ready for sacrifice, but, as in Shakespeare's play, it will be sacrificed only in the service of *Christian* marriage—a ritual sacrifice of paternal flesh offered for the propagation of Christian flesh.

Edgeworth tries to take the sting out of conversion by making it only figurative. The author can perform the act through "a twist in the plot" and thereby preclude the institutional procedures of religious conversion. Caught between her own convictions and the ideology of her culture, Edgeworth finds a halfway position that, while it satisfies the requirements of Christian ideology, ultimately fails the Jewish reader. Berenice's conversion is the only moment in the novel about which Rachel Mordecai complains, while Sir Walter Scott confesses, "I own I breathed more freely when I found Miss Montenero was not an actual Jewess." Berenice's eleventh-hour conversion certainly looks like proof that the deus ex machina of comedy is in fact a Christian god after all.

Berenice's conversion makes possible an ususually clear glimpse of what is, by its nature, necessarily masked—the process by which cultural ideology crosses over into, and becomes obscured in, literary form. In other words, the figurative conversion of the Jew in **Harrington,** like the figure of conversion in comic form generally, has theoretical significance insofar as we can read it as a trace or symptom of a masked procedure. But Berenice's conversion seems doubly obscured: not only is the conversion process itself masked but the history of such a process has never been recorded, and hence remains unknown to us. As a literary phenomenon, figurative conversion needs to be restored to the culture and the discourse within which it originates, for the failure to record the history of an ideology facilitates the means by which it reenters and remasters the consciousness of succeeding generations within a culture.

The origins of figurative conversion return us to the historic moment when the Christian community was formulating and constituting Jewish identity for public consumption for the first time. This period runs from the first through the fourth century, when the battle for hegemony between Christians and Jews ended at last through the establishment of Christianity as the religion of the state. The battle between conflicting communities, which we have been studying in the literary form known as comedy, we now encounter as a historic reality.

It is during this period that "the Jew" becomes a figure in a literature born of the attempt of one community to displace another. This act of displacement required an unusually intricate maneuver: to prove its own legitimacy, the Church had at once to undermine the authority of the Jewish people while maintaining (in fact, appropriating) the authority of Jewish texts. For this reason the battle for authority between the Church and Judaism took place within the arena of textual politics. The Church had to demonstrate that it had "inherited" (and thereby replaced) Judaism's role as the interpreter of those sacred texts that had been until now the source of Jewish authority in the pagan world. A rereading of Hebrew Scripture was then begun with two goals in mind: first, to authorize the legitimacy—even the historic primacy (as we will see)—of Christianity, not Judaism; second, to undermine Jewish authority through the construction of a fictitious figure, "the Jew." In this way Hebrew Scripture, the sacred book of the Jews, was used to defame the Jews: the *adversus judaeos* literature of this period argued that Hebrew Scripture proved that the Jews had demonstrated in numerous instances their incapacity to serve as the guardians of sacred Scripture—by misreading it, mistranslating it, even mutilating it. The battle for hegemony between Christianity and Judaism, then, became a battle over Jewish identity, or, more specifically, a battle over the representation of Jewish identity. The full transfer of power from one community to another, which in this case meant the full absorption of Judaism in Christianity, was represented in the act of naming by which the Church designated itself as the new Israel.

Figurative conversion became the central discursive strategy by which the Church rewrote Jewish identity and thereby rewrote its place in history. This became possible with the aid of a classificatory system that would redesignate the meaning of the name "Jew." In such texts as

the *Preparatio Evangelica* and the *Demonstratio Evangelica,* for example, Eusebius attempts to demonstrate the greater authority of Christianity by proving its greater antiquity. To do so, he rewrites Jewish history by a crucial redefinition of the names "Jew," "Hebrew," and "Christian." The immediate consequence of Eusebius's revisionary strategy is to make the Jews marginal in a history in which they once occupied the central position. The profound consequence is to alter the nature of Jewish identity not by adding or subtracting a local feature of this identity, but by thoroughly reinventing the definition of what a Jew was—that is, by a figurative conversion of the Jews as a people in history. Eusebius does this by drawing a false distinction between "Jews" and "Hebrews"; the change of names, the conventional sign of actual conversion, becomes our best clue to the fact that a figurative conversion has occurred in Eusebius's text. The Hebrews, according to Eusebius, not only predate the Jews, but are in fact the first Christians, primordial Christians. The Jews, on the other hand, have their historic beginning only with Moses (that is, with the Mosaic law), and play only a minor role—in fact, function only as a digression—in (Christian) history.

In this kind of discourse, so popular among the fourth-century Church fathers, the actual conversion of the Jews, what the Christian community seeks, is performed figuratively behind a double veil. First, the call for conversion is masked as no more than a call to return to a former state: the Jews are counselled merely to *return* to their faith, to the faith of Abraham, the Christian faith. In such a view, the "Jews" are merely "apostates," so that what the Church seeks is not their conversion but their reconversion—their Hebraization or Christianization, their return to their (Christian) roots: "Judaei veteres sperando futurum Christum redemptorem, Christiani erant. . . . Igitur apostatae habeantur necesse est" ["The Jews of old, through their hope of a future Christ Saviour, were Christians. Therefore they should now necessarily be regarded as apostates"]. Second, insofar as there is a call for actual conversion, it masks the fact that a figurative conversion has already taken place: the historic figures we normally take to be Jews, including Abraham and the prophets, are rewritten as, or converted into, Christians. Renaming then is not simply a practical procedure that attends the act of conversion, whereby the convert is renamed both generically (as Jew or Christian) and specifically (with a proper, or what is commonly called a Christian, name). Renaming is the method by which Jews were "converted" textually, authorially, by the early Church fathers.

I wish to claim that Abraham in Eusebius's text occupies the same position that Berenice occupies in Edgeworth's text: two characters whom the reader has assumed to be Jewish are revealed, through "a trick in the plot" (whether the plot of history or the plot of the novel), as Christians. The power of such conversions lies precisely in the reader's not recognizing them as such. They are strategically buried in the unfolding of a history—whether the divine plot of sacred history or the secular plot of narrative history—and thereby seem authorized by history, once history is correctly revised. The reader is simply asked to perform the act of recognition that will confirm the revisionary history. This authorial act by which the name Jew or Christian is suddenly relocated in order to rewrite the identity of an individual or a group, and thereby to revise a history, is the most potent and persistent discursive strategy in the history of the representation of Jewish identity. It is an act that is reborn time and again, embedded within a variety of discourses, always a sign of ideological struggle, but a sign under cover.

Harrington invents a way of subverting the procedure of figurative conversion by allowing the Jew to occupy a position outside the procedure, as a reader (instead of being trapped inside, as a textual figure). When Mr. Montenero performs his deconstructive reading of *The Merchant of Venice,* the Jew is reborn as a critic in a textual battle where his Jewish identity is at stake. He is reborn, in fact, to those debates, both historic and fictitious, in which the Jew was challenged to reclaim his interpretive authority over Hebrew Scripture and to disprove the anti-Semitic readings of Jewish identity that the Christian debater claimed to find in Hebrew Scripture itself. Now, in Edgeworth's text, as the textual critic of *The Merchant of Venice,* the Jew is given the chance to dismantle the holy scripture of English anti-Semitism.

In *Harrington,* when the Jew becomes the reader of Shakespeare's text, we get "the Jewish version of the story," which Harrington himself gets when he sees the play through Jewish eyes for the first time. Mr. Montenero's central strategy, as we have seen, is to place the play within its textual history and thereby to demonstrate the way in which it is a revision (or misrepresentation) of an earlier text. Mr. Montenero's reading of the play allows him to return to the scene of Shylock's trial as textual critic and as judge (like Portia, in fact), in order to claim that the true solution to the trial of Jewish identity comes not in an unraveling of the text of the bond (Portia's solution), but in an unraveling of the entirety of the text of *The Merchant of Venice* vis-à-vis an earlier text; in this light, Portia's famous solution is wasted on a misrepresentation, on—and in—an impure text. Whereas Portia's textual energies find a way to convict Shylock, Mr. Montenero's set Shylock free, centuries after the trial: Shylock, the ur-text of Jewish identity in England, was a *Christian* in the text that Shakespeare robbed and violated.

In such a case the power of the reader depends on the power of exposing the author, of unmasking the authorial or textual conversion that occurs behind the scenes of *The Merchant of Venice.* By explaining that the prototype for Shylock was in fact a Christian, and that the demand for a pound of flesh was originally a Christian act, Mr. Montenero restores the textual *and* the racial origins of Shylock. Mr. Montenero, then, rewrites the genealogy of the Jew as a *textual genealogy* and makes us ponder the strategies by which authors (re)constitute and fabricate racial identity. Montenero's method is to restore to this classic text both its textual history (Shakespeare's manipulation of a previous text) and its cultural history (Shakespeare's manipulation of an anti-Semitic audience). The history of the representation of Jewish identity in this way can be exposed as a system of misrepresentations based on the strategy of figurative conversion; in *The Merchant of Venice,* this conversion occurs in an unusually covert form, entirely behind the scenes, even before the first act of the drama begins. The fullest significance of Mr. Montenero's reading makes us ask: what invisible textual strategies are at work in the representation of Jewish identity?

In this way the act that Edgeworth herself performs, apparently covertly, in figuratively converting Berenice, is analyzed and unmasked by Mr. Montenero in his reading of *The Merchant of Venice.* But Mr. Montenero's critical strategy, when placed within the full historical and cultural framework to which it belongs, is far more resonant. Mr. Montenero, in a brilliantly ironic stroke, turns the tables on centuries of textual conversion by proving that Shylock is a Christian in Jew's clothing. While the predominant Christian textual strategy has been to convert Jewish identity, to designate Abraham and Berenice as Christians, Montenero bows to the pattern only to subvert it: he gives the Christians Shylock! And in doing so Mr. Montenero reveals racial identity as a code whose key is based in textual history—in the procedures by which texts get manipulated, expunged, rewritten, and reread, and then handed down in a system of transmission in which one community textually deauthorizes another community.

It is precisely such a picture of textual manipulation as the (secret) key to racial identity that Freud gives us in *Moses and Monotheism,* when he ostensibly performs the same act that Mr. Montenero performs, only for Moses instead of Shylock. Freud presents himself as a textual restorer, and thereby as a corrector of Jewish history, but in his vision the Jews themselves have manipulated the texts and figuratively converted non-Jewish identity. He argues that Moses was "an Egyptian whom the needs of a people [the Jews] sought to make into a Jew." Freud's revision of Jewish history runs this way: Moses, an Egyptian, converted the Jews to his own religion of monotheism, and then the Jews figuratively converted Moses into a Jew in the writing of their history. The key to Freud's revision (which he claims is only a return to historical truth) depends on deciphering the mutilated texts of Jewish history, especially Hebrew Scripture. Freud itemizes and analyzes the many textual mutilations the Jews authorized in order to claim Moses, circumcision, and monotheism as Judaic instead of Egyptian.

While Freud represents himself as a neutral party in this project, we now can recognize the act he performs from the vantage point of a profoundly political tradition of discourse: he is the author of a text that figuratively converts Jewish identity. Like Eusebius, he performs the textual conversion of a famous Jew in history; in fact, he completes what Eusebius began, adding Moses to the list of Abraham and the prophets. We begin to ask where can we locate Jewish identity. We have here a tradition of texts that slowly eradicates Jewish identity by attaching to it no famous names, no native leaders. Perhaps in the starling claim, "it was this one man Moses [an Egyptian] who created the Jews," Freud inadvertently reveals the truth not about the Jews but about the representation of Jewish identity: "the Jews" are a textual creation, invented and reinvented by a series of powerful individuals, authors, outsiders, each of whom is "a great foreigner" like the Egyptian Moses. Freud's own position in such a history of textual reinvention is embarrassing (as he admits in the opening sentence of his study), since he performs the act of an outsider as an insider: "To deprive a people of the man whom they take pride in as the greatest of their sons is not a thing to be gladly or carelessly undertaken, least of all by someone who is himself one of them."

By recognizing figurative conversion as a textual strategy whose forefathers are the Church fathers, and whose modern descendants include Freud, we can situate Edgeworth's novel—and the novel of Jewish identity generally—within the literary and cultural traditions that constitute the representation of Jewish identity both inside and outside of England, in ancient and modern times. Only in such a setting can we recognize, for example, the full force of George Eliot's figurative conversion of Daniel Deronda: in such a strategy we see that Eliot does not simply reverse Edgeworth's figurative conversion of Berenice but subverts the predominant technique by which Christian culture, from its beginnings, erases Jewish identity. In addition, Eliot makes her figurative conversion of Daniel a comment on the tradition of comedy by forcing this tradition to expand its conventional limits: when the climatic disclosure of the hero's true identity does not reveal a noble English ancestry but in fact cancels such an ancestry in Daniel's Jewish origins, Eliot rewrites the central plot of comedy. Eliot brilliantly manages to sustain the comic tradition within these new, expanded boundaries by fusing English comedy and Jewish history: Daniel is a second Moses, the trappings of his present role as "'an accomplished Egyptian'" giving him access to a kind of power that the Jew ordinarily does not have. In Eliot's revisionary comedy, a Jewish marriage marks at once the climax of the comedy and the regeneration of an ancient community—a Jewish community that leaves England behind as Daniel and Mirah journey to the East. In sum, in *Daniel Deronda* Eliot attempts to continue the project that Edgeworth began in **Harrington**: to revise the representation of Jewish identity and to revolutionize the function of comic form in England.

In exploring conversion as the literary and cultural master trope by which Jewish identity is represented and regulated, I have begun to write a revisionary history of the novel of Jewish identity by returning not simply to the specific English pre-text of this novelistic tradition, *The Merchant of Venice,* but also to the origins of figurative conversion in patristic literature. My comparison between ancient and modern literatures is not meant to erase the differences between these epochs but to challenge us to see the ways in which conversion as a literary and cultural technology is reinvented in succeeding periods—to see, for example, the ways in which the crisis over the Jew's political and religious status in nineteenth-century England often took the form of a renewed attempt at conversion. For the novel of Jewish identity responds to what I take

to be an especially ironic chapter in Anglo-Jewish history: what is commonly known as the Age of Emancipation for Jews coincides with the work of half a dozen newly established missionary societies dedicated to the conversion of the Jews. The pressure to convert was so strong, and entered the literary arena of nineteenth-century England so powerfully, that it produced a body of novels, written by Christians and Jewish apostates, urging Jews to convert, and a body of counternovels, written by English Jews, justifying Judaism and warning of the dangers of conversion.

The history I intend to write would explore both the revival of the cultural institution of conversion, and the origin and development of such competing novelistic traditions. Such a history would position the novel of Jewish identity within a special intertextual site in which Jewish figures not only from history (such as Abraham and Moses) but also from fiction are reauthored and converted. I have in mind, for example, the case of Scott's Rebecca, who resurfaces in William Makepeace Thackeray's *Rebecca and Rowena: A Romance Upon Romance* (1850) to declare to the entire Jewish community, by way of making herself fit to be Ivanhoe's bride, "'I am a Christian!'" In a powerful restoration of English comic form and the ideology of conversion, Thackeray remakes Rebecca into Jessica and reinstates the plot of *The Merchant of Venice.* In this light, charting the "progress" of the novel of Jewish identity means recording an ongoing intertextual struggle against the return not simply of Shylock and Jessica but of an ancient practice of textual reinscription and mutilation. The figure at the center of this practice is the convert—"the Jew" who originates in the Church fathers' revision of Hebrew Scripture and who becomes in time a palimpsest of reauthored identities. To write the history of this literary practice of re-representation is to expose its authorization in the institution of conversion.

Heather MacFadyen (essay date 1994)

SOURCE: "Lady Delacour's Library: Maria Edgeworth's *Belinda* and Fashionable Reading," in *Nineteenth-Century Literature,* Vol. 48, No. 4, March, 1994, pp. 423-39.

[*In the following discussion of* Belinda, *MacFadyen examines Edgeworth's depiction of the disruptive potential of adherence to fashion to a well-regulated domestic life.*]

In recent years literary scholars such as Mary Poovey and Nancy Armstrong have outlined the doctrines of feminine propriety and have highlighted the cultural importance of a domestic definition of femininity. The proper lady and the domestic woman are marked by their ability to regulate their own desires and the desires of other members of their circles. Such women privilege self-control over self-indulgence, the contained over the unbounded, order over chaos. Poovey and Armstrong, however, have also noted that this idealized notion of feminine goodness is persistently confronted with alternate interpretations of feminine identity. While sexual desire is the most common source of uneasiness, women's failure to regulate the economies of their households also troubles the proponents of domestic ideology. The affluence displayed on a woman's body or in her actions could be read both as a sign of her husband's status and as a sign of economic and sexual corruption. Not surprisingly, the proponents of domestic ideology viewed fashionable display with ambivalence, for such self-display made social status visible while depleting the economic basis of that status. The fashionable woman, like the aristocratic woman with whom she is associated, thus becomes a threat to domesticity.

Throughout her career Maria Edgeworth addressed the threat posed to domesticity by fashionability. Her most extended exploration of this topic appears in the eight works that make up the *Tales of Fashionable Life,* but the issue underlies most of her work and is crucial to one of her best-known novels, Belinda (1801). Readers have frequently found the eponymous heroine of the novel to be a tiresome distraction from the more appealing and irrepressibly witty woman of fashion, Lady Delacour. The reviewer for the *Monthly Review,* for instance, complained that Belinda "usurped the superior right of Lady Delacour to give the title to the work: for it is to the character and agency of the latter . . . that the tale owes its principle attractions." While the novel champions domesticity in its accounts of the courtships of Belinda Portman and Virginia St. Pierre, its primary goal is the transformation of the scintillating Lady Delacour from a fashionable woman into a domestic woman.

The disruptive potential of fashionability is clearly evident in Edgeworth's portrayal of the Delacour household. Lady Delacour's account of her unhappy marriage and dissipated life reveals that neither of the Delacours has a firm grasp of domestic economy. Both reject the self-regulation integral to domestic gender identities and enter "the fashionable world with a mutual desire to be as extravagant as possible." The consequent financial irregularities are accompanied by sexual irregularities as both Lady Delacour and Lord Delacour indulge themselves in successively more damaging incidents of financial and moral dissipation. Edgeworth uses a series of overlapping analogies of mind, body, and domestic sphere to represent these disruptions. Lady Delacour's diseased breast, for example, metonymically represents her diseased mind and her refusal to accept that legitimate femininity is defined by its domesticity and its ability to regulate a domestic circle. What gives the portrait of Lady Delacour's domestic failure its characteristically Edgeworthian accent is the prominence assigned to textual matters. Edgeworth supplements the familiar signs of domestic inadequacy—profligate spending, maternal inadequacy, and dubious sexual behavior—with a striking emphasis upon literary transgression. Indeed, Lady Delacour's fashionable success is dependent on her ability to use her literary skill to support her fashionable status.

The ability to assume a constantly shifting series of identities is the key to Lady Delacour's success in eliciting the publicity essential to her status as a fashionable woman, and she is therefore consistently characterized as an actress. While the novel is permeated with a theatrical motif, from the masquerade that opens it to the epilogue

that marks its closure, Lady Delacour supplements her obvious theatricality with frequent and ostentatious references to literary texts. A rough tally of the rates of allusion and quotation by the characters and the narrator of *Belinda* reveals that Lady Delacour outquotes them all, alluding to literary texts eight times more frequently. This concentration of literary allusion is not simply a function of Lady Delacour's dominance of the plot. Her deliberate proliferation of literary references through quotation, parody, and allusion is her most distinctive form of self-display. In Lady Delacour's efforts to maintain her social prominence through a display of her literary skills, Edgeworth develops a trope of fashionable reading.

The fashionable reader misuses her literary knowledge and skill to support a rapidly altering sequence of personas whose novelty and daring enable her to maintain her public preeminence. The fashionable reader shares a number of characteristics with her more common counterpart, the female reader. During the late eighteenth and early nineteenth centuries novel reading was persistently and negatively associated with women, and women's literary pleasure was generally regarded as a form of illicit sexual excitement. This widespread view generated a trope of female reading that asserts that women's reading is an act of the body, not the mind. Thus women's responses to literature are frequently represented as forms of gluttony, intoxication, or sexual arousal. Edgeworth frequently draws on the trope of female reading, but over the course of her canon she develops two alternate ways of viewing women's reading: the equally troubling trope of fashionable reading associated with Lady Delacour and the corrective trope of domestic reading associated with Belinda.

While Lady Delacour, a fashionable reader, uses texts to provide her with a series of nondomestic identities, the more orderly and more retiring Belinda, a domestic reader, uses her knowledge of literary matters to regulate her own desires and ultimately to regulate the desires of Lady Delacour. Because of the adept maneuvering of Mrs. Stanhope, her socially ambitious aunt, Belinda has been welcomed into Lady Delacour's household, where she encounters various challenges to her integrity. Belinda's ability to judge rightly is tested by the fascinating Lady Delacour and the intoxicating world she represents. Belinda's ability to resist Lady Delacour's temptations owes nothing to her aunt's instruction in "the art of rising in the world." Before Belinda became a ward of Mrs. Stanhope, she "had been educated chiefly in the country; she had early been inspired with a taste for domestic pleasures; she was fond of reading, and disposed to conduct herself with prudence and integrity." This indistinctly sketched domestic background has made her unfit for the metropolitan life of fashion. Although Belinda's "taste for literature" initially declines "in proportion to her intercourse with the fashionable world," she rapidly regains her taste for reading when she discovers the duplicity of that world at the masquerade that initiates much of the action of the novel. After inadvertently hearing Clarence Hervey briskly compare her to Packwood's ubiquitously advertised razor strops, Belinda leaves behind the world of routs, drums, and masquerades and retreats into a world of domestic reading. Belinda, in effect, refuses to acquiesce in her aunt's wish that she present herself as a commodity on the marriage market. She resists the indiscriminate circulation that is integral to the fashionable world and chooses instead to spend increasing amounts of time in Lady Delacour's library. While Belinda moves into the library, away from the sites of fashionable display, she does not closet herself in the secret space of self-indulgent reading. Instead of the romances and novels typically condemned by the trope of female reading, Belinda reads nonfiction by Adam Smith, Jean De La Bruyère, Anna Laetitia Barbauld, and John Aiken. When she does read fiction she picks up the blameless moral tales of Jean-François Marmontel and John Moore, writers to whom Edgeworth herself has often been compared. Such texts do not lend themselves to female reading. Belinda's ability to resist both the temptations of female reading and the charms of the fashionable world ultimately enables her to reform Lady Delacour, for domestic reading acts as a counter to the world of fashion and the flux that is its fundamental characteristic.

Both the trope of fashionable reading and the trope of female reading present women's reading as a breach of domestic femininity, and both represent the relationship of the female body to textuality as problematic. The trope of female reading emphasizes the secretive eroticism of the passive female reader. Female reading offers its practitioners an illicit and solitary sexual pleasure that leaves them vulnerable to seduction. The trope of female reading is represented in *Belinda* by Virginia St. Pierre, whose unsupervised novel reading overstimulates her adolescent sexual yearnings, creating the nightmares that torment her. Her novel reading produces a confused and confusing sexual arousal, but her disorder is largely a private matter. Virginia's story makes the case for the primacy of the domestic sphere by demonstrating the effect of excessive isolation upon Virginia's sexual imagination, while the story of Lady Delacour makes a similar case by exploring the effect of excessive publicity on Lady Delacour's body and family.

The trope of fashionable reading retains the problematic female body, but its emphasis falls upon the active public display of the female body. Edgeworth does link Lady Delacour's fashionable reading to a disruption in the libidinal economy of her marriage, but she insists that fashionable reading is not primarily an agent of sexual arousal. While female reading brings women lovers (whether real or imagined), fashionable reading brings them admirers. The female reader entertains lovers in a secret, erotic space, but the fashionable reader commands center stage, displaying her literary skill to ensure the publicity upon which her status within a system of fashionability rests. Thus, although Lady Delacour's flirtation with Clarence Hervey (a flirtation that relies heavily upon the manipulation of literary texts) is perceived by her husband as a sexual threat, it is not in essence erotic. Clarence is Lady Delacour's admirer, not her lover.

Edgeworth's trope of fashionable reading is associated, nevertheless, with a disruption of the sexual economy.

The displayed female body is a visible denial of domestic ideology, and much of Lady Delacour's fashionable reading is calculated to display either her own body or Belinda's. Lady Delacour's textual practices tend to draw Belinda into excessively public (though generally indirect) expressions of sexuality. The fashionable reader's insistence upon publicizing others at the same moment that she draws attention to herself is the foundation of many of the conflicts between Lady Delacour and Belinda during the first half of the novel. Lady Delacour's literary allusions, especially when used to characterize Belinda, are encoded expressions of the sexual ethic of the fashionable world, in which courtship is negotiated through publicity and in which marriage is primarily a financial arrangement. Fashionable adepts such as Lady Delacour and Mrs. Stanhope understand that publicity is an essential aspect of fashionable marriage, whether one is advertising an heiress or a less financially well-endowed woman.

Belinda, however, repudiates the display inherent in fashionable courtship and resists her aunt's and her chaperone's attempts to advertise her charms. Belinda's resistance to Lady Delacour's use of literary reference to encourage Clarence in his fitful courtship is evident in the episode that follows Belinda's refusal to be at home to him during one of Lady Delacour's absences. When Lady Delacour returns from her visit to the royal drawing room she finds Clarence languishing on her stoop. Upon learning that Belinda has refused to see him, Lady Delacour reassures him, insisting that "not at home is nonsense, you know." She then takes Clarence to Belinda's sanctuary, the library, crying as she goes, "Shine out, appear, be found, my lovely Zara!" The allusion to Voltaire's *Zaire* (1732) underlines Lady Delacour's insistence that Belinda be visible to Clarence and that she engage in the self-display essential to the fashionable world. Lady Delacour goes further in her attempt to publicize Belinda by proffering another literary allusion. Finding Belinda in the library, Lady Delacour remarks: "Here she is—what doing I know not—studying Hervey's Meditations on the Tombs, I should guess, by the sanctification of her looks." Lady Delacour ironically conveys her hidden preoccupation with death through this reference to James Hervey's *Meditations among the Tombs* (1746-47). More important, she uses the reference to suggest that Belinda is at some level interested in the scene's other Hervey.

This intersection of forced publicity, literary text, and courtship is repeated during the same visit when Lady Delacour attempts to enact "a second rape of the lock." In response to Lady Delacour's mimicry of the awkward movement of women in hoop skirts, Clarence declares that he can "manage a hoop as well as any woman in England." Clarence dons the appropriate clothing and plays Madame de Pomenars quite convincingly until Lady Delacour pulls the comb out of Belinda's hair and drops it on the floor. Clarence, befuddled by "the sight of the finest hair that he had ever beheld," bends to pick up the comb, "totally forgetting his hoop and his character." As a reward for his good-natured acceptance of the lost bet, Lady Delacour offers him a lock of Belinda's distracting hair.

Belinda, however, escapes the force of the allusion and its illegitimate advertisement of her sexual availability. Her response to Lady Delacour's display is a corresponding and resisting retreat. Belinda retires as soon as she can, but the "modest, graceful dignity" of her manners guarantees that she escapes "without even the charge of prudery."

Although Lady Delacour ostensibly uses literary references to promote a flirtation between Clarence and Belinda, the performances also call attention to Lady Delacour herself, setting up an uncomfortable triangular relationship. This triangle is most forcefully expressed in the sequence in which Lady Delacour appears dressed as Queen Elizabeth and Clarence casts himself as the Earl of Essex. The narrator announces that "both the actor and actress were highly animated, and seemed so fully possessed by their parts as to be insensible" to the implication of the scene they are playing out. The "deep blush" that appears on "Belinda's cheek, when Queen Elizabeth addressed her as one of her maids of honour, of whom she affected to be jealous," abruptly makes Clarence aware of the subtext of this masquerade. This charade is doubly revealing. Dr. X—, a rational physician, is able to read through Lady Delacour's disguise, for it paradoxically reveals the disease it is designed to hide. Dr. X— observes to Clarence and Belinda that Lady Delacour's feverish "gaiety" is not the sign of "a sound mind in a sound body." Further and more telling is the betraying ruff. The shadow cast by the ruff of Lady Delacour's costume trembles and reveals her hectic pulse to the discerning eye of Dr. X—, who chooses this moment to admonish Clarence about the frivolity of a life devoted to "the evanescent amusement of a drawing-room." He urges Clarence to strive to "be permanently useful to his fellow-creatures." This encouragement breaks the triangular flirtation, and Clarence begins to reform. He well knows that Lady Delacour is not in love with him, that "her only wish was to obtain his admiration." To encourage her reformation, therefore, he resolves to withdraw his admiration and "to show her that it could no longer be secured without deserving his esteem."

Clarence's assurance that he can correct Lady Delacour's flaws is somewhat impertinent, but his recognition that Lady Delacour needs a friend rather than an admirer is crucial to Edgeworth's point: the health of Lady Delacour's person and of her household requires that she replace her admirers with friends. Friendship, however, is the product of domestic not fashionable reading, and the course of Lady Delacour's recovery is dependent on her ability to perceive the difference between admiration and friendship. Thus the willingness of her former admirers to exchange fashionable reading for domestic reading is essential to her cure. Belinda Portman is the central figure in this process, and she gradually draws Lady Delacour away from self-display and toward the domestic literary practices exemplified in the Percival family. Belinda, in effect, must act as a "cordial," gradually healing Lady Delacour and her household.

Belinda's task is to unlock Lady Delacour's secrets, essentially the secret of her denied affection for her daughter, Helena, and for her husband. Belinda transforms the Delacour household by arranging the return of Helena, and with Helena comes an altered relationship to literary texts and to the question of self-display. Shortly after Clarence resolves to be Lady Delacour's friend rather than her admirer, Lady Delacour asks Belinda to "look over" some of the unread letters that have accumulated on her desk. Lady Delacour is surprised by Belinda's reaction to one of the letters. From Belinda's "countenance" she guesses that the letter must contain "something wondrous pathetic." When she learns that it is from Helena she dismisses the letter, telling Belinda to "read it to yourself, my dear—a school-girl's letter is a thing I abominate—I make it a rule never to read Helena's epistles." Belinda, however, possesses formidable "powers of persuasion," and she quickly convinces the seemingly indifferent mother to read her daughter's letters. Lady Delacour is pleased to discover that her daughter writes well, but she is less pleased by Helena's obvious affection for Lady Anne Percival. As Lady Delacour reveals her jealousy of Lady Anne, she also reveals that she has read this letter and previous letters with some care. Ultimately, it is less the content of Helena's letters that is important than the act of reading them, for in reading Lady Delacour enacts the maternal and domestic identity that is essential to proper femininity in Edgeworth's works.

When Helena enters her mother's house she brings with her the invisible but formidable influence of the exemplary Percival family. The Percivals themselves never enter the Delacour home, but Lady Anne and Henry Percival are indirectly responsible for its reform in that their family embodies the domestic literary practices essential to Lady Delacour's cure. As both Belinda and Clarence discover, no one person dominates the conversation in the Percival home. The entire family, including the children, participates in discussions. Furthermore, conversational skills are not used to display the individual's brilliance; rather, they are used to encourage the talents of others. The competition and the deceptive theatricality that mark the fashionable world of Lady Delacour are utterly absent.

The reunion of Lady Delacour and her daughter takes place in the privacy of the Delacour library during the half hour preceding a fashionable reading party, and the Sortes Virgilianæ sequence that follows the reading party is animated by the Percival influence. After the reading of Voltaire's *L'Ecossaise* (1760) Lady Delacour, Belinda, Helena, and Clarence idle away the time before the meal looking at the miscellaneous collection of books on the drawing-room table. Clarence takes up one of them, crying "Come, let us try our fate by the Sortes Virgilianæ." Lady Delacour, always eager for any game of chance, opens at random the proffered volume of Marmontel's tales. The book opens to "a description of the manner in which *la femme comme il y en a peu* managed a husband, who was excessively afraid of being thought to be governed by his wife." Lady Delacour can scarcely avoid the coincidence between the text and her own marital situation. When she finds Belinda's bookmark between the following pages, Lady Delacour assumes that Belinda and

Clarence have contrived the Sortes to provide her a less than subtle lesson.

Lady Delacour's fortuitous reading of Marmontel has indeed been contrived, but not in the obvious manner she supposes. Nor is she correct in her conjecture that Belinda's marker is a sign that she has been studying Marmontel in anticipation of becoming the second Lady Delacour. This moment of reading is contrived by Edgeworth as a means of embedding the Percival family model of maternal conduct in the heart of Lady Delacour's diseased household. The conjunction of Lady Delacour and "la femme comme il y en a peu" was first made by Lady Anne, during a dinner party earlier in the novel. On that occasion Lady Anne refuted an assertion that Lady Delacour was monstrous in her neglect of Helena by invoking both the rational principles of Marmontel and the more fanciful notion of enchantment. Lady Delacour's "enchantment will soon be at an end," she assured the company, "and she will return to her natural character. I should not be at all surprised, if Lady Delacour were to appear at once *la femme comme il y en a peu*." Thus the Sortes Virgilianæ gains its predictive power not from Lady Delacour's random selection of a passage but from its deliberate association with Lady Anne's rational domesticity. Lady Anne's indirect influence is augmented by the bookmark, which is a sign of Belinda's domestic reading, a reading marked by an absence of randomness as well as by its propriety.

The conversation that follows the Sortes Virgilianæ is dominated by Clarence's obvious efforts to persuade Lady Delacour to adopt a more appropriate maternal identity. He openly expresses his "admiration" of a fashionable duchess who had "stopped short in the career of dissipation to employ her inimitable talents in the education of her children; who had absolutely brought virtue into fashion by the irresistible powers of wit and beauty." While Lady Delacour dismisses his enthusiasm, advising him to "write a sentimental comedy, a comédie larmoyante, or a drama on the German model, and call it The School for Mothers," she is moved to express a bitter regret that it is too late for her to become the heroine of such a text. And indeed, until Lady Delacour is willing to reveal her secrets to the eye of her husband, she has no hope of reform.

Belinda, however, gradually persuades Lady Delacour to do just that. After Lady Delacour has been convinced that Belinda is not preparing to usurp her place in her husband's or her daughter's affections, she agrees to expose her breast to her husband and to Dr. X—. Each of these physical revelations is accompanied by a textual revelation, one also encouraged by Belinda. Soon after she bares her diseased breast to her husband and tells him the secret that has driven her onto the fashionable stage, Lady Delacour also opens her secret library to him. This secret library contains Clarence Hervey's letters, which she teasingly tells Belinda are "calculated to make you fall in love with the writer of them." Lord Delacour's almost-conquered jealousy of Clarence returns when he sees Lady Delacour opening Clarence's letters "one after another,

looking over them without seeming well to know what she was about" and hears her ask Belinda to put the letters in a "cabinet of curiosities" with a "secret lock" that Lady Delacour "alone can manage." In an aside, Belinda entreats her to open the secret of the letters to Lord Delacour, suggesting that he is not jealous of Lady Delacour's "person"—her body or her heart—but of her mind. Domestic harmony can be restored only when this final lock has been opened and this final secret told. By being opened up to the nominal supervision of a husband, Clarence's letters cease to belong to the world of fashion and enter into domestic circulation. Lady Delacour's demonstration of "confidence," "kindness," and "condescension" in this matter fixes Lord Delacour at home.

The transformation of Lady Delacour's fashionable household into an Edgeworthian domestic salon, however, requires that one final secret library be opened. As the time for her mastectomy approaches, Lady Delacour engages in a secret reading that recalls the solitary self-indulgence of the female reader. She takes to reading religious texts, and she is as ashamed of them as other heroines are of lewd novels. These "methodistical" books are "highly oratorical" and generally "of a mystical cast"; to Belinda, who happens upon them by chance, they are "scarcely intelligible." When Lady Delacour learns that Belinda has been examining them, she orders that the books "be locked up in my own bookcase" and the key returned to her.

Operating outside rational discourse and sociable domestic space, Lady Delacour's religious reading is linked to the motifs of disease and morbidity. Her religious mania comes upon her "by fits," generally when the effect of the opium is weakening and her mind is overwhelmed by "the most dreadful superstitious terrors—terrors the more powerful as they were secret." Secret and fearful, Lady Delacour's religious reading makes her vulnerable to manipulation and itself produces wrong interpretations, most clearly in the episode of Harriot Freke's final foray. Misled by gossip, Harriot believes that Lady Delacour has taken a lover. In an attempt to discover his identity and to frighten Lady Delacour, she dresses herself as a ghost and climbs over the garden wall. Confused by her reading, Lady Delacour readily believes that the vision she sees on three successive nights is a forerunner of her own death. Once she confesses this vision to Belinda and to Dr. X—, they are able to unmask Harriot and to expel her once and for all from Lady Delacour's life. The following morning Dr. X— determines that Lady Delacour's breast is not cancerous, and he points out that if she had "permitted either the surgeon or him to have *examined* sooner into the real state of the case, it would have saved herself infinite pain, and them all anxiety."

The third and final element of Lady Delacour's cure also underlines the importance of texts. Relieved of her fear for her health, Lady Delacour turns her attention to her family's library, complaining to Belinda that the books in the library are "in dreadful confusion." She notes that Lord Delacour "has really a very fine library," but instead of such a profusion of books she would prefer a more orderly collection: "I wish he had half as many books twice as well arranged: I never can find any thing I want." She turns from Belinda to Dr. X—, asking him to "recommend a librarian to my lord—not a chaplain, observe." Lady Delacour's interest in restoring order to the library is an implicit assumption of her role as the domestic superintendent of her husband's resources.

The novel's emphasis on the regulatory capacity of books might lead one to expect that Dr. X— will indeed provide a librarian, but instead he introduces a figure more suited to remove the residual effects of Lady Delacour's feverish descent into the obsessive reading of religious texts. The introduction of this figure, the chaplain Moreton, is framed by a literary text. Dr. X— begins by quoting the famous description of the Parson in Chaucer's Prologue to the *Canterbury Tales* (1387). Chaucer's model, he goes on to claim, is fully present in a contemporary minister, Mr. Moreton. Moreton himself then enters the story to complete Lady Delacour's cure, relieving her from "the terrors of methodism" and replacing them with "the consolations of mild and rational piety." With the elimination of Lady Delacour's secret remorse her transformation from fashionable reader to domestic reader is complete:

> She was no longer in continual anxiety to conceal the state of her health from the world. She had no secret to keep—no part to act; her reconciliation with her husband and with his friends restored her mind to ease and self-complacency. Her little Helena was a source of daily pleasure; and no longer conscious of neglecting her daughter, she no longer feared that the affections of her child should be alienated.

Lady Anne's prophecy has been fulfilled.

The effectiveness of Lady Delacour's adoption of domestic reading strategies is evident in the conclusion of the novel. Her manipulation of the sequence of events that closes the novel—the confrontation of Clarence and Virginia, the reunion of Virginia and her father, and the acceptance of Clarence as Belinda's suitor—is the occasion for one of Lady Delacour's most theatrical performances. This performance, however, is crucially differentiated from her earlier theatricals by its domestic intent. Following a brief debate about the proper way of ending the story of a female reader's confusion, a domestic reader's courtship, and a fashionable reader's reformation, Lady Delacour announces that she can "conclude the business in two lines." She closes the novel by placing her players "in proper attitudes for stage effect. What signifies being happy, unless we appear so?" She asks Captain Sunderland to kneel with Virginia "at her father's feet" and tells Mr. Hartley that he is "in the act of giving them your blessing." She assembles a second domestic tableau by informing Clarence that he has "a right to Belinda's hand" and that he "may kiss it too," for "it is the rule of the stage." When Lord Delacour enters with Helena, Lady Delacour turns to her own domestic circle, praising her husband's "good start of surprise" and instructing him to "stand still, pray; you cannot be better than you are: Helena, my love, do not let go your father's hand." Pleased with the three domestic tableaux, Lady

Delacour "comes forward to address the audience with a moral—a moral! Yes, 'Our *tale* contains a *moral;* and, no doubt, / You all have wit enough to find it out.'" The legitimacy of this literary display is guaranteed by Lady Delacour's domestic purpose. The theatrical tableaux she creates are not designed to display her person, but rather to display the harmony made possible by domesticity. The future happiness of Virginia, Belinda, and Lady Delacour is affirmed by their membership within these completed domestic circles.

The ability of Lady Delacour to use a previously disruptive theatricality to highlight the importance of domestic order has a secondary function. Just as the trope of female reading enables Edgeworth to confront the problems associated with women's literary consumption, her trope of fashionable reading enables her to explore the problems associated with women's literary production. Lady Delacour's nondomestic theatricality and her misuse of her literary skill articulate the improprieties implicit in a woman's assertion of public literary authority. Though transformed into a domestic reader, Lady Delacour has not lost her literary verve. As she herself says, she has been "*won,* not *tamed!*—A tame Lady Delacour would be a sorry animal, not worth looking at." By reforming Lady Delacour rather than silencing her, Edgeworth implies that a woman's literary skill can coincide with domestic propriety. Edgeworth's first portrait of a reformed fashionable reader thus suggests that a woman may possess both domestic and literary authority.

Teresa Michals (essay date 1994)

SOURCE: "Commerce and Character in Maria Edgeworth," in *Nineteenth-Century Literature,* Vol. 49, No. 1, June, 1994, pp. 1-20.

[*In the following essay, Michals examines "Edgeworth's idea of the relation between personality and property."*

In her time and in our own, Maria Edgeworth's reputation is oddly double. Read as a publicist for middle-class individualism, she is claimed for a progressive program; identified as a gifted apologist for paternalism, she is claimed for a conservative one. On one side of the question, critics like her biographer Marilyn Butler describe her as "the most thorough-going individualist writing outside the jacobin movement," while to others she is a committed paternalist to whom the very idea of "individual and inalienable rights" is deeply suspect. Contemporary reviewers present the same divided view, describing Edgeworth both as a dangerously secular utilitarian and as a reassuringly didactic moralist. In the discussion that follows I will argue that at the heart of these critical contradictions lies Edgeworth's idea of the relation between personality and property. Edgeworth embraces economic individualism without seeing individuals themselves as autonomous. For her the family has a corporate personality, one underwritten by the market value of its members' good characters rather than by its inheritance of land, the traditional basis of such a corporate personality. That is, the family rather than what she calls the "unconnected being" defines identity for Edgeworth, but this family survives only by drawing on the personal credit of its individual members.

If Ian Watt's analysis of the realist novel argues that the novel in all its factual detail makes the case for individualism, then Edgeworth seems a strong proponent of the individual. Watt links the rise of the novel with the rise of the autonomous individual through the device of the particularized character, the figure that the wealth of accurate circumstantial detail in the realist novel creates. He defines the novel as the peculiar product of a world of individuals, a form well suited to describe an "unplanned aggregate of particular individuals having particular experiences at particular times and at particular places." Watt also, of course, understands this individual as a representative figure; for example, Robinson Crusoe, taking endless inventory of his goods on his solitary island, is the *type* of the autonomous individual. However, Watt emphasizes as the novel's "primary criterion . . . truth to individual experience—individual experience which is always unique and therefore new."

Edgeworth's emphasis on the particular, however, differs significantly from Watt's emphasis on the uniqueness of individual experience. Her attention to precisely observed detail is often interpreted as a pioneering interest in realist technique, a technique that is itself seen, following Watt, as socially progressive because of the value it implicitly places on the particular lives of ordinary individuals. For Edgeworth, however, each individual is first and foremost a type within a system of classification that is at once moral and social. She thinks of a fictional character as the representative of a "class"; these classes of characters represent classes of the mass reading public that her novels are meant to influence. In a request to Walter Scott for "a bit of advice about a character," Edgeworth emphasizes "the consideration of whether there would be a sufficient *class* of people liable to be influenced by such motives as I should represent—not merely whether the individual character be possible or probable." "I think I have always aimed . . . at making my characters representatives of classes," she affirmed late in life. For Edgeworth, "class" can refer either to status or to character, either to a fixed social position based on the ownership of property or to a collection of personal traits shared by a group of people. Usually, however, it means both. As the market erodes the first sense of the word, Edgeworth supports it with the second. Throughout her writing the two senses of "class," as either character or status, tend to coincide with significant convenience: Irish tenants, for example, form a class in the sense of sharing a character for warm-hearted improvidence as well as in the sense of sharing a particular legal relation to the land that they farm. Similarly, in Edgeworth's fiction, members of the class of greedy, garrulous, childlike persons are also quite likely to be members of the class of servants.

The two narrators of Edgeworth's first novel, *Castle Rackrent* (1800), represent these two meanings of "class" with extraordinary fidelity, juxtaposing an old idea of inherited status with a new emphasis on individual character. Old Thady, an uneducated family steward, uses a traditional understanding of class as fixed status to narrate the bulk of *Castle Rackrent*. The fact that the Rackrents are drunken, litigious, violent, and wasteful does not alter Thady's respect for them as "the family"; their status is a function of their property, not of their personality. Thady's story, however, is introduced by a well-educated "editor" who explains "the manners of a certain class of the gentry of Ireland some years ago . . . to those who are totally unacquainted with Ireland." The editor's gloss is an act of translation, one that shifts the meaning of words like "class." Like Thady, this editor groups the Rackrents as a class, but he defines them by their vices rather than by their land:

> The race of the Rackrents has long since been extinct in Ireland; and the drunken Sir Patrick, the litigious Sir Murtagh, the fighting Sir Kit, and the slovenly Sir Condy, are characters which could no more be met with at present in Ireland, than Squire Western or Parson Trulliber in England.

The Rackrents' moral flaws constitute them as a recognizable "race," one doomed to extinction by its own irrationality. Despite the meticulously observed details that seem to distinguish one Rackrent from another, they are all finally examples of one uniform type: the class of comically archaic Irishmen.

Edgeworth's treatment of character as class looks like a socially conservative refusal to let Watt's autonomous individual emerge, an attempt to get Crusoe off his island and back into the thick of a hierarchically structured paternalist society. This moral is often made explicit in the crises of her stories; for example, when, after running away from his mentor, the young hero of **"Forester"** finds himself on the verge of being packed off to jail on a false charge of stealing a ten-guinea bank note, "he could not help reflecting, that an individual in society who has friends, and established character, and a *home,* is in a more desirable situation than an unconnected being who has no one to answer for his conduct" in ***Popular Tales*** [1804]. Edgeworth insists that each of her characters not only stands for a class of persons but also, more specifically, stands with a family; it is only as the representative of this larger group that an individual can be trusted, by other characters or by the reader. The eponymous heroine of ***Belinda*** (1801), for example, does not so much discover a unique individuality as pass through a string of corporate identities. She is saved from the respective machinations of two ancillary figures, her Aunt Stanhope and Lady Delacour, only by affiliating herself with a third family, the Percivals—who, despite their very sincere protestations of economic disinterest, only narrowly avoid succeeding where the Stanhopes and Delacours failed and marrying Belinda to their spendthrift ward.

Despite this politically conservative insistence on the impossibility of living as an "unconnected being," however, in economic terms Edgeworth was a progressive figure, a critic of land-based paternalism. Much of her fiction, like her management of her family's estate, is an experiment in the principles of free-market capitalism. Edgeworth's novels provide a practical guide both to the fictitious instruments of credit that the growing marketplace required, such as checks and bills of exchange, and to the larger theories that were thought to explain its workings as a whole—deep in rural Ireland, her characters quote Adam Smith. Learning to manage instruments of credit is a crucial lesson for Belinda, who at one point is saved from moral ruin only by forgetting to endorse a draft for 200 guineas. Moreover, despite Edgeworth's rejection of individualism, her novels and educational writings place a high value on a certain kind of personal independence. For example, she advises young men to avoid political life because it involves dependency: although "the forms of homage, and the rights of vassalage are altered . . . the feudal lord of ancient times could ill compete in power with the influence of the modern political patron" (**Patronage** [1804]).

To understand Edgeworth's position we must understand that the kind of independence she values and adapts for the uses of the marketplace has more to do with the status of an independent gentleman than with a belief in the absolute autonomy of the individual. A gentleman's independence is based on his independent property; Edgeworth imagines that what Forester calls "an established character and a *home*" can take the place of this property in supporting an individual in society. Her version of character reflects the traditional claim that the living and dead members of an aristocratic family have a corporate personality, one based on an unbroken, entailed inheritance of real property. In emphasizing that an individual always stands for and with a larger group, Edgeworth revises this claim, the "great mysterious incorporation" that Edmund Burke celebrates as a "sure principle of conservation," into an ideal suitable for a credit-based economy of middle-class entrepreneurs.

For Edgeworth the family is a kind of domestic corporation underwritten by the moral and financial credit of its living and dead members, by their collective character. She turns both financial assets and aristocratic honors into mere representations of character: "It appears to me highly advantageous," claims one of her spokesmen, "that *character,* in general, should descend to posterity as well as riches or honours, which are, in fact, often the representations, or consequences, in other forms, of different parts of character—industry, talents, courage" (**Patronage**).

Edgeworth's claim that a family's greatest asset is the credit-worthy character of its members reminds us that the eighteenth century is remarkable both for its increasing acceptance of impersonal market forces and for what Leonore Davidoff and Catherine Hall have called its "dearth of impersonal forms to encompass" market relationships. The family is one of the extremely personal forms through which business was carried out before the general acceptance of impersonal surrogates like the limited liability corporation. Similarly, as John Brewer points out, the idea of personal creditworthiness took on particular importance during the eighteenth century because of

that period's "acute shortage of specie"—its acute shortage of the tokens of impersonal exchange. The dependence of the market on credit facilitates Edgeworth's description of it as a supremely personal realm; typically, she insists that "high credit must surely give more pleasurable feelings than the mere possession of wealth," because of credit's foundation in personal bonds of trust (**Patronage**). Although we may think of personal character as a value that is opposed to the anonymity of the marketplace, as Smith was beginning to make that term understood, Edgeworth reveals it as the foundation of the market.

Edgeworth's novels about the marriage market reflect the complexity of creating and sustaining character in this larger credit-based marketplace. The marketplace required a credit-worthy self, or at least a credible self-presentation: "Presentation of self as sober, reliable, candid and constant was not merely a question of genteel manners, but a matter of economic survival," notes Brewer. The most troubling problem that credit raises, however, is not so much the possibility of misrepresenting the past—of lying about personal accomplishments or financial resources—but rather the importance of forming a plausible estimate of the future. Probability becomes an important measure of character because a marketplace of credit is essentially a "futures" market, one that buys and sells commitments to future action. The enthusiasm of Edgeworth's reviewers for "the charm of *probability* by which her stories are so strongly characterized" reflects this concern, for it was Edgeworth's characters rather than her plots that her contemporaries saw as significant: "This development of character is often so exquisitely managed, as to leave the readers of romance no regret for the shining improbabilities to which they have been accustomed." The ability to deploy the charm of probability at will, to become plausible to strangers, is the condition of entry for participation in the kind of informal credit economy inhabited by both the characters of **Belinda** and its author, who tirelessly warns readers against investing either emotionally or financially in shining improbabilities. The idea of character that defines the actors in this novel also supported the marketplace in which it was sold.

The growing economic concern with credit is reflected not only in the genre of the novel as a whole but also in the hardening up of the boundaries between the novel's subgenres; between those fictions that emphasize consistency, probability, and accuracy in circumstantial detail and those, such as the Gothic, that do not. In **Belinda** probability is clearly a question of literary genre as well as of economic discretion. Other characters praise Belinda for refusing to share in the shining improbabilities of the heroines of romance, for closing down a branch of tempting but improbable novelistic possibilities. When she reveals that there is no lover hidden in a suspiciously locked closet, for example, Belinda's prudence effectively shuts down the writing of romance:

> "My dear Miss Portman, you will put a stop to a number of charming stories by this prudence of yours— a romance called the Mysterious Boudoir, of nine

volumes at least, might be written on this subject, if you would only condescend to act like almost all other heroines, that is to say, without common sense."

Belinda's common sense prevents romances from being written at her expense. The nine volumes of "The Mysterious Boudoir" would contain a campaign of hostile publicity fatal to her "interests." "Demonstration is unanswerable even by enemies," claims a friend, agreeing to become an eyewitness to the emptiness of the locked closet rather than simply taking Belinda's word on the matter. He emphasizes the importance of controlling the impression that Belinda conveys to an infinite and anonymous mass of observers: "I will not sacrifice your interests to the foppery of my politeness. . . . I see no method so certain as that which you propose of preventing busy rumour."

Edgeworth echoes the emphasis of the credit-based market on the type of self one should present as well as on self-presentation. Her heroes and heroines are supremely sober, reliable, and constant, as Mrs. Barbauld notes in praising her for emphasizing the "severe and homely virtues of prudence and economy" over less market-oriented "splendid sentiments." Splendid sentiments belong to the romance's world of shining improbabilities, not to Edgeworth's world of plausible character: "Where have order, neatness, industry, sobriety, been recommended with more strength than in the agreeable tales of miss Edgeworth?" Barbauld asks. Despite Edgeworth's occasional references to Christianity, the reviewers' frequent criticisms of the "striking and much-to-be-lamented deficiency in every thing like religious principle" in her writing are justified by her language of calculation and by her emphasis on enlightened self-interest: "The use of education . . . is to teach men to see clearly, and to follow steadily, their real interests. All morality, you know, is comprised in this definition," remarks Mr. M'Leod in **"Ennui,"** a model steward who sadly quotes Adam Smith as his slovenly paternalist master corrupts the tenants with indiscriminate charity (in *Tales of Fashionable Life,* 1809).

Edgeworth's writing must be understood as a response to the lack of interest shown by large segments of the public in the idea of building a credible character. Her novels, educational handbooks, and tales form one answer to the social historian's question, "How could you educate a populace which included aristocrats who found it insulting to have to pay bills promptly and a labouring poor trapped in an erratic seasonal pattern of borrowing and spending," to the task of living "within a strictly regulated credit system?" In stories aimed at laborers and fashionable aristocrats of all ages, as well as at the erring children of the industrious middle classes, Edgeworth attacks just "this want of punctuality in money transactions, and this mode of treating contracts as matters of favour and affection" (**"The Limerick Gloves,"** in *Popular Tales*). In insisting on the absolute difference between contractual relations and "matters of favour and affection," Edgeworth might seem to insist on the absolute separation of the public and private spheres. Her model of the marketplace, however, remains a collection of re-

sponsible family members, able to function as economic agents only because they are able to draw on each other's moral and financial backing; in this sense not only marriage contracts but all contracts are seen to involve matters of favor and affection. Moreover, in emphasizing the issue of "punctuality" in relation to contract, Edgeworth emphasizes that her commitment to a market economy rests on this economy's commitment to future action.

Edgeworth's version of authorship also sees the market through the family. The rapid commercialization of England produced a literary marketplace vibrant enough to turn Edgeworth's novels into best-sellers; however, she consistently identifies as her most important readers not this newly anonymous audience but rather the "Committee of Education and Criticism of Edgeworthstown," the domestic circle on her family estate. Although Edgeworth's novels and tales were targeted at specific segments of her audience, carefully "adapted to different ages, sexes, and situations in life" (preface to *Popular Tales*), she describes them primarily as an extension of her large family's common interest in scientific education, as a restatement of their common knowledge of domestic matters. The prefaces that her father, Richard Lovell Edgeworth, wrote for her works at her request ensure that they leave the home only under his "parental protection" (preface to *Tales of Fashionable Life*). Similarly, the "Advertisement" that opens *Belinda* warns the public that although Edgeworth may be an author, she is not a novelist, not a commercial trafficker in "folly, errour, and vice": "The following work is offered to the public as a Moral Tale—the author not wishing to acknowledge a Novel." As Belinda is not a heroine, so *Belinda* is not a novel.

Like Edgeworth writing best-sellers in the name of her family, Belinda raises her value in the marriage market by displaying her eagerness to confine herself to a domestic circle. She dissociates herself from London's self-promoting entrepreneurs by insisting that not high society but rather "domestic life was that which could alone make her really and permanently happy." Clarence Hervey, the young man Belinda must marry by the end of the novel, first sees her as a minor and ephemeral commodity that is also a synecdoche for the new world of sophisticated marketing. "She was hawked about every where, and the aunt was puffing her with might and main," reports Clarence, comparing Belinda to the object of the indefatigable George Packwood's famous advertising campaign:

> "You heard of nothing, wherever you went, but of Belinda Portman and Belinda Portman's accomplishments: Belinda Portman and her accomplishments, I'll swear, were as well advertised as Packwood's razor strops."

"Do you forget that Belinda Portman and her accomplishments have already been as well advertised as Packwood's razor-strops," Belinda later reminds Lady Delacour, the reader, and Clarence. The bulk of the novel is tirelessly devoted to denying the reality of this connection between Belinda and self-promoting entrepreneurs like Packwood; nevertheless, Packwood's pioneering, extremely successful ads present the same version of the marketplace as do

Edgeworth's best-selling novels: in both, a credible character supplants property as the basis for commercial relations. Far from being a mere guarantee of eventual payment, "character" takes the place of cash in defining Packwood's relations with his customers: "Packwood's pride [is] in having customers of respectability . . . even the offer of ready cash on receipt will avail nothing, except they are of good fame and character," insists one of his ads. My point here is not so much that Edgeworth makes marriage look like the marketplace, but rather that she shows how the marketplace looked like marriage. That is, the informal structure of trade credit required that, like Belinda's courtship, market relations themselves be imagined as the domestic encounters of recognizable characters. The unstable, informal, and personal relationships that supported commercial ventures aspired to the respectability of family bonds.

Belinda's Aunt Stanhope, one of the novel's major villains, is also one of its clearest spokesmen for the idea of the family as a profitable corporation, as she schemes to marry Belinda to a series of feckless rich aristocrats. Aunt Stanhope is forever reversing the priority of character and its representations, as in her warning to Belinda that when a young lady loses her good character, all is lost: "all the money, &c. that has been spent upon her education is so much dead loss to her friends." Aunt Stanhope sees her family as a profitable and expanding enterprise. *Belinda* opens like a popular contemporary manual devoted to the "Art of Thriving": its first line introduces Aunt Stanhope as "a well-bred woman, accomplished in that branch of knowledge which is called the art of rising in the world." This is the register of Adam Smith, taking as an accepted norm "the natural effort which every man is continually making to better his own condition." Aunt Stanhope's self-interest, however, operates at one remove; her unceasing effort is most directly aimed at bettering the condition of her young relations: "She prided herself upon having established half a dozen nieces most happily, that is to say, on having married them to men of fortunes far superior to their own." Aunt Stanhope's relationship with her nieces is organized according to a kind of staggered contract: she pays now for the prospect of a future return. While Burke imagines the contract between generations as an entail, an agreement to keep a body of property intact, Aunt Stanhope sees a prospect of infinitely expanding profits: "You will, I trust . . . repay me when you are established in the world," she explains, lending Belinda a further 200 guineas for her London campaign. For Aunt Stanhope the family is neither the Burkean means of preserving a paternalist hierarchy through generations nor a private alternative to the unstable world of the marketplace, but rather a hybrid of the two—she is a speculator in domesticity.

Aunt Stanhope has made a "successful trade" of marrying her nieces to wealthy gentlemen, investing in the marriage market's principal commodity, genteel personal accomplishments. In *Practical Education* Edgeworth herself echoes Aunt Stanhope's basic assumption that the marriage market follows the rules of the larger marketplace, advising parents to consider Smith's law of supply and demand before investing heavily in their daughters' accomplish-ments: many other "parents are, and have been for some years, speculating in the same line; consequently, the market is likely to be overstocked, and, of course, the value of the commodities must fall." Belinda is widely assumed to be a silent partner in Aunt Stanhope's business, a speculator in her own accomplished and domestic character: "Young ladies who have the misfortune to be *conducted* by these artful dames, are always supposed to be partners in all the speculations, though their names may not appear in the firm," warns the narrator. Aunt Stanhope's indignation when her family is not so profitable as anticipated is a measure of the investment she has sunk into it: "there's [a niece] refused me a hundred guineas last week, though the piano-forte and harp I bought for her before she was married stood me in double that sum, and are now useless lumber on my hands; and she never could have had [her husband] without them. . . . " Having bargained the accomplishments of a young lady for the wealth of a husband, Aunt Stanhope now tries to fix a cash value for the symbols of those accomplishments, a piano-forte and harp.

Aunt Stanhope insists that the marriage market is a serious business, that those who enjoy the social season instead of viewing it as an opportunity for responsible economic action will pay the price: she warns that "nothing . . . can be more miserable than the situation of a poor girl, who, after spending not only the interest, but the solid capital of her small fortune in dress, and frivolous extravagance, fails in her matrimonial expectations (as many do merely from not beginning to speculate in time)." In summoning up this monitory figure of a tragically naive debutante who realizes too late that the buying she has imitated is actually a form of selling, Aunt Stanhope reveals that in the marriage market, responsible consumption is always self-merchandizing. In advising Belinda against "an ill-judged economy," Aunt Stanhope points out a central paradox of credibility: since trade credit was extended indefinitely, one was creditworthy just so long as one's creditors saw one as creditworthy, loans often being converted to debts only by a creditor's panic at signs of financial retrenchment. The expenditure required to maintain this very real sense of creditworthiness could rule out any hope of living within one's income, of remaining creditworthy in the sense of contracting only those debts that one might be able to pay. Aunt Stanhope advises Belinda to go into debt in order to demonstrate her creditworthiness:

> You will, of course, have credit with all her ladyship's tradespeople, if you manage properly. To know how and when to lay out money is highly commendable, for in some situations, people judge of what one can afford by what one actually spends.—I know of no law which compels a young lady to tell what her age or her fortune may be.

In opposing this idea of advertising oneself through personal expenditure, Belinda champions saving as a form of conspicuous nonconsumption.

Both the marriage market and the larger marketplace required one to constantly evaluate others in order to determine one's own value—a kind of work that Edgeworth also demands of her readers by presenting her novels as exercises in moral discrimination. Belinda and Clarence fall in love as much with their own ability to read character as with each other; their courtship is presented as a process of determining one's own value by determining that of the other. Clarence is "absolutely enchanted with . . . his own penetration in having discovered [Belinda's] real character," while Belinda, seeing Clarence's "character . . . in a new light," is "proud of her own judgment, in having discerned his merit." Because they will each derive their worth from that of whomever they incorporate with as a family, Belinda and Clarence are right to take conspicuous delight in conscientiously researching each others' "various excellencies and defects" before committing themselves either emotionally or financially. Edgeworth rewrites romance as rational investment in the marriage market, and investment as romance: this novel makes it seem only natural that the hero should first feel "in its fullest extent all the power [Belinda] had over his heart" in the moment of discovering that she has not actually shortchanged him by 200 guineas.

From Aunt Stanhope, obsessed with thriving on a small income, Belinda passes into the hands of Lady Delacour, obsessed with squandering a large one. While Aunt Stanhope treats Belinda as a fellow speculator in the marriage market, Lady Delacour urges her to become a consumer. From the table of contents onward, Lady Delacour's hyperbolic, mysterious guilt and supernatural alarms ("A Spectre"; "The Mysterious Boudoir") appear as miniature Radcliffean romances, playing against the exemplary virtues of the Percivals, who represent "Domestic Happiness" and "A Family Party." Lady Delacour introduces Gothic conventions into a domestic novel, disrupting both its tone of rational didacticism and its plot.

This disruption marks the point at which Edgeworth splits the commercial world into two separate and radically contradictory systems of representation. On the one hand the marketplace is a rational place governed by Adam Smith's predictable laws, laws that are at once moral and economic in their promise to reward prudent self-denial: Belinda's unwavering control of her own desires, for example, wins her a husband with a rent-roll worth £10,000 a year. On the other hand the marketplace is also a realm of open and insatiable consumer desire, a realm that Edgeworth describes through fantastic and improbable Gothic conventions. "The most dissipated and unprincipled viscountess in town," Lady Delacour is a thoroughly commercial version of the depraved and irresistible Gothic hero. Belinda thinks her "the most agreeable—no, that is too feeble an expression—the most fascinating person she had ever beheld," Lady Delacour tempts Belinda not with sex or satanism, however, but with the unholy pleasures of conspicuous consumption.

Lady Delacour has been ravaged by a life of financial dissipation, by "the pleasure of spending three fortunes." Her consumption has consumed her own body:

[She] held the candle so as to throw the light full upon her livid features. Her eyes were sunk, her cheeks hollow; no trace of youth or beauty remained on her death-like countenance, which formed a horrid contrast with her gay fantastic dress.

"You are shocked, Belinda." said she; "but as yet you have seen nothing—look here"—and baring one half of her bosom, she revealed a hideous spectacle.

This hideous spectacle is an apparently cancerous breast, which is taken to signify a variety of Lady Delacour's transgressions, from sexual infidelity to indifference toward her child. Although she is presented as a walking symbol of guilty corruption, however, Lady Delacour is innocent of these charges. She has in fact been set up by her author, framed as a Gothic villain. By the end of the novel Lady Delacour is acquitted of every violation of domestic principles but the wickedness of wildly overspending her income, the sin of refusing to behave like an economically rational being.

Despite her intelligence and general cynicism about human nature, Lady Delacour "know[s] nothing of business." She has ruined her character through using up her moral and financial credit:

"I was mighty well pleased to find, that by so easy an expedient as writing 'T. C. H. Delacour,' I could command money at will. I signed, and signed, till at last I was with all due civility informed that my signature was no longer worth a farthing."

Lady Delacour's unforgivable mistake is to assume that status can do the work of character. That is, she misunderstands the meaning of her own signature by imagining that it has value in representing who she is—or rather, who she has been—rather than in representing a real commitment to future action. In the social display that fostered the growth of the new consumer society, Edgeworth recognizes an old enemy: debt-ridden Lady Delacour is a Rackrent disguised as an elegant London hostess. Lady Delacour points to a basic identity between two different stages of history that, according to Edgeworth's scheme of development, ought to be far apart. In flaunting the fact that social status can be sold, and sold for a heap of flashy and ephemeral consumer goods, Lady Delacour reenacts the puzzling act of folly that Adam Smith points to as a founding moment of commerce—the breakup of feudal authority. The market itself grew out of the ridiculous "folly" of landed aristocrats oblivious to their true interests as well as out of the praiseworthy "industry" of merchants. "To gratify the most childish vanity was the sole motive of the great proprietors" in abandoning their feudal obligations, Smith fumes; "for a pair of diamond buckles perhaps, or for something as frivolous and useless, they exchanged . . . the price of maintenance of a thousand men for a year, and with it the weight and authority which it could give them" (*Wealth of Nations*).

Although both Smith and Edgeworth dislike frivolous and useless desires, however, the increasingly consumer-based society of the eighteenth century was built on them as well as on prudent self-denial. In her inassimilable extravagance Lady Delacour is a reminder of the desires that Edgeworth's heuristic blending of moral and financial credit must exclude. Her generic incongruity marks a tension between morality and economics, a tension that Edgeworth addresses more directly in **"The Dun,"** admitting that "there are political advocates for luxury, who assert, perhaps justly, that the extravagance of individuals increases the wealth of nations" (in *Tales of Fashionable Life*). Characteristically, Edgeworth resolves this tension between private vices and public benefits by invoking the ideal of credit. Extravagant consumption is bad, Edgeworth implies, because it leads to bad debts, debts that damage the creditor as well as the debtor; the need to reward industry requires that desires as well as "expenses [be] regulated." Edgeworth maintains that Lady Delacour's Gothic consumption is as destructive of British industry as it is of her own character.

As we have seen, Edgeworth's emphasis on the probable is part of her larger project of teaching a morality suited to a commercial world that purports to value estimates of future pleasure over present pleasure. Lady Delacour disrupts this scheme not only in her extravagant refusal to look to the future but also in the supreme improbability of her final moral and physical recovery. *Belinda* eventually reveals that the hideous spectacle of Lady Delacour's cancerous breast is indeed only a spectacle, as harmless as the wax figure of corruption hidden behind Udolpho's black veil. Lady Delacour's wound is, in fact, a mere bruise, received in a duel with another woman and aggravated by a quack doctor. In the course of a few pages, with a conscious improbability marked by an embarrassed footnote ("We spare the reader the medical journal of Lady Delacour's health for some months. Her recovery was gradual and complete," Lady Delacour rises from her deathbed, where she indulged in superstitious hallucinations, opium, and the horrors of morbid methodism, to become a model of domestic and financial propriety.

Edgeworth's emphasis on probable behavior and plausible desires reflects her attempt to transform commercial consumption, which seemed in the 1790s to be a passion as dangerous and irrational as Lady Delacour herself, into an orderly collection of moral and economic laws. Edgeworth's campaign to replace the fantastic unpredictability of the Gothic with the "probable" as the foundation of literary character also consolidates a shift toward credit as a privileged form of economic agency that began in the early eighteenth century. That is, Edgeworth's idea of character reflects the enabling belief about credit that, given a sufficiently consistent pattern of past action, one can form a reliable prediction of the future behavior of an individual. Edgeworth recognizes personal credit as the new basis of property, and predictability of character as the basis of credit. In her emphasis on controlling and manipulating one's public image, Edgeworth is a propagandist for the fictionalization of personal character that a market economy effects.

FURTHER READING

Biography

Harden, O. Elizabeth WcWhorter. *Maria Edgeworth*. Boston: Twayne Publishers, 1984, 149 p.
Concise biography and critical discussion of Edgeworth's major work.

Inglis-Jones, Elisabeth. *The Great Maria: A Portrait of Maria Edgeworth*. London: Faber and Faber, 1959, 265 p.
Biography based on unpublished papers including family correspondence.

Newby, P. H. *Maria Edgeworth*. Denver: Alan Swallow, 1950, 98 p.
Concise introduction to Edgeworth's life and work.

Criticism

Kelly, Gary. "Amelia Opie, Lady Caroline Lamb, and Maria Edgeworth: Official and Unofficial Ideology." In *Ariel* 12, No. 4 (October 1981): 3-24.
Examination of the ways the women novelists cited explored moral, social, and ideological issues in their fiction.

Ruoff, Gene W. "1800 and the Future of the Novel: William Wordsworth, Maria Edgeworth, and the Vagaries of Literary History." In *The Age of William Wordsworth: Critical Essays on the Romantic Tradition*, edited by Kenneth R. Johnston and Gene W. Ruoff, pp. 291-314. New Brunswick: Rutgers University Press, 1987.
Examines *Castle Rackrent* as a literary manifesto treating the cultural, political, and economic conflicts resulting from colonial exploitation.

Shaffer, Julie. "Not Subordinate: Empowering Women in the Marriage-Plot—The Novels of Frances Burney, Maria Edgeworth, and Jane Austen." *Criticism* XXXIV, No. 1 (Winter 1992): 51-73.
Examines ways that the novelists cited challenged the subordinate societal status of women in their fiction.

Tracy, Robert. "Maria Edgeworth and Lady Morgan: Legality versus Legitimacy." *Nineteenth-Century Fiction* 40, No. 1 (June 1985): 1-22.
Studies Edgeworth's efforts to craft her Irish regional novels to appeal to both Irish and English reader-ship.

Weekes, Ann Owens. "Maria Edgeworth: Domestic Saga." In her *Irish Women Writers: An Uncharted Tradition*.

Lexington: University Press of Kentucky, 1990, pp. 33-59.

Critical study positing biographical bases for characters and incidents in Edgeworth's fiction.

Additional coverage of Edgeworth's life and career is contained in the following sources published by Gale Research: *Dictionary of Literary Biography, Vol. 116; Nineteenth-Century Literature Criticism, Vol. 1;* and *Something about the Author, Vol. 21.*

Charles Fourier

1772-1837

(Full name François Marie Charles Fourier) French utopian social philosopher.

INTRODUCTION

Fourier was a French social theorist influenced by the failure of the French Revolution to equalize the distribution of property and wealth and by what he viewed as the negative effects of economic competition. Fourier developed theories of social organization that emphasized the indulgence of human passion as a means of attaining personal and social harmony. He gained a small following during his lifetime and achieved greater recognition in the 1840s, when the study of his work inspired the development of several communal living experiments, including Brook Farm in Massachusetts and the North American Phalanx in New Jersey.

Biographical Information

Born in 1772 in Besançon to a middle-class merchant family, Fourier completed his education at the Jesuit Collège de Besançon and in 1789 became an apprentice in a commercial concern in Lyons. In 1793, he invested and lost a small inheritance and was later imprisoned as a result of his association with the counterrevolutionary forces who were defeated during the Siege of Lyons. On his release from prison, Fourier served briefly in the army and later found work as a clerk, a cashier, and a bookkeeper. He began developing his utopian theories but was unable to devote his full attention to this work due to financial difficulties. Following his mother's death in 1812, he began receiving an annual stipend as well as financial support from followers. One of his early essays, "Harmonie universelle" (1803), briefly outlines his theory of social organization. In 1808 he completed *Théorie des quatre mouvements et des destinées générales,* his first thorough examination of the social problems of the time and his proposed solutions. After publishing several other works in an effort to interest people in his theories, Fourier and his disciples founded the journal *Le Phalanstère* in 1832. The publication was designed to elucidate Fourier's theories for the general public and to generate interest among possible investors. Some of Fourier's disciples, however, charged that Fourier was incapable of presenting his ideas in an accessible, appealing manner. The journal appeared for less than two years. After suffering from failing health for several years, Fourier died in 1837.

Major Works

Throughout his three major works—*Théorie des quatre mouvements et des destinées générales, Traité de l'Association domestique agricole* (1822), and *Le Nouveau Monde indus-*

triel et sociétaire (1829)—Fourier identified and analyzed the twelve human passions and argued that social institutions should provide the opportunity for the development of these passions. Commerce, he maintained, is morally harmful and should be replaced with a cooperative system of economy and life. Arguing for the equality of the sexes, he denounced marriage as a form of slavery and called for the practice of free love. Fourier also divided the development of humanity into a number of stages beginning with the state of Nature and ending with the ideal state, that of Harmony. Fourier identified the current state of humanity as Civilization, contending that while Civilization is full of evils, it contains the necessary forces to produce the ultimate state of Harmony. To achieve this state of Harmony, Fourier wrote, social organization must allow the free play of all of the human passions. Concurrent with the presentation of his theories regarding social organization, Fourier developed theories regarding the earth's physical development. Fourier argued that the planet was passing out of a state of infancy and that after Fourier's plans were adopted by the earth's inhabitants, it would enter into a new period of development in which lions would become servants of humanity and the sea would turn into lemonade.

Critical Reception

Despite the fantastical nature of some of Fourier's ideas, many scholars find matter for serious study in his social theories. While nineteenth-century critics noted the enthusiasm of Fourier's small but devoted following and conceded that the philosopher's influence was strong enough to reach America, they tended to dismiss his ideas as impractical and to decry his disregard for conventional morality. In 1842 one anonymous writer for the *Dial* argued that Fourier's system "treats man as a plastic thing," and in 1844 another critic from the same journal frowned on the absence of Christianity from Fourier's theories. Some modern critics have concentrated on the comparison of Fourier's theories with those of his socialist contemporaries Robert Owen and Saint-Simon (Claude-Henri de Rouvroy). Other critics, such as Leslie Goldstein, have examined the feminist aspects of Fourier's work. Carl Guarneri argues that even though interest in the community structure that Fourier outlined in his works diminished rapidly after the 1840s, communitarian values continued to be explored into the late nineteenth century through the work of landscape architect Frederick Law Olmstead, who designed municipal parks intended to display the harmonious balance between city and country, and novelist Edward Bellamy, whose novel *Looking Backward* (1888) envisaged the futuristic organization of labor around human desires.

PRINCIPAL WORKS

"Harmonie universelle" (essay) 1803

Théorie des quatre mouvements et des destinées générales (philosophy) 1808

Traité de l'Association domestique agricole (philosophy) 1822

Le Nouveau Monde industriel et sociétaire (philosophy) 1829

La Fausse Industrie (philosophy) 1835

Oeuvres complètes. 12 vols. (philosophy) 1966-68

Le Nouveau Monde amoureux (philosophy) 1967

CRITICISM

The Dial (essay date 1842)

SOURCE: "Fourierism and the Socialists," in *The Dial,* Vol. III, No. 1, July, 1842, pp. 86-90.

[*In the following excerpt, the anonymous critic praises the spirit of Fourier's social theory while expressing scepticism about its practicability.*]

The increasing zeal and numbers of the disciples of Fourier, in America and in Europe, entitle them to an attention which their theory and practical projects will justify and reward. In London, a good weekly newspaper (lately changed into a monthly journal) called *The Phalanx,* devoted to the social doctrines of Charles Fourier, and bearing for its motto, "Association and Colonization," is ed-

ited by Hugh Doherty. Mr. Etzler's inventions, as described in the *Phalanx,* promise to cultivate twenty thousand acres with the aid of four men only and cheap machinery. Thus the laborers are threatened with starvation, if they do not organize themselves into corporations, so that machinery may labor *for* instead of working *against* them. It appears that Mr. Young, an Englishman of large property, has purchased the Benedictine Abbey of Citeaux, in the Mont d'Or, in France, with its ample domains, for the purpose of establishing a colony there. We also learn that some members of the sect have bought an estate at Santa Catharina, fifty miles from Rio Janeiro, in a good situation for an agricultural experiment, and one hundred laborers have sailed from Havre to that port, and nineteen hundred more are to follow. On the anniversary of the birthday of Fourier, which occurred in April, public festivals were kept by the Socialists in London, in Paris, and in New York. In the city of New York, the disciples of Fourier have bought a column in the Daily Tribune, Horace Greeley's excellent newspaper, whose daily and weekly circulation exceeds twenty thousand copies, and through that organ are now diffusing their opinions.

We had lately an opportunity of learning something of these Socialists and their theory from the indefatigable apostle of the sect in New York, Albert Brisbane. Mr. Brisbane pushes his doctrine with all the force of memory, talent, honest faith, and importunacy. As we listened to his exposition, it appeared to us the sublime of mechanical philosophy; for the system was the perfection of arrangement and contrivance. The force of arrangement could no farther go. The merit of the plan was that it was a system; that it had not the partiality and hint-and-fragment character of most popular schemes, but was coherent and comprehensive of facts to a wonderful degree. It was not daunted by distance, or magnitude, or remoteness of any sort, but strode about nature with a giant's step, and skipped no fact, but wove its large Ptolemaic web of cycle and epicycle, of phalanx and phalanstery, with laudable assiduity. Mechanics were pushed so far as fairly to meet spiritualism. One could not but be struck with strange coincidences betwixt Fourier and Swedenborg. Genius hitherto has been shamefully misapplied, a mere trifler. It must now set itself to raise the social condition of man, and to redress the disorders of the planet he inhabits. The Desert of Sahara, the Campagna di Roma, the frozen polar circles, which by their pestilential or hot or cold airs poison the temperate regions, accuse man. Society, concert, co-operation, is the secret of the coming Paradise. By reason of the isolation of men at the present day, all work is drudgery. By concert, and the allowing each laborer to choose his own work, it becomes pleasure. "Attractive Industry" would speedily subdue, by adventurous, scientific, and persistent tillage, the pestilential tracts; would equalize temperature; give health to the globe, and cause the earth to yield 'healthy imponderable fluids' to the solar system, as now it yields noxious fluids. The hyaena, the jackal, the gnat, the bug, the flea, were all beneficent parts of the system; the good Fourier knew what those creatures should have been, had not the mould slipped, through the bad state of the atmosphere, caused, no doubt, by these same vicious imponderable fluids. All these shall be redressed by human culture, and the useful goat, and dog, and innocent poetical moth, or the wood-tick to consume decomposing wood, shall take their place. It takes 1680 men to make one Man, complete in all the faculties; that is, to be sure that you have got a good joiner, a good cook, a barber, a poet, a judge, an umbrella-maker, a mayor and aldermen, and so on. Your community should consist of 2000 persons, to prevent accidents of omission; and each community should take up 6000 acres of land. Now fancy the earth planted with fifties and hundreds of these phalanxes side by side,—what tillage, what architecture, what refectories, what dormitories, what reading rooms, what concerts, what lectures, what gardens, what baths! What is not in one, will be in another, and many will be within easy distance. Then know you and all, that Constantinople is the natural capital of the globe. There, in the Golden Horn, will be the Arch-Phalanx established, there will the Omniarch reside. Aladdin and his magician, or the beautiful Scheherzarade, can alone in these prosaic times, before the sight, describe the material splendors collected there. Poverty shall be abolished; deformity, stupidity, and crime shall be no more. Genius, grace, art, shall abound, and it is not to be doubted but that, in the reign of "Attractive Industry," all men will speak in blank verse.

Certainly we listened with great pleasure to such gay and magnificent pictures. The ability and earnestness of the advocate, and his friends, the comprehensiveness of their theory, its apparent directness of proceeding to the end they would secure, the indignation they felt and uttered at all other speculation in the presence of so much social misery, commanded our attention and respect. It contained so much truth, and promised in the attempts that shall be made to realize it so much valuable instruction, that we are engaged to observe every step of its progress. Yet in spite of the assurances of its friends, that it was new and widely discriminated from all other plans for the regeneration of society, we could not exempt it from the criticism which we apply to so many projects for reform with which the brain of the age teems. Our feeling was, that Fourier had skipped no fact but one, namely, Life. He treats man as a plastic thing, something that may be put up or down, ripened or retarded, moulded, polished, made into solid, or fluid, or gas, at the will of the leader; or, perhaps, as a vegetable, from which, though now a poor crab, a very good peach can by manure and exposure be in time produced, but skips the faculty of life, which spawns and scorns system and system-makers, which eludes all conditions, which makes or supplants a thousand phalanxes and New-Harmonies with each pulsation. There is an order in which in a sound mind the faculties always appear, and which, according to the strength of the individual, they seek to realize in the surrounding world. The value of Fourier's system is that it is a statement of such an order externized, or carried outward into its correspondence in facts. The mistake is, that this particular order and series is to be imposed by force of preaching and votes on all men, and carried into rigid execution. But what is true and good must not only be begun by life, but must be conducted to its issues by life. Could not the

conceiver of this design have also believed that a similar model lay in every mind, and that the method of each associate might be trusted, as well as that of his particular Committee and General Office, No. 200 Broadway? nay, that it would be better to say, let us be lovers and servants of that which is just; and straightway every man becomes a centre of a holy and beneficent republic, which he sees to include all men in its law, like that of Plato, and of Christ. Before such a man the whole world becomes Fourierized or Christized or humanized, and in the obedience to his most private being, he finds himself, according to his presentiment, though against all sensuous probability, acting in strict concert with all others who followed their private light.

Yet in a day of small, sour, and fierce schemes, one is admonished and cheered by a project of such friendly aims, and of such bold and generous proportion; there is an intellectual courage and strength in it, which is superior and commanding: it certifies the presence of so much truth in the theory, and in so far is destined to be fact.

But now, whilst we write these sentences, comes to us a paper from Mr. Brisbane himself. We are glad of the opportunity of letting him speak for himself. He has much more to say than we have hinted, and here has treated a general topic. We have not room for quite all the matter which he has sent us, but persuade ourselves that we have retained every material statement, in spite of the omissions which we find it necessary to make, to contract his paper to so much room as we offered him.

Mr Brisbane, in a prefatory note to his article, announces himself as an advocate of the Social Laws discovered by Charles Fourier, and intimates that he wishes to connect whatever value attaches to any statement of his, with the work in which he is exclusively engaged, that of Social Reform. He adds the following broad and generous declaration.

> It seems to me that, with the spectacle of the present misery and degradation of the human race before us, all scientific researches and speculations, to be of any real value, should have a bearing upon the means of their social elevation and happiness. The mass of scientific speculations, which are every day offered to the world by men, who are not animated by a deep interest in the elevation of their race, and who exercise their talents merely to build up systems, or to satisfy a spirit of controversy, or personal ambition, are perfectly valueless. What is more futile than barren philosophical speculation, that leads to no great practical results?

The Dial (essay date 1844)

SOURCE: "Fourierism," in *The Dial*, Vol. IV, No. IV, April, 1844, pp. 473-83.

[In the following essay, the critic offers a brief analysis of Fourier's philosophy as it was discussed at a convention held in Boston, Massachusetts, in late 1843 and early 1844.]

In the last week of December, 1843, and first week of January, 1844, a Convention was held in Boston, which may be considered as the first publication of Fourierism in this region.

The works of Fourier do not seem to have reached us, and this want of text has been ill supplied by various conjectures respecting them; some of which are more remarkable for the morbid imagination they display than for their sagacity. For ourselves we confess to some remembrances of vague horror, connected with this name, as if it were some enormous parasitic plant sucking the life principles of society, while it spread apparently an equal shade, inviting man to repose under its beautiful but poison-dropping branches. We still have a certain question about Fourierism, considered as a catholicon for evil, but our absurd horrors were dissipated, and a feeling of genuine respect for the friends of the movement ensured, as we heard the exposition of the doctrine of Association, by Mr. Channing, and others. That name already consecrated to humanity, seemed to us to have worthily fallen, with the mantle of the philanthropic spirit, upon this eloquent expounder of socialism; in whose voice and countenance, as well as in his pleadings for humanity, the spirit of his great kinsman still seemed to speak.

We cannot sufficiently lament that there was no reporter of the speech in which Mr. Channing set forth the argument derived from the analogy of nature, against the doctrine of community of goods to the exclusion of individual property. It was the general scope of the argument, to show that Life was forever tending to individuality of expression, and could not be refused the material order also, as a field for the scope of this tendency, and that individual property was the expression of this universal law; the lowest expression certainly, but still an expression. It would not be fair to give a garbled report of his masterly and delicate sketch of the ultimate result of denying this principle. He divided the truth on this subject to right and left, with the sword of pure spirit. Let it be sufficient to say, that only the ecstasy of self-love could understand it as casting personal reflections; and that it could not be expected to find an understanding heart with the ecstasy of destructiveness, which has seized many modern reformers.

But in the absence of reports of this and other speeches, we will give a sketch of Fourierism, as we gathered it from the debates of the Convention, and conversation with its friends; and then take the liberty of stating some qualifications, and limitations, which seem to have escaped the attention of its enthusiastic disciples. The general view upon which Fourier proceeds is this: that there is in the Divine Mind a certain social order, to which man is destined, and which is discoverable by man, according to his truth in thought to the two poles of Christian perfection, Love of God and Love of Man.

He assumes the fact, which will hardly be disputed, that the present social organizations are not this divine order; but that they perpetually and necessarily generate external evils, which so complicate the temptations of man, as to make innocence impossible, and virtue only the meed

of crucifixion; nor even attainable by that, except in instances of beings endowed with supernatural energy. For the proof of this fact, he appeals to all history and all experience.

Environed, as he felt himself also to be by this extreme disorder, yet Fourier had the courage to attempt to discover the Divine order, and labored forty years at the work. Brought up in mercantile life, and keeping this position, which enabled him to know personally the customs and laws of trade, as it is; and endowed with a genius for calculation, which, in the service of justice and benevolence, followed out the bearings of these customs and laws, and the effects of large monopolies upon the social happiness and moral character of the various men directly and indirectly affected by them; he yet, to use his own words, 'labored in distraction for seven years, before he obtained the clue.' At last, having seen that Labor stands, in the social world, for the analogous fact of motion in the physical, he pronounced the word *Attraction*, which arranged to his mind the universe of men, as once before, that same word, to a kindred genius, arranged the universe of matter.

The question then became, what is that social arrangement, so broad, and so elastic, that every man shall find, at every hour of the day, and every season of his life, *just that labor* which is to him attractive and not *repugnant*.

As Fourier places among the constituent passions of men every social charity, and even a passion for *self-sacrifice,* he could maintain that there is nothing done, and nothing to be done in the world, which might not find a willing agent, were circumstances properly arranged.

But to induce a desire after this arrangement, and evoke the ability to make it, mankind must have its scientific foundations, or harmony with the nature of things, made manifest to their reason. Man therefore must be analyzed into his constituent powers; and then the tendencies of each of these powers be studied out, and corresponding circumstances imagined, which should yield to each power its legitimate range; for such circumstances must necessarily be the Divine Order of Society to which man is destined.

Thus analyzed, man, according to Fourier, is constituted of twelve fundamental passions, consisting, firstly, of the five senses; secondly, of the four social passions, friendship, ambition, love, and the parental sentiment; and thirdly, of three intellectual powers, whose strange names, according to our best recollection, are Cabalism, Alternatism, and Emulation.

The training of these twelve powers into their appropriate activities, that each may contribute its share, both to the harmony of the Universe, and the unity of the individual, is what Fourier calls the social development of the passions.

This view of the constituency of man and the necessity of his training, may be made plainer perhaps by translating his language into that of another remarkable thinker, who seems to have had, fundamentally, the same view. Swedenborg says, that man's soul is made up of Loves, and every Love must find its Wisdom, the marriage unions of Love and Wisdom, being made manifest in Uses. The Angel of Love must find the Angel of Wisdom to whom it is betrothed, on penalty of becoming a devil, says Swedenborg. If the passions do not find their developments, by the law of groups and series, says Fourier, they become principles of disorder, and produce what we see now all around us,—*a world lying in wickedness and dead in sin.*

There is one of man's passions which has found its social development, so far as to become an illustration of the meaning of this theory with regard to all the rest; and this is the Passion of Hearing. Music is the Wisdom of this Passion; and the progress of this science has involved the large variety of musical instruments, and created the song, the chorus, the opera, the oratorio, and the orchestra. So, according to Fourier, each of the senses, each of the social passions, each of the intellectual powers, in finding its legitimate scope, must create a music in its sphere, with instruments corresponding, and weave men into groups corresponding with the chorus, the opera, the oratorio, and the orchestra. And there are intimations of this. The passion of Sight has created Painting, Sculpture, Architecture. And even what seem to be the humbler powers of Touch, Taste, Smell, have not failed to bring the tribute of their exactions to the comforts and elegancies of life, and the science of vitality.

One obvious and undisputed function of the senses, is to build up bodies, and contribute to physical well-being. But this is not all. There is another function which the senses have to perform, beside this obvious one; and also beside the transcendental one of creating harmonies in five different modes; even though we may admit that all these harmonies may rise to the spiritual elevation of that divine art which Beethoven has carried to the acme of symbolizing the highest intellectual, moral, and even religious exercises of the soul. This function is to perfect the Earth on which we live, and make it not only yield its treasures for physical well-being to every creature, but perform adequately its part in the Sidereal Universe.

At this point of Fourier's system, there opens upon us a quite poetical extent of view. Geologists and geographers have intimated to us heretofore, that the earth needs to be dressed and kept by men, in order not to become in several ways desert, and that the climates, which depend much more upon the state of the surface of the earth, than upon its relations with the sun, should be ameliorated. Fourier would demonstrate that *the cursing of the ground for man's sake,* sung of by the old Hebrew prophet, is no metaphor; but that, literally, man's falling below his destiny, has, as its natural consequence, the return of the earth to a state of chaos. He demonstrates, that, following out the suggestions of the senses of taste and smell, the human race must cultivate the whole vegetable creation, if not the animal, to a perfection which would involve an agricultural science, absolutely sublime in its extent; while the

spring-carriage, and easy railroad car, and every contribution the mechanical arts have made to the commodity of man, would fall among the meanest and vulgarest class of the innumerable results of seeking for the wisdom of the sense of Touch.

But is the earth to be restored to the state of Paradise, through the labors of man, merely to react upon his physical nature, and contribute to his personal enjoyments? By no means. But the earth thus cultivated and perfected, shall shine as a brighter star in the firmament of other worlds; shall hold, by its imponderable fluids, a more perfect relation with the sun, and through that star with the whole sidereal heavens.

It is hardly fair to Fourier to touch, without entering into his reasonings, upon a part of his system which is so original, and which requires, in order to be appreciated, at least all that he has himself said upon it.

If the development and training of the senses to results of science and art, have these wide bearings upon the sidereal universe, we may not doubt that Fourier makes the development and bearings of the social passions, open another captivating and exalting vista of thought.

The word Friendship, in this nomenclature, stands for the sentiment of humanity, in its widest and in its most delicate relations. Fourier attempts to show that to give this passion its scope, the social system, which is according to the divine order, will realize in its institutions all, and more than all, that declarations of the Rights of man have ever suggested; all that his hopes have aspired to and expressed, under the images of the Millennium and Fifth Monarchy.

And to balance this great liberty, the second social passion must have its scope. This passion, which he defines as the love of order, in graduating persons according to their comparative worth with relation to each other, he calls *Ambition;* thus casting out of this word its bad meaning,—for its object is no longer the exaltation of *self,* but of *worth.* It gives to every man and woman their exact place in the social scale, and justifies the idea of government. By the balance of the two passions of Friendship and Ambition, Liberty and Law will become, as they should do, the poles of a living political order.

The Passions of Love, and the Parental Sentiment, will also, when, through a general ease of circumstances, they are left free to find their legitimate exercises, dignify woman universally; and by consequence, purify the institution of marriage, and unfold the family, to their highest ends of refining, and sanctifying, and cherishing human beings, into the richest forms of life.

The Christian world, as it is, can hardly fail to acknowledge, that although Christianity has sanctified the *formula* of monogamy, yet the whole deep significance of that institution is yet to be widely appreciated. To marry from any consideration but the one of sentiment, must be considered a crime, before mankind will cease from that adultery of the heart, of which Christ warned his disciples.

Lastly, the three intellectual passions into which Fourier analyzes the Reason, have for their office to estimate the natures and ends of the foregoing nine passions, and interweave them into one web of life, according to their natures and ends; and then they will take the still higher range, of enjoying the divine order, and tracing in the happiness thence resulting, the image of God.

We see from the above rude outline, that Fourier thinks he has discovered the divine order, which is the true organization of society, by studying each of the twelve passions of man, with the same respect that the passion of hearing has been studied, in order to derive from thence the present living art of music. He thinks, that by following out the results of this study in practice, the earth would be cultivated and restored to the state of Paradise; with the superstructure thereon of a world of art, in harmony with the beauty of nature. Also, that political institutions would combine all desirable liberty, with all that can come from the observance of law, by distributing all men according to the gradation of their natures; and that individual families would be established in the purest and most powerful form; lastly, that the functions of Reason would be vindicated to their worthiest objects, of perpetually unfolding and keeping in order this great estate of man, internal and external.

If Fourier had done nothing but suggest to his race, that the divine order of society was a possible discovery, and thus have given a noble object to human investigations, and presented a worthy prize for human energy, in this direction, he would have done much. It is claimed, however, by those who have studied his works, that he has done a great deal more; that he has himself successfully worked at the practical problems; and the *Phalanx* which he has discovered in detail, is, as it were, a house already builded, into which men may go, and at once live, freed from a multitude of the evils that press upon the modern civilized state. A word or two in explanation of this Phalanx.

It is not a community of goods. It is a state of society which provides a public fund, as all societies do, and on a better security for its return in just proportions to those who produce it, but which admits of individual property as much as any partnership in trade. It is indeed a great partnership, in which the members throw in capital of three species, namely, labor, skill, and money, (which last is the representative of past labor and skill.) All these species of capital will draw a large interest, when the Phalanx is in operation; but in order to prevent any great inequality of the third species of capital, (money,) it is a fundamental law of the Phalanx that small sums shall draw interest in a larger ratio than large ones. The common property, accumulated by the Phalanx in its corporate capacity, shall be subject to the will of the members, expressed by ballot and otherwise; its general destination being to provide for all children, without distinction of rank or birth, an individually appropriate education, according to their genius and capacity; also to provide public conveniencies, and common comforts and amusements, and means of expressing their genius, to all the members.

The labor in the Phalanx will be organized upon scientific principles, i. e. by the law of groups and series, and individual genius and disposition will be the guide as to the distribution of the members into the several groups and series. The well being and good training of the laborer will never be sacrificed to the external object of the labor, for Fourier endeavors to demonstrate that, in the divine order, the necessity of such a sacrifice never can occur, even though all ends are answered.

The first objection that strikes a spiritual or intellectual person, at the presentation of Fourierism, is its captivating material aspect. A system which accepts the social passions, and even the senses of man in full, and puts them on the same ground with the functions of Reason, seems to be a dead-leveller.

Undoubtedly, at first sight, it is especially captivating to the sensualist. But, on a little investigation, it will be found to present no bed of roses for the sluggard, nor paradise for the mere epicure. The discharge of the external functions of the senses, involves the keenest and most health-giving labor, though a labor that must have all the characteristics of the chase, and other chosen amusements of manly men and women; nor can the labor fall upon any one to the degree of making a drudge.

Also, the abundance which this discharge of the external functions of the senses will bring forth from the earth, to the physical well-being of man, will leave him leisure to follow out the leadings of his social passions, which now are cramped and warped from their objects, by the necessity that rests upon every man to *scramble,* in order to get his sufficiency out of the present scarcity of provisions on the globe. For, undoubtedly, it is because poverty is in the world, and because all the accumulated riches, if divided, would not leave even a competence to each, that even the rich cannot get rid of this all-devouring instinct of hoarding, or getting more. Were every man assured of the necessities and comforts of life, where would be the stimulus to this morbid passion for gain, which consumes the civilized man, and makes him sacrifice the purity and warmth of his friendship, love, and parental sentiment?

But, then, the social passions, thus set free to act, do not carry within them their own rule, nor the pledge of conferring happiness. They can only get this from the free action upon them of the intellectual passions which constitute human Reason.

But these functions of Reason,—do they carry within themselves the pledge of their own continued health and harmonious action?

Here Fourierism stops short, and, in so doing, proves itself to be, not a life, a soul, but only a body. It may be a magnificent body for humanity to dwell in for a season; and one for which it may be wise to quit old diseased carcases, which now go by the proud name of civilization. But if its friends pretend, for what has been now described, any higher character than that of a body, thus turning men from seeking for principles of life essentially above organization, it will prove but another, perhaps a greater curse.

In being a body, however, it is as much entitled to consideration, as any other body which has been created. It has the presumptive advantage of being a creation of the Christian life. The question is, whether the Phalanx acknowledges its own limitations of nature, in being an organization, or opens up any avenue into the source of life that shall keep it sweet, enabling it to assimilate to itself contrary elements, and consume its own waste; so that, Phœnix-like, it may renew itself forever in great and finer forms.

This question, the Fourierists in the Convention, from whom alone we have learnt anything of Fourierism, did not seem to have considered.

But this is a vital point. Did our time and space permit, we should be tempted to follow out some curious analogies, suggested to us by reading Karl Ottfried Mueller's History of the Dorians. In looking over Fourier's analysis of human nature, as given above, we notice that every one of his passions, whether sensuous, social, or intellectual, was recognised as a *god,* by some separate tribe in antiquity. The Oriental religions, with the exception of the Hebrew, and the European also, consisted in deifications of the Forces and and the Functions of Being. The Dorians alone, in their fidelity to the beautiful individuality of their Apollo, gave to Grecian culture that polarity which is essential to a reproductive life; and made Greece what it is in the history of humanity.

But it is not our purpose to recommend the worship of Apollo to the Fourierists. The Word of God, the doctrine of the expiation, which even divinity must make, if it would act upon earth; all that Apollo beautifully intimated in his human form of superhuman beauty; in his destruction of the Pythoness; or in his pilgrimage to Tempe, where Jove made inquisition for blood; or in his reappearance from the Hyperborean land of perpetual summer, with wheat sheaves for men; all is symbolized and realized in Christ. And this is now the only name under heaven, by which men may be saved from spiritual death. Christian churches in the midst of a Phalanx, might be the Dorian cities of another Greece. Only let each member be at once subject and lawgiver, like a Lycurgus, pupil and master like a Pythagoras; like Lacedemon, fighting and conquering for self-preservation only, and the liberty of the conquered.

In a former article, we suggested the idea, that the Christian churches planted by the Apostles, were only initiatory institutions, to be lost, like the morning star, in the deeper glory of a kingdom of heaven on earth, which we then fancied Socialism would bring about.

Since then, by the study of ancient nationalities, and also of Neander's History of the Churches of Christ up to the time of Constantine, together with observations on the attempt at West Roxbury, we have come to see that initiatory churches will have an office as long as men are born children; and that a tremendous tyranny is necessarily involved by constituting society itself the VISIBLE church of Christ. Those who have ideas, and who, individually, and free from human constraining, have pledged themselves to live by them alone, or die, must be a select body, in the midst of the instinctive life that is perpetually arriving on the shores of Being, and which it is not fair or wise to catch up and *christen* before it can understand its position, and give its consent. We must be men before we are Christians, else we shall never be either Christians or men.

The life of the world is now the Christian life. For eighteen centuries, Art, Literature, Philosophy, Poetry, have followed the fortunes of the Christian idea. Ancient history is the history of the apotheosis of Nature, or natural religion; modern history is the history of an Idea, or revealed religion. In vain will any thing try to be, which is not supported thereby. Fourier does homage to Christianity with many words. But this may be *cant,* though it thinks itself sincere. Besides, there are many things which go by the name of Christianity, that are not it. Let the Fourierists see to it, that there be freedom in their Phalanx for churches, unsupported by its material organization, and lending it no support on its material side. Independently existing, within them, but not of them, feeding on ideas, forgetting that which is behind, petrified into performance,—and pressing on to the stature of the perfect man, they will finally spread themselves in spirit over the whole body.

In fine, it is our belief, that unless the Fourierist bodies are made alive by Christ, 'their constitution will not march'; and the galvanic force of reaction, by which they move for a season, will not preserve them from corruption. As 'the corruption of the best is the worst,' the warmer their friends are, the more awake should they be to this danger, and the more energetic to avert it.

We understand that Brook Farm has become a Fourierist establishment. We rejoice in this, because such persons as form that association will give it a fair experiment. We wish it God-speed. May it become a University where the young American shall learn his duties, and become worthy of this broad land of his inheritance.

E. S. Mason (essay date 1928)

SOURCE: "Fourier and Anarchism," in *The Quarterly Journal of Economics,* Vol. XLII, February, 1928, pp. 228-62.

[*In the following excerpt, Mason argues that many elements of Fourier's philosophy were "typically anarchist."*]

In the writings of Fourier are to be found . . . characteristics of anarchist thought, together with some interesting peculiarities of his own.

He is usually classified as a socialist in the histories of socialist and economic thought. To open a discussion, however, on the similarities and differences between socialism and anarchism, and to attempt to relate the thought of Fourier to various possible definitions of either term, would involve a long and unprofitable rehash of the literature of the subject. My idea of the relation of Fourier to anarchism will become clear through the following consideration of his writings.

Fourier's thought fits very easily into the anarchist use of the conception of the natural order. . . . This is true despite his sparing use of the terms "natural law" or "natural order." His order, or system, which is based on the natural "passions" or "springs of action" in men, is used to illuminate and to condemn the artificial and conventional weaknesses of existing society. To this end he draws, in common with his eighteenth-century predecessors, on a mythical state of nature which he christens "Eden," or "terrestial paradise," existing at a time previous to those four stages of human development—savagery, patriarchy, barbarism, and civilization—which were, and are, marked and marred by the use of authority and restraint. Whether or no he believed in the historical existence of this epoch, we have no means of knowing. Certainly he exhibits more evidence than this of an astonishing credulity in the course of the development of his system. This system, again in common with anarchist thought, pretends to be a scientific construction based on a careful study of human nature, and is, at the same time, the ideal order of the future.

The natural order of Fourier, with regard to its form and the uses to which he puts it, comes straight from the political and economic thought of the eighteenth century. Gonnard touches on this when he says:

> There are in Fourierism two characteristics which, if they were not combined with others of a totally different origin, would tempt us to call Fourier the last of the Physiocrats. For he, as they, is at the same time impressed with the idea that there is a certain order ordained by Providence and destined to guarantee the happiness of man, and that this beneficent order should be established primarily on an agricultural basis [*Histoire des Doctrines Economiques,* 1922].

Fourier's knowledge of eighteenth-century thought, however, can be described only as half-baked. Passing in his immediate circle as a master of erudition, he was really nourished in his thinking by a superficial reading of the French political philosophers themselves, and by such popularizatons of their writings as appeared in the papers and periodicals of his time. He caught and made his own their "general idea," and it is with respect to this general approach and framework only that his thought resembles theirs.

His use of a beneficent Providence in the fashioning of the natural order is even more pronounced than that of the Physiocrats. Here again, however, God has but set the universe in motion and left it to the reason of man, to science, to discover that order of society conformable to man's nature. This is the problem which Fourier has set

himself to solve and he appeals to God to put his stamp of approval on the solution.

> The little that has been said on this subject is sufficient to prove that the lever of primordial harmony [which Fourier has discovered] is not a process invented to amuse; it is an imitative method [imitative, that is, of nature], drawn in its entirety from the system of nature, and if one wishes to suspect its excellence, it will be necessary at the same time to suspect the mechanism of the Universe, and the wisdom of its learned creator.

Fourier shared the common anarchist admiration of the method and results of the natural sciences. The Newtonian conception of the physical world as a mechanical equilibrium, a universe in which every atom attracts every other atom, and of which the order of equilibrium is possible of statement in mathematical terms, had the same appeal to Fourier as to the political philosophers of the eighteenth century. He attempted, as they, the application of the same method to the study of society, the construction of a natural order in the social world. Fourier, as did his contemporary, St. Simon, paraded as the Newton of the social sciences, altho he was not nearly so successful as the latter in making his pose effective. The atoms of Fourier's social order were the passions or springs of action, and he laid down his system of "passional attraction" on the basis of what purported to be an exact and scientific study of the nature of these passions.

This system of Fourier's, as has been emphasized, was put to the same use as the conception of a natural order in the eighteenth century. It was opposed, that is, in the first place, to the conventional order of existing society. Fourier's attack upon civilization, and upon the false sciences which pretend to study the nature of human conduct, is unflagging. Brought up in a provincial mercantile milieu, losing the bulk of his property in his early twenties, and spending most of the remainder of his life as an obscure clerk and commercial traveller, Fourier had considerable opportunity to observe the workings of the competitive régime, and it filled him with disgust. Bourgeois conduct is a compound of hypocrisy and persistent cupidity. As with most radical reformers, whether socialist or anarchist, his writings are full of attacks on particular economic institutions and practices. But we are not concerned here with his particular criticisms, which are not much more, or less, penetrating than those of numerous nineteenth-century socialists. In general, it can be said that the fundamental reason for the ills of society, whether political, economic, or moral, is the existence of an order which suppresses and restrains man's natural passions.

All of these impulses are good. "The passions are the work of the eternal geometer: he does not proceed arbitrarily as do Plato and Seneca, repressing this passion and proscribing that. He has not created them uselessly; they have a purpose; and it is necessary to determine this by fixed rules." Existing society is a tissue of habits, customs, and conventions which represent a repression of passions the free expression of which awaits only the discovery and realization of the natural order. Ambition, a propensity which, in our present order, works in the main for evil, could be utilized, in a natural order, for good. Cupidity, justly condemned in our present dispensation, could be made productive of benefit for society and the individual. So, too, the passion for change and variety, disruptive now of all those activities dependent upon persistent application, the passion for intrigue and political maneuvering, destructive of coöperation and united effort, and many others, sources of evil, could be fitted into a societal framework which would make possible their useful application. Marriage, in particular, is a civilized relationship which represses more passions than it satisfies. Civilization itself is, then, an order of society which contrasts in almost every way with that order which is the law of nature.

Those eighteenth-century philosophers who have condemned civilization most savagely, and who are most impatient with existing political and moral philosophy, are praised by Fourier as foreshadowing his discoveries most clearly. Social thinkers preceding him are classified into two groups: the first, which has cleared the ground for future progress, "sophistes expectant," among whom may be named Socrates, Rousseau, and Voltaire, have opposed most clearly an ideal order of society to the existing one represented by civilization; the other, "sophistes obscurants," has taken the attitude that this is "the best of all possible worlds," that the ideal order is, perhaps, after all, not very different from the conventional. Unfortunately, most of our political and moral philosophy has been the work of the second group. Consequently, this political and moral philosophy, based upon and supporting, as it does, an order which represses and restrains the passions, must be thrown overboard. Fourier places small value on the body of knowledge which represents the slow accumulation of successive generations of scholars and thinkers. He was fond of that statement of Barthélemy, "These libraries, pretended treasure-houses of human knowledge, are only humiliating depositories of contradictions and errors," and would have rejoiced with Comte in the destruction of all books, with a certain few exceptions.

How does it happen that the thought of mankind on the subject of society has been so fruitless of results, so lacking in an understanding of the elementary basis of the natural order? It is simply "because people have neglected at all times the branches of study which would conduct them to it, the analytical and synthetic study of passional attraction. It was misunderstood by the Greeks and the Romans; it has been the same with moderns, servile imitators of antiquity." This failure to apply reason to the discovery of the natural order is particularly unpardonable in the eighteenth century, "which recommends incessantly the going from the known to the unknown, and which, laying down this precept for the method and manner of investigation, has obstinately refused to apply it to the study of man, has refused to go from material attraction, already known, to passional attraction, whose theory is yet to be known."

Fourier himself proceeds to an elucidation of human conduct with a great display of scientific method. He an-

nounces at the outset, and often reiterates, that this, his main work, is going to fall into the three general divisions of *Aperçu, Abrégé,* and *Traité.* That is, he intends to work out the natural order through a first, a second, and a third approximation, beginning with broad generalizations, commonly accepted, and proceeding to the undiscovered particulars. However, an examination of his book fails to uncover this systematic development of his material. The general framework of his system is very simple and his treatment of it is extremely repetitive. He applies his central idea of passional attraction to a large number of particular problems, but there is no continuous development of his thought from the simple equilibrium of a first approximation to the complex equilibrium of a third approximation.

Nevertheless, there is a definite attempt at an application of the inductive-deductive method of science. Fourier takes a consistently contractual view of society. The institutions and conventions of his society come about through the equilibration of calculable motives. The nature of these motives, as seen by Fourier, represents inductive generalizations of experience, his observations of the workings of human nature and of human institutions. And even in his most far-fetched constructions, he insists on the importance of the criterion of experience.

Fourier's conception of the meaning of science comes out clearly enough in his condemnation of contemporary social science. "Political science and economics are theories subversive of destiny, since they cause us to stagnate apathetically in an unorganized [*morcelée*] industrial society, or the state of barbarism and civilization, instead of making every effort to attain our true destiny, which is societal industry." It appears from this that the laws of science, as understood by Fourier, are, in the words of Veblen, "in the nature of canons of conduct governing nature rather than the generalizations of mechanical sequence"; or, in the words of Alfred Marshall, they are expression in the "imperative" rather than the "indicative" mood. Canons of conduct expressed in the imperative mood, they certainly were, but this does not mean, necessarily, that they were not also generalizations of mechanical sequence expressed in the indicative mood. Here again Fourier can be placed in that line of thought which included the Physiocrats, tho it is certainly not true to say, with Gonnard, that he is the last of that line. To view the natural order as a scientific hypothesis and as an ideal standard of conduct was not held by him to be incompatible, and for the same reasons which determined the attitude, on this matter, of his intellectual predecessors.

The method of approach which made it possible to reconcile these two uses of the idea was . . . the antithesis they drew between natural and conventional. Since the *whole* of existing relationships was not regarded as natural, the ideal order might be constructed without logical difficulty by inductive generalizations from a part of the existing or conventional order. The laws of this order could be, at the same time, statements of existing invariable relationships and canons of conduct. That there are difficulties to be found in this antithesis between natural and conventional, we have neither to reëmphasize nor to discuss.

Fourier's natural order, tho pretending to be constructed by the inductive-deductive methods of science, was considerably different from the natural order of his contemporaries, the economists and political scientists. For the most part it was deduced *a priori* from his theory of human nature, altho occasionally he finds an existing institution or custom which would bear incorporation in the ideal order. The passions or springs of action he approaches through his three approximations. The first detects three general groups of passions: (1) sensual susceptibilities to pleasure (in his own expression, the sensitive passions); (2) passions for coöperation, or, as he would say, for grouping (affective passions); and (3) a number of apparently heterogeneous passions which he designates as passions for serial organization (distributive passions), a term which I shall attempt to make clear. The second approximation divides the first group into the five senses—visual, olfactory, auditory, tactual, and the sense of taste. The second group is analyzed into passions for friendship, love, family relationships (familialism), and ambition. The third group contains the passion for intrigue, for variety, and what he calls the composite passion. In his third approximation these twelve passions become thirty-two. This number is significant, since it determines the ideal size of the *phalanstère,* or community.

However, most of his analytical and descriptive work is done with the second approximation. We can, therefore, fairly omit from this hurried consideration the first and third approximations. Furthermore, after naming the items of the first group, the senses, he pays them very little attention. The second group, the affective passions, which he also classifies as cardinal, or again, as industrial, is very important as securing harmony between the members of the various groups into which the phalanstère is to be divided. The third group is equally important in guaranteeing diversity between the interests and occupations of the groups themselves. It is in Fourier's analysis of the nature of these two groups of passions that we find the characteristic features of his system. He comes back again and again to the two cardinal elements of his system, homogeneity of interests and tastes within the group, diversity of tastes and interests between groups.

The general line of Fourier's thought with respect to the affective passions is easily seen. The human affections, love, friendship, and so forth, are springs of action of great potentiality. Civilization, when it does not actually restrain the expression of these passions in one way or another, provides inadequate avenues for their expression. The natural order of society will bring together, by an elaborate system of grouping, those of like interests and tastes, and make possible the cultivation of the affections. The possibility of giving expression to the affective passions through the association of like with like is an important means of realizing one of Fourier's primary aims, the attractiveness of labor.

The two other necessary conditions, which are fulfilled by an organization which will permit of an expression of the distributive passions, are (1) a division of labor minute enough to permit a worker to perform only that work which he is passionately desirous of performing; and (2) the providing of the possibility of a fairly frequent variation in employment; in Fourier's own words, an "organization by series," working in short "séances." "Work in series charms the senses because each group works on a thing which it has chosen with passion."

Consider the cultivation of apples, a function prosaic enough under present conditions. In the ideal state a man cultivates only that brand of apples in which he is most interested, and if he has no interest in apples, he works on something else. "He who is fond of green pippins refuses to work on trees bearing the yellow, and will have nothing to do with other apple trees." Furthermore, in his work he is associating only with friends of the green pippin. Even so, under ordinary conditions, continuous work among green pippins might become monotonous. But this, in the natural order, is impossible, for work of a given kind is carried on for not more than one and a half or two hours at a time, at the end of which a complete change of occupation is permissible.

This serial organization of labor with rapid variation of employment is a natural deduction from those human passions which Fourier has called distributive. Let us observe the passion for intrigue (*la passion cabaliste*). In civilization this passion is the source of little else than disorder. It is otherwise in a natural society. Why has God, demands Fourier, caused men and, still more, women to be lovers of intrigue? "Because in a societal order, every man, woman, and child must be a member of 30, 40, or 50 passional groups; must espouse warmly the party emotions, the cabals, and intrigues of the series." The group organization of society not only follows naturally as a deduction from human nature—it is the ideal order for the expression of those passions which make up human nature. "A general perfection of industry will be born, then, of that passion most condemned by the philosophers,—the cabalist or intriguing passion,—which has with us never attained the dignity of a passion, altho so deeply rooted in the philosophers themselves, who are the worst intriguers imaginable."

Let us consider also the passion for variety, called by Fourier *la papillonne,* or butterfly passion. Undoubtedly in our present industrial society, with its demands for prolonged and steady application, this penchant is productive of both poor work and unhappiness. If it were natural for work to be prolonged for 12 to 15 hours at a stretch, as it is today, God would certainly have given us a passion for monotony. That such is not a characteristic of human nature is but further evidence of the lack of reason in our present organization. "The human reason must endeavor to discover a social régime in affinity with the passions." And it is but a reasonable deduction from this passion for variety, that work should proceed in short and varied series.

The third of the principal distributive passions, the composite, called by Fourier the most beautiful of all, is the desire for a blending, in all activities, of the pleasures of the senses and the spirit. It enters into the plan of all the institutions of the ideal order, but none of these institutions or relationships springs from it alone. It is unnecessary to consider here the manifold applications of this composite passion.

This in rough outline is the framework of Fourier's natural order. It may be described as a system devised to give expression to the passions through an organization of life into groups of those having similar interests, to a number corresponding with the number of kinds of interest, which groups are continually forming and dissolving in response to the variability of the human passions. From what has been said it may be inferred that this system is actually an *a priori* deduction from Fourier's peculiar conception of human nature. Moreover, it would appear that this conception of human nature bears little relation to the uniformities of human conduct observable in society. This is true, even tho Fourier did find a few existing institutions, for example, certain coöperative ventures in dairy farming, which seemed to him to offer experiential verification of his theories; just as Kropotkin finds some existing institutions compatible with the principles of his anarchism.

This outline of Fourier's system should make it clear how, in common with other anarchists, he could start with his eighteenth-century predecessors, from the general premise of a natural order which aimed to be at the same time a statement of laws of persistent association of phenomena and a statement of canons of conduct of an ideal order, and arrive at an order of society whose structure was so radically different from theirs. The explanation, as I see it, has been stated above. Fourier appears to offer a very good example of the characteristics of anarchist thought there discussed.

Altho both the economists and the anarchists, including Fourier, fell into the error of accepting a conception of the natural order opposed to the customary, existing order, the antithesis was much more sharply drawn by the anarchists than by the economists. Altho both Fourier and the economists accepted the conception of a natural order which could be deduced *a priori* from a knowledge of human nature, this common premise, human nature, was an idea so abstract that, in giving it content, their respective lines of thought sharply diverge. Altho both groups accepted a conception of a natural order which was at once a scientific hypothesis and an ideal order, the preoccupation of the economists with the descriptive and analytical, and the preoccupation of Fourier and the anarchists with the ethical and evaluative, led, in the case of the former, to a final identification of the natural and the existing; in the case of the latter, to the perception of wide differences between the existing and the natural. In all these respects Fourier's thought was typically anarchist.

There can be no hope, in a paper of this size, of doing justice to Fourier. There is no reason, however, for letting this impossibility stifle a modest attempt, in conclusion, at interpretation and criticism.

The whole tenor of Fourier's thought is anarchistic. It is only by a vulgar interpretation of anarchism, that is, as meaning the advocacy of revolution by force and the destruction of all organization, that one can refuse to include him among the anarchists. The essential characteristics of anarchism, the accentuation of individual differences, the absence of authoritarian control, an organization of society based entirely upon individual agreement, are all to be found in Fourier. As one of the distinctly original radical thinkers of the nineteenth century, one of those instrumental in giving direction to main currents of radical thought, it is difficult to connect him closely with contemporary social reformers. Altho frequently associated by commentators with Robert Owen, he was in essentials, as has been seen very far removed from this English socialist. He was at one with his contemporary, St. Simon, only in his admiration for the method of the natural sciences, and in his optimism over the potential results of its application in the field of social studies.

Even among anarchists he stands alone in the extent to which he carries his conception of a possible harmony among conflicting interests. Economists conceive a world whose primary fact, the scarcity of desirable goods and services, necessitates conflict and competition throughout its complete compass. For the consumer, there is the necessity of choosing between conflicting, alternative commodities, of balancing utility against difficulty of attainment; for the producer, the choice between alternative and competing factors of production and methods of production; for every unit in the whole complicated economic mechanism, the continual necessity of choosing and, consequently, of going without. The system of Fourier involves no conflict or competition, no restraint of this desire in order to secure that. Its productive resources are distributed without regard to economic incentive, as the term is generally understood. Its commodities are produced and consumed in the correct amounts and at the proper time, without the necessity of pecuniary or other economic checks and balances. It is possible, by means of the reason, to discover an order which, by liberating the passions, will distribute human energy in exactly the right proportions between the various kinds of work to be done, and will, at the same time, make this work attractive. This order, for the same reasons, will ensure the consumption of exactly those commodities which have been produced.

Fourier would seem to depart from the theory of passional attraction in his remarks on the familiar economic problem of the distribution of income. He contemplates an allocation of 4/12 of the community's revenue to capital, 3/12 to talent (organizing ability), and 5/12 to labor. Apparently this is an appeal to economic incentive to guarantee the correct apportionment of the productive factors, but in appearance only. In reality, this is the distribution which happens to come about because of the nature of the human passions and the uses to which they will be put in the harmonious order.

This order not only secures an harmonious equilibrium in society between particular groups and interests which, in another society, would be conflicting; it also secures, through a complete expression of the passions, an equilibrium between otherwise conflicting interests within the human breast. Fourier, in common with other social philosophers, conspicuously Plato, envisaged society and the individual as parts of the same problem. Two problems, he says, face civilization and call for solution. "One turns on the art of adjusting the practice of virtue with the strength of the passions and with nature, with the love of wealth; the other, on the means of penetrating the great mystery, the system of nature and the harmony of the universe." The solution of one of them is the solution of both.

It differs curiously from the Platonic solution of both problems. Instead of the individual reason governing over and arbitrating between conflicting interests and passions in the man, restraining and repressing, adjusting and balancing, and, in the state, a body of reasonable men securing an harmonious equilibrium by a balancing and restraint of the interests of conflicting parties, we have an abdication of the reason. It is an equilibrium attained through expression of the passions rather than through repression and restraint of them. Once reason has found the key to the mechanism, there is nothing for it to do but efface itself. The first guarantee of the system of attraction to man is "the compass of permanent social revelation, in that the needle of attraction stimulates us continually through its impulses, as invariable in all times and places as the light of reason is variable and deceitful."

Fourier was a thoro-going romanticist. His accentuation of individual peculiarities and differences, his adulation of the primeval savage and a preëxisting terrestial paradise, his view of the perfectibility of man and society, his detestation of proportion and restraint, his dismissal of the reason in favor of the "natural" impulses of man, his refusal to admit the beneficent possibilities of adversity, all are romantic characteristics. Fourier represents Rousseauism grown rank and luxurious.

And in all his romanticism he is peculiarly modern. Gide has commented on Fourier's remarkable foresight—the resemblance of many of his plans and predictions with what has come to pass. He speaks of technological resemblances, for example, the similarity of Fourier's phalanstère to modern coöperative apartments; of his devices for centralized housekeeping and cooking, his forecasts of rapid transportation, and the like. But there is another and more important sense—the psychological—in which Fourier is modern. I have referred to it above as consisting in his emphasis on self-expression. It appears in his ideas on education, and takes the form of the adaptation of the subject-matter to the interests of the learner rather than the adaptation of these interests to the subject-matter. It appears in his ideas on the relation between the sexes. A good deal of modern so-called personnel work, vocational guidance, and the like, pursues the ends formulated by Fourier. Indeed, one can compare Fourier to a highly ingenious, if somewhat insane, personnel manager, devising a system of society adapted to the nature of the human material which God has seen fit to place at his disposal.

All this insistence on self-expression assumes that man has something to express. In Fourier's opinion this something is a great deal. Man by nature, untouched by society, springs from his mother's womb endowed with a complete set of interests, desires, and passions. There is no need of a patient cultivation of interests, no need of tempering and refining desire and passion through restraint and adversity, no need, or, for that matter, possibility, of a development of the higher capacities of the human spirit. It is these interests and desires which, already existing, must determine the nature of education and of society. The obvious objections which may be made to Fourier's insistence on self-expression have also their application to the modern over-accentuation of the need and possibilities of self-expression.

The industrial revolution passed Fourier by; he failed completely to appreciate its significance. One of the primary aims of Fourier's system was an expansion of the output of economic goods. Next to health, wealth contributes most to man's happiness. But his plans for the expansion of output called only for the elimination of waste in the use of existing technological equipment. He was an economist in that older sense of the word, meaning economizer. He advertised the economies of the division of labor with the enthusiasm of Adam Smith; but division of labor meant to him the simple form well illustrated in market-gardening, not the complex form associated with the machine technique. His phalanstère was based squarely on an agricultural régime and hand labor. In these respects he is exactly the opposite of his contemporary, Owen, who did understand the significance of the Industrial Revolution, and who attempted to include the advantages of the new industrial methods in his community schemes.

Despite, however, Fourier's manifest weaknesses, the fantastical nature of his proposals, the purely sensual character of his ideal order, his lack of understanding of the economic society in which he lived, there is the touch of genius in his work. His central idea of passional attraction, tho grotesquely overstated, provides a very profitable working vein for those engaged in extracting the secret of successful methods of human combination and cooperation. It implies psychological differentiation and analysis added to organization, and these were the things for which Fourier stood. He was interested in demonstrating also that organization does not necessarily involve an expansion of authoritarian control. Complexity of organization, and an effectiveness in the application of human energy, are compatible with an extensive sphere of individual autonomy. Individual freedom combined with an effective application of human energy—that is but another statement of Fourier's problem.

Russell E. Westmeyer (essay date 1940)

SOURCE: "Utopian Socialism: The French Utopian Socialists," in *Modern Economic and Social Systems*, Rinehart & Company, Inc., Publishers, 1940, pp. 27-42.

[*In the following excerpt, Westmeyer briefly describes the structure of Fourier's utopian society.*]

As a boy François Marie Charles Fourier (1772-1837) was an excellent student, but he left his school work for a business career and spent practically his entire life in mercantile activities. It is said that Fourier first had his attention called to the defects of the existing economic order when as a child of five he was punished for telling the truth about his father's goods. This was followed by other experiences, including one in which he had to order a cargo of rice thrown overboard because his employers had allowed it to rot rather than break the market. It seemed to Fourier that something was wrong with a system that encouraged parents to teach their children to lie and which permitted men to let food rot when it was badly needed, and after a time he set to work to figure out a social order which would make such things impossible.

"Unityism." Fourier believed that men were naturally good and only did wrong because their natural passions or emotions were restrained by existing society. From this he concluded that all of the misery and discord prevalent throughout the world could be eliminated by working out a new order of society which would allow free play to the human passions. But before such an order could be inaugurated it was first necessary to discover the true nature of the passions involved, and here Fourier's researches led him to the conclusion that human beings were subject to twelve passions, all of which fell conveniently into three groups. In the first group of passions he included the five appetites of the senses, hearing, seeing, feeling, tasting, and smelling; in the second he placed the four appetites of the soul, friendship, love, paternal or familial, and ambition; and in the third, three new passions which he had "discovered." These last were the distributive passions, *cabaliste,* or the desire for intrigue; *papillone,* the desire for change or variety; and *composite,* the passion for union. If all twelve of these passions were permitted free rein, the result would be the one mighty all-controlling passion of *uniteisme,* or "unityism," the love felt for others united in society.

The phalanx. In order to give free play to the passions and thus secure "unityism," or harmony, Fourier proposed the establishment of communities called phalanxes in whose members all of the enumerated passions or emotions would be represented. He calculated that the twelve passions could be combined in as many as eight hundred twenty different ways in as many individuals, and to secure complete harmony every possible combination ought to be represented in the workers of each phalanx. Making allowances for infants, the aged, and other non-workers, Fourier concluded that for complete harmony a phalanx should have a population of from eighteen hundred to two thousand. A smaller number would be possible but a larger number would cause discord.

Physically a phalanx may be described briefly as an area of about three square miles centered on a palace, a double line of continuous buildings about twenty-two hundred feet long, three stories high, and divided into a central portion and two wings. The center of the palace is described as being reserved for quiet occupations and includes a common dining room, a library, and council rooms. One of the wings is given over to noisy occupations while the other contains the living quarters for the four hundred families. Behind the palace are the agricultural areas and outbuildings, and somewhere nearby is a tower for signal communication with other phalanxes.

Economic organization of the phalanx. All workers in a phalanx with similar tastes form themselves into groups of seven or eight or nine, called series. Several series with related interests, usually from twenty-four to thirty-two, form a group, and the various groups unite to form a phalanx. The occupations found in a phalanx in order of their importance are: animal husbandry, agriculture, kitchen work, and manufacturing. Fourier believed that labor was naturally pleasant, and that it was only when man was forced to overwork or had to perform tasks he did not like that work became repulsive. Hence in the phalanx form of organization individual workers are permitted to work at what they please and may even change jobs if they desire. Fourier explains that the passion for change is so great that men may change tasks every two hours. Since young children have a marked passion for dirt, the phalanx utilizes this passion by having them clean the sewers and do the rest of the dirty work. Thus did Fourier make logical use of his theories in solving the problem of how to get the dirty work done.

An interesting feature of Fourier's phalanx form of organization is that it is not communistic, for he permits private capital and even the inheritance of capital. After a generous minimum of the common product is set aside for each member of the phalanx, the surplus is divided between labor, capital, and talent in the proportion of five-twelfths to labor, four-twelfths to capital, and three-twelfths to talent, the division being made by the officers of the phalanx. It is interesting to note that the highest pay goes to those performing the most necessary work and the smallest to those engaged in particularly agreeable work.

Productivity. Fourier believed that a four- or fivefold increase in productivity would follow the inauguration of the phalanx form of society. He believed that rivalry, similar to athletic rivalry, would develop between the different series and groups and that there would be competition to see which could produce the most. Also, the fact that a large number of men and women were working together would make possible a highly productive and economical division of labor. Furthermore, Fourier, like his predecessors, made no provision for idle or useless classes. And finally, because all of the members of a phalanx would be in complete harmony, there would be no necessity for soldiers, policemen, criminals, or lawyers, nor would there be any need for metaphysicians or political economists. Because of this a large number of individuals at the time engaged in uneconomic occupations would be free for more productive work. To the economy of associated effort the phalanx adds the economy of associated life, another factor which would greatly increase human productivity.

Victor Considerant's design for a Phalanstery as it appeared in Fourier's journal La Phalange, *Vol. I, 1836.*

It costs no more, said Fourier, to build a palace than to build four hundred separate and uncomfortable cottages. Other savings would accrue from carrying on cooking in common, the common housing of animals, common storage of food, and other forms of coöperative activity.

Fourier was convinced that further economies would be secured by the practical elimination of the ordinary activities of trade and commerce. He had once said that there were four epoch-making apples in human history, two of which, Eve's and Helen's, were bad and the other two, Newton's and his, were good. His apple was one of a dozen for which he paid in a shop many times what the farmer received, a fact which left a deep impression on him. Such expensive physical distribution does not enter into the phalanx form of organization, for Fourier provides for a convenient exchange of products between members, between phalanxes, and between nations. Fourier also pointed out that a coöperative enterprise like the phalanx avoids the waste of goods caused by industrial and commercial competition. Here he struck at one of the weakest spots in the modern economy, for competition, regardless of whatever advantages it may possess, exacts an enormous annual toll from consumers in the form of the higher prices necessary to meet the costs of competitive advertising, selling fees and commissions, duplication of facilities, crosshauling of freight, and the like.

Other features. Fourier looked upon each phalanx as a little republic governed by elected officials, but he did suggest a rather loose world-wide organization of phalanxes. Like some of his predecessors Fourier favored the emancipation of women, but at the same time his insistence that all passions and emotions be given free rein led him to advocate a system of free love quite at variance with the morals of his time. He was opposed to revolution as a means of bringing the new order into being, and revolution would be quite inconsistent with the system he proposed to set up. He believed that a single experiment would prove the desirability of his system, and he sought the aid of some wealthy philanthropist to accomplish such an experiment. Not having any close contacts with such persons, he announced publicly that he would be at home every day at noon to meet anyone disposed to furnish the million francs necessary to carry on the great experiment. He is said to have waited every day for twelve years, but needless to say no one ever came forward with such an offer.

Conclusion. Fourier's work is a peculiar amalgam of wisdom and foolishness. He appreciated the importance of having satisfied workers, both for the advance of productive efficiency and for human happiness, but the practicability of a system in which workers change jobs as often as every two hours is certainly open to question. His criticisms of the unnecessarily high costs of physical distribution and the tremendous wastes of competition are as pertinent today as they were at the time of which he was writing. Unlike the earlier writers, Fourier did not strive to set up a perfect community into which perfect men and women, alike as two peas, were to be fitted. Instead he realized that the practical social reformer must start with men as they are, and in this respect his writings mark an important step forward in the development of utopian thought. But, on the other hand, the idea of allowing free rein to the passions, the idea on which his whole system was built, led him into many difficulties, and some of the features of his system, particularly those dealing with marital relations, antagonized possible supporters. In any event, it is doubtful that perfect social unity could actually result from giving free rein to human passions. Chaos, not universal harmony, would be a more likely result.

Fourier never had a large following during his lifetime, but a few years after his death his ideas were introduced into the United States, and Fourierism became the basis of numerous attempts to establish ideal communities in this country. Although these communities had no particular effect on the development of economic and social reform in America, some of them met with surprising success. . . . Among Fourier's books may be mentioned ***History of the Four Movements, Treatise on Domestic and Agricultural Association,*** and ***The New Industrial World***.

Alice Felt Tyler (essay date 1944)

SOURCE: "Utopian Socialism in America," in *Freedom's Ferment: Phases of American Social History to 1860,* The University of Minnesota Press, Minneapolis, 1944, pp. 196-226.

[*In the following excerpt, Tyler discusses the formation of Fourierist phalanxes in the United States in the 1840s and 1850s.*]

FOURIERIST PHALANXES

Through a series of articles entitled "What Shall Be Done about Labor?" which he wrote for the *New Yorker,* Horace Greeley came in touch with Albert Brisbane, who had studied in Paris the theories of the French socialists, Saint-Simon and Charles Fourier. Greeley accepted many of Brisbane's ideas, and together they wrote for the *Future,* the *Tribune,* and also occasionally for the *Plebeian,* the *Democrat,* and the *Dial.* Brisbane was already the author of *The Social Destiny of Man,* an exposition of the doctrines of Fourier, and in 1843 he published *A Concise Exposition of the Doctrine of Association,* which became the Bible of American Fourierism. These two crusaders for social reorganization were joined by Parke Godwin, whose *Popular View of the Doctrines of Charles Fourier* brought those doctrines nearer the level of the common man.

Brisbane's philosophy was most clearly expressed in a quotation given in his wife's *Albert Brisbane: A Mental Biography:*

> Far away in the distant future I saw a globe resplendent, cultivated and embellished, transformed into the grandest and most beautiful work of art by the combined efforts

> of humanity. I saw upon it a race developed, perfected
> by the continued influence, generation after generation,
> of true social institutions; a humanity worthy of that
> Cosmic Soul of which I instinctively felt it to be a part.

Horace Greeley summarized his own social creed in the following terms: There should be no paupers and no surplus labor; unemployment indicates sheer lack of brains, and inefficiency in production and waste in consumption of the product of a national industry that has never worked to half its capacity have resulted in social anarchy; isolation is the curse of the laboring classes, and only in unity can a solution be found for the problems of labor; therefore, education is the great desideratum, and in association the future may be assured.

These views were in accord with Brisbane's somewhat loftier statement, but the two men in action were poor teammates. Brisbane was nonplused at the rapid spread of the idea of association in response to Greeley's newspaper campaign. He had expected years of hard work and a slow accumulation of capital before the first Fourierist phalanx could be established. He felt that no association could succeed until all "the faculties of the soul found adequate expression" within the community. Life within the phalanx must be more attractive in every way than that in the world outside. But Greeley was eager to try the associative idea in miniature as an immediate palliative for the hardships of depression.

[The] Brook Farm experiment in Fourierism was disappointing for Greeley and Brisbane and disastrous for the Farm. Many other short-lived phalanxes were formed—between forty and fifty in all: six each in New York and Pennsylvania, eight in Ohio, three in Massachusetts, two in New Jersey, and others in Illinois, Michigan, Wisconsin, Indiana, and Iowa. Their average duration was two years—and that only because one of them lasted twelve years.

Only two of these attempts merit further mention. The Sylvania Phalanx, established in 1842, was the first and had Greeley for its treasurer. Its site, selected by a landscape painter, a doctor, and a cooper, was some twenty-three hundred acres of land in northern Pennsylvania, where land was cheap because of barren soil and lack of access to markets. On the land were an old gristmill and three frame houses, which were expected to accommodate more than a hundred settlers from the New York and Albany working classes. Only four acres of the land were tillable, and the return on it in the one year of the settlement was eleven bushels of grain. The experiment cost Greeley five thousand dollars, which his heirs eventually recovered from the increased value of the timber growing on the original tract.

The North American Phalanx, founded in 1843, was the Fourierist colony that lasted for twelve years. Brisbane, Godwin, Greeley, Ripley, and Channing were all interested in it and much was written about it. Noyes called it the "test-experiment on which Fourierism practically staked its all in this country."

The site chosen was near Red Bank, New Jersey, where good farm land and easy access to markets were avail-

able. In September 1843 a few families took possession and began the construction of community buildings. Within a year the number of residents rose to ninety, and it was never much larger. Agriculture was expected to be the chief occupation of the association, but a gristmill was built and a few small industries were carried on under the Fourier system of groups and series. The original investment was eight thousand dollars; in 1852 the value of the property was estimated at eighty thousand dollars with an outstanding debt of less than twenty thousand. Greeley was probably correct in stating, when the colony disbanded in 1854, that financial failure was not the cause, for when all books were closed the stockholders were paid two thirds of the face value of their shares.

Each member was given the choice of the work he should perform, and each worked as much or as little as he chose. The wage scale varied, the highest rate, about ten cents an hour, going to "necessary but repulsive" labor and the lowest to agreeable work. Each worker was credited with the amount and kind of his or her labor each day and paid in full every month, any profits being divided annually. Rent was charged for lodging, and meals were served à la carte, with a small monthly dining room service charge. The earnings of phalanx members were low, but so were all living costs. The members were somewhat on the Brook Farm order and were for the most part congenial and happy. Many of them said in later years that the experience in the phalanx was the happiest part of their lives. But realization of Brisbane's ideal of a socially complete community was as distant in 1854 as in 1843.

All the many visitors to the North American Phalanx mention the pleasant friendly atmosphere, but they do not fail to state that plain living, no luxuries, and few comforts were the accompaniment of high thinking. Fredrika Bremer included a careful description of Red Bank in her *Homes of the New World*. She mentioned all the attractive features of cooperative housekeeping, economic security, and simple but comfortable living, but she concluded with the wail of the true individualist, that she would rather live "on the bleakest granite mountain of Sweden, alone by myself, and live on bread, and water, and potatoes . . . than in a Phalanstery on the most fertile soil, in the midst of associate brethren and sisters!"

The members of the phalanx must have at heart agreed with her. When their mill burned in 1854 and they met to consider Greeley's offer of a loan to finance rebuilding, some intrepid soul unexpectedly moved that they make no effort to rebuild but instead dissolve the phalanx, and much to their own surprise, the motion carried by a large majority. What a free people might choose to create in the way of association, they were equally free to undo, and the rejection of the principle was as voluntary as its adoption.

G. D. H. Cole (essay date 1953)

SOURCE: "Fourier and Fourierism," in *Socialist Thought: The Forerunners, 1789-1850,* Macmillan & Co., 1953, pp. 62-74.

[In the following excerpt, Cole offers a brief outline of Fourier's life and a detailed discussion of his philosophy, arguing that the most convincing aspects of Fourier's doctrine regard the organization of labor and social institutions around human desires.]

No two persons could well be more different in their approach to the social question than Saint-Simon and Fourier, though they were both precursors of Socialism. Saint-Simon loved vast generalisations and was dominated in all his thinking by the conception of unity. His approach was historical, on a world scale: he saw the coming industrial age as a phase in a grand progress of human development based on the expansion and unification of human knowledge. Fourier, on the other hand, set out always from the individual, from his likes and dislikes, his pursuit of happiness, his pleasure in creation, and his propensity to be bored. For Fourier, there was fundamental need that the work by which men had to live should be in itself pleasant and attractive, not merely beneficial in its results. It was necessary, too, to devise means for men, or rather families, to live together in societies which would be so organised as to satisfy the needs of the diverse bents and natures of the individuals concerned. Saint-Simon and his followers were always making vast plans in which the emphasis was laid on high output and efficient production, on large-scale organisation and comprehensive planning, and on the fullest use of scientific and technological knowledge. Fourier was not in the least interested in technology: he disliked large-scale production, mechanisation, and centralisation in all their forms. He believed in small communities as best for meeting the real needs of small men. It was no accident that Saint-Simon found many of his most enthusiastic disciples among the students and graduates of the École Polytechnique, whereas the Fourierists included a high proportion of persons who were hostile to the new developments of large-scale industry, and believed in the virtues of the simple life.

Fourier himself expressed a deep contempt for the followers of Saint-Simon in the days of Enfantin's pre-eminence. He said of them: 'I attended the service of the Saint-Simonians last Sunday. One cannot conceive how these sacerdotal play-actors can command so large a following. Their dogmas are inadmissible: they are monstrosities at which we must shrug our shoulders: to think of preaching in the nineteenth century the abolition of property and inheritance!' (from a letter written in 1831). Fourier thought he knew how to solve the problem of property without either abolishing it or destroying inheritance, which he regarded as natural, and as corresponding to a desire deeply implanted in the nature of men.

François-Marie-Charles Fourier (1772-1837) was born at Besançon, of a middle-class merchant family which lost most of its possessions during the Revolution. He had to earn his living as a clerk and commercial traveller, and to write his books in his leisure time. He worked out his ideas for himself, almost uninfluenced by any previous writer, starting from an analysis of human nature, and above all of the passions as affecting human happiness.

His fundamental tenet was that right social organisation must be based, not on curbing natural human desires, but on finding means for satisfying them in ways that would lead to harmony instead of discord. He was the opponent of all moralists who founded their systems on the notion of an opposition between the reason and the passions, or regarded social organisation as an instrument for compelling men to be good against their wills. He held human nature to be essentially unchanging from age to age, and thus denied the doctrine of many of his fellow-Utopians—especially Godwin and Owen—that character could be moulded into almost any shape by environment. Not that he stressed less than they did the importance of environment in the making or marring of human happiness: far from it. But the problem, as he saw it, was to establish a social environment that would fit human nature as it was, and not be designed to change it into something different.

Chester C. Maxey on Fourier's influence in the United States:

Fourier died in 1837, before his ideas had gained great momentum; but a zealous band of disciples took them up and spread them throughout the world. Looking backward upon Fourierism, it is difficult to understand the appeal of this obviously artificial and unearthly scheme to rational minds. But the fact remains, nevertheless, that thousands of intelligent people, including some of the foremost minds of the century, were persuaded that Fourierism was not only practicable, but practicable right now. Fourier converts were not content merely to preach the doctrines of their master; they must straightway put them into practice. A number of phalanxes were founded in France, and some of these developed into strong coöperative societies which still survive. It was in the United States, however, that Fourierism had its real splurge. On the American side of the Atlantic were millions of acres of cheap or free land, vast empires awaiting settlement, and plenty of people eager to try any new venture in colonization.

Chester C. Maxey, Political Philosophies, *revised edition, MacMillan Co., 1949.*

As things were, most men, Fourier considered, were compelled to waste the greater part of their energies in doing and making things which, instead of ministering to their happiness, bored and irked them and either fed imaginary wants or, when the products met real wants, fed them in an exceedingly wasteful manner. The waste of labour involved in competition, above all in distribution, which he knew most about, appalled him: he wanted men to have done with all the complicated processes of buying and selling on which they wasted their lives and to devise means of producing and consuming, by the simplest possible methods, only what they really enjoyed. He was not in the least an ascetic: he wanted everybody to have a good time, and in accordance with his theory of human nature, he recognised the pursuit of pleasure as a wholly legitimate end. For himself, he had a very keen pleasure in good, well-cooked food; and this, as we shall see, had a big influence on the shaping of his doctrine. It was natural to men, he thought, not only to enjoy the pleasures of the table, but also to enjoy doing whatever ministered to these pleasures—the growing and preparation of succulent food and drink. He cared much less how he was clothed or lodged, provided he was kept adequately warm and water-tight; and, accordingly, in his attitude to industrial production, he was governed by the feeling that such things as houses, furniture, and clothes should be made to last—of good craftsmanship, so that men would not need to be continually replacing them and thus condemning themselves to irksome labours when they might have been more pleasantly occupied. He hated shoddy goods, both because they were no fun to make and because they were wasteful of human effort; and he held that things wore out so fast mainly because, under the competitive system, the makers wanted them to wear out, in order to ensure a continuing demand. If goods were made well, as they should be for the satisfaction of the makers as well as the users, they would last long. Therefore, he did not see the need for any large amount of employment in industrial production: most of men's labour time, he held, could be better spent in producing and preparing pleasure-giving things to eat and drink.

It follows that the agriculture which Fourier regarded as the main occupation for men was thought of primarily as horticulture and the small-scale raising of stock and poultry. Fourier wanted a system of highly intensive land cultivation mainly for specialised products, to be raised by skilled manual operations. He thought little of main crops, or of production for exchange. He wanted his communities to produce nice things for their own eating—fruit and vegetables above all. He was very fond of salads. He believed that such intensive cultivation could yield an ample supply of provisions for the producers, including those who could not work on the land.

It was an essential part of Fourier's view that no worker should follow only a single occupation. Everyone, he considered, should work at many jobs, but at none for more than a short time. Within the working day, his settlers were to shift continually from one employment to another, so as never to feel the boredom of monotonous effort. They were to have free choice of occupations, within the wide range of alternatives open to them, attaching themselves voluntarily to such occupational groups— he called them *'séries'*—as they fancied. They were to enjoy their work because they chose it, because they were not held to it over long continuous periods, and because they could, as consumers of its product, clearly visualise its use. This variety of work for every person Fourier regarded as corresponding to the natural variety of human desires.

But who, in such a voluntarist society, was to do the 'dirty work'—a question that has been put often enough since to libertarian Socialists? Fourier had his answer. You had, he said, only to watch children at play to realise that they loved getting dirty and had a natural propensity to form 'gangs'. What, then, could be simpler than to recognise this natural tendency, let the children form their

gangs freely, and entrust to them the doing of such dirty work as could not be dispensed with by proper management? Repression of juvenile gangs was all wrong, because they gave expression to natural desires: the right course was to create for them a useful social function.

Fourier's conception of education was of a piece with this. He wanted the children to follow their natural bents, and to learn a variety of trades by attaching themselves freely to their elders in a sort of manifold apprenticeship. In all this, Fourier was an important anticipator of modern ideas of education, especially in its vocational aspects. He held that the best way to learn was to do, and that the way to make children want to learn was to give them the chance of doing. Given free choice, he said, they would pick up easily enough the kinds of knowledge towards which they had a natural attraction. Children, he said, have a natural taste both for making things and for imitating the doings of their elders; and these tastes provide the natural foundation for a right education in the arts of life.

All this rested on Fourier's preliminary analysis of human nature, which he never tired of elaborating. He thought he had discovered a working law of the distribution of men's propensities, and he set out to devise a form of social organisation that would conform to this law. The communities he advocated were to be of a size and structure designed to meet this requirement—neither too small to give every member a sufficient range of choice of occupations, nor any bigger than was necessary to meet this need. He fixed on the ideal of about 1600 persons, cultivating about 5000 acres of land. These figures were not meant to be rigid: in his later writings he went up to 1800 persons. Such numbers, he held, would suffice to give a normal distribution of tastes and temperaments and to ensure that the principle of free choice would not result in an unbalanced distribution of labour between different kinds of work. They would also yield a sufficient range of choice for the making of congenial friendships and for the avoidance of jostling between incompatibles too closely associated in everyday contacts.

Fourier's communities were to be called *phalanstères,* from the Greek word *phalanx.* They were to be housed in a great common building, or group of buildings, fully equipped with common services, including *crèches* where young children could be communally cared for. But the inhabitants were not to live in common any more than they chose. Each family was to have its own apartment and to be free to do as it pleased in keeping itself to itself or in making use of the communal restaurants and public rooms. Nor were these apartments (or the incomes of those who occupied them) to be all of equal size. They were to be adaptable to different tastes, requirements, and levels of income. Fourier was no advocate of absolute economic equality; nor did he object to unearned incomes derived from the possession of capital. On the contrary, he was prepared to pay special rewards for skill, responsibility, and managerial capacity, and also to allow interest on invested capital used for the development of the *phalanstère.* Indeed, he contemplated that every person would become an investor in the share-capital on a larger or smaller scale.

Here again he had a theory about the right distribution of the product of industry. In his earlier writings he proposed that, of the total value produced, five-twelfths should be paid out as a reward for ordinary labour, four-twelfths as the return on invested capital, and three-twelfths as remuneration for special talent, including payment for managerial services. Sometimes he varied these proportions, assigning half the total to labour and only two-twelfths to talent, but leaving the four-twelfths to capital unaltered. He did, however, see danger in allowing the unlimited accumulation of unearned income; and he proposed to keep this in check by varying the rate of return on capital according to the amount of the individual's holding. Thus, as any individual increased his investment, he would get less income from each additional share-holding. In effect, this was exactly the same as a progressive tax on unearned incomes; and the graduation which Fourier had in mind was pretty steep.

The *phalanstères* were to be set up and financed, not by the State or by any public agency, but by voluntary action. Fourier constantly appealed to possessors of capital to understand the beauty of his system, and the joys of living under it, and to come forward with the money needed to establish communities on the right lines. He advertised for capital-owners prepared to do this, asking them to meet him at a restaurant where, for years, he lunched in solitude, keeping a vacant place for the expected guest. None came. It was only after his death, and then mainly in the United States and, oddly enough, in Russia, Rumania, and Spain, that disciples came forward with a readiness to risk their money and their lives.

The proposed variations in the rate of return on capital, and the intention that every worker should be also a capital-owner, make Fourier's system a good deal less inegalitarian than it appears at first sight. But for flat equality he had no use: he believed it to be inconsistent with human nature. Men, he thought, have a natural desire to be rewarded according to their works, and it would be both wrong and foolish to attempt to thwart this desire.

Throughout, Fourier rested his proposals on a firm belief that they were in harmony, not only with human nature, but also with the will of God. It was God's doing that men had desires and passions; and accordingly these must have been given to men for good. Moreover, God has so arranged matters that the varieties of human bents and aversions actually correspond to what is needed for good living: the social philosopher has only to study these variations in order to compute the size of community in which men can happily share out the necessary tasks with full freedom for every man to follow his own bent. Thus, Fourier inherited the eighteenth-century proclivity for identifying God and nature, or at any rate for attributing to nature the attribute of being animated and directed by the divine will. He carried this view to the length of supposing that there were actually *no* desires natural to men that could not be made to contribute to the good life, if only the right outlets were found and made available. He was indeed the first exponent of the notion of 'sublimation', and held it in its most comprehensive form.

There is much in Fourier's writings that is fantastic—in his latest writings much that is plainly mad. It is unnecessary to dwell on these fantasies, which have no connection with the essence of his teaching. 'Anti-lions' and seas of lemonade have nothing to do with the merits or demerits of the phalansterian system: nor do such absurdities appear at all in most of his works. It is a great mistake merely to laugh Fourier out of court because he ended by going off his head. He was emphatically a serious social thinker who contributed much of permanent value, not only to Socialist and Co-operative ideas, but also to the solution of the entire problem of work and of the incentives and human relations connected with it. Fourier's fundamental theory is one of association founded on a psychological law. To employ his own phraseology, he believed himself to have discovered a social law of 'attraction', which was the complement to Newton's law of attraction in the material world. He held that God had made man for a social order, for life according to a 'Plan of God' which corresponded to God's will. The problem for men was to discover God's plan and to act in conformity with it. There was a correspondence, Fourier affirmed, between the planetary and the social world, and all men's passions, like all the stellar bodies, had their place in the system of human living. This realised, it comes to be understood that even the human passions hitherto regarded as evil are in fact good, and can be utilised for the benefit of humanity if they are given the right scope and set free from the perversions which have been induced in them by bad social organisation—bad, because not so balanced and adapted as to give men harmless scope for the satisfaction of their basic psychological needs. It is, accordingly, necessary to change not man's nature but his environment, and the clue to this change is the organisation of society in accordance with the principle of 'association'.

Fourier's system, then, rests on the belief that most forms of necessary labour can be made attractive if they are rightly organised, and that no one need or should be made to work at any particular job except of his own free will. In the *phalanstères* all work was to be shared on a voluntary basis by groups or *'séries'* of workers, between which there would arise a natural emulation in doing their jobs well. He did not, of course, believe that *any* kind of labour could be made attractive, even for short spells: what he did hold was that the kinds that were naturally unattractive were for the most part unnecessary and involved much more unpleasantness than their products were worth. That was why he wanted to keep down the amount of manufacturing labour by the elimination of unnecessary consumption and by making such things as clothes and furniture very durable. He believed that pleasure in work was a natural endowment of women as well as men, and wished women to have an equal freedom with men in choosing their jobs. Indeed, complete sex equality was to be established under the new order to which he looked forward.

Fourier had no taste for revolution, and was as cautious in his concrete proposals for innovation as he was daring in his speculative outlook. He did not call upon the State or any political body to organise his new system, though he held that when it had been established there would arise a loose federal structure, made up of federated *phalanstères* under a coordinating Governor, whom he called an Omniarch. If the *phalanstères* could not be established immediately, he was prepared to recommend a transitional form of organisation to which he gave the name of 'guaranteeism'—a modified community way of living, which could be set on foot by individual capitalists who were minded to experiment. The well-known Godin *Familistère* at Guise was inspired by Fourier's ideas and is an outstanding practical example of what he called 'guaranteeism'. It has been much visited, and often described. This half-way house he was prepared to accept, because he considered that it might be impossible for men to escape suddenly from the long period of corrupting influence under which they had been living.

Indeed, as we have seen, Fourier himself hoped that rich men would come and help him to start his *phalanstères*. Sometimes he appealed to kings, never to popular Governments, or to the poor, or to revolution. Like Owen, he was a community maker, who believed that he had only to lay his plans before men with enough insistence and reiteration for their attractions to prove invincible, if only men could be got to listen.

From volume to volume, over a period of nearly thirty years, Fourier reiterated his gospel without fundamental changes. His first book, ***Théorie des quatre mouvements,*** was published in 1808 and was followed by a series of others in which he repeated and expanded the same ideas with constantly varying terminology, so that a large number of words which have entered into the vocabulary of Socialist thinking can be traced back in one form or another to Fourier's writings. The most important of his later books were ***L'Association domestique agricole,*** subsequently renamed ***L'Unité universelle*** (1822); ***Le Nouveau Monde industriel et sociétaire*** (1829); and ***La Fausse Industrie*** (1835-6).

The variations of his terminology were endless. In his earlier writings he called his general system, sometimes 'Harmony' or 'Harmonism', sometimes 'Association', sometimes *'État Sociétaire'*, and sometimes *'Solidarité'*. Later, he spoke of it as *'Unité Universelle'*, or as *'Unitéisme'*, and occasionally as *'Collectisme'*. The half-way house towards it was sometimes *'Garantisme'* and sometimes *'Sociantisme'*; and sometimes these words meant two different degrees of approximation to the full content of his system. He also used both *'Mutualisme'* and *'Mutuellisme'*, in a somewhat general sense. For his communities he used the names *'phalange'* and *'phalanstère'*—the first with primary reference to the human group, the second to its habitation. *'Série'* primarily meant an associated group of workers, engaged on a common task.

Fourier's disciples were called, and called themselves, by a similar diversity of names—*Phalangistes, Fourieristes* (or, in America, 'Furyists', by their opponents), *École Sociétaire, Humanistes, Humaniens, Unistes, Associativistes, Sériistes, Sérisophistes,* and so on. In Great Britain, Hugh Doherty, the leader of the school, called Fourierism 'the Social System', and spoke of it also as 'Universalism', 'Humanisation', and 'Phalansterianism', and also as 'Solidarity'. In the United States, it was often called 'Associationism', sometimes 'Unityism' or 'Serialisation'; but the word most frequently used was 'Phalanx'. 'Collectivism' was also used as a description, and 'Mutualism' as a general term, not confined to Fourier's half-way proposals. Even this list by no means exhausts the variants. Apart from 'Fourierism', the words 'Association' and 'Harmony', and their derivatives, were perhaps the most often used.

Until near the end of his life Fourier found few disciples; but in the 1820s a small group gathered round him, and a sharp dispute began between his adherents and the Saint-Simonians. His following, as well as theirs, became much larger after the French Revolution of 1830, and the rivalry between the two 'Schools' was keen, each having a profound contempt for the other. Fourier accused the Saint-Simonians of stealing his ideas without acknowledgment, and they retorted with accusations that he was an impracticable dogmatist with no conception of progress or of the mission of science. Before long Fourierism began to exert some influence outside France. It was studied in Germany, as a variant of the new French social speculation, and it spread to England, where its adherents had to meet the rival doctrine of Owenite Socialism, to which it bore, in some respects, a close resemblance. Owenites and Fourierists had many arguments about the respective merits of their several doctrines, but often found themselves uniting against their common opponents. The Fourierists sometimes accused Owen of having stolen their master's ideas, which had appeared in print before his own; but there is no evidence that Owen had ever heard of Fourier when he published his principal writings. I think, however, that Fourierist ideas did have some influence on the later phases of Owenism, especially Queenwood, though they had none at all on his earlier projects of 'Villages of Co-operation'.

In Great Britain the leading exponent of Fourierism was Hugh Doherty, who translated and edited some of the master's writings, and produced in 1840 a Fourierist periodical, *The Morning Star*. The most important of the English Fourierist publications was the translation of a section of Fourier's main work, issued under the title, ***The Passions of the Human Soul*** (1851), and including a full summary of his doctrines, written by Hugh Doherty. The principal point at issue between the Fourierists and the Owenites arose out of their essentially different views of human nature. Fourier had insisted on its immutability, and on the need to establish a social environment that would fit in with it. The Owenites, on the contrary, wanted to establish an environment that would profoundly modify human nature. The difference was not absolute; for, as we shall see, Owen was well aware of the importance of native propensities as well as confident that their outcome in behaviour was almost infinitely malleable under environmental influences. Fourier, for his part, though he regarded human nature as unchanging and as involving a statistically certain and verifiable distribution of diverse propensities and desires, was as insistent as Owen on the need for an environment that would not change these propensities but direct them into the right channels. Nevertheless, the difference was important; for whereas Fourier stressed the supreme importance of making labour pleasant by adapting it to men's natural bents, Owen tended to rely on making men work well and happily by instilling into them a moral sense of their work as valuable in the common interest. Fourier, as much as Owen, emphasised the importance of educating children in good social habits and attitudes; but he put his main reliance, not on getting them to believe what it was in the general interest they should believe, but on guiding them to do, spontaneously and with pleasure in the doing, what their own desires, as well as the good of society, commanded. This was the aspect of Fourier's doctrine which attracted most such later libertarians as Kropotkin and William Morris.

[There] was clearly a great deal of wisdom in [Fourier's] insistence that men could live happily only if they were given large scope for the satisfaction of their natural desires and were not forced to live according to an artificial pattern of conduct devised by moralists in the name of reason.

— *G. D. H. Cole*

In the United States Fourierism gained a much greater hold than in Great Britain, or even in France. Its most influential American exponent was Albert Brisbane (1809-1890), who introduced the doctrine after the slump of 1837. His *Social Destiny of Man* was published in 1840. Horace Greeley of the *New York Tribune* supported Brisbane's efforts, and a number of colonies, at least twenty-nine, were founded on his principles in the 1840s. None, however, lasted more than a few years. Brisbane also greatly influenced C. H. Dana, Margaret Fuller, Nathaniel Hawthorne and Emerson. The famous Brook Farm Community of 1832, founded by a group of New England intellectuals, among whom was Margaret Fuller, has been described in Hawthorne's *Blithedale Romance*. It was largely Fourierist in inspiration, though it was not founded in strict conformity with his doctrine, as it rested on a basis of joint-stock ownership without the general participation of the settlers which Fourier had regarded as necessary. Brook Farm, like the more completely Fourierist communities, was not of long duration. It broke down through financial failure, the intellectuals whom it recruited proving to be of no great use at the manual labour on which it relied for support. Brisbane's North American *Phalanx* lasted till 1856, but thereafter the American Fourierist movement faded away. A description of these Fourierist communities can be found in any of the volumes describing American So-

cialist experiments; most recent of these is Mr. A. J. Bestor's *Backwoods Utopias.*

In France, Fourier's most important disciple was Victor-Prosper Considérant (1808-93). His chief works were: *La Destinée sociale,* 1834; *Manifeste de l'École Sociétaire,* 1841; *Le Socialisme devant le vieux monde,* 1848. Considérant was the editor of the two journals, *Le Phalanstère* and *La Phalange,* in which many of the principal later writings of the school appeared. In his earlier works Considérant advocated entire abstention from politics, holding that the old 'political' societies were doomed to perish and to be replaced by new community associations founded on an entirely voluntary basis. But later he abandoned this attitude, and began to urge the democratic parties to discard the 'political' for the 'social' point of view. In 1848 he was elected to the National Assembly, and took part in the Luxembourg Labour Commission over which Louis Blanc presided. After the defeat of the Revolution in France he went, on Brisbane's invitation, to the United States, and attempted to found a phalansterian settlement in Texas. This failed in 1854; and thereafter Considérant's views underwent a further modification. Abandoning the old hostility to scientific industrial development, he attempted to work out a version of Fourierism that would be reconcilable with the expansion of scientific knowledge. Born in 1808, he lived on until 1893.

Fourier's doctrine is evidently at its strongest in the attempt to show the need to adapt social institutions to actual human desires. Even if he went astray in supposing that every known passion could, given a right social environment, be found means of expression that would render it beneficial to humanity, there was clearly a great deal of wisdom in his insistence that men could live happily only if they were given large scope for the satisfaction of their natural desires and were not forced to live according to an artificial pattern of conduct devised by moralists in the name of reason. In particular, his application of this principle to the organisation of work was of much greater importance than has been assigned to it even to-day, under the growing influence of the Social Psychologists' new attention to industrial relations and conditions. His belief that work could be, and must be, a source of positive pleasure may be, and probably is, irreconcilable with the conditions of large-scale production and with the desire of engineers to treat men as if they were ill-made machines; but Socialism would have been a richer body of doctrine if it had paid a great deal more attention to this aspect of the 'labour problem'. Moreover, I have still to be convinced that Fourier was on the wrong track when he urged that nobody should be required to work continually at a single task or trade. It is well within the power of most persons, especially if they begin young, to acquire a quite sufficient dexterity at several quite different kinds of job; and I think Fourier was very much in the right in believing that the variety of employment thus made possible would render a great many people happier than they can be within the monotony of a single, not highly skilled, occupation. There are, no doubt, natural specialists who prefer to stick to a single job, or within a narrow range. But I wonder if there are many of them;

and I am certain there are not nearly so many as the organisation of modern industry assumes.

M. Beer (essay date 1957)

SOURCE: "The France of Napoleon and the Restoration," in *The General History of Socialism and Social Struggles*, Vol. I, Russell & Russell, Inc., 1957, pp. 103-33.

[*In the following excerpt, Beer discusses Fourier's conception of nature and human history.*]

WAR, IMPERIAL POLICY, AND COMMERCIAL SPECULATION

After the execution of Babeuf and Darthé and the banishment of Buonarroti and his comrades, the French socialist revolutionary movement disappeared from the surface of politics for three decades. The Directory repressed all opposition and prepared the way for the rule of Napoleon. In 1799 he overthrew the Directory, and in 1804 he was invested with imperial dignities. The French enjoyed equality—equality before the despotism which, however, filled their imaginations with bloody wars and glorious victories and their pockets with the chinking and paper results of commerce, of war contracts and war industry. For traders, speculators, money-lenders and stock-brokers the years of the Revolution and of the Napoleonic Wars were very lucrative and exciting. The buying-up of the confiscated property of the Church and of the *emigrés,* the rise in the prices of cereals, the capitalist monopolizing of native and overseas raw materials, especially in consequence of the blockade of French ports by the English fleet, made the rise of Napoleon to coincide with the rise of the French bourgeoisie.

Imperial policy supplanted all home and constitutional questions; the geographical conditions of imperialist successes, of economic prosperity and of military complications, and the significance of sea power, etc., were investigated with ardour. Even in Fichte's "Self-Sufficing Commercial State" we find noteworthy observations upon these subjects, tracing the antagonism between England and France to the insular position of the former. Yet more remarkable are the observations of Charles Fourier, who, among other things, infers from Japan's insular position that this Empire is destined to play a great maritime and economic part, and detects in it a future competitor of Russia with regard to China. Fourier also describes the wild orgies of swindling speculations, the predatory price manipulations, the Stock Exchange manœuvres of the financial magnates and merchants during that period. False war news was the means for causing a rise or fall in the French securities.

The French bourgeoisie enriched themselves and forgot the revolutionary struggles and constitutions as long as Napoleon's star shone undimmed, that is until about 1811.

CHARLES FOURIER

The intellectual product in the social sphere of this extraordinarily agitated time (1792-1810) was Charles Fourier (1772-1837), a man who combined exuberant imagination, boundless optimism and senseless vanity with acute intelligence, a gift of penetrating observation, and great courage. His was a character of wholly unequal parts. Originally a merchant and shop assistant, during his sojourn in the industrial centre of Lyons he was prompted to social criticism by the sharp competition and the disintegration of the economic life, which caused the downfall of many small existences—including his own—while the co-operative projects then published by L'Ange (Lange) seemed to point to a way out from the chaos. This gives us the whole of Fourier at a glance. As a destructive critic he attacked competition and disintegration; as a constructive reformer he advocated associated labour by means of co-operative joint-stock undertakings. He expounded his ideas in his work, *Quatre Mouvements,* which was, apparently, printed at Leipzig and was published in the year 1808. What he afterwards wrote was only by way of amplification and commentary.

His whole life's work is permeated by the following basic ideas. (1) Human motives and passions are on the whole good, and, given proper scope, would conduce to happiness: the social task consists in affording them this scope by means of appropriate social institutions. (2) Commerce is morally and materially pernicious, and corrupts human dispositions: it is the base soul of the civilization that is approaching its term and that will be replaced by the associated and co-operative mode of economy and life. (3) Marriage is general hypocrisy and involves the slavery of woman; it must be replaced by free love. (4) Civilization; the present stage in the history of mankind is full of evils; nevertheless it creates the forces requisite to raise mankind to the stage of association and harmony, where human motives will find scope for their free play and will create wealth, amenities and peace.

Fourier makes the claim that he has at length penetrated into the secrets of divine creation and of nature. What Columbus, Copernicus and Newton accomplished for the perception of the material world, he (Fourier) accomplished for the perception of the laws of movement of the organic and social world. He regards his "discovery" as more important than "all the scientific labours since the emergence of the human race." "Shall we lament," he asks, "that the Platos and Senecas, the Rousseaus and Voltaires and the whole of the spokesmen of ancient and modern ignorance—so far as their works are concerned with politics and moral philosophy—will vanish into oblivion?" He asks the philosophers what their ideology is good for:

> I, who am ignorant of the whole mechanism of thought, and have read neither Locke nor Condillac, have I not enough ideas to discover the whole system of general movement, of which you have only discovered a quarter, that is, the material part? And this, moreover, after 2,500 years of scientific efforts. Me alone will present and future generations have to thank for inaugurating their immense happiness. As possessor of the book of definitions, I disperse the political and moral-philosophical fog, and on the ruins of precarious sciences I build the theory of universal harmony.

These new truths were prompted by his reflexion upon the agricultural association which was put forward by L'Ange in 1793. Starting from this idea, Fourier believed he had discovered the whole mathematical secret of human determinations. The redemption of mankind depends upon the transition to association, to co-operation.

> And this transition will soon be accomplished. We shall be eye-witnesses of a spectacle which can never be repeated on this earth: the sudden transition from incoherence to social combination: it is the most dazzling effect of movement that can be executed on earth; the anticipation of it must compensate the present generation for all its calamities. Every year through which the metamorphosis extends will be worth centuries.

But enough of quotations. They fully confirm our description of Fourier as a man of unequal parts. Let us pass to his doctrines.

Fourier's conception of nature is that of the seventeenth and eighteenth centuries. All phenomena present themselves to him as mathematically executed movements. These movements—he says—are four in number: social, animal, organic and material. Newton discovered the law of material movement. It is the law of gravitation. Now the law of social movement has to be discovered. In social life individual passions conceal the law of movement. These passions are directed to definite ends, which are the "destinées sociales" (social objectives). If our passions are given their proper scope we need not hesitate to follow them, for in giving effect to them, in the "passional attraction," as Fourier is always asserting, we shall find our goal and the full satisfaction of our highest desires. Consequently the teaching of moralists and philosophers about the necessity of repressing our impulses and passions is extremely pernicious; these teachings have never availed anything; they remain ineffective, and their only result is the accumulation of libraries of books which are nothing but waste paper. The moralists were followed by the economists, who advocated commerce and, therefore, only gave an impetus to swindling, forestalling, bankruptcies and Stock Exchange manipulations, causing total demoralization and much misfortune.

There are three centres of attraction around which human passions gravitate.

(1) Sensual (or the five senses). (2) Intellectual passions (friendship, reverence, love, family feeling). (3) Refined passions (emulation, love of change or novelty, organization).

Thus the first group has five passions, the second group has four, the third has three—making twelve in all. These are like twelve needles, which drive the soul towards the three crucibles or goals of attraction. The most important is group 3, for these aim at general and social unity, but only provided they express themselves, not individually but in group organizations, in associations, and there find full scope.

From the mixture of the twelve passions arise the most diverse characters. A combination of twelve passions yields about eight hundred different characters, so that all perfection would be potential in an assembly of eight hundred men; and if these men were properly educated from childhood they would manifest the greatest talents: men like Homer, Cæsar, Newton, etc. "If, for example, the population of France, numbering thirty-six millions, be divided by eight hundred, we should find among them 45,000 individuals capable of equalling a Homer, a Demosthenes, a Molière, etc."

All this, however, is based upon the assumption that these passions and talents are developed under a co-operative mode of life and according to Fourier's ideas.

And this new order of mankind is coming. The stage of association follows the stage of civilization, which is now visibly approaching its end.

Mankind has so far passed through the following stages.—(1) State of Nature: The age of Paradise in the Garden of Eden, or Edenism, where there was freedom and equality and an abundance of fruits, fish and wild animals. In every relationship of life men lived in common and were organized in groups. (2) Savagery: Owing to the increase of the human race and the absence of deliberately rational unions, there arises a shortage of food, which provokes quarrels, attacks and plunderings. (3) Patriarchate: The strong and brutal set up families, degrade woman, and introduce exclusive property, as may be observed among all peoples who have lived or still live under the patriarchal order; in Biblical times among the Jews, and also in China and other parts of Asia. (4) Barbarism: that is the Middle Ages, where feudalism developed, the only good point of which was that many women were honoured. For the rest, feudalism developed the germs of civilization, commerce and industry. (5) Civilization: the utter incoherence and atomization of men, who regard each other as enemies and behave accordingly. Entire absence of organization; all the higher sensibilities destroyed by the commercial spirit—humanity, fatherland, justice, mutuality disappeared; forestallers; market fluctuations; crises; cheating; hypocrisy; enrichment of the rich; impoverishment of the poor; contempt for non-possessors; competition; disintegration; economic anarchy; disappearance of family feeling; the son struggling against the father; oppression of labour by capital; domination of government by the wealthy; rebellions and revolutions of the despairing—such are the characteristics of civilization. Woman in particular suffers thereunder; she is bought and sold, for marriage is nothing more than the purchase of girls, who from youth upwards are trained to look for a purchaser; but the sexual instinct will not be suppressed; the "honest" women have their house friends, the men their mistresses; cuckoldry and prostitution are the inevitable accompaniments of monogamic hypocrisy. Nevertheless, civilization has achieved some good: it has promoted science and technology, revealed the possibilities of raising the productivity of labour, and given the rich *entrepreneurs* the opportunity of conducting agriculture and manufacture upon more rational business lines.

It prepared the way for a commercial and industrial feudalism. A small number of the rich manage the economic forces of the country, or the State establishes comprehensive agricultural undertakings, where a certain degree of organization and co-ordination finds a place, and the workers are guaranteed an existence. Accordingly, civilization is followed by the sixth stage, which Fourier calls Guaranteeism—a sort of social and political epoch to serve as a transition to the seventh stage: to Socialism—Fourier calls this Sociantism—which will inaugurate complete harmony and happiness. Men will then dwell in phalansteries: in large hotels run on co-operative lines, and will work co-operatively in groups of 1,600 to 1,800 (twice 800 and something over, in order to ensure the best mixture of characters, where the three "refined passions"—emulation, variety and concentration of forces—will have full scope).

The socialization of the means of production was outside the range of Fourier's ideas. The phalansteries were to be free associations of capitalists, workers and talented officials, and the product of labour was to be divided in the following manner: Labour to receive five-twelfths, Capital four-twelfths, and Talent three-twelfths.

Free love, education of the children at the cost of the group, seven meals daily, opera and drama, joy of life—all this would be made possible by the phalanstery system, so that men might hope to attain an average age of 144 years and a height of seven feet.

Fourier was politically indifferent, hated the Revolution and the Jews, revered Napoleon, and was always seeking a great, rich, good man, who would take up his projects. His writings are only partly readable. The best exposition of Fourierism is given by Victor Considérant in his book *Destinée Sociale,* which appeared in 1837, the year of Fourier's death, and is dedicated to the King, Louis Philippe, the ruler and greatest proprietor of France. But this book contains more than Fourierism: it is a very important conspectus of the social critical work that was performed in France up till Marx's arrival in Paris (1843). . . .

Charles R. Crowe (essay date 1960)

SOURCE: "Fourierism and the Founding of Brook Farm," in *The Boston Public Library Quarterly,* Vol. 12, No. 2, April, 1960, pp. 79-88.

[*In the following essay, Crowe argues that Fourier's socialist ideology influenced the development of Brook Farm from the community's inception in 1841.*]

In the summer of 1843 a blaze of enthusiasm for the socialist ideas of Charles Fourier swept through the ranks of American reformers, and one hastily-formed phalanx after another began to appear in the backlands of Penn-

sylvania and New York. Late in the year when the New York Fourierists met in Boston with representatives of the Brook Farm, Northampton, and Hopedale communities, the Brook Farm delegation came out solidly in support of "scientific" socialism. The official conversion of Brook Farm to socialism came after the delegates returned to West Roxbury, filled with enthusiasm for Fourierist ideas. George Ripley, the community president, appointed a committee to draw up a new constitution in January 1844, and soon the community was rechristened a phalanx. While the leaders could hardly hope to furnish the required three hundred thousand dollars and the sixteen hundred and twenty members, they were determined to follow the gospel of Fourier to the fullest possible extent in other respects.

Within the phalanx, all activities were to be organized in groups for specific tasks, such as plowing or shoemaking, and the groups were to be integrated into "series" in the broad divisions of industry, agriculture, domestic work, education, and recreation. This apparently rigid organization was to be created and sustained by thoroughly democratic techniques: group leaders were to be elected weekly and series leaders chosen every two months with the consent of the elected community councils; no man was to be forced into employment which was disagreeable to him, for there was to be complete freedom of work choice from hour to hour; and every member was to be guaranteed full educational rights and reasonable leisure as well as complete social security.

The Brook Farmers accepted these ideals without reservation, and surpassed Fourier in their concern for human equality. Numerically, skilled and unskilled laborers predominated, but former ministers, teachers, farmers, clerks, and businessmen were present, and all lived together in a remarkably harmonious social relationship. Long before the formulation of the Communist maxim, "From each according to his ability: to each according to his need," the Brook Farmers made this ideal a social reality. Inner cohesion together with able leadership and an urgent sense of mission soon made Brook Farm a center for the New England labor movement, as well as a political Mecca for American Fourierists.

The Brook Farm newspaper, *The Harbinger,* made the influence of the community felt in reform circles everywhere; John Orvis and John Allen barnstormed across New England preaching the doctrines of Fourier to anyone who would listen; Ripley and Lewis Ryckman carried the ideology of Brook Farm into the New England Workingmen's Association; and Ripley gave practical aid to the ten-hour movement, the coöperative movement, and a number of other reform drives. Above all, the belief that their efforts would provide the future social pattern for mankind gave the communitarians an exhilarating sense of being in the vanguard of historical development.

Obviously, Brook Farm during the Fourierist period was a very serious reform enterprise. Vastly different descriptions have been written about early community life as the scene of Hawthorne's barnyard labors, the antics of the

"Transcendentalist heifer," Emerson's amusement at the dances where "clothespins fell merrily" to the floor from the pockets of dancing men, and, in general, the congenial Transcendentalist refuge for plain living and high thinking. Charm and vivacity were certainly a part of Brook Farm life, but was Emerson correct in describing the community as initially an escapist venture, no more than "a room at the Astor House reserved for the Transcendentalists"? The search for an answer to this question must begin with the writings and actions of the community's founder, George Ripley.

The ardent reformer of Brook Farm was not visible in the conservative young minister who began his career in 1826 at the Purchase Street Unitarian Church in Boston, but Ripley's private letters and published writings after 1834 are marked by a growing concern with reform in general and the welfare of the working classes in particular. As the misery created by the panic of 1837 increased and as the slums crept closer to the Purchase Street church, Ripley observed in his daily experience the growing evils of the industrial revolution. In 1840, disgusted by American society and disillusioned with his own church, he considered leaving the ministry and devoting his life to reform.

Despite an increasing awareness of social evils, Ripley did not become a militant social reformer overnight. As late as the spring of 1840 he qualified a favorable review of Edward Palmer's communistic denunciation of American society with the observation that "the heart must be set right" before plans for a general reformation of society could be seriously considered. For a time he thought of education as a key to reform and discussed with Emerson and Bronson Alcott the possibility of establishing a new and radically different kind of university. This was one of numerous projects considered during this time, for Ripley was, as James Freeman Clarke reported, "fermenting and effervescing to a high degree with . . . ideas."

By the fall of 1840 Ripley had resolved his doubts, and, rejecting Unitarianism, started a new life as a reformer. His farewell sermon began with an answer to the accusation that he had brought "politics" into the church. He insisted that the conscientious Christian must fight in the cause of social reform. The minister's responsibilities were especially heavy, for he was by the nature of his mission a man "hostile to all oppression of man by man" and constantly sympathetic to "the down-trodden and suffering poor." Ripley denounced the church-attending Philistines for denying Christian equality and failing to understand that the true Christian church was "a band of brothers who attach no importance whatever to the petty distinctions of birth, rank, wealth, and situation." He also advised his parishioners that if they and their kind had done their Christian duty there would be no oppression, slavery, war, executions, jails, violence, or ruthless business competition.

Even before the final parting from his church, Ripley was planning a reform community as an antidote for current social evils. The comments of many Boston intellectuals leave little room for doubt as to the seriousness of the West Roxbury venture. Samuel Osgood referred to Ripley's project as "a New Harmony," and Margaret Fuller revealed her conception of the community when she gave as her reason for refusing to join the Brook Farmers the belief that "we are not yet ripe to reconstruct society." Shortly after the community had been established, Osgood denounced "this cursed system of civilization" and praised Ripley for attempting to change it. Other sympathizers made similar remarks praising Ripley's reform efforts.

Those who are sometimes cited to suggest that Brook Farm was established as an educational experiment, a religious action, or a Transcendentalist escape into the wilderness that had little relevance to American society, when properly read often give evidence for the reformist nature of the community. John Humphrey Noyes, working on the mistaken notion that William Ellery Channing was indirectly responsible for the Brook Farm enterprise, did once describe the community as "a child of Unitarianism," but in *A History of American Socialisms,* he took Emerson to task for failing to understand fully Ripley's radical reform motives. Even Emerson, who was reluctant to praise and had privately referred to Brook Farm as "a Transcendentalist picnic," considered joining the community, admitted the seriousness and utility of Ripley's plans, and after refusing "painfully, slowly" and almost guiltily to join, took Bronson Alcott's family into his house as a substitute for the "bolder" venture. In later years Emerson paid tribute to Ripley's efforts to create a classless society by admitting that Brook Farm had been "a close union like that in a ship's cabin of persons in various conditions: clergymen, young collegians, merchants, mechanics, farmers' daughters . . . ."

Certainly Ripley's initial proposals for the new Jerusalem were quite specific. He wished to "insure a more natural union between intellectual and manual labor" by educating the worker and giving the intellectual physical labor to perform; to secure for workers "the fruits of their labor" which the capitalist in American society often plundered; to do away with class barriers; and to create a society of equals living in brotherly relation without poverty, ignorance, or social hatreds. The first community constitution did list several purposes, but obviously the central one was a determination

> to establish the external relations of life on a basis of wisdom . . . to apply the principles of justice and love to our Social Organization . . . to substitute a system of brotherly co-operation for one of selfish competition . . . to institute an attractive, efficient and productive system of industry . . . to diminish the desire of excessive accumulation by making the acquisition of individual property subservient to upright and disinterested uses.

From the very beginning the community represented an attempt to create a model for the total reformation of society, and the goals of the Brook Farm Institute and the Brook Farm Phalanx were almost identical. Socialism did, however, bring some new patterns. Fourierism gave Brook

Farmers a crusading spirit and a new sense of participation in a Providential movement which was world-wide in scope. The "Associationists" were stimulated intellectually by the possession of a cosmology and an infallible guide to "scientific" socialism. The Fourierist period was also characterized by flamboyant rites and symbols, plays and symbolic decorations, Fourier birthday celebrations, and the ritual devised for Christian socialism by the "religious associationists."

However, the early Brook Farmers had their costumes, rituals, and contempt for "civilizees," and the fact remains that the changes of 1844 were not really basic ones. From the beginning Brook Farm was intensely collectivistic and equalitarian. The rules of common and equal wages, diet, housing, leisure, and educational rights prevailed in 1841 as well as in 1844. While the formal structure of groups and series was lacking at first, organizational patterns were strikingly similar, and the same democratic attitudes existed permitting choice of employment and election of work leaders. Even Fourier's emphasis on social harmony and the integration of the individual personality was a cardinal principle in the early Brook Farm credo. J. T. Codman, perhaps the best reporter in that large and vocal company of former community members, stressed the continuity between the two phases of community history. "Integral education," "attractive industry," "honors according to usefulness," and "co-operative labor," Codman insisted, were accepted so readily because their essences had been a part of Brook Farm life long before the coming of Fourierism.

Surely the remarkable continuity between the "Transcendentalist" and the Fourierist periods requires an explanation. Was Brook Farm from the beginning a thinly veiled Fourierist Phalanx? Few scholars have been willing to consider this possibility, and a number of Ripley's contemporaries did not mention Fourier at all in discussing the origins of Brook Farm. John Humphrey Noyes was willing to concede only that "the beginnings of Fourierism may have secretly affected" the founders. One self-appointed propagandist for Brook Farm, Elizabeth Peabody, gave no credit to Fourier in her extensive accounts of the community. J. T. Codman admitted the striking similarity of Fourierist ideas to those advocated by Ripley in 1841, but he knew nothing of the circumstances surrounding the coming of Fourierism and, searching for an explanation, could only suggest that Ripley "had fallen unwittingly . . . on ideas that coincided with those of Charles Fourier. There was an agreement between them unknown at the start."

To make the matter more difficult, there were other possible sources for Ripley's communitarian ideas. In 1838 he visited the Shaker and Zoarite communities and was impressed by an air of common purpose, high community morale, and the lack of invidious distinctions which characterized life in these communities. This was an age of religious rebellion, and the "come-outer" impulse also played a part in the actions of the communitarians. Elizabeth Peabody, for whom Brook Farm meant "A Glimpse of Christ's Idea of Society," suggested that "in order to

live a religious and moral life worthy of the name," the Brook Farmers felt it "necessary to come out in some degree from the world, and to form themselves into a community of property." Finally there was a vein of Locofocoism in Transcendentalist ideology which helped to create a climax of opinion favorable to communal experiments.

Undoubtedly, all these forces influenced Ripley and his associates, but an adequate explanation of the Brook Farm way cannot be constructed from these materials, and the suggestions of Fourierist influence are too strong to be ignored. Moreover, adequate evidence exists to prove that Ripley was familiar with Fourier's ideas from an early date. His introduction to the subject may have come through Emerson, who discussed Fourierist concepts on the lecture platform in 1838 and returned repeatedly to the subject afterwards in the *Journals*. Since Ripley attended Emerson's lectures faithfully and saw him both socially and at meetings of the Transcendentalist Club, the conjecture is a likely one. Concrete and undeniable testimony on Ripley's early knowledge of Fourierism can be found in the writings of Samuel Osgood, a Boston intellectual on the fringes of the Transcendentalist movement, and Orestes A. Brownson, one of Ripley's closest friends. In September 1840 Osgood reported that "the New Light Socialists" were discussing Fourierism in formulating their communitarian plans. This opinion was confirmed early in 1842 by Brownson.

At a meeting of the Trancendentalist Club late in the summer of 1840 Ripley vigorously defended the socialist ideal, and in the October 1840 issue of *The Dial* he reviewed favorably Albert Brisbane's *The Social Destiny of Man,* which was to become the Bible of the American Fourierists. Ripley described Fourier as one of the greatest thinkers of all time on social problems and their solutions. While he maintained that too many details of this plan were adjusted to the peculiarities of the French character, he freely admitted that the ultimate reorganization of society would have to begin with the foundations provided by Fourier. By 1843 Ripley's socialism was so orthodox that Albert Brisbane and Horace Greeley brought him, at a conference in Albany, New York, into the inner circle of leaders who planned the most ambitious project of American Fourierism, the North American Phalanx.

In 1847 Ripley boasted that the first meeting in New England to discuss Fourierism was held in his house on Bedford Street during the fall of 1840. He also provided in 1844 an explanation of his failure to publicize Fourierist ideas during the early phase of Brook Farm history: "It has been thought that a steady endeavor to embody these ideas more and more perfectly in life would give the best answer, both to the hopes of the friendly and the cavils of the sceptical, and furnish in its results the surest ground for any larger effort . . . [Meanwhile] every step has strengthened the faith with which we set out."

Thus there can be no doubt that Ripley was versed in Fourierism and that the concepts of the French socialists had an impact on the formation of the community. The extent of the early influence can be seen in the easy transformation of the Brook Farm Institute into the Brook Farm Phalanx without accusations, resignations, or a single public protest—indeed, so far as the historian can tell, without private objections. At the same time it is obvious that if the community had been established along strictly Fourierist lines, more would have been written about the fact by Ripley, Emerson, and J. S. Dwight, and the conversion of 1844 would have been pointless.

The early Fourierist influence was real enough, but its precise forms are difficult to single out, particularly because of the Transcendentalist background of most Brook Farmers. There are a number of instances in which an idea or communal pattern can be traced to either Fourierism or Transcendentalism. Both Fourier and Emerson, for example, shared a concern for the maximum development of human nature, and the Brook Farmers might have drawn their inspiration from either. In other cases Fourierist origins are more easily discerned. Emerson objected to the splintering of the individual personality by modern specialization, and Ripley's passion for uniting the thinker and the worker may have had roots in Transcendentalist ideology. Still, Fourier and the Brook Farmers went beyond this. They wished to overcome class divisions and to make society as well as the individual personality a harmonious whole. Fourier and Ripley sought more than the best circumstances for spontaneous living; and their social objectives of free choice of employment for every member of society, ample wages for workers, and universal social security were hardly central objects of concern for the most famous Transcendentalists. Emerson wished to celebrate the aesthetic virtues of common things, but the determination of Ripley to dignify manual labor cannot be traced plausibly to Transcendentalism. Both the author of the first Brook Farm constitution and Fourier used the phrase "attractive labor," and so similar were the two explanations of the doctrine that only the Fourierist jargon kept them from being identical.

The ideology of the Brook Farm leaders was from the beginning closer to Fourierism than to Transcendentalism, and the force of "Associationist" dogmas grew gradually until the reorganization of the community as a Phalanx took place in 1844. While the Fourierist influence was weaker in 1841 than in 1844, it did exist and had great significance in Ripley's plan "to improve the race of man" by building a socialist community which would be "a beacon light over this country and this age."

Frank E. Manuel (essay date 1962)

SOURCE: "Charles Fourier: The Burgeoning of Instinct," in *The Prophets of Paris,* Cambridge, Mass.: Harvard University Press, 1962, pp. 197-248.

[*In the following excerpt, Manuel examines Fourier's arguments against civilization and the philosophy of his contemporaries.*]

DEATH TO PHILOSOPHY AND ITS CIVILIZATION

Fourier's basic method involved a deliberate total denial of all past philosophical and moralist schools. *Ecart absolu,* he called it. Its definition came early in the *Théorie des quatre mouvements,* a methodological addendum to the Cartesian doubt. "I assumed that the most certain means of arriving at useful discoveries was to remove oneself in every sense from the methods followed by the dubious sciences which never contributed an invention that was of the remotest utility to society and which, despite the immense progress of industry, had not even succeeded in preventing poverty; I therefore undertook to stand in constant opposition to these sciences." The accumulation of hundreds of thousands of volumes had taught mankind nothing. Libraries of tomes by pompous and sententious thinkers had not brought man one inch closer to happiness. His own theory of the passions occupied a position of unique importance in the history of scientific discoveries. It had not really mattered that men were ignorant of the movements of the planets before Copernicus, of the sexual system of plants before Linnaeus, of the circulation of the blood before Harvey, of the existence of America before Columbus; but every delay in the proof and inauguration of the system of passionate attraction was felt in the flesh of mankind. Each year wars destroyed a million lives and poverty at least twenty million more—procrastination took a heavy toll. Since most great revolutionary geniuses had been forced to pursue mean occupations, Fourier's own humble condition was no test of the merit of his system. Metastasio had been a porter, Rousseau a menial worker, Newton a clerk in the markets (*sic*). He now joined this august company by adopting the same underlying dialectical principle of *écart absolu* which had guided them—a complete reversal of the philosophical ideas which had held mankind enchained for three thousand years. "He isolated himself from all known pathways." *Ecart absolu* was developed independently later in the century by Nietzsche in quest of a new moral system, and the same formula reappeared again in Rimbaud. In recent years André Breton has correctly recognized in Fourier an important predecessor of his own surrealist school and has filially composed an *Ode à Fourier.*

The two abstract concepts of philosophy and morality could vie for supremacy as the blackest of Fourier's many bêtes noires. When the *Revue encyclopédique* finally deigned to publish an article on his works they were classified under the hated rubric "philosophy," much to the dismay of the loyal disciple Just Muiron, who on May 12, 1832, wrote to Clarisse Vigoureux: "Philosophy!! Oh! did the Master hit the ceiling? I am terribly afraid." And now in the second century after his death Fourier is again ill used by the fates—called a moralist and joined with his mortal enemies in a single volume. The respectworthy general ideas of eighteenth- and early nineteenth-century thought—virtue, enlightenment, emancipation, rationalism, positivism, industrialism—were for Fourier empty shibboleths, words instead of things. Progress, the grandest concept of them all, the crowning glory of Turgot and Condorcet, Saint-Simon and Comte, was an iniquitous deception because it pretended to improve civilization and this was patently impossible. Civilization had to be destroyed, it could not be amended. For Fourier civilized society was a prison: the *philosophes* were trying to ameliorate conditions in the prison, he to break its bars and escape.

In Fourier's imagery the historical world was at once stadial and cyclical. It was mankind's destiny to climb upward through a series of sixteen or so fixed epochs from the depths of savagery until the zenith was reached in harmony. Never at a loss when nomenclature had to be invented, Fourier's brain, junglelike in the fertility of its private language, devised a terminology for each of the stages in the series up the ladder and back again. The progression is not infinite, for after the passing of harmony man is ordained to trudge laboriously down sixteen steps to a societal form even more primitive than savagery, at which point he fortunately will disappear in a general dissolution of the earth. In the Fourierist dream a striving for progress in happiness is intimately associated with a vision of final destruction. Mankind was summoned to the worldly pleasures of the phalanstery but was offered no promise of eternity. The earth's delights were real but necessarily transitory: therefore *carpe diem*. With meticulous care Fourier estimated the approximate time periods originally allotted each of the sixteen successive upward stages in the historic calendar, but since the schedule was not inflexible it was possible to abbreviate intermediate periods and to accelerate the process from savagery to harmony. A heightened tempo of change was even more urgent in the Fourierist order than in Condorcet's, because man's total destiny on earth was so pathetically finite. Hastening to the felicity of harmony would lengthen the duration of the period of perfect happiness mankind might enjoy. To the degree that man was left to languish in a state of "civilization" or in preharmony interludes such as "guarantism" or "sociantism," whole generations were being robbed of their portion. The quantum of history was fixed; it could be passed either in misery or in supreme happiness. This was a human choice. Fundamentally the successful speeding-up of the pace of evolution depended upon the propagation of the correct theory, as it had with Condorcet and as it would with the major ideologists of the nineteenth century.

Fourier singled out the Jacobins as the historic archenemies of the human race, the misleaders of humanity into the blind alleys of false doctrine. They were the reactionaries who stood for the perfection of the purported moral values of civilization when its complete abolition was required. They preached the Stoic ethic of self-denial and the merits of competitive commerce when mankind craved pleasure and order; their cult of virtue was the essence of antiharmonious evil. Futile political revolution shed blood without even the redeeming feature of Napoleonic carnage—the prospect of the unification of mankind. In its pretense of discovering happiness in liberty, equality, fraternity, and the moderation of desire the Jacobin philosophy was the embodiment of anti-Fourier.

A counterpoint between the emotional and physical sufferings of man in the state of civilization and the perfect happiness attainable in the phalanstery runs through all of Fourier's works. As Burke well knew when he attempted to combat the French "reign of virtue," there is no way to refute a utopia. Try as you may to demonstrate that the ideal structure is impossible of realization, that evils will inevitably crop up to poison the harmony, that the proposed system is contrary to powerful interests, that it violates our knowledge of human nature and contradicts the wisdom of the ages, utopians like Fourier insistently direct you to take another look at the cheats of contemporary civilization, at the falsehoods which contaminate all human relationships in society as it is now constituted, and you recoil with horror, shouting as you join the movement, "Take me to the phalanstery!" The spirit of Jean-Jacques, the enemy of the *philosophes*, hovers over every line that Fourier wrote. The play of contrast between natural man and artificial man of the *Discourse on Inequality* is reflected in the antithesis of the happy man in the phalanstery and the wretched man of civilization.

Man's desire to fulfill the totality of his passionate nature was the will of God. Since nature and nature's God had bestowed passions upon man, they must be afforded absolute free expression. Even Rousseau usually avoided an extreme naturalist position by stopping at the bar of Stoic moderation. In Fourier's vocabulary moderation, along with liberty and equality, was a gross, pejorative word: to curb, to restrain, to repress a desire, was contrary to nature, hence the source of corruption. Nature never decreed moderation for everybody; surely nature never ordained moderation in all things for everybody. Fourier derided the philosophical moralists for their betrayal of the much-vaunted empirical method when they argued about what men *should* be like, what they *ought* to do, what sentiments they *ought* to have. Their discussions were chimerical nonsense, their morality high-flown dicta whose hypocritical authors never practiced their own preachments. Fourier began not with the rational principles of natural law but with an inquiry into what men actually wanted, their basic drives and passions. Despite the historical movement of mankind through the thirty-two stages up and down the ladder of progress, basic human passions had remained the same in all times and places and could be identified and described. Only the opportunities for the expression of the passions had differed from epoch to epoch. Since the passions were constant, human history was a study in varying degrees of repression.

Ever since the dawn of civilization three thousand years before, the external physical forces of nature had been sufficiently harnessed by man to allow for the total fulfillment of all the desires of all human beings on the planet; it had been theoretically possible during all those centuries for miserable mankind to leap out of civilization into harmony. The crisis of passionate man was thus not a novelty of the recent epoch of transition between feudal and industrial society. Gratuitous evil had been the lot of mankind ever since an equilibrium between desires and satisfactions had become abstractly possible. In the recent period, following the development of science and the wide extension of commercial relations, the gap between soci-

TABLEAU

DU COURS DU MOUVEMENT SOCIAL.

SUCCESSION et RELATIONS de ses 4 PHASES et 32 PÉRIODES.

Ordre des Créations futures.

(On ne pourra bien acquérir l'intelligence de ce Tableau que par l'étude des Chapitres suivans qui en donnent l'explication.)

PREMIÈRE PHASE. ENFANCE ou INCOHÉRENCE ASCENDANTE.   ANNÉES.

Sept périodes. Création subversive antérieure, déjà faite.

Reculement
  1.ᵉ SECTES CONFUSES. Ombre du bonheur.
  2.ᵉ Sauvagerie.
  3.ᵉ Patriarchat.
  4.ᵉ Barbarie.
Élan
  5.ᵉ Civilisation.
  6.ᵉ Garantisme.
  7.ᵉ SECTES ÉBAUCHÉES. Aube du bonheur.

— Saut des Chaos en Harmonie.

DEUXIÈME PHASE. ACCROISSEMENT ou COMBINAISON ASCENDANTE.

Neuf périodes.   8.ᵉ SECTES COMBINÉES SIMPLES. Aurore du bonheur.

Naissance de la Couronne boréale.

  9.ᵉ
  10.ᵉ
  11.ᵉ
  12.ᵉ
  13.ᵉ
  14.ᵉ
  15.ᵉ
  16.ᵉ

Ces sept périodes sont distinguées par SEPT CRÉATIONS HARMONIQUES, séparées par des intervalles d'environ 4000 ans.

1.ᵉ Création septigénérique et Plénitude ascendante.

APOGÉE DU BONHEUR.   Intermède ou Quiétude d'environ 8000 ans.

TROISIÈME PHASE.   DÉCLIN ou COMBINAISON DESCENDANTE.

Neuf périodes.
  17.ᵉ
  18.ᵉ
  19.ᵉ
  20.ᵉ
  21.ᵉ
  22.ᵉ
  23.ᵉ
  24.ᵉ

2.ᵉ Création septigénérique et Plénitude descendante.

Ces sept périodes sont distinguées par SEPT CRÉATIONS HARMONIQUES séparées par des intervalles d'environ 4000 ans.

Extinction de la Couronne boréale.

25.ᵉ SECTES COMBINÉES SIMPLES. Terme du bonheur.

— Saut d'Harmonie en Chaos.

QUATRIÈME PHASE. CADUCITÉ ou INCOHÉRENCE DESCENDANTE.

Sept périodes.   Création Subversive postérieure.

Retraite
  26.ᵉ SECTES ÉBAUCHÉES. Vestiges du bonheur.
  27.ᵉ Garantisme.
  28.ᵉ Civilisation.
  29.ᵉ Barbarie.
Agonie
  30.ᵉ Patriarchat.
  31.ᵉ Sauvagerie.
  32.ᵉ SECTES CONFUSES. Ombre du bonheur.

Fin du Monde animal et végétal, après une durée approximative de . . . 8000 ans.

VIBRATION ASCENDANTE — VIBRATION DESCENDANTE

CHAOS ASCENDANT. — HARMONIE ASCENDANTE. — HARMONIE DESCENDANTE. — CHAOS DESCENDANT.

A diagram of the history of human societies from the 1808 edition of Fourier's Théorie des quatre mouvements.

ety's potential capacity to appease desires and the restrictive self-denials imposed by civilization had become ever wider, not narrower. The progress of the arts and sciences had not been paralleled by an increase in gratification. The state of civilization had been protracted far beyond its alloted span of time—the period when it was extending human capacities; it had multiplied artificial restrictions, curtailed pleasure, extended repressions. Under civilization neither rich nor poor had realized their full measure of potential enjoyment.

Fourier had been advised by his more cautious disciples to withdraw his reflections on love in order to make his ideas on the organization of labor more palatable to philosophers, less outrageous to rational civilized society. But this was the very heart of the system of harmony. "Love in phalanstery is no longer, as it is with us, a recreation which detracts from work; on the contrary it is the soul and the vehicle, the mainspring, of all works and of the whole of universal attraction." Imagine asking Praxiteles to disfigure his Venus. "I'd rather break the arms of all the *philosophes* than those of my Venus; if they do not know how to appreciate her, I'll bury her rather than mutilate her." Let philosophy go to the depths of the Hell from which it came. Fourier would prefer to commit his theory to oblivion rather "than alter a single syllable" to please this nefarious clique. In his absolutism and his obsessions he was a worthy successor of Jean-Jacques. The philosophers must either accept the whole theory down to its minutest detail, the arrangement of the last mechanism of the passionate series—or nothing. There would be no compromise with philosophy and civilization. The system was a total truth which had to be preserved entire; modify its slightest aspect and it would be destroyed.

The *philosophes* were the infamous ones to be crushed; Fourier was the anti-Voltaire. Contemporary followers of the pretentious eighteenth-century moralists who believed in the perfectibility of reason had formed a cabal—he sounds Burkean in his imagining of the plot—to suppress invention in general and the one inventor in particular who could assure the happiness of mankind. The new philosophical superstition, the exaltation of reason at the expense of the passions, had to be obliterated to make way for the Fourierist truth. The morality preached by the philosophers of all ages had always been a hypocritical mask. Paris and London were the principal "volcanoes of morality" which each year poured forth on the civilized world veritable torrents of moral systems, and yet these two cities were the bastions of depravity. Athens and Sparta, the ancient centers of philosophy, had espoused pederasty as the path of virtue.

In the divine designation of insignificant Fourier as the bearer of the new doctrine of salvation there was a symbol, a correspondence with the ancient choice of a poor carpenter to defeat the scribes. "Finally to complete the humiliation of these modern titans," he wrote in the *Théorie des quatre mouvements,* "God decreed that they should be beaten by an inventor who is a stranger to the sciences and that the theory of universal movement should fall to the lot of an almost illiterate man; it is a store-clerk who

is going to confound these libraries of politics and morals, the shameful fruit of ancient and modern charlatanism. Well! It is not the first time that God has used a lowly man to humble the great and has chosen an obscure man to bring to the world the most important message."

The works of Fourier leveled the most circumstantial attack on the uses of civilization since Rousseau. What he lacked in style he made up in a profusion of detail. The cheats of ordinary commercial arrangements, the boredom of family life, the deceits of marriage, the hardships of the one-family farm and the miseries of pauperism in the great cities, the evils of naked competition, the neglect of genius, the sufferings of children and old people, the wastefulness of economic crises and wars, added up to a total rejection of civilization as a human epoch. Proof positive that it was quintessentially unnatural lay in the fact that children and savages, who were closest to nature, would have none of the ways of civilization until they were violently forced into its toils. The coercive mechanisms of society disguised as reason, duty, moderation, morality, necessity, or resignation did not work. In order to maintain its dominion the apparatus of mercantile trickery and morality called civilization had been constrained to rely upon more terrible contrivances: the executioner and his accessories the prisons and the bastilles. "Try to suppress these instruments of torture and the next day you will see the whole people in revolt abandoning work and returning to the savage state. Civilization is therefore a society that is contrary to nature, a reign of violence and cunning, and political science and morality, which have taken three thousand years to create this monstrosity, are sciences that are contrary to nature and worthy of profound contempt." The natural goal of man was an affluence of pleasures and riches, not penury, chastity, and self-sufficiency; order and free choice, not individualistic anarchy; instead of the negative philosophy of repression, the positive one of attraction. Civilized doctrines of "the wealth of nations" had merely succeeded in covering the immense majority of laborers with rags. The lot of ordinary people under civilization was worse than that of animals.

In *La Seconde boussole* Fourier arraigned the supposed achievements of the industrial revolution. "Men have been more wretched since the introduction of the steam engine and railroads than before." The steam carriage and the steam boar which rival the grasshoppers and the salmon in their velocity are beyond doubt fine trophies for man, but these prodigies are premature. Under existing conditions of civilized society they do not lead to the goal of augmenting in steady proportions the well-being of all social classes—rich, comfortable, middle, and poor. There is a gulf between our progress in material industry and our backwardness in industrial politics or the art of increasing the happiness of nations in proportion with the progress of their labors. We are retrogressing in the very branch of knowledge which is the most useful to man. Among the hardest-working nations, England, Ireland, and Belgium, the poverty-stricken class includes as many as thirty out of a hundred; in areas that are not industrialized, Russia, Portugal, the number of indigents is three out of a hundred, ten times less than in industrialized countries. In terms of genuine progress our social system is therefore a contradiction, an essentially absurd mechanism whose elements of potential good only result in evil. This is the art of transforming gold into copper, the fate of any business in which philosophical science has become involved. Philosophy has tried to direct monarchs and peoples. Where has it led them? We see sovereigns falling into debt, running to usurers, and vying with each other in ruining their states while the peoples who have been promised happiness experience a hard time getting work and bread and are never sure of having it on the morrow. These are the fruits of the science of deception called political and business economics. Let us therefore recognize false progress for what it is, mere nonsensical social change. "It has reached an impasse; it is in a vicious circle like a horse moving round and round without getting anywhere. . . . "

Fourier's writings became the *locus classicus* for descriptions of the evils of capitalism, the thievery of the stock market, the "corruption of commerce," the miseries of economic crises, the hoarding, the speculation. The civilized order was like a dinner table at which the guests fought with one another over every morsel, while if they lived amid the abundance of the phalanstery each man would graciously serve his neighbor. How could moralists pretend to be shocked by the intricate love relations in the state of harmony when they tolerated with equanimity the crowding of men and women into the attics of Lyons as if they were herrings in a barrel? Of all the consequences of industrial and commercial anarchy Fourier was most profoundly shocked by the squandering of natural resources and the products of the earth, because this represented an absolute diminution of potential pleasure for mankind. His witness of the dumping of boatloads of rice during a famine in order to sustain high prices assumed the same symbolic significance as his vision of the costly apple. The intermediaries in the contemporary social mechanism who were not directly related to production—housekeepers, soldiers, bureaucrats, merchants, lawyers, prisoners, philosophers, Jews, and the unemployed—were useless and parasitic; they lived at the expense of producers, savages, barbarians, and children.

Fourier's critique of civilization concentrated on the portrayal of its pervasive poverty. Virtually all men—not only the proletariat—are poor, because their passions are unfulfilled, their senses are not appeased, their amorous emotions are curbed, and their naturally complex social sensibilities can find outlets only in pitifully limited channels. As a consequence all men are bored. In civilization the distinction between the rich and the poor remains an important one because among the rich a small minority may even today enjoy a measure of satisfaction, while the poor are almost totally deprived. If the gastronomy of the rich is mediocre, the poor suffer hunger in an absolute sense. If the rich can at least partially alleviate their ennui by changing women and occupations and by satisfying their senses with music and beautiful sights, the poor man bound to his small agricultural plot is condemned to long hours of repetitive labor and is almost completely bereft of pleasures. A holding based on the organization of the family is far too circumscribed a unit for the contentment of man. While the most obvious distinction between the rich and the poor is economic, the concepts of richness and *luxe* (and its opposite poverty) acquired far broader connotations in Fourier. The idea of luxury has no pejorative overtones; richness is one of the basic desires of all men; it identifies a way of life in which there is a continual experience of a wide variety of sensations and in which the opportunities for gratification are ample. Real passionate richness is what Fourier is extolling, not mere richness of wish or fantasy; being rich implies active indulgence in sensuous delights. Fourier cleansed luxury of its Christian theological stigma and demoted poverty from its ideal position as a crowning virtue. "Poverty is worse than vice," he quoted from his Franche-Comtois peasant compatriots. In the state of civilization class conflict has become endemic because the poor who are ungratified hate the rich who seem to be fulfilled (though in reality they are not) and the rich are fearful of the poor who might deprive them of their pleasures. The view of the class system of domination as a form of instinctual repression—which Freud hinted at in his last works—was developed extensively by Fourier.

Family life, the key social institution of the civilized state, was Fourier's most compelling example of an unnatural institution holding men in its iron grip, bringing misery to all its members. While upon casual inspection the patriarchal monogamous family of the French appeared to establish a system under which the males were free to satisfy their sexual passions outside of the marital bond without suffering derogation and only the females were enslaved, the realities of contemporary marriage were oppressive to men and women alike. The legal fettering of women's desires had resulted in the invention of countless subterfuges to evade the law and in the diffusion of a general hypocritical spirit throughout society. Cuckoldry was rampant. Fourier's anatomy of modern adultery with its intricate categories and typologies—he identified some sixty-odd ideal situations, varying subtly with the temperaments of the threesome involved and their social status—is a triumph of psychological analysis which earned the plaudits of no less an observer of the human comedy than Honoré de Balzac. The husband is by no means the only sufferer and ridiculous figure in the drama, for the adulterers never appease their real passions and have to pay dearly for the mere semblance of contentment.

From his conversation with men boasting about their conquests, Fourier, not yet equipped with the delicate statistical techniques of contemporary sexologists from Indiana, arrived at the gross estimate that on the average each member of the female sex contracted six liaisons of fornication before marriage and six of adultery after marriage. But what about the exceptions, he asked rhetorically in a section of the *Traité de l'association domestique-agricole* piquantly entitled "Equilibre subversif." There goes a man who claims that he has taken a virgin to wife. He has, he says, good proofs. Maybe, if he married her young enough. But if she has not, before marriage, provided her quota of illicit loves to maintain the "subversive equilibrium," she will have to compensate by twelve liaisons of adulterous commerce after marriage. "No, says the husband, she will be chaste. I shall see to it. In that case it is necessary that her neighbor compensate by twenty-four infractions, twelve in fornication and twelve in adultery, since the general equilibrium requires twelve times as many illicit liaisons as there are men." Granted the relative accuracy of his informants, Fourier's computations were impeccable.

Daniel Bell on the appeal of Fourier:

In his writings one can see Fourier's deep and permanent longing for the eternal childhood of man which so many poets and Arcadians have celebrated. He resists relentlessly the expulsion from Eden and childhood's end. In Corinthians, Paul had put away childish things and seen through a glass darkly, but this "anti-Paul," with tinkling cymbals and a sounding brass, preached a new orgiastic chiliasm, the release of all restraints, the recurrent pleasures of childhood on earth. And this is the recurrent and permanent appeal of Charles Fourier.

Daniel Bell, in The Winding Passage: Essays and Sociological Journeys, 1960-1980, *Basic Books, Inc., 1980.*

Fourier's mordant descriptions of supposedly monogamous marital relations in a state of civilization were designed to silence those critics of free love in the state of harmony who had denounced its bestial materialism. Marriage in contemporary society, he wrote in the ***Théorie de l'unité universelle,*** is "pure brutality, a casual pairing off provoked by the domestic bond without any illusion of mind or heart. This is the normal way of life among the mass of the people. Dullened, morose couples who quarrel all day long are reconciled to each other on the bolster because they cannot afford two beds, and contact, the sudden pin-prick of the senses, triumphs for a moment over conjugal satiety. If this is love it is the most material and the most trivial."

The desires of most people are polygamous, witness the secret bacchanalia which take place in small villages and the virtual community of women which prevails among the rich. The great "passionate" lie of love in the state of civilization is rooted in the philosophical dogma that all men and women are the same in their wants. This is simply not true. Men and women have different love needs at various periods in their life cycle. Even persons of the same age group have widely divergent amorous tendencies ranging from the extreme of inconstancy—the Don Juan type among men—to the rare extreme of monogamy. To subject them equally to the same rigid law must inevitably yield a harvest of unhappiness for all.

The gospel of Fourier was the ultimate triumph of the expansive romantic ideal. True happiness consisted of plenitude and the enjoyment of an ever-increasing abun-dance of pleasure. Man's goal was not the attainment of illusory juridical rights but the flowering of the passions. Though civilization was originally an advance over savagery, patriarchy, and barbarism, in its present decadent state its superiority was not marked enough to attract either savages or barbarians. In the civilized world anarchic competition, monopoly, commercial feudalism, business speculation, were despoiling the earth, spreading misery, fostering thievery in the guise of commerce. Men with diverse passionate natures were constricted within the bonds of monogamous marriage, forcing them to seek other sexual pleasures clandestinely. Man had a progressive need for ever more multifarious luxuries of the table; such gastronomic pleasures were now denied to the vast bulk of the population and the destiny of a substantial portion was hunger. Men were bored by a dull family life under civilization, and at their parties and in their clubs there was a frantic though vain attempt to escape tedium, the corrosive enemy of the species.

Leslie F. Goldstein (essay date 1982)

SOURCE: "Early Feminist Themes in French Utopian Socialism: The St.-Simonians and Fourier," in *Journal of the History of Ideas,* Vol. XLIII, No. 1, January-March, 1982, pp. 91-108.

[*In the following excerpt, Goldstein examines the feminist aspects of Fourier's work while noting the limitations in his theories regarding the role of women in Fourierist communities.*]

Women's Rights vs. Women's Liberation—It is commonly noted that the feminist movement of the nineteenth and early twentieth centuries was a quest for women's rights, whereas the feminist movement of the late twentieth century is more properly denominated a quest for women's liberation. The central issues of the first wave of feminism were equality in legal and political rights and formal equality of opportunity. These feminists sought the opportunity to vote and hold public office, access to jobs and education, and equality of legal rights in marriage. The last included the rights of married women to own and earn property, to disobey their husbands, to sue for divorce (on grounds comparable to those available to their husbands), to obtain child custody after divorce, and to legal protection against physical abuse by their husbands. By the mid-twentieth century the goals of the women's rights movement had been, for the most part, written into the law of the United States and much of Western Europe. The 1960s, however, generated a new feminist movement which, while giving attention to some work of the first wave (e.g., seeking ratification of the E.R.A.), was predominantly concerned with women's liberation. A sample list of issues for the contemporary women's movement is "e.g., abolition of marriage, continuation of the nuclear family, payment for housewives, abolition of the housewife role, child care, abortion, access of women to predominantly male occupations, abolition of sex roles . . . " [*The Politics of Women's Liberation, 1975*]. Even the National Organization for Women (N.O.W.), which has a middleclass and mainstream image, emphasizes these new concerns: their

1968 "Bill of Rights" included insistence on child care centers, tax deductions for working parents for child care, jobtraining opportunities, and job-training allowances for poor women (presumably including poor mothers). In short, the core of today's feminism seems to be a concern for liberating women from traditional, sex-based division of labor *within* the family. This concern cuts across various ideological divisions within the movement and is the shared bond among its various segments whether they call themsleves "liberal feminists," "socialist feminists," "lesbian separatists," or "radical feminists." This paper is an exploration of some major intellectual origins of the women's liberationist ideology.

It is not difficult to find roots of the equal rights movement in the classic liberal principles of Hobbes and Locke. Finding the origin of the women's liberation movement is more difficult. A case can be made that Karl Marx, who insisted that the family needed to be "criticized in theory and revolutionized in practice," was a philosophic progenitor of the women's liberation movement. Marx, however, made no secret of his intellectual indebtedness to the utopian socialists of the early nineteenth century. He noted, for example, that Fourier before him had advocated abolition of the family. Fourier, in fact, is credited by modern scholars with having originated the word "féministe." But even before Fourier's ideas attracted widespread attention in France, those of his rivals, the Saint-Simonians, enjoyed quite a vogue. The Saint-Simonians, *unlike* their supposed mentor, Comte Claude Henri de Saint-Simon, openly espoused the cause of complete social and political equality for women. . . .

To be sure, the Saint-Simonians and Fourier were writing and being read during a period of enormous social ferment, a period in which a very wide variety of feminist ideas were "in the air." The attention that they devoted to the oppressive qualities of women's family role and the thoroughness and radicalness of their critique of that role, however, set them apart. These features of their work also identify it as a very appropriate starting point for one wishing to understand the history of women's liberation. . . .

Fourier and Women's Liberation—Like his contemporary Saint-Simonians, Charles Fourier called forthrightly for women's equality and freedom, condemned their servitude within the existing marriage institution, and railed against the double standard of sexual chastity. He too believed that all important jobs should be open to women on the basis of skill and aptitude rather than closed on account of gender. But unlike the Saint-Simonians, Fourier spoke of women as individuals, not as half the human couple. Fourier's concern was to liberate every human individual, man, woman, and child (whom he called the "third" or "neuter" sex), in two senses. First, through education he wished to free their faculties for maximum development. Education was to begin by age two and was to be handled by skilled experts (rather than haphazardly qualified parents), at community expense, for all, regardless of economic status or gender. Secondly, and more radically, Fourier sought the liberation of human passion

from all repression and frustration. He believed that if his utopia (Harmony) were established, every human problem could be eliminated: not only the obvious economic wants like hunger and need for shelter but also boredom, anxiety, and sexual frustration.

In fact, this distinction between productive faculties and consumption-oriented desires is somewhat alien to Fourier's thought. For him, in a sense, desires *were* stunted faculties needing development: our capacities for feeling, from the gastronomic to the sexual to the loving to the ambitious and conspiratorial, could—with proper techniques—be more fully developed and thus more freely enjoyed. Dulled for 2000 years in "Civilization" (his term for the current epoch), feelings would truly blossom in Harmony: people would live more than twice as long (on the average, one hundred and forty-four years); they would need to sleep only a few hours per night; and waking hours, filled with pleasures "so numerous, so fiery, so varied," would pass as one long ecstatic moment because the individual would live "in a sort of permanent frenzy." Whether one characterizes Fourier's goal with such elevated phrases as "a continuous . . . kaleidoscopic explosion of rapturous joy" or with the more down-to-earth phrases "permanent orgasm" and "eternal convulsion," the point is clear: his goals for improving human life extended far beyond ameliorating the lot of the poor and the unemployed and providing economic, professional, and political opportunities to women.

Fantastic though his vision was, the feminist message in that vision was an undeniably dominant theme. Fourier's feminist concerns figured in all of his major published works, from the *Théorie de Quatre Mouvements* in 1808 through the two-volume work (published shortly before his death in 1836-37), *La Fausse Industrie*. His thoughts on the importance of women's plight and on the nature of their oppression often have a contemporary ring, even more so than those of the Saint-Simonians. But, as with the Saint-Simonians, other of his major tenets will give serious pause to contemporary proponents of women's liberation.

Fourier announced repeatedly and in forceful terms that women in Civilization have been severely oppressed and particularly victimized. (Moreover, women were even more severely deprived in the stages prior to Civilization.) Their victimization and its solution are two-fold: women are deprived of economic-industrial and amorous fulfillment. Both deprivations are linked to the marriage institutions.

In fact, marriage for Fourier is at the hub of the two axes characterizing any cultural epoch: (1) the method for the social exchange of commodities (the economic system), and (2) the method of conjugal union between the sexes. Since marriage is both conjugal and economic, Fourier in earlier works stressed the determinative role of the amorous institutions:

> There is in each period a characteristic which forms the PIVOT OF THE MECHANISM and whose absence or presence determines the change of period. This trait is

always drawn from love. . . . As a general thesis, the Pivotal characteristic, which is always drawn from the amorous customs, brings about all the others; but the characteristics branching off to it do not give birth to the pivotal one, and lead only very slowly to a change of period. Barbarians could adopt up to twelve of the sixteen traits of Civilization [of which many are economic] and still remain Barbarians if they did not adopt the pivotal trait, *the civil liberty of an exclusive wife.*

It was this reasoning concerning the marriage institution, bolstered by the additional premise that "God recognizes as freedom only those liberties extended equally to both sexes," that underlay Fourier's famous italicized assertions that, "As a general thesis: *Social progress . . . occurs by virtue of the progress of women toward liberty, and social decline by virtue of decreases in the liberty of women.*" Thus, the alleviation of women's plight would perforce involve a beneficial transformation of those pivotal institutions of marriage and the family-based economy.

Within Civilization, women's economic and amorous deprivations were interwined. The typical lot of women, barred from most productive employment, was to be sold into conjugal servitude as soon as they reached marriageable age. For women outside the aristocracy, Fourier lamented that " . . . prostitution more or less prettied up is their only resort." The ever-present knowledge that she will have to attract a buyer-sponsor in the form of a husband had a terribly damaging effect on the personality of a growing girl, Fourier argued, and caused most women to develop vice-ridden characters, marked by servility and deviousness.

In Fourier's eyes, the anarchic arrangements of the present economic system produced even more waste and hardship for women than for men. Men faced poor working conditions, unemployment, employment in jobs unsuited to their faculties, and poverty—which produced hunger, ill-health, and despair. Most women not only endured the ills of poverty but also were pressured by gender prejudice out of almost every gainful employment except prostitution or marital subjugation. Once married, the rules were clear: lifetime bondage and obedience to a husband. Fourier even noted that in "civilized" England a husband could still sell his wife to another man.

Besides personal servitude in marriage, women in particular suffered its labor-wasting impact. The main flaw of a household-based economy was tremendous waste, primarily in duplication of functions. Fourier estimated that three-fourths of all women in cities, half of all women in the country, and three-fourths of all household servants—especially kitchen workers—could have their superfluous labor eliminated by the collective efficiency of Harmony.

Fourier's criticism of marriage, however, stressed its emotional and sexual deprivation, especially for women, much more than its economic deprivation. His typical critiques did not tell of wife-beating and household drudgery but focused on women's sexual repression. The nature of women's "oppression" was that "any word or thought consistent with the dictates of nature is imputed to women as a crime." Persecuted "when [they] obey Nature [women must] behave in ways contrary to their desires." This forces them to be fraudulent "in order to free their natural impulses." Thus, "seemly behavior on the part of the stronger sex is treated as a crime on the part of the weaker sex." After noting the solemn decision of the Council of Macon that women had no souls, Fourier points to a British example of legislation that in his judgment is "no less dishonoring" to women: a law permitting a husband to demand pecuniary damages from the acknowledged lover of his wife. In the Fourierist calculus, then, the denial of sexual freedom is equated with the denial of an immortal soul. When Fourier contrasts those nations that have dismally failed the "pivotal" test of "the extension of the privileges of women" with those which have not, he writes exclusively of sexual repression or its absence (amorous liberty).

The extension of women's liberty is the key to social progress. "Free love"—and Fourier did use the phrase—did not mean a cruelly anarchic every-person-for-him/herself version, for that would deprive many, especially the old and the ugly, of something as necessary as food. In Harmony, rather than monogamous marriage with its ever-present companion of widespread but dishonestly concealed infidelity that provides some with a wealth of gratification but leaves others emotionally starved, there would be a system of Amorous Guarantees or the Amorous Corporation. In this system, to a "social minimum" of fulfilling work and decent food, clothing, shelter, and entertainment would be added a "sexual minimum" of fulfilling sex.

In Fourier's Utopia people would live in communal households in village units called Phalanxes. Social motivation would be achieved through a complex incentive system based on Fourier's analysis of the 810 personality types—an incentive system that included differential economic rewards, including the right of bestowing inheritances, as well as psychological rewards (e.g., esteem, companionship) and sensual rewards (gastronomic, sexual, etc.). Jobs would be arranged so that work places were always pleasant and people only did tasks that were fun for them, never working at a single job long enough to get bored (i.e., more than two hours). Incentives would also be structured to ensure that everyone received sexual gratification. All physical needs would be satisfied; no one would work or make love out of economic necessity; life would be a constant delight. Outside the Phalanxes, massive economic development (e.g., irrigating the Sahara Desert) would be accomplished by volunteer industrial armies, lured from thousands of Phalanxes by Fourier's usual technique of "passionate attraction." The loveliest women would be attracted to the army, some in the virginal group of 15½ to 20 years old for whom the industrial "soldiers" would be contesting. To further attract recruits, the army would engage in nightly amorous festivities. Women would also serve in the ranks of "bacchantes, bayaderes, fakiresses, fairies, magicians, paladines, heroines, and other feminine jobs." The first three are Fourierist terms for amorous adventuresses who use sexual and affectionate wiles to console and distract dejected suitors who have failed in their quest for a beautiful virgin; the second two groups engage in amorous matchmaking; paladines and heroines have honorific titles for impressive accomplishments. What Fourier meant by "other feminine jobs." must be determined by inference.

On occasion, Fourier seems to intend to do away with the sexual division of labor:

> one half of the jobs . . . is to be reserved for women; one must avoid relegating them, as among us, to thankless functions, to the servile roles to which they are assigned by philosophy which pretends that woman is made only to scour pots and mend old clothes.

But then emphasis changes from egalitarian group quotas to somewhat more individualized variation:

> Although each branch of industry is especially suited to one of the sexes, such as needlework for women and plough-work for men, nonetheless nature loves mixtures, sometimes by halves, and some jobs by a quarter; she wants at least one eighth of the opposite sex in each function. . . . By means of this mixture in each job the feminine sex will form a useful rivalry with the masculine.

Yet Fourier, at other points, made it clear that he expected certain jobs to be performed only by females: the care of babies aged birth to two, needlework, and laundry. In Harmony, he says when the laundry is being cleaned "*women* will not ruin their hands by plunging them into icy or scalding water" (because there will be faucets to regulate the temperature), and he uses only a female term, i.e., laundresses, to describe the laundry workers.

Fourier's basic principles remained: each would work (according to taste and skill) at productive work under pleasant conditions. What varied was his specific conclusion as to how many members of a particular sex would be fulfilled, happy, and competent at needlework, laundry, and babycare. It was crucial that people not be channeled on the basis of gender into an occupation. Fourier even insisted that children aged birth to three should be dressed alike and raised alike so that only their true vocational talents would bloom, rather than a set of conventionally imposed ones. Although the modern reader may see Fourier as short-sighted in failing to realize that excluding male caretakers for the first two years of life might well have a channeling impact on children, one must grant that on the subject of occupation his heart seemed to be in a women's liberation place.

On women's role as bait for industrial armies, however, the problems with Fourier's outlook amount to far more than short-sightedness. To be sure, the "Vestal (virginal) quadrilles" sent by each of the 10,000-100,000 Phalanxes to these armies (in addition to the ten worker-soldiers to be sent) consisted of equal numbers of each sex, but the male half of the quadrille played a very different role from the female. Both were "the best and the brightest" from their respective Phalanxes, both received much honor and luxury and served to attract suitors from the oppo-site sex into the armies, but their attracting roles varied considerably. In Fourier's eyes the drawing power of a beautiful virgin was intrinsic:

> In young women 16-18 years old, nothing commands higher esteem than a virginity beyond doubt, a genuine, unvarnished decorum, an ardent devotion to useful and charitable duties. . . .

Female vestals would naturally be worshipped, and about thirty women per phalanx would be attracted to the role by its prestige and their own penchants. Males were different: they too would have respected "Vestal" roles in Harmony (unlike morally inconsistent Civilization where male virginity was scorned), but within each Phalanx only half as many males as females would be Vestals. Unlike females, youthful male virgins are not intrinsically respectable but seem to be needed in Harmony for two reasons: (1) to provide abstract moral consistency (God favors sex equality), and (2) to mediate between childhood and sexual maturity so that children at younger and younger ages are not prematurely tempted into sexual activity. Moreover, the intrinsic desirability of sexual purity does not attract young men into the Vestalate. Fourier feels the need to explain what sort of men would enter the Vestalate, and he lists three: (1) those who are so distracted and absorbed by the diversified fun of Harmony that they do not start thinking about sex until a later age than usual: (2) those who have their eye on a female Vestal and use this chance to get close to her; and (3) those who want to make a monarchical match for themselves. Royalty will select mates from the industrial army, and being a Vestal gives a young man an early chance to enter the army (to which admission is very competitive). In short, women Vestals are considered prizes *as such;* male Vestals are earning the chance to *become* considered a prize by joining the army where they can perform prodigious industrial feats or excel in competitive games.

Both men and women would be used as societal sex objects: "Love . . . will thus become one of the most brilliant mainsprings of the social mechanism." But the emphasis is on the use of *women* to attract *men* to labor: a cooperative, multi-phalanx "haying is followed by a meal attended by the loveliest women. . . . " Fourier's examples of vestals selecting mates from their various suitors always discuss women vestals, and his treatments of great industrial tasks typically estimate the number of *men* (*hommes*) needed for the job. He makes the point pretty bluntly: "the gathering of the most famous female vestals is one of the baits [*amorces*] which attracts young folks to these armies."

It is precisely this aspect of Fourier's thought that seems to open him to Karl Marx's criticism of "crude proposals" for "the community of women." Marx complained that these end up making woman into "a piece of communal and common property. . . . [W]oman passes from exclusive, private marriage to general prostitution." In Fourier's scheme, women's sexual services are bought by society as a whole to further industrial, or generally, economic, productivity. Fourier seems to argue implicitly that the use of sex for economic benefits to the community is

not demeaning if the sexual favors are granted to someone for whom one bears genuine affection or some sort of
penchant and if the sexual activity is not performed under
economic pressure. It is not at all clear that this answer is
adequate, however.

If all individuals are to coexist in freedom and equal dignity, it seems deeply problematic to compare lust for
another person with hunger for a piece of bread. This
outlook on sexual passion prompted Fourier to write in an
unpublished manuscript:

> [N]ature . . . has provided helpful knights even for individuals
> who are no longer of an age to be pleasing; here is the
> proof. . . . In 1816 a young man was tried in France for
> having raped six women aged 60 to 80. . . . They found
> him guilty and sentenced him but perhaps it would have
> been wiser to distribute pieces of his clothing as religious
> relics in order to propagate his good example. It is
> evidence that this young phoenix acted *out of need,*
> *and that need of this genre both in men and women*
> *can be pushed to the point of urgent necessity quite as*
> *much as that for food.* (Emphasis in original.)

Fourier dubbed this rapist of old women a knight (*"champion"*) presumably not because he "did them a favor" (in
the too-common misogynist formulation) but because he
exemplified two Fourierist principles: (1) that there was
adequate variety of passions in the natural world to fulfill
everyone's sexual needs (including old ladies') on a purely voluntary basis, and (2) that sexual passion was a *need*
just like hunger. Still, the example of rapist as hero is
revealing, for Fourier's tone takes him all too often to the
brink of depicting woman as the sexual servicer of society. And if he were ever to discover that his dream of
harmonious, free, passional fulfillment for all were unattainable, it is not at all clear that he would have rejected
as a next-best alternative the Marquis de Sade's dictum
that all humans have a right to total sexual gratification
and that any human desired sexually by another thus has
a *duty* to oblige.

One need not, however, take Fourier beyond his own stated position in order to criticize him. A world in which
human beings perform the societal role of serving as tac-
tile stimulant to other people is a world where some people are treating other people as less than human, as objects. That Fourier's scheme would give women the reciprocal right to treat men as sex objects does not succeed
in making the arrangement a humane one.

In certain respects, Fourier's vision took very important
strides toward arguing for women's liberation, as that term
is understood today. He advocated for women not only
legal and political equality but also educational equality
beginning in infancy and true equality of occupational
freedom. Women, even mothers, would be freed from the
specific duties of home and childcare. He also wished to
free women from the unfairness of the sexual double standard. It is true that certain aspects of his notion of the
perfect society, from a contemporary women's liberation
perspective, were less than perfect and tended to approach
a socialized version of Hugh Hefner's "Playboy philoso-

phy." It is also true that certain aspects of his vision were
sheer lunacy—e.g., his belief that the planets copulated
with one another, that the sea would turn into lemonade,
etc. These weaknesses, however, do not negate the contribution that his vision has made to the historical development of the women's liberation movement.

Conclusion—Although John Stuart Mill and Karl Marx,
as more coherent, rational, and careful thinkers, have
perhaps deserved the additional attention that they have
received as philosophers of feminism, and although the
religious mysticism of the Saint-Simonians and the quasi-
lunacy of Charles Fourier properly exclude them from the
ranks of "philosophers," the widespread neglect of these
utopian thinkers, particularly by historians of feminism,
has been undeserved. Although the women's liberation
ideology of the twentieth century did not spring full-blown
from the mind of any single nineteenth-century thinker, it
also is not lacking in roots within that earlier turbulent
era. Both the Saint-Simonians and Fourier himself contributed important seeds to the doctrine of women's liberation, seeds that lay dormant for many centuries but
that came to fruition in the more nurturant conditions of
the late twentieth century. Their seminal role in the history of feminism deserves acknowledgment.

Jonathan Beecher (essay date 1986)

SOURCE: "Publishing a Journal," in *Charles Fourier:
The Visionary and His World,* University of California
Press, 1986, pp. 431-53.

[*In the following excerpt, Beecher traces the development
of the journal created by Fourier and his disciples and
comments on the publication's significance.*]

The first months of 1832 were a time of great hope and
enthusiasm for Fourier and his disciples. The "conspiracy
of silence" that had so long impeded the spread of his
ideas was at last broken. The lectures and articles of Jules
Lechevalier and Abel Transon had made Fourierism known
to the world at large, and had also played an important
role in bringing about the conversion of a number of Saint-
Simonians. Fourier's older disciples were delighted by
these developments. From Metz Victor Considerant wrote
triumphantly about the "wonderful" news from Paris and
the "beautiful" prospects for the future. At Besançon Just
Muiron reveled in now being sought after by people who
had formerly laughed in his face when he had tried to talk
to them about Fourier's theory. At Dijon Gabriel Gabet
exulted. "At last the day of your glory has come," he
wrote Fourier, "the moment when your humiliated rivals
recognize the superiority of your genius." Fourier himself
does not seem to have been quite so overcome. But there
was a note of high hope in a letter he sent to Muiron three
days after Lechevalier's first lecture: "I have now reached
the decisive moment," he wrote. "I am near the denoue-
ment."

As winter turned into spring the news for Fourier and his
disciples continued to be good. Sympathetic articles on

Fourier and his thought began to appear in the Parisian press. And encouraging letters and even a few Fourierist "professions of faith" were received from a number of former Saint-Simonians who had been introduced to Fourier's doctrines by reading Transon's *Simple Ecrit* or Lechevalier's *Cinq leçons*. For the first time the Fourierists began to speak of themselves collectively as a "movement" or (more often) as the École Sociétaire. And now at last it seemed possible, not only to Fourier but also to his disciples, that an experimental test of his ideas might soon be made. It also seemed possible to realize one of Fourier's longstanding dreams: the publication of a journal devoted to the exposition and spread of his ideas.

For several years Fourier had believed that his efforts to find a benefactor and simply to provoke interest in his ideas would be greatly facilitated if he could count on the help of a journal such as the Saint-Simonian *Globe*. In the *Nouveau monde industriel* he had called for a benefactor to subsidize the creation of such a journal, and in the midst of his polemics with the Saint-Simonians he had several times paused to lament to Just Muiron that until he had a journal of his own, he could never adequately respond to the calumnies of his rivals.

In 1830 and 1831 Just Muiron's *Impartial* had given some publicity to Fourier's doctrine. But clearly this provincial *juste-milieu* biweekly newspaper could never serve as a very effective instrument for the dissemination of Fourier's ideas. Nor could the *Mercure de France*. The editors of this Parisian monthly had published a few articles sympathetic to Fourier's theory. They had taken his side in the quarrel with the Saint-Simonians. But as their own private correspondence shows, their interest in Fourier stemmed largely from a desire to add "spice" to their journal and to strike a modern and up-to-date pose. What Fourier wanted was a journal of his own, a journal that would serve as a vehicle for the publication by installments of a simplified exposition of the theory. By January of 1832 he and Considerant were exchanging letters on the subject.

> Our journal should be purely scientific [wrote Considerant]. It should not have to bother about day-to-day events. It should come out once a week and be eight pages long. At least half of it should always be devoted to the publication of the elementary method on which you are working now. Whenever you wish, the whole journal should be devoted to your writing. We will utilize the space that remains to speak about the need to organize association and to provoke public discussion on the subject. Only later, and after due preparation, will we turn to [your theories on] the study of man.

In his letters to Clarisse Vigoureux, Just Muiron talked about the journal in similar terms, noting that the publication in installments of Jules Lechevalier's lectures might be an excellent way to begin.

By March of 1832 Fourier and his disciples had agreed to begin raising funds for the publication of a weekly journal. Clarisse Vigoureux pledged two thousand francs to the enterprise. Another large contribution was received from a wealthy banker whom Fourier had recently met. With this money in hand it was possible to rent an office and to begin negotiations with a printer. By the end of April an office had been rented on the rue Joquelet, just around the corner from Brongniart's newly completed Bourse. With it came a large reception room and a small adjoining apartment. It was agreed that the apartment would be Fourier's new residence. When he moved into it in May 1832, he began the only extended period in his life when he lived in daily contact with his disciples and collaborated closely with them on a common enterprise.

The new journal, which first appeared on June 1, 1832, was called *Le Phalanstère, Journal pour la fondation d'une Phalange agricole et manufacturière associée en travaux et en ménage*. It was a weekly of eight large two-column pages, which its editors described as "consecrated to making known the advantages of domestic and agricultural association and the means discovered by Monsieur Fourier to create such an association." The aim of the journal was thus twofold. It was intended both to provide a forum for the elaboration of Fourier's ideas and to rally support for the establishment of a trial Phalanx. In their introductory statement Lechevalier and Considerant stressed the interconnection of Fourierist theory and practice and insisted that Fourierism was not merely a set of abstract ideas. Instead they brought "a fact to men eager for facts and realities." They continued:

> We are writing with a particular goal in mind, a goal that is particular even within the sphere embraced by our own ideas, because we are limiting ourselves to what is most immediately and . . . most easily practicable. . . . Our journal will not even contain the theoretical development of all our principles. Except for some necessary explanations, it will be quite simply the periodical prospectus for the degree of industrial association that we wish to establish.

Consistent with this initial statement, the emphasis in the first issue of the *Phalanstère* was on the realization of Fourier's ideas. Fourier himself contributed a long programmatic statement on the trial Phalanx, and a large part of the issue was given over to the publication of the official statutes of two share-holding companies the disciples proposed to create. One of them, a Society for the Foundation of an Agricultural and Industrial Phalanx, was intended to raise a capital of no less than four million francs for the trial Phalanx. The other, a Society for the Publication and Propagation of the Theory of Charles Fourier, sought to raise thirty thousand francs for the publication of the journal and of future writings by Fourier and the disciples.

Despite the professed desire of Fourier's disciples to concentrate on practical matters, there was little said in the early numbers of the *Phalanstère* concerning the actual establishment of a trial Phalanx. In fact, most of the articles that appeared in the journal during its first six months were devoted to broad and rather abstract restatements of Fourier's main ideas. The chief contributor was Fourier himself. About a third to a half of each issue was given over to contributions by him, most of which were what he liked to call "leçons particulières," essays on particular aspects of the theory ranging from architecture to cosmogony. Fourier of course had little to say about contemporary politics. But he did use the journal as a platform from which to launch renewed attacks on such "sophists" and "philanthropic comedians" as Owen, Saint-Simon, and their disciples. In this respect he was indefatigable, and almost every issue of the journal contained a new article on the "secret designs" of the Saint-Simonians, the "mindlessness of the philosophers," or the "war of the four rebellious sciences against the four faithful sciences."

Among Fourier's disciples, the chief contributors were Jules Lechevalier, Abel Transon, and Victor Considerant. Both Lechevalier and Considerant published long articles in serial form summarizing Fourier's economic views and his general theory of association. Transon published a number of shorter articles on particular points of theory, and he also took charge of much of the editorial work necessary to see each issue through the press. During the first six months there were also numerous occasional pieces and appreciations of Fourier's ideas by young military engineers who had been introduced to Fourier's doctrine by Victor Considerant while students at the Ecole d'Application at Metz. These articles were diverse in character and quality. But what they all had in common was the desire to make Fourier's theory accessible to a wider audience. The focus was on what one of the disciples described as Fourier's "industrial ideas" with minimal use of his private terminology and as little reference as possible to his cosmological and sexual views, or even to his theory of passionate attraction.

The efforts of the disciples to reach a wider audience were not unsuccessful. Already after just a few weeks of publication they could boast of having received a "fairly large number" of expressions of support from "individuals who had formerly studied and in part accepted Saint-Simonism." They could also report that Fourier's ideas were getting attention in the provincial press. But the success of the *Phalanstère* should not be exaggerated. In fact, its press run never greatly exceeded one thousand, and its total number of paid subscribers was probably less than half that. Furthermore, many of the subscribers to the *Phalanstère* had already developed at least some interest in Fourier's ideas before the appearance of the journal. Despite the expressed wishes of the disciples, much of what appeared in the journal simply could not have made much sense to someone not already familiar with Fourier's ideas.

Fourier's disciples recognized the limitations of the journal. One of the most outspoken of them, the Polytechnicien Nicolas Lemoyne, bluntly wrote that "the journal is indigestible." It deserved to be supported by the disciples. But it would "never have any other subscribers, or even any other readers, than the most fervent disciples. . . . It satisfies neither the Butterfly, nor the Cabalist, nor the Composite. Reading it is a task that only has a small amount of attraction even for someone who is already passionately committed to the Phalanstery." Not all the disciples found the *Phalanstère* to be indigestible. Indeed, one Bertin

could write in July 1832 that he was "devouring" each number of the journal with great interest; and others were equally enthusiastic. But those who attempted to use the journal as a means of arousing interest in Fourier's ideas among outsiders were generally disappointed. Thus a professor at the Collège de Nevers could write the editors in July that "up to now my efforts . . . to obtain subscribers for you have been totally futile. Nevers is a backward city like all the cities in the center of France." The story at Bordeaux was similar. "Here at Bordeaux," wrote Edouard Lanet to Lechevalier, "a few people, but a *very small number,* pay attention to your journal."

Most of the disciples agreed that the trouble with the *Phalanstère* was that it was too dry and too exclusively theoretical. As Lemoyne put it in a letter to Transon:

> In all of [our] publications, not excepting your own, my friend, or Considerant's, grandiose theoretical principles predominate over practical ideas. Even in the journal you are always inflexible theorists; you don't wish to make the slightest concession to commonplace ideas.

But according to many of the disciples there was another, graver problem. It concerned the role to be played on the journal by Fourier himself. Even his oldest and most loyal disciple, Just Muiron, had little confidence in Fourier's ability to make his ideas attractive, or simply accessible, to a wide audience. To the young Polytechniciens who embraced Fourierism in 1832, Fourier's limitations as a popularizer of his own ideas seemed even clearer. Within a few weeks after the establishment of the *Phalanstère* many of them had come to the conclusion that Fourier's contributions were a real liability to the journal. As one of them put it, "No one is less suited than [Fourier] to the propagation of his own ideas." Another was equally blunt: "Let him be the inspiration of the journal, but let him write less in it."

Fourier's disciples had many complaints about his contributions to the *Phalanstère*. They all deplored his periodic outbursts against the Saint-Simonians. They were also disturbed by his tendency to overwhelm his readers with unexplained theoretical allusions and bizarre terminology. "In the last number of the *Phalanstère,*" wrote one of them to Fourier anonymously, "you address yourself to the capitalists. You want them to bring you their money . . . and you talk to them about 'tribes' and 'choirs' and 'internal' and 'external' rivalry, about the 'three sexes,' about 'simple' and 'compound' impulsions, etc., etc. To understand all these things one has to have read your works. But you know very well that the capitalists have not read them." No less offensive to some of the disciples was Fourier's "extravagance" as a polemicist and the "vulgarity" of the tone that he assumed when he was making his best effort *not* to be obscure. As Nicolas Lemoyne put it in a letter to Pellarin: "I haven't dared show the last number of the journal to anyone on account of the articles by Fourier, and still this number is one of the most remarkable. Jules surpassed himself in it. Victor and [Baudet-]Dulary write perfectly well. But the note by Fourier on the grocers will be revolting to many people's feelings, even though the only thing one can criticize it for is bad literary taste. The article on the tragedy in forty acts is a buffoonery and isn't suited to our serious journal. Finally, some passages in the article by Fourier are incomprehensible for anyone besides a disciple."

Fourier was not interested in Lemoyne's notions of gravity, good writing, and good taste. He had his own ideas about journalism. In brief, he believed that a newspaper article should be piquant and entertaining and bold, and it should make a direct appeal to the interests of specific readers. Thus the articles that he published in the *Phalanstère* often bore catchy and arresting titles like **"The Torpedoes of Progress," "Eighty-five Model Farms and Eighty-five Follies," "The Grocers Dethroned,"** and **"The Emancipated Woman at last Found."** They included the same sort of bribes and extravagant claims that he had earlier dangled before individual "candidates." They were aggressive and rich in invective. And they went straight to the point. Here, for instance, is how Fourier began his article **"The Torpedoes of Progress."**

> What is your goal, braggarts who sing only of progress and association? You are insidiously seeking to suppress all attempts at real association and real progress.

When the disciples complained that this was crude and in poor taste, Fourier had an answer ready for them. It was the same answer that he had given in 1830 when Just Muiron had objected to the bad taste of Fourier's contributions to the *Impartial*: "Where have you learned that there has to be so much refinement and academic dressing among journalists? . . . Refinement is not required in journalistic or literary polemics. Voltaire was certainly a refined writer, but how many insults did he not spew forth against his enemies! Without going that far, one should try to hold to a middle course and speak with firmness to vandals and calumniators."

Not all of Fourier's disciples were blind to his gifts as a writer. Charles Pellarin, for example, could compare him to La Fontaine and Molière for his skill at "painting without embellishment the vices and inequities of civilization." Even a critic like Lemoyne was capable of appreciating the vein of "fantastical poetry" that ran through much of Fourier's work. But almost without exception, his disciples believed that he had no aptitude for journalism. Even those who appreciated the "poetry" in his major works feared that the bluntness and extravagance of his articles in the *Phalanstère* would compromise their efforts to get a hearing for his ideas. Eventually almost all of them came to agree with the views expressed by Victor Considerant in October of 1833 as he looked back on the *Phalanstère's* first year: "We needed a great deal of courage to keep on moving ahead with an awareness of the permanent harm [Fourier] was doing to his doctrine by his articles in the journal."

Given these feelings, it is not surprising that Fourier and the disciples were frequently at odds. In fact, the tension between them seems to have existed from the beginning of their collaboration on the *Phalanstère*. In the very first

issue the editors felt obliged to print a note apologizing for Fourier's insistence on accompanying his initial programmatic statement concerning the trial Phalanx with an elaborate "tableau" of the fifteen different "degrees or stages" of association. Since the nomenclature alone was enough to discourage any but the most valiant reader, the editors commented with embarrassment: "We do not claim that the totality of the tableau could be understood without extensive explanations that are a part of the general theory of Monsieur Fourier and not the special object of this publication." This was just the beginning. In July 1832, after Fourier had written an exceptionally vituperative article on the Saint-Simonians, Lechevalier and Transon had to publish a categorical rejection of his position.

> After having vainly tried to persuade Monsieur Fourier to adopt better ideas concerning the Saint-Simonian doctrine and its leaders, we believe it our obligation to declare on our own behalf as well as that of all the Saint-Simonians who have joined us that we do not by any means accept the terms of the preceding article. As an appreciation of the doctrine, the criticism of Monsieur Fourier seems to us to be far inferior to that which could be made with the help of all the great ideas set forth in the *Traité d'association* and the *Nouveau monde industriel*. In his judgments on men and on their intentions, we affirm that Monsieur Fourier is utterly mistaken.

Fourier himself does not seem to have been greatly troubled by his disciples' disavowal. The important thing for him was to be able to speak his mind about the Saint-Simonians; and if the disciples didn't like it, they could say so.

Fourier was more disturbed about the tendency of some contributors to the *Phalanstère* to write about his theory of association as if it were no more than a plan for an experimental farm. As he wrote in the journal in August 1832:

> Misled by the force of habit, our disciples frequently make mistakes, which it is important to prevent. Most of them want to attribute to the trial Phalanx the functions of a model farm that conducts experiments with livestock, tools, crop rotation, breeding, etc. They advise us to try a certain type of crop, a certain mode of planting. This is not the sort of innovation that we should be considering; we don't want too many irons in the fire. Our concern is the art of applying to productive work the passions and the instincts that small-scale subdivided industry is not able to utilize and that morality wishes to repress.

In private Fourier was blunter; and his letters to Muiron in the summer of 1832 were full of complaints concerning the "avortons maladroits" who were "using our journal as a steppingstone by which to gain some education at our expense."

Throughout the summer and fall of 1832 there continued to be friction between Fourier and his disciples. He was not happy with their watering-down of his theories. They in turn feared that his more outlandish ideas, his "bad taste," and his aggressiveness in polemic would alienate

The grave of Fourier in the Montmartre Cemetery.

social harmony." Again in September Lechevalier could speak of a "charming dinner" at which Fourier shined before an audience of disciples and journalists. "The director of *Le Breton* was there, as was Dubois of the Loire Inféries. We talked a great deal about Fourier's theory; and Fourier himself, who was present at the festivities, was just deliciously witty and full of verve. The incarnate Harmonian had a score to settle with Seigneur Fénelon."

The main responsibility for seeing the *Phalanstère* through the press each week rested in the hands of the disciples. But in addition to the articles he wrote, Fourier himself provided help with correspondence and bookkeeping. This was much needed. For few of the disciples had had any previous experience in business or journalism, and the first months in the life of the *Phalanstère* were difficult. Subscribers wrote from the provinces to complain that the journal was arriving irregularly; money kept mysteriously disappearing from the cash box; and an odd assortment of strangers and curiosity seekers kept flitting in and out of the new offices on the rule Joquelet. Through all of this Fourier seems to have been more successful than his disciples in maintaining his presence of mind. It was often he, rather than one of the disciples, who dealt with queries and complaints from subscribers. It was also Fourier, whose eye was more watchful than theirs in financial matters, who discovered where the money was going and confronted a thieving office boy with an itemized account of his misdeeds.

Within a few months after the establishment of the journal, its offices on the rue Joquelet had become a mecca not only for Fourier's disciples but also for their friends and for strangers who had taken an interest in his doctrine. Some of these eventually became true believers. There were also foreigners like the young American Albert Brisbane, the Romanian Teodor Diamant, the German Ludwig Gall, and the Italian Giuseppe Buccellati, all of whom were subsequently to popularize and apply Fourier's ideas in their own countries. Others came simply out of curiosity. The Fourierist gatherings never became as notorious as those of the Saint-Simonians, which Balzac had advertised in 1830 as more entertaining than the vaudevilles at the Théâtre des Variétés. But for a time at least in 1832 and 1833 the Fourierists were afflicted with what Victor Considerant described as a "legion of pests and parasites" whose coming and going gave the offices on the rue Joquelet a frivolous atmosphere, which was not appreciated by Fourier himself or by the older, provincial disciples. Thus Just Muiron could grumble, after a visit to Paris, about "la vaine Joqueleterie," and other provincial Fourierists could complain about the "dandies" of the rue Joquelet. Finally, it became necessary to set aside one evening a week for the reception of visitors who were interested in meeting Fourier or in finding out more about the doctrine.

Several of the visitors to the rue Joquelet in 1832 and 1833 left accounts of the impression that Fourier made on them. One that is well worth quoting is Albert Brisbane's portrait of the man.

potential supporters. Thus Fourier continued to chastize his disciples when he discovered that "errors" or "Saint-Simonian prejudices" had crept into their work. Again, in September, after Fourier had published an article on his cosmological theories, the editors found it necessary to point out solemnly that "the art of associating in industry, agriculture, and domestic life is independent of the phenomena of the creation and of everything that may be happening on the surface of the other planets."

Despite their recurrent disagreements, the personal relations between Fourier and his disciples remained relatively screne during the first five months of the *Phalanstère's* publication. The mere appearance of the journal did great things for Fourier's morale, and a few days after the publication of the first issue Clarisse Vigoureux could describe Fourier as a man who seemed "rejuvenated by fifteen or twenty years." Eventually the spell wore off, but for moments at least throughout the summer and fall of 1832 Fourier impressed his disciples with his hopefulness and enthusiasm and good humor. There was even a time in August when he seemed "charming" and when Jules Lechevalier could describe the reigning atmosphere in the offices on the rue Joquelet as one of "the best

When we became acquainted with [Fourier] in 1832, he was about sixty years old. He was of middle stature, being about five feet seven or eight inches in height; his frame was rather light, but possessing that elasticity and energy which denote strength of constitution and great intellectual activity. His complexion was fair, and his hair, when young, light brown. His forehead was very high, and rather narrow—appearing perhaps more so from its great height; the region about the eyebrows, where phrenologists locate the perceptive organs, was large and full, and the upper frontal part of the forehead . . . projected strongly and was extremely developed. . . . His eyebrows were thin; his eyes were large, and of a mingled blue and grey, the pupil extremely small, giving a look of great intensity to the face. His nose was large and high, and rather thin, projecting strongly at the upper part, and running straight to the point, which was quite sharp. His lips were extremely thin, closely compressed, and drawn down at the corners, which gave a cast of reserved and silent melancholy to his face. His features, except the mouth, were large and strongly marked, but delicately formed and moulded.

As we remember it, the expression of the countenance of Fourier was one of self-dependence, of great intensity, of determined energy, and of inflexible firmness and tenacity, but softened by thoughtfulness and profound contemplation. He was entirely unassuming in his manners; his dress was plain like that of a country gentleman, and he stooped slightly; his mien was that of a cold, unapproachable simplicity; he was thoughtful, reserved and silent, which, together with his natural firmness of character, counter-balanced his unpretending simplicity, and prevented all approach to familiarity, even on the part of his most devoted disciples. Not a shadow of vanity, pride, or haughtiness was perceptible to him; his own personality seemed sunk and lost in the vastness and universality of the great truths which he had discovered, and which he was the instrument of making known to man.

Alongside this sketch of Fourier as he appeared to Albert Brisbane in 1832, another must be set. Its author, Pierre Joigneaux, was a student at the Ecole Centrale when he met Fourier. He was also a republican and something of a neo-Babouvist at the time. Much later he wrote an autobiography in which he described what could happen when a visitor happened to penetrate beyond Fourier's mien of "cold, unapproachable simplicity."

One day a week, or rather an evening, but I don't remember which one, you were sure to meet Charles Fourier in the main room at the rue Joquelet. He was the god of that place, and the faithful, who held him in profound veneration, never failed to come each week to pay him their respects. The master was seated in a large armchair; the earliest disciples—Jules Lechevalier, Victor Considerant, Doctor Pellarin, and several others— didn't leave the antechamber. The supreme honor for neophytes like me consisted in parading before the master, bowing respectfully, and saying a few pretty words in order to get better ones back. Charles Fourier didn't seem to care a bit about entering into conversation with the visitors whom curiosity brought him in greater or lesser number. He remained motionless and apparently calm. His physiognomy was not encouraging; the curve of his nose was a little bit like the beak of a bird of prey.

You can imagine that I took the trouble to work up a little speech before going to the rue Joquelet, and I expected to be heartily congratulated for it. When I entered the room where Charles Fourier was enthroned and saw that I was alone, I told myself that it was the right moment for me to bestow my compliment and make my little comments and that I had better take advantage of it. So, screwing up my courage, I drew myself up before the master and complimented him on his works. After the compliments, which didn't seem to make much difference to him, I ventured my observations about the best ways and means to bring about the realization of the Phalanstery. My view was that at that time the government was doing nothing to promote social reform . . . and that what was needed therefore was to sweep away the political obstacle and to seek in the Republic support that we were unlikely to get from the monarchy. . . .

I was going to go on, but the old man bounded up from his armchair and cut me short: "So you're another one of those frightful Jacobins whom no violence can stop. . . . All you dream of doing is turning society upside down and making blood flow. . . .

Since I wasn't thinking of anything like that, I was stunned by the brick that had just dropped on my head. I was hoping for a compliment for my good intentions; I received something less encouraging. The statue had woken up, the master had lost his temper. Madame Gatti de Gamond, who was in the adjoining room, ran up, took me by the hand, led me gently out of the throne room, and explained to me that Monsieur Charles Fourier, after twenty-four years of study and research, had such firmly decided convictions that he could tolerate neither contradiction nor advice.

"Please believe, Monsieur," added Madame Gatti de Gamond, "that Monsieur Fourier will soon regret this outburst. Great geniuses have the right to a great deal of indulgence. . . . Whenever you have comments to make, doubts to be dissipated, or clarifications to obtain, I beg you to address yourself to the master's disciples, who will always give you a good reception and will be pleased to give you the explanations you need."

At the same time Madame Gatti de Gamond introduced me to Monsieur Victor Considerant and Monsieur Pellarin, who had no trouble in making me forget the violent attack of which I had been the object. They couldn't help laughing about it, and I laughed too.

Fourier wasn't always so harsh with those who came to meet him; and according to Charles Pellarin he was capable of being positively "charming to see and to listen to" when surrounded by his disciples or others whom he trusted. But even at his best Fourier was not an easy person. He always had what one of his followers described as "a great deal of absolutism in his character." And there were times when he turned on his disciples with just as much ferocity as he showed toward Joigneaux.

In November of 1832 a particularly bitter series of confrontations took place between Fourier and his disciples concerning the running of the *Phalanstère*. The documentation is sparse, and it is not wholly clear what happened or what caused it to happen. But it would seem that the root of the trouble was Fourier's growing fear of being entrapped or "enslaved" by his own disciples. For over twelve years he had been accumulating debts to Just Muiron and Clarisse Vigoureux. By 1832 they were virtually supporting him, and there were times when he could not stand the thought of it. "You are astonished that I speak of my debts," he wrote Muiron in February 1832, "I have not forgotten them. . . . Whatever you may say, I consider as a debt everything that should be envisaged as such." Two months later in a fit of anger Fourier turned on Clarisse Vigoureux and accused her and Muiron of "wishing to hold him in slavery." Muiron and Madame Vigoureux tried to minimize the importance of such outbursts, and the surviving documents do not tell us everything that we would want to know. But it seems clear that Fourier's feelings of dependency and enslavement were intensified by the creation of the *Phalanstère*. For it was his disciples who had provided the funds and it was they who controlled the journal. But that was not all. Fourier found it particularly galling to be told by the disciples what and how to write for the journal. Furthermore, he had begun to realize that what some of them wanted was for him to write nothing at all.

This was the background to Fourier's explosion of November 1832. His particular target was Victor Considerant, who wrote Clarisse Vigoureux a long and bitter letter about Fourier at the end of the month.

> You speak about divisions among us. Well, my God, there haven't been any [for some time]. . . . As for Monsieur Fourier, we simply let him alone. Do you know that he has twice become furious at me? On the first occasion, however, I behaved so gently that the gentle Transon, who was there, could not understand why I didn't send that bitter and unjust man packing. The cause of the second scene was simply that I told him in front of other people that it would not be worthy of him to write the kind of "amusing" articles that he said he wished to write for the journal. I have taken the utmost care to avoid having disputes with him. I speak to him very rarely and always with the greatest gentleness. If he says the opposite, he is lying and that's all there is to it.

Considerant went on to observe bitterly that he was "very glad" to report that Fourier had taken a dislike to him, for Fourier was "the very essence of injustice, jealousy, and . . . ingratitude." To be disliked by such a man was "an indication by which one knows that he has done something for the Phalansterian movement."

The letters containing Fourier's side of this story have been lost. But we can gain a sense of it from a letter written to him by Clarisse Vigoureux at the beginning of December.

> Just why do you seem so sad and discontent at a time when we have such high hopes? For a year things have been going better than any of us could have hoped. [Yet] you seem dissatisfied with all your disciples, you find fault with Victor. . . . Poor Victor, I once saw you acting so unfairly toward him that I want to tell myself that the same thing is happening again today. . . . But what distresses me most is the pain and the sadness that you feel. This weighs on my heart and almost on my conscience as if we were imperiously charged with the responsibility of making you happy until the moment when the human race has accepted you as its master. . . .

> Monsieur, do not keep making yourself embittered, but try to believe us when we tell you that such and such a means is appropriate with the civilized. Let me say again that you are too lofty for them to be able to understand you in all respects, and that you cannot descend to their level without losing the dignity that is necessary for success. That is why your intermediaries have been serving you. . . . But in the name of heaven, do not become so misled as to believe that we have any thought of trying to keep you away from the journal or from anything else. Isn't your science everything? In any case I could reply to you that you have been saying that since the founding of the journal, and the result is that nobody has written in it as much as you have.

Clarisse Vigoureux was speaking in good faith. But in fact Fourier's suspicions were well founded. Many of his disciples wanted very much to "keep him away from the journal." And as Madame Vigoureux was writing him from Besançon, the editors of the *Phalanstère* were considering changes in the journal the result of which would be to reduce Fourier's role in it.

The end of the year 1832 was marked by two new developments in the life of the Fourierist movement. One was the choice of a site for the first trial Phalanx. The other was an attempt on the part of the editors of the *Phalanstère* to make their journal less sectarian and to reach out to a wider public. . . . As for the changes the disciples wished to make in the journal, they seem to have been the subject of lengthy discussions in December 1832. Although the record is fragmentary, a long memorandum by Abel Transon gives a sense of the points at issue. To Transon's mind the most important problems with the journal were its pedestrian character and the lack of coordination among its collaborators. Too many articles consisted simply of general restatements of Fourier's theory. "Our goal," wrote Transon, "should be to give the journal . . . the same rank in public opinion that the old *Globe* held." What this would require, he believed, was more articles on scientific and literary topics and also a more concerted effort to show the relevance of Fourier's theory to specific social problems. "At the point we have now reached," he wrote, "we should give as little space as possible to big generalities. . . . It is of great importance for us to prove to the public that our theories are applicable to *particular* questions of [social] organization." Significantly, throughout this whole memorandum there was just one point at which Transon referred specifically to Fourier's role on the journal. "I suppose that [in undertaking these reforms] we should previously have indicated to Monsieur Charles Fourier the maximum length of his articles, which should be considered as distinct from our editorial policies." What

Transon was proposing in effect was that Fourier continue to write whatever he pleased but that its length be limited and the editorial policies of the journal be determined independently of Fourier.

Transon's proposals were adopted. Thus the final issue of the *Phalanstère* for 1832 contained the following announcement.

> Beginning on January 1, 1833, the publication of the *Réforme industrielle (ou le Phalanstère)* will no longer have as its unique object the exposition of the *societary theory.* This theory can in any case be studied in the works of Monsieur Fourier and his disciples.
>
> Henceforth, the articles in the journal, while continuing to have absolutely nothing to do with debates over questions of day-to-day politics, will focus primarily on those questions of general interest that fall under the rubric of industrial politics.

Readers of the journal were further informed that its size was to be expanded from eight to twelve pages and that henceforth scientific, literary, and artistic topics would be treated in the journal "whenever they have a social significance." At the conclusion of the same issue there was also a brief editorial note concerning Fourier: "The article Monsieur Fourier normally contributes to each issue could not appear today, the space allotted to it in the layout having been insufficient."

During the first few months of 1833 Fourier's disciples tried hard to make their journal livelier and more relevant to the concerns of the general public. They began to print book reviews and to write more articles on contemporary social problems and on current debates in medicine, education, and agriculture. At the same time they became more aggressively polemical in tone, engaging in journalistic disputes with the *Revue des deux mondes,* the *Tribune,* and the *Revue encyclopédique.* They also published large advertisements in popular Paris dailies such as the *National,* the *Temps,* the *Journal des débats,* and the *Constitutionnel.*

In the midst of all this Fourier simply went his own way. He kept turning out articles for the journal. But these articles were often the source of renewed conflict between him and the disciples. Not only were they repelled by his "bad taste" and "buffoonery," they also found the articles to be too long, and they were irritated by his habit of making changes and often large additions on the proofs at the last moment. "Despite all my observations," wrote Transon to Fourier at one point, "you continue to give your articles a length that is utterly out of proportion to the size of our journal." For a time the editors attempted to impose on Fourier a limit of four columns an issue. But this made no difference. His articles continued to be too long and too late. When a few lines of a late article had to be cut to fit the available space, Fourier, exploded. But when he was warned ahead of time that cuts would be necessary, his immediate reaction was to withdraw the article. This was something that the disciples found hard to accept, especially when it came on the day that the paper

was to go to press. "No, Monsieur," Transon protested on receiving a half-column addition to a five-column article. "you cannot wait until Thursday morning to give me that alternative. On Thursday morning the journal is done. Thursday morning *you cannot* withdraw an article the length of those you write on the pretext that it is mutilated if it can't be lengthened by half a column. Let's suppose you told me on *Monday* morning: 'I would prefer my article not to appear at all.' Then I would have time to find another. On Thursday that is impossible."

If Fourier was unhappy about his disciples' editing and cutting of his own articles, he was equally unhappy about much that he read in theirs. Repeatedly during the spring and summer of 1833 he wrote articles denouncing positions taken by his own disciples in the journal. In March of 1833 Charles Pellarin had devoted two articles to a discussion of analogies between Fourier's theory of the passions and the views of the phrenologists Gall and Spurzheim. Fourier replied by filling one-third of an entire issue with an angry discussion of "the kind of service that is rendered to me by certain bumbling friends who are assassinating me while they think they are increasing my reputation." A few weeks later an article on the Saint-Simonians by Aynard de la Tour-du-Pin drew from Fourier a more succinct but equally harsh reply entitled **"On a Panegyric of Theocracy and Mortmain."** Then again in early July another article appeared denouncing two "adventurous disciples"—Amédée Paget and Giuseppe Bucellati—whose articles were "studded with errors" and "completely imbued with Saint-Simonian formulas." "The two writers should not be astonished," wrote Fourier, "that the chief of the doctrine makes use of his right to point out heresies. This will be an instructive gloss for less experienced disciples."

The disciples' public response to all this was mild. In publishing Fourier's attack on Pellarin, for example, they added a conciliatory editorial note.

> Monsieur Fourier has deemed it appropriate to protest against the articles published in this journal on Gall's phrenological doctrine. It is entirely correct that he should make whatever use he wants of the right to distinguish his views from all others and to emphasize the differences that exist between him, *the inventor of the societary method,* and those who strive to introduce this great discovery into the domain of humanity.

They went on to acknowledge their sense of a "religious duty" to publish "without change" everything written by Fourier. But they insisted on their own right to persist in fulfilling what they understood as their duties as "intermediaries between Monsieur Fourier and the men of their time, between the societary theory and the other ventures in social science."

In private the disciples were less delicate. For they had become fed up by Fourier's repeated criticism. After June of 1833 Abel Transon and Victor Considerant simply ceased to write for the *Phalanstère.* Jules Lechevalier continued for a time, but his relations with Fourier grew strained. In July, after the attack on Paget and Bucellati, the latter wrote Fourier to protest the "ridicule" to which he had been subjected. "I do not believe," he added, "that nature has given you alone the right to investigate its laws." At the same time another disciple, who chose to remain anonymous, addressed a long letter to Fourier, complaining of the obscurity of Fourier's articles ("You teach algebra before arithmetic") and bluntly criticizing his treatment of his own disciples.

> It may surprise you to know that one of the writers who has succeeded in making himself best understood by the public (I am here speaking of uninitiated readers and beginners) is the same Monsieur A. Paget whom, in the interest of the orthodoxy of the journal, you felt obliged to reprimand publicly. I must point out that these reprimands seemed excessively severe and made a bad impression.

A few weeks later Victor Considerant summed up the feelings of many of the disciples when he wrote that the publication of the journal should be suspended. "It is of the utmost importance that Fourier should cease to have the means to publish articles by which he is destroying both himself and his theory in the eyes of the public."

By July of 1833 there was little left to the enthusiasm that Fourier and his disciples had felt a year earlier, at the time of the establishment of the *Phalanstère*. Funds were short, and the journal had never come close to paying its own way. Furthermore the attempt to establish a trial Phalanx at Condé-sur-Vesgre, which was supposedly the *raison d'être* of the journal, was running into serious difficulty. Finally, there was the widespread feeling among the disciples that the *Phalanstère* would never reach a large public so long as Fourier was free to write in it whatever he wished. For all these reasons there was considerable support for Considerant's proposal that the publication of the journal be terminated. But after some discussion the disciples decided simply to reduce its size. The decision was announced by Jules Lechevalier in an article that appeared on July 19. In this article Lechevalier observed that henceforth he and several of the other disciples would be submitting most of their work to journals whose circulation was wider than that of the *Phalanstère*. He went on, however, to pay tribute to "this insignificant journal that we founded by ourselves, without much help and with the most modest means." He promised that the *Phalanstère* would continue to be published and that it would "always be for us a sort of venerated birthplace, the sanctuary in which everything that has to do with the *science* and the *theory* will be carefully elaborated and proposed." These fine words notwithstanding, this article was Lechevalier's next to last contribution to the *Phalanstère*. Since many of the other contributors had already drifted away, and since by July of 1833 the energies of Considerant and Transon were engaged elsewhere, the responsibility for bringing out the journal was left in the hands of just two individuals. One was Charles Pellarin and the other was Fourier himself.

Between July 19 and August 16 Fourier and Pellarin managed to get out four rather modest issues of the journal. Then its publication was shifted to a monthly basis.

For another six months it continued to appear. But its circulation plummeted, and its articles—which bore such rousing titles as **"The Scientific Poltroons," "Mystification of the Sirens of Progress,"** and **"Commercial Speculation Offering a Net Profit of 300 Percent in Six Months"**—were all by Fourier. Abandoned by the disciples, the *Phalanstère* had ceased to be the organ of a movement.

In the last article that he wrote for the *Phalanstère* Jules Lechevalier attempted to justify the decision to reduce the journal's size and its frequency of appearance. He explained that these measures were prompted not only by a lack of funds or by the work to be done at Condé. The main reason, he said, was that "the primary effect we wanted [the *Phalanstère*] to have has been accomplished." According to Lechevalier, the journal had made it possible for "society" to "get wind of" Fourier's doctrines. The task that now confronted the disciples was "to seek to give a wider publicity to the same doctrines" through writing for more influential journals with a greater circulation. "If the *Phalanstère* had no other result than to bring us to this point, it would have already made a great contribution to the cause of ASSOCIATION."

This article may well have left an unpleasant taste in the mouths of many of the collaborators on the *Phalanstère*. People who were close to Lechevalier knew that his own desire to publish his writing elsewhere was prompted largely by personal ambition and by the waning of his interest in Fourierism. Most of the disciples were acutely aware of the limitations of the journal, and few can really have believed that it had "made a great contribution to the cause of association." On the contrary, many of them seem to have come away from the experience of collaborating on the journal with the feeling that little had been accomplished except for the fulfillment of an obligation toward Fourier. As Victor Considerant wrote in October 1833, the publication of the *Phalanstère* had enabled the disciples to give Fourier "the satisfaction that thirty-four years of torment [have] made him so ardently desire, the satisfaction of being at last able to make his voice heard by the public." But in the process, Considerant maintained, the disciples had learned that Fourier was unable to make himself *understood* by the public; and they had also discovered that he was an impossible person to work with on a cooperative enterprise.

Despite such comments, it would seem in retrospect that there was at least some justification for Lechevalier's positive verdict on the journal. If its circulation remained modest and if it never came close to "conquering Paris" as Fourier would have wished, the *Phalanstère* did significantly continue and extend the work of popularizing Fourier's ideas that had begun in the winter of 1831-1832. The lectures and articles of Jules Lechevalier and Abel Transon had begun the process. But their influence was felt largely in Paris and among former Saint-Simonians. What the *Phalanstère* did was to take Fourier's ideas to the provinces. Prior to the appearance of the journal there had been hardly a mention of Fourier or Fourierism in the French provincial press outside of Just Muiron's Besançon. A few months later the situation had changed radically. "We have every reason to be satisfied with the provincial press," the editors wrote in August 1832. "Spontaneously it has sought to give publicity to our opinions and to expound our ideas itself." This was no exaggeration. During the first year of the *Phalanstère's* existence articles on Fourier's ideas appeared in scores of provincial journals ranging from the *Sanglier des Ardennes* to the *Mémorial des Pyrenées,* from the *Abeille Picard* to the *Nouveau Contribuable de la Haute Vienne.* Some of these articles were original, but many were reprints taken directly from the *Phalanstère.* Thus Charles Pellarin could speak of one of his articles (on Breton agriculture) as having been so widely reprinted that "it literally made its own *tour de France."*

The editors of the *Phalanstère* attributed the relatively strong response to Fourier's ideas in the provinces to the fact that unlike Parisians, who were easily distracted by day-to-day events and political intrigues, provincial readers were able to take a longer view and to recognize that contemporary political discussion was trivial compared to the importance of the vital social question: how to provide for "the physical amelioration of the condition of the masses." There may be something to this, but clearly it is only a part of the story. For in the early 1830s there were other groups, notably the Saint-Simonians and their offshoots, who were calling attention to the primacy of the social question. If Fourierism had a following among the provincial bourgeoisie, it may be due as much to the answers it gave as to the questions it posed. It is possible that many of the *Phalanstère's* provincial readers were individuals whose social consciousness had been awakened by the Saint-Simonian movement, but who were then alienated by its religious excesses or relieved to discover (as the *Vigilant de Seint-et-Oise* put it) that Fourierism had the "profound" advantage over Saint-Simonism of showing greater deference to the rights of property and inheritance.

If the *Phalanstère* carried Fourier's ideas into the French provinces, it also enabled them to reach outside the comfortable middle-class milieu to which they had hitherto been confined. It seems clear that the vast majority of the journal's readers belonged to the professional bourgeoisie; they were army officers and engineers, doctors and lawyers, small-town functionaries and *rentires.* But in at least one part of France the *Phalanstère* did manage to reach a significant number of educated working-class readers. This was the city of Lyon, where Fourier himself had spent so many years, and where the longstanding interest of the silk workers in radical and utopian ideas was stimulated by the worsening of their economic position vis-à-vis the master merchants. The master weavers or *chefs d'atelier* at Lyon had their own newspapers, one of which, the *Echo de la Fabrique,* became something like a Fourierist organ in 1832 and 1833 and published more than a score of articles inspired by material that had previously appeared in the *Phalanstère.*

The importance of these developments should not be overestimated. The *Phalanstère* never acquired anything like the influence or the readership of the Saint-Simonian *Globe,* or of subsequent Fourierist journals such as the *Phalange* and the *Démocratie Pacifique.* It did, however, lay the groundwork for the success of these journals and, more generally, for the development of the Fourierist movement that was to become an important part of the ideological landscape in France during the 1840s. And its most immediate, tangible result was to give "Fourierism" a life of its own, a life independent not only of Fourier himself but also of his disciples in Paris. This was most evident at Lyon where, during the mid-1830s, an important Fourierist movement developed, and where, between 1835 and 1838, the *chef d'atelier* Michel Derrion made the first significant attempt to create cooperative institutions based on Fourier's ideas. But the story of the Lyon Fourierists, like that of the other isolated groups of disciples who emerged in Europe and America during the fifteen-year period that began with the publication of the *Phalanstère,* takes us farther beyond Fourier's biography than we can now go.

Carl J. Guarneri   (essay date 1991)

SOURCE: "The Fourierist Legacy," in *The Utopian Alternative: Fourierism in Nineteenth-Century America,* Cornell, 1991, pp. 384-405.

[*In the following excerpt, Guarneri examines the revival of Fourierism that took place during the latter half of the nineteenth century, arguing that by the end of the century, Fourier's "legacy" of communitarian ideals had completely faded.*]

Stephen Pearl Andrews bravely announced in 1871 that Fourierism was "not dead, merely sleeping." As the era of the Civil War closed, however, Fourierist phalanxes had ceased to be a vital option for American society. It was not just that such communities had failed or that northerners had rallied with confidence around their free-labor capitalist society, though these were immediate causes of Fourierism's demise. In the longer run the communitarian idea lost its salience when the fact became clear that urban-industrialism in its competitive capitalist form was here to stay. By the 1860s the institutions of individualism had become (according to J. F. C. Harrison) "so firmly based as to make efforts at challenging them appear quite impracticable," and the scale of urban settlements and manufacturing establishments had passed beyond the Fourierists' claim that a community of 1,620 persons could accommodate modern forms of production, consumption, and leisure. Communitarian projects appeared increasingly anachronistic. Organized as isolated colonies of true believers rather than "experiments carried out by interested citizens in the neighborhood where they already lived," they were denounced as escapist, tolerated as oddities, or else ignored completely. Communitarians themselves changed the meaning of their experiments by promoting them as mechanisms for settling the frontier, as islands of social justice in a hostile society, or as demonstrations of cooperative principles to be introduced into the larger society. As the century progressed, communitarianism became a "minor eddy" in a socialist stream whose "main channel" had once been Fourierist. In retrospect, the Fourierist movement appeared the last credible attempt to redirect American society into a communitarian path; its failure proved to be a crucial turningpoint in the nation's social history.

Yet if the miniature phalanxes of the 1840s were not the germs of a new social world, they did serve in subtle and gradual ways as agents of change. The experience of communal life, however short-lived, was not easily forgotten by committed members. As Paul Goodman once observed about such fragile experiments:

> Perhaps the very transitoriness of such intensely motivated intentional communities is part of their perfection. Disintegrating, they irradiate society with people who have been profoundly touched by the excitement of community life, who do not forget the advantages but try to realize them in new ways. . . . Perhaps these communities are like those "little magazines" and "little theatres" that do not outlive their first few performances, yet from them comes all the vitality of the next generation of everybody's literature [Goodman, *Communitas: Means of Livelihood and Ways of Life,* 1960].

To carry the Fourierists' case this far would exaggerate their later influence. Yet beginning in 1868 there occurred what Edward Spann calls "a modest revival" of Fourierism, sparked by publicity from their old critic John Humphrey Noyes, dislocations of the postwar recession and the Panic of 1873, and a general reawakening of northern radicalism during Reconstruction. Fourierist ideals helped inspire the next generation of dissenters, and alumni of the Associative "school" kept its vision alive in new contexts. Communitarianism remained an option for a few, but most postbellum Fourierists pressed the kind of transitional forms the movement had turned to in the late 1840s. Worker cooperatives, new currency schemes, model factories, cooperative apartment houses, and municipal parks seemed more appropriate than the phalanx to the scale and complexity of urban life in the later nineteenth century. These projects were a tacit rebuke to Fourier's theory of instant social reorganization through phalanxes, but they also demonstrated the enduring appeal of communitarian values. Promoting such schemes and attempting to attach a radical dimension to them was the Fourierists' chief legacy to the Gilded Age.

Not surprisingly, Fourier's first American apostle was also his last. The doggedly persistent Albert Brisbane remained active as an advocate of Fourierism long after the Civil War. Much of his time was taken up with promoting the host of inventions he conceived in the 1860s, including a greenhouse heater and a system of transport through pneumatic tubes. His continued study of Fourier often verged upon obscurity as he tried to formulate a "science of laws" or a "method of study" to bequeath to the next generation of social theorists. Yet Brisbane remained a committed Fourierist reformer, pledging the profits from his patents toward Fourierist propaganda or a new communal experiment and reaffirming in 1875 that he "acknowledge[d] but one Mind on this earth—the great Fourier." In private letters, manuscripts circulated among friends, two socio-

logical treatises, and several publications he continued to preach the master's theory, searching for a new way to restate it which would compel readers as he had been compelled by Fourier's writings in 1832. For three decades Brisbane churned out new communitarian proposals for frontier farms or eastern enclaves. Meanwhile, he hung around any reform movement which seemed to be gaining public support—free love, greenbackism, social science, worker cooperatives, Bellamyite Nationalism—trying to inject Fourierist influence into it. However compromised by his previous failures and his controversial private life, Brisbane's advocacy of Fourierism in the new era was a spur to other Associationist veterans almost to the time of his retirement to France in 1887, where he and Victor Considerant a decade earlier had enjoyed a tearful reunion among aging Fourierist associates. . . .

Looking Forward: Olmsted, the ASSA, and Bellamy

Among the most influential aspects of Fourierism for succeeding generations of reformers was its emphasis upon planning and design. Fourier's unitary dwelling showed the way toward an architecture that would take full advantage of technological advances as well as economies of scale, yet still express social values. Especially important was the way the phalanstery was intended to preserve individual and family privacy while also promoting free socializing of a diverse population. Without embracing the phalanstery itself, later architects reflected Fourierist design principles in their work. From model farms in Europe to collective workers' housing in the Familistère at Guise, from the Oneida Community's Mansion House to Le Corbusier's Unité d'Habitation in this century, architectural visionaries and social reformers adopted Fourierist conceptions to shape group living and working environments. In a less specific way, the phalanx's orderly blending of urban and rural forms and its provision for generous public spaces left an imprint upon urban planning in Europe and America.

The work of America's premier landscape architect and park designer, Frederick Law Olmsted, shows Fourierism's subtle influence on later shapers of the urban environment. As a gentleman farmer outside New York City, Olmsted became acquainted with Fourierist ideas in the 1840s through his friends Greeley, Godwin, and Marcus Spring. On his tour of English farms and cities in 1850, he met the British Fourierist Hugh Doherty, and after his return he stepped up contacts with the Associationist movement. In 1852 he penned a series of appreciative articles on the North American Phalanx, based on visits there, praising its "advantages of cooperation of labor," "united household of families," and diffusion of "moral . . . and aesthetic culture." Olmsted was a frequent guest at Spring's Raritan Bay Union and advised Victor Considerant on the location of his Texas colony. Though he never joined a phalanx or Fourierist club, Olmsted provided warm public testimonials to the Associationist movement.

Long after Fourierism disappeared as a distinguishable movement, Olmsted translated some of its key ideals into the design of America's largest and most important public parks. In New York's Central Park and elsewhere, Olmsted's plans reflected the Fourierist ideal of a harmonious counterpoint of city and country environments; the Fourierists' belief in varied group recreation as a basic human need; and their conviction that society had a duty to provide public facilities for communal activities. As an outdoor analogue to the phalanstery, the municipal park was a public meeting ground where social classes mingled and a communal spirit replaced selfish individualism. In 1870, in his most concise statement of the social ideal of city planning, Olmsted described New York's Central Park and Brooklyn's Prospect Park as "the only places in those . . . cities where . . . you will find a body of Christians coming together, . . . all classes largely represented, with a common purpose, not at all intellectual, competitive with none, disposing to jealousy or spiritual or intellectual pride toward none, each individual adding by his mere presence to the pleasure of all others, all helping to the greater happiness of each." Like public transit, sewers, and gas and water works, municipal parks demonstrated that city life was evolving from wasteful individualism toward efficient collective control of resources and technology. Olmsted found in antebellum Fourierism an ideal of social interdependence and a theory of historical development to give landscape architecture its largest meaning. Yet because his parks were meant to mitigate the effects of urban fragmentation and competition rather than overturn the society that produced them, they exemplified the evolution of utopian ideals into institutional reform in the late nineteenth century.

In this respect Olmsted's projects paralleled the civil service crusade championed by ex-Brook Farmer George W. Curtis and especially the reformist social science promoted by the American Social Science Association. Founded in 1865 by the Massachusetts humanitarian reformer Frank Sanborn, the ASSA was frankly philanthropic, intended to guide social development scientifically to harmony and equilibrium. Its leadership was composed mainly of influential New England educators, writers, and businessmen who believed that social questions were solvable through scientific inquiry; they organized investigations in four areas—education, health, economy, and jurisprudence—and made recommendations to policymakers. Behind their promotion of social science lay the urge to establish an impartial guide to "uplifting" the working classes and managing a conflict-free capitalist society. For a brief time Albert Brisbane was active in the New York City branch of the ASSA, into which he and Osborne Macdaniel, E. P. Grant, and John Orvis attempted to inject Fourierist social science. But their efforts failed, and the New York branch quickly evaporated.

The ASSA's brand of social science owed more to Herbert Spencer and Auguste Comte than to Fourier, and its policy efforts were directed at the un-Fourierist causes of free trade, civil service reform, and hard money. Nevertheless, its program struck a responsive chord among gentlemen reformers who had been touched by antebellum utopianism. Curtis was president of the organization for a time; Olmsted presented his planning philosophy before it; and ex-Associationist Walter Channing was active in its Health Department. The ASSA played an important transitional role in the professionalization of social science and the evolution of the concept from utopian blueprints to a reformist human engineering that stressed social interdependence and cooperation. Through men like Olmsted, Curtis, and Channing, faint echoes of Fourierism passed into "Mugwump" reform and were eventually transmitted, albeit in forms antebellum Fourierists would hardly have recognized, into the Progressive movement of the next generation.

Before this evolution was complete, there was one final revival of Fourierist ideals. The apex of utopian planning—and the endpoint of direct Fourierist influence upon later visionaries—came with the publication in 1888 of Edward Bellamy's novel *Looking Backward*. With his fictional solution to the crisis of American industrial capitalism, Bellamy achieved a level of popularity surpassing the Fourierist craze of the 1840s. When the book's hero, Julian West, wakes up in Boston in the year 2000 after sleeping for more than a century, he encounters a city peacefully transformed into a brave new socialist world of efficiency, abundance, and equality but otherwise reassuringly familiar. In *Looking Backward*'s odd mixture of technological advance and cultural conservatism, Fourierist elements were absorbed into a new synthesis, one that decisively superseded communitarianism and framed American dissenters' discussions for the next generation.

As a young man, Bellamy had been quite familiar with Fourierism. For eight months in 1871 and 1872—the height of the postbellum Fourierist revival—he began a journalistic career in New York City. At the *Evening Post,* where he did a brief stint, he probably met Parke Godwin, still intermittently on the editorial staff. It *is* known that Bellamy was introduced by his brother Frederick to Albert Brisbane, whose theories, according to Frederick, "interested him deeply." Brisbane's son reported that the aging Fourierist "closeted himself for long sessions" with the budding socialist. Later, Bellamy studied the history of antebellum communitarianism, which he considered "one of the most significant as well as most picturesque chapters of American history." He called his Nationalist program the heir of "the Brook Farm Colony and a score of phalansteries" that were *Looking Backward*'s "precursors" in spirit if not in exact form.

Several material features of Bellamy's Boston of 2000 were clear adaptations of Fourierist ideas and experiences. Probably the most obvious was the "industrial army," which Fourier had conceived as a vast mobile assemblage of workers committed to projects of construction rather than destruction. Bellamy, inspired by the Civil War and Prussian militarism, expanded the army to include the entire workforce, into which all citizens were drafted. His use of Fourier's term; the conviction that military organization could be harnessed for constructive purposes; the fascination with ceremony and parades; the belief that a proper job could be found for all human aptitudes; the idea of establishing an equilibrium between jobs and job seekers by adjusting work conditions to equalize "attractions"; reliance upon rivalry or "emulation" as a work incentive—all these reflect the influence of Fourier's "army" on Bellamy's utopia. Other borrowings worked their way down to architectural and technological details, such as Fourier's glass-covered street galleries and Brisbane's system of transport through pneumatic tubes.

Even more important, the overall conception of Bellamy's socialism as expressed in *Looking Backward* bore the unmistakable mark of Fourierism. Like the Fourierists, Bellamy planned social reconstruction as the peaceful and voluntary culmination of historical change. In Fourier's communitarian scenario the phalanx provided an abrupt leap to Harmony; yet in developing a historical theory to validate the phalanx, Fourier depicted the gradual evolution of society through stages that prefigure Bellamy's. His competitive Civilization corresponds to Bellamy's era before "the concentration of capital into greater masses." Then, just as Fourier foresaw a new feudalism emerging in the expansion of corporations, banks, and other "subversive" associations, Bellamy described his America as a time of growing popular "servitude" to pools and trusts. The socialist utopia was only one evolutionary step away, for by taking over the machinery of such combinations, the people eliminated oppression while reaping the rewards of technology and association. Following logically and inevitably from preceding social developments, Nationalism corresponded to the evolutionary version of Fourierism. Other aspects of Bellamy's vision that echoed Fourierist conceptions were his fascination with the practical economies of communal organization and his attempt to blend privacy and collectivism in socialist living arrangements.

The influence of the Fourierists penetrated even to the soul of Bellamy's socialism, as evidenced in his seminal essay "The Religion of Solidarity" (1874), which John L. Thomas has called "the psychological substructure" upon which *Looking Backward* was built. Parallels between this essay and the philosophy of Pierre Leroux, who introduced the word "solidarity" to the socialist vocabulary and whose metaphysics was championed by the antebellum Fourierists, seem too close to be accidental. Both Bellamy and Leroux began with human nature's split between individualistic and universal impulses. Both condemned individualism as the root cause of human problems, insisting that the key to human happiness lay in a mystical bond of fraternal love linking the individual with the species. So long as the individual was hindered from attaining "communion" (Leroux) or "merging" with humanity (Bellamy), his or her life would be one of tragic solitude, a condition both writers described through the metaphor of a prison. Heightened consciousness of our link to the universal could be glimpsed in fleeting, near-mystical experiences such as spiritual affinities (Bellamy) or intimations of immortality through reincarnation (Leroux), but future society would embody solidarity in daily relations animated by selflessness and sympathy. Though Bellamy's perspective is less theological than Leroux's, parallel arguments and the mutual use of "solidarity" to describe that quasi-religious unity between individual and humanity which prefigures and inspires the socialistic ideal, mark a strong

connection between two generations of romantic socialist idealism. Here again Albert Brisbane may have been the main link between antebellum and postbellum utopians, for his own writings of the period 1870-72 centered on human longings for unity with "the Cosmic universe" and proclaimed that in the future "the whole life of Man will become religious." At the very time he met Bellamy, Brisbane was recommending Leroux's theories to his Fourierist associates.

There were, of course, major differences between Bellamy's utopia and the Fourierists'. Two are particularly important for the light they shed on the popularity of *Looking Backward* and the fading relevance of Fourierism in the Victorian era. Fourier's utopia, with its passional psychology and its attack on bourgeois mores, was as much a program of cultural radicalism as of economic reform. In their ever changing rounds of work, play, and love, Harmonians would develop erotic and sociable impulses to a degree unimaginable under the repressions of Civilization. Though the official Associationist movement repudiated Fourier's free-love theories, there remained an air of spontaneity, experiment, even disreputability about the phalanxes; especially to younger antebellum radicals, utopian socialism implied a new lifestyle as well as a revamped economy. *Looking Backward* divorces socialism from this kind of cultural radicalism. Compared with the rich social life of Harmony, the world of Boston in the year 2000 is conservative, even insipid. Despite his intention to demonstrate solidarity, Bellamy retained much of the older ethic of individualism. If his Dr. Leete is representative, Bellamy's typical utopian citizen is remote and self-contained. Neighborhood clubhouses are hinted at and dining halls glimpsed in the novel, yet no social relationships—or any other interchanges—are depicted outside the small family circle. Antebellum communitarians envisoned utopians gathered almost daily in festive operas, parades, theatrical and religious rituals; Bellamy's Bostonians have radio concerts and church services piped into individual homes. Just as culture becomes connoisseurship, so too *Looking Backward* divorces production (in the industrial army) from consumption (through catalogue stores) and separates years of conscripted work from the freedom of leisure after age forty five. This impersonal and compartmentalized existence embodies Victorian middle-class privatism and consumerism far more than it reflects the antebellum communitarians' dream of a vital and integrated way of life.

Bellamy's version of home life in the year 2000 is an extreme version of what sociologists later called cultural lag. Somehow, a century of drastic political, economic, and technological evolution has left conventional middle-class mores intact. Despite abolishing individual housework, the new society retains Victorian ideals of familism and domesticity. Family members have the alternative of domestic servants and the private table, spend nearly all their time in their quarters, and move about discreetly and converse politely without intense emotions, whether of sorrow or joy. The genteel Dr. Leete, his admirably domestic daughter Edith, and their curiously dispassionate world provide a diametric opposite to the "passional attraction" of the Fourierists' "combined household." Bellamy deliberately set out to make socialism respectable in America and to separate it from subversive cultural ideas, including foreign theories and "all manner of sexual novelties." The popular success of his utopian vision was a measure of his achievement, but his depiction also indicated the distance he had traveled from the counterculture of his Fourierist predecessors.

Bellamy's Bostonians are calm and detached in part because a huge and impersonal bureaucracy has taken over their lives. Bellamy's second key divergence from Fourierists was his conviction that socialism was a matter of government ownership and the centralized direction of economic life, a condition to be achieved through political action. Its national focus and reliance upon legislation set Bellamy's brand of utopianism dramatically apart from the communitarian point of view. To be sure, a few aging ex-Fourierists showed up at Nationalist meetings, and Nationalist clubs in California and elsewhere incubated short-lived cooperative colonies. But the utopia of *Looking Backward* arrived through a political takeover of national business and financial institutions. The collective ownership of industrial enterprises through government, not their replacement by novel voluntary associations, was the socialist strategy appropriate to the industrial age. Bellamy explicitly repudiated the communitarian approach as obsolete. In the context of an entrenched large-scale, urban-industrial society, utopian colonies seemed escape hatches for true believers rather than plausible models for a chain-reaction overhaul of social relations: "We nationalists are not trying to work out our individual salvation, but the weal of all. . . . A slight amendment in the condition of the mass of men is preferable to elysium attained by the few."

Bellamy's centralized, bureaucratic polity—the state as "the Great Trust"—would have horrified antebellum communitarians, but it appeared reasonable in the late nineteenth century. To those who survived the nationalizing experience of the Civil War and witnessed the concentration of capitalists and laborers into contending national organizations, it seemed logical that popular government would expand to a corresponding dimension to save the republic from the specter of "plutocracy" or anarchy. It was Bellamy's call for action on a national scale rather than the Fourierists' decentralized communitarianism which set the agenda for the next generations of American radicals. As the legislative program implied in *Looking Backward* inspired the varied proposals of Populists, Progressives, and Socialists, the Fourierists' communitarian legacy finally passed into oblivion.

FURTHER READING

Biography

Pellarin, C. *The Life of Charles Fourier*. Translated by Francis George Shaw. W. H. Graham, 1848, 236 p.

Comprehensive biography of Fourier from which numerous biographical sketches were drawn by Fourier's disciples in the mid-nineteenth century.

Criticism

Altman, Elizabeth C. "The Philosophical Bases of Feminism: The Feminist Doctrines of the Saint-Simonians and Charles Fourier." *The Philosophical Forum* VII, No. 3-4 (Spring-Summer, 1976): 277-93.

Provides a brief examination of Fourier's and Saint-Simon's feminist philosophy, arguing that both schools of thought were reactions to the failure of liberalism to correct the injustices of industrial capitalism.

Bates, Ernst Sutherland. "The Fourierist Folly." In *American Faith: Its Religious, Political, and Economic Foundations*, pp. 374-89. New York: W. W. Norton & Company, 1940.

Examines several American experiments in community living, including Brook Farm, Hopedale, and Fruitlands, and discusses the influence of Fourier's writings on the development of these communities.

Beecher, Jonathan, and Bienvenu, Richard. An introduction to *The Utopian Vision of Charles Fourier*, by Charles Fourier, edited and translated by Jonathan Beecher and Richard Bienvenu. Boston: Beacon Press, 1971, 427 p.

Offers an overview of Fourier's life and thought.

Bowle, John. "Anarchists and Utopians: Godwin, Gourier, Owen." In *Politics and Opinion in the Nineteenth Century: An Historical Introduction*, pp. 134-51. New York: Oxford University Press, 1964.

Compares the utopian philosophies of William Godwin, Fourier, and Robert Owen.

Bowles, Robert C. "The Reaction of Charles Fourier to the French Revolution." *French Historical Studies* I, No. 3 (Spring, 1960): 348-56.

Presents Fourier's evaluation of the French Revolution and its political aftermath as a bitter and disappointed assessment.

Breton, André. *Ode to Charles Fourier*. Translated by Kenneth White. London: Cape Goliard Press, 1969, n.p.

Offers a view of Fourierism as grounds for the development of new ideas regarding social structure.

Riasanovsky, Nicholas V. *The Teaching of Charles Fourier*. Berkeley and Los Angeles: University of California Press, 1969, 256 p.

Offers a biographical account of Fourier's life in addition to an analysis of his philosophy.

Spencer, M. C. *Charles Fourier*. Edited by Maxwell A. Smith. Boston: Twayne, 1981, 184 p.

Analysis of the social aspects of Fourier's ideology and an evaluation of his literary significance.

John William Polidori

1795-1821

English novelist, dramatist, poet, and diarist.

INTRODUCTION

Author of *The Vampyre* (1819), the first published vampire novel in English, Polidori is best remembered for his association with more famous literary figures, including Lord Byron and Mary Wollstonecraft Shelley. *The Vampyre* was initially misattributed to Byron; although Polidori borrowed some plot elements from an abandoned narrative fragment by Byron, his novel is an original composition, establishing many of the literary conventions of the vampire theme that were followed by subsequent nineteenth-century authors, including Joseph Sheridan Le Fanu and Bram Stoker.

Biographical Information

Polidori was the oldest son of an English mother and an Italian father who had served as secretary to the Italian poet Vittorio Alfieri before emigrating to England. When he was nineteen Polidori became the youngest student to graduate with a medical degree from the University of Edinburgh. Too young to practice medicine in England, he offered his services as a private physician and was engaged in 1816 by Byron. Scandal surrounded Byron's recent separation from his wife; the poet was socially ostracized but still the focus of considerable critical and popular attention, and Byron's publisher offered to pay Polidori for a written account of the poet's activities. The pair traveled through France, Belgium, Germany, and Switzerland, where they encountered the Romantic poet Percy Bysshe Shelley. Shelley had abandoned his wife and eloped with Mary Wollstonecraft Godwin (later Shelley), ccompanied by her half-sister Claire Claremont, a former lover of Byron. Byron and Polidori leased the Villa Diodati on Lake Geneva; Shelley, Godwin, and Claremont took lodgings nearby and were frequent visitors. Although scholars dispute the account of a rainy night and "ghost-story-writing competition" giving rise to Mary Shelley's *Frankenstein; or, The Modern Prometheus* and Polidori's *Vampyre,* most concur that both works were conceived and started at the Villa Diodati during the summer of 1816. Polidori also began a second novel, later published as *Ernestus Berchtold; or, the Modern Oedipus* (1819). Byron's and Polidori's letters and diaries, as well as those of acquaintances and intimates of both, record minor disagreements and serious quarrels between them. In September Byron dismissed Polidori, who subsequently traveled to Italy, returning to England in 1817. For the next four years, he occasionally worked

as a doctor and published his two novels as well as two volumes of poetry. Many commentators, including Polidori's nephew William Michael Rossetti, assume that Polidori's death at age twenty-five was a suicide, but this remains unproven.

Major Works

The Vampyre may owe its existence in part to Byron: Polidori based some characteristics of his cultured, urbane supernatural antagonist on his employer, and some commentators speculate that the novel was first accepted for publication because Byron was thought to be the author. Nevertheless, Polidori's novel contains wholly original elements that significantly influenced subsequent genre fiction. In particular, Polidori shifted focus from a passive, suffering protagonist to the compelling, dynamic figure of the vampire himself. Further, Polidori may have been the first author in any language to cast the bestial vampire of legend into the form most familiar to modern readers: a sophisticated nobleman who exerts a sexual fascination over both male and female victims.

Critical Reception

Polidori remains a marginal literary figure, overshadowed by his renowned associates. Nevertheless, recent scholarship discerns much of merit and originality in *The Vampyre*. Genre enthusiasts still study this novel and identify it as a pivotal work of supernatural fiction.

PRINCIPAL WORKS

An Essay upon the Source of Positive Pleasure (essay) 1818
The Vampyre (novel) 1819
Ernestus Berchtold; or, The Modern Oedipus (novel) 1819
Ximenes, the Wreath, and Other Poems (poetry) 1819
The Fall of the Angels: A Sacred Poem (poetry) 1821
The Diary of Dr. John William Polidori (diary) 1911

CRITICISM

George Gordon, Lord Byron (letter date 1817)

SOURCE: An extract from a letter to John Murray on August 21, 1817, in *"So Late Into the Night": Byron's Letters and Journals, Vol. 5—1816-1817*, edited by Leslie A. Marchand, John Murray, 1976, pp. 257-61.

[*Byron kept closely in touch with his publisher John Murray during his travels. In 1817—nearly a year after Byron and Polidori had parted company—Murray wrote to Byron that "Polidori has sent me his tragedy! Do me the kindness to send by return of post a* delicate *declension of it, which I engage faithfully to copy." Byron responded with the humorous verse excerpted below, which is written in character as Murray, declining the drama on the grounds that play publication was proving unsuccessful financially.*]

You want a "civil and delicate declension" for the medical tragedy? Take it—

Dear Doctor—I have read your play
Which is a good one in it's way
Purges the eyes & moves the bowels
And drenches handkerchiefs like towels
With tears that in a flux of Grief
Afford hysterical relief
To shatter'd nerves & quickened pulses
Which your catastrophe convulses.
I like your moral & machinery
Your plot too has such scope for Scenery!
Your dialogue is apt & smart
The play's concoction full of art—
Your hero raves—your heroine cries
All stab—& every body dies;
In short your tragedy would be
The very thing to hear & see—

And for a piece of publication
If I decline on this occasion
It is not that I am not sensible
To merits in themselves ostensible
But—and I grieve to speak it—plays
Are drugs—mere drugs, Sir, nowadays—
I had a heavy loss by "Manuel"—
Too lucky if it prove not annual—
And Sotheby with his damned "Orestes"
(Which by the way the old Bore's best is,)
Has lain so very long on hand
That I despair of all demand—
I've advertized—but see my books—
Or only watch my Shopman's looks—
Still Ivan—Ina & such lumber
My back shop glut—my shelves encumber.—
There's Byron—too—who once did better
Has sent me—folded in a letter—
A sort of—it's no more a drama
Than Darnley—Ivan—or Kehama—
So altered since last year his pen is—
I think he's lost his wits at Venice—
Or drained his brains away as Stallion
To some dark-eyed & warm Italian;
In short—Sir—what with one & t'other
I dare not venture on another—
I write in haste, excuse each blunder
The Coaches through the Street so thunder.

. . . . .

Thus run our time and tongues away—
But to return Sir—to your play—
Sorry—Sir—but I can not deal—
Unless 'twere acted by O'Neill—
My hands are full—my head so busy—
I'm almost dead—& always dizzy—
And so with endless truth & hurry—
Dear Doctor—I am yours

John Murray.

The New Monthly Magazine (essay date 1819)

SOURCE: "Original Communications: Extract of a Letter from Geneva, with Anecdotes of Lord Byron, &c.," in *The New Monthly Magazine*, Vol. XI, No. LXIII, April 1, 1819, pp. 193-206.

[*The following excerpt is from an anonymous article mistakenly attributing the authorship of* The Vampyre *to Byron.*]

It appears that one evening Lord B., Mr. P. B. Shelly, the two ladies and the gentleman before alluded to [Polidori], after after having perused a German work, which was entitled *Phantasmagoriana;* began relating ghost stories; when his lordship having recited the beginning of *Christabel*, then unpublished, the whole took so strong a hold of Mr. Shelly's mind, that he suddenly started up and ran out of the room. The physician and Lord Byron followed, and discovered him leaning against a mantlepiece, with cold drops of perspiration trickling down his face. After having given him something to refresh him, upon enquiring into the cause of his alarm, they found that his wild imagination having pictured to him the bosom of one of the ladies with eyes (which was reported of a lady in the neighbourhood where he lived) he was obliged to leave the room in order to destroy the impression. It was afterwards proposed, in the course of conversation, that each of the company present should write a tale depending upon some supernatural agency, which was undertaken by Lord B., the physician, and Miss M. W. Godwin.

John W. Polidori (essay date 1819)

SOURCE: "Letter from Dr. Polidori," in *The New Monthly Magazine,* Vol. XI, No. LXIII, May 1, 1819, p. 332.

[*In the following letter, Polidori acknowledges Byron's influence but asserts his own authorship of* The Vampyre.]

MR. EDITOR,

As the person referred to in the Letter from Geneva, prefixed to the **Tale of the Vampyre,** in your last Number, I beg leave to state, that your correspondent has been mistaken in attributing that tale, *in its present form,* to Lord Byron. The fact is, that though *the groundwork* is certainly Lord Byron's, its developement is mine, produced at the request of a lady, who denied the possibility of any thing being drawn from the materials which Lord Byron had said he intended to have employed in the formation of his Ghost story.

I am, &c. JOHN W. POLIDORI.

European Magazine (essay date 1819)

SOURCE: A review of *Ernestus Berchtold; or, The Modern Oedipus,* in *European Magazine,* Vol. 76, December, 1819, pp. 534-37.

[*In the following review, the anonymous critic briefly describes the plot and subject matter of* Ernestus Berchtold.]

If it be one of the highest faculties of invention to combine the natural with the marvellous, and to develope the human character with the consistency of truth, in a sphere of action beyond the range of possibility, this extraordinary tale [*Ernestus Berchtold; or, The Modern Oedipus*] may claim no obscure place in the department of literature to which it belongs. In regard to the nature of its subject, it may be said to hold the same rank among novels which is assigned in the drama to the Oedipus Tyrannus of Sophocles, or to Horace Walpole's play, called *The Mysterious Mother* But the case of Ernestus Berchtold differs essentially from that of the Theban prince, and is less revolting in its circumstances than that which forms the basis of Lord Orford's masterly, but dreadful tragedy. That subjects of this kind are more fitted for narrative

than for dramatic representation, is a truth of which every reader will, we think, be convinced, who compares the impression left on his mind by the two plays above mentioned, with that which the present story is calculated to produce. It developes the origin and progress of an innocent love, which is blasted in its consummation by a sudden and accidental discovery, that the parties are connected through ties of consanguinity, incompatible with a more intimate union. No moderate degree of skill was required to detail such a story in a manner consistent with the purest delicacy, and at the same time to render it capable of exciting strong sympathetic emotions, and of conveying an important moral lesson. In his aim at these important objects, Dr. Polidori appears to have eminently succeeded; and it is gratifying to observe with what ease he has vanquished those difficulties in his subject, which might have dismayed a less daring spirit.

The scene opens in Switzerland, at the period when that country was invaded by the armies of revolutionary France. A considerable part of the outset of the story relates to the patriotic exertions of the brave mountaineers; and these are detailed by the author with that circumstantial minuteness, which might induce a belief that he had been a witness of the events he describes, and, perhaps, an actor in them.

Edinburgh Monthly (essay date 1820)

SOURCE:A review of *Ernestus Berchtold; or, the Modern Oedipus,* in *Edinburgh Monthly,* Vol. 4, No. XXIV, December, 1820, pp. 727-35.

[*In the following excerpt from a review of* Ernestus Berchtold, *the critic blames Polidori for the attribution of* The Vampyre *to Byron, describing that novel as a "vile abortion." The reviewer also excoriates writers of supernatural horror fiction, charging that Polidori inadequately developed the supernatural element of* Ernestus Berchtold *and marveling that such an untalented writer continues to publish. In a concluding offhand accusation of unoriginality against Polidori, the anonymous critic misattributes* Frankenstein; or, the Modern Prometheus *to Mr.* Shelley.]

Dr. Polidori is aware that he cannot decently appear before the public, without making certain explanations, touching a transaction, in which it is hard to say, whether dulness or impudence was most conspicuous. The publication of that vile abortion, **The Vampyre,** under the name of the greatest of living geniuses, was a wrong which we were among the first to expose, and which it will not be easy for the perpetrator to expiate. The attempt at explanation, made by him in his preface to [*Ernestus Berchtold; or, The Modern Oedipus*], is quite unsuccessful. This doctor tells us, that he left his Vampyre with a lady, that "from thence,—to use his own immaculate phraseology—it appears to have fallen into the hands of some person who sent it to the editor, in such a way as to leave it so doubtful from his words, whether it was his Lordship's (Lord Byron's,) or not, that I found some difficulty in vindicating it to myself. These circumstances," this worthy person adds, "were stated in a letter sent to the *Morning Chronicle,* three days after the publication of the tale—but, in consequence of the publishers representing to me, that they were compromised as well as myself, and that immediately they were certain it was mine, that they themselves would wish to make the *amende honorable* to the public, I allowed them to recal the letter which had lain some days at that paper's office." We have no doubt, our readers are satisfied, by the perusal of these passages, that Dr. Polidori is both a very candid and a very elegant writer.

We cannot imagine what mental disease could induce Lord Byron to endure for a moment the uncongenial dulness of such an author as this, or how he should have been betrayed into the foolery of writing the fragment published, along with *Mazeppa,*—a composition which might have formed no unworthy companion to the **Vampyre** itself. Dr. Polidori, indeed, can get up a flat and feeble tale of preternatural horrors, which, in the simple particular of revolting combinations, shall outdo the inspired ferocity of the noble bard himself—but so could any assignable blockhead, who ruminates within the purlieus of Grub Street. Nothing easier than to catch the common-place and the grossness of these things—nothing more difficult than to extract their poetry. The fact is, that all our unimaginative dealers in monstrous things, are just dull grown-up persons, who fearlessly resume the dress of infancy to propitiate the weaker portion of their fellow adults—while the secret of the disciples of the new morality—for they are kindred schools of one great establishment of dulness—is that they boldly appear among well clothed persons, *in puris naturalibus*—and give free utterance to the sentiments which linger about every imagination, but which it is the prime object of all moral training to subdue. There is nothing original or inventive about either; the one merely remembers what abler men would rather forget; the other only dares to express what better men blush even to feel. It may, and sometimes does happen, that men of great power stoop to a course so unworthy of them, and lavish on it the splendours of their genius; but even in their hands it fails of its aim—and while the display may extort our passing wonder, it will infallibly provoke our deep and lasting aversion.

The author before us is an avowed experimentalist in supernatural story; for he tells us, in his introduction, that he "had agreed to write a supernatural tale; and that does not," he adds, "allow of a completely every-day narrative." Now, we do not recollect to have seen a more tame or "every-day" narrative than this of **Ernestus Berchtold.** "I am afraid," the Dr. observes, "that though I have thrown the superior agency into the back ground as much as was in my power, still, that many readers will think the same moral, and the same colouring, might have been given to characters acting under the ordinary agencies of life,"— which is quite true; and the author himself confesses that it is so; but he "had agreed to write a supernatural tale." The *nec deus intersit* is thus intrepidly violated—but it is well; for if there had been in his story a single knot which it was beyond the dexterity of the most inexperienced

boarding-school miss to unite, Dr. Polidori is not the man to have called down a divinity adequate to its solution. . . .

We have already alluded to the fantastic descriptions, and bad rhetoric of this author—and were it worth while, we could select paragraphs without number in proof of our assertion,—but the task would be an unprofitable one.

The perusal of this volume has, we confess, left a painful impression on our minds of the extent to which the vice of scribbling is carried in this our age—mingled too with a reasonable share of compassion for those who are seduced by the glare of literary reputation, from the honest beaten paths of life—and whom it were real mercy to chastise in their wanderings, if any chastisement could reclaim them. When we say this, we are not forgetful of Swift's ingenious story of the mountebank in Leicester Fields, and the corpulent individual who—while he occupied with his own person the space which rightfully belonged to his neighbour—was the most vehement to complain of encroachment. We remember that we ourselves render no illiberal contribution to the general mass of printed intelligence—but our walk is less ambitious, and we should hope rather more useful, than that of persons who essay to climb the heaven of invention, and, like the author before us, tumble down with such melancholy and hideous ruin. It is indeed surprising, that while so many majestic spirits occupy the summits of the temple of fame, there should be found persons like the present, so presumptuous as to knock their addle pates against its base. The alternate pangs of difficult delivery and swift-coming disappointment, which they are fated to endure, render this class of persons the objects of the most sincere commiseration. The fancy of the poet alone can realize a Dr. Polidori in the agony of his supernatural parturitions, or the alternate anguish of deploring his still-born progeny.

> He gnawed his pen, then dashed it on the
>   ground,
> Sinking from thought to thought—a vast
>   profound,
> Plunged for his sense, but found no bottom
>   there,
> Yet wrote and floundered on in mere despair.
> Round him much embryo, much abortion lay,
> Much future ode, and abdicated play;
> Nonsense precipitate, like running lead,
> That slipped thro' cracks, and zig-zags of the
>   head,
> All that on folly, frenzy could beget,
> Fruits of dull heat, and sooterkins of wit.

And for what reason is all this folly acted by a plain dull man, vainly endeavouring to escape from his own native sphere? Why, for the laudable purpose of raking together the sweepings of the Minerva Press, and circulating libraries—of delighting and improving the world, by the delicate exhibition of a *partie quarrée* of incest—and of nicknaming a stupid story, the modern Œdipus, only we suppose because Mr. Shelly has chosen to designate one of *his* reveries the modern Prometheus.

Mary Wollstonecraft Shelley (essay date 1831)

SOURCE: An introduction to *Frankenstein; or, the Modern Prometheus,* by Mary Wollstonecraft Shelley, in *The Essential Frankenstein,* edited by Leonard Wolf, Plume, 1993, pp. 296-300.

[*Shelley's* Frankenstein, *one of the best-known horror novels of all time, was conceived and begun during the summer of 1816 , during the same sojourn during which Byron wrote the fragment from which Polidori developed* The Vampyre. *In the following excerpt from her introduction to the 1831 edition of* Frankenstein, *Shelley outlines the genesis of the two works, dismissing Polidori's initial literary effort. Subsequent scholarship has shown Shelley's account to be largely erroneous.*]

In the summer of 1816 we visited Switzerland and became the neighbours of Lord Byron. At first we spent our pleasant hours on the lake or wandering on its shores; and Lord Byron, who was writing the third canto of *Childe Harold,* was the only one among us who put his thoughts upon paper. These, as he brought them successively to us, clothed in all the light and harmony of poetry, seemed to stamp as divine the glories of heaven and earth, whose influences we partook with him.

But it proved a wet, ungenial summer, and incessant rain often confined us for days to the house. Some volumes of ghost stories translated from the German into French fell into our hands. There was the *History of the Inconstant Lover,* who, when he thought to clasp the bride to whom he had pledged his vows, found himself in the arms of the pale ghost of her whom he had deserted. There was the tale of the sinful founder of his race whose miserable doom it was to bestow the kiss of death on all the younger sons of his fated house, just when they reached the age of promise. His gigantic, shadowy form, clothed like the ghost in *Hamlet,* in complete armour, but with the beaver up, was seen at midnight, by the moon's fitful beams, to advance slowly along the gloomy avenue. The shape was lost beneath the shadow of the castle walls; but soon a gate swung back, a step was heard, the door of the chamber opened, and he advanced to the couch of the blooming youths, cradled in healthy sleep. Eternal sorrow sat upon his face as he bent down and kissed the forehead of the boys, who from that hour withered like flowers snapped upon the stalk. I have not seen these stories since then, but their incidents are as fresh in my mind as if I had read them yesterday.

"We will each write a ghost story," said Lord Byron, and his proposition was acceded to. There were four of us. The noble author began a tale, a fragment of which he printed at the end of his poem of Mazeppa. Shelley, more apt to embody ideas and sentiments in the radiance of brilliant imagery and in the music of the most melodious verse that adorns our language than to invent the machinery of a story, commenced one founded on the experiences of his early life. Poor Polidori had some terrible idea about a skullheaded lady who was so punished for peeping through a keyhole—what to see I forget: something very shocking and

wrong of course; but when she was reduced to a worse condition than the renowned Tom of Coventry, he did not know what to do with her and was obliged to dispatch her to the tomb of the Capulets, the only place for which she was fitted. The illustrious poets also, annoyed by the platitude of prose, speedily relinquished their uncongenial task.

An excerpt from *The Vampyre*

It happened that in the midst of the dissipations attendant upon a London winter, there appeared at the various parties of the leaders of the *ton* a nobleman, more remarkable for his singularities, than his rank. He gazed upon the mirth around him, as if he could not participate therein. Apparently, the light laughter of the fair only attracted his attention, that he might by a look quell it, and throw fear into those breasts where thoughtlessness reigned. Those who felt this sensation of awe, could not explain whence it arose: some attributed it to the dead grey eye, which, fixing upon the object's face, did not seem to penetrate, and at one glance to pierce through to the inward workings of the heart; but fell upon the cheek with a leaden ray that weighed upon the skin it could not pass. His peculiarities caused him to be invited to every house; all wished to see him, and those who had been accustomed to violent excitement, and now felt the weight of *ennui,* were pleased at having something in their presence capable of engaging their attention.

John William Polidori, in The Vampyre, *1819.*

Montague Summers (essay date 1928)

SOURCE: "The Vampire in Literature," in *The Vampire-His Kith and Kin,* 1928. Reprint by University Books, 1960, pp. 271-340.

[*A leading authority on Restoration drama and the supernatural, Summers wrote numerous studies of witchcraft, lycanthropy, and vampirism, and the literature thereof. In the following excerpt, he outlines the plot of* The Vampyre.]

In *The New Monthly Magazine,* 1 April, 1819, was published **The Vampyre: a Tale by Lord Byron,** which although it may seem to us—steeped in Le Fanu and M. R. James—a little old-fashioned, at the time created an immense sensation and had the most extraordinary influence, being even more admired and imitated on the Continent than in England. It was almost immediately known that actually the story did not come from the pen of Lord Byron, but had been written by Dr. John William Polidori, physician-companion to the poet. Byron had, as a matter of fact, been writing a work of the same title in imitation of Mrs. Shelley's *Frankenstein,* but he denied the authorship of this piece in the famous letter facsimilied in Galignani's edition of his works. As first printed, **The Vampyre** forms a part of extracts from "A letter from Geneva, with Anecdotes of Lord Byron." Here is to be read that among other things which the lady, from whom I procured these anecdotes, related to me, she mentioned the outline of a ghost story by Lord Byron. It appears that one evening Lord Byron, Mr. P. B. Shelley, the two ladies and the gentleman (the daughters of Godwin and Dr. Polidori) before alluded to after having perused a German work, which was entitled *Phantasmagoriana* began relating ghost stories; when his lordship having recited the beginning of Christabel, then unpublished, the whole took so strong a hold of Mr. Shelley's mind, that he suddenly started up and ran out of the room. The physician and Lord Byron followed, and discovered him leaning against a mantlepiece with cold drops of perspiration trickling down his face. After having given him something to refresh him, upon enquiring into the cause of his alarm, they found that his wild imagination having pictured to him the bosom of one of the ladies with eyes (which was reported of a lady in the neighbourhood where he lived) he was obliged to leave the room in order to destroy the impression. It was afterwards proposed in the course of conversation, that each of the company present should write a tale depending upon some supernatural agency, which was undertaken by Lord Byron, the physician, and Miss M. Godwin. My friend, the lady above referred to, had in her possession the outline of each of these stories, I obtained them as a great favour, and herewith forward them to you, as I was assured you would feel as much curiosity as myself, to peruse the *ébauches* of so great a genius, and those immediately under his influence.

Upon this the Editor has the following note: "We have in our possession the Tale of Dr.—— as well as the outline of that of Miss Godwin. The latter has already appeared under the title of *Frankenstein, or the modern Prometheus*; the former, however, upon consulting this author, we may, probably, hereafter give to our readers."

The Vampyre is introduced by several paragraphs which deal with the tradition. This preamble commences:

The superstition upon which this tale is founded is very general in the East. Among the Arabians it appears to be common; it did not, however, extend itself to the Greeks until after the establishment of Christianity; and it has only assumed its present form since the division of the Latin and Greek churches; at which time, the idea becoming prevalent, that a Latin body could not corrupt if buried in their territory, it gradually increased, and formed the subject of many wonderful stories, still extant, of the dead rising from their graves, and feeding upon the blood of the young and beautiful. In the West it spread, with some slight variation, all over Hungary, Poland, Austria, and Lorraine, where the belief existed, that vampyres nightly imbibed a certain portion of the blood of their victims, who became emaciated, lost their strength, and speedily died of consumptions; whilst these human bloodsuckers fattened—and their veins became distended to such a state of repletion as to cause the blood to flow from all the passages of their bodies, and even from the very pores of their skins.

The Editor then recounts the famous instance of Arnold Paul, and continues:

We have related this monstrous rodomontade, because it seems better adapted to illustrate the subject of the present observations than any other instance we could adduce. In many parts of Greece it is considered as a sort of punishment after death, for some heinous crime committed whilst in existence, that the deceased is doomed to vampyrise, but be compelled to confine his visitations solely to those beings he loved most while on earth—those to whom he was bound by ties of kindred and affection. This supposition is, we imagine, alluded to in the following fearfully sublime and prophetic curse from the *Giaour*.

But first on earth, as Vampyre sent,
Thy corse shall from its tomb be rent;
Then ghastly haunt thy native place,
And suck the blood of all thy race;
There from thy *daughter, sister, wife,*
At midnight drain the stream of life;
Yet loathe the banquet, which perforce
Must feed thy livid living corse,
Thy victims, ere they yet expire,
Shall know the demon for their sire;
As cursing thee, thou cursing them,
Thy flowers are withered on the stem.
But one that for *thy crime* must fall,
The youngest, best beloved of all,
Shall bless thee with a *father's* name—
That word shall wrap thy heart in flame!
Yet thou must end thy task and mark
Her cheek's last tinge—her eye's last spark,
And the last glassy glance must view
Which freezes o'er its lifeless blue;
Then with unhallowed hand shall tear
The tresses of her yellow hair,
Of which, in life a lock when shorn
Affection's fondest pledge was worn—
But now is borne away by thee
Memorial o thine agony!
Yet with thine own best blood shall drip
Thy gnashing tooth, and haggard lip;
Then stalking to thy sullen grave
Go—and with Ghouls and Afrits rave,
Till these in horror shrink away
From spectre more accursed than they.

After an allusion to Southey's *Thalaba,* Tournefort's *Travels,* and Dom Calmet's classical work, the editor concludes: "We could add many curious and interesting notices on this singularly horrible superstition, and we may, perhaps, resume our observations upon it at some future opportunity; for the present, we feel that we have very far exceeded the limits of a note, necessarily devoted to the explanation of the strange production to which we now invite the attention of our readers; and we shall therefore conclude by merely remarking, that though the term Vampyre is the one in most general acceptation, there are several other synonimous with it, which are made use of in various parts of the world, namely, Vroucolocha, Vardoulacha, Goul, Broucoloka, &c."

The story tells how at the height of a London season

> there appeared at the various parties of the leaders of the *ton* a nobleman, more remarkable for his singularities, than his rank. He gazed upon the mirth around him, as if he could not participate therein. Apparently, the light laughter of the fair only attracted his attention that he might by a look quell it, and throw fear into those breasts where thoughtlessness reigned. Those who felt this sensation of awe, could not explain whence it arose; some attributed it to the dead grey eye, which fixing upon the object's face, did not seem to penetrate, and at one glance to pierce through to the inward working of the heart; but fell upon the cheek with a leaden ray that weighed upon the skin it could not pass.

This original is invited to every house, and in the course of the winter he meets "a young gentleman of the name of Aubrey" he was an orphan left with an only sister in the possession of great wealth, by parents who died while he was yet in childhood." Aubrey is greatly fascinated by Lord Ruthven, for this is the name of the mysterious nobleman, and intending to travel upon the Continent he mentions this intention to my Lord, and is "surprised to receive from him a proposal to join him. Flattered by such a mark of esteem from him who, apparently, had nothing in common with other men, he gladly accepted it, and in a few days they had passed the circling waters."

As they travelled from town to town, Aubrey notices the peculiar conduct of his companion who bestows largess upon the most worthless characters, broken gamblers and the like, but refuse a doit to the deserving and virtuous poor. However the recipients of this charity "inevitably found that there was a curse upon it, for they all were either led to the scaffold or sunk to the lowest and the most abject misery." Eventually the travellers arrive at Rome, and here Aubrey receives letters from his guardians who require him immediately to leave his companion as since their departure from London the most terrible scandals, adulteries and seductions, have come to light. At Rome Aubrey is able to foil Lord Ruthven's plans, frustrating an intrigue designed to ruin a heedless young girl, and then he "directed his steps towards Greece, and, crossing the Peninsula, soon found himself at Athens." Here he lodges in the house of a Greek, whose daughter Ianthe is a paragon of the most exquisite beauty. As he sketches the ruins of the city she is wont to entertain him with Greek legend and tradition, and

> often, as she told him the tale of the living vampyre, who had passed years amidst his friends, and dearest ties, forced every year, by feeding upon the life of a lovely female to prolong his existence for the ensuing months, his blood would run cold, whilst he attempted to laugh her out of such idle and horrible fantasies; but Ianthe cited to him the names of old men, who had at last detected one living among themselves, after several of their relatives and children had been found marked with the stamp of the friend's appetite; and when she found him so incredulous, she begged of him to believe her, for it had been remarked, that those who had dared to question their existence, always had

> some proof given, which obliged them, with grief and heart-breaking to confess it was true. She detailed to him the traditional appearance of these monsters, and his horror was increased, by hearing a pretty accurate description of Lord Ruthven; he, however, still persisted in persuading her, that there could be no truth in her fears, though at the same time he wondered at the many coincidences which had all tended to excite a belief in the supernatural power of Lord Ruthven.

Before long it becomes evident that Aubrey is in love with Ianthe, "and while he ridicules the idea of a young man of English habits, marrying an uneducated Greek girl, still he found himself more and more attached to the almost fairy form before him." He endeavours to occupy his time with antiquarian excursions which lead him farther and farther afield, and at length he determines to proceed to a point beyond any he has as yet visited. When Ianthe's parents hear the name of the place he proposes to visit they most earnestly implore him on no account to return when once dusk has fallen, "as he must necessarily pass through a wood, where no Greek would ever remain after the day had closed, upon any consideration. They described it as the resort of the vampyres in their nocturnal orgies, and denounced the most heavy evils as impending upon him who dared to cross their path. Aubrey made light of their representations, and tried to laugh them out of the idea; but when he saw them shudder at his daring thus to mock a superior, the very name of which apparently made their blood freeze, he was silent."

Having given his promise to Ianthe that he will be back well before evening he sets out very early. The exploration, however, takes longer than he has supposed, and when he turns his horse homeward the darkness is already hurrying on urged by a terrific storm. The steed, alarmed at the battle of the elements dashes off at breakneck pace and only halts trembling and tired before a distant hovel in the heart of a solitary wood. "As he approached, the thunder, for a moment silent, allowed him to hear the dreadful shrieks of a woman mingling with the stiffled exultant mockery of a laugh, continued in one almost unbroken sound." With a terrific effort Aubrey burst open the door and rushing into the darkness

> found himself in contact with someone, whom he immediately seized, when a voice cried "again baffled," to which a loud laugh succeeded, and he felt himself grappled by one whose strength seemed superhuman: determined to sell his life as dearly as he could, he struggled; but it was in vain; he was lifted from his feet and hurled with enormous force against the ground; his enemy threw himself upon him, and kneeling upon his breast, had placed his hand upon his throat, when the glare of many torches penetrating through the hole that gave light in the day, disturbed him—he instantly rose and, leaving his prey, rushed through the door, and in a moment the crashing of the branches, as he broke through the wood was not longer heard.

Several peasants now hastened into the hut bearing flambeaus which illuminate the scene, and to the horror of all there is discovered hard by, the lifeless body of Ianthe. A curious dagger lies near, but her death was not the result of a blow from this weapon. "There was no colour upon her cheek, not even upon her lip; yet there was a stillness about her face that seemed almost as attaching as the life that once dwelt there:—upon her neck and breast was blood, and upon her throat were the marks of teeth having opened the vein:—to this the men pointed, crying, simultaneously struck with horror, 'a Vampyre, a Vampyre!'" It appears that Ianthe had followed the traveller to watch over his safety. Aubrey is carried back to the city in a raging fever, and the parents of the unfortunate girl die brokenhearted owing to so terrible a loss.

Whilst Aubrey lies ill Lord Ruthven arrives in Athens and establishing himself in the same house nurses the invalid with such care that past differences are forgotten, since Aubrey not only becomes reconciled to his presence but even seeks his company. Together they travel into the wildest interior of Greece, and here in some mountain pass they are attacked by brigands, from whose guns Lord Ruthven receives a shot in the shoulder. His strength strangely decreasing, a couple of days later it is plain to all that he is at the point of death. He now exacts a terrific oath that his companion shall conceal all that is known of him and that the news of his death shall not be allowed to reach England. "Swear!" cried the dying man, "Swear by all your soul reveres, by all your nature fears, swear that for a year and a day you will not impart your knowledge of my crimes or death to any living being in any way, whatever may happen, or whatever you may see." Aubrey binds himself most solemnly by the prescribed oath, and in a paroxysm of hideous laughter Ruthven expires.

According to a promise which has been obtained from the robbers by a heavy bribe the body was conveyed to the pinnacle of a neighbouring mount, that it should be exposed to the first cold ray of the moon which rose after his death. Aubrey insists that it shall be interred in the ordinary way, but when he is conducted to the place it is found that the body has disappeared, and in spite of the protestations of the band he is convinced that they have buried the corpse for the sake of the clothes. One circumstance, however, gives Aubrey much food for thought. Among the effects of the deceased he discovered a sheath of most curious pattern and make which exactly fits the dagger that had been found in the deserted hut upon the occasion of Ianthe's death.

Returning to England, as he retraces his journey through Rome to his horror Aubrey discovers that in spite of the precautions he had so carefully taken, Lord Ruthven succeeded only too well in his bad designs and now there is bitter sorrow and distress where once reigned peace and happiness. The lady had not been heard of since the departure of his lordship, and Aubrey instinctively divines that she has "fallen a victim to the destroyer of Ianthe."

Upon his arrival in London the traveller is greeted by his sister, whose presentation into society had been delayed until her brother's return from the Continent, when he might be her protector. "It was now, therefore, resolved that the next drawing room, which was fast approaching, should be the epoch of her entry into the busy scene." Upon this gay occasion the crowd was excessive, and as Aubrey heedless and distracted is watching the gay throng a voice which he recognizes only too well, whispers in this ear: "Remember your oath." Turning he sees Lord Ruthven standing near him. A few nights later at the assembly of a near relation among the crowd of admirers by whom his sister is surrounded—the most prominent of the throng—he again perceives the mysterious and horrible figure. Hurrying forward he seizes his sister's arm and requests her immediately to accompany him home. However, before they have had time to retire again does the voice whisper close to him: "Remember your oath!"

Aubrey now becomes almost distracted. He sees no remedy against a monster who has already once mocked at death. Even if he were to declare all that he knew it is probable that he would hardly be believed. Whenever he attends a social gathering his looks as he scans the company become so suspicious and strange that he soon acquires a reputation for great eccentricity. As the months go on his loathing and his fears drive him well-nigh to madness, so that eventually a physician is engaged to reside in the house and take charge of him. He is a little consoled by the thought that when the year and the day have passed he will at least be able to unburden his mind and be at any rate freed from his terrible oath. It so happens that he overhears a conversation between the doctor and one of his guardians who enlarges upon the melancholy circumstance of her brother being in so critical a state when Miss Aubrey is to be married on the following day. He instantly demands the name of the bridegroom and is told the Earl of Marsden. He requests to see his sister and in an hour or two she visits him. As they are conversing she opens a locket and shows him a miniature of the man who has won her affections. To his horror he perceives that it is a portrait of Lord Ruthven and falling into convulsions of rage he tramples it under foot. In twenty-four hours the period of his oath will have expired, and he implores them to delay the wedding at least for that time. Since there seems no good reason for doing this the request is disregarded, upon which Aubrey falls into so sad a state of utter depression succeeded by an outburst of fury that the physician concludes him to be not far removed from lunacy and doubles the restraint. During the night the busy preparations for the nuptial are ceaselessly continued. It appears that upon the pretext of being her brother's dearest friend and travelling companion Lord Ruthven had visited the house to inquire after Aubrey during his supposed derangement, and from the character of a visitor gradually insinuated himself into that of an accepted suitor. When the bridal party has assembled Aubrey, neglected by the servants, contrives to make his way into the public apartments which are decorated for the nuptials. Ere he can utter a cry, he is, however, at once perceived by Lord Ruthven who with more than human strength thrusts him, speechless with rage, from the room, at the same time whispering in his ear: "Remember your oath, and know, if not my bride to-day, your sister is dishonoured. Women are frail!" The attendants at once secure the unhappy man, but he can no longer support his distress. In his agonies a blood vessel breaks and he is incontinently conveyed to bed. This sad accident is kept from his sister; the marriage was solemnized, and the bride and bridegroom left London.

> Aubrey's weakness increased; the effusion of blood produced symptoms of the near approach of death. He desired his sister's guardians might be called, and when the midnight hour had struck, he related composedly what the reader has perused—he died immediately after.

> The guardians hastened to protect Miss Aubrey; but when they arrived it was too late. Lord Ruthven had disappeared, and Aubrey's sister had glutted the thirst of a Vampyre!

It were not easy to overestimate the astounding sensation which was caused by this story, and the narrative is certainly not without considerable merit, for in places the eerie atmosphere is well conveyed. Nor is it difficult to understand the extraordinary influence of the tale, since it introduced a tradition which had been long forgotten and which promised infinite possibilities in the way of that sensation and melodramatic calentures which the period craved. The first separate edition of *The Vampyre* appeared in 1819, and was published by Sherwood. The first issue of this, which is now very rare, contains a certain amount of preliminary matter concerning the Shelleys, Byron and Godwin. This was omitted in later issues, and according one often finds that copies of *The Vampyre* are described as First Edition, which is strictly quite correct, although they are the Second Issue, and naturally of far less value in a bibliographer's eyes. A large number of reprints increased with amazing rapidity and in the same year the novel was translated into French by Henri Faber, *Le Vampire, nouvelle traduite de l'anglais de Lord Byron,* Paris, 1819. In February, 1820, there followed under the aegis of Charles Nodier a very obvious imitation, or rather continuation by Cyprien Bérard, *Lord Ruthwen ou les Vampires.* "Roman de C. B. Publié par l'auteur de *Jean Sbogar* et de *Thérese Aubert.* Paris, 1820." In 1825, a new translation of Polidori's story was given by Eusebe de Salles. Nor was Germany behind hand, for *The Vampyre* was first translated in 1819: *Der Vampyr. Eine Erzahlung aus dem Englischen des Lord Byron. Nebst einer Schilderung seines Aufenthaltes in Mytilene.* Leipzig, 1819. In the following year there appeared at Frankfort a version by J.V. Adrian of Byron's poems and prose, wherein was included *Der Blutsuger.* In a collection of Byron's work the first volume of which was published at Zwickau in 1821, *The Vampyre* again found a place in volume V (1821), translated by Christian Karl Meifsner as *Der Vampyr.* The tale has also been included in various other continental collections and translations of Byron's work even until a recent date.

Yet it was well-known all the while that Polidori was the author of the story, but as Byron's was by far the greater name, so this sensational novella must be attributed to the cavaliero whose romantic adventures and the scandal of whose amours were thrilling the whole of Europe. Writing in the same year as the great poet's death Amédée Pichot of the University of Marseilles in his *Essai sur le génie et le caractere de Lord Byron* declared that this spurious issue "a autant contribué a faire connaître le nom de lord Byron en France, que ses poëmes les plus estimés." Publishers insisted upon *Le Vampire,* "nouvelle," being included among Byron's works, and it is said that Ladvocat was furious when it was represented to him that since it was openly acknowledge that Polidori had written *The Vampire,* the translation should properly be no longer given among the poet's work nor put forth under his name.

E. F. Bleiler   (essay date 1965)

SOURCE: "John Polidori and *The Vampyre,*" in *Three Gothic Novels,* edited by E. F. Bleiler, Dover Publications, 1966, pp. xxxi-xl.

[*In the following essay, Bleiler discusses the writing and publication of* The Vampyre *and assesses its influence.*]

By the beginning of 1816 it was inevitable that the great poet Lord George Gordon Byron and his wife Anne were to separate, and Byron announced his decision to leave England. As T. L. Peacock, Shelley's friend and correspondent, phrased it in *Nightmare Abbey,* "Sir, I have quarrelled with my wife; and a man who has quarrelled with his wife is absolved from all duty to his country. I have written an ode to tell the people as much, and they may take it as they list."

Byron caused a gigantic coach to be built containing in compressed form all conveniences for life on the Continent, including a bed, a library, a plate chest, and even a dining area. In this anticipation of a modern trailer, he planned to work his way across Europe to Switzerland, where he would meet the Shelleys, and from there proceed to Italy, and perhaps ultimately to points farther east. He hired a doctor to accompany him as both companion and medical attendant, a procedure that was not too unusual among more wealthy travellers.

The doctor himself, however, was unusual. He was John Polidori (1795-1821), the son of an Italian resident in London who had translated *The Castle of Otranto* into Italian; the uncle of the future Dante Gabriel and Christina Rossetti; and the youngest man ever to receive a medical degree from the University of Edinburgh. Intelligent, lively, enthusiastic, he was probably selected as much for his personality as for his qualifications in medicine and Italian. Byron was to learn not too much later that the intelligence was only a superficial glibness; that the liveliness could be succeeded by cycles of depression and sullenness; and that the enthusiasm very often emerged as irresponsible impetuosity. All in all Polidori stood to gain more than Byron would from their association. He had the honor of travelling as a near-equal with the most famous man in England. He had also been promised five hundred pounds or guineas by John Murray, Byron's publisher, for a full diary of Byron's activities.

Difficulties arose almost as soon as the two men reached the Continent, and the remainder of the trip soon became a succession of tantrums and retreats by Polidori. One incident will suffice to show the personalities of the two men: When the entourage reached Cologne and the Rhine, Polidori, who had been musing over the inequities of fate, said unexpectedly to Byron, "Pray, what is there excepting writing poetry that I cannot do better than you?" Byron calmly faced him and replied, "Three things. First, I can hit with a pistol the keyhole of that door. Secondly, I can swim across that river to yonder point. And thirdly, I can give you a damned good thrashing." Polidori stalked out of the room.

Just why Byron tolerated Polidori as long as he did is something of a mystery. One reason may be that Byron at times took a mildly sadistic delight in laughing at Polidori's mooncalf behavior. On a later occasion, in Switzerland, Byron and his friends discovered that Polidori was in love with a local girl and twitted him about it. Polidori immediately denounced Byron as a cold-hearted monster, and it was Byron's turn to fly into a rage.

The Byron party reached Geneva on May 25, 1816; there they met the Shelleys—the poet, his wife Mary Godwin Shelley, and Claire Clairmont (Mary's half-sister), who had been Byron's mistress in England and was anxious to resume the relationship. There is no record of the meeting of the two great poets, which took place on the shore of Lake Geneva on May 27th, but they seem to have been pleased enough with each other's company to spend considerable time together. The Shelleys settled at the Maison Chappuis in the first week of June, while several days later the Byrons leased the Villa Diodati, which was about fifteen minutes' walk away, through a vineyard.

The two companies saw much of each other, and while details are not known, certain areas of their conversation can be recreated. There was, it is true, a certain range of disagreement between the two poets: Byron, according to the notes of his friend Hobhouse, was contemptuous of Shelley's "vague Wordsworthianism," and Shelley, on the other hand, did not like Byron's feelings of class. As Shelley wrote to Peacock, Byron was "an exceedingly interesting person . . . but slave to the vilest and most vulgar prejudices, and as mad as the winds." But these feelings aside, the two parties got along famously, and days and evenings were spent together on or along the lake, or in their quarters. We know that Byron spoke much of the London literary men that he had met or knew by reputation, and that Shelley told of the Godwin circle. Both men were interested in contemporary science, particularly galvanism, which seemed to give a semblance of life to dead limbs, and there was speculation about the possibility of reviving the dead with electricity. Byron sang a wild Albanian song for the Shelleys, and in solitary moments wrote scraps of "Childe Harold" on odd pieces of paper, which he stuffed into his pockets.

Shelley and Byron, on the whole, talked. Polidori glared at Shelley, to whom he had taken a violent dislike. Mary Shelley listened shyly and quietly, while Claire Clairmont was visibly annoyed that the others, particularly the thick-skinned Polidori, would not leave her alone with Byron.

For the purposes of this introduction, the high point of this Geneva period in the lives of Byron and Shelley came during June 15th to 17th, give or take a day. The weather was miserable, rainy and cold, and the two parties spent most of their time in the Villa Diodati conversing. Mary Shelley describes this moment in her introduction to the second edition of *Frankenstein:*

> Some volumes of ghost stories, translated from the German into French fell into our hands. There was the "History of the Inconstant Lover," who, when he thought to clasp the bride to whom he had pledged his vows, found himself in the arms of the pale ghost of her whom he had deserted. There was the tale of the sinful founder of his race, whose miserable doom it was to bestow the kiss of death on all the younger sons of his fated house, just when they reached the age of promise. His gigantic, shadowy form, clothed like the ghost in *Hamlet* in full armour, but with the beaver up, was seen at midnight. . . . "We will each write a ghost story," said Lord Byron; and his proposition was acceded to. There were four of us. The noble author began a tale, a fragment which he printed at the end of his poem of Mazeppa. Shelley, more apt to embody ideas and sentiments in the radiance of brilliant imagery, and in the music of the most melodious verse that adorns our language, than to invent the machinery of a story, commenced one founded on the experiences of his early life. Poor Polidori had some terrible idea about a skull-headed lady, who was so punished for peeping through a keyhole—what to see I forget—something very shocking and wrong, of course; but when she was reduced to a worse condition than the renowned Tom of Coventry, he did not know what to do with her, and was obliged to dispatch her to the tomb of the Capulets, the only place for which she was fitted. The illustrious poets, also, annoyed by the platitude of prose, speedily relinquished their uncongenial task.

Despite Mary Shelley's comment about the "platitude of prose," Shelley had previously written two Gothic novels, *Zastrozzi, A Romance* (1810) and *St. Irvyne; or, The Rosicrucian, A Romance* (1811), both of which he had published privately. Nothing ever came of the Lake Geneva novel, however, and it is questionable if Shelley put anything on paper. Claire Clairmont's novel also came to nothing. Polidori started a novel, but abandoned it. His diary, however, contains a good summary of Byron's fragment and its planned continuation.

Strange experiences sustained the supernatural mood of these three or four days. One evening, while Byron was reciting lines from Coleridge's "Christabel," Shelley suddenly shrieked and ran from the room. The other followed him and found him near collapse, leaning against a fireplace. Podidori administered ether, which was considered a restorative in small doses, and Shelley then told of envisioning a woman, perhaps Mary Shelley, with eyes instead of nipples. Mary Shelley, too, shared the mood. As she lay half-asleep at night, the conversation of the previous day about Darwin's experiments in creating life, the possible revivification of the dead by electricity, and the impiety of it all swirled through her head. She dreamed the central situation of her *Frankenstein*. She awoke, and recognizing that what had terrified her might terrify others, began to write the novel *Frankenstein, or, The Modern Prometheus* which was published in 1818.

Byron seems to have worked on his novel for several days, writing it down in full text in a notebook. Polidori summarizes Byron's tale: after swearing his travelling companion to secrecy, a vampire, in modern Greece, undergoes a mock death and is buried. Some time later, the travelling companion returns to London and finds the vampire alive, preying on society. Bound by his oath, the traveller can say nothing. This summary, of course, fits both Byron's *Fragment* and Polidori's *Vampyre*.

After the supernatural soirées, which are probably more significant to us in restrospect than they were to the participants, life at the Villa Diodati proceeded along its usual emotional course. Polidori became more and more impossible as a companion. When Shelley beat him in a boat race, Polidori considered himself insulted and challenged Shelley to a duel. Shelley simply laughed, but Byron told Polidori that he, Lord Byron, had no conscientious objection to duels, and that he would be happy to take Shelley's place. Polidori sullenly retired. In his letter of June 17th, 1816 to Murray in England, Byron wrote about Polidori, "I never was much more disgusted with any human production than with the eternal nonsense, and tracasseries, and emptiness, and ill humour, and vanity of that young person."

By the end of the summer Byron recognized that Polidori's amusement value was less than his nuisance value, and dismissed him. Surprisingly enough, Polidori took his dismissal with good grace. When the Byron party removed to Milan, Polidori appeared and presented his compliments, and the two men met amicably. In the Opera, on October 28th, an incident occurred. Polidori found his vision blocked by a tall fur hat worn by an Austrian officer sitting in front of him, and requested the officer to remove it. Perhaps Polidori was less than polite, or perhaps he unwittingly insulted the military authorities. The officer asked Polidori to step outside. Polidori obliged, expecting a duel, but the officer simply had him arrested for disorderly conduct.

The French novelist Stendhal, who was present, has left a perceptive, detailed account of this incident. Byron and his Italian friends hastened to the guardhouse to effect Polidori's release, and a near riot took place. Polidori became scarlet with rage; Byron turned white. Finally one of Byron's Italian friends suggested that only *titolati* (titled persons) remain. The others left, and the *titolati* wrote their names on a card, guaranteeing Polidori's good behavior. Polidori was permitted to leave, but the next day he was ordered out of Milan, and nothing that Byron and his friends could do served to change the situation.

Exact dates are not available, but by the spring of 1817 Polidori had returned to England. He had originally planned to migrate to Brazil, but for one reason or another he settled at Norwich as a physician. He did not prosper in medicine or literature, despite several publications: *An Essay on the Source of Positive Pleasure* (1818); *Ximenes, The Wreath, and Other Poems* (1819); *Ernestus Berchtold, or The Modern Oedipus* (1819); and *The Fall of the Angels* (1820). In August 1821, what with gambling debts, his finances became desperate, and he committed suicide by poison. Byron's comment when he learned of Polidori's death was, "Poor Polly is gone."

Two and a half years before his death, however, Polidori had committed the single act that has ensured the preservation of his name. In the April 1819 issue of Colburn's *New Monthly Magazine* there appeared a short novel entitled *The Vampyre*. A long preface, which also discussed the Byron menage in Geneva, and referred to a correspondent there, attributed the story to Byron. As we now know, however, Polidori wrote *The Vampyre,* basing it on the novel that Byron was to have written at the Villa Diodati. Polidori's diary contains a summary of what Byron had planned to write.

Just what happened, or why it happened, is still not entirely clear, but a letter from John Murray to Lord Byron (April 27, 1819) provides some background, even though the interpretation of events may be biased:

> . . . a copy of a thing called *The Vampire,* which Mr. Colburn has had the temerity to publish with your name as its author. It was first printed in the *New Monthly Magazine,* from which I have taken the copy which I now enclose. The Editor of that Journal has quarrelled with the publisher, and has called this morning to exculpate himself from the baseness of the transaction. He says that he received it from Dr. Polidori for a small sum, Polidori saying that the whole plan of it was yours, and that it was merely written out by him. The Editor inserted it with a short statement to this effect; but to his astonishment Colburn cancelled the leaf on the day previous to its publication, and contrary to, and in direct hostility to his positive order, fearing that this statement would prevent the sale of this work in a separate form, which was subsequently done. He informs me that Polidori, finding that the sale exceeded his expectation, and that he had sold it too cheap, went to the Editor, and declared that he would deny it. . . .

In the following, May, issue of the *New Monthly,* a letter from Polidori was printed: "I beg leave to state that your correspondent has been mistaken in attributing that tale, in its present form, to Lord Byron. The fact is, that though the ground-work is certainly Lord Byron's, its development is mine, produced at the request of a lady, who denied the possibility of anything being drawn from the materials which Lord Byron had said he intended to have employed in the formation of his Ghost Story." Nevertheless, when the separate reprint of *The Vampyre* appeared, Colburn took no heed of either Byron's disavowal which appeared in *Gallignani's Messenger* (published in Paris) or Polidori's letter, and managed to insinuate that the story was by Byron.

A short time later, in the preface to his novel ***Ernestus Berchtold,*** which is a tragic novel about a Byronic egotist, Polidori made the following surprising claim about ***The Vampyre:***

> The tale here presented to the public is the one I began at Coligny, when *Frankenstein* was planned, and when a noble author having determined to descend from his lofty range, gave up a few hours to a tale of terror, and wrote the fragment published at the end of *Mazeppa*. . . . The tale which lately appeared, and to which his lordship's name was wrongfully attached, was founded upon the ground-work upon which this fragment was to have been continued. . . . it appears to have fallen into the hands of some person, who sent it to the Editor in such a way, as to leave it so doubtful from his words, whether it was his lordship's or not, that I found some difficulty in vindicating it to myself. These circumstances were stated in a letter sent to the *Morning Chronicle* three days after the publication of the tale, but in consequence of the publishers representing to me that they were compromised as well as myself, and that immediately they were certain it was mine, that they themselves would wish to make the *amende honorable* to the public, I allowed them to recall the letter which had lain some days at that paper's office.

At this point it is difficult to judge motivations, and we have no real way of knowing what Polidori's intentions really were. It would seem unlikely that a man as egotistical as Polidori would have been satisfied to see his own work printed under another man's name; it is reasonable to consider Colburn guilty. After stealing Byron's plot, Polidori may well have salved his conscience by his not inaccurate statement about authorship. He may have felt that theft was acceptable if one admitted it frankly—and he probably also needed the money. On the other hand an element of malice must also be assigned to Polidori's actions, for to a contemporary reader it would have been obvious that Ruthven the vampire is in part at least a fictionalization of Byron. Byron was an internationally notorious personality, known more at this time for his scandalous life than for his works. Many of Ruthven's characteristics fit well into the image of Byron that had been forming. Indeed, even the name Ruthven is significant, for Byron's former mistress Lady Caroline Lamb in her novel *Glenarvon* had attacked Byron under this name. This personal aspect of ***The Vampyre,*** though it is now nearly forgotten, must have added to Byron's rage, for he took personal attacks very seriously.

Yet despite the many disclaimers and apologies that saw print and probably passed in correspondence and conversation, ***The Vampyre*** was generally accepted as Byron's work and became enormously popular, particularly on the Continent. It was immediately translated into French, in three different versions, and into German at least twice. E. T. A. Hoffmann comments on Byron's "remarkable knack for the weird and horrible" in his *Serapion Brethren.* In 1824 A. Pichot published a critical essay on Byron, and came to the conclusion that ***The Vampyre*** had more to do with Byron's popularity in France than all his poetry.

Almost immediately ***The Vampyre*** appeared as a stage presentation in France, and by the early 1820's the theatrical life of Paris was almost obsessed by the vampire theme. Several versions of Polidori's play were on the boards at the same time, among the playwrights being such prominent literary figures as Eugène Scribe and Charles Nodier. As an amusing anticipation of modern motion picture practice, there were even plays entitled *The Three Vampires* and *Son of the Vampire.* Alexandre Dumas *père's* memoirs use a performance of Nodier's vampire play as background for an extended image of Parisian theatrical life. He summarizes the absurd story in detail, comments on the many errors and misunderstandings that permeated it, and describes with great vivacity the doings of the audience and the claque.

In the history of the English novel Polidori's *Vampyre* has interest beyond its literary merits. It is probably the first extensive vampire story in English, and it served as the model for many later developments.

For the remainder of the nineteenth century, fiction based on vampirism is heavily in debt to Polidori's work.

—E. F. Bleiler

Polidori's story returned toEngland when J. R. Planché translated Nodier's *Le Vampire* (which was supposed to be the best of the French productions) into English. As *The Vampire, or The Bride of the Isles,* it was performed at the English Opera House in London in 1820. Planché had objected strongly to setting the play in Scotland, but since Scottish situations were popular and the management had Scottish costumes to be used, Scotland it remained; the play was very successful. Later Planché had his own way when he staged an English adaptation of Marschner's opera *Der Wampyr* (which was also based on Polidori's story), and set the play in Hungary. Other vampire plays followed Planché's. To mention a typical specimen: *The Vampire Bride, or The Tenant of the Tomb* by George Blink is set in medieval times. The vampire Brunhilda, who had been brought back from death by magic, says in her tion. It was characteristic of Byron to remark that this notebook was once the household book of his former wife, and that he kept it as the sole example of her writing he owned, except for her signature on the bill of separation.

Murray published Byron's fragment at the end of *Mazeppa* in 1819 and there it has remained, forgotten and unread except by specialists. Yet it is an interesting work, full of the vitality that permeated Byron's remarkable letters, and we must regret that Byron did not finish it, or at least write more. It is still worth reading.

The origin and some conventions of the literary vampire:

In *The Giaour* (1813) Byron mentions vampires; three years later at Geneva, in company with Shelley, Dr. Polidori, and M. G. Lewis, he read some German ghost-stories and invited his friends each to write one. Thus Mrs. Shelley conceived *Frankenstein,* and Byron composed part of a 'tale of terror' which he had had in mind to write for some time (it was published in 1819 as *A Fragment*). Dr. Polidori elaborated this sketch, weaving into it suggestions from *Glenarvon,* the autobiographical novel in which Lady Caroline Lamb (1816) had represented Byron as the perfidious Ruthven Glenarvon, who was fatal to his mistresses and was finally carried away by the devil, who for the occasion assumed the shape of the victims' ghosts. In April 1819 Polidori's macabre tale, ***The Vampire,*** appeared in the *New Monthly Magazine* under Byron's name, through a misunderstanding on the part of the editor of the review, and Goethe, swallowing it whole, declared it to be the best thing the poet had written (Goethe himself, in the *Braut von Korinth,* 1797, had been the first to give literary form to the fearsome vampire legends which had arisen in Illyria in the eighteenth century). The hero of Polidori's ***Vampire*** is a young libertine, Lord Ruthven, who is killed in Greece and becomes a vampire, seduces the sister of his friend Aubrey and suffocates her during the night which follows their wedding. A love-crime becomes an integral part of vampirism, though often in forms so far removed as to obscure the inner sense of the gruesome legend.

Mario Praz, in The Romantic Agony, *Meridian Books, 1956.*

Christopher Frayling (essay date 1978)

SOURCE: An introduction to *The Vampyre: Lord Ruthven to Count Dracula,* edited by Christopher Frayling, Victor Gollancz Ltd., 1978, pp. 9-82.

[*Frayling is an English educator and critic who has written extensively on modern popular culture. In the following excerpt, he discusses Polidori's* Vampyre *in relation to several types of literary vampire in modern European fiction.*]

A Red Sea

The vampire is as old as the world. Blood tastes of the sea—where we all come from. Although we normally associate the myth with Eastern Europe or Greece, probably because of epidemics which emanated from those regions in the eighteenth century, traces of vampirism are to be found in most cultures. Blood drained by the Lamiae, emissaries of the Triple-Goddess Hecate: blood sucked by Lilith, the other woman in Adam's life; blood shed for dead Attis and mourning Cybele, the Great Mother; blood as taboo (the book of Genesis warns us not to eat "flesh with the life thereof, which is the blood thereof"); blood for healing, for fertility, for rejuvenation; blood as unclean; blood sacrifices to the Nepalese Lord of Death or

the Mongolian Vampire God. The pelican feeding her young with blood from her own breast. Drink ye all of this in remembrance of me. . . .

Attempts to trace the origins and development of the vampire myth have seldom been successful, perhaps because the lore is so synthetic. Montague Summers tried in two influential books—*The Vampire, His Kith and Kin* (1928) and *The Vampire in Europe* (1929)—to write a history of vampirism from earliest times to the present day, but succeeded only in showing how difficult it is to define the characteristics which exclusively belong to the vampire. The laboured analysis contained in these books was strangely digressive (this was not helped by the fact that Summers believed in vampirism 'to the letter') and the sources embroidered beyond all recognition (on one famous occasion, he mistook a popular penny-dreadful article for a scholarly dissertation). So Summers ended up telling a series of more or less nasty stories, with a couple of major detours to take in the complete works of Shakespeare and his beloved Restoration theatre. "Of recent years", he concluded, "the histories of vampirism in England are perhaps few, but this is not so much because they do not occur as rather that they are carefully hushed up and stifled." As a man who was professed to be 'no votary of the cinematograph', he would presumably have found the current interest in vampirism utterly baffling.

But the family tree of the card-carrying vampire of modern European fiction—the *grand saigneur,* combining the beauty of Milton's Satan with the haughtiness of Byron's Fatal Man—as opposed to the genesis of the myth itself, is relatively accessible. Some of the early Romantics, such as Burger, Goethe and Keats, based their vampire vision (loosely) on classical Greek and Roman manifestations. More often, vampire tales and poems in the nineteenth century (when the genre developed in two distinct directions) . . . were derived from folktales and eye-witness accounts of 'posthumous magic' in peasant communities, which dated from the period 1680-1760. Somehow, the inarticulate peasant vampires described by Tournefort and Calmet (folkloric) vampires who attacked sheep and cows as often as their relatives became the aristocratic hero-villains (like Milton's Satan, they tend to get all the good lines) of the Romantics.

Lord Ruthven

How this happened is a matter for dispute. Some commentators have attributed the upward social mobility of the vampire to mythologies surrounding certain members of the British aristocracy in post-Enlightenment Europe, and especially France. The stereotype can be traced to various sources: anecdotes about Lord Rochester and the Restoration Court (Byron listed the plays of Otway as one of the key influences on the public image he chose to adopt); tales about George Selwyn, whose hobby it apparently was (in an 'amateur' way, and for 'delight' rather than 'pleasure') to watch gruesome executions and tortures, or about Thomas Warton, who had similar tastes; the reputation of Sir John Lambert, who was said to have had bizarre views about cadaverous women ("he could only love girls who were dangerously thin . . . and he had a private collection of mummified ladies") and to have combed Revolutionary Paris for suitable specimens. The behaviour of these men could be legitimised by the popular Burkean principle that "the passions which turn on self-preservation, turn on pain and danger; they are delightful when we have an idea of pain and danger without being actually in such circumstances. . . . Whatever excites this delight, I call *sublime*."

More crucial than all these examples, perhaps, was the public image of Lord Byron himself (a calculated image, enshrining the principle that life could be treated as theatre, complete with satanic scowl which he admitted was lifted from the Gothick villians of Mrs Radcliffe). In Paris, at the time when Polidori's *The Vampyre* was first published, boulevard gossips were unwittingly contributing to the sales of the book (which canny editors insinuated was the work of Byron rather than his physician) by spreading the rumour that the English Milord had murdered his mistress and "enjoyed drinking her blood, from a cup made of her cranium". Goethe is on record as having suggested offhandedly that "there were probably one or two dead bodies in that man's past", and he thought that *The Vampyre* was "the English poet's finest work". The phenomenal sales in Paris of Lady Caroline Lamb's *Glenarvon* (her revenge, after a much-publicized affair with Byron which went spectacularly wrong) with an introduction which made explicit the association between the Satanic Clarence de Ruthven, Lord Glenarvon and Lord Byron ("Woe be to those who have ever loved Glenarvon!") simply reinforced such rumours. So did editions of Lady Blessington's *Conversations,* which claimed that Byron had said, "Do you know that when I have looked on some face that I love, imagination has often figured the changes that death must one day produce in it—the worm rioting on lips now smiling, the features and of health changed to the livid and ghastly tints of putrefaction . . . this is one of my pleasures of imagination." When Peter Schlemihl lost his shadow to the Devil, it can have surprised no one that it was at a party arranged by a member of the English aristocracy. No wonder Charles Robert Maturin began his Gothick novel *Melmoth the Wanderer* with an old Spanish woman screaming "No English . . . Mother of God protect us . . .Avaunt Satan".

Lady Caroline Lamb's *Glenarvon* was published in England on May 9th 1816, shortly after Byron left England for Geneva. Throughout the summer of 1816, Byron (who did not have immediate access to a copy) was increasingly apprehensive about what exactly Caroline Lamb had written about their affair: on June 23rd he asked, "what-and who-the devil is *Glenarvon?*"; on July 22nd he added, "I have not even a guess at the contents—except for the very vague accounts I have heard—and I know but one thing which a woman can say to the purpose on such occasions and that she might as well for her own sake keep to herself—which by the way they very rarely can"; he was particularly worried about the motto she had apparently chosen for her novel (adapted from his own *The Corsair*):

> He left a name to all succeeding times,
> Link'd with one virtue and a thousand crimes.

"If such be the posy," he wrote, "what should the ring be?"

By the beginning of August 1816, he had read the book; his immediate reaction was to consider himself 'libelled by her hate'. But by December of the same year, he had distanced himself enough from the whole affair to seem amused: "It seems to me that, if the authoress had written the *truth,* and nothing but the truth—the whole truth—the romance would not only have been more *romantic,* but more entertaining. As for the likeness," he added, rather uncharitably, "the picture can't be good—I did not sit long enough." Clearly, the question of the character of Clarence de Ruthven, Lord Glenarvon, had often been discussed during that extraordinary summer, and, for once, Byron was worried about what the public would make of his image. The association between Ruthven Glenarvon and the Satanic Lord is never made explicit in the book (at least, not in the English edition), but, by making her hero-villain pay for his 'thousand crimes' (at the end of the story, he is pursued by a phantom ship), Caroline Lamb was, as Byron feared, enjoying her revenge:

> the heart of a libertine is iron, it softens when heated in the fires of lust, but it is cold and hard inside.

> It was one of those faces which, having once beheld, we never afterwards forget. It seemed as if the soul of passion had been stamped and printed upon every feature. The eye beamed into life as it threw up its dark ardent gaze, with a look nearly of inspiration, while the proud curl of the upper lip expressed haughtiness and bitter contempt; yet, ever mixed with these fierce characteristic feelings, an air of melancholy and dejection shaded over and softened every harsher expression. (*Glenarvon*)

This, more than all the other villains, with their 'gaunt faces' and 'piercing eves', who epitomized the 'metamorphoses of Satan' in the Gothick novel, represents the prototype for the Byronic vampire. When Dr Polidori wrote *The Vampyre* in two or three mornings later that summer, he simply transposed the description to fit his 'Lord Ruthven' (history does not record what James, fifth baron Ruthven, thought about all this). In *The Vampyre,* the character of Lady Mercer seems to have been based on Caroline Lamb while, as we shall see, the unstable relationship between Aubrey and Ruthven during and after their Grand Tour (admiration, disillusionment, disgust) mirrors closely what Polidori felt about Lord Byron in the summer of 1816.

The Vampyre was first published in 1819 by Colburn (the publishers of *Glenarvon*) after Polidori had forgotten all about it. Not only was the story falsely attributed to Byron himself, but an Introduction was added (certainly not by Polidori) which cleverly related the story to the popular image of Byron as destructive libertine: the Noble Lord "never went to sleep without a pair of pistols and a dagger by his side"; the rumour that he had procured "in his house two sisters as the partakers of his revels" was, of course, "entirely destitute of truth"; and so on. Even after the question of authorship had been cleared up, publishers of Byron's works were reluctant to let *The Vampyre* go: in Paris, there were so many complaints by subscribers when the story was dropped from the second edition of Byron's *Works* ("we did not wish to speculate with the name of the English Lord"), that a corrected and revised version of Polidori's tale was reinstated in the third edition (1820) ("we have decided to give way to the pressure of numerous subscribers by resuscitating *The Vampyre*"). It was ironic, said one literary critic of the day, that it took 'an absurd story, not even by him' finally to establish the reputation of Lord Byron in France. For thirty years, up until the melodrama about Lord Ruthven written by Alexandre Dumas in 1851, which synthesized all previous variations on the theme, the close identification of *The Vampyre* with accepted mythologies about Lord Byron seriously limited the possibilities of character development within the genre.

The contribution of this stereotype in all its various incarnations (from Mrs Radcliffe's villains to the Byronic hero, from George Selwyn to Lord Byron himself) to the popular success of the vampire theme in the Paris and London of the 1820s was clearly decisive, and set the tone for the more ephemeral works in the genre.

Other commentators have located the crucial 'moment' in the development of the Byronic vampire even more specifically, not on the Paris boulevards, but by the shores of Lake Geneva, in a villa which had once been visited (appropriately enough) by Milton. The English and French tourists who observed the antics of the Byron and Shelley *ménages* (through telescopes) in summer 1816, and who reported bizarre happenings (including group sex) in the Villa Diodati, obviously *expected* something of the sort to be going on. And commentators ever since, by paraphrasing or quoting Mary Shelley's account of that 'wet, ungenial summer' (written fifteen years after the event) have ensured that the legend lives on. Unfortunately the traditional version of the conception of *The Vampyre* and *Frankenstein* is almost completely fictitious.

Mary Shelley, in her *Introduction* to the third edition of *Frankenstein* (the first cheap edition, 1831) told the following story about the events of summer 1816:

> Incessant rain often confined us for days to the house. Some volumes of ghost stories, translated from the German into French, fell into our hands. There was the tale of the sinful founder of his race, whose miserable doom it was to bestow the kiss of death on all the younger sons of his fated house, just when they reached the age of promise. . . . I have not seen these stories since then; but their incidents are as fresh in my mind as if I had read them yesterday.

> 'We will each write a ghost story,' said Lord Byron; and his proposition was acceded to. There were four of us. The noble author began a tale, a fragment of which he printed at the end of his poem of *Mazeppa*. Shelley . . . commenced one founded on the experiences of his early life. Poor Polidori had some terrible idea about a skull-headed lady, who was so punished for

peeping through a key-hole—what to see I forget—something very wrong and shocking of course. . . . The illustrious poets also, annoyed by the platitude of prose, speedly relinquished their uncongenial task. I buried myself *to think of a story*—a story to rival those which had excited us to this task. . . . *Have you thought of a story?* I was asked each morning, and each morning I was forced to reply with a mortifying negative. . . .

> Many and long were the conversations between Lord Byron and Shelley, to which I was a devout but nearly silent listener. During one of these, various philosophical doctrines were discussed, and among others the nature of the principle of life, and whether there was any probability of its ever being discovered and communicated. . . . Night waned upon this talk, and even the witching hour had gone by, before we retired to rest. When I placed my head on my pillow, I did not sleep. . . . On the morrow, I announced that *I had thought of a story.* . . . I certainly did not owe the suggestion of one incident, nor scarcely of one train of feeling, to my husband. . . .

By the time Mary Shelley wrote this, all the male members of the group had been dead for some years, and her story *Frankenstein* had become a box-office success on the stage: she herself had been to see the most famous melodramatization. Her stress on the Gothick elements of that 'ungenial summer' (the weather, the ghost stories, the discussion beyond 'the witching hour', the dream which made her contribution the most frightening of all) was probably calculated to increase sales of the popular edition. The *theatricality* of her account belies the complexity of the relationships which developed that summer. "There were four of us", she writes; in fact, there were five people present—Byron, Dr Polidori (Byron's physician), 'Claire' Clairmont, Shelley, and herself (then Mary Godwin). Too much laudanum, and the bad vibrations which had built up among the assembled company, combined to make the events of June 1816 a great deal more bizarre than Mrs Shelley allows.

The unstable 'Claire' (Mary's stepsister) had chased Lord Byron half way across Europe, so that she could be with him when their child was born; Byron was not pleased to see her. Apart from anything else, she insisted on 'prancing to me at all hours' (that, presumably, was why Byron 'could not exactly play the Stoic' with her). Although it was 'Claire's' idea that the Byron and Shelley *ménages* get together (for obvious reasons, since she was with the Shelley party), the resulting sequence of events did little to calm what Shelley had described as her 'horrible dismay'.

Polidori had been getting on Byron's nerves ever since they arrived in Ostend on April 25th: "I never was much more disgusted with any human production—than with the eternal nonsense—and tracasseries—and emptiness—and ill-humour—and vanity of that young person; he was exactly the kind of person to whom, if he fell overboard, one would hold out a straw to know if the adage be true that drowning men catch at straws". In addition to this clash of personalities it seems likely (from the evidence of his **Diary**) that Polidori was acting as Byron's accountant as well as his physician, perhaps at the publisher Murray's request. If so, it was a task for which Byron was not likely to thank him.

Shelley was finding it difficult to cope; in such an atmosphere 'the tempestuous loveliness of terror' could become a bit too much of a good thing. According to Polidori, whose diary is the only surviving journal actually written at the time, on June 18th (while the ghost-story session was still going strong) Shelley's overstrained nerves finally collapsed:

> Began my ghost-story after tea. Twelve o'clock, really began to talk ghostly. L. B. repeated some verses of Coleridge's *Christabel,* of the witch's breast; when silence ensued, and Shelley, suddenly shrieking and putting his hands to his head, ran out of the room with a candle. Threw water in his face, and after gave him ether. He was looking at Mrs S., and suddenly thought of a woman he had heard of who had eyes instead of nipples, which, taking hold of his mind, horrified him—

The lines from *Christabel* which pushed Shelley over the edge were these:

> Her silken robe and inner vest
> Dropped to feet, and full in view
> Behold! her bosom and half her side,
> Hideous, deformed and pale of hue

The image which took 'hold of his mind' so dramatically was, according to a later account, 'reported of a lady in the neighbourhood'. This was the evening which Mary Shelley blandly referred to as the one when "Shelley . . . commenced a story founded on the experiences of his early life".

If the *Introduction to Frankenstein* externalizes these extraordinary tensions, to make them the stage trappings of a Gothick melodrama (the result of tact, perhaps, or bad memory, or, less charitably, astute business acumen), the treatment of the famous ghost stories themselves is less explicable. For Mary Shelley, who constantly reminds us that the incidents she is describing are 'fresh in my mind', makes significant errors about each of these stories, including her own.

She claims, for example, that the idea to 'write a ghost story' was Byron's; in fact, it was taken from the first story of the collection *Fantasmagoriana* (published anonymously by Jean Baptiste Benoît Eyriès in 1812), one of the two tales from the 'ghost stories, translated from the German' mentioned by Mary in her *Introduction:*

> Every one is to relate a story of ghosts, or something of a similar nature . . . it is agreed amongst us that no one shall search for any explanation, even though it bears the stamp of truth, as explanations would take away all pleasure from ghost stories. (*Les Portraits de Famille,* from *Fantasmagoriana.*)

Mary Shelley goes on to describe *Les Portraits de Famille* (the first story that the Diodati party read) as a mixture of Horace Walpole's *Castle of Otranto,* and a tale of vampirism; the story itself bears little or no resemblance to her account. She suggests that the 'illustrious poets' found the prospect of sitting indoors and chatting (when they would have liked to have been exploring Rousseau territory around the Lake) 'uncongenial'. Byron paints a very different picture in the third canto of *Childe Harold's Pilgrimage* (completed ten days after the ghost-story session): he felt that 'confinement' would stimulate them all to "find room and food for meditation, nor pass by much, that may give us pause, if pondered fittingly".

But these are perhaps errors of emphasis: when Mary Shelley describes the stories which were told by Byron, Shelley, Polidori and herself (she never once mention's 'Claire's' contribution), she actually falsifies the evidence. Since her *Journal* for those crucial months has disappeared, and only two letters have survived (both predating June 15th-16th, when the events described in her retrospective account seem to have begun), it is impossible to establish how this happened. She states, for example, that Polidori "had some terrible idea about a skull-headed lady"; in fact, he told a version of his **Ernestus Berchtold,** published in 1819 with an introduction which stated that "the tale here presented to the public is the one I began at Cologny, when *Frankenstein* was planned". **Berchtold** has nothing whatever to do with skull-headed ladies, or Peeping Toms (it is about the incestuous love-affair of a young Swiss patriot), and such supernatural elements as there are, were introduced rather apologetically ("I had agreed to write a supernatural tale, and that does not allow of a completely everyday narrative"). She states that "Shelley . . . commenced one found on the experiences of his early life": Polidori's **Diary** (the entry for June 18th, part of which has already been quoted) tells us much more.

> He married; and, a friend of his liking his wife, he tried all he could to induce her to live him in turn. He is surrounded by friends who feed upon him, and draw upon him as their banker.

These strange references to Shelley's early life (the first to an incident involving his friend Hogg and Harriet his first wife, the second to the behaviour of William Godwin and Charles Clairmont, 'Claire's' brother) seem to date from the same evening as the *Christabel* incident, and must represent the 'experiences' which Shelley discussed, as his contribution to the ghost-story session. From his behaviour later in the evening, we know something about Shelley's state of mind at the time (he was to associate Mary Godwin with a bizarre folktale about breasts with eyes). For obvious reasons, Mary Shelley would have remembered what Shelley's 'tale of terror' was about (her father as vampire, perhaps); she decided, however, to suppress it in her *Introduction.* She states that "the noble author (Byron) began a tale, a fragment of which he printed at the end of his poem of *Mazeppa*"; the inference is that Byron only told the *beginning* of his tale, and that he always intended to publish a 'fragment' of it. In fact,

Byron only appended his 'fragment' to *Mazeppa* in self-defence, after the publication of Polidori's *Vampyre* (which was loosely derived from it). Polidori's summary of the story Byron told on June 17th 1816 suggests that rather more of Byron's story was told than Mary Shelley indicates: "It depended for interest upon the circumstances of two friends leaving England, and one dying in Greece, the other finding him alive, upon his return, and making love to his sister." The published 'Fragment' only refers to 'two friends leaving England, and one dying in Greece': Polidori must have remembered Byron telling the rest of the story (the part which shows it to have been a vampire tale *before* he began his 'adaptation'); presumably, Byron omitted the 'vampire' elements from his 'Fragment', in order to make the story he told seem as far removed as possible from *The Vampyre* (which, as we have seen, had been wrongly attributed to him on first publication).

But perhaps Mary Shelley's strangest mistakes occur when she is describing the genesis of her own story, *Frankenstein* (as James Rieger has recently pointed out): she states that she could not *think of a story* until well after all the other tales had been told (and after the illustrious poets had become 'annoyed by the platitude of prose'); that a conversation between Byron and Shelley about 'the nature of the principle of life' stimulated her waking dream about the scientist and his creation; and that she 'did not owe the suggestion of one incident' to her husband. All of these reminiscences are inaccurate. The conversation, which was about 'principles—whether man was thought to be merely an instrument', occurred on June 15th, and was between *Polidori* and Shelley. Polidori was something of an expert on this: not only had he published a dissertation on aspects of somnambulism and animal magnetism the previous year (on graduating from Edinburgh University) but, as recently as June 12th, had discussed these and related issues with a Dr Odier (another graduate from Edinburgh) who lived near by. If Mary Shelley's dream was stimulated by this discussion (there is always the possibility that the Polidori discussion stimulated another, later that evening, involving Byron, Shelley and Mary, with the physician not present), then she had already *thought of a story* by June 16th, the day on which Byron (after reading the *Fantasmagoriana*) suggested, "We will each write a ghost story." So, her story came first (Polidori's, in fact, was the last to be told). And Shelley had a hand in every stage of its writing: the surviving manuscript shows how he edited his wife's work, approved of her using passages from his *Mont Blanc* (a version of his 'philosophical hymn', in Mary's hand, has recently been discovered in Scrope Davis's chest) suggested the incident where Frankenstein travels to Scotland in order to create a mate for his Monster (a mate he subsequently 'aborts') and made important revisions to the final scene.

Mary Shelley's *Introduction* was written ten years after Shelley's death, and fifteen years after the events it describes. Clearly, she did not have a very accurate memory (despite her protestations) and she had every reason to be tactful about the weird events of June 1816. But her distortions and inaccuracies go beyond the relatively trivial question of whether or not she was factually correct. For she creates an *atmosphere* and a *legend,* both of which have coloured all subsequent accounts of the genesis of the vampire in modern literature. By surrounding the events with Gothick stage-effects and crudely derivative horror stories, she suggests that both *Frankenstein* and *The Vampyre* were directly related to the early Gothick novel; in fact, that 'wet, ungenial summer' sounded the death-knell of the Gothick just as surely as Jane Austen's more famous satire in Northanger Abbey. Shelley himself concluded that *Frankenstein* was much more than 'a mere tale of spectres or enchantment'. And when Polidori was seeking 'models' for his vampire, Lord Ruthven, he turned not only to Caroline Lamb's *Glenarvon* (scarcely a mainstream Gothick source), but also to 'the Italian Marquis', a villainous character in *La Morte Fiancée* (from the *Fantasmagoriana*): "His long and wan visage, his piercing look, had so little of attraction in them, that everyone would certainly have avoided him, had he not possessed a fund of entertaining stories." Like Ruthven, the Italian Marquis of the ghost-story specializes in destroying lesser mortals at the gaming table. Polidori found much more than stock Gothick effects in the *Fantasmagoriana* and the aristocratic *Vampyre* was more than just a cliché bogey man to him: two years later, he was to denounce rank, wealth and power as empty illusions, in his essay on the *Source of Positive Pleasure*. Unlike Mary Shelley (in her *Introduction*), he was interested in a great deal more than the clanking of chains.

Later derivatives of *The Vampyre* were to revert to Gothick clichés (although, since the genre was a late arrival on the scene, it had more life in it than all the bandits and necromancers of the early Gothick), but Polidori's 'original' is nearer to the clinical horror tales of the late nineteenth century than to the over-ripe terrors of Mrs Radcliffe and others. By hiding the romantic agonies which *all* the main participants endured, Mary Shelley denies the connection between these and the more fruitful developments in the genre (a look at the short 'tales of terror' she penned *after* that summer reveals her insensibility in this regard). Her omission of the more bizarre aspects of both the Byronic image and her husband's psychological state serves a similar purpose: the Fatal Man and the *femme fatale* had plenty of life left in them, as the development of the vampire genre was to show. She may have found the 'food for meditation' uncongenial, but neither Byron nor Shelley seems to have agreed. By making the story of the genesis of *Frankenstein* into a cliffhanger, she probably hoped to increase sales of her book, but in the process she suggests that the other contributions to the ghost-story session were a great deal less interesting than they in fact were; in particular, by ignoring the role which Polidori (a professional) played in conversations about 'various philosophical doctrines' (perhaps he was not considered 'illustrious' enough to ponder such issues 'fittingly'), and by misrepresenting his *Ernestus Berchtold* (and, indirectly, *The Vampyre*) as crude shudder-novels, she implicitly denies that Polidori's strange fusion of clinical realism with weird incidents has any validity. Again, the development of the vampire theme was to prove her very wide of the mark.

The vampire genre in the nineteenth century was to grow in two distinct, but related, directions: one owed much to Polidori's *Vampyre* (thus to the Byronic legend, as filtered through boulevard gossip), the other to Shelley's 'tempestuous loveliness of terror' (thus to the kind of psychosexual trauma which Byron's reading of Christabel—an archetypal *femme fatale*—induced). The Polidori strain was to be reincarnated in French and English melodramas of the 1820s, in a marathon penny-dreadful in the 1840s, as Count Azzo von Klatka the *Mysterious Stranger* and, eventually, as Count Dracula himself. The Shelley strain was to be reincarnated in works by Hoffman, Gautier, the decadents Baudelaire and Lautréamont, and, eventually, Bram Stoker. *Dracula, . . .* represents a *synthesis* of the two main developments in the genre. Both are distantly related to the late eighteenth-century Gothick: but, despite Mary Shelley, both managed to rework the tired clichés of the shudder-novel in interesting ways.

Burke had written: "to make anything very terrible, obscurity in general seems to be necessary"; the painter Fuseli went further when, in 1802, he defined the difference between the legitimate depiction of terror and the inadmissable depiction of horror. "We cannot sympathise with what we detest or despise, nor fully pity what we shudder at or loathe . . . mangling is contagious, and spreads aversion from the slaughterman to the victim." The Polidori/Byron/Ruthven vampire was to show that 'mangling' was not necessarily detestable or despicable (it could even be fun), although its possibilities for development were limited, and it could too easily be parodied. The Christabel/Shelley/Gautier vampire was to show that maybe Burke and Fuseli had a point after all.

Before the events of 1816, there had been isolated references to vampirism (or to the iconography of vampirism) in prose literature—such as the Ogre's seven little daughters, with their fresh complexions and "very big mouths, with long teeth, very sharp, very far apart" in Charles Perrault's *Hop O' My Thumb,* or the lost race of people at the earth's core who feed on the blood of their marital partners, in Giacomo Casanova's *Icosameron,* or the Baron d'Olnitz, who believes (literally) that 'love is like rabies' in Saint-Cyr's Sadian novel *Pauliska* (1798), or the Ghoul in Nights 945-948 of the *Thousand and One Nights,* who is despatched in a way which is (to my knowledge) unique in the literature, by a sharp kick in the testicles—and even sustained attempts to exploit the myth, by early Romantics from Germany such as Goethe and Tieck, but those who were involved in that 'wet, ungenial summer' succeeded in fusing the various elements of vampirism into a coherent literary genre (some might say a *cliché*) for the first time. The immediate consequence, for both Mary Shelley and Polidori, was that they wrote not as teenagers exploring the possibilities of fiction for the first time, but with the detached, tired sophistication of seasoned groupies. The long-term consequence can still be seen today, on television and cinema screens, any night, especially at the 'witching hour', all over the Western World. . . .

In essence, there were four archetypal vampires in nineteenth-century fiction: the Satanic Lord (Polidori and derivatives), the Fatal Woman (Tieck, Hoffman, Gautier, Baudelaire, Swinburne and Le Fanu), the Unseen Force (O'Brien, de Maupassant) and the Folkloric Vampire (Mérimée, Gogol, Tolstoy, Turgenev and Burton). One might add also the 'camp' vampire (Stenbock, Viereck, and perhaps Rymer), although he is parasitic of all the rest.

Clearly, the Polidori *Vampyre* spawned a fully-fledged literary genre, with well-defined rules and a series of plot formulae which could be manipulated to suit popular taste at any time between 1820 and 1850: the location might change (Ruthven was reincarnated in Greece, Italy, the Balkans, rural England and Scotland—he appeared north of the border, not because of any Byronic associations, but because the English Opera House was stuck with an extensive stock of unworn kilts) but the story remained more or less the same. The Ruthven phenomenon (perhaps the first literary formula in history to originate with elite culture, and, eventually, to feed into working class pulp literature) thus illustrates well what Tsvetan Todorov defines as a genre (in his *Introduction à la Littérature Fantastique,* 1970): "texts which do not represent a significant shift in ideas which are held at a given time about a type of literature" and "which do not normally qualify for inclusion in the history of literature, and thus pass into another category—known as 'popular' or 'mass' literature" seem peculiarly appropriate as examples for genre or formula analysis.

James B. Twitchell (excerpt date 1981)

SOURCE: "The Vampire in Prose," in *The Living Dead: A Study of the Vampire in Romantic Literature,* Duke University Press, 1981, pp. 103-41.

[*Twitchell is an American educator and critic who has written extensively on supernatural and horror literature and film. In the following excerpt, Twitchell praises* The Vampyre, *exonerates Polidori from the charge of plagiarism, and proposes possible biographical bases for some characters and incidents from the novel.*]

Whether or not **The Vampyre** would have survived on its own, had it not appeared to be Byron's work, is of course a moot point. It surely would not have gained such a wide readership, both in England and on the Continent (Goethe, for instance, claimed it was the best thing Byron ever wrote!), but it might well have launched the vampire into prose nonetheless. For it is a well-made tale, full of biographical intrigue, local color, melodrama, suspense, and, most important, a dynamic new protagonist who prefigures the wonderfully morose Melmoth the Wanderer. Polidori carefully prepares his reader for this new human terror by providing a brief history of the vampire and a catalogue of his peculiarities. In his Introduction he explains the rise of the vampire belief as it parallels the growth of Christianity, its use as a tool of territorial expansion and consolidation, and the physical characteristics of the vampire, embellishing the goriest parts: "[Once fed,] their veins become distended to such a state of repletion, as to cause the blood to flow from all the passages of their bodies, and even from the very pores of their skins." But his best argument is the stock of any ghost story—the teller's assertion and then proof that the demon he will describe is not imaginary but real. Polidori relates the history of Arnold Paul, a Hungarian vampire whose strange story had already been told in the 1732 *London Journal*. Paul, a Hungarian soldier, returned from the dead to ravage friends and family alike for some twenty days until he was finally disinterred, staked, decapitated, and burned. This is all a matter of record, says Polidori, and so begins his tale.

Just the briefest summary of Polidori's story will exonerate him from charges of plagiarism for, if anything, *The Vampyre* is more a slander of Byron than a plagiarism. Polidori's vampire is named Lord Ruthven, a name that had earlier been coined by Lady Caroline Lamb to satirize Byron in her novel *Glenarvon*. This novel, incidentally, had been published by the same Mr. Colburn in May 1816 and had caused Byron some initial anxiety, at least until he had read it. Polidori surely must have known how Byron would react to seeing that name, and doubtless thought it a clever send-up of his old employer. As we first meet Lord Ruthven in England he is a lady-killer in both the metaphorical and literal sense. His current victim is one Lady Mercer, who bears notorious resemblance to Byron's most eccentric pursuer, Lady Caroline Lamb (who had dressed in a page's uniform to insinuate her way into Byron's household):

> Lady Mercer, who had been the mockery of every monster shewn in drawing-rooms since her marriage, threw herself in his [Ruthven's] way, and did all but put on the dress of a mountebank, to attract his notice—though in vain;—when she stood before him, though his eyes were apparently fixed upon hers, still it seemed as if they were unperceived;—even her unappalled impudence was baffled, and she left the field.

As Lord Ruthven is quite literally dispensing with Lady Mercer, Mr. Aubrey, an idealistic ingenu, enters London society, seeking a place in the world. He is an orphan far from home and needing the guidance of a mature teacher. Unfortunately—for he is very impressionable—he meets the strange, melancholy Ruthven, and they become like father and son. Soon, however, Ruthven suffers some "nameless embarrassments" and hastily plans to leave England. Aubrey now too feels the need for a change of scenery and suggests that they set off together. Ruthven agrees, and they travel to the Continent, one for escape, the other ostensibly "to perform the Tour."

So far there seems little doubt that Polidori is paralleling his own fortunes with Aubrey's, and Byron's with Ruthven's. The comparison continues when Aubrey and Ruthven reach the Continent, for just as Polidori and Byron had grown irritated with each other, Aubrey now finds his companion not at all what he expected. For instance,

Ruthven's acts of generosity are strangely ambivalent:

> [He] was profuse in his liberality;—the idle, the vagabond, and the beggar, received from his hand more than enough to relieve their immediate wants. But Aubrey could not avoid remarking, that it was not upon the virtuous, reduced to indigence by the misfortunes attendant even upon virtue, that he [Ruthven] bestowed his alms;—these were sent from the door with hardly suppressed sneers; but when the profligate came to ask something, not to relieve his wants, but to allow him to wallow in his lust, or to sink him still deeper in his iniquity, he was sent away with rich charity.

By the time they reach Rome, Aubrey's suspicions become justified. Letters arrive from his guardians insisting that he part from his companion, for

> It had been discovered, that his [Ruthven's] contempt for the adultress had not originated in hatred of her character; but that he had required, to enhance his gratification, that his victim, the partner of his guilt, should be hurled from the pinnacle of unsullied virtue, down to the lowest abyss of infamy and degradation: in fine, that all those females whom he had sought, apparently on account of their virtue, had, since his departure, thrown even the mask aside, and had not scrupled to expose the whole deformity of their vices to the public gaze.

On the biographical level we are never told who this "adultress" is. Polidori seems content to let us have our choice: perhaps Lady Caroline Lamb, or even Annabella Milbanke. Aubrey, however, loses no time in severing the friendship and moves to other apartments. However, before he goes he informs Ruthven's current inamorata that she is in great danger. She too severs affairs with Ruthven, which only infuriates the literal lady-killer still more. We will never know whether Polidori had Claire Clairmont in mind as the continental victim of Ruthven/Byron, but since the other pieces so neatly fit, it is almost irresistible to so speculate.

Aubrey soon heads off to Greece, meeting on the way Ianthe, a sprightly young beauty who lives with her parents at the edge of the dark woods. It is Ianthe who first tells Aubrey of vampires, how they feed "upon the life of a lovely female," how they slowly destroy their victims, how they are totally without principle or compassion. She even describes their features: the hollow eyes, penetrating stare, pallid skin, lanky frame—all those features that Aubrey soon realizes apply to Lord Ruthven. But like the innocent adolescent of folklore, he is unable to anticipate consequences of an evil that he only intellectually knows exists.

One day Aubrey prepares to go off on an excursion and Ianthe, realizing that he will have to return through the woods at night, pleads with him to spend the night on the far side of the woods and not risk a possible vampire attack. Aubrey laughs at her suggestion, a laugh that has been since heard in almost every vampire story and film. It is the laugh of the foolish youngster who, once warned of the vampire, insists such things can never happen to him. Aubrey crosses the woods by day and starts to return that evening. Halfway through the forest he hears the "shrieks of a woman mingling with the stifled, exultant mockery of a laugh." He rushes to the source, a small dark cabin, heaves open the door, and is accosted by the blurred form of a man who throws him to the ground. Aubrey hears these muffled words, "Again baffled," but he does not understand the meaning. We do, for although Aubrey does not now realize it, the stranger is Ruthven and his "again baffled" refers to the fact that this is the second time that Aubrey has thwarted his desires. Aubrey would doubtless have been murdered were it not for the timely arrival of the local posse armed with torches. Fearing the bright lights, the mysterious figure departs, leaving behind a dazed Aubrey, a bejeweled dagger, and the body of a beautiful girl:

> There was no colour upon her cheek, not even upon her lip; yet there was a stillness about her face that seemed almost as attaching as the life that once dwelt there:—upon her neck and breast was blood, and upon her throat were the marks of teeth having opened the vein:—to this the men pointed, crying, simultaneously struck with horror, "A Vampyre! a Vampyre!"

The mutilated girl was Ianthe. What she was doing in the same woods that she knew to be haunted by vampires is anyone's guess.

Her parents are inconsolable, and die heartbroken; Aubrey weakens and soon becomes bedridden. Now, for some unaccountable reason, in a state of delirium he asks that Ruthven be sent for to nurse him back to health. The victim, like the moth to the flame, seems pathetically drawn to the source of his destruction. As it happens, Ruthven "chanced at this time to arrive at Athens" and is more than happy to aid a companion, even one who had earlier spurned him. As Aubrey improves, however, he is continually horrified by the weird juxtaposition of the sight of Ruthven on the one hand and his memory of the vampire on the other. But he is powerless to send the fiend away, either in memory or in reality.

Ruthven is hale and hearty while Aubrey recovers, but once Aubrey's convalescence is finished Ruthven returns to his original emaciated state. Whether or not Polidori is here introducing a psychological explanation of vampirism is unclear. As far as we know, Ruthven never actually drains Aubrey of blood; instead there is a continual battle for energy: Ruthven grows strong as Aubrey weakens, then Aubrey stabilizes and Ruthven slowly pales. Still, Aubrey never completely recovers his former strength, for he is forever haunted by the memory of his encounter with the vampire. Finally, hoping to dispel these unpleasant memories, he proposes to Ruthven that they visit some out-of-the-way sights in rural Greece. Ruthven naturally accedes.

While traveling through some nameless but remote spot, Aubrey and Ruthven are waylaid by robbers. Ruthven is badly wounded in his shoulder and two days later calls Aubrey to his side. Here he extracts a deathbed promise from Aubrey, a promise that has become a donnée of Gothic fiction:

> "Swear!" cried the dying man, raising himself with exultant violence, "Swear by all your soul reveres, by all your nature fears, swear that for a year and a day you will not impart your knowledge of my crimes or death to any living being in any way, whatever may happen, or whatever you may see."—His eyes seemed bursting from their sockets: "I swear!" said Aubrey; he sunk laughing upon his pillow, and breathed no more.

The next day, when Aubrey goes to bury the body, he finds that it has somehow mysteriously disappeared. He later learns that Ruthven had contracted with robbers to drag his corpse to a nearby mountain where it should be "exposed to the first rays of the moon." Once again, Polidori is introducing what will become a commonplace of vampire fiction, for this is the first time in any vampire story that moonlight's rejuvenative powers are mentioned. While sorting out Ruthven's possessions, Aubrey finds a strangely shaped jeweled sheath made to hold a dagger of the same size as the one he found next to Ianthe. Aubrey then finds an identical dagger, with caked blood still on it, and realizes the awful truth, the truth he has tried so hard not to admit—that Ruthven is beyond any doubt the vampire.

Aubrey never recovers from this shock. He returns to England for a long convalescence, a rest that is interrupted only by a "drawing room party" for his beautiful sister, the charming Miss Aubrey. Timidly standing at the edge of the festivities, he is seized by the arm. He turns—it is Lord Ruthven come back from the dead. Aubrey trembles; "Remember your oath," Ruthven whispers; and Aubrey becomes limp.

Polidori must have realized that the oath was the weakest link in the story, for to increase the pathos of Aubrey's condition, Polidori must make him an honorable man whose word is his bond, yet he must be courageous enough to realize that there can be no honor when dealing with fiends. Nobly Aubrey decides to break his oath and tell all about Ruthven, but ironically his own physical state is so pathetic and his powers of concentration so weak that all who hear the story, including the same trustees who had earlier warned him of Ruthven, consider it the tale of a madman.

As time passes Aubrey's condition worsens until he is revived by the news of his dear sister's impending wedding to a certain Earl of Marsden. Since he thinks she is free of Ruthven's attentions, his spirits are buoyed; however, chancing upon his sister's locket he finds that her intended husband is no other than the demonic Ruthven, now masquerading as the earl. Aubrey flies into a rage, ranting on about how his sister must forswear this demon, but his outburst only confirms what all have suspected—that Aubrey is insane.

As the wedding day approaches, Aubrey is placed in protective confinement. He bribes one of the servants to carry a last desperate appeal to his sister, but alas, the servant delivers the note to the very doctor who has confined him. The next day, in desperation, Aubrey escapes from his room, rushes downstairs to the ceremony. All set to blurt out the truth, he is clutched once again by his tormentor, who whispers,—"Remember your oath, and know if not my bride today, your sister is dishonoured. Women are frail!" Aubrey is no longer able to contain himself. With hideous appropriateness he bursts a blood vessel and is taken back to bed. He is incoherent until midnight; then exactly a year and a day after his oath, he calmly explains Lord Ruthven's true nature to the now-believing guardians. They rush to protect the innocent bride, "but when they arrived, it was too late. Lord Ruthven had disappeared, and Aubrey's sister had glutted the thirst of a *VAMPYRE!*"

So ends the first vampire story ever told in English prose. It is, finally, a far cry from Byron's projected story, yet Polidori seems to have Byron's outline in mind, at least in the beginning. He has introduced additional characters, new locations, and vivid details. And, with the exception of the oath, the story has a momentum of its own that is quite sufficient to carry even the most skeptical reader past such contradictions as why a vampire need carry a dagger, or what Ianthe is doing out in the woods at night. *The Vampyre* is also a far cry from the usual Gothic novel. There is none of the trite disinheritance plot and creaking cellar doors that had become almost a staple of the pulps; there is some "local color," and even an attempt at verisimilitude by having much of the action occur in Greece (considered a favorite ground for vampires); and there is no attempt to explain away terror with elaborate ratiocinations, but instead an acceptance of the supernatural on its own terms. Polidori's most important innovation, however, is the introduction of an active villain, a villain as eager to suck the life from his fictional compatriots as is the author to scare the life out of his audience.

Not only was Polidori the first to use the figure of the vampire in prose, but he also seems, like Coleridge and Keats, one of the first to understand its psychological possibilities. For Polidori seems to use the myth in part as an analogy to explain how people interact. To Ianthe and Miss Aubrey, Lord Ruthven is an actual vampire, a horrid demon, but to Aubrey, Ruthven is a parasite of a different sort, a psychological sponge. Ruthven never "attacks" Aubrey, never sucks his blood; yet there does seem to be some energy exchange between the two men. At their first meeting Aubrey is robust, Ruthven pale and thin. Ruthven then strengthens as the relationship deepens and becomes positively "healthy" on the continent, when he dispenses his perverse charity to those he knows will misuse it. But most interesting is what happens when Aubrey is taken ill, for it is Ruthven who nurses him back to health, letting energy now flow from strong character to weak. Polidori explains this strange energy flux:

> His lordship [Ruthven] seemed quite changed; he no longer appeared that apathetic being who had so astonished Aubrey; but as soon as his convalescence

began to be rapid, he again gradually retired into the same state of mind, and Aubrey perceived no difference from the former man, except that at times he was surprised to meet his gaze fixed intently upon him, with a smile of malicious exultation playing upon his lips: he knew not why, but this smile haunted him. During the last stage of the invalid's recovery, Lord Ruthven was apparently engaged in watching the tideless waves raised by the cooling breeze, or in marking the progress of those orbs, circling, like our world, the moveless sun;—indeed, he appeared to wish to avoid the eyes of all.

It is almost as if Ruthven were "playing with his food." The relationship between Aubrey and Ruthven becomes still more macabre when one considers the familial overtones. We are told that Aubrey comes to London to learn about the world. He is seeking a teacher, someone he can trust, a father. He is an orphan, and the paternal figure he finds is Lord Ruthven. Still this symbiosis between parent and child is never fully developed in Polidori's novella, as it is in, say, Coleridge's *Christabel*—there is only the hint of reciprocity, only the inkling of the interdependence between parent and child.

Ultimately Polidori's novel is remembered (if remembered at all) not for its possibly sophisticated psychology, but for two more mundane reasons. First, by the 1820s it had formally launched the vampire into prose fiction and drama; and second, its appearance under Byron's name had made it a "literary event." Soon after its initial appearance, *The Vampyre* was in such demand that the publishing firm of Sherwood, Nelly, and Jones issued it as a book, which in two years went to six printings and was translated into three French versions and two German ones. In retrospect, however, what made the book so sensational now seems best forgotten. The charge of plagiarism, made by people like Hobhouse and Murray, and buttressed by such statements from Byron as "I was never so disgusted with any human production than with the eternal nonsense . . . emptiness and ill humor, and vanity of that young person [Polidori]," overlooked Byron's insistence that "I have . . . a personal dislike to 'vampires,' and the little acquaintance I have with them would by no means induce me to divulge their secrets." Yet Polidori never escaped censure and a few years later, at the age of twenty-five, committed suicide. Paradoxically a close comparison of the two stories exonerates Polidori, for, if anything, he had written a more interesting, imaginative, and compelling tale than Byron's "Fragment of a Novel" ever promised to be.

Byron's "Fragment," published by John Murray in 1819, was attached to the end of *Mazeppa*, apparently more to prove Byron's wavering claim of being first to write a vampire story than to assert its literary importance. In Byron's story the ingenu is not only a participant, like Polidori's Aubrey, but narrator as well. He tells of his travels to the East accompanied by one Augustus Darvell. This Darvell is a man of fortune and family who, like Ruthven, is slightly older than the hero, and serves as both literal and figurative guide. As they travel, Darvell, who already was "prey to some curious disquiet," becomes "daily more enfeebled" until he seems almost to "waste away." The young narrator is understandably concerned as his companion becomes progressively more withdrawn and silent, but they still continue eastward. When they arrive at the ruins of Ephesus in Turkey, Darvell is simply too weak to continue, and so they camp near a cemetery. Here within sight of this "city of the dead" Darvell asks for water, but no water can be found. Darvell then, almost in a stupor, describes the exact spot of a concealed well not a hundred yards distant. The young narrator queries: "How did you know this?" and Darvell replies, "From our situation; you must perceive that this place was once inhabited, and could not have been so without springs: I have also been here before." Although Darvell is too weak to explain how or when he has been here before, he is strong enough to extract a promise from the narrator that he will never tell anyone of his death. As the young man swears a complex and solemn oath, Darvell removes a "seal ring" from his finger and gives it to his companion, telling him to fling it into the salt springs of the Bay of Eleusis at noon of the ninth day of the month and then to go to the ruins of the temple of Ceres and wait an hour. "Why?" both reader and narrator ask, but we are never told.

Now, inexplicably, a stork with a snake in her beak comes to perch on a gravestone near the expiring Darvell. When the young narrator tries to frighten the bird away, she only returns to the same spot. Strangely, the stork never eats her prey, and when Darvell is asked to explain he only replies, "It is not yet time." Just as he speaks the bird flies away and, as the narrator turns to tell his companion, he finds him dead. The body now, in most un-vampire-like fashion, starts rapidly to decompose, and so the narrator quickly starts digging at the appointed spot. As he does, "the earth suddenly gave way, having already received some Mahometan tenant." The narrator is bewildered, as we are too, for here Byron's fragment abruptly ends.

It is admittedly unfair to judge a completed work like Polidori's with a fragment like Byron's, but certain comparisons can be made. The stories do share Byron's projected outline: two friends travel from England to Greece, one dies and obtains from the other an oath of secrecy; but here the stories break apart. Byron's story is incomplete, while Polidori's has the young man return to England and later meet his former companion. So in a sense Polidori follows Byron's chronological outline, but he makes a crucial change with regard to character. Polidori's Ruthven is a vampire; Byron's Darvell simply is not. Nowhere in Byron's work is there anything other than a vague suggestion that Darvell is "a being of no common order." Twentieth-century critics have still echoed the nineteenth-century contention that Byron was going to write a vampire story, the rough draft of which is his "Fragment." But Byron never said he was going to write a vampire story, and the text of the "Fragment" seems to bear him out.

Had Byron wished to write a vampire story, one would expect him to have seeded his fragment with more sub-

stantial hints of Darvell's true character. Actually, Darvell seems simply another Byronic Hero who, like Lara or the Corsair or any of a host of others, is driven by some inner demon, some mysterious force, into a life of exile. And the central image in Byron's story—the stork with the snake in her beak—is nowhere to be found in vampire lore; it seems more reminiscent of Mayan or Aztec folklore than of middle European. Additionally, when the young narrator is told to fling the ring into the Bay of Eleusis "on the ninth day of the month at noon precisely (what month you please, but this must be the day)" and then to repair to some ruins and wait an hour, we are as baffled by this mumbo-jumbo as is the narrator. We know from such poems as The Giaour that Byron was familiar with vampire lore, so presumably he must have intended these instructions for some still unknown purpose. Finally the most crucial bit of evidence that Darvell is not a vampire is the rapid decomposition of his body, for this decay violates the most important principle of the vampire myth, namely the awful imperishability of the flesh.

So I suspect that Byron was not the originator of the vampire story, either in intention or execution. True, the general idea of the story was his, but the character of the vampire was not. Here history may have done Polidori an injustice, on the one hand exonerating him from the charge of plagiarism, while still maintaining that the introduction of the character was Byron's. Since the travelers, the oath, and the return from the dead, were all presumably Byron's ideas, it is understandable to conclude that the characterizations were also, but quite the opposite seems true. The characters—Ruthven, Aubrey, Lady Mercer, and Ianthe—are all clearly Polidori's, and so too is the literal and figurative use of the vampire. Polidori's innovation in the Gothic novel has been unfairly neglected, and while it may be hyperbolic to claim that had Polidori lived he "might now hold a place in the 19th century literary hierarchy slightly above Charlotte Brontë," it is certainly true that Polidori was able to add a character to the dusty pantheon of Gothic villains [James Rieger, "Dr. Polidori and the Genesis of *Frankenstein*"].

To a considerable extent, the vampire's subsequent durability in both the novel and the cinema is a testament to how Polidori first cast him in prose. It would be a mistake, I think, to see Polidori working outside the tradition of the Gothic, for although the publishing history of **The Vampyre** is startling, the work itself is solidly within the tradition of the Romantic *schauerroman*.

Patricia L. Skarda (essay date 1989)

SOURCE: "Vampirism and Plagiarism: Byron's Influence and Polidori's Practice," in *Studies in Romanticism*, Vol. 28, No. 2, Summer, 1989, pp. 249-69.

[*In the following essay, Skarda contends that the plot of* The Vampyre *and the personal histories of Byron and*

Polidori "demonstrate the essential vampirism inherent in the powerful influence of a strong talent on a weak one."]

> In our culture the most popular version of the vampire, which has spawned a multi-million-dollar movie industry, is the Romanian *nosferatu*, a blood-crazed living corpse that turns its victims into new vampires and can be combated with an odd, elaborate mixture of pagan and Christian remedies, including garlic, holy water, decapitation, a cross, a wooden stake driven through the heart, and (one of the more amusing and less exploited methods) tying the vampire up in his coffin with complicated knots. [*The Penguin Encyclopedia of Horror and the Supernatural,* edited by Jack Sullivan]

The first vampire story in English fiction told less about ghoulish rituals of blood-sucking and heart-staking than about the failure to actualize one man's dreams of literary fame. Today's vulgar vampires on film and video cassette sensationalize the complicated but poignant history of Lord Byron's spirit-stopping influence on John William Polidori, author of *The Vampyre; A Tale* (1819), the first vampire story in English prose, first published as though written by Byron. Both the fiction itself and the facts surrounding its invention, re-creation, and publication demonstrate the essential vampirism inherent in the powerful influence of a strong talent on a weak one. In *The Vampyre,* Polidori sought neither to idealize his precursor nor to compliment by simple imitation Byron's more capable imagination. Instead, Polidori ingeniously construed a story that describes by curious ritual and convoluted dream his own entrapment in the anxiety of influence. [In a footnote, the critic adds that "Polidori's *Vampyre* bears marked resemblance to Oscar Wilde's *Picture of Dorian Gray* as a study of the essentially vampiric effects of influence. Speaking to Dorian Gray, Lord Henry Wotton articulates the power of his influence over Dorian and, in so doing, he anticipates the evil influence Dorian later exerts over others: ' . . . to influence a person is to give him one's own soul. He does not think his natural thoughts, or burn with his natural passions. His virtues are not real to him. His sins, if there are such things as sins, are borrowed. He becomes an echo of someone else's music, an actor of a part that has not been written for him'."]

In writing out *The Vampyre* sometime between 17 June 1816, when Byron read the fragment of a quite similar tale to his guests at the Villa Diodati, and 1 April 1819, the date of first publication of the story, Polidori wrestled with Byron and Byron's poetry in a desperate attempt to clear an imaginative field for himself. Focusing principally on works by and about Byron, Polidori fashioned a version of a vampire tale more remarkable for its echoes than for its originality. His story of the vampire Lord Ruthven unquestionably draws on Byron's characterization of Childe Harold, the self-exile set apart from cultural and personal community, and on tropes and imagery in Byron's oriental tales, especially *The Giaour* (1813), Byron's early tale about murder for love. In Polidori's story, Ruthven—the name Lady Caroline Lamb gave to

the inheritor of Belfont Abbey in her scandalous novel *Glenarvon* (1816), a novel carefully read by Byron to Polidori at Diodati—appears mysteriously among the London aristocracy and inexplicably attracts both "the fair" and "female hunters," like Lady Mercer, a fictionalized Lady Caroline Lamb, "who threw herself in his way, and did all but put on the dress of a mountebank, to attract his notice." His principal conquest, however, is a young man Polidori calls Aubrey after John Aubrey (1626-97), a real antiquary and author of a collection of lives of eminent persons, first published in 1813. Aubrey is, in part, an image of Polidori, who was commissioned by Byron's publisher, John Murray, to keep a diary of Byron's activities and comments while travelling with the newsworthy poet. In the fictional substitute for the diary, Polidori describes the gradual initiation, isolation, seduction, and eventual death of Aubrey by Ruthven's vampiric supremacy. As Aubrey acts out his ambivalent acceptance and rejection of Ruthven, Polidori reveals his own sonship to the dominating literary father figure he both loves and hates, admires and criticizes. *The Vampyre*—supplemented by its attendant preface, introduction, and postscript—both masks and reveals the real and ideal Polidori and his personal and literary relationship with Byron.

Major Media Adaptation:

In the 1987 motion picture *Gothic,* Ken Russell directed Gabriel Byrne, Natasha Richardson, Julian Sands, and Timothy Spall as Polidori in an extravagant portrayal of the Byron-Shelley-Godwin-Claremont-Polidori ménage at the Villa Diodati.

In the tale, Aubrey, like Polidori, has more imagination than judgment; he confuses the dreams of poets with the realities of life and naïvely believes poverty to be picturesque and virtue to be universal. Fascinated by the aloof, self-absorbed Ruthven, Aubrey makes Ruthven, as Polidori had Byron, "into the hero of a romance," necessarily obscuring the person by imaginative fancy. Like one under a spell of his own making, Aubrey postpones giving up his "dreams" and sets out to realize them. He determines to make a Grand Tour, and Ruthven, in embarrassed financial circumstances, proposes to join him. Polidori here not only reverses the actual order of the invitation to travel, but he also promotes himself as an equal, forgetting for the fiction that Byron hired him as a travelling physician, not as a companion and certainly not as a peer. Clearly, Polidori exalts himself by endowing Aubrey with a famous travelling companion and with the financial security that the real twenty-year-old graduate of medical school could only dream of, but he also accurately acknowledges his own naïveté in Aubrey's "false notions of his talents and his merit." In Aubrey's powerlessness to control Ruthven's immoral escapades that seemed "the ruin of all," Polidori excuses the gambling of his last years and his failure in youth to be as successfully promiscuous as Byron was. What Polidori admired and sought to emulate in Byron becomes, in the fiction, reprehensible and subject to censure, while many of Polidori's own faults are transferred to Byron.

By the time that Aubrey vaguely discerns "something supernatural" in Ruthven, his sister and guardians confirm it as Ruthven's "evil power" and "irresistible powers of seduction." In life, Polidori records no explicit warnings about Byron's character from his family, but, writing to his own favorite sister Frances on 2 May 1816 from Brussels, Polidori praises Lord Byron and himself, adding a cautionary word about "passion" that seems to indicate earlier discussion or correspondence:

> I am very pleased with Lord Byron. I am with him on the footing of an equal, everything alike: at present here we have a suite of rooms between us. I have my sitting-room at one end, he at the other. He has not shown any passion; though we have had nothing but a series of mishaps that have put *me* out of temper though they have not ruffled his.

Polidori imitated his master by boasting of his equality and by adopting for himself the passion he expected to find in Byron, but, in fairness, Polidori records in his diary his honest disappointment in being reduced from one "ambitious for literary distinction" to becoming nothing more than "a tassel to the purse of merit," "a star in the halo of the moon." Like Aubrey, Polidori unquestionably aspired to Byron's fame, wealth, and popularity but met his own obscurity, indebtedness, and what Byron later identified as his "eternal nonsense—& tracasseries—& emptiness—& ill-humour—& vanity"—harsh words from a gentle and usually forgiving master.

Resolving to leave Ruthven, something Polidori never dreamed of doing but apparently wished he had, Aubrey spoils Ruthven's rendezvous with the daughter of an Italian countess. After laughing at Aubrey's inquiry as to his marital intentions, Ruthven quietly assents to a separation from Aubrey without mention of the girl in question. In fact, however, it was Polidori who was forced, after less than five months of service (23 April to 16 September 1816), to leave Byron, in part for inappropriate attentions to Mary Wollstonecraft Godwin. In the fiction, Polidori puts himself in Byron's place and provides far more serious moral grounds for dismissing Ruthven than Byron had for dismissing Polidori.

Polidori compensates for his own amorous failure by Aubrey's success, projecting in the fiction not only envy but appropriation of Byron's identity. Travelling alone, Aubrey unconsciously apes Ruthven by falling in love with a Greek peasant girl, Ianthe, auspiciously the nickname Byron gave to the Lady Charlotte Mary Harley (1801-1880), whose mother, Lady Oxford, loved him and whose beauty so charmed Byron that he dedicated to her an edition of *Childe Harold's Pilgrimage.* Polidori idealizes Ianthe's delicate beauty and guileless innocence as Byron had Lady Charlotte Mary Hartley's, but Polidori takes issue with Byron's image of her eye that "wild as the Gazelle's / Now brightly bold or beautifully shy, / Wins as it wanders, dazzles where it dwells." Gazelle's

eyes held such fascination for Byron that he repeats the image in *The Giaour* in his description of Leila's dark and charming eyes:

> Her eye's dark charm 'twere vain to tell,
> But gaze on that of the Gazelle,
> It will assist thy fancy well;
> As large, as languishingly dark,
> But Soul beam'd forth in every spark
> That darted from beneath the lid,
> Bright as the jewel of Giamschid.
> Yea, Soul, and should our prophet say
> That form was nought but breathing clay,
> By Alla! I would answer nay.

In *The Vampyre* Polidori more sensibly applies Byron's gazelle analogy to Ianthe's light-footed nimbleness, adding a clumsy attack on Byron's admiration for the gazelle's eyes:

> As she danced upon the plain, or tripped along the mountain's side, one would have thought the gazelle a poor type of her beauties; for who would have exchanged her eye, apparently the eye of animated nature, for that sleepy luxurious look of the animal suited but to the taste of an epicure.

Neither Polidori's context nor his characteristically discursive style excuses so tangential a comment. His own description suffers as he childes Byron as an epicure and reproaches his literary model for the ill-chosen image. This explicit correction inspires others, but Polidori proves to be a better parrot than critic of Byron.

In the same passage describing Ianthe, Polidori echoes Byron twice more. Supplementing Byron's refusal at that time to subscribe to the Mohammedan belief that women have no souls, Polidori writes that Ianthe might have served as model for a painter, "wishing to pourtray on canvass the promised hope of the faithful in Mahomet's paradise, save that her eyes spoke too much mind for any one to think she could belong to those who had no souls." In Byron's *Giaour,* reference to this Islamic tenet of faith contributes to the Moslem/Christian conflict that politicizes the protagonist's murder and confession; but in Polidori's "Vampyre" Mohammed's teaching on women's souls is an unnecessary aside functioning as clear evidence of unacknowledged borrowing. In like fashion, Polidori reduces Byron's extended comparison of Leila to the rare blue-winged Kashmeer butterfly, retaining for Ianthe only the physical activity of pursuing the butterfly. In Byron's text both images are provocative, but in Polidori's they are merely decorative. By limiting Byron's scope, Polidori eliminates his master's poetic and thematic vitality while muddling his own story with exotic but pointless Eastern allusions that blur his narrative and call attention to his source.

Polidori harvests images and phrases and setting from Byron's *Giaour* for the Ianthe in his *Vampyre* not merely because Byron's fields were fertile but because Polidori could not find his own. Since Polidori himself had no idyllic lover other than Byron on which to model Ianthe, he turned to Byron for more than legitimate inspiration. When his story required a romantic attachment that could equal or surpass the "vision of romance" in which Ruthven played Aubrey's hero, where should Polidori find materials appropriate to a story that, for whatever reason, purported to be Byron's own? In Byron's work, of course. Since the section on Ianthe lacked the authority of Byron's story, composed at Diodati and later published in fragmentary form at the end of *Mazeppa* (1819) as a formal disavowal of the ascription of *The Vampyre* to Byron, Polidori arrogated material from Byron with assumed impunity. Rather than be thrown on his own resources, Polidori turned naturally to the mentor who had encouraged his literary enterprises. Polidori succumbed to Byron's strangling enchantment because he was unable to displace Byron's dominating influence by using his own imagination.

Ianthe tells Aubrey all he is to know of vampires before she satisfies the monster's thirst and before Aubrey himself feels the vampire's "hands upon his throat." Light from the torches of rescuers saves Aubrey from certain death, but his grief brings on amnesic delirium that suffocates his good sense. Improbably, Ruthven arrives in Athens in time to nurse Aubrey to health. As Aubrey gradually improves, Ruthven stops ministering to his patient and returns to his prior state of apathy and isolation. Aubrey then inexplicably becomes "as much a lover of solitude and silence as Lord Ruthven." The fictional exchange of energies reveals actual identification. Just as Aubrey was nursed by Ruthven, so too was Polidori the doctor nursed through a fever and bad sprain by Byron; and just as Aubrey was reconciled to Ruthven, so was Polidori shocked by his own inadequacies into dipping again in Byron's *Giaour* for more tropes and incidental details.

Again Aubrey proposes travel and again Aubrey ignores the warnings of natives. Robbers overtake Aubrey and Ruthven in a narrow defile between mountains, a place unmistakably exaggerating the features of Byron's setting for the Giaour's mortal combat with Hassan, the jealous murderer of Leila. Byron's "small broken crags of granite gray" from "mountains" above a dry "river's wintry stream" become in Polidori's version "large masses of rock" from "neighbouring precipices" in a pass above the bed of a "torrent." By intensifying Byron's more poetic descriptions, Polidori prepares for the death of the vampire, not by Aubrey's hands, tied now by mysterious friendship, but by a robber's bullet that whistles close to the head in *The Vampyre* just as in The Giaour. In a long deathbed speech, though not quite as long as the Gaiour's, Ruthven elicits from Aubrey an oath of silence as to his crimes and his death for a year and day. Immediately after, Aubrey matches an ornamented sheath among Ruthven's effects with the dagger or "ataghan" found in the hut where Ianthe was killed. Although Polidori leaves unexplained why a competent vampire should need a knife, the illogical clue confirms Polidori's reliance on *The Giaour* as the source of details for Ruthven's death and for Aubrey's belief in vampires.

The story concludes as Polidori remembered Byron's did:

> Two friends were to travel from England into Greece; while there one of them should die, but before his death, should obtain from his friend an oath of secrecy with regard to his decease. Some short time after, the remaining traveller returning to his native country, should be startled at perceiving his former companion moving about in society, and should be horrified at finding that he made love to his former friend's sister.

Just beneath the surface of this groundwork is the taboo of incest, for the horror resides in making love to the sister not in taking her life. In the fiction, the fact that the sister, Aubrey's last possible companion, wants to marry the vampire heightens the frustration of Aubrey, who is condemned to silence by his oath and, more probably, by his fear of not being believed. Uncannily, Miss Aubrey resembles Ruthven, now reincarnated as the Earl of Marsden, in her "melancholy charm," but she is carefully distinguished from Ianthe in not being light of foot or attracted to a butterfly or blessed with animated eyes. Marsden apparently wins for himself more than her hand, for he warns Aubrey off on the day of wedding, saying "if not my bride to day, your sister is dishonoured'." They marry while Aubrey lies dying of a broken blood vessel; at midnight Aubrey tells his guardians of the real identity of Marsden and dies immediately. The guardians hurry to protect Miss Aubrey, but they arrive too late. The story ends on a wedding night reminiscent of *Frankenstein* but without the promise of the death of the monster: "Lord Ruthven had disappeared, and Aubrey's sister had glutted the thirst of the VAMPYRE!" The source of evil and influence lives on as victor leaving, as Byron did in Polidori's imagination, a wake of corpses, the most important of which became Polidori's own.

Modern readers, familiar with macabre accounts of demonic stalking vampires and heroic staking parties, are justifiably disappointed with Polidori's comparatively pale conclusion. So, apparently, was he, for he added, for the first edition, a six-page introduction to vampirism full of vampire deaths and superstitions not merely current but already published. Almost half of the introduction recounts the grisly death of a Hungarian vampire named Arnold Paul, reported in the *London Journal* of 7 January 1732, which Polidori cites, and which had been retold by Robert Southey in an extensive note to *Thalaba, the Destroyer* (1801). Polidori mentions Southey's *Thalaba* in his introduction but does not cite it or its note as his source. For his rendition of the story, Polidori depends alternately on the *Journal* for spelling and credibility and on Southey for elaboration of gruesome effects, often borrowed word for word. Polidori was directed to Southey's note by Byron's own note on vampires in *The Giaour,* from which Polidori quotes the celebrated vampire curse in lines 755-86. Although the introduction presumes to explain various superstitions associated with real or literary vampires, Polidori's story draws on so few of the vampiric characteristics or rituals mentioned, paraphrased, borrowed, or quoted that the tale seems to establish its own tradition, one not distinct from vampirism but obscured by now familiar blood images.

Polidori's vampire almost incidentally kills Ianthe and Miss Aubrey in order to take the life of Aubrey himself. Ruthven-Marsden does not suck Aubrey's blood, however: "his rage not finding vent, [Aubrey] had broken a blood-vessel." The rage itself implies connection between the envier Aubrey and the envied vampire, who displaces Aubrey as the sister's protector and insinuates himself into the sister's affections. As though under the vampire's power, the vessel bursts in an "effusion of blood" typical not of the vampiric victim but of the vampire itself, who, according to the reports in the *London Journal,* Southey's note, and Polidori's introductions, bleeds "from all the passages of their bodies, and even from the very pores of their skins . . . emitting at the mouth, nose, and ears, pure and florid blood." By carefully building Aubrey's rage and by cutting off all opportunities for its vent, Lord Ruthven vamps his primary victim: Aubrey. Aubrey, a vampire by infatuation and association with a man of his dreams is justified, then, in assuming responsibility for the deaths of both Ianthe and his sister. By satiating the vampire's thirst with the lifeblood of young women, Polidori obscures the more significant and more subtly incestuous seduction and death of Aubrey.

Aubrey's death, like publication of *The Vampyre* over Byron's name, marks the definitive result of unchecked imaginative influence. The ascription of *The Vampyre* to Byron, however it occurred, formalizes Polidori's misunderstanding of Byron's allusive and autobiographical methods. In casting Byron as the vampire Lord Ruthven, Polidori followed the suggestive lead not only of Lady Caroline Lamb but also of Byron himself.

Polidori learned his special kind of vampirism from Byron, who borrowed for his poetry frequently from his contemporaries and freely from the experiences of his own life. To Byron and, hence, to Polidori, both personal and professional borrowing was thought to flatter the originals. Byron compliments Southey on *Thalaba, the Destroyer* by drawing from it such details as the Muslim/Christian context and the vampire curse for his *Giaour.* For the multiple narrators and the fragmentary form of *The Giaour,* Byron is obliged to *The Voyage of Columbus* (1812) by Samuel Rogers. And for the oriental customs and scenery in *The Giaour* and other verse tales, Byron is indebted to William Beckford's *Vathek* (1786). The plot of *The Giaour,* Byron admits, was founded in part on his own rescue of a girl in Athens, who, according to strict Mohammedan law against infidelity, had been sewn in a sack and was about to be thrown into the sea. Both facts and rumors about Byron's role are reported in a letter Lord Sligo wrote at Byron's request telling what he knew and had heard of the episode. Byron circulated Lord Sligo's letter to counter some stories that Lady Caroline Lamb and others were spreading about the possibility that Byron himself was the lover of the girl or the murderer of her assassins. The story was expanded to illogical conclusions by Lady Caroline Lamb in *Glenarvon,* and Goethe, for one, believed more of Lady Caroline Lamb's version of Byron's unpardonable sins that he should have. In his review of *Manfred,* completed in 1817 but not published

until 1820, Goethe enthusiastically praises Byron's genius but he also confirms rumors of Byron's bloodguilt in the Athens affair and, more importantly, suggests that Byron modeled *Manfred* on *Faust.* Goethe did not actually call Byron a plagiarist, but readers of the review quickly applied the label and revelled in the additional scandal attached to the famous name of Byron. Goethe, however, regarded Byron's *Manfred* as tribute to himself and to his *Faust,* part of which was translated for Byron by Monk Lewis in August of 1816. Acknowledging Goethe's ambiguous notice of him, Byron responded with public generosity by humbly dedicating *Sardanapalus* (1821) to "the illustrious Goethe," the "liege lord" to Byron, "a literary vassal," "a stranger."

Byron's letters prove that he was inordinately sensitive to the charge of plagiarism, and in all his publications he was conscientious about noting his debts to his contemporaries and his poetic precursors. He appended notes to his poetry pointing out his conscious borrowings, and in letters and public notices he defended himself against charges of dependence or influence. But he could not stop the accusations or the forgeries or the "bookselling imposture[s]" that ascribed works to him. He had long fought battles of public opinion, from allegations of adultery and worse by his wife and of poetic self-portraits and immorality by his critics. What the public thought mattered mightily to Byron, and in matters of literary imitation or even emulation, he could be privately stern while remaining publicly gracious. Nonetheless, unconscious shaping and even verbal reminiscence reveal Byron's models: *Childe Harold's Pilgrimage* draws on Rousseau's *Confessions,* Fielding's *Tom Jones,* and even Spenser's *Faerie Queene* for its archaisms if not its scope. Wordsworth's influence on Canto III of *Childe Harold's Pilgrimage* seldom goes unremarked, and "Epistle to Augusta" has been persuasively elucidated as Byron's "personal response" to "Tintern Abbey." Without losing his particular poetic identity, Byron breathed in the revolutionary sublime of the spirit of the age even though he exhaled more irony than enthusiasm, more despair than hope. Although he faulted the Lake poets for sentimental excesses, he prided himself on excesses uniquely his own and, in a letter to Thomas Moore (2 February 1818), allied himself with Wordsworth, Coleridge, and Southey as well as with George Crabbe and Samuel Rogers:

> Our fame will be hurt by *admiration* and *imitation.* When I say *our,* I mean *all* (Lakers included), except the postscript of the Augustans. The next generation (from the quantity and facility of imitation) will tumble and break their necks off our Pegasus, who runs away with us; but we keep the *saddle* because we broke the rascal and can ride. But though easy to mount, he is the devil to guide; and the next fellows must go back to the riding-school and the manège, and learn to ride the "great horse."

Byron here distinguishes his contemporaries from imitative successors, implying by the intractable Pegasus on the run both the difficulty of the ride and the individuality

Villa Diodati on Lake Geneva, where Polidori began The Vampyre.

of current riders. Reading literature hot off the press and engaging in (often heated) discussions and correspondence with its authors need not and did not result in sameness or in plagiarism. Byron's echoes of the sense, sentiment, tropes, and images circulating in the *Zeitgeist* contribute to a symphony of sound explicitly Byron's own. Even in his defense of Pope and Dryden, unusual in his day, Byron romanticized or redefined them before reclaiming them. Byron's poetic fathers and his contemporaries were assimilated into his work, but he plowed his own imaginative fields.

Polidori, on the other hand, was forced not by incompetence but by dominance to dabble in Byron's. That the harvest was meager should come as no surprise. Polidori's refusal to wrestle with Byron's influence over him constitutes a surrender or a white flag before the battle begins. Embracing the strong poetic father smacks of incest far more threatening to the son than to the father, more threatening even than the incest implied in a brother's love or a vampire's seduction of a female victim. Polidori, like a willing rape victim, sacrifices himself in life and Aubrey in his fiction to the father-god he found in

Byron. By writing a spurious preface and a fictitious postscript for the earliest book editions of *The Vampyre,* Polidori immortalizes his ambivalent regard for Byron in testaments to his own brand of vampirism.

In the prefatory "Extract of a Letter from Geneva," reprinted in [a] 1966 edition of *The Vampyre; A Tale,* Polidori (or his thinly-masked female amanuensis or intimate friend) reverentially describes a pilgrimage to the shrine at Diodati. With "awe and respect," the speaker treads the same floor, sits in the same chair, and engages the same servant that Byron had in the summer of 1816 when Polidori was with him. The letter contains the same catalogue of names that Polidori records in his diary, complete with Byron's social slights and successes, and it supplies many of the historical and literary references that Byron made in *Childe Harold's Pilgrimage,* Canto III, from which three stanzas are quoted in full. Architectural details characteristic of Polidori alternate with opinions typical of Byron, including, thanks to an indiscreet servant, how Byron scheduled his day: "he retired to rest at three, got up at two, and employed himself a long time over his toilette; that he never went to sleep without a pair of pistols and a dagger by his side, and that he never eat animal food." The letter identifies the writer not merely as an admirer of Byron but as one who so identifies with the person of the poet as to follow in his literal footsteps even when he is absent. Self-consciously, the

---

Polidori's refusal to wrestle with Byron's influence over him constitutes a surrender or a white flag before the battle begins. Embracing the strong poetic father smacks of incest far more threatening to the son than to the father. . . . Polidori, like a willing rape victim, sacrifices himself in life and Aubrey in his fiction to the father-god he found in Byron.

—Patricia L. Skarda

---

writer tries to explain the depth of the research being conducted by admitting "I have my pleasure in thus helping my personification of the individual I admire, by attaining to the knowledge of those circumstances which were daily around him." Polidori is exalted in the letter as Byron's physician and sole companion, a dismissive gesture to Polidori's rivals for Byron's affection—Shelley, Mary Godwin, and Claire Clairmont (whose name is misspelled). As physician, Polidori is said to have helped calm Shelley, who ran from the reading of Coleridge's *Christabel* because he had imagined eyes on the bosom of one of the ladies, an incident vividly recorded in Polidori's *Diary*. The letter concludes by describing the ghost-story competition and by presuming to forward the outline of each of the stories to a nameless recipient as curious as the writer to "peruse the *ébauches* of so great a genius, and those immediately under his influence." The operative word is, of course, the last. Even if Polidori did not write the letter himself, though I am convinced by internal evidence that he did, the influence of Byron is clearly the focus and the purpose of the letter.

Byron took such hold of Polidori's imagination that he drafted a fanciful postscript to *The Vampyre,* called an *"Account of Lord Byron's Residence"* in 1812 on the island of Mitylene, a place visited by neither Byron nor Polidori. This account is decidedly more factitious than the *"Extract of a Letter from Geneva,"* but the narrating persona, a sailor, is more certainly Polidori. Byron's house is again elaborately described from prospect and floor-plan to the furnishings, decorations, books, and even the

books' marginal notes in Italian and Latin. Polidori here assigns his own particularity about architectural details and personal possessions to Byron. Another talkative servant repeatedly emphasizes Byron's reclusiveness and Christian practices, though Polidori was the Catholic. Byron is said to attend church "twice a week, besides Sundays," to give Greek Testaments to the children, and to be generous in his charities to the natives, even buying a piano-forte for the servant's beautiful daughter and teaching her to play it. In short, Byron is depicted as "a being on whose heart Religion hath set her seal, and over whose head Benevolence hath thrown her mantle," shocking endorsements for a man fictionalized as a vampire but exculpating ideals for the writer of such a fiction. The account concludes didactically: "To do good in secret, and shun the world's applause, is the surest testimony of a virtuous heart and self-approving conscience." The whitewash undoubtedly did more for Polidori's conscience than for Byron's. Whether satanic or angelic, Polidori's molds for Byron are consistently supernatural.

In the strict legal sense, Polidori was not quite a plagiarist because overall he relied more on Byron's person, ideas, and theories than on Byron's precise "mode of expression," protected even in 1819 by copyright law. But when the complete manuscript is considered, Polidori reveals himself, as many weak talents do, as consciously derivative where he ought to be unconsciously creative, and unconsciously imitative where he ought to be consciously independent of Byron and Byron's work. Instead of merely plagiarizing Byron, Polidori appropriates for himself and for his literary work Byron's "insignia" to mask the inadequacies and insignificance he reluctantly recognized in himself. Polidori so wished to be like Byron that he borrowed as he thought Byron borrowed; he exalted himself as he thought Byron did in his parade before his adoring public; he corrected Byron and his critics as indirectly as he thought Byron would have corrected himself, his reviewers, and the inveterate scandal-mongers; he recommended Byron's generosity as imaginatively as he assumed Byron had fictionalized himself; and he depicted Byron as a vampire without realizing that Byron's literary and personal influence had made Polidori one of a different order. Polidori's thefts are too obvious not to be conscious, but the full extent of his envy is not. Unwittingly, Polidori reveals his envy as he records his own suffocation, even his evisceration, in his fictional attack and in his non-fictional personification of his literary and moral model. The ambivalence with which Polidori perceives Byron as both evil and good testifies as much to Polidori's confusion about his own merits and abilities as to his misunderstanding of Byron.

Polidori's reliance on Byron's personality and literary abilities leaves him little if any imaginative space of his own. In the words of J. F. Ferrier on Coleridge, Polidori acts like a wasp or dungfly collecting the juice of flowers; but Byron is a bee, a "genius among flies, because he alone can put out his ideas in the shape of honey, and thereby make the breakfast-table glad." Polidori's plunder of Byron the man and Byron the poet goes beyond plagiarism to the bloodless vampirism of collecting rather than transforming the pollen of Byron's genius. The result is that without Byron, Polidori becomes nothing less than a vampire of an unacknowledged kind. *The Vampyre* with its critical apparatus is far more than a "roman à clef of some complexity" or a "cento of lines" from Byron [James B. Twitchell, *The Living Dead;* Samuel Taylor Coleridge, *Collected Letters*]. Taken as a whole, this first vampire story transforms Polidori's weaknesses into Byron's strengths and Byron's weaknesses into Polidori's strengths. Polidori had every reason to believe that Byron would be flattered by his doctor's clever indictment of his employer's excessive powers of influence and amused by Polidori's exoneration of the model for the vampire. When with Byron, Polidori knew firsthand Byron's reactions to parodies and to fraudulent attributions. In a letter to Rogers (29 July 1816), Byron dismisses Lady Caroline Lamb's *Glenarvon* by quoting Pope's *Horace Imitated,* saying simply "I have read *Glenarvon:* 'From furious Sappho scarce a milder fate /————by her love—or libelled by her hate.'" In a letter to Augusta Leigh, Byron is more caustic:

> If I understand you rightly, you seem to have been apprehensive—or menaced (like every one else) by that infamous Bedlamite [erased] [Caroline Lamb]—If she stirs against you, neither her folly nor her falsehood should or shall protect her. Such a monster as that *has no sex,* and should live no longer.

The novel heightened Byron's reputation as a living Byronic hero, but its caricatures did far more damage to the reputation of Lady Caroline Lamb than to Byron. To my knowledge, Byron said nothing publicly on the matter, though between July 22 and 29 in 1816 he read *Glenarvon* with Polidori, pointing out the truths as well as the vicious excesses of Lady Caroline Lamb's fiction. About the same time, Polidori himself brought to Byron's attention an advertisement for some lyrics attributed to Byron, and, in a letter to John Murray (22 July 1816), Byron responded by giving his publisher authority to write the disclaimer:

> I enclose you an advertisement—which was copied by Dr. P[olidori]—& which appears to be about the most impudent imposition that ever issued from Grub Street.— I need hardly say that I know nothing of all this trash— nor whence it may spring—'Odes to St. Helena— Farewells to England—&c. &c.'—and if it can be disavowed—or is worth disavowing you have full authority to do so.—I never wrote nor conceived a line of any thing of the kind—any more than of two other things with which I was saddled—something about 'Gaul' and another about 'Mrs. La Valette'— and as to the 'Lily of France' I should as soon think of celebrating a turnip.————On the 'morning of my Daughter's birth' I had other things to think of than verses—and should never have dreamed of such an invention—till Mr. Johnston and his pamphlet's advertisement broke in upon me with a new light on the Crafts & subtilties of the Demon of printing—or rather publishing. . . . I can forgive whatever may be said of or against me—but not what they make me say or sing for myself—it is enough to answer for what I have written—but it were too much for Job himself to bear what one has not.

Polidori undoubtedly noticed that Byron delegated the authority to sever himself from association with lame verse and that he ranted in a letter without asking to see the insipid verses ascribed to him. Would he not react similarly when *The Vampyre* came out?

Alas for Polidori, Byron did not sit idly by. In a letter to the editor of Galignani's *Messenger* (27 April 1819), an English newspaper in Paris, Byron unequivocally disavowed authorship of both *The Vampyre* and the account of his residence on Mitylene:

> Neither of these performances are mine—and I presume that it is neither unjust nor ungracious to request that you will favour me by contradicting the advertisement to which I allude.—If the book is clever it would be base to deprive the real writer—whoever he may be— of his honours;—and if stupid—I desire the responsibility of nobody's dullness but my own.—— You will excuse the trouble I give you,—the imputation is of no great importance,—and as long as it was confined to surmises and reports—I should have received it as I have received many others, in Silence.— But the formality of a public advertisement of a book I never wrote—and a residence where I never resided— is a little too much—particularly as I have no notion of the contents of the one—nor the incidents of the other.—I have besides a personal dislike to 'Vampires' and the little acquaintance I have with them would by no means induce me to divulge their secrets.————You did me a much less injury by your paragraphs about 'my devotion' and 'abandonment of Society for the Sake of religion'—which appeared in your Messenger during last Lent;—all of which are not founded on fact————but You see I do not contradict them———— because they are merely personal—whereas the others in some degree concern the reader.

Byron obviously knew vampires of Polidori's sort well, but he adopted the pose of the aggrieved author because at the time he was still waiting for Goethe's long-promised review of *Manfred,* and he knew the rumors of Goethe's suspicion of plagiarism in *Manfred* and immorality in *Don Juan.* Within a few weeks of publishing his official disclaimer of authorship, Byron read *The Vampyre* and all its critical apparatus. Then, in a letter to Murray, dated 15 May 1819, he specifically corrects several points in the *"Extract of a Letter from Geneva,"* including allegations of incest coming from having "two sisters as the partakers of his revels." Byron clearly regards the letter, the introduction to vampirism, the tale, and the account of his residence on Mitylene as coming from Polidori's pen. He calls Polidori's fabrication of life at the Villa Diodati "a blundering piece of exculpation," and he disavows authorship by sending Murray the fragment of his own vampire story as evidence of his own more distinguished prose.

Only after Polidori's death by suicide did Byron, in a conversation with Captain Medwin, admit that Polidori's "story" was his own. He had to disavow the story, he said, because of the absurdly idealized portraits of himself at Diodati and Mitylene:

The foundation of the story *was* mine; but I was forced to disown the publication, lest the world should suppose that I had vanity enough, or was egotist enough, to write in that ridiculous manner about myself.

The "vanity" and "egotism" Byron divorces himself from were precisely Polidori's greatest faults. He had, Byron admitted to Medwin, "entertained too sanguine hopes of literary fame."

Whatever his part in the publishing scam, Polidori did not seem to recognize the ridiculous portraits of himself in either the tale or in its preface and postscript; instead, he worked hard to advertise his own authorship. The day after publication, April 2, Polidori asserted his authorship in letters to the magazine publisher (Henry Colburn), the book publishers (Sherwood, Neely, and Jones), and to the editor of the *Morning Chronicle*. On April 5 Henry Colburn called on Polidori, promised him correction, and gave him a Judas price of thirty pounds, a minuscule sum for the profits of a book that in its first year went into five editions in London and three in both America and France. Curiously, none of these editions named Polidori as sole author though several omitted Byron's name; Colburn wisely changed the title page of his edition to read *The Vampyre; a tale related by Lord Byron to Dr. Polidori*. Modifying the title page could not save Polidori from being branded as "pirate, parasite, and liar" nor did it diminish the popularity of the tale and imitations in print and on stage. Regardless of how the manuscript came into the hands of the publisher, publication over Byron's name had little to do with transmission and everything to do with marketing.

The victimization of John William Polidori is not, in the end, solely his own fault, for he was vamped not only by Byron but also by his own publisher, reviewers, and by critics of the past and present. The suffering he endured from the ignominy of plagiarism guarantees him but a small measure of the fame to which he aspired. In his own right, however, he is an exemplary victim of a strong poet's influence and a vampire of a sort only now heralded.

Judith Barbour (essay date 1989)

SOURCE: "Dr. John William Polidori, Author of *The Vampyre*," in *Imagining Romanticism: Essays on English and Australian Romanticisms*, edited by Deirdre Coleman and Peter Otto, Locust Hill Press, 1992, pp. 85-110.

[*In the following essay, Barbour uses Polidori's* The Vampyre *to explore the figure of the vampire in the Romantic literary imagination.*]

I want to generalize an idea of the Romantic Imagination, in a period example, and as a crisis in authorial self-representation. The dominant trope in John William Polidori's *The Vampyre; a Tale* (1819) is the agon between evenly-matched male protagonist and male antagonist. This turning plot has antecedents in classical mythology and

Hebrew sacred story; even more important in English tradition is the Orphic and Hermetic belief in the travelling, flying or falling, sinking or rising, spirit which perpetuates itself across bodily and material entities and impediments, in a drive to fulfil its self-creating identity in material oblivion. Such a spirit is always proto-masculine in both Greek and Hebrew mythologies. The Orphic action of identity which Polidori fabulates as the bestiary of vampires is a locked flight, a dizzying and interminable jamming together of rival contenders for the material and bodily vehicles and channels of passage for the pre-generative/pregendered drive.

There are two vampires, but they are not father and son: their non-genetic relationship is the irresolute body of the vampire thematized in English Romantic fiction. *Iliad*, XVI, the battle to the death between Sarpedon and Patroklos: "They as two hook-clawed beak-bent vultures . . . go for each other." Next, Hektor against Patroklos, the slayer of Sarpedon, "As a lion overpowers a weariless boar in wild combat." But already Patroklos is finished, "broken by the spear and the god's blow"; Phoibos Apollo it was who "shrouded in a deep mist came in against him / and stood behind him, and struck his back and his broad shoulders." The agon between two equal men is overshadowed by a third who holds sway over the battle. What Homer writes down as Phoibos Apollo has a half-life in battle, and then an afterlife in dream, as Patroklos returns in *Iliad*, XXIII, to tell Achilles what he must do, "For all night long the phantom of unhappy Patroklos / stood over me in lamentation and mourning"; and so, "nine dogs of the table that had belonged to the lord Patroklos . . . / Of these he cut the throats of two, and set them on the pyre; / and so also killed twelve noble sons of the great-hearted Trojans / with the stroke of bronze, and evil were the thoughts in his heart against them."

The aerial battle of locked divinities is an invention of a historical moment—the Bourbon Restoration and the counter-Revolution or White Terror which followed the defeat of Bonaparte in 1815; it is a moment itself in a tropology, a metamorphic drive, which began its Romantic flight in the opening phases of the French Revolution and in the first creative outburst of feminist, democratic, and revisionist literature in the London of the 1790s. During the double but split generations, Revolution to Restoration, the prose fiction written by women, notably Wollstonecraft and Radcliffe, engaged with the aesthetics and sexual politics of the genres of epic poetry and tragic theatre through the mode of the Sublime.

The idea of the Sublime had been eagerly seized on by Dryden, from the mainly French translations of pseudo-Longinus, as the means by which the Protestant Revolution, in the period of its defeat by Restoration, might undergo the Orpheus passage and winter out the regeneration of its drive to identity in action. Cowley and Milton, from opposite factions in the earthly wars, were pitted in the sublime contention for textual and generic mastery, and a post-revolutionary aesthetic of the Sublime was opened.

When Samuel Johnson's "Literature" assumed responsibility for the education of the male youth of England it conserved for a time the platonic secular cult of the beautiful boy. The self-stimulation by beauty as a working of masculine desire, willing a recoil upon itself in order to shape and control the future of its art, provided a pedagogic role for literary educators, and a program of male homo-social congeniality. For first Romantics, William Blake especially, the Hebrew prophecies, and Milton's *Lycidas* and *Paradise Lost* enabled invention to master the contretemps between patriarchal genealogy ("Old" Testament), and the vegetative, sacrificial, and elegiac rites of passage of the chosen son through the material obstructions and bodily realizations of/to male primogeniture ("New" Testament). But pastoral elegy in *Lycidas,* like the "Roast Pork" of Charles Lamb's essay, demands the death of the beloved youth in order to sublimate unconsummated natural desire as cultural resurrection. And the war of Divine Succession in *Paradise Lost,* which tosses Lucifer over the battlements so as to impose the legitimate firstborn Messiah as Logos, is a grim mask of Christian allegory over the homeric tale of Hephaistos, crippled when Zeus pushed him over the ledge for trying to defend his mother from marital rape in Iliad, 1.

Johnson's augustan pact with Plato's scheme of sublimation was periodically refurbished, by Winckelmann to make room for sentimental pedophilia, by Rousseau to invest both roles, tutor and pupil, governor and ephebe, with self-interest. But the jacobin clamour for rights and the feminist claim for female education burst the varnished husk of platonic pedagogy. The belated and over-rehearsed *Biographia Literaria* of S. T. Coleridge reconstituted the platonic program, announcing for the secular theologians of the nineteenth-century academy a definition of cultural work as the education of a male clerisy in and by the propagation of the Christian-platonic Logos. Coleridge abstracted the two poles of the platonic paedia, so as to conflate the engendering thrust and the epiphanic emergence of the word. This bowdlerized version succeeded in the academy, and was ignored by the poets and mythmakers. 1817, the date of *Biographia,* thus forms a coda to a "ghost-story-writing competition" of 1816, in which Mary (Godwin) Shelley's insatiable Demon of Frankenstein and John William Polidori's satiated Vampyre of Lord Ruthven contend the intercourse of superior males under cover of the female darkness and ignorance.

The orthodox division of Old from New, Father from Son, Moses from Joshua, was pieced out by the strategies of the Sublime, formulated with impressive aplomb by Edmund Burke in his *Origin of Our Ideas of the Sublime and Beautiful* of 1757:

> ... there is no spectacle we so eagerly pursue, as that of some uncommon and grievous calamity; so that whether the misfortune is before our eyes, or whether they are turned back to it in history, it always touches with delight. This is not an unmixed delight, but blended with no small uneasiness. ... For sympathy must be considered as a sort of substitution, by which we are put into the place of another man, and affected in many respects as he is affected; so that this passion may either partake of the nature of those which regard self-preservation, and turning upon pain may be a source of the sublime; or it may turn upon ideas of pleasure. . . . Unite the greatest efforts of poetry, painting and music; and when you have collected your audience, just at the moment when their minds are erect with expectation, let it be reported that a state criminal of high rank is on the point of being executed in the adjoining square; in a moment the emptiness of the theatre would demonstrate the comparative weakness of the imitative arts, and proclaim the triumph of the real sympathy.

Burke's topic is the algolagnia so vividly realized in male-authored English fictions from Richardson's Clarissa to Lewis' Monk. Algolagnia crossed the Channel during the Revolution, solaced the Marquis de Sade in his incarceration, and acquired a rationale for the subjection of children and women (masochism) to men (sadism), the pragmatic upshot of the distinction within the aesthetic of the sublime between terror as the active proto-male drive to mastery, and horror as both passive condition and material obstruction and dissipation of the drive (*Aufhebung*).

This hierarchizing of terror and horror, articulated in the discourses of painting, sculpture and theatre by Jakob Lessing, Etienne Falconet, Anton Raphael Mengs, and Johann Heinrich Fuessli (Henry Fuseli), and attached to the neoclassical frame (iconostasis) of "Agamemnon veils his face to kill Iphigenia," was matched with a second strategy of perspectivizing, seen in its simplest expression in Burke's statement that from the outside, or from a distance, or from a safe vantage point, "without being actually in such circumstances," the metamorphic spectacle and metaphoric trope ("turn on") of pain and danger excite a non-passional, exclusively actional, "delight," which is "sublime." Fuseli provided the romantic iconostasis of perspectivized and hierarchized, i.e. sublimed intercourse between supernatural and natural, demonic and erotic, in his celebrated painting *The Nightmare* of 1781. His incubus of the boudoir is part-phallus, part-fetus, and wholly pre-gendered proto-male imposition upon a passive, wilting, but firm-fleshed female body.

The exploitation of the female body in and by horror was embarked on enthusiastically by Lewis for *The Monk* of 1796, and there is still some vulgar horror of the female in Polidori's **Vampyre** of 1819. Lewis is also a first for the combination of Mariolatry and blood, a mélange of anti-papist bigotry, and judaic anxieties about female menstruation and male spills of blood or semen. The "Bleeding Nun" is a voraciously sexed-up apparition, an old woman after a young man, in a parody nightmare, Fuseli's scene avenged. Lewis intensifies the male/female hierarchy of terror/horror as a precaution against this polluting vision, but by turning female horror against the younger man, representative of the son-successor, he only distracts the male victim of male terror. The "Nun's" element is the modern, post-Kantian Sublime of speed; she converts the respectable youth to perpetual motion. Trouble starts when he cannot do it without her. This shift in the tropes exposes the filial male/newcomer to a full female horror, which distracts and exhausts his powers in a mere coping with female flesh (which in aesthetic predications is a decoy and a distraction anyway). He succumbs to a lack or loss of perspective—an unsaying of the father-word through the woman-flesh to the son-word.

By coincidence, Monk Lewis was a house guest at the party in the Villa Diodati, Geneva, which Byron hosted in the summer of 1816. The young John William Polidori, recently engaged in Lord Byron's service as his personal physician, had an opportunity to read *Lycidas* on the scene of its inspiration, or to read *The Monk* in the company of its author. He undoubtedly did both, if not right then, as he was rather preoccupied with introducing the younger-still Mary Godwin to his own literary traditions, the Italian poets of the post-Renaissance, and the Italian patriots of the post-Napoleonic Risorgimento. Mary Godwin took up an interest in things Italian, just as this handsome tutor, who liked her to call him "brother," flung himself into English male games.

In *The Vampyre,* the hierarchical ranking of high male terror and low female horror, capitalized with vulgar precocity by Lewis, is diminished to a studious air of gentlemanliness. The male-to-male relation has sublime terror as its visionary or hallucinogenic text. Polidori moves in to close off recent defections from genre law. Caroline Lamb's infatuated libel on Byron in *Glenarvon* (1816), and even such irresistible productions as Coleridge's *The Rime of the Ancient Mariner* and *Christabel,* all read at Diodati while Polidori was one of the party, he places in isolation from the writing of the new, high, terror. The female body and all its juices is hierarchically subordinated to the male phallic body and its immaterial seminal power. Serial "shes," dimly lit and mute, facilitate repeated vampire strikes between the two male protagonists/antagonists, and each time a female victim is targeted and bled dry, the "dizzying locked flight" of the male duel continues.

The career of this vampire is brief to the point of anorexia. The amniotic barrier between father-and-son perspectives begins to leak, and to bleed into the son's perspective the stain of degendering. After Greece with Lord Ruthven, young Mr. Aubrey falls back from the frontline of action against the vampire, and assumes the domestic incest taboo as protector to his younger sister. The scene returns to conventional English society, where "protector" finds it hard to avoid ironic overtones as a sex-ploy of the patriarchy. The action of Aubrey in overseeing his sister's sexual and social initiation is cleared by the censor, who censures Ruthven's surveillance of both brother and sister. In a closing paroxysm of Aubrey's defenses he takes to exhausting bouts of writing, and by uncanny coincidence of written retrospect and fantasmic contact with the vampire, a spreading tinge of lead and advancing symptoms of internal wastage show that Aubrey has at last maneuvered himself within the exclusively male aura of the vampire.

Motives of prudence which substitute the female decoy/lure at the moment of anticipated strike are supplanted by motives of jealousy as Aubrey finds himself repeatedly

baffled in his desire for direct confrontation with Ruthven by the very female obstacles he has pushed in the path of Ruthven's advance. This marks not the collapse of son-to-father succession, but rather its systemic figural influence of horror and terror. For the succession to collapse entirely, there would have to be a transgressive thrust against the male-female hierarchizing which generates gender and genre, and facilitates the high drive of male-to-male identity through the superior path which at inferior levels is the terminus of the materially reproductive female body.

The writer/teller of the tale moves into confessional for the final episode, and forces the infection of vampirism into Aubrey's face and physique. This simultaneously realigns the female third party, Aubrey's sister, along the axis of the son's perspective in an oedipal confrontation. As the son, Aubrey, converts himself to vampiric libido by desperate self-exposure to the father/vampire (the medium is writing, the tactic is metamorphic and monstrous), so his sister is unmasked as the maternal/daughterly accomplice of Ruthven, seduced by him, abandoning her brother/son to abject horror, but only transferring her person to more such at Ruthven's whim. The catastrophe is posthumous to Aubrey's writing, although predicted by it: "Lord Ruthven had disappeared; and Aubrey's sister had glutted the thirst of a Vampyre!"

Dr. Polidori and Dr. Frankenstein

> April 24 [1816]. I left London . . . with Lord Byron, Scrope Davies Esq and J. Hobhouse, Esq. [*Diary of Dr. John William Polidori*]

The person who wrote *The Vampyre; a Tale,* published in 1819 as "by Lord Byron," was already entitled to sign himself "M.D." in 1815, the year before he wrote the story, but as he was too young at nineteen to obtain a practicing certificate in London, he offered himself, fresh from Edinburgh Medical School, to Byron, as personal physician accompanying his employer to the Continent in 1816. The April 1819 number of *New Monthly Magazine* attached Byron's name to the story, since the vampire of the tale is named "Lord Ruthven." Polidori owed the name as pseudonym for Byron to Caroline Lamb's *Glenarvon* of 1816, and Henry Colburn was both publisher of that novel and editor of the magazine.

In letters to the London papers, Polidori claimed authorship and denied complicity in the libel on Byron, but only tightened the links of association with Byron, by advertising his composition as a completion of a "ghost story" begun by Byron in 1816. The Italian world of letters preserved this connection till the end of the century; a Rome literary gazette in 1881 refers to *The Vampyre* as an anonymous composition "dietro un racconto fatto dal Byron a Ginevra" ["a sequel to a story by Byron composed at Geneva"]. However, Polidori also made reference to the audaciously successful *Frankenstein; or The Modern Prometheus* of 1818, a novel which in 1819 was still generally believed to be the work of Bysshe, not Mary Shelley. And this complicates the tale of origins of the *Vampyre,* since the teller of the tale is not always the owner of it. Polidori's public distance from his publicizer, Colburn, is thus traversed by the spreading rumors of political and sexual association among a group of English expatriates with Byron as their moving spirit. This was the "League of Incest and Atheism," according to the Tory journals, in which Byron and Percy Bysshe Shelley had women in common and wrote in a common cause (Republican Bonapartism).

The risk incurred by Polidori in associating his writing with Byron's was also a gamble that he could write himself into Byron's league, by emulating and casting into the shade the capabilities of the author of *Frankenstein.* It was quite in order for a male author to take out the double honors of copying and denigrating a recent success by a woman. In Mary Shelley's case, the entitling "Author of *Frankenstein*" was withheld by her literary adviser, her father William Godwin, until 1830, on the grounds that *Frankestein's* mass reputation as a "tale of terror" would detract from the serious claims of her historical novel, *Valperga,* for which Godwin had provided materials and from which he expected a financial return. It is now commonplace to hybridize *Frankenstein, Vampyre,* Victor, his Demon, the honorific title Doctor, both young authors, and the model for all their fictional monsters, Byron, himself a polyglot of Milton's Satan and Radcliffe's Montoni. The vampire is an imaginary hybrid bestiary of no genealogy or line of legitimate succession. The Italo-Scottish physician-poet who hybridized the author, Byron, and the text, the Byronic persona, into a tale of the uncanny, the return of the dead father in the living son, is legible only in the superscription "by Lord Byron."

The tale published in 1819 is narrated in the third person of the young protagonist, Aubrey, and his ultimately fatal association with the older aristocrat, Ruthven. The melodramas which were shortly to translate Polidori's original to the Paris stage, gave Aubrey a title to match Ruthven's—"Sir Aubrey"—and this is how the pair of travelling English Milords in the midsection of the story come across—as social equals, but as antagonistic chivalric types. This core relationship of a pair of men in radical conflict is also the starting point of Shelley's *Frankenstein;* but in the revised and amplified edition of 1831 a novelistic infusion of family and sexual relationships devolves the single, central effect of man-to-man confrontation.

Shelley was soon to write in *Mathilda* (1819) a tale of pure imagination, in which the idealized father-daughter relation at the core of Ann Radcliffe's fictions is revised as the agonistic incestuous confrontation of equals. The single step beyond *Frankenstein* is the uncanny return of the repressed father in the daughter's innermost (i.e., interpellated) self. Through her spectral or hysterical pregnancy, the son/son-in-law/innocent foreign suitor, are castrated. Mathilda is not the female mate of the Demon, who failed her resurrection in Scotland; she is, rather, the embodiment of the gap, break, or lapse of genre, between Victor Frankenstein's sublime self-idealization in Chapters 3-10, and the Demon's anarchic counterblast in Chapters 11-16, of *Frankenstein.*

It was Bysshe Shelley in a period of low ebb in 1816, following the birth of sons both to his estranged wife and to his current partner, and before the new friendship with Byron had had its stimulating effect on his writing, who urged Mary Godwin to expand and sublimate her short story into a modern novel. Among the suggestions made by Bysshe for this supplement were the futile flight to Scotland and the creation of a female mate for the Demon of Victor Frankenstein. Mary Shelley obediently set off these actions by "Victor," but in the fiction it is "Victor" himself who aborts them out of spite or fright. The ambivalences of Bysshe Shelley's readings of high sublime terror (for one, he read Plato with a roman-augustan prudishness) are glimpsed in Victor's high-toned philosophizing and his Demon's infantile sadism.

In *Frankenstein* the logic of a difference, and a differential between the two male figures locked at the centre of the tale, have agonistic intensity. Romance chivalry, and class-based sexual adventure, are tautly interwoven with a male adversarial plot. *Frankenstein* reveals, though it cannot judge between, the incompatible idealizations and conflicting identifications of the patriarchal genealogy: sublime terror in the father perspective on his future fulfillment in the son; and a revisionist counter-terror from the claimant to succession and possession in the male line. Shelley had to create for her Demon a pathetic and bathetic utterance which, far from usurping the supremacy of the genitor/male author, as Milton's Satan was forced to do, would persuade the all-powerful father institutionalized in the printed book to create a new and different, but autonomous and equal, human being. This utopian portent in the Demon's self-identifications, the first with the blind, defeated father of the cottage-dwellers, the second with the militant, satanic Victor of Chamouni, permanently too young to be a father, transforms Johnson's augustan fiction of male-male sublimation into the romantic repression of male-male desire, and into female-male difference.

Into Polidori's *Vampyre,* a whole train of borrowed and traditional designs disappears, and reappears marked and scorched by his unacclimatized jealousy and sad lack of English phlegm. Like the Demon of Frankenstein, he has been educated in English literature only to learn a quite un-Sophoclean set of curses. The job he had landed with Byron in 1816 was not the debut into society which his careful parents had wished for him. Sir Henry Halford, whom he approached for a reference, since his thesis had lacked the usual sponsor from within academe, was professionally eminent but also perhaps a risky referee. He had published some novel ideas about "The Influence of Some of the Diseases of the Body on the Mind," which sparked Polidori's interest for his 1815 thesis *De Morbo Oneirodynia* (lit. *"Of the disease of the woe in dreams"*), a study of nightmare, sleepwalking, and audio-visual hallucinations, with an epigraph from the sleepwalking scene in *Macbeth,* and a probing interest in the mind-body link. But Halford was out of Polidori's social orbit. Known to his colleagues as "the eel-backed baronet," he had been "indisputably at the head of London practice" since about 1800, was on Appointment to three English monarchs, and not long after Polidori's reference, succeeded in installing himself as President of the Royal College of Physicians until death ended all his appointments in 1844. If Polidori talked to impress the conversationalists of Diodati with his own professional prospects through his referee, Halford may have entered *Frankenstein* before he sat for *The Vampyre*. Another of Halford's publications is the 1813 "An Account of what appeared on opening the coffin of Charles 1": "He obtained possession of a portion of the fourth cervical vertebra, which had been cut through by the axe, and used it to show at his dinner table as a curiosity." Halford's career of professional elitism, and his handling of the royal martyr's remains, make Victor Frankenstein look good.

Polidori always insisted that he was employed by Byron in April 1816 to accompany his Lordship to the Continent as his personal physician, not as his secretary. Byron himself had a stake in the official description of Polidori's job, since he was modelling his departure for exile on that of Napoleon Bonaparte entering exile in St. Helena, accompanied by a personal physician. Benedictine schoolmasters and Edinburgh University tutors had accustomed Polidori to think very highly of the medical profession, as one in which Roman Catholic men could attain academic and social distinction, albeit not from Oxford or Cambridge. Polidori's diary presents the daily record of a timid but adhesive egoism, embroidering a notation of his parity of claim to social notice, esteem, protection, but above all, to parity of *literature*. The entry for September 5 (1816), "threatened to shoot S[helley] one day on the water," hardly gives away the fact, as it is now accepted, that Polidori had made a financial deal with Byron's publisher, John Murray, to write travelogue gossip about Byron and his friends. Polidori was, in short, a commissioned dealer in Byron literary stocks; but the gossip memoir would be that of a man of parts, a man of letters, among equals.

As soon as the travellers reached the field of Waterloo in Byron's lumbering coach, Polidori wrote to his sister Fanny, and on May 11 to Byron's very grand friend, John Cam Hobhouse, advertising his diagnoses of Byron's state of health, and the regimen under which he intended to place his Lordship. A few days later, to his father, Polidori wrote of "making great advances in the amendment of [Byron's] *corps délabre*." But this professionalism did not stop him from nudging Byron's attention for his own writings, where he was seething for praise. An ominous upset occurred in Dover, as the party with Byron waited to farewell the two travellers. Polidori's Aunt Charlotte later cut up his diary of 1816, and excised what he elsewhere hints was an attempt at suicide from one of his potent little bottles, after Hobhouse and Scrope Davies, not seeing why they should care about his feelings, had "smoked" the improvised performance of his tragedy, *Cajetan,* in manuscript.

This "martyrdom from an unexpected quarter," as real-life demoralization threatens to outdo fictional tragedy,

might have warned Byron that his young physician was reading his part from a hidden script. This was the romantic tale of the father of John William, Gaetano Polidori, who in 1785, "fresh as a drink of water" from his Benedictine schooling, had been employed by the Piedmontese patriot, tragic dramatist, and self-inventive autobiographer, Count Vittorio Alfieri. The relations between melancholy genius and ingenuous youth had been writ large in Alfieri's *Vita scritta da esso,* published posthumously in 1804, had filtered into Gaetano Polidori's amateurish Italian verse romances (published in Soho, London), and formed a family legend of patronage and *noblesse oblige* for the expatriate Polidori clan. In essence, it was a bond of service and reward between an aristocrat of poetry and his middle-class clerk, disciple, and mirror. It preserved an impeccable Italian style of courtliness, for Alfieri modelled each phase of his life story on the examples of Petrarch and Laura, Dante and Beatrice, and the classical tragedies revived by Goethe, while avoiding peremptorily any suggestion of French libertinism. Rousseau's more personal revelations, the French/Swiss cult of the politics of sexuality, were anathema to his patrician self-estimate.

To reinforce himself against modern doubt, Alfieri compressed everything after his thirty-third year into the last third of his autobiography, and lavished on his own portrait as child, adolescent, and youth, the repressed desires and their melancholy fruits which his life had ordered into sublimating fiction. Three strenuous attempts to locate "una mia unica donna" such as Laura/Beatrice, ended in "disinganno orribile," before she was found in the Countess of Albany, married, exiled, "Bonnie" Charles Edward Stuart's nobly burdened wife. Immediately thereafter, Alfieri transferred to his sister and her sons the burden and privilege of his aristocratic lineage, and retired from possessions and procreation to create a unique body of modern Italian, (Tuscan) tragic drama. Before the Napoleonic tide had receded from Italy, there was a liberal, nationalist literary language on its stage. For this enterprise, a complete relearning of a language to write in, Gaetano Polidori was Alfieri's Tuscan tutor, but also "un giovinotto pisano," a young liegeman from an Arrezo family, with a Benedictine schooling from the Pisan academy. Gaetano Polidori's apprenticeship ended properly when Alfieri parted with him to an approved English marriage and a livelihood translating the Italian Renaissance to Soho.

In 1816, untranslatable aspiration to relive his father's romance with the Italian Risorgimento—the Renaissance of the Renaissance—plunged John William Polidori into an unwinnable game with his English contemporaries. Only a few years later, with *Sartor Resartus,* the imaginary intercourse of male poet with male poet, which Polidori had missed so badly in life, became unwritable and anathematized in fiction, under the withering glare of Carlyle's misogyny and homophobia. The spectacle of the good Herr Eckermann as "the grasshopper," mythical bestiality of Tiresias who confessed to woman's sexual pleasure, closes off the prospect opened by Polidori's fabulous parasite. Worse still, the connection with the Edinburgh

Medical School has turned Editor Teufelsdrockh into a ferocious abortionist, plunging his hands again and again into a fat paper bag filled with little scraps of life.

Once Bitten, Never Shy

> "I saw their starv'd lips in the gloam
> With horrid warning/gaped wide (Keats' Letters)

There is a peculiarity about the vampire race—think of it as a kink in their tales—which dominates the telling of their serial half-lives. By the same token, there are no histories of vampires, only mangled autobiographies. A kind of volte-face in the narrative causes whoever is subjected to vampire attack to convert to vampirism and extend the line, spread the infection, or share the self-knowledge of vampire kind. This conversion is not of the Pauline or Augustinian kind, a profound involvement of ego and will which William Wordsworth was to use as a prophylactic against attacks of class and sex remorse. It is rather a spasmodic reversal of perspective, which dislodges the frail ego and frailer will for further falling flight from the centre of its world. The kink, then, or morbid intus-susception, is my theme for Polidori's **Vampyre**; and not the class description or family tree, which Montague Summers (*The Vampire: His Kith and Kin,* 1928) and Christopher Frayling (*The Vampire: Lord Ruthven to Count Dracula,* 1978) compile. Summers' plot of a genealogy, writes Frayling, "succeeded only in showing how difficult it is to define the characteristics which belong exclusively to the vampire." He might well have added that adhesiveness to the idea of genealogy—marriage, virgin bride, male primogeniture, and hoarded monumental wealth inclusive—is itself a mark of the vampire, given its consummate comic expression in Meredith's Sir Willoughby Patterne and his obsession with "my line."

Frayling tabulates vampire occurrences from 1728 (a male vampire who lies on top of dead bodies and bites them, in a devilish parody of the Jahwist's JHWH and Adam), to a Chinese girl vampire of 1913, which returns from the grave to drink the blood of the living, but "unlike its European counterpart . . . does not cause its victims to become vampires in their turn." This Chinese specimen is dated from just after the European "epidemics," in Frayling's note: this does not refer to plague-diseases introduced from the West, but to the waves of oral hysteria which accompany written records of vampires. An infection and pollution of women contextualizes a spectral, esoteric genealogy. The father-drive channels the patriarchal seed to its legitimate destination; but the son-successor recoils on and rebuts the linear directive, and further resorts to narrative excursions (through the female body, through maternal kin, through the "crossed hands" and "blinded eyes" of prophetic election) which bring a Jacob, not an Esau, to head the line.

The unnatural history of the English vampire begins with Thomas Chatterton's early jacobin uprising, *An Excelente Balade of Charitie,* in 1769. The three players in this miniature morality are a beggar and two priests on horseback. The two priests are contrasting chivalric types after *Canterbury Tales,* a glittering Sir Abbott, "His cope was all of Lincoln cloth so fine," and a sobersides limitour (or friar), "His cope and jape were grey, and eke were clean." The beggar is spurned by the first priest, charitably relieved by the second, and invokes an ambiguous judgment, "Or give the mighty will, or give the good man power." This powerful thaumaturge echoes in such Romantic cruxes as "the good want power, / The powerful goodness want" of Percy Bysshe Shelley. Wordsworth shut his ears to it by hearing instead—from Mary Wollstonecraft's *Letters from Sweden*—"The good die first." The democratic political force of Chatterton's plea wanders into elegy, as Wordsworth reads Wollstonecraft, and revives as political idealism as Shelley reads Wollstonecraft. The drooping or "dropping" pilgrim is a veritable apparition of famished want: "Look in his glommèd face, his sprite there scan; / How woe-begone, how withered, forwind, dead!" He may also be a threat to privileged ignorance, though his knowledge is only of death. A hint of Wat Tyler/Robin Hood in the stance of this beggar frightened Horace Walpole. In 1769, Walpole was approached in his very rich and secret life by Chatterton, on the hunt for a patron and a share of the spoils of art. The criminal associate of the vampire is the blackmailer. They have the same trick of mimicking their prey, by hints of a common language, or by insinuations of a shared taste.

This sense of menace in reserve is enhanced by naming the beggar in a string of secret names, or masks of furtive knowledge. Beggar, my term, is nowhere so named: "a hapless pilgrim, the almer, the mist alms craver, the dropping pilgrim." "Varlet . . . faitour" (from the abbott), and "unhaily pilgrim" (from the limitour), do not complete his character but energise his stance. "Haste to thy church-glebe-house, ashrewèd man! / Haste to thy kiste, thy only dortour bed," the implied bystander urges the beggar. The heroic presences in this text are not the players of the scene, but the language and the weather, as a "black tempest swol'n" bursts overhead, and is chased away by a contumacious sun, "And now the sun with the black clouds did strive, / And shetting on the ground his glary ray;" the abbot "spurred his steed," leaving the grammatical subject of "shetting" a puzzle for the jacobinical reader. These elemental energies imbue the mask of poverty and the mask of privilege with a splendid antagonism, which diminishes the charitable friar to the limiting role of middle-class conscience. Instead of a middle, human ground, the centre of the stage presents the caparisoned horse of the aristocratic younger son/Abbott: "The trammels of his palfrey pleased his sight, / For the horse-milliner his head with roses dight." Chatterton plays on "milliner" for (female) prostitute; the overdetermined image functions as elegant arabesque and as sign of the surplus economy which is art/which "Art" is.

The vampire image maintains unstable associations with a class threat identified as resentment from both sides of the class barrier, but turbulent and spasmodic in expression, since the psychology of resentment is ambivalent dejection. Frayling chronicles a drift away from peasant types and superstitions, and a vampire rising towards "aristocratic settings." But Romanticism did not merely scrub up the vampire from Chatterton's rustic democrat to Southey's haunted highborn Thalaba. Chatterton's text already has the makings of an intimate exchange of energies, as well as of an elemental electricity of antagonism, between the beggar and the aristocrat. This leaves the reformist conscience in the middle of nowhere.

Wordsworth's "The Leechgatherer" of 1802, in Chatterton's (and Spenser's) ballad metre, is a masterly renovation and exquisite hollowing out of Chatterton. The "marvellous Boy" Chatterton, in bad company with older and bolder Burns, is consigned to a pre-Shakespearean wildness, like that of Marlowe's Faustus: "Cut is the branch that should have grown full straight." Prepotent, mythic virility is these singers' prelingual air, and the Wordsworth poet pays them their history as his own autobiography. The old man who confronts the poet, in fact and in Dorothy Wordsworth's journal account a beggar, is drawn into the human middle to be relieved of his burden of language for a survival in strength. Amid other reversals of image and meaning, the middle of the way as the poet contemplates marriage and his thirty-third year is replenished with extreme youth, extreme age, the antediluvian past and the apocalyptic future, and yet all simply is, there to be read, as Gray had read the stones of the "mute, inglorious Milton" of Stoke Poges.

Of the postwar Romantics, Keats could not, in spite of his hopes, find again a Chatterton whose reserve of power could crest Wordsworth's melting class/language harmonies. Keats knew enough to know that he had to plunge deeper than Wordsworth himself, in a bid to repeat what had bidden Wordsworth to outbid Prospero's sea-plunge. "La Belle Dame sans Merci" of April 1819 (the same month as *The Vampyre*) drops resentment for melancholy, as the "knight-at-arms" reveals his doom at the hands of wild child woman and the infernal fathers. But this tangent of sex guilt from class anger was then trimmed back by Leigh Hunt, who changed the chivalrous hail, "Oh, what can ail . . . ?" (to the "knight-at-arms") for the opprobrious salute, "Oh, what can ail thee, wretched wight?" For his pains, Keats has fetched Chatterton's hapless proletarian, "Poor in his view, ungentle in his weed / Long bretful of the miseries of need," just from the wayside to the poor-house.

Byron shakes off the claims of Sassenach imaginary politics to return to Southey's swashbuckler vampire of *Thalaba* (1798), and Radcliffe's Montoni from *The Mysteries of Udolpho* (1794), whose disaffections are satanic, highmettled, and, above all, continent of words: since words stoop to serve desire. The theatrical pose of folded arms, made famous by Napoleon, puts the Byron persona above the question and keeps his name out of lesser mouths. Caroline Lamb hurls her novel *Glenarvon* at this figure of impassivity, and Polidori does not need to be very clever to frame her in this futile gesture. His opening gambit in *The Vampyre* is to wedge himself, as social equal and male fellow-traveller, between Lord Ruthven and Lady Mercer. Hauteur stares down impertinence. But Byron in life refused the gesture; and Polidori in writing is incapa-

ble of the pertinent egoism which views the social comedy or the battlefield with folded arms.

The unlikely couple, John William Polidori and Caroline Lamb, brought to its close in their Man of Moods, Lord Ruthven of Glenarvon, a triennial cycle (1816-19) of clerkly treason to the cause of democratic and women's rights. Ruthven incarnates the enemies of the bourgeoisie in one booted package, and nullifies them all at the same time. His hunger can only be insatiable greed, his pride can only be aristocratic arrogance, and his sexuality can only be lustful violence. Lamb and Polidori share these views of Ruthven from beneath his bootsole. The rhetoric of English liberty, which Chatterton had splendidly voiced in 1769, suffered massive censorship in the reaction against Jacobinism which made a monster of the French uprising. Anger and fear agitate the depths of Dr. Frankenstein, but hardly ripple the surface of Lord Ruthven. Political conflict has been smoothly incorporated into a moral scheme of righteous resentment. No social claim touches Ruthven, so jealously guarded by his inventors; but no individual claim touches him either, for he is imperviously exterior. The punishments of life—old age, disease, impotence, death—cannot be aimed or deflected by an allegory where one's fellow-author is the very devil.

Document 1. Fragment of a Novel (1816)

The only fragment of autographed autobiography of a certified Vampire in English is *Fragment of a Novel* (1816), published by particular request of its author, Lord Byron, by his publishers, John Murray of Albemarle Street, as an attachment to Byron's verse tale *Mazeppa* in 1819.

Byron chose to publish this fragment as a way of declining an offer of authorship of a prose tale, *The Vampyre,* published earlier in 1819, but publicly acknowledged by one Dr. John William Polidori as having been written by himself, in completion of a sketch, or broken-off attempt, at a tale of terror, by his Lordship. Marion Campbell has made an interesting opening on the topic of one man's completion of another man's text. In her example, Chapman's completion of Marlowe's *Hero and Leander,* the editorial thrust in Marlowe's colophon, "Desunt Nonnulla" ("not a jot is lacking"), announces the male master who fathers on the female text a phallic completion, "hangs a hook on it," in vulgar parlance.

According to Polidori, it had been at Byron's suggestion that a house party of English tourists in Geneva, in the summer of 1816, should compete with each other to produce a tale of "ghosts." Polidori was later to be backed up in this part of his statement by Mary Shelley, in her Author's Introduction to the third edition of *Frankenstein* in 1831. But no one other than Polidori himself ever declared that Byron's prose tale was to be the tale of a vampire; and Byron took full advantage of his right of retort in print, to expunge from the published *Fragment* in 1819 any telltale marks of the beast.

Here is how Polidori recalled in print his impression of Byron's recital: "It depended for interest upon the circumstance of two friends leaving England, and one dying in Greece, the other finding him alive, upon his return, and making love to his sister." It was naughty of Byron to publish the take without that last precautionary phase. He had other uses for it than to censor his homosexual scene of action.

The story begun by Byron on June 17, 1816, was well-calculated to make Polidori writhe, though for no better reason than that its so-English assumptions of confidence between two Englishmen, "we had been educated at the same schools and university," probed the wound of his half-English antecedents. The narrator is the younger man, over whom the older man, Augustus Darvell, a sitting portrait of Byron, has obtained an effortless ascendancy, yet an ascendancy so beautifully sublimated by both that it leaves the younger man in undisputed self-possession. At ease within a network of shared pedagogical assumptions the two men linger over the omens that Darvell's natural death is fast approaching, but that he has sown the seed of his preternatural return from natural death in the willing apprehension of his youthful companion. It was perhaps Polidori's greatest mistake to kill his vampire, Ruthven, with a stray bullet from an ambush. It surely has to be the internal ebbing of the phallic father which seeks and finds both release and a flood-tide of renewed identity in the vehicle-body of the chosen successor.

For his Vampyre, Polidori wilfully misreads his alter ego, worthy Aubrey, into the part for the younger man of Byron's pair, obviously designed by Byron for Bysshe Shelley. Polidori is in too much of a rush to note that the name "Augustus" may be bequeathed by the fictional Darvell to Darvell's *ephebe,* as that of his spirit-bride, "Augusta." Evidently, Polidori read fictional genders as natural. Augustus and (is it?) Augusta in Byron seal a solemn pact by glancing aside together at a fabulous chimera, a stork with a snake in its beak, before the older man gracefully dies. Canto 1 of Percy Bysshe Shelley's *The Revolt of Islam,* first published as *Laon and Cythna* in late 1817, bore into print the first fruits of Shelley's friendship with Byron. The story gives redirection to the pact sealed between Augustus and his *ephebe,* into the fabulous chimera of aerial locked flight between a Bonaparte imperial eagle and a Demogorgon anarchist/feminist snake, followed by a brother-sister (homosocial but heterosexual) love-death. But this utopian elaboration is less uncanny than Byron's fragment, since the defeated snake, who falls into a boat and onto a bosom, is able to replenish itself heterosexually, taking the male part with a real woman. *Mazeppa* in 1819 refuses Bysshe's utopian vision of the female and democratic replenisher; Mazeppa's maddened horse carries its rider beyond what the West can seemingly desire.

On the evening following Byron's storytelling, and (if Polidori got the dates and anecdotes in his diary straight), while the invitation from Byron to join him in a pact against Western bourgeois chivalry was still ringing in a number of ears, Bysshe Shelley startled them all by seeing a vision of a woman "he had heard of who had eyes instead of nipples." Polidori, for once mindful of what he

was there for, administered a slosh of cold water and a dose of ether to the shrieking poet. In return, Bysshe Shelley let Polidori into his own life-history, for their recorded "conversation (June 15) about principles" moved on . . . to more confidential exchanges: "He married; and a friend of his liking his wife, he tried all he could to induce her to like him in turn. He is surrounded by friends who feed upon him, and draw upon him as their banker."

This wet summer of 1816 saw Polidori agog at the relationships, seen and guessed at, between Byron, Shelley, and the two stepsisters (Mary Godwin and Claire Clairmont) accompanying Shelley—"one of them LB's." Polidori could not hope to control the right tone for that "friend of his liking his wife, he tried all he could to induce her to like him in turn." Nor could he penetrate the magic circle, or tough outer hide, which the two English men enjoyed together, and together teased him with, while the two young women lent themselves to party games. *The Vampyre* scrambles together the torment and titillation of all these half-confessions, half-confidences, insidiously half-meant invitations. None was more insidious than the "curse of Hassan's mother on the Giaour" in Byron's verse-tale of 1813, *The Giaour.* This terrific curse turns the pale stranger for the duration of its spell into a Vampire dripping with blood from the mouth where he has sucked dry his sister, wife, and daughter. Terrific it is, but it is well-guarded against fundamentalist or autobiographical interpretations, since it is in the high sublime genre of prosopopeia, a self-destroying impersonation, whose generic origins lie in the curse-prophecy before battle; the bestknown example is the doubled-back curse on the mother of Sisera in the prosopopeia of the prophetess Deborah in *Judges,* 5. Polidori fell into a gambler's trap when he read this vampire aria in verse as an invitation to respond in kind and in person.

A muffed game, and the exacerbation of his unsporting instincts which resulted, can still be discerned in his text of 1819. The libel of the "vampire" tag on Byron's public reputation is extravagant. The supreme fiction of terror within the gossip fiction of the "tale of terror" persists in eluding and refusing itself to its self-mutilating pursuer. English male poets needed only to "look askance" at certain figures, fabulous chimeras or imaginary bestialities, like Coleridge's lesbian snake and dove; "And with the dove it heaves and stirs / Swelling its neck as she swells hers." Polidori could not leave off until he had caught, full in the face, Byron's meaning when he read those lines and Shelley's feelings when he rushed shrieking from the room on hearing them. The very figures designed to confabulate unspoken feelings and missing meanings, assumed for Polidori the aspects of both insult and threat.

Document 2. The Vampyre; a Tale (1819)

The first full-blown vampire strike in English is this, from ***The Vampyre; a Tale,*** by Dr. John William Polidori:

> He shut his eyes, hoping that it was but a vision arising
> from his disturbed imagination; but he again saw the

same form, when he unclosed them, stretched by his side. There was no colour upon her cheek, not even upon her lip; yet there was a stillness about her face that seemed almost as attaching as the life that once dwelt there:—upon her neck and breast was blood, and upon her throat were the marks of teeth having opened the vein:—to this the men pointed, crying, simultaneously struck with horror, "A Vampyre! a Vampyre!"

The disturbance of imagination brought on by vampire attack is horror, the greater of two evils, but the inferior aesthetic effect, in the idea of the sublime after Edmund Burke. Horror exposes the human subject to insult, and demoralizes a captive audience with the taste of their own decay. In the episode recounted, the local peasants are struck in common ("simultaneously") with panic; horror is endemic in the ignorant classes, who provide its victims while they circulate its effects. These peasants have blundered in on an encounter of sublime terror enacted by two socially superior men, English milords in the wild hinterland of Greece, c. 1813. As Greek peasants in Turkish territory, their intrusion is not a vigilante raid but an unorchestrated chorus of victimized, impotent serfs. The female victim of ritual murder to whose corpse they attach the label of horror is a local Greek peasant girl, Ianthe, and femaleness is a metonym for their common castration, as they move in, "the glare of many torches penetrating through the hole that gave light in the day," and fail to catch the perpetrator of terror. Horror is only the aftermath, the incurable symptom, of terror, and the name "Vampyre" does not lead from the visible corpse back to the invisible striker. The slightly unidiomatic "attaching" is a catachresis—"almost as attacking"—to square the circular, fugitive links between "the lifeless corpse . . . stretched at his side," and the fatal blow which stretched her thus. The difference between a living and a dead body is metonymized as the parallel stretching of a live male viewer and a female corpse whom he struggles to see as the carrier of an effectual, saving difference, a different fate for the female body in horror.

The problem of representation which is least negotiable is that of the living human body as the same body dead. Paul de Man argues that representation is captive to belatedness, that textual inscription and literal-graphic inditing are always out of synchronicity. The sense of a blow always already fallen in textual inscription, and of an archaic impress of things in character (E. R. Dodds's sense of the Homeric *ate,* the "cry" of this or that character), absents meaning from the terms of nostalgia or amelioration between dead body and late living person. The literal mark of deposition is a defacing and disfiguring continuum in the launching and the landing of an unmitigated difference.

Inside the scene of horror, the Englishman Aubrey shuts and opens his eyes as his only active contribution to his own rescue from horror; and in the struggle against discomposure / decomposition, he is able to levitate his active, ongoing consciousness above the inanimate female corpse at his side, and grope his way back to daylight consciousness and the upright stance of masculine reason. Aubrey pays his dues to nostalgia, "of her who had lately been to him the object of so many bright and fairy visions, now fallen with the flower of life that had died within her"; and to class and gender guilt, "When [the girl's parents] ascertained the cause of their child's death, they looked at Aubrey, and pointed to the corpse. They were inconsolable; both died broken-hearted." But he is only superficially engaged in this duel of ironies, of self-absentings and self-presentings. Truly speaking, he has been brought back unwillingly from the psychic flight and secret dreaming of terrible power; his lip-service to the mutilated corpse simply stands in for impotent straining after the vanished antagonist. He, no more than the dead woman, can attach, let alone attack, the terror which took its flight as soon as "help" (really, helplessness) broke in.

The elaborate anatomizing of the corpse's symptoms/stigmata—showy blood, secretive holes and ambiguous marks ("of teeth having opened the vein") is an irony to overmaster his precautions, as he pores over the exterior of a female body in ignorance of the internal takeover of his own consciousness. The narrative underlines this ironic inference by reversing (at this mid-point in the tale) the relationship between the younger Englishman and his somewhat older travelling companion, Lord Ruthven. Aubrey hitherto has studied Ruthven, indeed understudied him, in an effort to polish his own social presence, but also with a view to checking and reforming Ruthven's morals. After the death of Ianthe, Aubrey has lost the initiative with Ruthven, and discovers that every move he makes is shadowed by Ruthven, so that Aubrey's moves have in effect become mere feints. The girl's body has performed as lure for the vampire to attack; but it has also performed as lure for Aubrey to anatomize, and by switching his gaze from Ruthven to Ianthe, far from searching out in her the leads back to her attacker, Aubrey has exposed his own back to infiltration by terror.

This climactic episode in the vampire's den spans a double-scene of sublime male-male terror and sublime male-female horror. The sequence of reading from pages 14 to 15 is misleading, since it overcomes the gap between terror and horror, as Aubrey consciously struggles to overcome it, but as it may not in truth be overcome by any continuing self-conscious narration. The realm of terror is sealed off from the aftermath in the scene of horror by Aubrey's very struggles to retain his priority of seeing over the dead woman. He only sets self-preservation in motion, and is released to levitate to normal consciousness and its conventional class and gender superiorities.

John William Polidori was never in Greece; Byron's *The Giaour* of 1813 provides a sketchy pretext for the Greek scenes in ***The Vampyre;*** and Aubrey's action in leading the way to Greece for Ruthven to follow may be seen both as a retort to the Giaour's political pretensions to act Messiah for the Greek nation, and as a relief mechanism for having to portray Aubrey as an Englishman ignorant of European Continental high culture. The ambiguous status of Englishmen travelling on Turkish firmans in occupied Greece becomes for Polidori's fiction a double-sided chiasmic play of sameness and difference. Aubrey and Ruthven are both foreigners in this territory, and Aubrey's need to reestablish the shattered conventions which will ensure that he survives the vampire attack, makes it impossible that he should win back to the scene in which he confronted the terror as an equal and intimate; since the confrontation is inconceivable in the local terms which are the only guarantee of Englishmen's safe passage. Aubrey must cling to his common Englishness and common maleness with Ruthven in order to survive the panic horror, and get by on difference from the locals.

As Aubrey moves toward the woodman's hovel, "Suddenly his horse took flight, and he was carried with dreadful rapidity through the entangled forest"; but when the vampire assailant is disturbed, his impact in flight has a stunning violence: "he instantly rose, and, leaving his prey, rushed through the door, and in a moment the crashing of the branches, as he broke through the wood, was no longer heard." This is a flight in full phallic intactness, and for Aubrey's mere horse, the assailant assumes the form of a centaur, as in Byron's *Mazeppa*. Within the hovel, stunningly loud and interrupted noise, pitch blackness, and the sudden glare of lights, stifling pressure under the assailant, and the sudden rush with which he evacuates the scene (this last a motif of Fuseli's vampire paintings), are an ensemble of effects of the Burkean sublime, working as sensations/deprivations of sense, to increase the pressure against consciousness, and lift the threshhold of deafness and blindness. As well, these flickering sensations have psychological value as correlates of Aubrey's abysmal experience with the terror of confrontation and the horror of impotence: "Aubrey, incapable of moving, was soon heard from without." For just one step in the dark two male antagonists grapple: "He found himself in contact with someone . . . his enemy threw himself upon him, and kneeling upon his breast, had placed his hands upon his throat—when . . . " and the eye begins to see once more in horror.

Crucially, the scene of terror is a coitus interruptus, a sex-gender copulation, always interruptedly taking place between two parties and a shadowy third. It is only in the aftermath that three identifiable persons are segregated as raped, dead female, male rapist/murderer fled, and stunned male would-be rescuer. And this is the recit, the accountable retrospect, permitted to Aubrey after he has drifted back up to the daylight world of mortal bodies and heterosexual arrangements. The aesthetic pointing of the sublime scenario renders an illusion of movement from the noise/darkness/action of male terror, to the daylight/immobilized/bloodied body of female horror. The male protagonist, always the "hither side" of narratorial space, experiences the guilty relief of passive intactness at the sight of the scapegoated female body. The aporia or gap of astonishment, cutting off this invalid Aubrey from his aphrodisiac antagonist, gapes wide as vampire and vampire-hunter recoil into defensive mutual repressions. An immobile levitation for Aubrey is in illusory interchange with the backward charge of the vampire through the thickets. I recall the climax of Beckford's *Vathek,* as male

and female demoniacs spring apart into separate cauldrons of energetic hatred. The continuation past this point of Polidori's tale is a failure of conception. The equality with Ruthven sought by Aubrey has now arrived for him, as surely as for the seekers of *Vathek,* yet the knell of self-recognition (in *Vathek,* the yell!) never sounds; the voracious mouth of the vampire gapes forever where Aubrey cannot see it.

Byronic influence on the first vampire in English literature:

In one important way, Byron's presence in the introduction of the vampire into popular culture should not go unnoticed. Byron, no doubt inadvertently, first coupled the folklore nosferatu with his own magnificent creation—himself. The character of the Byronic hero, that lusty libertine in the open shirt that Byron made such a part of his verse dramas and life dramas, is simply the vampire with a pedigree. This figure is the eternal searcher for sexual happiness, even if he has to destroy women in the process. Before Bram Stoker finally transformed the barbaric nosferatu into the suave Dracula, Byron had already started the metamorphosis. Polidori may even have realized this, for he consciously patterned Ruthven (a name already coined by Lady Caroline Lamb to satirize Byron in her novel *Glenarvon*) on Byron in order to take a poke at his erstwhile employer. On one level *The Vampyre* is clearly a roman à clef with the innocent Aubrey being Polidori himself.

James B. Twitchell, in Dreadful Pleasures: An Anatomy of Modern Horror, *Oxford University Press, 1985.*

D. L. Macdonald (essay date 1991)

SOURCE: *"Ernestus Berchtold; or, The Modern Oedipus,"* in *Poor Polidori: A Critical Biography of the Author of "The Vampyre,"* University of Toronto Press, 1991, pp. 204-23.

[*In the first full-length critical biography of Polidori, Macdonald acknowledges Polidori's marginal status as a literary figure, but suggests that Polidori's life and works, as well as his relationships with more renowned contemporaries, are worthy of scholarly study. In the following excerpt from that work, Macdonald examines the novel* Ernestus Berchtold.]

Most of *Ernestus Berchtold* is made up of the oral autobiography, or confession, of the younger of the two title characters. It begins in 1778, with the arrival of his mother and an elderly male companion in Beatenberg, a village north of the Thunersee (Polidori passed it on his walk to Milan in 1816). The village priest takes the travellers in. The old man, who has been wounded, dies; the woman, who is pregnant, gives birth to twins, a boy and a girl, and then also dies. Their only servant runs away, taking with him everything but a locket containing a portrait of the mother. Since there is no hope of tracing the family of the orphans, the priest gives them to his sister to raise. The boy is named after him; the girl is named Julia.

Young Ernestus grows up among the grim sublimities of the Swiss landscape. He rarely visits the nearby towns, having little sympathy for 'the petty interests, which pervade human breasts in the narrow sphere of a miserable provincial town' (this looks like an allusion to Polidori's experiences in the narrow sphere of Norwich).

Father Berchtold takes charge of the boy's education, and inspires him, as Polidori declared his own father had inspired him, with tales of the classical heroes. Looking back, Ernestus realizes: 'there was a material defect in my education . . . my imagination was stimulated, while my judgment was not called forth, and I was taught to admire public instead of private virtues.' The unfortunate consequences of this defect are not immediately apparent. When word of the French Revolution reaches the village, Ernestus, like Polidori under the influence of Byron, is momentarily inspired, but the French intervention in Switzerland soon disillusions him—and gives him an occasion to practise the public virtues of the ancients.

The priest does his best to restrain Ernestus's patriotic enthusiasm, arguing that 'in consequence of the tardiness and imbecility of the rulers of Switzerland, in spite of the courage and daring of its peasantry, it was doomed to become an easy prey to France,' a judgment which reflects Polidori's disillusionment with the government of Geneva in 1816, rather than the situation in 1798. At that time, there were actually popular unrisings against the governments of a number of the cantons, including that of Bern, in which Beatenberg is situated. The French certainly encouraged these uprisings, but they did not originate them. Only after a number had occurred did they intervene to establish the Helvetic Republic.

Ernestus follows the advice of the older Berchtold until one day, when he is out hunting chamois, he hears a young woman singing:

> In unison with my feelings at that moment, the notes sometimes broke out into the wildest tones of defiance; at others, suddenly sinking, they seemed uncertain and soothing. I dared not look around; I felt as if entranced, and I imagined I heard the voice of these mountains, mocking the invaders, then sinking into despondence.

She approaches with her father. Their names (though we do not learn them until much later) are Louisa and Count Filiberto Doni. Although they are Italians, Louisa asks Ernestus why he is idle when his country needs him. Ernestus immediately determines to join the forces of resistance.

Again, this is only marginally relevant to the historical situation. Switzerland did not really exist as a country in 1798; it was more independent than Italy, but not much more united. The cantons were more or less autonomous.

It was the supporters of the Helvetic republic and of the French who advocated a unitary state; the cantons that resisted did so because they did not wish to be included. No one supposed that in the Europe of 1798, such resistance would mean independence; everyone realized, as Talleyrand remarked, that 'Switzerland today must be either Austrian or French.' It is strange that Polidori, hater of Austrians and lover of ambivalence, should pass over this; he may simply have been unaware of it.

The rest of the first part of the novel is devoted to Ernestus's adventures in the unsuccessful campaign against the French and their supporters. It is based largely on the stories Polidori heard from the old Swiss priest who also provided a model for the older Berchtold. Distortions and all, it is an effective and unsentimental piece of military fiction, reminiscent of Polidori's account of his battle against the six Genevan carters.

Ernestus is decorated for valour; he twice saves the life of a young Italian volunteer, Olivieri, who (as we learn much later) is Louisa's brother. Ernestus is captured and escapes; finally, when all is lost, he is betrayed, captured again, and imprisoned in the Château de Chillon—'once the prison of Bonniva, now destined to be my own,' as he explains for the benefit of readers who may have forgotten the relationship between Polidori and Byron. Louisa manages to have a knife and a file smuggled into the prison and a boat left below its walls, and Ernestus escapes. Despite the danger, he returns to Beatenberg, only to find that Father Berchtold has died and that he and Julia have been invited to live with the Doni family in Milan.

With the move to Milan, the novel turns from the military and the political, and the public virtues Ernestus has acquired from his education, to the domestic and familial, and the private virtues he has yet to acquire. It does not even mention the waves of invasion, revolution, and counter-revolution that washed back and forth across Lombardy at the turn of the century. (Olivieri later joins a gang of Gothic banditti, not a lodge of Carbonari.)

The spirit of her mother has begun appearing to Julia in dreams, warning her obscurely of some danger that threatens her and Ernestus. But at first all seems to go well. Doni, who is not only extremely rich but also generous and wise, supervises Ernestus's neglected education; Ernestus spends most of his time reading with Louisa, and their love for each other naturally grows.

In the evenings they attend the salon of Doni, who is careful not to allow the conversation to be wasted on trivialities, directing it instead to such topics as the existence and powers of God and of spirits, or the reality and nature of virtue. These high-minded seminars, however, paradoxically begin to undermine Ernestus's morale because of the defects of his education: 'Berchtold had educated me in doctrines, without teaching me the foundation upon which they were built; he thought it impiety to question them.' Now that he hears them questioned nightly, he is confused and distressed. He confides his perplexities to Louisa and Julia; Louisa is able to assuage them, but Julia comes to share them.

He also begins to come under the influence of Olivieri, who appears to less advantage in the salons of Milan than on the battlefields of Switzerland—and who appears to be another caricature of Byron, less grotesque than Lord Ruthven but in some ways even less pleasant (Polidori's portrayal of him anticipates in detail Mary Shelley's portrayal of the Byronic Lord Raymond in *The Last Man* [1826]):

> whether it were that he had constantly met with mean and weak companions, or that conscious of his own bad qualities, he had thence estimated the value of man's professions, he always seemed to view the human character in a darker hue than was warranted by truth, and to have formed his mind into a general contempt for mankind as a mass, and a determination, if ever an occasion offered, of rising at their expence, considering them but as tools to work with. His manners were at first always engaging, and rather pleasing, but this seemed irksome to him, and he gave way to an imperious, assuming air in conversation, which soon disgusted his friends. His ideas of a life after death seemed strangely childish, he did not believe in an immortality, yet he had so strong a love of fame, that there was no reputation he did not covet. He sometimes formed visions of a throne raised upon the blood of his countrymen spilt in civil war; at times, of the fame of a benefactor to debtors and galley slaves. He sought at the same time for the applause of the philosophers and the drunkard, the divine, and the libertine. Things, of which, even at the moment of action he was ashamed, were often done by him in the view of proving himself capable of excelling even in vice.

Olivieri cannot bear to be excelled in virtue any more than in vice. Doni often holds Ernestus, up to him as an example, so Olivieri decides to corrupt him. Thus the relationship between Ernestus and Olivieri matches that between Aubrey and Ruthven: in both cases, a naive young man travels into a foreign country and comes under the influence of an older and more sophisticated but evil companion. This recalls, from Polidori's point of view, the relations between Polidori and Byron, but the naive young hero and the sophisticated older villain are also wholly conventional Gothic characters.

Ernestus is safe from Olivieri as long as he is also under the influence of Louisa, but eventually she is called away to attend a sick relative, and Olivieri takes Ernestus to La Scala. There he gets into less spectacular but more serious trouble than Polidori did. First he grows accustomed to loose company; then he begins to gamble; finally, deeply in debt and in despair, he takes to drinking and debauchery.

When Louisa returns, she begs Ernestus to reform, but he does not dare ask Doni for enough money to pay off all his debts. Olivieri tempts him into trying his luck just once more—'as I acknowledged myself incapable of paying the whole, it would be as well to owe a greater as a

lesser sum'—and soon he is more deeply entangled than ever. Polidori's account of the temptation, fall, reform, and relapse of Ernestus the gambler makes painful reading: whether or not it is based on his own experience, it gives a plausible and vivid portrayal of the process that a compulsive gambler of our time has described as 'diluted suicide.' This slow death is, like the compulsive travelling of the vampire, a demonstration of life. (Byron, though not a great gambler himself, remarked: 'I have a notion that Gamblers are as happy as most people—being always *excited*;—women—wine—fame—the table—even Ambition—*sate* now & then—but every turn of the card—& cast of the dice—keeps the Gambler alive—besides one can Game ten times longer than one can do any thing else.') Its intense and exclusive focus on the present moment, its repetitiousness and inconsequentiality (faro, the game mentioned in both *The Vampyre* and *Ernestus Berchtold,* is among the simplest and most repetitious of card games) also function as a denial of continuity, and so as a defence against the horror of incest, which is contingent on the continuities of kinship.

In the depths of his addiction, Ernestus begins to suspect that Louisa, whom he has given little enough reason to remain faithful to him, may have fallen in love with Count Wilhelm, a German visitor to the city. His suspicions prove to be unfounded; in fact, Count Wilhelm contributes almost nothing to the plot of the novel. Instead (as the *Literary Gazette* pointed out), he functions as yet another caricature of Byron. Polidori's continual harping on his troubled relationship with his employer suggests the compulsive self-exposure characteristic of melancholia—and, like the latter, it contains an element of aggression, for it allows him to expose Byron too. Wilhelm is not monstrous, like Ruthven, or even immoral, like Olivieri; he is only insufferable:

> He was speaking with elegance upon the fallen glories of some sunken nation; when he had ended, and the conversation had became more general, he raised his eyes, and affecting surprize, he seemed ashamed of having attracted so much notice, though he did not blush, for the hue of his features seemed invariable. He retreated to a corner of the room, left vacant by the pressure of the company towards the spot he had just occupied. He there bent down his head, as if abstracted in thought; but looking under his eye-brows, he was evidently engaged in remarking the effect he had made upon the company. He again gradually got a circle round him, and again was apparently carried away by the great powers of his mind, and held forth upon some subject, and then once more retreated.

Wilhelm's elegant moralizing over the fallen glories of sunken nations alludes satirically to *Childe Harold* and also, perhaps, to Gaetano's insistence on a classical education for his sons.

Instead of falling in love with Wilhelm, Louisa has fallen ill with consumption. Afraid that she is dying, Doni agrees to her plea that he pay Ernestus's debts again, and Ernestus reforms again, this time for good. Doni forgives him. Then, to their surprise, Ernestus and Julia happen to see

Doni talking with a spirit. They have heard rumours that he is a magician, and that this is the source of his immense wealth. Now they know the rumours to be true.

Julia, it turns out, has been seduced and abandoned by Olivieri. She spies on Doni in the hope of learning the secret of his magic power and of using it to win back her lover. This is the only incident in the novel that bears even the slightest resemblance to Mary Shelley's anecdote 'about a skull-headed lady, who was so punished for peeping through a keyhole.' But Julia does not peep through a key-hole, and, as W. M. Rossetti remarks, 'Her head, after this inspection, remains exactly what it was before.' She does learn Doni's secret, but the spirits refuse to help her on the grounds that she is already damned for her affair with Olivieri, and so has nothing to offer them.

Julia and Olivieri both disappear. Julia has a child, and, dying, she sends for Ernestus to ask him to take care of it. She lives only long enough to tell him her story. Olivieri becomes the leader of a gang of banditti near Strasbourg, where he is captured. Ernestus tries to rescue him, but Olivieri is fatally wounded during their escape. He lives only long enough to hear that Julia and Ernestus have both forgiven him.

All these disasters have aggravated Louisa's illness, but finally, after another pointless contretemps with Count Wilhelm, she and Ernestus are married. They secretly order portraits of Doni and of Ernestus's mother (the latter based on the picture in the locket), thinking that Doni will be pleasantly surprised. He is certainly surprised: he recognizes the portrait of Ernestus's mother and collapses. He lives long enough to write his confessions. Ernestus reads them, and gives Louisa the merest hint of their contents; the shock is too much for her.

At this point, Ernestus breaks off; the rest of the novel is made up of the written confessions of Doni. He tells how, as a poor young man, he fell in love with a German woman, Matilda Ernach, but was rejected—he believed—because of his poverty. So he went to Alexandria to make his fortune. There he met a young German, Huldebrand, who turned out to be the real reason for his rejection by Matilda. He went into business with Huldebrand, secretly hoping to find some way of ruining and supplanting him. Eventually, the two of them joined an expedition to India. Polidori treats the oriental themes which were still fashionable—and which had made Byron famous—as unsentimentally as he does the theme of war: 'I travelled through [Asia] careless about the scenery or inhabitants; the whole of my attention was engaged in my endeavours to acquire wealth.' This also deflates the orientalist romanticism of Polidori's cousin Eliza Arrow, and the pretensions of the Honourable East India Company, for whom the Arrows worked.

Their expedition was a success, but on their way home, Doni and Huldebrand were attacked by Arabs, robbed of all they had gained, and taken prisoner. During the fight, Doni tried to save the life of an old Armenian, who, though mortally wounded, was so grateful that he offered Doni a chance to regain his wealth by making one of two Faustian pacts with the powers of darkness:

> He told me that either I could only call for a certain sum at a time, and that at each time, some human domestic infliction, worse than the preceding, would fall upon me, or that, I at once, could gain unlimited power, and constant domestic prosperity, on the condition of giving myself up for ever to the will of a malignant being.

Doni sensibly chose the first alternative and soon had enough money to buy his freedom from the Arabs. He left Huldebrand a prisoner—and, he believed, dying of thirst (he even refused to bring him water)—returned to Milan, told Matilda that her beloved was dead, and after a suitable period of mourning, married her.

After Olivieri and Louisa were born, however, Huldebrand returned, presumably as the first of Doni's domestic inflictions. Matilda left Doni—with Huldebrand, he thought, but actually with her father Ernach. Doni pursued them and fired on their carriage, wounding Ernach. Matilda and Ernach, of course, made it as far as Beatenberg.

Doni explains the disasters that Ernestus has already narrated as the result of his summoning the demon for more money, first to pay Ernestus's gambling debts, then in the hope of ransoming Olivieri. On the latter occasion, the demon 'announced to me that I had exhausted my spells, and that after this infliction, as nothing round me would remain, on which he could breathe his pestilential breath, he would no longer obey my summons.' And on seeing the portraits, 'the demon's threat I found had indeed been fulfilled. Your mother's portrait was Matilda's. Olivieri had seduced, you married a daughter of Matilda, of Matilda's husband, and I was the murderer of her father.' Doni has turned out, disastrously, to be not a foster-father but a real father, not a Taylor or di Breme or Vacca but a Gaetano. And, one might add, Ernestus has succeeded in killing his father by ordering the pictures.

Speculation about parallels between the incestuous relations in *Ernestus Berchtold* and Polidori's own life would be groundless. Polidori was evidently very fond of his sister Frances, and her son D. G. Rossetti reports that she considered Polidori her favourite brother. But there is certainly no evidence of anything incestuous in their relations. Incest was a common theme even for writers who had not spent time in Byron's company; and both *The Vampyre* and *Ernestus Berchtold* celebrate purely fraternal affection as well as deplore the forces, internal and external, that threaten it. The horror of incest does not affect only those who actually indulge in it.

The difficult relations between Polidori and Gaetano may have contributed more directly to those between Ernestus and Doni. Ernestus's guilt at having to ask Doni for money to pay his gambling debts may reflect Polidori's feelings about his dependency, whether or not it reflects his feelings about gambling. Olivieri's flamboyant filial rebellion may reflect the way Polidori wished he could feel and act as a son. On the other side, Polidori may well have felt that his thrifty father had sacrificed his family's happiness for money; he may even have thought that his father was like Doni's demon, laying on his son, each time he asked for money, the domestic infliction of a lecture worse than the last time. And the final collapse of Doni, like that of Gustavus in **Ximenes,** may be a judgment on Gaetano. It is at least striking that Polidori should have given his tragedy and his novel such neatly balanced subtitles as **The Modern Abraham** and **The Modern Oedipus**.

The identity of Ernestus's auditor and Ernestus's reasons for confiding in him are left unclear. Although he is often directly addressed, he is never named. His function, however, is clear: to foreground Ernestus's difficulties of narration.

The most significant of these difficulties are emotional. Near the beginning of his story, Ernestus concedes: 'You may think I rest too much upon these instants of my life; but I dread to narrate my miseries; the recalling to memory anguish and grief racks my heart; but I have begun, and you shall hear the whole.' Similarly, he often apologizes for his inability to describe either Louisa herself or his feelings for her. The former may be merely a conventional tribute to her beauty; the latter seems to have something to do with his dread of narrating the miseries those feelings have involved him in.

Dread and misery frequently interrupt Ernestus's narrative. In a passage on Louisa's love for Doni, he sighs: 'Oh, if that smile had fallen upon myself, as it then fell upon her father, if I had only felt its cheering influence without that burning passion it has excited in this breast; but I must not anticipate my narration.' After his account of the funeral of the older Berchtold, he describes him as 'but the first victim' of the curse on himself: 'My love has left me, a scattered pine amidst this desolate scene, but first it has destroyed all who were bound to me, my love has proved,—but I must preserve my strength,—I have horrors to relate . . .' Eventually, Ernestus is entirely unable to continue, so he gives his listener Doni's written confession instead. All these hesitations suggest the strength of the obstacles—Freud would call them resistances—in the path to truth. That Ernestus overcomes them suggests the strength of his determination to reveal the truth—or, to put it less grandly, of his melancholic compulsion to self-exposure, which matches that of his creator. Doni's determination is equally strong: it does not even occur to him not to write his confessions, though the effort kills him and though he knows they will 'blast' his only remaining son and daughter, who are not to blame for the 'horrors' he has to tell them.

One might say that their determination to reveal the truth is as strong as that of Oedipus. Certainly the resistances both have to overcome are similar in kind. All Ernestus's hesitations have to do with his incest; he has no difficulty in confessing to his gambling, drinking, and fornication, though, unlike the incest, they are his fault. The same resistances operate as powerfully within his narrative. The spirit of Matilda cannot tell Julia precisely what danger it is that threatens her and her brother: 'it was a vague threat, that seemed the more terrific, because it could not be decidedly represented to the mind.' This terrific vagueness assimilates, even more explicitly than *Manfred* does, the horror of incest to the sublimity of the obscure. The reviewer of the novel for the *Edinburgh Monthly Review* displays some understanding of the assimilation, though he (like Carlyle) uses clothing, rather than silence or darkness, as his symbol for repression, and comes down squarely on the side of repression: 'the secret of the disciples of the new morality . . . is that they boldly appear among well clothed persons, *in puris naturalibus*—and give free utterance to the sentiments which linger about every imagination, but which it is the prime object of all moral training to subdue.'

The unspeakability of incest is already assumed in *Oedipus Tyrannus*. Tiresias, it turns out, has known the truth all along, but has preferred to 'shroud it all in silence.' The old shepherd who gave the infant Oedipus to a Corinthian instead of killing him has to be threatened with torture before he will talk. The messenger who reports the suicide of Jocasta and the mutilation of Oedipus interrupts himself in a way that will become standard long before Polidori's time: Oedipus is

> shouting,
> 'Loose the bolts, someone, show me to all of
>   Thebes!
> My father's murderer, my mother's—'
> No, I can't repeat it, it's unholy.

Parricide is apparently less unholy, or at least less unspeakable, to the messenger. Even Oedipus himself, after his heroic struggle has brought the truth to light, cuts himself off: 'No more— / it's wrong to name what's wrong to do.'

In Beaumont and Fletcher's *A King and No King* (1611)—which Byron may have had in mind when he cited 'some of the best of our old English writers' as precedents for his treatment of incest in *Parisina* and for his intended treatment of it in *The Bride of Abydos*—Arbaces is in love with Panthaea, whom he believes to be his sister, but he 'cannot utter it.' He tells his faithful retainer Mardonius to take her a message, but insists that he deliver it in sign language—moreover, he refuses to reveal what it is. His discretion is justified: when Mardonius finally realizes what the message is, he refuses to deliver it. The title of Walpole's *The Mysterious Mother* (1768), a play Byron called 'a tragedy of the highest order,' alludes to 'this secret sin; this untold tale, / That art cannot extract, nor penance cleanse.' In Alfieri's *Myrrha* (1786), which Byron cited as another precedent for *The Bride of Abydos* and *Parisina,* and which, when he saw it performed in 1819, affected him so powerfully that he had convulsions, the action revolves entirely around the attempts of Myrrha's family to persuade her to tell her secret—her incestuous love for her father. She never does so: she stabs herself after only hinting at it. In his memoirs, Alfieri explains how he approached the technical problems unspeakability creates for the dramatist: 'I perceived that it was necessary to display, by action alone, what is related in Ovid, and that the heroine must execute her purpose without divulging it.' In Schiller's *Don Carlos* (1787), which Byron also cited, Carlos's confessor refers to 'The sacred mystery of your secret grief,' and Carlos interrupts himself as he begins to reveal it: 'O, I know—/ But hush!—no more of that!'

Polidori's more famous contemporaries followed this convention carefully. Byron decided that *The Bride of Abydos* (1813) was *'two centuries* at least too late for the subject.' So he left it not only unmentioned but non-existent: the lovers turn out to be only cousins, though not until after they reveal their love. In *Parisina* (1815), Lord Azo hears his wife, Parisina, repeat a name in her sleep: 'And whose that name?—'tis Hugo's,—his—/ In sooth he had not deemed of this!' Hugo is Azo's illegitimate son. His punishment is as unspeakable as his crime: Azo tells Parisina that 'thou, frail thing! shalt view his head—/ Away! I cannot speak the rest.' In the end, both lovers become nameless:

> Hugo is fallen; and, from that hour,
> No more in palace, hall, or bower,
> Was Parisina heard or seen:
> Her name—as if she ne'er had been—
> Was banished from each lip and ear,
> Like words of wantonness or fear;
> And from Prince Azo's voice, by none
> Was mention heard of wife or son . . .

The review in *Literary Panorama* (like that of **Ernestus Berchtold** in the *Edinburgh Monthly Review*) followed suit by describing the subject of the poem as 'adultery not to be named.' In *Manfred* (1817), the hero's lover is described by his servant as 'The Lady Astarte, his—Hush! who comes here?' Percy Shelley had to revise incest out of *Laon and Cythna* (1818; the revised version is called *The Revolt of Islam*), as Byron had revised it out of *The Bride of Abydos.* He could hardly remove it from *The Cenci* (1819), but incest is never explicitly mentioned in the play, as Mary Shelley was careful to point out in a note. Beatrice tells Orsino not to ask what she has suffered, 'for there are deeds / Which have no form, sufferings which have no tongue.' Later, she characterizes her father's deed as 'expressionless,' as one of 'The crimes which mortal tongue dare never name.' As in *Parisina* (though not as in *Oedipus Tyrannus*), the punishment for incest is as unspeakable as the crime: Cenci's son Giacomo complains: 'he who is our murderous persecutor / Is shielded by a father's holy name, / Or I would—' and then *'stops abruptly.'*

Ernestus Berchtold does not deal with incest in nearly so innovative a way as **The Vampyre** deals with vampirism. It does contain an unusually complete compendium of the motifs associated with its theme, and since not all of them are compatible, it is characteristically ambivalent: it presents incest, for example, as both ennobling and lethal.

Insofar as it is ennobling, incest, as Polidori presents it, depends on the two complementary processes that Freud calls identification and idealization. Identification compensates for 'the real or emotional loss of a loved object' by 'introjection of it into the ego'; it is one of the ways in which the ego ideal is formed. Ernestus and Julia have lost their beloved mother, but her spirit continues to hover over them and give them advice, precisely like an ego ideal. Introjection is also, more specifically, a characteristic of melancholia. The motivation for it, Freud suggests, is the same fixated desire that also informs the imagery of vampirism: 'The ego wants to incorporate this object into itself, and, in accordance with the oral or cannibalistic phase of libidinal development in which it is, it wants to do so by devouring it.'

In idealization, 'the object serves as a substitute for some unattained ego ideal of our own. We love it on account of the perfections which we have striven to reach for our own ego,' and project part of our ego ideal onto it. When Ernestus first encounters Louisa, he is already full of 'indignation at the conduct of men, who sacrificed to personal interest the safety of their country.' Her song is in unison with his feelings, but she makes him introject his indignation. He enlists at once. She sings to him again outside the Château de Chillon—at first in 'melancholy notes' which 'seemed to sympathize with my sorrows,' then in 'livelier notes,' so that 'hope breathed upon my heart.' He finds the strength to escape. She saves him from vice in Milan just as she has roused him from idleness in Switzerland. He repeatedly refers to her as his guardian or ministering angel. He has clearly projected onto her the ideal he derived from their mother, a process made easier by the moral resemblance (Polidori is careful not to make it a physical resemblance) between Louisa and her mother: Matilda's

> presence was commanding, but her voice was persuasive; its tones struck the heart and produced those emotions, which all remember, none can express, the feeling, as if we had been always virtuous, and were worthy of listening to the voice of a being superior to ourselves . . . Louisa was her counterpart . . .

And it is Louisa's voice that first and most powerfully inspires Ernestus. The novel's analysis of idealizing love is thus both more detailed and, paradoxically, less critical than that in the *Essay*. Louisa is the unique and unattainable ideal for which the compulsive seducer tries to substitute an endless series of objects of desire; unfortunately, she turns out not to be unattainable.

The Mysterious Mother also associates incest with idealization. Years before the action of the play, the Countess of Narbonne has used a bed trick to sleep with her son, Edmund. In horror at her sin, she has sent him into exile: like a romantic vampire, he has become a restless wanderer. She has given birth to a daughter, whom she has named Adeliza and brought up as an orphan. When Adeliza tells her that she has met a young knight, the Countess playfully accuses her ward of loving him. The innocent Adeliza confesses:

Yes, with such love as that I feel for thee.
His virtues I revere: his earnest words
Sound like the precepts of a tender parent:
And, next to thee, methinks I could obey him.

The young knight, of course, is Edmund.

Ambrosio, the eponymous villain of *The Monk* (1796), owes some of his seductive power to a similar process. He is the long-lost son of Elvira and the brother of Antonia; he first appears to them as the embodiment of their ideals. His speaking voice harmonizes with their inner feelings, as Louisa's singing voice does with Ernestus's. Elvira remarks:

His fine and full-toned voice struck me particularly; but surely, Antonia, I have heard it before. It seemed perfectly familiar to my ear; either I must have known the abbot in former times, or his voice bears a wonderful resemblance to that of some other, to whom I have often listened. There were certain tones which touched my very heart, and made me feel sensations so singular, that I strive in vain to account for them.

Antonia has felt the same effect, but disagrees about the cause: 'I suspect that what we attribute to his voice really proceeds from his pleasant manners, which forbid our considering him as a stranger.' He will eventually strangle his mother, and rape and stab his sister.

Since Olivieri does not resemble his mother, Julia's affair with him does not have an ennobling effect on her. Olivieri's relations with Ernestus, however, do initially add to the effect Louisa has on him (though later, in Milan, their influences are opposed). As Freud points out, 'the first stirrings of a love of liberty and a sense of justice' are often inspired by sibling rivalry—a dominant trait in Olivieri's character, as Ernestus later realizes. So, in defence of Swiss liberty, they 'often joined and tried to vie with each other in acts of daring and courage.'

Incestuous love is also often linked to the love of liberty, in literature if not in psychoanalytic theory. In Ford's *'Tis Pity She's a Whore* (1615-33?), yet another work that Byron cited as a precedent for *The Bride of Abydos*, Giovanni makes the simplest argument for the link: that the prohibition of incest is a mere convention, a pointless repression against which it is right to rebel. The supposedly nameless crime is a mere matter of names:

                  Shall a peevish sound,
    A customary form, from man to man,
    Of brother and of sister, be a bar
    'Twixt my perpetual happiness and me?

Giovanni's argument is intended to be sophistical. But Shelley makes essentially the same point in his preface to *Laon and Cythna*: the presentation of incestuous love is intended 'to break through the crust of those outworn opinions on which established institutions depend,' and 'to strengthen the moral sense, by forbidding it to waste its energies in seeking to avoid actions which are only

crimes of convention.' Shelley, one might say, saw the beauty as well as the horror of incest. He wrote to Maria Gisborne in 1819: 'Incest is like many other incorrect things a very poetical circumstance. It may be the excess of love or hate. It may be [as in *Laon and Cythna*] the defiance of everything for the sake of another which clothes itself in the glory of the highest heroism, or it may be [as in *The Cenci*] that cynical rage which, confounding the good and the bad in existing opinions breaks through them for the purpose of rioting in selfishness and antipathy.' The cynical way in which Manfred, in *The Castle of Otranto* (1765), and the widow Sandal, in *Melmoth the Wanderer* (1820), manipulate the fear of incest (Manfred wants his marriage annulled as incestuous so that he can make another incestuous marriage) suggests that Walpole and Maturin also were willing to entertain the idea that this fear was at least partly a matter of convention.

Ernestus may break this convention, but he never questions it. For him, Louisa is the embodiment of a wholly conventional ideal, the personification of conscience. She may be like Cythna, who inspires (or re-inspires) Laon by singing hymns to liberty, which harmonize with his feelings because he composed them himself. But she is more like Elizabeth of Valois in *Don Carlos*. Elizabeth feels no desire except 'the pure desire / To call heroic virtue into life.' She repeatedly tells her stepson Carlos (on wholly conventional grounds) not to wish for the consummation of their love, but to sublimate it in devotion to the freedom of Flanders, which his father is oppressing.

Byron associates incest both with the love of liberty and with conscience, but not at the same time. The shadowy Astarte shared Manfred's implicitly subversive or at least heterodox 'quest of hidden knowledge,' but she was not a conscience: 'Her faults were mine—her virtues were her own,' and she seems to have been content to leave it that way. In *Cain* (1821), Adah is Cain's conscience, but a conservative conscience. She defends incest against Lucifer's insinuations on the grounds of precedent: it is, after all, the only form of sexual love that has been known so far. And she appeals to Cain in the name of their love and of their children not to go on the quest for hidden knowledge to which Lucifer has tempted him:

Shall they not love and bring forth things that
    love
Out of their love? have they not drawn their
    milk
Out of this bosom? was not he, their father,
Born of the same sole womb, in the same hour
With me? did we not love each other? and
In multiplying our being multiply
Things which will love each other as we love
Them? — And as I love thee, my Cain! go not
Forth with this spirit; he is not of ours.

(It is worth pointing out that Byron praised Augusta Leigh precisely for not being his conscience: 'Thy soft heart refused to discover / The faults which so many could find.' And she seems to have had no interest in questing for hidden knowledge.)

When the literary treatments of incest bother—or venture—to justify their condemnation of it, they usually do so on the grounds that it is narcissistic (*The Cenci* is unusual in treating it as we are now coming to understand it, as a matter of power relations—just as it is unusual in treating what is by far the most common form of it). Ernestus does not: his idealizing love for Louisa is implicitly narcissistic, since it projects an ideal of his own onto her, but he does not seem to believe, or to be willing to admit, that there is anything wrong with this. And since, in order to minimize the implausibility of his plot, Polidori has made Louisa physically unlike either her mother or her brother, he has denied himself the conventional symbol for narcissism.

The physical likeness of the incestuous lovers is already prominent in *'Tis Pity She's a Whore,* where Giovanni exposes his narcissism by arguing: 'Wise Nature first in your creation meant / To make you mine: else't had been sin and foul / To share one beauty to a double soul.' But the *locus classicus* of the symbol for English literature is the narrative of Sin in the second book of *Paradise Lost* (1674), which associates incest with rebellion in order to discredit rebellion. At an assembly of the rebel angels, Sin sprang from Satan's head, 'Likest to thee in shape and count'nance bright'; at first, the angels were amazed and afraid, 'but familiar grown, / I pleas'd' them all, especially Satan himself, 'who full oft / Thyself in me thy perfect image viewing / Becam'st enamor'd.'

Like Satan, the hero of Chateaubriand's 'René' (1802) falls in love with the daughter of his own brain, 'the ideal creature of some future passion.' He prays that she might be born from his side, like Eve (of whom Milton's Sin is a kind of proleptic parody), only to realize, too late, that she is already incarnate in his sister. The scheming monks who are the villains of *The Mysterious Mother* direct Adeliza's thoughts to a 'mental spouse,' Christ, hoping that she will become a nun, so that the countess's money will go to the Church. But this ideal lover turns out to be incarnate in Edmund. Lewis's Ambrosio falls in love with a portrait of the Virgin, who turns out to be incarnate in the novice Rosario, who turns out to be a woman, Matilda, who turns out, in the end, to be a demon. The sequence thus begins with a symbolic incest and then moves on to homosexuality, here another trope for narcissism. When she first reveals her gender, Matilda reassures the monk: 'Think not, Ambrosio, that I come to rob your bride of your affections.' She is referring to his mental spouse, Religion; she is lying, and after seducing him herself, she tempts him to literal incest with Antonia.

In Percy Shelley's adolescent romance *St. Irvyne; or, The Rosicrucian* (1811), narcissism leads Olympia to a forbidden and fatal, though not incestuous, love:

> Nourished by restless imagination, her passion soon attained a most unbridled height: instead of conquering a feeling which honour, generosity, virtue, all forbade ever to be gratified, she gloried within herself at having found one on whom she might with justice fix her burning attachment; for though the object of them had never before been present to her mind, the desires for that object, although unseen, had taken root long, long ago.

Alastor (1815), the most radical of these narratives of narcissism, dispenses entirely with any incarnate object of desire. Its hero falls in love with a maiden in a dream, whose voice, like Louisa's or Ambrosio's, is 'like the voice of his own soul / Heard in the calm of thought,' and whose concerns are also his own:

> Knowledge and truth and virtue were her theme,
> And lofty hopes of divine liberty,
> Thoughts the most dear to him, and poesy,
> Himself a poet.

He spends the rest of the poem pursuing her—that is, withdrawing more and more deeply within himself, neglecting the sublime scenery with which Shelley has surrounded him as he has rejected the love of a real Arab maiden. He does respond to one natural scene, a pool bordered by narcissi, 'whose yellow flowers / For ever gaze on their own drooping eyes, / Reflected in the crystal calm'; he briefly longs to deck his hair with them. By another pool, he poses as Narcissus himself:

> His eyes beheld
> Their own wan light through the reflected lines
> Of his thin hair, distinct in the dark depth
> Of that still fountain; as the human heart,
> Gazing in dreams over the gloomy grave,
> Sees its own treacherous likeness there.

Eventually, like Narcissus, he wastes away and dies.

But according to Shelley, there is nothing wrong with his mind's desire 'for intercourse with an intelligence similar to itself,' only with the pursuit of it in solitude. The fragment 'On Love' postulates this kind of narcissism as a prerequisite for any reciprocity. In *St. Irvyne,* the poet Fitzeustace is, like the Poet in *Alastor,* a male Olympia, 'a love-sick swain, without ever having found . . . a *congenial* female,' but then he is lucky enough to meet the congenial Eloise St. Irvyne. Laon and Cythna are mental and physical doubles: she is repeatedly described as his shadow, the only difference being that the shadow is lovelier, and paradoxically brighter, than the original.

Astarte, too, is exactly like Manfred, only better. She is what Shelley in 'On Love' calls 'a mirror whose surface reflects only the forms of purity and brightness.' Manfred is curiously insistent about this, stressing her superiority as if he were trying to transform a narcissistic idealization into a real differentiation:

> She was like me in lineaments—her eyes—
> Her hair—her features—all, to the very tone
> Even of her voice, they said were like to mine;
> But softened all, and tempered into beauty:
> She had the same lone thoughts and wanderings,
> The quest of hidden knowledge, and a mind
> To comprehend the Universe: nor these

Alone, but with them gentler powers than mine,
Pity, and smiles, and tears—which I had not;
And tenderness—but that I had for her;
Humility—and that I never had.
Her faults were mine—her virtues were her
    own—

The next lines suddenly undercut this attempt, for they not only characterize incest as inevitably fatal but, through their mirror imagery and repetitions (which are rhetorical mirrorings), ascribe its fatality to narcissism: 'I loved her, and destroyed her! . . . / Not with my hand, but heart, which broke her heart; / It gazed on mine, and withered.' She seems to have committed suicide: this at least would be a suitably introverted death, and would account for Manfred's feeling guilty for her death without being responsible for it.

In most of the other literary treatments of incest, it is equally fatal. In Milton, of course, Sin gives birth to Death. Giovanni begins by asking his sister to stab him, and ends by cutting out her heart. The mysterious mother stabs herself with her son's dagger, and he leaves to seek death in the crusades. Don Carlos is arrested by the Inquisition. Zuleika, the Bride of Abydos, asks Selim to stab her but instead dies of a broken heart as he is shot by her father. Despite Shelley's defiance of convention, Cythna must join Laon on his funeral pyre (in a striking anticipation of the climax of *Die Götterdämmerung*). Beatrice Cenci and her stepmother conspire to murder her father and are executed for it. In Mary Shelley's *Mathilda* (1819), the father drowns and the daughter, after considering suicide, dies of consumption, like Louisa.

Ernestus Berchtold makes explicit the horror of incest that lies behind ***The Vampyre's*** presentation of sexuality as fatal; consequently, it presents sexuality as more emphatically fatal and love as more emphatically pure or asexual. Louisa is too pure to be corrupted by sex like Ruthven's victims; she dies of it instead. Literally, she dies of consumption, but Ernestus ascribes her illness to her love for him and insistently applies sexual metaphors to it: he has sown 'the seeds of death' in her.

Polidori is apologetic about the role of the supernatural in his novel. His introduction tries to explain it away as simply one of the conditions of the Diodati pact:

> A tale·that rests upon improbabilities, must generally disgust a rational mind; I am therefore afraid that, though I have thrown the superior agency into the back ground as much as was in my power, still, that many readers will think the same moral, and the same colouring, might have been given to characters acting under the ordinary agencies of life; I believe it, but I had agreed to write a supernatural tale, and that does not allow of a completely every-day narrative.

A number of the reviews quoted Polidori against himself, and complained of the 'merely irrelevant hints at supernatural agency,' as the *Monthly Review* called them, adding: 'we are surprised to find how busy the evil spirits

have been in producing misfortunes which we had been satisfied with ascribing to the influence of evil passions.' The *Edinburgh Monthly Review* made the same point with the sarcastic comment: 'it is well; for if there had been in his story a single knot which it was beyond the dexterity of the most inexperienced boarding-school miss to untie, Dr. Polidori is not the man to have called down a divinity adequate to its solution.' In fact, the attribution of unnatural love to apparently supererogatory supernatural causes is conventional. The fate of Oedipus is the consequence of a curse placed on Laius. Myrrha expiates her mother's hubristic denial of homage to Venus. The two brothers of Schiller's *The Bride of Messina* (1803)—who, by an unfortunate coincidence, both fall in love with their long-lost sister—expiate the crime of their father, who married a bride intended for his father.

Other incest narratives also blame the parents for the incest of the children, but in a more frankly natural way. It is hardly surprising that Don Carlos cherishes an incestuous passion for his stepmother, since he was engaged to her before his father appropriated her. Byron copies this plot element in *Parisina* (it is not in the historical sources for the poem), and makes the bastard Hugo argue that, if he has been prone to sexual excess, it is because his father's 'guilty love' produced 'too like a son.' The Countess of Narbonne and Count Cenci, of course, are still more directly responsible for their children's incest.

In both cases, the responsibility of the parents is made explicit. In ***Ernestus Berchtold*** it is not, or not by Ernestus. Doni blames himself abundantly, but his son always speaks of him with the highest respect. For Ernestus, Doni's responsibility remains absolutely unmentionable, like the element of convention in sexual morality and the element of narcissism in his own love for Louisa. One might say that they remain unconscious, unanalysed residues, so that Ernestus remains possessed by an obsessive guilt for something that is not his fault. In short, the working-out of the curse on Ernestus, which Polidori feared would disgust the rational mind, serves to dramatize the workings of the irrational mind.

The reviews of the novel were more favourable than those of ***The Vampyre,*** though most deplored its subject and several had not forgiven its author either for the earlier tale or for its ascription to Byron. The *Edinburgh Monthly Review,* the most severe, would concede only that 'Dr. Polidori, indeed, can get up a flat and feeble tale of preternatural horrors, which, in the simple particular of revolting combinations [that is, incest], shall outdo the inspired ferocity of the noble bard [Byron, of course] himself—but so could any assignable blockhead, who ruminates within the purlieus of Grub Street.' The *Literary Gazette* regretted 'the semi-sentimental semi-supernatural productions to which we are now so prone—the prose Byroniads which infect the times,' but allowed that Polidori's work was 'well constructed and ably written,' and its 'story as horrible as the greatest lovers of raw-head and bloody-bones can desire.' The *Monthly Review* thought that the 'considerable powers of imagination' displayed in the novel proved Polidori 'capable of writing in a higher and purer strain.' The *European Magazine,* the most generous, thought 'this extraordinary tale may claim no obscure place in the department of literature to which it belongs,' and even suggested that it was preferable to *Oedipus Tyrannus* and *The Mysterious Mother,* on the grounds that 'subjects of this kind are more fitted for narrative than for dramatic representation.' In a printed narrative, the unspeakable can remain, literally, unspoken.

In fact, the novel has hardly succeeded in claiming a place in any department of literature. In November 1819, Polidori wrote to Frances: 'Your reading my *Ernestus Berchtold* so many times has nothing wonderful in it Madam for one Lady a *young pretty—accomplished* lady has learnt a great deal of it by heart.' But there cannot have been many such young ladies. In August 1820, Longman and Company wrote to Polidori, informing him that only 199 copies of the novel had been sold, and asking him if he wanted to buy the rest of the edition.

Polidori speaks from beyond the grave?

William Michael Rossetti recorded a possible contact with Polidori's spirit in his séance diary for 25 November 1865. (At this type of séance, the spirit was supposed to answer questions by rapping on the table, once for yes and twice for no. More complicated answers had to be spelled out: the sitters would recite the alphabet over and over, and the spirit would rap when they reached the right letter.) One of the sitters asked:

'Is there a spirit who will communicate with me?'—Yes.—Who?—Uncle John.—He said: 'I had no uncle of that name.' I then said: 'Is it my Uncle John?'—Yes. I asked for the surname, by the alphabet, but could not get it. Then: Is it an English surname?—No.—Foreign?—Yes.—Spanish, German, etc., etc., Italian?—Yes.—I then called over five or six Italian names, coming to Polidori.—Yes.—Will you tell me truly how you died?—Yes.—How?—Killed.—Who killed you?—I.—There was a celebrated poet with whom you were connected: what was his name?—Bro. This was twice repeated, or something close to it the second time. At a third attempt, 'Byron.'—There was a certain book you wrote, attributed to Byron: can you give me its title?—Yes.—I tried to get this title [*The Vampyre*] several times, but wholly failed.—Are you happy?—Two raps, meaning not exactly.

William Michael Rossetti, quoted in Poor Polidori: A Critical Biography of the Author of *The Vampyre, University of Toronto Press, 1991.*

Vijay Mishra (essay date 1994)

SOURCE: "Gothic Fragments and Fragmented Gothics," in *The Gothic Sublime,* State University of New York Press, 1994, pp. 83-116.

[*In the following excerpt, Mishra discusses Polidori's* The Vampyre *and* Ernestus Berchtold *as exemplary of a particular type of Gothic fiction: a deliberately inconclusive work intended to arouse fear, astonishment, or delight that appears fragmentary because it is not resolved.*]

There is a class of Gothic texts that I would want to refer to as symptoms of the form insofar as it raises problems hidden "by the completeness of works that have attained the status of 'texts'." If in literary terms transcendence always implies a way of totalizing so that the work of art itself triumphs over the contradictions rendered in the social formations depicted in the text (the Marxist sublime), then the extreme version of its negation would be texts that are so ruptured, so rent apart, that they signify the ultimately uncanonizable in literature. These barely theorized Gothic symptoms (or texts) signify, discursively, the impossibility of any order of the *a priori,* whether thematic or structural, and resist the inscription of the Real in them by foregrounding features that Jameson was to describe as characteristics of postmodernism: "new types of syntax or syntagmatic relationships." I have in mind those extreme instances of Gothic fragments that Robert D. Mayo believed belonged to a "distinctly different genre" ["Gothic Romance in the Magazines," *PMLA,* September, 1950]. The paradigmatic text of this form was Mrs. Barbauld's "Sir Bertrand," which spawned countless imitations in the magazines. In all these fragments the aim was simply to arouse fear, astonish, and delight, and as fragments they were inconclusive narratives. But we need not commit ourselves totally to Mrs. Barbauld's definition of the Gothic fragment, because fragments are really versions or symptoms of the extreme otherness of the Gothic sublime, which emerges, in these fragments, as the embodiment of what Slavoj Zizek has aptly called the "void, the emptiness created by the symbolic structure" implicit in the fragments [*The Sublime Object of Ideology*]. My use of the term *fragment* is, therefore, slightly different from its traditional generic definition (as in Mayo, for instance). Apart from "Sir Bertrand," all the other texts discussed in this chapter are fragments only insofar as they characterize a particular type of tendency in the Gothic. Wordsworth's *Gothic Tale* and Byron's "A Fragment" were simply left incomplete by their respective authors. Mary Shelley's *Mathilda,* in its manuscript form, strikes one as a kind of a palaeographic sublime in which a daughter's agitated writing (the marks of ink on paper, writing as pure signifier) draws on the handwriting of the absent historical father, William Godwin. Goethe's melancholy sublime, *Werter,* is a text that invades these fragments and offers a prior model, a simulacrum, sets of "intensities," that infiltrate the discourse of the Gothic by entering its interstices and providing it with a narrative of nostalgia and loss.

Polidori's narratives, notably **The Vampyre** and **Ernestus Berchtold,** comprise another type of "fragment" we discuss here. **The Vampyre** is a conscious writing out of a fragment, a re-working of a precursor, that in turn becomes itself fragmented as a text written in the shadow of Byron. **Ernestus Berchtold** is a horrifying tale of incest, in many ways even a cruel text, as it terrorizes the mind of the reader with a narrative that aims at radically lifting the censorship of the superego and indeed, making its claims to a superior moral ground redundant. Polidori's attempts to give form, find a totality, through a perverse writing that encourages capaciousness and plenitude, are symptomatic of the genre of fragments, as we use that term here. In this respect **Ernestus Berchtold's** realist design and formal patterning simply hide its fissures, its incapacity to "contain" its themes within narrative. The thematic core of this text, an extreme form of incestuous coupling, the absolute *imaginary* relation, as defined by Lacan, is then played out in *Mathilda,* the text with which this chapter ends.

In both Byron and Polidori, the narrative on the theme of Calmet's vampires introduces a "love-crime," the rape/death of a woman on her wedding night. This murder and violation is related to a perverse fascination, on the part of the narrator, with the vampire-hero (developed more fully in Bram Stoker's *Dracula*) who is "sick unto death." The sublime vampire gets recast as Frankenstein's monster who will also violate Frankenstein's bride on her wedding night. The conjunction of love and death that we noted with reference to Walpole and Matthew Gregory Lewis takes a more extreme form in these fragments as the life force, through the structures of the "Uncanny," duplicates itself in its absolute opposite, the principle of death. Gothic fragments and fragmented Gothics are thus explorations of a psychology that threatens the subject with another form of the sublime. This sublimity is marked either by the sentimentalist's obsession with death (in a version of the proto-oceanic sublime), as in *Werter* and *Mathilda,* or by the victim's fascination with a (heroic) representative of death. As we examine the texts, it should become clear that the two versions (the sentimentalist and the heroic) in fact collapse into one another, dissolving all these texts into fragments of the Gothic "unspeakable," the absolute negation of the soaring, ultimately defiant, subject of the positive Romantic sublime.

One of the underlying characteristics of these fragments is the desire for the Other which is, however, never fulfilled. Because desire is insatiable, it is indicated in the Gothic fragments either by an incapacity to complete the narrative ("I almost reached my destination" form) or by a failure to work through the moment of trauma. These fragments are therefore marked by constant deferrals, reformulations, tautologies, recurrences, return to beginnings, repetition, exhaustion, excess, and so forth, as the thinking self is invaded by the desiring self. Desire, of course, cannot be fulfilled or represented, since we don't really know, in Zizek's words, "What desire should I desire?" In short, the form that the narratives take is predicated on a Gothic sublime that, like the Lacanian Real, escapes inscription. But the subject's orientation in terms of this sublime points to its own lack as a signifiable entity. It is this lack that drags the subject (as the ideal ego) to the theme of incest, which is one of the grand narratives of the imaginary identity of self and Other through the metaphorics of the double and the mirror. The suture implied here of this impossible act of totalization can only lead to an even further regression. Again, the subject in the Gothic sublime ceases to soar; the mind

fails to supply it with the technology of transcendence because, in spite of the intervention of the law of reason, the attraction of dissolution in the sublime is so overpowering that the subject does not metaphorically glance back at the Law for permission for this momentary fascination with the sublime. The abyss is embraced, but not contemplatively, as in the Indian sublime. . . .

Byron's physician Dr. John William Polidori (whose excessive gambling led him to commit suicide at the age of twenty-six) is remembered chiefly as the person who left behind a brief account of the night of June 16, 1816, when five individuals, three singularly gifted, began to write their ghost stories. Two of them—Claire Clairmont and Percy Bysshe Shelley—defaulted; Byron produced an outline of a tale about a vampire-villain, whereas the remaining two, Mary Godwin Shelley and Polidori, in fact completed their tasks. Though we know very little about the reactions of the members of this group to each others' compositions, Byron is reported to have said to Mary Shelley, "You and I will publish ours together" on the night of the telling of the ghost stories. Later, in a letter dated April 27 (1819) to Mrs. Maria Gisborne (née Reveley), who was an old acquaintance of both William Godwin and Thomas Holcroft, Mary called the plot of Byron's (Polidori's) story "very dramatic & striking." What Mary Shelley and Polidori finally completed are by no means equal, and comparisons between *Frankenstein* and **The Vampyre** are often made only to complete an extended footnote. . . . [My aim here] is to examine the nature of Gothic fragments further through Polidori's and Byron's versions of the vampire tale.

Byron's own fragment (under the title "A Fragment") first appeared as an appendix to the first edition of Byron's *Mazeppa, A Poem.* It begins as a letter dated June 17, 1816 (which corresponds exactly to the day after the telling of the ghost stories referred to by Polidori), but the story itself is located in the century before, though how far before we can't be at all certain. The opening words, "In the year 17—," constitute a common literary device, which we encounter in *Frankenstein* as well. This is followed by the first-person narrator declaring that he set out to travel through "countries not hitherto much frequented" with a friend, Augustus Darvell. An older person, the latter was, we are told, a man of fortune who belonged to an "ancient family." He has, however, a strange attraction about him, a capacity, charismatic no doubt but probably fiendish, to draw people toward him even though one always feels terribly uncomfortable in his presence. One is never sure, after all, whether his behavior has a cause— "ambition, love, remorse, grief"—or whether it is "a morbid temperament akin to disease." As Byron proceeds from the simple and totally explicable elements of romance to the unconscious world of the Gothic his account of Darvell becomes more and more complicated: "these were so contradictory or contradicted." It takes the narrator, ultimately, to an equation so crucial in the Gothic between mystery and evil:

> Where there is mystery, it is generally supposed that there must also be evil: I know not how this may be,

but in him there certainly was the one, though I could not ascertain the extent of the other.

In spite of Darvell's aloofness, their differences in age, and the obvious presence of an abiding, uncomfortable enigma, the narrator is drawn to him. The attraction, in a replay of the uncanny recognition of one's own double, is so powerful (though implicitly doomed) that the narrator is not satisfied until Darvell agrees to be his travelling companion. Attracted by Darvell's "shadowy restlessness," he finds himself in a dreadful predicament when Darvell asks him to take an oath:

> This is the end of my journey, and of my life—I came here to die: but I have a request to make, a command— for such my last words must be—You will observe it?

The command in fact is, on the surface, innocuous enough: "conceal my death from every human being." After some hesitation, he swears to do so, and Darvell looks considerably relieved. He dies uttering, "Tis well!" and asks the narrator to bury him that evening at the spot where an ominous bird was perched. Having bound the narrator to an oath full of alarming possibilities, an oath that is fraught with self-extinction as it traps the subject into the *imaginary* realm of duplication or nondifference, the fragment ends with the words:

> Between astonishment and grief, I was tearless.

Since the Gothic is an already-told tale, a relic of the already-occurred event, in some ways these consciously incomplete Gothic fragments demonstrate a feature of the genre that is part of its occluded structure. In short, the fragment is itself a theory of the Gothic as it exposes the hidden agenda of the form. All dream texts are similarly incomplete fragments that require efforts of interpretation before they can be completed. To read the Gothic fragment is thus tantamount to reading the real, repressed Gothic form. Of course, we can construct, even without the help of Polidori, the inevitable ending of the narrative. In Byron's outline of the story—glimpsed from references in Mary Shelley's journals and letters, and in Polidori's own *The Vampyre* and diary—Darvell returns from the dead to seduce the narrator's own sister. And the enigma, the evil force, that binds the plot here is the oath which cannot be broken. Because of this she can't be forewarned that Darvell (as his name suggests) is the *devil himself*. The narrative inversion/perversion here is interesting because Darvell's interdiction turns around to haunt the honorable, realist subject. Where Darvell knows the true nature of the Gothic narrative (that honor is an ideological device), the narrator, trapped in the discourse of realism, mistakes illusion for truth. The positive sublime finally constructs a world that is meaningful; the negative Gothic sublime, only the mutilated and castrated subject who willingly submits.

The complete version of this narrative is to be found in Polidori's *The Vampyre*. The figure of Darvell now functions as the sign of the loss of individual identity, of difference, as in fact the sublime object of the Gothic

Other, the object of desire. As we see repeatedly, what the Gothic subject desires is the death of selfhood, a guilty absorption in the censored object. The Gothic narrative here plays on a version of the theme of the Faustian pact, an attraction to the Other, from which there can be no escape. Literature has many versions of this pact, but all seem to be a variation on the pact with the Devil. Polidori takes up this theme and transforms Byron's Darvell/Devil into a vampire. This transformation and the reasons for it are explained in Polidori's introduction. His starting points are stories about "the dead rising from their graves, and feeding on the blood of the young and beautiful." Drawing on an account in the *London Journal* of March 1732, Polidori recounts the case of a Hungarian who was "tormented by a vampyre," but who attempted to get rid of the vampire by "eating some of the earth out of the vampyre's grave, and rubbing himself with his blood." The source of the *London Journal*'s information was Augustine Calmet's work on vampires. Polidori might have been familiar with English translations of Calmet's work, though it is more likely that he came to Calmet through reviews in the periodical literature.

For the purposes of our analysis the crucial section of Calmet's work may be found in volume 2, chapters 7-35. Apparently in Moravia it was common enough "to see men who had died some time before, present themselves in a party, and sit down to table with persons of their acquaintance without saying anything; but that nodding to one of the party, who would infallibly die some days afterwards." These specters, when driven through with "stakes," would utter "very loud cries, and a great quantity of bright vermilion blood" would flow from them. If we compare Calmet's observations with Polidori's introductory remarks in *The Vampyre*, it soon becomes clear that he is either quoting directly from this text or, as I think more likely, quoting extracts from Calmet cited elsewhere. In a region in the vicinity of Transylvania the Heyducq people call the ghosts from the dead vampires who suck the blood of the living to nourish themselves. While the victims debilitate, and perish, these vampyres "fill themselves with blood in such abundance that it is seen to come from them by the conduits, and even oozing through the pores." The life of a certain Heyducq, Arnald Paul (Polidori's "Arnold Paul" in his introduction) is then recounted. This Arnald Paul was crushed to death, but some weeks later inexplicable "vampyre" deaths occur, which recall to the people's mind Arnald Paul's own claim that in the frontiers of Turkish Serbia, he had been visited by vampires. He'd cured himself (since those sucked by vampires in turn suck others on their death) "by eating earth from the grave of the vampyre, and smearing himself with his blood; a precaution which, however, did not prevent him from becoming so after his death, since, on being exhumed forty days after his interment, they found on his corpse all the indications of an arch-vampire" (Polidori in fact quotes the entire passage verbatim.) The Hadnagi, or bailiff, ordered that sharp stakes be driven through his heart. But when the stake was pierced through his body he uttered "a frightful shriek, as if he had been alive: that done, they cut off his head, and burnt the whole body." The vampire, being neither dead nor alive, contains within him both the principles of life and death (Eros and Thanatos) and parodies the religious belief in life after death. The vampire is a ghastly/ghostly parody, a monstrous subversion that mocks a fundamental tenet of Christianity: that Christ alone returned from the dead.

Drawing on Calmet, Polidori is able to fill out the general outline of Byron's narrative. Whereas the relationship between Darvell and his victim (Lord Ruthven and Aubrey, in Polidori) remains unchanged, we are given a fuller account of Lord Ruthven's disturbed state of mind: there is a "curse on him" and there is something "supernatural" about his person. Such is the strength of this sublime object that during the continental journey Aubrey refuses to accept that his beloved Ianthe was actually murdered by Lord Ruthven (the "Vampyre") even though a dagger left behind perfectly matches one of Lord Ruthven's sheaths. Since the Father's Law (Lord Ruthven is another version of the Gothic patriarch) must be obeyed, Aubrey can only relapse into a state of delirium, from which he recovers only to be led by Lord Ruthven toward his own death in an Orientalist fantasy. As in Lord Byron's "A Fragment," the dying Ruthven extracts a terrible promise. "I would do any thing," says Aubrey, and binds himself to Ruthven by taking an oath.

> "Swear!" cried the dying man, raising himself with exultant violence, "Swear by all your soul reveres, by all your nature fears, swear that for a year and a day you will not impart your knowledge of my crimes or death to any living being in any way, whatever may happen, or whatever you may see."—His eyes seemed bursting from their sockets: "I swear!" said Aubrey; he sunk laughing on his pillow, and breathed no more.

Although Ruthven's demand does not have the "Orientalist" promise of numerological fulfillment—this Orientalist fantasy/promise would unlock a different or alternative meaning, if pursued far enough—it corresponds nevertheless, in essence, to Darvell's demand in Byron's "A Fragment." There is clearly a much older, and complex, tradition of narrative based on "enigmas" of this kind; though here one of the discoveries of that narrative—promise followed by pact and exchange—is not explicitly stated. The silence is a pact based on notions of honor and friendship, but Aubrey gets nothing in return, and, in fact, loses not only his beloved (which he has done anyway) but also his sister. The promise is thus ambiguously directed at a ritual, an exchange, through silence, of a sister. But the exchange remains one way only; unlike Faust's pact, where knowledge is imparted, and unlike the godly promise of a beatitude, all we get is a fiercely binding promise, and its own equally inexplicable logic.

Polidori's narrative then moves toward the sacrifice of a sister whose desecration and rape by Lord Ruthven anticipates the sister/bride's rape by the Monster in *Frankenstein*. Because the oath has such binding force (an interdiction, a taboo, a threat) it subverts the logic of the su-

perego. Instead of controlling the libido, it releases it; the sister is offered as a sacrifice and Aubrey becomes an accomplice in this act of barbarism. It is only after the deadly hour of the oath has elapsed that Aubrey narrates his tale, only to die immediately afterward. By then "Lord Ruthven had disappeared, and Aubrey's sister had glutted the thirst of a VAMPYRE!"

Contemporary periodical literature by and large ignored Polidori. When there is a reference to this tale, it is in the context of Byron's works. Thus, when *Mazeppa* and *Don Juan* were reviewed in the July 1819 issue of the *Monthly Review*, Polidori is mentioned in passing with reference to *Mazeppa*. The only significant contemporary examination of Polidori's **The Vampyre** is to be found in the *Monthly Review* of May 1819, which gives an account of the plot together with copious quotations. Thus, the ten pages devoted to the book—technically one of the longer reviews in the journal that year—hide a singular disinterestedness in the work itself. In fact, the reviewer seems to be more interested in the scientific literature on "vampyres" than in the special problems of either demonology or fantasy. Thus, Polidori's "error" in describing the vampire antihero (a "deadly hue, which never gained a warmer tint") is set against scientific accounts that refer to the complexion of "vampyres" as "florid, healthy, and full of blood." Echoing the critical discourses on *Frankenstein*, which was reviewed by the same critic in April 1818, the reviewer argued that works like these "produced . . . for a temporary and social purpose" cannot be subjected to close critical scrutiny. The concept of peripheral or marginal writing, or *"terrorist"* writing, as one reviewer called it, has always been set against books of permanent value in periodical literary criticism. The use of the term *terrorist,* which is italicized for both emphasis and, perhaps, semantic deviation, is used here in the satirical sense in which it was used by a correspondent to refer to Ann Radcliffe's "fashion to make *terror* the *order of the day,* by confining the heroes and heroines in old gloomy castles, full of spectres, apparitions, ghosts, and dead men's bones."

Polidori's tale of obsession and demonology was not new—Calmet had done the background work and Byron had effectively written the plot. But he did combine in his works the two essential characteristics of the Gothic that go back to Walpole: horror and incest. In Walpole these two themes made their way into a heterogeneous set (*The Castle of Otranto* and *The Mysterious Mother*). By a neat repetition of the same process, in Polidori the two themes are distributed through **The Vampyre** and **Ernestus Berchtold**. The levels of genealogical duplication and uncanny identifications that signify the order of the *imaginary* become a powerful feature of Polidori's narratives. The sublime, as we begin to understand it in these fragments, now takes the form of the kind of unities of self and other theorized in Lacan. Polidori's little-known tale of double incest is about as good a proof-text of this theory as any. We therefore turn to **Ernestus Berchtold** next.

The epigraphs to Polidori's **Ernestus Berchtold** juxtapose two radically different poets, Dryden and Byron. From

Dryden a passage from *Oedipus* is quoted; from Byron, a passage from *The Giaour,* one of Polidori's favorite poems. The theme of the novel is thus implicit in these two quotations—Dryden's predictable condemnation of humanity trying to unravel (much to its grief) the mysteries of "heavenly justice," Byron's much more passionate concern with individual guilt and transgression. In the introduction, Polidori concedes his own lack of talent as a writer. He "cannot boast of the horrible imagination of the one, [Mary Shelley] or the elegant classical style of the latter [Byron]." Polidori is also conscious of the criticism directed against supernatural tales—that they are not realistic, their moral vision is blinkered or flawed, and so on—but he would nevertheless want to defend his own work by the old trick of claiming that the actions of the characters are not different from those found in everyday life.

Incestuous coupling has a peculiar fascination for the Gothic, since the consequence of this coupling is not, as in realist fiction, a matter of moral anxiety; rather, the consequence is "structural" in that it threatens and splinters human history through an alternative history that is pre*symbolic*. As in Walpole's *The Mysterious Mother,* the tale of incest becomes indistinguishable from the Gothic of horror because both begin to share the same concerns about history, that is, an urge (though admittedly "failed") toward the dissolution of difference, and a confrontation, in representational terms, with the extremes of experience. The incestuous sublime thus repeats an essential feature of both the unity of the self and Other in the *imaginary* and the subject's plunge into the horrifying abyss of personal genealogy in which the distinctions so carefully made in *The Castle of Otranto* collapse. [Genealogy] is the true narrative of *Ernestus Berchtold* . . . .

The formal marriage of Ernestus and Louisa is paralleled by the illicit union of Olivieri and Julia, who are also half brother and sister. This genealogical duplication is then extended to cover a duplication in the narrative procedure itself. Doni, the father of Louisa and Olivieri, writes down his secret life (which includes a Faustian pact with an Arab based on the exchange of happiness for money) as a way of lifting the lid on his dark and unspeakable history. The narrator, the character Ernestus, finally leaves Doni's manuscript with the person to whom the text has been narrated all along because he is unable to articulate this "real [but monstrous] history," of which he is a source and a participant. He therefore tells the narratee, or the infra reader:

> I cannot tell you more; read that damning tale, and then you may know what I dare, nay, dare not rest on. My history is quickly ended.

As in the Gothic generally, there are two histories at work here. One is the history of the grand narrative, the history of events that may be quickly and decisively plotted. The other is history as unspeakable genealogy that transforms human history into a pathology, as indicated in the final words of the novel (which are in fact Doni, the father's):

But you married; I dreamt of happiness, on Louisa's birthday accompanied you to your room, and the demon's threat I found had indeed been fulfilled. Your mother's portrait was Matilda's. Olivieri had seduced, you married a daughter of Matilda, of Matilda's husband, and I was the murderer of her father.

Such is the frightening nature of this admission that the passage cited above, composed in a slightly awkward syntax, is part of a coda to the text, given ostensibly as documentary evidence without any authorial/editorial intrusion. This coda, entitled "The Life of Count Filiberto Doni," insinuates an objective history that the Gothic cannot possibly accept. The unspeakable genealogical sublime fragments, rips apart, shatters the Gothic by writing out the narrative of the *imaginary* ideal in the double, the sexual relationship of the frighteningly harmonious whole. In all these Gothic fragments and fragmented Gothics the agenda is the same: not the subject's momentary entry into the sublime under the law of reason, but his dissolution in a version of the oceanic experience.

This reading was, of course, totally lost on the contemporary reviewers. In the February 1820 issue of the *Monthly Review,* for instance, *Ernestus Berchtold* is damned with faint praise: the work is "gloomy and sceptical," but Polidori is encouraged to write more since "he is capable of writing in a higher and purer strain." In the preface to the novel, Polidori had covered himself by claiming that the characters were all under a demonic influence. Clearly, Polidori had consciously told a lie; he had repressed in his critical preface the real, disturbing, narrative of his work by doing precisely what so many other Gothic writers had done before: issuing a disavowal that contradicts the text itself. The *Monthly Review,* however, continued to read Polidori in largely realist terms by rebuking him for adopting an apparatus (the exchange of knowledge for wealth with the mysterious Arab) that added nothing more to the text.

> The story displays considerable powers of imagination, but conveys merely irrelevant hints at supernatural agency; so that, in the explanation which follows it, we are surprised to find how busy the evil spirits have been in producing misfortunes which we had been satisfied with ascribing to the influence of evil passions.

The fascination with "evil passions," notably incest and "evil spirits," has been one of the more powerful underlying themes of the Gothic. Indeed, as we found out in Walpole's *The Mysterious Mother,* these themes are the underside, the soft underbelly, of the surface horrors of all Gothic texts. In Polidori, as in Mary Shelley's *Mathilda,* the conjunction of the two makes explicit the final and unremitting "horror" of the Gothic. It was a theme that had been played out by Polidori in a poem entitled *"Chatterton to His Sister."* The construction of an imaginary sister for Chatterton allowed Polidori to enter into the theme of an illicit passion, which surfaced much more explicitly in the Ernestus-Louisa/Julia/Oliviera affairs some months later.

FURTHER READING

Bibliography

Viets, Henry R. "The Printings in America of Polidori's *The Vampyre* in 1819." *Papers of the Bibliographic Society of America* 62, No. 3 (1968): 434-35.

    Account of the genesis and first publication of Polidori's work, followed by descriptions of three United-States editions that appeared the same year.

————. "The London Editions of Polidori's *The Vampyre.*" *Papers of the Bibliographic Society of America* 63 (1969): 83-103.

    Lengthy anecdotal account of the composition and publication of *The Vampyre.* Viets includes information on pirated editions, foreign-language editions, and stage adaptations.

Biography

Macdonald, D. L. *Poor Polidori: A Critical Biography of the Author of "The Vampyre."* Toronto: University of Toronto Press, 1991, 333 p.

    The first full-length treatment of Polidori's life and literary career. Includes an extensive primary and secondary bibliography that cites unpublished and privately held papers as well as published sources. A chapter from this work is excerpted in the entry above.

Rieger, James. "Dr. Polidori and the Genesis of *Frankenstein.*" *Studies in English Literature, 1500-1900* III, No. 4 (Autumn 1963): 461-72.

    Debunks the account of the story-writing session that is popularly believed to have been the genesis of Polidori's *Vampyre* and Mary Shelley's *Frankenstein.* Rieger posits an earlier date of genesis for Shelley's novel and maintains that Polidori played a more central and intellectual role in the Diodati ménage than most commentators grant him.

Viets, Henry R. "John William Polidori, M.D., and Lord Byron— A Brief Interlude in 1816." *The New England Journal of Medicine* 264, No. 11 (16 March 1961): 553-57.

    Account of the time Polidori spent with Byron in Switzerland, including a brief biographical sketch of Polidori and a description of the "ghost-story scheme" that resulted in *The Vampyre.* Viets presents Polidori as volatile and mentally unstable.

————. "'By the Visitation of God': The Death of John William Polidori, M.D." *British Medical Journal* 2 (30 December 1961): 1773-75.

Recounts the circumstances surrounding Polidori's death, quoting extensively from coroner's inquest documents as well as diaries and letters. Viets finds nothing to support the avowal, made by Polidori's nephew William Michael Rossetti and subsequent commentators, that Polidori committed suicide.

Criticism

Foust, Ronald. "Rite of Passage: The Vampire Tale as Cosmogonic Myth." In *Aspects of Fantasy: Selected Essays from the Second International Conference on the Fantastic in Literature and Film,* edited by William Coyle, pp. 73-84. Westport, Conn.: Greenwood Press, 1986.

    Notes that *The Vampyre* "both initiates the modern vampire story and adumbrates the major elements that will become the archetypal staples of the form."

Punter, David. "Gothic and Romanticism: Blake, Coleridge, Shelley, Byron, Keats, John Polidori, Mary Shelley." In his *The Literature of Terror: A History of Gothic Fictions from 1765 to the Present Day,* pp. 99-129. London: Longman, 1980.

    Notes that many characteristics of the Romantic-era male vampire in literature are embodied in Polidori's antagonist Ruthven.

Twitchell, James B. "The Rise and Fall and Rise of Dracula." In *Dreadful Pleasures: An Anatomy of Modern Horror,* pp. 105-59. New York: Oxford University Press, 1985.

    Discusses *The Vampyre* in relation to other vampires in literature and film.

West, Paul. *Lord Byron's Doctor.* New York: Doubleday, 1989, 277 p.

    Historical novel that provides a fictional account of Polidori's life from the time he departed for Europe with Byron in 1816 until his death five years later.

Wolf, Leonard. Introduction to *The Essential Frankenstein, Including the Complete Novel by Mary Shelley,* edited by Leonard Wolf, pp. 1-20. New York: Plume, 1993.

    Explicates the complex relationships between Polidori, Lord Byron, Claire Claremont, Mary Wollstonecraft Shelley, and Percy Bysshe Shelley. An account of the story-writing session at the Villa Diodati is extensively footnoted. Wolf suggests that Mary Shelley's 1831 account of the evening (excerpted in the entry above) represents her compression of events that occurred over several days, weeks, or months.

Additional coverage of Polidori's life and works is contained in the following source published by Gale Research: *Dictionary of Literary Biography, Volume 116.*

Arthur Schopenhauer

1788-1860

German philosopher.

INTRODUCTION

Believing himself to be the only worthy successor to Immanuel Kant, Schopenhauer was one of the leading German metaphysicians of the nineteenth century. Schopenhauer conceived of Kant's *ding an sich* as an absolute Will that causes and impels all appearances in the phenomenal (and unreal) world. Schopenhauer incorporated Hindu and Buddhist thought into his philosophy and crystallized the pessimism of the late nineteenth century in his rejection of the apparent world and his endorsement of asceticism.

Biographical Information

Schopenhauer was born in Danzig (now Gdansk). His father, a businessman, and his mother, a popular novelist, moved the family to Hamburg when Danzig was annexed to Prussia in 1793. The elder Schopenhauer died in 1805, probably by suicide. To honor a promise to his father, Schopenhauer began a business career, but after a year, he convinced his mother to let him continue his education at the gymnasium in Gotha, where he studied Greek and Latin. After being expelled for improper conduct, Schopenhauer moved to Weimar, where his mother had established a literary salon frequented by Johann Wolfgang von Goethe and other literary figures. In 1809, Schopenhauer enrolled in the University of Göttingen, where he studied medicine and, later, philosophy. While there, the skeptic Gottlob Ernst Schulze encouraged him to read Plato and Kant. The orientalist Friedrich Mayer also introduced him to the *Upanishads* and various Buddhist texts. Continuing his studies at the University of Berlin in 1811, Schopenhauer attended lectures by professed Kantians Johann Gottlieb Fichte and Friedrich Schleiermacher. Schopenhauer resented what he considered to be their misinterpretation of Kant; thus he began a lifelong antagonism toward academic philosophy. Schopenhauer left Berlin when the Prussians rose against the French in 1813. He submitted his dissertation, *Über die vierfache Wurzel des Satzes vom zureichenden Grunde* (*On the Fourfold Root of the Principle of Sufficient Reason*), to the University of Jena, where he graduated in 1813. The work was praised by Goethe, and Schopenhauer returned to Weimar to collaborate with him on a study of anti-Newtonian color theory. Goethe disapproved of Schopenhauer's manuscript, however, so Schopenhauer independently published *Über das Sehn und die Farben* in 1816. After quarreling with his mother, Schopenhauer left Weimar in 1814 and never saw her again. From 1814 to 1818 Schopenhauer lived in Dresden and wrote his most acclaimed work, *Die Welt als Wille und Vorstellung* (*The World as Will and Representation*). The book gar-

nered little critical interest when it was published in 1818, but with three of his works already published, Schopenhauer was awarded a lectureship in philosophy at the University of Berlin in 1820. Scheduling his lectures to coincide with those of Georg Wilhelm Friedrich Hegel, whom he despised, Schopenhauer tried to discredit him and proselytize his admirers. Hegel was then at his most popular, however, and with no audience for Schopenhauer, he was soon dismissed. Schopenhauer lived in Italy for ten years before returning to Berlin to answer a charge of battery against a woman. He moved to Frankfurt-am-Main in 1831 to escape a cholera epidemic—from which Hegel died—and rarely left Frankfurt after 1833. Schopenhauer continued to write and became fairly popular when he published *Parerga und Paralipomena* in 1851. Critical recognition followed, and by the time of his death in 1860, Schopenhauer was one of the best known philosophers in Europe.

Major Works

Schopenhauer considered his first published work—*Über die vierfache Wurzel des Satzes vom zureichenden Grunde*—to be the proper introduction to his thought. In it, Schopenhauer contended that human knowledge presupposes the unprovable assumption that everything must have a ground or reason. Schopenhauer's greatest achievement, *Die Welt als Wille und Vorstellung*, published in 1818, outlines his contention that the world is but a phenomenal expression of the irrational and all-encompassing Will. The Will enslaves the human intellect to such impulses as the emotions, the sex drive, and the subconscious. According to Schopenhauer, people ought to transcend appearances through artistic contemplation and negate the Will through asceticism. Later works generally bolster his central metaphysical arguments. For example, his *Über den Willen in der Natur* (*The Will in Nature*) insists that his philosophy is supported by the empirical sciences, and *Die beiden Grundprobleme der Ethik* (*On the Basis of Morality*) addresses the problem of freedom and determinism. In 1844 he published a revised edition of *Die Welt als Wille und Vorstellung*, with fifty supplementary chapters, almost doubling the size of the 1818 edition.

Critical Reception

Critics largely ignored Schopenhauer's writings until late in his life. The essays of *Parerga und Paralipomena* were more approachable than the intimidating *Die Welt als Wille und Vorstellung* and appealed to popular pessimistic sentiment. Positive reviews, especially a *Westminster Review* article from 1853, popularized Schopenhauer's philosophy and evinced favorable reactions throughout Europe. Schopenhauer's main influence thus was posthumous, but appealed to such artists, cultural critics, and philosophers as Thomas Mann, Friedrich Nietzsche, Leo Tolstoy, Richard Wagner, and Ludwig Wittgenstein. Although twentieth-century analytic philosophers have shown little interest, Schopenhauer infused modern thought with a pessimism and irrationalism that helped shape nineteenth- and twentieth-century letters.

PRINCIPAL WORKS

Über die vierfache Wurzel des Satzes vom zureichenden Grunde: Eine philosophische Abhandlung [*On the Fourfold Root of the Principle of Sufficient Reason*] (philosophy) 1813
Über das Sehn und die Farben: Eine Abhandlung (philosophy) 1816
Die Welt als Wille und Vorstellung: Vier Bücher, nebst einem Anhange, der die Kritik der Kantischen Philosophie enthält [*The World as Will and Idea*; also published as *The World as Will and Representation*] (philosophy) 1818; revised edition, 1844
Über den Willen in der Natur: Eine Erörterung der Bestätigungen, welch die Philosophie des Verfassers, seit ihrem Auftreten, durch die empirischen Wissenschaften erhalten hat [*The Will in Nature: An Account of the Corroborations Received by the Author's Philosophy from the Empirical Sciences*; also published as "On the Will in Nature"] (philosophy) 1836
Die beiden Grundprobleme der Ethik, behandelt in zwei akademischen Preisschriften [*On the Freedom of the Will* and *On the Basis of Morality*] (philosophy) 1841
Parerga und Paralipomena: Kleine philosophische Schriften [*Parerga and Paralipomena: Short Philosophical Essays*] (philosophy) 1851
Arthur Schopenhauers sämmtliche Werke (philosophy) 1873-74

CRITICISM

John Oxenford (essay date 1853)

SOURCE: "Iconoclasm in German Philosophy," in *The Westminster Review*, Vol. III, No. 2, January 1, 1853, pp. 388-407.

[*An English critic and playwright, Oxenford was a well-known translator of Goethe when the following article appeared in* The Westminster Review *in 1853. One of the first writings to have introduced Schopenhauer to the English-speaking world, "Iconoclasm in German Philosophy" was also translated into German; it was widely read in Germany, sparked reactions in France and Italy, and garnered Schopenhauer a number of admirers. In the article, Oxenford outlines Schopenhauer's metaphysics, contextualizing Schopenhauer in relation to Kant and his academic contemporaries.*]

Few, indeed, we venture to assert, will be those of our English readers who are familiar with the name of Arthur Schopenhauer. Fewer still will there be who are aware that the mysterious being owning that name has been working for something like forty years to subvert that whole system of German philosophy which has been raised by the university professors since the decease of Immanuel Kant, and that, after his long labour, he has just succeeded in making himself heard—wonderfully illustrating that doctrine in acoustics which shows how long an interval may elapse between the discharge of the cannon and the hearing of the report. And even still fewer will there be who are aware that Arthur Schopenhauer is one of the most ingenious and readable authors in the world, skilful in the art of theory building, universal in attainments, inexhaustible in the power of illustration, terribly logical and unflinching in the pursuit of consequences, and—a most amusing qualification to every one but the persons "hit"—a formidable hitter of adversaries.

The list of works at the head of this article will show how long this most eccentric of philosophers has laboured, and how continuous his labours have been. In 1813 he propounded a new theory of cause and effect; and the philosophical world of Germany said—nothing. Six years afterwards came out the grand work, *Die Welt als Wille und Vorstellung,* in which a whole metaphysical theory was developed with a force and clearness which Germany had not seen since the days of Kant, but still the same world (with a solitary exception) said—nothing. We marvel not that the Schopenhauer temper, which, we opine, from certain polemical treatises, is not of the mildest, was a little ruffled. All over Germany were professorlings dotted about, receiving their snug salaries, and, without a spark of genius in their composition, retailing the words of some great master of philosophic art, and complimenting each other, as each brought out his trifling modification of a system which had been slightly modified from some previous modification, and yet could not Schopenhauer get a word of notice—not so much as a little abuse. There were histories of philosophy, and compendia of philosophy, and philosophical journals, but none could be found diffusing the knowledge of Schopenhauer's emanations. At last a chance presents itself—who shall say from what quarter the good wind will blow?—the Royal Norwegian Scientific Society offers a prize for the best treatise on the Freedom of the Will, and in the year 1829 this is gained by Schopenhauer. Surely Germany, with its known predilection for rank, will recognise the adjudication of a crown of honour by a royal society—a scientific society, too, even though Drontheim be not universally regarded as the modern Athens. But no, even this would not do. The prophet was only great out of his own country. In vain did he demonstrate that, in the ordinary sense of the word, freedom of will was a mere chimera, exploded years ago, and in vain did Scandinavia applaud, professional Germany ignored the existence of Schopenhauer, his pamphlet, the Royal Scientific Society, and Norway itself, and went on teaching "absolute freedom," and preaching "categorical imperatives," just as if the energetic Schopenhauer had never brought pen and paper into visible contact. Still did Schopenhauer work on, not through good and evil report, but through what was much more disheartening—no report at all. His last publication, ***Parerga und Paralipomena,*** a collection of philosophical papers illustrative of his own system, but perfectly readable without previous knowledge of it, is even more vigorous, and gives more signs of independent thought than the work of his youth, which saw the light forty years ago. And at last we find that the neglected philosopher is known, and, to some extent, appreciated. The history of German philosophy published by Professor Fortlage in 1852—a book highly respectable of its kind—devotes a not over short chapter to the examination of Schopenhauer, as one of the remarkable phenomena of the present day, and though the professor differs from the non-professor, the difference is courteous. Two articles in the last number of J. H. Fichte's philosophical *Zeitschrift* still more clearly show that Schopenhauer, if he is not liked, is, at any rate, deemed formidable.

But if there is really something remarkable about Schopenhauer, why this forty years' obscurity? That is the question, above all others, which Schopenhauer himself is prepared to answer. Because, he will tell you, he is not a professor of philosophy, is not a philosopher by trade, has no academical chair, and there has been an understanding among all the university philosophers to put down any man who is not one of their craft. The Hegelians may differ from the Herbartians, and the Herbartians from the Hegelians, and both from the Schellingites, and all from the Schleiermacherians, and the small branches that spring from the huge trees may jostle against each; but all this

is done civilly, and the adversaries compliment each other on learning, or profundity, or acuteness, or comprehensiveness, however they may dissent from theories propounded. On the other hand, woe to the luckless student of philosophy who, having devoted himself to the wisdom of the Oriental world, to the dialectic of the Greeks, to the acuteness of the French, to the hard, common sense of the English, and, above all, to his own reflections, shall dare to come forward with the result of his labours, unless he shall have secured a license to speculate. As far as the promulgation of his views is concerned, he shall be doomed to solitary confinement, and every operation by which his opinion could find its way to the public shall be effectually stopped up.

Of course the cry of Schopenhauer, that German philosophy as taught by the successors of Kant, is not founded on any honest investigation of the truth, but is a mere trade, by which the professor hopes to secure a living for his wife and family, may be interpreted as no more than another form of the ancient fox's declaration, that the "grapes are sour." Schopenhauer, not receiving any encouragement from the acknowledged *magnates* of philosophy, bespatters the whole system to which they owe their authority. That vexation and disappointment had some share in producing the virulence with which he attacks the philosophers in high places is likely enough, but, at the same time, it is by no means certain that a word spoken in anger is altogether inappropriate; and, unfortunately, too many philosophical works of modern Germany encourage the suspicion that the animadversions of Schopenhauer are not altogether unfounded.

Let any impartial Englishman, who has gone through an ordinary course of logic, who has studied mathematics to a degree sufficient to make him understand the methods of demonstration—who has read the metaphysicians of his own country, and we will even add, the leading works of Immanuel Kant—let this Englishman, we say, take any one of Hegel's so-called scientific works, and honestly ask himself, whether this is the style in which a work intended to convey instruction ought to be written. The general drift of the system, with its optimism, its liberalism, its apparently comprehensive grasp, may please him; the universal attainments of the author may command his admiration; but, apart from these considerations, let him still ask himself, whether the system is really a system at all—whether the reasonings are reasonings at all—whether the links that seem to connect proposition with proposition really do anything of the kind. If he be not of presumptuous temper, he will for awhile be modest, and fancy that the measure of the author's profundity exceeds that of his own power of penetration; but if he reflects that he has been tolerably able to follow the chain of reasoning in every existing science, but just this one science of German metaphysics, as propounded by the schools of Schelling and Hegel, and that the process employed in the highest mathematics does not, after all, differ so very much from that which is used in ordinary conversation, modesty will at last grow a little weary; and the student will begin to suspect that he has looked up to his preceptor with something beyond a due measure of veneration. Let him next proceed to take up one of those compendia of Hegelian philosophy, by means of which some disciple of the great master offers to render the fountain-head of wisdom more approachable to the uninitiated; he will now find matters grown worse. Hegel himself, independently of his system, had a certain quantity of illustrative information and remark, which was much more valuable than the thing illustrated—just as in picture-books, the pictures are generally far superior to the letter-press—and these were appended as a sort of perpetual comment to the dry skeleton of the system. But when the Hegelian usher becomes the preceptor, he can only give the master's doctrine in a shorter, and consequently drier form, while he proves the unfructifying nature of the philosophy itself by showing that he can scarcely utter a word in a different order from that in which it is set down in the original book. The theories of Plato, of Locke, of Kant, need not be described according to a certain fixed outline, utterly destructive of all individual peculiarity, but the interpreter may infinitely vary his mode of exposition, and give full play to any descriptive power with which he may be blessed. It is not so with the philosophy of Hegel; his system, if it is really to be taught, like any other science, requires a thorough re-writing: but his disciples, far from doing anything of the kind, merely repeat his words, without a syllable of elucidation. Anything more profitless than the second-rate works belonging to the various schools of German philosophy cannot be found in the whole compass of literature. Having taken a sufficient dose of this filtered wisdom, let our supposed impartial Englishman, who has now gone through the most dreamy series of unconvincing arguments that imagination can reach, now seek to know the obstacle which renders impossible all union between his own reasoning and the reasoning in the books before him. He is bluntly told by the school that he is not endowed with a "speculative spirit;" or if he has preferred the region of Schelling to that of Hegel, that he is without a certain preternatural form of intuition, which must be assumed as indispensable to philosophical study.

At this point, unless his own self-depreciation be of the most abnormal kind, he will indeed be a little staggered. The faculties that have carried him hitherto through the most various branches of learning and science, fail him now; and he finds a sort of ratiocination proposed to him which he could not use for any one purpose of his life— nay, which he could not even describe without talking, parrot-like, out of one of his books. At this juncture, when faith is wavering, let him take up some strong page of Arthur Schopenhauer, and lo! an uneasy suspicion, which has been for some time floating in his mind, will begin to assume a tangible shape. It will not be as though Schopenhauer, in his invectives against Hegel and Schelling, taught him anything new, but as though a sudden conviction was awakened in his own bosom. We are not prepared to go the length of Schopenhauer in saying that all the teaching of the modern professors is a mere matter of salary; but of this we are certain, that the parties he attacks have laboured to the utmost of their power to support him in his notion.

Polemic philosophers are often more skilful in *de*struction than in *con*struction, displaying a world of acuteness in picking out the weak places of an adversary's edifice, but a singular want of care and precision in raising their own. Schopenhauer is the very reverse of all this. Far from dissecting the theories of Schelling and Hegel, he gives them a volley of abuse, as though he did not consider them worth the pains of an argument at all; and then he patiently builds up his own system, supporting it as he goes on by perfectly intelligible arguments; his real refutation of all other systems consisting in the confidence with which he points to his own. Appealing to the common sense of his readers, to induce them to leave off listening to a number of strange words of most vague signification, he reduces several terms to the meaning which they bore before the time of Kant; and he propounds a theory with which they may agree or not, but which they can hardly fail to understand. The general fault of German metaphysicians is, that they do not even afford you a fair ground of attack. The systems are so strangely reasoned out, and the words are so uncertain in their import, that you do not know when you are fighting with shadows and when with substance. Struck with admiration at a strange sort of ingenuity, or disgusted by an increasing obscurity, in either mood you venture on no contest at all, but simply remain unconvinced. Now Schopenhauer gives you a comprehensible system, clearly worded; and you may know, beyond the possibility of a doubt, what you are accepting, and what you are rejecting. Never did author less attempt to impose upon his reader.

> **Arthur Schopenhauer is one of the most ingenious and readable authors in the world, skilful in the art of theory building, universal in attainments, inexhaustible in the power of illustration, terribly logical and unflinching in the pursuit of consequences, and . . . a formidable hitter of adversaries.**
>
> **—*John Oxenford***

Let us, however, hasten to remove a false impression we have probably made. It may be imagined that we are wholly condemning the so-called successors of Kant, and wholly extolling Schopenhauer, and therefore we would have it speedily understood, that all we have said applies not to the doctrine taught, but to the manner of teaching. The tendencies of the modern German philosophers, however they may differ among themselves, are liberal and ennobling in the highest degree; and whether they be—as their enthusiastic disciples believe them—exalted geniuses, inspired with the love of truth, or mere members of a profitable craft, they are still important organs for the diffusion of lofty ideas, which sometimes take the form of an elevated system of morality, sometimes have for their aim the foundation of an all-comprehensive scheme of science. Their rallying cry, however strange the language in which it may be couched, is still "progress!" and therefore they are still the pedantic sympathizers with the spirit of modern civilization. It is not in their doctrines, in their ultimate tendency, that the impartial English thinker finds so much to object to, as in the constant mistake (in his eyes) of abstractions for actual existences, of no-reasonings for reasonings, of words for things. That many of the newest German philosophers, although brought up in the schools of twenty years back, have themselves come to a conviction that all is not right in this particular, is sufficiently shown by the productions of those authors, who now group themselves around the younger Fichte, and display a befitting reverence for what we may call a sane mode of thinking. Let any one compare the last numbers of the *Zeitschrift für Philosophie,* edited by J. H. Fichte, with the old *Jahrbücher der wissenschaftlichen Kritik,*—that organ of the Hegelian school, in which an ordinary novel could not be reviewed without the employment of a whole arsenal of technical weapons,—and he will be struck with the improvement which has taken place.

On the other hand, while Schopenhauer's teaching is the most genial, the most ingenious, and—we would add, the most amusing that can be imagined, the doctrine taught is the most disheartening, the most repulsive, the most opposed to the aspirations of the present world, that the most ardent of Job's comforters could concoct. All that the liberal mind looks forward to with hope, if not with confidence—the extension of political rights, the spread of education, the brotherhood of nations, the discovery of new means of subduing stubborn nature—must be given up as a vain dream, if ever Schopenhauer's doctrine be accepted. In a word, he is a professed "Pessimist"; it is his grand result, that this is the worst of all possible worlds; nay, so utterly unsusceptible of improvement, that the best thing we can do is to get rid of it altogether, by a process which he very clearly sets forth.

At the commencement of his theory, Schopenhauer appears as a compounder of Kant with Berkeley; and here we may observe, that though he ultimately proves to be a mystic, in the St. Antony sense of the word, he first comes forward as a special admirer of the common sense of the English. Hobbes, Berkeley, and Priestley, whose existence has been almost ignored by the modern German teachers, are at his fingers' ends, and he cites them not only as kindred souls, but as authorities. All that he says while first setting forth the delusions of the visible world, and denying the freedom of the will (in which latter process he is much indebted to Priestley) seems so fair and above-board, that the unsuspecting reader has no suspicion of the dire result which is at hand. Berkeley has gone further than Kant (who lamely endeavoured to refute him) in denying the reality of the world around him, while Kant constituted an *à priori* system, situated in the mind itself, of which Berkeley had no notion. Nothing could be easier than to reconcile the two systems, and Fichte had already set the example of denying the reality of that mysterious *Ding-an-sich,* (thing in itself,) which Kant stationed behind his phenomena. Indeed, there are many points of affinity between Schopenhauer and Fichte, not-

withstanding the former's strong abuse of the latter; and in an early critique of Herbart upon Schopenhauer (the solitary exception already referred to) which stands out as a single star amid the general darkness, the notion seemed to be that a clearer Fichte was in the philosophical field.

As this article is chiefly intended for those who are in some degree acquainted with German philosophy, we may assume that our readers are so far familiar with Kant's theory, as to be aware that he considered time and space as mere forms of the mind, through which it received the impressions of outward things, but which had no existence in the things themselves; and that he moreover supposed certain general laws, as for instance, that of cause and effect, likewise to have their seat in the mind alone, so that it was under these laws that all judgments must be formed. Space, time, and the "categories"—the media through which sensible objects are revealed, and the laws under which they objects of thought as well as sense, are therefore, *à priori,* in the same way—to use a common simile—as if we said that a green tint spread over the face of nature, would come, *à priori,* to a man destined to wear green spectacles for life. Here arises the fundamental difficulty, which prevents the thinkers of the English school from accepting the teaching of the German. The Englishman, when declaring that experience is the sole source of knowledge, will not make any exception in favour of laws, however general, or axioms, however evident; while the Germans, however they may differ on other points, are agreed on this; that the mind itself independently of experience, is a source of knowledge. With Kant, however, the difference from the English is less important than with his successors. They indeed endeavour to establish theories which would carry men far beyond the limits of nature, but *his* theory of *à priori* forms has a confining, not an extending tendency. The "categories" seated in the mind are merely of value, on the supposition that objects are presented upon which they can be employed, and we have no right to employ them when the world of sense leaves off. To return to the simile, the man with the green spectacles must not imagine that because lighted nature wears a green tint, darkness will appear green likewise. According to consistent Kantism, physical theology, with its high priests Durham and Paley, and its paraphernalia of Bridgewater Treatises, is but an amiable absurdity, based on an illegitimate extension of the law of cause and effect to an object which lies beyond its jurisdiction. Theoretically speaking, man, according to Kant, has no right either to affirm or deny the existence of a God, of an immaterial soul, or, indeed, of any entity, that lies beyond the observation of the senses. Theoretically, Kantism is negative atheism, though by his "*practical* reason" Kant re-admits at the back door the ideas which have been ignominiously thrust forth from the portico.

The theoretical part of Kant's system is, with certain modifications, adopted by Schopenhauer; that is to say, he accepts the ideality of time and space, but he reduces the twelve categories, which Kant deduced from the forms of propositions set down in the common logic of the schools, to the simple law of cause and effect, which, however, appears in various shapes. Now, it is that end-less chain by which all the phenomena of the visible world are connected, (the law of cause and effect, properly so called,) now it is the connexion which exists between the premises and the conclusion of an argument. But, what-ever shape it takes, it is the law by which the mind is compelled to think, when it contemplates the objects of the external world.

The faculty which acts under this law of cause and effect, is called by Schopenhauer the *understanding,* and he as-cribes to its operation much that has been hitherto re-ferred (by Kant among others) to the senses alone. And we may here observe of Schopenhauer generally, that, differing from a great many of his countrymen, who de-light to flounder in abstraction, and shrink, as it were, by instinct, from familiar illustration, he always displays a most laudable industry in collecting facts, which may serve to set forth his views in a new light. Zoological records, transactions of learned societies, classical poets of vari-ous languages, even newspaper anecdotes, are all ran-sacked with zeal, and the treasures they afford are used with discrimination. It is to the acuteness with which he pounces on a happy illustration, that Schopenhauer is justly indebted for the peculiar charm of his writings.

The understanding (*Verstand*), according to Schopenhau-er, who is the reverse of a Cartesian in this respect, is possessed by man, in common with other animals, though it varies in degrees of acuteness. It has no power of gen-eralization; but its functions are confined to single imme-diate objects, and the man who knows that a mutton-chop will cause a cessation of hunger, is just in the same pre-dicament as a horse, who practically affirms the same thing of a bunch of hay. Practical cleverness, ingenuity, in short, most of the facilities for "getting on in the world" depend, in a great measure, on the acuteness of the under-standing, in assigning each single effect to its proper cause, and an habitual tendency to make mistakes in this partic-ular, constitutes ordinary stupidity.

In the definition of the reason (*Vernunft*), Schopenhauer greatly differs from all his contemporaries. With them, reason is a comprehensive faculty, which, scorning the finite, displays itself by grasping, or contemplating, or suspecting the infinite, or the absolute, or the uncondi-tioned, (according to the particular vocabulary which the philosopher adopts,) but which is subjected to the special inconvenience, that many an unprejudiced thinker will be inclined to suspect that it does not exist at all. What is meant by the understanding is always intelligible enough, but when an ordinary German philosopher begins to talk about the reason, his discourse generally rises into the misty sublime. The warning of Kant, who saw the ambi-tious flights of the reason in the regions of science, that it was not to be received as a theoretical instructor, has been but little heeded, and reason has been made to hatch forth any monstrosity that the philosophical head may fancy. With Schopenhauer the reason takes even an hum-bler position than with Kant, who, placing it at the head of his moral system, and thus giving it a high practical exaltation, led the way to that strange apotheosis of ab-stract forms, which we find in his late successors, though he himself would have protested against it. What Schopen-hauer says on this subject [in *Die Welt als Wille und Vorstellung*] may serve as a specimen of his dispassion-ate style:—

Besides that class of perceptions, which we have already considered, that is to say, those which might be reduced to space, time, and matter, if we regard the object, or to pure sensuousness and understanding, if we regard the subject, there is in man alone, among all the inhabitants of the earth, another faculty of knowledge, another mode of consciousness, which, with anticipatory correctness, has been called *reflection.* For it is, indeed, a reflex, something deduced from that intuitive knowledge, but it nevertheless has a nature totally different from that of the rest, and knows nothing of their forms, while, with respect to it, the law of cause and effect, that prevails over all objects, here wears a perfectly different aspect. This new consciousness—this consciousness raised to a higher power—this distinct reflection of everything intuitive in the non-intuitive conceptions of reason, it is this alone which endows man with that circumspection, which so completely distinguishes his own consciousness from that of animals, and which causes his whole earthly career to be so different from that of his irrational brethren.

He is equally their superior in pain and in suffering. They live in the present alone; he, at the same time, in the future and the past. They satisfy their immediate wants; he makes artificial preparations for the future, nay, for times which he will not live to see. They are exposed to the impressions of the moment, to the operation of immediate motives; he is determined, by abstract conceptions, independent of the present day. He, therefore, executes well-digested plans, or acts according to fixed maxims, without regard to secondary circumstances and the casual impressions of the moment. He can thus, for instance, calmly devise artificial means for his own death, can make himself impenetrable by dissimulation, can carry a secret with him to the grave, and, lastly, has a real choice between several motives. . . . The brute animal, on the other hand, is determined by present impressions; fear of immediate punishment can alone curb its desires, till at last fear becomes a custom, and in that shape determines the animal, under the name of 'training,' or 'breaking in.' The animal has feeling and intuition; man, besides this, *thinks* and *knows; the will* is common to both. The animal communicates its feelings by sounds and gestures, while man communicates (or conceals) his thought by speech. Speech is the first product and the necessary implement of his reason. Hence, in the Greek and Italian languages, speech and reason are designated by the same word. . . . The German word for reason, '*Vernunft,*' comes from the verb '*vernehmen,*' which is not synonymous with '*hören,*' to hear, but signifies a perception of the thought conveyed by words. It is by the help of speech alone that reason attains its most important results, such as the harmonious action of a number of individuals,—the organized co-operation of thousands—civilization—states; then again science— the preservation of early experiences—the combination of objects into one general conception—the communication of truth—the diffusion of error—thought and poetical creation—religious dogmas and superstitions. The animal knows nothing of death till it actually comes to him; man consciously approaches his death every hour, and this gives life itself a doubtful aspect in the eyes of one who has not perceived that constant annihilation is the character of life throughout. It is chiefly on this account that man has systems of philosophy and religion, though whether that which we commend above all in his actions, namely, rectitude of conduct and nobleness of disposition is the result of either of them is uncertain. On the other hand, among the productions which most certainly belong to them, and therefore to reason alone, may be mentioned the whimsical absurdities of the philosophers of different schools, and the strange and sometimes cruel customs of the priests of different religions.

Reason, though creating the broad distinction between man and beast, and though originating so much that is ennobling and debasing to human nature, is nothing more, according to Schopenhauer, than the power of forming, what Locke calls, "abstract ideas;" and so far the old English and the modern German philosopher agree as much as possible. With all its marvels, reason can still do nothing but arrange the impressions already given by intuition, and far from being a source of new knowledge, it merely takes up at second-hand the knowledge already acquired in another shape. As a means of power, reason certainly raises man above the rest of the animal creation; but as a means of knowledge intuition is the safer of the two. At this point of Schopenhauer's doctrine, a theory of mathematics, which will remind some readers of Gassendi, is introduced. The geometricians, who have followed in the wake of Euclid, are all, he thinks, so far mistaken, that they have neglected the more certain method of intuition, which lay open to them, in the construction of their figures, and have based the demonstrations of their propositions on logical reasoning, which is, at best, but a surrogate. Kant having established the truth, that space is an *à priori* form of intuition, and Schopenhauer having adopted it, the latter proceeds to give hints how a system of geometry may be contrived, in which not only the truth but the cause . . . of the propositions may be proved. We have not room enough to expatiate on this mere episode of the theory, but would just remark that the demonstration he most relies on for a specimen is taken from the *Meno* of Plato.

The whole visible world then is nothing but a mass of consistent unreality. Space, time, and the law of casuality, are all of them mere forms of the mind, which have nothing to do with the real nature of things, but merely concern them so far as they become objects of a perceiving subject. The law of causality being that under which the mind is compelled to think it is a contradiction in terms to talk about a First cause. Every cause is in its turn the effect of another cause, and as for a real *bonâfide* beginning, why seek for anything of the kind when the whole world is a delusion—the "veil of Maya," as the Indian sages call it, and as Schopenhauer, whose religious faith wavers between Brahminism and Buddhism, loves to call it after them. As for the way in which those who think

otherwise are treated by our choleric sage, that may serve as a specimen of his *passionate* manner:—

Now what has been done by our good, honest, German professors of philosophy, who prize mind and truth above everything,—what has been done by them, I say, for that dearly-beloved cosmological proof, after Kant, in his *Critique of Reason*, had dealt it a mortal blow? Then good counsel was a costly commodity, for (and this the worthies know, though they wont say so) *causa prima*, like *causa sui*, is a mere contradiction in terms, although the former expression is much oftener used than the latter, and is generally uttered with a very serious and even solemn air. Nay, many persons, English reverends in particular, turn about their eyes, in a most edifying manner, when with emphasis and emotion they talk of that contradiction in terms—a First cause. They know well enough that a First cause is just as inconceivable as a spot, where space comes to an end, or the moment when time had a beginning. For every cause is a change, with respect to which we must of necessity ask after the preceding change, which brought it about, and so on—*in infinitum,—in infinitum!* Nay, not even a first state of matter, from which all the others would proceed, is conceivable. For if this state had in itself been the cause, they must have existed from all eternity, so that the present state would not only have begun just now. If, on the other hand, it began to be causal at a certain time, something must have changed it at that time, so as to terminate its repose. In this case some foreign agent must have approached, a change must have taken place, after the cause of which (that is to say, after a preceding change) we must immediately inquire, and thus we are again on the ladder of causes, and are whipped on higher and higher by the inexorable laws of casuality—*in infinitum, in infinitum*. The law of causality is not so accommodating as to allow itself to be treated like a backney-coach, which we may send home as soon as we have completed our journey. It is rather like the living broom in Göthe's *Zauberlehrling*, which when once set in activity will never stop moving about and drawing more water, so that only the old conjuror himself can make it quiet again. But alas! our gentlemen are no conjurors. What have they done then, these noble upright friends of truth, who are only waiting for real merit to proclaim it to the world, as soon as it shows itself, and who, when an individual appears, who really *is*, what they only pretend to be, far from wishing to stifle his works by a crafty silence or timid concealment, become, on the contrary, the heralds of his fame, as certainly—ay, as certainly as folly loves understanding. What now have these gentlemen done with their old friend the cosmological demonstration, now so hardly pressed, and laid upon its back. Oh, they imagined a right cunning device. 'Friend,' they said to the cosmological demonstration, 'you are in a sad plight, a sad plight indeed, since your unlucky encounter with that old hard-headed fellow of Königsberg—aye, in as sad a plight as your two brothers, the ontological and physico-theological demonstrations. Never mind, we will not desert you—in fact, you know we are paid to assist you,—but—it cannot be helped—you must change your name and dress, for if we call you by your own name, everybody will run away. In your *incognito*, we will take you under the arm, and introduce you into society, only mind—*incognito* it must be. Your object shall henceforth bear the name of the 'Absolute,'—that sounds foreign, imposing and genteel. We are good judges, as to how far gentility goes with the Germans. Every one knows what is meant, and thinks himself wise into the bargain.

The above extract is characteristic in more respects than one. It shows that odd mixture of sarcasm, invective, and commonsense argument, which constitutes the polemic style of Schopenhauer, and, at the same time, allows that private pique, which is never wholly forgotten, to appear in the form of bitter irony.

The whole world being thus disposed of in a theory not materially different from that of Kant, Schopenhauer arrives at his own proper soil. Hitherto he has ostensibly worked on the teaching of others, his own additions being rather episodical than otherwise; but now comes the flash of true originality.

It will be remembered that after Kant has explained away the phenomenal world, by making space and time mere forms of the perception, and the categories mere forms of the understanding, he leaves an indefinable something, to which he gives the name of the "thing in itself," (*Ding an sich,*) that is to say, the thing considered by itself apart, irrespective of its contemplation by the perceiving mind. This is susceptible of a negative definition only; it lies beyond the boundaries of our knowledge, and all that we can say of it is, that we neither know, nor can know, anything about it. Thus, in the case of a rose, its extension belongs to the form of intuition (space); its arrangement, under any conceivable category, even that of unity—in fact, its existence as a distinct object at all, belongs to the understanding; but there is still something separate from these, which is represented by the mere sensations, the peculiar smell and colour of the rose, and this is the manifestation of the "great unknown." The admission that there is still a residue after the world of sense has been explained away, constitutes a marked difference between Kant and Berkeley: but this difference was removed by Fichte, who having little respect for the unapproachable mystery left by his predecessor, declared the "thing in itself" to be no more than a mere creation of the mind.

This doctrine of Fichte is especially impugned by Schopenhauer. Having already established the position, that causality is a mere law for connecting phenomena with each other, he at once shows the fallacy of using emanation or any other form of this law as a means of explaining independent existences. The mind cannot be the cause of the "thing in itself," because neither of these being phenomena, they both lie beyond the reach of the jurisdiction of causality.

What, then, is the "thing in itself?" "The Will," answers Schopenhauer, with an air of evident triumph; "and this answer is the great discovery of my life." The world, as a collection of invisible objects, is but a series of phenomena, of dreams—nay, of such mere dreams, that it is hard to define the difference between sleeping and wak-ing; but the world in itself is one enormous will, constantly rushing into life. When we are conscious of external objects, only one side of them is revealed to us—namely, the outward side; whereas, when we become our own object, we are conscious of ourselves not only as phenomena, but as will, which is no phenomenon; and here we have the key to the whole mystery, for arguing by analogy, we may extend this will, which in us is accompanied by consciousness, to the whole world, including even its unconscious parts and inhabitants.

We shall now make use of the knowledge that we have of the essence and operation of our own bodies, as a key to the essence of every phenemenon in nature, and with respect to those objects which are not our own body—and therefore are not revealed to us in a double manner, but as outward representations only—form a judgment according to the analogy of that body and essence, that as, on the one hand, they are phenomena, like itself, so, on the other hand, when we set aside their existence as phenomena of the subject, that which remains must, in its own essence, be the same as that which in ourselves we call the will. For what other sort of existence in reality should we ascribe to the rest of the corporeal world? Whence procure the elements out of which such a world could be composed? Besides the will and the phenomena nothing is known to us, or even conceivable. When we would ascribe to the corporeal world, which only exists in our own perceptive faculty, the greatest reality of which we are aware, we ascribe to it that reality which everyone finds in his body, for that to us is more real than anything else. But when we analyze the reality of this body and its actions, we find, beyond its existence as one of our phenomena, nothing but the will; herein is the whole of its reality, and we can never find any other sort of reality, which we can ascribe to the corporeal world. If, therefore, the corporeal world is to be something more than a mere phenomenon of our minds, we must say, that besides this visible existence, it is in itself, and in its own essence, that which we immediately find in ourselves as the Will . . . We must, however, distinguish from the veritable essence of the Will that which does not belong to it, but only to its appearance in the world of phenomena, of which there are many degrees; as, for instance, its accompaniment by knowledge, and its consequent determination by motives. This belongs not to its essence, but merely to its clearest manifestations, in the form of animal and man. When I say, therefore, that the power which impels the stone towards the earth is, in its own essence, apart from all manifestation, the Will, I do not mean to express the absurdity, that the stone is conscious of a motive of action, because the will appears accompanied by consciousness in man.

Nevertheless, gravitation, electricity, and, in fact, every form of action, from the fall of an apple to the foundation of a republic, is an expression of the will and nothing more. The world is essentially will and nothing more, developing itself in a series of manifestations, which rise in a graduated scale, from the so-called laws of matter, to that consciousness, which in the inferior animals reaches the state of sensibility and understanding (in Schopenhauer's sense), and in man reaches that higher state called reason. In the earlier stages its manifestations have a more general aspect; one stone is but numerically distinct from another of the same species, but distinctiveness increases as they ascend in the scale, and when they attain the form of man, each individual is perfectly distinct from all the rest, and that phenomenon, which we call "character," is produced.

However, Schopenhauer does not stop in laying down a huge abstraction, to which he gives the name of the will,—and which in this undefined condition would be little else than a pompous cipher, but he proceeds to mark out the line of its operations, and this perhaps is the most ingenious part of his theory. The old Platonic Ideas occur to his mind, and these not only answer his purpose, but the way in which he uses them gives him a greater affinity to the ancient philosopher of Greece, than is exhibited by any of his contemporaries, though the name of Plato is often enough in their mouths. The Ideas of Plato, which some of our metaphysicians of the last century termed "Universals,"—those supernatural forms of which sensible objects participate, though they themselves are never revealed to mortal eyes in all their purity—those eternal essences, which never pass away, though the individuals through which they are imperfectly revealed, rise and perish in rapid succession,—those "ideas," which have puzzled so many philosophers, and caused so much paper to be covered with fruitless controversy, are interpreted by Schopenhauer to be the various stages at which the manifestation of the will occurs. In every science there is something assumed, which is used to explain or classify various phenomena, but which is not explained in its turn, being deemed, as far as that particular science is concerned, inexplicable. Thus in mechanics gravitation is assumed, but not deduced, and in history, a human will capable of being acted upon by motives is a necessary postulate. The various phenomena of the world are expressive of certain essential laws and attributes, which being forced to appear under the form of space, assume an individuality, which does not intrinsically belong to their own nature. The individual stone may pass away, or may be absorbed into another state of existence, but impenetrability and gravity, which constituted its essential nature,—its "real realities," as Coleridge would say, remain immovable, untouched by the wreck of countless individualities. The "Ideas" thus hold a middle place between the will, as "Thing in itself," and the phenomena, being the points at which the will enters into the phenomenal region. Many of our readers, who have considered all we have hitherto described as tolerable common sense, will probably be inclined to smile at this part of the doctrine, as the vision of a German dreamer. But they will smile much less, if they are familiar with the sort of philosophical atmosphere in which Schopenhauer has been forced to move, during the dynasties of Schelling and Hegel. At any rate, we perfectly know, what Schopenhauer means by his ideas,—but who can say as much for the Absolute Idea of Hegel?

There is no causal connexion between the will and its manifestations, for as Schopenhauer has already explained, causality has no jurisdiction beyond the world of phenomena; but the body is the will itself in its manifested form, and to explain this view in a detail, which we have not space to follow, all sorts of aid are borrowed from physiological science, the different organs of the body being explained according to this hypothesis, and the human brain being the visible representative of human reason. A very ingenious theory of art is likewise connected with this interpretation of "Ideas."

At this stage of the theory, Schopenhauer's moral doctrine may be conveniently introduced. Virtue, which, in his view, is better taught by the sages of Hindostan than by the Jewish or Christian theologians, is based on a practical acknowledgment, that the whole world is but a manifestation of the same will as ourselves—that the various men and animals around us, are so closely connected with us, on account of their common substance, that to say they are "akin" is but a feeble expression. "Thou thyself art this," is the moral maxim of the Hindoo teacher, who points to the surrounding world, as he declares this identity—and the one virtue is sympathy. This is likewise the moral doctrine of Christianity, when it commands its professor to love his neighbour as himself, but Christianity is so far less perfect than Hindooism, that it does not, in its command of universal love, include the brute creation. Hence cruelty to animals—a vice which Schopenhauer holds in the greatest abhorrence, frequently praising the exertions of the English "Prevention" society—is far more common in Christian countries than in the East.

In a moral disquisition, which he wrote some years ago, in answer to a prize question, proposed by the Royal Society of Copenhagen, and which did *not* gain the premium—(our philosopher was not so fortunate in Denmark as in Norway), Schopenhauer displays a great deal of humour, while he ridicules the moral ideal and the "categorical imperative" set up by Kant. There is no doubt that the stern moralist of the Kantian school,—if he was ever anything more than an *ens rationis,* like the wise man of the Stoics,—who would never trust a single generous impulse, but would be diving into abstract principles of action, while the supplicant for charity died of starvation before his eyes,—must have been a singularly disagreeable personage, and that Kant in endeavouring to elevate the dominion of reason, underrated a very essential element in human nature.

The bad man, according to Schopenhauer, is he in whom the "will to live," gains such predominance in its individual form, that he ignores the rights of his fellow-manifestations altogether, and robs and murders them, as seems meet for his own advantage. The just man, who is just, and nothing more, stands higher in the moral scale than the bad man, but he has not reached Schopenhauer's idea of virtue. He so far shows a sympathy with his fellow-creatures that he does not encroach upon their rights, but he is equally unwilling to go out of his way to do them any substantial good. He is a sort of man who pays his taxes and his church-rates, keeps clear of the Court of Requests, and is only charitable when he has an equivalent in the shape of an honourable place in a subscription list.

The good man, as we have already seen, is he whose heart beats with sympathy for all creatures around him, practically if not theoretically acknowledging them as manifestations of the same great Will as himself. He loves every living being, from his neighbour down to a turtle-dove; and as the laws of inanimate nature are still manifestations of the one Will, he may consistently imitate the example of the man in the old story, who looked upon the overloading of a wheelbarrow with one leg as an instance of cruelty to animals. But do not imagine that the Schopenhauer ideal is reached yet. Above the bad man, the just man, the good man, and the whole rabble of vice and virtue, there comes a more august personage yet, who however needs a few preliminary remarks to introduce him.

Just as ignorant persons, who have a smattering knowledge of Berkeley, think that the good bishop regarded the whole world as a creation of the fancy, and that they can refute his disciples by giving them an actual (not a metaphorical) rap on the knuckles, so doubtless there may be wiseacres, who will fancy that as Schopenhauer has declared the will to be the real essence of the world, and every human being a manifestation of that will, every human being is in a state of the most perfect freedom. Quite the reverse! With respect to the individual will, Schopenhauer is an absolute necessitarian, holding that the action of a certain motive on a certain character is as sure of producing a certain result, as an operation of agent upon patient in the sphere of mechanics. What may be a motive to one person may not be a motive to another, for the characters may be different; but given the character and the motive, the result is infallible. The absolute will, which lay beyond the jurisdiction of causality, has forced itself into the world of phenomena in an individual shape, and it must take the consequences, that is to say, a subjugation to that law of cause and effect by which the whole world of phenomena is governed, and which is equally potent in the discharge of a pistol and the performance of a virtuous action. The "character," which is the Idea of the human individual, just as gravitation is one of the Ideas of matter, is born with him, and cannot be altered. The knowledge of the individual may be enlarged, and consequently he may be put in a better track, by learning that his natural desires will be more gratified if he obeys the laws of society, than if he rises against them; but the character remains the same, although the cupidity which would have made a gamester or a highwayman, may become a constituent element in an honest tradesman. Thus every man brings his own depravity into the world with him, and this is the great doctrine of original sin, as set forth by Augustine, expounded by Luther and Calvin, and applauded by Schopenhauer, who, though a freethinker in the most complete sense of the word, is absolutely delighted with the fathers and the reformers, when they bear witness to human degradation. The world of phenomena is a delusion—a mockery; and the fact of being born into such a world is in itself an evil. So though the immediate apostles of Christianity—so thought the anchorites of the desert—so thought Calderon when he wrote his play of *Life is a Dream,* which Schopenhauer quotes with especial unction,—and, above all, so say the teachers of Hindostan. If a contrary doctrine is held in Europe, it is the mere result of Judaism, which with its doctrine of a First Cause and its system of temporal rewards—that is to say, its optimism—Schopenhauer regards with the contempt of a consistent Kantist, and the hatred of a profound misanthrope. Christianity, he thinks, is a result of Hindooism, which became corrupted in its passage through Palestine, and he is excessively wroth with those missionary societies who send back to India the adulterated form of a doctrine which the natives already possess in greater purity.

And now we may introduce Schopenhauer's ideal. The artist comes in for a large share of his respect, for he, without regard to selfish motives, contemplates the ideas which form the substrata of the world of phenomena, and reproduces them as the beautiful and the sublime. The good man, with his huge sympathy, is another estimable being; but higher still is he, who, convinced of the illusion of the world, is resolved to destroy it, as far as he is concerned, by extinguishing the will to live. Suicide will not answer this purpose. Suicide is a dislike of a particular chain of circumstances, which it endeavours to break through, but it is no alienation of the individual desires from life in general. Asceticism, that gradual extinction of all feelings that connect us with the visible world—the life of the anchorite in the Egyptian desert—of the Quietist of the time of Louis XIV.—of the Indian Fakeer, who goes through years of self-torture,—this is the perfection of Schopenhauer. The particular theological creed under which these saints performed their austerities is a matter of trivial importance,—they are all alike in the one grand qualification of holiness; they receded from the visible world and gradually extinguished the "will to live," till death, commonly so called, came as the completion of their wishes.

In this asceticism consists the only possible freedom of the will. While acting in the world of phenomena the will becomes entangled in the law of causality, but now it recedes back to a region when that law can operate no more, and where it is consequently free. The freedom of the will is, in a word, annihilation, and this is the greatest boon that can be desired.

When Lord Byron had brought his hero, Childe Harold, to the borders of the sea, he closed his poem; and now that we, *auspice* Schopenhauer, have brought our readers to the shores of absolute nothing, we close our article. Except so far as a commendation of the author's *style* is concerned, we intend it as an article of description—nothing more; and those who construe any of our remarks into an acceptance of such a system of ultra-pessimism, have totally misapprehended our meaning. At the same time we shall be greatly surprised if our brief outline of this genial, eccentric, audacious, and, let us add, terrible writer, does not tempt some of our readers to procure for themselves a set of works, every page of which abounds with novel and startling suggestions. We only wish we could see among the philosophers of modern Germany a writer of equal power, comprehensiveness, ingenuity and erudition, ranged on a side more in harmony with our own feelings and convictions, than that adopted by this misanthropic sage of Frankfort.

Friedrich Nietzsche (essay date 1874)

SOURCE: "Schopenhauer as Educator," translated by William Arrowsmith, in *Unmodern Observations*, edited by William Arrowsmith, Yale University Press, 1990, pp. 147-226.

[*One of the most important figures of the nineteenth century, Nietzsche was, among other things, a forerunner of existentialism, the first philosopher to recognize nihilism as a historical phenomenon, and an influential psychological theorist. In the following excerpt, which was originally published in 1874, Nietzsche criticizes his academic contemporaries and insists that the true philosopher is one who, like Schopenhauer, explores "the suffering of truthfulness."*]

A traveler who had visited many countries and peoples and several continents, was asked what trait he had discovered to be common to all men, and replied: a tendency to laziness. Some will think that he might have answered more accurately and truthfully: they are all afraid. They hide behind customs and opinions. Basically every man knows quite well that he is on this earth only once, a *unicum,* and that no accident, however unusual, could ever again combine this wonderful diversity into the unity he is. He knows this, but hides it like a bad conscience. Why? From fear of his neighbor who demands convention and wraps himself inside it. But what compels an individual to fear his neighbor, to think and act as part of a herd, rather than joyously being himself? Modesty perhaps, in a few rare cases. But with the vast majority it is convenience and indolence—in short, that inclination to laziness observed by our traveler. He is right; men are

more lazy than fearful, and above all they fear the burdens that unconditional honesty and nakedness would impose upon them. Artists alone despise this aimless drifting about in borrowed manners and superimposed opinions, and they expose the secret, everyone's bad conscience, the principle that every man is a unique miracle. They dare to show us how man, down to each twitch of his muscles, is himself, himself alone, and what is more, that in this rigorous coherence of his uniqueness, he is beautiful and worthy of contemplation, as new and incredible as any work of nature, and anything but boring. When the great thinker despises men, it is their laziness he despises; it is laziness that makes them seem massproduced, indifferent, unworthy of association and instruction. The man who does not want to belong to the mass has only to stop being lazy with himself. Let him follow his conscience, which cries out to him: "Be yourself! You are none of those things you now do, think, desire."

Day and night every young soul hears this cry and trembles at it; for when it thinks of its true liberation, it has an intimation of the happiness destined for it from eternity. But so long as it remains bound in the shackles of opinion and fear, nothing can help it attain this happiness. And without this liberation how bleak and meaningless life can become! There is no drearier and more repulsive creature in nature than the man who has evaded his own personal destiny, his eyes squinting left and right, behind him, everywhere. In the end a man like this can no longer be touched or grasped because he is all shell and no kernel, a shabby, puffed up, painted garment, a gaudy ghost that can arouse no fear and certainly no compassion. And if it is rightly said that the lazy man kills time, then we must ensure that a time that entrusts its salvation to public opinion—which is to say, to private lazinesses—should itself be killed, and killed for good, by which I mean stricken from the history of the true liberation of life. Imagine the revulsion of later generations in coping with the legacy of a time governed not by living men, but by publicly opining mockeries of men—which is why our own age may for some distant posterity be the darkest and least known, because least human, chapter of history. I walk through the new streets of our towns and I think how a century from now not one of all these frightful houses built for themselves by the breed of public opiners will be left standing, and how the opinions of those builders will have collapsed as well. How hopeful, by contrast, are all those who feel that they are no citizens of this time. For if they were, they would join in "killing the time" and perishing with it—whereas they want rather to quicken the age to life, so that they may go on living in this life.

But even if the future allowed us no hope, our remarkable existence in this Now—the inexplicable fact that we are living now and yet have had endless time in which to appear; that we possess nothing but a brief today in which we are to show how and for what purpose we came to exist at just this moment—this gives us the strongest encouragement to live according to our own standards and law. We are accountable to ourselves for this existence of ours; and this is why we want to be the real helmsmen of our lives and keep them from resembling the mindless result of chance. One's life must be lived with a certain danger and boldness since one will always, at best and at worst, lose it. Why cling to your clod of earth, to your trade, who heed what the neighbors say? It is so provincial to obligate oneself to views which a few hundred miles away are no longer obligatory. East and West are lines chalked by someone before our eyes in order to mock us with our own timidity. I will make the effort, says the young soul, to attain freedom. Should that effort be hindered simply because two countries happen to hate each other and go to war, or because an ocean lies between two continents, or because a religion that did not even exist two thousand years ago is being everywhere taught? All this is not yourself, the young soul says to itself. Nobody can build you the bridge over which you must cross the river of life, nobody but you alone. True, there are countless paths and bridges and demigods that would like to carry you across the river, but only at the price of your self; you would pledge your self, and lose it. In this world there is one unique path which no one but you may walk. Where does it lead? Do not ask; take it. Who was it who said, "A man never rises higher than when he does not know where his road may take him"?

But how can we find ourselves again? How can man know himself? He is a dark and veiled thing; and whereas the hare has seven skins, man could skin himself seventy-times-seven times and still not say, "This now is you yourself, this is no longer skin." Besides, it is an agonizing, dangerous enterprise to dig down into yourself, to descend forcibly by the shortest route the shaft of your being. A man may easily do himself such damage that no doctor can cure him. And again, why should it be necessary, since everything bears witness to our being—our friendships and hatreds, the way we look, our handshakes, the things we remember and forget, our books, our handwriting? But there is a way by which this absolutely crucial inquiry can be carried out. Let the young soul look back upon its life and ask itself: what until now have you truly loved, what has raised up your soul, what ruled it and at the same time made it happy? Line up these objects of reverence before you, and perhaps by what they are and by their sequence, they will yield you a law, the fundamental law of your true self. Compare these objects, see how one completes, enlarges, exceeds, transforms the other, how they form a ladder on which you have so far climbed up toward yourself. For your true nature does not lie hidden deep inside you but immeasurably high above you, or at least above that which you customarily consider to be your ego. Your true educators and molders reveal to you the true original meaning and basic stuff of your nature, something absolutely incapable of being educated and molded, but in any case something fettered and paralyzed and difficult of access. Your teachers can be nobody but your liberators. And that is the secret of all education; it does not provide artificial limbs, wax noses, or corrective lenses—on the contrary, what might provide such things is merely a parody of education. Education is rather liberation, the clearing away of all weeds, rubble, and vermin that might harm the delicate shoots, a radiance of light and warmth, the kind rustling fall of rain at

night; it is imitation and adoration of nature where nature is maternal and mercifully minded; it is perfection of nature when it prevents nature's fits of cruelty and mercilessness and converts them to good, when it throws a veil over nature's stepmotherly disposition and sad incomprehension.

Admittedly, there are other means of finding oneself, of coming to oneself out of that stupor in which we customarily float as though in a dark cloud. But I know of no better way than to reflect on one's own educators and molders. And this is why I want to bring to mind the one teacher and severe taskmaster of whom I boast: *Arthur Schopenhauer*. And after him to recall others.

To describe what an event it was for me when I first looked at Schopenhauer's writings, I might linger briefly on an idea that in younger days occurred more frequently and touched me more urgently than almost any other. When in earlier years I used to indulge in wishful thinking, I thought that fate would spare me the dreadful task and effort of educating myself: at the right moment I would find a philosopher to be my teacher, a true philosopher whom I could obey without further thought because I could trust him more than myself. And I would ask myself: by what principles would he educate? And I mused on what he might say of the two educational precepts in vogue today. The first of these requires the teacher to recognize his student's particular forte quickly, and then to direct all his energies, all his sunlight and sap, to just that point in order to help that unique excellence ripen and bear. In contrast, the other precept requires the educator to elicit and foster all existing abilities and bring them into harmonious rapport. Are we then to force a boy with a decided bent for the goldsmith's art into music? Are we to side with Benvenuto Cellini's father, who constantly drove his son back to that "delicious little horn"— or "that damned piping," as the boy called it? In the case of natural gifts as vigorous and clearly defined as Cellini's, such a tack is obviously wrong; and it may be that the maxim of harmonious education applies only to weaker natures, in which there is a whole swarming hive of needs and bents, but which, taken singly or collectively, do not amount to much. But where do we find harmonious wholeness and polyphonic unity in a single nature, if not in men like Cellini, men in whom everything—all insight, desire, love, hatred—coverage toward a single career, a single radical strength, where, because of the compelling and ruling power of this center, a harmonic system of movements—movements radiating out in every direction, back and forth, upwards and downwards—is created.

And so the two precepts are perhaps not contradictory? Perhaps the first merely declares that man should have a center, the second that he should have a circumference? The teacher-philosopher of my daydreams would, then, not only discover the focal strength but would also know how to keep it from destroying the other talents. His educational task, as I imagined it, would rather be to transform the whole man into a solar and planetary system with its own life and movement, and to discover the laws of its higher mechanics.

But in the meantime my philosopher failed to put in an appearance, and I tried one thing after another. I discovered how pathetic we moderns are in comparison with the Greeks and Romans, even in this matter of taking the aims of education seriously and strictly. With a need like this in your heart, you can visit all Germany, and in particular German universities, and not find what you are seeking. Much simpler, much humbler wants than these go unfulfilled here. For instance, if a German wants to become an orator, or to enter a school for writers, he will nowhere find either master or school; it does not yet seem to have dawned on anyone in Germany that speaking and writing are arts that cannot be acquired without the most rigorous discipline and years of painstaking apprenticeship. Yet nothing more plainly and shamefully reveals the arrogant complacency of our contemporaries than the shabbiness—half stinginess, half mindlessness—of the demands they make of teachers and educators. Even among our most respectable and best-informed people, absolutely anybody will do as a family tutor, and how common it is for some motley conclave of noddies and fossils to be called a gymnasium and found *good.*

And consider what we settle for in the highest institution of learning, the university! What leaders, what institutions, when we compare them with the difficulty of their task of educating a man to be a man! Even the celebrated way in which German scholars attack their discipline clearly reveals that they think more of their scholarship than of humanity; that they have been trained like a lost battalion to sacrifice themselves to their disciplines in order to lure new generations to make the same sacrifice. If the practice of scholarship is neither guided nor controlled by any higher educational principle but granted always greater freedom on the grounds of "the more, the better," it is surely just as pernicious to the scholar as the economic doctrine of laissez-faire is to the morality of whole nations. Who nowadays recognizes that the scholar's education, if we are not to sacrifice or desiccate his humanity in the process, poses an extremely ticklish problem? But if we merely note the countless numbers of men whose natures, by a mindless and premature surrender to scholarship, have been warped or endowed with a hump, the problem leaps to the eye. But there is more important evidence of the total absence of higher education—more important, more perilous, above all more general. If it is immediately apparent why at present no orator, no writer can be educated—because there are no teachers for them; if it is almost as clear why a scholar is nowadays doomed to being warped or deformed—because he is to be educated by scholarship, an inhuman abstraction; if this is so, then we must ask ourselves: Where among our contemporaries can we—educated and uneducated, noble and humble—find moral examples and men of true distinction, visible embodiments of all creative morality in this age? That meditation on moral questions which in every age has been the concern of every noble society—what has become of it? There are no longer men of that distinction, meditation of that sort no longer exists. The truth is that we are living off the inherited moral capital accumulated by our forefathers, a capital we no longer know how to increase but only to squander. Such matters are in our

society either not discussed or discussed with revolting naturalistic amateurishness and inexperience. We have reached the point at which our schools and teachers simply ignore moral education or content themselves with mere formalities. And *virtue* is a word that finds no echo among the thoughts of teachers and students, a musty word at which people smile—and woe to you if you fail to smile, since that makes you a hypocrite!

Explanation of this faintheartedness, this low watermark of all moral forces, is difficult and involved. But certainly nobody who considers the influence of victorious Christianity on the morals of the ancient world can ignore the counter-reaction of Christianity in its time of decline—and further decline is its likely fate in our time. Through its lofty idealism Christianity so far surpassed the moral systems of antiquity and the naturalness prevalent in all of them, that mankind grew indifferent to that naturalness and became disgusted with it. But afterwards, when men still knew the higher and the better, but could no longer achieve it, they found they could no longer return to the high and the good—to that ancient moral virtue—despite their desire to do so. Modern man lives in this oscillation between Christianity and antiquity, between a cowardly and deceitful Christian approach to morals and a classicizing approach equally timid and self-conscious, and he suffers by so doing. The inherited fear of the natural and, on the other side, its renewed fascination for him; his longing for stability somewhere; the impotence of his intellect as it stumbles back and forth between the good and the better—all this produces a restlessness, a confusion in the modern soul, that condemns it to joyless sterility. Never were moral teachers more needed, and never was there smaller likelihood of finding them. The time when doctors are most needed, the age of great epidemics, is also the time when doctors themselves are in the greatest danger; and where are the doctors of modern man who are sufficiently strong and sure-footed to support another man and lead him by the hand? Over the best men of our time there hangs a somber, paralyzing gloom, an everlasting discontent over the battle between pretense and honesty that is being fought in their breasts, a restless failure of self-confidence, and for this reason they are quite incapable of showing others the way and, as teachers, providing a stern discipline.

In short, it was a debauchery in wishful thinking when I imagined that I could find a true philosopher as my teacher, a man who could raise me above the inadequacy of the age and once again teach me to be *simple and honest* in thought and life—that is, to be *unmodern,* in the deepest sense of the word. For modern man has become so multiple and complex that he is necessarily dishonest every time he speaks, asserts an opinion, and wants to act accordingly.

These were the distress, the needs, and desires I was feeling when I first encountered Schopenhauer.

I am among those readers of Schopenhauer who, from the moment they finish the first page, know for certain that they will read every page he wrote, listen to every word he uttered. My faith in him was immediate, and it is no less today than it was nine years ago. I understood him as though he had written expressly for me, to put it arrogantly and foolishly, but understandably. This is why I have never found a paradox in Schopenhauer, though here and there a minor error. For what are paradoxes but assertions that inspire no confidence because the author made them without conviction, because he wants to glitter, or mislead, and in general *seem*? Schopenhauer never wants to shine in this showy way. He writes for himself, and no man wants to be self-deceived, least of all a philosopher who has made this his law: Deceive nobody, not even yourself! Do not deceive even with those polite social deceptions which are part of almost every conversation, and which our writers almost unconsciously imitate; still less with the more conscious deceits of the public platform, and the artificial techniques of rhetoric. But Schopenhauer speaks to himself; or, if we have to imagine an audience, imagine a son being advised by his father. It is a straightforward, brusque, good-natured speech, addressed to someone who listens lovingly. We lack writers of this sort. The vigorous well-being of the speaker surrounds us at the first sound of his voice; it is like entering a forest of tall trees; we breathe deeply and suddenly we feel well again. Here, we feel, the air is always bracing; here is that inimitable naturalness and lack of affectation of men at home with themselves, and masters of a very rich home at that—the exact opposite of those writers who are stunned if they somehow manage something witty, and whose style is therefore somewhat nervous and unnatural. So, when Schopenhauer speaks, there is literally nothing to remind us of the scholar with his natural stiffness and awkwardness, his hollow chest, and his jerky, embarrassed, or pompous gait. On the other hand, Schopenhauer's rough, almost bearish spirit teaches us not so much to regret as to abhor the smoothness and polished grace of the good French writers; certainly nobody will find in him that pseudo-French tinsel on which German writers so preen themselves. In places, Schopenhauer's way of expressing himself reminds me somewhat of Goethe, but of no other German model whatever. For he knows how to say profound things simply, to be moving without rhetoric, to speak technically without pedantry; and from what German could we have learned this lesson? He is also quite free of Lessing's mannered subtlety, excessive sprightliness, and—if I may use the word—quite un-German style; and this is a great merit in him, since Lessing is, of all writers in prose, the most seductive model. The highest praise I can give his style is to apply to it his own saying: "A philosopher must be very honest in order to dispense with poetical and rhetorical devices."

That honesty matters and may even be a virtue is one of those private opinions prohibited in this age of public opinion. So I shall not have praised Schopenhauer, but merely characterized him, if I say once more that he is honest, even as a writer. So few writers are honest that we should really distrust all writers. I know of only one writer whom, in point of honesty, I can rank with Schopenhauer, and even above him, and that is Montaigne. The fact that such a man has written truly adds to the joy of living on this earth. At any rate, since my first encounter with this freest and most vigorous of spirits, I feel moved to say of him what he said of Plutarch: "No sooner do I look at him than I sprout a leg or a wing." If my task were to make myself at home on this earth, it is to him that I would cleave.

Schopenhauer shares with Montaigne another quality besides honesty: a genuinely cheering cheerfulness. *Aliis laetus, sibi sapiens.* There are two very different kinds of cheer. The true thinker invariably cheers and quickens, whether he expresses his seriousness or his playfulness, his human insight or divine indulgence; he does this not with gloomy gestures, trembling hands, and tearful eyes, but surely and simply, with courage and strength, perhaps somewhat cavalierly and harshly, but in any event as a conqueror. And it is this that provides the most profound and intense cheer—to see the victorious god amid all the monsters he has fought. By contrast, the cheerfulness we sometimes meet in mediocre writers and small-time thinkers makes us miserable on reading them: the way I felt, for instance, with the "cheerfulness" of David Strauss. There is truly something shameful in having such cheerful contemporaries, because they expose to posterity the nakedness of our age and the people in it. These cheerlings do not even see the suffering and monsters which, as thinkers, they pretend to see and fight. And because their cheerfulness is deceptive, it provokes irritation; it tends to mislead us into believing that a victory has been won. Basically, there is good cheer only where there is victory, and this applies just as much to the works of true thinkers as to any work of art. Even if the subject is as grave and terrible as the problem of existence, the work will have a depressing and painful effect only when the half-thinker and the half-artist have smothered it in the fumes of their own inadequacy. On the other hand, nothing more joyful, nothing better, can happen to a man than to be close to one of those victorious spirits who, because they have thought most deeply, must therefore love precisely what is most alive, and who, because they are wise, are finally disposed to what is beautiful. They really speak. They neither stammer nor parrot; they truly move and live, not in the sinister masquerade in which men are accustomed to live. And so, when we are close to them, we feel human and natural at last, and would like to cry out with Goethe, "How wonderful and precious is a living thing! How suited to its condition, how truly, how vividly it *is*!"

I am describing only the first, almost physiological, impression Schopenhauer made on me, the uncanny outflowing of inner power from one living thing to another that takes place at the first, gentlest contact. And analyzing that impact in retrospect, I find it composed of three elements: the impression of his honesty, his cheerfulness, and his steadfastness. He is honest because he speaks and writes to himself and for himself; cheerful because he has conquered with his thought the most difficult thing of all; and steadfast because that was his nature. His power rises like a flame on a windless day, straight up, easily and undisturbed, steady, unflickering. Wherever he is, he finds his way, without our ever noticing that he had sought it; he moves along as steadily and nimbly and inevitably as though propelled by the law of gravity. And anyone who has felt what it means, in this age of stunted freaks and hybrid humanity, to discover a completely integrated, harmonious, free, and uninhibited nature—a man who, like a door, swings freely on his hinges—will understand my joy and astonishment on discovering Schopenhauer. In him I felt that I had found that teacher and philosopher I had so long been searching for. Granted, he existed only as a book, and this was a great deprivation. And so I made greater efforts to look behind the book and imagine the living man whose great testament I was reading, and who promised that his heirs would be only those who wanted to be and were able to be more than readers—that is, his sons and disciples.

A philosopher matters to me according to his ability to be an example. There is no doubt that by force of his example he can draw whole nations after him; the history of India, which is virtually the history of Indian philosophy, proves it. But the example must be evinced not merely in his books, but in his visible life, in the way the Greek philosophers taught—through their facial expressions, demeanor, dress, food, and habits, rather than through what they said or wrote. How utterly we Germans still lack this courageous manifestation in our philosophical life!

Here the body is very gradually being liberated, whereas the mind was long ago emancipated; and yet it is an illusion to think that the mind can be free and independent unless this acquired freedom from limitation—which is basically a creative limitation, self-imposed—is manifested from morning till night in every glance and footstep. Kant clung to the university, submitted to authority, sustained the pretense of religious faith, put up with colleagues and students; so it is only natural that his example has begotten university professors and professorial philosophy. Schopenhauer thinks very little of the learned classes; he keeps aloof; he strives for independence from state and society—this is his example, the model he sets—to start with the most superficial aspects. But many stages in the emancipation of the philosophical life are still unknown among the Germans, and they cannot for long remain that way. Our artists live more boldly and honestly; and the mightiest example presented to our eyes—that of Richard Wagner—shows that, if the genius wants to bring to light the higher order and the truth that live in him, he must not flinch from a fight to the death with established forms and rules. That "truth," however, of which our professors chatter so much, appears a mousy little creature from whom nothing unruly or exceptional need be feared—a cozy, good-natured little thing who constantly assures all the established powers that she will cause nobody any trouble; after all, she is only "pure knowledge." In sum, I would say that philosophy in Germany must more and more forget about being "pure knowledge." And this is precisely the example set by the man Schopenhauer.

But it is a miracle, nothing less, that Schopenhauer should have become this human example. Outwardly and inwardly he was assailed by pressures and dangers so frightful that they would have crushed or broken a weaker nature. There was, it seems to me, a strong likelihood that the man Schopenhauer might have perished, leaving at best a residue of "pure knowledge," and this only in the best of circumstances. More likely, neither man nor knowledge.

The dangers that most commonly threaten exceptional men who live in a society bound to convention have been described by [Walter Bagehot in *Physics and Politics*]: "Unusual characters of this kind are at first cowed, then they turn melancholy, then sicken, and finally die. A Shelley could not have lived in England, and a race of Shelleys would have been impossible." Our own Hölderlin and Kleist, and countless others, died of their own unconventionality and could not endure the climate of what is called "German culture"; only natures of iron—like Beethoven, Goethe, Schopenhauer, and Wagner—can stick it out. But even these natures reveal, in any number of traits and wrinkles, the effect of this utterly exhausting agony and struggler: their breathing becomes labored, their tone too easily tends to be violent. A knowledgeable diplomat, who had barely set eyes on Goethe and exchanged a few words with him, observed to a friend: "Voilà un homme qui a eu de grands chagrins!"—which Goethe translated as, "There's a man who worked himself to death." And he adds, "If there is no way we can erase from our features the marks of the sufferings we endured and the activities we brought to conclusion, it is no wonder that every surviving remnant of us and our struggles should bear the same traces." And this is Goethe, whom our culture-philistines point out as the happiest of Germans in order to prove from his example that it must be possible to be happy in their midst—with the implied corollary that it is unforgivable for a man to feel unhappy and alone among them. For this reason they have, with great cruelty, advanced and put into practice the theory that every case of loneliness implies a secret guilt.

Poor Schopenhauer too, of course, has a secret guilt on his conscience and in his heart, the guilt of valuing his philosophy more highly than he valued his contemporaries. Besides, he was unfortunate enough to have learned from Goethe that in order to save the life of his philosophy he had to protect it at any cost from the indifference of his contemporaries. For there is a kind of inquisitorial censorship which, according to Geothe, the Germans have brought to perfection: glacial silence. At least it was for this reason that most of the first edition of Schopenhauer's masterpiece had to be pulped. The looming danger that his great project might be doomed by indifference produced in Schopenhauer a terrible, almost uncontrollable anxiety; not one worthy supporter made an appearance. It is saddening to watch him searching for any sign of recognition; and his final piercing cry of triumph that he was actually being read (*legor et legar*) is somehow painfully moving. It is precisely those traits in which the philosopher's dignity is absent that reveal the suffering man, in anguish over his most precious possession; he is tormented by the fear of losing his small fortune and, along with it perhaps, his ability to maintain his pure, classical attitude toward philosophy. And so, in his yearning for trusting and sympathetic companions, he frequently made mistakes, only to return sadly to his faithful dog. He was in every respect a solitary; not a single truly like-minded friend consoled him; and here, between one and none, as between something and nothing, lies an infinity. No one who has real friends knows what real loneliness is, not even if the whole world is against him.

But I see my reader does not know what solitude is. Wherever powerful societies, governments, public opinion, and religions have existed—in short, wherever tyranny existed—the solitary philosopher has been hated. For philosophy offers an asylum where no tyranny can penetrate, the cavern of inwardness and the labyrinth of the heart. And this angers the tyrants. There the solitary ones take refuge; but there too lies their greatest danger. These men who have internalized their freedom must also live in the external world, must be visible, must let themselves be seen. By virtue of birth, domicile, country, chance, and the importunity of others, they are bound by countless human ties. Similarly, all sorts of opinions are attributed to them simply because these are the dominant opinions; every attitude that is not denial is construed as assent; every gesture that does not destroy is taken as approval. They know, these solitary, free-spirited people, that in some way they always appear different from their own sense of themselves. Whereas all they want is truth and honesty, they are tangled in a web of misunderstandings; and despite their own passionate desires they cannot keep a dense fog of wrong opinions, compromises, half-truths, charitable silences, and misinterpretations from settling over everything they do. And so a cloud of melancholy gathers on their brows, for these natures hate the necessity of pretense worse than death; and this continuous bitterness makes them volcanic and menacing. Every so often they take revenge for their enforced self-concealment and the reserve imposed upon them. They emerge from their caves with a ferocious look; their words and actions are explosions, and they can destroy themselves. Schopenhauer lived in this way, dangerously.

Solitaries of this kind need love above everything else; they must have companions with whom they can be as open and simple as they are with themselves, in whose presence the strain caused by silence and hypocrisy is absent. Remove their companions and you create a growing danger. Heinrich von Kleist was destroyed by this lack of love, and the most dreadful antidote that can be applied to exceptional men is to drive them so deeply into themselves that their re-emergence is invariably a volcanic eruption. And yet there is always some demigod who can bear to live under such frightful conditions, and to live victoriously. If you want to hear his solitary song, listen to Beethoven's music.

Solitude: this is the first danger in whose shadow Schopenhauer developed. The second danger is called despair of truth. To this danger every thinker who takes the philosophy of Kant as his starting point is susceptible, providing that in his sufferings and desires he is a whole and vigorous man and not merely a clacking machine for thinking and calculating. We all know very well the shameful situation implied by this assumption; in my opinion, any-

way, Kant vitally affected and radically transformed only a very few people. True, the work of this quiet scholar is said, as we can read on all sides, to have revolutionized every field of intellectual life. But I cannot believe it. For I see no signs of it in people themselves, who would have had to be revolutionized before any whole field of inquiry. And if Kant began to have a popular effect, we would be aware of it in the form of a corrosive and destructive skepticism and relativism. Only in the case of the noblest and most active spirits—those who could never persist in doubt—would there come that shattering upheaval and despair of all truth which, in the case of Kleist, were the effect of Kant's philosophy. "It was only recently," writes Kleist in his moving way, "that I encountered the philosophy of Kant, and now I must tell you one of its ideas, without indulging my fear that it will shatter you as deeply and as painfully as it did me. 'We cannot decide whether what we call truth really is truth, or whether it only seems so. If the latter, then the truth we gather here is nothing after we die, and all our efforts to win a property that can follow us to the grave are useless. If this pointed thought does not pierce your heart, do not smile at another man who feels himself wounded in the sacred inmost depths of his being. My highest, my only purpose has vanished, and I have no other left.'" Alas, when will men again feel things with the naturalness of Kleist? When will they learn again to measure the meaning of a philosophy in "the sacred inmost depths of their being"?

> This is how, from the outset, Schopenhauer's philosophy should be interpreted: individually, by each individual for himself alone, to acquire insight into his own misery, and need, and limitations, and to know the remedies and consolations—that is, the sacrifice of the ego, submission to the noblest goals, above all to justice and compassion.
>
> —*Friedrich Nietzsche*

Yet this is what is above all needed if we are to evaluate what, after Kant, Schopenhauer might mean to us—that is, the leader who guides us up from the cave of skeptical disillusion or critical renunciation to the peaks of tragic contemplation, the night sky with its infinity of stars overhead, and who first trod this path himself. This is his greatness, that he confronts the picture of life as a whole in order to interpret it in its wholeness, whereas the acutest intellects cannot liberate themselves from the mistaken notion that this interpretation is best mediated by a painstaking analysis of the colors and canvas on which the picture is painted—only to conclude perhaps that the texture of the canvas is extremely intricate and that the chemistry of the paints resists analysis! To understand the picture, you must first divine the painter: this Schopenhauer knew. But now the whole scholarly guild is engaged in understanding that canvas and those colors, but not the painting. In fact, one could say that only he who has the overall picture of life and existence firmly in view can make use of the individual fields of learning without suffering damage; and that without a comprehensive view as a controlling norm, the disciplines are merely guidelines leading nowhere, which makes the course of our life even more confused and labyrinthine. It is in this, as I observed earlier, that Schopenhauer's greatness lies; he pursues the picture as Hamlet pursues the ghost, without letting himself be diverted like the scholars, or tangled in a web of scholastic abstractions, which is the fate of uncontrolled dialecticians. If the study of these stunted philosophers is appealing, it is because they immediately stumble on just those points in the structure of a great philosophy where scholarly pros and cons, commentary, doubts, and contradictions are permitted, and thereby evade the demand made by every great philosophy, which as a whole says only and always: This is the picture of all life; learn from it the meaning of your own life. And conversely too: Read your own life and, by so doing, understand the hieroglyphs of universal life.

And this is how, from the outset, Schopenhauer's philosophy should be interpreted: individually, by each individual for himself alone, to acquire insight into his own misery, and need, and limitations, and to know the remedies and consolations—that is, the sacrifice of the ego, submission to the noblest goals, above all to justice and compassion. He teaches us to distinguish between real and apparent means of promoting human happiness: how the acquisition of wealth, respectability, or erudition cannot pluck the individual out of his deep disgust at the worthlessness of his existence; and how the aspiration towards all these good things acquires meaning only by a lofty and transfiguring common goal—to acquire power in order to assist our own *physis* and correct somewhat its folly and awkwardness. At first, only for oneself; but through one's self, finally for all. Admittedly, this is an aspiration that leads, profoundly and cheerfully, to resignation. For what, and how much, after all, can still be improved, in the individual and in general!

Applying these words directly to Schopenhauer, we touch upon the third danger, the one most peculiar to him, imbedded in the whole structure and makeup of his nature. Every man usually discovers a limitation in himself, in both his talents and his moral will, which fills him with longing and melancholy. And just as consciousness of sin makes him yearn for what is holy, so, as an intellectual creature, he has a deep longing for his own personal genius. All true culture is rooted in this longing. And if I equate culture with man's yearning to be *reborn* as saint and genius, I know that one need not be a Buddhist to understand this myth. Where we come across talent without this longing, in scholarly circles or among those who call themselves cultured, we feel revulsion and disgust. For we suspect that these people, with all their intelligence, do not foster, but impede a developing culture and the generating of genius—which is the aim of all culture. They exhibit a hardening, of no greater value than the cold arrogance of conventional righteousness, which is so far removed from true holiness and drives men away from it.

Schopenhauer's nature contained an unusual and extremely dangerous duality. Few thinkers have felt so strongly, with such incomparable certainty, their own in-dwelling genius; and his genius made him the supreme promise—that the furrow cut by his ploughshare in the soil of modern mankind would be the deepest furrow of all. So he knew that half of his nature was fulfilled and satisfied, conscious of its power and without other cravings; and he therefore carried out his calling with the greatness and dignity of a man who had victoriously fulfilled himself. In the other half of his nature there was a violent yearning; we intuit it at once when we hear how he turned away, pain in his eyes, from the portrait of Rancé, the great founder of the Trappist order, with these words: "It is a matter of grace." For the genius yearns more deeply for holiness because he has seen, from his high vantage point, farther and more clearly than any other man into the reconciliation of knowledge and being, into the realm of peace and the denial of the will, across to the shore beyond, of which the Hindu sages speak. But this is precisely the miracle: how inconceivably whole and unbreakable Schopenhauer's nature must have been, that this yearning could neither destroy nor harden it! Each man will comprehend this according to his stature and nature; none of us will grasp it all, in all its gravity.

The more one ponders the three dangers I have described, the more astonishing appears Schopenhauer's vigor in defending himself from them, and the fact that he emerged from the struggle healthy and unbroken. With many scars and open wounds to be sure, and in a mood that may seem overly harsh and at times excessively pugnacious. Even the greatest man is shorter than his own ideal. But despite scars and flaws, Schopenhauer can surely stand as a model to men. We might even say that what in him was imperfect and all too human brings us closer to him in the most human sense, since we view him as a sufferer and fellow-sufferer, not merely on the remote heights of genius.

These three constitutional dangers that threatened Schopenhauer threaten us all. Every man carries within him a creative uniqueness, as the core of his being; and when he becomes aware of this uniqueness, a strange radiance surrounds him, the aura of the unusual. To most men this awareness is intolerable because, as I observed earlier, they are lazy, and because each man's uniqueness shackles him to burdens and troubles. For the exceptional man who burdens himself with these shackles, there is no doubt that life loses almost everything we hope to have from it when we are young—joy, security, amusement, honors. The fate of solitude is the gift he receives from other men; live where he will, the desert and the cave are instantly with him. So let him take care that he is not forced to submit, that he does not become depressed and melancholy. And let him therefore surround himself with the examples of good, courageous warriors, like Schopenhauer.

But the second danger that threatened Schopenhauer is not uncommon. It sometimes happens that nature equips a man with keenness of vision; his thoughts readily take the ambiguous way of dialectic. How easy it is for him, by giving free rein to his talent, to perish as a human being and lead merely a ghostly existence in the realm of "pure knowledge." Or alternatively, because he is accustomed to seeking the pros and cons of things, he begins to doubt the truth itself and to live without courage or confidence, denying and doubting, gnawed by remorse, discontented, in half-hopes and anticipated disappointment. [According to Goethe's *Faust,*] "Even a dog wouldn't want a life like that!"

The third danger is moral and intellectual hardening. Man breaks the bond that linked him to his ideal. He ceases to be productive in this or that field, to reproduce himself; culturally speaking, he is either a menace or useless. The uniqueness of his nature has become an indivisible, isolated atom, a frozen stone. In this manner a man can be destroyed through his uniqueness just as he can perish through fear of his uniqueness; he can perish through his self as he can by surrendering himself, through yearning as by hardening. And living means, in short, to be in danger.

Besides these constitutional dangers to which Schopenhauer would have been exposed in whatever century he lived, there are also dangers that beset him from his *own time*. And this distinction between constitutional and historical dangers is essential if we are to grasp what is exemplary and educational in Schopenhauer. Imagine the philosopher's gaze as it muses on existence: he wants to make a fresh assessment of its value. For this has always been the peculiar work of all great thinkers, to be the legislators of the weights and measures and coinage of things. What an obstacle to his work when the humanity he sees before him is in fact a blighted, wormeaten fruit! What a great supplement of value must be added to the worthlessness of our times, if he is to do justice to existence in general. If there is any value in studying the history of past or foreign peoples, it is especially valuable to the philosopher who wants to deliver an accurate judgment on the whole destiny of man—not merely on the average lot of man, but also and above all on the highest fate that can befall a single individual or whole peoples. But the present is importunate; it manipulates and determines the philosopher's eye, despite his resistance; and it is unintentionally overvalued in the final reckoning. This is why the philosopher must take pains to assess his own time in comparison with others; and by overcoming the present for himself, also overcome the present in the picture he draws of life, making it inconspicuous and, as it were, painting it over.

This is a difficult, indeed almost impossible, assignment. The judgment of the ancient Greek philosophers on the value of existence means so much more than a modern judgment because all around them and before their eyes they had life itself in luxuriant realization, and because with them the thinker's intuition was not troubled, as it is with us, in the conflict between the craving for freedom, beauty, and greatness of life, and the drive for truth which asks only: What is the cumulative value of existence? It is important for every age to know what Empedocles, living in an age when Greek culture was in full exuberant

flush and lust for life, has to say about existence. His judgment carries great weight, especially since he is not contradicted by a single contrary judgment by any other great philosopher of that same great period. He speaks more clearly than the rest, but basically—that is, if we keep our ears open a little—they are all saying the same thing. A modern thinker, as I said, will always suffer from an unfulfilled desire: he will insist first on being shown life again, real, red-blooded, healthy life, in order to pass judgment on it. He will think it necessary, at least for himself, to be a living man before he can dare to think that he will be a good judge. It is for this reason that the modern philosophers are among the staunchest champions of life and the will to live, and that they long to escape from their own enervated age and yearn for culture, a transfigured physis. This yearning, however, is also their *danger;* in them the reformer of life and the philosopher, that is, the judge of life, are in conflict. Whichever way the victory goes, it is a victory that implies a defeat. And how did Schopenhauer escape this danger too?

If we like to think of every great man as a true child of his times, and he clearly suffers from all its maladies more strongly and sensitively than smaller men, then the struggle of such a great man *against* his times is apparently only a senselessly self-destructive struggle against himself. But only apparently. For his war is with that quality in his own age which prevents him from being great, which for him means simply being free and wholly himself. It follows that his hostility is actually directed against something that is clearly in him but which is not truly himself; that is, against the impure, chaotic confusion of forever irreconcilable and uncombinable things, against the false fusion in him of the contemporary and the timeless. And in the end the putative child of the age proves himself to be only its stepchild. Thus Schopenhauer, from early youth on, struggled against that false, vain, and unworthy mother—his own age—and by expelling her from himself, he purified and healed his nature and recovered the health and purity that were properly his. For this reason Schopenhauer's writings should be used as a mirror of the age; and it is surely no flaw in the mirror if everything modern appears in it only as a disfiguring sickness, as emaciated pallor, sunken eyes, and worn features, as the recognizable maladies of the stepchild. His yearning for a vigorous nature, for sane and simple humanity, was a yearning for himself; and as soon as he had overcome his own times within himself, he was bound to look with astonishment upon the genius within himself. Now the secret of his being was disclosed to him; the aim of his stepmotherly age to conceal his genius from him was thwarted, and the realm of transfigured physis was revealed. Now, when he turned with fealess eyes to the question "What is life finally worth?" he no longer had to pass judgment on a chaotic and anemic age and its life of hypocritical obscurity. He really knew that there was something far higher and purer than contemporary life to be found and achieved on this earth, and that he who knows and appraises existence only in its hateful contemporary guise does it a bitter injustice. No, genius itself is now called to witness, so we may hear whether it, the supreme fruit of existence, can perhaps justify life as a whole. The man, magnificent and creative, must answer the question: "Do you affirm this life in the depths of your being? Does it suffice you? Will you be its advocate and redeemer? A single sincere 'Yes!' from you—and life, now so terribly accused, will be set free." What answer will he give? The answer given by Empedocles.

Let this last hint remain unexplained for the moment. I am now concerned with a very comprehensible matter, namely, to explain how all of us *can,* with Schopenhauer's help, educate ourselves *against* the age—because through him we have the advantage of really *knowing* this age of ours. That is, if knowing our age is an advantage! In any case it may no longer be even possible a few centuries from now. I take pleasure in the thought that man may soon grow sick and tired of books and writers as well, and that one day the scholar may take stock, write his will, and leave orders for his corpse to be cremated amidst his books—especially his own. And if the forests keep on thinning away, might there not be an age in which libraries will be treated like wood, straw, and brush? Most books, after all, are born from the smoking heads of scholars, and to smoke they shall return. If they lack fire, then fire will punish them for it. A later century may perhaps view this age of ours as a *saeculum obscurum* because its products served to keep the furnaces constantly burning. In that case, how fortunate we are that we can know this age of ours. For if there is any sense at all in studying our own times, it is a fortunate thing to study it as thoroughly as possible, so that no further doubt will remain. And it is just this opportunity that Schopenhauer provides.

Admittedly, our good fortune would be a hundred times greater if this inquiry showed that there had never been a period as proud and promising as our own. And even now in some corner of the world, like Germany, there are people so naive that they are ready to believe such things, and even to declare in all seriousness that the world has been set right in the last two years, and that anyone who has grave and grim misgivings about existence has been refuted by the "facts." And the "fact" is that the founding of the new German Reich is the decisive blow that demolishes all "pessimistic" philosophizing—this simply can't be denied! Opinions of this sort, widely held and fostered above all in the universities, must be dealt with by anyone who asks about the significance of the philosopher as educator in our times. And this is our answer: It is a shame and a disgrace that such nauseatingly obsequious flattery of the idols of the age could be uttered and repeated by presumably decent and intelligent people—proof that we no longer grasp the vast difference in seriousness between philosophy and a newspaper. People of this sort have lost every last shred of religious and philosophical conviction, and have exchanged them, not for optimism, but for journalism, the wit and unwisdom of the day—and the dailies. Any philosophy founded on the belief that the problem of existence has been changed or solved by a political event is a parody of philosophy and a sham. Many states have been founded since the world began; it is an old story. How could a political innovation suffice

to make men contented dwellers on this earth at last? If anyone sincerely believes this to be possible, let him make himself heard. He truly deserves to be appointed professor of philosophy at a German university, like [Hans Joachim Friedrich] Harms at Berlin, Jürgen Meyer at Bonn, and [Phillip Moriz] Carrière at Munich.

In this matter we are experiencing the consequences of a doctrine lately preached from every rooftop, that the state is the highest purpose of mankind, and that man has no higher duty than service to the state. In this I see a relapse, not into paganism, but into stupidity. It may be that a man who views service to the state as his highest duty actually knows no higher duty. Still, this is precisely why there are higher men and higher duties, and one of these duties (which to me at least seems higher than service to the state) calls for the destruction of stupidity in every form, which means this stupidity too. I am therefore concerned here with those men whose teleology extends father than the welfare of the state, that is, with philosophers, and with them only as regards a world fairly independent of the welfare of the state—namely, the world of culture. Of the many links in the mesh composing the human community, some are gold, others gilt.

How, then, does our philosopher view culture in this age? Very differently, of course, from those professors of philosophy who are so delighted with the state and the present state of affairs. If he reflects on the universal frenzy and the accelerating tempo, the disappearance of contemplation and simplicity, it almost seems to him as though he were seeing the symptoms of the complete destruction, the total extirpation of culture. The flood of religion recedes, leaving swamps or puddles behind; the nations veer apart once again in the most violent hostility, impatient to massacre one another. The various fields of learning, pursued without moderation and in the blindest laissez-faire, are fragmenting and dissolving every established belief. Educated classes and nations alike are being swept away by a gigantic and contemptible economy of money. Never has the world been more worldly, never has it been poorer in love and goodness. In all this secular turmoil, the educated are no longer a beacon or sanctuary; day by day they become increasingly restless, mindless, and loveless. Everything, contemporary art and scholarship included, serves the approaching barbarism. The educated man has degenerated into culture's greatest enemy by denying the general malaise with lies and thereby impeding the physicians. They take offense, these poor, spineless rascals, when you speak of their weakness and oppose their pernicious falsehood. They would very much like to persuade you that they have surpassed all past centuries, and so they walk about with affected gaiety. Their manner of pretending happiness has something touching about it, since their happiness is so utterly incomprehensible. We have to resist the temptation to ask them what Tannhäuser asked Bitterolf [in Wagner's *Tannhäuser*]: "Poor thing, what pleasure have you ever known?" But, alas, we know better, we know otherwise. Over our heads lies a wintry sky, and we live on a high mountain, in danger and in need. Every pleasure is brief, and the pale sunlight steals down to us from the white peaks. Then a burst of music, and old man cranks a hurdy-gurdy, the dancers whirl around—the wanderer looks and shudders. Everything is so wild, confining, bleak, and hopeless. And then, suddenly, a note of joy, of pure, thoughtless joy! But the early evening mist is already closing in, the music dies, the wanderer's steps crunching on the snow. As far as his eye can reach, there is nothing to be seen but the bleak and terrible face of Nature.

But if it is one-sided to stress the faintness of line and dullness of color in this picture of modern life, the other side is no more comforting but, if anything, more alarming. True, there are forces here, tremendous forces, but wild, primitive, and completely pitiless. One looks at them as one might look at the cauldron in the witches' kitchen, with terrible suspense. At any moment it may erupt in flame and thunder, announcing horrible apparitions. For a century now we have been expecting radical upheavals. And although an attempt has recently been made to offset the modern world's profound tendency to explosion or collapse through the cohesive power of the so-called national state, yet for a long time to come the effect of the state will be to increase the general insecurity and danger. The fact that individuals behave as though they were ignorant of these anxieties does not mislead us; their very restlessness shows how much they are aware of them. They think about themselves more obsessively and exclusively than men have ever done before. They build and plant only for their own day; and the quest for happiness will never be greater than when its quarry must be taken today or tomorrow, because the day after tomorrow the hunting season may be over forever.

We live in the age of atoms, of atomistic chaos. In the Middle Ages the opposing forces were more or less held together, and to some degree assimilated to each other, through the strong pressure exercised by the Church. But when the bond breaks and the pressure slackens, each force rises up against the other. The Reformation declared many matters to be *diaphora*—areas exempt from control by religious considerations. This was the price religion had to pay for its existence, just as Christianity itself, threatened by a far more religious ancient world, paid a similar price to ensure its survival. Since then the gulf has steadily widened. At present almost everything on earth is determined by the grossest and most malignant forces, by the selfishness of financial profiteers and by military despots. The state, controlled by the latter, attempts—as does the egotism of the money-makers—to reorganize everything, beginning with itself, and to become the bond and pressure linking all those opposed forces. It wants, that is, the same idolatry that men once accorded the Church. With what success? We will know before too long. For today at any rate we are still in the icy, glacial stream of the Middle Ages; the thaw has begun, and a disastrously powerful movement is under way. Floe piles on floe, the shores are flooded and endangered. The revolution, the atomistic revolution, cannot be avoided. But what are the smallest indivisible particles of human society?

There is no doubt that humanity is in almost greater danger during the advent of periods like this than during the actual collapse and chaos of revolution, and that the terrible suspense and greedy exploitation of the moment stimulate every vileness and selfish instinct in the human soul, whereas a real danger, above all a great universal calamity, usually makes men braver and better. Who then, amidst these dangers besetting our age, will pledge his services as sentinel and champion of *humanity,* to the sacred and inviolable temple-treasure gradually amassed by so many different generations? Who will raise the *image of man* when everyone feels in himself the worm of selfishness and a jackal terror, and has fallen from that image into bestiality or even robot automatism?

There are three images of man that modern times have successively raised, whose contemplation will for a long time inspire mortals to transfigure their own lives. These are Rousseau's Man, Goethe's Man, and Schopenhauer's Man. The first of these has the greatest luster and is certain to have the widest popular influence; the second is only for the few, that is, for contemplative thinkers in the grand style, and is misunderstood by the mob. The third can only be contemplated by truly active men; only they can gaze at it without coming to grief, since it undoes contemplative men and terrifies the mob. From the first image came a force that incited, and still incites, violent revolutions. For in every socialist tremor and upheaval, it is always Rousseau's Man who is stirring, like old Typhon underneath Etna. Oppressed and half-crushed by class arrogance and the cruelty of wealth, corrupted by priests and bad education, humiliated in his own eyes by absurd customs, man in his misery calls out to "holy Nature," and suddenly he feels that she is as remote from him as any Epicurean god. So deeply has he sunk into the chaos of the unnatural that his prayers fail to reach her. Scornfully, he casts off all the showy finery—his arts and sciences, the refinements of his life, which he had only recently regarded as his most human possessions. He beats his fists against the wall in whose shadow he has degenerated; he cries out for light, sunshine, the forests, the mountains. And as he exclaims, "Only Nature is good, only the natural is human," he despises himself and yearns to transcend himself—a condition in which the soul is ready for frightful decisions, but which also summons from the depths her noblest and rarest powers.

Goethe's Man is a less threatening force; in some sense he is even the corrective and sedative antidote to just those dangerous excitements to which Rousseau's Man is exposed. Goethe himself in his younger days passionately embraced the gospel of kindly Nature; his Faust was the highest and boldest image of Rousseau's Man, at least insofar as it portrayed the former's lust for life, his discontent and yearning, his converse with the demons of the heart. But look now what emerges from all those gathering clouds—certainly no lightning! In this fact the new image of Man, Goethe's Man, stands revealed. One would have thought that Faust would be led through life, menaced on all sides, the tireless rebel and liberator, the power that negates out of love; he would be the true and proper genius, as it were religious and daemonic, of revolution, in sharp contrast to his quite undaemonic companion; and this, despite the fact that he cannot rid himself of his companion and makes use of him even while loathing the latter's evil and destructive skepticism—which is the tragic destiny of every rebel and liberator. But we are wrong to expect anything of the kind. In this respect Goethe's Man diverges from Rousseau's Man, for he hates all violence, any sudden leap—which means any action; and in this way Faust the world-liberator turns into something like a mere world-traveler. Before the eyes of this insatiable observer every domain of life and nature goes floating by, all past epochs, arts, mythologies, all the sciences. His deepest desire is aroused and satisfied; even Helen can no longer hold him. And now must come the moment for which his mocking companion has been furtively waiting. At a certain place on earth the flight comes to an end, the wings fall away, and Mephistopheles stands at his side. When the German ceases to be Faust, his greatest danger is that of becoming a philistine and falling into the clutches of the devil, from which only heavenly powers can save him. Goethe's Man is, as I said earlier, a contemplative in the grand manner; he survives in this world only by gathering for his nourishment everything great and memorable in the past and the present, so he lives on, even though living only from one desire to another. He is not the active man. On the contrary, if at some point he adapts himself to existing categories of activity, we can be certain that nothing will come of it, as nothing came of Goethe's passion for the theater. Above all, we can be certain that no "order" will be overthrown. Goethe's Man is a conservative and conciliatory force—but in danger, as I said, of degenerating into a philistine, just as Rousseau's Man can easily become a Catilinarian. Add just a little more muscularity and natural wildness to Goethe's Man, and all his virtues would be greater. It looks as though Goethe knew where the danger and the weakness of his man lay, and he hints at it in Jarno's words to Wilhelm Meister [in *Wilhelm Meister's Apprenticeship*]: "You are disgruntled and bitter, and that is all to the good; if someday you got really angry, that would be better still."

And so, to put it bluntly, we must for once be really wicked, in order to make things better. And the image of Schopenhauer's Man should encourage us in this task. *Schopenhauer's Man voluntarily imposes upon himself the suffering of truthfulness,* and this suffering serves to destroy his individual will and to prepare him for that total upheaval and reversal of his nature whose attainment is the real meaning of life. To others, this blunt, outspoken truthfulness looks like the effect of malice, for they think it is their humanitarian duty to preserve their mediocrity and half-truths, and that those who wreck their childish little games in this way must be wicked. To such a man they are tempted to say what Faustus said to Mephistopheles: "To the eternally active, healing, and creative energy, you oppose your devil's fist," and the man who wants to live, according to Schopenhauer, must resemble Faustus more than Mephistopheles—that is, to the myopic modern eye which detects signs of wickedness in any negation. But there is a species of negation and destruction which is the exact expression of that powerful yearning for holiness and salvation of which Schopenhauer has been, to profane and secularized people like ourselves,

the first philosophical teacher. All existence that can be denied deserves to be denied; and being truthful means believing in an existence which could not in any way be denied, which is true in itself and exempt from falsehood. This is why the truthful man feels that his activity has a metaphysical meaning, explicable according to the laws of another, higher life; and, in a deeper sense, affirmative, even though everything he does appears to be destructive and a violation of the laws of that higher life. In this respect, his activity necessarily means constant suffering. But, like Meister Eckehart, he knows that "suffering is the swiftest steed to carry you to perfection."

I like to think that anyone whose soul was confronted by such an ideal of life would feel his heart expand and within him a burning desire well up to become such a Schopenhauerian man. That is, to be disinterested and wonderfully serene as regards himself and his personal welfare; in intellectual pursuits, filled with a fierce, consuming fire, far removed from the cold and contemptuous neutrality of what is called "pure scholarship" exalted high above sulky and peevish contemplation; always ready to sacrifice himself as the first victim of the truth he has discovered; and deeply conscious of the sufferings that must necessarily result from his truthfulness. Admittedly, he destroys his own earthly happiness through his courage; he must be an enemy to those he loves and to the institutions that gave him birth; he is permitted to spare neither men nor things, even though he suffers with them in their injuries. He will be misunderstood and for a long time regarded as an ally of forces he despises; and despite his aspiration to justice, he will have to be unjust when judged by human standards. But he can comfort and encourage himself with these words which Schopenhauer, his great educator, once used: "A happy life is impossible; the highest life attainable by man is *a heroic life.* This is the life of the man who, for whatever motive and in any way, fights against immense difficulties for the benefit of all and who finally conquers but receives little or no reward. So, at the end, he finds himself like the prince in Gozzi's *Re Corvo,* turned to stone, but in a noble stance and with magnanimous features. His memory lives on, and it is honored like that of a hero; his will, mortified by a lifetime of toil and trouble, by lack of success and the world's ingratitude, is absorbed into Nirvana."

This heroic life, with the complete mortification it implies, clearly bears no relation whatever to the petty ideas of those who discuss it most. They celebrate the memory of great men and imagine that the great man is great in the same way that they are small, quite as though greatness were a gift designed for one's own pleasure, or through some mechanism and in blind obedience to this inner compulsion, with the implication that the man who has not received the gift, or who feels no compulsion, has just as much right to be small as the other man to be great. But *gift* and *compulsion*—these are contemptible words by whose means one tries to escape an inner voice and which are insulting to the man who has heeded this voice, that is, to the great man, since he is the last person in the world to accept gifts or suffer compulsion, even though he knows as well as any little man that he could find an easy life and a soft berth if only he took the conventional, courteous way with himself and his fellow man. For all human arrangements are directed towards this end—that, through constant distraction of thinking, life may not be *felt*. Why does the hero so passionately desire the opposite, namely, to feel life, which is the same thing as suffering from life? Because he sees that others would like to defraud him of himself, that there is a kind of conspiracy to lure him out of his cave. And so he balks, pricks up his ears, and decides: "I will remain my own!" It is a frightful decision; only gradually does he come to realize this. For now, in fact, he must descend into the depths of existence with a string of curious questions on his lips. Why am I alive? What lesson am I to learn from life? How did I become what I am, and why do I suffer from being what I am? He tortures himself, and observes that nobody else tortures himself in this way. On the contrary, the hands of his fellow men are stretched passionately towards the fantastic events provided by the political theater where men strut about in a hundred masks—young men, old men, fathers, citizens, priests, officials, and merchants, all utterly preoccupied with their common comedy and not at all with themselves. To the question "Why are you alive?" they would answer, proudly and promptly, "To *become* a citizen, or a scholar, or a statesman." And yet they *are* something which can never become anything else, and why are they precisely this? And alas, why not something better?

The man who regards his life as merely a point in the evolution of a race, a state, or a field of knowledge, the man who therefore wants to belong wholly to the history of Becoming, has not mastered the lesson given him by existence and must therefore set about learning it over. This eternal Becoming is a fiction, a puppet-play over which man forgets himself, a distraction in the true sense of the word, which disperses the individual to the four winds; the endless silly game which Time, the great baby, plays before our eyes, and with us. The heroism of truthfulness lies in our someday refusing to be Time's toy. In Becoming, everything is hollow, false, shallow, and contemptible; the riddle which man must solve, he can only solve in Being, in being what he is and not something else, in the immutable. Now he begins to investigate how deeply he is involved with Becoming, and how deeply with Being, and a fearful task confronts his soul—that of destroying all Becoming, of exposing to the light all falseness in things. He too wants to know everything, but to know it in a different way from Goethe's Man, not for the sake of a noble delicacy, or to preserve himself and delight in the multiplicity of things. On the contrary, he himself is the first sacrifice he offers. The heroic man scorns his own misery or well-being, his virtues and vices; he scorns to make himself the measure of things. He no longer hopes for anything more from himself, and in all things wants to look down into this hopeless abyss. His strength lies in forgetting himself; when he thinks of himself, it is to measure the distance between himself and his goal, and it is as though what he saw behind and below him were a wretched pile of rubble. With all their might the ancient thinkers sought for happiness and truth—

and what a man must seek, he will never find: such is the malicious law of Nature. But he who seeks untruth in everything and willingly makes unhappiness his companion, will perhaps experience another miracle of disillusionment. Something inexpressible, of which happiness and truth are merely idolatrous imitations, approaches him, the earth loses its gravity, the events and powers of the world seem like a dream, and everything, as on a summer evening, sheds a radiance around him. It seems to the beholder as though he were just waking, and the cloudy wisps of a fading dream were playing around him. But these too will drift away. And then it is day.

But I promised to depict Schopenhauer as *educator,* according to my own experience. Hence, it is simply not enough to offer an image, and an inadequate one at that, of the ideal man who holds sway in Schopenhauer and around him, his Platonic Idea, as it were. The most difficult task remains, that is, to show how a new round of duties is to be derived from this ideal, and how we can make contact with this boundless ideal through ordinary activity; in short, to show that this ideal *educates*. Otherwise, we might suppose it was nothing more than an enchanting, even intoxicating vision vouchsafed us in isolated moments, only to abandon us immediately, leaving us even more alone and prey to even deeper disgust. Now it is clear that our acquaintance with this ideal *begins* in this way, with these startling alternations of light and darkness, intoxication and disgust, and that in this respect we are repeating an experience as old as the ideals themselves. But we must not remain standing at the threshold, but proceed quickly past the initial stages.

We must therefore ask, seriously and purposively, whether it is possible to bring that incredibly lofty goal so close to us that it educates us while drawing us upwards. By so doing, we may avoid fulfilling in our own respect Goethe's great words [in *Wilhelm Meister's Apprenticeship*]: "Man is born to a limited position; he is able to grasp simple, proximate, and definite goals, and he gets used to employing those means that are immediately available to him. But when he escapes his limits, he knows neither what he wants nor what he ought to do. And it makes no difference whether he is distracted by the multiplicity of objects or driven into ecstasy by their loftiness and nobility. For him it is always a misfortune when he is impelled to strive for something with which he cannot connect himself by means of ordinary activities originating in himself." And with a good semblance of justice, this same objection might be brought against Schopenhauer's Man, whose nobility and loftiness may carry us beyond ourselves, with the result that we are once again removed from all communities of active men; the coherence of duties, the flow of life vanish. One man may perhaps accustom himself to unhappy self-division and to living by a double standard, that is, in conflict with himself, insecure in either part of himself, and hence becoming daily more weak and sterile; whereas another man on principle rejects all activity in common with others and scarcely notices when others act. The risks are always great when excessive hardship is imposed upon a man and he can *fulfill* no duties at all. Stronger natures may be destroyed in this way; weaker men—that is, the majority—sink into contemplative laziness and finally, through laziness, lose even the habit of contemplation.

In reply to these objections, I admit that our work has barely begun, and that from my own experience there is only one fact that I perceive and know for certain. And that is that, starting out from that ideal image, it is possible to impose on you and me a chain of duties capable of being fulfilled, and that some of us already feel the weight of that chain. But before I can state categorically the formula under which I would like to subsume this new round of duties, certain preliminary considerations are in order.

At all times men of greater profundity have felt compassion for animals, since animals suffer from life yet lack the strength to turn the sting of suffering against themselves and thereby achieve a metaphysical understanding of their existence. Moreover, the sight of senseless suffering is deeply revolting. This is why in many places on earth the belief arose that the souls of guilty men had been implanted in these animal bodies, and that senseless suffering, at first sight so outrageous, resolves itself intelligently and meaningfully as punishment and penance under eternal justice. Obviously it is a harsh punishment to live like an animal, in hunger and desire, and yet to achieve no awareness of this life. And no harsher fate can be imagined than that of the beasts of prey who are driven through the desert by the most devouring torment, seldom ever satisfied; and even when it is, the satisfaction turns into pain in the flesh-tearing struggle with other animals, or in nauseating greed and satiety. To cling to life wildly and blindly with no prospect of higher reward; and far from knowing that one is being punished and why, but rather craving this punishment as if it were a happiness, with the stupidity of a frightful desire—this is what it means to be an animal. And if all nature aspires to man, it is to show us that man is necessary in order to redeem nature from the curse of animal existence; and that in man existence at last owns a mirror in whose depths life no longer appears as senseless, but in its metaphysical meaning.

But consider this question carefully: Where does the animal stop, where does man begin? That man who is Nature's sole concern? So long as we crave life as if it were happiness, we have not succeeded in lifting our gaze above the animal's horizon; we merely desire with greater awareness what the animal pursues from blind instinct. But this is how it is with most of us for the greater part of our lives. We rarely transcend our animal existence; we ourselves are the animals that seem to suffer senselessly.

But there are moments *when are understand this*. The clouds break, and we see how we, together with all of nature, aspire toward Man as something standing high above us. In that sudden blaze of light, we look with terror around us and behind us. There they go, the delicate beasts of prey, and we are there among them. The immense commotion of men over the great desert of the earth, the cities and states men found and the wars they wage, their restless conclaves and dispersions, their chaotic collisions and mutual imitations, their reciprocal overreachings and down-treadings, their shrieks of pain and howls of triumph—all this is a continuation of our animal existence; almost as though man had been deliberately created to regress and cheated of his metaphysical disposition; as if Nature, having for so long yearned and labored for man, now recoiled from him with a shudder, preferring to return to the unconsciousness of instinct. Alas, Nature needs knowledge, and is terrified of the knowledge she needs; and so the flame flickers uncertainly as though afraid of itself, seizing on a thousand things before seizing on the one thing which above all else Nature needs to know.

In isolated moments we all know that we have deliberately complicated the arrangements of our lives only in order to evade our real task. We know how happy we would be to hide our heads somewhere—as though our hundred-eyed conscience could not find us there; and how ready we are to surrender our selves to the state or money-making, to social life or scholarship, only in order to get rid of them; and that even in our everyday work we slave more fiercely and busily than necessary in order to earn a living because it seems even more necessary to avoid reflection. The haste is universal because everyone is running from himself. And because we want to seem contented and to disguise our misery from the more acute observers, the timid concealing of this haste is no less universal. Also universal is the need for fresh-sounding words in order to adorn life with a kind of riotous festivity. We all know that peculiar state when disagreeable memories suddenly invade our minds, and we try to expel them by violent sounds and gestures. But the sounds and gestures of common life allow us to perceive that we are always in such a state, fearful of memory and inward experience. What bothers us so, what is this mosquito that will not let us sleep? The air around us is filled with spirits; every instant of life wants to tell us something, but we refuse to listen to this ghostly voice. When we are alone and quiet, we fear that something will be whispered into our ear, and for this reason we hate the quiet and drug ourselves with social life.

As I said earlier, there are moments when we understand all this, and we look with astonishment at the dizzy haste, and anguish, and the whole dreamlike quality of our life, which seems to be afraid of waking, which dreams more intensely and restlessly as the moment of waking approaches. But at the same time we feel that we are too weak to bear these moments of deep introspection, and that we are not the men toward whom all of Nature presses for her redemption. It is no small achievement that we can now and then lift our heads and see the stream into which we have sunk so deeply. And even this—this emerging and waking for a fleeting instant—we cannot manage by our own strength. We have to be lifted up—and who are those who lift us up?

They are those true *men, those no-longer animals, the philosophers, artists, and saints*. In their appearance and through their appearance, Nature, who makes no leaps, makes her only leap, a leap of joy! For the first time she feels that she has reached her goal, the point at which she intuits that she will have to unlearn her goals, and that she has staked too much on the game of life and Becoming. She is transfigured by this knowledge, and a gentle twilight weariness which men call "beauty" suffuses her face. What these transfigured features now express is the great *illumination* of existence, and the highest wish possible to mortals is to share, constantly and with open ears, in this illumination. When we think of everything that Schopenhauer, for instance, must have *heard* in the course of his life, we may well say to ourselves later: "Oh, these deaf ears of mine, this dull head, this feeble intellect of mine, this shrunken heart, how I despise everything I call my own! I cannot fly, only flutter my wings! To look up without the capacity to rise! To know, almost to take, the way that leads to the philosopher's immeasurably free vision, and then to reel back after a few steps! If only that greatest of all wishes could be fulfilled for one day, how gladly would we give the rest of our lives in exchange for it! To climb as high as any thinker ever climbed, into the icy purity of the Alpine air where there is no longer any fog or veiling mist, where the underlying structure of things is revealed, stark and rigid, but in absolute clarity! Merely at the thought the soul becomes solitary, infinite. But if the soul's great wish were granted; if its gaze fell on things below, sheer and radiant as a ray of light; if shame, anxiety, and desire could vanish—what words could describe the state of mind, that new, enigmatic, motionless emotion with which the soul—like Schopenhauer's soul—would settle and diffuse itself over the whole immense hieroglyph of existence and the petrified doctrine of Becoming—not as black night but as a blazing crimson light streaming out over the world? And obversely, what a fate it would be to have so clear an intuition of the philosopher's special destiny and blessedness that one might sense the uncertainty and despair of the nonphilosopher, the man who desires but has no hope! To feel that one is fruit on the tree, fruit that cannot ripen because there is too much shade, and to see only a little way off the sunlight that one lacks!"

The torture would be enough to make such a mis-gifted man envious and malicious, if he were capable of envy and malice. More probably, it will end by his turning his soul in another direction so that it will not be devoured by vain desire. And it is at this point that he will *discover* a new round of duties.

I am now in a position to reply to the question I raised earlier: whether it is possible, through ordinary, self-originating activity, to establish a relation with the great ideal represented by Schopenhauer's Man. Above all, one fact is certain: these new duties are not the duties of a single individual; rather, by their means, one belongs to a mighty community welded together not by external forms and laws, but by a fundamental idea. This is the fundamental idea of *culture,* insofar as culture imposes only one duty on each of us: *to promote the production of the philosopher, the artist, and the saint, within us and in the world, and thereby to labor for the perfection of Nature.* Just as Nature needs the philosopher, so she also needs

the artist, for a metaphysical purpose, that is, for her own illumination, so that she may at last be presented with a pure and perfected image of what she never sees in the confusion of Becoming—and by so doing achieve self-consciousness. It was Goethe who, with arrogant profundity, observed that all of Nature's efforts are useful only insofar as the artist finally guesses the meaning of her stammering, meets her half-way, and expresses the real meaning of her efforts. "I have often said," he once exclaimed, "and I will say it again and again, that the *causa finalis* of the world's business and human affairs is dramatic poetry. For otherwise the stuff is completely useless."

And for this reason Nature finally has need of the saint, in whom the individual ego has entirely melted away and whose life of suffering is no longer, or hardly any longer, felt individually, but rather as a profound sensation of likeness, compassion, and unity with every living thing; the saint in whom the miracle of transformation takes place, and on whom the play of Becoming leaves no trace—that last, supreme humanization for which all Nature, in search of its redemption, strives. There is no doubt that we are all bound by kinship to the saint as we are bound by kinship to the philosopher and the artist. There are moments and sparklings, as it were, struck from that most brilliant and amorous fire, by whose light we no longer understand the word *I*. Beyond our being there lies something which in those moments becomes here and now, and this is why we desire from the bottom of our hearts to make bridges between here and that which lies beyond.

In our customary state we can of course contribute nothing to the production of the redeeming man, and we therefore *hate* ourselves in this state—a hatred which is the root of that pessimism which Schopenhauer had to re-teach our age, but which is as ancient as the aspiration to culture. The root, but not the flower; the foundation, but not the gable; the start of the road, not the goal: for someday we must learn to hate something else, something larger than our individual self with its wretched limitations and its restless turmoil. In that exalted state we shall have learned to love something different from what we now love. Only when, either in this life or in some later incarnation, we have been welcomed into that exalted order of philosophers, artists, and saints, will there be new goals assigned to our love and hatred. In the meantime we have our tasks and our round of duties, our hatred and our love. For we know what culture is. Applied culture requires us to prepare for and promote the production of Schopenhauer's Man by learning what impedes his coming and removing it from his path—in sum, requires us to fight tirelessly against everything that has held us back from the highest fulfillment of our existence, preventing us from becoming such Schopenhauerian man. . . .

It often seems as though an artist and a fortiori a philosopher are in their age *by accident,* as hermits and wanderers who have straggled away and been left behind. Simply try to understand, with real sympathy, how great, personally and in everything, Schopenhauer is—and how absurdly small his effect has been. Nothing can be more humiliating to an honest contemporary than to see the casual position which Schopenhauer occupies in this age, and by what forces—and nonforces—his impact has until now been curtailed. The first obstacle, to the everlasting shame of our literary age, was his longstanding lack of readers; then, when readers came, the inadequacy of his first public supporters. Even worse, I think, was the insensitivity of modern men to books, which they absolutely refuse to take seriously. And now, gradually, a new danger has appeared, arising from various efforts to adapt Schopenhauer to this insipid period by applying him as a seductive, exotic spice, a sort of metaphysical pepper. It was in this way that he gradually won renown and fame so that at present, I believe, his name among some people is better known than Hegel's. Nonetheless, he is still a hermit; he still has had no real effect. Those who can least claim the honor of having presented his influence are the yapping literary jackals who opposed him, first of all because so few people have the patience to read them, and, secondly, because those who do are immediately led to Schopenhauer. Who, after all, would let a mule-driver prevent him from riding a fine horse, no matter how loudly the driver praised his mule at the horse's expense?

Those who are conscious of the folly afflicting the age might consider how to come to its assistance. But their task will be to make Schopenhauer's work known among free spirits and those who suffer deeply from the age, and to organize them into a coherent force that will counteract Nature's past and present inability to put her philosophers to use. They will come to see that the obstacles that prevent a great philosophy from having an effect are one and the same as those that impede the appearance of a great philosopher. So their task might be defined as preparing for the rebirth of Schopenhauer, that is, of the philosophical genius. From the beginning what has slowed the spread of his work and influence, and what will in every possible way oppose the rebirth of the philosopher, is, in a word, the imbecility of modern human nature. And so all those destined for greatness must waste incredible energy in order to save themselves from this imbecility. The world into which they now come is smothered in cant. By which I do not necessarily mean religious dogmas only, but such claptrap notions as "progress," "general education," "nationalism," "modern state," "struggle of church and state." We might, in fact, observe that all general terms nowadays are prinked out with such arty unnaturalness that a more enlightened posterity will charge our age in particular with being twisted and deformed, quite despite our noisy boasting about our "health." According to Schopenhauer, the beauty of ancient vases is that they express with such simplicity exactly what they are meant to be and do. And the same holds true of all other ancient utensils. We feel that if Nature had created vases, amphoras, lamps, tables, chairs, helmets, breastplates, armor, and so on, *this* is how they would look. If, however, we consider how everybody these days handles his utensils—politics, art, religion, and education (not to mention, for obvious reason, our "pots" and vases)—we find that men express themselves with a certain barbaric capriciousness and excess, and that such crackbrained ideas and moronic needs are the great vogue of the age. *These* are the leaden pressures which, invisibly and inexplicably, so often force down the hand of the genius while he tries to guide his plow, with the result that even his highest achievements bear to some degree the marks of the violent upward straining required by their creation.

If I turn now to the conditions under which, in the luckiest cases, the born philosopher might avoid being overwhelmed by the imbecility of the age, I am struck by a remarkable fact. It is that these are, at least partly, the same general conditions in which Schopenhauer grew up. There were, of course, unfavorable conditions. The lunatic quality of the age, for instance, came frightfully close to him in his mother's vanity and literary pretentiousness. But his father's proud, free, republican character saved him, as it were, from his mother and gave him the chief thing a philosopher needs: dogged, rugged virility. His father was neither a civil servant nor a scholar; he traveled with his young son in numerous foreign countries, all very helpful to someone destined to know men, not books, and to revere the truth, not governments. Schopenhauer quickly became insensitive to, or too sensible for, national limitations. He was at home in England, France, Italy, and he felt marked sympathy with the spirit of Spain. On the whole, he did not consider it an honor to be born in Germany; I cannot say whether he would have felt differently under our new political conditions. He believed, as everyone knows, that the sole purpose of the state was to provide defense from abroad, defense from within, and defense from the defenders; and that to assign the state any other purpose might easily endanger its true purpose. And for this reason, to the horror of so-called liberals, he bequeathed his property to the orphans and widows of the Prussian soldiers who had fallen in 1848 in the struggle to maintain order. Henceforth, the ability to understand the state and its duties in simple terms is more and more likely to be seen as a sign of superior intelligence. For the man with the *furor philosophicus* will have no time for the *furor politicus,* and will wisely refrain from reading newspapers every day, and above all serving in a party, though he will not for an instant hesitate to take his place when real danger threatens his country. All states in which men other than politicians must concern themselves with politics are badly organized and deserve to perish of too many politicians.

Schopenhauer was also extremely fortunate in not being destined and educated for scholarship. For some time, although reluctantly, he actually worked in a commercial office, and throughout his youth he breathed the freer air of a large trading house. A scholar can never become a philosopher. Even Kant could not manage it and, despite the innate power of his genius, remained to the very end in chrysalis state. Those who think these words are unfair to Kant do not know what a philosopher is—not only a great thinker but a genuine human being. And when has a scholar ever turned into a genuine human being? Anyone who lets concepts, opinions, past events, and books come between himself and things, who in the broadest sense is born to history, will never see things for the first time and will never himself be one of those prodigies that have never been seen before. But both these traits must be present in the philosopher, since most of what he teaches he has to draw from himself and because he himself is his own image and compendium of the whole world. If a man sees himself through the opinions of others, it is no surprise if he sees in himself nothing but—other people's opinions! And this is how scholars live, see, and are.

Schopenhauer, in contrast, had the indescribable good fortune not only to observe genius at close range, in himself, but also outside himself, in Goethe. And this double reflection instructed him and made him wise with regard to all scholarly goals and culture. Through this experience, he knew how the strong, free man to whom every artistic culture aspires should be formed. How, after a vision like this, could he have still wanted to deal with what is called "art" in the learned or hypocritical way of modern man? He had, after all, glimpsed something far higher: an awful scene of otherworldly judgment in which all life, even the highest and most perfected, was laid in the scales and found wanting. He had seen the saint as the judge of existence. We cannot determine at what age Schopenhauer saw this vision of life in the form in which he tried to describe it in his later writing. We can show that the young man, and perhaps even the child, had already seen this tremendous vision. Everything he later acquired from life, and books, and every field of knowledge, was for him little more than color and means by which to express it. Even Kant's philosophy he used mainly as an extraordinary rhetorical device for expressing that vision more clearly. Buddhist and Christian mythology at times served the same purpose. For Schopenhauer there was only one task, and a thousand ways of accomplishing it. There was one meaning and countless hieroglyphs to express it.

It was one of the splendid conditions of his existence that he could really live for such a task, according to his motto—*vitam impendere vero*—and that he was never weighed down by the vulgarities associated with poverty. It is well known how magnificently he thanked his father for this. But without such good fortune, the contemplative man in Germany pursues his spiritual vocation usually at the expense of the purity of his character, as a "deferential tramp," greedy for honor and position, circumspect and pliable, obsequious to influential people and his betters. Regrettably, Schopenhauer insulted them in nothing quite so much as his failure to resemble them. . . .

Now if thinkers of this sort are dangerous, it is obvious why our academic thinkers are harmless; their thoughts grow as tranquilly in the soil of tradition as ever a tree bore apples. They inspire no terror, they throw open no doors, and to all their hustle and bustle we might raise the same objection Diogenes made when he heard a philosopher praised: "What great deed has he ever done? All his life he practiced philosophy and never yet *disturbed* a soul." And surely this should be the epitaph of a university philosophy: "It never disturbed a soul." But this is the sort of praise we might give an old woman, not the goddess of truth. So it is hardly surprising that those who know the goddess only as an old woman are hardly men themselves and are rightly ignored by men of power.

But if this is how matters stand in our times, then the dignity of Philosophy is trampled in the dust, and she seems in fact to have become absurd or irrelevant. For this reason all her true friends are obliged to bear witness against this confusion and to prove that it is not Philosophy but her false servants and unworthy worthies who are absurd and irrelevant. Better yet, let them prove in their actions that the love of truth is mighty and terrible.

Schopenhauer proved it—and he will go on proving it more and more with every passing day.

Friedrich Nietzsche (essay date 1887)

SOURCE: "What Do Ascetic Ideals Mean?" in *The Birth of Tragedy and The Genealogy of Morals,* translated by Francis Golffing, Anchor Books, 1956, pp. 231-99.

[*In the following excerpt from* The Genealogy of Morals, *which was originally published in 1887, Nietzsche contends that although Schopenhauer's aesthetic theory seemingly stresses disinterestedness, Schopenhauer instead considered art as a means to intellectual empowerment.*]

Schopenhauer made use of the Kantian version of the esthetic problem, though he certainly did not look upon it with the eyes of Kant. Kant had thought he was doing an honor to art when, among the predicates of beauty, he gave prominence to those which flatter the intellect, i.e., impersonality and universality. This is not the place to inquire whether Kant did not attack the whole problem in the wrong way; all I wish to point out here is that Kant, like all philosophers, instead of viewing the esthetic issue from the side of the artist, envisaged art and beauty solely from the "spectator's" point of view, and so, without himself realizing it, smuggled the "spectator" into the concept of beauty. This would not have mattered too much had that "spectator" been sufficiently familiar to the philosophers of beauty, as a strong personal experience, a wealth of powerful impressions, aspirations, surprises, and transports in the esthetic realm. But I am afraid the opposite has always been the case, and so we have got from these philosophers of beauty definitions which, like Kant's famous definition of beauty, are marred by a complete lack of esthetic sensibility. "That is beautiful," Kant proclaims, "which gives us disinterested pleasure." Disinterested! Compare with this definition that other one, framed by a real spectator and artist, Stendhal, who speaks of beauty as "a promise of happiness." Here we find the very thing which Kant stresses exclusively in the esthetic condition rejected and canceled. Which is right, Kant or Stendhal?—When our estheticians tirelessly rehearse, in support of Kant's view, that the spell of beauty enables us to view even *nude* female statues "disinterestedly" we may be allowed to laugh a little at their expense. The experiences of artists in this delicate matter are rather more "interesting"; certainly Pygmalion was not entirely devoid of esthetic feeling. Let us honor our estheticians all the more for the innocence reflected in such arguments—Kant, for example, when he descants on the peculiar character of the sense of touch with the ingenuousness of a country parson! To come back to Schopenhauer, who was so much closer to the arts than Kant but who yet could not escape from the spell of Kant's definition—how are we to account for his view?

Schopenhauer interpreted the term "disinterested" in a wholly personal way, basing it on an experience which he must have had quite regularly. There are few things about which he speaks with such assurance as the effect of esthetic contemplation. He claims that it counteracts the sexual "interest" (like lupulin and camphor), and he never tires of glorifying this release from the will as the great boon of the esthetic condition. One might even be tempted to ask whether he did not derive his basic conception of Will vs. Idea (the notion that only the Idea can deliver us from the Will) from a generalization of that sexual interest. (In all questions pertaining to Schopenhauer's philosophy we must never leave out of account that it was conceived by a young man of twenty-six; so that it partakes not only of the specific character of Schopenhauer but of the specific traits of that period of life.) Listen, for instance, to one of the most explicit of all the countless passages he has written extolling the esthetic condition (*The World as Will and Idea, I*) and you will hear the suffering, the happiness, the gratitude behind the words. "This is the painless condition which Epicurus praised as the highest good and the condition of the gods. For a moment we are delivered from the wretched urgency of the will; we celebrate the day of rest in the treadmill of volition; the wheel of Ixion stands still. . . . " What vehemence in these words, what images of pain and endless disgust! What an almost pathological time confrontation in the terms, "the moment" as against the "wheel of Ixion," the "treadmill of volition," the "wretched urgency of the will"! But assuming that Schopenhauer was one hundred per cent right in his own case, we might still ask what has really been gained for our understanding of the nature of beauty? Schopenhauer has described one effect of beauty, that it acts as a sedative of the will, but can it even be claimed that this is a regular effect? As I have pointed out, Stendhal, no less sensual a man than Schopenhauer but more happily constituted, stresses a very different effect of beauty: "it promises happiness." For him it is precisely the excitement of the will, of "interest," through beauty that matters. And might one not urge against Schopenhauer himself that he was quite wrong in seeing himself as a Kantian, that he had failed to understand Kant's definition as its author intended it? That he too responded to beauty from an interested motive, even out of the strongest, most personal interest, that of the tortured man seeking release from his torment? If we now return to [the] question, "What does it mean when a philosopher pays homage to the ascetic ideal?" we receive our first clue: he craves release from a torture.

Let us not immediately pull a long face at the word *torture;* there is plenty to offset it, to mitigate it—there will even be something left over to laugh about. We must take account of the fact that Schopenhauer, who treated sexuality (including woman, that *instrumentum diaboli*) as a personal enemy, absolutely required enemies to keep him in good spirits; that he loved atrabilious words, that he

fulminated for the sake of fulminating, out of passion; that he would have sickened, become a *pessimist* (which he was not, much as he would have liked to be) had he been deprived of his enemies, of Hegel, of woman, of sensuality, of the human will to survival. You may be certain that without these Schopenhauer would not have stayed, he would have run away. It was his enemies who kept him alive. Just as with the ancient Cynics, his rage was his balm, his recreation, his compensation, his specific against tedium, in short, his happiness. This much in regard to what is most personal in the case of Schopenhauer; but there is, on the other hand, something typical about it too, and this brings us back to our main issue. Wherever there have been philosophers, from India to England (to indicate the opposite extremes of speculative orientation), there has prevailed a special philosopher's resentment against sensuality; Schopenhauer is only the most eloquent, and, for him who has ears to hear, the most delightful exponent of that resentment. There likewise exists a properly philosophical prejudice in favor of the ascetic ideal, let us make no mistake about it. Both dispositions, as I have said, are *typical;* if a philosopher lacks them, we may be sure that he is spurious. What does that *mean?* For it is our duty to interpret such a state of affairs, which in itself simply stands there stupidly to all eternity, like every thing-in-itself. Every animal, including *la bête philosophe,* strives instinctively for the optimum conditions under which it may release its powers. Every animal, instinctively and with a subtle flair that leaves reason far behind, abhors all interference that might conceivably block its path to that optimum. (The path I am speaking of does not lead to "happiness" but to power, to the most energetic activity, and in a majority of cases to actual unhappiness.) Thus the philosopher abhors marriage and all that would persuade him to marriage, for he sees the married state as an obstacle to fulfillment. What great philosopher has ever been married? Heracleitus, Plato, Descartes, Spinoza, Leibniz, Kant, Schopenhauer—not one of them was married; moreover, it is impossible to imagine any of them married. I maintain that a married philosopher belongs in comedy, and as for that great exception, Socrates, it would almost seem that the malicious Socrates got married in a spirit of irony, precisely in order to prove that contention. Every philosopher would speak as Buddha spoke when he was told that a son had been born to him: "Rahula has been born to me; a fetter has been forged for me" (Rahula means "little daemon"). Every free spirit would be set thinking, provided he had ever stopped thinking, just as it once happened to Buddha: "'Close and oppressive is life in a house, a place of impurity; to leave the house is freedom' and, thus meditating, he left the house." The ascetic ideal suggests so many bridges to independence that a philosopher cannot help rejoicing as he listens to the story of all those resolute men who one day made up their minds to say "no" to every form of servitude and went forth into a desert—even if they were really only strong mules, and as far as possible from being strong spirits. What, then, does the ascetic ideal betoken in a philosopher? The reader will have guessed my answer before now. Asceticism provides him with the condition most favorable to the exercise of his intelligence. Far from denying "existence," he affirms his existence, and his alone, perhaps even to the point of *hubris: pereat mundus, fiat philosophia, fiat philosophus, fiam!* . . .

The case of Schopenhauer should be viewed in the light of this interpretation. Contact with beauty released the central energy of his nature (i.e. his profound speculative energy), making it explode and thus, at a stroke, assume mastery of his consciousness. Yet I do not mean by this to exclude the possibility that the peculiar sweetness and richness proper to the esthetic condition may stem from its sensual ingredient—just as the "idealism" of nubile girls may be traced to the same source. It may well be that the emergence of the esthetic condition does not suspend sensuality, as Schopenhauer believed, but merely transmutes it in such a way that it is no longer experienced as a sexual incentive. . . .

H. N. Gardiner (essay date 1888)

SOURCE: "Schopenhauer as a Critic of Religion," in *The Andover Review,* Vol. X, No. LV, July, 1888, pp. 1-23.

[*In the following essay, Gardiner outlines and evaluates Schopenhauer's objections to religion and explores his life to suggest some factors that may have sparked his anti-religious fervor.*]

[In James Martineau's *A Study of Religion* (1888),] the story is told of an eminent English Positivist, that, listening to an account of the argument in Mr. Fiske's *Destiny of Man,* he gave silent attention until the inference was being drawn of personal inimortality, when he brake in with the exclamation: "What! John Fiske say that? Well; it only proves what I have always maintained, that you cannot make the slightest concession to metaphysics without ending in a theology!"

Whatever truth there may be in the opinion thus expressed that metaphysics culminates, by a logical necessity, in theology, it is certain that every system of metaphysics is bound, by the very nature of its pretensions, to assume some definite attitude towards religion. For religion and metaphysics both concern themselves, in the last resort, with essentially the same objects, having both alike to do with ultimate reality and human destiny, on which profoundest of themes each, in its own way, professes to give to man the profoundest views attainable. Rightly, therefore, will the question be put to metaphysics which Marguerite put to the philosophic Faust, "What thinkest thou of God?" and rightly, too, will metaphysics pronounce judgment on religion, and declare *its* views of things to be true or false or uncertain.

A comparison of religious ideas with the results of a given philosophy not only makes clear the spirit and temper of the latter, but may also be of no small advantage to religion; for whether the views in question substantially agree or widely differ, in any case, the serious consideration of the free criticisms and subtler apprehensions of philosophy can hardly fail to clarify and deepen faith, or

at least to stimulate to a more thorough investigation of its grounds. It is in view of these advantages that I have attempted, in what follows, an examination of some "religious aspects" of the philosophy of Schopenhauer. No system of modern times assumes a more definite or hostile attitude towards religion than this brilliantly expounded metaphysics, half pantheistic, half atheistic, of the great German pessimist. The reason for this lies in the intensely practical outcome of the whole speculation, which was clearly designed as a philosophy of redemption to take the place, at any rate among the educated, of the fast disappearing beliefs of religion. The matter is not without a timely interest. Just a hundred years after the birth of its author, the philosophy of the *World as Will and Idea* celebrates its triumphs as probably the most influential system of German metaphysics since the breaking up of Hegelianism. Such a system the friends of religion cannot well afford to ignore.

I shall confine myself chiefly to the opinions **"On Religion"** collected together in the fifteenth chapter of the second volume of *Parerga and Paralipomena*. The first and most important section of this chapter contains, in the form of a dialogue, a general examination and criticism of religion much after the manner of Hume. One of the speakers, Demopheles, undertakes to defend religion for the masses on practical grounds. His principle is utility, and the ends which religion attains in the practical sphere completely outbalance, he urges, any theoretical exceptions which might be taken to the means. These ends are: first, the satisfaction of man's metaphysical need, the need "which arises from the pressing problem of our existence, and from the consciousness that there must be, beyond the physical of the world, somehow a metaphysical, an unchangeable, serving as the basis for continual change." Religion meets this need, bringing to men truth, yes, the deepest truth, in a form adapted to the common apprehension, allegorical, mysterious, overawing, therefore, and with an authority secured by antiquity and tradition, as is necessary to its practical effectiveness. In the second place, it appeals to the ever-present moral consciousness of men, affording to it that external support and confirmation, "without which it could not easily maintain itself in the struggle with so many temptations." In thus restraining violence, and wisely controlling conduct generally, religion forms the very bulwark of the social order, while Christianity in particular holds forth ideals which reveal the true ethical import of human life in all its depth and seriousness. Finally, religion brings to man, amid great and innumerable sorrows, comfort and consolation, in death especially unfolding to him the whole of its beneficent power. Accordingly, it "is like one who takes a blind man by the hand and leads him, . . . the great thing is, not that he himself should see everything, but that he should reach his destination."

These points are developed, with repetitions and varying emphasis, now here, now there, according to the occasions presented by the free movement of the dialogue.

Philalethes, the other speaker, represents the theoretical and philosophical consciousness. His motto is: *"Vigeat veritas et pereat mundus."* He objects to religion as a popular metaphysics, because, while presenting the truth allegorically, everything has to be taken (as Demopheles also allows) *sensu proprio.* But *sensu proprio* the doctrines are false. The friend of truth, therefore, must reject and condemn them. But the naked truth, stripped of its allegorical dressing up, would be philosophy, and no longer religion. If the principle *simplex sigillum veri* is here unavailing, and the common people cannot be made to understand the profound truths of philosophy, they can at least be brought to so much better insight as to see that what they now regard as true is false, and so be saved from error; and this gain fully justifies the attacks which philosophers and men of science are constantly making on the popular creeds. In regard to the second point, the influence of religion on morals, it is admitted that, in some respects, such influence is both powerful and good. It is not, however, by any means, as has been claimed, the bulwark of civil order, which is much more dependent on the law and the magistrate than on motives of religion. "Suppose," says Philalethes, "that now suddenly, by public proclamation, all criminal laws were declared null and void: I think that neither you nor I would have the courage, under the protection of religious motives, to go home alone only from here. But if, in like manner, all religion were declared to be untrue, we should continue to live as before, without any particular increase of our cares and precautions, under the protection of the laws only." Moreover, the principle contended for is false. It is not true that the end justifies the means. From the standpoint of truth, the *fraus* is to be reprobated, no matter how *pia.* Nor, surely, does moral worth ever belong to deeds, whose source is really and purely superstition. As to Christianity, the ethical import of life which it teaches is, indeed, great, and belongs to it alone—that is to say, in the Occident; but it is never to be forgotten, on the other hand, that, being a monotheistic religion, it is necessarily intolerant, since a single God is, from his very nature, a jealous God, that allows life to no other. Its history, therefore, is a history of bigotry and persecution, of hypocrisy and deceit, of torture and the stake, and of crimes unmentionable, justifying, in part at least, the Spanish proverb, "Behind the cross stands the devil." As regards morality, therefore, the service of religion is largely problematical, while its disadvantages, or even the deeds of violence which have followed it, are manifest. Granted, finally, that the consolations of religion constitute, as they do, its greatest glory, what, it must be urged, can that comfort be worth over which forever hangs the Damocles-sword of disillusioning?

"Religion," says Demopheles at the end, "like Janus, or, better, like Yama, the Brahman's god of death, has two faces, and indeed, like this, one very friendly, the other very forbidding; we have each been looking at one of them." To this Philalethes assents, and the dialogue closes.

In considering this discussion, one cannot but be struck by the fact that Schopenhauer throughout appears able to apprehend religion in no other way than as folk-metaphysics, and that he judges it entirely from the standpoint of his own metaphysics, to which it is, in almost every

particular, opposed. It seems to be assumed that religion is and can be only an affair of the uneducated. Much is said of the opposition between religion and philosophy, but the long line of thinkers whose philosophy has culminated in a religious philosophy are simply ignored. Emphasis is laid on the conflict between religion and science, but the many eminent men of science who, not satisfied to regard blind physical force as ultimate, have turned with reverent hearts to the personal God, are silently passed over. Science is simply set over against faith, reasoned metaphysics against folk-metaphysics, with which religion is straightway identified. The abuses which have been practiced in the name or under the cloak of religion, even those which were without or even against its sanction, these are all heaped together as a reproach upon "religion." No attempt whatever is made to grasp religion in its idea or essence; it is taken up in a purely empirical way as a complex of phenomena, chiefly sociological. The endeavor to make religion appear rational is treated by Schopenhauer in other of his writings as a piece of sophism, for which professors of philosophy receive pay from the government. *All* religion is *necessarily* allegorical, and therefore false. Even Demopheles in the dialogue knows of no better defense of it than as a metaphysical theory adapted to the capacities of the common people and to be respected for its practical effectiveness.

It might be objected, perhaps, at this point that religion is not adequately characterized as metaphysics at all, since the system of beliefs, which constitute what may be called the cognitive part of it, does not of itself constitute its essence. The very belief in God, we are told, need not be religious; for "God" may be simply a scientific hypothesis having no more religious value than a mathematical symbol or a formula like Taylor's theorem. In order to be religious, the belief must determine the life, and a manifold of sentiments and activities must be unfolded, whose peculiar character is derived from relation to a supreme object at once of thought and of veneration.

This is true; and it is also true that religious beliefs do not exist primarily in the form in which they are taken up in the reflective consciousness. But whether in this abstract consciousness or imbedded in the medium of feeling and inwrought into the activities of will, they nevertheless do exist and involve, implicitly or otherwise, a metaphysical theory which challenges comparison with the views of philosophy obtained in other ways. In the end, therefore, nothing is gained if, as Schopenhauer claims, the ideas which determine life religiously are without foundation. If this were true, then the history of religion would be simply a history of folly. Here, then, if at all, is the point where Schopenhauer must be met. Are the ideas of religion capable of justification? Is the folk-metaphysics also good metaphysics? Or is there and can there be a good metaphysics which is also available for purposes of religion? It is noteworthy that Schopenhauer at least recognizes that religion is not to be treated merely as an artificial appendage to human life, but as having its immovable foundation in the "ineradicable metaphysical need" of our nature. This, doubtless, is not enough. The permanent foundation of religion lies not alone in this theoretical requirement, but also in the equally ineradicable feeling of individual dependence on unseen reality and in the coördinate impulse to realize personal life in union with it. But what specially concerns us here is the metaphysical element in religion, and the question whether that element is susceptible of rational development.

Viewing the matter thus, we shall have no difficulty in finding in these caustic criticisms of Schopenhauer much that is profitable and pertinent. I refer especially to his characterization of religious doctrines as allegorical. That they are necessarily so, as Schopenhauer maintains, is not to be conceded, but that they are largely so in the form which religion assumes as "folk-metaphysics" can hardly, I think, be questioned. For not only have the exigencies of language, built up, in the first instance, in relation to sensible phenomena, made all allusions to the supersensible doubly symbolical, but there is here a constant tendency for symbol and idea to run together. The larger part of the metaphysical conceptions connected with the religious life of mankind has ever been and is still mythological. How difficult it is to eliminate the myth when we attempt to grasp the facts and forces of a world transcending the sense-world is illustrated by the practice of even so great a genius as Plato, who used it repeatedly as an artistic form in which to set forth doctrines too sublime, apparently, for treatment in terms of abstract thinking. Nor would it be difficult to discover a similar spirit in the professed metaphysics of later times. Small wonder, therefore, if even the more spiritual religions, especially in the popular apprehension of them, have not been able wholly to escape it. This is true, among others, of Christianity. The Bible is full of symbolical expressions and figurative descriptions, especially concerning God and the processes and results of human redemption, which, taken literally, must be judged, from the standpoint of the modern consciousness, to be pure fiction. In the Middle Ages, the dogmas of religion were apprehended in accordance with the prevalent cosmography; the divine drama was adapted to the physical theatre. The opposition of the Church to scientific speculations in the fifteenth and sixteenth centuries was, from it own point of view, most logical. The Copernican theory not only contradicted a literal interpretation of the Bible, it necessitated at the same time a revolution in the manner of holding the faith. The heaven above the crystalline sphere, which Aristotle had posited as the outer limit of the material world and which the schoolmen believed in, disappeared. It was no longer possible seriously to think of a throne of God above the stars whence Christ had come down to the earth to redeem it, and where He now sits in glorified body, the effulgent centre of angelic hierarchies. The earth itself, far from being the centre of a universe created especially for its benefit, was discovered to occupy only a secondary place among the planets, and transformed itself into a mere star-speck floating in the infinitude of space. With such a conception, even the most fundamental of the Church's assumptions, the assumption, namely, that God had taken upon Himself human form and for man's salvation had suffered and died, constituting the Church a treasury of supernatural grace and investing it with a plero-

ma of miraculous powers, appeared highly questionable—little did the earth seem fitted for such superlative distinction. And as heaven vanished above, so hell disappeared beneath, and the doctrines of future retribution and personal immortality, in the old form of holding them, became impossible. That the old drama is not adapted to the new theatre is evident. Nevertheless, the literal materialism of mediæval conceptions still continues to leaven much of our popular theology. If, influenced by the fact of the human birth, the number of those who think of the coming of Christ to the earth in a spatial fashion is fewer than formerly, the number of those is still great who think in this manner of his ascension to heaven. From the same point of view, the great majority of Christians, apparently, still look forward to the second advent as a coming of Christ in the clouds with cohorts of angels, and verily believe that this sublime spectacle will be seen by every human eye (Rev. i. 7)—in contravention of all the laws of optics and of his own express declaration that the event predicted was to take place in the lifetime of some of his immediate followers (Mark ix. 1; cf. Mt. xxiv. 34). The same literalism prevails in popular conceptions of the resurrection, whence the horror with which cremation is regarded among the uneducated; while in respect to the final judgment, scarcely a doubt seems yet to have been stirred among orthodox believers that it will take place on a day appointed in the assembled presence of men and angels, and that each will *hear* the very *words* of Christ which will solemnly declare the world's drama to be ended and separate out for different localities the good and the bad forever. These doctrines, held in this way, simply contradict the views which necessarily connect themselves with our enlarged conceptions of the physical universe. But there are others which to a trained moral consciousness are even more abhorrent. Such, for example, is the popular misconception of the doctrine of the Atonement. As a "plan" of salvation "devised" in the council chambers of the Eternal, an "arrangement agreed upon" between Father and Son, it is an utter artificiality; as a "scheme" by which the guilty might escape through the infliction of the precise equivalent of their just penalty on the innocent, it is the worst sort of legal fiction. Matthew Arnold is undoubtedly right in characterizing such a supposed transaction "as sheer mythology, at bottom, as Saturn's devouring his children or Pallas springing from the head of Zeus." Assuredly all of these doctrines have meaning, but the form of presenting them is, as Schopenhauer says, allegorical; and every truthful man must desire to penetrate as far as possible into the meaning of the allegory, to think truly and to feel as he thinks.

We live in an age of change. No one who is sympathetic to the spiritual forces which control the intellectual movement of our times carries with him into mature life the beliefs of his childhood unaltered. The change may be a gradual transformation or an outspoken revolt. The poetry of youth may merge imperceptibly into "the light of common day," which, however "common," is at least capable of dispelling illusions; or the present may prove a rupture with the past attended with unutterable anguish and pathos. If the latter be the case, there is at any rate one consolation which earnest seekers after truth have in all ages of the world experienced, the consciousness of at least being on the right road.

> Ein guter Mensch, in seinem dunkeln Drange
> Ist sich des rechten Weges wohl bewusst.
> (*Faust*. Prolog im Himmel. Der Herr.)

This process, now, cannot be arrested. It is idle to attempt to permanently allay doubt with palliatives; it can only be met satisfactorily with reasons. Just as, in the age of the Sophists, when skeptical inquiry was undermining the foundations of all religion and morality derived from tradition and authority, the great and pious Socrates sought, not to deny the right of skepticism, but to so far affirm it as to make it skeptical of itself, and by a still deeper investigation to bring explicitly into consciousness the inherent rationality of the accepted order,—so the leaders of religious thought to-day must recognize every serious doubt of a dogma not seen to be rational, and every hesitancy to accept as true what does not seem to the doubter to rest upon sufficient evidence, as legitimate, in reliance on the scriptural prihciple, "the spirit searcheth all things, even the deep things of God," and must seek to present the essential truth of religious conceptions in a form harmonious with our growing knowledge of the world. This, happily, is what a goodly number of some of the best and wisest of our religious teachers are trying to do. They are trying to make the content of the faith, in the best sense of the word, rational; to substitute for the letter, spirit, for mechanical conceptions, vital, for artificialities, reality. This is why their appeal to the freshest minds of to-day is so powerful; they speak as having authority, and not as the scribes, for their authority is the internal one of essential reasonableness, and not the merely external one of constituted custom. Such men hold in their spirit the keys of the future. The preacher or teacher professing to declare the counsels of the Almighty with no other evidence of his claim than his bare assertion, or the assertions of those who have preceded him, may flourish for a time, possibly for a long time, but his authority is doomed as soon as it becomes recognized, as in the end it must, that every man, by the inherent rationality of his nature, is justified in rejecting it.

No one, probably, will claim, without evident self-deception, that he has succeeded in realizing in his own consciousness a system of religious beliefs which is in all respects rational, one, that is, whose inner conformity to the nature of things is in all respects manifest. The nature of things is itself altogether too vast for our comprehension; its very rationality, apart from certain broad and general principles, is a postulate, which we are bound indeed to make, if we will have any comprehension of it at all, but which is only within comparatively narrow limits verified. Much, therefore, necessarily remains matter of conjecture, hypothesis, belief. And much, doubtless, will ever remain so. We see many things only as in a mirror, darkly. The very imperfections of our knowledge suggest that there are many things in the objective order

of the world, of the full bearings and relations of which we have as yet but the most inadequate insight. Nevertheless, it is a great thing to be clearly conscious of the goal; the further consciousness that the intelligence which seeks to attain it is no fixed mathematical quantum, but a developing rational life, may serve perhaps as a salutary check upon our impatience that it is not attained sooner. The next thing is to clearly apprehend the right method of approach. This, if I mistake not, must be, in the main, strictly philosophical, the attempt to realize the truth of things in its completeness. No part of experience must be treated as though it were the whole. It will not do, for example, to follow here the abstract method of the natural sciences, which, while disclosing many important things about the world as an object known, necessarily ignore the most wonderful fact of all, the knowing of this object. The subject must also come to its rights, not only the cognitive, but the feeling and willing subject,—the subject of joys and sorrows, of needs and aspirations; the subject whose inspirations flash meteor-like upon the dark enigmas of existence, and whose ideals of science, art, conduct, and, among others, somehow to be accounted for, of religion, mark its intrinsic excellence. Nor is this all. The individual subject is, on its part, as truly an abstraction as the known object we call nature. Each individual, besides having relations through the body with the whole of external nature, stands, through the medium of language and social institutions, in relation to other individuals, in the family, in society, in the state, and is what he is, and becomes what he becomes, only in and through such relations. But they, though we commonly speak of them as our "environment," are anything but an environment in the sense in which the sea environs an island or the atmosphere the earth. They are spiritual and unique, and all merely mechanical analogies utterly fail to comprehend them. In some way, the individual life becomes a sharer in a more universal life, and is this individual only as it thus participates. There is an interpenetration of the universal in the individual, and an intussusception on the part of the individual of the universal. And not only so. Not only does each individual here and now stand in relation to other individuals here and now, but the whole life of the present is indissolubly connected with both the past and the future. It is only in the abstract science of mathematics that the world bears a purely static aspect; everywhere else it is a world of movement, of history. Particularly is this true in the affairs of men. The men and institutions of to-day are the product, in a sense, of the men and institutions of yesterday, of all past generations of men, of a long line of generations of organisms lower than man, of long ages of geological changes connected with chemical and physical processes lower still, of the primeval star-dust, and of what was before the star-dust; and not only the product, but, in some sense, the bearers, incorporating into their own life all other life; mirroring, as Leibniz, from another standpoint, figuratively expressed it, the entire universe; in one aspect most particular, in another most universal. This truth, if it be a truth, is important; for connecting man with man in society and with humanity in history, and uniting man with nature in a present which assimilates the past and gives birth to the future, it presents to us the world as an ordered system, each part of which involves the whole, and this without any loss of individuality, but rather as a necessary condition of individuality. The world thus appears as a concrete organism, vital, and, since we can assign no limits to its content, infinite. But to conceive the world so would seem necessarily to involve the conception of Theism, since the principle of unity for such a world cannot be anything mechanical like the *partes extra partes* of figurate space, but must be ideal, like the life of the plant or the unity of consciousness; it must be Intelligence, since no lesser principle can constitute the required unity of real and ideal, nor connect into a series the succession of temporal phenomena; and it must be Power, and if Intelligence, intelligent Power, that is, Will, since the whole world-order, in its continued on-going, is the evident manifestation of energy. But however this may be, however we may be compelled to think of our Highest Principle, the point to be insisted on is this, that religion, which grew originally out of a conscious relation of the individual life to the deepest reality apprehended in the universe in the feeling of dependence, must mould its conceptions of that reality, and of all that connects itself with our relations to it in accordance with the principles which increasing intelligence finds more and more clearly revealed, not only in one department of being abstracted from the rest, but in the organic structure of the universe. Only so will it be possible to repel the bitter taunt of Schopenhauer [in *Parerga and Paralipomena*] that knowledge and faith are "like wolf and sheep caged together, and knowledge is the wolf which threatens to eat up its neighbor."

Schopenhauer's views of Christianity are highly paradoxical, interesting, therefore, but not very important. The historical Christ he regarded, with Reimarus, as originally a demagogue, who, failing in the attempt to make himself king of the Jews, succeeded in getting himself transformed, after he was dead, from an earthly king into a heavenly. The details of the gospel narratives are mythical. Christian doctrine is a great allegory, which, having grown up on occasion of external and contingent circumstances, was finally put into shape by the systematizing genius of Augustine. Augustinianism, therefore, and not "primitive Christianity," is Christianity in its completeness. The doctrines themselves are derived principally from two heterogeneous sources, optimistic Judaaism and pessimistic Buddhism; but their centre of gravity is decidedly in the latter. The devil is here a highly important personage. He is "the prince of this world" (John xii. 32), and a much-needed counterpoise to the all-goodness, all-wisdom, and all-power of God. So thoroughly is Schopenhauer convinced of the Indian origin of the essential doctrines of Christianity, that he not only appeals in proof to "its thoroughly Indian ethics leading to asceticism, to its pessimism, and its avatar," but finds his theory especially confirmed by the expression "the wheel of generation," which he compares with the wheel of the transmigration of souls, frequently referred to in the writings of Buddhism. He even goes so far as to suggest that the name John may be derived from "Saniassi,"—"from his Saniassi-life in the wilderness!" To account for the connection, he is inclined to attribute an element of truth to the story of the flight into Egypt, where Jesus, he thinks, might have become acquainted with Hinduism through intercourse with Egyptian priests.

These dict are, at the best, but bold and stimulating suggestions; they certainly do not present themselves as reasoned conclusions on the broad basis of historical investigation. The point most worth considering, perhaps, is the oft-repeated assertion of the connection of Christianity and Buddhism. That the two religions present in many particulars striking similarities, cannot be questioned. So obvious, indeed, are these resemblances that missionaries have been led, at times, to look on Buddhism as a counterfeit of Christianity invented by the devil in order to obstruct the progress of the gospel. It is quite possible, of course, perhaps even probable, that each religion may have developed similarly under similar conditions in entire independence. But it is also possible that there may have been at some period a historical connection. This is a matter which can only be settled by investigations considerably more elaborate than those we find in Schopenhauer, but it is, after all, one purely historical, and any serious attempt to make out the connection will at all times meet with ready welcome among candid scholars, whatever may be their judgment as to its success. But granting all this, granting even that the dependence is on the side of Christianity and that we may be obliged to recognize, in the end, along with Jewish and Hellenic also Buddhistic influences in its formation, it would still be a long way from this to the identification of the inner spirit of Christianity with that of Buddhism. Schopenhauer's procedure here is anything but judicious. Having first assumed that Christianity is Augustinian dogmatics, he then expounds the latter as an allegorical setting forth of the essential doctrines of Buddhism. "At bottom," he says, "and apart from mythologies on both sides, Buddha's *Sansara* and *Nirwana* are identical with the two *civitates* of Augustine, . . . the *civitas terrena* and *cœlestis,*"—which is about as reasonable as if one should say that, since each narrates the story of a theft, there is no essential difference between Pope's *Rape of the Lock* and the Greek *Iliad*. Christianity is, in fact, no more identical with Augustinianism that it is with Pelagianism or any other -ism. Its forms are as variable as the forms of nature: one of its most eminent characteristics is that it can adapt itself to the ever-changing conditions and ever-growing capacities of humanity. Its spirit is its only really essential element—the spirit of Christ, which is the spirit of divine love in human hearts redeeming man from sin unto holiness and unto God. This spirit is world-wide different from that of Buddhism. True, Christianity has its pessimistic aspect. The world, as it conceives it, is no play-ground. There is evil enough in it—lust and avarice, pride and prejudice, hypocrisy and envy, malice and convetousness, evils of the heart more terrible far than physical sufferings. No danger of overlooking the natural corruption of human nature. And in accordance with this, a morality is demanded, the very first condition of which is self-abnegation. It is true, Christianity has for its symbol an instrument of torture and proclaims unweariedly, as the profoundest law of the moral universe, that salvation is only possible through sacrifice. But this is only one aspect of it. For if the keynote of Christian morality is the paradox, "Whoso loseth his life shall find it," the emphasis is before all else on the finding. The identification with Buddhism is thoroughly superficial. Buddhism is essentially a religion of negation; the "will-to-be," as Schopenhauer expressed it, must be denied, all desire suppressed, the flesh crucified, that at the last, after numberless transmigrations, the soul may lose itself, merged, unconscious as in a swoon, in the unruffled, changeless essence of the All. Christianity, on the contrary, is emphatically a religion of affirmation. Its negative element involves an even more characteristic positive. It not only asserts, with Buddhism, that the individual life is, as such, of evil, but it teaches that, in negating this partial, isolated, false life of self, which is alienation from God and therefore sinful, the true self is not lost but realized. If it demands, as the indispensable prerequisite to the attainment of blessedness, unqualified surrender of the self to God, it is only that God may implete the poverty of the life apart from Him with divine fullness. If it enjoins renunciation of the world, it is in the sense of a moral attitude unconditionally necessary to a being destined for immortality, whose ends, therefore, cannot be realized in the fleeting phenomena of time. The world that is negated is the world of sense, of the things that perish with the using; and the form of negation is not absolute, for while denied as ends, the service which they render is in no way underestimated as means. The spirit of Christianity, therefore, is not the asceticism of the body,—"the Son of Man came eating and drinking,"—but the asceticism of the spirit, which turns away from the world as the unsatisfying source of delusions and misery when it is regarded as ultimate, and turns to God as the true Fountain of Happiness and the Giver of Eternal Life. Stated philosophically, both religions agree that the individual can only find the end of his being in union with the universal; but with Buddhism this union destroys individuality, while with Christianity it perfects it. Nor is the ground of this difference far to seek. It lies in the essential difference in the mode in which the universal is apprehended. With Buddhism, it is abstract; with Christianity, it is concrete. With Buddhism, the ultimate Principle is indeterminate Being; with Christianity, it is the Personal God. Buddhism, in a word, is Pantheistic; Christianity, Theistic. Hence union with the universal is in Buddhism absorption, loss of identity; in Christianity it is full preservation of the individual life in a kingdom of free spirits, a realm of persons above whom and in whom rules forevermore the Spirit of personal, Eternal Love.

But it is precisely this theistic conception which which Schopenhaner in the strongest terms repudiates as the source of all error and confusion. His account of it, however, is anything but satisfactory. He regards monotheism, for example, as the mere personification of nature,—an opinion neither historically deduced nor philosophically grounded, and false in both regards. No one, he says, has done so much harm to Theism as Copernicus. Astronomy, having taken away heaven, has taken away God also, since "a personal being, as every God necessarily is, that has no place, but is everywhere and nowhere, . . . cannot be imagined, and therefore cannot be believed in."

He even goes so far as to say that all worship of a personal Being is idolatrous, as much so as the worship of fashioned wood, and that whether a man sacrifices his sheep, or his inclinations, is, at bottom, not so very different. What in all this is not pure arbitrariness rests obviously on a misunderstanding. Theism is confounded with Deism, the God who is Spirit, whom all space manifests but none contains, with the local deity who sits above the clouds on a great white throne, and finally appears upon the pictures as an old man with a beard.

We see, then, in Schopenhauer, a critic who rejects all religion as superstition; who regards Christianity, so far as it is true at all, as merely a disguised Buddhism; who looks on Theism as puerile and all worship of a personal God as idolatry; and who pronounces the conflict between Science and Faith to be a *bellum ad internecionem*. Add to this his denial of personal immortality and his bitter repudiation of supernatural revelation as a claim made by the cunning of priests, taking advantage of the ineradicable metaphysical need of men, combined with their ignorance, to the ends of ecclesiastical and civil power, and we have in outline a position than which none would seem to be more radically in conflict with the current religious conceptions of our time.

> No system of modern times assumes a more definite or hostile attitude towards religion than this brilliantly expounded metaphysics, half pantheistic, half atheistic, of the great German pessimist.
>
> —*H. N. Gardiner*

As, now, the attitude towards religion generally, like that towards theories in speculation, depends no less, and in most cases rather more, on subjective disposition and contingent circumstances than on strictly objective insight, so, if we should inquire into the causes which led to this determined opposition to religion on the part of Schopenhauer, we should doubtless find them as well in the personal traits and surroundings of the philosopher as in the professedly objective considerations of his philosophy. I can here only refer to one or two salient points which appear to me not a little instructive.

And, first, while it would be odious and is far from my intention to suggest insanity, there can be no doubt, I think, that Schopenhauer inherited from both sides of his family an unbalanced nature which frequently led to an unbalanced judgment both of men and of things. His grandmother on his father's side was crazy, and after the death of her husband under legal guardianship; his uncle Andreas, her eldest son, was half-witted from his youth; her second son became so through excesses, and gave to a melancholy life, lived in separation from his family in the company of vulgar clowns, a somewhat merry ending by leaving behind to his brothers and sisters "their rightful portion," and to other persons many thousands—all on paper. The grandfather on the mother's side was, in spite of many excellent qualities, a man of uncontrollable temper. "Just at the time when least expected," so writes his daughter, "the most trifling occasion could rouse him to a wild passion of anger, which, to be sure, was quickly over. At such times, the whole house trembled before his voice of thunder, and the entire household, even to dog and cat, ran frightened out of his way." Yes, even the philosopher's own father, whose intelligence and far-seeing industry, combined with extraordinary energy of will, marked a character of no common strength and independence, suffered at times from mental aberration, particularly towards the latter part of this life, when increasing deafness had made him moody and suspicious. It was generally supposed at the time that he committed suicide: all that is certainly known is that he fell from an opening in the warehouse into the canal and was drowned. But Schopenhauer's biographer [Wilhelm Gwinner], who narrates the circumstance, says that he knows a number of things told by the widow and son, which leave little doubt that the rumor was well founded.

This taint in the blood made itself painfully evident in the conduct and opinions of Schopenhauer. He was a born misanthrope. A lively imagination excited a naturally suspicious nature almost to the pitch of madness, so that the evil which he feared, he seemed at times to see bodily before him. One evening, when he was only six years old, his parents, on returning home from a walk, found him in the greatest despair, having imagined himself suddenly abandoned by them forever. A student in Berlin, he believed himself for a long time to be consumptive. At the breaking out of the war of 1813, he imagined that he had been pressed into the service. In Verons he was seized with the idea that he had taken poisoned snuff. When in 1833 he was about to leave Mannheim, he was overcome, without any external occasion whatever, with an unspeakable feeling of dread. For years he was plagued with fear of a criminal process; and if any noise arose in the night, he would jump out of bed and seize dagger and pistols, which he kept constantly loaded. His valuables were concealed in all sorts of out-of-the-way places about his rooms; some could only be found with difficulty in spite of the Latin indications of their whereabouts in his will. And as he had lived in constant dread of being cheated, so that he might not be cheated at the last he gave orders that his body should be allowed to lie longer than was customary, to make the reality of his death perfectly sure.

It was a favorite doctrine with Schopenhauer that genius is allied to madness, and he regarded himself, not wholly without reason, as a genius of the very first rank. He also considered a certain amount of misanthropy as a necessary ingredient of every more talented nature, and held with Chamfort that the beginning of wisdom is the fear of man. From the solitary heights of genius, in the proud consciousness of superiority, he looked down no less with scorn than with pity on the great herd of the uncultivated, the "pack of humanity," the "bipeds," the "Philistines," "nature's wares," as he was wont to term them, and more and more, without perhaps intending it, grew into the habit of judging all things by reference to himself. This isola-

tion he felt very keenly when he found his philosophy, which he describes as "a superb edifice destined for the centuries," completely neglected for over thirty years. This neglect was the source of great embitterment. He could find no other way to account for it than that of a formal conspiracy on the part of the university professors to prevent him a hearing. Hence his outbursts against the paid professors, who, having to earn their living by their teaching, naturally, he thought, prefer position to truth; especially his attacks on the "three great Sophists," Fichte, Schelling, and Hegel, and more especially on Hegel, whom he could regard in no other light than that of a common charlatan. These invectives are marked by anything but Attic urbanity; on the contrary, they are at times right coarse and vulgar. And when he saw Hegelian philosophy trapped out with the accoutrements of religious phraseology and vaunting itself as the champion of religions orthodoxy, a man of Schopenhauer's volcanic temperament would hardly be likely to find his feelings towards the latter very strongly conciliated.

Another circumstance which contributed, I think, to Schopenhauer's alienation from religion was the absence of anything like what we should call religious training in his own family. The father's ambitions appear to have been wholly secular: Arthur was to become a merchant of position and an accomplished man of the world. True, the remark in a letter that it was quite good that Arthur should be confirmed and attend the morning lectures in Theology from a man whose favorite author was Voltaire shows a character singularly free from prejudice; but there is no evidence that he ever gave to religion any very hearty support. Naturally we might look for more positive influence from the mother; but between mother and son was altogether too little sympathy, and hers was a nature far too shallow. At Weimar, where after the death of her husband she held a sort of literary court, she would not have him, then a youth of twenty, live in the same house with her. An impartial critic would probably not lay all the blame to the charge of the mother. "So long as thou art what thou art," she writes him, "I would make any sacrifice rather than agree to this. I am not blind to thy good qualities, and what repels me lies not in thy disposition, thy inner being, but in thy outer, thy views, thy judgments, thy habits,—in short, as concerning the external world, I can agree with thee in nothing. Thy melancholy, too, oppresses me and puts me out of humor, without helping thee at all. See, dear Arthur, thou wert only with me a few days on a visit, and every day there were violent scenes about nothing, and again about nothing, and each time I breathed free again only after thou wert gone, because thy presence, thy complaints about unavoidable things, thy gloomy looks, thy bizarre judgments, which were spoken by thee like oracles allowing of no objection, oppressed me, and still more the everlasting struggle within with which I violently repressed everything that I might say in reply in order not to give occasion to fresh contention. I am living now very quietly; for years I have not had an unpleasant moment which I do not owe to thee." Evidently Schopenhauer's was not a character finely calculated to promote peace and happiness. But here was just the trouble: Johanna Schopenhauer was ready to sacrifice everything to the maintenance of her personal even though cultivated pleasure. Her strange and gifted son she did not understand; she made no effort to understand him. On reading the title of his first work, *On the Fourfold Root of the Law of Sufficient Reason,* she said to him contemptuously that that, she supposed, was a work for apothecaries! Anselm Feuerbach, who met her in the year 1815, has preserved the following notice: "Hofräthin Schopenhauer, a rich widow. Makes a profession of learning. Authoress. Talks much and well; intelligent; without heart or soul. Self-satisfied, courting applause and constantly smiling at herself. God preserve us from women whose spirit has run to mere intellect. The seat of true womanly culture is alone in the woman's heart." This characteristic, according to Schopenhauer, who read it many years afterwards, hits the mark only too accurately. A woman with intellect but without heart, self-complacent and delighting in flattery, could hardly be regarded as an instrument fitted by nature for the spiritual guidance of a young pessimist. When he writes her, as a boy, from his boarding-school in England of the misery to which the compulsory inactivity of an English Sunday subjected him, she only laughs at him, recollecting the many struggles she had had to get him to do anything on Sundays and feast-days, because they were to him "days of rest," "and now thou hast of Sunday rest sufficient and enough;" while the wish, which this bitter personal experience occasioned, that "truth with its torch might burn through the Egyptian darkness in England," she only takes note of to criticise as a form of expression: "How canst thou expect truth to do any such thing? A darkness can be illumined, but burn it truly cannot. This is what in English is called *bombast*."

This experience in England was, without doubt, no insignificant factor in Schopenhauer's anti-religious education. He was then fifteen. He had just come from France, where the movement and freedom of a warm-blooded people had exercised all the fascination of which a nature such as his, and especially at that period of his life, would be susceptible. He now found himself in a totally different atmosphere, thrown, as never before, upon his own resources, and bound down to the rigid discipline of a clergyman's boarding-school, governed in accordance with the strictest principles of orthodoxy, theoretical as well as practical. Against all this he vigorously rebelled. Violent outbursts of indignation reach from time to time his parents, who are traveling for six months in the North, but the only response they meet with is such as that already spoken of from his mother, together with sundry exhortations, perhaps, to make himself more agreeable, and diligently to practice himself in the English language. But the stiff formality of English society never ceased to be repulsive to him, and the whole English religious life, as he saw it, wore to him no other aspect than, in the language of Carlyle, "dead, damnable, putrescent cant." To a school-friend he writes that his stay in England has made him hate the whole nation. This hatred, however, was by no means as universal as the expression might lead one to suppose. There was, in fact, no people to whom he felt himself, on the whole, so spiritually allied as the English. He prided himself on his knowledge of

their language, conducted his accounts in it, read regularly the London *Times,* preferred Englishmen to all others as traveling companions, and in many ways affected English style, even to matters of dress and the cut of his beard. But his embitterment against English bigotry and priestcraft, which dated from the experience at the Wimbledon boarding-school, remained unabated to the very last. "If you will see," he writes [in *Parerga and Paralipomena*], "with your own eyes and near at hand what the early infection of belief can do, look at the English. See this nation, favored by nature above all others and furnished more than all others with intelligence, spirit, judgment and strength of character, see it, sunk deep beneath all others, nay, made absolutely contemptible by its stupid superstition about the Church, which, along with its other endowments, seems actually like a chronic illusion, a monomania. For this they have simply to thank the fact that education is in the hands of the clergy, who take care so to indoctrinate them in earliest youth with all the articles of faith, that there veritably results a partial atrophy of the brain, which then manifests itself all through life in that silly bigotry with which even people, in other respects highly intelligent and talented, among them degrade themselves, and leave us wholly at a loss to know what to make of them." In another passage he illustrates his contention that religion tends frequently to regard supposed duties towards God as a surrogate for duties towards man by English views of the Sabbath. "Look at England," he exclaims, "where audacious priestly cunning lyingly identifies the Christian Sunday, which was established in opposition to the Jewish Sabbath, by Constantine the Great, with the latter; and it does this in order to transfer Jehovah's ordinances for the Sabbath, that is, the day when Omnipotence, wearied with six days' work, was obliged to rest—whence it is *really the last* day of the week—over to the Christian's Sunday, the *dies solis,* this first day which gloriously opens the week, this day of pious meditation and rejoicing. As a consequence of this fraud, "Sabbath-breaking," or "the desecration of the Sabbath," that is, every employment, even the slightest, that is useful or pleasant, all play, all music, all knitting, every worldly book on Sunday, is regarded in England as a grievous sin. Must not the common man there believe that, if he only keeps up "a strict observance of the holy Sabbath and a regular attendance on divine worship," as his spiritual guides tell him, if, that is, he is only inviolately and right thoroughly lazy on Sunday and does not fail to sit two hours in church to listen for the thousandth time to the "same Litany and join *a tempo* in mumbling the responses—he may well reckon elsewhere on indulgence for this or that license which he may occasionally allow himself"? Many other passages to the like effect could be quoted, in which the judgment might appear as harsh and unsympathetic, and to pious ears, perhaps, as shocking as in those just given, but which none the less seize upon and forcibly present an aspect of truth, blindness to which would be utter folly. Enough, however, has been cited to convey the very distinct impression of the perversion to religious influences which a stupid and rigid formalism can effect when violently thrust *ab extra* upon a nature incorrigibly rebellious at the start against all control merely external. What would have been the result if, early in life, Schopenhauer had met with a presentation of religion more simple and sympathetic, we can but conjecture. Certainly, he was not wanting in those deeper mystical elements to which such a presentation is wont most strongly to appeal. As it was, he found religion everywhere, and in England more especially, identified with creed and ceremony, and went his way to wage a life-long warfare against what seemed to him, and no doubt to some extent was, superstition and bigotry, worthy only of ridicule and contempt.

I cannot bring these personal allusions to a close without refering, finally, to one other circumstance, which seems to me of no slight importance to a proper understanding of Schopenhauer's position: I mean the moral self-contradiction which he realized in his own spirit. There can be no question that Schopenhauer's is the most paradoxical philosophy of modern times; indeed, it may be doubted if in the whole history of thought there has ever appeared a system which not only ran so completely counter to natural instincts and the current views of things, but involved so many obvious internal contradictions. The inconsistencies within the system itself have been so frequently pointed out that to repeat them here, even if space allowed, would be but to slay the slain. Nor have unfriendly critics failed to call attention to the glaring inconsistency between the doctrine and the life, the self-renunciation and asceticism demanded by the former and the irascibility, self-overestimation, and very comfortable habits of Schopenhauer himself. But what has not been so often noticed is Schopenhauer's own consciousness of this contradiction, his deep sense of the inner conflict in his own spirit. Between the intellect and the will, which no one has so sharply distinguished, nor, with such fatal consequences, divided, existed in him an internecine warfare which allowed of no peace, a conflict all the more violent because of the surpassing strength of both contestants as they were brought together on the filed of consciousness of one such man of genius. By the insight of the intellect, it was declared to be necessary, in order to escape the terrible evils of existence, that the will-to-be, which is the source of existence, and, with existence, of evil, should be completely negated: it must be given its quietus, and must altogether cease; but the will-to-be was in Schopenhauer peculiarly potent: he was a man of strong passions and of a self-asserting individuality altogether remarkable. He found in himself no means of bringing this conflict to an issue. It was a burden upon his spirit, a source of fresh conflict and of a deepened sense of isolation. "Never," writes [Gwinner],—"never shall I forget my friend as he once saw at my house Rancé's picture of the abbot of La Trappe, and, turning away with a gesture of pain, said: That is matter of grace!" And he himself tells of similar emotions experienced in the presence of the picture of St. Jerome in the Dresden Gallery. Who does not know something of what these experiences mean? Schopenhauer has but more intensely realized, because more richly endowed than most men, the universal moral struggle of humanity and the universal longing for redemption. Inevitably do his experiences suggest those of another, who centuries earlier also discovered in himself a double nature, the flesh warring against the spirit and

the spirit against the flesh, and amid the desire for good evil ever present. This man too found no power in himself strong enough to decide the issue, but, looking upon it as "matter of grace," cried out in anguish of soul, "Who shall deliver me from the body of this death?" How like the experiences, and how world-wide different the conclusions! For while Schopenhauer, seeking salvation only as cessation of the conflict, and recognizing no redeeming efficacy but that of his own will to negate will, confessedly fails utterly in that, St. Paul, yielding himself to the inspiration of a Divine Love, finds strength made perfect in his weakness and, in "the spirit of life which is in Christ Jesus," unfailing in its joyousness, goes forth, clothed with power, as with the sun, to a life of heroic and successful service. Schopenhauer knows nothing of this heroism; life is to him either a tragedy to weep over or a comedy to laugh at. He knows nothing of the experience which produced it; had he known it, he would not have proclaimed so superficially as he did that willing existence is necessarily painful, nor have declared happiness to be merely absence of pain, and therefore capable of full realization only as a state of apathy. And his criticisms of religion, no longer wholly from without, would have gained through intimate acquaintance infinitely in justness, while losing the characteristics which they share in common with his philosophy generally of contradiction and excess.

T. Bailey Saunders (essay date 1890)

SOURCE: "Translator's Preface," in *The Wisdom of Life, Being the First Part of Arthur Schopenhauer's Aphorismen zur Lebensweisheit*, by Arthur Schopenhauer, translated by T. Bailey Saunders, S. Sonnenschein & Co., 1890, pp. v-xxvi.

[In the following essay, Saunders comments on Schopenhauer's pessimism.]

Of Schopenhauer—as of many another writer—it may be said that he has been misunderstood and depreciated just in the degree in which he is thought to be new; and that, in treating of the Conduct of Life, he is, in reality, valuable only in so far as he brings old truths to remembrance. His name used to arouse, and in certain quarters still arouses, a vague sense of alarm; as though he had come to subvert all the rules of right thinking and all the principles of good conduct, rather than to proclaim once again and give a new meaning to truths with which the world has long been familiar. Of his philosophy in its more technical aspects, as matter upon which enough, perhaps, has been written, no account need be taken here, except as it affects the form in which he embodies these truths or supplies the fresh light in which he sees them. For whatever claims to originality his metaphysical theory may possess, the chief interest to be found in his views of life is an affair of form rather than of substance; and he stands in a sphere of his own, not because he sets new problems or opens up undiscovered truths, but in the manner in which he approaches what has been already revealed.

He is not on that account less important; for the great mass of men at all times requires to have old truths imparted as if they were new—formulated, as it were, directly for them as individuals, and of special application to their own circumstances in life. A discussion of human happiness and the way to obtain it is never either unnecessary or uncalled for, if one looks to the extent to which the lives of most men fall short of even a poor ideal, or, again, to the difficulty of reaching any definite and secure conclusion. For to such a momentous inquiry as this, the vast majority of mankind gives nothing more than a nominal consideration, accepting the current belief, whatever it may be, on authority, and taking as little thought of the grounds on which it rests as a man walking takes of the motion of the earth. But for those who are not indifferent—for those whose desire to fathom the mystery of existence gives them the right to be called thinking beings—it is just here, in regard to the conclusion to be reached, that a difficulty arises, a difficulty affecting the conduct of life: for while the great facts of existence are alike for all, they are variously appreciated, and conclusions differ, chiefly from innate diversity of temperament in those who draw them. It is innate temperament, acting on a view of the facts necessarily incomplete, that has inspired so many different teachers. The tendencies of a man's own mind—the Idols of the Cave before which he bows—interpret the facts in accordance with his own nature: he elaborates a system containing, perhaps, a grain of truth, to which the whole of life is then made to conform; the facts purporting to be the foundation of the theory, and the theory in its turn giving its own colour to the facts.

Nor is this error, the manipulation of facts to suit a theory, avoided in the views of life which are presented by Schopenhauer. It is true that he aimed especially at freeing himself from the trammels of previous systems; but he was caught in those of his own. His natural desire was to resist the common appeal to anything extramundane—anything outside or beyond life—as the basis of either hope or fear. He tried to look at life as it is; but the metaphysical theory on which his whole philosophy rests made it necessary for him, as he thought, to regard it as an unmixed evil. He calls our present existence an infinitesimal moment between two eternities, the past and the future, a moment—like the life of Plato's "Dwellers in the Cave,"—filled with the pursuit of shadows; where everything is relative, phenomenal, illusory, and man is bound in the servitude of ignorance, struggle and need, in the endless round of effort and failure. If you confine yourself, says Schopenhauer, only to some of its small details, life may indeed appear to be a comedy, because of the one or two bright spots of happy circumstance to be found in it here and there; but when you reach a higher point of view and a broader outlook, these soon become invisible, and Life, seen from the distance which brings out the true proportion of all its parts, is revealed as a tragedy—a long record of struggle and pain, with the death of the hero as the final certainty. How then, he asks, can a man make the best of his brief hour under the hard conditions of his destiny? What is the true Wisdom of Life?

Schopenhauer has no pre-conceived divine plan to vindicate; no religious or moral enthusiasm to give a roseate hue to some far-off event, obliging us in the end to think that all things work together for good. Let poets and theologians give play to imagination! he, at any rate, will profess no knowledge of anything beyond our ken. If our existence does not entirely fail of its aim, it must, he says, be *suffering;* for this is what meets us everywhere in the world, and it is absurd to look upon it as the result of chance. Still, in the face of all this suffering, and in spite of the fact that the uncertainty of life destroys its value as an end in itself, every man's natural desire is to preserve his existence; so that life is a blind, unreasoning force, hurrying us we know not whither. From his high metaphysical standpoint, Schopenhauer is ready to admit that there are many things in life which give a short satisfaction and blind us for the moment to the realities of existence,—pleasures as they may be called, in so far as they are a mode of *relief;* but that pleasure is not positive in its nature nor anything more than the negation of suffering, is proved by the fact that, if pleasures come in abundance, pain soon returns in the form of satiety; so that the sense of illusion is al that has been gained. Hence, the most a man can achieve in the way of welfare is a measure of relief from this suffering; and if people were prudent, it is at this they would aim, instead of trying to secure a happiness which always flies from them.

It is a trite saying that happiness is a delusion, a chimæra, the *fata morgana* of the heart; but here is a writer who will bring our whole conduct into line with that, as a matter of practice; making pain the positive groundwork of life, and a desire to escape it the spur of all effort. While most of those who treat of the conduct of life come at last to the conclusion, more or less vaguely expressed, that religion and morality form a positive source of true happiness, Schopenhauer does not professedly take this view; though it is quite true that the practical outcome of his remarks tends, as will be seen, in support of it; with this difference, however—he does not direct the imagination to anything outside this present life as making it worth while to live at all; his object is to state the facts of existence as they immediately appear, and to draw conclusions as to what a wise man will do in the face of them.

In the practical outcome of Schopenhauer's ethics—the end and aim of those maxims of conduct which he recommends, there is nothing that is not substantially akin to theories of life which, in different forms, the greater part of mankind is presumed to hold in reverence. It is the premises rather than the conclusion of his argument which interest us as something new. The whole world, he says, with all its phenomena of change, growth and development, is ultimately the manifestation of Will—*Wille und Vorstellung*—a blind force conscious of itself only when it reaches the stage of intellect. And life is a constant self-assertion of this will; a long desire which is never fulfilled; disillusion inevitably following upon attainment, because the will, the thing-in-itself—in philosophical language, the *noumenon*—always remains as the permanent element; and with this persistent exercise of its claim, it can never be satisfied. So life is essentially suffering; and the only remedy for it is the freedom of the intellect from the servitude imposed by its master, the will.

The happiness a man can attain, is thus, in Schopenhauer's view, negative only; but how is it to be acquired? Some temporary relief, he says, may be obtained through the medium of Art; for in the apprehension of Art we are raised out of our bondage, contemplating objects of thought as they are in themselves, apart from their relations to our own ephemeral existence, and free from any taint of the will. This contemplation of pure thought is destroyed when Art is degraded from its lofty sphere, and made an instrument in the bondage of the will. How few of those who feel that the pleasure of Art transcends all others could give such a striking explanation of their feeling!

But the highest ethical duty, and consequently the supreme endeavour after happiness, is to withdraw from the struggle of life, and so obtain release from the misery which that struggle imposes upon all, even upon those who are for the moment successful. For as will is the inmost kernel of everything, so it is identical under all its manifestations; and through the mirror of the world a man may arrive at the knowledge of himself. The recognition of the identity of our own nature with that of others is the beginning and foundation of all true morality. For once a man clearly perceives this solidarity of the will, there is aroused in him a feeling of *sympathy* which is the mainspring of ethical conduct. This feeling of sympathy must, in any true moral system, prevent our obtaining success at the price of others' loss. Justice, in this theory, comes to be a noble, enlightened self-interest; it will forbid our doing wrong to our fellow-man, because, in injuring him, we are injuring ourselves—our own nature, which is identical with his. On the other hand, the recognition of this identity of the will must lead to commiseration—a feeling of sympathy with our fellow-sufferers—to acts of kindness and benevolence, to the manifestation of what Kant, in the *Metaphysic of Ethics,* calls the only absolute good, *the good will.* In Schopenhauer's phraseology, the human will, in other words, . . . the love of life, is in itself the root of all evil, and goodness lies in renouncing it. Theoretically, his ethical doctrine is the extreme of socialism, in a large sense; a recognition of the inner identity, and equal claims, of all men with ourselves; a recognition issuing in . . . universal benevolence, and a stifling of particular desires.

It may come as a surprise to those who affect to hold Schopenhauer in abhorrence, without, perhaps, really knowing the nature of his views, that, in this theory of the essential evil of the human will— . . . the common selfish idea of life—he is reflecting and indeed probably borrowing what he describes as the fundamental tenet of Christian theology, that *the whole creation groaneth and travaileth in pain,* standing in need of redemption. Though Schopenhauer was no friend to Christian theology in its ordinary tendencies, he was very much in sympathy with some of the doctrines which have been connected with it. In his opinion the foremost truth which Christianity proclaimed to the world lay in its recognition of pessimism,

its view that the world was essentially corrupt, and that the devil was its prince or ruler. It would be out of place here to inquire into the exact meaning of this statement, or to determine the precise form of compensation provided for the ills of life under any scheme of doctrine which passes for Christian: and even if it were in place, the task would be an extremely difficult one; for probably no system of belief has ever undergone, at various periods, more radical changes than Christianity. But whatever prospect of happiness it may have held out, at an early date of its history, it soon came to teach that the necessary preparation for happiness, as a positive spiritual state, is *renunciation,* resignation, a looking away from external life to the inner life of the soul—*a kingdom not of this world.* So far, at least, as concerns its view of the world itself, and the main lesson and duty which life teaches, there is nothing in the theory of pessimism which does not accord with that religion which is looked up to as the guide of life over a great part of the civilised world.

What Schopenhauer does is to attempt a metaphysical explanation of the evil of life, without any reference to anything outside it. Philosophy, he urges, should be *cosmology,* not *theology;* an explanation of the world, not a scheme of divine knowledge: it should leave the gods alone—to use an ancient phrase—and claim to be left alone in return. Schopenhauer was not concerned, as the apostles and fathers of the Church were concerned, to formulate a scheme by which the ills of this life should be remedied in another—an appeal to the poor and oppressed, conveyed often in a material form, as, for instance, in the story of Dives and Lazarus. In his theory of life as the self-assertion of will, he endeavours to account for the sin, misery and iniquity of the world, and to point to the way of escape—the denial of the will to live.

Though Schopenhauer's views of life have this much in common with certain aspects of Christian doctrine, they are in decided antagonism with another theory which, though, comparatively speaking, the birth of yesterday, has already been dignified by the name of a religion, and has, no doubt, a certain number of followers. It is the theory which looks upon the life of mankind as a continual progress towards a state of perfection, and humanity in its nobler tendencies as itself worthy of worship. To those who embrace this theory, it will seem that because Schopenhauer does not hesitate to declare the evil in the life of mankind to be far in excess of the good, and that, as long as the human will remains what it is, there can be no radical change for the better, he is therefore outside the pale of civilisation, an alien from the commonwealth of ordered knowledge and progress. But it has yet to be seen whether the religion of humanity will fare better, as a theory of conduct or as a guide of life, than either Christianity or Buddhism. If any one doctrine may be named which has distinguished Christianity wherever it has been a living force among its adherents, it is the doctrine of renunciation; the same doctrine which in a different shape and with other surroundings, forms the spirit of Buddhism. With those great religions of the world which mankind has hitherto professed to revere as the most ennobling of all influences, Schopenhauer's theories, not perhaps in their details, but in the principle which informs them, are in close alliance.

Renunciation, according to Schopenhauer, is the truest wisdom of life, from the higher ethical standpoint. His heroes are the Christian ascetics of the Middle Age, and the followers of Buddha who turn away from the Sansara to the Nirvana. But our modern habits of thought are different. We look askance at the doctrines, and we have no great enthusiasm for the heroes. The system which is in vogue amongst us just now objects to the identification of nature with evil, and, in fact, abandons ethical dualism altogether. And if nature is not evil, where, it will be asked, is the necessity or the benefit of renunciation—a question which may even come to be generally raised, in a not very distant future, on behalf of some new conception of Christianity.

And from another point of view, let it be frankly admitted that renunciation is incompatible with ordinary practice, with the rules of life as we are compelled to formulate them; and that, to the vast majority, the doctrine seems little but a mockery, a hopelessly unworkable plan, inapplicable to the conditions under which men have to exist.

In spite of the fact that he is theoretically in sympathy with truths which lie at the foundation of certain widely revered systems, the world has not yet accepted Schopenhauer for what he proclaimed himself to be, a great teacher: and probably for the reason that hope is not an element in his wisdom of life, and that he attenuates love into something that is not a real, living force—a shadowy recognition of the identity of the will. For men are disinclined to welcome a theory which neither flatters their present position nor holds out any prospect of better things to come. Optimism—the belief that in the end everything will be for the best—is the natural creed of mankind; and a writer who of set purpose seeks to undermine it by an appeal to facts is regarded as one who tries to rob humanity of its rights. How seldom an appeal to the facts within our reach is really made! Whether the evil of life actually outweighs the good,—or, if we should look for better things, what is the possibility or the nature of a Future Life, either for ourselves as individuals, or as part of some great whole, or, again, as contributing to a coming state of perfection?—such inquiries claim an amount of attention which the mass of men everywhere is unwilling to give. But, in any case, whether it is a vague assent to current beliefs, or a blind reliance on a baseless certainty, or an impartial attempt to put away what is false,—hope remains as the deepest foundation of every faith in a happy future.

But it should be observed that this looking to the future as a complement for the present is dictated mainly by the desire to remedy existing ills; and that the great hold which religion has on mankind, as an incentive to present happiness, is the promise it makes of coming perfection. Hope for the future is a tacit admission of evil in the present; for if a man is completely happy in this life, and looks upon happiness as the prevailing order, he will not think so much of another. So a discussion of the nature of happiness is not thought complete if it takes account only of our present life, and unless it connects what we are now and what we do here with what we may be hereafter. Schopenhauer's theory does not profess to do this; it promises no positive good to the individual; at most, only relief; he breaks the idol of the world, and sets up nothing in its place; and like many another iconoclast, he has long been condemned by those whose temples he has desecrated. If there are optimistic theories of life, it is not life itself, he would argue, which gives colour to them; it is rather the reflection of some great final cause which humanity has created as the last hope of its redemption. . . .

Still, hope, it may be said, is not knowledge, nor a real answer to any question; at most, a makeshift, a moral support for intellectual weakness. The truth is that, as theories, both optimism and pessimism are failures; because they are extreme views where only a very partial judgment is possible. And in view of the great uncertainty of all answers, most of those who do not accept a stereotyped system leave the question alone, as being either of little interest, or of no bearing on the welfare of their lives, which are commonly satisfied with low aims; tacitly ridiculing those who demand an answer as the most pressing affair of existence. But the fact that the final problems of the world are still open, makes in favour of an honest attempt to think them out, in spite of all previous failure or still existing difficulty; and however old these problems may be, the endeavour to solve them is one which it is always worth while to encourage afresh. For the individual advantages which attend an effort to find the true path accrue quite apart from any success in reaching the goal; and even though the height we strive to climb be inaccessible, we can still see and understand more than those who never leave the plain. The sphere, it is true, is enormous—the study of human life and destiny as a whole; and our mental vision is so ill-adapted to a range of this extent that to aim at forming a complete scheme is to attempt the impossible. It must be recognised that the data are insufficient for large views, and that we ought not to go beyond the facts we have, the facts of ordinary life, interpreted by the common experience of every day. These form our only material. The views we take must of necessity be fragmentary—a mere collection of *apercus,* rough guesses at the undiscovered; of the same nature, indeed, as all our possessions in the way of knowledge—little tracts of solid land reclaimed from the mysterious tocean of the unknown.

But if we do not admit Schopenhauer to be a great teacher,—because he is out of sympathy with the highest aspirations of mankind, and too ready to dogmatise from partial views,—he is a very suggestive writer, and eminently readable. His style is brilliant, animated, forcible, pungent; although it is also discursive, irresponsible, and with a tendency to superficial generalisation. He brings in the most unexpected topics without any very sure sense of their relative place; everything, in fact, seems to be fair game, once he has taken up his pen. His irony is noteworthy; for it extends beyond mere isolated sentences, and sometimes applies to whole passages, which must be read *cum grano salis.* And if he has grave faults as well as excellences of literary treatment, he is at least always witty and amusing, and that, too, in dealing with subjects—as here, for instance, with the Conduct of Life—on which many others have been at once severe and dull. It is easy to complain that though he is witty and amusing, he is often at the same time bitter and ill-natured. This is in some measure the unpleasant side of his uncompromising devotion to truth, his resolute eagerness to dispel illusion at any cost—those defects of his qualities which were intensified by a solitary and, until his last years, unappreciated life. He was naturally more disposed to coerce than to flatter the world into accepting his views; he was above all things *un esprit fort,* and at times brutal in the use of his strength. If it should be urged that, however great his literary qualities, he is not worth reading because he takes a narrow view of life and is blind to some of its greatest blessings, it will be well to remember the profound truth of that line which a friend inscribed on his earliest biography: *Si non errasset fecerat ille minus,* a truth which is seldom without application, whatever be the form of human effort. Schopenhauer cannot be neglected because he takes an unpleasant view of existence, for it is a view which must present itself, at some time, to every thoughtful person. To be outraged by Schopenhauer means to be ignorant of many of the facts of life.

In this one of his smaller works, ***Aphorismen zur Lebensweisheit,*** Schopenhauer abandons his high metaphysical standpoint, and discusses, with the same zest and appreciation as in fact marked his enjoyment of them, some of the pleasures which a wise man will seek to obtain,—health, moderate possessions, intellectual riches. And when, as in this little work, he comes to speak of the wisdom of life as the practical art of living, the pessimist view of human destiny is obtruded as little as possible. His remarks profess to be the result of a compromise—an attempt to treat life from the common standpoint. He is content to call these witty and instructive pages a series of aphorisms; thereby indicating that he makes no claim to expound a complete theory of conduct. It will doubtless occur to any intelligent reader that his observations are but fragmentary thoughts on various phases of life; and, in reality, mere *aphorisms*—in the old, Greek sense of the word—pithy distinctions, definitions of facts, a marking-off, as it were, of the true from the false in some of our ordinary notions of life and prosperity. Here there is little that is not in complete harmony with precepts to which the world has long been accustomed; and in this respect, also, Schopenhauer offers a suggestive comparison rather than a contrast with most writers on happiness.

The philosopher in his study is conscious that the world is never likely to embrace his higher metaphysical or ethical standpoint, and annihilate the will to live; nor did Schopenhauer himself do so except so far as he, in common with most serious students of life, avoided the ordinary aims of mankind. The theory which recommended universal benevolence as the highest ethical duty, came, as a matter of practice, to mean a formal standing-aloof—the *ne plus ultra* of individualism. / The Wisdom of Life, as the practical art of living, is a compromise. We are

here not by any choice of our own; and while we strive to make the best of it, we must not let ourselves be deceived. If you want to be happy, he says, it will not do to cherish illusions. Schopenhauer would have found nothing admirable in the conclusion at which the late M. Edmond Scherer, for instance, arrived. *L'art de vivre,* he wrote in his preface to Amiel's *Journal, c'est de se faire une raison, de souscrire au compromis, de se prêter aux fictions.* / Schopenhauer conceives his mission to be, rather, to dispel illusion, to tear the mask from life;—a violent operation, not always productive of good. Some illusion, he urges, may profitably be dispelled by recognising that no amount of external aid will make up for inward deficiency; and that if a man has not got the elements of happiness in himself, all the pride, pleasure, beauty and interest of the world will not give it to him. Success in life, as gauged by the ordinary material standard, means to place faith wholly in externals as the source of happiness, to assert and emphasize the common will to live, in a word, to be *vulgar.* He protests against this search for happiness—something subjective—in the world of our surroundings, or anywhere but in a man's own self; a protest the sincerity of which might well be imitated by some professed advocates of spiritual claims.

It would be interesting to place his utterances on this point side by side with those of a distinguished interpreter of nature in this country [Sir John Lubbock], who has recently attracted thousands of readers by describing *The Pleasures of Life;* in other words, the blessings which the world holds out to all who can enjoy them—health, books, friends, travel, education, art. On the common ground of their regard for these pleasures there is no disagreement between the optimist and the pessimist. But a characteristic difference of view may be found in the application of a rule of life which Schopenhauer seems never to tire of repeating; namely, that happiness consists for the most part in what a man is in himself, and that the pleasure he derives from these blessings will depend entirely upon the extent to which his personality really allows him to appreciate them. This is a rule which runs some risk of being overlooked in the operation of dazzling the mind's eye by a description of all the possible sources of pleasure in the world of our surroundings; but Sir John Lubbock, in common with every one who attempts a fundamental answer to the question of happiness, cannot afford to overlook it. The truth of the rule is perhaps taken for granted in his account of life's pleasures; but it is significant that it is only when he comes to speak of life's troubles that he freely admits the force of it. *Happiness,* he says, in this latter connection, *depends much more on what is within than without us.* Yet a rigid application of this truth might perhaps discount the effect of those pleasures with which the world is said to abound. That happiness as well as unhappiness depends mainly upon what is within, is more clearly recognised in the case of trouble; for when troubles come upon a man, they influence him, as a rule, much more deeply than pleasures. How few, even amongst the millions to whom these blessings are open—health, books, travel, art—really find any true or permanent happiness in them!

While Schopenhauer's view of the pleasures of life may be elucidated by comparing it with that of a popular writer like Sir John Lubbock, and by contrasting the appeals they severally make to the outer and the inner world as a source of happiness; Schopenhauer's view of life itself will stand out more clearly if we remember the opinion so boldly expressed by the same English writer. *If we resolutely look,* observes Sir John Lubbock, *I do not say at the bright side of things, but at things as they really are; if we avail ourselves of the manifold blessings which surround us; we cannot but feel that life is indeed a glorious inheritance.* There is a splendid excess of optimism about this statement which well fits it to show up the darker picture drawn by the German philosopher.

Finally, it should be remembered that though Schopenhauer's picture of the world is gloomy and sombre, there is nothing weak or unmanly in his attitude. If a happy existence, he says,—not merely an existence free from pain—is denied us, we can at least be heroes and face life with courage: *das höchste was der Mensch erlangen kann ist ein heroischer Lebenslauf.* A noble character will never complain at misfortune; for if a man looks round him at other manifestations of that which is his own inner nature, the will, he finds sorrows happening to his fellow-men harder to bear than any that have come upon himself. And the ideal of nobility is to deserve the praise which Hamlet—in Shakespeare's Tragedy of Pessimism—gave to his friend:

> Thou hast been
> As one, in suffering all, that suffers nothing.

But perhaps Schopenhauer's theory carries with it its own correction. He describes existence as a more or less violent oscillation between pain and boredom. If this were really the sum of life, and we had to reason from such a partial view, it is obvious that happiness would lie in *action;* and that life would be so constituted as to supply two natural and inevitable incentives to action, and thus to contain in itself the very conditions of happiness. Life itself reveals our destiny. It is not the struggle which produces misery, it is the mistaken aims and the low ideals—*was uns alle bändigt, das Gemeine!*

A. J. Ayer on Schopenhauer's importance:

While there are a few philosophers whose name is more widely known than that of Schopenhauer, the study of his writings, at least in this country, has fallen largely into neglect. A not unfounded distrust of his metaphysics has led to the false assumption that there is nothing of philosophical importance to be learned from him. [However,] even Schopenhauer's extravagances very often proceed from sharp philosophical insights. In particular, admirers of Wittgenstein may be surprised to discover the extent to which his thought was influenced by Schopenhauer's.

A. J. Ayer, "Editorial Forward," in Schopenhauer, *Penguin Books, 1963.*

Josiah Royce (essay date 1892)

SOURCE: "Schopenhauer," in *The Spirit of Modern Philosophy,* Houghton Mifflin Company, 1920, pp. 228-64.

[*Royce was an American philosopher whose works include* The World and the Individual *(1900) and* Lectures on Modern Idealism *(1919). Royce's neo-Hegelian idealism conceives of reality as fragmentary manifestations of an absolute mind; only when the individual understands the unity of the ideal absolute can perfection be attained. In the following excerpt from a lecture originally published in 1892, Royce contextualizes Schopenhauer's metaphysics with regard to idealism versus realism and evaluates Schopenhauer in relation to Hegel.*]

I need hardly remark in the presence of this audience that the name of Schopenhauer is better known to most general readers, in our day, than is that of any other modern Continental metaphysician, except Kant. The reputed heretic has in this field the reward of his dangerous reputation, and I scarcely know whether to fear or to rejoice, as I now approach the treatment of so noteworthy and significant a man, at the position in which Schopenhauer's fame puts his expositor. In one respect, of course, my task is rendered easier by all this popular repute of my hero. Of his doctrine most of us have heard a good deal, and many of us may have followed to a considerable extent his reasoning; at all events we have become acquainted, at least by hearsay, with the fact that his outcome was something called Pessimism. And thus, in dealing with him, I am not voyaging with you in seas unknown to all but the technical students of philosophy. . . . On the other hand, the kind of reputation that his writings have very naturally won is decidedly against me when I undertake to treat him with genuinely philosophical fairness. It is so much easier to be edifying than to face with courage certain serious and decidedly tragic realities! Let me be frank with you, then, at the outset about my difficulty. It is, plainly stated, simply this: You have heard that Schopenhauer is a pessimist. You, meanwhile, are surely for the most part no pessimists. Therefore, as we approach Schopenhauer, you want me, in your secret hearts, if not in your expressed wishes, to refute Schopenhauer. Now refutation is . . . a thing of only very moderate service in the study of philosophy. We may refute a great thinker's accidental misjudgments; we can seldom refute his deeper insights. And as I must forthwith assure you, and shall very soon show you, Schopenhauer's pessimism is actually expressive of a very deep insight into life. This insight is indeed not a final one. We must transcend it. But surely you would justly discover me in a very unphilosophical, and in fact very unworthily self-contradictory, attitude if now . . . I should suddenly, at this point of my discourse, assume the airs of a champion of the faith against the infidels, and should fall to hewing and hacking at Schopenhauer with genuinely crusading zeal. In fact it is not my calling to do anything of the sort. I always admire the crusaders, but my admiration is due rather to their enthusiasm than to their philosophical many-sidedness; rather to the vitality of their faith than to the universality of their comprehension. I fear that if I should try to join myself unto them they would not accept me without reserve. I cannot therefore treat Schopenhauer as a crusader would treat him. He is to me a philosopher of considerable dignity, whom we could ill spare from the roll of modern thinkers; whom I do not by any means follow as disciple, but to whom I owe, in common with other philosophical students, a great deal, for his skillful analysis and for his fearlessly clear assertion of his own significant temperament.

But as to pessimism itself, Schopenhauer's famous doctrine, as to this terrible view that life is through and through tragic and evil, what is my attitude towards that? I must, you will probably say, either accept it, and then must avow it in manly fashion, or I must reject it. And if I reject it, then I am bound to refute it. My answer to the question is not far to seek. As an actual fact I do accept, and avow with perfect freedom, what to many gentle minds seems, as I am aware, a pessimistic view of life; namely, precisely the view that . . . we found Hegel maintaining and expanding into his marvelously ingenious and technical doctrine of what he called *Negativität* as the very essence of the passionate spiritual existence. The spiritual life isn't a gentle or an easy thing. It is indeed through and through and forever paradoxical, earnest, enduring, toilsome; yes, if you like, painfully tragic. Whoever hopes to find it anything else, either now or in some far-off heaven, hopes unquestionably in vain. If that is pessimism,—and in one sense, namely, in the sense in which many tender but thoughtless souls have used the phrase, it is pessimism, being opposed to the gentle and optimistic hopes of such,—then I am now, and always shall be, in that very sense no optimist, but a maintainer of the sterner view that life is forever tragic. In so far as Schopenhauer has sought to make this plain, I follow him unhesitatingly, and honor him for his mercilessness. Why I do so I shall try to make plain before this lecture is done. In so far, however, as Schopenhauer held that the tragedy of life disheartens every spirit that has once come to know the truth, I as plainly and absolutely reject so much of his outcome. The world is, on the whole, very nearly as tragic as Schopenhauer represents it to be. Only spirituality consists in being heroic enough to accept the tragedy of existence, and to glory in the strength wherewith it is given to the true lords of life to conquer this tragedy, and to make their world after all divine. The way to meet Schopenhauer's pessimism is, not to refute its assertions, but to grapple practically with its truths. And if you do so, you will find as the real heart and significance of Schopenhauer's own gloomy thought, a vital, yes, even a religious assurance, which will make you thank God, that . . . the very ice and cold, the very frost and snow, of philosophy praise and magnify him forever. . . .

The general character and worth of this contribution I must first describe, and in doing so I shall follow in the main the view of a recent German writer on the history of philosophy, namely, [Wilhelm] Windelband, to whose well-known book, *Die Geschichte der neueren Philosophie* [1878-80], [this lecture owes] not a little. Modern idealism, as it developed since Kant, was from the first an effort to discover the rationality of our world through an analysis of the nature of consciousness. Such analysis was the problem that Kant bequeathed to his successors. For Kant showed that we know the world only in terms of consciousness and its laws, so that the understanding is the creator of the show nature that stands before our senses. Fichte tried to solve this Kantian problem by proving that it is the moral law which is the very heart and essence of our consciousness, so that our seemingly outer world is there as a means whereby we can do our work and win our deeper self. The romanticists, however, felt that consciousness was no more exhaustively expressed by the moral will than by any other humane interest of the self. Thus, there entered into philosophy a reign of caprice, to which even Hegel did not put an end. Once understand the nature of this caprice, and you will see the place which Schopenhauer's system is to hold in the development of doctrine.

Were it not, says all idealism, were it not that I am just such a conscious being as I am, my world would be a wholly different one from the world that I see. To know the real nature of my world I must therefore understand my own deeper self. Is there anything fixed, stable, necessary, about my nature? If so, then I am necessarily forced to exist in just this sort of world. But if I am essentially of no one fixed and necessary nature, then at any moment my whole world might alter. The ordinary realism of common sense doesn't fear this, doesn't feel the necessity of an ultimate appeal to anything stable or fixed about me as the real source of truth, because ordinary realism holds that the truth is there beyond me, as something knowable to all people of good intelligence, in the hard and fast matter of the world of sense. There is the moon yonder. For ordinary realism, the moon is as permanent as nature makes it, and stays there whether any one knows it or not. Hence, in order to ask whether there is anything stable about the world, ordinary realism has to put no questions to the inner life. But the very essence of idealism it is to say, *My* moon, the moon that I see and talk about, the moon of my own world of outer show and of empirical knowledge, is just one of my ideas. *You* see the *same* moon only in so far as in *your* world, in your inner life, there is a fact truly corresponding to what I call the moon in my inner life. Therefore, if you and I are to continue to see the same moon, that must be because both of us have some common and necessary deeper nature, a true and abiding oneness of spirit, that forces us to agree in this respect as to our inner life. Hence, not the abiding matter of the moon, as something that should stay there when you and I had both departed, but some common law that holds for your spirit as for mine, is the basis for the seeming permanence and common outer reality of the moon for us. The moon has the same sort of objective existence that, for instance, at this moment, my lecture has. The lecture exists as thought in me, and as experience in you. But because of a certain community of our thoughts, we all of us have the same lecture more or less present to us. We all of us, moreover, regard the lecture as an outer reality, and we therefore seem to be as much in presence of an objective fact as if the lecture were made of real atoms, instead of ideas. Or again, for the idealistic view, the existence of the events in matter, or of any other external events, resembles the existence at any instant of the price of a stock in the stock-market, or the credit of a great firm in the commercial world. A consensus of the thoughts of the buyer and sellers exists at any moment, which, however well founded, or again however arbitrary and changing this consensus may be, is expressed for the instant as if it were a hard and fast material thing in a genuinely outer world. In fact, prices and credits are ideas, and exist in the show-world of market values and of commercial securities, being but the projections of the various ideas of people as these at any moment agree to express themselves. Even so, then, just as this lecture is at this instant a fact because our minds agree in making it so, and just as the price of the stock, or the credit of the great firm, is an often irresistible fact, to which the individual dealer must yield in so far as his own financial might isn't equal to altering it, even so the moon yonder is likewise for us all an outer fact, because we are forced to agree in regarding it as outer. But our agreement itself is a fact of the deeper life of our common selfhood.

Such common ideas being, then, the idealist's true world, his problem it is to determine whether there is any deeper and impersonally human necessity which guarantees that our ideas *shall* thus in any wise agree. This necessity must be sought, if at all, in our own hidden nature. Constructive idealists have always sought it in that common band of rationality which, as they conceive, so links us all together that we are organically related parts or moments of one deeper self. This self, which shall express itself in you, in me, in everybody, is to link your experience to mine in such fashion that we shall see related outer worlds. Because this self in you constructs a show-space in three dimensions, and does a similar thing for me, therefore we alike look out into the depths of space, where the same stars seem to glitter for us all. Unity, fixity, assurance, we get, if we get such prizes at all, only by virtue of that rational and spiritual unity that is beneath our lives. Can the philosopher find the true heart and essence of this our common selfhood? If he can, then idealism becomes a system. We are, then, all in one world of truth. The outer world is indeed show, but no illusion; and our life has an organic fixity, a lawful completeness about it, such as every philosophy longs for.

But now, unfortunately, when idealists set about deducing this unity and consistency of the spiritual world from some deep inner principle, their reflection always leaves us in one great respect dissatisfied. We very certainly, namely, can never deduce from the idea of our common spirituality the idea of any particular sense thing, such as the moon. Or, to repeat one of my former illustrations, idealists can't tell us *why* we are spiritually or rationally bound all alike to perceive a starry world, wherein there shall be a belt of telescopic asteroids between the orbits of Mars and Jupiter. Such facts idealists get, like their neighbors, from daily experience or from science. Idealists may say in general, as Fichte said, that the moral law needs a world of outer experience as the material for its embodiment. They cannot show why just *this* material is needed. There remains, then, an element of brute fact, a residuum, if you choose, of spiritual caprice, in their world

of the all-embracing self. Perhaps we have, as they say, the one deeper self in common, perhaps this deeper self has rational grounds for building in us all alike just this world of sense, of moons, of asteroids, of comets, of jelly-fish, and of all the rest, only there is still, from our finite point of view, a vast element of at least apparent caprice about the entire universe of the spirit as thus built. And all idealists have to recognize this fact of the seeming capriciousness of the external order. The universal reason builds the world, says idealism; but then does not the universal reason seem to build many irrational facts into its world? You see then the difficulty. Our common spiritual nature is to guarantee the truth of our common experience. Unless this nature has some hard and fast necessity in it, of which we can form an adequate conception, there is no satisfaction in our philosophy. But when we try to develop this idea of the universal necessity of the world of our common selfhood, we come once more against an element of the most stubborn caprice. Idealism seems to be an insight as suggestive and inspiring as it is limited. The nature of this divine self has something seemingly irrational about it. Our attempted account of the world in terms of the universal reason therefore remains so far a mere programme, a postulate, almost a dogma. And yet dogmas were just what our philosophy had all along been trying to reduce and to rationalize.

In view of this common perplexity of all the idealistic systems, there were certain to arise, upon the historical basis of the Kantian theory, philosophies that not only accepted the perplexity, but that magnified it, that referred it to the very nature of the quasi-mental reality behind the world of sense, and that declared: "Deeper than reason, in this world of the ideal existence, is the caprice which once for all expresses itself in the wealth of nature's facts." Of such systems Schopenhauer's philosophy is the classic representative. Not that Schopenhauer was in this general tendency alone. Windelband very properly classes under the same head Schelling's later theologico-philosophical speculations . . . along with two or three other doctrines. Windelband calls them all by the common name *Irrationalismus*. A doctrine of this sort, upon a Kantian basis, must run somewhat as follows: The world as we see it exists only in our ideas. We all have a common outer show-world because we all possess a common deeper nature, wherein we are one. You are essentially the same ultimate being that I am. Otherwise we should not have in common this outer projected world of seeming sea waves, star clusters, and city streets. For, as ideas, those things have no outer basis. As common to us all, they must have a deep inner basis. Yet this their basis can't be anything ultimately and universally rational. For in so far as we actually have reason in common, we think necessary, clearly coherent, exactly interrelated groups of ideas, such, for instance, as the multiplication table. But about the star clusters and the sea waves there is no such ultimate rational unity and coherency. Natural laws only bind such things together, in the fashion that Kant so prettily explained, in case the phenomena to be bound together are once for all there. Why, given sea waves and star clusters and city streets, we should be bound to think them as in *some* sort of interconnection,

Kant has told us. Only no such laws of nature can explain why there should be the phenomena there that are thus to conform to law. This is capricious. This is due to our common but irrational nature. The world of the true idealism isn't so much the world of the rational and divine self, as it is the world of the deep unreason that lies at the very basis of all of our natures, of all our common selfhood. Why should there be any world at all for us? Isn't it just because we are all actually minded to see one? And isn't this being minded to see a world as ultimately and brutally unreasonable a fact as you could name? Let us find for this fact, then, a name not so exalted as Fichte's high-sounding speech would love. Let us call this ultimate nature of ours, which forces us all alike to see a world of phenomena in the show forms of space and time, simply our own deep common Will. Let us drop the divine name for it. Will, merely as such, isn't precisely a rational thing; it's capricious. It wills because it does will; and if it wills in us all to be of such nature as to see just these stars and houses, then see them we must, and there is the end of it.

Thus stated, you have an irrationalism on an idealistic basis, a doctrine that may be summed up in three propositions;—

1. The world has existence only as we see it.

2. What facts we are to see can only be learned from experience, and cannot be found *a priori* through any absurd transcendental deductions of the so-called essence of any absolute spirit.

3. The deepest ground, however, for all these seen facts, and for the community of our various visible worlds, is the common and single World-Will, which, expressed in all of us equally, forces us to see alike, but does so simply because this is the particular caprice that it happens to have, so that it embodies itself for us and in us as just this show-world, rather than any other, because such is its fashion of willing.

The obvious value of such a theory is that it is at once idealistic in its analysis of the presuppositions of life, just to the direct and irresistible reality of the facts of experience, and disposed, after all, to go deeper than experience in its search for the ultimate truth of the world. Final it certainly is not in this form. But it has an obvious advantage over the sort of caprice that, as we saw, was characteristic of the philosophy of the romantic school. Their caprice was the fickleness of private and individual choice. For them you can change, as it were, at any moment of time, your show-world. For them the man of genius makes whatever world he chooses. But for this theory of Schopenhauer's there is but one caprice, and that is the caprice of the World-Will itself, which once for all has hit upon this particular world of facts in time and in space. For us, in our individual capacity, there is no further caprice. We are in presence of this world now, because we ourselves are embodiments of the world-will. We cannot help the fact any longer. Experience is experience; fact is fact; the show is going on for us all alike;

the world-will has chosen; but it has not chosen at any point in time. Hence in the world, as it is in time, there is no further caprice, only fact. Time itself is indeed not any ultimate reality. Time belongs to the show-world, and is there like any other fact or form of things, because the world-will fancies such a form for the things of sense. But just for this very reason, we, as individuals, are just where we are, and the realities of sense and of science, although susceptible of so deep and mysterious an interpretation as this, are as inevitable and as objective for us as ever the most naive and unreflectively superficial realism made them. As against such realism our doctrine possesses depth, philosophical keenness of analysis, idealistic insight. As against the romantic idealism, our doctrine has the advantage of objectivity and fixity. Just because our common temporal existence is part of the caprice of the World-Will, this temporal existence itself has for us individuals reality and fixity.

So much for the theoretical side of our author's doctrine. On the practical side, in respect, namely, of his pessimism, we shall find Schopenhauer in a very interesting historical relation to Hegel. In fact, as we shall learn, our author's pessimism is but another aspect of the same insight into the paradoxical logic of passion which we have discovered at the heart of Hegel's doctrine. It is true that Schopenhauer's World-Will, this blind power that, according to him, embodies itself in our universe, appears in his account, at first, as something that might be said to possess passion without logic. Yet this first view of the World-Will soon turns out to be inadequate. The very caprice of the terrible principle is seen, as we go on, to involve a sort of secondary rationality, a logic, fatal and gloomy, as well as deeply paradoxical, but still none the less truly rational for all that. Schopenhauer's world is, in fact, tragic in much the same sense as Hegel's. Only, for Schopenhauer the tragedy is hopeless, blind, undivine; while for Hegel it is the divine tragedy of the much-tried Logos, whose joy is above all the sorrows of his world. Were this difference between these two thinkers merely one of personal and speculative opinion, it might have little significance. But since it involves, as we shall find, one of the most truly vital problems of our modern life, one which meets us at every step in our literature and in our ethical controversies, we shall find it well worth our while to study the contrast more closely. . . .

Schopenhauer's principal work, *Die Welt als Wille und Vorstellung,* is in form the most artistic philosophical treatise in existence, if one excepts the best of Plato's *Dialogues.* In its first edition it was divided into four books; a later edition added in a second volume comments upon all four. Of these books, the first summarizes the Kantian basis of Schopenhauer's own doctrine. The world is, first of all, for each and for all of us, just our *Vorstellung,* our Idea. It is there because and while we see it; it consists in its detail of facts of experience. These, however, are, for our consciousness, always interpreted facts, seen in the sense forms of space and of time, and within these forms, perceived through and by virtue of our universal form of comprehension, namely, the principle of causation. When I experience anything, I inevitably seek for a cause in space and in time for this experience. When I find such a cause, I localize the experience as an event manifesting some change in something there in space and in time; but these forms of space and of time, as well as this principle of causation, are all alike simply formal ideas in me. Kant's great service lay, in fact, in his proving the subjectivity, the purely mental nature, of such forms. The space and time worlds, with all that they contain, exist accordingly for the knowing subject. No subject without an object, and no object without a subject. I know in so far as there is a world to know; and the world yonder exists in so far as I know it. In vain, moreover, would one seek for any thing in itself really outside of me as the cause of my experiences. For cause is just an idea of mine, useful and valid for the events of the show world, but wholly inapplicable to anything else. Within experience the law of causation is absolute, because such is my fashion of thinking experience and of perceiving the localized things of sense. But beyond experience what validity, what application, can one give to the principle of causation? None. There is no cause to be sought beyond my own true nature for my own experiences.

But what *is* this my nature? The second book answers the question. My nature, you must observe, is something very wealthy. It does not indeed *cause* my experiences, in any proper sense; for cause means only an event that in time or in space brings another event to pass; and there is nothing that, in time or in space, brings to pass my own deepest, timeless, and spaceless nature. As phenomenon in time, my body may move or die, as other events determine; but my deepest nature is so superior to space and time that, as we have just shown, space and time are in fact *in me,* in so far as they are my forms of seeing and of knowing. Therefore my true nature neither causes, nor is caused; but, as one now sees, it in truth *is,* comprises, embodies itself in, all my world of phenomena. Hence you see how wealthy my true nature must be in its implications. Yes, in a deeper sense, you also, in so far as you truly exist, must have the same deepest nature that I have. Only in space and in time do we seem to be separate beings. Space and time form, as Schopenhauer says, the dividing principle of things. In an illusory way they seem to distinguish us all from one another; but abstract space and time, with all their manifold and illusory distinctions of places and moments, and the real world collapses into one immanent nature of things. Since my own deepest nature is beneath and behind the time form of the apparent world, it follows that, in an essential and deep sense, I am one with all that ever has been or that ever will be, either millions of ages ago or millions of ages to come. And as for space, there is no star so remote but that the same essential nature of things which is manifest in that star is also manifest in my own body. Space and time are, as the Hindoos declared, the veil of Maya or Illusion, wherewith the hidden unity of things is covered, so that, through such illusion, the world appears manifold, although it is but one.

To answer, therefore, the question, What is the nature of things? I have only to find what, apart from my senses

and my thought, is my own deepest essence. And of this I have a direct, an indescribable, but an unquestionable awareness. My whole inner life is, namely, essentially my will. I long, I desire, I move, I act, I feel, I strive, I lament, I assert myself. The common name for all this is my will. By will, of course, Schopenhauer does not merely mean the highest form of my conscious choice, as some people do. He means simply the active nature of me, the wanting, longing, self-asserting part. This, in truth, as even the romantic idealists felt, lies deeper than my intellect, is at the basis of all my seeing and knowing. Why do I see and acknowledge the world in space and in time? Why do I believe in matter, or recognize the existence of my fellow-men, or exercise my reason? Is not all this just my actual fashion of behavor? In vain, however, do I seek, as the idealists of Fichte's type often pretended to seek, for an ultimate reason why I should have this fashion of behavior. That is a mere fact. Deeper than reason is the inexplicable caprice of the inner life. We want to exist; we long to know; we make our world because we are just striving to come into being. Our whole life is as ultimate and inexplicable an activity as are our particular fashions of loving and of hating. *So* I am; this is the nature of me,—to strive, to long, to will; and I cannot rest in this striving. My life is a longing to be somewhere else in life than here, where I am.

Here, then, is the solution of our mystery in so far as it can have a solution. The world is the Will. In time and space I see only the behavior of phenomena. I never get at things in themselves; but I, in my timeless and spaceless inner nature, in the very heart, in the very germ, of my being, am not a mere outward succession of phenomena. I am a Will,—a will which is not there for the sake of something else, but which exists solely because it desires to exist. Here is the true thing in itself. The whole world, owing to the utter illusoriness of time and space, has collapsed into one single and ultimate nature of things. This nature, immediately experienced in the inner life, is the Will. This Will, then, is that which is so wealthy that the whole show world is needed to express its caprice. Look, then, on the whole world in its infinite complication of living creatures and of material processes. These, indeed, are remote enough from your body. Seen in space and time, you are a mere fragment in the endless world of phenomena, a mere drop in the ocean, a link in an endless chain. But look at the whole world otherwise. In its inmost life and truth it must be one, for space and time are the mere forms in which the one interest of the observer is pleased to express itself. Look upon all things, then, and it can be said of you as, once more, the Hindoos loved to say, "The life of all these things,—*That art Thou.*"

Schopenhauer himself was fond of quoting this well-known phrase of the Hindoo philosophy as expressing the kernel of his own doctrine. New about his philosophy was, he felt, the synthesis that he had made of Kant's thought and the Hindoo insight; but with this insight itself he essentially agreed. "The inmost life of things is one, and *that life art thou.*" This sentence expresses to his mind the substance of the true thought about the world. Let us, then, quote a paragraph or two from one of the Hindoo philosophic classics called the *Upanishads,* much read and loved by Schopenhauer, to illustrate his view. In the passage in question a teacher is represented as in conversation with his pupil, who is also his son.

'Bring me,' says the father, 'a fruit of yonder tree.' 'Here it is, O Venerable One.' 'Cut it open.' 'It is done.' 'What seest thou therein?' 'I see, O Venerable One, very little seeds.' 'Cut one of them open.' 'It is done, Venerable One.' 'What seest thou therein?' 'Nothing, Venerable One.' Then spake he: 'That fine thing which thou seest not, my well beloved, from that fine thing (that life) is, in truth, this mighty tree grown. Believe me, my well beloved, *what* this fine (substance) is, of whose essence is all the world, that is the Reality, that is the Soul,—*That art Thou,* O vetaketu.'

'This bit of salt, lay it in the (vessel of) water, and come again to-morrow to me.' This did he. Then spake (the teacher): 'Bring me that salt which yesterday even thou didst lay in the water.' He sought it and found it not, for it was melted. 'Taste the water here. How tastes it?' 'Salt.' 'Taste it there. How tastes it?' 'Salt.' 'Leave the vessel and sit at my feet.' So did he, and said, '(The salt) is still there.' Then spake the teacher: 'Verily, so seest thou the truly Existent not in bodies, yet is it truly therein. What this fine substance is of whose essence is all the world, that is the Reality, that is the Soul,—*That art Thou,* O vetaketu.'

'Just as, O my well beloved, a man whom they have led away out of the land of the Gandharis with eyes blindfolded, and have loosed him in the wilderness,—just as he wanders eastwards or westwards, southwards or northwards, because he has been led hither blindfolded and loosed blindfolded, but after some one has taken off the blind from his eyes, and has said, "Yonder lies the land of the Gandharis; yonder go," he, asking the way in village after village, instructed and understanding, comes home at last to the Gandharis,—even so, too, is the man who here in the world has found a teacher; for he knows "to this (world) I belong only until I am delivered; then shall I come to my home." What this fine (substance) is, of whose essence is all the world, that is the Reality, that is the Soul,—*That art Thou,* O vetaketu.'

Here, one sees, is the Hindoo way of getting at the substance. It is also Schopenhauer's way. Look for the substance within, in your own nature. You will not see it without. It is the life of your own life, the soul of your own soul. When you find it, you will come home from the confusing world of sense-things to the heart and essence of the world, to the reality. *That art Thou.*

Since for Schopenhauer this soul of your soul is the capricious inner will, there is no reason to speak of it as God or as Spirit; for these words imply rationality and conscious intelligence. And intelligence, whose presence in the world is merely one of the caprices of this will itself, finds itself always in sharp contrast to the will, which it can contemplate, but which it can never explain. However, of contemplation there are various stages, determined in us phenomenal individuals by the various sizes and powers of our purely phenomenal brains. Why any

intelligence exists at all, and why it is phenomenally associated with a brain, nobody can explain. The will thus likes to express itself. That is the whole story. However, once given the expression, this intelligence reaches its highest perfection in that power to contemplate the whole world of the will with a certain supreme and lofty calm, which, combined with an accurate insight into the truth of the will, is characteristic of the temperament of the productive artist. Art is, namely, the embodiment of the essence of the will as the contemplative intelligence sees it. And to art Schopenhauer devotes his third book. The will has certain ultimate fashions of expressing itself, certain stages of self-objectification, as Schopenhauer calls them. These, in so far as contemplation can seize them, are the ultimate types, the Platonic ideas, of things, all endlessly exemplified in space and time by individual objects, but, as types, eternal, time-transcending, immortal. They are the ultimate embodiments of passion, the eternal forms of longing that exist in our world. Art grasps these types and exhibits them. Architecture, for instance, portrays the blind nature-forces, or longings, of weight and resistance. Art is, then, the universal appreciation of the essence of the will from the point of view of a contemplative onlooker. Art is, therefore, disinterested, embodying passion, but itself not the victim of passion. Of all the arts, according to Schopenhauer, Music most universally and many-sidedly portrays the very essence of the will, the very soul of passion, the very heart of this capricious, world-making, and incomprehensible inner nature of ours. Hence music is in some respects Schopenhauer's favorite art. Music shows us just what the will is,—eternally moving, striving, changing, flying, struggling, wandering, returning to itself, and then beginning afresh,—all with no deeper purpose than just life in all its endlessness, motion, onward-flying, conflict, fullness of power, even though that shall mean fullness of sorrow and anguish. Music never rests, never is content; repeats its conflicts and wanderings over and over; leads them up, indeed, to mighty climaxes, but is great and strong never by virtue of abstract ideas, but only by the might of the will that it embodies. Listen to these cries and strivings, to this infinite wealth of flowing passion, to this infinite restlessness, and then reflect,—*That art Thou;* just that unreposing vigor, longing, majesty, and—caprice.

Of all Schopenhauer's theories, except his pessimism itself, this theory of art has become the most widely known and influential. As he stated it, it was, indeed, evidently the notion, not of the systematic student of any art, but of the observant amateur of genius and sensibility. It lacks the professional tone altogether. Its illustrations are chosen whimsically from all sorts of directions. The opposition between will and contemplation reaches for the first time its height at this point in the system. On one side, the world of passion, throbbing, sorrowing, longing, hoping, toiling, above all, forever fleeing from the moment, whatever it be; on the other side, the majesty of artistic contemplation, looking in sacred calm upon all this world, seeing all things, but itself unmoved. Plainly, in this contemplative intellect the will has capriciously created for itself a dangerous enemy, who will discover its deep irrationality.

This enemy is none other than that Wagnerian Brünhilde, who is destined to see, through and through, the vanity of the world of the will, and who, not indeed without the connivance of the high gods of the will themselves, is minded to destroy the whole vain show in one final act of resignation. There arise from time to time in the world, thinks Schopenhauer, holy men, full of sympathy and pity for all their kind, full of a sense of the unity of all life, and of the vanity of this our common and endless paradox of the finite world. These men are called, in the speech of all the religions, saints. Whatever their land or creed, their thought is the same. Not the particular griefs of life, not the pangs of cold and hunger and of disease, not the horrors of the baseness that runs riot in humanity,—not these things do they weigh in the balance with any sort of precision or particularity, although these things, too, they see and pity. No, the source of all these griefs, the will itself, its paradox, its contradictory longing to be forever longing, its irrational striving to be forever as one that suffers lack,—this they condemn, compassionate, and—resign. They do not strive or cry. They simply forsake the will. Life, they say, *must* be evil, for life is desire, and desire is essentially tragic, since it flees endlessly and restlessly from all that it has; makes perfection impossible by always despising whatever it happens to possess, and by longing for more; lives in an eternal wilderness of its own creation; is tossed fitfully in the waves of its own dark ocean of passion; knows no peace; finds in itself no outcome,—nothing that can finish the longing and the strife.

And this hopelessly struggling desire,—so the saints teach to each one of us in our blindness,—*That art Thou.* The saints pity us all. Their very existence is compassion. They absent them from felicity awhile, that they may teach us the way of peace. And this way is what? Suicide? No, indeed. Schopenhauer quite consistently condemns suicide. The suicide desires bliss, and flees only from circumstance. He wills life. He hates only this life which he happens to have. No, this is not what the saints teach. One and all they counsel, as the path of perfection, the hard and steep road of Resignation. That alone leads to blessedness, to escape from the world. Deny the will to live. Forsake the power that builds the world. Deny the flesh. While you live be pitiful, merciful, kindly, dispassionate, resisting no evil, turning away from all good fortune, thinking of all things as of vanity and illusion. The whole world, after all, is an evil dream. Deny the will that dreams, and the vision is ended. As for the result, "we confess freely," says Schopenhauer, in the famous concluding words of the fourth book of his first volume, "what remains, after the entire annulling of the will, is, for all those who are yet full of the will, indeed nothing. But, on the other hand, for those in whom the will has turned again, and has denied itself, this our own so very real world, with all her suns and Milky Ways, is—Nothing."

The estimate of the doctrine which we now have before us will be greatly aided if we bear in mind the nature of its historic genesis. The problem bequeathed by Kant to his successors was, as we have seen throughout both this and the preceding discussion, the problem of the relation of the empirical self of each moment to the total or universal self. This problem exists alike for Hegel and for Schopenhauer. Hegel undertakes to solve it by examining the process of self-consciousness. This process, developed according to his peculiar and paradoxical logic, which we [venture] to call the Logic of Passion, shows him that in the last analysis there is and can be but one self, the absolute spirit, the triumphant solver of paradoxes. Sure of his process, Hegel despises every such mystical and immediate seizing of the Universal as had been characteristic of the romanticists. With just these romanticists, however, Schopenhauer has in common the immediate intuition whereby he seizes, not so much the universal self as, in his opinion, the universal and irrational essence or nature that is at the heart of each finite self, and of all things, namely, the Will. Yet when he describes this will, after his intuition has come to grasp it, he finds in it just the paradox that Hegel had logically developed. For Hegel, self-consciousness is, as even Fichte already had taught, essentially the longing to be more of a self than you are. Just so, for Schopenhauer, if you exist you will, and if you will you are striving to escape from your present nature. It is of the essence of will to be always desiring a change. If the Will makes a world, the Will as such will be sure, then, thinks Schopenhauer, to be endlessly dissatisfied with its world. For, once more, when you will, the very essence of such will is discontentment with what is yours now. I no longer make that an object of desire which I already possess. I will what I have not yet, but hope to get, as a poor man wills wealth, but a rich man more wealth. I will the future, the distant, the unpossessed, the victory that I have not yet won, the defeat of the enemy who still faces me in arms, the cessation of the tedium or of the pain that besets me. Do I attain my desire, my will ceases, or, which is the same thing, turns elsewhere for food. Curiously enough, this, which is precisely the thought that led Hegel to the conception of the absolutely active and triumphant spirit, appears to Schopenhauer the proof of the totally evil nature of things. Striving might be bearable were there a highest good, to which, by willing, I could attain, and if, when I once attained that good, I could rest. But if will makes the world and is the whole life and essence of it, then there is nothing in the world deeper than the longing, the unrest, which is the very heart of all willing. Doesn't this unrest seem tragic? Is there to be no end of longing in the world? If not, how can mere striving, mere willing, come to seem bearable? Here is the question which leads Schopenhauer to his pessimism. Precisely the same problem made Hegel, with all his appreciation of the tragedy of life, an optimist. Hegel's Absolute, namely, is dissatisfied everywhere *in* his finite world, but is triumphantly content *with* the whole of it, just because his wealth is complete.

An historical lecture like the present one has not to decide between the metaphysical claims and rights of the Schopenhauerian immediate intuition of the Universal and the Hegelian logic. As theories of the absolute, these two doctrines represent conflicting philosophical interests whose discussion would belong elsewhere. Our present concern is the more directly human one. Of the two attitudes towards the great spiritual interests of man which these systems embody, which is the deeper? To be sure, even this question cannot be answered without making a confession of philosophical faith, but that I must here do in merely dogmatic form.

For my part, I deeply respect both doctrines. Both are essentially modern views of life, modern in their universality of expression, in their keen diagnosis of human nature, in their merciless criticism of our consciousness, in their thorough familiarity with the waywardness of the inner life. The century of nerves and of spiritual sorrows has philosophized with characteristic ingenuity in the persons of these thinkers,—the one the inexorable and fairly Mephistophelian critic of the paradoxes of passion, the other the nervous invalid of brilliant insight. We are here speaking only of this one side of their doctrines, namely, their diagnosis of the heart and of the issues of life. How much of the truth there is in both, every knowing man ought to see. Capricious is the will of man, thinks Schopenhauer, and therefore endlessly paradoxical and irrational. Paradoxical is the very consciousness, and therefore the very reason, of man, finds Hegel; and therefore, where there is this paradox, there is not unreason, but the manifestation of a part of the true spiritual life,—a life which could not be spiritual were it not full of conflict. Hegel thus absorbs, as it were, the pessimism of Schopenhauer; while Schopenhauer illustrates the paradox of Hegel.

But if both doctrines stand as significant expressions of the modern spirit, a glance at our more recent literature—at the despairing resignation of Tolstoi, with its flavor of mysticism, and at the triumphant joy in the paradoxes of passion which Browning kept to the end—will show us how far our romancers and poets still are from having made an end of the inquiry as to which doctrine is the right one. My own notion about the matter, such as it is, would indeed need for its full development the context of just such a philosophical argument as I have declined to introduce [now]. As constructive idealist, regarding the absolute as indeed a spirit, I am in sympathy with Hegel's sense of the triumphant rationality that reigns above all the conflicts of the spiritual world. But as to Schopenhauer's own account of life, I find indeed that his pessimism is usually wholly misunderstood and unappreciated, as well by those who pretend to accept as well by those who condemn it. What people fail to comprehend concerning these deep and partial insights which are so characteristic of great philosophers is that the proper way to treat them is neither to scorn nor to bow down, but to experience, and then to get our freedom in presence of all such insights even by the very wealth of our experience. We are often so slavish in our relations with doctrines of this kind! Are they expressed in traditional, in essentially clerical language, . . . then the form deceives us often into accepting mystical resignation as if it were the whole of spirituality, instead of bearing, as it does bear, much the same relation to the better life that sculptured marble bears to breathing flesh. But if it is a Schopenhauer, a notorious heretic, who uses much the same speech, then we can find no refuge save in hating him and his gloom. In fact,

pessimism, in its deeper sense, is merely an ideal and abstract expression of one very deep and sacred element of the total religious consciousness of humanity. In fact, finite life is tragic, very nearly as much so as Schopenhauer represented, and tragic for the very reason that Schopenhauer and all the counselors of resignation are never weary of expressing, in so far, namely, as it is at once deep and restless. This is its paradox, that it is always unfinished, that it never attains, that it throbs as the heart does, and ends one pulsation only to begin another. This is what Hegel saw. This is what all the great poets depict, from Homer's wanderings of the much tossed and tried Odysseus down to "In Memoriam" of Tennyson, or the "Dramatic Lyrics" of Browning. Not only is this so, but it must be so. The only refuge from spiritual restlessness is spiritual sluggishness; and that, as everybody is aware, is as tedious a thing as it is insipid. For the individual the lesson of this tragedy is always hard; and he learns it first in a religious form in the mood of pure resignation. "I cannot be happy; I must resign happiness." This is what all the Imitations and the Schopenhauers are forever and very justly teaching to the individual. Schopenhauer's special reason for this view is, however, the deep and philosophical one that at the heart of the world there seems to be an element of capricious conflict. That fact was what drove him to reject the World Spirit of the constructive idealists, and to speak only of a World-Will. But is this the whole story? No; if we ever get our spiritual freedom, we shall, I think, not neglecting this caprice which Schopenhauer found at the heart of things, still see that the world is divine and spiritual, not so much in spite of this capriciousness, as just because of it. Caprice isn't all of reason; but reason needs facts and passions to conquer and to rationalize, in order to become triumphantly rational. The spirit exists by accepting and by triumphing over the tragedy of the world. Restlessness, longing, grief,—these are evils, fatal evils, and they are everywhere in the world; but the spirit must be strong enough to endure them. In this strength is the solution. And, after all, it is just endurance that is the essence of spirituality. Resignation, then, is indeed part of the truth,—resignation, that is, of any hope of a final and private happiness. We resign in order to be ready to endure. But courage is the rest of the truth,—a hearty defiance of the whole hateful pang and agony of the will, a binding of the strong man by being stronger than he, a making of life once for all our divine game, where the passions are the mere chessmen that we move in carrying out our plan, and where the plan is a spiritual victory over Satan. Let us thank Schopenhauer, then, for at least this, that in his pessimism he gives us an universal expression for the whole negative side of life. If you will let me speak of private experience, I myself have often found it deeply comforting, in the most bitter moments, to have discounted, so to speak, all the petty tragedies of experience, all my own weakness and caprice and foolishness and ill fortune, by one such absolute formula for evil as Schopenhauer's doctrine gives me. It is the fate of life to be restless, capricious, and therefore tragic. Happiness comes, indeed, but by all sorts of accidents; and it flies as it comes. One thing only that is greater than this fate endures in us if we are wise of heart; and this one thing endures forever

An excerpt from *The World as Will and Representation* (1818)

Before us there is certainly left only nothing; but that which struggles against this flowing away into nothing, namely our nature, is indeed just the will-to-live which we ourselves are, just as it is our world. That we abhor nothingness so much is simply another way of saying that we will life so much, and that we are nothing but this will and know nothing but it alone. But we now turn our glance from our own needy and perplexed nature to those who have overcome the world, in whom the will, having reached complete self-knowledge, has found itself again in everything, and then freely denied itself, and who then merely wait to see the last trace of the will vanish with the body that is animated by that trace. Then, instead of the restless pressure and effort; instead of the constant transition from desire to apprehension and from joy to sorrow; instead of the never-satisfied and never-dying hope that constitutes the life-dream of the man who wills, we see that peace that is higher than all reason, that ocean-like calmness of the spirit, that deep tranquillity, that unshakable confidence and serenity, whose mere reflection in the countenance, as depicted by Raphael and Correggio, is a complete and certain gospel. Only knowledge remains; the will has vanished. We then look with deep and painful yearning at that state, beside which the miserable and desperate nature of our own appears in the clearest light by the contrast. Yet this consideration is the only one that can permanently console us, when, on the one hand, we have recognized incurable suffering and endless misery as essential to the phenomenon of the will, to the world, and on the other see the world melt away with the abolished will, and retain before us only empty nothingness. In this way, therefore, by contemplating the life and conduct of saints, to meet with whom is of course rarely granted to us in our own experience, but who are brought to our notice by their recorded history, and, vouched for with the stamp of truth by art, we have to banish the dark impression of that nothingness, which as the final goal hovers behind all virtue and holiness, and which we fear as children fear darkness. We must not even evade it, as the Indians do, by myths and meaningless words, such as reabsorption in *Brahman*, or the *Nirvana* of the Buddhists. On the contrary, we freely acknowledge that what remains after the complete abolition of the will is, for all who are still full of the will, assuredly nothing. But also conversely, to those in whom the will has turned and denied itself, this very real world of ours with all its suns and galaxies, is—nothing.

Arthur Schopenhauer, in The World as Will and Representation, *Dover Publications, 1969.*

in the heart of the great World-Spirit of whose wisdom ours is but a fragmentary reflection. This one thing, as I hold, is the eternal resolution that if the world *will* be tragic, it *shall* still, in Satan's despite, be spiritual. And this resolution is, I think, the very essence of the Spirit's own eternal joy.

William Caldwell (essay date 1896)

SOURCE: "The Positive Aspects of the System," in *Schopenhauer's System in Its Philosophical Significance,* William Blackwood and Sons, 1896, pp. 486-521.

[In the following excerpt, Caldwell outlines Schopenhauer's unique metaphilosophy.]

What is significant for philosophy in Schopenhauer is not so much the mere principle of will, which he sought to substitute for the *idea* of rationalistic metaphysic, as the simple fact of the attempted substitution. Strictly speaking, life cannot be grasped by thought as reducible, in the way of the old ontology, to some one or two entities. Whenever Schopenhauer talks of the will as if it were a thing in itself, we become distrustful of him. The chief safeguard of the will as a principle in philosophy lies in the fact of its being an impulse or an attempt, a fusion of all actual and imaginable entities into one grand effort to become all reality. The mind, in trying to grasp reality, must grasp it expansively and broadly and freely as something that is continually changing and evolving—must grasp it, in short, as an *effort* after a fuller and richer life. In doing so, it will become conscious of the fact that the very effort to attain to a philosophical synthesis of things is nothing that possesses an absolute significance in itself, nothing in connection with which we should look for definite returns or results, but is rather itself to be construed as part of the effort put forth by the human personality to attain to a more stable and permanent position in the fabric of reality than is apparently possessed by material things and by the lower animals. We *think* things in order that we may act better and preserve our individuality in the system of things. Just as we cannot understand art without cultivating in ourselves the artistic impulse, and just as we cannot know the moral ideal without (as Aristotle suggested) cultivating in ourselves the habits and the insight of the good man, so we cannot *understand* philosophy without cultivating the philosophical *impulse,* without appreciating philosophy as itself a supreme effort of man to make more sure of his existence in a world where everything seems to have the mark of finitude upon it. Philosophy represents the highest effort of man to find and to secure for himself an established place in the cosmic process of change and development. The philosopher should be a man who has the emotional and volitional capacity to appreciate every side of life, and *along with* that the power of thought to reduce the varied forms of his experience and the different aspects of the cosmos to their simplest terms. In this way he will be enabled to *think* reality and to *think* himself and to trace the roots of his action in his own organism and in the organisms that preceded his own. As soon as we see that the world is one will, we can relate ourselves to the whole universe and make our "dead self" in unconscious nature a "stepping-stone" to higher things.

Schopenhauer's suggestiveness, in short, extends as far as the dynamic or volitional philosophy of life will carry us. His *quietism* in art and ethics and religion cannot be taken to be the last phase of his thought. It has a meaning undoubtedly, the great meaning, in fact, that in art and religious aspiration we already see the world spiritualised or made subservient to the purposes of intelligent human beings. For [as Goethe wrote]

Was im Leben uns verdriesst
Man im Bilde gern geniesst.

Indeed, the outcome of quietism, as of religious faith in general, is that we must have the courage to proclaim *as real* what we experience in art and in religion, and must deliberately place our artistic and religious intuitions, the world of beauty and of goodness, above the world of the senses and of the scientific understanding, although we may not have the *knowledge* and the critical ability to justify this procedure with our understanding.

Arthur O. Lovejoy (essay date 1911)

SOURCE: "Schopenhauer as an Evolutionist," in *The Monist,* Vol. XXI, No. 2, 1911, pp. 195-222.

[*In the following essay, Lovejoy contends that Schopenhauer, especially in his later writings, proposes doctrines akin to Darwin's evolution.*]

The Absolute of the philosophy of Schopenhauer is notoriously one of the most complicated of all known products of metaphysical synthesis. Under the single, and in some cases highly inappropriate, name of "the Will" are merged into an ostensible identity conceptions of the most various character and the most diverse historic antecedents. The more important ingredients of the compound may fairly easily be enumerated. The Will is, in the first place, the Kantian "thing-in-itself," the residuum which is left after the object of knowledge has been robbed of all of the "subjective" forms of time and space and relatedness. It is also the Atman of the Vedantic monism, the entity which is describable solely in negative predicates, though at the same time it is declared to sum up all of the genuine reality that there is in this rich and highly colored world of our illusory experience. The Will is, again, the "Nature" of Goethe; it is the "vital force" of the late eighteenth and early nineteenth century vitalists in biology; and it is even the physical body of man and animals, in contrast with the mind. It is likewise the absolutely alogical element in reality, the "non-rational residuum," of the last period of Schelling's philosophy; and it is an apotheosis of that instinctive, naive, spontaneous, unreflective element in human nature, which had been glorified by Rousseau and, in certain of his moods, by Herder. It is Spinoza's "striving of each thing *in suo esse perseverare.*" It is the insatiable thirst for continued existence which the Buddhist psychology conceives as the ultimate power that keeps the wheel of existence in motion, and it is an hypostasis of the Nirvana in which Buddhism conceives that thirst to be extinguished.

Though thus singularly manifold, these elements are not all necessarily incongruous *inter se.* But, apart from minor discrepancies among them, they all fall into at least two groups, having attributes which obviously cannot be harmonized as characterizations of one and the same entity. The Will, in Schopenhauer, has manifestly a positive and a negative aspect: it is thought of now in concepts to which the name Will is truly pertinent, now in concepts to which that name is singularly unsuitable. In so far as the "Will" is a designation for the thing-in-itself, or for the Vedantic Absolute, it is a being which is not only

itself alien to time and to space and to all the modes of relation, unknowable, ineffable, but is also *ipso facto* incapable of accounting for, or of being manifested in, a world of manifold, individuated, striving and struggling concrete existences. It is merely the dark background of the world of experience; it is the One which remains while the many change and pass. From the point of view of the world of the many and of change, it is literally nothing. To the understanding it is necessarily as inaccessible, and, indeed, as self-contradictory and meaningless, as is the Unknowable of Herbert Spencer,—of which it is, indeed, the twin brother, not to say the identical self. This kind of negative and inexpressible Absolute is a sufficiently familiar figure in the philosophy of all periods. Schopenhauer assuredly did nothing original in reviving it. What was original in his work was that he baptized this Absolute with a new, and startlingly inappropriate, name; and that he gave it this name because, in spite of himself, he was really interested in quite another kind of "ultimate reality" of which the name was genuinely descriptive.

The other aspect of Schopenhauer's "Will" is, of course, that in which it appears, as Spencer's Unknowable intermittently appears, as a real agency or tendency in the temporal world, as a power which is not merely behind phenomena, but also is manifested *in* phenomena; and, more especially, as a blind urge towards activity, towards change. towards individuation, towards the multiplication of separate entities—each of them instinctively affirmative of its own individual existence and also of the character of its kind—towards the diversification of the modes of concrete existence, and towards a struggle for survival between these modes. When Schopenhauer speaks of the Will as a *Wille sum Leben,* it is sufficiently manifest that what he has before his mind is not in the least like the Oriental Brahm, "which is without qualities" and without relations and without change. It is, of course, true that Schopenhauer imagined that he had mitigated the baldness of the incongruity between the two aspects of the Will by calling the one reality and the other mere phenomenon, by insisting that the first sort of characterization tells us, so far as human language can, what the Will is in itself, while the second form refers only to the illusory appearance which the Will presents when apprehended by the understanding. But, as a matter of fact, it is quite clear that the characteristics of the world of phenomena, as Schopenhauer habitually thinks of it, are explicable much more largely by the nature of the Will than by the nature of the Understanding. Schopenhauer is fond of reiterating, for example, that space and time constitute the *principium individuationis;* but they are so only in the sense that they provide a means for logically defining individuality. It is very apparent that there is nothing in the abstract notion of either space or time which can explain why that pressure towards individuation, that tendency towards the multiplication of concrete conscious individuals, should exist. It is, after all, the Will that must be conceived to be responsible for its own objectification in a temporal and spatial universe; for, even from Schopenhauer's own point of view, there is nothing in the conception of the forms under which the Will gets objectified which can account for the necessity of such objectification. It was with the Will in its concrete sense, and in its restless, temporal movement, that Schopenhauer was more characteristically concerned; it was the ubiquity and fundamental significance of this trait of all existence which constituted his personal and novel *aperçu.*

Now the conception of the Will as a force or tendency at work in the world of phenomena is manifestly a conception which might have been expected to lead the author of it into an evolutionistic type of philosophy. Since the will is characterized as *ein endloses Streben,* as *ein ewiges Werden,* as *ein endloser Fluss,* and since we are told of it that "every goal which it reaches is but the starting point for a new course," its manifestations or products might, it would seem, most naturally be represented as appearing in a gradual, progressive, cumulative order. The phrase "will to live" readily, if not inevitably, suggests a steady movement from less life to more life and fuller, from lower and less adequate to higher and more adequate grades of objectification. But did Schopenhauer in fact construe his own fundamental conception in this way? An examination of his writings with this question in view makes it appear probable that at the beginning of his speculative activity he did not put an evolutionistic construction upon the conception of the Will; but it makes it very clear that in his later writings he quite explicitly and emphatically adopted such a construction, connecting with his metaphysical principles a thorough-going scheme of cosmic and organic evolution. Singularly enough, this significant change in Schopenhauer's doctrine upon a very fundamental point, has, so far as I know, not hitherto been fully set forth. Not only the most widely read histories of philosophy, but even special treatises on Schopenhauer's system, represent his attitude towards evolutionism wholly in the light of his early utterances; and even where his later expressions upon the subject are not forgotten, their plain import has often been denied, upon the assumption that they must somehow be made to harmonize with the position taken in his early and most famous treatise.

In *Die Welt als Wille und Vorstellung* Schopenhauer is preoccupied chiefly with the negative and "other-worldly" aspect of his philosophy. His emphasis may, upon the whole, be said to be laid upon the consideration that the world of objects is but an illusory presentation of the Will, rather than upon the consideration that the Will is, after all, the kind of entity that presents itself in the guise of a world of objects and of minds. With this preoccupation, Schopenhauer delights to dwell upon the timelessness of the true nature of the Will. Yet, since even in his most mystical and nihilistic moments he is obliged to remember that the Absolute does somehow take upon itself a temporal form, this emphasis upon the eternity of true being did not of itself forbid his representing the temporal side of things as a gradual process of expansion and diversification. The passages in which Schopenhauer speaks of the timelessness of the Will ought not to be quoted, as they sometimes have been quoted, as constituting in themselves any negation of a developmental conception of the world in time; for such passages are not pertinent to the world in time at all. It is rather a subsid-

iary and somewhat arbitrary detail of his system, which he uncritically took over from Schelling, that leads Schopenhauer in this period to pronounce in favor of the constancy of organic species. Between the Will as a timeless unity and the changing world of manifold phenomena he interpolates a world of Platonic Ideas, or archetypal essences of phenomena. This world, it is true, has only an ideal existence; it has, in a sense, not even the degree of reality that phenomenal objects have. But it has an important functional place in Schopenhauer's scheme of doctrine; since the Ideas, so to say, lay down the limits of diversity within which the phenomena may vary. Each individual being is in some degree different from every other, and the name of them is legion. But the generic forms, the kinds of individuals that there may be, are determined by the natures of the Ideas.

Now these Ideas relate primarily to the kinds of natural processes which Schopenhauer regards as the hierarchically ordered grades of the objectification of the Will,—mechanism, chemism, organism, etc. But it is evident that Schopenhauer also includes among the Ideas the timeless archetypes of each species of organism. Even from the fact that, upon Schopenhauerian principles, the pure form of each species is eternal, as it behooves a Platonic Idea to be, it could not necessarily be inferred by any cogent logic that the temporal copies of these forms need be changeless. Schopenhauer none the less does appear to draw, in a somewhat arbitrary manner, the inference that species must be everlasting and immutable. He writes, in the Supplement to the third book of *Die Welt als Wille und Vorstellung* (second edition, 1844):

> That which, regarded as pure form, and therefore as lifted out of all time and all relations as the Platonic Idea, is, when taken empirically and as in time, the species; thus the species is the empirical correlate of the Idea. The Idea is, in the strict sense, eternal, while the species is merely everlasting (*die Idee ist eigentlich ewig, die Art aber von unendlicher Dauer*), although the manifestation of a species may become extinct upon any one planet.

So again (in the chapter on "The Life of the Species," *ibid.,* chapter 42) Schopenhauer writes:

> This desire [of the individuals of a species to maintain and perpetuate the characteristic form of their species], regarded from without and under the form of time, shows itself in the maintenance of that same animal form throughout infinite time (*als solche Tiergestalt eine endlose Zeit hindurch erhalten*) by means of the continual replacement of each individual of that species by another;—shows itself, in other words, in that alternation of death and birth which, so regarded, seems only the pulse-beat of that form (. . . *species*) which remains constant throughout all time (*jener durch alle Zeit beharrenden Gestalt*).

These passages seem to be fairly clear in their affirmation of the essential invariability of species.

In *Der Wille in der Natur* in 1854 we find Schopenhauer passing a partly unfavorable criticism upon Lamarck, which at first sight undeniably reads as if he at that date still retained the non-evolutionistic position of his earlier treatise. He has been asserting that the adaptive characters of organisms are to be explained neither by design on the part of a creative artificer, nor yet by the mere shaping of the organism by its environment, but rather through the will or inner tendency of the organism, which somehow causes it to have the organs which it requires in order to cope with its environment. "The animal's structure has been determined by the mode of life by which the animal desired to find its sustenance and not *vice versa.* . . . The huntsman does not aim at the wild boar because he happens to have a rifle: he took the rifle with him, and not a fowling piece, because he intended to hunt boars; and the ox does not butt because it happens to have horns, it has horns because it intends to butt." This, of course, sounds very much like a bit of purely Lamarckian biology; and Schopenhauer is not unmindful of the similarity.

> This truth forces itself upon thoughtful zoologists and anatomists with such cogency that, unless their mind is purified by a deeper philosophy, it may lead them into strange error. Now this actually happened to a very eminent zoologist, the immortal De Lamarck, who has acquired undying fame by his discovery of the classification of animals into vertebrates and invertebrates, so admirable in profundity; for he quite seriously maintains and tries to prove at length that the shape of each animal species, the weapons peculiar to it, and its organs of every sort adapted for outward use, were by no means present at the origin of that species, but have, on the contrary, come into being gradually *in the course of time* and through continued generation, in consequence of the exertions of the animal's will, evoked by the nature of its situation and environment,—i. e., through its own repeated efforts and the habits to which these gave rise.

Schopenhauer then goes on to urge certain purely biological objections, which may for the moment be passed over, to what he conceives to be the Lamarckian hypothesis. The most serious misconception on Lamarck's part, however, he declares to arise from an incapacity for metaphysical insight, due to the unfortunate circumstance that that naturalist was a Frenchman.

> De Lamarck's hypothesis arose out of a very correct and profound view of nature; it is an error of genius, which, in spite of all its absurdity, yet does honor to its originator. The true part of it should be set down to the credit of Lamarck himself, as a scientific inquirer; he saw rightly that the primary element which has determined the animal's organization is the will of the animal itself. The false part of it must be laid to the account of the backward state of metaphysics in France, where the views of Locke and his feeble follower, Condillac, still hold their ground, and where, accordingly, bodies are supposed to be things in themselves, and where the great doctrine of the ideality of space and time and of all that is represented in them. . . . has not yet penetrated. De Lamarck, therefore, could not conceive his construction of living beings otherwise than as in time and succession. . . .

> The thought could not occur to him that the animal's will, as a thing in itself, might lie outside time, and in that sense be prior to the animal itself. Therefore he assumes the animal to have first been without any clearly defined organs, and indeed without any clearly defined tendencies, and to have been equipped only with perceptions. . . . But this primary animal is, in truth, the Will to Live; as such, however, it is metaphysical, not physical. Most certainly the shape and organization of each animal species has been determined by its own will according to the circumstances in which it needed to live; not, however, as a thing physical, in time, but on the contrary as a thing metaphysical, out of time.

As it stands this passage, apart from its context, unquestionably is most naturally interpreted as a rejection, not merely of the details of Lamarck's hypothesis, but also of the general doctrine of a gradual transformation of species in time. Its import has been so understood by a number of expositors of Schopenhauer. Thus Kuno Fischer writes [in *Arthur Schopenhauer*, 1893]: "Schopenhauer blames De Lamarck for representing animal species as evolved through a genetic and historical process, instead of conceiving of them after the Platonic manner." So Rádl [in *Geschichte der biologischen Theorien*]: "Schopenhauer speaks in praise only of the Lamarckian doctrine that the will is the cause of organic forms; Lamarck's genetic philosophy, on the other hand, he rejects." But these writers have neglected to observe that, only a few pages later in the same treatise, Schopenhauer sets down an unequivocal though brief affirmation of the origination of species from one another through descent; and does so on the ground that without such an hypothesis the unity of plan manifest in the skeletal structure of great numbers of diverse species would remain unintelligible. In other words, Schopenhauer argues in favor of transformism by pointing to one of the most important and familiar evidences of the truth of the theory of descent, *viz.,* the homologies in the inner structure of all the vertebrates. In the neck of the giraffe, for example, (he remarks) we find, prodigiously elongated, the same number of vertebrae which we find in the neck of the mole contracted so as to be scarcely recognizable. This unity of plan, argues Schopenhauer, requires to be accounted for; and it can *not* be accounted for as one of the aspects of the general adaptation of organisms to their environment. For that adaptation might in many cases have been as well, or better, realized by means of a greater diversity in the architectural schemes of species having diverse environments and instincts.

> This *common anatomical factor* (*Element*) which, as has been already mentioned, remains constant and unchangeable, is so far an enigma,—namely, in that it does not come within the teleological explanation, which only begins after that basis is assumed. For in many cases a given organ might have been equally well adapted to its purpose even with a different number and arrangement of bones. . . . We must assume, therefore, that this common anatomical factor is due, partly to the unity and identity of the Will to Live in general, partly to the fact that the original forms of the various animals have arisen one out of another (*dass die Urformen der Tiere eine aus der andern*

hervorgegangen sind), and that it is for this reason that the fundamental type of the whole line of descent (*Stamm*) has been preserved.

And Schopenhauer himself adds a reference to a passage in the **Parerga and Paralipomena** (to be examined below) in which, at much greater length, his own particular form of organic evolutionism is expounded.

Now, abundant in contradictions though Schopenhauer was, it is difficult to suppose that he can have expressed, within half a dozen pages, diametrically opposed views upon a perfectly definite and concrete question of natural science, in which he manifestly took an especial interest,—and that he can, in spite of his habit of carefully revising each edition of his works, have left such a piece of obvious self-contradiction standing in the final version of **Der Wille in der Natur**. If, now, bearing this in mind, we revert to the criticism of Lamarck which has not unnaturally misled hasty readers of Schopenhauer, we shall see that what is criticized is *not* necessarily the doctrine of the derivation of species from earlier species by descent, but only a specific theory of the manner in which "the Will" works in the formation of species. Lamarck, at least as Schopenhauer understood him, placed behind every organ or function of all animals, as its cause and temporal antecedent, a *felt* need, a conscious desire, leading it to the activities by means of which that organ is developed. To this Schopenhauer objects, in the first place, that the hypothesis implies that if we should go back to the beginning of the series of animals we should come to a time in which the ancestor of all the animals existed *without any organs or functions at. all,* in the form of a *mere* need, a desire pure and simple;—which implication he regards as reducing the hypothesis to an absurdity. This is an entirely pertinent criticism upon Lamarck's explanation of specific characters as the results of use and disuse of organs, in so far as that explanation is taken as the sole explanation. The criticism applies, not only to the origination of animal organs and functions in general, but also to the origination of any particular class of organs and functions. It is difficult to see how an animal, yearn it never so strongly, can develop an organ out of its needs merely as such; or how it can modify by use or disuse a type of organ of which it is not yet in possession. Given the rudiments of an eye, with a specific visual sensibility, and it is at least abstractly conceivable that the persistent utilization of such a rudimentary organ might somehow lead to its further development; but some sort of eye must necessarily first be given. In other words, Lamarckianism (as apprehended by Schopenhauer) did not sufficiently recognize that the primary thing in species-forming must be the appearance (through obscure embryogenetic processes with which conscious needs and desires can have nothing to do) of suitable congenital variations. The essence of Lamarck's error, as Schopenhauer sees it, is that, according to the French naturalist, "it is the will which arises out of knowledge," i. e., out of the animal's temporally antecedent consciousness of its own need; whereas, in fact, "the will did not proceed from the intellect, nor did the intellect exist, together with the animal, before the will made its appearance." We cannot even say

Schopenhauer as a young man.

that the will, in the sense of a definite concrete volition, existed before the production of the organ requisite to make the fulfilment of the given kind of volition possible in an animal species. In short, Schopenhauer's doctrine was that the timeless Will, working in time in the form of a blind purposiveness, gives rise to the organs and the potencies of new species by producing new congenital characters *before* any felt need for and endeavor after those characters have arisen; while Lamarck's doctrine, as Schopenhauer believed, was that an actual (though doubtless vague) awareness of need, and a concrete movement of conation, temporally precede the production of each new character or organ. The two doctrines were really distinct; but (as will presently more fully appear) the one was as definitely evolutionistic as the other.

It was, furthermore, an objection in Schopenhauer's eyes to Lamarck's theory (and would have doubtless been urged by him as an objection to the Darwinian theory) that it supposed species to have been formed by the gradual enlargement and accumulation of characters too small and trivial at their first emergence to be functionally significant, or useful in the struggle for survival. He says,

> Lamarck overlooks the obvious objection. . . . that, long before the organs necessary for an animal's preservation could have been produced by such endeavors as these carried on through countless generations, the whole species must have died out from the want of them.

Schopenhauer, after his definite adoption of evolutionism, always insisted not only upon the primacy of the fact of variation in the explanation both of species-form and of adaptation, but also upon the doctrine that, though one species descends from another, it descends *ready-made.* In other words—and in twentieth-century words—Schopenhauer was, in his view concerning species, a mutationist, though one of a somewhat extreme and peculiar sort.

In interpreting the bearing of Schopenhauer's comments on Lamarck in *The Will in Nature* I have, of course, been guided not only by the context of that passage, but also by the passage in the *Parerga and Paralipomena* to which, as has been mentioned, he himself refers his reader for a fuller exposition of his views on the question of species. The latter passage occurs in the small treatise (Chapter VI of *Parerga and Paralipomena*) entitled *Zur Philosophie und Wissenschaft der Natur,* perhaps the most important of its author's later writings, but one which has been amazingly neglected by the historians of philosophy and even by writers of special monographs on Schopenhauer. With the publication of this work (1850) he quite unmistakably announced—what remained his final view—that the philosophy of nature to which his metaphysics of the Will properly led was of a frankly and completely evolutionistic type. Since this part of the *Parerga and Paralipomena* (unlike most of the rest of that collection) has, so far as I know, never been done into English, I shall, in setting forth the teachings of it, for the most part simply give a translation of Schopenhauer's own words.

Organic life originated, Schopenhauer declares, by a *generatio aequivoca* of the organic (under certain definite physical conditions) out of the, inorganic; indeed, he believed, with singular scientific naïveté, that spontaneous generation is an everyday occurrence, taking place "before our eyes in the sprouting of fungi from decaying vegetable matter." But only the simplest forms can have been thus produced.

Generatio aequivoca cannot be conceived to occur in the higher grades of the animal kingdom as it does in the lowest. The form of the lion, the wolf, the elephant, the ape, or that of man, cannot have originated as do the infusoria, the entozoa and epizoa;—cannot have arisen directly from the sea-slime coagulated and warmed by the sun, nor from decaying organic substances. The genesis of these higher forms can be conceived of only as a *generatio in utero heterogeneo,*—such that from the womb, or rather from the egg, of some especially favored pair of animals, when the life-force of their species was in them raised to an abnormal potency, at a time when the positions of the planets and all the atmospheric, telluric and astral influences were favorable, there arose, exceptionally, no longer a being of the same kind as its parents, but one which, though of a closely allied kind, yet constituted a form standing one degree higher in the scale. In such a case the parent would for once have produced not merely an individual but a species. Processes of this sort naturally can have taken place only after the lowest animals had appeared in the usual manner and had prepared the ground for the coming races of animals.

The reader will observe in the account of the conditions requisite for the production of these exceptional births traces of Schopenhauer's queer weakness for occultism; but the condition which he chiefly insists upon is less remote from the range of conceptions sanctioned by modern natural science. The productive potency of organisms, "which is only a special form of the generative power of nature as a whole," undergoes this "abnormal heightening" when it encounters antagonistic forces, conditions tending to restrict or destroy it; "it grows with opposition." This tendency, for example, manifests itself in the human race in times of war, pestilence, natural catastrophes, and the like; and in such periods of special intensification of the power of reproduction, that power, Schopenhauer seems to conceive, shows also a greater instability and variability, a tendency to the production of new forms which thereafter remain constant. Now, says Schopenhauer,—adopting the geological system of Cuvier,—a renewal of life through *generatio aequivoca,* followed by an increasing multiplication of diverse descendant species, must have taken place "after each of those great revolutions of the earth, which have at least thrice extinguished all life upon the globe so that it required to be produced anew, each time with more perfect forms, i. e., with forms more nearly approximating our existing fauna. But only in the series of animals that have come into being subsequently to the last of these great catastrophes, did the process rise to the pitch of producing the human race,—though the apes had already made their appearance in the preceding epoch."

We have seen Schopenhauer in *The Will in Nature* declaring in favor of the theory of descent on the ground that it affords the only possible explanation of the homologies of the skeletons of the vertebrates. In the present writing he still more emphatically declares in favor of it on the ground of the argument from recapitulation,—of the parallelism of the ontogenetic and the phylogenetic series.

The batrachians visibly go through an existence as fishes before they assume their characteristic final form, and, according to a now fairly generally accepted observation, all embryos pass successively through the forms of lower species before attaining to that of their own. Why, then, should not every new and higher species have originated through the development of some embryo into a form just one degree higher than the form of the mother that conceived it? This is the only reasonable, i. e., the only rationally thinkable, mode of origination of species that can be imagined.

Schopenhauer was thus, as I have already said, not only an evolutionist in his biology but also a mutationist; his speculations are prophetic of the theory of De Vries rather than that of Darwin. But the scale on which he supposed these "discontinuous variations" to occur is calculated to make our contemporary mutationists stare and gasp; the changes of form which he assumed are saltatory indeed. He writes:

We are not to conceive of this ascent as following a single line, but rather as mounting along several lines side by side. At one time, for example, from the egg of a fish an ophidian, and afterwards from the latter a saurian arose; but from some other fish's egg was produced a batrachian, from one of the latter subsequently a chelonian; from a third fish arose a cetacean, possibly a dolphin, some cetacean subsequently giving birth to a seal, and a seal finally to a walrus. Perhaps the duckbill came from the egg of a duck, and from that of an ostrich some one of the larger mammals. In any case, the process must have gone on simultaneously and independently in many different regions, yet everywhere with equally sharp and definite gradations, each giving rise to a persistent and stable species. It cannot have taken place by gradual, imperceptible transitions.

The implication with respect to the simian descent of man Schopenhauer does not shirk:

> We not wish to conceal from ourselves the fact that, in accordance with the foregoing, we should have to think of the first men as born in Asia from the pongo (whose young are called orangoutangs) and in Africa from the chimpanzee—though born men, and not apes. . . . The human species probably originated in three places, since we know only three distinct types which point to an original diversity of race—the Caucasian, the Mongolian and the Ethiopian type. The genesis of man can have taken place only in the old world. For in Australia Nature has been unable to produce any apes, and in America she has produced only long-tailed monkeys, not the short-tailed, to say nothing of the highest, i. e., the tailless apes, which represent the next stage before man. *Natura non facit saltus.* Moreover, man can have originated only in the tropics; for in any other zones the newly generated human being would have perished in the first winter. . . . Now in the torrid zones man is black, or at least dark brown. This, therefore, without regard to diversities of race is the true, natural and distinctive color of the human species; and there has never existed a race white by nature.

Schopenhauer does not leave us without a hint as to the writer from whom he learned his evolutionism; though—never generous in his acknowledgments, and always prepared to think the worst of the English—he is a good deal more copious in criticism than in appreciation of that writer.

> The conception of a *generatio in utero heterogenco* which has here been expounded was first put forward by the anonymous author of the *Vestiges of the Natural History of Creation* (6th ed., 1817), though by no means with adequate clearness and definiteness. For he has entangled it with untenable assumptions and gross errors, which are due in the last analysis to the fact that to him, as an Englishman, every assumption which rises above the merely physical—everything metaphysical, in short—is forthwith confused with the Hebraic theism, in the effort to escape which, on the other hand, he gives an undue extension to the domain of the physical. Thus an Englishman, in his indifference and complete barbarism with respect to all speculative philosophy or metaphysics, is actually incapable of any spiritual (*geistig*) view of Nature; he knows no

middle ground between a conception of it as operating of itself according to rigorous and, so far as possible, mechanical laws, and a conception of it as manufactured according to a preconceived design by that Hebrew God whom he speaks of as its "Maker." The parsons, the English parsons, those slyest of all obscurantists, are responsible for this state of things.

This can scarcely be considered a very clear and coherent criticism of Robert Chambers. But the passage makes it appear highly probable that it was through becoming acquainted, late in the eighteen-forties, with the mutationist evolutionism of Chambers's *Vestiges,* that Schopenhauer was led to adopt and to develop in his own fashion a similar doctrine.

These transformist opinions in biology were, in the treatise *Zur Philosophic und Wissenschaft der Nature,* merely a part of a thorough-going scheme of evolutionism, which included a belief in the development of the chemical elements out of an original undifferentiated *Urstoff,* in the gradual formation of the solar system, and in an evolutionary geology. His cosmogony Schopenhauer takes over from Laplace. The general outlines of the history of our planet, as he conceives them in the light of the geology of Cuvier, are set forth in a passage which is interesting enough to be worth quoting at length:

> The relation of the latest results of geology to my metaphysics may be briefly set forth as follows: In the earliest period of the globe, that preceding the formation of the granitic rocks, the objectification of the Will to Live was restricted to its lowest phases—i. e., to the forces of inorganic nature—though in these it manifested itself on the most gigantic scale and with blind impetuosity. For the already differentiated chemical elements broke out in a conflict whose scene was not merely the surface but the entire mass of the planet, a struggle of which the phenomena must have been so colossal as to baffle the imagination. . . . When this war of the Titans had spent its rage, and the granite rocks, like gravestones, had covered the combatants, the Will to Live, after a suitable pause and an interlude in which marine deposits were formed, manifested itself in its next higher stage—a stage in sharpest contrast with the preceding—namely, in the dumb and silent life of a purely plant-world. . . . This plant-world gradually absorbed carbon from the atmosphere, which was thus for the first time made capable of sustaining animal life. Until this was sufficiently accomplished, the long and profound peace of that world without animals continued. At length a great revolution of Nature put an end to this paradise of plants and engulfed its vast forests. Now that the air had been purified, the third great stage of the objectification of the Will began, with the appearance of the animal world: in the sea, fishes and cetaceans; on land, only reptilia, though those were of colossal size. Again the curtain fell upon the cosmic stage; and now followed a still higher objectification of the Will in the life of warm-blooded animals,—although these were chiefly pachydermata of genera now extinct. After another destruction of the surface of the globe, with all the living things upon it, life flamed up anew, and the Will to Live objectified itself in a world of animals exhibiting a far greater number and diversity of forms,

of which the genera, though not the species, are still extant. This more complete objectification of the Will to Live through so great a multiplicity and variety of forms reached as high as the apes. But even this, the world just before ours, must needs perish, in order that the present population of the globe might find place upon fresh ground. And now the objectification of the Will reached the stage of humanity.

An interesting incidental consideration, in view of all this, is that the planets which circle round the countless suns in all space—even though some of them may be still in the merely chemical stage, the scene of that frightful conflict of the crudest forces of Nature, while others may be in the quiet of the peaceful interlude— yet all contain within themselves those secret potencies from which the world of plants and animals must soon or late break forth in all the multiplicity of its forms. ... But the final stage, that of humanity, once reached, must in my opinion be the last, for this brings with it the possibility of the negation of the Will, whereby there comes about a reversal of the whole inner tendency of existence (*der Umkehr vom ganzen Trciben*). And thus this *Divina Commedia* reaches its end. Consequently, even if there were no physical reasons which made certain a new world-catastrophe, there is, at all events, a moral reason, namely, that the world's continuance would be purposeless after the inmost essence of it has no longer need of any higher stage of objectification in order to make its deliverance (*Erlösung*) possible.

It is thus clear that by 1850 Schopenhauer had reformulated his conception of the "objectification of the Will" in thoroughly evolutionistic terms and had incorporated into his philosophy a complete system of cosmogony and phylogeny. It was at about the same time that Herbert Spencer was beginning to imagine the outlines and primary principles of the *Synthetic Philosophy,* which has commonly passed for the first comprehensive attempt by any nineteenth-century philosopher to generalize the conception of evolution and to give to it the principal role in his system. The two doctrines may, in truth, not uninstructively be set side by side. They exhibit, in the first place, a degree of resemblance which is likely to be overlooked by those who can not discern, beneath diversities of terminology and of emphasis, identities of logical essence. In both systems, for example, the ultimate nature of things is placed beyond the reach of temporal becoming. Spencer's evolutionary process belongs only to the realm of "the knowable," Schopenhauer's to the world of the Will as objectified behind the one stands, as true reality, the Unconditioned, alien to all the characters of human experience and all the conceptions of human thought; behind the other stands the Will as it is in itself, timeless, indivisible, ineffable. In other words, both systems consist of an evolutionary philosophy of nature projected against the background of an essentially mystical and negative metaphysics. Yet each, as I have already remarked, regards its supratemporal and indeterminate Absolute as the very substance and sum of the world in time; and each is prone to the same inconsistency, that of practically treating this same Absolute as the real ground and explanation of becoming and as a power at work in

the temporal movement of things. In the degree of emphasis which they lay upon this negative element in their doctrine, the two philosophers, no doubt, greatly differ. Spencer closes the door upon it after half a dozen chapters, and then forgets it for whole books at a time,— reverting to it only at the moments when his logic seems, in the deduction of the laws of "the knowable," to be on the point of breaking down.

Schopenhauer, too, can forget the obscure background of existence when he is absorbed in the concrete phenomena of evolution; but he takes it, on the whole, more seriously, and draws the veil from before it more frequently. And the more closely Kantian affinities of his epistemology create for him a difficulty in adjusting his evolutionism to his metaphysics which Spencer seemingly escapes,—though he escapes it only by an evasion. Since, for Schopenhauer, space and time are subjective forms of perception, premental evolution, the formation of planetary systems and of planets themselves before the emergence of consciousness, necessarily has for him an especially equivocal ontological status.

> The geological processes which took place before there was any life on earth were present in no consciousness;. ... from lack of a subject, therefore, they had a merely objective existence, i. e., they were not at all. But what is meant then by speaking of their having been (*Dagewesensein*)? The expression is at bottom purely hypothetical, it means that *if* any consciousness had been present in that primeval period, it *would have* then observed those processes. To them the regress of phenomena leads us back; and it therefore lay in the nature of the thing in itself to manifest itself in such processes [i. e., if there had been any consciousness for it to manifest itself to].

When Spencer declares that our conceptions of space and time are modes of thought produced *in us* somehow by the Unconditioned, but not ascribable to that entity itself, he involves himself in a similar difficulty about early geological time, and implies an identical way of dealing with the difficulty; but so far as, I can recall, he does not anywhere directly face the question.

The points of resemblance between the system of Schopenhauer and that of Spencer, however, consist chiefly in the general fact that both were evolutionists, and that their evolutionist cosmology had much the same sort of metaphysical setting. In its spirit, as in its details, Schopenhauer's evolutionism was essentially different from Spencer's. He is, but for some faint foreshadowings in the philosophy of certain of the Romantics, the first representative of a tendency in evolutionistic philosophy that is essentially hostile to the tendency of which Spencer is the representative. Spencer's enterprise is neither more nor less than a resumption of that which Descartes had undertaken in 1633, in his suppressed treatise on "The World"; the nineteenth-century philosopher, like the one of the seventeenth century, conceives it possible to deduce from the laws of the motion of the parts of a conservative material system the necessity for the gradual development of such a world as we now find. Spencer's evolutionism, in short, is, or rather attempts to be, thoroughly mechanistic. And in the course of the whole process, therefore, (though Spencer frequently forgets this) no real novelties can appear except novelties in the spatial arrangement of the particles of matter. Even these novelties are only the completely predetermined consequences of the sum of matter and energy originally present in the universe, and of the laws of relative motion. The whole cosmic history is solely a process of redistribution of matter and change of direction in motion. It is for this reason that M. Bergson is fond of saying of Spencer that his system contains nothing that really has to do with either becoming or evolution; "he had promised to trace out a genesis, but he has done something quite different; his doctrine is an evolutionism only in name."

Schopenhauer's evolutionism of the ever-expanding, self-multiplying Will, however, is radically anti-mechanistic. For it the universe, even the physical universe, can not be a changeless closed system, in which no truly new content ever emerges. The primary characteristic of the Will is that it is never satisfied with the attained, and therefore ever goes on to further attainment. Its objectification, in the latest phase of Schopenhauer's thought, becomes necessarily progressive and cumulative. In short, a philosophy which conceives the genesis and movement of the temporal world in terms of the Will necessarily gives a very different account of the biography of the cosmos from that presented by a philosophy which aspires to tell the whole story in terms of mechanics and in accord with the principle that the ultimate content of nature never suffers increase or diminution. This latter program Spencer, it is true, realizes very imperfectly. In the later volumes of the *Synthetic Philosophy the First Principles* seem often pretty completely forgotten. There are not a few strains of what may be called the romantic type of evolutionism in Spencer. But in him these strains are incongruous with the primary postulate of his system; in Schopenhauer they are the characteristic note of the whole doctrine.

This contrast between the two types of evolutionism found in these two writers is due in part to certain features in their respective doctrines which arose without dependence upon their evolutionism. They had essentially opposed preconceptions about the program and possibilities of science. Spencer was from his youth obsessed with the grandiose idea of a unification of all knowledge. All truths were eventually to be brought under some "highest generalization which is true not of one class of phenomena, but of all classes of phenomena, and which is thus the key to all classes of phenomena." This, of course, meant the theoretical possibility of the reduction of the more complex sciences to the simpler ones—of physiology to chemistry, of chemistry to physics, and of all physics to the mechanics of molecules. This intellectual process of explanation of the more complex by the simpler and more generalized type of phenomena was the counterpart, and in truth a necessary implication, of the objective process of evolution of simple into more complex arrangements of the matter of the universe. Schopenhauer, on the other hand, from the beginning insisted upon the irreducibility

of the several sciences to one another, and most emphatically upon the uniqueness and autonomy of biology. When science, he writes, "in the quest for causal explanations (aetiology) declares that it is its goal to eliminate all ultimate forces except one, the most general of all (for example, impenetrability) which science flatters itself upon thoroughly understanding: and when, accordingly, it seeks to reduce (*zurückzuführen*) by violence all other forces to this single force, it then destroys its own foundation and can yield only error instead of truth. If it were actually possible to attain success by following this course, the riddle of the universe would finally find its solution in a mathematical calculation. It is this course that people follow when they endeavor to trace back physiological effects to the form and composition of the organism, this perhaps to electricity, this in turn to chemism, and this finally to mechanism." Just why Schopenhauer adopted this doctrine of the irreducibility and discontinuity of scientific laws at a period when he apparently had not adopted evolutionism, is not wholly clear. He seems to have been partly led to such a view by his conception of the Platonic Ideas. Since for each of the broad divisions of science, which correspond to grades of objectification of the Will, there is a separate Idea, Schopenhauer seems to have felt that the distinctness of the several Ideas forbade the supposition of the complete reducibility of the laws of one science to those of a prior one. But inasmuch as the whole notion of the Platonic Ideas is a logically irrelevant part of the Schopenhauerian system, this explanation does not carry us very far. Whatever his reasons, the fact remains that Schopenhauer attached the utmost importance to his contention that, at the points where one typical phase of the Will's self-manifestation passes over into a higher one, new modes of action, essentially different kinds of being, must be recognized. Consequently, when he eventually arranged the grades of the Will's objectification in a serial, temporal order, thus converting his system into an evolutionism, this contention made his evolutionism one which implied the repeated production of absolute novelties in the universe, and the supervention from time to time of natural laws supplementary to, if not contradictory of, the laws or generalizations pertinent to the phenomena of a lower order.

Another detail of Schopenhauer's body of doctrine which likewise antedates the evolutionistic transformation of his system but yet has an important relation to certain subsequent developments in the philosophy of evolution, was his peculiar form of teleology. He was equally opposed, on the one hand, to the conception of design as an explanation of the adaptive characters of organisms, and on the other hand to the mechanistic elimination of all purposiveness from nature. Between these two extremes he endeavored to find room for a teleology dissociated from anthropomorphism. The Will moves towards ends determined by its own inner nature, though it does not foresee these ends. It triumphs over obstacles in its way, and circumvents obstructions; but it does so blindly and without conscious devices. This notion of a blind purposiveness, which more than any other philosopher Schopenhauer may be said to have introduced into the current of European philosophy, has come in our own day to be a familiar conception in the interpretation of the meaning of evolution, especially in its biological phase. Here again Schopenhauer is the precursor of Bergson. That contemporary too rejects what he calls *le finalisme radical* not less than the radical mechanistic doctrine, while insisting upon the indispensability of some notion of finality in any attempt to comprehend the development of organisms. From this point of view Bergson has objected, upon grounds altogether similar to those which have been noted in Schopenhauer's reference to Lamarck, to the Lamarckian tendency to identify the cause of the production of new characters with "a conscious effort of the individual"; while he at the same time regards Lemarekianism as approaching far nearer than does Darwinism with its essentially mechanistic interpretation of organic evolution to a correct representation of the developmental process. Like Schopenhauer, M. Bergson adopts, as the biological theory most congenial to his metaphysics of the *poussée vitale,* a combination of the doctrines of orthogenesis and of mutation. The later writer may or may not have been influenced by the earlier one, but there can be no doubt that in Schopenhauer we find the first emphatic affirmation of the three conceptions most characteristic of the biological philosophy of *L'évolution créatrice.*

It is a somewhat curious circumstance that the trait in Schopenhauer's conception of the action of the "objectified" Will which has hitherto most attracted the notice of writers on the history of biology is closely related to the fundamental conception of precisely that sort of organic evolutionism to which he was most opposed. The universal prevalence of a struggle for existence among organisms was eloquently set forth by Schopenhauer forty years before Darwin published the *Origin of Species.* But it seems never to have occurred to Schopenhauer to regard this struggle as an explanation of the formation of species and the adaptation of organisms to their environments. Why he was unlikely to do so is evident from all that has been already said. The Darwinian hypothesis makes of species and their adaptive characteristics merely the result of a sort of mechanical pressure of external forces. Slight promiscuous variations, due probably to fortuitous displacements in the molecules of the germ-cell, are conserved or eliminated in the course of the jostle for survival, according as they do or do not fit the individuals possessing them to keep a footing in that turmoil. But such a doctrine assigns to the organism itself, and to its inner potencies, an essentially passive rôle; development is, as it were, extorted from living things by external circumstances, and is not a tendency expressive of all that is most characteristic in the nature of organisms as such. The metaphysician whose ruling conception was that of a cosmic life-force was debarred by the dominant temper of his thought and the deepest tendency of his system from any such account of the causes and the meaning of that progressive diversification of the forms of life, the reality of which he clearly recognized. Thus, though Schopenhauer incidentally shows certain affinities with Darwinism, he is much more truly to be regarded as the protagonist in nineteenth century philosophy—at just the time when Darwin was elaborating a mechanical biology and Spencer a would-be mechanistic cosmogony—of that oth-

er form of evolutionism which [M. René Berthelot] has described as "a sort of generalized vitalism. He was thus the first important representative of the tendency which, diversely combined with other philosophical motives, and expressed with varying degrees of logical coherency, has been chiefly represented since his time by such writers as Nietzsche, Bernard Shaw, Guyau, E. D. Fawcett, and Bergson. The romantic evolutionism of all these writers is, it is true, innocent of the pessimistic coloring of Schopenhauer's philosophy; but the pessimism of Schopenhauer was always connected rather with those preconceptions in his doctrine which were really survivals from older systems, than with that vision of the Will as creatively at work in the temporal universe which was his real contribution to the modern world's stock of metaphysical ideas. When his philosophy had been converted, as we have seen that it was converted even by himself, into an evolutionism, it was already ripe for the elimination of the pessimistic strain.

Irwin Edman (essay date 1928)

SOURCE: An introduction to *The Philosophy of Schopenhauer,* edited by Irwin Edman, The Modern Library, 1928, pp. v-xiv.

[*Edman has edited works by Plato, Schopenhauer, and John Dewey. In the following excerpt, Edman comments on Schopenhauer's writing style and popular appeal.*]

The popularity of Schopenhauer with a large unacademic public is easily explained. Part of the explanation is to be found in the extraordinarily vivacious and luxurious discourse that was his medium. He is one of the great German prose writers, and even in translation there is the tang of sense, the pungency of realistic observation in his pages. But there is something more. He seems to the reflective layman to have hit upon the inner essence and divined the essential tragedy of human existence. His philosophy is not the closet dialectic of the schools, though even in the dialectical branches of thought he is nobody's fool; it is philosophy in the old and appealing meaning of wisdom of life. The plain man here recognises something he has long felt and never articulated. This philosophy is the alert, half-sad, half-cynical harvest of a candid eye. That is why lawyers and men of the world, acquainted with the disillusioned realms of experience, why adolescents just waking up from their own dreams, have found in Schopenhauer a philosophy they could feel at home with. Schopenhauer's philosophy is the Pathétique Symphony of nineteenth-century thought. Like that popular piece of musical *Weltschmerz,* it has its limitations. These any technical student of philosophy is free to point out, as is also any classical critic of the romantic temperament. There is at once in [Schopenhauer's writing] a high hand with the philosophical respectabilities and a soft luxuriance with grief that are the despair of the sober technician in philosophy and the reposeful classicists in literature. But below the carelessness of technique and the irony and pity there is a high, impeccable and irrefutable insight. The Western world has nowhere found a more complete exposition of the essence of things as it appears to those who live by impulse, and the tragedy of things for those who know that impulse must always be partially frustrated, and the life that generates impulse ultimately doomed. Instead of trying, as so many philosophers have tried, to resolve the discords of experience into a smooth and illusory coherence, Schopenhauer faced those discords and built his philosophy upon them. This disillusioning feat of picturesque honesty has impressed those who have found most other philosophies systems of obscure optimism. . . .

He was the first one, too, in the history of thought emphatically to insist on the primacy of will over intellect, on the instrumental character of mind in life and in philosophy. He started a movement to which James, Bergson, and Dewey owe not a little. And he combines in his writings the elements of three usually distinct and disparate personalities, a man of the world, a man of thought, and a man of letters. The net result in his case was one of the unparalleled works of art in the history of philosophy; *The World as Will and Idea* remains a piece of speculative literature by a writer with the imagination of a poet and the precision of an observing realist. It was his imagination that, borrowing its materials from Kantian idealism, constructed a highly romantic metaphysical world; it was his realism that gave him a sense of the suffering, injustices, and disillusions of life. It is this combination that has made him appeal at once to the perpetual adolescence of life and to hard-headed middle-aged realists. He remains one of the very great second-raters in the history of European thought, and a permanent exposition of that mood which beginning with the self frets at an unsatisfactory cosmos, and in the midst of which it does not seek what seems impossible happiness, but from which it tries to escape to a heaven of quietude and peace. It is a quaint irony that Schopenhauer, at heart a cynical epicurean, should have become the *vade mecum* of the Æsthete and the spiritual ascetic. In whatever quarrels one may find with his philosophy, his prose will always remain immitigably convincing.

Will Durant on Schopenhauer's writing style:

What strikes the reader at once upon opening *The World as Will and Idea* is its style. Here is no Chinese puzzle of Kantian terminology, no Hegelian obfuscation, no Spinozist geometry; everything is clarity and order; and all is admirably centered about the leading conception of the world as will, and therefore strife, and therefore misery. What blunt honesty, what refreshing vigor, what uncompromising directness! Where his predecessors are abstract to the point of invisibility, with theories that give out few windows of illustration upon the actual world, Schopenhauer, like the son of a business man, is rich in the concrete, in examples, in applications, even in humor. After Kant, humor in philosophy was a startling innovation.

Will Durant, in The Story of Philosophy, *Pocket Library, 1933.*

Thomas Mann (essay date 1939)

SOURCE: "Schopenhauer," in *Essays of Three Decades,* translated by H. T. Lowe-Porter, Alfred A. Knopf, 1947, pp. 372-410.

[*Mann was a German novelist, short story and novella writer, essayist, and critic who acknowledged a deep indebtedness to Schopenhauer's philosophy. In the following essay, Mann overviews Schopenhauer's metaphysics, ethics, and aesthetics and evaluates their historical significance.*]

The Pleasure we take in a metaphysical system, the gratification purveyed by the intellectual organization of the world into a closely reasoned, complete, and balanced structure of thought, is always of a pre-eminently Æsthetic kind. It flows from the same source as the joy, the high and ever happy satisfaction we get from art, with its power to shape and order its material, to sort out life's manifold confusions so as to give us a clear and general view.

Truth and beauty must always be referred the one to the other. Each by itself, without the support given by the other, remains a very fluctuating value. Beauty that has not truth on its side and cannot have reference to it, does not live in it and through it, would be an empty chimera— and "What is truth?" Our conceptions, created out of the phenomenal world, out of a highly conditioned point of view, are, as a critical and discriminating philosophy admits, applicable in an immanent, not in a transcendent sense. The subject-matter of our thinking, and indeed the judgments we build up on it, are inadequate as a means of grasping the essence of things in themselves, the true essence of the world and of life. Even the most convinced and convincing, the most deeply experienced definition of that which underlies the manifestation, does not avail to get at the root of things and draw it to the light. What alone encourages the spirit of man in his persistent effort to do this is the necessary assumption that our own very being, the deepest thing in us, has the same universal basis, that it must of necessity root therein; and that accordingly we may be able to draw from it some data wherewith to clarify the relation of the world of phenomena with the true essence of things.

That sounds modest. It is not far removed from the Faustian "and see that we can nothing know!" And all the bumptiousness of philosophy with its "intellectual point of view" and "absolute thought" sounds like *hubris* and silly bounce beside it. In fact, if its origins in the critical and national school are united with a choleric and polemic temper, it may come about that the grim and contemptuous word "wind-baggery" will be levelled against such arrogance, against a philosophy of "absolute knowledge." And yet the school of thought thus assailed has some right to return the compliment. For with the devaluation of all objective knowledge, with the statement that it offers us nothing but phenomena; with doubts about the intellect as an adequate, trustworthy instrument of knowledge; even with the justification of all philosophizings, only on the ground that our most intimate self—something quite different and much earlier in time than the intellect—must have at its very root a connection with universal foundations; with all these considerations there enters a subjective factor into our conception of the knowledge of truth, an element of the intuitive, of equation with the emotional, or even an imbalance on the side of passion and pathos, which from the point of view of pure mind might merit the epithet "wind-baggery." At least, in so far as an *artist's* conception of the world, including not only the head but the whole man with heart and senses, body and soul, merits the same severe epithet. The world of emotions and passions, that is the same as the world of beauty, in accordance with the mysterious law which binds feeling and form, makes feeling ever crave form, yes, makes them in origin one: a conception of the world born in passion lived and suffered with the whole human being, will always bear the stamp of the beautiful. It will know nothing of the sense-destroying dryness and boredom of pure intellectual speculation; it will emerge as a soul-novel, as a symphony of ideas, wonderfully composed, developed from one single thought kernel, existing everywhere—in a word, as a work of art, working by virtue of all art's magic. And just as the anguished yearning for favour and grace, for a deep affinity between suffering and beauty is resolved in form, just so it is beauty that vouches for its truth.

The philosophy of Arthur Schopenhauer has always been regarded as pre-eminently creative, as an artist-philosophy *par excellence*. Not because it is so markedly or so extensively a philosophy of art—actually its Æsthetics occupies somewhat more than a quarter of the whole work. Nor yet because its style is so perfectly, consistently clear, so rounded, its presentation and language so powerful, so elegant, so unerringly apposite, so passionately brilliant, so classically pure, so magnificently and blithely severe—like never any other in the history of German philosophy. All this is only "phenomenal"; it is merely the inevitable and inborn beauty of form expressed in the essence, the inner nature of this kind of thinking, an emotional, breath-taking nature, playing between violent contrasts, between instinct and mind, passion and redemption—in short, a dynamic artist-nature, which cannot reveal itself in any other way than as the personal creation of truth, convincing by virtue of its having been lived and suffered.

That is why this philosophy has found among artists and the initiated in art its most enthusiastic admirers and fanatical converts. Tolstoy called Schopenhauer "the genius *par excellence* among men." For Richard Wagner, who was introduced to him by the poet Georg Herwegh, the teaching of Schopenhauer was "a gift from heaven," the greatest boon, the most illuminating, productive, stimulating, intellectual experience he ever had, nothing more and nothing less than a revelation. Nietzsche, whose mission it was to bring art and knowledge, science and passion, even nearer to each other, to make truth and beauty mingle together, even more tragically and thrillingly than Schopenhauer before him; Nietzsche saw in this man his great teacher and master. Still young, he had dedicated to him one of the *Thoughts out of Season:* "Schopen-

hauer as Teacher." And especially at the time of his adulation of Wagner, when he wrote *The Birth of Tragedy,* he moved entirely in Schopenhauerian trains of thought. Even after this great self-conqueror had renounced both Wagner and Schopenhauer, in itself a decisive event in the history of the human intellect, he never ceased to love where he had ceased to believe, and in the late work *Ecce Homo,* that almost frighteningly *spirituelle* last phosphorescence of his over-stimulated and solitary career, there is a page on *Tristan* that reveals no estrangement but, on the contrary, much passion. Indeed, this spirit, as noble as it was unsparing towards itself, offered up to the end the most explicit homage to the great figure of the philosophic shaper of his youth. One may say that his thinking and teaching after he had "got over" Schopenhauer were a continuation and interpretation of his teacher's world-picture instead of an actual departure from it.

The history of Schopenhauerian thought goes back to the sources of the life of thought in our Western world, whence issue European science and European art, and in which the two are still one. It goes back to Plato. (The Greek philosopher taught that the things of this world have no real existence; they are always becoming, they never *are*.) They are of no avail as objects of actual knowledge, for that can subsist only in what is in and of itself and always in the same way; whereas they, in their multiplicity and their purely relative, borrowed existence, which might as well be called non-existence, are never anything but the subject of an opinion based on sense-experience. They are shadows. The only things that have real existence, that always are and never pass away, are the actual originals of those shadows, the eternal *ideas,* the primeval forms of all things. These are not multiple, being by their very nature each unique, each the archetype, the shadows or imitations of which are merely like-named, ephemeral, individual things of the same kind. Ideas do not, like these, come up and die away; they are timeless and truly existent, not becoming and passing like their perishable imitations. Of them alone, then, can there be actual knowledge, as of that which always and in every respect *is*. Concretely: *the* lion, that is the idea; *a* lion, that is pure seeming, and it follows that it cannot be the object of pure knowledge. The banal objection may be raised that only the phenomenal image of the single "empirical" lion affords us the possibility of getting any knowledge not only of the lion as such, but certainly of the lion as idea. But precisely the immediate intellectual subordination of the experience got from the phenomenal image of the single lion, to the *"leonitas,"* the *idea* lion, the pure and general thought-image of the animal; the subsumption of every special and temporal perception in the general and intellectual, thus an achievement in abstraction, the penetration of every conditioned and transitory actuality, the deepening and clarifying of mere *seeing* till it becomes the contemplation of the absolute, unclouded and abiding truth, which is behind and above the manifold single manifestations and to whose name these answer—that is the philosophical challenge which Plato made to the humanity of his time.

We see that this thinker knew how to derive a far-reaching significance from the distinction between the definite and the indefinite article; he made of it a learned paradox. For paradoxical it certainly is, to say that knowledge can only refer to the invisible, the thought-about, perceived in the mind; it is paradoxical to explain the visible world as a phenomenon, which, in itself worthless, has a reality and meaning only through that of which it is an expression. The reality of the actual—only a loan from the mind! That was nothing—or only a bewilderment—to an ordinary human understanding! But in this *"épater le bourgeois"* always lay the mission and the satisfaction, the lofty martyrdom of knowledge in this earth; always she found her pain and pleasure in disobliging the ordinary common sense of men, in standing the popular truth on its head, in making the earth go round the sun, whereas any normal senses can see it does the reverse; in perplexing mankind, in beguiling and bedevilling them, by telling them truths that run contrary to what their senses tell them. But this happens when someone aims to teach the mind of man, to lead it to higher things, making it capable of new achievements. What Plato, with his far-reaching exposition of the difference between the definite and the indefinite article, introduced into the early Occidental world, was the scientific spirit.

Obviously, it is the scientific spirit and training that teach us to subordinate to the idea the multiplicity of phenomena; that attribute truth and genuine reality to it alone and adhere to the contemplative abstraction and spiritualization of knowledge. Because of this discriminating distinction between the phenomenon and the idea, between the empiric and the intellectual, between the world of truth and the world of appearance, between the temporal and the eternal, the life of Plato was a very great event in the history of the human spirit; and first of all it was a scientific and a moral event. Everyone feels that something profoundly moral attaches to this elevation of the ideal as the only actual, above the ephemeralness and multiplicity of the phenomenal, this *devaluation* of the senses to the advantage of the spirit, of the temporal to the advantage of the eternal—quite in the spirit of the Christianity that came after it. For in a way the transitory phenomenon, and the sensual attaching to it, are put thereby into a state of sin: he alone finds truth and salvation who turns his face to the eternal. From this point of view Plato's philosophy exhibits the connection between science and ascetic morality.

But it exhibits another relationship: that with the world of art. According to such a philosophy, time itself is merely the partial and piecemeal view which an individual holds of ideas—the latter, being outside time, are thus eternal. "Time"—so runs a beautiful phrase of Plato—"is the moving image of eternity." And so this pre-Christian, already Christian doctrine, with all its ascetic wisdom, possesses on the other hand extraordinary charm of a sensuous and creative kind; for a conception of the world as a colourful and moving phantasmagoria of pictures, which are transparencies for the ideal and the spiritual, eminently savours of the world of art, and through it the artist as it were first comes into his own. He it is who may

owe his bond to the world of images and appearances—be sensually, voluptuously, sinfully bound to them, yet be aware at the same time that he belongs no less to the world of the idea and the spirit, as the magician who makes the appearance transparent that the idea and spirit may shine through. Here is exhibited the artist's mediating task, his hermetic and magical role as broker between the upper and the lower world, between idea and phenomenon, spirit and sense. Here, in fact, we have what I may call the cosmic position of art; her unique mission in the world, the high dignity—which flings dignity away—of her functioning, can be defined or explained in no other way. The moon-symbol, the cosmic parable of all mediation, is art's own. To the old world, to primitive humanity, the planet was strange and sacred in its double meaning, in its median and mediating position between the solar and the earthly, the spiritual and the material world. Femininely receptive in relation to the sun but masculinely begetting in relation to the earth, the moon was to them the impurest of the heavenly, the purest of the earthly bodies. It did belong to the material world, but assumed therein the highest, most spiritual position, passing over into the solar, so hovering on the borders of two worlds, at once parting and uniting them, guarding the unity of the All, interpreter between mortal and immortal. Just *this is the position of art between spirit and life.* Androgynous like the moon, female in its relation to spirit, but masculine and begetting in life, the materially impurest manifestation of the heavenly, transitorily the purest and incorruptibly most spiritual of the earthly sphere, in its nature it is that of a moon-enchanted mediator between the two spheres. This mediating position is the source of its irony.

Plato as artist. I hold that a philosophy is effective not only—sometimes least of all—by reason of its ethical teaching, by the doctrine which it links to its interpretation of the world and its experience of it; but also and especially through this very experience itself. This indeed—not the spiritual and ethical concomitant of its doctrine of truth and salvation—is the essential, primary, and personal part of a philosophy. If one divorce from a philosopher his philosophy, there is much left; and it would be a pity if there were not. Nietzsche, the intellectually apostate pupil of Schopenhauer, wrote of his master:

> What he *taught* is put aside;
> What he *lived,* that will abide—
> Behold a man!
> Subject he was to none.

If the philosophy of Schopenhauer, which I am about to discuss, its validity and dynamic power, will never be quite abandoned, yet it proved as liable to abuse as the ascetic, scientific, and creatively fruitful message of Plato. I refer here to the exploitation that Schopenhauer suffered at the hands of a colossally gifted artist, Richard Wagner—of this perhaps more at another time. But whosesoever the blame, it certainly does not lie at the door of Schopenhauer's other teacher and inspirer, who contributed to the structure of his system. I mean, of course,

Kant. Kant's bent was exclusively and positively on the side of mind—very much aloof from art, but by so much the closer to critique.

Immanuel Kant, the critic of pure knowledge, rescued philosophy from the speculation into which it had retreated and brought it back into the realm of the human intellect; made this his field and delimited the reason. At Königsberg in Prussia, in the second half of the eighteenth century, he was teaching something very like the premises laid down two thousand years before by the Athenian thinker. Our whole experience of the world, he declared, is subject to three laws and conditions, the inviolable forms in which all our knowledge is effectuated. These are time, space, and causality. But they are not definitions of the world as it may be in and for itself, of *das Ding an sich*, independently of our apperception of it; rather they belong only to its appearance, in that they are nothing but the forms of our knowledge. All variation, all becoming and passing away, is only possible through these three. Thus they depend only on appearance and we can know nothing through them of the "thing in itself," to which they are in no way applicable. This fact applies even to our own ego: we apprehend it only as manifestation, not as anything that it may be in itself. In other words, time, space, and causality are mechanisms of the intellect, and we call immanent the conception of things which is vouchsafed to us in their image and conditioned by them; while that is transcendent which we might gain by applying reason upon itself, by critique of the reason, and by dint of seeing through these three devices as mere forms of knowledge.

This is Kant's fundamental concept; and as we can see, it is closely related to Plato's. Both explain the visible world as phenomenal; in other words, as idle-seeming, which gains significance and some measure of reality only by virtue of that which shines through it. For both Plato and Kant the true reality lies above, behind, in short "beyond" the phenomenon. Whether it was called "idea" or *"das Ding an sich"* is relatively unimportant.

Both these concepts penetrated deeply into Schopenhauer's thought. He early elected the exhaustive study of Plato and Kant (Göttingen, 1809-11) and placed above all others these two philosophers so widely separated in time and space. The almost identical results they arrived at seemed best calculated to support and justify, to help construct the image of the world which he bore within himself. No wonder, then, that he called them the two greatest Occidental philosophers. He took from them what he could use, and it gratified his craving for the traditional that he could so well use it; although owing to his entirely different constitution—so much more "modern," storm-tossed, and suffering—he made out of it something else altogether.

What he took was the "idea" and the *"Ding an sich."* But with the latter he did something very bold, even scarcely permissible, though at the same time with deeply felt, almost compulsive conviction: he defined the *Ding an sich*, he called it by name, he asserted—though from Kant himself you would never have known—that he knew what it was. It was the will. The will was the ultimate, irreducible, primeval principle of being, the source of all phenomena, the begetter present and active in every single one of them, the impelling force producing the whole visible world and all life—for it was the will to live. It was this through and through; so that whoever said "will" was speaking of the will to live, and if you used the longer term you were guilty of a pleonasm. The will always willed one thing: life. And why? Because it found it priceless? Because it afforded the experience of any objective knowledge of life? Ah, no. All knowledge alike was foreign to the will; it was something independent of knowledge, it was entirely original and absolute, a blind urge, a fundamentally uncaused, utterly unmotivated force; so far from depending on any evaluation of life, the converse was the case, and all judgments were dependent upon the strength of the will to live.

The will, then, this "in-itself-ness" of things, existing outside of time, space, and causality, blind and causeless, greedily, wildly, ruthlessly demanded life, demanded objectivation; and this objectivation occurred in such a way that its original unity became a multiplicity—a process that received the appropriate name of the *principium individuationis* (the principle of individuality). The will, avid of life, to wreak its desire objectivated itself in accordance with the *principium,* thus dispersing itself into the myriad parts of the phenomenal world existing in time and space; but at the same time it remained in full strength in each single and smallest of those parts. The world, then, was the product and the expression of the will, the objectivation of the will in space and time. But it was at the same time something else besides: it was the *idea,* my idea and yours, the idea of each one and each one's idea about himself—by virtue, that is, of the discerning mind, which the will created to be a light to it in the higher stages of its objectivation. We must understand aright this matter of the "higher stages." Schopenhauer, that is, a mystic as well as an exceedingly modern mind, fed and nourished on natural science, interpolated into his cosmogony of the will and the endless multiplicity of its emanations the concept of evolution. He did it out of affection for that philosophical factor which he took over from Plato and the ideas. He assumed, or established in the multiplicity of objectivations of the will, an order of rank, a series of stages, and in this way he won or he preserved the ideas—for when you looked at these they were no other than a series of stages of objectivations of the will. Taken singly, they were not a quite adequate objectivity of the will, because they were clouded by the forms of our knowledge. In fact we should not recognize any "exemplars," any occurrences, any change, any multiplicity, but only the existing, the pure and immediate objectivations of the will in its various stages, and the world, to speak with the schoolmen, would accordingly be a *"nunc stans,"* an abiding now of unclouded and everlasting ideas. Thus in the upper stages of its individuation, even in animals and especially in the human being, the highest and most complicated of all, the will, to give itself aid, comfort, enlightenment, and security, kindled the light of the intellect which should make an idea or representation of the world. Note that it was not the intellect that brought forth the will; the converse was the case, the will brought forth the intellect. It was not intellect, mind, knowledge, that was the primary and dominant factor; it was the will, and the intellect served it. And how could it have been otherwise, since, after all, enough knowledge even for the objectivation of will belonged to a later stage and without will simply had no chance to appear? In a world entirely the work of will, of absolute, unmotivated, causeless, and unvaluated life-urge, intellect had of course only second place. Sensibility, nerves, brain, were—just like the other parts of the organism and quite specifically like the sex organs, the opposite pole of the discerning brain—an expression of the will at a given phase of its objectivation. And the idea, coming into being through the will, was just as much intended to serve it and just as little an end in itself as were those other parts. This relation between will and mind, this premise of Schopenhauer that the first is only the tool of the second, has about it much that is humiliating and deplorable, much that is even comic. It puts in a nutshell the whole tendency and capacity of mankind to delude itself and imagine that its will receives its direction and content from its mind, whereas our philosopher asserts the direct opposite, and relegates the intellect—aside from its duty of shedding a little light on the immediate surroundings of the will and aiding it to achieve the higher stages of its struggle for life—to a position as mere mouthpiece of the will: to justify it, to provide it with "moral" motivations, and, in short, to rationalize our instincts.

Thus the Christian philosophers of the Middle Ages, whom the Devil had carried off when they retreated from the position that the reason existed for the sole purpose of making an apologia for faith. Kant ought to have heard that. And still Schopenhauer, who had taken from Kant the *"Ding an sich"* and from Plato the "ideas," was convinced that he was Kantian and Platonist in such an evaluation of the reason.

It was a remarkably pessimistic valuation. Indeed, all the textbooks tell us that Schopenhauer is first the philosopher of the will and second the philosopher of pessimism. But actually there is no first and second, for they are one and the same, and he was the second because and by virtue of his being the first; he was necessarily pessimist because he was the philosopher and psychologist of the will. Will, as the opposite pole of passive satisfaction, is naturally a fundamental unhappiness, it is unrest, a striving for *something*—it is want, craving, avidity, demand, suffering; and a world of will can be nothing else but a world of suffering. The will, objectivating itself in all existing things, quite literally wreaks on the physical its metaphysical craving; satisfies that craving in the most frightful way in the world and through the world which it has brought forth, and which, born of greed and compulsion, turns out to be a thing to shudder at. In other words, will becoming world according to the *principium individuationis,* and being dispersed into a multiplicity of parts, forgets its original unity and, although in all its divisions it remains essentially one, it becomes will a

million times divided against itself. Thus it strives against itself, seeking its own well-being in each of the millions of its manifestations, its place in the sun at the expense of another, yes, at the expense of all others, and so constantly sets its teeth in its own flesh, like that dweller in Tartarus who avidly devoured his own members. This is meant in a literal sense. Plato's "ideas" have in Schopenhauer become incurably gluttonous. As stages of the objectivation of the will, space, time, and matter fall upon each other. The plant world has to serve as nourishment for the animal, each animal for another as prey and food, and thus the will to live gnaws forever at itself. And lastly man sees the whole created for his use but in his turn makes frightfully explicit the abomination of the struggle of all against all, the division of the will against itself. We express all this in the phrase *homo homini lupus.*

Everywhere that Schopenhauer takes occasion to talk of the anguish of the world and the rage for life of the will's multiple incarnations (and he talks much and explicitly about them), his extraordinary native eloquence, his genius as a writer, reach their utmost height of icy brilliance. He speaks with a cutting vehemence, in accents of experience and all-embracing knowledge that horrify and bewitch us by their power and veracity. Certain pages display a fierce and caustic mockery of life, uttered as it were with flashing eyes and compressed lips, and in showers of Greek and Latin quotations: a pitiful-pitiless coruscation of statement, citation, and proof of the utter misery of the world. All this is far from being so depressing as one would expect from the pitch of acuity and sinister eloquence it arrives at. Actually it fills the reader with strange, deep satisfaction, whose source is the spiritual rebellion speaking in the words, the human indignation betrayed in what seems like a suppressed quiver of the voice. Everyone feels this satisfaction; everyone realizes that when this great writer and commanding spirit speaks of the suffering of the world, he speaks of yours and mine; all of us feel what amounts almost to triumph at being thus avenged by the heroic Word.

Poverty, need, concern for the mere preservation of life—these come first. Then, when they are painfully allayed, come sexual urge, the sufferings of love, jealousy, envy, hatred, fear, ambition, avarice, illness—and so on and on, without end. All the evils whose source is the inner conflict of the will come out of Pandora's box. And what is left at the bottom? Hope? Ah, no. Satiety, tedium. For between pain and satiety every human being is tossed to and fro. The pain is positive, the pleasure merely the absence of pain—a negative, passing over at once into boredom, just as the tonic to which the melodic labyrinth leads back, just as the harmony in which disharmony issues, would bore us intolerably if they went on and on. Are there real satisfactions? They exist. But compared with the long torture of our desires, the endlessness of our requirements, they are short and scant, and to one gratified desire there are at least ten that remain unstilled. Moreover, the appeasement itself is only apparent, for the fulfilled desire soon makes a new vacancy—the first is now a known error, the second still unknown. No achieved object of desire can give lasting satisfaction. It is like alms thrown to a beggar, which merely linger out from day to day his miserable life. Happiness? It would be in repose. But precisely this is impossible for him who feels desire. To flee, to pursue, to fear disaster, to covet pleasure—it is all one: preoccupation with the will's incessant demands fills and animates the consciousness without cease, and thus the subject of the willing lies ever on Ixion's turning wheel, takes up water in the sieve of the Danaides, and plays the ever toiling Tantalus.

Scenes of torture and Tartarus, such as the case of Thyestes, who, raging with hunger, devoured his won members. Then is life a hell? Not quite; only approaching it, a foretaste. Hellish, certainly; since it is fixed, to start with, that every expression of the will to live has always something of the infernal about it, being itself a metaphysical stupidity, a frightful error, a sin, *the* sin. Do we feel the Christian, the Platonic note? Plato's already slightly ascetic and pessimistic devaluation of the senses by the soul, wherein alone reside all salvation and truth—here it is most grimly reasserted and reinforced; in two thousand years it has received an imprint of suffering and complaint foreign to the early Occidental: the actual world is the product of an arch-sinful, arch-stupid act of will, which never should have taken place; and if it has never become completely and formally a hell, that is because the will's will to live has not been vehement enough. If it were a little stronger still, had been a little more will to live, the hell would have been perfect, That sounds like a modification of the pessimism, but it is just a new jab, a biting rebellion against life and the accursed will—akin to that jest which Schopenhauer once permitted himself when he said life everywhere precariously balances on the edge of the still barely possible; this world is the worst of all conceivable worlds; for if it were even a little worse it could not be at all. He reminds one often of Voltaire. Sometimes because of the lucid and perfect form and triumphant wit. But he is superior to the Frenchman in a certain rich reconditeness in the depth and power of his intellectual life. Witness the doctrine of redemption which he has built into, which emerges from, his philosophy of the will; witness the longing for redemption. But yet: there *is* release from miseries and mistakes, from the errors and penalties of this life. This gift is laid in the hand of the human being, the highest and most developed objectivation of the will and accordingly the most richly capable of suffering. Would you think the gift might be death? Not at all. Death belongs utterly and entirely to the sphere of the phenomenal, the empirical, the sphere of change. It has no contact with transcendent and true actuality. What is mortal in us is merely the individuation; the core of our being, the will, which is the will to live, remains entirely unassailed, and can, *if it continue to affirm itself,* find out fresh avenues of approach to life. Herein, may I say in passing, resides the folly and immorality of suicide: in its futility. For the individual denies and destroys only his individuation, not the original error, the will to live, which in suicide is only seeking a route to more complete realization. So, then, not death. Redemption bears quite another name and has quite a different conditioning. One does not suspect the mediator who is to be thanked for this blessing when it comes. It is the intellect.

But the intellect—is it not the creature of the will, its instrument, its light in the darkness, destined only for its service? It is, and so remains. And yet—not always, not in all cases. Under peculiar, happy—ah, verily, under blissful—conditions; in exceptional circumstances, then, the servant and poor tool may become the master of his master and creator, may get the better of him, emancipate himself, achieve his own independence, and, at least at times, assert his single sovereignty, his mild, serene, and all-embracing rule. Then the will, put aside and shorn of power, falls into a bland and peaceful decline. There is a state where the miracle comes to pass, that knowledge wrenches itself free from will, the subject ceases to be merely individual and becomes the pure, will-less subject of knowledge. We may call it the Æsthetic state. This is one of the greatest and profoundest of Schopenhauer's perceptions. And however frightful the accents he commands in describing the tortures of the will and the domination of the will, in equal degree his prose discovers seraphic tones, his gratitude speaks with surpassing exuberance, when abundantly and exhaustively he discourses of the blessings of art. The intellectual formulation and interpretation of this, perhaps Schopenhauer's most personal experience, he owes to his teachers, Plato and Kant. "Beautiful," Kant had declared, "is what happens without *interest.*" Without interest. That, for Schopenhauer, and rightly, meant without reference to the will. The Æsthetic gratification was pure, disinterested, free from will, it was "idea" in the most intensive, most hopeful sense of the word; it was clear, unclouded, profoundly satisfied contemplation. And why was it that? Here Plato came in, with the latent Æstheticism of his philosophy of ideas. Ideas. They it was for which, in the Æsthetic state, phenomena, the mere images of eternity, became transparent. The eyes opened upon ideas; and here was the great, pure, sunny, objective contemplation by which alone the genius, and even he only in his creative hours and moments, and with him his audience, was justified of his Æsthetic achievement.

Well, and so it is the intellect that opens the way to such contemplation. Yes, the intellect, wrenched free from the will, became pure and disinterested knowledge. Needless to say, in art the word "intellect" does not apply in the narrow sense of the word; not thought, abstraction, understanding brought about the blessed state. Art could not be taught, it was a free gift of intuition. Intellect was therein only so far in play as it was intellect that made the world *idea.* One needed to know nothing about the metaphysical bearings of things, nothing of appearance and idea, of Kant or Plato, to be a part of art. It was philosophy's business to expound the nature of Æsthetics and make it accessible to abstract thought—though it would have to be a philosophy with more understanding and actual *experience* of art than any we have had in the past or present. It knew and taught that the eye of art was that of creative objectivity—and if we recall here what was said earlier about the mediating services of art being the source of irony, we perceive that irony and objectivity belong together and are one.

Apollo, god of the Muses, "he who shoots his arrows from afar," is a god of distance, of space, not of pathos and pathology or involvement, a god not of suffering but of freedom. He is an objective god, the god of irony. In irony, then, as Schopenhauer saw it, in creative objectivity knowledge was freed from its bondage to will, and the attention was no longer blurred by any motive. We reached a state of selfless resignation, where reference was had to things as sheer ideas, no longer as purposes; and a peace heretofore unknown was all at once vouchsafed us. "It is," says our author, "wholly well with us. It is the painless state praised by Epicurus as the highest good and the state of the gods; we are, for that moment, released from the base urge of the will, we celebrate the sabbath of our toil in the prison-house of will, the wheel of Ixion stands still."

Famous, oft-quoted words, lured from this bitter and tormented soul by the vision of the beautiful and the peace it purveyed. Are they true? But what is truth? An experience that finds such words to describe itself must be true, must be justified by the power of its feeling. Or should we believe that these words of sheer and boundless gratitude were coined to describe a relative, at bottom a merely negative, happiness? For happiness anyhow is negative, it is the surcease of torment; and even in all our glad objective contemplation of Æsthetic ideas it cannot be other than the same. Schopenhauer, in the choice of the images he is inspired to use, unequivocally reveals the fact. This happiness too is temporal, transitory. The creative state, so he found, the sojourn among images irradiated by the idea—these would not bring the final redemption. The Æsthetic state was but the prior stage to a perfected one, in which the will, not permanently satisfied in the Æsthetic, would be once for all outshone by knowledge, would void the field and be annihilated. The consummation of the artist would be the saint.

Alongside of his Æsthetics Schopenhauer places his system of ethics. He elevates ethics and thrones it above the other; for ethics was the doctrine of the conversion of the will in man, the highest stage of its objectivation; the theory of the will's self-abnegation by virtue of the insight into the frightful fallibility and worthlessness of the suffering world which was its effect and mirror, its objectivation—thus by virtue of the fact that the will to life came to understand itself as something to be definitely and absolutely rejected. How was that possible? How could a denial of the will come out of life, which was after all through and through a will to life? It became possible because the world was the result of an act of will and such an act could be nullified and cancelled by another act of will in the opposite direction. This was what knowledge did, tearing itself loose from will, renouncing its subservience, freed from its as it were cosmic slavery; and this act was the final activity, the inmost content of the ethics which made the transition.

What, after all, is ethics? It is the philosophy of the actions of human beings, the teaching of good and evil. The teaching? Then was the will, blind, causeless, and senseless as it was, teachable? Certainly not. Certainly virtue

was not a thing to be taught; any more than was art. Just as a man could not become an artist by having explained to him the essence of the creative state, so he could not shun evil and ensue good by instruction in the nature of the one and the other, which Schopenhauer, as a philosopher, was ready to do. At all events, abstraction might be useful; and was, in the form of this or that dogma of various religions, the exoteric garb of esoteric wisdom, the garment of truth, truth, so to speak, for the people. The rational motive of a good deed did not so much matter, if the good deed was done. But it was done out of feeling, out of an intuitive recognition of truth, based upon penetration, on "seeing through," precisely as did the Æsthetic state, on which subject Schopenhauer would presently give more detailed explanations. Just now he laid stress on making it clear that ethics could not be a codex of moral teachings, consisting of prescriptions for the will. No prescriptions could be issued to the will. It was free, absolute, all-powerful. Freedom, indeed, dwelt in the will alone, thus it existed wholly in transcendence, never in the empiric world, which was the objectivation of the world subsisting in time, space, and causality. Here everything was strictly causal, bound and determined by cause and effect. Freedom, like the will, was beyond and on the other side of the phenomenal, but there it was present and dominant, and therein lay the freedom of the will. As so often, the situation respecting freedom was just contrary to that conceived by ordinary common sense. It lay not in doing but in being, not in *operari* but in *esse*. In *doing,* indeed, then, inevitable necessity and determinacy reigned; while *being* was originally and metaphysically free. The human being who performed a culpable action had indeed so *acted* of necessity, as a being existing in the realm of the empiric, and under the influence of definite motives. But he could have *been* different; and his fear, his pangs of conscience, also had reference to his being, not his doing.

A bold, deeply felt, and at the same time a harsh thought. It is one of the most remarkable and, to a considered judgment, most compelling intuitions in Schopenhauer's construction of truth. What it rescued from empiricism for transcendence and timelessness and there in mysterious security preserved was a pair of moral and aristocratic concepts, to which Schopenhauer undoubtedly clung, and which he would unwillingly have seen go down in absolute determinism: they are guilt and merit. But their persistence depended upon the freedom of the will—and how many struggles there had already been on this point! However, it was always temporal freedom that was meant, freedom of the will within the phenomenon and with reference to the empirical character of man, as man himself experienced it in his own destiny and represented it to others as pleasant or unpleasant. So soon as the will had objectivated itself, become phenomenon, and entered into the individuation, then there was not trace of freedom left and accordingly neither praise nor blame. The human being behaved as being the individual he was, he had to behave under the influence of definite motives; but his doing and faring, the course his life took, his destiny, these were only the experience which he—along with others of his essence, his "intelligible" character, existing outside of and behind the manifestation—went through; and this character was like the whole world the product of a free act of will. In everything the will appeared precisely as it decided in itself and outside of time. The world was only the mirror of this will, and everything in it belonged to the expression of that which it willed, and was so just because it so willed. Accordingly, every being led his life with the strictest justice, and not only life, but the life peculiar to him, his individuality; and in all that befell him, yes, in all that could befall him, everything happened exactly right.

A harsh, cruel thought—arrogant, offensive, ruthless. To accept it runs contrary to our feelings—and yet it is precisely our feelings that are challenged by its mysticism. For it has at the bottom of it a mystic truth, by virtue of which the twin conceptions of merit and demerit, far from being invalidated, become even more profound and awe-inspiring. They are, of course, divorced thereby from the moral sphere as such. But aristocratic intellects, not much concerned with considerations of "justice," have always been inclined to favour this divorce. Goethe liked to talk of "inborn merits," an absurd phrase from any logical or ethical point of view. For "merit" is entirely and by definition an ethical concept; whereas what is inborn—be it beauty, talent, wit, refinement, or, in the sphere of outward destiny, good fortune—can thus not logically be merits. In order to speak of merit in this sense it must be the issue of choice, the expression of a will antecedent to the phenomenon. And this is just what Schopenhauer asserts when he harshly and haughtily declares that each of us, blest or unblest, gets exactly what he deserves.

But this aristocratic complaisance at injustice and the varied lot of mortals is soon enough resolved in the most peremptory and democratic equality; simply because the variations—and even the differentiation itself—are shown to be an illusion. Schopenhauer calls this illusion by a name drawn from Hindu metaphysics, which he greatly admires because of its pessimistic harmony with his own account of the world: he calls it the "veil of Maya." But much earlier he had, as Occidental scholars do, clothed it in Latin, thus: he says that the great illusion of inequality and injustice in the character, situation, and fate of individuals rests on the *principium individuationis*. Variation, inequality, are only attributes of multiplicity in time and space. That is to say, they are mere appearance, the notion which we, as individuals, thanks to the organization of the intellect, have of a world which in reality is the objectivation of the will to live, in the general and in the particular, in you and in me. But the individual, with his strong sense of being separate and set apart from the universe, does not recognize this—how could he, when the conditioning of his knowledge, the "veil of Maya," enfolding his vision and the outlying world, prevents him from getting sight of the truth? The individual does not see the essence of the truth. The individual does not see the essence of things, which is one, but its manifestations, which he beholds as separate and differing, yes, even opposed: pleasure and pain, the tormentor and the tor-

mented, the joyous life of one and the other's wretched lot. You affirm, that is, for yourself, the one, and deny with special reference to yourself, the other. The will, which is your origin and essence, makes you demand good fortune and the enjoyment of existence. You stretch out your hands for them, you press them to you, and it escapes your notice that when you thus affirm these as goods, you affirm at the same time all the evils, all the torments in the world and press them no less to your heart. The evil that you do thereby, the evil that you inflict; on the other hand, your indignation at the world's injustice, your envy, yearning, and desire, your cosmic craving—all these come from the delusion of multiplicity, the false belief that you are not the world and the world is not you. All this comes from the illusion of Maya, from the illusory distinction between the I and the you.

Thence, likewise, comes your fear of death. Death is only the setting right of an error, a confusion—for every individual is a confusion. Death is nothing but the disappearance of an imaginary partition-wall shutting off the I you are enclosed in from the rest of the world. You believe that when you die this rest of the world will go on existing, while you, horrible to say, will be no more. But I say to you, this world, which is your idea, will no longer be; whereas you, precisely that in you which, because it is the will to live, fears death and rejects it, *you* will remain, will live. For the will, out of which you have your being, will always know how to find the gate of life. To it all eternity belongs; and together with life, which it recognizes as time, though actually it is perpetual present, time too will be vouchsafed you again. Your will, so long as it wills, is always sure of life, with all its torments and blisses. Better it were for you if it were not.

Meanwhile you live, as he who you are. You see and love, you look and long, you covet the unknown image of your desire—ah, so strange and different from yourself!—you suffer for it, you long to draw it to your heart, to draw it into you, to *be* it. But to be a thing is something quite different, and incomparably more grievous and onerous than to see it. The longing set up by the idea is all a delusion. You yourself are given to yourself, your body is given to you, as idea, as all the rest of the world is. But at the same time it is given to you as will—the only thing in the world that is given you at the same time as will. Everything else is for you only idea. The universe is, so to speak, a play, a ballet; all your natural, instinctive convictions tell you that it has nothing like the same reality as you, the spectator, have; that it is not to be taken with anything like the same seriousness as you yourself are. Trapped in the *principium individuationis,* shrouded in the veil of Maya, the ego sees all other forms of life as masks and phantoms, and is simply incapable of ascribing anything like the same importance or seriousness to them as to itself. Are not you the only actually existent thing, are you not all that matters? You are the navel of the world; if it be well with you, if the afflictions of this life be kept as far from you as possible, its blisses as near, that is the one vital thing. What happens to others is nothing by comparison. It does you neither good nor harm.

Such is the conviction of native, unbroken, and quite unenlightened egoism: absolute prepossession with the *principium individuationis.* To see through this principle, to divine its illusory, truth-shrouding character; to begin to perceive that the I and the you are indistinguishable the one from the other; to have the emotional intuition that the will is the same in the one and the all: such is the beginning and the essence of ethics. In other words, it deals with this knowledge, this emotional intution, and describes its beneficent results, but it does not and cannot teach it, for just as little as Æsthetics in the abstract ever made an artist, just so little can virtue be learned or taught. Man experiences it, as that Indian novice did before whose eyes a great spirit brought all the creations in the world, living and lifeless, and at each one said: *tat twam asi*—this is you. In this word, this insight, a gift of the intution, lies all virtue, righteousness, all goodness and nobility—and in its ignorance, like a madness, the opposite of all that: namely, *evil.* Evil is that man who, so soon as no other outer power prevents him, inflicts evil. I mean a man who, not content with affirming the will to life as manifested in his own body, also denies the will manifest in other individuals and seeks to destroy their existence as soon as it is in the way of his own efforts. A wild, untamed will, one not content with the affirmation of his own body, speaks in the bad character. But there is above all so profound a prejudice in favour of the manifestation and the *principium individuationis* that it clings with iron grip to the distinctions fixed by the *principium* between its own person and all others. And accordingly it considers the existence of others wholly foreign to its own, severed from it by a deep abyss. It regards them as empty shells, and cherishes a profound conviction that reality is an attribute of itself alone. And thus we arrive at the definition of the *good* man; particularly when we contemplate the transitional type between it and the bad man: the *just* man. Justice is already a penetration of the *principium individuationis,* but to a lesser degree, more negative than positive, the rejection of wrong. The just man, in the assertion of his own will, does not go so far as the denial of the will represented in other individuals. He refrains from inflicting suffering on others in order to increase his own well-being. The principle of individuation is not to him as it is to the wicked man, an absolute dividing wall; rather in what he does and leaves undone he shows that he recognizes his own being, the will to life, as a thing apart, likewise in other beings, manifestations given him only as idea, and finds himself in them at least in so far as to make him guard himself from injuring them. That is a great deal; and it is always at once a great deal more: real goodness is already bound up with it. Let no one consider it weak! The good man is by no means an originally weaker manifestation of the will than is a bad one—unless he is merely good-natured, which does not come to much. No, it is knowledge that in him triumphs over the will. What knowledge? But it is clear; it is that the difference between him and others rests on an illusion which tempts to evil, is a deceiving manifestation, that the *in itselfness* of his own manifestation is also that of the unknown: namely, the will to life, which embodies itself in everything, animals as well and all nature, wherefore he will not even misuse a beast.

But here one must not stop at negatives or speak in them: goodness is positive. It performs the service of love. Its motive is profoundly emotional: were it not to do so, it would seem to itself like a man who starves today in order tomorrow to have more than he can eat. Just so it would seem to the good man to let others famish while he lived in abundance. For such a one the veil of Maya has become transparent; he has lost the great illusion whereby will, in its multiple manifestations, here starves and suffers, there enjoys, because it is after all the same will, and the same torture, which he thus both invokes and suffers. Love and goodness are *sympathy*—in recognition of the *"Tat twam asi"* (the "This thou art"), when the veil of Maya is lifted. Spinoza said: *"Benevolentia nihil aliud est, quam cupiditas ex commiseratione orta"* ("Goodness is nothing else than love born of sympathy"). But from this it is clear that as justice can rise to heights of goodness, so goodness in its turn can rise to greater heights: not only to most disinterested love and most magnanimous self-sacrifice, but verily to saintliness. For a man with such knowledge of love will regard the suffering of everything living as his own suffering, and make his own the pain of all the world. He sees the whole: sees life as an internal conflict; and continual pain, suffering humanity, suffering animal world, and the knowledge of the essence of things in themselves combine to lay a quieting hand upon his will. In him will turns away from life. Obliged, in his sympathetic understanding, to deny life, how then can he affirm even in himself the will to live, life being but the work, mirror, and expression of will? Thus to recognize, thus to resolve, means renunciation, means the ultimate quietism. And so it comes about that virtue passes over into *ascesis;* and this is a paradox, truly a high and great one: an individuation of the will here rejects the essence manifesting and expressing itself in its very own body. Its acts give the lie to its manifestation, they openly controvert it. That temporary, releasing subdual of the will, on which rests the happiness of the Æsthetic state—it is completed in the renouncing, the ascetic, the saint. In him knowledge has forever made itself mistress over the will, entirely eclipses and cancels it. He bears the sins of the world, he atones for them, he is priest and sacrifice at once. As the body expresses altogether the will, so the sex organs express the assertion of the will above and beyond the individual life. The ascetic rejects the satisfactions of sex. His chastity is the sign that with the life of the body likewise the life of the will abrogates itself. What is the mark of the saint? That he does nothing of all that he would like to do, and does all that he does not like to do. We know some amazing spiritual examples of this attitude: we have seen it practised by born ascetics and priestly self-tormentors, who amid dithyrambic glorification of the power-drunken will celebrated the passion of their lives by doing nothing they would gladly have done and everything by which they injured themselves—pupils every one of the philosopher Schopenhauer and that properly only when they no longer willed to be. . . . If ascetic chastity were to become a general practice, it would bring about the end of the human race. And since all manifestations of the will are one, with man, the highest of these, would also fall away his feebler reflection, the animal kingdom. All knowledge would fail, and since without subject there is no object, all the rest of the visible world would dissolve and melt away. Man is the potential redeemer of nature. The mystic Angelus Silesius says:

O man, all living love thee; there is much press
  about thee,
All run to thee that they may reach their god.

If ascetic chastity were to become a general practice, it would bring about the end of the human race. And since all manifestations of the will are one, with man, the highest of these, would also fall away his feebler reflection, the animal kingdom. All knowledge would fail, and since without subject there is no object, all the rest of the visible world would dissolve and melt away. Man is the potential redeemer of nature.

—Thomas Mann

Here, in rough outline, is the content of Arthur Schopenhauer's chief work, to which he gave the title *The World as Will and Idea*—a highly objective title, which yet in three words completely expresses not only the content of the book but also the man who created it, in his mighty darkness and just as mighty light, his profound sensuality and pure, austere intellectuality, his passion and his urge for redemption. It is a marvel of a book, whose thought, reduced to the shortest formula in the title and present in every line, is only one, and in the four sections or, better put, symphonic movements of which it is built up, reaches complete and all-sided development—a book based on itself, penetrated with itself, corroborating in itself in that it is and does what it says and teaches: everywhere you open it, it is all there, but to realize itself in time and space needs the whole manifoldness of its appearance unfolded in more than thirteen hundred printed pages in twenty-five thousand lines of print, whereas actually it is *a nunc stans,* the abiding presence of his thought, so that the verses from the *Divan* apply to it as to nothing else:

Dein Lied ist drehend wie das Sterngewölbe,
Anfang und Ende immerfort dasselbe,
Und, was die Mitte bringt, ist offenbar
Das, was am Ende bleibt und Anfangs war.

    Thy song rolls round as doth the starry
sphere,
      End and beginning one for evermore,
      And when the turning middle doth
appear,
      'Tis still what end and what beginning
are.

It is a work of such cosmic completeness and inclusive power of thought that one has a strange experience: if you have been occupied with it a long time, then everything else, everything, read in between or immediately afterwards seems strange, unenlightened, wrong, arbitrary, undisciplined by truth. . . . Truth? Is it then so true? Yes, in the sense of the highest and most compelling sincerity. But the adjective implies a modification. Does it contain and convey truth? Schopenhauer has not asserted that so clearly and incisively, not with the almost blasphemous pretension with which Hegel did it when he told his pupils: "Gentlemen, I can say: I not only speak the truth, I am the truth!" The corresponding summing up of Schopenhauer runs: "Mankind has learned from me something it will never forget." I find that better bred, more modest, as well as more acceptable. And when we are speaking about truth, it is a matter of acceptableness. Truth, it seems to me, is not bound to words, does not coincide with a definite wording; perhaps that may even be its chief criterion. That one never forgets what Schopenhauer says may be due to the fact that it is not just dependent on the words he uses for it, that one might use other words—and still a kernel of feeling would remain, an experience of truth so acceptable, so immune to attack, so right, as never before found in philosophy. One can live and die by it—particularly die: I would venture to assert that Schopenhauerian truth, its acceptableness, is fit to stand alone in the last hour, without effort, without strain of thought, even without words. Not for nothing does he say: "Death is the real inspiring genius or *musagetes* of philosophy. . . ." Indeed, without death, there would scarcely be any philosophizing. He is a great seer and sayer of death—the famous chapter in the second volume of *The World as Will and Idea,* "On Death and Its Relation to the Indestructibility of Our Being in Itself," belongs to the finest, one might say the profoundest (though he is always so profound) things he has written. And this expression goes together with his ethical pessimism, which is more than a doctrine, which is a character, a creative state of mind, a prevailing atmosphere, for which the still youthful Nietzsche confesses his love when he says: "I found pleasurable in Wagner what I do in Schopenhauer: the ethical air, the Faustian flavour, Cross, Death, and Grave." It is the prevailing intellectual atmosphere of the second half of the nineteenth century—the air of youth and home for those of us past sixty. In some ways we may have got out from under it; but that we preserve a grateful loyalty this little essay bears witness. Music too belongs to this ethical-pessimistic atmosphere: Schopenhauer was very musical, I have often called his great work a symphony in four movements; and in the third, devoted to the "object of art," he celebrates music as no other thinker has ever done, ascribing to her a quite special place, not beside but above the other arts, because she is not like them, the image of the phenomenon, but immediately the image of the will itself, and thus to all the physical of the world she depicts the metaphysical, to all appearance the thing itself. This philosophy leads one to the speculation that here too the intellect serves the will, and that Schopenhauer did not love music because he subscribed such a metaphysical significance to her, but rather because he loved her. But this love, so much is certain, has immediate spiritual relationship with his expertise in the things of death, and he might well have said that "without death there would scarcely have been any making of music."

Whoever is interested in life, I said in *The Magic Mountain,* is particularly interested in death. That is the trail of Schopenhauer, deeply imprinted, valid throughout life. It would also have been Schopenhauerian if I had added: "Whoever is interested in death seeks life in it"; and I did say it, if less epigrammatically, as a very young German, when it was a matter of bringing Thomas Buddenbrook, the hero of my early novel, down to his death; and I granted him to read that great chapter On Death who myself as a young writer, twenty-three or twenty-four years old, was just fresh from its impact. It was a great joy and I have taken occasion in my recollections to speak of it, and tell how I needed not to keep an experience like this to myself; that a beautiful opportunity at once came, to bear witness, to return thanks; that there was straightway a place to use it creatively. To him, the suffering hero of my novel of bourgeois life, which was the task, the burden, the virtue, the home and blessing of my young years, I gave the dear experience, the high adventure; I poured it into his life, just close to the end, I wove it into the narrative and made him find life in death, liberation from the bonds of his wearied individuality, freedom from a role in life which he had regarded symbolically and presented with courage and capacity, but which had never satisfied his spirit or his hopes and had been a hindrance to him in achieving something other and better. Schopenhauer is certainly something for the young, on the ground that his philosophy is the conception of a young man. When **The World as Will and Idea** appeared in 1818—the first volume, which contained his system—he was a man of thirty; but it had taken four years to work it out, and the intellectual experiences which therein crystallized undoubtedly lie still further back; he was, when his book took shape in him, scarcely older than I when I read it. He grew to be an old man—developing and perfecting it, collecting the commentary, obstinately and tirelessly confirming and testing what was a gift of his youth, so that he affords the singular spectacle of an old man who in uncanny loyalty concerns himself up to his last moment with the work of his youth. But this it remained, in its very essence; and not for nothing does Nietzsche draw attention to this early conception when he says that a man has the philosophy proper to his years, and that Schopenhauer's world—poem has the stamp of the time of life when the erotic predominates. And the feeling for death, may one add; for young folk are much more familiar with death, and know much more about it, than the old, because they know more about love. The erotic of death, as a musical, logical system of thought, born of an enormous tension of mind and senses—a tension whose issue and leaping spark is precisely eroticism: such is the parallel experience of youth in its encounter with this philosophy, which it understands not morally but vitally, personally—not because of its doctrine, I mean its preachment, but because of its essence—and with which they are well agreed.

"Where shall I be when I am dead?" asks Thomas Buddenbrook. "Ah, it is so brilliantly clear, so overwhelmingly simple! I shall be in all those who have ever said, do ever or ever shall say 'I'—*especially, however, in all those who say it most fully, potently, and gladly!*"

"Somewhere in the world a child is growing up, strong, well-grown, adequate, able to develop its powers, gifted, untroubled, pure, joyous, relentless, one of those beings whose glance heightens the joy of the joyous and drives the unhappy to despair. *He* is my son. He is I, myself, soon, soon; as soon as Death frees me from the wretched delusion that I am not he as well as myself.

"Have I ever hated life—pure, strong, relentless life? Folly and misconception! I have but hated myself, because I could not bear it. I love you. I love you all, you blessed, and soon, soon, I shall cease to be cut off from you all by the narrow bonds of myself; soon will that in me which loves you be free and be in and with you—in and with you all."

I shall be forgiven, I hope, for citing again this youth-lyric of mine, inspired by the intoxication of the twenty-year-old young man after drinking that metaphysical magic potion. I can testify that the organic shock it meant can only be compared with the one which the first contact with love and sex produces in the young mind—and the comparison is not fortuitous. But the passage is quoted to show that one can think in the *sense* in a philosopher without in the least thinking according to his sense; I mean that one can avail oneself of his thoughts—and thus can think as he would by no means have thought. Here, indeed, one thought who had read Nietzsche as well as Schopenhauer and carried the one experience over into the other, setting up the most extraordinary mixture with them. But my point is the naïve misuse of a philosophy which precisely artists are "guilty" of, and which I had in mind when I said that a philosophy is often influential less through its morality or its theory of knowledge, the intellectual bloom of its vitality, than by this vitality itself, its essential and personal character—more, in short, through its passion than its wisdom. In this way artists often become "betrayers" of a philosophy, and thus was Schopenhauer "understood" by Wagner, when he put his erotic mystery play as it were under the protection of Schopenhauer's metaphysics. The thing in Schopenhauer that worked on Wagner, in which the latter recognized himself, was the explanation of the world in terms of "will," the instinct, the erotic conception of the world (sex as "focus of the will") by which the *Tristan* music and its cosmogony of yearning are conditioned. It has been denied that *Tristan* was influenced by the philosophy of Schopenhauer—correctly in so far as the "denial of the will" comes in question: for it deals of course with a love-poem; and in love, in sex, the will asserts itself the most strongly. But precisely as a love-mystery the work is to the last degree Schopenhauerian in its coloration. In it, as it were, the erotic honey, the intoxicating essence, is sucked out of Schopenhauer's philosophy, but the wisdom left behind.

So artists go about to deal with a philosophy—they "understand" it in their way, an emotional way: for art needs to come only to emotional, to passionate experiences, not to moral ones, whereto philosophy, as a schoolmistress, felt herself at all times obligated. Even though no state-endowed "university philosophy," even though "subject to none," yet it was desirable for her moral conclusions to agree with the reigning morality—in the Occident, of course, Christianity; as a product of wisdom she did well to correspond to the religious result and confirm it. One might oneself be an atheist—and Schopenhauer was; if one is only a metaphysician it is always possible to arrive at results from another angle, which strengthen desirably the claims of religious morality. Schopenhauer had the good fortune, he discovered the possibility of arriving at highly moral results from highly sensual and passionate experiential premises; to a doctrine of compassion and redemption in agreement with Christianity—deducing it from the illusory nature of life, the delusion of the *principium individuationis:* compassion, Christlike love, the abrogation of egoism as the result of knowledge, which sees through the deception of the I and the you, the veil of Maya. Such a harmony cannot surprise the philosopher if he, like Schopenhauer, institutes a parallelism between religion and philosophy and sees in that "metaphysics for the people," which, as it is calculated for the great masses of humanity, can offer truth only in allegorical form, whereas philosophy offers it neat. He himself says: "The moral result of Christianity, up to the most exalted asceticism, one finds in my work rationally based and in association; whereas in Christianity they are based on sheer fables. Faith in these disappears more and more; thus people will be forced to turn to my philosophy." But the notion that in religion and philosophy there is only a matter of exoteric and esoteric truth, of which the one has become inacceptable so that the other must substitute for it—this notion does not prevent even for the philosopher's conscience the conclusion that it is not the religious morality that needs confirmation by philosophy, but the other way round; and for me there exists no doubt that a philosopher finds himself reassured by the agreement of the moral issues of his world-theory with the teachings of religion; and that Schopenhauer too feels himself legitimated as a philosopher thereby. "Subject he was to none." But for instance his train of thought led him to an ethical condemnation of suicide, because in it the will to life asserts itself, instead of refusing; and for that he was grateful to his train of thought: "the priest says just about as much only in a little different words."

At bottom he was lucky. He came into conflict with religion as little as with the state, and that thanks to the disdain with which it treated him; and which made him see in the Hegelian state-worship the greatest of all philistinism. For his part he judged the state as a necessary evil, and assured of his uncritical and forbearing disinterestedness those "who have the heavy task of governing men—that is, of upholding law and order, peace and quiet among many millions of one species, in the great majority boundlessly egotistic, unfair, dishonest, envious, malicious, and very limited and wrong-headed to boot; and of protecting the few who have any possessions against the innumerable numbers of those who own nothing but their physical strength." That sounds both grim and exhilarating—we feel a certain amount of agreement. But does not this conception of the state as an institution for the protection of property approach as nearly to "philistinism," though from another side, as Hegel's apotheosis of the state as the apex of all human striving and as "absolutely perfected ethical organism"? We know the inhuman horrors of a doctrine by which it would be the destiny of a man to be consumed in the state; know it from its consequences, for fascism as well as communism come from Hegel, and Schopenhauer himself had lived to see the theoretic prolongation of Hegelian state absolutism into communism. But however greatly we sympathize with the indignation which he felt at state totalitarianism, by which, as he said, "the lofty goal of our existence is quite ravished from our sight," the totality of the human, of which the political and social is a part, seems not to be better served by the philosopher-small-capitalist's renunciation of any interference with this sphere, the intellect's renunciation of all political passion, in the words of the jingle: *"Ich danke Gott an jedem Morgen, dass ich nicht brauch fürs heil'ge röm'sche Reich zu sorgen"* ("Each day I thank what Gods there be I need not care about the H R E")—lines which might well be applied to true philistinism and shirking of responsibility; they make us marvel how an intellectual fighter like Schopenhauer could make them his own.

It does not of course suffice as an explanation of a "disinterested contemplation" of the state, very close to the utterest political conservatism, to speak of Schopenhauer's deeply concerned interest in the preservation of the small but for a young bachelor philosopher adequate property inherited from his father, a Danzing merchant. It was a justifiable and at bottom highly intellectual interest; for this bourgeois property, to whose caretaker in naïve loyalty he degraded the state, was his one and all, his prop and support in this contemptible world; it gave him social freedom, the independence and solitude that he needed for his work; and the more incapable he felt of earning his bread himself in some official capacity, the more grateful he was all his life to the departed Heinrich Floris Schopenhauer for the priceless inheritance he bequeathed. But his unpolitical, anti-political—that is to say, conservative—position has of course a deeper root; it springs from his philosophy, for which an improvement and leading upward of the world as the manifestation of a principle evil and reprehensible in itself, the will, is utterly out of question, and which aims at redemption, not at liberation. How should a philosophy know much about how to deal with the idea of political freedom, to which freedom lies beyond the manifestation? But, above all, the political indifference of this philosophy is explained by its objectivism, by the value for salvation which it ascribes to objective contemplation and to it alone. For Schopenhauer's genius is nothing more nor less than objectivity—that is, the power of sustaining itself purely in a contemplative attitude, only as recognizing subject, as "clear world-eye." Here he makes contact with Goethe, whom he boundlessly admired, and to whose decisive influence the a-political character of German culture goes back.

Philosophy, declares Schopenhauer, asks not the whither, the whence, the wherefore, but only the what of the world; it has for object the nature of the world, manifesting itself in all relations, but itself never subject to them, always itself; and the ideas of the same. From such knowledge proceeds, like art, also all philosophy—from it finally also issues that mental constitution which leads to holiness and to the redemption of the world. Art and philosophy, then, are quietist (for pure objectivism is quietism). They will on no account alter anything, they will only look at it. So that Schopenhauer has not a good word for "progress," and even less for the political activity of the people, the revolution. His behaviour in the '48 was grimly, comically petty—one cannot put other words to it. His heart was not at all with those who fanatically enough hoped at that time to give a direction to German public life which might have meant a happier turn to the whole of European history down to our day, and which was to the interest of every intellectual man—the democratic direction. He called "the people" simply the *"souveraine canaille,"* and ostentatiously lent his "goggles" to the officer who from Schopenhauer's house was reconnoitring the men on the barricades, that he might better direct the fire. Yes, in his will he appointed as his universal legatee "the fund established in Berlin for the support of the invalided Prussian soldiers and their families, survivors of those who fell to uphold and restore law and order in Germany in the struggles of the insurrection and revolt of 1848-49."

Again, his anti-revolutionary position is based on his conception of the world; not only logically and theoretically, but also as a matter of temperament. It is fundamental, it belongs to his system of morals, his ethical pessimism, to that atmosphere of "Death, Cross, and Grave" which out of psychological necessity is averse to rhetoric, to the freedom-pathos and to the cult of humanity. It is anti-revolutionary out of pessimistic ethic, out of hatred for the indecent optimism of the present-day demagogy of progress; and, all in all, there is about it the atmosphere of a certain only too familiar, only too reminiscently indigenous German intellectual middle-classness—German precisely because it is intellectual, and because its inwardness, its conservative radicalism, its absolute remoteness from all democratic pragmatism, its "pure genius," its foolhardy unfreedom, its profound lack of policy, is a specifically and legitimately German possibility. In this world Arthur Schopenhauer belongs, a middle-class citizen with the stigmata of genius, which lift his figure into the eccentric, but bourgeois indisputably, in the most intellectual and personal sense. One need only look at his life, his Hanseatic merchant origin. The settled life of the elderly man, in Frankfurt am Main, dressed always with old-fashioned elegance, his angular, pedantic, immutable, and punctilious daily course; his care for his health on the basis of sound physical knowledge—"Not pleasure but absence of pain does the reasonable man seek"—his exactness as a capitalist (he wrote down every penny, and in the course of his life doubled his patrimony by shrewd husbandry); the calm tenacity, sparingness and evenness of his methods of work (he produced for print exclusively during the first two hours of

his morning and wrote to Goethe that loyalty and uprightness were the qualities he carried over from the practical into the theoretic and intellectual sphere, which made up the essence of his achievements and successes); all that testifies as strongly for the bourgeois nature of his human side as it was the expression of his bourgeois intellectualism that he so decisively rejected the romantic Middle Ages, priestly humbug, and knight-errant mummery, and considered that he based himself entirely on classical humanism; although—

But here we have a whole host of althoughs, which bring into question Schopenhauer's humanism and classicism, and seem rather to indicate that he should be called a romantic, or in any case to make one distinguish among the elements of his complex nature. In the narrower learned sense, as expert and scholar of ancient languages and literature, Schopenhauer was certainly a pre-eminent humanist; when as a young man destined by his father for trade, he had felt a compelling urge for learning, he had been bought off by an extended educational tour of Europe, and then after the death of his father changed over to study after all. He had lived in Weimar with his mother, the Frau Councillor and novelist Johana Schopenhauer, a good friend of Goethe, and under the guidance of a young high-school teacher had zealously studied Greek and Latin and amazed his master with his torrential progress. He wrote fluent Latin, and the innumerable quotations in his writings from the ancient authors display a classical reading and knowledge as intimate as it is extended. When he quotes from the Greek he appends a flawless Latin translation. But his literary culture was by no means solely humanistic; it extended over the product of all Europe in all centuries, for his proficiency in modern languages dated from earlier than the classic, and his books are seasoned with quotations from English, French, Italian, and Spanish writers, as well as from German, especially from Goethe and from the mystics, almost more than from the classics. That gives him something cosmopolitan, superprofessional, learned, world-literary; and correspondingly his philological and humanistic equipment is rounded out by a real and objective knowledge of natural science, for which he had laid the foundation as a young student at Göttingen, and in the perfecting of which he busied himself all his life, as he needed it to support and empirically confirm his metaphysics.

Above all, Schopenhauer is a classical humanist, on the Æsthetic side, in his theory of the beautiful: his hypothesis that genius is conditioned as the highest objectivity is altogether Apolline and Goethian; he invokes Goethe, he thinks he stands on his side; he feels himself a *"Classiker"* and is, very extensively, in his thinking and judgments, particularly in the German-bourgeois humanistic sense I spoke of, which makes him despise feudal honorific claptrap as well as the pietistic reactionary tendencies, the neo-Catholicism of his own time. He respects the Christian allegory as a pessimistic religion of redemption, but of the various *"Landesreligionen"* (established religions) he speaks altogether with philosophic superiority; and his religious "gift," in such a strongly metaphysical mind, must be called weak on the whole; one has only to read what he has to say here and there about faith and the service of God or the gods—it is not less rationalistic than, let us say, Freud's remarks on the religious "illusion."

In all this Schopenhauer is the humanist, altogether addressed to the classical and rational. I will go further and state that most importantly of all—all his misanthropy notwithstanding and all that he says about the corrupt condition of life in general and the distortions of the spirit of man in particular; notwithstanding his despair over the wretched social state one is born into as a human being—Schopenhauer is humanly full of pride and reverence as he contemplates the "crown of creation." To him the words mean, just as they did to the author of Genesis, man, the highest and most developed objectivation of the will. This most significant form of Schopenhauer's humanism perfectly—if by implication—accords with his political scepticism, his anti-revolutionarism. Man, according to him, is to be reverenced because he is the *knowing* creature. All knowing, of course, is fundamentally subject to the will out of which it sprang just as the head springs from the trunk. In the animal kingdom, indeed, this subjection of the intellect is never overcome. But look at the difference between man and beast in this relation between head and trunk. In the lower animal kingdom they are completely grown together, and in all animals the head is inclined to the earth, where lie the objects of the will; yes, even in the higher animals head and trunk are much more one than in man, whose head (Schopenhauer here uses the German word *Haupt,* to make the distinction clear) appears to be independently set on the shoulders, and uses the body to carry it, instead of being subject to it. This human advantage is shown pre-eminently in the Apollo Belvedere. The god of the Muses carries his mobile, wideeyed head so easily on his shoulders that it seems to have escaped from the body and to need to take no further interest in it.

What association of ideas could be more humanistic than this? Not for nothing does Schopenhauer choose the statue of the god of the Muses as the image of human dignity. Art, knowledge, and the dignity of human suffering are here envisaged as one—a profound and significant perception of our pessimistic humanist. And since humanism in general is prone to rhetoric and the wearing of rose-tinted spectacles, we have here something quite new, and, I venture to assert, something in the realm of ideas considerably in advance of its time. In the human being, the highest objectivation of the will, the latter is most brightly irradiated by knowledge. But in equal measure as knowledge arrives at clarity, the consciousness is heightened, the suffering increases, and thus in man it reaches its highest point. Even in individuals it varies in degree. "The degree of suffering," says Nietzsche, "is determined by the position in the hierarchy." Here Nietzsche betrays his ultimate dependence upon Schopenhauer's aristocratic theory of man's noble vocation to suffer. And in particular the highest type of man, the genius. It is this vocation that gives rise to the two great possibilities that Schopenhauer's humanism envisages for man. They are: art, and consecration. Only the human being possesses

the possibility of the Æsthetic state, as "disinterested" contemplation of the idea; to humanity alone is it given to achieve the final redemption, the renunciation of the will to live, as the artist mounts to the still loftier stage of ascetic saintliness. To man is vouchsafed the opportunity to right the wrong, to reverse the great error and mistake of being; to get the supreme insight that teaches him to make the suffering of the whole world his own and can lead him to renunciation and the conversion of the will. And so man is the secret hope of the world and of all creatures; towards whom as it were all creation trustfully turns as to its hoped-for redeemer and saviour.

This is a conception of great mystical beauty. It expresses a humane reverence for the mission of man, such as outweighs all misanthropy and supplies the corrective to all Schopenhauer's loathing of humanity. To me the importance of it lies in this union of pessimism and humanism, revealed to us by the philosopher: the intellectual experience he affords us that the one in no wise excludes the other, and that in order to be a humanist one does not need to be a rhetorical flatterer of humanity. I am not much disturbed by the question of the *truth* of Schopenhauer's interpretations, in particular his exposition, taken over from Kant, of the beautiful and the Æsthetic state, the famous "disinterestedness" over which Nietzsche, so much more advanced in psychological subtlety, not unjustly made merry. Nietzsche, the Dionysiast, turned against the moralization of art and the artist life, whose heightening and perfecting was to produce the ascetic and saint; against the alleged negativism of the productive and receptive Æsthetic zeal as the liberation from the torment of the will; against the negation of pleasure altogether, thus against pessimism itself, which for him lay in the confrontation of a "true world" and a "world of appearance" of which even in Kant he had already scented and pointed out. He noted without comment (the commentary is still wanting) that Kant declared: "These statements of Count Nerri [an eighteenth-century Italian philosopher] I subscribe to with full conviction: *il solo principio motore dell' uomo è il dolore. Il dolore precede ogni piacere non è un essere positivo.*" Was that so contrary to the meaning of the writer wherein one reads: "Desire is a form of pain"? In any case it was against his anti-Christian conviction, which simply will not, for the sake of earth and life, agree to any "real world" at all. Which does not alter the fact that, precisely in Æsthetics, he never denies his descent from Schopenhauer, even in the time of his apostasy. For when it says, in **The World as Will and Idea,** "that the essence of life itself, the will, existence itself, is a constant suffering, partly pathetic, partly terrible; on the other hand, the same as idea alone, simply looked at, or repeated through art, free from torment, makes a *significant spectacle (bedeutsames Schauspiel),*" Nietzsche is dealing with the justification of life entirely as an *Æsthetic spectacle* and manifestation of beauty, not otherwise than Schopenhauer deals with "disinterestedness"; in that he only gives Schopenhauer's thought the intellectual turn into the anti-moral, drunken and affirmative, into a dionysism of justification of life, wherein truly Schopenhauer's moral, life-denying pessimism can be recognized only with difficulty, but yet which survived, in another coloration, with other labels and altered demeanour. Indisputably, a man can become the opponent of a thinker and yet remain intellectually his pupil. For instance, does a man cease to be Marxist by standing the Marxian doctrine on its head and deriving certain economic principles from the ideological and religious instead of the reverse? In the same way, Nietzsche remained a Schopenhauerian. He is protected from the dubious title of optimist by the conception of the hero implicit in his dionysism, which springs from pessimism. One hesitates to speak of optimism, where what we are dealing with is really a bacchantic pessimism, a form of assent to life which is not primary and naïve but rather a conquest, a notwithstanding, won from suffering. But we find the heroic in Schopenhauer too: "Happiness is impossible; the highest attainable is a heroic life."

But we should be careful not to take too literally or seriously Schopenhauer's humanistic attitude or his classical, Apolline pronouncements. In his case, as in many others, we must distinguish between the person and the opinion, the human being and his judgments. What warns us is Schopenhauer's extremist position, a grotesque and dualistic antithesis in his nature, a *romanticism* (in the most colourful sense of the word) which removed him further from the Goethian sphere than he would ever have let himself even dream of. I said that Schopenhauer adhered to the Kantian when he defined the Æsthetic state as the tearing itself free of knowledge from will, whereby the subject ceases to be a mere individual and becomes a pure will-less subject of knowledge. But Kant, with his unemotional nature, would never have hit upon describing *"das Ding an sich"* as will, instinct, sinister passion, from which the artist state gained temporary deliverance; and his Æsthetics of "without interest" is not the moral issue of a romantic and emotional dualism of will and idea, a world-conception of the contrast between sensuality and asceticism with all the terrors and dæmonic tortures of one side and all the satisfactions of the other; but, by comparison, the coolest intellectuality. Ascetism means killing off. But with Kant there was not much to kill, he would never have found, to describe the Æsthetic state, the vehement images of extravagant gratitude that flocked into Schopenhauer's mind. Asceticism belongs to a world of romantic contrasts and has as premise frightful experiences of the will, instinct and passion, and deep suffering therefrom. The saint as consummation of the artist is the discovery of Schopenhauer, philosopher of the instincts and the emotion—not the thought-world of Kant, which, while certainly ruthless, was far more moderate-tempered; the fearfully, brilliantly intellectual tensions of Schopenhauer's world of contrast, with its two poles of brain and genitals, were entirely foreign to it.

Seldom has a book had a more expressive, more exhaustive title than Schopenhauer's chief work, his only work, in truth, developing his own original train of thought. All else that he wrote in a lifetime of seventy-two years only forms an assiduously collected accompaniment and reinforcement to it. *The World as Will and Idea*. That is not only the theme, in its most compendious formulation: it is the man, the human being, his personality, his life, his

suffering. The compulsive force of this man, and in particular his sexual urge, must have been enormous—cruel and tortuous as are the mythological figures he employs to describe the bondage to the will. It must have opposed with such equal power the compulsive force of his urge for knowledge, his lucid and mighty intellectuality, as to produce a frightfully radical duality and conflict, with a correspondingly profound craving for release; and to issue in intellectual denial of life itself, the impeachment of his own essence as evil, erroneous, and culpable. Rightly, if in an elevated sense, one may call this tortuous and grotesque. Sex is to Schopenhauer the focal point of the will; in its physical objectivation the opposite pole of the brain, which represented knowledge. Obviously, his capacity in both spheres went far beyond the average; though that in itself would only speak for the intensity and range of his nature. What makes him a pessimist, a *denier* of the world, is just the contradictory and hostile, exclusive and anguishing relation of the two spheres to each other. We need not, though it would be easy to do so, fail to understand his pessimism as the intellectual product of that very richness and power. Here is a bipolar nature, full of contrasts and conflicts, tortured and violent; after its own pattern it must experience the world: as instinct and spirit, passion and knowledge, "will" and "idea." But suppose he had learned to reconcile them in his genius, in his creative life. Suppose he had understood that genius does not at all consist in sensuality put out of action and will unhinged, that art is not mere objectivation of spirit, but the fruitful union and interpenetration of both spheres, immensely heightening to life and more fascinating than either can be by itself! That the essence of the creative artist is nothing else—and in Schopenhauer himself was nothing else—than sensuality spiritualized, than spirit informed and made creative by sex! Goethe's interpretation and experience differed from the pessimist's; it was happier, healthier, more blithely "classic," less pathologic (I use the word in an intellectual, unclinical sense)—less romantic, shall I say? For Goethe, sex and spirit (mind) were the highest, most provocative charms in life. He wrote: *"Denn das Leben ist die Liebe, und des Lebens Leben—Geist"* ("For life is love, and spirit the life of life"). But in Schopenhauer genius intensified both spheres until they took refuge in the ascetic. To him, sex is of the Devil, a diabolic distraction from pure contemplation; knowledge is that denial of sex which says: "If thine eye offend thee, pluck it out." Knowledge as "peace of the soul," art as a sedative and liberating condition of pure contemplation unmarred by will; the artist as a half-way stage to sainthood, divorced from the will to live: that is Schopenhauer. And again, in so far as this conception of mind and art is objective, it approaches Goethe's, it has a classic cast. But being exaggerated and ascetic, it is definitely romantic, in one sense of the word, which would not have appealed to Goethe at all—as witness his attitude to Heinrich von Kleist. And accordingly with similar feelings he may have read *The World as Will and Idea;* agreeing in some places, but in the main rejecting, affected hypochondrically—and have laid it by, shaking his head; as a matter of fact, we know that after a beginning of sympathetic curiosity he did not finish it.

The distance between one great man and another, which is the result of inevitable egotism, must not mislead us. Goethe too united, in his happier way, the classic and the romantic in himself—that, indeed, is one of the formulas to which one may reduce his greatness. It is no different with Schopenhauer: the combination of the two intellectual strains is rather to be reckoned to the advantage than the detriment of his greatness—in so far, that is, as greatness is reconciling, comprehensive, summing up an epoch. Schopenhauer combines much, his theory contains many elements: idealistic, scientific, yes, pantheistic; and that his personality is strong enough to bind these elements together, such as the classic and romantic, to blend them together into something new and unique so that there is no occasion to speak of eclecticism, that is the decisive thing.

But, after all, terms and antitheses like "classic" and "romantic" do not apply to Schopenhauer. Neither the one nor the other is adequate to describe a mentality later in time than those for whom those terms once played their role. He stands nearer to us than do the minds who in their day were occupied with such distinctions and ranged themselves accordingly. Schopenhauer's mental life, the dualistic, overstrained irritability and fever of his genius, is less romantic than it is modern. I should like to enlarge upon this distinction, but content myself with making it refer in general to a state of mind the increasing strain of which became only too marked in our Western world in the century between Goethe and Nietzsche. In this respect Schopenhauer stands between the two, he makes a bridge between them: more "modern," more suffering and difficult than Goethe, but much more "classic," robust, and healthy than Nietzsche. From which it is clear that optimism and pessimism, the affirmation or denial of life, have nothing to do with health and illness. Illness and health, accordingly, have to be used with great caution as criteria or valuations. They are biological conceptions, whereas the nature of man is not exhausted in the biological. But it would be hard to assert that Nietzsche's Dionysiac, anti-Christian enthusiasm was personally something healthier and more robust than Schopenhauer's resentment against life—or that, objectively or intellectually, he brought more health into the world. Much too much, in the way of confusion, did Nietzsche labour with this biological contrast; he summoned up a false idea of healthiness which tramples on the spiritual factor that might today heal Europe. But he himself indicates a step further in suffering, in subtlety and modernity—particularly in the quality in which, more explicitly than any other, he is the pupil of Schopenhauer—I mean as a psychologist.

Schopenhauer, as psychologist of the will, is the father of all modern psychology. From him the line runs, by way of the psychological radicalism of Nietzsche, straight to Freud and the men who built up his psychology of the unconscious and applied it to the mental sciences. Nietzsche's anti-Socratism and hostility to mind are nothing but the philosophic affirmation and glorification of Schopenhauer's discovery of the primacy of the will, his pessimistic insight into the secondary and subservient relation of mind to will. This insight, certainly not humane in the classical sense, that the intellect is there to do the pleasure of the will, to justify it, to provide it with motivations, which are often very shallow and self-deluding—in fine, to rationalize the instincts—conceals a sceptical and pessimistic psychology, an analysis of relentless penetration. And it not only prepared the way for what we call psychoanalysis, it was already just that. At bottom all psychology is the unmasking, the acute, ironic, naturalistic perception of the riddling relation that obtains between the reason and the instincts. A little dialogue in the *Wahlverwandtschaften* well illustrates this underhand game our natures play. Edouard, already in love after his first meeting with Ottilie, is made by Goethe to say: "She is an entertaining person." To which his wife replies: "Entertaining? She never opened her mouth." Schopenhauer must certainly have enjoyed this passage. It is a pleasant, blithely classic illustration of his own thesis, that one does not want a thing because it is good, but finds it good because one wants it.

He himself says, for instance: "Still, it must be remarked that in order to deceive himself, a man will prepare for himself apparently inadvertent errors, which are in fact secretly deliberate acts. For we deceive and flatter nobody with such ingeniousness as ourselves." In this casual remark are whole chapters, yes, volumes of analytic unmasking of psychology *in nuce*—as later so often, in Nietzsche's aphoristic writings, Freudian revelations are anticipated as by a flash of lightning. In an address in Vienna I pointed out that Schopenhauer's sinister domain of the will is entirely identical with what Freud calls the unconscious, the "id"—as, on the other hand, Schopenhauer's intellect entirely corresponds to the Freudian ego, that part of the soul which is turned outwards to the world.

This essay is an attempt to evoke today a figure little known to the present generation; and to reconsider and recapitulate his concepts. Its object is to reassert the idea of the connection between pessimism and humanism. I should like to hand on to a world where human feeling is today finding itself in sore straits the knowledge of this combined melancholy and pride in the human race which make up Schopenhauer's philosophy. His pessimism—that is his humanity. His interpretation of the world by the concept of the will, his insight into the overweening power of instinct and the derogation of the one-time godlike reason, mind, and intellect to a mere tool with which to achieve security—all this is anti-classic and in its essence inhumane. But it is precisely in the pessimistic hue of his philosophy that his humanity and spirituality lie; in the fact that this great artist, practised in suffering and wielding the prose of a great humane cultural epoch in our history, lifts man out of the biological sphere of nature, makes his own feeling and understanding soul the theatre where the will meets its reverse, and sees in the human being the saviour of all creation. Therein lie both his humanity and his intellectuality.

The twentieth century has in its first third taken up a position of reaction against classic rationalism and intellectualism. It has surrendered to admiration of the unconscious, to a glorification of instinct, which it thinks is overdue to life. And the bad instincts have accordingly been enjoying a heyday. We have seen instead of pessimistic conviction deliberate malice. Intellectual recognition of bitter truth turns into hatred and contempt for mind itself. Man has greedily flung himself on the side of "life"—that is, on the side of the stronger—for there is no disputing the fact that life has nothing to fear from mind, that not life but knowledge, or rather mind, is the weaker part and one more needing protection on this earth. Yet the anti-humanity of our day is a humane experiment too in its way. It is a one-sided answer to the eternal question as to the nature and destiny of man. We palpably need a corrective to restore the balance, and I think the philosophy I here evoke can do good service. I spoke of Schopenhauer as modern. I might have called him futurist. The chiaroscuro harmonies of his human traits, the mixture in him of Voltaire and Jakob Böhme, the paradox of his classic, pellucid prose, employed to lighten the darkest and lowest purlieus of being; his proud misanthropy, which never belies his reverence for the idea of the human being; in short, what I called his pessimistic humanity seems to me to herald the temper of a future time. Once he was fashionable and famous, then half-forgotten. But his philosophy may still exert a ripe and humanizing influence upon our age. His intellectual sensitivity, his teaching, which was life, that knowledge, thought, and philosophy are not matters of the head alone but of the whole man, heart and sense, body and soul; in other words, his existence as an artist may help to bring to birth a new humanity of which we stand in need, and to which it is akin: a humanity above dry reason on the one hand and idolatry of instinct on the other. For art, accompanying man on his painful journey to self-realization, has always been before him at the goal.

Radoslav A. Tsanoff (essay date 1942)

SOURCE: "The Moral Gospel of Pessimism," in *The Moral Ideals of Our Civilization,* E. P. Dutton & Co., 1942, pp. 389-405.

[*In the following excerpt, Tsanoff outlines Schopenhauer's criticisms of Kant's moral law and contrasts Schopenhauer's "pessimistic ethics of redemption" with Kant's a priori metaphysic of morals.*]

In [Schopenhauer's] view of human life, a life of insatiate greeds preying on each other, of wretched and futile desires, what meaning could morality have? A moral philosophy which ignored these basic facts of human nature and motivation would be vain irrelevance. In the fourth book of *The World as Will and Idea* Schopenhauer, probing the dismal outcome of his metaphysics of the Will-to-live, had traced the large outlines of a pessimistic ethics of redemption. In his work *The Basis of Morality,* he takes up more systematically this problem: "Is the fountain and basis of Morals to be sought for in an idea of morality which lies directly in the consciousness (or conscience), and in the analysis of the other ethical conceptions which arise from it? or is it to be sought in some other source of knowledge?" This question is ostensibly the same as that which had confronted Kant in his *Fun-*

damental Principles of the Metaphysics of Morals, and Schopenhauer's first task was accordingly a criticism of the Kantian ethics. Despite his manner of treatment, severe in the case of Kant, contemptuous towards Kant's followers, especially Fichte, Schopenhauer's critique of the ethics of duty is among the most searching, and it is also an indispensable introduction to his own theory of morals.

Kant undertakes to establish moral philosophy on a basis of 'pure practical reason.' Ethics is not a statement and statistical summary of what men do, but a universal pronouncement of what they ought to do, irrespective of their actual practice. This first false step, according to Schopenhauer, vitiates the entire procedure of Kant's ethics. For how are we warranted in declaring what 'ought' to be done, even though it never is actually done? Unless such a rescript is based on the facts of human life, though it may maintain solemnly a lofty authority above and beyond experience, it is finally vain and ineffectual pretense. If, however, it does find its substance and force in effective compulsion, then it is only a disguise of the old morality of rewards and punishments, social or theological legalism, a spurious ethics in a new solemn garb.

Stating his criticism in terms of Kant's own terminology, Schopenhauer would maintain that a categorical imperative, the conception of an unconditional obligation, is completely unthinkable (he also calls it nonsensical). But a hypothetical imperative, obligation deriving its force on motives by appeal to consequences, would be compulsion, therefore not moral. The conclusions seem to be that ethics cannot disregard actual human conduct, and that morality cannot adequately be expressed in terms of law and obligation. Both of these inferences Schopenhauer undertakes to develop and maintain against Kant.

It is because Kant cannot find morality in experience that he would dictate it categorically from above. But emptied out of any specific content, the alleged law of reason would have only its bare lawfulness to recommend it. So Kant finds that the moral imperative affirms simply its own universality and necessity. *The* duty appears to be to act dutifully, as we have it in Kant's maxim. The mere appeal to universality does not yield a distinctively moral response, and is thus barren as a moral principle. Schopenhauer maintains in fact that Kant's alleged disinterested categorical imperative finds its actual fuller statement in terms of the very egoism which Kant had initially and solemnly disdained. Though Kant insists on disinterested dutiful motivation,—speak the truth though the heavens fall,—yet he declares as a certain conclusion that in a rational universe the heavens will not fall through veracity, that it is undutiful conduct which proves self-defeating in the end. Lying is wrong, for according to Kant's maxim, it could not be made a universal law; were it universalized, no one would believe me or else "would pay me back in my own coin." Duty is bound to prevail and virtue to find its confluence with happiness, man's immortality providing the scope for it, and God assuring the adjustment of goodness to good fortune in the realm of ends. [Schopenhauer writes:] "In spite of [Kant's] grand *a priori* edifice, Egoism is sitting on the judge's seat, scales in hand."

Kant's arguments vindicating veracity, benevolence, justice in terms of his own maxim may not all warrant Schopenhauer's interpretation of them as ultimately implying egoistic motivation; but Schopenhauer appears to be sustained in his basic claim that, if the moral imperative is to have any substance and concrete significance, it must be in some sense rooted in experience, and find its sanction in human nature. In this criticism of Kant's ethics, the fundamental principle and method of Schopenhauer's moral philosophy are revealed: "Ethics has to do with actual human conduct, and not with the *a priori* building of card houses—a performance which yields results that no man would ever turn to in the stern stress and battle of life, and which, in face of the storm of our passions, would be about as serviceable as a syringe in a great fire."

We require a basis of morality that will apply to living men and women, not to mere 'rational beings.' We should accordingly analyze human conduct, to distinguish the various incentives to action and discover if any motive of moral worth obtains.

This investigation of moral value in terms of motivation indicates another respect in which Schopenhauer differs from Kant. Kant distinguishes the freedom of moral acts from the causal necessity of all events in the world of phenomena. Against this distinction, Schopenhauer insists on regarding all human acts as determined. An action is moral not because it is free but because of the kind of motivation which determines it. Good actions, if goodness there be, cannot be actions in any supersensible realm, but in the same world of experience and as truly subject to determination as any events whatever. Motivation is only another variety of the operation of antecedents on consequents: more complex and less immediate but none the less necessary. Every specific action of ours is determined by antecedent factors or motives, and these again by others. But all of them together are as they are ultimately because they are ours, expressions of our being. What I do follows from what I am. I should act differently only if I were another.

But why am I as I am? To this question no answer is forthcoming. The essence of me and of you operates under the conditions of space and time and is accordingly determined; but itself as the Will-to-live, the ultimate dynamic of all, is beyond determination and free. Freedom thus does not characterize any specific action, but the inexplicable root and kernel of all being. In reaching the limits of all determination we meet the unfathomable.

Proceeding now to distinguish various motives and their determination of actions, Schopenhauer notes that in the very nature of the case men are moved to act by considerations of weal or woe, of oneself or of others. It is wholly against nature to pursue one's own woe: so three incentives remain as objectives of action: one's own weal,

another's woe, another's weal. Schopenhauer pronounces the first two of these three incentives antimoral; no good can come from them, yet together they exhaust well-nigh all of human conduct: Egoism and Malice. The 'maxim' of egoistic action is: Help no one, but so far as it is to your advantage, hurt others. The malicious man acts on the maxim: Help no one, but as much as you can, hurt others. Malice and selfishness thus agree in utterly disregarding the well-being of others; but selfishness is preeminently concentrated on pursuing one's own advantage. The egoist would destroy the world without a qualm, *if* the destruction served his own purpose. But utterly indifferent to the needs of others, the selfish man would not lift a finger to hurt another, if he saw no advantage accruing to himself. Assure yourself that he has no further profit in molesting you, and you may rest in peace. So where no one else enters to interfere with the egoist's gain, he might pursue his own way interfering with no one, and his acts would then be morally neutral. But the malicious and spiteful man has made it his special joy to see others suffer; he is not happy unless he is hurting others, and would risk hurt and even destruction if he could gratify fiendish ill-will. These two incentives lead to all the vices of human life. [Schopenhauer writes:] "From *Egoism* we should probably derive greed, gluttony, lust, selfishness, avarice, covetousness, injustice, hardness of heart, pride, arrogance, etc.; while to malice might be ascribed disaffection, envy, ill-will, spitefulness, pleasure in seeing others suffer, prying curiosity, slander, insolence, petulance, hatred, anger, treachery, fraud, thirst for revenge, cruelty, etc."

To counteract these vicious motives in human nature and to yield moral worth, if moral worth there be in men, another motive power is needed, and indeed there is only one other, *Compassion*. This is a motive aiming at the well-being of others, refraining from the infliction of any harm. Its maxim is, Hurt no one, but so far as you can, help others. Only when it genuinely springs from within can it check the egoism that normally sways the will; otherwise, laws, religious restraints, rewards and punishments, self-respect, human dignity, and categorical imperatives are of no avail. Only when the lot of others so affects me that without any ulterior considerations I come to participate in the sufferings of others and seek to relieve them, only then is my conduct truly compassionate and then only is it good. The essence of moral value is in the overcoming of selfish desire. In this respect goodness shares the same basic character with other values, with the impersonal objectivity of truth and with the desireless contemplation which, according to Schopenhauer, is the essence of art, the perception and expression of beauty.

Compassion may be either negative or positive: the two cardinal virtues are thus Justice and Lovingkindness. The just man follows the first part of the maxim, Hurt no one. He does not shift onto the shoulders of others the burdens which life piles on us all. The lives of others are not made the more miserable because of his living, and when he dies the sigh that men breathe is not a sigh of relief. Respecting the rights of others, fulfilling his assumed obligations, doing his share whether compelled or not, the just man has always others in as clear a view as himself and makes no one else his victim or his tool. But lovingkindness, positive compassion, moves us to active promotion of the well-being of others; the compassionate soul responds to the cry of distress and, forgetting all thought of personal advantage, seeks to alleviate suffering wherever found. All actions which men acknowledge as good are, according to Schopenhauer, reducible to justice or lovingkindness, are thus forms of negative or positive compassion. Uncommon as these virtues in their genuine forms are, we may yet observe that justice is a more characteristically masculine virtue; women incline less to justice than to lovingkindness.

But what is the essence and the basis of compassion? Schopenhauer seems to find its two moments in the two components of the word, the same in various languages, Sympathy, Compassion, *Mitleid*. The compassionate man *suffers,* and he suffers *with* others. The impassable gulf which separates the selfish and the malicious from their neighbors is effaced in sympathy. A deepening conviction of oneness with others is the ground-note in all compassionate action. And this conviction is tragic; it is a communion in woe. Life is a distress; the distress cannot be escaped at another's expense; the distress is essentially due to the will-driven desire for the gratification of self, the egoism which makes men rivals and foes of each other. Compassion is the practical recognition of the illusion and the evil of self-engrossment; it is therefore the evidence of a deep insight into the tragic enigma of existence. [Schopenhauer writes]: "To be just, noble, and benevolent is nothing else than to translate my metaphysics into action." Compassion, alone good, points beyond itself; justice and lovingkindness, relieving the distress of others, lead the moral saint to relieve and to renounce the essential distress, the will-driven life itself, to curb and deny the Will-to-live. Thus compassion culminates in asceticism. It is not suicide that Schopenhauer has in mind when he advocates the denial of life; for suicide registers the victory of unquenched desire, not its subjugation. Not cessation of living is the goal, but extinction of craving. The prevailing mood of Christian asceticism, and even more, Buddhist quietism dominates Schopenhauer's conclusion. The man who has renounced desire and self has left the sweep and whirlpool of seeking and effort. He finds and attains the desireless, selfless calm of Nirvana.

This ascetic-quietist culmination of compassion has been criticized as involving racial self-annihilation and so the self-extinction of morality. Should all humanity adopt Kant's ethics of duty, the world might become an assembly of stern Puritans; but at the altars of Schopenhauer's ascetic ideal, mankind could continue to worship for just one generation. Yet this is not the main defect; it only serves to indicate it. Schopenhauer criticizes severely Kant's dismissal of experience in his ethics; but on what experience has he based his own theory of morality? In his account of human character as egoistic or malicious, he professes to draw inevitable inferences from his metaphysics of the Will-to-live. Though we may not share his pessimistic portrayal of the facts of human life, we recognize it as what is to be expected from his account of the

nature of reality. But all the more surprising is his gospel of compassion and self-effacement. If the ultimate reality manifests itself at the human level as insatiate greed, how is sympathetic conduct possible? If the Will-to-live is the source and dynamic of all existence, then how can denial of the will take place?

Schopenhauer openly recognizes that a truly compassionate act is the rarest thing in the world, but insists that it alone is good; even as Kant declares the purely dutiful act virtuous, even though such an act had never been performed. Both find morality beyond the common run of experience: Kant, in the dutiful loyalty to the moral law; Schopenhauer, in the will-curbing sympathy and self-renunciation. But while Kant's account of human experience and of natural order does not make provision for the categorical imperative, it does not exclude it. Kant's Realm of Ends transcends the causal nexus, but does not nullify it. That it expands and deepens it, or reveals its fuller fruition, was the claim of the Post-Kantian idealists. Schopenhauer, however, unlike Kant, does have a theoretical metaphysics, and if the nature of ultimate reality as explained in the doctrine of the Will-to-live, involves human selfishness, how can it admit of a single case of genuinely compassionate action? Schopenhauer himself is aware of this basic difficulty in his system, and also of the specific perplexity in which it involves his ethics. [Schopenhauer writes:] "Every purely beneficent act, all help entirely and genuinely unselfish, being, as such, exclusively inspired by another's distress, is, in fact, if we probe the matter to the bottom, a dark enigma, a piece of mysticism put into practice; inasmuch as it springs out of, and finds its true explanation in, the same higher knowledge that constitutes the essence of whatever is mystical."

It is not Schopenhauer's ethical exaltation of compassion which is most important here. Considered only in this way, his moral theory, a pessimistic variety of the ethics of benevolence, invites a variant of the familiar criticisms. Not Schopenhauer's laudation of sympathy, but his recognition of it in his system is the significant point, for this moral gospel involves and demands a revision of the irrationalistic-pessimistic metaphysics of the Will-to-live. The familiar concluding words of his masterpiece are crucial here: "To those in whom the will has turned and has denied itself, this our world, which is so real, with all its suns and milky-ways—is nothing." The aesthetics and the ethics of Schopenhauer disclose capacities in human nature for disinterested contemplation, for justice and lovingkindness; they indicate an insight into human nature and reality beyond insatiate greed and beyond the Will-to-live. The self is not inevitably selfish; it can be compassionate, even self-effacing.

We may now see in a new light Schopenhauer's criticism of Kant's maxim as egoism in disguise. The dutiful act is not selfish in the damaging sense of the term used by Schopenhauer, but fully self-expressive. The self-recognition of moral character reveals that the 'ought' is the expression of man's truest and deepest self, a fellow-member with all other persons in the Realm of Ends; in which he wills for himself only what he would will for others, freedom of realized personality in loyal devotion to ideals. . . . But Schopenhauer's gospel of salvation, in ethics and aesthetics alike, reveals the need of revision in his metaphysics on which they were supposed to rest. In his gospel of salvation he reached a wisdom more final than the pessimism. In the doctrine of disinterested contemplation and of the world-renouncing insight of the moral saint, was involved a revised account of the role of intelligence, as not inevitably and finally the tool of the Will-to-live, and therefore an advance beyond the initial irrationalism.

Bertrand Russell (essay date 1945)

SOURCE: "Schopenhauer," in *A History of Western Philosophy, and Its Connection with Political and Social Circumstances from the Earliest Times to the Present Day,* Simon and Schuster, 1945, pp. 753-59.

[*One of the preeminent thinkers of the twentieth century, Russell wrote a number of important works in philosophy, including* Principia Mathematica *(1910-13), a highly influential study in mathematical logic that he co-authored with Alfred North Whitehead. In the following essay, Russell briefly describes Schopenhauer's life and the relative importance of his ideas in the history of philosophy.*]

Schopenhauer (1788-1860) is in many ways peculiar among philosophers. He is a pessimist, whereas almost all the others are in some sense optimists. He is not fully academic, like Kant and Hegel, nor yet completely outside the academic tradition. He dislikes Christianity, preferring the religions of India, both Hinduism and Buddhism. He is a man of wide culture, quite as much interested in art as in ethics. He is unusually free from nationalism, and as much at home with English and French writers as with those of his own country. His appeal has always been less to professional philosophers than to artistic and literary people in search of a philosophy that they could believe. He began the emphasis on Will which is characteristic of much nineteenth- and twentieth-century philosophy; but for him Will, though metaphysically fundamental, is ethically evil—an opposition only possible for a pessimist. He acknowledges three sources of his philosophy, Kant, Plato, and the Upanishads, but I do not think he owes as much to Plato as he thinks he does. His outlook has a certain temperamental affinity with that of the Hellenistic age; it is tired and valetudinarian, valuing peace more than victory, and quietism more than attempts at reform, which he regards as inevitably futile.

Both his parents belonged to prominent commercial families in Danzig, where he was born. His father was a Voltairian, who regarded England as the land of liberty and intelligence. In common with most of the leading citizens of Danzig, he hated the encroachments of Prussia on the independence of the free city, and was indignant when it was annexed to Prussia in 1793—so indignant that he removed to Hamburg, at considerable pecuniary loss. Schopenhauer lived there with his father from 1793

to 1797; then he spent two years in Paris, at the end of which his father was pleased to find that the boy had nearly forgotten German. In 1803 he was put in a boarding-school in England, where he hated the cant and hypocrisy. Two years later, to please his father, he became a clerk in a commercial house in Hamburg, but he loathed the prospect of a business career, and longed for a literary and academic life. This was made possible by his father's death, probably by suicide; his mother was willing that he should abandon commerce for school and university. It might be supposed that he would, in consequence, have preferred her to his father, but the exact opposite happened: he disliked his mother, and retained an affectionate memory of his father.

Schopenhauer's mother was a lady of literary aspirations, who settled in Weimar two weeks before the battle of Jena. There she kept a literary salon, wrote books, and enjoyed friendships with men of culture. She had little affection for her son, and a keen eye for his faults. She warned him against bombast and empty pathos; he was annoyed by her philanderings. When he came of age he inherited a modest competence; after this, he and his mother gradually found each other more and more intolerable. His low opinion of women is no doubt due, at least in part, to his quarrels with his mother.

Already at Hamburg he had come under the influence of the romantics, especially Tieck, Novalis, and Hoffmann, from whom he learnt to admire Greece and to think ill of the Hebraic elements in Christianity. Another romantic, Friedrich Schlegel, confirmed him in his admiration of Indian philosophy. In the year in which he came of age (1809), he went to the university of Göttingen, where he learnt to admire Kant. Two years later he went to Berlin, where he studied mainly science; he heard Fichte lecture, but despised him. He remained indifferent throughout the excitement of the war of liberation. In 1819 he became a *Privatdozent* at Berlin, and had the conceit to put his lectures at the same hour as Hegel's; having failed to lure away Hegel's hearers, he soon ceased to lecture. In the end he settled down to the life of an old bachelor in Dresden. He kept a poodle named Atma (the world-soul), walked two hours every day, smoked a long pipe, read the London *Times,* and employed correspondents to hunt up evidences of his fame. He was anti-democratic, and hated the revolution of 1848; he believed in spiritualism and magic; in his study he had a bust of Kant and a bronze Buddha. In his manner of life he tried to imitate Kant except as regards early rising.

His principal work, ***The World as Will and Idea,*** was published at the end of 1818. He believed it to be of great importance, and went so far as to say that some paragraphs in it had been dictated by the Holy Ghost. To his great mortification, it fell completely flat. In 1844 he persuaded the publisher to bring out a second edition; but it was not till some years later that he began to receive some of the recognition for which he longed.

Schopenhauer's system is an adaptation of Kant's, but one that emphasizes quite different aspects of the [*Cri-*

tique of Pure Reason] from those emphasized by Fichte or Hegel. They got rid of the thing-in-itself, and thus made knowledge metaphysically fundamental. Schopenhauer retained the thing-in-itself, but identified it with will. He held that what appears to perception as my body is really my will. There was more to be said for this view as a development of Kant than most Kantians were willing to recognize. Kant had maintained that a study of the moral law can take us behind phenomena, and give us knowledge which sense-perception cannot give; he also maintained that the moral law is essentially concerned with the will. The difference between a good man and a bad man is, for Kant, a difference in the world of things-in-themselves, and is also a difference as to volitions. It follows that, for Kant, volitions must belong to the real world, not to the world of phenomena. The phenomenon corresponding to a volition is a bodily movement; that is why, according to Schopenhauer, the body is the appearance of which will is the reality.

But the will which is behind phenomena cannot consist of a number of different volitions. Both time and space, according to Kant—and in this Schopenhauer agrees with him—belong only to phenomena; the thing-in-itself is not in space or time. My will, therefore, in the sense in which it is real, cannot be dated, nor can it be composed of separate acts of will, because it is space and time that are the source of plurality—the "principle of individuation," to use the scholastic phrase which Schopenhauer prefers. My will, therefore, is one and timeless. Nay, more, it is to be identified with the will of the whole universe; my separateness is an illusion, resulting from my subjective apparatus of spatio-temporal perception. What is real is one vast will, appearing in the whole course of nature, animate and inanimate alike.

So far, we might expect Schopenhauer to identify his cosmic will with God, and teach a pantheistic doctrine not unlike Spinoza's, in which virtue would consist in conformity to the divine will. But at this point his pessimism leads to a different development. The cosmic will is wicked; will, altogether, is wicked, or at any rate is the source of all our endless suffering. Suffering is essential to all life, and is increased by every increase of knowledge. Will has no fixed end, which if achieved would bring contentment. Although death must conquer in the end, we pursue our futile purposes, "as we blow out a soap-bubble as long and as large as possible, although we know perfectly well that it will burst." There is no such thing as happiness, for an unfulfilled wish causes pain, and attainment brings only satiety. Instinct urges men to procreation, which brings into existence a new occasion for suffering and death; that is why shame is associated with the sexual act. Suicide is useless; the doctrine of transmigration, even if not literally true, conveys truth in the form of a myth.

All this is very sad, but there is a way out, and it was discovered in India.

The best of myths is that of Nirvana (which Schopenhauer interprets as extinction). This, he agrees, is contrary to Christian doctrine, but "the ancient wisdom of the human race will not be displaced by what happened in Galilee." The cause of suffering is intensity of will; the less we exercise will, the less we shall suffer. And here knowledge turns out to be useful after all, provided it is knowledge of a certain sort. The distinction between one man and another is part of the phenomenal world, and disappears when the world is seen truly. To the good man, the veil of Maya (illusion) has become transparent; he sees that all things are one, and that the distinction between himself and another is only apparent. He reaches this insight by love, which is always sympathy, and has to do with the pain of others. When the veil of Maya is lifted, a man takes on the suffering of the whole world. In the good man, knowledge of the whole quiets all volition; his will turns away from life and denies his own nature. "There arises within him a horror of the nature of which his own phenomenal existence is an expression, the kernel and inner nature of that world which is recognized as full of misery."

Hence Schopenhauer is led to complete agreement, at least as regards practice, with ascetic mysticism. Eckhard and Angelus Silesius are better than the New Testament. There are some good things in orthodox Christianity, notably the doctrine of original sin as preached, against "the vulgar Pelagianism," by Saint Augustine and Luther; but the Gospels are sadly deficient in metaphysics. Buddhism, he says, is the highest religion; and his ethical doctrines are orthodox throughout Asia, except where the "detestable doctrine of Islam" prevails.

The good man will practise complete chastity, voluntary poverty, fasting, and self-torture. In all things he will aim at breaking down his individual will. But he does not do this, as do the Western mystics, to achieve harmony with God; no such positive good is sought. The good that is sought is wholly and entirely negative:

> We must banish the dark impression of that nothingness which we discern behind all virtue and holiness as their final goal, and which we fear as children fear the dark; we must not even evade it like the Indians, through myths and meaningless words, such as reabsorption in Brahma or the Nirvana of the Buddhists. Rather do we freely acknowledge that what remains after the entire abolition of will is for all those who are still full of will certainly nothing; but, conversely, to those in whom the will has turned and has denied itself, this our world, which is so real, with all its suns and milky ways—is nothing.

There is a vague suggestion here that the saint sees something positive which other men do not see, but there is nowhere a hint as to what this is, and I think the suggestion is only rhetorical. The world and all its phenomena, Schopenhauer says, are only the objectification of will. With the surrender of the will,

> . . . all those phenomena are also abolished; that constant strain and effort without end and without rest at all the grades of objectivity, in which and through which the world consists; the multifarious forms

succeeding each other in gradation; the whole manifestation of the will; and, finally, also the universal forms of this manifestation, time and space, and also its last fundamental form, subject and object; all are abolished. No will: no idea, no world. Before us there is certainly only nothingness.

We cannot interpret this except as meaning that the saint's purpose is to come as near as possible to non-existence, which, for some reason never clearly explained, he cannot achieve by suicide. Why the saint is to be preferred to a man who is always drunk is not very easy to see; perhaps Schopenhauer thought the sober moments were bound to be sadly frequent.

Schopenhauer's gospel of resignation is not very consistent and not very sincere. The mystics to whom he appeals believed in contemplation; in the Beatific Vision the most profound kind of knowledge was to be achieved, and this kind of knowledge was the supreme good. Ever since Parmenides, the delusive knowledge of appearance was contrasted with another kind of knowledge, not with something of a wholly different kind. Christianity teaches that in *knowledge* of God standeth our eternal life. But Schopenhauer will have none of this. He agrees that what commonly passes for knowledge belongs to the realm of Maya, but when we pierce the veil, we behold not God, but Satan, the wicked omnipotent will, perpetually busied in weaving a web of suffering for the torture of its creatures. Terrified by the Diabolic Vision, the sage cries "Avaunt!" and seeks refuge in non-existence. It is an insult to the mystics to claim them as believers in this mythology. And the suggestion that, without achieving complete non-existence, the sage may yet live a life having some value, is not possible to reconcile with Schopenhauer's pessimism. So long as the sage exists, he exists because he retains will, which is evil. He may diminish the quantity of evil by weakening his will, but he can never acquire any positive good.

Nor is the doctrine sincere, if we may judge by Schopenhauer's life. He habitually dined well, at a good restaurant; he had many trivial love-affairs, which were sensual but not passionate; he was exceedingly quarrelsome and unusually avaricious. On one occasion he was annoyed by an elderly seamstress who was talking to a friend outside the door of his apartment. He threw her downstairs, causing her permanent injury. She obtained a court order compelling him to pay her a certain sum (15 thalers) every quarter as long as she lived. When at last she died, after twenty years, he noted in his accountbook: "Obit anus, abit onus" ["The old woman dies, the burden departs"]. It is hard to find in his life evidences of any virtue except kindness to animals, which he carried to the point of objecting to vivisection in the interests of science. In all other respects he was completely selfish. It is difficult to believe that a man who was profoundly convinced of the virtue of asceticism and resignation would never have made any attempt to embody his convictions in his practice.

Historically, two things are important about Schopenhauer: his pessimism, and his doctrine that will is superior to knowledge. His pessimism made it possible for men to take to philosophy without having to persuade themselves that all evil can be explained away, and in this way, as an antidote, it was useful. From a scientific point of view, optimism and pessimism are alike objectionable: optimism assumes, or attempts to prove, that the universe exists to please us, and pessimism that it exists to displease us. Scientifically, there is no evidence that it is concerned with us either one way or the other. The belief in either pessimism or optimism is a matter of temperament, not of reason, but the optimistic temperament has been much commoner among Western philosophers. A representative of the opposite party is therefore likely to be useful in bringing forward considerations which would otherwise be overlooked.

More important than pessimism was the doctrine of the primacy of the will. It is obvious that this doctrine has no necessary logical connection with pessimism, and those who held it after Schopenhauer frequently found in it a basis for optimism. In one form or another, the doctrine that will is paramount has been held by many modern philosophers, notably Nietzsche, Bergson, James, and Dewey. It has, moreover, acquired a vogue outside the circles of professional philosophers. And in proportion as will has gone up in the scale, knowledge has gone down. This is, I think, the most notable change that has come over the temper of philosophy in our age. It was prepared by Rousseau and Kant, but was first proclaimed in its purity by Schopenhauer. For this reason, in spite of inconsistency and a certain shallowness, his philosophy has considerable importance as a stage in historical development.

On Schopenhauer's character as it affected his writing:

His pessimism seems to have been in Schopenhauer's life, and he was born with a gift for looking on the dark side of things. His teachings have little practical value, however interesting they may be to the student of the history of opinions. Yet he is one of those original and deep-searching men who can never be ignored, and who draw others to them by the very novelty and daring of their speculations. All he writes is interesting, and much of it true in a manner perversely one-sided and warped by the natural bias of his mind.

A review of The World as Will and Idea, *in* The Critic and Good Literature, *February 2, 1884.*

Frederick Copleston, S. J. (essay date 1946)

SOURCE: "Schopenhauer, Other Thinkers, Christianity," in *Arthur Schopenhauer: Philosopher of Pessimism,* 1946. Reprint by Search Press, 1975, pp. 190-212.

[*Professor emeritus at the University of London, Copleston is a highly respected historian of philosophy who is best known for his nine-volume* History of Philosophy *(1946-1974). In the following excerpt from his book-length study of Schopenhauer, first published in 1946, Copleston argues that Schopenhauer's ontology precludes interpretation as an evolutionary system and that his ethics and psychology are internally inconsistent.*]

If one reads *Die Welt als Wille und Vorstellung* as a work of literature, one certainly finds oneself compensated for the energy expended in covering so many pages by passages of striking beauty, while, if one reads it as an extreme theoretical expression of the pessimistic mood with which not a few are now and again afflicted, it has a certain impressiveness and appears to possess a simple consistency; but, if studied from the strictly philosophical standpoint, internal inconsistencies very soon reveal themselves and the total system appears bizarre and fantastic in the extreme, so that one feels tempted to dismiss it as a mere imaginative creation or even as the product of a disordered mind. The thought may then occur to the reflective mind that the work of so celebrated a man as Schopenhauer cannot possibly be devoid of real philosophical value and that if one stripped away the terminological and rhetorical extravagances, one could discover underneath the husk a kernel of deep import. The author of this book acknowledges that he himself resolved to make this attempt, not in the course of the exposition itself but after its completion (since one is scarcely justified in presenting as a man's philosophy what one thinks he was 'getting at', without paying any attention to the way in which the philosopher himself presented his thought, and so running the risk of reading into his thought what was not there or treating as irrelevant what he would by no means have considered irrelevant). Further consideration, however, convinced him that it is not possible to do this in any systematic way, for reasons which will presently become apparent. . . . [The] author proposes to justify his conviction that it is not possible to give a systematic, coherent and consistent 'esoteric' philosophy, which could legitimately be attributed to Schopenhauer or accepted as what he was really 'getting at'. We must remember that Schopenhauer professed his sure belief that his philosophy was *true,* and he undoubtedly meant that it was true *as he presented it:* he did not regard what we might consider mere fantastic extravaganzas as irrelevant to the system or as unimportant overloading.

It might easily occur to someone that by changing the term 'Will' to 'Energy', or 'Force', one might present the philosophy of Schopenhauer as an evolutionary system more or less according to pattern; and it might justifiably be pointed out that, although Schopenhauer had a special reason for employing the term 'Will', he never meant to postulate a willing subject: the metaphysical Will was for him entirely impersonal, a fundamental energy, that lies at the base of, and forms, the world. A little reflection, however, will suffice to show that, even if one thought that an evolutionary system was the philosophic notion underlying the mythology of the Will, it is impossible to bring the Schopenhauerian philosophy within the framework of any such scheme, not at any rate without leaving out of account parts of the philosophy that were by no means unimportant in the mind of their creator. In the first place, are we to think of Schopenhauer's Will as

material or immaterial? To say that it is material would be scarcely accurate, since matter, in so far as we can attach any intelligible meaning to the term, is dependent on the *subjective* forms of space and time: the Will objectifies itself in material objects only in dependence on the *a priori* constitution of the human consciousness. It objectifies itself immediately in the Ideas; but these are, in themselves, outside space and time and cannot be called material in any ordinary sense; they are certainly not conceived as extended. Moreover, Schopenhauer called them the 'Platonic Ideas', and the latter at least were not material, so far as their own essence was concerned. On the other hand, although the Will is not extended in space and does not endure in time, it cannot be termed spiritual, for it is in itself irrational, and how can it be spiritual, if it is irrational, without intellect? As non-spiritual, therefore, the Will cannot be conceived as God (and Schopenhauer repudiated any such interpretation by his utter rejection of both theism and pantheism), while, as nonmaterial, it cannot be consistently interpreted as material force or energy. Moreover, even if we did identify the Will with material force or energy, how could we go on to extract a consistent evolutionary doctrine out of Schopenhauer's philosophy? The Will is said to objectify itself, it is true: but the individual objectifications of Will are Maya, illusion. The Will manifests itself, objectifies itself, at various grades; but the individual objectifications are the 'idea' of an individual subject, are dependent on consciousness. The first book of the *World,* i.e., the doctrine that the world is *Vorstellung,* 'my idea', renders impossible any realist evolutionary interpretation of the philosophy as a whole. We may say that the idealistic side of the philosophy is out of place and can be dismissed; but Schopenhauer certainly did not think that it was irrelevant or of little importance, and it would be a queer evolutionary philosophy in which the whole phenomenal world was declared to be 'my idea'. Again, one would naturally suppose that change, motion, duration, were essential to an evolutionary system; but time is *subjective* according to Schopenhauer.

Supposing that we choose to interpret the metaphysical Will as Life, as an *élan vital.* Immediately we come up against Schopenhauer's doctrine that the Will is not itself Life, but the Will to live: life as we know it is indeed the manifestation of Will, but it is illusory, Maya. And how can we reconcile any theory of 'creative evolution' with Schopenhauer's philosophy? Even if we were prepared, in despite of the philosopher, to regard the 'Platonic Ideas' as no more than abstractions or formulæ, as it were, of the various succeeding evolutionary grades, we should still come up against the theory that time is subjective and the fact that 'evolution' for Schopenhauer is ideal rather than real; the empirically real is Maya, and one grade cannot develop into another in real duration, apart from the perceiving subject. The *Origin of Species* was published in 1858 and shortly before his death Schopenhauer, judging the Darwinian theory according to an extract in *The Times,* described it in a letter (March 1st, 1860) as 'downright empiricism'. He meant, of course, that Darwin left out of account the inner and hidden force that manifests itself in the struggle for existence and that adaptation to environment, natural selection, etc., are nothing but external conditions; but, if one were to tack on empirical Darwinism to the metaphysic of the Will, what would one do with the idealism of Schopenhauer and the doctrine of Maya, factors which would scarcely fit in either with Darwinism as such or with the emergent evolution of, e.g., Lloyd Morgan? As for Henri Bergson, the idea of real duration is essential to his philosophy of the world and, whatever may have been his precise position in regard to *space,* he did not accept the Kantian doctrine of *time,* which Schopenhauer certainly did. Moreover, it is clear from the later developments of Bergson's thought that the *élan vital,* considered biologically, is an effect of Creative Life itself, God, whereas for Schopenhauer, the Will is not the 'cause' of life nor is it God, so that, to put it very crudely, we have to get the rabbit out of the hat without any recourse to the conjuror. The Will objectifies itself, but its objectifications are Maya: the Will is blind and irrational, but it knows itself, as it were, through its phenomenon; it objectifies itself in a multiplicity of individuals at various grades, yet the multiplicity of individuals are but the 'idea' of an individual subject that is itself a phenomenon; it is not Idea, yet it manifests itself in Ideas: it is not itself Life, but the Will to live, and it denies itself, destroys itself, through the phenomenon. How is it possible to present a clear, consistent and systematic account of the Will that would bear any near resemblance to the system of Herbert Spencer or the empirical evolutionism of Darwin or the creative evolution of Bergson or the materialistic emergent evolution of the Marxists and which would at the same time be recognized by Schopenhauer as in any real sense a faithful transcription of his doctrine?

Similarly, it is difficult to obtain any coherent and systematic psychology from the pages of Schopenhauer. The intellect is declared to be essentially the servant of will: in other words, the biological function of intelligence would seem to be stressed. At the same time, however, intelligence is supposed to be capable of formulating a conceptual philosophy, which is true and objective, whereas one would expect to find all the emphasis laid on the biological value of 'fictions' and an anticipation of the theory of the late [Hans] Vaihinger. One cannot have it both ways: either intelligence is essentially practical in function, essentially the servant of will, and objective philosophical truth is unobtainable (at least, it could never be *known* to be the truth), or the intelligence has *ab initio* a speculative, as well as a practical function. That it has a practical or biological function, no one, of course, if he has any sense, would deny: but, if you start out by saying that the intelligence comes into being originally simply to serve a biological function, that it is in origin essentially and exclusively the servant of will, then, whatever 'superfluity' it may develop in the course of evolution, you could never be certain that any one of its conclusions or formulated theories was any more than a biologically-useful fiction—in fact you could never be sure that the doctrine that the intellect is the servant of will is itself anything more than a biologically-useful fiction. Moreover, the discursively and rationally expressed philosophical system of Schopenhauer is not supposed to

be the mediation of a supra-intellectual intuition, but rather of an infra-intellectual 'intuition', an immediate consciousness that is common to all, and which can scarcely be differentiated from instinct: yet instinct, one would think, is essentially biological and practical in function. Schopenhauer may refer the ways of instinct, as seen in insects, for example, to the cunning of the Will to live; but how can the mere Will to live have any 'cunning'? In any case, how is it ever going to be demonstrated that the whole intellectual life of man, including that of Schopenhauer, is any more than the result of the Will's cunning, that objective truth is not simply a *lusus imaginations?*

Nor, again, can we obtain any coherent ethic or theory of value from the philosophy of Schopenhauer. It is quite true that he speaks with respect of what he regarded as true virtue and holiness, and that in this sense he asserted values, sanctity and virtue, and held up an ascetic ideal; but . . . these values are negatively conceived and, given his metaphysic and characterization of the Will, the supreme value should be non-existence. With Plato the supreme value, the Idea of the Good, was the supremely real, and indeed, if values are not in some sense objective and real, it is very hard to see how they can be values. Yet with Schopenhauer all is either Will or objectification of Will, and the Will, together with its manifestation, is evil, is that which should be denied. He asserted that the world had an ethical significance, an assertion that implies a positive theory of value; but at the same time his pessimistic philosophy left no room for a positive theory of value. Moreover, while many philosophies of conduct have stressed self-denial, this has meant self-denial of lower impulses, e.g. control of the passions, in order that man's true nature may be asserted and developed without hindrance. If Epictetus counselled control of the passions, he insisted at the same time on a positive ethic; if Spinoza regarded the power of the 'passive emotions' as constituting man's servitude, he emphasized the 'active emotions' and the supreme attitude of the *amor intellectualis Dei*; if Plato urged men to curb the headstrong and recalcitrant steed, he insisted on the positive tendance of the soul and the integration of man's faculties in the service of his true end; above all, if Christianity inculcates the necessity of the 'denial of self', it certainly does not mean to imply that man should deny his inner self, that man should renounce his being as an individual man, for self-denial is not an end in itself, but is to be practised with a view to attaining a positive end, the highest possible perfection of man's being and activity, first of all in the supernatural order, yet also, if subordinately, in the natural order. For Schopenhauer, however, self-denial means denial of one's inner nature, not only denial of one's phenomenal individuality, but also denial of one's innermost essence, identity with Will, and the highest peak of holiness is the completest denial of one's own being and of ultimate reality, so that value increases and holiness increases in proportion as complete frustration is approached—truly a paradoxical position. Again, Schopenhauer, as we have seen, asserted a doctrine of character-determinism, a doctrine which, if consistently maintained, is incompatible with ethical discrimination and moral judgments based on a standard of value. Yet, after asserting determinism, he admits freedom, as a *deus ex machina,* in exceptional cases. Moreover, if character-determinism were true, would it not, at the very least, cast doubt on the objective validity of the Schopenhauerian philosophy and *Weltanschauung?* That philosophy is a philosophy of pessimism, and presumably, on Schopenhauer's own theory, it would be the outcome of his pessimistic character, would stand in direct relation to his character and could not be considered as expressing absolute truth. In any case, it would seem impossible to obtain any real theory of value on Schopenhauer's premises. I do not wish to affirm that his moral theory is entirely worthless, of course, for he does at least evince respect for disinterested sympathy and love and for the ascetic life and this respect does him credit, even if his reasons for showing that respect and his explanation of virtue and holiness are unacceptable: it is not everyone who has an ideal of conduct as lofty and sublime as that of Schopenhauer. Moreover, even if there were no God and theology were void of all objective foundation, the unprejudiced mind would have to admit that the world would be the poorer without the lives of St. Francis, St. Peter Claver, the Curé d'Ars. A 'philanthropic' millionaire is not exactly the same thing as a saint. But, while I am far from saying that the ideal of conduct depicted by Schopenhauer is entirely worthless, I do affirm that his system gives no adequate foundation to the implied positive values and is incompatible with them, for sanctity is *in fact* something very positive.

John Bowle (essay date 1954)

SOURCE: "The Cult of the Irrational: Schopenhauer: Nietzsche," in *Politics and Opinion in the Nineteenth Century: An Historical Introduction,* Oxford University Press, Inc., 1954, pp. 365-81.

[*Bowle wrote a number of studies of European history and politics, including* Western Political Thought *(1947) and* The Unity of European History *(1948). In the following excerpt, Bowle outlines Schopenhauer's political philosophy.*]

The introspection displayed by Schopenhauer and Nietzsche was already apparent in Herder and Hegel and the Romantic writers of their day. As this romanticism developed, it had often achieved benevolence and sensibility—in hatred of oppression, humanitarian reform, the championship of small nationalities, the emancipation of the slaves. But there was another side to the picture; the obsession with self, the cult of farouche egotism, of utter despair.

It could, of course, prove politically demoralizing. When this romanticism, and its disillusionment, was bound up with philosophy, and when that philosophy was German, sad results might be expected. Driven to its logical conclusion, the new outlook could lead not to the transcendental humanism of Hegel, that heady substitute for religion, but to a blistering atheism and a suicidal despair. Life, it could be argued by soured romantics, was intrinsically evil; love was a cheat; politics a game for fools.

When such views were expressed with violent originality and startling eloquence by a philosopher of genius, his influence could be formidable. The romantic youth of late nineteenth-century Germany, in particular, always alert for a new pessimistic philosophy, were swayed by the writings of Schopenhauer like ripe wheat before the wind. The views of this philosopher lead to a despair of politics, to an exaltation of elites who claimed the right to practise a morality different from that of the people. Even to a horror of life and scorn of humanitarian motives which helped to darken the political scene in the later nineteenth century. Unlike other subsequent prophets of despair, Schopenhauer was an authentic philosopher; a profound and brilliant writer whose views command respect. It was the effect of these opinions on intellectuals obsessed by philosophical abstractions which was to be deplored.

A well-to-do eccentric of compelling personality and striking appearance, Schopenhauer had brought to the problems of his age the attack and confidence of the eighteenth century and a more than eighteenth-century subtlety of mind. He had grown up under the influence of Byron and the romantics, whom he frequently quotes. He was also one of the first Europeans to be well versed in Indian philosophy, with its political abnegations and desire for escape from the world of appearance. Following Kant, he accepted the limitations of mind before phenomena, anticipated modern views on the importance of the subconscious, attempted to fuse matter and spirit in emergent will, and regarded intelligence as a by-product of the blind process of life. Here is a cult of Will, but it is not a Good Will. Kant, he believed, advocated a 'slave morality' as an escape from correct conclusions. The world is an enigma and philosophy strictly empirical, dictated by experience. A blind will to live sustains the world and in man the Life-Force first attains full consciousness. 'Man is the only creature that is astonished at his own existence.' He is the only 'metaphysical animal'—the intelligent monkey. Hence the popular need for religion, which is the poetry and philosophy of the people. The greatest spirits are beyond such compensations, and beyond the rules of ordinary morality. Like Spinoza, Schopenhauer regarded the world as a totality, but he does not find the world good. Man is the culmination of life, since a more intelligent being could not bear to live. There is, of course, no personal survival, but while individuals perish, the unknowing (*unbewusstlos*) Life Force drives inexorably on. Hence Schopenhauer's detestation of what he regarded as the vulgarity of optimistic demagogues. 'They have come', he wrote [in *Parerga und Paralipomena*], 'through hatred of Christianity to pretend that the world is an end in itself, and that life . . . makes for happiness, that the howling colossal suffering . . . is due to governments, and that without them there would be Heaven on earth.' 'Howling colossal suffering'—here is the key to Schopenhauer's deepest mind. The Eastern remedy of self-transcendence was his answer. This may be achieved by contemplation, by 'Menschenliebe'—a detached pity. And also by asceticism which cheats life of its purpose. Though Schopenhauer disapproves of it, his followers found the idea of suicide attractive, at once an affirmation of annihilation of will. Had not Byron written

Count o'er the joys thine eyes have seen,
Count o'er thy days from anguish free;
And know, whatever thou hast been,
'Tis something better—not to be.

The basic human instinct is sex. This fraud keeps the whole hideous process alive. The instinct is the heart of the will to live; the concentration of the whole being. 'That is why,' he wrote, 'I call the sex organs the seat of the Will.' Here is the undying core of Life; the root and connection of the whole species, impersonal, animal, profound. But Nature recks nothing of individuals, and love is the future generation clamouring for life. Sexual relations are brutally impersonal; for the pleasure of a few 'epileptic moments' the individual is permanently trapped. The looks of lovers are sinister; 'the meditation of the . . . species'. They are furtive traitors, plotting to perpetuate pain. The 'drunkenness of the species' attains its end, regardless of the artificialities of romantic love. Not since the brave times of Tertullian and St. Augustine had such eloquent denunciations of normal instinct been put about.

This adolescent and sensational despair naturally made Schopenhauer's works widely notorious, and greatly contributed to their influence. It won popularity among those reacting from the extremities of romantic love, as well as among those who desired to appear sophisticated—both always a considerable proportion of articulate youth. For here was a philosophical justification for Byronic disillusionment. Here, said Schopenhauer's admirers, is a true realism, facing the appalling facts of battle, pestilence, loneliness and despair. Here, the cheating sophistries of romantic sentimentalists and the coarse optimism of fatuous reformers are unmasked. It was easy for Dante to describe Hell: when it came to describing Paradise he had little material for his imagination. The world, said Schopenhauer, like Hobbes before him, is a chaos of blind conflicting Wills, and they reflect the laws of man's own being.

The political influence of such a philosophy was naturally deleterious. Since life was an evil enigma, an Eastern quietism, remote from politics, should be attained. To these forerunners of existentialism, irresponsibility was the beginning of wisdom. 'Im *esse* nicht im *operari* liegt die Freiheit'—'In being not in doing Freedom lies.' Appeals to duty or to utility were alike meaningless; the best that could be hoped is for politics not to interfere with private life. This embittered outlook tended to a characteristic despair of politics. For this nineteenth-century prophet infected with his brilliant pessimism a wide circle of admirers. In particular, his distinction between the common herd, whom he called the 'clockworks of nature', and the fine-drawn minority of master minds—of pioneers, beyond conventional morality and religion, who sensed the tragedy of Time—foreshadowed the doctrines of Nietzsche. Morality can only be attained by exceptionally talented individuals; 'It is as foolish to believe that our systems of morals and ethics will produce virtuous characters and saints as to think that our aesthetics will create poets, musicians and painters.' History, in such a view, is largely meaningless, a catalogue of suffering.

This outlook was violently opposed to the main current of nineteenth-century opinion. Hegel, Saint-Simon, Comte, Marx, the post-Darwinian political philosophers, as well as the liberal democrats, the psychologists, historians and anthropologists, were deeply committed to the idea of Progress. Schopenhauer defied them all.

Meanwhile his political scepticism made an appeal to liberal romantics, disillusioned after their failures in 1848. Since unhappiness is inevitable, aesthetic contemplation, detachment, and a certain distant pity were the proper reaction of a civilized man. With this detached view, he could write [in the **Parerga**]: 'the question of the sovereignty of the people comes down ultimately to this—if anyone has the right to govern the people against its Will? I do not see how this can reasonably be admitted. Therefore, absolutely, the people is sovereign; but it is a sovereign that is a perpetual "minor", which must always remain in tutelage, and cannot even exercise its rights without running the greatest dangers. For like all minors, it easily becomes the plaything of cunning rascals, who are, therefore, termed demagogues'. It follows that an absolute hereditary monarchy is the best form of government. But in any case, the individual cannot expect to find fulfilment in anything so vulgar as the state. Hence, among other reasons, Schopenhauer's detestation of Hegel. A spectator in politics, he cared mainly for the preservation of property and order.

Such, in a brief sketch, were the doctrines of this original pessimist. Rich, healthy and talented, his extreme sensibility to suffering and his capacity to face the worst implications of advanced mid-nineteenth-century opinion, plunged him in stormy gloom. His sensitive pessimism can certainly make the robust confidence of a Herbert Spencer or a Buckle look Philistine. Though he won little influence among his contemporaries, his effect on later generations was lasting. Here was an appeal to the self pity of disillusioned romantics, to the desire for separation from the herd, to a bold treatment of sexual morality, startling at the time. Had he been insulated in the Latin obscurity of medieval or sixteenth-century theological controversy, his opinions would have had no more effect than those of most heretics. With access to the full publicity of the nineteenth century, his influence was highly subversive. But it was never negligible. Apart from his influence on Nietzsche, by his definition of the idea of creative will he anticipated Bergson, and by his understanding of the sub-conscious he anticipated Freud.

Georg Lukács (essay date 1954)

SOURCE: "The Bourgeois Irrationalism of Schopenhauer's Metaphysics," in *Schopenhauer: His Philosophical Achievement,* edited by Michael Fox, The Harvester Press, Sussex, 1980, pp. 183-93.

[*A Hungarian literary critic and philosopher, Lukács is a leading proponent of Marxist thought. In the following excerpt, which originally appeared in his* The Destruction of Reason *(1954), Lukács contends that Schopenhauer's "purification" of Kant and his resulting idealism effect complacency toward social improvement and pacifies objectors to the established capitalist order.*]

It is a well-established fact that on all crucial philosophical questions, Kant occupies a shifting, equivocal position. With matchless lucidity Lenin characterized Kant's position between materialism and idealism [in *Materialismus und Empiriokritizismus,* 1952]:

> The basic feature of Kantian philosophy is the reconciling of materialsim and idealism, a compromise between the two, a systematic binding together of heterogeneous, mutually contradictory philosophical orientations. When Kant assumes that something outside of us, some thing-in-itself corresponds to our ideas, he is a materialist. When he states that this thing-in-itself is unknowable, transcendent and from the Beyond, he is making an idealist stand. By acknowledging experiences and sensations as our sole source of knowledge he gives his philosophy a bent towards sensualism and beyond sensualism, under specific conditions, to materialism as well. By acknowledging the a-priority of space, time, causality, etc., Kant gives his philosophy an idealist bent.

In this crucial respect the whole of German classical philosophy marks a major step backwards in relation to Kant. Fichte already 'purifies', to use Lenin's term, Kantian philosophy of its materialist fluctuations and creates a purely subjective idealism. Schopenhauer's epistemology was always moving in this direction. It too, as we are about to see, reduced Kant's fluctuations to Berkeley's consistently subjective idealism.

But Kant's position was variable, provisional not only as regards this question, a crucial one for philosophy in general, but also on the question of dialectics. The contradictions which became manifest in mechanical-metaphysical thinking at the end of the eighteenth century (Diderot, Rousseau, Herder, etc.) come to a head with Kant. His comprehension of contradiction as a point of departure, as a logical and epistemological basis, is a tendency to be found throughout his *œuvre*—although never taken to its conclusion or consistently worked out. Granted, with Kant all these preliminary moves still end in the reinstatement of metaphysical thinking and in a philosophical agnosticism. But . . . even these inconsequential moves became . . . starting-points for the development of dialectics in Germany. . . .

. . . Schopenhauer's 'purifying' of Kant's materialist inconstancies, his reduction of Kantian to Berkeleyan epistemology, not only marks the establishing of a consistent subjective idealism, but also implies a striving to eradicate all dialectical elements from Kantian philosophy and to replace them with an irrationalism based on intuition, with an irrationalist mysticism. . . .

In his critique of Kantian philosophy, Schopenhauer investigates the central problem of consistent subjective idealism in a very determined manner. He charges Kant above all with having failed to 'deduce the merely rela-

tive existence of the phenomenon from the simple, so apparent and undeniable truth *No object without subject,* in order thus to portray the object as dependent on the subject from its very root, as determined by the latter and hence a mere phenomenon which does not exist in itself, unconditionally, because it will always exist only in relation to a subject.'

He formulated the same idea even more firmly, if anything, in his first book, **On the Fourfold Root of the Thesis of Adequate Ground:**

> Just as the object is posited with the subject (since the very word is otherwise meaningless), and likewise the subject with the object, and to be a subject is therefore tantamount to having an object, and to be an object tantamount to being known by the subject: in exactly the same way, the subject is posited along with an object *determined in any way* as *knowing it in just that way*. To that extent it does not matter whether I say that objects have such and such determinants pertinent and peculiar to them, or that the subject perceives in such and such ways; it does not matter whether I say that objects are to be divided into such classes, or that such differing powers of recognition are peculiar to the subject.

In this respect, then, Schopenhauer goes back firmly to Berkeley and defends him against Kant: 'That important thesis to whose merit Kant did not do justice Berkeley had already made the keystone of his philosophy, thereby creating a lasting memorial to himself, although he did not himself draw the appropriate inferences from the thesis and was consequently partly not understood, and partly not sufficiently heeded.' Hence he rejected the second, revised edition of the *Critique of Pure Reason* as a falsification of Kant's true tendencies and always adhered to the first edition when interpreting Kant. This sharp contrast which Schopenhauer drew between the first and second edition of Kant's *magnum opus* has played a major part in Kant philology. But the crucial question has to do not with philological history but with philosophy. We have noted how Schopenhauer viewed Kant's relationship to Berkeley. Now Kant wrote in the preface to the second edition of the *Critique of Pure Reason* that he had added a 'refutation of idealism' (aimed against Berkeley) which he justified thus:

> However innocuous idealism may be considered with regard to the basic purposes of metaphysics, (though in fact it is not innocuous), it is still scandalous for philosophy and universal human reason to have to accept merely *on trust* the existence of things outside of ourselves (since, after all, we obtain all the actual material for knowledge from our inner mind), and—should it occur to anyone to cast doubt on this—not to be able to answer with any satisfactory proof.

Thus what Schopenhauer regarded as Kant's great, though inconsistently sustained philosophical feat, Kant himself termed 'scandalous for philosophy'.

This firm adoption of the course of Berkeleyan subjective idealism would in itself ensure Schopenhauer the place of an important forerunner in reactionary bourgeois philosophy. For when Mach and Avenarius adopted Berkeley's epistemology afresh, just as fully in essence but using a much more veiled form of expression, they continued along the lines which started with Schopenhauer. Lenin too ascertained the affinity in his Mach critique: 'One is above not only materialism but also the idealism of "any" Hegel, but not averse to flirting with an idealism in the spirit of Schopenhauer!'

But in two respects Schopenhauer outstripped his successors. On the other hand he supported unreservedly Berkeley's solipsistic subjectivism and idealism; it was still wholly alien to him to mask his idealism as a 'third road' between idealism and materialism, as an 'elevation' above this antithesis. On the other hand he did not content himself, like Mach and Avenarius, with a mere agnosticism, but developed that mysticism and irrationalism inherent (consciously or not) in all consistent idealism overtly from it with thorough-going logic. In this, likewise, he came nearer to Berkeley than to his own successors. There is, admittedly, the important historical difference that his development of subjective idealism merges it not with Christian religion, as Berkeley's did, but with . . . religious atheism. . . .

Now in order to find an epistemological rationale for this, Schopenhauer does not repudiate the existence of things-in-themselves in general but simply puts an irrationalist-mystical interpretation on them by equating the thing-in-itself with the will, exaggerated and mysticized irrationalistically. He wrote:

> Phenomenon means idea and nothing further: all idea, of whatever kind, all *object* is *phenomenon*. But the *thing-in-itself* is *will* alone: as such it [i.e. the will—Translator] is never idea but different from idea *toto genere:* it is that of which all idea, all object constitutes the manifestation, the visible nature, the *objectivity*. It is the most intrinsic element, the core of each separate entity and equally of the whole: it appears in every blindly operating force of Nature; it appears also in man's deliberate actions; the great difference between the two concerns only the degree of manifestation, not the essence of what is manifesting itself.

Thus Schopenhauer, like Schelling previously, presents us with two diametrically opposite modes of comprehending reality: an inessential one (that of objective reality as really given) and a genuine, essential one (that of mystical irrationalism). But . . . the young Schelling rejected with this conjunction only conceptual (discursive) knowledge of reality. With his intellectual intuition he was striving to comprehend, albeit in a confusedly mystical manner, the essence of the same reality, the motive forces of evolution as a universal principle behind all reality. Schopenhauer, on the contrary, automatically discredited all scientific knowledge and created a far deeper rift between knowledge of the phenomenal world and that of the thing-in-itself than Schelling did in even his late period when he opposed positive to negative philosophy. For here we are dealing with two different kinds of reality, or rather with reality and non-reality, and the difference between these is exactly reflected in the two kinds of cognition.

In part this is connected with their different epistemologies. Schelling was an objective, Schopenhauer a subjective idealist. For Schelling, in consequence, the objectivity of reality is still somehow present, although in a form that was growing more and more distorted through mystical irrationalism. His early conception of the identical subject-object especially is a mystificatory form of expressing the notion that human consciousness is, on the one hand, the product of natural evolution and that on the other hand, the achieving of this identity in intellectual intuition implies a knowledge, an elevation of this objective natural process into self-consciousness. With Schopenhauer, however, the association between subject and object is constituted quite differently from the outset. We have already quoted Schopenhauer's statements in this regard: they culminate in the thesis that there can be no object without subject, and that what we call reality (the world of appearance) is identical with our ideas. He therefore identifies himself with the Berkeleyan *Esse est percipi.*

From this it follows that for Schopenhauer—as later for Mach, Avenarius, Poincaré, etc.—the external world cannot have any real objectivity that is independent of human consciousness; that cognition—this too agrees with Machism—possesses only a purely practical significance in the 'struggle for existence', the preservation of the individual and the species. Schopenhauer wrote:

> Therefore knowledge in general, rational as well as merely intuitive, proceeds in the first place from the will itself and belongs to the essence of the higher stages of its objectivation as a mere *mekhane*, a means of preserving the individual and the species as much as every bodily organ. Originally determined, then, to serve the will and to accomplish its purposes, it remains entirely the servant of the will almost continuously: this is the case in all animals and in nearly all human beings.

Without further ado Schopenhauer was able to deduce from this epistemological viewpoint that in the case of phenomena, the mode of comprehension thus determined is incapable in principle of telling us anything about their essence. He divided knowledge of the external world into morphology and aetiology. Of the former he said, 'This presents us with innumerable shapes for our ideas, infinitely manifold and yet related through an unmistakable family resemblance, shapes which on this plane remain strange to us and, if regarded simply from this angle, look like baffling hieroglyphs.' Aetiology 'teaches us that, according to the law of cause and effect, one particular state of matter brings about the other, and has thereby accounted for it and done its task.' But this has not had any bearing on the knowledge of objective reality. Schopenhauer sums up his epistemology as follows:

> But this does not enlighten us in the least about the inner essence of any of those phenomena. This is called *natural force* and lies outside the realm of aetiological explanation which gives the name of *natural law* to the immutable constancy of the occurrence of such a

force's externalization, as long as the conditions it knows are present. But this natural law, these conditions and this occurrence, in respect of a particular place at a particular time, are all that it knows and ever can know. The actual force externalized, the inner essence of the phenomenon occurring according to those laws will remain for ever a mystery, quite strange and unknown, in the case of both the simplest and most complex phenomenon. . . . In consequence, even the most thorough aetiological explanation of the whole of Nature would actually never be anything beyond a catalogue of inexplicable forces and a reliable list of the rules whereby manifestations of those forces occur in time and place, succeed and give way to one another. It would however have to leave the inner essence of the forces manifested for ever unexplained, because the law it obeys does not go that far, but stops with the phenomenon and its classifying.

Here we can distinctly see both the purely bourgeois character of Schopenhauer's epistemology and the energy with which it anticipates irrationalist philosophy's later development. Schopenhauer's close contact with eighteenth-century English philosophers, with Berkeley and Hume, stems chiefly from the fact that they were trying to meet the ideological needs of a bourgeoisie which had already gained control economically, by means of a compromise with the land-owning class and the religious views of the old powers. For that reason, they tried to create an epistemology which did not, on the one hand, obstruct the free development of natural science indispensable to capitalist production (unlike, for instance, the religious ideas of feudal or semi-feudal philosophy which affected science itself). On the other hand, the epistemology they were seeking repudiated all philosophical consequences of scientific developments liable to hamper the compromise made with the ruling powers of the *ancien régime* by a bourgeoisie mostly inclining to reaction. This attitude's purely bourgeois character is manifest in the fact that the decisive argument for banishing such consequences is once again an indirect one. They are not dismissed (as in feudal or semi-feudal philosophy) because they fail to agree with Christian dogmas, but on account of their 'unscientific nature' and because they cross frontiers defined by epistemology as impassable for the intellectual apprehension of the phenomenal world. Schopenhauer's anticipatory character, his 'genius', is indicated by the fact that he recognized his trend of bourgeois development in backward Germany at the start of the nineteenth century; that in the political unawareness—socially, matters still stood quite differently—of the German bourgeoisie of his age, he clearly surmised and raised to a high stage of generalization tendencies which only gained the upper hand in Germany and all over the Continent after the defeat of the 1848/49 revolution.

As we have seen, this perception of the phenomenal world could only possess, in Schopenhauer's opinion, a practical, pragmatist significance. He now countered it with apprehension of the essence of things-in-themselves, apprehension of will. At this point the irrationalist mysticism in his philosophy becomes fully evident. Even for the mode of perceiving the phenomenal world, Schopenhauer stresses the outstanding role played by intuition. Schelling's intellectual intuition which, as we know, was for him solely the mode of knowing things-in-themselves—in sharp contrast to that of perceiving phenomena—he made a universal principle governing every kind of knowledge. [Schopenhauer wrote:] 'Accordingly our everyday, *empirical intuition* is an *intellectual* one, and to *this* is due the predicate which Germany's philosophical windbags have attached to a purported intuition of imagined worlds in which their favoured *absolutum* performs its evolutions.'

Naturally this irrationalist principle of intuition makes an even bolder appearance in knowledge of the thing-in-itself, the will. Apprehension of this will occurs, as regards each man as an individual, purely intuitively and directly 'as something, namely, which is directly known to that Everyone which the word "will" denotes.' That this entails a complete solipsism, a denial of the reality of our fellow-men and the external world in general, Schopenhauer can contest only with sophistry and the tools of Schelling's philosophy, the philosophy he otherwise challenges so strongly. We judge the existence of our fellow-beings, Schopenhauer says, 'according to the analogy of that body', that is, according to our own, and in both instances we distinguish between idea (phenomenon) and will (thing-in-itself). The same method is then used to apply the will by analogy to the entire phenomenal world as to its underlying Being-in-itself. Schopenhauer expounds this analogizing, this extension of human will to the whole cosmos as follows:

> It must however be observed that here, all we need is a *denominatio a potiori* through which, for that very reason, the concept of will is expanded further than before. Perception of the identical in different manifestations and of the incongruous in similar ones is, as Plato so often comments, the very precondition of philosophy. Until now, however, we have not recognized the identity, with the will, of the essence of every single force straining and operating in Nature. Hence we have not regarded the manifold phenomena as the different species of the same genus which they are but have taken them for heterogeneous: that is also why there could not be a word to denote the concept of this genus. Hence I give the genus the name of its most admirable species, a nearer, immediate knowledge of which leads us to indirect knowledge of all other species.

This analogizing, needless to say, again occurs in an intuitive way, on the basis of direct knowing:

> But the word *will,* which is supposed to reveal the innermost essence of each thing in Nature like an open sesame, by no means signifies an unknown quantity, something that is reached by drawing conclusions; it signifies rather something which is directly perceived and so well known that we know and understand what will is far better than anything else, anything whatever. Hitherto the concept *will* was subsumed under the concept *force;* but I do the exact opposite and ask for every force in Nature to be conceived as will.

So here Schopenhauer anthropologizes the whole of Nature with the help of plain analogy, which he loftily declares to be myth, and hence truth.

Here we are neither able nor disposed to analyse in all its details the philosophical system which arose in this way. We shall only indicate those crucial elements in which the new irrationalism of Schopenhauer—which had a tremendously strong bearing on nineteenth-century philosophy—found expression. From Schopenhauer's return to Berkeley as we have traced it so far, it necessarily follows that for Schopenhauer, space, time and causality are purely subjective forms of the phenomenal world and can never be applied to things-in-themselves, to will as Schopenhauer grasped it. Kant's fluctuating position derived from the fact that here, he was similarly striving for a sharp dichotomy, but was forever trying to escape from the prison of this metaphysical dualism in the course of his concrete accounts. These steps taken by Kant towards a dialectical view of phenomenon and essence (objective reality, thing-in-itself) were mostly hesitant and equivocal. Schopenhauer radically abolished them and used the dualism, carried through in a more consistently metaphysical, anti-dialectical argumentation, to bring about a total irrationalisation of the world of things-in-themselves.

Let us take an important case in natural philosophy. Schopenhauer said:

> Force itself lies right outside the chain of causes and effects, which presupposes time, by having meaning only in relation to it: but the former also lies outside time. The particular variation always has an equally particular variation, but not the force, to the cause whose externalization it is. For just that which always gives a cause its efficacy, however many times it occurs, is a natural force and as such groundless, i.e. it lies right outside the causal nexus and the domain of the thesis of ground, and is perceived philosophically as the immediate objectivity of the will, which is entire Nature's In-itself.

Thereupon, the whole of Nature is turned into a mystery, although all the particular changes needed for capitalist praxis may be comprehended in terms of causal laws and used on behalf of production. But philosophically speaking, everything is inexplicable and irrational: 'It is as inexplicable to us that a stone should fall to the earth as that an animal should move.' And by pursuing this idea to its logical conclusion, Schopenhauer arrived at findings very close to the reactionary mysticism of imperialist natural philosophy, which they anticipate in methodology. Let us remember from Spinoza's deterministic statements that a stone flying through the air, if it had consciousness, would imagine that it was flying of its free will—a graphic image to illustrate the illusion of free will. . . . Schopenhauer . . . refers to Spinoza's image but completely reverses its philosophical meaning by adding that

> the stone would be right. The push is the same for the stone as the motive for me, and what is manifested in the stone's case as cohesion, gravity, persistence in

> the assumed state is, in esoteric essence, the same as that which I recognise in myself as will and which the stone too would recognise as will, were it to acquire perception.

Schopenhauer, of course, was not familiar with today's bourgeois atomic physics, but he would surely have assented enthusiastically, at least from the methodological angle, to the a-causal movements of electrons and 'free will' in the movement of particles.

The results of this metaphysical-irrationalist splitting asunder of phenomenon and essence emerge even more clearly in the human world. Since Schopenhauerian will lies beyond the operational field of space, time and causality, and since he regards the individuation principle as thereby dissolved, every will is identical with will itself. This has very important human (ethical) consequences:

> Only the *inner* processes, as far as they concern the *will,* have true reality and are real events; because will alone is the thing-in-itself. In each microcosm there lies the whole macrocosm, and the latter contains no more than the former. Diversity is phenomenon, and the external processes are mere configurations of the phenomenal world, hence possessing no direct reality or meaning, which they only have indirectly through their relation to the will of individuals.

This, therefore, is not merely to say that it is exclusively the inner factor which counts in every deed. That is also implied in Kant's 'categorical imperative', albeit with the important difference that Kant was always striving to give his pure abstract ethics a social content as well, and in order to achieve this he did not flinch from sophistic methods, from an unconscious abandonment of his own methodological starting-point. With Schopenhauer, on the contrary, we are dealing with inwardness pure and simple, with the philosophical and ethical devaluation of every action, every real deed. But over and beyond this, the identity of macrocosm and microcosm, of the essential world and the pure inwardness of the *individuum* is also implied in the passage just quoted. Certainly, the path to this is an *askesis,* a dismissal of the cruelties of existence, a vision of the inner identity of all beings, and therefore a surmounting of ordinary egotism. On all these issues Schopenhauer speaks in a wide-ranging, picturesque and often witty manner. But we must never forget that—again in abrupt contrast to Kant and indeed to all the genuine moralists of the past—he regards his own ethics as optional for the philosopher expounding and justifying them. Why, then, should they be obligatory for his readers and followers? But if they are not so, all that these 'sublime' ethics leave us with is the inflation of the individual to a cosmic potency and a philosophical *carte blanche* to look down on all social activity in a superior way. . . .

Schopenhauer designed a world-picture in which neither the phenomenal cosmos nor that of the things-in-themselves knew change, development or history. The former, to be sure, consisted of a ceaseless changing, an apparent becoming and expiring, a changing moreover that was subject to a fatalistic necessity. But this becoming and expiring was still static in essence: a kaleidoscope in which alternating combinations of the same components give the direct, uninitiated beholder the illusion of constant change. And anyone possessing real philosophical insight must be aware that behind this brightly coloured veil of surface phenomena continually succeeding one another, there is hidden another world without space, time and causality, a world regarding which it would be pointless to speak of history, development or even progress. This initiated mind, wrote Schopenhauer, 'will not share people's belief that time produces something really new and momentous, that through it or in it something sheerly real will come into existence. . . . '

For Schopenhauer, therefore, history does not exist. 'For we are of the opinion,' he wrote,

> that everyone is still infinitely far from a philosophical knowledge of the world who presumes it possible to grasp its essence in some *historical* way, however finely clothed it is; but that is the case as soon as any *Becoming* or Having Become or In the Process of Becoming (*Werdenwerden*) occurs in his view of the world's essence in itself and any Earlier or Later has the slightest significance. . . . For all such historical philosophy, however superior its manner, takes *time* for a condition of things-in-themselves as though Kant had never existed, and hence stops at what Kant terms phenomenon as opposed to thing-in-itself. . . . it is just knowledge which is accommodated by the thesis of sufficient reason that never takes us to the inner essence of things but only pursues phenomena into infinity, moving without purpose or goal. . . .

In principle, said Schopenhauer, history can never become the object of a science; it is 'false not only in the exposition but in its essence'. Hence for Schopenhauer there exists no difference in history between important and trivial, major and minor; only the individual is real, whereas the human race is an empty abstraction.

Thus only the individual, isolated in a world without meaning, is left over as the fateful product of the individuation principle (space, time, causality). An individual, certainly, that is identical with the world-essence by virtue of the aforestated identity between microcosm and macrocosm in the world of things-in-themselves. This essence, however, located as it is beyond the valid sphere of space, time and causality, is consequently—nothingness. Hence Schopenhauer's *magnum opus* logically ends with the words: 'Rather we freely acknowledge that what is left after the complete annulment of the will is, for all those who are still full of will, assuredly nothingness. But conversely also, for those in whom will has turned and denied itself, this very real world of ours with all its suns and Milky Ways is—nothingness.'

And at this point, with our survey of the most important problems of Schopenhauer's philosophy completed, we ask once again: what is the social task it fulfils? Or, to put this question from another angle: what is behind its widespread and lasting influence? Here pessimism is not by itself an adequate answer. . . . Schopenhauer's philoso-phy rejects life in every form and confronts it with nothingness as a philosophical perspective. But is it possible to live such a life? (Let us mention only in passing that Schopenhauer—in line with Christianity, here as on the question of original sin—rejected suicide as a solution to the meaninglessness of existence.) If we consider Schopenhauer's philosophy *as a whole,* the answer is undoubtedly yes. For the futility of life means above all the individual's release from all social obligations and all responsibility towards men's forward development, which does not even exist in Schopenhauer's eyes. And nothingness as the pessimist outlook, as life's horizon, is quite unable, according to Schopenhauer's ethics, . . . to prevent or even merely to discourage the individual from leading an enjoyable contemplative life. On the contrary: the abyss of nothingness, the gloomy background of the futility of existence only lends this enjoyment an extra piquancy. Further heightening it is the fact that the strongly accented aristocratism of Schopenhauer's philosophy lifts its adherents (in imagination) way above the wretched mob that is short-sighted enough to battle and to suffer for a betterment of social conditions. So Schopenhauer's system, well laid-out and architecturally ingenious in form—rises up like a modern luxury hotel on the brink of the abyss, nothingness and futility. And the daily sight of the abyss, between the leisurely enjoyment of meals or works of art, can only enhance one's pleasure in this elegant comfort.

This, then, fulfils the task of Schopenhauer's irrationalism: the task of preventing an otherwise dissatisfied sector of the intelligentsia from concretely turning its discontent with the 'established order', that is, the existing social order, against the capitalist system in force at any given time. This irrationalism thereby reaches its central objective—no matter how far Schopenhauer himself was aware of it: that of providing an indirect apologetic of the capitalist social order.

Max Horkheimer (essay date 1960)

SOURCE: "Schopenhauer Today," translated by Robert Kolben, in *The Critical Spirit: Essays in Honor of Herbert Marchuse,* edited by Kurt H. Wolff and Barrington Moore, Jr., Beacon Press, 1967, pp. 55-71.

[*Horkheimer was a German-born American sociologist and philosopher. In the following essay, which was originally delivered as a lecture on the one-hundredth anniversary of Schopenhauer's death, Horkheimer addresses Schopenhauer's philosophies of history and politics, declaring that "Schopenhauer is the teacher for modern times."*]

Arthur Schopenhauer regarded fame with no less detachment than the majority of thinkers who finally gained it. Public recognition left him so indifferent that when he partook of it at last he did not even have to belittle it, either to himself or to others. He could relish the signs of future veneration and even succumb to the temptation of agreeing with Seneca's optimistic judgment that fame follows merit unfailingly. What great respect for the course of history! Only rarely did the philosopher show so much confidence in the verdict of a humanity, whose cultural decline he prophetically thought more plausible than its progress. As if there could be any certainty that among those forgotten there were no great men: indeed, hardly any age has demonstrated the universality of forgetting as clearly as has the present. In spite of our infinitely refined instruments of perception and its communication—not just because of them—only very few of those are remembered (let alone the thoughts they put on paper) who in Germany gave their lives in a lone attempt to put an end to the national disaster. They are of no lesser stature than their predecessors who were famous. They are gone. For Schopenhauer, however, justice from posterity was guaranteed, as it were, by that same history which in other respects he hated. Posterity was his longing, his utopia. Nietzsche, his successor, was not thus fooled. "I do not want any disciples," he says in *Ecce Homo*. "I am terribly afraid of being canonized one day. People will understand why I publish this book before: it is to keep them from playing tricks on me." He was convinced that fame is as despicable as the public opinion which awards it.

In regard to one's contemporaries, in regard to "up-to-dateness," Schopenhauer agrees with the author of *Thoughts Out of Season*. One of the prime conditions of greatness, he writes in the **Parerga,** is to have no respect at all for one's contemporaries, including their opinions and views, and the praise and blame resulting from them. What is "up-to-date" in this sense is what happens to be considered valid as a result of the interaction between material, relatively spontaneous, interests and manipulated, secret, and avowed ones. Truth itself, on the other hand, lies hidden, according to Democritus, deep in a well, and, according to Schopenhauer, it gets a rap on the knuckles when it tries to come out. In any case, it has had to hide itself again and again, depending on the state of events, as Voltaire puts it in his allegory. Up-to-date literature, whether conceived with an eye to the market by instinct or routine, serves the established order. Even the notion that opposes it is incorporated, assimilated, decontaminated. The controlled consumption of consumer and cultural goods in a boom period is a match for everything. The late stage of society is in all cultural matters at once cunning and unassuming, modest and insatiable—in this respect similar to antiquity in its decline. It manages to incorporate as its own ornament even criticism, negative art, resistance. The less of a chance the historical situation gives great works actually to inspire human action, the fewer the obstacles to their publication; the more diligence scholars apply to them, the less significant is the effect of their writing.

Schopenhauer's work is not free from such "up-to-dateness." Still, it has suffered from it less than the work of other great philosophers, probably because it is so ill-suited to education for efficiency, even academic efficiency. For that, it rejects too many pet ideas of employees of Culture and Education; it calls neither for Decision, nor for Engagement, nor for the Courage to Be. Schopenhauer does not compensate for the low wages

society doles out to the guardians of the spirit by the consciousness of an office that is supposed to be superior to other trades. His work makes no promises. Neither in heaven nor on earth, neither for developed nor for underdeveloped peoples does it hold out that to which leaders of every political or racial hue claim to be guiding their faithful. The apparently comforting title, **"On the Indestructibility of Our True Being through Death,"** announces a chapter that brings despair rather than solace. It is hardly fit to gain friends among the molders of public opinion, except perhaps by the element of denial, for it seems to attribute harshness to existence by showing that existence is necessarily harsh. But Schopenhauer does so little to clothe the negative in a semblance of meaning that he can hardly lead to resignation and conformism.

> Anyone who would have dared, in Schopenhauer's day or even at the turn of the century, to predict the course of history up to the present moment would certainly have been decried as a blind pessimist. Schopenhauer was a clairvoyant pessimist.
>
> *—Max Horkheimer*

Yet he saw things too clearly to exclude the possibility of historical improvement. The ending of almost all manual labor, especially of hard physical labor, is something he foresaw more precisely than most of the economists of his day. But he also suspected what could result from such a change. He took technical, economic, and social improvements into account, but from the very beginning he also perceived their consequences: blind devotion to success and a setback for a peaceful course of events. In sum, I might say, he saw the dialectic of such progress. Not unlike some left-wing Hegelians, who in this respect contradicted their teacher, he decidedly rejected the idea of the State's divinity. To Schopenhauer the good state is nothing else than the quintessence of a reasonable self-interest; its sanctions protect individuals from each other and its own citizens from other states. The state is no moral institution; it rests on force. "At the highest stage," he says, agreeing with the founders of socialism, "mankind would need no state." But he saw no prospect of this ever happening. He deified nothing, neither state nor technology. The development of the intellect rests on that of needs. Hunger, the urge to power, and war have been the greatest promoters of knowledge. The idealistic fable of the ruse of reason, which extenuates the horrors of the past by pointing to the good ends they served, actually babbles out the truth: that blood and misery stick to the triumphs of society. The rest is ideology.

In the century since Schopenhauer's death, history has had to admit that he saw straight into its heart. In spite of all the internal injustice in the various nations around the middle of the last century, there was still something like a European solidarity, a kind of urbane intercourse among nations, a good deal of discretion and even respect on the part of great nations towards small ones. Since his death, history has entered a new phase, progressing from a balance of power to ruthless competition among nations. Stiffer competition spurred technology, and the armaments race began. Rulers and ministers of state were in uniform. The anarchy of nations and the arms race inevitably led to the age of world wars, which in turn eventually resulted in the frantic urge for power in all nations of the world. This was Schopenhauer's prognosis. Struggles among individuals and social groups, domestic competition and concentration of power are supplemented and outdistanced by competition and concentration of power abroad. Schopenhauer shows what it is all about. Material interests, the struggle for existence, prosperity, and power are the motor; history is the result.

Schopenhauer did not offer philosophic rationalizations for his experiences of terror and injustice, even in countries with the most humane administrations. History frightened him. Violent political change which in recent times is usually brought about with the aid of nationalistic enthusiasm, he detested. Not having lived to see the decay of absolutism in its acute phase, with its torture and witch-hunting, burnings at the stake and other methods of qualified execution, he was not interested in a change of system. He would rather, as Goethe writes in the *West-Östliche Diwan,* converse "with clever men, with tyrants" than set out for the dictatorship of the "unified" people in the company of demagogues and fanaticized masses. His hatred of "patriots" springs immediately from the threat to his economic independence, resulting from nationalistic rebellions, but indirectly and theoretically, this hatred is aimed altogether at nationalism and the nationalistic age, which was then beginning. The fanaticism of unity and the violence it announced repelled him. He suffered from the same lack of enthusiasm for the so-called wars of liberation of Prussia as Goethe, and from the same fear of the French revolution of 1830 as Hegel. The great enlighteners of mankind have been very wary of The People as the highest value. Lessing once suggested that men should learn to recognize the stage when patriotism ceases to be a virtue.

"The Nation"—that was the word with which the new forces, opposed to absolutism, stirred up the people. Schopenhauer gave the Germans credit for not indulging, on the whole, in national pride as the English were doing, only one in fifty of whom was prepared to accept criticism of the "stupid and degrading bigotry" of their nation. Of course, later the Germans made up for it all the more, and Schopenhauer was startled to meet in Germany with this kind of demagogy, with "this game of insidious swindlers." For centuries thinkers had denounced mass suggestion and its identical opposite, the inaccessibility of seduced masses, as well as the ferocity of those who have come off badly—all as the result of domination. National pride, like the pride of individuals, is easily injured, even if the wound does not show for a long time. The revenge that follows is blind and devastating. There was a time when fanaticism was a distorted and misunderstood religion. Since St. Just and Robespierre it has taken on the form of exaggerated nationalism, which the

strong men in the saddle, when the going is a bit rough, can conveniently call up to rationalize murky instincts. When in an ominous historical moment those in power, no matter how different from one another in other respects, have nothing more to offer to quell the dissatisfaction of the people, they can always let loose on them the peddlers of a nationalistic community, of this mirage of Utopia, and feed them the sugar pill of cruelty. But since historians are not altogether wrong in distrusting generalizations and reflect on differences rather than similarities (as did Schopenhauer) among ruling systems and sociopsychological mechanisms, the reign of terror which broke out in Europe in the first half of the twentieth century, not to speak of Asia and Africa, seemed to be an accident. Anyone who would have dared, in Schopenhauer's day or even at the turn of the century, to predict the course of history up to the present moment would certainly have been decried as a blind pessimist. Schopenhauer was a clairvoyant pessimist.

His fear of the beginning enthusiastic nationalism is a sign of his modernity: to take no bribes from the *Zeit-geist.* He regarded world history sceptically, denouncing it as "the unchanging and permanent," indeed as the unhistorical. Not that he overlooked variations in social injustice, characteristic of various ages and stamping the majority of the people as either slaves or serfs. As to poverty and slavery, he says in **Parerga:** "The fundamental difference is that slaves owe their origin to violence; the poor, to cunning." The reason for this perverted state of society, he continues, for "the general struggle to escape misery, for sea-faring that costs so many lives, for complicated trade interests, and finally for the wars resulting from all this," is at bottom greediness for that superabundance which does not even make men happy. At the same time, such barbarism cannot be abolished, for it is the reverse side of refinement, an element of civilization. Schopenhauer did not remain behind the sociological knowledge of his day—he was faithful to the Enlightenment.

His judgment of the historical situation is based on his theoretical philosophy. Among European philosophers, he pointed to Plato and Kant as his forerunners. What they have in common with him is the gap between the essence of things, that which in itself is, and the world in which men move. What men perceive, what strikes them, how they see everything, depends on their intellectual apparatus and their senses, which in turn depend on the conditions of their biological and social existence. The countryside has a different aspect to the farmer assessing its fertility, to the hunter on the lookout for game, to the fugitive seeking a hiding place, to the wanderer, the painter, the strategist, not to mention people of different cultures. And how much more different will it appear to an animal, tame or wild, bird or gnat, not only with regard to color, sound, and smell, but also to form and relations. Just as things in space and time are conditioned by the perceiving subject, so are space and time themselves, which are the spectacles, as it were, worn by all who can see, hear, and feel. Pascal once said that to a creature in an infinitesimal, microscopic world which we cannot even perceive, millennia may pass in one of our seconds—thus a human millennium might appear but a moment to some superhuman being. Empirical scientific knowledge, vital to progress, the technical miracles which are the result of observation and which can increase or reduce life's span, are therefore not truth itself but only the semblance of truth. Plato and Kant described the relation between the two spheres, essence and appearance, differently. To Plato, truth was a realm of ordered concepts, and things were their transitory images. Kant taught that the thing-in-itself—that is, being as it exists in eternity, apart from human or animal perspectives—furnishes the subject with the matter necessary for cognition, with the sensible facts, out of which the intellect, with its ordering functions, produces the unitary world, just as a machine processes raw material into the finished product.

This concept of transcendental apperception, with its power and its "file boxes"—the head-office, one might say, of the intellect—was modeled on factory and business management. The intellect manufactures something conceptually solid out of the flux of perceptions, as a factory produces commodities. Over and above the ordering functions, the categories are, so to speak, the goals toward which they work: the ideas of freedom, eternity, and justice, which show the intellect the direction it must take. That these can be found in reason, that they even constitute reason in a certain sense, is Kant's ground for the hope that knowledge, and with it that which is to be known, will attain truth at a point of infinity, and that truth is not merely a means but the fulfillment.

Kant's subtle rescue of utopia was preceded on the European continent by rationalistic systems, which might be regarded as a series of attempts to save, against losing odds, the perfection of eternal being from the onslaught of the new science that was trying to explore appearance. After the end of scholasticism these attempts continued in the seventeenth century with the help of bourgeois reason. The innate ideas from which these systems develop are halfway between Plato's Ideas and Kant's categorical functions. They claim evidence, and evidence is to guarantee the truth, good and sufficient in itself, vis-à-vis the changing, terrifying reality, which since the sixteenth century and the overseas discoveries was marked by social upheavals and religious wars resulting from them. The need for something constructive, something permanent as the meaning behind all change was the motive power of philosophy. In spite of methexis, Plato had left essence and appearance unreconciled: Ideas were everything, transient things nothing. After the coming of Christianity, the world required justification, whether by faith or by concepts.

Rationalism was undermined by scientific thinking, which had been imported from England, where, thanks to the growth of trade and self-government in the towns, the citizens had slowly adapted to reality in a long drawn-out process; where political consciousness took form as a kind of resignation that accorded with religious consciousness; where convention became a religious matter and religion a civic one, and abstract concepts without facts had long

lost their prestige. Conceptual realism had made way for nominalism: facts came into their own right, and concepts were mere names. The Magna Charta asserted itself in the theory of knowledge; empiricist philosophy and the mental attitude attendant on it came to be accepted without much friction. But on the Continent this shift took place as a distinct break. The order whose term had come was here realized only much later, and whatever fails to occur at its proper time occurs with violence. Empiricism and the materialism related to it imply criticism, not only of the dominant philosophy and the original perfection of things which it had proclaimed, but also of the conditions of the world, of social and political reality. A new vision of the future world replaced the old: a universal rational society. From St. Augustine to Bossuet history had been understood as progress, as the history of salvation, in which the messianic kingdom was the necessary goal. Translating this into the secular sphere, Holbach and Condorcet saw social history as the path to earthly fulfillment. The dualism had remained: the better, future world was the meaning toward which men oriented themselves. The one thing which the empiricism of the European Enlightenment had in common with the rationalism it superseded was that the image of the future was couched in concepts which were as if innate and could dispense with empirical verification: liberty, equality before the law, protection of the individual, property. The remaining ideas that transcended facts, especially those of positive theology, fell before the empirical-sensualistic critique.

Schopenhauer's revolutionary philosophic achievement rests above all on the fact that in the face of pure empiricism he held to the original dualism that had been the basic theme of European philosophy up to Kant, but that, nevertheless, he did not deify the world-in-itself, the real essence. Since the time of Aristotle, Plato's great disciple, European thinking had held to the principle that the more real, steadfast, and eternal a being was, the greater its goodness and perfection. I know of no philosophic dogma as widely accepted as this one. Men were to orient themselves toward that which was most real: being-in-itself. Philosophy deduced the meaning and laws of transitory life from the eternal, thus expressing or implying satisfaction of all strivings and a reward for all good deeds. Only good could result from being at one with the most real, the best, the most powerful. In a more modern fashion, philosophers tried to base hope on human reason, that hope which formerly rested on the authority of the father and on revelation.

This is the philosophic conviction and at the same time the function of philosophy with which Schopenhauer broke. The highest, the most real, the metaphysical being to which philosophers had directed their view, away from the changing world of existing objects, is *not* at the same time the good. Degrees of reality are not degrees of perfection. Looking at the positively infinite, at the unconditional does not teach man how he should act; it is impossible to refer to the authority of being when one wishes a guide toward a decent course of action. The true essence which is at the bottom of all external things, the thing-in-itself as opposed to appearance, is something that everyone can discover within himself, if only he looks clearly enough and knows how to interpret the experiences of his own nature. It is the insatiable desire for well-being and enjoyment, a desire which wells up every time it has been satisfied, and not the reasons the intellect finds for such strivings, that make up the ineradicable reality of all that is alive, of existence altogether. In the struggle with nature and with men, the intellect serves as a weapon by providing rationalizations with which individuals, interest groups, and nations try to accommodate their demands to the moral precepts in force. The intellect is a function of the struggle for existence in individuals and in the species; it is kindled by resistance and vanishes with resistance.

Schopenhauer's theory of consciousness as a small part of the psyche, by which it is used as a tool—not to mention his many particular observations of normal and pathological psychology—anticipates the basic principle of modern psychoanalysis. The basis for his theory is the ever-flowing source of stimuli: unappeasable will. Each breath is followed by a silence that is already the desire for the next breath, and each moment which passes without satisfying this desire increases the need and its awareness, until they finally fade out. Breathing stands for life. So do eating and drinking: those cut off from them must fight for them, and the higher the stage of development of the living creature, the more subtle and insatiable the struggle becomes. Need and endless striving, kindled again and again, make up the content of history and determine man's relationship to Nature. If the air were not free but the result of work, men would fight for it as they do for land, and they could not do otherwise. Today it already seems as though they might actually have to fight for air. If there ever was an era that could confirm Schopenhauer's views, it is the period since the turn of the twentieth century, when reliance on progress was questioned least. For Schopenhauer the good is far more the ephemeral, thought, and appearance, than that which keeps reproducing itself.

Nevertheless he acknowledged himself a man of the eighteenth century. He was bitter toward the profundity of the "facetious philosophers" (a profundity widely disseminated today, too, in our schools and universities), who slandered "the greatest men of the last century, Voltaire, Rousseau, Locke, Hume . . . those heroes, those ornaments and benefactors of humanity." He complained that the venerable word "Enlightenment . . . has become a sort of term of abuse." He identified himself most deeply with the fight against superstition, intolerance, and rationalistic dogmatism. What seemed to him suspect about the Enlightenment, even paradoxical, was the identification of what today or in the future exists in all its power—let alone of gory history—with what ought to be. As the epitome of the good, not even the idea of a future mankind whose members were not trying to exterminate each other, was an adequate compromise for him. He is no good as a reference for the prophets of secular salvation and of even less use to the defenders of the status quo. In the face of theology, metaphysics, and positive philosophy of all kinds, Schopenhauer withdrew philosophic

sanction from the solidarity of those who are suffering, from the community of men lost in the universe, but without thereby advocating harshness. As long as there are hunger and misery on earth, he who can see will have no peace. In *Thoughts Out of Season,* Nietzsche quoted with enthusiasm the following passage from Schopenhauer's *Parerga:* "That man leads a heroic life who somehow or other, in spite of overwhelming difficulties and with little or no recompense, fights and eventually wins the battle for what will be of some benefit to all mankind." The more lucid thinking is, the more will it drive towards the abolition of misery; and yet any assurance that this is the ultimate meaning of existence, the end of pre-history, the beginning of reason is nothing but an endearing illusion. The heroic, even the holy life, without ideology, is the consequence of suffering and rejoicing with others, of sharing in the lives of others; perceptive men cannot stop fighting horror until they die. The famous idea that, by devoting themselves completely to transcending egoistic aims, morally great individuals can step out of the cycle of reincarnations has nothing to do with positive bliss. Happiness itself is negative. Even the last utopian escape which his teacher Kant, the greatest German *Aufklärer,* wanted to offer—the idea of the ultimate purpose that human history was to fulfill—was to Schopenhauer, in the face of the horror of this earth, only rationalistic deception; the eudemonistic concept of "the Highest Good" was still more so. Enlightened thought has no need of such illusions.

Basically, the classical idealism of Kant's successors, too, abandoned utopia. In that, they are like Schopenhauer. They regard the discrepancy between the world as it is and as it ought to be as overcome once this discrepancy is canceled in thought. Utopia survives only in rarefied form as the deified subject. The world as it appears is no longer that produced and constituted by men, as in Kant, but instead, as in Fichte, the result of free-floating action or, as in Schelling, the result of self-confirming primordial being. The thing-in-itself is identified with the subject, yet not as the negative but as the unconditioned positive. Hegel saw it as the living concept, the infinite movement, in which an antithesis between thing and thought shows itself as conditioned. But although Schopenhauer hated Hegel, he is not so far from him. The life of the concept, of the Hegelian Absolute, is the contradiction, the negative, the painful. What Hegel calls concept—the system of philosophical determinations that arise out of each other and are in eternal movement—is nothing but the rise and decline of what this system comprehends. The great achievement of Hegel's philosophy lies in the very fact that the concept does not exist outside and independently of what disappears and, as it does, is preserved in the concept. The consolation offered by his "wicked optimism" is in the end the insight into the necessary interweaving of the concepts into the whole, into that brittle unity that is called system. Hegel's recognition of logical structure in the worlds of nature and man, as emphasized in his doctrine of nature and objective mind, is by no means as far removed from Schopenhauer's aesthetic and philosophical reflections as Schopenhauer was inclined to think. Hegel speaks of substantive determination, of the absolute final purpose of world history; ultimately, world history moves towards the absolute mind, the philosophic system, towards mere insight into the whole. On the real course of history, on the other hand, Hegel says: "When we look at this spectacle of the passions and see the consequences of their violence, of the unreason associated not only with them but also, and even primarily, with good intentions and just aims; when we see the attendant wickedness and evil, the ruin of the most flourishing kingdoms which the human mind has produced; then we can only be filled with sorrow over this transitoriness and, insofar as this destruction is not only the work of nature but of the will of men, we must end up in moral grief, in a revolt of the good spirit, if such is in us, against such a spectacle."

Decay and permanence, the dying of the particular and the being of the universal, are one. Hegel is far away from Fichte's positive pathos, even farther from his *Instructions for a Blessed Life* which, to be sure, had lost all eudemonistic attraction even for the author of the *Speeches to the German Nation*. In the destruction of false comfort, Schopenhauer goes a shade beyond Hegel by refusing to recognize, as the ground for deifying existence, the consistency of a system that encompasses the world and thus the development of mankind to the point where philosophic insight becomes possible. The social whole, too, the institutions in which the mind comes into its own, as in art and philosophy, must pass. The absolute mind adheres to the objective and subjective mind of nations, and their fate is to perish, like any group or individual, like anything finite. Reconciliation, the identity of opposites reached through thought, is no real reconciliation, whether it occurs in the present or future state of mankind. The violent stroke of genius by which Hegel, the last great systematizer of philosophy, rescued the positivity of the absolute by including agony and death in it, fails because insight is tied to the living subject and must perish with him.

Hegel's teaching shows that the positivity that distinguishes him from Schopenhauer cannot ultimately stand up. The failure of a logically stringent system in its highest form in Hegel, means the logical end of attempts at a philosophic justification of the world, the end of the claim of philosophy to emulate positive theology. All these attempts rest directly or indirectly on the idea of the world as the work or expression of true mind. But if the world, in its essence and in its actual condition, is *not* necessarily connected with mind, philosophic confidence in the very existence of truth disappears. In that case, truth can be found only in perishable men themselves and is as perishable as they are. Even thinking about transitoriness loses the lustre of the more-than-transitory. Merely faith remains; the attempt to rationalize it was doomed to failure.

Schopenhauer's thinking is infinitely modern, so modern, in fact, that young people have it by instinct. This thinking knows about the contradiction of autonomous truth and is profoundly irritated by it. Philosophy does not move beyond real history. Young people no longer accept thinking that is philosophically out of date. If an attempt is made to pass over or mask the contradictions in which thought inevitably gets entangled, the young lose faith not only in the truthfulness of their elders but in the whole culture in which they participate and whose shares, for many internal reasons, have in any case dropped in value. Technology makes memory superfluous. The young have little reason left to believe the old and their reference to eternal commandments. They try to manage without them. At many universities in America and even in Eastern countries logical positivism has won out, supplanting philosophy. It takes thought itself as mere function, as business. There is no fundamental difference between the production of mathematical formulas and their application in technology and industry. Positivism presents the result implied in the failure of positive philosophy. We need not worry about philosophic truth, as it does not exist anyhow. That is the short-circuit which Schopenhauer's work avoids. He is driven by the passion for truth and, like Spinoza, devoted his life to this passion without making a job of it. But his philosophy gives perfect expression to what young people today feel: that there is no power that can transcend truth—indeed, that truth carries in it the character of powerlessness. According to Schopenhauer, positivism is right against metaphysics because there is nothing unconditional which might guarantee truth or from which it could be deduced. But theological metaphysics is right against positivism because every spoken statement cannot help but make an impossible claim not only concerning an anticipated effect, concerning success, as positivism believes, but also concerning truth in its proper sense, whether or not the speaker intends this. Without thinking about truth and thereby of what it guarantees, there can be no knowledge of its opposite, of the abandonment of mankind, for whose sake true philosophy is critical and pessimistic—there cannot even be sorrow, without which there is no happiness.

According to Schopenhauer, philosophy does not set up any practical aims. It criticizes the absolute claims of programs without itself proposing one. The vision of organizing the earth in justice and liberty, the basis of Kantian thought, has turned into the mobilization of nations and the uprising of peoples. Every revolt following the great French Revolution has reduced the substance of its humanistic content and increased nationalism—or so it appears. The greatest drama of the perversion of faith in humanity into intransigent cult of the state was offered by socialism itself. The revolutionaries of the International fell victim to nationalistic leaders. A certain state of humanity, venerated as the true one, is an aim among others for which men may justifiably sacrifice themselves. But if it is hypostatized as the absolute aim, then, by definition, there is no authority, neither divine commandment, nor morality, nor even—and I think this is no less important—the personal relation called friendship, which could control it. Every finite being—and humanity is finite—which gives itself airs as the ultimate, the highest, the unique, becomes an idol with a demonic ability to change its identity and take on another meaning. The history of many recent revolutions, in contrast to the theory of Marx, offers frightening examples. Before they seized power, the aim of Lenin and most of his friends was a society of freedom and justice, yet in reality they opened the way to a terroristic totalitarian bureaucracy which certainly does not come closer to freedom than the empire of the Czar. The transition of the new China into sheer barbarism is obvious.

The new idol is the collective *We*. It is not the only one. Insofar as conditional aims or motives for life generally are presented to young people as if they were unconditional, they are met with the scorn of those who have become wise or with mock enthusiasm. They see through the conventionality of arguments for a respectable life that are not founded, as Schopenhauer advocated, on simple common sense and, ultimately, on penal law. Young people can see the unscrupulous practices of moral, adult persons. And just because they accept from their elders only their practical nimbleness but not their pathos, because they understand the Idea only as a set of rationalizations, they have nothing with which to oppose mass deception. If it is expedient to accept it, it would be merely stupid to resist it. Added to this is an unavowed yearning, a feeling of insufficiency, and defiance, which by repeating evil, unconsciously tries to provoke the good, so that it will show itself even if it is lethal. A skeptical generation is no more immune to participation in misdeeds than is one of believers. Instead, their disillusioned life, despite all pressures toward a career, engenders the pervasive feeling of meaninglessness in which false faith has a fertile soil. In order to resist it, there would have to be a longing for that which is different, a longing that would have passed through culture without, however, having been victimized by any of its hardened forms.

Now I can be clearer about why Schopenhauer is the teacher for modern times. The doctrine of blind will as an eternal force removes from the world the treacherous gold foil which the old metaphysics had given it. In utter contrast to positivism, it enunciates the negative and preserves it in thought, thus exposing the motive for solidarity shared by men and all beings: their abandonment. No need is ever compensated in any Beyond. The urge to mitigate it in *this* world springs from the inability to look at it in full awareness of this curse and to tolerate it when there is a chance to stop it. For such solidarity that stems from hopelessness, knowledge of the *principium individuations* is secondary. The more sublime and the less rigid a man's character is, the more indifferent will he be about how near to his own ego, or how far from it, a given situation is, and the less will he distinguish between such nearness and distance when his work deals with them; nor can he give up his labors, even if they become those of Sisyphus. To stand up for the temporal against merciless enternity is morality in Schopenhauer's sense. This morality is not influenced either—for if it were, it would remain calculation—by the Buddhist myth of reincarnation, according to which after a man dies, the soul, timeless and spaceless, is supposed to find the body that corresponds to its stage of purification. The merciless structure of eternity could generate a community of the abandoned, just as injustice and terror in society result in the community of those who resist. Persecution and hunger dominate the history of society even today. If young peo-

ple recognize the contradiction between the possibilities of human powers and the situation on this earth, and if they do not allow their view to be obscured either by nationalistic fanaticism or by theories of transcendental justice, identification and solidarity may be expected to become decisive in their lives. The road leads through knowledge, not only of science and politics, but also of the great works of literature.

What Schopenhauer declared about individuals—that they are an expression of the blind will to existence and wellbeing—is at present becoming apparent with regard to social, political and racial groups in the whole world. That is one of the reasons why his doctrine appears to me as the philosophic thought that is a match for reality. Its freedom from illusions is something it shares with enlightened politics; the power of conceptual expression, with theological and philosophic tradition. There are few ideas that the world today needs more than Schopenhauer's—ideas which in the face of utter hopelessness, because they confront it, know more than any others of hope.

Patrick Gardiner (essay date 1963)

SOURCE: "The Possibility of Metaphysics," in *Schopenhauer: His Philosophical Achievement,* edited by Michael Fox, The Harvester Press, Sussex, 1980, pp. 37-49.

[*Gardiner is an English critic, editor, and educator. In the following essay, which originally appeared in his* Schopenhauer *(1963), Gardiner examines Schopenhauer's distinction between philosophy and religion, and describes his approach to characterizing the* Ding an sich.]

'A Man becomes a philosopher by reason of a certain perplexity, from which he seeks to free himself . . . But what distinguishes the false philosopher from the true is this: the perplexity of the latter arises from the contemplation of the world itself, while that of the former results from some book, some system of philosophy which lies before him.' Schopenhauer was not alone in characterizing the metaphysical frame of mind as being essentially one of original perplexity or (as he refers to it elsewhere) wonder; wonder 'concerning the world and our own existence, inasmuch as these press upon the intellect as a riddle, the solution of which therefore occupies mankind without intermission.' To be impressed by the fact that things are as they are and not otherwise, to find it strange or marvellous that there should be anything at all: this, Schopenhauer and others have wished to insist, is the mark of a certain type of outlook, a certain type of temperament, not shared by all; and for one unable to understand or enter into such an attitude, for whom 'the world and existence appear as a matter of course', the theories and doctrines propounded by metaphysicians would seem, not merely unintelligible in themselves, but without ground, without reason; the metaphysical quest itself would seem an enigma, and he could only view with indifference attempts to solve what to him must appear as nonexistent problems and difficulties. All the same, Schopenhauer believed that total inability to feel the force of fundamental questions such as those that have in one way or another occupied the attention of philosophers throughout the ages is in fact rare. The kind of approach to the world he had in mind was not, he thought, confined to the relatively sophisticated; it was also to be found among the simple and ignorant, although it was true that it manifested itself in exceedingly different forms. Such an attitude towards experience is, in other words, deeply founded in our character and make-up as human beings, and accounts for the continuous survival of metaphysical thinking as an activity capable of retaining its hold upon the human mind and imagination; it is 'the pendulum which keeps the clock of metaphysics in motion'.

To say that there is a deeprooted tendency in human nature to ask ultimate questions about the world as a whole or to raise issues about the meaning and purpose of human existence is one thing; it is another to explain this tendency; and it is another thing again to justify it. So far as explanation was concerned, Schopenhauer put forward a number of different considerations at various places in his writings, all of which could be said to suggest possible sources of the disposition to regard the world as a problem that demanded solution. There was, however, one point upon which he laid special emphasis. It concerns the knowledge men have of the inevitability of death, together with their awareness of 'the suffering and misery of life'. The combination of the two was regarded by him as providing perhaps the most powerful stimulus to the desire to find a metaphysical interpretation of existence. 'If our life were endless and painless, it would perhaps occur to no one to ask why the world exists and is just the kind of world it is; but everything would just be taken as a matter of course.' But death and suffering are undeniable realities. It might of course be the case that, even so, we should not be troubled in this way if the world were (as some philosophers have claimed) 'an absolutely necessary existence'. For then it would be something which embraced within itself 'not only all actual but all possible existence, so that, as Spinoza indeed declares, its possibility and its actuality would be absolutely one.' We should then regard it as something which could not but exist, and which moreover could not be conceived of as being different from what it is: its existence and character could in no sense be thought away, and the same would apply to our own place in and relations to the world. Hence there could be no question of our regarding it as 'remarkable, problematical, and indeed as the unfathomable and ever-disquieting riddle': on the contrary, we should 'necessarily be as little conscious of its existence *as such,* i.e., as a problem for reflection, as we are of the incredibly fast motion of our planet.' Such ideas, however, quite apart from the logical difficulties they raise, seem to be manifestly untrue to what we instinctively realize to be the case. We can conceive of the world's being other than it is, we can conceive that it might not have existed at all—there is no impossibility in doing either. Hence questions about the grounds and sense of the world are free to arise, and they seem naturally to force themselves upon us at every stage: 'not merely that the world exists, but still more that it is such a wretched world'—this is the torturing problem of metaphysics.

Among other things, considerations of the type described help to explain (Schopenhauer thinks) why systems which assume or attempt to establish the reality of continued existence after death always excite the keenest interest and receive the greatest general approval. Such systems usually involve additional claims concerning the existence of creative or superintending agencies lying above or outside the world—gods, for example. But it should not be thought that it is this which always gives them their principal attraction and appeal. True, men have in general come to view theistic beliefs and beliefs in personal immortality as being inseparably connected with one another. But they are logically quite distinct; and if in fact one could establish the reality of immortality, in a way that did not require the postulation of a deity capable of preserving us in being after we die, the enthusiasm which many people at present feel for their gods would, Schopenhauer suggests, quickly cool. And for similar reasons he argues that 'materialistic' or 'sceptical' systems and theories, which seek to deny or cast doubt upon the validity of immortality doctrines, have never been able to achieve a wide or lasting hold upon men's minds.

From all this it might be supposed that Schopenhauer was primarily concerned to offer an account of what prompts *religious* rather than *philosophical* speculation about the nature of the world. He certainly believed that the religious and philosophical urges in man both spring from the disquiet human beings feel when they contemplate the reality which confronts them, the conditions that govern their lives and experience. Philosophy, like religion, arises from the demand for an 'interpretation of life', and unless this is recognized, the main philosophical systems of the past cannot be understood, since it is impossible to cut them loose from the profound psychological and moral needs they are in one way or another concerned to satisfy. But, while insisting on the importance of the foregoing, he was far from wishing to assimilate philosophy to religion. To say that certain forms of thinking ultimately stem from a common root is not to imply that they may not differ profoundly in other respects; and, although Schopenhauer was (somewhat confusingly) prepared to call both religion and philosophy 'metaphysics', he none the less drew a very definite distinction between them. Thus religion may be termed the 'metaphysics of the people', on analogy with the 'poetry of the people' (ballads, for instance) and the 'wisdom of the people' (proverbial wisdom). Its evidence and credentials lie 'outside itself', in the sense that it depends upon 'revelation, which is authenticated by signs and miracles', rather than upon thought and reflection: on this account it is above all intended for what Schopenhauer considers to be the great majority of mankind, 'who are not capable of thinking but only of believing' and who are not moved by reasons but only by authority. When it comes to argument, he suggests that the upholders of religious doctrines tend to fall back upon threats of some kind (the *ultima ratio theologorum*), whether these be threats of eternal punishment in some other sphere or ones of a more immediate and mundane character—'the stake or things like it'. To say this, however, is not to deny that religions may serve a useful purpose in human life and society, nor is it even to withold from them any kind of validity. Certainly to treat them as expressing truths in any straightforward sense leads to insuperable difficulties; one is confronted by fantastic assertions, together with dogmas which 'cannot even be distinctly thought.' It must be allowed, too, that most religions tend to flourish at periods when the general level of knowledge is low and when, because of the prevalence of ignorance and superstition, it is easier to accept what they say at its face value: 'like glow-worms, they need darkness in order to shine.' At such times men's desires for what it is not in their power to obtain, and their fears of things they cannot by their own efforts defend themselves against, make them more than ever ready to cling to the hope that there may exist supernatural agencies which can be induced to intervene on their behalf by prayer or entreaty: thus the appeal which many religious doctrines undeniably possess is to be ascribed to human passion or desire rather than to rational or intellectual conviction. But it is possible, all the same, to look at religious beliefs in another and less unsympathetic way; and from this point of view Schopenhauer put forward the suggestion, familiar in our own day but less so in his, that religions are most plausibly interpreted as 'allegories'. So conceived, they may be viewed, for instance, primarily in ethical terms, as ways of impressing upon us in a vivid and memorable form the moral relations in which we stand to one another; hence many religious dogmas can be said primarily to relate to the earthly field of conduct and social existence. As he made one of the disputants say in his imaginary dialogue, **On Religion,** 'There must be . . . a public standard of right and virtue, it must always flutter high overhead. In the end it is all one and the same what heraldic figures appear on it, provided only they signify what is meant.'

Nor is this all. Religions may also, in their own strange fashion, be regarded as giving voice to the obscure sense we are wont to have that 'behind the physical in the world there must be a metaphysical'—a feeling which, in ordinary terms, we find it almost impossible to express or clearly articulate. From this standpoint the fact that many religious statements seem to involve absurdities, or even downright contradictions, need no longer be a source of surprise. Rather, it may well appear to be an understandable feature of such assertions; for inasmuch as religion endeavours to concern itself with an order of things beyond the scope of everyday experience and discourse, 'not only the contradictory but also the comprehensible dogmas [of religious teaching]' are really nothing more than 'allegories and accommodations to the human power of comprehension.' On this interpretation, we exhibit a misunderstanding of the role and purpose of religion if we demand lucidity and rationality; the point of its teachings is to make people *feel* certain things which lie beyond the grasp of their purely intellectual faculties, and in order to perform this function it uses whatever imaginative resources may lie to hand.

Schopenhauer maintains, however, that with philosophy things are very different. The latter has its evidence 'in itself', and by this he partly means that, in so far as philosophy constitutes an attempt to solve the problems which the world and our existence in it present, it must do so in a way that is open to reflective appraisal and does not involve a blind appeal to authority or revelation. It is of the essence of philosophical inquiry that results should be *arrived at* in a clear and intelligible manner, even if the truths the philosopher seeks to communicate are themselves *au fond* simple ones (as Schopenhauer more than once suggests they will be—*Simplex sigillum veri*). Moreover, it is stressed that philosophical conclusions and assertions are always put forward as being in the strictest sense true—true *sensu proprio* as contrasted with *sensu allegorico*—and must be evaluated as such. If this is so, it is obvious that only confusion and muddle will follow upon a failure to distinguish clearly between religious and philosophical modes of thinking and speaking—as the history of metaphysical speculation amply and continually demonstrates. For, on the one hand, philosophers have regularly shown a disposition to bring about some kind of fusion of the two, with the consequence that they have carried over concepts and ideas from one field to the other without giving thought to the question of the legitimacy of such a procedure. And, on the other hand, representatives of established religions have in their turn encroached upon the sphere of philosophy, with the undisguised purpose of securing 'inner' or rational authentication for their teachings in a manner that would show these teachings to be *sensu proprio* true: e.g. the belief that the universe has been created by a personal god with certain intelligible purposes in view must be exhibited as being at least as worthy of acceptance as the belief that it contains thousands of stars. Such an ambition, Schopenhauer thinks, may well strike one as pointless and unnecessary: an established religion does not *need* the help of philosophy—has it not already everything on its side, 'revelation, documents, miracles, prophecies, the protection of government . . . the consent and reverence of all', and (last but not least) 'the invaluable privilege of being able to imprint its doctrines on the mind at the tender age of childhood, whereby they become almost innate ideas'? Yet he was of course perfectly aware that these ironical concessions would not satisfy a believer who wished to see the propositions of his faith finally and indisputably established in the form in which they were popularly understood and accepted: the fact remained, nevertheless, that any attempt to meet such a demand could only result in a type of undertaking that both in intention and spirit was incompatible with the nature and scope of philosophy as truly conceived. For philosophy could not be regarded as an instrument to be utilized in the service of something other than itself, nor treated as a means of giving additional support to contentions already subscribed to on independent grounds; the tenets of religion could never justifiably be viewed by a philosopher as something *given,* which it was his task to establish and vindicate. Although the conclusions to which he was led as a result of his own reflection might be analogous, in *some* respects, to ideas which—in a veiled and figurative form—found expression in certain religious doctrines, it was essential that he should have reached them freely and independently, uninfluenced by any desire to provide a basis for a previously accepted creed or dogma. And this was to say, among other things, that his procedure should be quite different from that which Schopenhauer accused the university professors of his time of following. For they, having fallen under the spell of Hegel's 'verbiage', had evolved the practice of borrowing familiar dogmas and notions from the religion of their country, and of dressing these up in the obscure jargon of the 'Absolute': as a result, they were to be found talking of 'nothing but God, explaining how, why, wherefore, by what voluntary or involuntary process, he created or brought forth the world, showing whether he is within or without it, and so forth, just as if philosophy were theology and as if it sought for enlightenment concerning God, not concerning the world.' But what was the excuse for all this? In the Christian religion the existence of a deity is presupposed at the start, being regarded as something beyond serious question. Philosophy, on the other hand, 'has no articles of faith', and, as a form of investigation which should aim at the truth *sensu proprio* and should do so in a clear and intelligible manner, it has no right to concern itself with entities and agencies the very nature of which is obscure. German professors, however, showed no appreciation of this; instead of volunteering an explanation of exactly what it was they were referring to when they held forth upon their favourite themes, they preferred to keep it hidden behind an 'edifice of words', so that scarcely a tip could be seen.

Observations of this sort concerning the relation between religious and philosophical thinking are to be found in all Schopenhauer's main writings. Central to them is the belief that religions are not what they are all too often taken to be, repositories of knowledge about things that lie 'outside the world', for of such things there *can* be no knowledge. At the same time he thought that it could not be denied that the assumption that they are repositories of such knowledge has exercised an immense influence upon the direction taken by philosophical speculation, and that it is only possible fully to understand a great deal of traditional metaphysical theorizing with this in mind. Certainly it seems to be true that many metaphysical systems have in fact been constructed in the confidence that they can establish conclusions of the highest importance for ethics and religion, thereby silencing sceptics and reassuring the faithful; to this extent Schopenhauer may well have been justified in stressing the manner in which theological interests had tended to affect the pattern taken by such thinking. But whether or not his diagnosis is accepted as correct, it is in the light of his rejection of the idea that philosophy should try to provide a theoretical foundation for theological dogmas that his own conception of the proper scope and aims of philosophical reflection is most conveniently approached. . . .

A stage has now been reached where it is possible to outline the position from which Schopenhauer's own philosophical system developed. In view of his declared acceptance of the main implications of Kant's anti-speculative theses, one might have expected his procedure to have been one of faithfully carrying forward the Kantian programme; one might have supposed that he would have set aside as hopeless any undertaking remotely savouring of ancient metaphysical ambitions, and that

he would instead have restricted himself to the further investigation and analysis of the pervasive forms and categories in terms of which, according to Kant, we interpret our experience. The fact that Schopenhauer, as it turned out, did not confine himself within such limits may be explained by a variety of considerations, not all of which can be discussed at this point. There was, however, one special feature of Kant's philosophy to which Schopenhauer himself assigned a central place in explaining the evolution of his own ideas. This was the Kantian doctrine of the *Ding an sich,* or 'thing-in-itself'. . . .

In a general way Schopenhauer thought that his own theory provided the key to the overall problem of the relation between phenomena and things-in-themselves which haunts Kant's philosophy like an uneasy ghost. For this relation can now be given an interpretation that avoids the difficulties inherent in Kant's formulations. For Schopenhauer, 'our *willing* is the one opportunity which we have of understanding simultaneously from within any event which exhibits itself outwardly, consequently the one thing which is known to us *immediately,* and not, like all the rest, merely given in idea': thus the restriction of our knowledge to perceptible phenomena, which otherwise holds universally, does not apply in the case of myself; and Schopenhauer further argues that in recognizing my perceptible body as being at the same time will, I am conscious of what is is 'in itself'—the will 'reveals itself to everyone directly as the in-itself of his own phenomenal being.' But we should not be justified, simply on the grounds that we are immediately aware of this double aspect of things in the case of our own bodies alone, in supposing that it is only here that the distinction between phenomenal existence and thing-in-itself can validly be applied. If a person were to assume this, he would be implying that his own body was unique among all the objects with which he was or could be perceptually acquainted; it alone would be 'will' as well as 'idea', and hence he would be committed to the position that it was 'the only real individual in the world.' Such a view is one that Schopenhauer labels 'theoretical egoism', regarding it as the counterpart of what in another context may be described as 'practical egoism', this being the kind of attitude which a man manifests when in his dealings with his fellows he treats himself alone as a person entitled to serious consideration. Schopenhauer is prepared to allow that 'theoretical egoism' cannot be disproved by logical argument; he claims, however, that it has never in fact been regarded in philosophy as more than a sophistical pretence—as a serious conviction it could only be found in a madhouse, standing in need of a cure rather than a refutation, and it may therefore be safely disregarded. What he says on this subject is perhaps worth noticing in the light of the 'solipsistic' beliefs that are sometimes attributed to him. It is, I think, true that he never, for example, properly faced the philosophical problem of our knowledge of other people conceived of as animated beings with an inner life like our own, or took account of the difficulties which some of his own theoretical presuppositions might be held to raise in this regard. But however that may be, he certainly did not wish to be understood as saying that a man could legitimately suppose those about him to be mere products or projections of his own individual consciousness; such notions are indeed incompatible with the main tenets of his system as he subsequently develops it.

Schopenhauer maintains that we are in fact bound to think of the world we inhabit, which includes other human beings to all intents and purposes like ourselves, as being more than mere phenomenon or 'idea'; and it is this obscure consciousness which finds expression in various well-known philosophical 'solutions' of the problem of the external world. Nevertheless, the problem has been misconceived, the inarticulate dissatisfaction that gives rise to it misapprehended and misinterpreted. Philosophers have obsessively looked for something in essentials *like* what we normally take to be reality (i.e. phenomenal objects and events) but at the same time different in that what is so sought must be thought of as lacking any *sensible* properties; yet such a quest necessarily involves absurdities and contradictions. So far as the existence of physical objects is concerned, the world we perceive is not to be regarded as 'illusion', but rather lies 'open for sense and understanding' and 'presents itself with naïve truth as that which it is.' What in the depths of our being we feel, however, is that all appearances to the contrary, the rest of the world in some way shares the same fundamental nature which through direct inner experience we know to be ours. And in this sense the old philosophical conundrum can be given a meaningful interpretation: moreover, it can be answered. For each of us is aware in his own case that he is not merely phenomenon but also 'will'.

By thus appealing to personal experience as providing the key to the inner nature of the world as a whole, Schopenhauer thought that he had circumvented the kind of objection it is reasonable to bring against the Kantian doctrine of the 'thing-in-itself'. For in the first place it seemed to him obvious that my knowledge of myself as will is different in kind from my knowledge of myself as idea or representation. What I am unaware of in self-consciousness is not, it is true, something separate from what I am aware of when I look at my body and observe its movements, if by this it is implied that I have to do with two different entities or with two different sets of occurrences. The point is, however, that when I am conscious of myself as will I am not conscious of myself *as an object;* I am only conscious of myself under the latter aspect when I perceive myself at the same time as a body, for my body is the 'objectification' of my will. Thus to regard the 'thing-in-itself' as will is not to be committed to a belief in duplicate skeletal objects underlying the objects of sense-perception, with all the attendant difficulties such a position involves. For 'will' is not the name of any sort of object: questions concerning the shape or size of the will, for instance, are evidently out of place, and it is even misleading to ascribe 'unity' to it—'it is itself one, though not in the sense that an object is one, for the unity of an object can only be known by contrast to a possible multiplicity.' Nor is it right to speak of will as a *cause,* for example of its causing bodily behaviour; Schopenhauer's doctrine that an act of will and a corresponding movement of the body are not two distinct events, but the same event considered under different aspects, rules out the application of causal terminology here. Thus on Schopenhauer's account of the 'thing-in-itself' there is no problem to be faced concerning the justification of extending the causal principle beyond the sphere of perceptible phenomena, for the will is not such that it does or could function as the cause of such phenomena—its relation to them is of quite another kind. Finally, on Schopenhauer's theory, the 'thing-in-itself' is not wholly beyond our reach, inexperienceable and therefore unknowable, since we at least have access to it in our own self-awareness:

> . . . a *way from within* stands open for us to that essential inner nature of things, to which we cannot penetrate *from without;* as it were, a subterranean passage . . . which, as if by treachery, places us at once within the fortress which it was impossible to take by assault from without.

Now to suggest that we may validly extrapolate from the content of our own inner self-knowledge to that of our fellow human beings, whose appearance, behaviour, modes of expression, and so forth largely resemble our own, is one thing; but surely to ascribe what we find through self-conscious reflection upon our own inner experience to everything else in the phenomenal world, conscious and non-conscious, animate and inanimate alike, is a very different matter? And that, of course, is so. Schopenhauer's theory involves an explicit extension of concepts and modes of description beyond the areas within which they are normally restricted in their use, so that they come to cover *all* objects of experience. It is precisely this feature of his system which gives it the peculiar kind of comprehensiveness naturally associated with metaphysical theories, of whatever kind; a comprehensiveness which cuts across accepted classifications and divisions in a fashion so total and all-embracing that it seems to rule out the possibility of the theory's being challenged by reference to particular considerations or observations of the sort relevant at the level of common sense or empirical science.

Schopenhauer would not have wished to deny that his theory was metaphysical in this sense. The fact that the world presents itself to us 'as a riddle' returning again and again to torment us, and that the puzzlement and disquiet with which its existence and nature fill us do not appear to be such that they could be removed by any information the empirical sciences may be able to offer—these are matters, he implies, to be taken seriously; they cannot be simply brushed aside on the grounds that philosophers have notoriously failed in their attempts to satisfy us with regard to them. Kant was admittedly able to show why his predecessors had always failed, by exposing the emptiness of all claims to knowledge transcending the limits of possible experience. But why, once again, should it be assumed that all metaphysics must be 'transcendent' in character? May it not be that philosophers have been misled into making their preposterous claims by insufficiently recognizing the resources provided by experience, and in particular inner experience, as a means of interpreting the world? With this in mind, Schopenhauer wrote:

> I . . . say that the solution of the riddle of the world must proceed from the understanding of the world itself; that . . . the task of metaphysics is not to pass over the experience in which the world exists, but to understand it thoroughly, because outer and inner experience is . . . the principal source of all knowledge; that therefore the solution of the riddle of the world is only possible through the proper connexion of outer with inner experience, effected at the right point . . .

Along what general lines, on this interpretation, will metaphysics proceed? Since its function is not conceived to be one of transcending experience, it is not wedded to the idea that it must proceed by purely deductive reasoning, basing itself solely upon *a priori* concepts and formal principles. The latter conception of philosophical method, springing as it does from the belief that 'only what we know *before* all experience can extend beyond all possible experience,' breaks down when it is seen that the only concepts and principles which can properly be said to be *a priori* in the requisite sense are (as Kant showed) ones whose legitimate employment is tied to empirical contexts. And in point of fact philosophers who have in their theorizing striven to conform to the conception in question have tended, despite their professions, covertly to introduce into their premises certain experiential ideas and judgments; without, however, realizing that this makes it impossible for them to move through deduction to their desired goal, since 'nothing can follow from a proposition except what it already really says itself.' Whatever their pretensions, the systems offered only too often represent no more than tautologous transformations of propositions (definitional or factual) assumed at the outset to be true. Once, on the other hand, it is honestly realized that philosophy cannot be a purely formal or deductive discipline, envisaged on the model of certain idealized sciences, and also that its fundamental datum can be nothing else but experience, the metaphysician need no longer be deceived concerning the scope of his activity; he will, moreover, be in a position to approach the problem presented by existence in a more discerning and perspicacious manner, unbefuddled by abstract conceptions, and less ready to treat as profound truths about the nature of things which are often in fact no more than superficial trivialities suggested by certain partial aspects of ordinary life and knowledge.

For philosophy should properly be concerned with the interpretation of what Schopenhauer calls 'experience in general'; and that alone, quite apart from other considerations, is sufficient to distinguish it from empirical inquiries of the ordinary sort, to which—if its claims to be an *a priori* study are denied—there might be an inclination to assimilate it. The observational sciences treat of findings which lie within definable and specific limits; further, the fact that new discoveries are constantly being made within their various separate domains involves the continual revision and reappraisal of old theories, the provision of new ones. By contrast, philosophy is not

dependent in this manner upon results obtained in particular areas of investigation; it is not 'confirmable' or 'falsifiable' in the sense in which an empirical hypothesis may be said to be so. One should not, however, infer from this that a philosophical interpretation of the world must necessarily be 'vacuous', that there is no way in which it can intelligibly be said to conform or fail to conform to experience. Schopenhauer compares such an interpretation to the deciphering of a 'cryptograph', arguing that just as an explanation of something written in cipher is in a certain sense justified by 'the agreement and connexion in which all the letters of that writing are placed by this explanation', so 'a deciphering of the world' is shown to be acceptable 'through the agreement with each other in which it places the very diverse phenomena of the world, and which we do not perceive without it.' Such a deciphering must 'prove itself from itself', this proof being 'the mark of genuineness'; what is interpreted in terms of it must so to speak 'come out right.' It was an interpretation of this kind that Schopenhauer believed that he had provided in his own theory, a theory which, taking as its 'subject and source' not particular experiences but the 'totality of all experience' and employing as its primary concepts notions which already have a specific meaning within that totality, offered a solution to the 'riddle of the world' such that once it was grasped it could be directly recognized as being correct; in the light of it, phenomenal existence in general could be seen to possess a determinate and pervasive inward significance, present in all its multifarious manifestations. And while always insisting that his theory was in no sense comparable to a scientific hypothesis, in some of his later work Schopenhauer implied that what he had written might even be said to have obtained a kind of indirect 'corroboration' from the fact that certain recent empirical investigators, particularly when interpreting the functions and development of living organisms, had adopted modes of viewing and representing natural phenomena strikingly close to those suggested by his own system. He stressed, however, that metaphysics conceived on the pattern outlined must on no account be presumed capable of answering every question we may find ourselves wanting to ask about the ultimate character and explanation of reality. Its scope was restricted to the world and our experience of the world; if anyone demanded elucidations which went beyond this, he was asking for something which could be neither thought nor understood—'something that the human intellect is absolutely incapable of grasping and thinking.' It followed that any philosopher who took it upon himself to afford such a solution, and who spoke of knowing the final ground or origin of things by reference to that which lies 'outside the world' and beyond all possible experience, alluding to it as 'the Absolute', or by some other equally mystifying expression, could not be accorded serious consideration. He would be merely playing tricks. . . .

Paul Gottfried (essay date 1974)

SOURCE: "Arthur Schopenhauer as a Critic of History," in *Journal of the History of Ideas,* Vol. XXXVI, No. 2, April-June 1975, pp. 331-38.

[*In the following essay, Gottfried examines Schopenhauer's philosophy of history, contrasting it with that of Hegel and the Judeo-Christian tradition.*]

During the second half of the nineteenth century, educated Europeans, particularly Germans, respected Schopenhauer primarily as a formal philosopher and stylist. His most enthusiastic readers also knew that he was interested in history, and his most fervent admirers defended his views on this subject. György Lukács, the Marxist scholar, with much justification, speaks of him as "the intellectual leader of the German bourgeoisie" in the generation following 1848. The spoiled revolutions of that year supposedly destroyed the idealism of many liberal reformers. At the same time, those capitalists who feared the possibility of a proletariat uprising, searched for antisocial ideologies. Both groups rejected the Hegelianism still dominant in the German universities and spurned its paradigm of a rationally organized society. Moreover, they declared their belief in Schopenhauerian pessimism, which denied the feasibility of social improvement and the rationality of man.

While this explanation for Schopenhauer's fame may be clearly jaundiced, it raises some points worthy of consideration. The master himself, in a biographical sketch of the 1850's, remarked on the inverse proportion between his reputation and that of Hegel. In 1867 Foucher de Careil, a Parisian publicist, devoted a whole book [*Hegel et Schopenhauer*] to discussing the bearing of this polar relationship upon his own contemporaries. More and more there was the need for a middle course between the "advocates of the great pantheist and historical optimist" (Hegel) and those of the "atheistic disparager of life who disdained history as a dream . . . and who considered law only as a measure of each man's power" (Schopenhauer).

The Hegelians, however, continued to think of themselves as occupying the vital center of German thought throughout the sixties. In 1864 Rudolf Haym, one of their most respected academic members, published a pamphlet [*Arthur Schopenhauer*] attacking Schopenhauer as a "colossal egoist" and his disciples as lackeys. Alternating acute criticism of Schopenhauer's argumentation with assaults on his vanity, he ended up by denouncing him for his disregard for historical forces. His call for a total extirpation of the will only reflected his contempt for the "heritage of our race." It also betrayed his hope of seeing "the whole occidental culture being swallowed up by the putatively superior Orient."

Eduard von Hartmann, a popular pessimist and author of *The Philosophy of the Unconscious* (1867), likewise upbraided Schopenhauer for his scorning of the historical process. His own cosmology was based upon an unfolding dialectic of will and reason—what he called the unconscious and conscious. On the basis of his speculation he aspired to bring together the advocates of the great optimist with those of the "atheistic disparager of life." Like the latter he spoke of happiness as a footless illusion, and he looked forward to an age, which he believed was fast approaching, when mankind would firmly resist the blandishments of the will. Nonetheless, like Hegel, he regarded history as the best means for grasping the purpose of existence. For the triumph of reason over will would be an historical moment, the point toward which all human suffering and disillusionment were impelling the race. Both an evolutionary perspective and the awareness of universal moral progress were indispensable for Hartmann's plan of cosmic redemption, which he predicted men would embrace collectively, not individually as in Schopenhauer. So compelling was his faith in the future, moreover, that he proclaimed himself a chastened Hegelian. He cautioned other *soi-disant* pessimists against a teacher "who, because of his unbalanced contempt for history, ignored all progress and development." Such attitudes made Schopenhauer "a stranger to Western culture," a mystic whose true home was on the Ganges, not on the Rhine.

All the same, some of Hartmann's readers discerned an emphatically pessimistic element in the Schopenhauerian approach to history. In 1876, Johannes Huber, a Hegelian, wrote a commentary on pessimistic thought [*Der Pessimismus*] to demonstrate the continuities, as well as discrepancies, between Hegel and Schopenhauer. According to him, both thinkers believed that "epochs of unhappiness far exceeded those of contentment" and that the human condition was generally quite wretched. While Hegel viewed life teleologically and therefore rationally, he stressed no less than Schopenhauer the dominance of the will in the conduct of world historical figures. Equally remarkable is the fact that Schopenhauer, although a voluntarist, taught his own conception of Hegel's "cunning of reason." According to his contention the human mind, notwithstanding its original servitude to the will, could bring the will to self-destruction through the adoption of precepts of self-denial. In any case, the historicizing of pessimism which Hartmann claimed to have accomplished, had already begun with Schopenhauer. The pessimist had drawn far more out of Hegel than he himself was willing to acknowledge.

By the same token, Julius Frauenstädt, Schopenhauer's closest friend and most prolific commentator, linked his rising fame in the sixties to a "scientific" reshaping of historical theory. The second book of his *chef d'oeuvre,* **The World as Will and Idea,** proposed to show how volition asserted itself by means of an ascending hierarchy of being. The result was a chain that moved from nature through the animal world and finally up to man at the top. The stresses throughout on instinct and the struggle for survival seemed to anticipate the insights of Darwinian biology, far better than the rational world order of the Hegelians. Further, the evolutionary climb, which Schopenhauer so eloquently described, bore witness to the need for mortifying the will. Only by exposing nature and history as the rule of force could the scientist become a spiritual teacher.

This ethically based pessimism soon appealed to historians as well as to moralists. In 1871 Jacob Burckhardt delivered his lectures "Fortune and Misfortune in History" to prove "the prevalence of grief (*Schmerz*)" in human affairs. In writing to his friend Friedrich von Preen in 1875, he spoke of "the philosopher's mission" to discredit "that bumptious and brutal optimism now trickling down to the working class." Paul Deussen, the historian of philosophy, felt equally attracted to the "moral core" of pessimism. In his two-volume study of world religions and philosophies [*Allgemeine Geschichte der Philosophie,* 1920], he paid lengthy tribute to Schopenhauer for having tried to merge Eastern religion with Western intellectuality.

From the foregoing discussion, one may conclude that Schopenhauer made a number of statements indicating his interest in history and historical trends, and that some scholars, even historians, studied them with enthusiasm. In order to analyze their content, however, it is necessary to recall his relationship to Hegelian thought. For that polarity which his critics noticed between his philosophical perceptions and those of Hegel marked their observations about history too. Indeed such a focus may help provide the context for understanding most of his opinions regarding this topic.

The first expansive reference to history in his works comes in the first volume, second section, of *The World as Will and Idea,* written sometime in 1817. The discussion here centers around the structure of consciousness; and the argument is advanced that both sensory and intellectual perceptions came about through the mediation of four types of relationships. All of them are derived from the same causative principle, which Schopenhauer calls sufficient reason. In its connection to physical phenomena this principle operates as mechanical causality, and permits one to perceive the succession of conditions situated within time and space. A second form of sufficient reason forms the basis for judgments, joining otherwise transitory perceptions by means of unifying categories. In mathematics the same law of relationship is also operative. Here it defines the connections between units of time and space, and makes possible the construction of arithmetic and geometric axioms. Finally, sufficient reason allows one to investigate the sources of motivation and to explain the link between human behavior and its observable causes.

This fourth form of relationship is particularly critical for Schopenhauer, for it supplies the bridge between the world of idea and the will. The subject, in probing his own actions, knows "his inner self" with more immediacy than in any other form of cognition. In a sense then, he "sees causality from within." Historians supposedly deal with the external side of the same relationship. Since their study regards "the deeds accomplished by men as its problem," they approach socially important conduct through the appropriate mode of sufficient reason. Because of their rigorous use of causation, historians were for Schopenhauer, at least in 1817, as much practitioners of "science" (*Wissenschaft*) as mathematicians.

It is essential to keep in mind that the philosopher, by speaking of history as a science, was conceding to it a place of intellectual respectability. But his comments on

this point cut in more than one way. Granted that history purveys a knowledge of significant relationships, it does so only by banking on sufficient reason; that is, by relying on a principle which shows the world not as it actually was, but rather how the mind chooses to organize it. Furthermore, the German idealists from Kant on down, maintained that human consciousness offered merely a simulacrum of reality, but never its true form.

In the second book of his major study, Schopenhauer designates the will as that which preexists and determines the realm of appearance. He then goes on to suggest how this cosmic will reveals itself independently of sufficient reason. He does this by examining artistic inspiration. The successful creative artist rises above his own bodily appetites to contemplate nature without the intrusion of his personality. Out of this detachment comes access to the will, whose presence is reflected in every drive and instinct and in the eternity of all suffering. Art then yields a truer knowledge of life than the data of history, which lead "not to the thing in itself, but only to its appearance within the individual." Thus history, in contradistinction to art, proves "as alien to the idea as the shape to the cloud it delineates—the foam to a brook or the tree and flower to ice."

Despite these epistemological restrictions, the historian "sometimes allows us to grasp it [the inner nature of man] with artistic eyes." Yet, here too, his achievements are placed in disparaging contrast to those of the poet. Unlike the historian "who takes them both as they come," the poet "thrusts meaningful characters into meaningful situations with discrimination and intent." The reason for this cognitive inequality is not far to seek. Whereas history bases its findings on "the truth of appearance," poetry points to "the truth of the idea that merely speaks through appearance."

The second volume of *The World as Will and Idea*—written some twenty-five years after the first—continued to make history into a foil for art. Thus the author, citing Aristotle's *Poetics,* insists that "poetry is more useful and philosophical than history." History is now criticized not only as being a pale imitation of art, but as being a generally dispensable means for understanding those relationships which human consciousness contrived. Its status changes from being science to mere "knowing (*Wissen*)." For, while science is built on "general concepts (*umfassende Begriffe*)," history "simply grasps particulars to crawl forward on the basis of the empirical." Schopenhauer underscores this point by comparing history to philosophy, which he regards as a science:

> Philosophy is concerned with what is general and universal. Whereas history teaches us that in every age different conditions have prevailed, philosophy endeavors to furnish us with the insight that in all times the same things were, are, and will be present.

Here Schopenhauer is obviously frowning upon the study of history. A look at his *Parerga and Paralipomena,* a miscellany of essays published in 1851, further confirms this impression. There history is defined as "a favorite subject for those who wish to learn something without taking the trouble which the sciences impose on our understanding." Any attempt, moreover, to liken it to philosophy, he condemns as "absurd." A more plausible analogue to history is allegedly zoology, for "one pertains to the classification of species, the other to that of individuals and their deeds." Elsewhere Schopenhauer satirically reduces the chronicles of nations to variations on the following kind of event: "As soon as a people feels any exuberance of strength, it leaps upon its neighbor simply to take possession of their labor and to spare itself the need of living by its own."

Why, one might ask, did the aging pessimist turn with such obvious vehemence against historical learning? The reason becomes clear in the light of what Frauenstädt regarded to be his single overriding obsession: namely, the war against Hegel. The *Parerga* offers surly comments on Hegel's "stultifying bogus philosophy" in the process of making its criticism of history. Such epithets are not confined to these pages. In fact denunciations of Hegelian ideas abound elsewhere in his writings, and furnish much of their stylistic pungency. Several explanations can be given to account for these excesses. For one thing, Schopenhauer spent most of his life overshadowed by a thinker whose views deeply offended him. His professorial career, which lasted only a few months, came abruptly to a halt at Berlin in 1819, a victim to Hegel's enduring popularity as a lecturer. His literary endeavors proved equally fruitless until less than a decade before his death (in 1860), owing to the persistent Hegelian influence among German thinkers and academics.

Admittedly personal frustrations were significant in lending ardor to his anti-Hegelianism. Indeed, the expressions of this bitterness could be found elsewhere. Perhaps his growing disdain for history owed some of its intensity to his irrepressible hatred for the much celebrated "philosopher of history." And yet one must guard against simplistic explanations. His objections to Hegel were marked by rivalrous passion, but they were also grounded in the awareness of an unbridgeable philosophical difference between himself and the greatest modern interpreter of redemptive history.

For Hegel the movement of human events furnished the process whereby universal reason brought the world into conformity with itself. For Schopenhauer, on the other hand, no more scandalous error existed than the view of history as a "planned totality." By identifying reality with the fictions of human reason, its exponents "took the appearance of the world for its essence." Schopenhauer, of course, held no brief for the Hegelian attempt to show the world's descent from a rational design. His skepticism was intellectually as well as viscerally based. The Hegelian dictum that "what is is rational" was something far less cogent than its defender believed it to be. Kant, in his *Critique of Pure Reason,* had already confuted the case for universal design, and now Hegel predicated his whole system upon it, as if Kant had never written. But even more, Hegel evidenced no understanding for the depth

and prevalence of earthly misery. "Since everything tends ultimately toward the good," Hegelianism, like the rigidly providential outlooks of the Jews and Moslems, made no allowances for human tragedy. Suffering and evil only remained as passing inconveniences or as the birth pangs of an age whose blessings were still not apparent. The Hegelians also devised an eschatological excuse for their insensitivity to misfortune. They proclaimed worldly happiness as the inescapable end of all social development: a Pollyanna optimism which they tried to justify by equating their otherwise elusive goal with the pretensions of their own time and class. Thus felicity, which seemed to Schopenhauer an "empty, deceptive, and erroneous thing," was supposed to arise out of "constitutions, legislation, steamships and telegraphs."

The tenor of Schopenhauer's remarks about the Hegelian philosophy of history would indicate a steady broadening of his target. At first he aimed his shafts against a hated rival, then against the rival's system of thought, and finally against the root assumptions from which that system sprang, i.e., the ideas of historical progress and the rational nature of reality. Arthur Hübscher, in [*Biographie eines Weltbildes*], attributes much of his debate with the Hegelians to a "radical denial of historicism." If the term "historicism" means an absolute faith in the power of historical change to solve social and moral problems, then Hübscher is arguing from strength. The second volume of *The World as Will and Idea* vividly contrasts Hegelianism with a "true philosophy of history." What the latter should teach is the perception that "throughout all endless change and turmoil, [one] confronts the same unalterable being, who acts in the same way today as he did yesterday and always." To the historicist belief in human malleability there is now opposed a concept of unchanging essence, and with it comes a sociological definition of man. The creature here conceptualized is torn between his will and moral sense; as long as he experiences the intensity of most men's passions, his natural condition is to suffer.

Such notions seem to transmit the aura of Greek tragedy, and it is understandable that Schopenhauer preferred the classical historians to their Christian and modern counterparts. His books are replete with references to Thucydides, Tacitus, and Pliny; Herodotus appears to have been his favorite historian. Concerning the last, he wrote that "by studying Herodotus it is possible to learn enough history for a lifetime." He also believed that the study of the Persian Wars offered "the constituents of all later history: the activities, agonies, and fate of the whole human race."

The Greeks' sense of fate and of the immutability of the human condition attracted Schopenhauer to their chronicles as well as to their drama. These affinities would suggest the applicability of a contrast even more crucial for our analysis than the one between Schopenhauer and Hegel. It concerns the stark opposition between the historical pessimism pervading Schopenhauer's books and the Judaeo-Christian concept of Providence. The father of modern pessimism was almost boastfully conscious of the gulf he created between himself and the Christian world. His revulsion for the "Jewish optimism" underlying the Christian view of history, his contempt for its teleology and its time-centered notion of revelation, all left him an opponent of much of the Western religious tradition.

Many of his early disciples tried almost desperately to ignore this aspects of his thought. His first biographer, a devout Lutheran, Wilhelm Gwinner, emphasized the Christian foundation of his ethic of self-denial. The same view soon became a recurrent theme in the writings of other Schopenhauerians, especially in the tracts of Deussen and Richard Wagner. And more than one reluctant agnostic followed Burckhardt in regarding pessimism as a non-theological expression for his own cultural Christianity.

Perhaps the young Nietzsche was the first to understand the drift of Schopenhauer's historical thinking. In *Schopenhauer as Educator* (1874) he pursued its implications with reckless determination. Here he spoke of the "philosopher, artist, and saint" as the only justifications for world history. With the emergence of such figures, "nature, which hardly ever leaps, makes its one leap, and a joyous one at that." Significantly, however, Nietzsche divorced the appearance of moral and artistic genius from any historical process. Like Schopenhauer's spiritual athletes, his too were the exceptional men in any age, doomed to solitary existences and reviled by their generation. It was thus natural for such figures as Schopenhauer "to despise human nature as he found it." Or, to assail the spokesmen of historical progress for associating cultural advancement with the increasing contentment of the masses.

What led the pessimist astray, however, was his refusal to recognize the beneficent effect of suffering. Rather than having recommended the quiescence of the will, Schopenhauer should have taken more seriously an aphorism which he himself wrote for the **Parerga:** "A happy life is impossible; the highest man can achieve is a heroic destiny." Such a destiny is only possible for those who cease to look for happiness either for themselves or in history. In *The Birth of Tragedy* written two years earlier, Nietzsche had expressed admiration for the pre-Socratic Greeks for having affirmed "life even in its most alien and trying problems." It was the decadent Socrates who had deprived them of their "fitness for delicate and arduous suffering" by teaching that the "virtuous are happy." Now Nietzsche tries to wed his exuberant fatalism to an ethic of solitude. Again the possibility of spiritual improvement is related to the exclusion of universal design. "Whoever undertakes life as a point in time," says one of his maxims, "misunderstands it."

Karl Löwith, in his book *From Hegel to Nietzsche,* plots the disintegration of the Hegelian world view in the generation succeeding Hegel's death (in 1831). With much detail, he demonstrates how the concepts of universal reason and ordered history gave way, on the one side, to the Christian personalism of Kierkegaard and, on the other, to the pagan fatalism of Nietzsche. His scheme succeeds in tracing the beginnings of existentialist thought to the critical responses which arose to challenge Hegelian

philosophy. But what it fails to do is to acknowledge Schopenhauer's contribution toward this development. His critiques of the Hegelian and Christian cosmologies foreshadowed the Nietzschean exaltation of *moira* and set the tone for the absurdist universe of modern existentialism. Finally, his attack on the Hegelian interpretation of history pointed toward that existentialist denial of all predetermined time, which [Ludwig Marcuse in *Pessimismus,* 1953] has called "the veiled triumph of pessimism."

FURTHER READING

Bibliography

Cartwright, David. "An English-Language Bibliography of Works on Schopenhauer." *Schopenhauer—Jahrbuch* 68 (1987): 257-66.
> Bibliography of Schopenhauer criticism written in English.

Cartwright, David, and Luft, Eric von der. "Bibliographies." In *Schopenhauer: New Essays in Honor of His 200th Birthday,* edited by Eric von der Luft, pp. 327-404. Lewiston: Edwin Mellen Press, 1988.
> Bibliographies of Schopenhauer's works through 1988 and an extensive selection of recommended secondary material.

Hübscher, Arthur. *Schopenhauer—Bibliographie.* Stuttgart-Bad Canstatt: Frommann-Holzboog, 1981, 331 p.
> German bibliography of Schopenhauer criticism, concentrating on his aesthetics and his influence on later literary figures.

Laban, Ferdinand. *Die Schopenhauer-Literatur. Bersuch einer chronologischen Übersicht derselben.* 1880. Reprint. New York: Burt Franklin, 1970, 123 p.
> German bibliography of Schopenhauer's writings, and biographies and critical articles on Schopenhauer, arranged chronologically through 1880.

Biography

Bridgwater, Patrick. *Arthur Schopenhauer's English Schooling.* London: Routledge, 1988, 392 p.
> Biography of Schopenhauer that focuses on his trip to England in 1803 and his subsequent enrollment at Wimbledon School. The book includes Schopenhauer's English diary and letters written to him during his stay.

Hübscher, Arthur. *The Philosophy of Schopenhauer in Its Intellectual Context: Thinker against the Tide.* Edited by Joachim T. Baer and David E. Cartwright. Lewiston: Edwin Mellen Press, 1989, 528 p.
> Historical examination of Schopenhauer's philosophy, depicting his life and influences, his contemporaries, his unique system and philosophical approach, and his effect on later figures.

Safranski, Rüdiger. *Schopenhauer and the Wild Years of Philosophy*. Translated by Ewald Osers. London: Weidenfeld and Nicolson, 1989, 385 p.

> Biography of Schopenhauer that outlines his life and articulates his ideas. Safranski also examines Schopenhauer's influences, compares him to his contemporaries, and explores his influence on later philosophers.

Criticism

Atwell, John E. *Schopenhauer: The Human Character*. Philadelphia: Temple University Press, 1990, 259 p.

> Investigates Schopenhauer's conception of the "human character," discussing such topics as the body and its relationship to the will, free will and determinism, and moral responsibility.

Ausmus, Harry J. "Schopenhauer and Christianity—A Preliminary Examination." *Illinois Quarterly* 36, No. 4 (April 1974): 26-42.

> Argues that Schopenhauer's doctrine is fundamentally Christian in outlook.

Caldwell, William. *Schopenhauer's System in Its Philosophical Significance*. Edinburgh: William Blackwood and Sons, 1896, 538 p.

> Discussion of Schopenhauer's epistemology, aesthetics, ethics, and philosophy of religion as they relate to his metaphysics.

Copleston, Frederick. *Arthur Schopenhauer, Philosopher of Pessimism*. London: Search Press, 1975, 216 p.

> Contextual analysis of Schopenhauer's system, with particular emphasis on his ethics and aesthetics.

Dauer, Dorothea W. *Schopenhauer as Transmitter of Buddhist Ideas*. Berne: Herbert Lang & Co. Ltd., 1969, 39 p.

> Enumerates the ways in which Schopenhauer's philosophy is essentially Buddhist in nature.

Fox, Michael, ed. *Schopenhauer: His Philosophical Achievement*. Sussex: Harvester Press, 1980, 276 p.

> Collection of important essays on Schopenhauer's philosophy, including overviews and comparative studies.

Gardiner, Patrick. *Schopenhauer*. Baltimore: Penguin Books, 1963, 312 p.

> Overview of Schopenhauer's philosophy, beginning with his explanation of the philosophical impulse; proceeding through his ontology, epistemology, ethics, and aesthetics; and concluding with Schopenhauer's treatment of the metaphysical.

Goodale, Ralph. "Schopenhauer and Pessimism in Nineteenth-Century English Literature." *Publications of the Modern Language Association of America* XLVII, No. 1 (March 1932): 241-61.

> Argues that, contrary to some accounts, Schopenhauer had merely a contributory influence on the pessimism apparent in nineteenth-century English literature.

Hamlyn, D. W. *Schopenhauer: The Arguments of the Philosophers*. London: Routledge & Kegan Paul, 1980, 181 p.

> Outlines the whole of Schopenhauer's argumentation, from the epistemology of *The Fourfold Root* to the ethics resulting from his systematic ontology.

———. "Schopenhauer on Action and the Will." In *Idealism Past and Present,* edited by Godfrey Vesey, pp. 127-40. Cambridge: Cambridge University Press, 1982.

> Analysis of Schopenhauer's argument that Kant's *Ding an sich* is the Will.

Janaway, Christopher. *Self and World in Schopenhauer's Philosophy*. Oxford: Clarendon Press, 1989, 378 p.

> Overview of Schopenhauer's philosophy, with particular emphasis on his adaptation of Kant.

Luft, Eric von der, ed. *Schopenhauer: New Essays in Honor of His 200th Birthday*. Lewiston: Edwin Mellen Press, 1988, 459 p.

> Collection of essays written in English, French, and German that address different aspects of Schopenhauer's philosophy and discuss his influence on such figures as Wittgenstein, Thomas Hardy, Marcel Proust, and Tolstoy.

Magee, Bryan. *The Philosophy of Schopenhauer*. Oxford: Clarendon Press, 1983, 400 p.

> Examines Schopenhauer's ontology. Appendices relate Schopenhauer to the Neo-Kantians, Wittgenstein, and Wagner.

Saltus, Edgar Evertson. *The Philosophy of Disenchantment*. Boston: Houghton, Mifflin and Company, 1885, 233 p.

> Explores pessimistic philosophy generally but emphasizes Schopenhauer's role in its development, calling him "the high priest of pessimism."

Stern, J. P. "The Aesthetic Re-interpretation: Schopenhauer." In *Re-interpretations: Seven Studies in Nineteenth-Century German Literature*, pp. 156-207. New York: Basic Books, 1964.

> Examines Schopenhauer's aesthetics, claiming that his views greatly affected subsequent conceptions of art and the artistic process.

Wagner, Gustav Friedrich. *Schopenhauer-Register*. Rev. ed. Edited by Arthur Hübscher. Stuttgart: Fr. Frommann, 1960, 530 p.

> German concordance to Schopenhauer's works.

Additional coverage of Schopenhauer's life and career is contained in the following source published by Gale Research: *Dictionary of Literary Biography*, Vol. 90.

Paul Verlaine

1844-1896

(Full name: Paul Marie Verlaine; also wrote under the pseudonym Pablo de Herlagñez) French poet, essayist, autobiographer, and short story writer.

For additional information on Verlaine's career, see *Nineteenth-Century Literature Criticism,* Volume 2.

INTRODUCTION

A poet renowned for the fluidity and impressionist imagery of his verse, Verlaine succeeded in liberating the musicality of the French language from restrictions imposed by classical, formal structure through his use of innovative rhythms and meters. Fascinated by the visual aspects of form and color, Verlaine attempted to capture in his poems the symbolic elements of language by transforming emotion into subtle suggestion. Verlaine eschewed theorizing; yet, he believed that the function of poetry is to be evocative rather than descriptive. Although Verlaine's decadent lifestyle has often deflected attention from his literary activity, he is, for his aesthetic and intuitive verse, seen as a creative precursor of the French Symbolists.

Biographical Information

An only child, Verlaine was born in Metz to middle-class parents. After the family moved to Paris in 1851, Verlaine attended the Lycée Bonaparte (now Condorcet), earning his baccalaureate along with prizes in Latin and rhetoric. Upon graduating he took a clerical position with the city government, which allowed him ample opportunity to frequent cafes and compose poetry. At this time he associated with a group of young poets known as La Parnasse, or the Parnassians. The Parnassians adopted Théophile Gautier's doctrine of "Art for Art's Sake" and included Leconte de Lisle and Charles Baudelaire. Verlaine married in 1870, but the following year he met and became involved with the young poet Arthur Rimbaud. Verlaine abandoned his wife to travel throughout Europe with Rimbaud. Their affair ended in 1873 when Verlaine shot Rimbaud during a drunken quarrel. Verlaine was arrested and sentenced to serve two years in prison. While incarcerated, he underwent a religious conversion to Catholicism. After his release, he worked intermittently as a teacher. He died in 1896.

Major Works

Verlaine's *Poèmes saturniens* (1866; *Saturnian poems*) was a volume true to the Parnassian ideals of emotional detachment, impeccable form, and stoic objectivity. Well-received by his fellow poets, it did not sell well. With *Fêtes galantes* (1869; *Gallant Parties*) Verlaine moved away from Parnassian restrictions, creating through the

use of unconventional meter, rhyme, and imagery what critics have described as "impressionistic music." According to many commentators, this volume first revealed Verlaine's poetic talents in their pure form and later established him as a precursor of the Symbolist movement. Verlaine celebrated his marriage with *La bonne chanson* (1870, *The Good Song*). During his prison term Verlaine wrote *Romances sans paroles* (1874; *Songs without Words*), a collection of verse strongly influenced by his life with Rimbaud, and *Sagesse* (1881; *Wisdom*), a group of poems about his religious crisis and conversion. Verlaine followed with a trilogy celebrating his religious growth: *Amour* (1888; *Love*), *Parallèlement* (1889; *Parallels*), and *Bonheur* (1891; *Happiness*). In all three collections Verlaine continued to develop his highly personal poetic voice.

Critical Reception

While many critics consider Verlaine one of the harbingers of the French Symbolists due to the impressionistic and evocative nature of his poetry, he denied belonging to any particular movement. Much attention has been given to Verlaine's use of familiar language in a musical and visual manner and to his ability to evoke rather than demand a response from his readers. Since his own time, sensationalistic writing about Verlaine's personal life has often derailed discussion of his numerous collections of verse and his poetic genius. Despite the many attacks on his character, Verlaine is considered a consummate poet whose extraordinary talent for fluid verse, figurative and suggestive language, and impressionistic imagery have assumed legendary stature. It was Verlaine, most critics agree, who was responsible for releasing French poetry from its technical severity and for bringing out the musicality inherent in the French language.

PRINCIPAL WORKS

Poèmes saturniens [Saturnian Poems] (poetry) 1866
Les Amies [as Pablo de Herlagñez] (poetry) 1868
Fêtes galantes [Gallant Parties] (poetry) 1869
La bonne chanson [The Good Song] (poetry) 1870
Romances sans paroles [Songs without Words] (poetry) 1874
Sagesse [Wisdom] (poetry) 1881
Jadis et naguère (poetry) 1884
Les poètes maudits (essays) 1884
Les Memoires d'un veuf (prose poetry) 1886
Amour [Love] (poetry) 1888
Parallèlement [Parallels] (poetry) 1889
Bonheur [Happiness] (poetry) 1891
Chansons pour elle (poetry) 1891
Hombres (poetry) 1891
Mes hôpitaux (essays) 1891
Liturgies intimes (poetry) 1892
Dans les limbes (poetry) 1893
Elégies (poetry) 1893
Mes prisons (essays) 1893
Odes en son honeur (poetry) 1893
Confessions [Confessions of a Poet] (autobiography) 1895
Poems of Paul Verlaine (poetry) 1895
Chair (poetry) 1896
Invectives (poetry) 1896
Oeuvres complètes [Complete Works]. 5 vols. (poetry, short stories, essays, and autobiography) 1898-1903
Oeuvres posthumes. 3 vols. (poetry, essays, and letters) 1911-29

CRITICISM

Geoffrey Brereton (essay date 1956)

SOURCE: "Paul Verlaine," in *An Introduction to the French Poets: Villon to the Present Day,* 1956. Reprint by Methuen and Company, 1957, pp. 174-85.

[*In the following excerpt, Brereton briefly outlines Verlaine's artistic development and literary influence.*]

The deplorable Verlaine—for so, from the moral point of

view, he must be considered—traversed in his life various psychological crises which, if lived experience alone were decisive, should have yielded poetry comparable to Baudelaire's. Yet, for all his self-inclusion among the *poètes maudits* or "doomed poets" of the eighties, Verlaine is not a Satanic, or even a tragic, figure. It is not possible to take him so seriously, nor does he often demand it. When he does, one is inclined to smile rather than to participate. It is always "pauvre Lélian" in trouble again, never a clairvoyant fellow man playing on one's own fears and vices. Certainly he can sometimes be touching, with oblique, unexpected strokes which awaken a momentary sentiment, a probably literary nostalgia, but do not last. Their effect can be quite pleasing.

He is not to be criticized for the fact that he is relatively superficial. It was part of a valid conception of poetry which he evolved to harmonize with his own temperament. He aimed at other effects than the effect in depth. His work marks the beginning of Symbolism, and if he is now more usually classed as an impressionist, in this instance the one led to the other. In any case, in spite of his openly personal and "intimate" style, he marks very clearly the end of Romanticism as poets from [Alphonse] Lamartine to [Victor] Hugo had conceived it. The *moi* in Verlaine no longer performs the same function as in them. It is more like the "I" in [Clément] Marot, or even in La Fontaine. It is, though on several levels higher, the "I" of the crooner and not of the guide or prophet who leads us by the hand into our own natures. . . .

Verlaine, whose reputation to-day stands considerably lower than that of his friend [Arthur Rimbaud] was an excellent poet in his own right. His work follows a curve which is clear enough in outline. There is a first phase of imitation and experiment, containing some poems stamped with the contemporary impersonality and even "impassibility", though stamped with a feather if one compares them with the massive castings of Leconte de Lisle. Then follows the truly feathery phase of **La Bonne Chanson** and **Romances sans paroles**—which is the characteristic Verlaine at his best. After this he embarks on his long adventure into piety, which must be described as a one-sided flirtation with a God whom he knew only through such edifying works as the eight-volume *Catechism of Perseverance* which the prison chaplain gave him to read. Verlaine, of all people, could never take fire through a duenna and the result in his poetry is too often the cultivation of the hackneyed symbol or else that tearful diffuseness which was always the defect of his virtues. His faith, in any case, brought no stiffening into either his concepts or his vocabulary—and how much that was needed is evident in nearly all the poems he published in the last eight years of his life. Not that these are unreadable. The mordant shaft, the humour, the direct sensuality, the touching piety, the growingly conscious but sometimes amateurish echoes of [François] Villon, still give life to the occasional poem if not to the mass. But really by this time Verlaine had disintegrated, and what flies about us as we progress through his increasingly fluffed-out verse is no longer feathers but kapok. To the student of the literary scene of the nineties, such collections as

Dédicaces, Invectives and *Epigrammes* have an immense interest. They are highly ingenious as verse and sometimes very funny. But that is incidental to whatever pleasure one may take in poetry.

When he was first published, Verlaine was described by a hostile critic, Barbey d'Aurevilly, as: "A puritan Baudelaire—an unfortunate and comic combination, without the brilliant talents of M. Baudelaire, and with reflections here and there of M. Hugo and Alfred de Musset. . . .

The religious poems in *Sagesse* have moved many Catholics and in a few of his best sonnets Verlaine is not greatly inferior to the French religious poets of the late Renaissance. Yet his dialogue with the Creator lacks animation: one misses both the battle of doubt and the ecstatic resignation of the true mystic. Biographically, of course, it soon became apparent that neither of these was for Verlaine. As he goes downhill his characteristics become over-stressed. The aery vagueness of his youth becomes a middle-aged flabbiness; his bright-eyed sensuality becomes grossness; his glancing allusions, just chatter. The volume *Amour* contains a moving sequence of poems on Lucien Létinois, here regarded as an adopted son. His reflections after Lucien's death might be compared to Hugo's meditations after the death of his daughter Léopoldine. At first the contrast, the complete lack of "eloquence" and emphasis, is refreshing. Here grief speaks naturally. . . .

But it becomes obvious that "naturalness" is not enough. Who is this speaking—a poet who can either ennoble or illuminate the occasion, or an old woman, loquacious, sentimental, and querulously pious? Only pathos is communicated and other poets have accustomed us to expect more from poetry.

Nevertheless, Verlaine's work as a whole still interests for its power of sentimental and visual suggestion, its flickering use of imagery, its easy-going rhythms and language. If Hugo had once "put a red cap on the old dictionary", Verlaine went much further, writing argot and slang as freely as he evidently spoke them. This enlivens but also dates him. The current slang of the eighteen-eighties—except for a few words which are always with us—has faded while not yet acquiring the historical interest of, say, Villon's slang. His poetic stock, for a long time quoted over-highly, has now fallen much lower than [Stéphane] Mallarmé's or Rimbaud's. Yet his influence on twentieth-century poetry has been as great as either of theirs. It is felt from [Guillaume] Apollinaire to [Louis] Argon, while his vein if not precisely his influence can be discovered in many of the poets who have rejected the appearance of conscious art to give the first place to *fantaisie.*

A. E. Carter (essay date 1969)

SOURCE: "Paul Verlaine," in *Verlaine: A Study in Parallels,* University of Toronto Press, 1969, pp. 228-40.

[*In the following essay, Carter surveys Verlaine's career.*]

Had anyone present at the funeral been asked why he admired the dead man, he would probably have answered that Verlaine carried on the work of Baudelaire, added new themes and techniques to French poetry, and freed it from the shackles of tradition. Such was his reputation during his last years. . . .

If we view these opinions nowadays with a rather sceptical eye it is not because they are false, but because they imply a kind of progress: that after Verlaine, and through him, French verse would be better than ever. Eighty years have passed, and such has not been the case. The exact reverse is closer to the truth: Verlaine, with [Arthur] Rimbaud and [Stéphane] Mallarmé, was the last great French poet. There have been poets in France since he lived, but none of them reach his stature. Not through lack of talent; they were simply lesser men. Much the same thing has happened in England, where Housman and Eliot, brilliant in so many ways, cannot match the sheer bulk and force of the great Victorians. And when all is said, were Verlaine's innovations really as extraordinary as his contemporaries thought? Most of them, examined with care, turn out to be rather trifling: he sometimes composed in lines of 5, 9, 11, 13, and even 17 syllables, instead of the more usual 8, 10, or 12. It was the *impair* he recommended in "**Art poétique. . . .** "

And in obedience to another precept of the same poem, he demanded greater freedom of rhyme, by which he meant the right to rhyme weakly or adequately instead of richly.

In some of his best work he follows these rules (if we can call them that): five of the nine pieces of **Ariettes oubliées** are written in *impair,* and the rhymes are often weak . . . , depending on vowel sounds alone with no supporting consonant. But his precepts lose something of their force when we discover that three of the other poems in the same section, including the most "Verlainian" of all (**"Il pleure dans mon coeur"**) are not in *impair* and frequently have adequate rhymes. And this is true of most of his work: **"Mon Rêve familier," "Chanson d'automne," "Mon Dieu m'a dit,"** all of *Fêtes galantes* except three (**"Mandoline," "Colombine," "Ensourdine"**)—verse with less of heaviness and pose than anything else he produced. The claim that *impair* and weak rhyme can be used to blur the contours of sense and produce a vague and dreamy impression is one of those paradoxes a clever man invents and others believe. Unless a poem is already vague and dreamy, it is unlikely that any technique will make it so. **"Art poétique,"** as Verlaine himself admitted, was a song; he never intended it to be taken too seriously.

He also liked to override the traditional caesura when he wrote alexandrines. Sometimes it is displaced, falling elsewhere than at the sixth syllable; more rarely deliberately bridged by a single word (*enjambement sur la césure*) as in **"Et la tigresse épouvantable d'Hyrcanie"** of *Fêtes galantes.* But reverence for the caesura was never an absolute, even in classical days. There may not be an example of *enjambement sur la césure* in Racine, but his tragedies contain numerous lines where the essential pause occurs elsewhere than at the sixth syllable. And for that matter, Victor Hugo had claimed credit for this particular "reform" long before Verlaine wrote (**"Réponse à un acte d'accusation"**). More important was Verlaine's use of *rejet* or "overflow" at the end of his lines. He was perhaps the first French poet to use this trick with entire success, and it enabled him to obtain effects of great beauty. . . .

Verlaine practised it with a skill so perfect that one suspects it must have corresponded to a fundamental need of heart and ear. And his more experimental work (*Fêtes galantes, Romances sans paroles*) does not contain the most striking examples. They are found in **Sagesse** where they fit the context admirably well, creating a tone of ecstatic adoration, particularly in the **"Mon Dieu m'a dit"** cycle. The ease and grace of such poems as **"Clair de lune," "La Lune blanche,"** and **"Mon Rêve familier,"** are, I think, more apparent than real. Because such poems express nothing in particular, tell no story, and are mere translations of mood and sensation, we suppose their technique to be as vague, hazy, and harmonious as the impression that technique creates. But on examination, they turn out to obey most of the regulations, such as alternate masculine and feminine rhymes, and lines of equal syllabification. For this reason alone they are triumphs of poetic art. French prosody is touchy and demanding; a poet who can obey all its rules and still give an impression of shimmering and evanescent reverie is a genius indeed.

There is little else to say of Verlaine as an innovator. When theory was in question he was much less daring, much more of a traditionalist, than his fiery young admirers supposed. . . .

Moréas concluded that he was an obstinate Parnassian, who had never progressed further than Baudelaire, with no influence on contemporary poetry, and the end of a line rather than a beginning; a man without ideas, theories, or a reasoned programme.

Coming from a second-rater like Moréas (second-rate by comparison with Verlaine), such criticism appears remarkably brash. But it has some truth. Verlaine's importance in literature, whether French or universal, arises from neither his technical experiments nor his influence on later writers. The experiments were means of self-expression, vehicles for his genius, but not the genius itself. And, unlike Baudelaire, he did not found a line of poets and his influence, when it existed, was almost invariably bad. . . .

There is no rhetoric in Verlaine, only a series of devices for avoiding it. *Enjambement* was one device, used particularly at the end of the lines. Rhetoric is for strong nerves, not for a sensibility preoccupied with the past, eternally alive to the suggestions of memory. Verlaine dwelt in recollections of his first years; the escapades of his life and the beauties of his verse were both manifes-

tations of the same wish-neurosis, the same desire for a *jouissance de néant meilleure que toute plénitude*. Hence his style, hence the eternal parallels between life and art: they were mutually nostalgic and even hallucinogenic. And hence too (since reality and illusion are very different things), his constant failure to adjust to ordinary living and the catastrophes that attended all his sentimental adventures. . . .

His books were the direct and inevitable results of his temperament: artificial refuges, constructed according to the emotional habits he had contracted under the bell-glass of Elisa's [Moncomble, his cousin] affection. Each shows the persistence of memory in a man who never grew up, each is an attempt to adjust reality to the data memory supplies. All recreate in some form or other the never-forgotten paradise: ideal love (*Poèmes saturniens*); an eighteenth-century dreamworld (*Fêtes galantes*); harmonic suggestion (*Romances sans paroles*); union with God (*Sagesse, Bonheur*); life with Rimbaud or Létinois (*Parallèlement, Amour*); a flesh-padded universe of willing beauties (*Chansons pour Elle, Chair, Femmes, Hombres*). All the best poems spring from an involuntary nervous tremor, provoked by sensation; it cracks the glass of reality and the old obsession rises like a djin from a bottle. And always, behind the glimmering illusion, flows the chill wind of insecurity, the terror of time and death.

Verse of this kind, evolving from such capricious sources, inevitably has serious limitations, not the least of which is a disconcerting tendency to dry up, leaving the poet with no other resource than silence or uninspired labour. He is never free from the matrix of infancy, and even at its best, his work is often morbid and green-sick. At times he even distrusts his own genius: Verlaine sought to evade his more than once—as when he rushed into marriage, terrified by his passion for Lucien Viotti; or spent his year with Rimbaud lamenting the security he had lost; or again when, overtaken by disaster and locked in a cell, he alternated between exquisite inspiration (**"Le ciel est par-dessus le toit"**) and the copious mediocrity of the *récits diaboliques*. Paralysed by subconscious trauma, he was not only powerless to face the present, but, at times, even to take advantage of his own sublime gifts: they half-frightened him. He was torn between opposites; he wanted illusion and reality, spiritual adventure with Rimbaud (iconoclasm, liberty, "amours de tigre," the flaming blue eyes and the demi-god's body) and also the bourgeois comforts of home, complete with hot tea, a good fire, and a natty little woman. That is to say, he wanted them all until he got them. Then, like Emma Bovary, he wanted something else. There was no end to his powers of self-deception. It would perhaps be an exaggeration to attribute all this to the childhood fixation. But that was the initial flaw, the minute fissure in the dyke which, enlarged by other pressures, admitted a whole sea of anarchic passion. He was never happy with either side of his nature: Mathilde bored him; Rimbaud filled him with guilt and remorse. Neither reconciled dream and action. Neither could, since the dream was so distorted by illusion as to correspond to nothing factual. This memory obsession is one of Romanticism's most poisonous and seductive legacies. The tough, classical centuries—the seventeenth, the eighteenth—had no past; they lived three-dimensionally. A fourth dimension, time, has since been included. It is no passive addition, like a new room in a house, but rather tends to control and even corrupt the other three, as though it were less a room that a hypogeum of badly embalmed corpses, wafting their stench throughout the building. There is a good deal of this kind of smell in Verlaine, unmitigated by any intellectual ventilation. His art belongs to the general reinterpretation of aesthetic values which set in with the waning of scientific positivism. It gave us Impressionist painting, the music of Debussy, Fauré, and Duparc, the poetry of Mallarmé, and the prose of Marcel Proust, not to mention the philosophy of Henri Bergson. Both Proust and Bergson were sensationists; Proust, certainly, was as much fascinated by the past as Verlaine himself. All three used sensation to unchain memory and put it to work in a creative or divinatory way. In more senses than one, Verlaine's poetry is another "recherche du temps perdu," a further example of "matière et mémoire."

But there was an essential difference: Proust and Bergson were less interested in sensation as an end than as a means; they used it to reach a better understanding of illusion and reality. Their aims were objective; they were intent on plumbing the mysteries of consciousness, personality, and the creative process. There was no such purpose in Verlaine. The lack of it was one reason for his break with the Symbolists. They wanted a programme, and he had none. He lived instinctively. In his deepest work (*Sagesse*) the ideas were not his own but those supplied by the Athanasian Creed. He wandered into unknown country almost by accident, and made no attempt to chart it. He never turned on reality the penetrating gaze of a Baudelaire or the fiery glance of a Rimbaud. His nature was submissive and masochistic—"feminine," as he told [F. A.] Cazals.

He was Baudelaire's disciple; he borrowed some of his ideas and techniques, but only those which heighten sensation, like the theory of *correspondances*. The two men had no other point of contact. The dark world of despair and unrest which yawns throughout *Les Fleurs du mal* was not for Verlaine, nor the refusal to accept half-answers, nor the heroic cynicism of "Le Voyage." . . .

[Verlaine] had a prodigious lyric talent, and not many poets can rival him for sheer virtuosity, not even Baudelaire or Rimbaud. But it was the virtuosity of a child prodigy who never ceased being a child prodigy. The more we read him, the more we perceive that his achievements depended on this fundamental immaturity. His shiftlessness, his tantrums, his inability to resist seduction, and his raw sensitivity were all essential to his verse, even his religious verse. Raw sensitivity is a prerogative of childhood; no amount of sophistication could have given birth to the poignant sincerity of *Sagesse* or the alluring music of *Romances sans paroles*. . . . He wrote according to the dictates of a nervous erethism forever alert to the half-felt and the intangible: perfume, sound, colour, light and shade, remembered sexuality. Once involved with a subject demanding objectivity, he was beyond his depth

and laboured in vain. As far as such a thing is possible, he was a poet of the echo—echoes of dead voices, silent music, joy realized through sadness.

It was a limited range; these are the qualities of frustration, with nothing epic or tragic about them. The past lay across his talent like a fallen column on a growth of acanthus:

> Pour soulever un poids si lourd,
> Sisyphe, il faudrait ton courage . . .

And Verlaine was no Sisyphus. Even had he been, the obstruction was too massive; he would have spent his forces in sterile effort. There was no escape but the one he chose—illusion, the *affreux soulagement* of sex and alcohol, the quest for self-oblivion in the personalities of others. He was divided against himself, split into "parallels" by the cumbrous burden. And since parallels never meet, there could be no fusion, no supreme revelation like *Les Fleurs du mal*. A sadder fate than Baudelaire's, because so totally unheroic. Yet defeat under such conditions was not absolute. It even had elements of victory. The crushed plant was not dead: year after year it sent up its shoots and its leaves, mysterious and indestructible; and with what exquisite foliage it bordered and concealed the unyielding stone!

Joanna Richardson (essay date 1971)

SOURCE: "Prince of Poets (1893-96)," in *Verlaine,* The Viking Press, 1971, pp. 323-61.

[*In the following excerpt from her seminal biography of Verlaine, Richardson discusses Verlaine's poetry in the context of his era.*]

Verlaine published his first book at a moment when French poetry was dominated by the Pernassians: by a belief in technical perfection and by the creed of impassibility. Verlaine was a technician of consummate skill, he understood the value of discipline; but he could not be impassible. He was, by his nature, from the first, the most responsive and personal of poets.

> To be a poet [he maintained, at the end of his life], I think one must live intensely, in every way—and remember it . . .

> As I see it, then, the poet must be absolutely sincere, but completely conscientious as a writer. He must hide nothing of himself; but, in his honesty, he must show all the dignity which can be expected of him. He must show his concern for this dignity, as far as he can, if not in the perfection of form, at least in the imperceptible but effective effort towards this high and demanding ideal: I was going to say this virtue.

> A poet—myself—has attempted this task. Perhaps he has failed, but he has certainly done all he can to come out of it with honour.

Verlaine, in his best work, had practised this creed. He had lived intensely, and no poet had recorded his life more consistently. At times, it is true, he had hinted rather than recorded, he had suppressed when he might have told, he had spoken when he might have been silent. He had been ambiguous and exhibitionist, he had occasionally played a part. But his life and his poetry cannot be separated, and he reflects his changing moods, his inconsistencies, his spiritual progress, as much as his permanent qualities and his weaknesses; and this he does in a way that no French poet had done before him. Beside the poems of Verlaine, the more personal poems of Hugo sound like theatrical rhetoric, the melancholy and piety of Lamartine sound dated, academic and unconvincing. Musset had lived intensely, as a poet should; but Musset, as Verlaine emphasised, had not given himself completely in his work, and Musset had not been a perfect artist, for he had not laboured to achieve perfect form.

Of all his predecessors in French poetry, it was Baudelaire who was Verlaine's spiritual ancestor. There was a manliness, an intellectual depth, a spiritual power in Baudelaire with which Verlaine was simply not endowed. Verlaine could not rise to the majesty of the poems which Baudelaire addressed to Mme Sabatier; and he did not approach the fierce, exotic passion of the poems to Jeanne Duval. Baudelaire's despair and grief, his anguish of soul, were more bitter and more profound. But there remains a remarkable affinity between their poems of mood. Verlaine was instinctively in sympathy with him. **Poèmes saturniens** was a tribute to this poetic kinship. Verlaine, like Baudelaire, recognised the correspondences between the arts, and between the senses; Verlaine, like Baudelaire, recorded the inescapable *mal du siècle*.

> The profound originality of Charles Baudelaire is, to my mind [Verlaine had written], his powerful presentation of the essential modern man: . . . the physical man of to-day, as he has been made by the refinements of an excessive civilisation: modern man, with his sharpened, vibrant senses, his painfully subtle mind, his intellect steeped in tobacco, his blood burned up by alcohol . . . It is, I repeat, Charles Baudelaire who presents the sensitive man, and he presents him as a type, or, if you like, as a *hero* . . . The future historian of our age should study *Les Fleurs du mal* with pious attention. It is the quintessence, the extreme concentration of a whole element of this century.

This was not only an acute assessment of Baudelaire; it proved to be an unconscious self-portrait. Where Baudelaire had recorded the Parisian of the 1840s and 1850s, Verlaine recorded the man of the following generation: the man who lived through the Franco-Prussian War, the Siege of Paris, the Commune and the Republic, the outbursts of anarchy, the moods of defeat, disgust and despair, the aimlessness, the excessive chauvinism. A hundred different and often conflicting influences were felt. It was an increasingly philistine and materialistic age which judged success, American fashion by money. It was the age of 'carnal spirit and unhappy flesh', which welcomed Naturalism and the novels of Zola. It was also the age of

aesthetes like Robert de Montesquiou and Huysmans' Des Esseintes. There were influences from abroad: the influence of English aestheticism, of German music, of Russian nihilism. There were disturbing signs of technical progress. The generation of Verlaine lived in the disarray of a stage of transition; as Raynaud observed: 'It was a searching, artistic, refined, but unstable generation; and, drawn by diverse influences, it struggled desperately, in the general débâcle, in search of some or other certainty . . . Verlaine is the voice of this generation . . . He reflects its vain agitation, its incoherence and its ungovernable impotence.'

He did so in a manner that was entirely his own. If Baudelaire had inspired him at the start of his career, Rimbaud had reminded him that poetry must be distilled till it became a new language and expressed the hitherto unknown. Rimbaud—like Baudelaire—had entered Verlaine's life with marvellous precision. He was not only supreme in Verlaine's emotional existence, he was also his poetic kin.

Baudelaire and Rimbaud were Verlaine's literary mentors. Verlaine's own life, brief though it was, embraced a world of experience. He lived feverishly, and, as he told Vance Thompson, he wrote *en fièvre*. As Arthur Symons recognised:

> Few men ever got so much out of their lives, or lived so fully, so intensely, with such a genius for living. That, indeed, is why he was a great poet. Verlaine was a man who gave its full value to every moment, who got out of every moment all that that moment had to give him. It was not always, not often, perhaps, pleasure. But it was energy, the vital force of a nature which was always receiving and giving out, never at rest, never passive, or indifferent, or hesitating . . . He sinned, and it was with all his humanity; he repented, and it was with all his soul. And to every occurrence of the day, to every mood of the mind, to every impulse of the creative instinct, he brought the same unparalleled sharpness of sensation.

As a literary critic, Verlaine had introduced Mallarmé, Rimbaud and Corbière to the French public; and **Les Poètes maudits,** with his eager, repeated appreciations of Rimbaud, and his early assessment of Baudelaire, were his most significant contributions to criticism. The twenty-seven biographies of poets and men of letters which he wrote for the series *Les Hommes d'aujourd'hui* were often generous, but they were not profound. Verlaine, as he said himself, was not a critic, he was a man of feeling.

As a writer of prose, he is little more than an unreliable source for the biographer or the literary historian. Charles Le Goffic wrote: 'His prose works, rough and strange, with a syntax dictated only by the impression of the moment, will always surprise those who have not heard him talk. They will delight the others: they were exactly like his conversation, unpredictable, with all its brackets and parentheses. In a few minutes it went through every shade of mischievousness and passion.'

As a poet, he had done service to modern literature. He had restored the free use of metre: given back to poets the unfettered use of their instrument of work. He had deliberately broken every rule of prosody, used every metre from five to thirteen syllables; he had used combinations of metres which had not been used since the sixteenth century. He had done as he pleased with cesuras and *enjambements,* with masculine and feminine rhymes. He had introduced foreign words, and vulgarisms. He had refined the French language until it became a new instrument in his hands. *'Suggestion,'* said [Stephane] Mallarmé. 'That is the dream. It is the perfect use of this mystery which constitutes the symbol.' Verlaine used his marvellous technical powers, as well as his instincts, to record suggestion. Only his two literary mentors, and, perhaps, Gérard de Nerval, or Mallarmé, understood the art of mystery and suggestion like Verlaine. He understood it in his first book, in **"Monrêve familier"**; he understood it, perfectly, in **"Kaléidoscope"** in *Jadis et Naguère,* where a broken mosaic of memories crowds upon him, some apparently trivial, some serious, all of them invested with an undefined, disturbing significance.

> Ce sera comme quand on rêve et qu'on s'éveille!
> Et que l'on se rendort et que l'on rêve encor
> De la même féerie et du même décor,
> L'été, dans l'herbe, au bruit moiré d'un vol
> d'abeille . . .

No-one else catches, like Verlaine, this infinitely fragile state between dreaming and waking, between imagination and reality. He expresses a thought before it is formulated, an instinct before it is recognised, an emotion which has yet to be acknowledged. 'In many short poems which are like the tremors of a soul, caught as they pass, it is hardly Verlaine who is talking any more, it is some or other human soul, impersonal, intemporal, it is almost the soul of things gaining awareness of itself in the soul of a man.'

The best of Verlaine's landscapes are, again, the landscapes of the soul, the **"Paysages tristes"** of *Poèmes saturniens,* some of the *'Ariettes oubliées'* in *Romances sans paroles,* and certain poems in *Sagesse:* **"Le son du cor s'afflige vers les bois . . . ,"** or **"L'échelonnement des haies"**. **"Bournemouth"**, in *Amour,* is both a landscape and an impression of serenity. Symons wrote wisely that, to Verlaine, 'physical sight and spiritual vision, by some strange alchemical operation, were one'. *Fêtes galantes,* which was one of the most accomplished of his books, contains a series of tiny pictures of an eighteenth-century world; and yet these are not mere transpositions of art. They give a brilliant suggestion of theatre, of elegant and artificial revelry, of fugitive pleasures watched by a hard and brooding destiny. They are charming, in the style of [Antoine] Watteau, delicately licentious, in the manner of [Jean] Fragonard; and yet they are undoubtedly disturbing. They create an atmosphere as much as a scene.

> Votre âme est un paysage choisi

Arthur Rimbaud at seventeen, shortly after his first meeting with Verlaine.

> Que vont charmant masques et berga masques . . .

There is a poem written by Verlaine on the threshold of manhood: a poem which he alone could have written. It is at once the landscape of a soul, and a microcosm of the world which Watteau and his contemporaries painted. It is the first poem in *Fêtes galantes*. The last poem, **"Colloque sentimental"**, concentrates within itself a world of anguish: an anguish half explained, yet completely told. It is a marvel of suggestive power.

No French poet has recorded certain moods with the exquisite touch of Verlaine: the vague melancholy of *Chanson d'automne* and **"Il pleure dans mon cœur . . ."**; the vast peace of **"La lune blanche . . ."**, written for Mathilde [Manté, his wife]: a poem which was music long before French composer [Gabriel] Fauré discovered it. In such poems as these, and in **"C'est l'extase langoureuse . . ."**, which he wrote for Rimbaud, and in the poem of infinite regret which he wrote, in prison: **"Le ciel est, par-dessus le toit . . . ,"** Verlaine is unequalled in French literature. Simple in word and form, he seems to write almost without effort. In their own inherent melody, in their emotive power, his lyrics come as close as any poems have ever come to music.

As a poet of love, Verlaine is uneven. The Lesbian poems

of the early years are written with gentle tact, under the influence of Baudelaire. The poems he addressed to Mathilde generally suggest a suitor who is trying to conform. The poems to his mistresses, in his later years, were set down when his mind was dulled, his inspiration gone. They are sometimes trivial, sometimes crude; only rarely (one recalls a fragment in *Le Livre posthume*) does Verlaine remind us that he was a great poet. Verlaine wrote no poem to a woman which, in intensity of feeling, approached the poem that he wrote on the rumour of Rimbaud's death. **"Laeti et Errabundi"** was not simply a record of physical passion, it was a tribute to the only complete relationship in his life.

In 1923 Georg Brandes, the Danish critic, wrote: 'The historian . . . will probably point out the ground swell which seems to be bearing modern French literature towards Rome and Catholicism. It seems to me at the moment to be almost entirely ultra-Catholic; it had already been so since the conversion of Verlaine . . . To-day Paul Claudel is setting the tone for French literature, and it is the same tone.' It was ironic that Claudel should be mentioned. At the thought of Verlaine and Rimbaud, he reached instinctively for his chaplet; and he found hypocrisy in *Sagesse*. Perhaps, as a religious poet, Verlaine has been overestimated. His religious poems lack the conviction of some of his love poems, the originality of his landscapes and his poems of mood. Some critics maintain that his dialogue with God in *Sagesse* is the height of his poetic achievement; yet, honest though his conversion was, there remains a certain convention about the work. It was remarkable that *Sagesse* appeared when Naturalism was at its height; it was remarkable that he should write a book religious in inspiration. And yet the poems in *Sagesse* which one now recalls are not the more theological pieces: they are, yet again, the poems of mood and suggestion, the recollection of forbidden pleasures.

'*L'art, mes enfants, c'est d'être absolument soi-même.*' So Verlaine had explained in *Bonheur*. No poet had been more himself than Verlaine. He recorded all his life, all his raptures and regrets, all his bitterness, licentiousness and melancholy, all his humour, violence, weakness, and simplicity. Verlaine's was at times a subtle simplicity. It was that of a child; it was also that of a consummate poet.

For his genius is not in doubt. French poetry was changed by Verlaine. As [Emile] Verhaeren said: 'He fused himself so profoundly with beauty, that he left upon it an imprint which was new and henceforth eternal.'

C. Chadwick (essay date 1973)

SOURCE: "Verlaine and His Critics," in *Verlaine,* The Athlone Press, 1973, pp. 113-21.

[In the following excerpt, Chadwick traces the early critical reception of Verlaine's poetry.]

Critical opinion of Verlaine's work varied enormously throughout his career, not always in direct ratio to the quality of his poetry. A good example of this is provided by a review of *Poèmes saturniens* by Barbey d'Aurevilly who, in revenge perhaps for the scathing comments *Les œuvres et les Hommes* had received the previous year, dismissed Verlaine as "un Baudelaire puritain . . . sans le talent net de M. Baudelaire, avec des reflects de M. Hugo et d'Alfred de Musset ici et là. Tel est M. Paul Verlaine. Pas un zeste de plus". He was of course right to recognise the influence of older writers in *Poèmes saturniens* but he was wrong to condemn the volume as being entirely derivative. His refusal, or inability, to recognise any original talent in *Poèmes saturniens* was so deep-rooted that he even quoted disparagingly the final line of **"Mon Rêve familier"**, one of the most successful poems in the volume, in order to make a cheap jibe at Verlaine: "'Il a dit quelque part, en parlant de je ne sais qui—cela du reste n'importe guère—'Elle a l'inflexion des voix chères qui se sont tues". Quand on écoute M. Verlaine, on désirerait qu'il n'eût jamais d'autre inflexion que celle-là".

Other critics, however, were more perceptive. Jules de Goncourt wrote to Verlaine: "Merci pour vos vers. Ils rêvent et peignent. Mélancolies d'artistes ciselées par un poète . . . Vous avez ce vrai don: la rareté de l'idée et la ligne exquise des mots". Leconte de Lisle too recognised the technical skill that Verlaine had displayed: "Vos *Poèmes* sont d'un vrai poète, d'un artiste très habile déjà et bientôt maître de l'expression". Banville and Sainte-Beuve both stressed the originality of *Poèmes saturniens*—"Vous visez à faire ce qui n'a pas été fait", said the latter, whilst the former wrote: "Je suis certain que vous êtes un poète et que votre originalité est réelle". In support of their compliments, unfortunately, both of them picked out poems which are by no means the best or the most original in *Poèmes saturniens,* Banville expressing a preference for the three rather trivial poems **"Femme et Chatte"**, **"Jésuitisme"** and **"La Chanson des Ingénues"** and Sainte-Beuve choosing two of the most clearly derivative poems in the whole volume, **"César Borgia"** and **"La Mort de Philippe II"**. It may be, therefore, that their flattering comments should be taken with a grain of salt as simply the polite remarks inevitable in letters of thanks for the copies of his first volume of verse that Verlaine had sent them.

Nevertheless, *Poèmes saturniens* had attracted favorable attention in literary circles and Verlaine's feet seemed firmly set on the ladder leading to success. He took a further step up this ladder with the publication of *Fêtes galantes* in 1869 which brought from Victor Hugo the comment: "Que de choses délicates et ingénieuses dans ce joli petit livre". *La Bonne Chanson,* however, had the misfortune to be printed just before the outbreak of the Franco-Prussian war in September 1870 and it was not published, in the sense of being made available to the public, until 1872 when hostilities had finally ended after the bitter civil strife of the Commune. By then Rimbaud had arrived in Paris and the relationship between him and Verlaine undoubtedly harmed the latter's reputation, particularly after July 1872 when the two poets left Paris to live together in London until the quarrel between them in

July 1873. Verlaine's subsequent arrest and eighteen months' imprisonment in Belgium meant that he was still further ostracised as far as literary circles in Paris were concerned. . . . [He] himself wrote, in a poem composed in prison in 1874:

> Las! je suis à l'Index et dans les dédicaces
> Me voici Paul V . . . pur et simple . . .

It is not therefore surprising that when **Romances sans Paroles** was published in March 1874 it was a disastrous failure and was completely ignored by the press and by the public. Eighteen months later, in October 1875, the poems Verlaine sent for inclusion in the third volume of *Le Parnasse Contemporain* were rejected by the editorial committee made up of Banville, Coppée and Anatole France. Since Verlaine had figured in the first two volumes in 1866 and 1869 this was a particularly cruel rebuff, and a particularly undeserved one as the admirable sonnet **"Beauté des femmes . . . "**, later included in *Sagesse,* is known to have been one of the poems submitted and the others probably included those written at the beginning of Verlaine's imprisonment, which are generally agreed to be among his finest work. But this was not the view expressed by Anatole France who rejected the poems with the words: "Non. L'auteur est indigne et les vers sont des plus mauvais qu'on ait vus".

Sagesse suffered the same fate as **Romances sans Paroles** when it was published in 1881. By then Verlaine had been away from Paris for almost ten years, so long a lapse of time that Zola, in an article which also appeared in 1881, referred to him as if he were dead: 'M. Verlaine, aujourd'hui disparu, avait débuté avec éclat par les Poèmes saturniens. Celui-là a été une victime de Baudelaire, et on dit même qu'il a poussé l'imitation pratique du maître jusqu'à gâter sa vie'.

It was not until the following year, 1882, when Verlaine returned to Paris and began to mingle once again in literary circles that he started to re-establish his reputation as a poet. . . .

In 1885 Banville wrote, with regard to *Jadis et Naguère* which had just been published: "Parfois vous côtoyez de si près le rivage de la poésie que vous risquez de tomber dans la musique. Il est possible que vous ayez raison", an often quoted remark which admirably defines much of Verlaine's poetry, although it is less applicable to *Jadis et Naguère* than to earlier volumes. It was this musicality of Verlaine's poetry which was now constantly stressed. "There are poems of Verlaine" wrote his English admirer, Arthur Symons, in 1899, "which go as far as verse can go to become pure music". But Symons also emphasised another feature of Verlaine's poetry: "a simplicity of language which is the direct outcome of a simplicity of temperament. These two aspects of simplicity and musicality had already been noted in a striking way by one of the leading French critics of the day, Jules Lemaître, who said of Verlaine, in an essay first published in *La Revue Bleue* in January 1888 and included the following year in the fourth volume of a series entitled *Les Contemporains:*

"C'est un barbare, un sauvage, un enfant . . . seulement cet enfant a une musique dans l'âme et, à certains jours, il entend des voix que nul avant lui n'avait entendues". Anatole France quoted this remark with approval in an article in *Le Temps* in 1890 (later published in *La Vie Littéraire* in 1899) and added: "Il y a quelque chance qu'on dise un jour de lui ce qu'on dit aujourd'hui de Françpis Villon auquel il faut bien le comparer: 'C'était le meilleur poète de son temps'".

But in thus making such lavish amends for his unnecessarily harsh rejection of the poems Verlaine had submitted to him some fifteen years before, Anatole France was perhaps being over-generous. The second half of the nineteenth century in France was particularly rich in poets and two of them, Rimbaud and Mallarmé, have a stronger claim than Verlaine to be considered as "les meilleurs poètes de leur temps".

In his Symbolist Manifesto published in *Le Figaro* on 18 September 1886 Jean Moréas had defined Verlaine's contribution to Symbolism as having been to "briser les cruelles entraves du vers". At that time it was no doubt true that Verlaine seemed to have done more than anyone to break the cruel bonds of versification, because Rimbaud's work was as yet scarcely known and was in fact not so much as mentioned by Moréas. But it is now apparent that Rimbaud went much farther than Verlaine in breaking away from traditional patterns of rhyme and rhythm. Verlaine's innovations were limited to a liking for the octosyllabic line rather than the alexandrine, the introduction, in a number of poems, of the 'vers impair', the extensive use of 'enjambement' and a preference for weak rather than rich rhymes. But Rimbaud, after following in the elder poet's footsteps for a brief period early in 1872, at the beginning of their relationship, soon overtook Verlaine as regards freedom of form and abandoned verse altogether in favour of prose poetry in his *Illuminations*. Similarly Mallarmé, after beginning as a Parnassian, like Verlaine, and then, again like him, moving towards a more evocative kind of poetry in *L'Après-midi d'un Faune,* went far beyond any degree of freedom of form that Verlaine had attempted. In *Un Coup de Dés,* written in 1897, the year after Verlaine's death and the year before his own, Mallarmé used different kinds of lettering and distributed his words irregularly over the unit of the double page as part of his attempt to achieve the effect at which he was aiming in this highly original and complex work. And even in his apparently more conventional poems, such as the sonnets he wrote in the last ten years of his life, Mallarmé's twisted and tortured syntax, which enables him to give to his poems an extraordinary richness and density, makes Verlaine appear as a comparatively timid innovator.

As regards the content of their poetry too, there is no doubt that Rimbaud and Mallarmé, who were intellectually far superior to Verlaine, were pre-occupied with matters beyond the comprehension of 'pauvre Lélian'. In Rimbaud's *Une Saison en Enfer* 'la vierge folle' (who is, of course, Verlaine) says of l'époux infernal' (who is, of course, Rimbaud): 'J'étais sûre de ne jamais entrer dans son monde. A côté de son cher corps endormi, que d'heures des nuits j'ai veillé, cherchant pourquoi il voulait tant s'évader de la réalité'. To escape from reality into an ideal world, or rather to create an ideal world through the medium of poetry, was also the aim of Mallarmé who, according to Moréas, gave to Symbolism its 'sens du mystère et de l'ineffable'. Rimbaud and Mallarmé were therefore both Symbolists of the transcendental kind, endeavouring to penetrate beyond the superficial forms of the real world to the ideal forms of an infinite and eternal world. But Verlaine was a Symbolist of the human kind, concerned solely with the reflection of inner feelings in the objects of the outer world of reality. It is true that in some of the religious poems of *Sagesse* he conjures up a vision of an ideal world parallel with that conjured up by Rimbaud in his *Illuminations* or by Mallarmé in "Prose pour des Esseintes", but precisely because this was a Christian and therefore traditional vision it lacked the novelty and the excitement of the ideal worlds towards which Rimbaud and Mallarmé aspired and had less appeal in an increasingly secular society.

Verlaine himself realised that he did not belong to Symbolism in its transcendental sense and in Jules Huret's *Enquête sur l'évolution littéraire* in 1891 he replied to the journalist's request for a definition of Symbolism in the following uninhibited passage, typical of his conversational style in his last years:

> Vous savez, moi, j'ai du bon sens; je n'ai peut-être que cela, mais j'en ai. Le Symbolisme? . . . comprends pas . . . Ça doit être un mot allemand, hein? Qu'est-ce que cela peut bien vouloir dire? Moi, d'ailleurs, je m'en fiche. Quand je souffre, quand je jouis ou quand je pleure, je sais bein que cela n'est pas du symbole. Voyez-vous, toutes ces distinctions-là, c'est de l'allemandisme: qu'est-ce que cela peut faire à un poète ce que Kant, Schopenauer, Hegel et autres Boches pensent des sentiments humains! Moi, je suis FranÇais, vous m'entendez bien, un chauvin de Franæais, avant tout. Je ne vois rien dans mon instinct qui me force à chercher le pourquoi du pourquoi de mes larmes; quand je suis malheureux, j'écris des vers tristes, c'est tout.

He also recognised in the same article, that he did not share the advanced views on prosody of the younger generation of Symbolists.

> J'ai élargi la discipline du vers, et cela est bon; mais je ne l'ai pas supprimée! Pour qu'il y ait vers, il faut qu'il y ait rythme. A présent on fait des vers à mille pattes! Ça n'est plus des vers, c'est de la prose, quelquefois même ce n'est que du charabia.

It was for these two reasons—the comparatively unadventurous nature of both the content and the form of his poetry, his inability to speculate on the 'pourquoi du pourquoi' of things and his reluctance to break completely with traditional forms of versification—that Verlaine's reputation, which had stood so high in his last years, soon suffered a steep decline. In February 1896, the month after his death, the magazine *La Plume* organised a second *enquête* parallel to the one Jules Huret had carried

out half a dozen years before but this time centred on Verlaine, and already certain reservations were expressed. "Il ouvrit la fenêtre" was the opinion of the eccentric *femme de lettres* Rachilde who had been a close friend of Verlaine's for many years. Another close friend, Mallarmé, described Verlaine as having been caught up in "le conflit de deux époques, une dont il s'extrait avec ingénuité, réticent devant l'autre qu'il suggère". A third contributor to the *enquête* however, Charles Maurras, was not content with veiled criticisms about Verlaine having merely opened windows, or having failed to complete the transition from one period to another; he expressed his view much more openly: "Paul Verlaine laisse un grand nom; mais je ne sais s'il laisse une æuvre".

A few years later, with the arrival of Surrealism and the emphasis it laid both on the search for a world beyond reality and on total freedom of form, Verlaine's reputation sank still lower and André Breton, the leader of the Surrealists, for whom Rimbaud was the dominant figure of the earlier generation, stated categorically that "la surestimation de Verlaine a été la grande erreur de l'époque symboliste".

Even an admirer of Verlaine such as Pierre Martino who, in 1924 wrote what is still probably the best study of the poet as a poet, agreed that Verlaine did not share the general ambition of the Symbolists to "renouveler les thèmes poétiques et changer l'horizon même de la poésie" and that "sa timidité dans le maniement des procédés nouveaux d'expression rhythmique, ses défiances à l'égard du vers libre tracent une espèce de lignefrontière qui sépare très nettement son æuvre de celles qui eurent les préférences de la génération symboliste".

Thirty years later another Verlaine enthusiast, Antoine Adam conceded that, as far as the attitude of the public was concerned there was still "une réticence que l'on sent générale", and in 1955 A. M. Schmidt, in *La Litterature Symboliste*, revealed the extent to which he shared this reticence by hesitating to rank Verlaine alongside his fellow poets Mallarmé and Rimbaud and by finding a curiously non-committal adjective to describe his poetry: "Moins grand sans doute que Mallarmé et Rimbaud . . . Verlaine a composé d'inimitables poèmes".

Yet although this view of Verlaine as a poet of the second rank as compared with his two great contemporaries is now generally accepted, it may well be that our continued admiration for the latter springs more from what they attempted than from what they achieved. Rimbaud's insistence that 'les inventions d'inconnu réclament des formes nouvelles' and Mallarmé's ceaseless struggle to find a means of expression that would enable him to create a non-existent world led both of them, in their different ways, 'aux limites extrêmes de la poésie', as R. Jasinski put it [in *Histoire de la littérature Française*, 1947]. One could indeed go farther and claim that they went not merely to the extreme limits but even beyond the boundaries of poetry, for it now seems certain, after the vast amount of work that has been done on Rimbaud and Mallarmé over the last thirty years, that some of their work is destined to remain inaccessible even to the most perceptive and sympathetic reader.

It is when one turns away, perhaps with a certain impatience, from extreme originality of this kind, towards the poetry of Verlaine, that one wonders whether the latter's more modest achievements may perhaps stand the test of time better than the bolder attempts of his two contemporaries. 'Notre vingtième siècle, si intellectuel, est porté vers l'exégèse des œuvres où des problèmes d'interprétation se posent', wrote Eléonore Zimmermann in one of the most recent studies of Verlaine. It may be that future years will adopt a different approach and will set greater store by Verlaine's unique gift for subtly conveying the infinite sadness of things. The heartsickness of hope deferred, the sense of lost youth, the suicidal loneliness of a rainy day, the fall of autumn leaves, the grief of separation, the stillness of moonlight, the melancholy of sunset, the dream that remains no more than a dream, simply the sadness of being sad—no one else has succeeded as well as Verlaine in re-creating these emotions in those who read his poetry.

Philip Stephan (essay date 1974)

SOURCE: "Verlaine's Decadent Manner," in *Paul Verlaine and the Decadence, 1882-90,* Manchester University Press, 1974, pp. 124-40.

[Here, Stephan describes some decadent elements and themes in Verlaine's works.]

For a quarter of a century now it is *Fêtes galantes* and *Romances sans paroles* that Verlaine critics have esteemed the most highly. Phenomenological critics have examined the psychological tensions of *Fêtes galantes,* where Verlaine seeks to compensate for the amorous frustrations of real life by projecting an imaginary world of *commedia dell' arte* figures enjoying an endless orgy of desire and gallantry unmarred by sexual achievement. *Romances sans paroles* is seen as a universe shimmering with sensations which hover for ever just this side of extinction. In his rendering of their *fadeur,* in his translations of these sensations into musical-verbal equivalents, Verlaine has developed a brilliant mode of communication with his reader, for these *equivalences sensorielles* which he holds at arm's length with *c'est* and similar impersonal constructions are no more than arm's length from the reader, either, so that our perception and Verlaine's meet at a midpoint of common communication. Dream and sensation—and music is the sensation *par excellence* for communicating the data of other senses—are the chief elements of this highly original formula.

In a happy fusion of biographical and textual criticism, this interpretation of Verlaine's creative endeavour posits the role played by his emotional imbalance. The dream *région où vivre* of his poetry depends on the poet's biographical need to sublimate the dissatisfactions of his real existence. When Verlaine did achieve a satisfactory, if temporary, resolution of his emotional problems, as dur-

ing his engagement to Mathilde Mauté and after his conversion to Catholicism, the effect on his inspiration was unhappy, Hence the critics' denigration of *La Bonne Chanson* and of parts of *Sagesse,* which they call prosaic, banal, unimaginative, and given to conceptualism and allegory, for Verlaine's dream *poétique* does not permit his singing a real and present attainment. His own contemporaries placed a high value on the sincerity, and emotional intensity of *Sagesse,* and intellectual currents such as the Catholic aspect of decadence and the idealism of symbolism further nourished their high estimate of this work. Modern criticism, on the other hand, has condemned Verlaine's verse beginning with *Sagesse*—after his mystic experience of 1874 would be a more accurate expression—so that for some readers the term *la conversion de Sagesse* has become almost a pun, denoting both a religious experience and a changed poetic theory.

It is true that, while Verlaine always wrote some bad poetry, he wrote more and more of it after his prison term at Mons in 1873-75, and that as he used up his supply of unpublished early verse in *Jadis et naguère, Amour,* and *Parallèlement* his collections of verse become increasingly dreary. The same is true of his contributions to periodicals during the decade of the 1880's: except for an occasional early poem, titles like **"Un Crucifix"**, **"Saint Benoît Joseph Labre"**, or **"La Mort de S. M. le Roi Louis II de Bavière"** reveal all too eloquently the limited scope of his poetic imagination. It was unusual for him to collect his poems of the previous two or three years and to publish them immediately, as was the case with *Fêtes galantes, La Bonne Chanson,* and *Romances sans paroles*. On the contrary, his normal practice was to collect poems composed over a number of years into variegated and uneven volumes like *Poèmes saturniens, Sagesse,* or *Jadis et naguère*. Hence the critic must select poems for discussion according to their date of composition, their similarity to other poems, or some other criterion which suits his purpose. To single out those poems composed between 1880 and 1890 which reveal decadent characteristics, therefore, is no more presumptuous than to discuss any other aspect of Verlaine's work. Jacques Borel's studies of *Jadis et naguère* and *Parallèlement* for the latest editions of Verlaine's complete works [*Oeuvres complètes,* 1960, and *Oeuvre poétiques complètes,* 1962] draw attention to hitherto unnoticed aspects of his verse of this period. The subtlety with which Borel analyses the 'ambiguity' of Verlaine's simultaneous rejection, in 1884-87, both of his earlier work based on a *poétique* of dream and of sensation, and of the new-found religious orthodoxy which causes him to reject it, suggests that Verlaine's poetry after *Sagesse* is ripe for reappraisal. When Borel calls *Parallèlement,* rather than some earlier collection, 'le dernier sans doute des recueils intèressants', it has the effect of prolonging Verlaine's creative period for another fifteen years, thus proposing for our examination poems which perhaps deserve more attention than they have received.

On 26 May, 14 July and 18 August 1883, then, Verlaine published eight poems in *Le Chat Noir* under the collective title 'Vers à la manière de plusieurs' ('Le Poète et la

Sketch of Verlaine by Félix Régamey, 1872.

muse' was added to this series in *Jadis et naguère* only in 1884). While most of these were composed in the 1860's or early 1870's, **'L'Aube à l'envers',** and perhaps **'Madrigal'** and **'Langueur'** too, were composed after his return to Paris in 1882, and in any case the first two illustrate his decadent manner. In spite of the importance traditionally attached to it, **'Langueur'** is not particularly representative of Verlaine's decadent manner, and possibly, as Eléanor Zimmermann argues [in *Magies de Verlaine,* 1967], it was composed in 1872-74, with the **'Ariettes oubliées',** rather than after his contacts with the decadent milieu. Still, the poem is useful as an indication of the direction his poetry would take.

While other poets of the period chose the homosexual as the epitome of classical decadence, for Verlaine decadence was aestheticism, represented by the poet who composes acrostic verses as victorious armies of barbarians march past, just as Nero is said to have fiddled while Rome burned. It is appropriate that Verlaine, who sought to fix in verse the nuances of *langueur,* should choose lethargy and superficiality as attributes of decadence: 'O n'y pouvoir, étant si faible aux voeux si lents, / O n'y vouloir fleurir un peu cette existence!' The tone of languid, careless aestheticism recalls Nero's 'Qualis artifex pereo', The 'style d'or' (today we speak rather of 'Silver

Age' Latin) is rendered by the excessive anaphora of the last eight lines and by the use of diminutives: *L'Ame seulette, fleurir un peu, mourir un peu.* Diminutive endings were a feature of vulgar Latin, as is evident from the number of modern Romance words derived from them rather than from standard classical forms (e.g. *oreille auricula auris*). Could Verlaine have had in mind the emperor Hadirna's poem to his departing soul, the charm of which is due largely to its use of affectionate diminutive endings?

'L'Aube à l'envers', a landscape of the modern industrial city, and **'Madrigal'** are examples of Verlaine's new manner, a *poétique* based on style and diction. **'Madrigal'** also illustrates the elaborate imagery and a somewhat obscure allusiveness which comprise this manner:

> Tu m'as, ces pâles jours d'automne blanc, fait
>   mal
> A cause de tes yeux où fleurit l'animal,
> Et tu me rongerais, en princesse Souris,
> Du bout fin de la quenotte de ton souris,
> Fille auguste qui fis flamboyer ma douleur
> Avec l'huile rancie encor de ton vieux pleur!
> Oui, folle, je mourrai de ton regard damné.
> Mais va (veux-tu?) l'étang là dort insoupçonné,
> Dont du lys, nef qu'il eût fallu qu'on acclamât,
> L'eau morte a bu le vent qui coule du grand
>   mât.
>
> T'y jeter, palme! et d'avance mon repentir
> Parle si bas qu'il faut être sourd pour l'ouïr.

The pond is a typically decadent setting. In lines 1-3 and 9-10 closely connected grammatical elements are separated by interrupting phrases. The vocabulary is elaborately chosen: in line 1 *pâle* (before its noun!) and *blanc* repeat each other; *quenotte* and *souris* in line 4 are colloquial terms, *nef* in line 9 and *ouïr* in line 13 are archaic. The poem concludes with an antithetical *pointe,* that one must be deaf to hear his softly uttered repentance. Esoteric vocabulary terms are drawn not from a single class but from several lexical categories, so that comparatively few such items suffice to give an impression of pronounced strangeness. *Souris* (smile) puns with *souris* (mouse), and their use as rhyme words draws attention to the pun. Of the numerous alliterations and assonances we notice line 5, with its '*Fi*lle auguste qui *fis f*lamboyer . . . ' and 'l'hu*i*le ranc*i*e' in the following line; in line 9 the combination of [k] and [y] render the line cacophonous and even hard to pronounce. In the phrase 'Mais va (veux-tu!)' *veux-tu* is a colloquial expression for reinforcing an imperative; the three vowels [a], [oe], and [y] form a progressive closing and tightening of the mouth; this tensioning of the vocal organs is set off and contrasted by the open, relaxed, and harmonious vocables immediately following: *l'etang là dort.* (Such cacophony, caused by the repetition of plosives and of tense, shrill vowels like [oe] [y], [i], and often followed by more relaxed and musical vocables, is a distinctive feature of Verlaine's decadent manner.) Lines 9 and 10 are very confused grammatically: the proper sequence is 'l'étang, dont l'eau a bu le vent qui coule du grand mât du lys, (lequel est une] nef qu'il eût fallu qu'on acclamât'. This involved and invert-ed grammatical construction, and the accumulation of *de's* (lines 4 and 9-10), are but two of several factors which in combination create an impression of obscurity. Here, as in other poems addressed to his exwife, Mathilde Mauté, or to Arthur Rimbaud, Verlaine does not explain the bio-graphical frame of reference, whence an air of mystery and of private association which are troubling to the un-initiated reader. In the poem at hand, the girl to whom the poem is addressed is compared, to a mouse, and this fig-ure is completed by the animality of her look and by the gnawing teeth of her smile; it is not necessary to know that the girl is Mathilde Mauté, nor the circumstances of their separation. The next figure, however, is hermetic: a lily floating on a pond is compared to a ship, and the water in the pond has drunk the wind flowing from the mainmast. While appreciating the tone of dark foreboding which this figure adds to the poem, still we should like to see it clarified. While Verlaine is never hermetically ob-scure, nevertheless confused grammar, allusiveness, and complex imagery do produce a murkiness of expression which is unusual in his verse and hence distinctive of his decadent manner.

About two years later, in May and June of 1885, *Lutece* published a group of six poems, collected subsequently in *Parallèlement* under the heading 'Lunes', which also il-lustrate Verlaine's decadent manner:

> Je veux, pour te tuer, ô temps qui me dévastes,
> Remonter jusqu'aux jours bleus des amours
>   chastes
> Et bercer ma luxure et ma honte au bruit doux
> De baisers sur Sa main et non plus dans Leurs
>   cous.
> Le Tibère effrayant que je suis à cette heure,
> Quoi que j'en aie, et que je rie ou que je pleure,
> Qu'il dorme! pour rêver, loin d'un cruel
>   bonheur,
> Aux tendrons pâlots dont on ménageait l'honneur
> Es-fêtes, dans, après le bal sur la pelouse,
> Le clair de lune quand le clocher sonnait douze.
>
>   ['Lunes, 1']

Again, in lines 1 and 6 we have a harsh alliteration of plosives, the mysterious allusions to *Sa main* (Mathilde's) and *Leurs cous* (those of the street-walkers with whom he was living), a classical allusion to Caesar Tiberius in line 5, and, in the last four lines, a combination of interrupted word-order and of choice vocabulary (*tendrons, ès, pâlots*). We recognise in these poems traits which we have come to regard as typically decadent: exaggerated alliterations and assonances, all manner of word plays, impressionist style, conversational mannerisms of language, classical allusions, the presence of a pond and of flowers, and, in **'L'Aube à l'envers'**, a modern, urban landscape. 'Lunes I, III, IV, and V hint at the depravity of some decadent poetry.

The figures of the lily compared to a ship in **'Madrigal'** and of Tiberius, to whom the poet compares himself in 'Lunes, 1', are examples of the elaborate, sometimes hermetic imagery which distinguishes Verlaine's manner in *Parallèlement*, but which is not otherwise typical of decadent verse. In **'Fernand Langlois'** the poet's heart is compared to a lock which Langlois patiently opens, in **'Autre Explication'** there are the tropes of constancy (compared to a prostitute), the cuttlefish, and the hour. Curiously, it is in two of the *Poèmes saturniens,* **'Cré-puscule du soir mystique'** and **'Le Rossignol',** with their decadent ponds, flowers, and birds, that we find a previ-ous instance of such extended imagery. In **'Le Rossignol'** the poet's memories are likened to a flock of birds swoop-ing down on the tree of his heart, mirrored in the water of Regret; and the nightingale is the poet's first love. On the other hand, his practice in these poems of capitalising words taken in a symbolic sense is a common one in decadent verse; in *Les Déliquescences* **'Pour avoir péché'** and **'Platonisme'** parody this Baudelairean device.

As with decadent verse in general, an intensification of his usual traits distinguishes **'Madrigal'** and 'Lunes' from Verlaine's earlier verse and makes them appear as self-parodies. Recent critics who have drawn attention to this parodying quality in Verlaine's poetry of the 1880's sug-gest that the very intention of the 'Lunes' cycle, and of **'A la manière de Paul Verlaine'** in particular, is to re-ject his earlier manner by making fun of it. . . . Ver-laine's relationship with the decadents was an ambivalent one, since he did not take the decadence very seriously, and it is therefore always possible that the target of his caricatural poems was decadence itself as well as his own earlier manner. If so, in the perverse logic of decadence, which was fascinated by what it loathed, such poems are all the more decadent!

It is in any case certain that Verlaine consciously adopted decadent mannerisms during the 1880's. His use of Lat-inisms and classical allusions corroborates this point. Although his unpublished verse included three schoolboy translations from Latin, which he apparently valued enough to save, in the 110 poems of *Poèmes saturniens, Fêtes galantes, La Bonne Chanson,* and *Romances sans pa-roles* there are only five containing Latin phrases or allu-sions to classical antiquity—and two of these reflect merely his Parnassian affectation of Greek mythology. In con-trast, of the 128 poems of *Jadis et naguère, Amour,* and *Parallèlement,* we count twelve—almost one in ten—containing Latin expressions or classical allusions; this proportion would undoubtedly be still greater if we ex-cluded poems composed before 1880.

Collating two versions of the same poem provides further corroboration. **'L'Aube à l'envers'** is clearly contempo-rary with Verlaine's residence at Boulogne-sur-Seine in the summer of 1882, while the second version, **'Nouv-elles Variations sur le Point-du-Jour',** published in *Lutèce* at the very end of 1885, must be an elaboration of the first poem.

> L'Aube à l'envers
>
> Le Point-du-Jour avec Paris au large,
> Des chants, des tirs, les femmes qu'on 'rêvait',

La Seine claire et la foule qui fait
Sur ce poème un vague essai de charge.

On danse aussi, car tout est dans la marge
Que fait le fleuve à ce livre parfait,
Et si parfois l'on tuait ou buvait,
Le fleuve est sourd et le vin est litharge.

Le Point-du-Jour, mais c'est l'Ouest de Paris!
Un calembour a béni son histoire
D'affreux baisers et d'immondes paris.

En attendant que sonne l'heure noire
Où les bateaux-omnibus et les trains
Ne partent plus, tirez, tirs, fringuez, reins!

Already the poem is distinctly decadent on account of its naturalist subject, with commuter steamers and trains the play on *Point-du-Jour,* which means 'daybreak' as well as designating a landmark to the west of Paris, and the artificiality implicit in the book trope of line 6. It is precisely these elements that Verlaine expands in the later version:

Nouvelles Variations sur le Point-du-Jour

Le Point du Jour, le point blanc de Paris,
Le seul point blanc, grâce à tant de bâtisse
Et neuve et laide et que je t'en ratisse,
Le Point du Jour, aurore des paris!

Le bonneteau fleurit 'dessur' la berge,
La bonne tôt s'y déprave, tant pis
Pour elle et tant mieux pour le birbe gris
Qui lui du moins la croit encore vierge.

Il a raison, le vieux, car voyez donc
Comme est joli toujours le paysage:
Paris au loin, triste et gai, fol et sage,
Et le Trocadéro, ce cas, au fond,

Puis la verdure et le ciel et les types
Et la rivière obscène et molle, avec
Des gens trop beaux, leur cigare à leur bec:
Epatants ces metteurs-au-vent de tripes!

The basic play on words now fills the first stanza with variants: *Le Point du Jour, le point blanc, Le seul point blanc; Point du Jour, aurore des paris; Paris-paris.* These are followed up with homonyms: tant *de bâtisse,* t'en *ratisse; Le* bonneteau, *La* bonne tôt. Popular locutions abound, such as *je t'en ratisse, à leur bec, dessur, birbe, Il a raison, le vieux, les types,* and in general the diction is rhetorically self-conscious. In lieu of the book and margin figure, Verlaine has introduced the old man who seduces the young maid (in the sense of *bonne,* since he spells out that she is no longer *vierge!*), a decadent motif. *La Seine claire* has been replaced by *La rivière obscène et molle,* in which the adjectives somehow make us think of putrefaction and of flabby degeneracy. While even the 1882 version could be contrasted with Verlaine's landscapes in *Poèmes saturniens* or *Romances sans paroles,*

the revisions of the 1885 version have emphasised those qualities which *Les Déliquescences* and minor poems like them have led us to call decadent. . . .

The most general conclusion to be made concerning Verlaine's decadent style is simply that it incorporates pell-mell all manner of previous tendencies: exotic and esoteric vocabulary, colloquialisms, impressionist style, original syntax, As critics from Gautier to A. E. Carter have pointed out, concern with language and with new forms of diction is an essential element of decadence. The progressive exaggeration of his own personalised diction over a twenty-year period, perhaps even for the sake of self-parody, parallels the development of decadent poetry. In its final form Verlaine's asyndetic style reduces the sentence to a series of word groups, the alliterations of plosives have a staccato effect which literally detaches some syllables from their context, interjections are set off by dashes or parentheses, and strong caesuras destroy the entity of the poetic line. Thus the whole of a poem, stanza, or line disintegrates into isolated, autonomous fragments, and this fragmentations of the whole into its parts is typical of decadent style. The conversational tendency in Verlaine's style, and the development of the friendship theme, with its apostrophes to Mathilde and Rimbaud, its frequent poems addressed to personal acquaintants (nine in *Amour* alone; consider also the very title of *Dédicaces*), with a poem such as **'A Fernand Langlois'** (especially stanzas 6-8), which is structured on a conversational situation, recall the language of the naturalist novel, similar poems we saw in early issues of *La Nouvelle Rive Gauche* and *Le Chat Noir,* some poems of Jean Lorrain, and, of course, Corbière and Laforgue. Verlaine, to be sure, lacks the latter's pungent, humorous irony, and in no case do we see their influence on his verse. On the other hand, Claude Cuénot seems to have missed the point when he condemns the vulgar, slangy quality of Verlaine's late verse; such language, like his divergent use of both popular and literary diction, is simply a feature of the decadent preoccupation with language for its own sake.

To look now at themes, Verlaine's changing attitudes toward homosexuality and toward licentious verse in general can perhaps be ascribed to his decadent manner as well as to personal considerations. In July of 1883 he omitted from 'Vers à la manière de plusieurs' the compromising 'Le Poète et la muse'. Now, although the nature of his relationship with Rimbaud had always been known—so much so that in 1874 it was Lepelletier who had to dissuade him from dedicating *Romances sans paroles* to Rimbaud—from the time of his imprisonment until after his return to Paris Verlaine maintained a firm and tactful silence on the whole subject of perversion (indeed, until his death he always denied that their relationship had been sexual). But in March of 1884 he published the compromising **'Vers pour être calomnié'**, followed in December by **'La Dernière Fête galante'**, with its revealing conclusion, 'O que nos coeurs . . . / Dès ce jourd'hui réclament . . . / L'embarquement pour Sodome et Gomorrhe!'. Then the publication of **'Explication'** and **'Autre Explication'** in *Lutèce* for 19-23 July 1885 initiated a series of poems in which during the next several years he was to write ever more openly of his relationship with Rimbaud and even to justify homosexuality. Jacques Borel argues convincingly for the psychological reasons which, when he was preparing *Parallèlement,* induced Verlaine to take up again the Rimbaud theme, with its candour and its exaltation of ' . . . ceux-là que sacre le haut Rite' ('Ces passions qu'eux seuls . . .'): nostalgia for the mystic exhilaration of their adventure, or the false rumours of Rimbaud's death in 1887, which inspired at least one poem. Similar considerations apply to a reprise of the theme of female eroticism; Verlaine's early penchant for erotic verse appears in *Les Amies* (1868) and in the indecent poems appended to *La Bonne Chanson* (1870). But these were clandestine works, and less than two decades later he was openly publishing poems of this sort.

Perhaps there was no longer the same need for prudence. While until 1882 Verlaine had good reason to maintain his pose as a respectable gentleman misunderstood by his contemporaries, by 1884 he had little to gain from further claims to respectability. For one thing, the truth was by now widely known; for another, after his dismissal from the Collège de Rethel, after the rejection of his application for re-employment in the city administration, and in view of the impossibility of rejoining Mathilde (who remarried in 1885), it was apparent that he was to be permanently excluded from conventional, self-respecting bourgeois life. On the other hand, with the growth of his 'legend' and with his decision to stake everything on a full-time literary career, he had rather more to gain than to lose by frankly accepting the role of an incorrigible if penitent sinner, as richly endowed with the grace of poetry as he was deprived of that of common morality. But to admit past indiscretions is not the same as singing current offences. Would not Verlaine's new-found candour also have been brought about by the decadent milieu, with its treatment of vice, its preference for perversion because it is unnatural, and its implication that Paris rivalled Rome as a centre of debauchery? Since Baudelaire, since *A Rebours,* since the more lurid decadent novels like Péladan's *Le Vice suprême,* homosexuality was becoming less taboo and more, if not acceptable, at least tolerated in avant-garde circles. The first issue of *Le Décadent,* for example, contains an instalment of Luc Vajarnet's *La Grande Roulotte,* in which the lesbian attachment of Countess Jeanne and her chambermaid Mariette is presented in such detail as to be erotically stimulating to male readers. Against this background we can understand Verlaine's including in *Parallèlement* poems such as '**Sur une statue de Ganymède**', '**Ces passions qu'eux seuls nomment encore amours**', and '**Laeti et errabundi**'. Heterosexual love, which, if less original, still figures prominently in the decadent aesthetic, was handled quite freely, to the point where *La Plume* saw some of its issues seized by the police. In comparison to his relative shyness in 1883, Verlaine's plans for *Parallèlement* are revealing. Although the first edition already included *Filles* and *Les Amies,* for a projected new edition he wanted to include '**Nous ne sommes pas le troupeau**', '**Billet à Lily**' (from the pornographic volume *Femmes*), '**Le Bon**

Disciple' (from *Hombres*), as well as 'un dialogue entre éphèbes et vierges à la Virgile; le cadre me permettra les dernières hardiesses. Inititulé Chant alterné.' The use of a classical setting as an excuse for licentious verse is particularly indicative . . . , for this common practice of decadent poets reflects their fundamental interpretation of Greco-Roman antiquity.

Bishop on Verlaine's development as a poet

Verlaine's art is, despite its grace and wit, predicated upon consummate control of formal and expressive means. Work and art were synonymous for him to the end of his life. Madrigals, odes, elegies, sonnets, he half-realized, however, were soon to become things of the past. He himself toys, half-mockingly, with assonance, while deeming rhyme to be central to poetry and holding free, blank verse to be inadequately equipped to survive on poetic grounds. . . . [However,] he recognizes the principles of liberty and new possibility at stake, and senses the legitimacy of new claims. Indeed, it is important to stress, too, in conclusion, the significance of an almost entirely overlooked element of his oeuvre, the publication, in 1886, of *Les Mémoires d'un veuf/Memoirs of a Widower*. Verlaine's tentative foray into the realm of *poème en prose*—his allusion to Baudelaire's "Les Bons Chiens," from *Le Spleen de Paris,* is explicit in his own **"Chiens"** / **"Dogs"** and, although some texts retain an initially hesitant *entrée en matiere,* many others are very fine prose poems answering all criteria that poets and others have established for their evaluation. . . . [They] show us a poet open upon the future poetic options of the world that, in part, will come to reign.

Michael Bishop, in Nineteenth-Century French Poetry, *Twayne Publishers, 1993.*

Joanna Richardson (essay date 1974)

SOURCE: An introduction to *Verlaine: Selected Poems,* translated by Joanna Richardson, Penguin Books, 1974, pp. 15-28.

[*In the following excerpt, Richardson provides a critical overview of Verlaine's verse, reputation, and contribution to literature.*]

Romances sans paroles, which many consider to be [Verlaine's] finest book, reflects his persistent love for Mathilde; it also bears the ineffaceable mark of Rimbaud. It was Rimbaud whom Verlaine followed as he created an original, unacademic language. Rimbaud advocated pictorial simplicity, a return to popular sources, to simple refrains and simple rhythms. Verlaine followed his guidance, bringing some of his poems close to popular songs, seeking a new simplicity and a new complexity. Just as Rimbaud freed Verlaine from bourgeois domesticity, from suburban mediocrity, so he shook him free from certain literary conventions, and swept him into a splendid adventure: the search for a new poetry. In some ways, Rimbaud was only appealing to instincts and beliefs which were already present: to Verlaine's sympathy for the simple and the popular, to his love of technical experiments, his lifelong pleasure in exploring and exploiting language and syntax, his interest in expressing moods. Verlaine was already a supreme poet of mood; under Rimbaud's influence he attempted to eliminate himself from his work, to record mood and atmosphere without the intervention of self. This was the ultimate refinement of poetry. . . .

[While in prison, Verlaine] wrote **'Kaléidoscope.'** As the title suggests, it is a collection of impressions, with no logical connection. Here, before Proust, Verlaine experiences those rare, mysterious, transient moments which have more savour than the actual events which they revive. The setting of the poem cannot be identified. In the last verse, he destroys any lingering vestige of reality, and leaves the whole poem, suspended, in a dream. Like certain poems by Rimbaud, **'Kaléidoscope'** catches a world beyond the world. It is in this sort of poem that Verlaine shows the extent of his powers. . . .

The profound charm of *Sagesse* lies in its obsession with the past. Verlaine's contrition is frail, but it intensifies the forbidden pleasures of the past, the enduring obsession with Rimbaud. When he wrote *Sagesse,* he honestly believed that he had entered the path of salvation; he had been tempted, but determined that he would not now turn back. But one must distinguish between the man's intentions and the very depth of his soul, which he could not help revealing in poetry. The essential reality is not edifying. There are a few moments in *Sagesse* when the convert bathes in the purifying love of Christ; and there are many times when he re-lives and regrets the forbidden past. Verlaine was not a hypocrite—but *Sagesse* presents the two contestants in the unequal fight which God would lose. . . .

Verlaine spent his final years in the cafés and hospitals of Paris. Perpetual drinking and squalid living, illness and disease, had made him, now, a wreck of a human being. His homosexual days were virtually over, but he was torn between two middle-aged women of dubious morals, and for one of them he wrote *Le Livre posthume*. Here, for a brief moment, his poetic gift returned. But, for the most part, he turned out sadly pedestrian verse; his inspiration had gone, and he was living on his past. . . .

[In January 1896, shortly after Verlaine died,] in *Le Figaro*, Émile Zola enlarged on the theme of Verlaine, the man apart. Far from Verlaine as he had been in his literary principles and his achievement, he spoke of him with admiring sympathy, and with vehement conviction.

> Sad, delightful Verlaine has gone to the land of great eternal peace, and already a legend is growing over his grave.

> He was, we are told, a solitary, disdainful of the crowd, a man who lived in the lofty dream of his work, without any kind of concession or compromise . . . This is quite untrue . . . Verlaine did not disdain society, it was society which rejected him. He became an unwilling creature apart, an involuntary 'exile' . . . Indeed, so little did he spurn honours and distinctions that, quite seriously, he wanted to stand for the Académie . . . If he refused everything, as they have said, that was because nothing was offered him . . .

> And who knows if misery did not diminish him? Of course the fatal negligence of his life helped to give his poetry that freedom of movement which is its original contribution to literature. But . . . I should like to imagine him happy, well off, comfortable, an Academician, having had the leisure to produce all his fruit, like the tree which a kindly destiny shelters from the onslaughts of frost and wind. Certainly he would have left a more complete and more extensive work.

The critic Charles Le Goffic disagreed with Zola: he considered that Verlaine had been genuinely indifferent to honours, and that he had chosen independence. Independent he had certainly been; he had always stood apart, and, as Le Goffic emphasized, the years had not changed him.

> Until the end he lived outside the rules of prosody and behaviour. And this independent bohemianism was neither an attitude nor the accepted consequence of his errors: he could (and some have tried to make him do so) make honourable amends, conform to the outward conventions of bourgeois life. He preferred to die his old vagabond self, indifferent to status and to official celebrity: he was honestly uninterested. At the height of his glory he remained a good soul, he broke with none of those he had known in his days of ill-fortune, and he refused to discriminate. He is a singularly *déclassé* figure . . . But this *déclassé* had a humble heart; this unnatural Catholic made the sweetest gesture of submissive and repentant piety before the Blessed Virgin; this poet found in the delights of a fallen angel some lines of mortal beauty. His art was great enough, and controlled enough, to efface itself, and to break the bounds of a confining prosody until it became a light and volatile music, a tremor and a cry. There it was that he set himself apart from other poets, and there it is that he remains inimitable and the most wonderful example of the helotism of genius to present to lettered youth in every age.

Some critics insisted that Verlaine had been a perpetual child; others acclaimed him as 'the dear father of us all, a good old grandfather . . . In him,' wrote one, 'we proudly honour the great French Christian poet'. Verlaine remained controversial; but now, by common consent, he had entered into glory. It was decided to erect a memorial in the Jardin du Luxembourg; Mallarmé and Rodin presided over the memorial committee. In 1897, the year after Verlaine's death, Mallarmé declared: 'We know that he is smiling in immortality, and that he is now beside La Fontaine and Lamartine'. Verlaine must indeed have been smiling. At the Académie française, José-Maria de Heredia, the Parnassian poet, was singing his praises. In Brussels, Émile Verhaeren proclaimed the greatness of 'the wandering

Lélian, whose thumping and imperious stick seems like a symbol on the paths of literature'.

Verhaeren was among Verlaine's most understanding admirers. That April [1896], in *La Revue blanche,* there appeared the generous appreciation which was to be reprinted in his *Impressions:*

> After the death of Victor Hugo, it was the death of Verlaine which afflicted French literature most deeply . . . Whatever the worth of Banville and Leconte de Lisle, they seem to be tributaries; they do not shine enough with a personal fire . . .

> Paul Verlaine proves himself to be quite different. If the **Poèmes saturniens** are still impregnated with Parnassian traditions, if the **Fêtes galantes** seem to drive from 'La Fête chez Thérèse', which Victor Hugo arranged in his *Contemplations,* the **Romances sans paroles** and, above all, **Sagesse,** affirm their independence in French literature. These works are no longer subjects, they are sovereigns. They live with a new and special art . . .

> Verlaine never knew calm . . . His being is always shaken by anguish or pacified by prayer; he is always burning with vices, or with virtues . . . He is a man as profoundly as he is a Christian. And it is his double nature that, as a great poet, he has sung, expressed and immortalized . . .

> He spiritualized the language; he was tempted by shades of meaning, and by the fragility of phrases. He composed some which were exquisite, fluid, tenuous.

> They seem scarcely a tremor in the air; the sound of a flute in the shadows in the moonlight; the vanishing of a silk dress in the wind; the trembling of glass and crystal on a dresser. Sometimes all that they contain is the docile gesture of two hands coming together . . .

> It will be the original glory of Paul Verlaine to have conceived, lived and created a work of art which, alone, reflects and enlarges the rebirth of faith—that rebirth which we have seen in recent years . . .

> There are moralists who reproach Verlaine for his dissipated and sinful life. One really wonders if it should be deplored, as soon as one recalls the cries of repentance, of gentleness, humility and sacrifice with which he redeemed it.

Other critics were less admiring and less charitable. A psychiatrist, discussing decadent poetry, considered that 'Verlaine was a disturbed man of genius, a progenerate rather than a degenerate, but he had strange deviations and strange weaknesses . . . One is too well aware of the sick man behind the poet.' Several critics confused their moral and aesthetic judgements. In his study *What is Art?,* [Leo] Tolstoy wrote, in puritan mood:

> I cannot refrain from dwelling on the extraordinary

glory of these two men, Baudelaire and Verlaine, who are recognized today, throughout Europe, as the greatest geniuses of modern poetry. How can the French . . . attribute such vast importance, and accord such enormous glory, to these two poets, who are so imperfect in manner and so vulgar and so low in matter? . . . The only explanation which I can see is this: that the art of the society in which they produce their works is not something serious and important, but a mere amusement . . .

> Baudelaire and Verlaine have invented new forms, they have, moreover, spiced them with pornographic details which nobody before them had deigned to use. And that was all that was needed to make them acknowledged as great writers by the critics and the upper classes.

Despite Tolstoy's moral strictures and left-wing criticism, it was clear that Verlaine now enjoyed a European reputation. In 1899, Georges Rodenbach, the Belgian Symbolist poet, declared that Verlaine's conversion had been 'a struggle between Jesus and a childlike Pascal. And in this sublime crisis were born the eternal poems of *Sagesse,* the most moving confession of the soul in all modern literature'. Rodenbach maintained his belief in Verlaine's immortality. His faith was shared by the publisher who, in 1899-1900, brought out the five volumes of Verlaine's *Oeuvres complètes* (followed, in 1903, by his *Oeuvres posthumes*). Achille Segard, who had known Verlaine, declared that he had 'established a new form of sensibility, and in it . . . a whole generation rediscovered, enlarged and clarified, the very image of its common soul'. Ernest Raynaud, the historian of Symbolism, wrote that he understood 'all the phenomena of modern neurasthenia . . . No one translated, better than Verlaine, the atrophy which comes from excessive activity, excessive nervous tension, the abuse of life and its stimulants. In his poetry, the apotheosis of transient sensation, Verlaine contrived to catch the indiscernible.'

As the twentieth century began, the familiar trend in Verlaine criticism continued. While men of letters recognized his individual gifts and his influence, the more conventional critics continued to take a moral stand and to show a violent personal resistance to his work. Now that it was no longer possible to ignore Verlaine, people denied his genius with fury. One remains astonished by the tone of the discussion, the degree of anger and invective which sober writers allowed themselves to show. In 1901, René Doumic reviewed his *Oeuvres complètes* in the *Revue des deux mondes.*

> We have been invited to do something which few of us had done: to read Verlaine in his entirety. This reading . . . makes us appreciate the equal banality of the man and of his work. And so it could not be recommended too warmly to literary novices who would take their elders' word and be tempted to believe in Verlaine's genius. This reading will prevent them from being, in their turn, the victims of a kind of gigantic joke and the dupes of an insolent mystification . . .

Far from being a beginning, the art of Verlaine is the last convulsion of a dying poetry. This poetry is merely Romanticism which has lost its vigour . . . One had only to see Verlaine ambling round the streets to think of the old Romantics in the days of the Bousingots, who were proud to go around the town in clothes which made them noticed, and believed that eccentric dress possessed some secret virtue. The careful disorder and the contrived irregularity of this costume is simply another form of dandyism. Verlaine knew it and he was prepared to admit it. He was not unaware that decent dress would make him lose much of his personality . . .

Verlaine is the frantic representative of intimate poetry thus conceived in conformity with the *credo* of Romanticism. One could not mention any work in which the self has so far been displayed with such boastful cynicism.

It is to be feared that one day Verlaine will be completely forgotten. He has collected his admirers, some of them men of good faith. His poetry has found an echo in certain souls which therefore saw in it something of themselves. This example will be quoted to show into what deliquescence moral ideas and artistic feelings have, at a certain date and in a certain group, very nearly dissolved, lost themselves and foundered. . . .

As a poet, he had done service to modern literature. He had restored the free use of metre, given back to poets the unfettered use of their instrument of work. He had deliberately broken every rule of prosody. He had used his marvellous technical powers, as well as his instincts, to record suggestion. No one else catches, like Verlaine, the infinitely fragile state between dreaming and waking, between imagination and reality. He expresses a thought before it is formulated, an instinct before it is recognized, an emotion which has yet to be acknowledged. As Fernand Gregh observed: 'In many short poems, which are like the tremors of a soul, caught as they pass, it is hardly Verlaine who is talking any more, it is the human soul, impersonal, intemporal, it is almost the soul of things gaining awareness of itself in the soul of a man.' No French poet has recorded certain moods with the exquisite touch of Verlaine. Simple in word and form, he seems to write almost without effort. In their own inherent melody, in their emotive power, his lyrics come as close as any poems have ever come to music.

As a poet of love, he is uneven. As a religious poet, he has perhaps been over-estimated. But 'l'art, mes enfants, c'est d'être absolument sois-même'. So he had explained. No poet had been more himself than Verlaine. He recorded all his life, all his raptures and regrets, all his bitterness, licentiousness and melancholy, all his humour, violence, weakness and simplicity. Verlaine's was at times a subtle simplicity. It was that of a child. It was also that of a consummate poet.

Henri Peyre (essay date 1974)

SOURCE: "The Tragic Impressionism of Verlaine," in *What Is Symbolism?*, translated by Emmett Parker, Uni-

versity of Alabama Press, 1980, pp. 48-62.

[*Peyre is a French-born critic who has lived and taught in the United States for most of his career. One of the foremost American critics of French literature, he has written extensively on modern French literature in works that blend superb scholarship with a clear style accessible to the non-specialist reader, most notably in* French Novelists of Today *(rev. ed. 1967). Below, he discusses stylistic aspects of Verlaine's verse that are frequently labeled symbolist and impressionist. Peyre's commentary was originally published as* Qu'est-ce que le symbolisme? *in 1974*]

[Verlaine] wrote too much, and many mediocre things. Those less prolific than he, like Coleridge or Baudelaire, or those who died while still writing, or who disappeared young, like Rimbaud and Keats, have in the last resort found themselves more fortunate. What is worse, Verlaine repeated himself; J. S. Bach, Antonio Vivaldi, Goethe himself, Hugo, and Claudel did the same; the latter taking the precaution of frequently contradicting himself. Verlaine often fell into vulgarity or into inconsequential platitudes. But criticism came to the final conclusion that there were some very fine works, fervent with youthfulness, in the poems of the fiftyish Victor Hugo and even in the works of the elderly Tennyson, or in the last canvases of [Claude] Monet and [Pierre] Renoir. In Verlaine's case, it has taken much longer to revise lazily arrived at opinions that set the final limit of his important production at **Romances without Words** (1874; he was then thirty years old) or, at the furthest extent, at the religious verses and the laments emitted in prison and collected in **Wisdom,** written between 1875 and the date of their publication in book form in 1881. But the greater Verlaine, certainly the most tragic, is the one of the fifteen or so pieces in the volumes that followed: **Long Ago and Not so Long Ago** (1885), **Love** (1888), **In Parallel** (1889). And the very last of his poems, from 1895, **"Mort,"** is not the least moving or the least artistically orchestrated.

If being called a "symbolist" meant above all to have recourse to symbols and to insinuate that a mysterious meaning resided behind the appearances of expression, Verlaine would be a symbolist only occasionally. But Verlaine occupies a considerable place, both in the history of the symbolist movement (his **"Art poétique"** and his sonnet on decandence have served much more effectively as rallying banners than all the manifestoes) and in the spiritual and technical enrichment of French poetry that occurred between 1870 and 1890. One often forgets today that it was he first of all, through his work and his early innovations, who initially fascinated the adolescent Rimbaud and contributed to showing him his way; the younger man very quickly showed more fierce boldness than the older one. Even then, Verlaine, so malleable and unresisting, revealed a certain independence in refusing to let himself be seduced by the voyant's theories and in accepting to serve as the target for his sarcasms. He understood that neither free verse nor the biblical *verset* nor the poem-in-prose suited him, and that objective poetry, if he had been capable of it, was not in itself superior to the other. Nevertheless, and better than any of those who are called symbolists (Mallarmé included), Verlaine proclaimed the superhuman or inhuman genius of his young friend. In truth, in several of his judgments or his remarks uttered somewhat casually on Baudelaire, on Poe (by whom he refused to be captivated), and later in his admittedly hasty articles on the *poètes maudits*, Verlaine revealed flair and perspicacity. As others have already remarked, he remained faithful to poetry and to a rather elevated idea of art, refusing to abandon literature as Rimbaud did, or to toy with it in graceful "futile petitions" or witty quatrains that might be deciphered by the postman.

With respect to the psychological imbalance that is at the source of his poetry, Verlaine let it be understood more than once that he knew very well what was involved there, even if he lacked the will and perhaps the desire to discipline himself. "I have the rage to love. My so weak heart is mad," he pathetically admits in the fifth of his pieces entitled **"Lucien Létinois"** in *Love*. His avowal in a letter to Cazalis has often been cited: "I am a feminine person, which explains many things." Antoine Adam, as early as 1936, in one of the most subtle and most convincing studies in which psychoanalysis has served literary appreciation, then Guy Michaud in his *Message poétique du symbolisme* in 1947, have shown how well Verlaine's work can be elucidated by the deciphering of his temperament and by a character analysis of the poet's self. He knew himself to be profoundly, and no doubt incurably, "double," vacillating between the faun and the angel, the occasional tiger and the small child crying out his need to be commanded and loved. The perspicacity of his self-image is keen in a different way from that of many so-called personal poets, from Lamartine or Musset to Laforgue. He knew the strength of that "amativeness" within him that he could not resist. There is yet to be extracted from his prose and poetic works (in the former, often under the cover of characters into whom he projects his own self or behind whom he conceals himself, Gaspard Hauser or the condemned husband rising up from Hell in **"Grace"**) a self-portrait of Verlaine that would be astonishingly accurate.

Verlaine's work is so closely entangled in his life that critics who have devoted themselves to it have hardly been able to avoid explications based on his heredity, his parents' indulgence, the keen awareness of his ugliness ("They did not find me handsome," Gaspard Hauser says of women), a first love for his cousin Eliza, broken off by death, and finally, homosexuality. Sensual rage and ecstatic rapture alternated in him, or rather coexisted, along with gentleness and contrition. Antoine Adam has shown what one can read into declarations by way of which the poet seems to rediscover old symbols of sexuality that on one occasion profess guilt and on another pride themselves on being unorthodox. "A falcon I soar, and I die a swan," he exclaims in the most inverted and daringly inverse of his sonnets, **"The Good Disciple."** He finds it delightful to abdicate, to allow himself to be engulfed in the vertiginous sensation of the swing that rocks him, of the carousel horse that turns, of the jig that he dances. He knows that he is like the dead leaf carried off by some ill wind, like the butterfly, like the pilotless vessel. At the moment, that forgetfulness is delightful, that langorousness is voluptuous and propitious to dreaming. Afterward, reality will take its revenge and remorse will gnaw him:

> Le ver est dans le fruit, le réveil dans le rêve
> Et le remords est dans l'amour: telle est la loi.

> The worm is in the fruit, the awakening in the
>   dream,
> And within love is remorse: such is the law of
>   things.

From this vertigo, from these bouts of repetance, will spring forth, however, confessional poems scarcely less bitter than those of Baudelaire, almost as uninhibited in their unabashed display of a dislocated self as the avowals of Dostoevski's characters. In marriage, in his liaison with the imperious dominator that Rimbaud was, in conversion, sometimes even in a childish patriotism, in promises to himself (set down in his diary) to "pray morning and night" and to attend mass everyday, Verlaine would seek the stability to which he aspired. All in vain. He was never really to find that discipline except in his craft as a poet and in the constraints he was able to impose on himself.

"This innocent," Paul Valéry, the most conscious and least undisciplined of verse writers, wrote of Verlaine, "is an organized primitive. . . . Never was there a more subtle art than this art that supposes that in it one flees from another and not that one precedes him." In the area of language, first of all, Verlaine joins the example to the precept, or rather furnishes examples well before formulating the precept, by wringing the neck of eloquence. Eloquence, to be sure, did not die of it; from "The Drunken Boat" to the "Five Great Odes" and the remarkable poets of 1950 or 1960, it survives and creates the merit of several of the most moving works of French poetry. But Verlaine broke with the somewhat encompassing unity of tone and style that characterized *Les Fleurs du Mal* almost as much as the works of Hugo or Leconte de Lisle. There is nothing stilted in him. He dared introduce familiar speech, popular turns of phrase, and even low-class words (*peuple*) in his verses, to write as one speaks among friends—"You! you've got your head someplace else" ("Toi! t'as du vague à l'âme"), to use "ca" repeatedly instead of "cela," to omit the pronoun before the third-person verb in the present tense ("faut pas"), to introduce the exclamatory "tiens" or "hein," or call wooden horses "dadas." Historians of the symbolists' language, such as Charles Bruneau, have pointed out provincialisms in the poet's verses, popular archaisms, the unselfconscious omission of "ne," which, in a negative expression, should precede the "pas," charming grammatical inaccuracies such as "faisez le beau" (for "faites le beau"), "plus pire" (for "pire" or "plus mauvais"). Odd poetic effects sometimes result from these insolent manipulations of speech, as in the celebrated lines of **"Reversibilities."**

> Ah, dans ces mornes séjours
> Les Jamais sont les Toujours!
>
> Ah, in these dreary abodes
> The Nevers are the Always!

Similar effects are achieved with other adverbs, "Encores" or "Déjàs," put in the plural like substantives.

The French reader is so accustomed to demanding a certain purity of tone and to taking offense in numerous ways at the mixing of the genres, that Verlaine's semivulgarisms clash with the need for dignity and even for formality that he brings to the reading of poets. Verlaine, without affectation and with a knowing dose of humor and poetic vision, as an amused observer of others than himself, achieves an almost unique success in nineteenth-century poetry in pieces like **"It's Jean de Nivelle's Dog"** or **"Brussels: Wooden Horses."** The symbolic meaning of this last piece does not have to be emphasized by the poet, desirous of losing himself in the circular motion. Adroitly, following a few lighthearted lines ("It's wonderful what a buzz you get, going to that silly circus"), in the final stanza he dares evoke poetically the coming of night that sees the departure of the soldier and the maidservant, their Sunday diversion at the carnival ended:

> Tournez, tournez! le ciel en velours
> D'astres en or se vêt lentement.
>
> Turn, turn! the sky, velvet-clad,
> Slowly adorns itself with golden stars.

He would later advise the poet to avoid "impure laughter," which French poets have traditionally—and quite regrettably—in fact avoided in their works, especially the romantics. But Verlaine in practice frequently accepted it and did not judge it impure. Laforgue, Apollinaire, and various "fantasy poets" of our century were not to forget this precedent.

But still more than in the area of language and style (although an in-depth study of Verlainian metaphors deserves to be undertaken and ought to prove rich in possibilities), it is through his metrics that the poet showed himself to be a sometimes innovator and a very great master. As early as 1931-32 a very keenly precise article by P. Mathieu in the *Revue d'Histoire littéraire* analyzed the various lasting changes that Verlaine had brought to French prosody, still timorous among the romantics (Hugo excepted) and with Baudelaire. A book by Eléonore Zimmermann, impressive in its sharp subtlety and its erudition, has analyzed Verlaine's work very closely in its musicality, its stylistic methods, as much as in its inspiration and its affinities with other forms of poetic expression, notably that of Rimbaud.

The example of his more deliberately revolutionary young friend, it is readily admitted, prompted the author of

Romances without Words (1873) to put behind him what had been facile and traditional in his previous collections. Verlaine himself, always generous in that regard, stated this to be the case. To tell the truth, it is not at all certain that the elder of the two poets, frightened by the audaciousness of the younger man, and especially by his theories (which he considered demoniacal), was not made more cautious because of that. Verlaine was already, before knowing Rimbaud, the author of Sapphic love poems published in Brussels in 1867 under a quite transparent pseudonym, and also of the collection entitled *Fêtes galantes,* judged by the schoolboy Rimbaud in Charleville, as early as August 25, 1870, "most strange, very odd and truly . . . adorable." Free verse, in any case, suited Verlaine no more than Mallarmé, Apollinaire, or Valéry, and he did not deceive himself on that score. Aggravated at the end of his career by the innovations of young poets who seemed to reject him, he spoke out as a conservative embittered against those who thus claimed "to lay a hand on verse."

More than any other, nevertheless, Verlaine worked to alter the profound character of the alexandrine by multiplying the number of ternary lines, by boldly varying the cesura, by accumulating odd run-on lines that broke out of the verse mold and came close to certain prose poems: dialogues with God or Christ in *Wisdom,* an astounding piece in the same volume that invokes the voices of Pride, Hate, and the Flesh in order to entreat them to die and to make way for the voice of Prayer and "the terrible Voice of Love." He will vilify rhyme in a celebrated line from his **"Art poétique."** The most skillful of rhymers (and the most discreet of them when he wanted to be), Verlaine makes light of rhyme at other times, forming couplets that end with the two words "choisi" and "quasi," "gai" and "guet," playing with bizarre words ("up-chucked" ["débagoulé"], "tribades"), in the hardly edifying **"Saturnian Poem"** from *In Parallel*. Above all, he modifies the alexandrine while rendering it more supple with such virtuosity that the ear no longer knows if it is hearing ten, eleven, or thirteen syllables or where the verse line, segmented by run-on lines and odd divisions, begins or ends. Verlainian metrics often seem to reject any kind of syllabication and are based on combinations of very expert stresses, so expert that they often fall on conjunctions or on particles astonished to find themselves thus ennobled. With a daring that few French poets have had, Verlaine took delight in composing poems made up of odd-syllable lines: five syllables ("In the Interminable," in which frequent recurrences of rhymes reinforces the impression of monotonous boredom), of seven or nine syllables (the former very frequent and most often admirably successful, as in **"Wooden Horses"** and **"Art poétique"**). But it is mastery of the eleven-syllable line, for example in the most grandiose of all Verlaine's poems (*Crimen Amoris*), and in the thirteen-syllable line (**"A Tale"** in *Love;* less happily in the pious poetry of 1893 that begins with "Little Jesus who already suffers in your flesh"). Often, running every risk, Verlaine triumphantly won. Ronsard had been able to endow certain heptasyllabic poems with a hesitant and seductive grace; but it is Verlaine who imposed upon French ears both this line and the nine-syllable line from this or that "forgotten arietta." After him, Frenchmen have recited "It is the langorous Ecstasy" or "I detect through a Murmur" quite as familiarly as though it were a matter of one of Villon's or Gautier's lines, or one from Baudelaire's "To Her Who Is too Gay." The very new stress combinations of the Verlainian hendecasyllables (two groups of four syllables and one of three in a number of lines from **Crimen Amoris**), the fragmentations of the verse line when the poet uses the article les to form the rhyme, the words that the article announces ("seven sins") being, for the eye alone, carried over to the following line, makes the poet the first in France who cannot be reduced to a system based on syllabic count. With him, French versification at last proclaims that it rests on individual combinations and not on a mechanical counting of syllables. Later in his career, the aged poet was to feel himself outdistanced by the young symbolists of 1885 and made fun of their innovations. But since Rimbaud was not known, and since Mallarmé remained a traditionalist in matters of versification, it was Verlaine who had made their attempts possible.

Verlaine's mind was without doubt not the most disposed to construct coherent and rigorous doctrines. Nonetheless, and paradoxically, no French poem in the latter quarter of the nineteenth century and for some years to come in the twentieth, not even Baudelaire's "Correspondences," has had more striking effect as a poetic manifesto than **"Art poétique,"** composed in 1873-74 and published in 1882 in a review and in 1885 in the volume *Long Ago and Not So Long Ago.* In that volume the poet sets forth, in the form of precepts (or rather of advice), what his work, from before 1873 (and even before he had known Rimbaud), had put into practice. Did he write it under Rimbaud's influence? It is generally stated that he did, but gratuitously, and without doubt by way of a too elementary simplification of the very mysterious concept of "influence." Other recollections that some have thought to find there (from Shakespeare's *Twelfth Night,* for example) are even more problematical. The piece, if worthwhile for its content and its doctrinal statements, is no less significant for the emotions with which it is charged (this defense of freedom and imagination by a prisoner) and for the exquisite art of its vocabulary and its rhythm. . . .

Verlaine states first of all, not in a didactic counsel but in an impassioned cry, the primacy of music in poetry, and foreshadows, without knowing it, the symbolists and their successors, Pierre Louÿs and Paul Valéry, who chose later to consider music as the rival necessary to despoil to the profit of poetry. Image, symbol, are at one blow relegated to a secondary level. This music will be above all that finer, newer one born of the odd-syllable line that melts away as did poor Lélian's will and that rejects pose and affectation, and weighty stability if, indeed, Verlaine meant to play with the double meaning of the verb *qui pose.* That kind of ambiguity Verlaine calls "misapprehension" ("méprise"), and he recommends it: it forces upon the reader an active way of reading that Mallarmé was soon to demand by asking the reader to seek out the

key to poetic mystery. In the very graceful third stanza, by way of three metaphorical evocations, Verlaine offers a few illustrations of this mystery while taking care himself, as one of the clearest of poets, to use the adjective *clear* ("clair"). For, Valéry was to say later, what is more obscure and more profound than clarity? In the same stanza, the adjective *trembling* ("tremblant") is no less important; beauty for the poet is inconceivable without mobility or without vibration.

Like the painters who, shortly after the composition of this poem, were in 1874 to take to themselves the term *impressionists,* by which people had thought to ridicule them, Verlaine forcefully lays claim to the nuance, mother of dreams and of soft spiritual harmonies in place of color. At the home of Nina de Villars, he had often encountered Manet who asserted: "The principal character of a painting is light." The prosaicness of the artful conceit and of clever wittiness is banished, though not that form of it that comes from recourse to the familiar that Verlaine practiced. Eloquence is vilified in the well-known outcry. Rhyme, which Verlaine in practice never renounced (although he may have treated it with disrespect), is condemned if it is too rich. Before everything else, let poetry be escape, adventure, unceasing aspiration towards the new: let it suggest, like music, the unexpressed; it does not reject precision, but prefers it to be limited and to serve as a foil to ambiguity.

This pursuit of vagueness that is "muted" ("en sourdine"—also the title of one of the poems from *Fêtes galantes*), of the half-light, of grisaille, or "morning twilight" ("crépuscule du matin," the orginal title of **"L'Angélus du matin"**) or of evening twilight—is quite another matter and much more than a technique for Verlaine. It translates his rejection of brutality, of the too-neat choice between the flesh and the soul, between angelism and the mire, between the drunken man's brutality and childlike gentleness, and even between one sex and the other. Verlaine's poems on lesbians are much more than an erotic game on a theme that Gautier, Baudelaire, and many others since Sappho had touched upon. The **"Songs of the Ingénues"** in Verlaine's first collection, these artless young women who know themselves to be "the future lovers of libertines," allude to the hero of sexual transvestitism, the gracious and cunning Faublas. Another piece, in *Les Fêtes galantes,* has as its title **"The Ingénus,"** male this time, but their words are "specious," the autumn evening is "equivocal," and even their sex is vague, as are the commentators of many poems who are undecided whether to read Mathilde or Arthur behind works like **"Forgotten Arietta"** or even **"Water Color,"** in which the author dreams of letting his head roll upon a young breast. In more than one domain, Verlaine spontaneously translates the deep secret of his vacillating nature by avoiding the clear-cut, the decisive, the choice that was later to disturb the Gide of *Fruits of the Earth* because it forces one to renounce what one has not chosen and some potentiality within oneself. In his old age, and like so many others turned conservative (Baudelaire, also weary, had indeed conceded to his younger friend Manet that he was foremost, but "in the decrepitude of his art"), Verlaine treated his **"Art poétique"** lightly in 1890, while sounding this warning—tinged however with a rare modesty—to the young: "Do not take my **'Art poétique'** at face value; after all it is only a song." At that time he made himself the apostle of common sense, especially against the dogmatic doctrines of the technicians. That **"Art poétique,"** so undidactic, so lilting and mocking, remains the only one still alive among the ten or fifteen poems of the same, or almost the same, title that, since Gautier and Mallarmé, French poets have written (Tristan Klingsor, Francis Jammes, Max Jacob, J.-M. Bernard, André Salmon, Jean Cocteau, André Spire, and various surrealists).

Around this period in his life, between 1871 and 1874, Verlaine was equally seminal in creating (or nearly so, if Victor Hugo's poems that can be called impressionist, such as "Evening Things" in *The Art of Being a Grandfather* are excepted), in the poetic domain, literary impressionism. Here again, his originality seems complete. He was scarcely touched by the example of Edmond and Jules de Goncourt, and very little by that of the painters, even those like Monet and Pissaro whom he might have been able to see in London in 1871 or in Ignace Fantin-Latour's studio. The very tempting and very dangerous parallels that critics strive periodically to propose between the three forms of impressionism—pictorial, musical, literary—do not help very much. The practitioners of these three art forms are conditioned by the techniques of expression, the medium, the autonomy peculiar to each of them. It is more natural to expect of the poet that he pierce or tear away the veil that he draws over reality or over the canvas on which he traces it, and touch upon the secret or the import that lies beyond. The exaggerated claims to the synthesis of the arts and to an ambitious and heady orphism count among the least fortunate aftereffects of the symbolist movement. The transpositions of art dear to Gautier and even the synesthetic effects described in the tercets of the celebrated Baudelairian sonnet scarcely went beyond the picturesque or the piquant. It would amount to a kind of purism, however, to seek to raise an insurmountable barrier between writers, painters, and musicians who, in Paris especially, live, discuss, and create in close proximity to one another. Prudently, in the last great article that he had written on Delacroix, Baudelaire had observed that the arts are incapable of taking one another's place, but that they could in our times "reciprocally lend one another new strengths."

Verlaine did not venture to formulate the theory of any certain literary impressionism. He wrote from London to Edmond Le Pelletier at the end of 1872, when he was making an effort to learn more about English art (for which he cared little, but which he was perhaps to like better in the long run): "In the meantime, like Mérat, I am collecting impressions." After so much classic, romantic, and Parnassian poetry that explained, proclaimed, reasoned, or, in any case, went beyond sensations, Verlaine, out of temperament, had preferred to let himself be lightly touched and sometimes invaded by landscapes and objects, refusing to interpret them or to ask them their secret. The frequency of expressions of his ignorance, of his uncertainty, of his refusal to know, is revealing:

"what?" "who?" "we don't know why," "I am unaware." Often he avoids organizing sketchy details in an ordered landscape, not from lack of skill, for he is the author of one of the best composed landscapes there is, in the very beautiful poem contained in the collection *Love,* **"Bournemouth,"** but because he wanted only to enumerate, to juxtapose, while omitting verbs and adjectives, as in the graceful Belgian landscape entitled **"Walcourt,"** composed in lines of four syllables with two tonic accents. Realism? Not precisely, for this reality is permeated with phantoms **"Charleroi"**); the sounds of wind, of some forge, the whistling of grass in cold blasts, trains that thunder, even odors; all of these are "sinister," and the poet renders this shuddering of things and of his entire being. Above all, everything there moves, runs, flees. Few poets have so well rendered in French this feeling of something ephemeral, disturbing, in which the self is dissolved, which Joseph Eichendorff, Nikolaus Lenau, or an impressionist like Edward Moerike have captured in the German language. **"Simple Frescoes"** in heptasyllables and in entirely feminine rhymes, in *Romances without Words,* is a slender, graceful, and disturbing masterpiece:

> La fuite est verdâtre et rose
> Des collines et des rampes,
> Dans un demi-jour de lampes
> Qui vient brouiller toute chose.

> The flight is greenish and pink
> Of hills and slopes,
> In a dim lamp's light
> That comes to confuse all things.

In *Romances without Words* as well, and also in heptasyllables, the untitled piece that opens with "The ordered ranks of the hedgerows" (**"L'Echelonnement des haies"**) is one of the most original works of Verlaine the impressionist. The verb *unfurls* ("moutonne") brings together from the start the plain dissected by hedgerows and the image of foamy waves. Everything is in movement—hills, trees, young horses in the fields, lambs, and the swirling rain. No feeling, no lament is suggested. The masterpiece of this type is doubtless "In the Interminable/Tedium of the plain," in pentasyllables. The word *tedium* ("ennui") brings together the impression received by the poet and the feeling of dreary monotony that weighs upon his soul. The blackness of the sky is interpreted through comparisons, to the moon, for example, that seems to live and die. The oaks appear to float like storm clouds in the grisaille that blends together sky and earth; the thoughts of the poet, who does not want to complain in his own name, transfers to imaginary animals, in the form of questions, his internal desolation. The real is grasped but never immobilized or materialized. Verlaine does not try to take hold of this reality as Rimbaud does, to incorporate it into a construction of his own like a demiurge recreating the world. He does not seek, like a voyant, to supplement it with a superreality. He translates the astonishment of his sometimes childlike soul and that headiness born of the void into which he feels himself perpetually upon the point of sinking. Beyond external notations that are a form of realism (but a magic realism in the manner of the German romantics), one denotes Verlaine's effort to forget himself, to escape life's wounds and his feeling of guilt—from before the time of the pistol shot and the prison at Mons.

It would be idle to exaggerate the similarities between Verlaine the poet and this or that one among the painters who were his contemporaries. He is not, like them, a colorist; he does not have their luminosity or the serene patience of their attention to the out-of-doors. More than they, he feels himself to be a musician and inclined towards gently soothing reveries. There is in truth a literary impressionism that runs parallel to the need to harden and stiffen reality that was typical of Flaubert and Maupassant. The Goncourts are the prose authors who had the clearest awareness of it and who, in passages that one would prefer to isolate from the rest of their work, have given remarkable samples of it in prose. Mallarmé, as early as March 1865, wrote to Henri Cazalis, alluding to his "Hérodiade": "I have discovered there an intimate and unique way of sketching and noting very fugitive impressions." Hugo, we know, called him, in a surprisingly exact remark: "My dear impressionist poet." There are those who sometimes seek to limit Verlainian impressionism to a brief period in his career—1872-74—and to convince themselves that afterwards he went beyond it. He certainly changed, and he understood the danger of monotony that that kind of art runs. But there remains much of this feeling of the fluidity of all things and of what is elusive, in poems from which neither the inner life nor feelings in which impressions complement one another are banished. Other than the very well-known sonnet of the summer of 1873, "Hope gleams . . . " (*Wisdom*), in which impressions and discreet symbols are wedded (a piece of straw that is perhaps grace, a wasp that could be woman, consoling water, the pebble in a hollow place), several of Verlaine's most beautiful poems are still impressionistic, but composed rather than juxtaposed and incorporating within them the dramatic element of time that flies and that overlays impressions of the present with nostalgia for the past and anguish before the future. We would include among these poems that ought to be the very first to represent Verlaine in an anthology of French impressionistic poetry: **"The Morning Angelus"** from *Long Ago and Not So Long Ago* (published under a different title in the first issue of *Le Parnasse Contemporain*), **"Kaleidoscope"** from the same collection that dates from the prison years (October 1873), and, later, that subtle poem on the imagination that bears the title **"Limbo"** in *In Parallel* (1889).

Artists and art critics who, around 1885, turned away from pictorial impressionism, like the very remarkable and short-lived Albert Aurier, reproached it with being a surface art, a kind of realism too slavishly submissive to the visible appearance and the color of things and landscapes, uninterested in the absolute and in being. The pursuit of that absolute and the disdain for the concrete and the fleshly did not always succeed, moreover, for the English pre-Raphaelites, for the philosophical painters of Germany, or even for Gustave Moreau, Odilon Redon, and Puvis de Chavennes in their less good moments. But if, in effect, the absence of the tragic can be deplored among painters such as Monet, Renoir, or Alfred Sisley (whose daily existence amid poverty and among general incomprehension nonetheless skirted tragedy more than once), this reproach cannot be addressed to Verlaine. More than Rimbaud, who was less gnawed by remorse and less haunted by the flesh than Verlaine, more than Mallarmé whose torment was metaphysical and literary, Verlaine lived tragically; it is he who could most accurately be seen as a parallel to Van Gogh. **"Kaleidoscope," "Bournemouth,"** and **"There,"** another poem inspired by the section of London called "Angels," stand among the greatest poems in French of throbbingly painful memories, of anguish, and of visionary dreams welling up out of reality. In the first of these pieces, past and future are confounded in an irresistible whirlwind, as often in Verlaine. The setting is that of the large city that had fascinated the two friends vagabonding among the streets of the British metropolis, though here it is a "dream city," a "magic city" (lines one and nine). The rupture, the one's scorn for the pitiful "mad virgin," the other's exasperation, and, then, his "cellular" life emerge. Will he be able to relive the past? "A slow awakening after many metempsychoses?" The poet sees again in his mind the vulgarity of the city and its hideous festivities, which were nonetheless dear to him; of the future he expects nothing. He calls upon death, but directly, without romantic rhetoric. Will it be the awakening from a dream, the dream of life, "life's unquiet dream" to use Shelley's phrase? Then, again, the descent into the dream and into the same pitiable weaknesses?

> Ce sera comme quand on rêve et qu'on s'éveille,
> Et que l'on se rendort et que l'on rêve encor
> De la même féerie et du même décor,
> L'été, dans l'herbe, au bruit moiré d'un vol
>   d'abeille.

> That will be as when one dreams and when one
>   awakens
> And goes back to sleep and dreams once again
> Of the same fairy tale and the same setting
> In the summertime, in the grass, to the
>   shimmering hum of a flight of bees.

The word *kaleidoscope* contains within itself the adjective that signifies "beautiful," and Verlaine tried to see as beautiful, through the darkness of what lay in wait for him, his dream of the future. He cannot believe in it. He knows himself to be the slave of his destiny, and he bows his head. "It will be so ineluctable that one will think to die of it." A few years later, he wrote **"Bournemouth,"** when he was teaching in England. In his *Confessions* of 1894, he recalled that visit and the landscape. Modestly, he added: "I also wrote an entirely insignificant poem, entitled '**Bournemouth**,' that people are quite pleased to find good." Octave Nadal was to say correctly of that admirable work, which is symbolist in more ways than one: "It is the roar, the death rattle, and the stubbornness of the sea that find their correspondences in the tortured and patient heart of the poet." Claudel, who had had the courage in his youth, when it was not fashionable to do so, to celebrate Verlaine, declared in his later days (in his *Improvised Mémoirs* from his eighty-second year) that this poem was "one of the most beautiful pieces of French poetry." With a worthy independence of taste, he added, rightly in our eyes, that it was not in his Catholic collection, *Wisdom,* but in *Love* (published in 1888) that Verlaine had attained the summit of his art.

"There," from the same collection, entirely stamped with the memories of London, and transpierced by the passage of grace while he recalls his "old sins," a symbolist poem in its own way, is discreetly haunted by Rimbaud's memory. It is in the twenty or so poems that form the Rimbaud cycle that Verlaine attains the tragic. These pieces range from a few ariettas from the beginning of their liasion to the most immodest lines, **"Verses for Being Vilified,"** and **"Lusts"** in *Long Ago and Not so Long Ago,* and to the two pathetic sonnets of *Dedications* (1890), addressed to Rimbaud (the second, inserted later in *Dedications,* is from 1893) **"Mortal, Angel AND Demon," "You, dead, dead, dead."**

People have evinced distaste for certain of these poems. There are those, in fact, like numbers IV, V, and VI of the **"Old Coppées,"** interlarded with slang and very free in their language, that wallow in obscenity. The inverse sonnet **"The Good Disciple"** flaunts insolently, as no poem in any other language has dared, the physical ecstasy sought by the two companions. But the very brutality of that frankness which seeks to make a display of itself only barely hides Verlaine's secret remorse, recalling past pleasures and knowing with what regrets and what abandonment they were followed. **"Laeti et errabundi"** is a poem otherwise radiant with beauty in its boasting. Verlaine, so feminine himself, and whom the need for feminine tenderness and understanding always pursued, takes pleasure in crying out his disdain for orthodox love: " . . . detached / From women taken pity upon / And from the last of prejudices." No doubt he is echoing certain of the mocking remarks about his need for women and grace, and on the subject of his very real suffering at the time of his divorce, that his young partner must have often repeated. The piece is swept away by an inflamed outburst; it closes with the admirable verses in which the poet celebrates his forever absent friend as a "god among the demigods" and refuses to believe him dead. "He lives his life," and that exalting love burns his veins and radiates in his brain. Verlainian eroticism is one of the most ardent and the most splendidly expressed in all literature, equaled by neither the Marquis de Sade nor Jean Genêt in prose nor Victor Hugo or Pierre Louÿs in poetry. Verlaine is the poet of the flesh, as he was at other times and in other pieces, the poet of virginal reveries and of the soul's longings.

But this exaltation of the flesh is very far from being joy alone. Verlaine knows that desire is insatiable, and he recalls this in another very beautiful piece of insolent avowal ("These passions they alone still call love"); he boasts of being the apostle of that reinvented love. He knows as well, however, the weariness and disgust of both rapture and sensual satisfaction. In his boldest collection, *In Parallel,* he included two sonnets of **"Explanation"** in which he confessed "satiety to be an obscene

machine," and a **"Saturnian poem"** in which he depicts himself sinking into the mire, jeered at by hooligans in the street, fallen to the lowest degree of abject humiliation.

It is in certain ones of these poems from the Rimbaud cycle that Verlaine reached the depths and the summit of the tragic, on a par with Baudelaire, and better than any other poet from what is called the symbolist movement. It has become fashionable to declare as outmoded the verse tale, of which Musset, Keats, and Matthew Arnold in England had given some very fine examples. It is not even certain that these verse tales, a kind of indirect lyricism avoiding the self and its laments, may not be preferable, in Musset's case, to the "Nights" and "Hope in God." More than one poetry lover, rejecting passing fashions, may have regretted that French symbolism and its immediate successors should have abandoned poetic domains where free rein could be given to narrative account, drama, inventive fantasy, and humor. Poetry did not as a matter of course gain anything in being reduced to lapidary aphorisms and to abrupt discontinuity. To be sure, some banalities slip into the hundreds of alexandrines of **"Grace"** or **"Final Impenitence"** (*Long Ago and Not so Long Ago*.) But Verlaine embodies therein the torment that is his during those years when he is unable to resign himself to the abandon upon which Rimbaud has decided and to bury his memories of complete joy experienced with him. The claims of the flesh are less plainspoken than in the more directly personal and vulgar pieces in the late-published collection, *Flesh,* in which the poet wants to make himself believe that the pagan times regretted by Lucretius can be reborn, the bodies of lovers embracing one another in the forests like does and stags. The battle between the Devil and salvation, the headiness of knowing oneself to be damned, and the vague feeling that it is to the damned (as in the novels of François Mauriac and Julien Green) that grace prefers to go, renders these tales lugubrious and tragic. **"Don Juan Duped,"** in decasyllables, shouts blasphemies: "The Flesh is holy, we must worship it," and contains something of the fearful boldness within revolt of Balzac's novella *The Elixir of Long Life.* But the masterpiece of the genre, and perhaps Verlaine's masterpiece, is the great symbolic and apocalyptic poem to which he gave the Latin title **"Crimen amoris."** Verlaine recounted in *My Prisons* how he composed this diabolical tale in the early days of his incarceration, using a small piece of wood and on paper having served to wrap his meager food ration. He later reworked it a great deal. Some Baudelairian memory wandered about his brain when he incarnated in his sixteen-year-old friend (Verlaine several times attributed that age to the urchin-genius who invaded his life in 1871) the most beautiful of angels, Lucifer. In an oriental palace in the midst of an orgy where the Seven Deadly Sins flaunt themselves, during the course of an enchanted night, the adolescent suddenly appears. There, he cries out impudently his rebellious will against conventional morality, against narrow and timorous love, against God: "Oh, I shall be he who will create God!" He wants to marry the Seven Deadly Sins to the Three Theological Virtues, good and evil, heaven and hell. He lights an immense cauldron

Verlaine in 1892.

of fire in which "Satan, his brothers and his sisters" die as (in certain of the *Illuminations*) the victims of the capricious prince die. He offers to some new and maleficent divinity this sacrificial conflagration.

Punishment comes in a lugubrious twilight of the gods and of men. "The sacrifice had not been accepted." Verlaine cries out the terror that his friend's monstrous pride inspired in him. In a very beautiful finale, the night becomes once again serene, an "evangelical" softness (Verlaine used this adjective) has succeeded the harsh Rimbaldian colors: black, red, gold. Nature once again at peace "professes / The clement God who will guard us from evil." Verlaine, fraught with fear, aspires to punishment and peace. He cannot brace himself to go beyond "morality, that weakness of the intellect" vilified by his friend, and resolutely bypass the distinction between good and evil, the better and the worse. He already senses the submission, if not the denial, to which his friend was to resign himself, far from the Western world, and, on his deathbed, having perhaps murmured childishly, "Then, it was evil." The form of the poem of twenty-five stanzas (one less than the "Femmes damnées" of Baudelaire of which it makes one think), Verlaine's most brilliantly colored and most dramatic, and the originality of his

hendecasyllabic lines divided after the fourth syllable, then after the seventh—sometimes the sixth—make it the most successful of Verlaine's works and perhaps the most tragic of all the poetry that is called symbolist.

Enid Rhodes Peschel (essay date 1981)

SOURCE: An introduction to *Four French Symbolist Poets: Baudelaire, Rimbaud, Verlaine, Mallarmé,* translated by Enid Rhodes Peschel, Ohio University Press, 1981, pp. 1-65.

[*In the following excerpt, Peschel presents a detailed analysis of two of Verlaine's poems, "Moonlight" and "Crimen Amoris," describing tensions that exist beneath the calm surface of the text.*]

"Your soul is a selected landscape," Verlaine begins **"Moonlight,"** the first of the lovely and unsettling, happy and sad, populated and lonely poems of his *Fêtes galantes*. This poem, which sets the ambiguous scene for that entire book, is emblematic of much of Verlaine's other poetry as well:

> Your soul is a selected landscape that maskers
> And bergamasche go about beguiling

Playing the lute and dancing and quasi
Sad beneath their fantastical disguises.

While singing in the minor mood
Triumphant love and life that is opportune,
They do not seem to believe in their good
    fortune
And their song mingles with the moonlight,

With the calm moonlight sad and beautiful,
That makes the birds dream in the trees
And the fountains weep with ecstasy,
The great svelte fountains amid the marble
    statues.

Here, a landscape and a soulscape are equated. Perceptions in Verlaine's poetry are paramount, for just as a person's soul reflects or incorporates a "selected landscape," so a landscape will reflect or incorporate the person perceiving it. The soul in the first stanza is another person's soul (a woman's soul, perhaps, or perhaps *your* soul, the reader's soul, as you enter this world of gallant festivals). But that soul also reflects, in some profound and important ways, the poet's soul, for it is he who is depicting its inner depths. In that soul, the site of a masked ball, people are actors and dancers, "maskers and bergamasche." Their masks, which both conceal what they are and reveal what they might like to be or what they play at being, suggest theater and artifice, charm and disguise, enchantment and deceit. Are these phantomlike figures only acting the roles of lovers, or do they—or can they—love in reality? The word "bergamasche" is richly suggestive. While Verlaine seems to imply dancers by it, the word actually means some fast dances (or the music for those dances) similar to the tarantella, the rapid, whirling southern Italian dance for couples. "Bergamasche" therefore evoke exoticism, eroticism, and a whirling, swirling frenzy: the kind of dizzy, intoxicating and disequilibriating motion in which Verlaine so often delights (e.g. see **"Mandolin"** and **"Brussels: Merry-Go-Round"**).

Subtly now, indications of malaise are insinuated. The actors, dancers and musicians "go about beguiling" the soul they inhabit, enchanting, captivating and charming it for good—but perhaps for evil. Suddenly a chill ripples through. For the end of the first stanza reveals that amid all the charm and gaiety of the masked ball, the gallant figures are "quasi / Sad beneath their fantastical disguises." Words about seeming, that by their nature question the existence and very essence of what is seen and what is said, are one of the hallmarks of Verlaine's poetry. For him, things rarely *are;* instead, they *seem to be,* which means that they almost always suggest the lurking presence of something else, of something alien perhaps, or even opposite. These figures, clothed in their "disguises," seem sad, almost sad. What are they disguising? Are they really sad, or is that the poet's projection of himself onto the scene? In any case, a note of melancholy is sounded here. Too, the word "fantastical" insinuates a disturbing tone, for while it means fantastic—of the mind or the imagination—it also may imply something strange, or weird or grotesque.

In the second stanza, the poet continues his impressionistic medley of sights that are both precise and hazy, and of sounds that are simultaneously soothing and unsettling. Now the nature of everything evoked is questioned, for although the figures sing what would seem to be victorious, favorable and timely ("Triumphant love and life that is opportune"), still they sing these "in the minor mood," suggesting the melancholy and plaintive sounds associated with the minor key. Once again, a motif of seeming questions everything. Phrased now in a negative way ("They do not seem to believe in their good fortune"), the words cast doubt not only on the singers' feelings, but also on the nature of their fortune.

Finally, their song mingles with the moonlight: the microcosm of this soul inhabited by people and a landscape mingles fully with the macrocosm—with the universe, with "the calm moonlight sad and beautiful." The word "calm," like motifs of seeming, is a key word for Verlaine, a word that almost invariably veils an underlying malaise or frenzy, at times even a feeling of despair. "Calm" is often a mask or veil that Verlaine uses to cover, or to try to cover, a face of anguish. "Calm in the twilight that / The high branches make above, / With this profound silence let's / Completely imbue our love," he begins **"With Muted Strings,"** another of the *Fêtes galantes* which, like several poems in that collection, proceeds from ostensible calm to a cry of anguish: "And when the solemn evening / Falls from the black oaks, / Voice of our hopelessness, / The nightingale will sing."

The moonlight in **"Moonlight"** is at once "sad and beautiful": beauty for Verlaine implies the presence of sadness. So, too, does his notion of "ecstasy," for the very intensity of this emotional rapture leads inevitably to its loss (see, for example, **"Mandolin," "With Muted Strings"** and **"Sentimental Colloquy"**). In **"Moonlight,"** where "the fountains weep with ecstasy," the trancelike state is so overpowering that the joy expresses itself in tears: tears of rapture that recall sorrow and pain.

This brief examination of **"Moonlight"** suggests that Verlaine's poetry, which might appear calm or simple on the surface, is actually much more complex, extremely rich in underlying tensions and implications. Even such an apparently carefree piece as **"Streets"** (a poem inspired by Verlaine's and Rimbaud's stay in London) contains an inner anguish, despite its exclamatory refrain sounded five times, "Let's dance the jig!" For, from the poet's evocation of the woman's "mischievous eyes," to his exclaiming that the way she had of "making a poor lover grieve" was "really . . . charming indeed!", to his recalling in the last stanza that the times and talks they had had together were the "best" of his "possessions," certain impressions of pain and of melancholy have filtered through. When the refrain is sounded a final time after the last stanza, the poet's call to dance the jig seems like an attempt to shake off, by means of this fast, gay and springy dance, the loneliness, nostalgia and sadness that have been welling within him. "The desired lightness of motion and emotion is there; but almost inadvertently, the presence of thought, tinged by regret, has been insinuated. 'Let's dance the jig' contains at the end an echo of remembrance more than an invitation to joy," writes Henri Peyre [in *French Symbolist Poetry*].

The incessant interplay between quiet and disquiet continues throughout Verlaine's poetry, contributing to its uniqueness and its melancholy beauty, and to its powers to enchant and to disturb. Thus, *"Crimen amoris,"* one of Verlaine's most fascinating and ambitious poems, modulates from a swirling and violently agitated vision into a melodious and peaceful soulscape at the end. It is almost as though for Verlaine the excess of one emotion calls for, and must be balanced by, its opposite. But for the reader well-attuned to the ceaseless struggles going on in Verlaine's tortured psyche, the calm vision at the end of *"Crimen amoris"* contains echoes of the agitations that preceded and—we know from Verlaine's life—would follow.

"Crimen amoris" is Verlaine's one-hundred-line vision of Rimbaud as a sixteen-year-old prophet, an "evil" angel, a "Satan," who also, in certain ways, resembles Jesus. It is written in lines of eleven syllables, a rhythm that is somewhat jarring to the French reader reared on classical alexandrines. But just because of the line's unevenness and its sense of imbalance, the *vers impair* is so well suited to this poem and to Verlaine's equivocal nature.

The "crime" takes place in Persia, in Ecbatana (the ancient name of Hamadan in present-day Iran). The location adds exotic, mythical and religious dimensions to the tale. As the poem opens, "Beautiful demons, adolescent Satans," celebrate "the festival of the Seven Sins." Their glorification of sensuous and sensual pleasures ("ô how beautiful / It is! All desires beamed in brutal fires") is, of course, a rebellion against the church. Their festival, as described lyrically, excitedly—delightedly—by the poet, is melodious, amorous, luxurious, and filled with "Goodness." Verlaine's words capture its splendor, rapture, fierceness and excitement, its tender erotic ecstasies that bring on tears, its cosmic proportions and powers of enchantment:

> Dances to the rhythms of epithalamiums
> Were swooning in long sobs quite tenderly
> And beautiful choirs of men's and women's
>   voices
> Were rolling in, palpitating like waves of the
>   sea,
>
> And the Goodness that issued from these things
>   was so potent
> And so charming that the countryside
> Around adorned itself with roses
> And night appeared in diamond.

In stanza 5, Rimbaud, "the handsomest of all those evil angels," appears. Because he is deeply distressed, the other Satans try to cheer him. Finally, in stanzas 10-14, he addresses them, proclaiming a "gospel of blasphemy" that is at the same time a "metaphysical rebellion." "'Oh! I

will be the one who will create God!'" he begins his scandalous and prophetic pronouncements. He then delineates his dream of abolishing the concept of sin, for sins, he says, will henceforth be rejoined to virtues. And he announces that he will sacrifice himself—make himself sacred thereby—for the sake of others, and for the sake of "universal Love": "'through me now hell / Whose lair is here sacrifices itself to universal love!'" This, therefore, is his "Crime of Love": his vision of a new and revolutionary Love, of a total and completely unrestricted Love, of a Love that is universal, all-embracing, erotic, emotional and spiritual. But this Love is also a rebellion that implies, among other things, Verlaine's and Rimbaud's homosexual love. It is a physical and metaphysical revolt against the teachings of Catholicism, and so is a "crime" in the eyes of society and the church. The title is, therefore, an indictment against Rimbaud (and Verlaine). But it may also be interpreted as an indictment against the church and state that condemn a complete and free and universal Love.

The sacrifice, flame-licked, tortured, but exalted, begins in stanzas 15-18, with repeated intimations that death and destruction are imminent as the other Satans follow their visionary prophet:

> And the dying Satans were singing in the
>   flames. . . .
>
>   . . . . .
>
> And he, with his arms crossed in a haughty air,
> With his eyes on the sky where the licking fire
>   climbs along,
> He recites in a whisper a kind of prayer,
> That will die in the gaiety of the song.

Suddenly, the song ends, for "Someone had not accepted the sacrifice." Everything is then destroyed, and all becomes "but a vain and vanished dream . . . " (stanza 21). But does that dream really disappear?

The four last stanzas are lyrical and calm, a gentle song after the exploding visions in the twenty-one that preceded. Yet calmness in Verlaine's poetry is so often a veil cast over an inner agitation that one cannot but wish to look more closely here. In stanza 22, the entire ambiance is veiled, wavering, almost palpitating; something seems to be rising from just below the surface. One senses a soul behind the scene. The plain is "evangelical," "severe and peaceful." The word "severe" might indicate an underlying strain. The tree branches, "vague like veils," suggest angels—or ghosts. They also "look like wings waving about," intimating angels' wings perhaps, or perhaps wings of birds that wish to fly—to flee.

In the next stanza, all seems calm. "The gentle owls float vaguely in the air / Quite embalmed with mystery and with prayer." But the word "embalmed" . . . suggests, along with sweet scents, intimations of death. "At times a wave that leaps hurls a flash of lightning." This sentence at the end of the stanza startles: its fire is reminiscent of the flames of the Satanic festival.

In stanza 24, a "soft shape" rises from the hills "Like a love defined unclearly still, / And the mists that from the ravines ascend / Seem an effort towards some reconciled end." In the context of Verlaine's other poetry, the word "seem" is somewhat troubling. While here it seeks to define nature in terms of the divine, still the word does raise a question, for it is certainly possible that the mists might not *be* "an effort towards some reconciled end."

The last stanza is clearly an invocation to Christ—a "heart," and a "soul," and a "word" (the Word), and a "virginal love":

> And all that like a heart and like a soul,
> And like a word, and with a virginal love,
> Adores, expands in an ecstasy and beseeches
> The merciful God who will keep us from evil.

The word "ecstasy" is used here in its religious sense, but for Verlaine, as we saw earlier, the notion of ecstasy leads almost invariably to feelings of loss, or pain or sadness. Two other words clearly inject some uneasiness into the apparently serene soulscape of this last stanza: "beseeches" ("réclame") and "evil" ("[le] mal"). The word "beseeches" stresses urgency and need. It means "to ask for earnestly," "to implore" and "to beg for." This is a heartfelt and a pressing prayer. One senses at this point the poet's profoundest longings for peace and for a pure love: for a "virginal love" that would counter the "crime of love," and for a "virginal love" that would be free from sexuality. The poet's calling upon God to help him in his distress is typical of Verlaine's religious poetry. It is also significant, I believe, that he does not beseech a "God who will lead us to good" but rather a "God who will keep us from evil." This is, in the closing quiet of **"Crimen amoris,"** a muffled cry of anguish. The fact that Verlaine ends his poem on the word "evil" suggests that "evil" will continue to torment—and to attract—him. In fact, judging from the length of the poem, and from the beauty and power of the description of the Satanic festival, that "evil" undoubtedly continued to allure Verlaine, even as he wrote the poem and sought to condemn the "Crime of Love."

Verlaine's poems mediate ceaselessly therefore, between gaiety and sadness, hope and fear, quiet and disquiet. It is as though just below their melodious and apparently simple surfaces, a silent scream is waiting to be released. In his poetry, as Festa-McCormick notes, "The tragic shows through the surface, as it shows through the surface in certain impressionist paintings or in Watteau's so melancholy picture ["The Embarkation for Cythera"] in which the voyagers seem sadly satiated or disenchanted with the pleasure for which they are embarking." Verlaine's moods and language, his mysterious music "with muted strings," his choice of rhythms, rhymes and words that continually question the scene's—and therefore the soul's—serenity, combine to create a state of uneasy calm, a vision of happiness or pleasure that may be undermined at any moment. One can sense in Verlaine's poetry, as in his life, both control and loss of control. For his soulscapes

are permeated with a kind of restless repose and with tremors of the ephemeral or otherworldly which seek to convey calm or hope or joy, but which almost invariably insinuate hidden presences of pain or sorrow, as well. And always in Verlaine's poetry there is "Music before anything else. . . . " Never overpowering or thunderous in its orchestration, his music, lute-like, or like the music of other stringed instruments, is melodious, lyrical and seductive, an integral part of his poetry of moods and sensations. Through its sounds and its rhythms, his poetry filters into you, caresses you, possesses you, lulls you and disturbs you, subtly. You are taken into its beauty and its uneasiness, almost unawares. Verlaine's malaise, through his music, becomes your own disquietude. And his poetry, that "One wants to think caressing . . . both delights / And distresses simultaneously."

Susan Taylor-Horrex (essay date 1988)

SOURCE: "Impossible Lands: Themes in *Fêtes galantes*" and "Themes in *Romances sans paroles*," in *Verlaine: "Fêtes galantes" and "Romances sans paroles,"* Grant & Cutler Ltd., 1988, pp. 24-63.

[*Below, Taylor-Horrex analyzes the themes of love, active versus passive modes of loving, and irresponsibility versus responsibility in Verlaine's collections of verse* Fêtes galantes *and* Romances sans paroles.]

In essence, Verlaine's poems treat the theme of the divided self: in **Fêtes galantes** the passive versus the active self, in **Romances sans paroles** the irresponsible versus the responsible self. As such, **Fêtes galantes** and **Romances sans paroles** take a different approach from **La Bonne Chanson** and **Sagesse** which treat the theme of the weak self to be saved, respectively, by marriage to Mathilde [Mauté] and returning to God, and where the conflict is somewhat externalised. With **Fêtes galantes** and **Romances sans paroles** the conflict remains firmly located within the poet's self.

Not surprisingly then, in comparison with these other collections, **Fêtes galantes** and **Romances sans paroles** have a predominantly emotional rather than intellectual content.

Fêtes galantes and **Romances sans paroles** deal with the theme of the divided self specifically in the area of love. In an important respect all the poems in the collections treat love. It is the central theme. Some poems present a related theme but this always refers back, directly or indirectly, to the dominant theme of love. The thematic pattern of both collections is, then, multidimensional as distinct from exclusively linear and progressive.

This is not to say that the thematic presentation is static, a random assortment of emotional moods. Both collections present a range of shifting emotional nuances, and both collections are shaped by an evolution in the nature of Verlaine's conflict with himself and consequently in his way of loving. The development from passive versus active self to a clearer confrontation of the irresponsible with the responsible self (already hinted at in *Fêtes galantes*) will equally be the argument of my discussion of the themes of *Fêtes galantes* and *Romances sans paroles*. Change is rarely satisfyingly straightforward. We often come full circle before we are able to move forward. And change does not necessarily mean improvement. This is perhaps the deepest exemplification of Verlaine's *other* 'art poétique', 'L'art, mes enfants, c'est d'être absolument soi-même.' . . .

In *Fêtes galantes* there are three distinct aspects; echoes of the paintings of [Antoine] Watteau and of the poetry of Hugo, and the themes of love and passivity. I shall consider these aspects as three 'layers' in the poems and show that, in a small number of poems, these three layers merge so as to be indistinguishable. This kind of merging, I believe, is the hallmark of Verlaine's distinctive poetry, a form of pure poetry, which creates its own world and terms of reference and is the vital link with Verlaine's poetic art of the finest poems of *Romances sans paroles*.

In one important respect the title of *Fêtes galantes* is its theme, for it denotes the complex nature of the detached perspective on love, that least detached of emotions. Verlaine's title is commonly attributed to the influence of Watteau's eighteenth-century genre of painting of the same name, and to Victor Hugo's poem, "La Fête chez Thérèse" (*Les Contemplations,* I, 22, 1840, published 1856). Watteau (1684-1721) is credited with having developed the genre of the *fête galante*. Broadly speaking, by the beginning of the eighteenth century, the *fête galante* was an idealised country scene peopled by aristocratic figures, originally the new élite of the city which, under the Regency, and in rivalry with the court after the death of Louis XIV, went to the 'country' (in reality the Paris suburbs) to 'commune with nature'. . . .

Watteau's art enjoyed a revival of interest in the midnineteenth century; Hugo, [Théodore] Banville, [Théophile] Gautier and especially Baudelaire responded to it. The revival was doubtless one element of the more general reaction against an age of materialism, of bourgeois mediocrity, the impulse towards the lowest common denominator of imaginative understanding. It was after all the age which could prosecute *Les Fleurs du mal* and *Madame Bovary*. Poems on the *fête galante* theme were also written by Banville, Gautier and Baudelaire. It is well documented that Verlaine enjoyed Watteau's painting and, especially, responded to the Goncourt brothers' [Edmond and Jules] studies of eighteenth-century art. . . .

[An] underlying assumption of *Fetes galantes* is the notion of the mask which conceals the feeling person. . . . Above all the onlooking Pierrot of Watteau's painting encapsulates Verlaine's own distancing of himself from the world of emotions which is the substance of *Fêtes galantes*. Indeed a number of critics have traced the probable pictorial originals of some of Verlaine's *Fête galante* poems. What matters of course is what Verlaine made of these and doubtless other related inspirations. Clearly he

responded to the Watteau who used the artifice of the *fête galante* to explore essential and natural truths of the human condition. Obviously this 'impersonality' would appeal to a young poet still closely identified with the Parnassian movement. Watteau's figures appear to seek harmonious happiness with the right partners; some succeed, some fail. The couples, partners in dance and song, symbolise the psychological truths of harmony and fulfilment; the distant, isolated figures, the absence of this fulfilment. The apparently lighthearted *fête galante* mode explores with complete seriousness the life of the emotions. The paradox does not stop here. This life itself brings with it numerous ambiguities. The very artificiality which has revealed these essential human truths and aspirations also asks the spectator such questions as 'can these scenes of harmony be trusted; is such harmony possible, and if so, how long does it last?' The apparent *légèreté* of the paintings, an aspect too readily seized upon and used to dismiss Watteau, *is* only apparent. We have only to consider the central female figure in L'Embarquement pour Cythère moving away from the island, her head turned wistfully towards the paradise she is leaving, to understand this.

Verlaine responded, then, to Watteau's use of the impersonal stylised mode as a means of seriously exploring the intensely personal world of love and its disappointments. Watteau achieves an impersonal, some would say objective, means of studying that which is most personal. He gave Verlaine an example of how he might usefully distance himself from the emotions he knows most intimately; usefully because in *Fêtes galantes* the emotional confusion is located in the conflict between active and passive modes of loving. . . .

I suggest that *Fêtes galantes* can be considered as a coherent collection of poems with a definite structure, that of an emotional life, much as we find in Hugo's *Les Contemplations* or Baudelaire's *Les Fleurs du mal*. The first and last poems of *Fêtes galantes* ("Clair de lune" and "Colloque sentimental") function as a kind of framework to the ever-changing picture of emotional life on the canvas of the remaining twenty poems. These two poems operate to achieve a 'distance' comparable to that of Watteau's paintings. This is in no way a verbal transcription of Watteau's mode of painting. "Clair de lune" is, literally, a scene setter. All the main elements of the collection are present in this poem and indeed the first line 'Votre âme est un paysage choisi', is the key to the collection. Firstly, the landscape is identified with the soul, the poet's and, quite possibly, our own. The scenes depicted in the remaining poems will ultimately be statements about the poet's and our own emotional landscape. Secondly, it is a 'paysage *choisi*'; it has a particularity, a uniqueness, a stylisation; in short, an artificiality which will permit an exploration of the natural life of the emotions. . . .

[In] **"Clair de lune"** a stylised world is established, one which is then further transformed. This is the artificial, transfigured, self-enclosed *fête galante* world of which the remaining poems are a part. Never again are we reminded that this world is the poet's/our own soul. We are invited once and for all to enter fully into this world.

"Colloque sentimental" repeats the ambiguity of the opening poem. One of the characters in the dialogue appears to doubt that any part of the couple's experience of 'bonheur' ever happened. At the very least s/he does not remember. There is additional uncertainty: the characters seem like ghosts; and by whom are they overheard? It is not altogether certain they *were* heard. All might equally have been imagined by the poet/reader. In this sense, then, the poem casts a further ambiguity, this time retrospective, over the entire collection. The suggestive power of the emotions is all the stronger for this uncertainty. In a sense the very quality of our existence is put in doubt. So equally there may be a move back on the part of the disbelieving character from the enclosed *fête galante* world to a familiar reality. We seek refuge from uncertainty in the certain reality of disbelief. An emotional shift such as this is entirely appropriate to what is ultimately a thematic ambiguity.

Each of the poems [in *Fêtes galantes*] deals with love from a particular angle. In fact the themes, that is, emotional attitudes towards love, cover a very wide range, from lighthearted enjoyment to despairing isolation. Moreover, these related themes are dealt with in groups of poems, so that a number of aspects of the same theme are offered in a kaleidoscopic presentation. "Pantomime" and "Sur l'herbe" give a specifically lighthearted picture of the playfulness of relationships, in Watteauesque terms. The *commedia dell'arte* characters engage in the playful stages of 'l'amour naissant'. Colombine, in "Pantomime", feels love dawning. The lover in "Sur l'herbe" indulges in the stock language of adoring the loved one. This lightheartedness is picked up later in "En bateau."

In "L'Allée", "A la promenade", "Dans la grotte", "Cortège" and "Les Coquillages", Verlaine intensifies this idealised love game into a stylised sensual idealism which includes the erotic. "L'Allée" offers a detailed portrait of a woman loosely based on the *blason* device, used in the sixteenth century and dating back, via the poets of the Middle Ages, to Antiquity. It is a device whereby a woman's beauty is detailed from head to toe. . . .

In "A la promenade" the poem following "L'Allée", the same scene is entered more intimately, for it is presented from the point of view of one of the lovers. . . .

"Dans la grotte" employs consciously archaic eighteenth-century poetic diction to express the lover's complete submission to the pain of love in this idealised love world. . . .

"Cortège" and "Les Coquillages" present essentially the same stylised loving in even more elaborate terms. "Cortège", clearly inspired by Watteau's painting of the same name, nonetheless captures the quintessential artificiality of the scene in such a way that the pet monkey gazing at the woman's décolletage and the negro attendant peeping at his mistress's ankles function like six-teenth-century emblems to symbolise repressed desire strong enough to be lust. Such feelings are spoken in the first person in the erotic poem "Les Coquillages", clearly modelled on eighteenth-century erotic poetry, such as "Le Sein" from *Tableaux* by Parny.

Matters taken a stage further are presented in the theme of emotional and sensual surrender in "Les Ingénus", "Mandoline" and "En sourdine". In "Les Ingénus" Verlaine depicts the emotional surrender in the early stages of a relationship. . . .

"Mandoline" captures the precise moment when the lovers, their exquisite clothes, their style their happiness, their shadows, all blend perfectly with the moonlight, the music, the quivering breezes. This precise moment of total harmony of sensations, emotions, physicality, is encapsulated in intense movement. . . .

With the poem "Cythère" the ideal world of total surrender is achieved. Cythera, the island of Aphrodite's temple, has long been a favoured subject of painters and poets, Watteau and Baudelaire among them. Verlaine is writing very much within this tradition. The poem's theme is ideal love, a world of passivity, of complete sensual gratification. . . .

The theme of love has so far been presented as a mainly positive and pleasurable experience. Nonetheless, love's less attractive aspects are at least hinted at in some of these poems, "Cythère" for example. Other poems deal more directly with these issues. . . .

[L]ove does not last. The longest poem, "En patinant", uses the familiar device of the passing seasons to depict the passing of love. In this poem there is a further dimension, the idea of manipulation. . . .

Failure, despair, and fear are dealt with more directly in "Le Faune", "L'amour par terre" and "Colloque sentimental". Like its more positive counterpart, "Mandoline", "Le Faune" fixes the precise moment when the lover realises that love will not last. . . .

Despair of love lasting is polarised into the themes of innocence and corruption in "Fantoches" and "Colombine". In 'Fantoches' the evil *commedia* characters Scaramouche and Polichinelle seemingly plot in the moonlight while Colombine steals away to her handsome lover. Love asserts itself over evil and, it is hoped, will assuage the lovers' distress. In "Colombine", on the other hand, Colombine is presented as an evil manipulator of her innocent lovers. . . .

Across the collection, the distinctive theme of love is developed in an equally distinctive way. There is a deepening emotional richness. In general the poems up to "En patinant" are fairly straightforward depictions of a happy, lighthearted love. "En patinant" marks a turning point; with the theme of manipulation, the darker side of love is introduced. From this point on, the poems are more complex with the additional dimension of the more negative aspects of love discussed above. This interplay of positive and negative aspects of love, I suggest, is the source of the richness of the later poems as of the essential thematic progression.

If we take together the three *commedia*/Watteauesque poems, **"Pantomime"**, **"Fantoches"** and **"Colombine"**, it is possible to see this symbolised in the way the character of Colombine is developed. In **"Pantomime"**, Colombine is surprised by love; she is tender and gentle. In **"Fantoches"** she actively seeks her lover, whilst in **"Colombine"** she has become a cruel manipulator, she is active rather than passive, and this activity is perceived as malign. As a *commedia* character, she symbolises, from a safe distance, somewhat in the manner of Watteau's artificiality, the range of emotions associated with love and which *Fêtes galantes* explores. As a character associated with love, the Colombine figure may be considered to represent the increasingly complex treatment of love across the collection.

"A la promenade", **"A Clymène"** and **"Les Indolents"** suggest a *modus vivendi* in the face of this despair, this 'fate'. . . .

The stance adopted with its logic, 'Le rare est le bon. Donc mourons' is specifically amoral with its implied (conventional) equation of death with sex. The tone of the poem is no less so. . . .

"A la promenade" and **"A Clymène"** approach the theme of amorality from a different angle. In **"A la promenade"** we are told quite simply that the lovers are 'Cœurs tendres, mais affranchis du serment'. As in Watteau's paintings, they are absolved of all responsibilities and are free to pursue their pleasures, their search for the right partner in defiance of fate. The lived reality of such a world is the theme of the beautiful poem, **"A Clymène"**. As in **"En sourdine"** the poem traces the process of invoking passivity, of relaxing control. This time the power of the loved one is specifically in the domain of sensations. Here too Verlaine self-consciously uses Baudelairian *correspondances*. (Baudelaire's sonnet "Correspondances explores the symbolic connections of perfume, sound and colour.) In **"A Clymène"** the effect on the poet's senses, backed up by the 'authority' of another poet's experience, is offered as a *justification* of the poet's surrender. The repeated construction 'Puisque' leading to the final 'Ainsi soit-il!' which, translated, means 'Amen', has, as in "Les Indolents", a semblance of logic. In addition the strikingly liturgical quality of the verse seems to offer further justification. Amorality, then, a refusal of responsibility, some would say decadence, a seizing of the moment, is both an aspect of love and may well be a way of dealing with love's transience. The 'Ainsi soit-il' which closes **"A Clymène"** is more than the quasi-religious acquiescent welcoming of love that it may first appear to be. As I have suggested above, the syntax of 'Puisque . . . Ainsi soit-il' offers a justification, a legitimisation of amorality. The world of **"Les Indolents"** operates on just such a legitimised assumption. . . .

A critic has referred to this amorality as 'libertinage sophistiqué'. This seems to me accurate, but I believe the amorality to be a great deal more than this. As such it is the principle connection with Verlaine's vision of love in *Romances sans paroles*. In **"Les Ingénus"** the amoral is specifically a freedom from commitment. . . . It may equally be viewed as a special world where such commitments are irrelevant, if not rejected. Certainly this last attitude would constitute the darker side of freedom. Another way of considering the matter would be to suggest that it is a world of irresponsibility, attempted, if not chosen. The amoral, then, may usefully be seen as the irresponsible. Verlaine's investigation of the nature of love has led him to the verge of taking responsibility, a point beyond which he has chosen not to go. The amoral *fête galante* world strongly and permanently hints at a world of irresponsibility as a way of life.

It is in this context that I want to suggest that beneath the overt theme of love there lies a theme less directly expressed; it is the theme of passivity. Each poem can be seen as an evocation of a state of passivity. In a fundamental sense this is the key to Verlaine's poetic vision and art. This theme is *suggested* throughout the collection and is the mood through which the dominant theme of love is filtered. In Verlaine's case the evocation of states of passivity may usefully be viewed as the aesthetic counterpart of his own lived refusal to take responsibility for himself, his actions, his moods, his decisions. It is an astounding and, in some ways, a horrendous transmutation of lived experience into art. The impossible lands of *Fêtes galantes,* as indeed of *Romances sans paroles,* have their genesis in that which is only too possible.

As with the theme of love, the states of passivity cover a wide range. **"Les Coquillages"**, **"Dans la grotte"** and **"A Clymène"** evoke the pleasure of letting go, of achieving the perfect passivity of physical pleasure. As suggested, the theme of **"En sourdine"** is the process of bringing about a state of passivity, here a form of receptivity to nature, in such a way that the individual and nature become one on some plane of exquisite pleasure, which is detailed further in **"A Clymène"** J. P. Richard refers to this process as the removal of 'le moi conscient' of the thinking self, to allow the world of sensations alone to come into being. Passivity too can be discerned in the theme of manipulation; the victims are passive in **"En patinant"**. Passivity is equally the inability or refusal to do anything about this manipulation and the resultant isolation (**"Fantoches"**). It is vulnerability in **"En bateau"**, fear and loss of control over one's destiny (**"Le Faune"**). Above all, in **"A la promenade"**, **"A Clymène"** and **"Les Indolents"**, passivity is manifested in amorality which is legitimised into a way of life in the *fête galante* world; refusal of commitment is proposed as an ethos. It is a serious proposition and one which Verlaine explores much further in *Romances sans paroles*.

This layering of themes, one overt, one suggested, is, of course, appropriate to the presentation of mainly non-intellectual themes. I want to go further and suggest that the *way* the themes are presented also emerges as a theme in its own right. These structures are the nearest the poems get to being 'intellectual'. After all, the world of emotions has to be set down. For the sake of clarity, four distinctive modes of presenting the emotions can be discerned.

Firstly, in **"Pantomime"** and **"A la promenade"**, for instance, Verlaine uses the device of contrast. Pierrot's practical activity of eating is contrasted with Colombine's passive reception of love to underline the theme of isolation, and the contrast between callousness and feeling, corruption and innocence, conventional masculine and feminine principles. The word 'contraste' is actually used in **"A la promenade"** to emphasise the enigmatically playful quality of idealised love scene. The woman's cold gaze is contrasted with her generous smile. . . .

This contrast between appearance and reality is tightened into a paradox in a number of poems, notably **"L'Allée"**, and **"Dans la grotte"**. Paradox, the second mode, is obviously of the essence of the *fête galante* world, dealing as it does with artificial appearance and emotional truth. **"L'Allée"**, which precedes **"A la promenade"**, is a purely external portrait of the lovers of the latter poem. . . .

"A Cythère", **"Mandoline"** and **"En sourdine"** present a world within the world of *Fêtes galantes,* the third mode. **"A Cythère"** is the pure, perfect world of sensations. This plane of rarefied existence is doubtless the world experienced, in movement, by the characters in **"Mandoline"** as they 'Tourbillonnet dans l'extase'. In its more relaxed form this world is that to which the lovers aspire in **"En sourdine"**. . . .

[The] fourth mode, I term a dialectic. In the abstract, dialectic may be defined as follows: one emotional state is taken to the extreme point where it brings into being its opposite emotion. This is comparable to the essence of Mallarmé's Symbolist undertaking, 'après avoir trouvé le Néant, j'ai trouvé le Beau'; it is only by encountering total negation that the poet can imagine its opposite, 'l'Idéal'. Verlaine's dialectic, of course, operates on an emotional level. The happiness in **"En sourdine"** cannot last. In addition, the letting go of the thinking self runs so close to self-annihilation that the conscious self reasserts itself. And this takes the form of despair in **"En sourdine"**, despair at the loss of the conscious self, or equally at not being able to escape its control, at not being able to achieve the emotional ideal of total passivity. Certainly there is too the despair of the deeper parts of the emotional self which are usually suppressed. . . .

On a more mundane level, a mode of presentation such as this conveys the understandable fear that happiness will not last. **"Le Faune"** demonstrates this very clearly. There is too, something here of the dynamic of the self-fulfilling prophecy. Each of these suggested approaches has its truth. Not surprisingly, there is overall a greater incidence of this dialectical presentation of the theme in the second half of the collection **"Mandoline"**, **"A Clymène"**, **"Les Indolents"**, **"Colombine"**, **"En sourdine"**), which is obviously a factor in the greater complexity noted in the thematic development of the collection.

I suggested earlier that the way the theme is presented constitutes a theme in its own right. The three 'layers' of themes in *Fêtes galantes,* love, passivity and the mode of presentation, blend in **'En sourdine'**. Here the willed gradual surrender and resultant despair, which is nothing other than vulnerability, is a dialectical process. Emotions work like this. The world of **"En sourdine"** is more recognisable than that of **"Cythère"** for instance. In **"En sourdine"** we are invited to participate in the gradual process of passivity, in **"Cythère"** to witness an idealised world. This art of merging layers in **"En sourdine"** marks an important link with the poetic art of *Romances sans paroles*.

The significant connections between *Fêtes galantes* and *Romances sans paroles* are the themes of love and passivity, their links with the positing of an amoral world where responsibility is refused, and the expression of this in a form of pure poetry. As such *Fêtes galantes* contains elements of this, Verlaine's art of symbolist impressionism. By using the *fête galante* mode, Verlaine has explored these issues in a safe, detached way. He distances himself from the highly personal and confused emotions to clarify the conflict between active and passive modes of loving. In *Romances sans paroles* the same issues are examined in a more personal way, and so, more deeply. In so far as **"En sourdine"** expresses the experience of willed passivity more intimately than the other poems in the collections. it is the key connecting poem between the two collections. In *Fêtes galantes,* Verlaine is an onlooker, gazing at the Watteauesque painterly poems which he creates. He is a spectator. In *Romances sans paroles,* the more specifically musical poems, Verlaine is more profoundly engaged. **"En sourdine"**, with its stated musicality, points the way.

. . . . .

As with *Fêtes galantes,* the themes of *Romances sans paroles* are predominantly emotional states. To the familiar themes of love and passivity is added that of freedom. . . . I shall consider three ways in which *Romances sans paroles* develops from *Fêtes galantes;* firstly, the use of the *Romances sans paroles* mode with its subdivisions, secondly the resultant double perspective of external reality and inner emotional reality which permeates the collection, and finally how the presentation of the themes focuses the conflict noted in *Fêtes galantes* between active and passive ways of loving into the issue of responsibility versus irresponsibility, the issue which, I believe, accounts for the uneven quality of the poetry in this collection. There is, quite simply, a marked contrast between a 'poésie pure' of delicious passivity, free from moral values, a poetry of presentation (as distinct from representation), and a poetry of unsubtly expressed emotions, clearly autobiographical in nature. *Fêtes galantes* presents a wholly imagined inner world where ethos and emotional state are unified in the specifically pure, amoral world of **"A la promenade"**, **"A Clymène"** and **"Les Indolents"**. In *Romances sans paroles* this is not the case.

Romances sans paroles explores further the *fête galante* world and, as it were, tests out these imaginary lands. As we shall discover, the lands are visited and yet it is impossible to remain there. Emotions and ethos are ultimately found to be in conflict. This is because Verlaine is forever torn between the pull of freedom and the temptation of security, and refuses to *choose* one or the other. I consider that this unresolved gap between the delicious emotional state, its pain as well as its pleasure, and the ethical basis on which it is founded, generates the best and worst of Verlaine's poetic art and is the hallmark of *Romances sans paroles*. In view of this it seems to me crucial to adopt two approaches to the collection: firstly that of 'poésie pure', poetry in its own right, and secondly a biographical approach in the case of a number of poems, specifically the fourth and sixth **"Ariettes oubliées"**, **"Birds in the night"**, **"Child wife"**, **"A Poor Young Shepherd"** and **"Beams"**. Apart from the **"Ariettes oubliées"**, these poems contain little that I consider to be of purely aesthetic merit. They are largely versified self-pity and/or anger directed towards Mathilde [Mauté, his wife].

In *Fêtes galantes* Verlaine dealt with the themes of love, passivity and amorality in a detached way, through the *fête galante* world. *Romances sans paroles* is distinctly less detached in its treatment of these themes. In the place of the **fête galante** framework there is the mode of the *Romances sans paroles,* wordless songs, which are subdivided into **"Ariettes oubliées"**, **"Paysages belges"**, **"Simples fresques"** and **"Aquarelles"**, that is, musical as well as pictorial modes, linked by the notion of the significance of the unexpressed. While *Romances sans paroles* clearly refers to Mendelssohn's 'Songs without words', the 'Romance' is also a sung elegy, emotional in substance and without complicated dramatic presentation. The genre itself conveys the idea of musicality, of experiences that transcend the limitations of words, a questioning of the power of words. . . . There is too the idea that there is no name for the experience which *Romances sans paroles* collectively portrays. This is less to do with morality, or its absence, than to suggest the uniqueness of a love affair, of which homosexuality is but one element. In short, another plane of existence is involved, as in *Fêtes galantes*. In *Fêtes galantes* this world of delicious passivity was lived vicariously through the *commedia* characters, with the notable exception of **"En sourdine"** where the experience is considerably less limited by the specific figures. In *Fêtes galantes* there is an outer reality, that of the *fête galante* world, and an inner reality, the truth of human emotions. With *Romances sans paroles* the outer reality is the fact and circumstances of the relationship with [Arthur] Rimbaud, and Mathilde; the inner reality, the intimate experience of this relationship, what it felt like. The experience is neither vicarious nor transposed beyond recognition. Both realities are the poet's. There is, then, no one clear mode to give specificity to the experience. On the contrary, like music, it is evoked in the very process of its unfolding. **"En sourdine"** came nearest to this kind of poetry in *Fêtes galantes*. The mode of the *Romances sans paroles* is entirely appropriate to this art of symbolist impressionism which presents, not represents.

Within this overall genre it seems to me worth considering the titles of the separate sections. **"Ariettes oubliées"**, the first section, contains the quintessentially Verlainian poetry. The 'Ariette' certainly refers to the musical comedy, *Ninette à la cour,* by the eighteenth-century dramatist, Favart, from which the opening epigram is taken. Rimbaud discovered these plays in the library at Charleville. As the name implies, an 'Ariette' is a small aria. Its distinctive quality is an unaccompanied melody. The melody is the theme, that is, the ephemeral quality of the emotions, possibly a reason for the use of the diminutive. The melody's accompaniment derives from the words' rich suggestiveness, connotative, phonological and metrical. Given the fact that Verlaine named this particular section later (they were originally to have been called *Romances sans paroles*), there is, as Bornecque suggests, a retrospective view; the experience of the relationship, of its emotional essence, has been *forgotten* by Rimbaud.

"Paysages belges" obviously recalls the setting of *Fêtes galantes,* 'Votre âme est un paysage choisi' (**"Clair de lune"**). The equivalence between landscape and emotions now applies in reverse; the Belgian landscape is that of the poet's soul, it is seen through the poet's emotional being. This section is a continuation of the emotional world of **"Ariettes oubliées"** and is more outward looking. The subdivision, **"Simples fresques"** (fresco art implies painting directly on to wet plaster), suggests the seizing of the bare essential elements of the experience, in the form of sparse landscape details. It is the art of the precise nuance and of the rapid gesture. **"Aquarelles"** continues the painting mode. The water colours may be considered the visual equivalent of **"Ariettes oubliées"**. The pictorial detail of the landscape is fused with the emotional landscape. There is a shift in emphasis from music in the first section, to painting in the final section, which denotes a move away from the completely personal world of emotions and sensations in its complex unfolding process (**"C'est l'extase"**, **"Ariette"** I) to a world where details from a 'recognisable' external world depict a particular emotional attitude (**"Green"**). . . .

Each section is linked with a place visited by Verlaine and Rimbaud. **"Paysages belges"** obviously recalls Belgium, **"Birds in the night"** and **"Aquarelles"** are from the London experience, while **"Ariettes oubliées"** probably covers the entire experience, certainly the early Paris-based relationship, and that on a far more essential level. It is the 'paysage intérieur' of merging emotions and sensations, Verlaine's own *Cythère,* the journey to and from the island of ideal love. A number of critics assign each section to a particular person in Verlaine's life at this time. The general consensus appears to be thus: **"Ariettes oubliées"**—nostalgia for Mathilde; **"Paysages belges"**—Rimbaud; and **"Aquarelles"**—return to Mathilde. I see an emotional truth and logic in this. After all, Verlaine found it difficult to leave Mathilde and presumably to live, for him, a more adult, homosexual life. On balance, though, I believe the sections signify in a different manner. Each division presents a different location for a particular stage in the relationship with Rimbaud, beginning with the self-enclosed world of emotions ("**Ariettes**"), the life of adventure in Belgium ("**Paysages belges**") and then London ("**Aquarelles**"). Cutting across these sections is the conflict between the reluctance to leave Mathilde and security, and the tempting freedom with Rimbaud. Verlaine's attacks on Mathilde are, after all, externalised fear and cowardice. The straightforward circumstantial adventure is accompanied by a far more complex refusal of this freedom. Even so, each section has its own coherence, recalling the 'blocks' of poems in *Fêtes galantes*; for instance "Ariettes oubliées" presents kaleidoscopic perspectives on the physical, emotional and artistic relationship, ranging from sensual pleasure through the 'morality' of the situation, to regret at the loss of the stable conventional marriage that freedom has demanded.

The collection as a whole has rather less coherence. There is the overall pattern of a decline in emotional intensity and subtlety. The collection begins with the exquisite "**C'est l'extase**", the assertion of the reality of the least tangible of experiences, and ends with "**Beams**", with its theme of surrender in love. However, in "**Beams**" the presentation is utterly conventional and Hugolian in tone. There are two possible explanations for the decline. Firstly, the inevitable diminution of intense experience. Secondly, there may well be some cynical mockery, ever the perspective of Verlaine in exile. Certainly a poem such as "**Beams**" bears a strong resemblance to the less impressive poems from *La Bonne Chanson* and later *Sagesse*. Whatever the truth of the matter, the fact remains that the poetry in *Romances sans paroles* ranges from the exquisite to the banal and the ludicrous.

It seems to me too that a double perspective operates. Just as the *fête galante* world, by its very nature, ultimately doubts the existence of the harmony it depicts, so *Romances sans paroles* is pervaded by an atmosphere of retrospective fatalistic melancholy, a strong sense of past, present, and future preconditioned by the past, far more marked than in *Fêtes galantes* (cf. "**Le Faune**", "**L'Amour par terre**"). Accordingly there is a greater awareness of the gap between ideal and reality than in *Fêtes galantes*. In "**C'est l'extase**", for instance, the moment of sublime happiness is immediately questioned 'C'est la nôtre, n'est-ce pas?' Many of the poems are permeated by this fatalistic doubt. Some are entirely composed of it, for instance the eighth "**Ariette**", "**Dans l'interminable . . .**" From the beginning in *Romances sans paroles* there is the certainty that harmonious happiness will not last. In the light of this and for the sake of clarity, I shall discuss each section separately with respect to the treatment of the themes of love, passivity and freedom.

In "**Ariettes oubliées**" the theme of love is not articulated as such. Instead the poems variously explore finely nuanced facets of the state of being in love. The theme of passivity too pervades this section in the sense that, with the exception of IV, the poems are about a sensual and emotional state in which the poet finds himself. The theme of passivity is united with the theme of freedom, for the

poems evoke an attitude of complete surrender, a letting go, including the fearful dimensions of such a situation. Together, then, the nine "**Ariettes**" present the essence of the Verlainian emotion of total surrender to love; each poem constitutes an aspect of the entire experience which is thus unfolded in its finely nuanced, ever-changing process. The "**Ariette**", "**C'est l'extase**" is one of the best examples of this. . . .

Just as the first poem evoked sensual perfection and doubts, and the second a spiritual ideal and certain doubts, so poem III completes this opening cycle of experience. It is a poem of melancholy. The tragedy is that the poet does not know why he is so desolate:

> C'est bien la pire peine
> De ne savoir pourquoi
> Sans amour et sans haine
> Mon coeur a tant de peine!
>
> (13-16)

This, the essence of despair, has an unresolved quality which focuses and expresses directly that of I, the demand for reassurance, and of II, the certainty of imperfection.

Together, the first three "**Ariettes**" convey the entire and extreme range of Verlaine's experience, which is consistently presented as an unfolding process: we are taken through the process with the poet. The remaining "**Ariettes**" are rather more varied in that they treat specific aspects of this experience and differ considerably in tone. With the possible exception of VI, poems IV-IX deal with the various forms of pain the relationship inevitably entails.

"**Ariette**" VI is of quite a different order. It is Verlaine's version of Rimbaud's 'Ma Bohème', a half mocking poem of joyous wandering. . . .

Compared with "**Ariettes oubliées**", the "**Paysages belges**" are generally more outward-looking, as the title suggests. The themes of love, passivity and freedom are present in the poet's receptivity to the Belgian landscape, which, of course, is simultaneously his emotional landscape. In contrast to the "**Ariettes**" which unfolded sensations and emotions, "**Paysages, belges**" tend to pile up sensations in a manner which resembles Rimbaud's poems of sensations, *Illuminations*. "**Voyance**" includes pure receptivity to sensations. Nonetheless the poems are never exclusively verbal impressionism. They have their emotional depth.

"**Walcourt**" and "**Charleroi**", like "**Bruxelles: Simples fresques**", form diptychs which depict the pleasure and the pain of the exile in freedom. The mood of "**Walcourt**" recalls that of "**Ariette**" VI with its jolly conclusion to the brief and rapid description of the town through which Verlaine and Rimbaud walked on their way to Brussels in 1872, . . . and which led him to compare the two friends with happy wanderers, whereas usually the wandering Jew is seen as a tragedy. On the other hand, the opening line of **"Charleroi"**, 'Dans l'herbe noire / Les Kobolds vont' echoes the eighth **"Ariette"**, 'Dans l'interminable / Ennui de la plaine' just as the questioning, 'On sent donc quoi?' echoes that of **"Ariette"** V, 'Qu'est-ce que c'est que ce berceau soudain?'. In both instances despair is manifested in an unbridged gap between the senses, emotions and the faculty of understanding. In **"Le piano . . . "** the poet's memory fails to recall the origin of the sensations; in **"Charleroi"** the intellect fails to understand both the sensations and their source. The situation becomes worse still in the first of the "Bruxelles" poems, **"Simples fresques"**: there is a near-failure of feeling. Like the fresco which fades with time, the poem deals with the passing of time, and so, of love *and* memory. . . .

However, the defiance of passing time and of failure of emotions is not guaranteed, for the achievement of emotional happiness is uncertain. The first **"Fresque"** had questioned whether the experience had ever happened, so frail is memory. The desperate tone of **"Fresque"** II conveys more of an unfulfilled wish than of certainty. The doubts and ambiguities posed in the ninth **"Ariette"** persist.

"Chevaux de bois" is quite different in theme, tone and length from the other poems in **"Paysages belges"**. Its loud, exciting evocation of a fairground scene anticipates the early twentieth-century simultaneity of Apollinaire's and Cendrars's poetry of urban life. . . .

The closing poem, **"Malines"**, constitutes a farewell to this cycle of poems, depicting as it does scenes glimpsed from a train. The poem is characterised by silence especially after the noisy activity of **"Chevaux de bois"**. The train's carriages are rooms for intimate communication:

> Chaque wagon est un salon
> Où l'on cause bas et d'où l'on
> Aime à loisir cette nature
> Faite à souhait pour Fénelon.
>
> (17-20)

And communication is but part of a more general harmony ('cette nature'). The allusion to Fénelon's doctrine of quietism completes the picture of silent harmony. This, an emotionally gentle close to the cycle, gives a note of completion contrasting with the section **"Aquarelles"** which follows after the vicious interlude of **"Birds in the night"** in which Verlaine criticises his young wife. The Belgian experience has been explored and understood: that of London will remain unresolved. In **"Aquarelles"** the theme of freedom is treated rather differently from the two previous sections. There is less consistent welcoming of freedom. In **"Green"** and **"Spleen"**, love and passivity take the form of a full and open receptivity to the fleeting, essential moment in the emotional life. . . .

In **"Spleen"** the poet is slave to his emotions.

In contrast, the London-based **"Streets"**, I and II, present respectively a lighthearted farewell to the loved one and

a vivid street scene in London. The poems' joyful energy conveys a momentary freedom, real or imagined, from the loved one, be it freedom from wanting Mathilde or from the depths of surrender to Rimbaud. It does not matter. What does matter is the mature understanding that happy memories are the positive reward of this freedom:

> Mais je trouve encore meilleur
> Le baiser de sa bouche en fleur,
> Depuis qu'elle est morte à mon coeur.
>
> (10-12)

"Streets" II is an example of the clear, fresh vision that emotional freedom can bring, . . . The poem, entirely a painted scene, and comparable in this to some of Rimbaud's *Illuminations,* is one of the few where the landscape (or, in this case, townscape) is free from any signs of reference to an inner landscape. This absence itself of course informs us of the poet's freedom from distress. Nothing interferes with his detailed and original observations of the world around him. Passivity can be this constructive receptivity to the external world. Here absence of love is seemingly the condition of freedom.

Together **"Child wife"**, **"A Poor Young Shepherd"** and **"Beams"** are about love. They enact, respectively, the process of leaving Mathilde, the early stages of love and the playful surrender to a new lover. The tone of these poems is markedly different from that of the other poems in the collection, with the exception of **"Birds in the night"**, although it is marginally prefigured in **"Streets"**. The three poems have a Hugolian tone of declamation: love from a great distance and an impressive height. The child wife is told, 'Et vous n'aurez pas su la lumière et l'honneur / D'un amour brave et fort' (17-18). It is a stance of love, not the experience of love: 'Elle se retourna, doucement inquiète / De ne nous croire pas pleinement rassurés' (**"Beams"** 13-14). The emotions were raw at the beginning of this third cycle (**"Green"**, **"Spleen"**), now they are hardened. The issue of freedom has been 'resolved' by evasion into externalised imagined scenes of parting, courtship and acquiescence to a new love, as it has into a poetic style which contrasts to the point of parody with the authentic Verlainian style.

In discussing *Fêtes galantes,* I referred to three themes, love, passivity and the mode of treatment, and suggested that the blending of these three in 'En sourdine' made that poem a significant link with *Romances sans paroles*. In *Romances sans paroles* the themes of love, passivity and freedom blend with the mode of treatment. In **"Ariette"** II (**"Je devine . . . "**) the unfolding presentation is appropriate to the theme of spiritual love; so too, and at the other extreme, is the chronological narrative of the popular song genre, to the unsubtle and strong emotions expressed in **"Birds in the night"**. Running through the entire collection is a further layer. It is the pattern of emotional harmony and discord, a moving away from or towards one of these polarities. Some of the poems begin in a state of harmony and move towards discord. Thus **"Ariette"** V (**"Le piano que baise . . . "**) opens with a full evocation of finely nuanced sensations and progresses towards troubled questioning. **"Ariette" IX ("L'ombre des arbres")** on the other hand remains harmonious in its consistent evocation of disappointment. Harmony does not necessarily imply happiness, although the harmonious joy in **"Walcourt"** does involve both.

It is illuminating to consider the first and last three poems of ***Romances sans paroles*** in the light of this emotional pattern. As I have shown, the first three **"Ariettes"** constitute a small cycle of poems in their own right, for they deal with the full range of Verlainian experience, sensual ecstasy, spiritual ideals and despair, all of which are expressed as an unfolding experiential process. The last three poems, **"Child wife"**, **"A Poor Young Shepherd"** and **"Beams"** also constitute an independent cycle of poems in their externalised stance of parting and loving anew. As such both `cycles' offer vignettes of the Verlainian experience, both are harmonious in their tonal consistency. The first cycle is authentic, the second, an unconvincing pose. However, unlike **"Colloque sentimental"** (***Fêtes galantes***), the lack of conviction in the second cycle does not cast a retrospective ambiguity over the whole collection. Instead it opens up questions concerning the diminution of the poems' quality, and so, the uneven quality of the poetry in the collection as a whole.

The key factor is the theme of freedom. If we consider the poems in their order of arrangement, which is not necessarily the order of composition, a picture emerges. In the first three **"Ariettes"** freedom is of the essence of the experience, for the poems convey the poet's acceptance of the positive and negative aspects of the experience. The reassurance he seeks in **"C'est l'extase"**, the doubt itself, is part of the experience, as is the failed spiritual perfection in **"Je devine . . . "** and the failure to understand the source of despair in **"Il pleure . . . "** In the last three poems Verlaine adopts a *pose* of freedom, leaving a woman, beginning a new relationship; even the acquiescent love in **"Beams"** is playful. Put another way, the first three **"Ariettes"** do not question the ethical basis for this freedom, the situation is enjoyed and accepted for what it is; by the stage of the last three poems, the matter has been confronted and sidestepped.

So there is an unresolved conflict in the collection between emotional freedom and its ethical basis. This, the crucial and poignant discord, cuts across the collection and is the source of its tension. This discord concerns the issue of a *Chosen* irresponsibility. In ***Fêtes galantes*** Verlaine justifies his amorality, and **"Ariettes"** IV and VII, **"Birds in the night"** and **"Child wife"** deal with the same matter, this time in the form of an irresponsibility not chosen, together with the attendant guilt and indictment of the beloved. These poems, circumstantially autobiographical, contrast with the other poems in the collection by dealing with specifically ethical matters. **"Ariettes"** IV and VII present respectively the homosexual life with Rimbaud and the leaving of Mathilde, representing conventional heterosexual security; bohemianism versus social integration. In offering a justification for 'amorality', **"Ariette"** IV develops the theme of **"A Clymène"** (***Fêtes galantes***). In this **"Ariette"** Verlaine's justifica-tion is an uncharacteristically assertive demand for forgiveness, 'Il faut . . . nous pardonner les choses'. It is obviously possible to read this line as referring to some undisclosed violation of an unstated code. Indeed the vagueness is the very condition to which he refers; homosexual love was inadmissible in nineteenth-century France and, as Oscar Wilde put it, 'dared not speak its name'. There is possibly a sense of sin in the choice of the word 'pardonner', given Verlaine's subsequent reconversion to Catholicism during his imprisonment in Mons prison after the shooting incident, and in view of the fact that he was given the maximum sentence of two years' hard labour, less for shooting at Rimbaud than for practising sodomy with a minor. In **"Ariette"** IV, Verlaine insists on a life of freedom which, given the reference to the poets as 'filles', is doubtless passive in the sense of rejecting coventional notions of masculinity. Depending on one's point of view, the seventh **"Ariette"** (**"O triste . . . "**) captures, as I have suggested, the paradox of being separated without being separate; equally it could convey the self-pity of a man who cannot have his cake and eat it.

"Birds in the night" evokes a similarly ambiguous response. It is by far the longest poem in the collection, narrating the poet's emotional life with a woman from the beginning of the relationship to a parting which clearly does not constitute the end of the relationship. The overt theme of the poem is the poet's forgiveness of the woman. I do not doubt the sincerity of this, given Verlaine's collections of poems such as ***La Bonne Chanson*** and ***Sagesse*** I find the criterion of sincerity difficult with respect to poetry and prefer to leave it aside as being ultimately unuseful for assessing the merits of a poem. In the final analysis the poem should stand on its own. Letting **"Birds in the night"** do just that, I find it has little aesthetic merit, with its banal verse form, rhyme scheme and relentless list of undoubtedly powerful but nonetheless crassly expressed emotions. And indeed I find that in the place of any such merit the emotional content intrudes itself. This is the point: the poem refuses any response of the order which we are accustomed to give to most of the poems in the collection. Instead it presents itself with a tone of appalling self-pity and cowardly self-justification. The same is true of **"Child wife"** which begins, 'Vous n'avez rien compris à ma simplicité'. As with **"Birds in the night"**, the fact that Verlaine obviously believes such assertions is ultimately irrelevant. For the overt theme of self-pity and cruel criticism of Mathilde's understandably annoying childish behaviour is contradicted by a tone of quite staggering indictment of the young wife. The poem ends with a grandiose and ludicrous Hugolian utterance indicating all that the young wife has missed through her failure to understand her husband. Presumably the Hugolian echoes are further justification for the criticism of the wife. Hugo's life is doubtless the ideal to which all poets *and* wives should aspire. Adèle Hugo had, after all, 'understood' *her* husband's infidelities.

These four poems, autobiographical, and expressing the tension between freedom and security, are Verlaine's 'Saison en enfer'. ***Fêtes galantes*** had presented an ethos of freedom from responsibility in the transposition to the imaginary *fête galante* world. In ***Romances sans paroles*** the matter is focused into a choice between a free, 'immoral' life with Rimbaud or a life of conventional security with Mathilde. Verlaine seems to choose neither; or rather he *refuses to choose*. In the last analysis, the direction chosen is irrelevant; what matters is the choice between responsibility and amorality. Verlaine does not even choose to be amoral; this is the ultimate, and damaging, irresponsibility. His change of lifestyle with Rimbaud has hardly proved to be the free amoral world imagined in ***Fêtes galantes***. The promise of the *fête galante* world has not been realised. The poet is faced instead with the consequences of his chronic refusal to choose; they are aesthetic as well as ethical consequences.

The quality of the poetry in ***Romances sans paroles*** is patchy compared with that of ***Fêtes galantes***. Verlaine's best art is written under the successfully self-deceiving illusion of acceptance that love is passive irresponsibility. Moreover, in these poems, particularly the **"Ariettes"**, the positive and negative dimensions of the situation are maturely explored. However, in the poems where no such illusions are created, and where a more recognisably personal matter intrudes, Verlaine simply misses the essence of the moment in question. So, it is when he deals with the serious source of his delicious irresponsibility and which he ultimately evades by blaming Mathilde for everything, that the poetry borders on the banal. In such poems Verlaine misses the core of the emotion: 'Tout le reste est littérature'. This, the last line from **"Art poétique"**, Verlaine's own criticism of 'unmusical' poetry, judges, sadly, its own author. With Verlaine's critique in mind, together with his own dramatic lapses from this ideal of musicality, it is time to turn our attention to the large question of music in ***Fêtes galantes*** and ***Romances sans paroles,*** beginning with Verlaine's art of versification.

Sainte-Georges de Bouhélier on Verlaine's death:

My throat was constricted. When I reached the dead man's rooms, and met friends I knew, I burst into tears. Even if I had lost a relation, I shouldn't have felt more grief.

The room itself had been hung with black, but the little canary in its gilded cage was singing desperately. In the dining-room I found Eugénie [Verlaine's mistress]. . . . When I appeared, she went hysterical, wept bitterly, and insisted that what had happened hadn't been her fault. I hadn't yet accused her of anything, but she forestalled me. And then she told me how the poor man had died.

'A moment ago,' she continued, without transition, 'an Englishman arrived. He wanted a memento of Paul at any price. I let him take a pen-holder. Do you know how much he paid me? A louis. What do you think of that?'

Obviously she was astounded. She was now looking through the drawers to rummage out things to sell. I learned afterwards that she had had to go to a local stationer's to buy pencils and pen-holders. She did not want to be taken unawares.

Sainte-Georges de Bouhélier, in Le Printemps d'une Génération, *Éditions Nagel, 1946*

Laurence M. Porter (essay date 1990)

SOURCE: "Verlaine's Subversion of Language," in *The Crisis of French Symbolism,* Cornell University Press, 1990, pp. 76-112.

[*In the following excerpt, Porter comments on Verlaine's antilinguistic stance and subversion of language.*]

Verlaine has been neglected in recent years. The brevity of his poems; their songlike, informal diction; their paucity of metaphor and allusion; and their lack of those intellectual themes that are commonly held to characterize true "Symbolism"—from the beginning, all these features have tempted critics to judge his verse agreeable but minor. His alcoholism and the poetic decline of his final fifteen years, which he spent as a sodden derelict, have reinforced the trend to slight or to dismiss his work. Until recently even critics who have looked closely at his poems have tended to obscure our sense of the evolution of Verlaine's poetry by treating it in terms of what they perceive to be general, overarching tendencies such as "fadeur" (insipidity) or "naiveté," to say nothing of the all too familiar "musicality." A fine recent collection of French essays is disparagingly titled *La Petite Musique de Verlaine* [SEDES, 1982]. Once one has described Verlaine's "music" by counting syllables and noting repetitions of sounds, there seems to be little more to say. Like Lamartine, he has been damned with faint praise.

If one seriously addresses the question of Verlaine's musicality, it seems intuitively obvious that repetition and regularity are more "musical" than their absence. In actual music composed before the modern era, a high percentage of the measures occur more than once—only one-third or one-quarter of the total may be different—whereas in a literary work few if any sentences are repeated. Zola need use the same sentence only half a dozen times in a long novel such as *La Bête humaine* before critics start comparing it to a Wagnerian leitmotif. A modest amount of repetition in literature, then, has the same effect as the considerable amount of repetition in music. The phrases that echo frequently in a poem such as Verlaine's **"Soleils couchants"** attract all the more attention because they do not belong to a conventional pattern of recurrence in a fixed form such as the rondeau or the ballade.

No one, however, has yet done a statistical study to determine whether Verlaine deploys obvious forms of repetition—rich rhyme, internal rhyme, anaphora, epiphora, refrains, reduplication of single words, alliteration, and assonance—more frequently than less "musical" poets. Baudelaire and Mallarmé, in fact, seem to use more rich rhymes than does Verlaine; Baudelaire more often repeats lines. Nor has anyone done an empirical study to determine whether poems identified as "musical" by naive and by sophisticated audiences actually contain more repetitive devices than do other poems. No one, in short, has rigorously characterized "musicality" in language in linguistic terms. And no one who wishes to ascribe "musicality" to the verse of Verlaine and the other Symbolists has come to terms with the fact that all these poets were lamentably illiterate and incompetent as composers, as performers, and even as passive listeners to music. While awaiting the outcome of the empirical and statistical studies of the future, we can best treat the problem of literary "musicality" by recognizing that "musicality" serves merely as a metaphor for the relative prominence of phonemic and verbal repetition; for allusions to, evocations of, and descriptions of things musical; for the foregrounding of rhythm, which is the essence of music; for vagueness of denotation; and for the suppression of overt narrative progression. (These last two traits often figure together in descriptions of that critical artifact called "literary impressionism.") Taken all together, these features do not help to distinguish Verlaine's poetry from that of many of his contemporaries.

One can obtain a more fruitful definition of Verlaine's "musicality" by observing what I consider to be a primary rule in literary criticism: once you have singled out a certain motif or a feature for analysis, seek its polar opposite. It is not the motif of "musicality" alone but the structure formed by thesis (here, "musicality"), antithesis (whatever for Verlaine may seem opposed to "musicality"), and the relationship between them which characterizes the creative individuality of the poet. This structure defines his imagination (in linguistic terms, his poetic "competence") and its expression (in linguistic terms, his poetic "performance") in a way that one isolated element such as "musicality," shared by many poets, could not possibly do.

Mistrusting the act of communication, each of the major French Symbolist poets focuses his principal suspicion on one particular, discrete point along the axis of communication. What Verlaine's good early verse does is to call into question the signifying capacities of the verbal medium itself. He fears lest the very ground of his utterances be meaningless or at least vitiated by the way it is ordinarily treated. The problem is not merely that he finds words inadequate to treat transcendent subjects (Mallarmé's difficulty) but rather that he finds words unreliable, period. Since he still wishes to write poetry, he has no recourse other than to exalt the "je ne sais quoi," the "imprécis," and to expatiate upon the topos of inexpressibility.

Antoine Adam, a noted critic of Verlaine, does not take the poet's antilinguistic stance too seriously. He invokes [in *The Art of Paul Verlaine,* 1963] the testimony of Edmond Lepelletier, who saw Verlaine daily at the time of his early publications and claimed that lyrical expressions of love and sadness in the *Poèmes saturniens* and the *Fêtes galantes* were mere poses in a person interested primarily in dogmatic poetics. He cites two lines from **"Aspiration"** (1861) to suggest that the critique of love language in ensuing collections may derive as much from misogyny as mistrust of communication: "Loin de tout ce qui vit, loin des hommes, encor / Plus loin des femmes". Far from all that lives, far from men, and yet / Farther from women). Referring specifically to the *Fêtes galantes,* Adam claims: "This poetry of an all-embracing mel-

ancholy dimension is, however, meant to be a game. . . . The poet amuses himself. . . . Baudelaire's sober doctrine [in Verlaine's **"A Clymène"**] becomes a pretext for subtle combinations of hues and fragrances. The enjambments that set off the ironical charge of a phrase, and the rhymes—profuse, unusual, employed in a hundred original ways—these are part of the fun."

But in an interpretation similar to my own, Jacques-Henry Bornecque, who studied this crucial collection in much more detail, maintains that it traces a sequence of moods declining toward pessimism and despair. Verlaine contaminates with his own sadness the playful Regency world (1715-23) into which he had hoped to escape. His other writings of the same period include many macabre pieces that express his disgust with his contemporaries. Bornecque observes, "In those verse or prose pieces that are not 'fêtes galantes,' Verlaine does not disguise his feelings: he gives free rein to his peevishness as to his anguish, regularly and obviously swinging between aggressive bitterness and the despairing detachment which is the ebb tide of the former." He cites many examples, notably the sinister short story "Le Poteau," which reveals a certain affinity with Baudelaire's "Vin de l'assassin." The death of Verlaine's beloved Elisa Moncomble four days before the composition of the first two "Fêtes galantes" seems decisive. Bornecque characterizes the collection as the work of a convalescent—a convalescent, one could add, with nothing to live for.

Sensitive though he is to Verlaine's moods, Bornecque overlooks the poet's mistrust of language, so characteristic of the Symbolist crisis. Unlike the other major French Symbolist poets, Verlaine focuses this mistrust on the linguistic medium itself, instead of on the acts of conceiving and communicating a message. He subverts the notion of the essential "humanness" of language by playfully (and of course figuratively) replacing human speakers with nonhuman ones. And by making utterances flatly contradict the situations to which they refer, Verlaine challenges our assumption that language provides reliable information. Many instances can be found in the prose works, particularly the **Mémoires d'un veuf**. There **"Bons bourgeois"** describes a family quarrel: after an exchange of insults, "la parole est à la vaisselle maintenant" (now the crockery [which the family members start throwing at each other] does the talking). Afterward the lady of the house excuses herself to her visiting country relative by saying CELA N'ARRIVE JAMAIS" (that never happens). **"Ma Fille"** cancels its own language when after an idealized description the narrator announces, "Heureusement qu'elle n'a jamais existé et ne naîtra probablement plus!" (Fortunately she never lived and probably will not be born in the future!). In another story, Pierre Duchâtelet has a conversation with his wife in which he lies to conceal his imminent departure for a ten-day mission to a battle zone; on his return he finds a letter saying simply, "Monsieur— Adieu pour toujours" (Sir: Farewell forever). And if we read allegorically, considering the hand as the writer's instrument . . . , we could even say that artistic self-expression destroys its subject and is itself doomed to a sudden death. Such an interpretation illuminates Verlaine's tale **"La Main du Major Muller"** (from *Histoires comme ça*), where the preserved hand that had to be amputated after a duel comes to life, poisons its owner, and then quickly rots.

The most compelling corroborative evidence for Verlaine's dour linguistic self-consciousness, however, comes from the master article of all his literary criticism (and one that should be much better known): his response to another great Symbolist poet, Baudelaire. This piece appeared in the November 16, 1865, issue of *L'Art*. Of three individual lines cited as models, two treat nonverbal communication: "Le regard singulier d'une femme galante" (the odd glance of a promiscuous woman) and "Un soir l'âme du vin chantait dans les bouteilles" (One evening the soul of the wine was singing inside the bottles). From the five wine poems, in other words, the one line that Verlaine cites is one that gives a voice to a nonhuman entity. And from the "Tableaux parisiens" section, likewise, Verlaine singles out this passage:

> Et, voisin des clochers, écouter en rêvant
> Leurs hymnes solennels emportés par le vent . . .
>
> . . . . .
>
> Je verrai l'atelier qui chante et qui bavarde.

(And, next to the bell towers, to listen dreamily / To their solemn hymns carried off by the wind / . . . / I shall see the workshop singing and chattering.)

After beginning the essay with the declaration that "le public est un enfant mal élevé qu'il s'agit de corriger" (the public is a badly brought up child: you have to chastise it), Verlaine gives as examples of appropriate behaviors instances of silencing: the poem **"Semper eadem"** with its repeated "Taisez-vous!" (Quiet!) and elsewhere the command to the beloved, "Sois charmante, et tais-toi" (Be charming, and be still). Far more is at stake here than mere playfulness.

Whereas narrative and drama represent what is meaningful to at least several people or to a collective culture, the lyric represents what is meaningful to only one person. Poetry is half a conversation, a soliloquy or apostrophe to a being that is nonhuman, absent, or dead, and therefore incapable of responding in words. When we say "Rose, thou art sick," we don't expect an answer. In those instances where the interlocutor is not suppressed, poetry becomes "dramatic lyric" that shades into theater. In the lyric situation, where the single speaking voice is the norm, Verlaine sometimes imposes one of two marked choices. Either he uses free direct discourse—a conversation that does not identify the speakers—to multiply the sources of meaningfulness to the point where each interferes with the other and they blur; or else he introduces nonverbal elements so as to subvert meaningfulness at its source; or he does both at once, as in the paradigmatic **"Sur l'herbe"** of the *Fêtes galantes*.

When Verlaine does depict the normal one-sided conversation, he undermines its meaningfulness as much as he can without sacrificing coherence. He tries to express his radical skepticism regarding the power of words to signify by undermining their status and seeming to replace them with something else. For him this something else is musicality: not a flight into a balmy vagueness, but the cutting edge of his satiric attack on the verbal ground of our relationships. By using uncommon "rythmes impairs" (five-, seven-, nine-, eleven-, or thirteen-syllable lines) instead of the octosyllables, decasyllables, or alexandrines that were to dominate French poetry through the 1920s, Verlaine again makes a "marked choice"; he selects a form of expression that violates our expectations through the absence or the excess of a certain quality. He foregrounds the supreme musicality of rhythm at the expense of the other elements of poetry. Since the essence of music lies in rhythm more than in melody, harmony, intensity, or timbre, a poetry that calls attention to its rhythm makes that element a rival of the verbal poetry rather than its adjunct. Similarly, from the *Fêtes galantes* on, internal rhyme and assonance become more common in Verlaine's poetry, constituting a marked choice of sound repetition in excess of what one would ordinarily expect and thus suggesting, once again, an antiverbal musicality. More obviously, of course, words seem to become ancillary in Verlaine's texts when he uses them to denote, connote, or describe music and the visual arts. He subverts language by using words to evoke indefinable states of vagueness and confusion; to designate situations in which the words themselves are trivial, insincere, or absurd; and to characterize acts whereby words cancel themselves or serve to impose silence. To produce a mere catalogue of such devices would be a facile and not very enlightening exercise. But as it happens, examining them in context can illuminate the structure of individual collections of verse and clarify the trajectory of Verlaine's entire career.

The section titled "Melancholia" in Verlaine's first collection of verse, the *Poèmes saturniens* (1867), presents the dilemma of the breakdown of signification thematically, by depicting the lyric self's nostalgia for a past time when love language was still meaningful. Distancing himself from his nostalgia in the last section of the *Poèmes saturniens,* the lyric self shifts to a parody of love language from "La Chanson des ingénues" on; such parody persists to the end of the *Fêtes galantes* (1869). As the historical Verlaine strives to return to a conventional life, *La Bonne Chanson* (1870) transiently adopts a conventional, affirmative poeticizing. The *Romances sans paroles* (1872) revert to undermining signification, but they show rather than tell. A supreme discursive *prise de conscience* affirming vagueness and musicality as the highest poetic goals appears in "L'Art poétique" of 1874 (published only when *Jadis et naguère* appeared in 1882). This statement itself, however, is subverted by verbal excess, for there is a fundamental paradox in specifying how to be allusive.

Verlaine's Symbolist crisis, then, as I would define it, lasted from 1866 to 1874. After his conversion in prison, he seems to have become dedicated to betraying his earlier self. He reverts to a wholly conventional prosodic practice and to a thematic questioning, typical of Romanticism, of the codes and contexts of traditional beliefs rather than a questioning of the efficacy of the communicative process itself. Some thirty-two poems from his earlier years, previously unpublished in collections, appear in the later collections (notably in *Jadis et naguère*, which contains twenty-seven of them) but without exception they lack the critical bite of those already published—the reason Verlaine had set them aside in the first place. A few pieces in *Parallèlement* (1889), composed probably between 1884 and 1889, again present a lyric self alienated from love and his own words and sinking into a preoccupation with mere physicality. But these poems appear superficial; they degenerate into self-parody; and they convey none of the fundamental questioning of signification characteristic of Verlaine's "Symbolist" period. Verlaine's 1890 article "**Critique des *Poèmes saturniens***" rejected everything he had written before *Sagesse* in 1881—in other words, nearly everything most critics still find important. . . .

Our faith in the referentiality of language—that there exists a real link between the signifier and a signified—depends upon our faith in intersubjectivity, the belief that we share a common code and that each signifier means the same thing to us as to the significant others in our lives. Once Verlaine had experienced "l'incommunicabilité," the impossibility of communication, he attacked the belief in referentiality in three distinct ways in his poetry. At times, as in the theater of the absurd, he depicted a dialogue of the deaf, as in **"Colloque sentimental,"** where each signifier has different referents for different people. At other times he exalted "musicality" over verbality: thus he was attracted to the libretti of Favart, which he studied with Rimbaud, because they provided the model for a form intermediate, so to speak, between language and music, insofar as the importance of the words was minimized by the necessity of tailoring them to the prepotent musical form. Verlaine's marked choice of unusual rhythms augmented the ostensible importance of the "musical"—that is, the rhythmic—dimension of his verse by calling attention to its rhythms so they could not be taken for granted. As Verlaine, like the other Symbolists, was not himself musical and was in fact rather unfamiliar with music, the inspiration that music could provide for his verse had to remain limited. Yet his fascination with musicality represented a positive response to the experience of the emptiness of language, for it implied that one can shift out of an unreliable system into another system that is self-contained. When you name musical notes, for example, your referents are elements of a preexisting structure independent of language; their "meanings" are precisely non-referential, consisting as they do in internal relationships between the parts of a musical composition.

The pessimistic mode of Verlaine's assault on signification, the one with which he ended, was the specular, narcissistic short circuit in which all signifiers voiced by the poet refer back to the poet himself. In his earlier collections of verse, images of the moon symbolize this condition. The heavenly body corresponds to the poet's body (e.g., the Pierrot's white face explicitly mimics the appearance of the moon), and the moon also recalls the fantasized maternal breast, surviving in the preconscious as the dream screen and existing only to gratify the needs of the imperial self. In the weaker later verse, the confessional tradition back into which Verlaine sinks narrativizes this pessimistic solution of narcissism. If you cannot communicate with others, then you must commune with your own emptiness.

FURTHER READING

Biography

Hanson, Lawrence, and Hanson, Elizabeth. *Verlaine: Fool of God.* New York: Random House, 1957, 394 p.
    A sensitive and sympathetic biography that treats Verlaine's works as a natural outgrowth of his personality.

Harris, Frank. "Talks with Paul Verlaine." In *Contemporary Portraits,* pp. 269-82. New York: Mitchell Kennerly, 1915.
    Personal recollections of Verlaine and his wife, providing insights into both their characters.

Richardson, Joanna. *Verlaine.* New York: Viking, 1971, 432 p.
    A critical biography, scholarly and readable.

Criticism

Bishop, Michael. "Verlaine." In *Nineteenth-Century French Poetry,* pp. 221-54. New York: Twayne Publishers, 1993.
    A detailed stylistic and thematic analysis which includes discussion of such topics as the body, women, aspirations, hope, self-renewal, gods, loves, parallels, unity, and innocence in Verlaine's verse.

Carter, A. E. *The Idea of Decadence in French Literature: 1830-1900.* Toronto: University of Toronto Press, 1958, 154 p.
    Discusses Verlaine in the context of the Decadent movement, commenting on Verlaine's ideas of homosexuality.

Cohn, Robert Greer. "Rescuing a Sonnet of Verlaine: 'L'espoir luit . . .'." *Romantic Review* LXXVII, No. 2 (March 1987): 125-30.
    Examines religious and stylistic elements in Verlaine's sonnet.

King, Russell S. "Verlaine's Verbal Sensation." *Studies in Philology* 72, No. 2 (April 1975): 226-36.
    Linguistic study of Verlaine's poetry with a concentration on Verlaine's unique use of verbs and adjectives.

————"The Poet As Clown: Variations on a Theme in Nineteenth-Century French Poetry." *Orbis Litterarum* 33, No. 3 (1978): 238-52.
    A comparative study of the clown as symbol of the poet

in the poetry of Verlaine, Théodore de Banville, Charles Baudelaire, and Stéphane Mallarmé.

Milech, Barbara. "'This Kind': Pornographic Discourses, Lesbian Bodies, and Paul Verlaine's *Les Amies.*" In *Men Writing the Feminine: Literature, Theory, and the Question of Genders,* edited by Thaïs E. Morgan, pp. 107-22. Albany: State University of New York Press, 1994.

A scholarly exploration of *Les Amies,* a set of six sonnets on lesbian love, using Foucauldian and feminist theory.

Nalbantian, Suzanne. "The Symbolists: The Failing Soul." In *The Symbol of the Soul from Holderlin to Yeats: A Study in Metonomy,* pp. 66-85. New York: Columbia University Press, 1977.

Describes how Verlaine and other Symbolists treat the soul as a static and material entity, incapable of transcendence.

Rifelj, Carol de Dobay. "Familiar and Unfamiliar: Verlaine's Poetic Diction." *Kentucky Romance Quarterly* 29, No. 4 (1982): 365-77.

Discusses Verlaine's poetic diction, particularly his use of colloquial and even vulgar and slang expressions

——————"Verlaine: Wringing the Neck of Eloquence." In *Word and Figure: The Language of Nineteenth Century French Poetry,* pp. 100-31. Athens: Ohio University Press, 1987.

Examines Verlaine's use of colloquial diction, metaphor, and figurative language in his verse.

Schmidt, Paul. "Visions of Violence: Rimbaud and Verlaine." In *Homosexualities and French Literature,* edited by George Stambolian and Elaine Marks, pp. 228-42. Ithaca, NY: Cornell University Press, 1979.

An analysis of the sadomasochistic homosexual relationship between Verlaine and Rimbaud as evidenced through their verse.

Sonnenfeld, Albert. "The Forgotten Verlaine." *Bucknell Review* XI, No. 1 (December 1962): 73-80.

Investigates the anti-lyrical strain often found in Verlaine's verse, attributing it to the poet's need for irony and his feelings of inadequacy.

Stephan, Philip. "Paul Verlaine." In *European Writers: The Romantic Century,* Vol. 7, edited by Jacques Barzun, pp. 1619-43. New York: Charles Scribner's Sons, 1985.

Informative biographical and critical overview.

Walker, Hallam. "Visual and Spatial Imagery in Verlaine's *Fêtes galantes.*" *Publications of the Modern Language Association of America* 87, No. 5 (October 1972): 1007-15.

Analyzes the visual and spatial elements of Verlaine's poetry.

Additional coverage of Verlaine's life and career is contained in the following sources published by Gale Research: *Nineteenth-Century Literature Criticism,* Volume 2; and *Poetry Criticism,* Volume 2.

Nineteenth-Century Literature Criticism

Cumulative Indexes
Volumes 1-51

How to Use This Index

The main references

Calvino, Italo
      1923-1985.....CLC 5, 8, 11, 22, 33, 39,
                                      73; SSC 3
---

list all author entries in the following Gale Literary Criticism series:

BLC = *Black Literature Criticism*
CLC = *Contemporary Literary Criticism*
CLR = *Children's Literature Review*
CMLC = *Classical and Medieval Literature Criticism*
DA = *DISCovering Authors*
DC = *Drama Criticism*
HLC = *Hispanic Literature Criticism*
LC = *Literature Criticism from 1400 to 1800*
NCLC = *Nineteenth-Century Literature Criticism*
PC = *Poetry Criticism*
SSC = *Short Story Criticism*
TCLC = *Twentieth-Century Literary Criticism*
WLC = *World Literature Criticism, 1500 to the Present*

The cross-references

See also CANR 23; CA 85-88;
   obituary CA 116
---

list all author entries in the following Gale biographical and literary sources:

AAYA = *Authors & Artists for Young Adults*
AITN = *Authors in the News*
BEST = *Bestsellers*
BW = *Black Writers*
CA = *Contemporary Authors*
CAAS = *Contemporary Authors Autobiography Series*
CABS = *Contemporary Authors Bibliographical Series*
CANR = *Contemporary Authors New Revision Series*
CAP = *Contemporary Authors Permanent Series*
CDALB = *Concise Dictionary of American Literary Biography*
CDBLB = *Concise Dictionary of British Literary Biography*
DLB = *Dictionary of Literary Biography*
DLBD = *Dictionary of Literary Biography Documentary Series*
DLBY = *Dictionary of Literary Biography Yearbook*
HW = *Hispanic Writers*
JRDA = *Junior DISCovering Authors*
MAICYA = *Major Authors and Illustrators for Children and Young Adults*
MTCW = *Major 20th-Century Writers*
NNAL = *Native North American Literature*
SAAS = *Something about the Author Autobiography Series*
SATA = *Something about the Author*
YABC = *Yesterday's Authors of Books for Children*

Literary Criticism Series
Cumulative Author Index

Barfoot, Joan 1946- . . . . **CLC 18**
See also CA 105

Baring, Maurice 1874-1945 . . . . **TCLC 8**
See also CA 105; DLB 34

Barker, Clive 1952- . . . . **CLC 52**
See also AAYA 10; BEST 90:3; CA 121;
129; MTCW

Barker, George Granville
1913-1991 . . . . **CLC 8, 48**
See also CA 9-12R; 135; CANR 7, 38;
DLB 20; MTCW

Barker, Harley Granville
See Granville-Barker, Harley
See also DLB 10

Barker, Howard 1946- . . . . **CLC 37**
See also CA 102; DLB 13

Barker, Pat 1943- . . . . **CLC 32**
See also CA 117; 122

Barlow, Joel 1754-1812 . . . . **NCLC 23**
See also DLB 37

Barnard, Mary (Ethel) 1909- . . . . **CLC 48**
See also CA 21-22; CAP 2

Barnes, Djuna
1892-1982 . . . **CLC 3, 4, 8, 11, 29; SSC 3**
See also CA 9-12R; 107; CANR 16; DLB 4,
9, 45; MTCW

Barnes, Julian 1946- . . . . **CLC 42**
See also CA 102; CANR 19; DLBY 93

Barnes, Peter 1931- . . . . **CLC 5, 56**
See also CA 65-68; CAAS 12; CANR 33,
34; DLB 13; MTCW

Baroja (y Nessi), Pio
1872-1956 . . . . **TCLC 8; HLC**
See also CA 104

Baron, David
See Pinter, Harold

Baron Corvo
See Rolfe, Frederick (William Serafino
Austin Lewis Mary)

Barondess, Sue K(aufman)
1926-1977 . . . . **CLC 8**
See also Kaufman, Sue
See also CA 1-4R; 69-72; CANR 1

Baron de Teive
See Pessoa, Fernando (Antonio Nogueira)

Barres, Maurice 1862-1923 . . . . **TCLC 47**
See also DLB 123

Barreto, Afonso Henrique de Lima
See Lima Barreto, Afonso Henrique de

Barrett, (Roger) Syd 1946- . . . . **CLC 35**

Barrett, William (Christopher)
1913-1992 . . . . **CLC 27**
See also CA 13-16R; 139; CANR 11

Barrie, J(ames) M(atthew)
1860-1937 . . . . **TCLC 2**
See also CA 104; 136; CDBLB 1890-1914;
CLR 16; DLB 10, 141; MAICYA;
YABC 1

Barrington, Michael
See Moorcock, Michael (John)

Barrol, Grady
See Bograd, Larry

Barry, Mike
See Malzberg, Barry N(athaniel)

Barry, Philip 1896-1949 . . . . **TCLC 11**
See also CA 109; DLB 7

Bart, Andre Schwarz
See Schwarz-Bart, Andre

Barth, John (Simmons)
1930- . . . . . . **CLC 1, 2, 3, 5, 7, 9, 10, 14,
27, 51, 89; SSC 10**
See also AITN 1, 2; CA 1-4R; CABS 1;
CANR 5, 23, 49; DLB 2; MTCW

Barthelme, Donald
1931-1989 . . . . . . **CLC 1, 2, 3, 5, 6, 8, 13,
23, 46, 59; SSC 2**
See also CA 21-24R; 129; CANR 20;
DLB 2; DLBY 80, 89; MTCW; SATA 7;
SATA-Obit 62

Barthelme, Frederick 1943- . . . . **CLC 36**
See also CA 114; 122; DLBY 85

Barthes, Roland (Gerard)
1915-1980 . . . . **CLC 24, 83**
See also CA 130; 97-100; MTCW

Barzun, Jacques (Martin) 1907- . . . . **CLC 51**
See also CA 61-64; CANR 22

Bashevis, Isaac
See Singer, Isaac Bashevis

Bashkirtseff, Marie 1859-1884 . . . **NCLC 27**

Basho
See Matsuo Basho

Bass, Kingsley B., Jr.
See Bullins, Ed

Bass, Rick 1958- . . . . **CLC 79**
See also CA 126

Bassani, Giorgio 1916- . . . . **CLC 9**
See also CA 65-68; CANR 33; DLB 128;
MTCW

Bastos, Augusto (Antonio) Roa
See Roa Bastos, Augusto (Antonio)

Bataille, Georges 1897-1962 . . . . **CLC 29**
See also CA 101; 89-92

Bates, H(erbert) E(rnest)
1905-1974 . . . . **CLC 46; SSC 10**
See also CA 93-96; 45-48; CANR 34;
MTCW

Bauchart
See Camus, Albert

Baudelaire, Charles
1821-1867 . . . . . **NCLC 6, 29; DA; PC 1;
SSC 18; WLC**

Baudrillard, Jean 1929- . . . . **CLC 60**

Baum, L(yman) Frank 1856-1919 . . . **TCLC 7**
See also CA 108; 133; CLR 15; DLB 22;
JRDA; MAICYA; MTCW; SATA 18

Baum, Louis F.
See Baum, L(yman) Frank

Baumbach, Jonathan 1933- . . . . . . **CLC 6, 23**
See also CA 13-16R; CAAS 5; CANR 12;
DLBY 80; MTCW

Bausch, Richard (Carl) 1945- . . . . . . **CLC 51**
See also CA 101; CAAS 14; CANR 43;
DLB 130

Baxter, Charles 1947- . . . . **CLC 45, 78**
See also CA 57-60; CANR 40; DLB 130

Baxter, George Owen
See Faust, Frederick (Schiller)

Baxter, James K(eir) 1926-1972 . . . . **CLC 14**
See also CA 77-80

Baxter, John
See Hunt, E(verette) Howard, (Jr.)

Bayer, Sylvia
See Glassco, John

Baynton, Barbara 1857-1929 . . . . . . **TCLC 57**

Beagle, Peter S(oyer) 1939- . . . . **CLC 7**
See also CA 9-12R; CANR 4; DLBY 80;
SATA 60

Bean, Normal
See Burroughs, Edgar Rice

Beard, Charles A(ustin)
1874-1948 . . . . **TCLC 15**
See also CA 115; DLB 17; SATA 18

Beardsley, Aubrey 1872-1898 . . . . . **NCLC 6**

Beattie, Ann
1947- . . . . **CLC 8, 13, 18, 40, 63; SSC 11**
See also BEST 90:2; CA 81-84; DLBY 82;
MTCW

Beattie, James 1735-1803 . . . . **NCLC 25**
See also DLB 109

Beauchamp, Kathleen Mansfield 1888-1923
See Mansfield, Katherine
See also CA 104; 134; DA

Beaumarchais, Pierre-Augustin Caron de
1732-1799 . . . . **DC 4**

**Beauvoir, Simone (Lucie Ernestine Marie
Bertrand) de**
1908-1986 . . . . **CLC 1, 2, 4, 8, 14, 31, 44,
50, 71; DA; WLC**
See also CA 9-12R; 118; CANR 28;
DLB 72; DLBY 86; MTCW

Becker, Jurek 1937- . . . . **CLC 7, 19**
See also CA 85-88; DLB 75

Becker, Walter 1950- . . . . **CLC 26**

Beckett, Samuel (Barclay)
1906-1989 . . . . . . **CLC 1, 2, 3, 4, 6, 9, 10,
11, 14, 18, 29, 57, 59, 83; DA; SSC 16;
WLC**
See also CA 5-8R; 130; CANR 33;
CDBLB 1945-1960; DLB 13, 15;
DLBY 90; MTCW

Beckford, William 1760-1844 . . . . **NCLC 16**
See also DLB 39

Beckman, Gunnel 1910- . . . . **CLC 26**
See also CA 33-36R; CANR 15; CLR 25;
MAICYA; SAAS 9; SATA 6

Becque, Henri 1837-1899 . . . . **NCLC 3**

Beddoes, Thomas Lovell
1803-1849 . . . . **NCLC 3**
See also DLB 96

Bedford, Donald F.
See Fearing, Kenneth (Flexner)

Beecher, Catharine Esther
1800-1878 . . . . **NCLC 30**
See also DLB 1

Beecher, John 1904-1980 . . . . **CLC 6**
See also AITN 1; CA 5-8R; 105; CANR 8

Beer, Johann 1655-1700 . . . . **LC 5**

Beer, Patricia 1924- . . . . **CLC 58**
See also CA 61-64; CANR 13, 46; DLB 40

Berrigan, Daniel 1921-............ **CLC 4**
See also CA 33-36R; CAAS 1; CANR 11,
43; DLB 5

Berrigan, Edmund Joseph Michael, Jr.
1934-1983
See Berrigan, Ted
See also CA 61-64; 110; CANR 14

Berrigan, Ted.................... **CLC 37**
See also Berrigan, Edmund Joseph Michael,
Jr.
See also DLB 5

Berry, Charles Edward Anderson 1931-
See Berry, Chuck
See also CA 115

Berry, Chuck.................... **CLC 17**
See also Berry, Charles Edward Anderson

Berry, Jonas
See Ashbery, John (Lawrence)

Berry, Wendell (Erdman)
1934-............. **CLC 4, 6, 8, 27, 46**
See also AITN 1; CA 73-76; DLB 5, 6

Berryman, John
1914-1972 ...... **CLC 1, 2, 3, 4, 6, 8, 10,
13, 25, 62**
See also CA 13-16; 33-36R; CABS 2;
CANR 35; CAP 1; CDALB 1941-1968;
DLB 48; MTCW

Bertolucci, Bernardo 1940-........ **CLC 16**
See also CA 106

Bertrand, Aloysius 1807-1841 .... **NCLC 31**

Bertran de Born c. 1140-1215 ..... **CMLC 5**

Besant, Annie (Wood) 1847-1933 ... **TCLC 9**
See also CA 105

Bessie, Alvah 1904-1985.......... **CLC 23**
See also CA 5-8R; 116; CANR 2; DLB 26

Bethlen, T. D.
See Silverberg, Robert

Beti, Mongo................ **CLC 27; BLC**
See also Biyidi, Alexandre

Betjeman, John
1906-1984 .... **CLC 2, 6, 10, 34, 43**
See also CA 9-12R; 112; CANR 33;
CDBLB 1945-1960; DLB 20; DLBY 84;
MTCW

Bettelheim, Bruno 1903-1990 ...... **CLC 79**
See also CA 81-84; 131; CANR 23; MTCW

Betti, Ugo 1892-1953 .... **TCLC 5**
See also CA 104

Betts, Doris (Waugh) 1932-.... **CLC 3, 6, 28**
See also CA 13-16R; CANR 9; DLBY 82

Bevan, Alistair
See Roberts, Keith (John Kingston)

Bialik, Chaim Nachman
1873-1934 .... **TCLC 25**

Bickerstaff, Isaac
See Swift, Jonathan

Bidart, Frank 1939- .... **CLC 33**
See also CA 140

Bienek, Horst 1930-........... **CLC 7, 11**
See also CA 73-76; DLB 75

Bierce, Ambrose (Gwinett)
1842-1914(?) .... **TCLC 1, 7, 44; DA;
SSC 9; WLC**
See also CA 104; 139; CDALB 1865-1917;
DLB 11, 12, 23, 71, 74

Billings, Josh
See Shaw, Henry Wheeler

Billington, (Lady) Rachel (Mary)
1942- .... **CLC 43**
See also AITN 2; CA 33-36R; CANR 44

Binyon, T(imothy) J(ohn) 1936- .... **CLC 34**
See also CA 111; CANR 28

Bioy Casares, Adolfo
1914- ... **CLC 4, 8, 13, 88; HLC; SSC 17**
See also CA 29-32R; CANR 19, 43;
DLB 113; HW; MTCW

Bird, Cordwainer
See Ellison, Harlan (Jay)

Bird, Robert Montgomery
1806-1854 .... **NCLC 1**

Birney, (Alfred) Earle
1904- .... **CLC 1, 4, 6, 11**
See also CA 1-4R; CANR 5, 20; DLB 88;
MTCW

Bishop, Elizabeth
1911-1979 ...... **CLC 1, 4, 9, 13, 15, 32;
DA; PC 3**
See also CA 5-8R; 89-92; CABS 2;
CANR 26; CDALB 1968-1988; DLB 5;
MTCW; SATA-Obit 24

Bishop, John 1935-............... **CLC 10**
See also CA 105

Bissett, Bill 1939-................ **CLC 18**
See also CA 69-72; CAAS 19; CANR 15;
DLB 53; MTCW

Bitov, Andrei (Georgievich) 1937-... **CLC 57**
See also CA 142

Biyidi, Alexandre 1932-
See Beti, Mongo
See also BW 1; CA 114; 124; MTCW

Bjarme, Brynjolf
See Ibsen, Henrik (Johan)

Bjornson, Bjornstjerne (Martinius)
1832-1910 .... **TCLC 7, 37**
See also CA 104

Black, Robert
See Holdstock, Robert P.

Blackburn, Paul 1926-1971 ...... **CLC 9, 43**
See also CA 81-84; 33-36R; CANR 34;
DLB 16; DLBY 81

Black Elk 1863-1950 .... **TCLC 33**
See also CA 144; NNAL

Black Hobart
See Sanders, (James) Ed(ward)

Blacklin, Malcolm
See Chambers, Aidan

Blackmore, R(ichard) D(oddridge)
1825-1900 .... **TCLC 27**
See also CA 120; DLB 18

Blackmur, R(ichard) P(almer)
1904-1965 .... **CLC 2, 24**
See also CA 11-12; 25-28R; CAP 1; DLB 63

Black Tarantula, The
See Acker, Kathy

Blackwood, Algernon (Henry)
1869-1951 .... **TCLC 5**
See also CA 105; DLB 153

Blackwood, Caroline 1931- .... **CLC 6, 9**
See also CA 85-88; CANR 32; DLB 14;
MTCW

Blade, Alexander
See Hamilton, Edmond; Silverberg, Robert

Blaga, Lucian 1895-1961 .... **CLC 75**

Blair, Eric (Arthur) 1903-1950
See Orwell, George
See also CA 104; 132; DA; MTCW;
SATA 29

Blais, Marie-Claire
1939- .... **CLC 2, 4, 6, 13, 22**
See also CA 21-24R; CAAS 4; CANR 38;
DLB 53; MTCW

Blaise, Clark 1940-............... **CLC 29**
See also AITN 2; CA 53-56; CAAS 3;
CANR 5; DLB 53

Blake, Nicholas
See Day Lewis, C(ecil)
See also DLB 77

Blake, William
1757-1827 .... **NCLC 13, 37; DA;
PC 12; WLC**
See also CDBLB 1789-1832; DLB 93;
MAICYA; SATA 30

Blasco Ibanez, Vicente
1867-1928 .... **TCLC 12**
See also CA 110; 131; HW; MTCW

Blatty, William Peter 1928-......... **CLC 2**
See also CA 5-8R; CANR 9

Bleeck, Oliver
See Thomas, Ross (Elmore)

Blessing, Lee 1949-.............. **CLC 54**

Blish, James (Benjamin)
1921-1975 .... **CLC 14**
See also CA 1-4R; 57-60; CANR 3; DLB 8;
MTCW; SATA 66

Bliss, Reginald
See Wells, H(erbert) G(eorge)

Blixen, Karen (Christentze Dinesen)
1885-1962
See Dinesen, Isak
See also CA 25-28; CANR 22; CAP 2;
MTCW; SATA 44

Bloch, Robert (Albert) 1917-1994... **CLC 33**
See also CA 5-8R; 146; CAAS 20; CANR 5;
DLB 44; SATA 12

Blok, Alexander (Alexandrovich)
1880-1921 .... **TCLC 5**
See also CA 104

Blom, Jan
See Breytenbach, Breyten

Bloom, Harold 1930- .... **CLC 24**
See also CA 13-16R; CANR 39; DLB 67

Bloomfield, Aurelius
See Bourne, Randolph S(illiman)

Blount, Roy (Alton), Jr. 1941- ..... **CLC 38**
See also CA 53-56; CANR 10, 28; MTCW

Bloy, Leon 1846-1917............ **TCLC 22**
See also CA 121; DLB 123

Bradley, John Ed(mund, Jr.)
1958- . . . . **CLC 55**
See also CA 139

Bradley, Marion Zimmer 1930-. . . . . **CLC 30**
See also AAYA 9; CA 57-60; CAAS 10;
CANR 7, 31; DLB 8; MTCW

Bradstreet, Anne
1612(?)-1672 . . . . . . **LC 4, 30; DA; PC 10**
See also CDALB 1640-1865; DLB 24

Brady, Joan 1939- . . . . **CLC 86**
See also CA 141

Bragg, Melvyn 1939- . . . . **CLC 10**
See also BEST 89:3; CA 57-60; CANR 10,
48; DLB 14

Braine, John (Gerard)
1922-1986 . . . . **CLC 1, 3, 41**
See also CA 1-4R; 120; CANR 1, 33;
CDBLB 1945-1960; DLB 15; DLBY 86;
MTCW

Brammer, William 1930(?)-1978 . . . . **CLC 31**
See also CA 77-80

Brancati, Vitaliano 1907-1954. . . . . **TCLC 12**
See also CA 109

Brancato, Robin F(idler) 1936- . . . . . **CLC 35**
See also AAYA 9; CA 69-72; CANR 11,
45; CLR 32; JRDA; SAAS 9; SATA 23

Brand, Max
See Faust, Frederick (Schiller)

Brand, Millen 1906-1980. . . . . **CLC 7**
See also CA 21-24R; 97-100

Branden, Barbara . . . . **CLC 44**

Brandes, Georg (Morris Cohen)
1842-1927 . . . . **TCLC 10**
See also CA 105

Brandys, Kazimierz 1916- . . . . **CLC 62**

Branley, Franklyn M(ansfield)
1915- . . . . **CLC 21**
See also CA 33-36R; CANR 14, 39;
CLR 13; MAICYA; SAAS 16; SATA 4,
68

Brathwaite, Edward Kamau 1930-. . . **CLC 11**
See also BW 2; CA 25-28R; CANR 11, 26,
47; DLB 125

Brautigan, Richard (Gary)
1935-1984 . . . . **CLC 1, 3, 5, 9, 12, 34, 42**
See also CA 53-56; 113; CANR 34; DLB 2,
5; DLBY 80, 84; MTCW; SATA 56

Braverman, Kate 1950- . . . . **CLC 67**
See also CA 89-92

Brecht, Bertolt
1898-1956 . . . . . . **TCLC 1, 6, 13, 35; DA;
DC 3; WLC**
See also CA 104; 133; DLB 56, 124; MTCW

Brecht, Eugen Berthold Friedrich
See Brecht, Bertolt

Bremer, Fredrika 1801-1865 . . . . . **NCLC 11**

Brennan, Christopher John
1870-1932 . . . . **TCLC 17**
See also CA 117

Brennan, Maeve 1917- . . . . **CLC 5**
See also CA 81-84

Brentano, Clemens (Maria)
1778-1842 . . . . **NCLC 1**
See also DLB 90

Brent of Bin Bin
See Franklin, (Stella Maraia Sarah) Miles

Brenton, Howard 1942-. . . . . **CLC 31**
See also CA 69-72; CANR 33; DLB 13;
MTCW

Breslin, James 1930-
See Breslin, Jimmy
See also CA 73-76; CANR 31; MTCW

Breslin, Jimmy . . . . **CLC 4, 43**
See also Breslin, James
See also AITN 1

Bresson, Robert 1901-. . . . . **CLC 16**
See also CA 110; CANR 49

Breton, Andre 1896-1966. . . **CLC 2, 9, 15, 54**
See also CA 19-20; 25-28R; CANR 40;
CAP 2; DLB 65; MTCW

Breytenbach, Breyten 1939(?)- . . **CLC 23, 37**
See also CA 113; 129

Bridgers, Sue Ellen 1942- . . . . **CLC 26**
See also AAYA 8; CA 65-68; CANR 11,
36; CLR 18; DLB 52; JRDA; MAICYA;
SAAS 1; SATA 22

Bridges, Robert (Seymour)
1844-1930 . . . . **TCLC 1**
See also CA 104; CDBLB 1890-1914;
DLB 19, 98

Bridie, James . . . . **TCLC 3**
See also Mavor, Osborne Henry
See also DLB 10

Brin, David 1950-. . . . . **CLC 34**
See also CA 102; CANR 24; SATA 65

Brink, Andre (Philippus)
1935- . . . . **CLC 18, 36**
See also CA 104; CANR 39; MTCW

Brinsmead, H(esba) F(ay) 1922- . . . . **CLC 21**
See also CA 21-24R; CANR 10; MAICYA;
SAAS 5; SATA 18, 78

Brittain, Vera (Mary)
1893(?)-1970 . . . . **CLC 23**
See also CA 13-16; 25-28R; CAP 1; MTCW

Broch, Hermann 1886-1951. . . . . . . **TCLC 20**
See also CA 117; DLB 85, 124

Brock, Rose
See Hansen, Joseph

Brodkey, Harold 1930-. . . . . **CLC 56**
See also CA 111; DLB 130

Brodsky, Iosif Alexandrovich 1940-
See Brodsky, Joseph
See also AITN 1; CA 41-44R; CANR 37;
MTCW

Brodsky, Joseph . . **CLC 4, 6, 13, 36, 50; PC 9**
See also Brodsky, Iosif Alexandrovich

Brodsky, Michael Mark 1948- . . . . . **CLC 19**
See also CA 102; CANR 18, 41

Bromell, Henry 1947-. . . . . **CLC 5**
See also CA 53-56; CANR 9

Bromfield, Louis (Brucker)
1896-1956 . . . . **TCLC 11**
See also CA 107; DLB 4, 9, 86

Broner, E(sther) M(asserman)
1930- . . . . **CLC 19**
See also CA 17-20R; CANR 8, 25; DLB 28

Bronk, William 1918-. . . . . **CLC 10**
See also CA 89-92; CANR 23

Bronstein, Lev Davidovich
See Trotsky, Leon

Bronte, Anne 1820-1849. . . . . **NCLC 4**
See also DLB 21

Bronte, Charlotte
1816-1855 . . . **NCLC 3, 8, 33; DA; WLC**
See also CDBLB 1832-1890; DLB 21

Bronte, (Jane) Emily
1818-1848 . . . . **NCLC 16, 35; DA; PC 8;
WLC**
See also CDBLB 1832-1890; DLB 21, 32

Brooke, Frances 1724-1789 . . . . **LC 6**
See also DLB 39, 99

Brooke, Henry 1703(?)-1783 . . . . **LC 1**
See also DLB 39

Brooke, Rupert (Chawner)
1887-1915 . . . . **TCLC 2, 7; DA; WLC**
See also CA 104; 132; CDBLB 1914-1945;
DLB 19; MTCW

Brooke-Haven, P.
See Wodehouse, P(elham) G(renville)

Brooke-Rose, Christine 1926-. . . . . . **CLC 40**
See also CA 13-16R; DLB 14

Brookner, Anita 1928- . . . . . **CLC 32, 34, 51**
See also CA 114; 120; CANR 37; DLBY 87;
MTCW

Brooks, Cleanth 1906-1994 . . . . . **CLC 24, 86**
See also CA 17-20R; 145; CANR 33, 35;
DLB 63; DLBY 94; MTCW

Brooks, George
See Baum, L(yman) Frank

Brooks, Gwendolyn
1917- . . . . . . **CLC 1, 2, 4, 5, 15, 49; BLC;
DA; PC 7; WLC**
See also AITN 1; BW 2; CA 1-4R;
CANR 1, 27; CDALB 1941-1968;
CLR 27; DLB 5, 76; MTCW; SATA 6

Brooks, Mel . . . . **CLC 12**
See also Kaminsky, Melvin
See also AAYA 13; DLB 26

Brooks, Peter 1938-. . . . . **CLC 34**
See also CA 45-48; CANR 1

Brooks, Van Wyck 1886-1963. . . . . . **CLC 29**
See also CA 1-4R; CANR 6; DLB 45, 63,
103

Brophy, Brigid (Antonia)
1929- . . . . **CLC 6, 11, 29**
See also CA 5-8R; CAAS 4; CANR 25;
DLB 14; MTCW

Brosman, Catharine Savage 1934-. . . . **CLC 9**
See also CA 61-64; CANR 21, 46

Brother Antoninus
See Everson, William (Oliver)

Broughton, T(homas) Alan 1936- . . . **CLC 19**
See also CA 45-48; CANR 2, 23, 48

Broumas, Olga 1949- . . . . **CLC 10, 73**
See also CA 85-88; CANR 20

Brown, Charles Brockden
1771-1810 . . . . **NCLC 22**
See also CDALB 1640-1865; DLB 37, 59,
73

Brown, Christy 1932-1981. . . . . **CLC 63**
See also CA 105; 104; DLB 14

Brown, Claude 1937- . . . . **CLC 30; BLC**
See also AAYA 7; BW 1; CA 73-76

Brown, Dee (Alexander) 1908- . . **CLC 18, 47**
See also CA 13-16R; CAAS 6; CANR 11, 45; DLBY 80; MTCW; SATA 5

Brown, George
See Wertmueller, Lina

Brown, George Douglas
1869-1902 . . . . **TCLC 28**

Brown, George Mackay 1921- . . . . **CLC 5, 48**
See also CA 21-24R; CAAS 6; CANR 12, 37; DLB 14, 27, 139; MTCW; SATA 35

Brown, (William) Larry 1951- . . . . . . **CLC 73**
See also CA 130; 134

Brown, Moses
See Barrett, William (Christopher)

Brown, Rita Mae 1944- . . . . . **CLC 18, 43, 79**
See also CA 45-48; CANR 2, 11, 35; MTCW

Brown, Roderick (Langmere) Haig-
See Haig-Brown, Roderick (Langmere)

Brown, Rosellen 1939- . . . . **CLC 32**
See also CA 77-80; CAAS 10; CANR 14, 44

Brown, Sterling Allen
1901-1989 . . . . **CLC 1, 23, 59; BLC**
See also BW 1; CA 85-88; 127; CANR 26; DLB 48, 51, 63; MTCW

Brown, Will
See Ainsworth, William Harrison

Brown, William Wells
1813-1884 . . . . **NCLC 2; BLC; DC 1**
See also DLB 3, 50

Browne, (Clyde) Jackson 1948(?)- . . . **CLC 21**
See also CA 120

Browning, Elizabeth Barrett
1806-1861 . . . . . **NCLC 1, 16; DA; PC 6; WLC**
See also CDBLB 1832-1890; DLB 32

Browning, Robert
1812-1889 . . . . **NCLC 19; DA; PC 2**
See also CDBLB 1832-1890; DLB 32; YABC 1

Browning, Tod 1882-1962 . . . . **CLC 16**
See also CA 141; 117

Brownson, Orestes (Augustus)
1803-1876 . . . . **NCLC 50**

Bruccoli, Matthew J(oseph) 1931- . . **CLC 34**
See also CA 9-12R; CANR 7; DLB 103

Bruce, Lenny . . . . **CLC 21**
See also Schneider, Leonard Alfred

Bruin, John
See Brutus, Dennis

Brulard, Henri
See Stendhal

Brulls, Christian
See Simenon, Georges (Jacques Christian)

Brunner, John (Kilian Houston)
1934- . . . . **CLC 8, 10**
See also CA 1-4R; CAAS 8; CANR 2, 37; MTCW

Bruno, Giordano 1548-1600 . . . . **LC 27**

Brutus, Dennis 1924- . . . . **CLC 43; BLC**
See also BW 2; CA 49-52; CAAS 14; CANR 2, 27, 42; DLB 117

Bryan, C(ourtlandt) D(ixon) B(arnes)
1936- . . . . **CLC 29**
See also CA 73-76; CANR 13

Bryan, Michael
See Moore, Brian

Bryant, William Cullen
1794-1878 . . . . **NCLC 6, 46; DA**
See also CDALB 1640-1865; DLB 3, 43, 59

Bryusov, Valery Yakovlevich
1873-1924 . . . . **TCLC 10**
See also CA 107

Buchan, John 1875-1940 . . . . **TCLC 41**
See also CA 108; 145; DLB 34, 70; YABC 2

Buchanan, George 1506-1582 . . . . **LC 4**

Buchheim, Lothar-Guenther 1918- . . . **CLC 6**
See also CA 85-88

Buchner, (Karl) Georg
1813-1837 . . . . **NCLC 26**

Buchwald, Art(hur) 1925- . . . . **CLC 33**
See also AITN 1; CA 5-8R; CANR 21; MTCW; SATA 10

Buck, Pearl S(ydenstricker)
1892-1973 . . . . **CLC 7, 11, 18; DA**
See also AITN 1; CA 1-4R; 41-44R; CANR 1, 34; DLB 9, 102; MTCW; SATA 1, 25

Buckler, Ernest 1908-1984 . . . . **CLC 13**
See also CA 11-12; 114; CAP 1; DLB 68; SATA 47

Buckley, Vincent (Thomas)
1925-1988 . . . . **CLC 57**
See also CA 101

Buckley, William F(rank), Jr.
1925- . . . . **CLC 7, 18, 37**
See also AITN 1; CA 1-4R; CANR 1, 24; DLB 137; DLBY 80; MTCW

Buechner, (Carl) Frederick
1926- . . . . **CLC 2, 4, 6, 9**
See also CA 13-16R; CANR 11, 39; DLBY 80; MTCW

Buell, John (Edward) 1927- . . . . **CLC 10**
See also CA 1-4R; DLB 53

Buero Vallejo, Antonio 1916- . . . **CLC 15, 46**
See also CA 106; CANR 24, 49; HW; MTCW

Bufalino, Gesualdo 1920(?)- . . . . **CLC 74**

Bugayev, Boris Nikolayevich 1880-1934
See Bely, Andrey
See also CA 104

Bukowski, Charles
1920-1994 . . . . **CLC 2, 5, 9, 41, 82**
See also CA 17-20R; 144; CANR 40; DLB 5, 130; MTCW

Bulgakov, Mikhail (Afanas'evich)
1891-1940 . . . . **TCLC 2, 16; SSC 18**
See also CA 105

Bulgya, Alexander Alexandrovich
1901-1956 . . . . **TCLC 53**
See also Fadeyev, Alexander
See also CA 117

Bullins, Ed 1935- . . . . **CLC 1, 5, 7; BLC**
See also BW 2; CA 49-52; CAAS 16; CANR 24, 46; DLB 7, 38; MTCW

Bulwer-Lytton, Edward (George Earle Lytton)
1803-1873 . . . . **NCLC 1, 45**
See also DLB 21

Bunin, Ivan Alexeyevich
1870-1953 . . . . **TCLC 6; SSC 5**
See also CA 104

Bunting, Basil 1900-1985 . . . . **CLC 10, 39, 47**
See also CA 53-56; 115; CANR 7; DLB 20

Bunuel, Luis 1900-1983 . . **CLC 16, 80; HLC**
See also CA 101; 110; CANR 32; HW

Bunyan, John 1628-1688 . . **LC 4; DA; WLC**
See also CDBLB 1660-1789; DLB 39

Burckhardt, Jacob (Christoph)
1818-1897 . . . . **NCLC 49**

Burford, Eleanor
See Hibbert, Eleanor Alice Burford

Burgess, Anthony
. **CLC 1, 2, 4, 5, 8, 10, 13, 15, 22, 40, 62, 81**
See also Wilson, John (Anthony) Burgess
See also AITN 1; CDBLB 1960 to Present; DLB 14

Burke, Edmund
1729(?)-1797 . . . . **LC 7; DA; WLC**
See also DLB 104

Burke, Kenneth (Duva)
1897-1993 . . . . **CLC 2, 24**
See also CA 5-8R; 143; CANR 39; DLB 45, 63; MTCW

Burke, Leda
See Garnett, David

Burke, Ralph
See Silverberg, Robert

Burney, Fanny 1752-1840 . . . . **NCLC 12**
See also DLB 39

Burns, Robert 1759-1796 . . . . **PC 6**
See also CDBLB 1789-1832; DA; DLB 109; WLC

Burns, Tex
See L'Amour, Louis (Dearborn)

Burnshaw, Stanley 1906- . . . . . **CLC 3, 13, 44**
See also CA 9-12R; DLB 48

Burr, Anne 1937- . . . . **CLC 6**
See also CA 25-28R

Burroughs, Edgar Rice
1875-1950 . . . . **TCLC 2, 32**
See also AAYA 11; CA 104; 132; DLB 8; MTCW; SATA 41

Burroughs, William S(eward)
1914- . . . . **CLC 1, 2, 5, 15, 22, 42, 75; DA; WLC**
See also AITN 2; CA 9-12R; CANR 20; DLB 2, 8, 16, 152; DLBY 81; MTCW

Burton, Richard F. 1821-1890 . . . . **NCLC 42**
See also DLB 55

Busch, Frederick 1941- . . . **CLC 7, 10, 18, 47**
See also CA 33-36R; CAAS 1; CANR 45; DLB 6

Bush, Ronald 1946- . . . . **CLC 34**
See also CA 136

Bustos, F(rancisco)
See Borges, Jorge Luis

Bustos Domecq, H(onorio)
See Bioy Casares, Adolfo; Borges, Jorge Luis

Butler, Octavia E(stelle) 1947- . . . . . **CLC 38**
See also BW 2; CA 73-76; CANR 12, 24,
38; DLB 33; MTCW

Butler, Robert Olen (Jr.) 1945- . . . . . **CLC 81**
See also CA 112

Butler, Samuel 1612-1680 . . . . **LC 16**
See also DLB 101, 126

Butler, Samuel
1835-1902 . . . . . . **TCLC 1, 33; DA; WLC**
See also CA 143; CDBLB 1890-1914;
DLB 18, 57

Butler, Walter C.
See Faust, Frederick (Schiller)

Butor, Michel (Marie Francois)
1926- . . . . **CLC 1, 3, 8, 11, 15**
See also CA 9-12R; CANR 33; DLB 83;
MTCW

Buzo, Alexander (John) 1944- . . . . . . **CLC 61**
See also CA 97-100; CANR 17, 39

Buzzati, Dino 1906-1972 . . . . **CLC 36**
See also CA 33-36R

Byars, Betsy (Cromer) 1928- . . . . **CLC 35**
See also CA 33-36R; CANR 18, 36; CLR 1,
16; DLB 52; JRDA; MAICYA; MTCW;
SAAS 1; SATA 4, 46, 80

Byatt, A(ntonia) S(usan Drabble)
1936- . . . . **CLC 19, 65**
See also CA 13-16R; CANR 13, 33;
DLB 14; MTCW

Byrne, David 1952- . . . . **CLC 26**
See also CA 127

Byrne, John Keyes 1926-
See Leonard, Hugh
See also CA 102

Byron, George Gordon (Noel)
1788-1824 . . . . . . **NCLC 2, 12; DA; WLC**
See also CDBLB 1789-1832; DLB 96, 110

C. 3. 3.
See Wilde, Oscar (Fingal O'Flahertie Wills)

Caballero, Fernan 1796-1877 . . . . . **NCLC 10**

Cabell, James Branch 1879-1958 . . . **TCLC 6**
See also CA 105; DLB 9, 78

Cable, George Washington
1844-1925 . . . . **TCLC 4; SSC 4**
See also CA 104; DLB 12, 74

Cabral de Melo Neto, Joao 1920- . . . **CLC 76**

Cabrera Infante, G(uillermo)
1929- . . . . **CLC 5, 25, 45; HLC**
See also CA 85-88; CANR 29; DLB 113;
HW; MTCW

Cade, Toni
See Bambara, Toni Cade

Cadmus and Harmonia
See Buchan, John

Caedmon fl. 658-680 . . . . **CMLC 7**
See also DLB 146

Caeiro, Alberto
See Pessoa, Fernando (Antonio Nogueira)

Cage, John (Milton, Jr.) 1912- . . . . . **CLC 41**
See also CA 13-16R; CANR 9

Cain, G.
See Cabrera Infante, G(uillermo)

Cain, Guillermo
See Cabrera Infante, G(uillermo)

Cain, James M(allahan)
1892-1977 . . . . **CLC 3, 11, 28**
See also AITN 1; CA 17-20R; 73-76;
CANR 8, 34; MTCW

Caine, Mark
See Raphael, Frederic (Michael)

Calasso, Roberto 1941- . . . . **CLC 81**
See also CA 143

Calderon de la Barca, Pedro
1600-1681 . . . . **LC 23; DC 3**

Caldwell, Erskine (Preston)
1903-1987 . . . . **CLC 1, 8, 14, 50, 60;**
SSC 19
See also AITN 1; CA 1-4R; 121; CAAS 1;
CANR 2, 33; DLB 9, 86; MTCW

Caldwell, (Janet Miriam) Taylor (Holland)
1900-1985 . . . . **CLC 2, 28, 39**
See also CA 5-8R; 116; CANR 5

Calhoun, John Caldwell
1782-1850 . . . . **NCLC 15**
See also DLB 3

Calisher, Hortense
1911- . . . . **CLC 2, 4, 8, 38; SSC 15**
See also CA 1-4R; CANR 1, 22; DLB 2;
MTCW

Callaghan, Morley Edward
1903-1990 . . . . **CLC 3, 14, 41, 65**
See also CA 9-12R; 132; CANR 33;
DLB 68; MTCW

Calvino, Italo
1923-1985 . . . . . **CLC 5, 8, 11, 22, 33, 39,**
73; SSC 3
See also CA 85-88; 116; CANR 23; MTCW

Cameron, Carey 1952- . . . . **CLC 59**
See also CA 135

Cameron, Peter 1959- . . . . **CLC 44**
See also CA 125

Campana, Dino 1885-1932 . . . . **TCLC 20**
See also CA 117; DLB 114

Campbell, John W(ood, Jr.)
1910-1971 . . . . **CLC 32**
See also CA 21-22; 29-32R; CANR 34;
CAP 2; DLB 8; MTCW

Campbell, Joseph 1904-1987 . . . . **CLC 69**
See also AAYA 3; BEST 89:2; CA 1-4R;
124; CANR 3, 28; MTCW

Campbell, Maria 1940- . . . . **CLC 85**
See also CA 102; NNAL

Campbell, (John) Ramsey
1946- . . . . **CLC 42; SSC 19**
See also CA 57-60; CANR 7

Campbell, (Ignatius) Roy (Dunnachie)
1901-1957 . . . . **TCLC 5**
See also CA 104; DLB 20

Campbell, Thomas 1777-1844 . . . . **NCLC 19**
See also DLB 93; 144

Campbell, Wilfred . . . . **TCLC 9**
See also Campbell, William

Campbell, William 1858(?)-1918
See Campbell, Wilfred
See also CA 106; DLB 92

Campos, Alvaro de
See Pessoa, Fernando (Antonio Nogueira)

Camus, Albert
1913-1960 . . . . **CLC 1, 2, 4, 9, 11, 14, 32,**
63, 69; DA; DC 2; SSC 9; WLC
See also CA 89-92; DLB 72; MTCW

Canby, Vincent 1924- . . . . **CLC 13**
See also CA 81-84

Cancale
See Desnos, Robert

Canetti, Elias
1905-1994 . . . . **CLC 3, 14, 25, 75, 86**
See also CA 21-24R; 146; CANR 23;
DLB 85, 124; MTCW

Canin, Ethan 1960- . . . . **CLC 55**
See also CA 131; 135

Cannon, Curt
See Hunter, Evan

Cape, Judith
See Page, P(atricia) K(athleen)

Capek, Karel
1890-1938 . . . . . **TCLC 6, 37; DA; DC 1;**
WLC
See also CA 104; 140

Capote, Truman
1924-1984 . . . . . . **CLC 1, 3, 8, 13, 19, 34,**
38, 58; DA; SSC 2; WLC
See also CA 5-8R; 113; CANR 18;
CDALB 1941-1968; DLB 2; DLBY 80,
84; MTCW

Capra, Frank 1897-1991 . . . . **CLC 16**
See also CA 61-64; 135

Caputo, Philip 1941- . . . . **CLC 32**
See also CA 73-76; CANR 40

Card, Orson Scott 1951- . . . . **CLC 44, 47, 50**
See also AAYA 11; CA 102; CANR 27, 47;
MTCW

Cardenal (Martinez), Ernesto
1925- . . . . **CLC 31; HLC**
See also CA 49-52; CANR 2, 32; HW;
MTCW

Carducci, Giosue 1835-1907 . . . . **TCLC 32**

Carew, Thomas 1595(?)-1640 . . . . **LC 13**
See also DLB 126

Carey, Ernestine Gilbreth 1908- . . . . **CLC 17**
See also CA 5-8R; SATA 2

Carey, Peter 1943- . . . . **CLC 40, 55**
See also CA 123; 127; MTCW

Carleton, William 1794-1869 . . . . . . **NCLC 3**

Carlisle, Henry (Coffin) 1926- . . . . . . **CLC 33**
See also CA 13-16R; CANR 15

Carlsen, Chris
See Holdstock, Robert P.

Carlson, Ron(ald F.) 1947- . . . . **CLC 54**
See also CA 105; CANR 27

Carlyle, Thomas 1795-1881 . . **NCLC 22; DA**
See also CDBLB 1789-1832; DLB 55; 144

Carman, (William) Bliss
1861-1929 . . . . **TCLC 7**
See also CA 104; DLB 92

Carnegie, Dale 1888-1955 . . . . **TCLC 53**

Carossa, Hans 1878-1956 . . . . **TCLC 48**
See also DLB 66

Carpenter, Don(ald Richard)
1931- . . . . **CLC 41**
See also CA 45-48; CANR 1

Chapman, Graham 1941-1989 . . . . . . **CLC 21**
See also Monty Python
See also CA 116; 129; CANR 35

Chapman, John Jay 1862-1933 . . . . . **TCLC 7**
See also CA 104

Chapman, Walker
See Silverberg, Robert

Chappell, Fred (Davis) 1936- . . . . **CLC 40, 78**
See also CA 5-8R; CAAS 4; CANR 8, 33;
DLB 6, 105

Char, Rene(-Emile)
1907-1988 . . . . **CLC 9, 11, 14, 55**
See also CA 13-16R; 124; CANR 32;
MTCW

Charby, Jay
See Ellison, Harlan (Jay)

Chardin, Pierre Teilhard de
See Teilhard de Chardin, (Marie Joseph)
Pierre

Charles I 1600-1649 . . . . **LC 13**

Charyn, Jerome 1937- . . . . **CLC 5, 8, 18**
See also CA 5-8R; CAAS 1; CANR 7;
DLBY 83; MTCW

Chase, Mary (Coyle) 1907-1981 . . . . . . **DC 1**
See also CA 77-80; 105; SATA 17;
SATA-Obit 29

Chase, Mary Ellen 1887-1973 . . . . **CLC 2**
See also CA 13-16; 41-44R; CAP 1;
SATA 10

Chase, Nicholas
See Hyde, Anthony

Chateaubriand, Francois Rene de
1768-1848 . . . . **NCLC 3**
See also DLB 119

Chatterje, Sarat Chandra 1876-1936(?)
See Chatterji, Saratchandra
See also CA 109

Chatterji, Bankim Chandra
1838-1894 . . . . **NCLC 19**

Chatterji, Saratchandra . . . . **TCLC 13**
See also Chatterje, Sarat Chandra

Chatterton, Thomas 1752-1770 . . . . **LC 3**
See also DLB 109

Chatwin, (Charles) Bruce
1940-1989 . . . . **CLC 28, 57, 59**
See also AAYA 4; BEST 90:1; CA 85-88;
127

Chaucer, Daniel
See Ford, Ford Madox

Chaucer, Geoffrey
1340(?)-1400 . . . . **LC 17; DA**
See also CDBLB Before 1660; DLB 146

Chaviaras, Strates 1935-
See Haviaras, Stratis
See also CA 105

Chayefsky, Paddy . . . . **CLC 23**
See also Chayefsky, Sidney
See also DLB 7, 44; DLBY 81

Chayefsky, Sidney 1923-1981
See Chayefsky, Paddy
See also CA 9-12R; 104; CANR 18

Chedid, Andree 1920- . . . . **CLC 47**
See also CA 145

Cheever, John
1912-1982 . . . . . . **CLC 3, 7, 8, 11, 15, 25,**
64; DA; SSC 1; WLC
See also CA 5-8R; 106; CABS 1; CANR 5,
27; CDALB 1941-1968; DLB 2, 102;
DLBY 80, 82; MTCW

Cheever, Susan 1943- . . . . **CLC 18, 48**
See also CA 103; CANR 27; DLBY 82

Chekhonte, Antosha
See Chekhov, Anton (Pavlovich)

Chekhov, Anton (Pavlovich)
1860-1904 . . . . . **TCLC 3, 10, 31, 55; DA;**
SSC 2; WLC
See also CA 104; 124

Chernyshevsky, Nikolay Gavrilovich
1828-1889 . . . . **NCLC 1**

Cherry, Carolyn Janice 1942-
See Cherryh, C. J.
See also CA 65-68; CANR 10

Cherryh, C. J. . . . . **CLC 35**
See also Cherry, Carolyn Janice
See also DLBY 80

Chesnutt, Charles W(addell)
1858-1932 . . . . **TCLC 5, 39; BLC; SSC 7**
See also BW 1; CA 106; 125; DLB 12, 50,
78; MTCW

Chester, Alfred 1929(?)-1971 . . . . . . **CLC 49**
See also CA 33-36R; DLB 130

Chesterton, G(ilbert) K(eith)
1874-1936 . . . . **TCLC 1, 6; SSC 1**
See also CA 104; 132; CDBLB 1914-1945;
DLB 10, 19, 34, 70, 98, 149; MTCW;
SATA 27

Chiang Pin-chin 1904-1986
See Ding Ling
See also CA 118

Ch'ien Chung-shu 1910- . . . . **CLC 22**
See also CA 130; MTCW

Child, L. Maria
See Child, Lydia Maria

Child, Lydia Maria 1802-1880 . . . . **NCLC 6**
See also DLB 1, 74; SATA 67

Child, Mrs.
See Child, Lydia Maria

Child, Philip 1898-1978 . . . . **CLC 19, 68**
See also CA 13-14; CAP 1; SATA 47

Childress, Alice
1920-1994 . . **CLC 12, 15, 86; BLC; DC 4**
See also AAYA 8; BW 2; CA 45-48; 146;
CANR 3, 27; CLR 14; DLB 7, 38; JRDA;
MAICYA; MTCW; SATA 7, 48, 81

Chislett, (Margaret) Anne 1943- . . . . **CLC 34**

Chitty, Thomas Willes 1926- . . . . . . **CLC 11**
See also Hinde, Thomas
See also CA 5-8R

Chivers, Thomas Holley
1809-1858 . . . . **NCLC 49**
See also DLB 3

Chomette, Rene Lucien 1898-1981
See Clair, Rene
See also CA 103

Chopin, Kate . . . . **TCLC 5, 14; DA; SSC 8**
See also Chopin, Katherine
See also CDALB 1865-1917; DLB 12, 78

Chopin, Katherine 1851-1904
See Chopin, Kate
See also CA 104; 122

Chretien de Troyes
c. 12th cent. - . . . . **CMLC 10**

Christie
See Ichikawa, Kon

Christie, Agatha (Mary Clarissa)
1890-1976 . . . . . . **CLC 1, 6, 8, 12, 39, 48**
See also AAYA 9; AITN 1, 2; CA 17-20R;
61-64; CANR 10, 37; CDBLB 1914-1945;
DLB 13, 77; MTCW; SATA 36

Christie, (Ann) Philippa
See Pearce, Philippa
See also CA 5-8R; CANR 4

Christine de Pizan 1365(?)-1431(?) . . . . **LC 9**

Chubb, Elmer
See Masters, Edgar Lee

Chulkov, Mikhail Dmitrievich
1743-1792 . . . . **LC 2**
See also DLB 150

Churchill, Caryl 1938- . . . **CLC 31, 55; DC 5**
See also CA 102; CANR 22, 46; DLB 13;
MTCW

Churchill, Charles 1731-1764 . . . . **LC 3**
See also DLB 109

Chute, Carolyn 1947- . . . . **CLC 39**
See also CA 123

Ciardi, John (Anthony)
1916-1986 . . . . **CLC 10, 40, 44**
See also CA 5-8R; 118; CAAS 2; CANR 5,
33; CLR 19; DLB 5; DLBY 86;
MAICYA; MTCW; SATA 1, 65;
SATA-Obit 46

Cicero, Marcus Tullius
106B.C.-43B.C. . . . . **CMLC 3**

Cimino, Michael 1943- . . . . **CLC 16**
See also CA 105

Cioran, E(mil) M. 1911- . . . . **CLC 64**
See also CA 25-28R

Cisneros, Sandra 1954- . . . . . . **CLC 69; HLC**
See also AAYA 9; CA 131; DLB 122, 152;
HW

Clair, Rene . . . . **CLC 20**
See also Chomette, Rene Lucien

Clampitt, Amy 1920-1994 . . . . **CLC 32**
See also CA 110; 146; CANR 29; DLB 105

Clancy, Thomas L., Jr. 1947-
See Clancy, Tom
See also CA 125; 131; MTCW

Clancy, Tom . . . . **CLC 45**
See also Clancy, Thomas L., Jr.
See also AAYA 9; BEST 89:1, 90:1

Clare, John 1793-1864 . . . . **NCLC 9**
See also DLB 55, 96

Clarin
See Alas (y Urena), Leopoldo (Enrique
Garcia)

Clark, Al C.
See Goines, Donald

Clark, (Robert) Brian 1932- . . . . **CLC 29**
See also CA 41-44R

Clark, Curt
See Westlake, Donald E(dwin)

Clark, Eleanor 1913- . . . . CLC 5, 19
See also CA 9-12R; CANR 41; DLB 6

Clark, J. P.
See Clark, John Pepper
See also DLB 117

Clark, John Pepper
1935- . . . . CLC 38; BLC; DC 5
See also Clark, J. P.
See also BW 1; CA 65-68; CANR 16

Clark, M. R.
See Clark, Mavis Thorpe

Clark, Mavis Thorpe 1909- . . . . CLC 12
See also CA 57-60; CANR 8, 37; CLR 30;
MAICYA; SAAS 5; SATA 8, 74

Clark, Walter Van Tilburg
1909-1971 . . . . CLC 28
See also CA 9-12R; 33-36R; DLB 9;
SATA 8

Clarke, Arthur C(harles)
1917- . . . . . . CLC 1, 4, 13, 18, 35; SSC 3
See also AAYA 4; CA 1-4R; CANR 2, 28;
JRDA; MAICYA; MTCW; SATA 13, 70

Clarke, Austin 1896-1974. . . . . CLC 6, 9
See also CA 29-32; 49-52; CAP 2; DLB 10,
20

Clarke, Austin C(hesterfield)
1934- . . . . CLC 8, 53; BLC
See also BW 1; CA 25-28R; CAAS 16;
CANR 14, 32; DLB 53, 125

Clarke, Gillian 1937- . . . . CLC 61
See also CA 106; DLB 40

Clarke, Marcus (Andrew Hislop)
1846-1881 . . . . NCLC 19

Clarke, Shirley 1925- . . . . CLC 16

Clash, The
See Headon, (Nicky) Topper; Jones, Mick;
Simonon, Paul; Strummer, Joe

Claudel, Paul (Louis Charles Marie)
1868-1955 . . . . TCLC 2, 10
See also CA 104

Clavell, James (duMaresq)
1925-1994 . . . . CLC 6, 25, 87
See also CA 25-28R; 146; CANR 26, 48;
MTCW

Cleaver, (Leroy) Eldridge
1935- . . . . CLC 30; BLC
See also BW 1; CA 21-24R; CANR 16

Cleese, John (Marwood) 1939- . . . . . CLC 21
See also Monty Python
See also CA 112; 116; CANR 35; MTCW

Cleishbotham, Jebediah
See Scott, Walter

Cleland, John 1710-1789 . . . . LC 2
See also DLB 39

Clemens, Samuel Langhorne 1835-1910
See Twain, Mark
See also CA 104; 135; CDALB 1865-1917;
DA; DLB 11, 12, 23, 64, 74; JRDA;
MAICYA; YABC 2

Cleophil
See Congreve, William

Clerihew, E.
See Bentley, E(dmund) C(lerihew)

Clerk, N. W.
See Lewis, C(live) S(taples)

Cliff, Jimmy. . . . . CLC 21
See also Chambers, James

Clifton, (Thelma) Lucille
1936- . . . . CLC 19, 66; BLC
See also BW 2; CA 49-52; CANR 2, 24, 42;
CLR 5; DLB 5, 41; MAICYA; MTCW;
SATA 20, 69

Clinton, Dirk
See Silverberg, Robert

Clough, Arthur Hugh 1819-1861. . NCLC 27
See also DLB 32

Clutha, Janet Paterson Frame 1924-
See Frame, Janet
See also CA 1-4R; CANR 2, 36; MTCW

Clyne, Terence
See Blatty, William Peter

Cobalt, Martin
See Mayne, William (James Carter)

Cobbett, William 1763-1835 . . . . . NCLC 49
See also DLB 43, 107

Coburn, D(onald) L(ee) 1938- . . . . . . CLC 10
See also CA 89-92

Cocteau, Jean (Maurice Eugene Clement)
1889-1963 . . . . CLC 1, 8, 15, 16, 43; DA;
WLC
See also CA 25-28; CANR 40; CAP 2;
DLB 65; MTCW

Codrescu, Andrei 1946- . . . . CLC 46
See also CA 33-36R; CAAS 19; CANR 13,
34

Coe, Max
See Bourne, Randolph S(illiman)

Coe, Tucker
See Westlake, Donald E(dwin)

Coetzee, J(ohn) M(ichael)
1940- . . . . CLC 23, 33, 66
See also CA 77-80; CANR 41; MTCW

Coffey, Brian
See Koontz, Dean R(ay)

Cohan, George M. 1878-1942 . . . . . TCLC 60

Cohen, Arthur A(llen)
1928-1986 . . . . CLC 7, 31
See also CA 1-4R; 120; CANR 1, 17, 42;
DLB 28

Cohen, Leonard (Norman)
1934- . . . . CLC 3, 38
See also CA 21-24R; CANR 14; DLB 53;
MTCW

Cohen, Matt 1942- . . . . CLC 19
See also CA 61-64; CAAS 18; CANR 40;
DLB 53

Cohen-Solal, Annie 19(?)- . . . . CLC 50

Colegate, Isabel 1931- . . . . CLC 36
See also CA 17-20R; CANR 8, 22; DLB 14;
MTCW

Coleman, Emmett
See Reed, Ishmael

Coleridge, Samuel Taylor
1772-1834 . . NCLC 9; DA; PC 11; WLC
See also CDBLB 1789-1832; DLB 93, 107

Coleridge, Sara 1802-1852 . . . . NCLC 31

Coles, Don 1928- . . . . CLC 46
See also CA 115; CANR 38

Colette, (Sidonie-Gabrielle)
1873-1954 . . . . . . TCLC 1, 5, 16; SSC 10
See also CA 104; 131; DLB 65; MTCW

Collett, (Jacobine) Camilla (Wergeland)
1813-1895 . . . . NCLC 22

Collier, Christopher 1930- . . . . CLC 30
See also AAYA 13; CA 33-36R; CANR 13,
33; JRDA; MAICYA; SATA 16, 70

Collier, James L(incoln) 1928- . . . . . CLC 30
See also AAYA 13; CA 9-12R; CANR 4,
33; CLR 3; JRDA; MAICYA; SATA 8,
70

Collier, Jeremy 1650-1726. . . . . LC 6

Collier, John 1901-1980
See also CA 65-68; 97-100; CANR 10;
DLB 77; SSC 19

Collins, Hunt
See Hunter, Evan

Collins, Linda 1931- . . . . CLC 44
See also CA 125

Collins, (William) Wilkie
1824-1889 . . . . NCLC 1, 18
See also CDBLB 1832-1890; DLB 18, 70

Collins, William 1721-1759 . . . . LC 4
See also DLB 109

Colman, George
See Glassco, John

Colt, Winchester Remington
See Hubbard, L(afayette) Ron(ald)

Colter, Cyrus 1910- . . . . CLC 58
See also BW 1; CA 65-68; CANR 10;
DLB 33

Colton, James
See Hansen, Joseph

Colum, Padraic 1881-1972. . . . . CLC 28
See also CA 73-76; 33-36R; CANR 35;
CLR 36; MAICYA; MTCW; SATA 15

Colvin, James
See Moorcock, Michael (John)

Colwin, Laurie (E.)
1944-1992 . . . . CLC 5, 13, 23, 84
See also CA 89-92; 139; CANR 20, 46;
DLBY 80; MTCW

Comfort, Alex(ander) 1920- . . . . CLC 7
See also CA 1-4R; CANR 1, 45

Comfort, Montgomery
See Campbell, (John) Ramsey

Compton-Burnett, I(vy)
1884(?)-1969 . . . . . . CLC 1, 3, 10, 15, 34
See also CA 1-4R; 25-28R; CANR 4;
DLB 36; MTCW

Comstock, Anthony 1844-1915 . . . . TCLC 13
See also CA 110

Conan Doyle, Arthur
See Doyle, Arthur Conan

Conde, Maryse 1937- . . . . CLC 52
See also Boucolon, Maryse
See also BW 2

Condillac, Etienne Bonnot de
1714-1780 . . . . LC 26

Condon, Richard (Thomas)
1915- . . . . CLC 4, 6, 8, 10, 45
See also BEST 90:3; CA 1-4R; CAAS 1;
CANR 2, 23; MTCW

Congreve, William
    1670-1729 ... LC 5, 21; DA; DC 2; WLC
    See also CDBLB 1660-1789; DLB 39, 84

Connell, Evan S(helby), Jr.
    1924- .... CLC 4, 6, 45
    See also AAYA 7; CA 1-4R; CAAS 2;
    CANR 2, 39; DLB 2; DLBY 81; MTCW

Connelly, Marc(us Cook)
    1890-1980 .... CLC 7
    See also CA 85-88; 102; CANR 30; DLB 7;
    DLBY 80; SATA-Obit 25

Connor, Ralph .... TCLC 31
    See also Gordon, Charles William
    See also DLB 92

Conrad, Joseph
    1857-1924 .... TCLC 1, 6, 13, 25, 43, 57;
                          DA; SSC 9; WLC
    See also CA 104; 131; CDBLB 1890-1914;
    DLB 10, 34, 98; MTCW; SATA 27

Conrad, Robert Arnold
    See Hart, Moss

Conroy, Pat 1945- .... CLC 30, 74
    See also AAYA 8; AITN 1; CA 85-88;
    CANR 24; DLB 6; MTCW

Constant (de Rebecque), (Henri) Benjamin
    1767-1830 .... NCLC 6
    See also DLB 119

Conybeare, Charles Augustus
    See Eliot, T(homas) S(tearns)

Cook, Michael 1933- .... CLC 58
    See also CA 93-96; DLB 53

Cook, Robin 1940- .... CLC 14
    See also BEST 90:2; CA 108; 111;
    CANR 41

Cook, Roy
    See Silverberg, Robert

Cooke, Elizabeth 1948- .... CLC 55
    See also CA 129

Cooke, John Esten 1830-1886 ..... NCLC 5
    See also DLB 3

Cooke, John Estes
    See Baum, L(yman) Frank

Cooke, M. E.
    See Creasey, John

Cooke, Margaret
    See Creasey, John

Cooney, Ray .... CLC 62

Cooper, Douglas 1960- .... CLC 86

Cooper, Henry St. John
    See Creasey, John

Cooper, J. California .... CLC 56
    See also AAYA 12; BW 1; CA 125

Cooper, James Fenimore
    1789-1851 .... NCLC 1, 27
    See also CDALB 1640-1865; DLB 3;
    SATA 19

Coover, Robert (Lowell)
    1932- .. CLC 3, 7, 15, 32, 46, 87; SSC 15
    See also CA 45-48; CANR 3, 37; DLB 2;
    DLBY 81; MTCW

Copeland, Stewart (Armstrong)
    1952- .... CLC 26

Coppard, A(lfred) E(dgar)
    1878-1957 .... TCLC 5
    See also CA 114; YABC 1

Coppee, Francois 1842-1908 ...... TCLC 25

Coppola, Francis Ford 1939- ..... CLC 16
    See also CA 77-80; CANR 40; DLB 44

Corbiere, Tristan 1845-1875 ..... NCLC 43

Corcoran, Barbara 1911- .... CLC 17
    See also AAYA 14; CA 21-24R; CAAS 2;
    CANR 11, 28, 48; DLB 52; JRDA;
    SAAS 20; SATA 3, 77

Cordelier, Maurice
    See Giraudoux, (Hippolyte) Jean

Corelli, Marie 1855-1924 .... TCLC 51
    See also Mackay, Mary
    See also DLB 34

Corman, Cid .... CLC 9
    See also Corman, Sidney
    See also CAAS 2; DLB 5

Corman, Sidney 1924-
    See Corman, Cid
    See also CA 85-88; CANR 44

Cormier, Robert (Edmund)
    1925- .... CLC 12, 30; DA
    See also AAYA 3; CA 1-4R; CANR 5, 23;
    CDALB 1968-1988; CLR 12; DLB 52;
    JRDA; MAICYA; MTCW; SATA 10, 45

Corn, Alfred (DeWitt III) 1943- .... CLC 33
    See also CA 104; CANR 44; DLB 120;
    DLBY 80

Corneille, Pierre 1606-1684 .... LC 28

Cornwell, David (John Moore)
    1931- .... CLC 9, 15
    See also le Carre, John
    See also CA 5-8R; CANR 13, 33; MTCW

Corso, (Nunzio) Gregory 1930- ... CLC 1, 11
    See also CA 5-8R; CANR 41; DLB 5, 16;
    MTCW

Cortazar, Julio
    1914-1984 ...... CLC 2, 3, 5, 10, 13, 15,
                          33, 34; HLC; SSC 7
    See also CA 21-24R; CANR 12, 32;
    DLB 113; HW; MTCW

Corwin, Cecil
    See Kornbluth, C(yril) M.

Cosic, Dobrica 1921- .... CLC 14
    See also CA 122; 138

Costain, Thomas B(ertram)
    1885-1965 .... CLC 30
    See also CA 5-8R; 25-28R; DLB 9

Costantini, Humberto
    1924(?)-1987 .... CLC 49
    See also CA 131; 122; HW

Costello, Elvis 1955- .... CLC 21

Cotter, Joseph Seamon Sr.
    1861-1949 .... TCLC 28; BLC
    See also BW 1; CA 124; DLB 50

Couch, Arthur Thomas Quiller
    See Quiller-Couch, Arthur Thomas

Coulton, James
    See Hansen, Joseph

Couperus, Louis (Marie Anne)
    1863-1923 .... TCLC 15
    See also CA 115

Coupland, Douglas 1961- .... CLC 85
    See also CA 142

Court, Wesli
    See Turco, Lewis (Putnam)

Courtenay, Bryce 1933- .... CLC 59
    See also CA 138

Courtney, Robert
    See Ellison, Harlan (Jay)

Cousteau, Jacques-Yves 1910- ..... CLC 30
    See also CA 65-68; CANR 15; MTCW;
    SATA 38

Coward, Noel (Peirce)
    1899-1973 .... CLC 1, 9, 29, 51
    See also AITN 1; CA 17-18; 41-44R;
    CANR 35; CAP 2; CDBLB 1914-1945;
    DLB 10; MTCW

Cowley, Malcolm 1898-1989 .... CLC 39
    See also CA 5-8R; 128; CANR 3; DLB 4,
    48; DLBY 81, 89; MTCW

Cowper, William 1731-1800 ...... NCLC 8
    See also DLB 104, 109

Cox, William Trevor 1928- ... CLC 9, 14, 71
    See also Trevor, William
    See also CA 9-12R; CANR 4, 37; DLB 14;
    MTCW

Coyne, P. J.
    See Masters, Hilary

Cozzens, James Gould
    1903-1978 .... CLC 1, 4, 11
    See also CA 9-12R; 81-84; CANR 19;
    CDALB 1941-1968; DLB 9; DLBD 2;
    DLBY 84; MTCW

Crabbe, George 1754-1832 .... NCLC 26
    See also DLB 93

Craig, A. A.
    See Anderson, Poul (William)

Craik, Dinah Maria (Mulock)
    1826-1887 .... NCLC 38
    See also DLB 35; MAICYA; SATA 34

Cram, Ralph Adams 1863-1942 .... TCLC 45

Crane, (Harold) Hart
    1899-1932 .... TCLC 2, 5; DA; PC 3;
                          WLC
    See also CA 104; 127; CDALB 1917-1929;
    DLB 4, 48; MTCW

Crane, R(onald) S(almon)
    1886-1967 .... CLC 27
    See also CA 85-88; DLB 63

Crane, Stephen (Townley)
    1871-1900 .... TCLC 11, 17, 32; DA;
                          SSC 7; WLC
    See also CA 109; 140; CDALB 1865-1917;
    DLB 12, 54, 78; YABC 2

Crase, Douglas 1944- .... CLC 58
    See also CA 106

Crashaw, Richard 1612(?)-1649 ...... LC 24
    See also DLB 126

Craven, Margaret 1901-1980 .... CLC 17
    See also CA 103

Crawford, F(rancis) Marion
    1854-1909 .... TCLC 10
    See also CA 107; DLB 71

Crawford, Isabella Valancy
    1850-1887 .... NCLC 12
    See also DLB 92

Deren, Eleanora 1908(?)-1961
See Deren, Maya
See also CA 111

Deren, Maya .... **CLC 16**
See also Deren, Eleanora

Derleth, August (William)
1909-1971 .... **CLC 31**
See also CA 1-4R; 29-32R; CANR 4;
DLB 9; SATA 5

Der Nister 1884-1950........... **TCLC 56**

de Routisie, Albert
See Aragon, Louis

Derrida, Jacques 1930-........ **CLC 24, 87**
See also CA 124; 127

Derry Down Derry
See Lear, Edward

Dersonnes, Jacques
See Simenon, Georges (Jacques Christian)

Desai, Anita 1937- .... **CLC 19, 37**
See also CA 81-84; CANR 33; MTCW;
SATA 63

de Saint-Luc, Jean
See Glassco, John

de Saint Roman, Arnaud
See Aragon, Louis

Descartes, Rene 1596-1650 .... **LC 20**

De Sica, Vittorio 1901(?)-1974 ..... **CLC 20**
See also CA 117

Desnos, Robert 1900-1945....... **TCLC 22**
See also CA 121

Destouches, Louis-Ferdinand
1894-1961 .... **CLC 9, 15**
See also Celine, Louis-Ferdinand
See also CA 85-88; CANR 28; MTCW

Deutsch, Babette 1895-1982 .... **CLC 18**
See also CA 1-4R; 108; CANR 4; DLB 45;
SATA 1; SATA-Obit 33

Devenant, William 1606-1649 .... **LC 13**

Devkota, Laxmiprasad
1909-1959 .... **TCLC 23**
See also CA 123

De Voto, Bernard (Augustine)
1897-1955 .... **TCLC 29**
See also CA 113; DLB 9

De Vries, Peter
1910-1993 .... **CLC 1, 2, 3, 7, 10, 28, 46**
See also CA 17-20R; 142; CANR 41;
DLB 6; DLBY 82; MTCW

Dexter, Martin
See Faust, Frederick (Schiller)

Dexter, Pete 1943-............ **CLC 34, 55**
See also BEST 89:2; CA 127; 131; MTCW

Diamano, Silmang
See Senghor, Leopold Sedar

Diamond, Neil 1941- .... **CLC 30**
See also CA 108

di Bassetto, Corno
See Shaw, George Bernard

Dick, Philip K(indred)
1928-1982 .... **CLC 10, 30, 72**
See also CA 49-52; 106; CANR 2, 16;
DLB 8; MTCW

Dickens, Charles (John Huffam)
1812-1870 ...... **NCLC 3, 8, 18, 26, 37,
50; DA; SSC 17; WLC**
See also CDBLB 1832-1890; DLB 21, 55,
70; JRDA; MAICYA; SATA 15

Dickey, James (Lafayette)
1923- .... **CLC 1, 2, 4, 7, 10, 15, 47**
See also AITN 1, 2; CA 9-12R; CABS 2;
CANR 10, 48; CDALB 1968-1988;
DLB 5; DLBD 7; DLBY 82, 93; MTCW

Dickey, William 1928-1994 ...... **CLC 3, 28**
See also CA 9-12R; 145; CANR 24; DLB 5

Dickinson, Charles 1951-......... **CLC 49**
See also CA 128

Dickinson, Emily (Elizabeth)
1830-1886 .. **NCLC 21; DA; PC 1; WLC**
See also CDALB 1865-1917; DLB 1;
SATA 29

Dickinson, Peter (Malcolm)
1927- .... **CLC 12, 35**
See also AAYA 9; CA 41-44R; CANR 31;
CLR 29; DLB 87; JRDA; MAICYA;
SATA 5, 62

Dickson, Carr
See Carr, John Dickson

Dickson, Carter
See Carr, John Dickson

Diderot, Denis 1713-1784 .... **LC 26**

Didion, Joan 1934-..... **CLC 1, 3, 8, 14, 32**
See also AITN 1; CA 5-8R; CANR 14;
CDALB 1968-1988; DLB 2; DLBY 81,
86; MTCW

Dietrich, Robert
See Hunt, E(verette) Howard, (Jr.)

Dillard, Annie 1945-............ **CLC 9, 60**
See also AAYA 6; CA 49-52; CANR 3, 43;
DLBY 80; MTCW; SATA 10

Dillard, R(ichard) H(enry) W(ilde)
1937-...................... **CLC 5**
See also CA 21-24R; CAAS 7; CANR 10;
DLB 5

Dillon, Eilis 1920-1994........... **CLC 17**
See also CA 9-12R; 147; CAAS 3; CANR 4,
38; CLR 26; MAICYA; SATA 2, 74

Dimont, Penelope
See Mortimer, Penelope (Ruth)

Dinesen, Isak.......... **CLC 10, 29; SSC 7**
See also Blixen, Karen (Christentze
Dinesen)

Ding Ling...................... **CLC 68**
See also Chiang Pin-chin

Disch, Thomas M(ichael) 1940-... **CLC 7, 36**
See also CA 21-24R; CAAS 4; CANR 17,
36; CLR 18; DLB 8; MAICYA; MTCW;
SAAS 15; SATA 54

Disch, Tom
See Disch, Thomas M(ichael)

d'Isly, Georges
See Simenon, Georges (Jacques Christian)

Disraeli, Benjamin 1804-1881 .. **NCLC 2, 39**
See also DLB 21, 55

Ditcum, Steve
See Crumb, R(obert)

Dixon, Paige
See Corcoran, Barbara

Dixon, Stephen 1936-..... **CLC 52; SSC 16**
See also CA 89-92; CANR 17, 40; DLB 130

Dobell, Sydney Thompson
1824-1874 .... **NCLC 43**
See also DLB 32

Doblin, Alfred .... **TCLC 13**
See also Doeblin, Alfred

Dobrolyubov, Nikolai Alexandrovich
1836-1861 .... **NCLC 5**

Dobyns, Stephen 1941-............ **CLC 37**
See also CA 45-48; CANR 2, 18

Doctorow, E(dgar) L(aurence)
1931- ..... **CLC 6, 11, 15, 18, 37, 44, 65**
See also AITN 2; BEST 89:3; CA 45-48;
CANR 2, 33; CDALB 1968-1988; DLB 2,
28; DLBY 80; MTCW

Dodgson, Charles Lutwidge 1832-1898
See Carroll, Lewis
See also CLR 2; DA; MAICYA; YABC 2

Dodson, Owen (Vincent)
1914-1983 .... **CLC 79; BLC**
See also BW 1; CA 65-68; 110; CANR 24;
DLB 76

Doeblin, Alfred 1878-1957........ **TCLC 13**
See also Doblin, Alfred
See also CA 110; 141; DLB 66

Doerr, Harriet 1910- .... **CLC 34**
See also CA 117; 122; CANR 47

Domecq, H(onorio) Bustos
See Bioy Casares, Adolfo; Borges, Jorge
Luis

Domini, Rey
See Lorde, Audre (Geraldine)

Dominique
See Proust, (Valentin-Louis-George-Eugene-)
Marcel

Don, A
See Stephen, Leslie

Donaldson, Stephen R. 1947-....... **CLC 46**
See also CA 89-92; CANR 13

Donleavy, J(ames) P(atrick)
1926- .... **CLC 1, 4, 6, 10, 45**
See also AITN 2; CA 9-12R; CANR 24, 49;
DLB 6; MTCW

Donne, John
1572-1631 .... **LC 10, 24; DA; PC 1**
See also CDBLB Before 1660; DLB 121,
151

Donnell, David 1939(?)-........... **CLC 34**

Donoghue, P. S.
See Hunt, E(verette) Howard, (Jr.)

Donoso (Yanez), Jose
1924- .... **CLC 4, 8, 11, 32; HLC**
See also CA 81-84; CANR 32; DLB 113;
HW; MTCW

Donovan, John 1928-1992 .... **CLC 35**
See also CA 97-100; 137; CLR 3;
MAICYA; SATA 72; SATA-Brief 29

Don Roberto
See Cunninghame Graham, R(obert)
B(ontine)

Doolittle, Hilda
      1886-1961 ..... **CLC 3, 8, 14, 31, 34, 73;**
                                    DA; PC 5; WLC
   See also H. D.
   See also CA 97-100; CANR 35; DLB 4, 45;
   MTCW

Dorfman, Ariel 1942- .... **CLC 48, 77; HLC**
   See also CA 124; 130; HW

Dorn, Edward (Merton) 1929- ... **CLC 10, 18**
   See also CA 93-96; CANR 42; DLB 5

Dorsan, Luc
   See Simenon, Georges (Jacques Christian)

Dorsange, Jean
   See Simenon, Georges (Jacques Christian)

Dos Passos, John (Roderigo)
      1896-1970 ...... **CLC 1, 4, 8, 11, 15, 25,**
                                    34, 82; DA; WLC
   See also CA 1-4R; 29-32R; CANR 3;
   CDALB 1929-1941; DLB 4, 9; DLBD 1;
   MTCW

Dossage, Jean
   See Simenon, Georges (Jacques Christian)

Dostoevsky, Fedor Mikhailovich
      1821-1881 ...... **NCLC 2, 7, 21, 33, 43;**
                                    DA; SSC 2; WLC

Doughty, Charles M(ontagu)
      1843-1926 .... **TCLC 27**
   See also CA 115; DLB 19, 57

Douglas, Ellen .... **CLC 73**
   See also Haxton, Josephine Ayres;
   Williamson, Ellen Douglas

Douglas, Gavin 1475(?)-1522 .... **LC 20**

Douglas, Keith 1920-1944 .... **TCLC 40**
   See also DLB 27

Douglas, Leonard
   See Bradbury, Ray (Douglas)

Douglas, Michael
   See Crichton, (John) Michael

Douglass, Frederick
      1817(?)-1895 .... **NCLC 7; BLC; DA;**
                                    WLC
   See also CDALB 1640-1865; DLB 1, 43, 50,
   79; SATA 29

Dourado, (Waldomiro Freitas) Autran
      1926- .... **CLC 23, 60**
   See also CA 25-28R; CANR 34

Dourado, Waldomiro Autran
   See Dourado, (Waldomiro Freitas) Autran

Dove, Rita (Frances)
      1952- .... **CLC 50, 81; PC 6**
   See also BW 2; CA 109; CAAS 19;
   CANR 27, 42; DLB 120

Dowell, Coleman 1925-1985 .... **CLC 60**
   See also CA 25-28R; 117; CANR 10;
   DLB 130

Dowson, Ernest Christopher
      1867-1900 .... **TCLC 4**
   See also CA 105; DLB 19, 135

Doyle, A. Conan
   See Doyle, Arthur Conan

Doyle, Arthur Conan
      1859-1930 ...... **TCLC 7; DA; SSC 12;**
                                    WLC
   See also AAYA 14; CA 104; 122;
   CDBLB 1890-1914; DLB 18, 70; MTCW;
   SATA 24

Doyle, Conan
   See Doyle, Arthur Conan

Doyle, John
   See Graves, Robert (von Ranke)

Doyle, Roddy 1958(?)- .... **CLC 81**
   See also AAYA 14; CA 143

Doyle, Sir A. Conan
   See Doyle, Arthur Conan

Doyle, Sir Arthur Conan
   See Doyle, Arthur Conan

Dr. A
   See Asimov, Isaac; Silverstein, Alvin

Drabble, Margaret
      1939- .... **CLC 2, 3, 5, 8, 10, 22, 53**
   See also CA 13-16R; CANR 18, 35;
   CDBLB 1960 to Present; DLB 14;
   MTCW; SATA 48

Drapier, M. B.
   See Swift, Jonathan

Drayham, James
   See Mencken, H(enry) L(ouis)

Drayton, Michael 1563-1631 .... **LC 8**

Dreadstone, Carl
   See Campbell, (John) Ramsey

Dreiser, Theodore (Herman Albert)
      1871-1945 ...... **TCLC 10, 18, 35; DA;**
                                    WLC
   See also CA 106; 132; CDALB 1865-1917;
   DLB 9, 12, 102, 137; DLBD 1; MTCW

Drexler, Rosalyn 1926- .... **CLC 2, 6**
   See also CA 81-84

Dreyer, Carl Theodor 1889-1968 .... **CLC 16**
   See also CA 116

Drieu la Rochelle, Pierre(-Eugene)
      1893-1945 .... **TCLC 21**
   See also CA 117; DLB 72

Drinkwater, John 1882-1937 ...... **TCLC 57**
   See also CA 109; DLB 10, 19, 149

Drop Shot
   See Cable, George Washington

Droste-Hulshoff, Annette Freiin von
      1797-1848 .... **NCLC 3**
   See also DLB 133

Drummond, Walter
   See Silverberg, Robert

Drummond, William Henry
      1854-1907 .... **TCLC 25**
   See also DLB 92

Drummond de Andrade, Carlos
      1902-1987 .... **CLC 18**
   See also Andrade, Carlos Drummond de
   See also CA 132; 123

Drury, Allen (Stuart) 1918- .... **CLC 37**
   See also CA 57-60; CANR 18

Dryden, John
      1631-1700 ... **LC 3, 21; DA; DC 3; WLC**
   See also CDBLB 1660-1789; DLB 80, 101,
   131

Duberman, Martin 1930- .... **CLC 8**
   See also CA 1-4R; CANR 2

Dubie, Norman (Evans) 1945- ...... **CLC 36**
   See also CA 69-72; CANR 12; DLB 120

Du Bois, W(illiam) E(dward) B(urghardt)
      1868-1963 ...... **CLC 1, 2, 13, 64; BLC;**
                                    DA; WLC
   See also BW 1; CA 85-88; CANR 34;
   CDALB 1865-1917; DLB 47, 50, 91;
   MTCW; SATA 42

Dubus, Andre 1936- ... **CLC 13, 36; SSC 15**
   See also CA 21-24R; CANR 17; DLB 130

Duca Minimo
   See D'Annunzio, Gabriele

Ducharme, Rejean 1941- .... **CLC 74**
   See also DLB 60

Duclos, Charles Pinot 1704-1772 ..... **LC 1**

Dudek, Louis 1918- .... **CLC 11, 19**
   See also CA 45-48; CAAS 14; CANR 1;
   DLB 88

Duerrenmatt, Friedrich
      1921-1990 ...... **CLC 1, 4, 8, 11, 15, 43**
   See also CA 17-20R; CANR 33; DLB 69,
   124; MTCW

Duffy, Bruce (?)- .... **CLC 50**

Duffy, Maureen 1933- .... **CLC 37**
   See also CA 25-28R; CANR 33; DLB 14;
   MTCW

Dugan, Alan 1923- .... **CLC 2, 6**
   See also CA 81-84; DLB 5

du Gard, Roger Martin
   See Martin du Gard, Roger

Duhamel, Georges 1884-1966 .... **CLC 8**
   See also CA 81-84; 25-28R; CANR 35;
   DLB 65; MTCW

Dujardin, Edouard (Emile Louis)
      1861-1949 .... **TCLC 13**
   See also CA 109; DLB 123

Dumas, Alexandre (Davy de la Pailleterie)
      1802-1870 .... **NCLC 11; DA; WLC**
   See also DLB 119; SATA 18

Dumas, Alexandre
      1824-1895 .... **NCLC 9; DC 1**

Dumas, Claudine
   See Malzberg, Barry N(athaniel)

Dumas, Henry L. 1934-1968 ..... **CLC 6, 62**
   See also BW 1; CA 85-88; DLB 41

du Maurier, Daphne
      1907-1989 ...... **CLC 6, 11, 59; SSC 18**
   See also CA 5-8R; 128; CANR 6; MTCW;
   SATA 27; SATA-Obit 60

Dunbar, Paul Laurence
      1872-1906 ...... **TCLC 2, 12; BLC; DA;**
                                    PC 5; SSC 8; WLC
   See also BW 1; CA 104; 124;
   CDALB 1865-1917; DLB 50, 54, 78;
   SATA 34

Dunbar, William 1460(?)-1530(?) .... **LC 20**
   See also DLB 132, 146

Duncan, Lois 1934- .... **CLC 26**
   See also AAYA 4; CA 1-4R; CANR 2, 23,
   36; CLR 29; JRDA; MAICYA; SAAS 2;
   SATA 1, 36, 75

Duncan, Robert (Edward)
1919-1988 .... **CLC 1, 2, 4, 7, 15, 41, 55;**
PC 2
See also CA 9-12R; 124; CANR 28; DLB 5,
16; MTCW

Duncan, Sara Jeannette
1861-1922 .... **TCLC 60**
See also DLB 92

Dunlap, William 1766-1839 ...... **NCLC 2**
See also DLB 30, 37, 59

Dunn, Douglas (Eaglesham)
1942- .... **CLC 6, 40**
See also CA 45-48; CANR 2, 33; DLB 40;
MTCW

Dunn, Katherine (Karen) 1945- ..... **CLC 71**
See also CA 33-36R

Dunn, Stephen 1939- .... **CLC 36**
See also CA 33-36R; CANR 12, 48;
DLB 105

Dunne, Finley Peter 1867-1936.... **TCLC 28**
See also CA 108; DLB 11, 23

Dunne, John Gregory 1932-........ **CLC 28**
See also CA 25-28R; CANR 14; DLBY 80

Dunsany, Edward John Moreton Drax
Plunkett 1878-1957
See Dunsany, Lord
See also CA 104; DLB 10

Dunsany, Lord................ **TCLC 2, 59**
See also Dunsany, Edward John Moreton
Drax Plunkett
See also DLB 77, 153

du Perry, Jean
See Simenon, Georges (Jacques Christian)

Durang, Christopher (Ferdinand)
1949- .... **CLC 27, 38**
See also CA 105

Duras, Marguerite
1914- ...... **CLC 3, 6, 11, 20, 34, 40, 68**
See also CA 25-28R; DLB 83; MTCW

Durban, (Rosa) Pam 1947-........ **CLC 39**
See also CA 123

Durcan, Paul 1944-........... **CLC 43, 70**
See also CA 134

Durkheim, Emile 1858-1917 ...... **TCLC 55**

Durrell, Lawrence (George)
1912-1990 .... **CLC 1, 4, 6, 8, 13, 27, 41**
See also CA 9-12R; 132; CANR 40;
CDBLB 1945-1960; DLB 15, 27;
DLBY 90; MTCW

Durrenmatt, Friedrich
See Duerrenmatt, Friedrich

Dutt, Toru 1856-1877.......... **NCLC 29**

Dwight, Timothy 1752-1817...... **NCLC 13**
See also DLB 37

Dworkin, Andrea 1946- .... **CLC 43**
See also CA 77-80; CAAS 21; CANR 16,
39; MTCW

Dwyer, Deanna
See Koontz, Dean R(ay)

Dwyer, K. R.
See Koontz, Dean R(ay)

Dylan, Bob 1941- ...... **CLC 3, 4, 6, 12, 77**
See also CA 41-44R; DLB 16

Eagleton, Terence (Francis) 1943-
See Eagleton, Terry
See also CA 57-60; CANR 7, 23; MTCW

Eagleton, Terry .... **CLC 63**
See also Eagleton, Terence (Francis)

Early, Jack
See Scoppettone, Sandra

East, Michael
See West, Morris L(anglo)

Eastaway, Edward
See Thomas, (Philip) Edward

Eastlake, William (Derry) 1917-..... **CLC 8**
See also CA 5-8R; CAAS 1; CANR 5;
DLB 6

Eastman, Charles A(lexander)
1858-1939 .... **TCLC 55**
See also NNAL; YABC 1

Eberhart, Richard (Ghormley)
1904- .... **CLC 3, 11, 19, 56**
See also CA 1-4R; CANR 2;
CDALB 1941-1968; DLB 48; MTCW

Eberstadt, Fernanda 1960-........ **CLC 39**
See also CA 136

Echegaray (y Eizaguirre), Jose (Maria Waldo)
1832-1916 .... **TCLC 4**
See also CA 104; CANR 32; HW; MTCW

Echeverria, (Jose) Esteban (Antonino)
1805-1851 .... **NCLC 18**

Echo
See Proust, (Valentin-Louis-George-Eugene-)
Marcel

Eckert, Allan W. 1931- .... **CLC 17**
See also CA 13-16R; CANR 14, 45;
SATA 29; SATA-Brief 27

Eckhart, Meister 1260(?)-1328(?) .. **CMLC 9**
See also DLB 115

Eckmar, F. R.
See de Hartog, Jan

Eco, Umberto 1932-........... **CLC 28, 60**
See also BEST 90:1; CA 77-80; CANR 12,
33; MTCW

Eddison, E(ric) R(ucker)
1882-1945 .... **TCLC 15**
See also CA 109

Edel, (Joseph) Leon 1907-...... **CLC 29, 34**
See also CA 1-4R; CANR 1, 22; DLB 103

Eden, Emily 1797-1869 .... **NCLC 10**

Edgar, David 1948-.............. **CLC 42**
See also CA 57-60; CANR 12; DLB 13;
MTCW

Edgerton, Clyde (Carlyle) 1944- .... **CLC 39**
See also CA 118; 134

Edgeworth, Maria 1767-1849... **NCLC 1, 51**
See also DLB 116; SATA 21

Edmonds, Paul
See Kuttner, Henry

Edmonds, Walter D(umaux) 1903-.. **CLC 35**
See also CA 5-8R; CANR 2; DLB 9;
MAICYA; SAAS 4; SATA 1, 27

Edmondson, Wallace
See Ellison, Harlan (Jay)

Edson, Russell .... **CLC 13**
See also CA 33-36R

Edwards, Bronwen Elizabeth
See Rose, Wendy

Edwards, G(erald) B(asil)
1899-1976 .... **CLC 25**
See also CA 110

Edwards, Gus 1939-............. **CLC 43**
See also CA 108

Edwards, Jonathan 1703-1758.... **LC 7; DA**
See also DLB 24

Efron, Marina Ivanovna Tsvetaeva
See Tsvetaeva (Efron), Marina (Ivanovna)

Ehle, John (Marsden, Jr.) 1925-.... **CLC 27**
See also CA 9-12R

Ehrenbourg, Ilya (Grigoryevich)
See Ehrenburg, Ilya (Grigoryevich)

Ehrenburg, Ilya (Grigoryevich)
1891-1967 .... **CLC 18, 34, 62**
See also CA 102; 25-28R

Ehrenburg, Ilyo (Grigoryevich)
See Ehrenburg, Ilya (Grigoryevich)

Eich, Guenter 1907-1972 .... **CLC 15**
See also CA 111; 93-96; DLB 69, 124

Eichendorff, Joseph Freiherr von
1788-1857 .... **NCLC 8**
See also DLB 90

Eigner, Larry...................... **CLC 9**
See also Eigner, Laurence (Joel)
See also DLB 5

Eigner, Laurence (Joel) 1927-
See Eigner, Larry
See also CA 9-12R; CANR 6

Eiseley, Loren Corey 1907-1977..... **CLC 7**
See also AAYA 5; CA 1-4R; 73-76;
CANR 6

Eisenstadt, Jill 1963-............. **CLC 50**
See also CA 140

Eisenstein, Sergei (Mikhailovich)
1898-1948 .... **TCLC 57**
See also CA 114

Eisner, Simon
See Kornbluth, C(yril) M.

Ekeloef, (Bengt) Gunnar
1907-1968 .... **CLC 27**
See also CA 123; 25-28R

Ekelof, (Bengt) Gunnar
See Ekeloef, (Bengt) Gunnar

Ekwensi, C. O. D.
See Ekwensi, Cyprian (Odiatu Duaka)

Ekwensi, Cyprian (Odiatu Duaka)
1921- .... **CLC 4; BLC**
See also BW 2; CA 29-32R; CANR 18, 42;
DLB 117; MTCW; SATA 66

Elaine...................... **TCLC 18**
See also Leverson, Ada

El Crummo
See Crumb, R(obert)

Elia
See Lamb, Charles

Eliade, Mircea 1907-1986 .... **CLC 19**
See also CA 65-68; 119; CANR 30; MTCW

Eliot, A. D.
See Jewett, (Theodora) Sarah Orne

Eliot, Alice
See Jewett, (Theodora) Sarah Orne

Eliot, Dan
See Silverberg, Robert

Eliot, George
1819-1880 ..... **NCLC 4, 13, 23, 41, 49;
DA; WLC**
See also CDBLB 1832-1890; DLB 21, 35, 55

Eliot, John 1604-1690 .... **LC 5**
See also DLB 24

Eliot, T(homas) S(tearns)
1888-1965 ..... **CLC 1, 2, 3, 6, 9, 10, 13,
15, 24, 34, 41, 55, 57; DA; PC 5; WLC 2**
See also CA 5-8R; 25-28R; CANR 41;
CDALB 1929-1941; DLB 7, 10, 45, 63;
DLBY 88; MTCW

Elizabeth 1866-1941 .... **TCLC 41**

Elkin, Stanley L(awrence)
1930-1995 ...... **CLC 4, 6, 9, 14, 27, 51;
SSC 12**
See also CA 9-12R; 148; CANR 8, 46;
DLB 2, 28; DLBY 80; MTCW

Elledge, Scott. .... **CLC 34**

Elliott, Don
See Silverberg, Robert

Elliott, George P(aul) 1918-1980..... **CLC 2**
See also CA 1-4R; 97-100; CANR 2

Elliott, Janice 1931-............. **CLC 47**
See also CA 13-16R; CANR 8, 29; DLB 14

Elliott, Sumner Locke 1917-1991 ... **CLC 38**
See also CA 5-8R; 134; CANR 2, 21

Elliott, William
See Bradbury, Ray (Douglas)

Ellis, A. E. .... **CLC 7**

Ellis, Alice Thomas. .... **CLC 40**
See also Haycraft, Anna

Ellis, Bret Easton 1964-........ **CLC 39, 71**
See also AAYA 2; CA 118; 123

Ellis, (Henry) Havelock
1859-1939 .... **TCLC 14**
See also CA 109

Ellis, Landon
See Ellison, Harlan (Jay)

Ellis, Trey 1962-................. **CLC 55**
See also CA 146

Ellison, Harlan (Jay)
1934-......... **CLC 1, 13, 42; SSC 14**
See also CA 5-8R; CANR 5, 46; DLB 8;
MTCW

Ellison, Ralph (Waldo)
1914-1994 .... **CLC 1, 3, 11, 54, 86;
BLC; DA; WLC**
See also BW 1; CA 9-12R; 145; CANR 24;
CDALB 1941-1968; DLB 2, 76;
DLBY 94; MTCW

Ellmann, Lucy (Elizabeth) 1956-.... **CLC 61**
See also CA 128

Ellmann, Richard (David)
1918-1987 .... **CLC 50**
See also BEST 89:2; CA 1-4R; 122;
CANR 2, 28; DLB 103; DLBY 87;
MTCW

Elman, Richard 1934-............. **CLC 19**
See also CA 17-20R; CAAS 3; CANR 47

Elron
See Hubbard, L(afayette) Ron(ald)

Eluard, Paul. .... **TCLC 7, 41**
See also Grindel, Eugene

Elyot, Sir Thomas 1490(?)-1546 ..... **LC 11**

Elytis, Odysseus 1911-......... **CLC 15, 49**
See also CA 102; MTCW

Emecheta, (Florence Onye) Buchi
1944-................. **CLC 14, 48; BLC**
See also BW 2; CA 81-84; CANR 27;
DLB 117; MTCW; SATA 66

Emerson, Ralph Waldo
1803-1882 ...... **NCLC 1, 38; DA; WLC**
See also CDALB 1640-1865; DLB 1, 59, 73

Eminescu, Mihail 1850-1889 ..... **NCLC 33**

Empson, William
1906-1984 .... **CLC 3, 8, 19, 33, 34**
See also CA 17-20R; 112; CANR 31;
DLB 20; MTCW

Enchi Fumiko (Ueda) 1905-1986.... **CLC 31**
See also CA 129; 121

Ende, Michael (Andreas Helmuth)
1929-..................... **CLC 31**
See also CA 118; 124; CANR 36; CLR 14;
DLB 75; MAICYA; SATA 61;
SATA-Brief 42

Endo, Shusaku 1923-..... **CLC 7, 14, 19, 54**
See also CA 29-32R; CANR 21; MTCW

Engel, Marian 1933-1985.......... **CLC 36**
See also CA 25-28R; CANR 12; DLB 53

Engelhardt, Frederick
See Hubbard, L(afayette) Ron(ald)

Enright, D(ennis) J(oseph)
1920-.................... **CLC 4, 8, 31**
See also CA 1-4R; CANR 1, 42; DLB 27;
SATA 25

Enzensberger, Hans Magnus
1929-..................... **CLC 43**
See also CA 116; 119

Ephron, Nora 1941-.......... **CLC 17, 31**
See also AITN 2; CA 65-68; CANR 12, 39

Epsilon
See Betjeman, John

Epstein, Daniel Mark 1948- .... **CLC 7**
See also CA 49-52; CANR 2

Epstein, Jacob 1956-............. **CLC 19**
See also CA 114

Epstein, Joseph 1937-............. **CLC 39**
See also CA 112; 119

Epstein, Leslie 1938-............. **CLC 27**
See also CA 73-76; CAAS 12; CANR 23

Equiano, Olaudah
1745(?)-1797 .... **LC 16; BLC**
See also DLB 37, 50

Erasmus, Desiderius 1469(?)-1536.... **LC 16**

Erdman, Paul E(mil) 1932-........ **CLC 25**
See also AITN 1; CA 61-64; CANR 13, 43

Erdrich, Louise 1954-......... **CLC 39, 54**
See also AAYA 10; BEST 89:1; CA 114;
CANR 41; DLB 152; MTCW; NNAL

Erenburg, Ilya (Grigoryevich)
See Ehrenburg, Ilya (Grigoryevich)

Erickson, Stephen Michael 1950-
See Erickson, Steve
See also CA 129

Erickson, Steve .... **CLC 64**
See also Erickson, Stephen Michael

Ericson, Walter
See Fast, Howard (Melvin)

Eriksson, Buntel
See Bergman, (Ernst) Ingmar

Ernaux, Annie 1940- .... **CLC 88**
See also CA 147

Eschenbach, Wolfram von
See Wolfram von Eschenbach

Eseki, Bruno
See Mphahlele, Ezekiel

Esenin, Sergei (Alexandrovich)
1895-1925 .... **TCLC 4**
See also CA 104

Eshleman, Clayton 1935-........... **CLC 7**
See also CA 33-36R; CAAS 6; DLB 5

Espriella, Don Manuel Alvarez
See Southey, Robert

Espriu, Salvador 1913-1985......... **CLC 9**
See also CA 115; DLB 134

Espronceda, Jose de 1808-1842... **NCLC 39**

Esse, James
See Stephens, James

Esterbrook, Tom
See Hubbard, L(afayette) Ron(ald)

Estleman, Loren D. 1952-......... **CLC 48**
See also CA 85-88; CANR 27; MTCW

Eugenides, Jeffrey 1960(?)-........ **CLC 81**
See also CA 144

Euripides c. 485B.C.-406B.C. .... **DC 4**
See also DA

Evan, Evin
See Faust, Frederick (Schiller)

Evans, Evan
See Faust, Frederick (Schiller)

Evans, Marian
See Eliot, George

Evans, Mary Ann
See Eliot, George

Evarts, Esther
See Benson, Sally

Everett, Percival L. 1956-......... **CLC 57**
See also BW 2; CA 129

Everson, R(onald) G(ilmour)
1903-..................... **CLC 27**
See also CA 17-20R; DLB 88

Everson, William (Oliver)
1912-1994 .... **CLC 1, 5, 14**
See also CA 9-12R; 145; CANR 20; DLB 5,
16; MTCW

Evtushenko, Evgenii Aleksandrovich
See Yevtushenko, Yevgeny (Alexandrovich)

Ewart, Gavin (Buchanan)
1916-.................... **CLC 13, 46**
See also CA 89-92; CANR 17, 46; DLB 40;
MTCW

Ewers, Hanns Heinz 1871-1943 ... **TCLC 12**
See also CA 109

Ewing, Frederick R.
See Sturgeon, Theodore (Hamilton)

Exley, Frederick (Earl)
1929-1992 .... **CLC 6, 11**
See also AITN 2; CA 81-84; 138; DLB 143;
DLBY 81

Eynhardt, Guillermo
See Quiroga, Horacio (Sylvestre)

Ezekiel, Nissim 1924-............ **CLC 61**
See also CA 61-64

Ezekiel, Tish O'Dowd 1943- .... **CLC 34**
See also CA 129

Fadeyev, A.
See Bulgya, Alexander Alexandrovich

Fadeyev, Alexander.............. **TCLC 53**
See also Bulgya, Alexander Alexandrovich

Fagen, Donald 1948-............. **CLC 26**

Fainzilberg, Ilya Arnoldovich 1897-1937
See Ilf, Ilya
See also CA 120

Fair, Ronald L. 1932-............ **CLC 18**
See also BW 1; CA 69-72; CANR 25;
DLB 33

Fairbairns, Zoe (Ann) 1948- .... **CLC 32**
See also CA 103; CANR 21

Falco, Gian
See Papini, Giovanni

Falconer, James
See Kirkup, James

Falconer, Kenneth
See Kornbluth, C(yril) M.

Falkland, Samuel
See Heijermans, Herman

Fallaci, Oriana 1930-............ **CLC 11**
See also CA 77-80; CANR 15; MTCW

Faludy, George 1913-............ **CLC 42**
See also CA 21-24R

Faludy, Gyoergy
See Faludy, George

Fanon, Frantz 1925-1961..... **CLC 74; BLC**
See also BW 1; CA 116; 89-92

Fanshawe, Ann 1625-1680......... **LC 11**

Fante, John (Thomas) 1911-1983 ... **CLC 60**
See also CA 69-72; 109; CANR 23;
DLB 130; DLBY 83

Farah, Nuruddin 1945-....... **CLC 53; BLC**
See also BW 2; CA 106; DLB 125

Fargue, Leon-Paul 1876(?)-1947 ... **TCLC 11**
See also CA 109

Farigoule, Louis
See Romains, Jules

Farina, Richard 1936(?)-1966 .... **CLC 9**
See also CA 81-84; 25-28R

Farley, Walter (Lorimer)
1915-1989 .... **CLC 17**
See also CA 17-20R; CANR 8, 29; DLB 22;
JRDA; MAICYA; SATA 2, 43

Farmer, Philip Jose 1918-....... **CLC 1, 19**
See also CA 1-4R; CANR 4, 35; DLB 8;
MTCW

Farquhar, George 1677-1707 .... **LC 21**
See also DLB 84

Farrell, J(ames) G(ordon)
1935-1979 .... **CLC 6**
See also CA 73-76; 89-92; CANR 36;
DLB 14; MTCW

Farrell, James T(homas)
1904-1979 .... **CLC 1, 4, 8, 11, 66**
See also CA 5-8R; 89-92; CANR 9; DLB 4,
9, 86; DLBD 2; MTCW

Farren, Richard J.
See Betjeman, John

Farren, Richard M.
See Betjeman, John

Fassbinder, Rainer Werner
1946-1982 .... **CLC 20**
See also CA 93-96; 106; CANR 31

Fast, Howard (Melvin) 1914- ...... **CLC 23**
See also CA 1-4R; CAAS 18; CANR 1, 33;
DLB 9; SATA 7

Faulcon, Robert
See Holdstock, Robert P.

Faulkner, William (Cuthbert)
1897-1962 ..... **CLC 1, 3, 6, 8, 9, 11, 14,
18, 28, 52, 68; DA; SSC 1; WLC**
See also AAYA 7; CA 81-84; CANR 33;
CDALB 1929-1941; DLB 9, 11, 44, 102;
DLBD 2; DLBY 86; MTCW

Fauset, Jessie Redmon
1884(?)-1961 .... **CLC 19, 54; BLC**
See also BW 1; CA 109; DLB 51

Faust, Frederick (Schiller)
1892-1944(?) .... **TCLC 49**
See also CA 108

Faust, Irvin 1924-................. **CLC 8**
See also CA 33-36R; CANR 28; DLB 2, 28;
DLBY 80

Fawkes, Guy
See Benchley, Robert (Charles)

Fearing, Kenneth (Flexner)
1902-1961 .... **CLC 51**
See also CA 93-96; DLB 9

Fecamps, Elise
See Creasey, John

Federman, Raymond 1928- ...... **CLC 6, 47**
See also CA 17-20R; CAAS 8; CANR 10,
43; DLBY 80

Federspiel, J(uerg) F. 1931-........ **CLC 42**
See also CA 146

Feiffer, Jules (Ralph) 1929-.... **CLC 2, 8, 64**
See also AAYA 3; CA 17-20R; CANR 30;
DLB 7, 44; MTCW; SATA 8, 61

Feige, Hermann Albert Otto Maximilian
See Traven, B.

Feinberg, David B. 1956-1994..... **CLC 59**
See also CA 135; 147

Feinstein, Elaine 1930-............ **CLC 36**
See also CA 69-72; CAAS 1; CANR 31;
DLB 14, 40; MTCW

Feldman, Irving (Mordecai) 1928-.... **CLC 7**
See also CA 1-4R; CANR 1

Fellini, Federico 1920-1993 ..... **CLC 16, 85**
See also CA 65-68; 143; CANR 33

Felsen, Henry Gregor 1916- .... **CLC 17**
See also CA 1-4R; CANR 1; SAAS 2;
SATA 1

Fenton, James Martin 1949-....... **CLC 32**
See also CA 102; DLB 40

Ferber, Edna 1887-1968.......... **CLC 18**
See also AITN 1; CA 5-8R; 25-28R; DLB 9,
28, 86; MTCW; SATA 7

Ferguson, Helen
See Kavan, Anna

Ferguson, Samuel 1810-1886..... **NCLC 33**
See also DLB 32

Fergusson, Robert 1750-1774 .... **LC 29**
See also DLB 109

Ferling, Lawrence
See Ferlinghetti, Lawrence (Monsanto)

Ferlinghetti, Lawrence (Monsanto)
1919(?)- .... **CLC 2, 6, 10, 27; PC 1**
See also CA 5-8R; CANR 3, 41;
CDALB 1941-1968; DLB 5, 16; MTCW

Fernandez, Vicente Garcia Huidobro
See Huidobro Fernandez, Vicente Garcia

Ferrer, Gabriel (Francisco Victor) Miro
See Miro (Ferrer), Gabriel (Francisco
Victor)

Ferrier, Susan (Edmonstone)
1782-1854 .... **NCLC 8**
See also DLB 116

Ferrigno, Robert 1948(?)-......... **CLC 65**
See also CA 140

Feuchtwanger, Lion 1884-1958 ..... **TCLC 3**
See also CA 104; DLB 66

Feuillet, Octave 1821-1890 ...... **NCLC 45**

Feydeau, Georges (Leon Jules Marie)
1862-1921 .... **TCLC 22**
See also CA 113

Ficino, Marsilio 1433-1499 .... **LC 12**

Fiedeler, Hans
See Doeblin, Alfred

Fiedler, Leslie A(aron)
1917- .... **CLC 4, 13, 24**
See also CA 9-12R; CANR 7; DLB 28, 67;
MTCW

Field, Andrew 1938-............. **CLC 44**
See also CA 97-100; CANR 25

Field, Eugene 1850-1895 .... **NCLC 3**
See also DLB 23, 42, 140; MAICYA;
SATA 16

Field, Gans T.
See Wellman, Manly Wade

Field, Michael .... **TCLC 43**

Field, Peter
See Hobson, Laura Z(ametkin)

Fielding, Henry
1707-1754 .... **LC 1; DA; WLC**
See also CDBLB 1660-1789; DLB 39, 84,
101

Fielding, Sarah 1710-1768 .... **LC 1**
See also DLB 39

Fierstein, Harvey (Forbes) 1954- ... **CLC 33**
See also CA 123; 129

Figes, Eva 1932-................ **CLC 31**
See also CA 53-56; CANR 4, 44; DLB 14

Finch, Robert (Duer Claydon)
1900- .... **CLC 18**
See also CA 57-60; CANR 9, 24, 49;
DLB 88

Findley, Timothy 1930- . . . . **CLC 27**
See also CA 25-28R; CANR 12, 42;
DLB 53

Fink, William
See Mencken, H(enry) L(ouis)

Firbank, Louis 1942-
See Reed, Lou
See also CA 117

Firbank, (Arthur Annesley) Ronald
1886-1926 . . . . **TCLC 1**
See also CA 104; DLB 36

Fisher, M(ary) F(rances) K(ennedy)
1908-1992 . . . . **CLC 76, 87**
See also CA 77-80; 138; CANR 44

Fisher, Roy 1930- . . . . **CLC 25**
See also CA 81-84; CAAS 10; CANR 16;
DLB 40

Fisher, Rudolph
1897-1934 . . . . **TCLC 11; BLC**
See also BW 1; CA 107; 124; DLB 51, 102

Fisher, Vardis (Alvero) 1895-1968. . . . **CLC 7**
See also CA 5-8R; 25-28R; DLB 9

Fiske, Tarleton
See Bloch, Robert (Albert)

Fitch, Clarke
See Sinclair, Upton (Beall)

Fitch, John IV
See Cormier, Robert (Edmund)

Fitzgerald, Captain Hugh
See Baum, L(yman) Frank

FitzGerald, Edward 1809-1883 . . . . **NCLC 9**
See also DLB 32

Fitzgerald, F(rancis) Scott (Key)
1896-1940 . . . . . . **TCLC 1, 6, 14, 28, 55;**
DA; SSC 6; WLC
See also AITN 1; CA 110; 123;
CDALB 1917-1929; DLB 4, 9, 86;
DLBD 1; DLBY 81; MTCW

Fitzgerald, Penelope 1916-. . . **CLC 19, 51, 61**
See also CA 85-88; CAAS 10; DLB 14

Fitzgerald, Robert (Stuart)
1910-1985 . . . . **CLC 39**
See also CA 1-4R; 114; CANR 1; DLBY 80

FitzGerald, Robert D(avid)
1902-1987 . . . . **CLC 19**
See also CA 17-20R

Fitzgerald, Zelda (Sayre)
1900-1948 . . . . **TCLC 52**
See also CA 117; 126; DLBY 84

Flanagan, Thomas (James Bonner)
1923- . . . . **CLC 25, 52**
See also CA 108; DLBY 80; MTCW

Flaubert, Gustave
1821-1880 . . . . **NCLC 2, 10, 19; DA;**
SSC 11; WLC
See also DLB 119

Flecker, (Herman) James Elroy
1884-1915 . . . . **TCLC 43**
See also CA 109; DLB 10, 19

Fleming, Ian (Lancaster)
1908-1964 . . . . **CLC 3, 30**
See also CA 5-8R; CDBLB 1945-1960;
DLB 87; MTCW; SATA 9

Fleming, Thomas (James) 1927- . . . . **CLC 37**
See also CA 5-8R; CANR 10; SATA 8

Fletcher, John Gould 1886-1950 . . . **TCLC 35**
See also CA 107; DLB 4, 45

Fleur, Paul
See Pohl, Frederik

Flooglebuckle, Al
See Spiegelman, Art

Flying Officer X
See Bates, H(erbert) E(rnest)

Fo, Dario 1926-. . . . . **CLC 32**
See also CA 116; 128; MTCW

Fogarty, Jonathan Titulescu Esq.
See Farrell, James T(homas)

Folke, Will
See Bloch, Robert (Albert)

Follett, Ken(neth Martin) 1949- . . . . **CLC 18**
See also AAYA 6; BEST 89:4; CA 81-84;
CANR 13, 33; DLB 87; DLBY 81;
MTCW

Fontane, Theodor 1819-1898 . . . . . **NCLC 26**
See also DLB 129

Foote, Horton 1916-. . . . . **CLC 51**
See also CA 73-76; CANR 34; DLB 26

Foote, Shelby 1916- . . . . **CLC 75**
See also CA 5-8R; CANR 3, 45; DLB 2, 17

Forbes, Esther 1891-1967. . . . . **CLC 12**
See also CA 13-14; 25-28R; CAP 1;
CLR 27; DLB 22; JRDA; MAICYA;
SATA 2

Forche, Carolyn (Louise)
1950- . . . . **CLC 25, 83, 86; PC 10**
See also CA 109; 117; DLB 5

Ford, Elbur
See Hibbert, Eleanor Alice Burford

Ford, Ford Madox
1873-1939 . . . . **TCLC 1, 15, 39, 57**
See also CA 104; 132; CDBLB 1914-1945;
DLB 34, 98; MTCW

Ford, John 1895-1973. . . . . **CLC 16**
See also CA 45-48

Ford, Richard 1944-. . . . . **CLC 46**
See also CA 69-72; CANR 11, 47

Ford, Webster
See Masters, Edgar Lee

Foreman, Richard 1937-. . . . . **CLC 50**
See also CA 65-68; CANR 32

Forester, C(ecil) S(cott)
1899-1966 . . . . **CLC 35**
See also CA 73-76; 25-28R; SATA 13

Forez
See Mauriac, Francois (Charles)

Forman, James Douglas 1932-. . . . . . **CLC 21**
See also CA 9-12R; CANR 4, 19, 42;
JRDA; MAICYA; SATA 8, 70

Fornes, Maria Irene 1930-. . . . . . **CLC 39, 61**
See also CA 25-28R; CANR 28; DLB 7;
HW; MTCW

Forrest, Leon 1937- . . . . **CLC 4**
See also BW 2; CA 89-92; CAAS 7;
CANR 25; DLB 33

Forster, E(dward) M(organ)
1879-1970 . . . . . **CLC 1, 2, 3, 4, 9, 10, 13,**
15, 22, 45, 77; DA; WLC
See also AAYA 2; CA 13-14; 25-28R;
CANR 45; CAP 1; CDBLB 1914-1945;
DLB 34, 98; DLBD 10; MTCW;
SATA 57

Forster, John 1812-1876 . . . . **NCLC 11**
See also DLB 144

Forsyth, Frederick 1938-. . . . . . **CLC 2, 5, 36**
See also BEST 89:4; CA 85-88; CANR 38;
DLB 87; MTCW

Forten, Charlotte L. . . . . **TCLC 16; BLC**
See also Grimke, Charlotte L(ottie) Forten
See also DLB 50

Foscolo, Ugo 1778-1827. . . . . **NCLC 8**

Fosse, Bob . . . . **CLC 20**
See also Fosse, Robert Louis

Fosse, Robert Louis 1927-1987
See Fosse, Bob
See also CA 110; 123

Foster, Stephen Collins
1826-1864 . . . . **NCLC 26**

Foucault, Michel
1926-1984 . . . . **CLC 31, 34, 69**
See also CA 105; 113; CANR 34; MTCW

Fouque, Friedrich (Heinrich Karl) de la Motte
1777-1843 . . . . **NCLC 2**
See also DLB 90

Fourier, Charles 1772-1837 . . . . . . **NCLC 51**

Fournier, Henri Alban 1886-1914
See Alain-Fournier
See also CA 104

Fournier, Pierre 1916-. . . . . **CLC 11**
See also Gascar, Pierre
See also CA 89-92; CANR 16, 40

Fowles, John
1926- . . . . . . **CLC 1, 2, 3, 4, 6, 9, 10, 15,**
33, 87
See also CA 5-8R; CANR 25; CDBLB 1960
to Present; DLB 14, 139; MTCW;
SATA 22

Fox, Paula 1923-. . . . . **CLC 2, 8**
See also AAYA 3; CA 73-76; CANR 20,
36; CLR 1; DLB 52; JRDA; MAICYA;
MTCW; SATA 17, 60

Fox, William Price (Jr.) 1926-. . . . . **CLC 22**
See also CA 17-20R; CAAS 19; CANR 11;
DLB 2; DLBY 81

Foxe, John 1516(?)-1587 . . . . **LC 14**

Frame, Janet . . . . **CLC 2, 3, 6, 22, 66**
See also Clutha, Janet Paterson Frame

France, Anatole . . . . **TCLC 9**
See also Thibault, Jacques Anatole Francois
See also DLB 123

Francis, Claude 19(?)- . . . . **CLC 50**

Francis, Dick 1920- . . . . **CLC 2, 22, 42**
See also AAYA 5; BEST 89:3; CA 5-8R;
CANR 9, 42; CDBLB 1960 to Present;
DLB 87; MTCW

Francis, Robert (Churchill)
1901-1987 . . . . **CLC 15**
See also CA 1-4R; 123; CANR 1

Frank, Anne(lies Marie)
    1929-1945 .... **TCLC 17; DA; WLC**
    See also AAYA 12; CA 113; 133; MTCW;
    SATA-Brief 42

Frank, Elizabeth 1945-........... **CLC 39**
    See also CA 121; 126

Franklin, Benjamin
    See Hasek, Jaroslav (Matej Frantisek)

Franklin, Benjamin 1706-1790... **LC 25; DA**
    See also CDALB 1640-1865; DLB 24, 43,
    73

Franklin, (Stella Maraia Sarah) Miles
    1879-1954 .... **TCLC 7**
    See also CA 104

Fraser, (Lady) Antonia (Pakenham)
    1932- .... **CLC 32**
    See also CA 85-88; CANR 44; MTCW;
    SATA-Brief 32

Fraser, George MacDonald 1925-.... **CLC 7**
    See also CA 45-48; CANR 2, 48

Fraser, Sylvia 1935-............. **CLC 64**
    See also CA 45-48; CANR 1, 16

Frayn, Michael 1933-...... **CLC 3, 7, 31, 47**
    See also CA 5-8R; CANR 30; DLB 13, 14;
    MTCW

Fraze, Candida (Merrill) 1945-..... **CLC 50**
    See also CA 126

Frazer, J(ames) G(eorge)
    1854-1941 .... **TCLC 32**
    See also CA 118

Frazer, Robert Caine
    See Creasey, John

Frazer, Sir James George
    See Frazer, J(ames) G(eorge)

Frazier, Ian 1951-................ **CLC 46**
    See also CA 130

Frederic, Harold 1856-1898...... **NCLC 10**
    See also DLB 12, 23

Frederick, John
    See Faust, Frederick (Schiller)

Frederick the Great 1712-1786...... **LC 14**

Fredro, Aleksander 1793-1876..... **NCLC 8**

Freeling, Nicolas 1927- .... **CLC 38**
    See also CA 49-52; CAAS 12; CANR 1, 17;
    DLB 87

Freeman, Douglas Southall
    1886-1953 .... **TCLC 11**
    See also CA 109; DLB 17

Freeman, Judith 1946-............ **CLC 55**

Freeman, Mary Eleanor Wilkins
    1852-1930 .... **TCLC 9; SSC 1**
    See also CA 106; DLB 12, 78

Freeman, R(ichard) Austin
    1862-1943 .... **TCLC 21**
    See also CA 113; DLB 70

French, Albert 1943- .... **CLC 86**

French, Marilyn 1929-...... **CLC 10, 18, 60**
    See also CA 69-72; CANR 3, 31; MTCW

French, Paul
    See Asimov, Isaac

Freneau, Philip Morin 1752-1832.. **NCLC 1**
    See also DLB 37, 43

Freud, Sigmund 1856-1939 ...... **TCLC 52**
    See also CA 115; 133; MTCW

Friedan, Betty (Naomi) 1921-...... **CLC 74**
    See also CA 65-68; CANR 18, 45; MTCW

Friedman, B(ernard) H(arper)
    1926- .... **CLC 7**
    See also CA 1-4R; CANR 3, 48

Friedman, Bruce Jay 1930-.... **CLC 3, 5, 56**
    See also CA 9-12R; CANR 25; DLB 2, 28

Friel, Brian 1929-........... **CLC 5, 42, 59**
    See also CA 21-24R; CANR 33; DLB 13;
    MTCW

Friis-Baastad, Babbis Ellinor
    1921-1970 .... **CLC 12**
    See also CA 17-20R; 134; SATA 7

Frisch, Max (Rudolf)
    1911-1991 ..... **CLC 3, 9, 14, 18, 32, 44**
    See also CA 85-88; 134; CANR 32;
    DLB 69, 124; MTCW

Fromentin, Eugene (Samuel Auguste)
    1820-1876 .... **NCLC 10**
    See also DLB 123

Frost, Frederick
    See Faust, Frederick (Schiller)

Frost, Robert (Lee)
    1874-1963 .... **CLC 1, 3, 4, 9, 10, 13, 15,
        26, 34, 44; DA; PC 1; WLC**
    See also CA 89-92; CANR 33;
    CDALB 1917-1929; DLB 54; DLBD 7;
    MTCW; SATA 14

Froude, James Anthony
    1818-1894 .... **NCLC 43**
    See also DLB 18, 57, 144

Froy, Herald
    See Waterhouse, Keith (Spencer)

Fry, Christopher 1907-....... **CLC 2, 10, 14**
    See also CA 17-20R; CANR 9, 30; DLB 13;
    MTCW; SATA 66

Frye, (Herman) Northrop
    1912-1991 .... **CLC 24, 70**
    See also CA 5-8R; 133; CANR 8, 37;
    DLB 67, 68; MTCW

Fuchs, Daniel 1909-1993 .... **CLC 8, 22**
    See also CA 81-84; 142; CAAS 5;
    CANR 40; DLB 9, 26, 28; DLBY 93

Fuchs, Daniel 1934-.............. **CLC 34**
    See also CA 37-40R; CANR 14, 48

Fuentes, Carlos
    1928-...... **CLC 3, 8, 10, 13, 22, 41, 60;
        DA; HLC; WLC**
    See also AAYA 4; AITN 2; CA 69-72;
    CANR 10, 32; DLB 113; HW; MTCW

Fuentes, Gregorio Lopez y
    See Lopez y Fuentes, Gregorio

Fugard, (Harold) Athol
    1932- .... **CLC 5, 9, 14, 25, 40, 80; DC 3**
    See also CA 85-88; CANR 32; MTCW

Fugard, Sheila 1932- .... **CLC 48**
    See also CA 125

Fuller, Charles (H., Jr.)
    1939- .... **CLC 25; BLC; DC 1**
    See also BW 2; CA 108; 112; DLB 38;
    MTCW

Fuller, John (Leopold) 1937-....... **CLC 62**
    See also CA 21-24R; CANR 9, 44; DLB 40

Fuller, Margaret .... **NCLC 5, 50**
    See also Ossoli, Sarah Margaret (Fuller
    marchesa d')

Fuller, Roy (Broadbent)
    1912-1991 .... **CLC 4, 28**
    See also CA 5-8R; 135; CAAS 10; DLB 15,
    20

Fulton, Alice 1952-.............. **CLC 52**
    See also CA 116

Furphy, Joseph 1843-1912....... **TCLC 25**

Fussell, Paul 1924-.............. **CLC 74**
    See also BEST 90:1; CA 17-20R; CANR 8,
    21, 35; MTCW

Futabatei, Shimei 1864-1909..... **TCLC 44**

Futrelle, Jacques 1875-1912 ...... **TCLC 19**
    See also CA 113

Gaboriau, Emile 1835-1873...... **NCLC 14**

Gadda, Carlo Emilio 1893-1973 .... **CLC 11**
    See also CA 89-92

Gaddis, William
    1922-..... **CLC 1, 3, 6, 8, 10, 19, 43, 86**
    See also CA 17-20R; CANR 21, 48; DLB 2;
    MTCW

Gaines, Ernest J(ames)
    1933-......... **CLC 3, 11, 18, 86; BLC**
    See also AITN 1; BW 2; CA 9-12R;
    CANR 6, 24, 42; CDALB 1968-1988;
    DLB 2, 33, 152; DLBY 80; MTCW

Gaitskill, Mary 1954-............. **CLC 69**
    See also CA 128

Galdos, Benito Perez
    See Perez Galdos, Benito

Gale, Zona 1874-1938 .... **TCLC 7**
    See also CA 105; DLB 9, 78

Galeano, Eduardo (Hughes) 1940-... **CLC 72**
    See also CA 29-32R; CANR 13, 32; HW

Galiano, Juan Valera y Alcala
    See Valera y Alcala-Galiano, Juan

Gallagher, Tess 1943-.... **CLC 18, 63; PC 9**
    See also CA 106; DLB 120

Gallant, Mavis
    1922-........... **CLC 7, 18, 38; SSC 5**
    See also CA 69-72; CANR 29; DLB 53;
    MTCW

Gallant, Roy A(rthur) 1924- .... **CLC 17**
    See also CA 5-8R; CANR 4, 29; CLR 30;
    MAICYA; SATA 4, 68

Gallico, Paul (William) 1897-1976 ... **CLC 2**
    See also AITN 1; CA 5-8R; 69-72;
    CANR 23; DLB 9; MAICYA; SATA 13

Gallup, Ralph
    See Whitemore, Hugh (John)

Galsworthy, John
    1867-1933 .... **TCLC 1, 45; DA; WLC 2**
    See also CA 104; 141; CDBLB 1890-1914;
    DLB 10, 34, 98

Galt, John 1779-1839............ **NCLC 1**
    See also DLB 99, 116

Galvin, James 1951-.............. **CLC 38**
    See also CA 108; CANR 26

Gamboa, Federico 1864-1939..... **TCLC 36**

Gandhi, M. K.
    See Gandhi, Mohandas Karamchand

Gandhi, Mahatma
　　See Gandhi, Mohandas Karamchand

Gandhi, Mohandas Karamchand
　　1869-1948 . . . . **TCLC 59**
　　See also CA 121; 132; MTCW

Gann, Ernest Kellogg 1910-1991 . . . . **CLC 23**
　　See also AITN 1; CA 1-4R; 136; CANR 1

Garcia, Cristina 1958- . . . . **CLC 76**
　　See also CA 141

Garcia Lorca, Federico
　　1898-1936 . . . . **TCLC 1, 7, 49; DA;**
　　　　　　　　　　DC 2; HLC; PC 3; WLC
　　See also CA 104; 131; DLB 108; HW;
　　MTCW

Garcia Marquez, Gabriel (Jose)
　　1928- . . . . **CLC 2, 3, 8, 10, 15, 27, 47, 55,**
　　　　　　　　68; DA; HLC; SSC 8; WLC
　　See also AAYA 3; BEST 89:1, 90:4;
　　CA 33-36R; CANR 10, 28; DLB 113;
　　HW; MTCW

Gard, Janice
　　See Latham, Jean Lee

Gard, Roger Martin du
　　See Martin du Gard, Roger

Gardam, Jane 1928- . . . . **CLC 43**
　　See also CA 49-52; CANR 2, 18, 33;
　　CLR 12; DLB 14; MAICYA; MTCW;
　　SAAS 9; SATA 39, 76; SATA-Brief 28

Gardner, Herb . . . . **CLC 44**

Gardner, John (Champlin), Jr.
　　1933-1982 . . . . . **CLC 2, 3, 5, 7, 8, 10, 18,**
　　　　　　　　　　　28, 34; SSC 7
　　See also AITN 1; CA 65-68; 107;
　　CANR 33; DLB 2; DLBY 82; MTCW;
　　SATA 40; SATA-Obit 31

Gardner, John (Edmund) 1926- . . . . . **CLC 30**
　　See also CA 103; CANR 15; MTCW

Gardner, Noel
　　See Kuttner, Henry

Gardons, S. S.
　　See Snodgrass, W(illiam) D(e Witt)

Garfield, Leon 1921- . . . . **CLC 12**
　　See also AAYA 8; CA 17-20R; CANR 38,
　　41; CLR 21; JRDA; MAICYA; SATA 1,
　　32, 76

Garland, (Hannibal) Hamlin
　　1860-1940 . . . . **TCLC 3; SSC 18**
　　See also CA 104; DLB 12, 71, 78

Garneau, (Hector de) Saint-Denys
　　1912-1943 . . . . **TCLC 13**
　　See also CA 111; DLB 88

Garner, Alan 1934- . . . . **CLC 17**
　　See also CA 73-76; CANR 15; CLR 20;
　　MAICYA; MTCW; SATA 18, 69

Garner, Hugh 1913-1979 . . . . **CLC 13**
　　See also CA 69-72; CANR 31; DLB 68

Garnett, David 1892-1981 . . . . **CLC 3**
　　See also CA 5-8R; 103; CANR 17; DLB 34

Garos, Stephanie
　　See Katz, Steve

Garrett, George (Palmer)
　　1929- . . . . **CLC 3, 11, 51**
　　See also CA 1-4R; CAAS 5; CANR 1, 42;
　　DLB 2, 5, 130, 152; DLBY 83

Garrick, David 1717-1779 . . . . **LC 15**
　　See also DLB 84

Garrigue, Jean 1914-1972 . . . . **CLC 2, 8**
　　See also CA 5-8R; 37-40R; CANR 20

Garrison, Frederick
　　See Sinclair, Upton (Beall)

Garth, Will
　　See Hamilton, Edmond; Kuttner, Henry

Garvey, Marcus (Moziah, Jr.)
　　1887-1940 . . . . **TCLC 41; BLC**
　　See also BW 1; CA 120; 124

Gary, Romain . . . . **CLC 25**
　　See also Kacew, Romain
　　See also DLB 83

Gascar, Pierre . . . . **CLC 11**
　　See also Fournier, Pierre

Gascoyne, David (Emery) 1916- . . . . **CLC 45**
　　See also CA 65-68; CANR 10, 28; DLB 20;
　　MTCW

Gaskell, Elizabeth Cleghorn
　　1810-1865 . . . . **NCLC 5**
　　See also CDBLB 1832-1890; DLB 21, 144

Gass, William H(oward)
　　1924- . . . **CLC 1, 2, 8, 11, 15, 39; SSC 12**
　　See also CA 17-20R; CANR 30; DLB 2;
　　MTCW

Gasset, Jose Ortega y
　　See Ortega y Gasset, Jose

Gates, Henry Louis, Jr. 1950- . . . . . . **CLC 65**
　　See also BW 2; CA 109; CANR 25; DLB 67

Gautier, Theophile
　　1811-1872 . . . . **NCLC 1; SSC 20**
　　See also DLB 119

Gawsworth, John
　　See Bates, H(erbert) E(rnest)

Gaye, Marvin (Penze) 1939-1984 . . . **CLC 26**
　　See also CA 112

Gebler, Carlo (Ernest) 1954- . . . . **CLC 39**
　　See also CA 119; 133

Gee, Maggie (Mary) 1948- . . . . **CLC 57**
　　See also CA 130

Gee, Maurice (Gough) 1931- . . . . **CLC 29**
　　See also CA 97-100; SATA 46

Gelbart, Larry (Simon) 1923- . . . **CLC 21, 61**
　　See also CA 73-76; CANR 45

Gelber, Jack 1932- . . . . **CLC 1, 6, 14, 79**
　　See also CA 1-4R; CANR 2; DLB 7

Gellhorn, Martha (Ellis) 1908- . . **CLC 14, 60**
　　See also CA 77-80; CANR 44; DLBY 82

Genet, Jean
　　1910-1986 . . . **CLC 1, 2, 5, 10, 14, 44, 46**
　　See also CA 13-16R; CANR 18; DLB 72;
　　DLBY 86; MTCW

Gent, Peter 1942- . . . . **CLC 29**
　　See also AITN 1; CA 89-92; DLBY 82

Gentlewoman in New England, A
　　See Bradstreet, Anne

Gentlewoman in Those Parts, A
　　See Bradstreet, Anne

George, Jean Craighead 1919- . . . . . . **CLC 35**
　　See also AAYA 8; CA 5-8R; CANR 25;
　　CLR 1; DLB 52; JRDA; MAICYA;
　　SATA 2, 68

George, Stefan (Anton)
　　1868-1933 . . . . **TCLC 2, 14**
　　See also CA 104

Georges, Georges Martin
　　See Simenon, Georges (Jacques Christian)

Gerhardi, William Alexander
　　See Gerhardie, William Alexander

Gerhardie, William Alexander
　　1895-1977 . . . . **CLC 5**
　　See also CA 25-28R; 73-76; CANR 18;
　　DLB 36

Gerstler, Amy 1956- . . . . **CLC 70**
　　See also CA 146

Gertler, T. . . . . **CLC 34**
　　See also CA 116; 121

Ghalib 1797-1869 . . . . **NCLC 39**

Ghelderode, Michel de
　　1898-1962 . . . . **CLC 6, 11**
　　See also CA 85-88; CANR 40

Ghiselin, Brewster 1903- . . . . **CLC 23**
　　See also CA 13-16R; CAAS 10; CANR 13

Ghose, Zulfikar 1935- . . . . **CLC 42**
　　See also CA 65-68

Ghosh, Amitav 1956- . . . . **CLC 44**
　　See also CA 147

Giacosa, Giuseppe 1847-1906 . . . . . . **TCLC 7**
　　See also CA 104

Gibb, Lee
　　See Waterhouse, Keith (Spencer)

Gibbon, Lewis Grassic . . . . **TCLC 4**
　　See also Mitchell, James Leslie

Gibbons, Kaye 1960- . . . . **CLC 50, 88**

Gibran, Kahlil
　　1883-1931 . . . . **TCLC 1, 9; PC 9**
　　See also CA 104

Gibson, William 1914- . . . . **CLC 23; DA**
　　See also CA 9-12R; CANR 9, 42; DLB 7;
　　SATA 66

Gibson, William (Ford) 1948- . . . **CLC 39, 63**
　　See also AAYA 12; CA 126; 133

Gide, Andre (Paul Guillaume)
　　1869-1951 . . . . **TCLC 5, 12, 36; DA;**
　　　　　　　　　　　　SSC 13; WLC
　　See also CA 104; 124; DLB 65; MTCW

Gifford, Barry (Colby) 1946- . . . . **CLC 34**
　　See also CA 65-68; CANR 9, 30, 40

Gilbert, W(illiam) S(chwenck)
　　1836-1911 . . . . **TCLC 3**
　　See also CA 104; SATA 36

Gilbreth, Frank B., Jr. 1911- . . . . **CLC 17**
　　See also CA 9-12R; SATA 2

Gilchrist, Ellen 1935- . . **CLC 34, 48; SSC 14**
　　See also CA 113; 116; CANR 41; DLB 130;
　　MTCW

Giles, Molly 1942- . . . . **CLC 39**
　　See also CA 126

Gill, Patrick
　　See Creasey, John

Gilliam, Terry (Vance) 1940- . . . . **CLC 21**
　　See also Monty Python
　　See also CA 108; 113; CANR 35

Gillian, Jerry
　　See Gilliam, Terry (Vance)

Gilliatt, Penelope (Ann Douglass)
1932-1993 .... CLC **2, 10, 13, 53**
See also AITN 2; CA 13-16R; 141;
CANR 49; DLB 14

Gilman, Charlotte (Anna) Perkins (Stetson)
1860-1935 .... TCLC **9, 37;** SSC **13**
See also CA 106

Gilmour, David 1949-............ CLC **35**
See also CA 138, 147

Gilpin, William 1724-1804...... NCLC **30**

Gilray, J. D.
See Mencken, H(enry) L(ouis)

Gilroy, Frank D(aniel) 1925-........ CLC **2**
See also CA 81-84; CANR 32; DLB 7

Ginsberg, Allen
1926- ...... CLC **1, 2, 3, 4, 6, 13, 36, 69;**
DA; PC **4;** WLC **3**
See also AITN 1; CA 1-4R; CANR 2, 41;
CDALB 1941-1968; DLB 5, 16; MTCW

Ginzburg, Natalia
1916-1991.........CLC **5, 11, 54, 70**
See also CA 85-88; 135; CANR 33; MTCW

Giono, Jean 1895-1970......... CLC **4, 11**
See also CA 45-48; 29-32R; CANR 2, 35;
DLB 72; MTCW

Giovanni, Nikki
1943- ...... CLC **2, 4, 19, 64;** BLC; DA
See also AITN 1; BW 2; CA 29-32R;
CAAS 6; CANR 18, 41; CLR 6; DLB 5,
41; MAICYA; MTCW; SATA 24

Giovene, Andrea 1904-............ CLC **7**
See also CA 85-88

Gippius, Zinaida (Nikolayevna) 1869-1945
See Hippius, Zinaida
See also CA 106

Giraudoux, (Hippolyte) Jean
1882-1944 .... TCLC **2, 7**
See also CA 104; DLB 65

Gironella, Jose Maria 1917-....... CLC **11**
See also CA 101

Gissing, George (Robert)
1857-1903 .... TCLC **3, 24, 47**
See also CA 105; DLB 18, 135

Giurlani, Aldo
See Palazzeschi, Aldo

Gladkov, Fyodor (Vasilyevich)
1883-1958 .... TCLC **27**

Glanville, Brian (Lester) 1931- ...... CLC **6**
See also CA 5-8R; CAAS 9; CANR 3;
DLB 15, 139; SATA 42

Glasgow, Ellen (Anderson Gholson)
1873(?)-1945 .... TCLC **2, 7**
See also CA 104; DLB 9, 12

Glaspell, Susan (Keating)
1882(?)-1948 .... TCLC **55**
See also CA 110; DLB 7, 9, 78; YABC 2

Glassco, John 1909-1981 .... CLC **9**
See also CA 13-16R; 102; CANR 15;
DLB 68

Glasscock, Amnesia
See Steinbeck, John (Ernst)

Glasser, Ronald J. 1940(?)-........ CLC **37**

Glassman, Joyce
See Johnson, Joyce

Glendinning, Victoria 1937-........ CLC **50**
See also CA 120; 127

Glissant, Edouard 1928-........ CLC **10, 68**

Gloag, Julian 1930- .... CLC **40**
See also AITN 1; CA 65-68; CANR 10

Glowacki, Aleksander
See Prus, Boleslaw

Glueck, Louise (Elisabeth)
1943-................ CLC **7, 22, 44, 81**
See also CA 33-36R; CANR 40; DLB 5

Gobineau, Joseph Arthur (Comte) de
1816-1882 .... NCLC **17**
See also DLB 123

Godard, Jean-Luc 1930-.......... CLC **20**
See also CA 93-96

Godden, (Margaret) Rumer 1907-... CLC **53**
See also AAYA 6; CA 5-8R; CANR 4, 27,
36; CLR 20; MAICYA; SAAS 12;
SATA 3, 36

Godoy Alcayaga, Lucila 1889-1957
See Mistral, Gabriela
See also BW 2; CA 104; 131; HW; MTCW

Godwin, Gail (Kathleen)
1937- .... CLC **5, 8, 22, 31, 69**
See also CA 29-32R; CANR 15, 43; DLB 6;
MTCW

Godwin, William 1756-1836...... NCLC **14**
See also CDBLB 1789-1832; DLB 39, 104,
142

Goethe, Johann Wolfgang von
1749-1832 .... NCLC **4, 22, 34;** DA;
PC **5;** WLC **3**
See also DLB 94

Gogarty, Oliver St. John
1878-1957 .... TCLC **15**
See also CA 109; DLB 15, 19

Gogol, Nikolai (Vasilyevich)
1809-1852 .... NCLC **5, 15, 31;** DA;
DC **1;** SSC **4;** WLC

Goines, Donald
1937(?)-1974 .... CLC **80;** BLC
See also AITN 1; BW 1; CA 124; 114;
DLB 33

Gold, Herbert 1924-....... CLC **4, 7, 14, 42**
See also CA 9-12R; CANR 17, 45; DLB 2;
DLBY 81

Goldbarth, Albert 1948-......... CLC **5, 38**
See also CA 53-56; CANR 6, 40; DLB 120

Goldberg, Anatol 1910-1982 .... CLC **34**
See also CA 131; 117

Goldemberg, Isaac 1945-.......... CLC **52**
See also CA 69-72; CAAS 12; CANR 11,
32; HW

Golding, William (Gerald)
1911-1993 .... CLC **1, 2, 3, 8, 10, 17, 27,
58, 81;** DA; WLC
See also AAYA 5; CA 5-8R; 141;
CANR 13, 33; CDBLB 1945-1960;
DLB 15, 100; MTCW

Goldman, Emma 1869-1940...... TCLC **13**
See also CA 110

Goldman, Francisco 1955-........ CLC **76**

Goldman, William (W.) 1931-.... CLC **1, 48**
See also CA 9-12R; CANR 29; DLB 44

Goldmann, Lucien 1913-1970 ...... CLC **24**
See also CA 25-28; CAP 2

Goldoni, Carlo 1707-1793 .... LC **4**

Goldsberry, Steven 1949-.......... CLC **34**
See also CA 131

Goldsmith, Oliver
1728-1774 .... LC **2;** DA; WLC
See also CDBLB 1660-1789; DLB 39, 89,
104, 109, 142; SATA 26

Goldsmith, Peter
See Priestley, J(ohn) B(oynton)

Gombrowicz, Witold
1904-1969 .... CLC **4, 7, 11, 49**
See also CA 19-20; 25-28R; CAP 2

Gomez de la Serna, Ramon
1888-1963 .... CLC **9**
See also CA 116; HW

Goncharov, Ivan Alexandrovich
1812-1891 .... NCLC **1**

Goncourt, Edmond (Louis Antoine Huot) de
1822-1896 .... NCLC **7**
See also DLB 123

Goncourt, Jules (Alfred Huot) de
1830-1870 .... NCLC **7**
See also DLB 123

Gontier, Fernande 19(?)-.......... CLC **50**

Goodman, Paul 1911-1972.... CLC **1, 2, 4, 7**
See also CA 19-20; 37-40R; CANR 34;
CAP 2; DLB 130; MTCW

Gordimer, Nadine
1923- .... CLC **3, 5, 7, 10, 18, 33, 51, 70;**
DA; SSC **17**
See also CA 5-8R; CANR 3, 28; MTCW

Gordon, Adam Lindsay
1833-1870 .... NCLC **21**

Gordon, Caroline
1895-1981 ... CLC **6, 13, 29, 83;** SSC **15**
See also CA 11-12; 103; CANR 36; CAP 1;
DLB 4, 9, 102; DLBY 81; MTCW

Gordon, Charles William 1860-1937
See Connor, Ralph
See also CA 109

Gordon, Mary (Catherine)
1949- .... CLC **13, 22**
See also CA 102; CANR 44; DLB 6;
DLBY 81; MTCW

Gordon, Sol 1923-................ CLC **26**
See also CA 53-56; CANR 4; SATA 11

Gordone, Charles 1925-.......... CLC **1, 4**
See also BW 1; CA 93-96; DLB 7; MTCW

Gorenko, Anna Andreevna
See Akhmatova, Anna

Gorky, Maxim............. TCLC **8; WLC
See also Peshkov, Alexei Maximovich

Goryan, Sirak
See Saroyan, William

Gosse, Edmund (William)
1849-1928 .... TCLC **28**
See also CA 117; DLB 57, 144

Gotlieb, Phyllis Fay (Bloom)
1926-.................... CLC **18**
See also CA 13-16R; CANR 7; DLB 88

Gottesman, S. D.
See Kornbluth, C(yril) M.; Pohl, Frederik

Gottfried von Strassburg
    fl. c. 1210- . . . . **CMLC 10**
  See also DLB 138

Gould, Lois . . . . **CLC 4, 10**
  See also CA 77-80; CANR 29; MTCW

Gourmont, Remy de 1858-1915. . . . **TCLC 17**
  See also CA 109

Govier, Katherine 1948- . . . . **CLC 51**
  See also CA 101; CANR 18, 40

Goyen, (Charles) William
    1915-1983 . . . . **CLC 5, 8, 14, 40**
  See also AITN 2; CA 5-8R; 110; CANR 6;
    DLB 2; DLBY 83

Goytisolo, Juan
    1931- . . . . **CLC 5, 10, 23; HLC**
  See also CA 85-88; CANR 32; HW; MTCW

Gozzano, Guido 1883-1916 . . . . **PC 10**
  See also DLB 114

Gozzi, (Conte) Carlo 1720-1806 . . **NCLC 23**

Grabbe, Christian Dietrich
    1801-1836 . . . . **NCLC 2**
  See also DLB 133

Grace, Patricia 1937- . . . . **CLC 56**

Gracian y Morales, Baltasar
    1601-1658 . . . . **LC 15**

Gracq, Julien . . . . **CLC 11, 48**
  See also Poirier, Louis
  See also DLB 83

Grade, Chaim 1910-1982 . . . . **CLC 10**
  See also CA 93-96; 107

Graduate of Oxford, A
  See Ruskin, John

Graham, John
  See Phillips, David Graham

Graham, Jorie 1951- . . . . **CLC 48**
  See also CA 111; DLB 120

Graham, R(obert) B(ontine) Cunninghame
  See Cunninghame Graham, R(obert)
    B(ontine)
  See also DLB 98, 135

Graham, Robert
  See Haldeman, Joe (William)

Graham, Tom
  See Lewis, (Harry) Sinclair

Graham, W(illiam) S(ydney)
    1918-1986 . . . . **CLC 29**
  See also CA 73-76; 118; DLB 20

Graham, Winston (Mawdsley)
    1910- . . . . **CLC 23**
  See also CA 49-52; CANR 2, 22, 45;
    DLB 77

Grant, Skeeter
  See Spiegelman, Art

Granville-Barker, Harley
    1877-1946 . . . . **TCLC 2**
  See also Barker, Harley Granville
  See also CA 104

Grass, Guenter (Wilhelm)
    1927- . . . . . **CLC 1, 2, 4, 6, 11, 15, 22, 32,**
                49, 88; DA; WLC
  See also CA 13-16R; CANR 20; DLB 75,
    124; MTCW

Gratton, Thomas
  See Hulme, T(homas) E(rnest)

Grau, Shirley Ann
    1929- . . . . **CLC 4, 9; SSC 15**
  See also CA 89-92; CANR 22; DLB 2;
    MTCW

Gravel, Fern
  See Hall, James Norman

Graver, Elizabeth 1964- . . . . **CLC 70**
  See also CA 135

Graves, Richard Perceval 1945- . . . . **CLC 44**
  See also CA 65-68; CANR 9, 26

Graves, Robert (von Ranke)
    1895-1985 . . . . . . **CLC 1, 2, 6, 11, 39, 44,**
                   45; PC 6
  See also CA 5-8R; 117; CANR 5, 36;
    CDBLB 1914-1945; DLB 20, 100;
    DLBY 85; MTCW; SATA 45

Gray, Alasdair (James) 1934- . . . . . . **CLC 41**
  See also CA 126; CANR 47; MTCW

Gray, Amlin 1946- . . . . **CLC 29**
  See also CA 138

Gray, Francine du Plessix 1930- . . . **CLC 22**
  See also BEST 90:3; CA 61-64; CAAS 2;
    CANR 11, 33; MTCW

Gray, John (Henry) 1866-1934 . . . . **TCLC 19**
  See also CA 119

Gray, Simon (James Holliday)
    1936- . . . . **CLC 9, 14, 36**
  See also AITN 1; CA 21-24R; CAAS 3;
    CANR 32; DLB 13; MTCW

Gray, Spalding 1941- . . . . **CLC 49**
  See also CA 128

Gray, Thomas
    1716-1771 . . . . . . **LC 4; DA; PC 2; WLC**
  See also CDBLB 1660-1789; DLB 109

Grayson, David
  See Baker, Ray Stannard

Grayson, Richard (A.) 1951- . . . . **CLC 38**
  See also CA 85-88; CANR 14, 31

Greeley, Andrew M(oran) 1928- . . . . **CLC 28**
  See also CA 5-8R; CAAS 7; CANR 7, 43;
    MTCW

Green, Brian
  See Card, Orson Scott

Green, Hannah
  See Greenberg, Joanne (Goldenberg)

Green, Hannah . . . . **CLC 3**
  See also CA 73-76

Green, Henry . . . . **CLC 2, 13**
  See also Yorke, Henry Vincent
  See also DLB 15

Green, Julian (Hartridge) 1900-
  See Green, Julien
  See also CA 21-24R; CANR 33; DLB 4, 72;
    MTCW

Green, Julien . . . . **CLC 3, 11, 77**
  See also Green, Julian (Hartridge)

Green, Paul (Eliot) 1894-1981 . . . . . . **CLC 25**
  See also AITN 1; CA 5-8R; 103; CANR 3;
    DLB 7, 9; DLBY 81

Greenberg, Ivan 1908-1973
  See Rahv, Philip
  See also CA 85-88

Greenberg, Joanne (Goldenberg)
    1932- . . . . **CLC 7, 30**
  See also AAYA 12; CA 5-8R; CANR 14,
    32; SATA 25

Greenberg, Richard 1959(?)- . . . . **CLC 57**
  See also CA 138

Greene, Bette 1934- . . . . **CLC 30**
  See also AAYA 7; CA 53-56; CANR 4;
    CLR 2; JRDA; MAICYA; SAAS 16;
    SATA 8

Greene, Gael . . . . **CLC 8**
  See also CA 13-16R; CANR 10

Greene, Graham
    1904-1991 . . . . **CLC 1, 3, 6, 9, 14, 18, 27,**
              37, 70, 72; DA; WLC
  See also AITN 2; CA 13-16R; 133;
    CANR 35; CDBLB 1945-1960; DLB 13,
    15, 77, 100; DLBY 91; MTCW; SATA 20

Greer, Richard
  See Silverberg, Robert

Gregor, Arthur 1923- . . . . **CLC 9**
  See also CA 25-28R; CAAS 10; CANR 11;
    SATA 36

Gregor, Lee
  See Pohl, Frederik

Gregory, Isabella Augusta (Persse)
    1852-1932 . . . . **TCLC 1**
  See also CA 104; DLB 10

Gregory, J. Dennis
  See Williams, John A(lfred)

Grendon, Stephen
  See Derleth, August (William)

Grenville, Kate 1950- . . . . **CLC 61**
  See also CA 118

Grenville, Pelham
  See Wodehouse, P(elham) G(renville)

Greve, Felix Paul (Berthold Friedrich)
    1879-1948
  See Grove, Frederick Philip
  See also CA 104; 141

Grey, Zane 1872-1939 . . . . **TCLC 6**
  See also CA 104; 132; DLB 9; MTCW

Grieg, (Johan) Nordahl (Brun)
    1902-1943 . . . . **TCLC 10**
  See also CA 107

Grieve, C(hristopher) M(urray)
    1892-1978 . . . . **CLC 11, 19**
  See also MacDiarmid, Hugh
  See also CA 5-8R; 85-88; CANR 33;
    MTCW

Griffin, Gerald 1803-1840 . . . . **NCLC 7**

Griffin, John Howard 1920-1980 . . . . **CLC 68**
  See also AITN 1; CA 1-4R; 101; CANR 2

Griffin, Peter 1942- . . . . **CLC 39**
  See also CA 136

Griffiths, Trevor 1935- . . . . **CLC 13, 52**
  See also CA 97-100; CANR 45; DLB 13

Grigson, Geoffrey (Edward Harvey)
    1905-1985 . . . . **CLC 7, 39**
  See also CA 25-28R; 118; CANR 20, 33;
    DLB 27; MTCW

Grillparzer, Franz 1791-1872 . . . . . . **NCLC 1**
  See also DLB 133

Grimble, Reverend Charles James
  See Eliot, T(homas) S(tearns)

Grimke, Charlotte L(ottie) Forten
1837(?)-1914
See Forten, Charlotte L.
See also BW 1; CA 117; 124

Grimm, Jacob Ludwig Karl
1785-1863 .... NCLC 3
See also DLB 90; MAICYA; SATA 22

Grimm, Wilhelm Karl 1786-1859 .. NCLC 3
See also DLB 90; MAICYA; SATA 22

Grimmelshausen, Johann Jakob Christoffel
von 1621-1676 .... LC 6

Grindel, Eugene 1895-1952
See Eluard, Paul
See also CA 104

Grisham, John 1955- .... CLC 84
See also AAYA 14; CA 138; CANR 47

Grossman, David 1954- .... CLC 67
See also CA 138

Grossman, Vasily (Semenovich)
1905-1964 .... CLC 41
See also CA 124; 130; MTCW

Grove, Frederick Philip .... TCLC 4
See also Greve, Felix Paul (Berthold
Friedrich)
See also DLB 92

Grubb
See Crumb, R(obert)

Grumbach, Doris (Isaac)
1918- .... CLC 13, 22, 64
See also CA 5-8R; CAAS 2; CANR 9, 42

Grundtvig, Nicolai Frederik Severin
1783-1872 .... NCLC 1

Grunge
See Crumb, R(obert)

Grunwald, Lisa 1959- .... CLC 44
See also CA 120

Guare, John 1938- .... CLC 8, 14, 29, 67
See also CA 73-76; CANR 21; DLB 7;
MTCW

Gudjonsson, Halldor Kiljan 1902-
See Laxness, Halldor
See also CA 103

Guenter, Erich
See Eich, Guenter

Guest, Barbara 1920- .... CLC 34
See also CA 25-28R; CANR 11, 44; DLB 5

Guest, Judith (Ann) 1936- .... CLC 8, 30
See also AAYA 7; CA 77-80; CANR 15;
MTCW

Guevara, Che .... CLC 87; HLC
See also Guevara (Serna), Ernesto

Guevara (Serna), Ernesto 1928-1967
See Guevara, Che
See also CA 127; 111; HW

Guild, Nicholas M. 1944- .... CLC 33
See also CA 93-96

Guillemin, Jacques
See Sartre, Jean-Paul

Guillen, Jorge 1893-1984 .... CLC 11
See also CA 89-92; 112; DLB 108; HW

Guillen (y Batista), Nicolas (Cristobal)
1902-1989 ..... CLC 48, 79; BLC; HLC
See also BW 2; CA 116; 125; 129; HW

Guillevic, (Eugene) 1907- .... CLC 33
See also CA 93-96

Guillois
See Desnos, Robert

Guiney, Louise Imogen
1861-1920 .... TCLC 41
See also DLB 54

Guiraldes, Ricardo (Guillermo)
1886-1927 .... TCLC 39
See also CA 131; HW; MTCW

Gumilev, Nikolai Stephanovich
1886-1921 .... TCLC 60

Gunn, Bill .... CLC 5
See also Gunn, William Harrison
See also DLB 38

Gunn, Thom(son William)
1929- .... CLC 3, 6, 18, 32, 81
See also CA 17-20R; CANR 9, 33;
CDBLB 1960 to Present; DLB 27;
MTCW

Gunn, William Harrison 1934(?)-1989
See Gunn, Bill
See also AITN 1; BW 1; CA 13-16R; 128;
CANR 12, 25

Gunnars, Kristjana 1948- .... CLC 69
See also CA 113; DLB 60

Gurganus, Allan 1947- .... CLC 70
See also BEST 90:1; CA 135

Gurney, A(lbert) R(amsdell), Jr.
1930- .... CLC 32, 50, 54
See also CA 77-80; CANR 32

Gurney, Ivor (Bertie) 1890-1937 ... TCLC 33

Gurney, Peter
See Gurney, A(lbert) R(amsdell), Jr.

Guro, Elena 1877-1913 .... TCLC 56

Gustafson, Ralph (Barker) 1909- .... CLC 36
See also CA 21-24R; CANR 8, 45; DLB 88

Gut, Gom
See Simenon, Georges (Jacques Christian)

Guthrie, A(lfred) B(ertram), Jr.
1901-1991 .... CLC 23
See also CA 57-60; 134; CANR 24; DLB 6;
SATA 62; SATA-Obit 67

Guthrie, Isobel
See Grieve, C(hristopher) M(urray)

Guthrie, Woodrow Wilson 1912-1967
See Guthrie, Woody
See also CA 113; 93-96

Guthrie, Woody .... CLC 35
See also Guthrie, Woodrow Wilson

Guy, Rosa (Cuthbert) 1928- .... CLC 26
See also AAYA 4; BW 2; CA 17-20R;
CANR 14, 34; CLR 13; DLB 33; JRDA;
MAICYA; SATA 14, 62

Gwendolyn
See Bennett, (Enoch) Arnold

H. D. .... CLC 3, 8, 14, 31, 34, 73; PC 5
See also Doolittle, Hilda

H. de V.
See Buchan, John

Haavikko, Paavo Juhani
1931- .... CLC 18, 34
See also CA 106

Habbema, Koos
See Heijermans, Herman

Hacker, Marilyn 1942- .... CLC 5, 9, 23, 72
See also CA 77-80; DLB 120

Haggard, H(enry) Rider
1856-1925 .... TCLC 11
See also CA 108; DLB 70; SATA 16

Hagiwara Sakutaro 1886-1942 .... TCLC 60

Haig, Fenil
See Ford, Ford Madox

Haig-Brown, Roderick (Langmere)
1908-1976 .... CLC 21
See also CA 5-8R; 69-72; CANR 4, 38;
CLR 31; DLB 88; MAICYA; SATA 12

Hailey, Arthur 1920- .... CLC 5
See also AITN 2; BEST 90:3; CA 1-4R;
CANR 2, 36; DLB 88; DLBY 82; MTCW

Hailey, Elizabeth Forsythe 1938- ... CLC 40
See also CA 93-96; CAAS 1; CANR 15, 48

Haines, John (Meade) 1924- .... CLC 58
See also CA 17-20R; CANR 13, 34; DLB 5

Haldeman, Joe (William) 1943- ..... CLC 61
See also CA 53-56; CANR 6; DLB 8

Haley, Alex(ander Murray Palmer)
1921-1992 .... CLC 8, 12, 76; BLC; DA
See also BW 2; CA 77-80; 136; DLB 38;
MTCW

Haliburton, Thomas Chandler
1796-1865 .... NCLC 15
See also DLB 11, 99

Hall, Donald (Andrew, Jr.)
1928- ....CLC 1, 13, 37, 59
See also CA 5-8R; CAAS 7; CANR 2, 44;
DLB 5; SATA 23

Hall, Frederic Sauser
See Sauser-Hall, Frederic

Hall, James
See Kuttner, Henry

Hall, James Norman 1887-1951 ... TCLC 23
See also CA 123; SATA 21

Hall, (Marguerite) Radclyffe
1886(?)-1943 .... TCLC 12
See also CA 110

Hall, Rodney 1935- .... CLC 51
See also CA 109

Halleck, Fitz-Greene 1790-1867 .. NCLC 47
See also DLB 3

Halliday, Michael
See Creasey, John

Halpern, Daniel 1945- .... CLC 14
See also CA 33-36R

Hamburger, Michael (Peter Leopold)
1924- .... CLC 5, 14
See also CA 5-8R; CAAS 4; CANR 2, 47;
DLB 27

Hamill, Pete 1935- .... CLC 10
See also CA 25-28R; CANR 18

Hamilton, Alexander
1755(?)-1804 .... NCLC 49
See also DLB 37

Hamilton, Clive
See Lewis, C(live) S(taples)

Hamilton, Edmond 1904-1977 .... CLC 1
See also CA 1-4R; CANR 3; DLB 8

Hamilton, Eugene (Jacob) Lee
See Lee-Hamilton, Eugene (Jacob)

Hamilton, Franklin
See Silverberg, Robert

Hamilton, Gail
See Corcoran, Barbara

Hamilton, Mollie
See Kaye, M(ary) M(argaret)

Hamilton, (Anthony Walter) Patrick
1904-1962 . . . . CLC 51
See also CA 113; DLB 10

Hamilton, Virginia 1936- . . . . CLC 26
See also AAYA 2; BW 2; CA 25-28R;
CANR 20, 37; CLR 1, 11; DLB 33, 52;
JRDA; MAICYA; MTCW; SATA 4, 56,
79

Hammett, (Samuel) Dashiell
1894-1961 . . . . CLC 3, 5, 10, 19, 47;
SSC 17
See also AITN 1; CA 81-84; CANR 42;
CDALB 1929-1941; DLBD 6; MTCW

Hammon, Jupiter
1711(?)-1800(?) . . . . NCLC 5; BLC
See also DLB 31, 50

Hammond, Keith
See Kuttner, Henry

Hamner, Earl (Henry), Jr. 1923- . . . CLC 12
See also AITN 2; CA 73-76; DLB 6

Hampton, Christopher (James)
1946- . . . . CLC 4
See also CA 25-28R; DLB 13; MTCW

Hamsun, Knut . . . . TCLC 2, 14, 49
See also Pedersen, Knut

Handke, Peter 1942- . . CLC 5, 8, 10, 15, 38
See also CA 77-80; CANR 33; DLB 85,
124; MTCW

Hanley, James 1901-1985 . . . CLC 3, 5, 8, 13
See also CA 73-76; 117; CANR 36; MTCW

Hannah, Barry 1942- . . . . CLC 23, 38
See also CA 108; 110; CANR 43; DLB 6;
MTCW

Hannon, Ezra
See Hunter, Evan

Hansberry, Lorraine (Vivian)
1930-1965 . . . . . . CLC 17, 62; BLC; DA;
DC 2
See also BW 1; CA 109; 25-28R; CABS 3;
CDALB 1941-1968; DLB 7, 38; MTCW

Hansen, Joseph 1923- . . . . CLC 38
See also CA 29-32R; CAAS 17; CANR 16,
44

Hansen, Martin A. 1909-1955 . . . . . TCLC 32

Hanson, Kenneth O(stlin) 1922- . . . . CLC 13
See also CA 53-56; CANR 7

Hardwick, Elizabeth 1916- . . . . CLC 13
See also CA 5-8R; CANR 3, 32; DLB 6;
MTCW

Hardy, Thomas
1840-1928 . . . . . . TCLC 4, 10, 18, 32, 48,
53; DA; PC 8; SSC 2; WLC
See also CA 104; 123; CDBLB 1890-1914;
DLB 18, 19, 135; MTCW

Hare, David 1947- . . . . CLC 29, 58
See also CA 97-100; CANR 39; DLB 13;
MTCW

Harford, Henry
See Hudson, W(illiam) H(enry)

Hargrave, Leonie
See Disch, Thomas M(ichael)

Harjo, Joy 1951- . . . . CLC 83
See also CA 114; CANR 35; DLB 120;
NNAL

Harlan, Louis R(udolph) 1922- . . . . . CLC 34
See also CA 21-24R; CANR 25

Harling, Robert 1951(?)- . . . . CLC 53
See also CA 147

Harmon, William (Ruth) 1938- . . . . . CLC 38
See also CA 33-36R; CANR 14, 32, 35;
SATA 65

Harper, F. E. W.
See Harper, Frances Ellen Watkins

Harper, Frances E. W.
See Harper, Frances Ellen Watkins

Harper, Frances E. Watkins
See Harper, Frances Ellen Watkins

Harper, Frances Ellen
See Harper, Frances Ellen Watkins

Harper, Frances Ellen Watkins
1825-1911 . . . . TCLC 14; BLC
See also BW 1; CA 111; 125; DLB 50

Harper, Michael S(teven) 1938- . . CLC 7, 22
See also BW 1; CA 33-36R; CANR 24;
DLB 41

Harper, Mrs. F. E. W.
See Harper, Frances Ellen Watkins

Harris, Christie (Lucy) Irwin
1907- . . . . CLC 12
See also CA 5-8R; CANR 6; DLB 88;
JRDA; MAICYA; SAAS 10; SATA 6, 74

Harris, Frank 1856(?)-1931 . . . . . . TCLC 24
See also CA 109

Harris, George Washington
1814-1869 . . . . NCLC 23
See also DLB 3, 11

Harris, Joel Chandler
1848-1908 . . . . TCLC 2; SSC 19
See also CA 104; 137; DLB 11, 23, 42, 78,
91; MAICYA; YABC 1

Harris, John (Wyndham Parkes Lucas)
Beynon 1903-1969
See Wyndham, John
See also CA 102; 89-92

Harris, MacDonald . . . . CLC 9
See also Heiney, Donald (William)

Harris, Mark 1922- . . . . CLC 19
See also CA 5-8R; CAAS 3; CANR 2;
DLB 2; DLBY 80

Harris, (Theodore) Wilson 1921- . . . . CLC 25
See also BW 2; CA 65-68; CAAS 16;
CANR 11, 27; DLB 117; MTCW

Harrison, Elizabeth Cavanna 1909-
See Cavanna, Betty
See also CA 9-12R; CANR 6, 27

Harrison, Harry (Max) 1925- . . . . . . CLC 42
See also CA 1-4R; CANR 5, 21; DLB 8;
SATA 4

Harrison, James (Thomas)
1937- . . . . CLC 6, 14, 33, 66; SSC 19
See also CA 13-16R; CANR 8; DLBY 82

Harrison, Jim
See Harrison, James (Thomas)

Harrison, Kathryn 1961- . . . . CLC 70
See also CA 144

Harrison, Tony 1937- . . . . CLC 43
See also CA 65-68; CANR 44; DLB 40;
MTCW

Harriss, Will(ard Irvin) 1922- . . . . . . CLC 34
See also CA 111

Harson, Sley
See Ellison, Harlan (Jay)

Hart, Ellis
See Ellison, Harlan (Jay)

Hart, Josephine 1942(?)- . . . . CLC 70
See also CA 138

Hart, Moss 1904-1961 . . . . CLC 66
See also CA 109; 89-92; DLB 7

Harte, (Francis) Bret(t)
1836(?)-1902 . . . . TCLC 1, 25; DA;
SSC 8; WLC
See also CA 104; 140; CDALB 1865-1917;
DLB 12, 64, 74, 79; SATA 26

Hartley, L(eslie) P(oles)
1895-1972 . . . . CLC 2, 22
See also CA 45-48; 37-40R; CANR 33;
DLB 15, 139; MTCW

Hartman, Geoffrey H. 1929- . . . . CLC 27
See also CA 117; 125; DLB 67

Hartmann von Aue
c. 1160-c. 1205 . . . . CMLC 15
See also DLB 138

Haruf, Kent 19(?)- . . . . CLC 34

Harwood, Ronald 1934- . . . . CLC 32
See also CA 1-4R; CANR 4; DLB 13

Hasek, Jaroslav (Matej Frantisek)
1883-1923 . . . . TCLC 4
See also CA 104; 129; MTCW

Hass, Robert 1941- . . . . CLC 18, 39
See also CA 111; CANR 30; DLB 105

Hastings, Hudson
See Kuttner, Henry

Hastings, Selina . . . . CLC 44

Hatteras, Amelia
See Mencken, H(enry) L(ouis)

Hatteras, Owen . . . . TCLC 18
See also Mencken, H(enry) L(ouis); Nathan,
George Jean

Hauptmann, Gerhart (Johann Robert)
1862-1946 . . . . TCLC 4
See also CA 104; DLB 66, 118

Havel, Vaclav 1936- . . . . CLC 25, 58, 65
See also CA 104; CANR 36; MTCW

Haviaras, Stratis . . . . CLC 33
See also Chaviaras, Strates

Hawes, Stephen 1475(?)-1523(?) . . . . . LC 17

Hawkes, John (Clendennin Burne, Jr.)
1925- . . . . . . CLC 1, 2, 3, 4, 7, 9, 14, 15,
27, 49
See also CA 1-4R; CANR 2, 47; DLB 2, 7;
DLBY 80; MTCW

Hawking, S. W.
See Hawking, Stephen W(illiam)

Hersey, John (Richard)
  1914-1993 . . . . . . **CLC 1, 2, 7, 9, 40, 81**
  See also CA 17-20R; 140; CANR 33;
  DLB 6; MTCW; SATA 25;
  SATA-Obit 76

Herzen, Aleksandr Ivanovich
  1812-1870 . . . . **NCLC 10**

Herzl, Theodor 1860-1904 . . . . **TCLC 36**

Herzog, Werner 1942- . . . . **CLC 16**
  See also CA 89-92

Hesiod c. 8th cent. B.C.- . . . . **CMLC 5**

Hesse, Hermann
  1877-1962 . . . . **CLC 1, 2, 3, 6, 11, 17, 25,**
                        69; DA; SSC 9; WLC
  See also CA 17-18; CAP 2; DLB 66;
  MTCW; SATA 50

Hewes, Cady
  See De Voto, Bernard (Augustine)

Heyen, William 1940- . . . . **CLC 13, 18**
  See also CA 33-36R; CAAS 9; DLB 5

Heyerdahl, Thor 1914- . . . . **CLC 26**
  See also CA 5-8R; CANR 5, 22; MTCW;
  SATA 2, 52

Heym, Georg (Theodor Franz Arthur)
  1887-1912 . . . . **TCLC 9**
  See also CA 106

Heym, Stefan 1913- . . . . **CLC 41**
  See also CA 9-12R; CANR 4; DLB 69

Heyse, Paul (Johann Ludwig von)
  1830-1914 . . . . **TCLC 8**
  See also CA 104; DLB 129

Heyward, (Edwin) DuBose
  1885-1940 . . . . **TCLC 59**
  See also CA 108; DLB 7, 9, 45; SATA 21

Hibbert, Eleanor Alice Burford
  1906-1993 . . . . **CLC 7**
  See also BEST 90:4; CA 17-20R; 140;
  CANR 9, 28; SATA 2; SATA-Obit 74

Higgins, George V(incent)
  1939- . . . . **CLC 4, 7, 10, 18**
  See also CA 77-80; CAAS 5; CANR 17;
  DLB 2; DLBY 81; MTCW

Higginson, Thomas Wentworth
  1823-1911 . . . . **TCLC 36**
  See also DLB 1, 64

Highet, Helen
  See MacInnes, Helen (Clark)

Highsmith, (Mary) Patricia
  1921-1995 . . . . **CLC 2, 4, 14, 42**
  See also CA 1-4R; 147; CANR 1, 20, 48;
  MTCW

Highwater, Jamake (Mamake)
  1942(?)- . . . . **CLC 12**
  See also AAYA 7; CA 65-68; CAAS 7;
  CANR 10, 34; CLR 17; DLB 52;
  DLBY 85; JRDA; MAICYA; SATA 32,
  69; SATA-Brief 30

Higuchi, Ichiyo 1872-1896 . . . . **NCLC 49**

Hijuelos, Oscar 1951- . . . . . . **CLC 65; HLC**
  See also BEST 90:1; CA 123; DLB 145; HW

Hikmet, Nazim 1902(?)-1963 . . . . **CLC 40**
  See also CA 141; 93-96

Hildesheimer, Wolfgang
  1916-1991 . . . . **CLC 49**
  See also CA 101; 135; DLB 69, 124

Hill, Geoffrey (William)
  1932- . . . . **CLC 5, 8, 18, 45**
  See also CA 81-84; CANR 21;
  CDBLB 1960 to Present; DLB 40;
  MTCW

Hill, George Roy 1921- . . . . **CLC 26**
  See also CA 110; 122

Hill, John
  See Koontz, Dean R(ay)

Hill, Susan (Elizabeth) 1942- . . . . **CLC 4**
  See also CA 33-36R; CANR 29; DLB 14,
  139; MTCW

Hillerman, Tony 1925- . . . . **CLC 62**
  See also AAYA 6; BEST 89:1; CA 29-32R;
  CANR 21, 42; SATA 6

Hillesum, Etty 1914-1943 . . . . **TCLC 49**
  See also CA 137

Hilliard, Noel (Harvey) 1929- . . . . . . **CLC 15**
  See also CA 9-12R; CANR 7

Hillis, Rick 1956- . . . . **CLC 66**
  See also CA 134

Hilton, James 1900-1954 . . . . **TCLC 21**
  See also CA 108; DLB 34, 77; SATA 34

Himes, Chester (Bomar)
  1909-1984 . . . . **CLC 2, 4, 7, 18, 58; BLC**
  See also BW 2; CA 25-28R; 114; CANR 22;
  DLB 2, 76, 143; MTCW

Hinde, Thomas . . . . **CLC 6, 11**
  See also Chitty, Thomas Willes

Hindin, Nathan
  See Bloch, Robert (Albert)

Hine, (William) Daryl 1936- . . . . **CLC 15**
  See also CA 1-4R; CAAS 15; CANR 1, 20;
  DLB 60

Hinkson, Katharine Tynan
  See Tynan, Katharine

Hinton, S(usan) E(loise)
  1950- . . . . **CLC 30; DA**
  See also AAYA 2; CA 81-84; CANR 32;
  CLR 3, 23; JRDA; MAICYA; MTCW;
  SATA 19, 58

Hippius, Zinaida . . . . **TCLC 9**
  See also Gippius, Zinaida (Nikolayevna)

Hiraoka, Kimitake 1925-1970
  See Mishima, Yukio
  See also CA 97-100; 29-32R; MTCW

Hirsch, E(ric) D(onald), Jr. 1928- . . . **CLC 79**
  See also CA 25-28R; CANR 27; DLB 67;
  MTCW

Hirsch, Edward 1950- . . . . **CLC 31, 50**
  See also CA 104; CANR 20, 42; DLB 120

Hitchcock, Alfred (Joseph)
  1899-1980 . . . . **CLC 16**
  See also CA 97-100; SATA 27;
  SATA-Obit 24

Hitler, Adolf 1889-1945 . . . . **TCLC 53**
  See also CA 117; 147

Hoagland, Edward 1932- . . . . **CLC 28**
  See also CA 1-4R; CANR 2, 31; DLB 6;
  SATA 51

Hoban, Russell (Conwell) 1925- . . **CLC 7, 25**
  See also CA 5-8R; CANR 23, 37; CLR 3;
  DLB 52; MAICYA; MTCW; SATA 1,
  40, 78

Hobbs, Perry
  See Blackmur, R(ichard) P(almer)

Hobson, Laura Z(ametkin)
  1900-1986 . . . . **CLC 7, 25**
  See also CA 17-20R; 118; DLB 28;
  SATA 52

Hochhuth, Rolf 1931- . . . . **CLC 4, 11, 18**
  See also CA 5-8R; CANR 33; DLB 124;
  MTCW

Hochman, Sandra 1936- . . . . **CLC 3, 8**
  See also CA 5-8R; DLB 5

Hochwaelder, Fritz 1911-1986 . . . . . . **CLC 36**
  See also CA 29-32R; 120; CANR 42;
  MTCW

Hochwalder, Fritz
  See Hochwaelder, Fritz

Hocking, Mary (Eunice) 1921- . . . . . **CLC 13**
  See also CA 101; CANR 18, 40

Hodgins, Jack 1938- . . . . **CLC 23**
  See also CA 93-96; DLB 60

Hodgson, William Hope
  1877(?)-1918 . . . . **TCLC 13**
  See also CA 111; DLB 70, 153

Hoffman, Alice 1952- . . . . **CLC 51**
  See also CA 77-80; CANR 34; MTCW

Hoffman, Daniel (Gerard)
  1923- . . . . **CLC 6, 13, 23**
  See also CA 1-4R; CANR 4; DLB 5

Hoffman, Stanley 1944- . . . . **CLC 5**
  See also CA 77-80

Hoffman, William M(oses) 1939- . . . **CLC 40**
  See also CA 57-60; CANR 11

Hoffmann, E(rnst) T(heodor) A(madeus)
  1776-1822 . . . . **NCLC 2; SSC 13**
  See also DLB 90; SATA 27

Hofmann, Gert 1931- . . . . **CLC 54**
  See also CA 128

Hofmannsthal, Hugo von
  1874-1929 . . . . **TCLC 11; DC 4**
  See also CA 106; DLB 81, 118

Hogan, Linda 1947- . . . . **CLC 73**
  See also CA 120; CANR 45; NNAL

Hogarth, Charles
  See Creasey, John

Hogg, James 1770-1835 . . . . **NCLC 4**
  See also DLB 93, 116

Holbach, Paul Henri Thiry Baron
  1723-1789 . . . . **LC 14**

Holberg, Ludvig 1684-1754 . . . . **LC 6**

Holden, Ursula 1921- . . . . **CLC 18**
  See also CA 101; CAAS 8; CANR 22

Holderlin, (Johann Christian) Friedrich
  1770-1843 . . . . **NCLC 16; PC 4**

Holdstock, Robert
  See Holdstock, Robert P.

Holdstock, Robert P. 1948- . . . . **CLC 39**
  See also CA 131

Holland, Isabelle 1920- . . . . **CLC 21**
  See also AAYA 11; CA 21-24R; CANR 10,
  25, 47; JRDA; MAICYA; SATA 8, 70

Holland, Marcus
  See Caldwell, (Janet Miriam) Taylor
  (Holland)

Hollander, John 1929- . . . . . . **CLC 2, 5, 8, 14**
See also CA 1-4R; CANR 1; DLB 5;
SATA 13

Hollander, Paul
See Silverberg, Robert

Holleran, Andrew 1943(?)- . . . . **CLC 38**
See also CA 144

Hollinghurst, Alan 1954- . . . . **CLC 55**
See also CA 114

Hollis, Jim
See Summers, Hollis (Spurgeon, Jr.)

Holmes, John
See Souster, (Holmes) Raymond

Holmes, John Clellon 1926-1988 . . . . **CLC 56**
See also CA 9-12R; 125; CANR 4; DLB 16

Holmes, Oliver Wendell
1809-1894 . . . . **NCLC 14**
See also CDALB 1640-1865; DLB 1;
SATA 34

Holmes, Raymond
See Souster, (Holmes) Raymond

Holt, Victoria
See Hibbert, Eleanor Alice Burford

Holub, Miroslav 1923- . . . . **CLC 4**
See also CA 21-24R; CANR 10

Homer
c. 8th cent. B.C.- . . . . . . **CMLC 1, 16; DA**

Honig, Edwin 1919- . . . . **CLC 33**
See also CA 5-8R; CAAS 8; CANR 4, 45;
DLB 5

Hood, Hugh (John Blagdon)
1928- . . . . **CLC 15, 28**
See also CA 49-52; CAAS 17; CANR 1, 33;
DLB 53

Hood, Thomas 1799-1845 . . . . **NCLC 16**
See also DLB 96

Hooker, (Peter) Jeremy 1941- . . . . . . **CLC 43**
See also CA 77-80; CANR 22; DLB 40

Hope, A(lec) D(erwent) 1907- . . . . **CLC 3, 51**
See also CA 21-24R; CANR 33; MTCW

Hope, Brian
See Creasey, John

Hope, Christopher (David Tully)
1944- . . . . **CLC 52**
See also CA 106; CANR 47; SATA 62

Hopkins, Gerard Manley
1844-1889 . . . . **NCLC 17; DA; WLC**
See also CDBLB 1890-1914; DLB 35, 57

Hopkins, John (Richard) 1931- . . . . . . **CLC 4**
See also CA 85-88

Hopkins, Pauline Elizabeth
1859-1930 . . . . **TCLC 28; BLC**
See also BW 2; CA 141; DLB 50

Hopkinson, Francis 1737-1791 . . . . . . **LC 25**
See also DLB 31

Hopley-Woolrich, Cornell George 1903-1968
See Woolrich, Cornell
See also CA 13-14; CAP 1

Horatio
See Proust, (Valentin-Louis-George-Eugene-)
Marcel

Horgan, Paul (George Vincent O'Shaughnessy)
1903-1995 . . . . **CLC 9, 53**
See also CA 13-16R; 147; CANR 9, 35;
DLB 102; DLBY 85; MTCW; SATA 13

Horn, Peter
See Kuttner, Henry

Hornem, Horace Esq.
See Byron, George Gordon (Noel)

Hornung, E(rnest) W(illiam)
1866-1921 . . . . **TCLC 59**
See also CA 108; DLB 70

Horovitz, Israel (Arthur) 1939- . . . . . **CLC 56**
See also CA 33-36R; CANR 46; DLB 7

Horvath, Odon von
See Horvath, Oedoen von
See also DLB 85, 124

Horvath, Oedoen von 1901-1938 . . . **TCLC 45**
See also Horvath, Odon von
See also CA 118

Horwitz, Julius 1920-1986 . . . . **CLC 14**
See also CA 9-12R; 119; CANR 12

Hospital, Janette Turner 1942- . . . . . **CLC 42**
See also CA 108; CANR 48

Hostos, E. M. de
See Hostos (y Bonilla), Eugenio Maria de

Hostos, Eugenio M. de
See Hostos (y Bonilla), Eugenio Maria de

Hostos, Eugenio Maria
See Hostos (y Bonilla), Eugenio Maria de

Hostos (y Bonilla), Eugenio Maria de
1839-1903 . . . . **TCLC 24**
See also CA 123; 131; HW

Houdini
See Lovecraft, H(oward) P(hillips)

Hougan, Carolyn 1943- . . . . **CLC 34**
See also CA 139

Household, Geoffrey (Edward West)
1900-1988 . . . . **CLC 11**
See also CA 77-80; 126; DLB 87; SATA 14;
SATA-Obit 59

Housman, A(lfred) E(dward)
1859-1936 . . . . . . **TCLC 1, 10; DA; PC 2**
See also CA 104; 125; DLB 19; MTCW

Housman, Laurence 1865-1959 . . . . . **TCLC 7**
See also CA 106; DLB 10; SATA 25

Howard, Elizabeth Jane 1923- . . . **CLC 7, 29**
See also CA 5-8R; CANR 8

Howard, Maureen 1930- . . . . . **CLC 5, 14, 46**
See also CA 53-56; CANR 31; DLBY 83;
MTCW

Howard, Richard 1929- . . . . . . **CLC 7, 10, 47**
See also AITN 1; CA 85-88; CANR 25;
DLB 5

Howard, Robert Ervin 1906-1936 . . . **TCLC 8**
See also CA 105

Howard, Warren F.
See Pohl, Frederik

Howe, Fanny 1940- . . . . **CLC 47**
See also CA 117; SATA-Brief 52

Howe, Irving 1920-1993 . . . . **CLC 85**
See also CA 9-12R; 141; CANR 21;
DLB 67; MTCW

Howe, Julia Ward 1819-1910 . . . . . **TCLC 21**
See also CA 117; DLB 1

Howe, Susan 1937- . . . . **CLC 72**
See also DLB 120

Howe, Tina 1937- . . . . **CLC 48**
See also CA 109

Howell, James 1594(?)-1666 . . . . **LC 13**
See also DLB 151

Howells, W. D.
See Howells, William Dean

Howells, William D.
See Howells, William Dean

Howells, William Dean
1837-1920 . . . . **TCLC 7, 17, 41**
See also CA 104; 134; CDALB 1865-1917;
DLB 12, 64, 74, 79

Howes, Barbara 1914- . . . . **CLC 15**
See also CA 9-12R; CAAS 3; SATA 5

Hrabal, Bohumil 1914- . . . . **CLC 13, 67**
See also CA 106; CAAS 12

Hsun, Lu
See Lu Hsun

Hubbard, L(afayette) Ron(ald)
1911-1986 . . . . **CLC 43**
See also CA 77-80; 118; CANR 22

Huch, Ricarda (Octavia)
1864-1947 . . . . **TCLC 13**
See also CA 111; DLB 66

Huddle, David 1942- . . . . **CLC 49**
See also CA 57-60; CAAS 20; DLB 130

Hudson, Jeffrey
See Crichton, (John) Michael

Hudson, W(illiam) H(enry)
1841-1922 . . . . **TCLC 29**
See also CA 115; DLB 98, 153; SATA 35

Hueffer, Ford Madox
See Ford, Ford Madox

Hughart, Barry 1934- . . . . **CLC 39**
See also CA 137

Hughes, Colin
See Creasey, John

Hughes, David (John) 1930- . . . . **CLC 48**
See also CA 116; 129; DLB 14

Hughes, (James) Langston
1902-1967 . . . . . **CLC 1, 5, 10, 15, 35, 44;**
BLC; DA; DC 3; PC 1; SSC 6; WLC
See also AAYA 12; BW 1; CA 1-4R;
25-28R; CANR 1, 34; CDALB 1929-1941;
CLR 17; DLB 4, 7, 48, 51, 86; JRDA;
MAICYA; MTCW; SATA 4, 33

Hughes, Richard (Arthur Warren)
1900-1976 . . . . **CLC 1, 11**
See also CA 5-8R; 65-68; CANR 4;
DLB 15; MTCW; SATA 8;
SATA-Obit 25

Hughes, Ted
1930- . . . . **CLC 2, 4, 9, 14, 37; PC 7**
See also CA 1-4R; CANR 1, 33; CLR 3;
DLB 40; MAICYA; MTCW; SATA 49;
SATA-Brief 27

Hugo, Richard F(ranklin)
1923-1982 . . . . **CLC 6, 18, 32**
See also CA 49-52; 108; CANR 3; DLB 5

Hugo, Victor (Marie)
1802-1885 . . **NCLC 3, 10, 21; DA; WLC**
See also DLB 119; SATA 47

Huidobro, Vicente
See Huidobro Fernandez, Vicente Garcia

Huidobro Fernandez, Vicente Garcia
1893-1948 . . . . **TCLC 31**
See also CA 131; HW

Hulme, Keri 1947- . . . . **CLC 39**
See also CA 125

Hulme, T(homas) E(rnest)
1883-1917 . . . . **TCLC 21**
See also CA 117; DLB 19

Hume, David 1711-1776 . . . . **LC 7**
See also DLB 104

Humphrey, William 1924- . . . . **CLC 45**
See also CA 77-80; DLB 6

Humphreys, Emyr Owen 1919- . . . . . **CLC 47**
See also CA 5-8R; CANR 3, 24; DLB 15

Humphreys, Josephine 1945- . . . . **CLC 34, 57**
See also CA 121; 127

Hungerford, Pixie
See Brinsmead, H(esba) F(ay)

Hunt, E(verette) Howard, (Jr.)
1918- . . . . **CLC 3**
See also AITN 1; CA 45-48; CANR 2, 47

Hunt, Kyle
See Creasey, John

Hunt, (James Henry) Leigh
1784-1859 . . . . **NCLC 1**

Hunt, Marsha 1946- . . . . **CLC 70**
See also BW 2; CA 143

Hunt, Violet 1866-1942 . . . . **TCLC 53**

Hunter, E. Waldo
See Sturgeon, Theodore (Hamilton)

Hunter, Evan 1926- . . . . **CLC 11, 31**
See also CA 5-8R; CANR 5, 38; DLBY 82;
MTCW; SATA 25

Hunter, Kristin (Eggleston) 1931- . . . **CLC 35**
See also AITN 1; BW 1; CA 13-16R;
CANR 13; CLR 3; DLB 33; MAICYA;
SAAS 10; SATA 12

Hunter, Mollie 1922- . . . . **CLC 21**
See also McIlwraith, Maureen Mollie
Hunter
See also AAYA 13; CANR 37; CLR 25;
JRDA; MAICYA; SAAS 7; SATA 54

Hunter, Robert (?)-1734 . . . . **LC 7**

Hurston, Zora Neale
1903-1960 . . . . **CLC 7, 30, 61; BLC; DA;**
SSC 4
See also BW 1; CA 85-88; DLB 51, 86;
MTCW

Huston, John (Marcellus)
1906-1987 . . . . **CLC 20**
See also CA 73-76; 123; CANR 34; DLB 26

Hustvedt, Siri 1955- . . . . **CLC 76**
See also CA 137

Hutten, Ulrich von 1488-1523 . . . . **LC 16**

Huxley, Aldous (Leonard)
1894-1963 . . . . . **CLC 1, 3, 4, 5, 8, 11, 18,**
35, 79; DA; WLC
See also AAYA 11; CA 85-88; CANR 44;
CDBLB 1914-1945; DLB 36, 100;
MTCW; SATA 63

Huysmans, Charles Marie Georges
1848-1907
See Huysmans, Joris-Karl
See also CA 104

Huysmans, Joris-Karl . . . . **TCLC 7**
See also Huysmans, Charles Marie Georges
See also DLB 123

Hwang, David Henry
1957- . . . . **CLC 55; DC 4**
See also CA 127; 132

Hyde, Anthony 1946- . . . . **CLC 42**
See also CA 136

Hyde, Margaret O(ldroyd) 1917- . . . **CLC 21**
See also CA 1-4R; CANR 1, 36; CLR 23;
JRDA; MAICYA; SAAS 8; SATA 1, 42,
76

Hynes, James 1956(?)- . . . . **CLC 65**

Ian, Janis 1951- . . . . **CLC 21**
See also CA 105

Ibanez, Vicente Blasco
See Blasco Ibanez, Vicente

Ibarguengoitia, Jorge 1928-1983 . . . . **CLC 37**
See also CA 124; 113; HW

Ibsen, Henrik (Johan)
1828-1906 . . . . . . **TCLC 2, 8, 16, 37, 52;**
DA; DC 2; WLC
See also CA 104; 141

Ibuse Masuji 1898-1993 . . . . **CLC 22**
See also CA 127; 141

Ichikawa, Kon 1915- . . . . **CLC 20**
See also CA 121

Idle, Eric 1943- . . . . **CLC 21**
See also Monty Python
See also CA 116; CANR 35

Ignatow, David 1914- . . . . . . **CLC 4, 7, 14, 40**
See also CA 9-12R; CAAS 3; CANR 31;
DLB 5

Ihimaera, Witi 1944- . . . . **CLC 46**
See also CA 77-80

Ilf, Ilya . . . . **TCLC 21**
See also Fainzilberg, Ilya Arnoldovich

Immermann, Karl (Lebrecht)
1796-1840 . . . . **NCLC 4, 49**
See also DLB 133

Inclan, Ramon (Maria) del Valle
See Valle-Inclan, Ramon (Maria) del

Infante, G(uillermo) Cabrera
See Cabrera Infante, G(uillermo)

Ingalls, Rachel (Holmes) 1940- . . . . . **CLC 42**
See also CA 123; 127

Ingamells, Rex 1913-1955 . . . . **TCLC 35**

Inge, William Motter
1913-1973 . . . . **CLC 1, 8, 19**
See also CA 9-12R; CDALB 1941-1968;
DLB 7; MTCW

Ingelow, Jean 1820-1897 . . . . **NCLC 39**
See also DLB 35; SATA 33

Ingram, Willis J.
See Harris, Mark

Innaurato, Albert (F.) 1948(?)- . . **CLC 21, 60**
See also CA 115; 122

Innes, Michael
See Stewart, J(ohn) I(nnes) M(ackintosh)

Ionesco, Eugene
1909-1994 . . . . **CLC 1, 4, 6, 9, 11, 15, 41,**
86; DA; WLC
See also CA 9-12R; 144; MTCW; SATA 7;
SATA-Obit 79

Iqbal, Muhammad 1873-1938 . . . . . **TCLC 28**

Ireland, Patrick
See O'Doherty, Brian

Iron, Ralph
See Schreiner, Olive (Emilie Albertina)

Irving, John (Winslow)
1942- . . . . **CLC 13, 23, 38**
See also AAYA 8; BEST 89:3; CA 25-28R;
CANR 28; DLB 6; DLBY 82; MTCW

Irving, Washington
1783-1859 . . . . **NCLC 2, 19; DA; SSC 2;**
WLC
See also CDALB 1640-1865; DLB 3, 11, 30,
59, 73, 74; YABC 2

Irwin, P. K.
See Page, P(atricia) K(athleen)

Isaacs, Susan 1943- . . . . **CLC 32**
See also BEST 89:1; CA 89-92; CANR 20,
41; MTCW

Isherwood, Christopher (William Bradshaw)
1904-1986 . . . . **CLC 1, 9, 11, 14, 44**
See also CA 13-16R; 117; CANR 35;
DLB 15; DLBY 86; MTCW

Ishiguro, Kazuo 1954- . . . . . . **CLC 27, 56, 59**
See also BEST 90:2; CA 120; CANR 49;
MTCW

Ishikawa Takuboku
1886(?)-1912 . . . . **TCLC 15; PC 10**
See also CA 113

Iskander, Fazil 1929- . . . . **CLC 47**
See also CA 102

Ivan IV 1530-1584 . . . . **LC 17**

Ivanov, Vyacheslav Ivanovich
1866-1949 . . . . **TCLC 33**
See also CA 122

Ivask, Ivar Vidrik 1927-1992 . . . . . . **CLC 14**
See also CA 37-40R; 139; CANR 24

Jackson, Daniel
See Wingrove, David (John)

Jackson, Jesse 1908-1983 . . . . **CLC 12**
See also BW 1; CA 25-28R; 109; CANR 27;
CLR 28; MAICYA; SATA 2, 29;
SATA-Obit 48

Jackson, Laura (Riding) 1901-1991
See Riding, Laura
See also CA 65-68; 135; CANR 28; DLB 48

Jackson, Sam
See Trumbo, Dalton

Jackson, Sara
See Wingrove, David (John)

Jackson, Shirley
1919-1965 . . . . **CLC 11, 60, 87; DA;**
SSC 9; WLC
See also AAYA 9; CA 1-4R; 25-28R;
CANR 4; CDALB 1941-1968; DLB 6;
SATA 2

Jacob, (Cyprien-)Max 1876-1944 . . . **TCLC 6**
See also CA 104

Jacobs, Jim 1942- . . . . **CLC 12**
See also CA 97-100

Jacobs, W(illiam) W(ymark)
1863-1943 .... **TCLC 22**
See also CA 121; DLB 135

Jacobsen, Jens Peter 1847-1885 .. **NCLC 34**

Jacobsen, Josephine 1908- .... **CLC 48**
See also CA 33-36R; CAAS 18; CANR 23, 48

Jacobson, Dan 1929- .... **CLC 4, 14**
See also CA 1-4R; CANR 2, 25; DLB 14; MTCW

Jacqueline
See Carpentier (y Valmont), Alejo

Jagger, Mick 1944-............... **CLC 17**

Jakes, John (William) 1932- ...... **CLC 29**
See also BEST 89:4; CA 57-60; CANR 10, 43; DLBY 83; MTCW; SATA 62

James, Andrew
See Kirkup, James

James, C(yril) L(ionel) R(obert)
1901-1989 .... **CLC 33**
See also BW 2; CA 117; 125; 128; DLB 125; MTCW

James, Daniel (Lewis) 1911-1988
See Santiago, Danny
See also CA 125

James, Dynely
See Mayne, William (James Carter)

James, Henry
1843-1916 ...... **TCLC 2, 11, 24, 40, 47; DA; SSC 8; WLC**
See also CA 104; 132; CDALB 1865-1917; DLB 12, 71, 74; MTCW

James, M. R.
See James, Montague (Rhodes)

James, Montague (Rhodes)
1862-1936 .... **TCLC 6; SSC 16**
See also CA 104

James, P. D. .... **CLC 18, 46**
See also White, Phyllis Dorothy James
See also BEST 90:2; CDBLB 1960 to Present; DLB 87

James, Philip
See Moorcock, Michael (John)

James, William 1842-1910..... **TCLC 15, 32**
See also CA 109

James I 1394-1437 .... **LC 20**

Jameson, Anna 1794-1860 .... **NCLC 43**
See also DLB 99

Jami, Nur al-Din 'Abd al-Rahman
1414-1492 .... **LC 9**

Jandl, Ernst 1925- .... **CLC 34**

Janowitz, Tama 1957- .... **CLC 43**
See also CA 106

Jarrell, Randall
1914-1965 .... **CLC 1, 2, 6, 9, 13, 49**
See also CA 5-8R; 25-28R; CABS 2; CANR 6, 34; CDALB 1941-1968; CLR 6; DLB 48, 52; MAICYA; MTCW; SATA 7

Jarry, Alfred
1873-1907 .... **TCLC 2, 14; SSC 20**
See also CA 104

Jarvis, E. K.
See Bloch, Robert (Albert); Ellison, Harlan (Jay); Silverberg, Robert

Jeake, Samuel, Jr.
See Aiken, Conrad (Potter)

Jean Paul 1763-1825 .... **NCLC 7**

Jefferies, (John) Richard
1848-1887 .... **NCLC 47**
See also DLB 98, 141; SATA 16

Jeffers, (John) Robinson
1887-1962 .... **CLC 2, 3, 11, 15, 54; DA; WLC**
See also CA 85-88; CANR 35; CDALB 1917-1929; DLB 45; MTCW

Jefferson, Janet
See Mencken, H(enry) L(ouis)

Jefferson, Thomas 1743-1826 .... **NCLC 11**
See also CDALB 1640-1865; DLB 31

Jeffrey, Francis 1773-1850....... **NCLC 33**
See also DLB 107

Jelakowitch, Ivan
See Heijermans, Herman

Jellicoe, (Patricia) Ann 1927- ...... **CLC 27**
See also CA 85-88; DLB 13

Jen, Gish .... **CLC 70**
See also Jen, Lillian

Jen, Lillian 1956(?)-
See Jen, Gish
See also CA 135

Jenkins, (John) Robin 1912- .... **CLC 52**
See also CA 1-4R; CANR 1; DLB 14

Jennings, Elizabeth (Joan)
1926- .... **CLC 5, 14**
See also CA 61-64; CAAS 5; CANR 8, 39; DLB 27; MTCW; SATA 66

Jennings, Waylon 1937-.......... **CLC 21**

Jensen, Johannes V. 1873-1950.... **TCLC 41**

Jensen, Laura (Linnea) 1948- ...... **CLC 37**
See also CA 103

Jerome, Jerome K(lapka)
1859-1927 .... **TCLC 23**
See also CA 119; DLB 10, 34, 135

Jerrold, Douglas William
1803-1857 .... **NCLC 2**

Jewett, (Theodora) Sarah Orne
1849-1909 .... **TCLC 1, 22; SSC 6**
See also CA 108; 127; DLB 12, 74; SATA 15

Jewsbury, Geraldine (Endsor)
1812-1880 .... **NCLC 22**
See also DLB 21

Jhabvala, Ruth Prawer
1927- .... **CLC 4, 8, 29**
See also CA 1-4R; CANR 2, 29; DLB 139; MTCW

Jiles, Paulette 1943-.......... **CLC 13, 58**
See also CA 101

Jimenez (Mantecon), Juan Ramon
1881-1958 .... **TCLC 4; HLC; PC 7**
See also CA 104; 131; DLB 134; HW; MTCW

Jimenez, Ramon
See Jimenez (Mantecon), Juan Ramon

Jimenez Mantecon, Juan
See Jimenez (Mantecon), Juan Ramon

Joel, Billy .... **CLC 26**
See also Joel, William Martin

Joel, William Martin 1949-
See Joel, Billy
See also CA 108

John of the Cross, St. 1542-1591 .... **LC 18**

Johnson, B(ryan) S(tanley William)
1933-1973 .... **CLC 6, 9**
See also CA 9-12R; 53-56; CANR 9; DLB 14, 40

Johnson, Benj. F. of Boo
See Riley, James Whitcomb

Johnson, Benjamin F. of Boo
See Riley, James Whitcomb

Johnson, Charles (Richard)
1948- .... **CLC 7, 51, 65; BLC**
See also BW 2; CA 116; CAAS 18; CANR 42; DLB 33

Johnson, Denis 1949-............. **CLC 52**
See also CA 117; 121; DLB 120

Johnson, Diane 1934-........ **CLC 5, 13, 48**
See also CA 41-44R; CANR 17, 40; DLBY 80; MTCW

Johnson, Eyvind (Olof Verner)
1900-1976 .... **CLC 14**
See also CA 73-76; 69-72; CANR 34

Johnson, J. R.
See James, C(yril) L(ionel) R(obert)

Johnson, James Weldon
1871-1938 .... **TCLC 3, 19; BLC**
See also BW 1; CA 104; 125; CDALB 1917-1929; CLR 32; DLB 51; MTCW; SATA 31

Johnson, Joyce 1935-............ **CLC 58**
See also CA 125; 129

Johnson, Lionel (Pigot)
1867-1902 .... **TCLC 19**
See also CA 117; DLB 19

Johnson, Mel
See Malzberg, Barry N(athaniel)

Johnson, Pamela Hansford
1912-1981 .... **CLC 1, 7, 27**
See also CA 1-4R; 104; CANR 2, 28; DLB 15; MTCW

Johnson, Samuel
1709-1784 .... **LC 15; DA; WLC**
See also CDBLB 1660-1789; DLB 39, 95, 104, 142

Johnson, Uwe
1934-1984 .... **CLC 5, 10, 15, 40**
See also CA 1-4R; 112; CANR 1, 39; DLB 75; MTCW

Johnston, George (Benson) 1913- ... **CLC 51**
See also CA 1-4R; CANR 5, 20; DLB 88

Johnston, Jennifer 1930-.......... **CLC 7**
See also CA 85-88; DLB 14

Jolley, (Monica) Elizabeth
1923- .... **CLC 46; SSC 19**
See also CA 127; CAAS 13

Jones, Arthur Llewellyn 1863-1947
See Machen, Arthur
See also CA 104

Jones, D(ouglas) G(ordon) 1929-.... **CLC 10**
See also CA 29-32R; CANR 13; DLB 53

Jones, David (Michael)
1895-1974 . . . . **CLC 2, 4, 7, 13, 42**
See also CA 9-12R; 53-56; CANR 28;
CDBLB 1945-1960; DLB 20, 100; MTCW

Jones, David Robert 1947-
See Bowie, David
See also CA 103

Jones, Diana Wynne 1934- . . . . **CLC 26**
See also AAYA 12; CA 49-52; CANR 4,
26; CLR 23; JRDA; MAICYA; SAAS 7;
SATA 9, 70

Jones, Edward P. 1950- . . . . **CLC 76**
See also BW 2; CA 142

Jones, Gayl 1949- . . . . **CLC 6, 9; BLC**
See also BW 2; CA 77-80; CANR 27;
DLB 33; MTCW

Jones, James 1921-1977 . . . . **CLC 1, 3, 10, 39**
See also AITN 1, 2; CA 1-4R; 69-72;
CANR 6; DLB 2, 143; MTCW

Jones, John J.
See Lovecraft, H(oward) P(hillips)

Jones, LeRoi . . . . **CLC 1, 2, 3, 5, 10, 14**
See also Baraka, Amiri

Jones, Louis B. . . . . **CLC 65**
See also CA 141

Jones, Madison (Percy, Jr.) 1925- . . . **CLC 4**
See also CA 13-16R; CAAS 11; CANR 7;
DLB 152

Jones, Mervyn 1922- . . . . **CLC 10, 52**
See also CA 45-48; CAAS 5; CANR 1;
MTCW

Jones, Mick 1956(?)- . . . . **CLC 30**

Jones, Nettie (Pearl) 1941- . . . . **CLC 34**
See also BW 2; CA 137; CAAS 20

Jones, Preston 1936-1979 . . . . **CLC 10**
See also CA 73-76; 89-92; DLB 7

Jones, Robert F(rancis) 1934- . . . . **CLC 7**
See also CA 49-52; CANR 2

Jones, Rod 1953- . . . . **CLC 50**
See also CA 128

Jones, Terence Graham Parry
1942- . . . . **CLC 21**
See also Jones, Terry; Monty Python
See also CA 112; 116; CANR 35

Jones, Terry
See Jones, Terence Graham Parry
See also SATA 67; SATA-Brief 51

Jones, Thom 1945(?)- . . . . **CLC 81**

Jong, Erica 1942- . . . . . . **CLC 4, 6, 8, 18, 83**
See also AITN 1; BEST 90:2; CA 73-76;
CANR 26; DLB 2, 5, 28, 152; MTCW

Jonson, Ben(jamin)
1572(?)-1637 . . . . **LC 6; DA; DC 4; WLC**
See also CDBLB Before 1660; DLB 62, 121

Jordan, June 1936- . . . . **CLC 5, 11, 23**
See also AAYA 2; BW 2; CA 33-36R;
CANR 25; CLR 10; DLB 38; MAICYA;
MTCW; SATA 4

Jordan, Pat(rick M.) 1941- . . . . **CLC 37**
See also CA 33-36R

Jorgensen, Ivar
See Ellison, Harlan (Jay)

Jorgenson, Ivar
See Silverberg, Robert

Josephus, Flavius c. 37-100 . . . . . . **CMLC 13**

Josipovici, Gabriel 1940- . . . . **CLC 6, 43**
See also CA 37-40R; CAAS 8; CANR 47;
DLB 14

Joubert, Joseph 1754-1824 . . . . **NCLC 9**

Jouve, Pierre Jean 1887-1976 . . . . . **CLC 47**
See also CA 65-68

Joyce, James (Augustine Aloysius)
1882-1941 . . . . **TCLC 3, 8, 16, 35, 52;
DA; SSC 3; WLC**
See also CA 104; 126; CDBLB 1914-1945;
DLB 10, 19, 36; MTCW

Jozsef, Attila 1905-1937 . . . . **TCLC 22**
See also CA 116

Juana Ines de la Cruz 1651(?)-1695 . . . **LC 5**

Judd, Cyril
See Kornbluth, C(yril) M.; Pohl, Frederik

Julian of Norwich 1342(?)-1416(?) . . . . **LC 6**
See also DLB 146

Juniper, Alex
See Hospital, Janette Turner

Just, Ward (Swift) 1935- . . . . **CLC 4, 27**
See also CA 25-28R; CANR 32

Justice, Donald (Rodney) 1925- . . **CLC 6, 19**
See also CA 5-8R; CANR 26; DLBY 83

Juvenal c. 55-c. 127 . . . . **CMLC 8**

Juvenis
See Bourne, Randolph S(illiman)

Kacew, Romain 1914-1980
See Gary, Romain
See also CA 108; 102

Kadare, Ismail 1936- . . . . **CLC 52**

Kadohata, Cynthia . . . . **CLC 59**
See also CA 140

Kafka, Franz
1883-1924 . . . . **TCLC 2, 6, 13, 29, 47, 53;
DA; SSC 5; WLC**
See also CA 105; 126; DLB 81; MTCW

Kahanovitsch, Pinkhes
See Der Nister

Kahn, Roger 1927- . . . . **CLC 30**
See also CA 25-28R; CANR 44; SATA 37

Kain, Saul
See Sassoon, Siegfried (Lorraine)

Kaiser, Georg 1878-1945 . . . . **TCLC 9**
See also CA 106; DLB 124

Kaletski, Alexander 1946- . . . . **CLC 39**
See also CA 118; 143

Kalidasa fl. c. 400- . . . . **CMLC 9**

Kallman, Chester (Simon)
1921-1975 . . . . **CLC 2**
See also CA 45-48; 53-56; CANR 3

Kaminsky, Melvin 1926-
See Brooks, Mel
See also CA 65-68; CANR 16

Kaminsky, Stuart M(elvin) 1934- . . . **CLC 59**
See also CA 73-76; CANR 29

Kane, Paul
See Simon, Paul

Kane, Wilson
See Bloch, Robert (Albert)

Kanin, Garson 1912- . . . . **CLC 22**
See also AITN 1; CA 5-8R; CANR 7;
DLB 7

Kaniuk, Yoram 1930- . . . . **CLC 19**
See also CA 134

Kant, Immanuel 1724-1804 . . . . . . **NCLC 27**
See also DLB 94

Kantor, MacKinlay 1904-1977 . . . . . . **CLC 7**
See also CA 61-64; 73-76; DLB 9, 102

Kaplan, David Michael 1946- . . . . . . **CLC 50**

Kaplan, James 1951- . . . . **CLC 59**
See also CA 135

Karageorge, Michael
See Anderson, Poul (William)

Karamzin, Nikolai Mikhailovich
1766-1826 . . . . **NCLC 3**
See also DLB 150

Karapanou, Margarita 1946- . . . . **CLC 13**
See also CA 101

Karinthy, Frigyes 1887-1938 . . . . . . **TCLC 47**

Karl, Frederick R(obert) 1927- . . . . . **CLC 34**
See also CA 5-8R; CANR 3, 44

Kastel, Warren
See Silverberg, Robert

Kataev, Evgeny Petrovich 1903-1942
See Petrov, Evgeny
See also CA 120

Kataphusin
See Ruskin, John

Katz, Steve 1935- . . . . **CLC 47**
See also CA 25-28R; CAAS 14; CANR 12;
DLBY 83

Kauffman, Janet 1945- . . . . **CLC 42**
See also CA 117; CANR 43; DLBY 86

Kaufman, Bob (Garnell)
1925-1986 . . . . **CLC 49**
See also BW 1; CA 41-44R; 118; CANR 22;
DLB 16, 41

Kaufman, George S. 1889-1961 . . . . . **CLC 38**
See also CA 108; 93-96; DLB 7

Kaufman, Sue . . . . **CLC 3, 8**
See also Barondess, Sue K(aufman)

Kavafis, Konstantinos Petrou 1863-1933
See Cavafy, C(onstantine) P(eter)
See also CA 104

Kavan, Anna 1901-1968 . . . . . . **CLC 5, 13, 82**
See also CA 5-8R; CANR 6; MTCW

Kavanagh, Dan
See Barnes, Julian

Kavanagh, Patrick (Joseph)
1904-1967 . . . . **CLC 22**
See also CA 123; 25-28R; DLB 15, 20;
MTCW

Kawabata, Yasunari
1899-1972 . . . . . **CLC 2, 5, 9, 18; SSC 17**
See also CA 93-96; 33-36R

Kaye, M(ary) M(argaret) 1909- . . . . . **CLC 28**
See also CA 89-92; CANR 24; MTCW;
SATA 62

Kaye, Mollie
See Kaye, M(ary) M(argaret)

Kaye-Smith, Sheila 1887-1956 . . . . . **TCLC 20**
See also CA 118; DLB 36

Kinsella, Thomas 1928- .... **CLC 4, 19**
See also CA 17-20R; CANR 15; DLB 27;
MTCW

Kinsella, W(illiam) P(atrick)
1935- .... **CLC 27, 43**
See also AAYA 7; CA 97-100; CAAS 7;
CANR 21, 35; MTCW

Kipling, (Joseph) Rudyard
1865-1936 ...... **TCLC 8, 17; DA; PC 3;**
SSC 5; WLC
See also CA 105; 120; CANR 33;
CDBLB 1890-1914; DLB 19, 34, 141;
MAICYA; MTCW; YABC 2

Kirkup, James 1918- .... **CLC 1**
See also CA 1-4R; CAAS 4; CANR 2;
DLB 27; SATA 12

Kirkwood, James 1930(?)-1989 ...... **CLC 9**
See also AITN 2; CA 1-4R; 128; CANR 6,
40

Kis, Danilo 1935-1989 .... **CLC 57**
See also CA 109; 118; 129; MTCW

Kivi, Aleksis 1834-1872 .... **NCLC 30**

Kizer, Carolyn (Ashley)
1925- .... **CLC 15, 39, 80**
See also CA 65-68; CAAS 5; CANR 24;
DLB 5

Klabund 1890-1928 .... **TCLC 44**
See also DLB 66

Klappert, Peter 1942- .... **CLC 57**
See also CA 33-36R; DLB 5

Klein, A(braham) M(oses)
1909-1972 .... **CLC 19**
See also CA 101; 37-40R; DLB 68

Klein, Norma 1938-1989 .... **CLC 30**
See also AAYA 2; CA 41-44R; 128;
CANR 15, 37; CLR 2, 19; JRDA;
MAICYA; SAAS 1; SATA 7, 57

Klein, T(heodore) E(ibon) D(onald)
1947- .... **CLC 34**
See also CA 119; CANR 44

Kleist, Heinrich von
1777-1811 .... **NCLC 2, 37**
See also DLB 90

Klima, Ivan 1931- .... **CLC 56**
See also CA 25-28R; CANR 17

Klimentov, Andrei Platonovich 1899-1951
See Platonov, Andrei
See also CA 108

Klinger, Friedrich Maximilian von
1752-1831 .... **NCLC 1**
See also DLB 94

Klopstock, Friedrich Gottlieb
1724-1803 .... **NCLC 11**
See also DLB 97

Knebel, Fletcher 1911-1993 .... **CLC 14**
See also AITN 1; CA 1-4R; 140; CAAS 3;
CANR 1, 36; SATA 36; SATA-Obit 75

Knickerbocker, Diedrich
See Irving, Washington

Knight, Etheridge
1931-1991 .... **CLC 40; BLC**
See also BW 1; CA 21-24R; 133; CANR 23;
DLB 41

Knight, Sarah Kemble 1666-1727 ..... **LC 7**
See also DLB 24

Knister, Raymond 1899-1932 ..... **TCLC 56**
See also DLB 68

Knowles, John
1926- .... **CLC 1, 4, 10, 26; DA**
See also AAYA 10; CA 17-20R; CANR 40;
CDALB 1968-1988; DLB 6; MTCW;
SATA 8

Knox, Calvin M.
See Silverberg, Robert

Knye, Cassandra
See Disch, Thomas M(ichael)

Koch, C(hristopher) J(ohn) 1932- ... **CLC 42**
See also CA 127

Koch, Christopher
See Koch, C(hristopher) J(ohn)

Koch, Kenneth 1925- .... **CLC 5, 8, 44**
See also CA 1-4R; CANR 6, 36; DLB 5;
SATA 65

Kochanowski, Jan 1530-1584 .... **LC 10**

Kock, Charles Paul de
1794-1871 .... **NCLC 16**

Koda Shigeyuki 1867-1947
See Rohan, Koda
See also CA 121

Koestler, Arthur
1905-1983 .... **CLC 1, 3, 6, 8, 15, 33**
See also CA 1-4R; 109; CANR 1, 33;
CDBLB 1945-1960; DLBY 83; MTCW

Kogawa, Joy Nozomi 1935- .... **CLC 78**
See also CA 101; CANR 19

Kohout, Pavel 1928- .... **CLC 13**
See also CA 45-48; CANR 3

Koizumi, Yakumo
See Hearn, (Patricio) Lafcadio (Tessima
Carlos)

Kolmar, Gertrud 1894-1943 ...... **TCLC 40**

Komunyakaa, Yusef 1947- .... **CLC 86**
See also CA 147; DLB 120

Konrad, George
See Konrad, Gyoergy

Konrad, Gyoergy 1933- ...... **CLC 4, 10, 73**
See also CA 85-88

Konwicki, Tadeusz 1926- ..... **CLC 8, 28, 54**
See also CA 101; CAAS 9; CANR 39;
MTCW

Koontz, Dean R(ay) 1945- .... **CLC 78**
See also AAYA 9; BEST 89:3, 90:2;
CA 108; CANR 19, 36; MTCW

Kopit, Arthur (Lee) 1937- .... **CLC 1, 18, 33**
See also AITN 1; CA 81-84; CABS 3;
DLB 7; MTCW

Kops, Bernard 1926- .... **CLC 4**
See also CA 5-8R; DLB 13

Kornbluth, C(yril) M. 1923-1958 .... **TCLC 8**
See also CA 105; DLB 8

Korolenko, V. G.
See Korolenko, Vladimir Galaktionovich

Korolenko, Vladimir
See Korolenko, Vladimir Galaktionovich

Korolenko, Vladimir G.
See Korolenko, Vladimir Galaktionovich

Korolenko, Vladimir Galaktionovich
1853-1921 .... **TCLC 22**
See also CA 121

Kosinski, Jerzy (Nikodem)
1933-1991 .... **CLC 1, 2, 3, 6, 10, 15, 53,**
70
See also CA 17-20R; 134; CANR 9, 46;
DLB 2; DLBY 82; MTCW

Kostelanetz, Richard (Cory) 1940- .. **CLC 28**
See also CA 13-16R; CAAS 8; CANR 38

Kostrowitzki, Wilhelm Apollinaris de
1880-1918
See Apollinaire, Guillaume
See also CA 104

Kotlowitz, Robert 1924- .... **CLC 4**
See also CA 33-36R; CANR 36

Kotzebue, August (Friedrich Ferdinand) von
1761-1819 .... **NCLC 25**
See also DLB 94

Kotzwinkle, William 1938- .. **CLC 5, 14, 35**
See also CA 45-48; CANR 3, 44; CLR 6;
MAICYA; SATA 24, 70

Kozol, Jonathan 1936- .... **CLC 17**
See also CA 61-64; CANR 16, 45

Kozoll, Michael 1940(?)- .... **CLC 35**

Kramer, Kathryn 19(?)- .... **CLC 34**

Kramer, Larry 1935- .... **CLC 42**
See also CA 124; 126

Krasicki, Ignacy 1735-1801 .... **NCLC 8**

Krasinski, Zygmunt 1812-1859 .... **NCLC 4**

Kraus, Karl 1874-1936 .... **TCLC 5**
See also CA 104; DLB 118

Kreve (Mickevicius), Vincas
1882-1954 .... **TCLC 27**

Kristeva, Julia 1941- .... **CLC 77**

Kristofferson, Kris 1936- .... **CLC 26**
See also CA 104

Krizanc, John 1956- .... **CLC 57**

Krleza, Miroslav 1893-1981........ **CLC 8**
See also CA 97-100; 105; DLB 147

Kroetsch, Robert 1927- ...... **CLC 5, 23, 57**
See also CA 17-20R; CANR 8, 38; DLB 53;
MTCW

Kroetz, Franz
See Kroetz, Franz Xaver

Kroetz, Franz Xaver 1946- .... **CLC 41**
See also CA 130

Kroker, Arthur 1945- .... **CLC 77**

Kropotkin, Peter (Aleksieevich)
1842-1921 .... **TCLC 36**
See also CA 119

Krotkov, Yuri 1917- .... **CLC 19**
See also CA 102

Krumb
See Crumb, R(obert)

Krumgold, Joseph (Quincy)
1908-1980 .... **CLC 12**
See also CA 9-12R; 101; CANR 7;
MAICYA; SATA 1, 48; SATA-Obit 23

Krumwitz
See Crumb, R(obert)

Krutch, Joseph Wood 1893-1970 .... **CLC 24**
See also CA 1-4R; 25-28R; CANR 4;
DLB 63

Krutzch, Gus
See Eliot, T(homas) S(tearns)

Latsis, Mary J(ane)
See Lathen, Emma
See also CA 85-88

Lattimore, Richmond (Alexander)
1906-1984 .... CLC 3
See also CA 1-4R; 112; CANR 1

Laughlin, James 1914- .... CLC 49
See also CA 21-24R; CANR 9, 47; DLB 48

Laurence, (Jean) Margaret (Wemyss)
1926-1987 .. CLC 3, 6, 13, 50, 62; SSC 7
See also CA 5-8R; 121; CANR 33; DLB 53;
MTCW; SATA-Obit 50

Laurent, Antoine 1952- .... CLC 50

Lauscher, Hermann
See Hesse, Hermann

Lautreamont, Comte de
1846-1870 .... NCLC 12; SSC 14

Laverty, Donald
See Blish, James (Benjamin)

Lavin, Mary 1912- ...... CLC 4, 18; SSC 4
See also CA 9-12R; CANR 33; DLB 15;
MTCW

Lavond, Paul Dennis
See Kornbluth, C(yril) M.; Pohl, Frederik

Lawler, Raymond Evenor 1922- .... CLC 58
See also CA 103

Lawrence, D(avid) H(erbert Richards)
1885-1930 ...... TCLC 2, 9, 16, 33, 48;
DA; SSC 4, 19; WLC
See also CA 104; 121; CDBLB 1914-1945;
DLB 10, 19, 36, 98; MTCW

Lawrence, T(homas) E(dward)
1888-1935 .... TCLC 18
See also Dale, Colin
See also CA 115

Lawrence of Arabia
See Lawrence, T(homas) E(dward)

Lawson, Henry (Archibald Hertzberg)
1867-1922 .... TCLC 27; SSC 18
See also CA 120

Lawton, Dennis
See Faust, Frederick (Schiller)

Laxness, Halldor .... CLC 25
See also Gudjonsson, Halldor Kiljan

Layamon fl. c. 1200- .... CMLC 10
See also DLB 146

Laye, Camara 1928-1980 ... CLC 4, 38; BLC
See also BW 1; CA 85-88; 97-100;
CANR 25; MTCW

Layton, Irving (Peter) 1912- ..... CLC 2, 15
See also CA 1-4R; CANR 2, 33, 43;
DLB 88; MTCW

Lazarus, Emma 1849-1887 .... NCLC 8

Lazarus, Felix
See Cable, George Washington

Lazarus, Henry
See Slavitt, David R(ytman)

Lea, Joan
See Neufeld, John (Arthur)

Leacock, Stephen (Butler)
1869-1944 .... TCLC 2
See also CA 104; 141; DLB 92

Lear, Edward 1812-1888 .... NCLC 3
See also CLR 1; DLB 32; MAICYA;
SATA 18

Lear, Norman (Milton) 1922- ...... CLC 12
See also CA 73-76

Leavis, F(rank) R(aymond)
1895-1978 .... CLC 24
See also CA 21-24R; 77-80; CANR 44;
MTCW

Leavitt, David 1961- .... CLC 34
See also CA 116; 122; DLB 130

Leblanc, Maurice (Marie Emile)
1864-1941 .... TCLC 49
See also CA 110

Lebowitz, Fran(ces Ann)
1951(?)- .... CLC 11, 36
See also CA 81-84; CANR 14; MTCW

Lebrecht, Peter
See Tieck, (Johann) Ludwig

le Carre, John .... CLC 3, 5, 9, 15, 28
See also Cornwell, David (John Moore)
See also BEST 89:4; CDBLB 1960 to
Present; DLB 87

Le Clezio, J(ean) M(arie) G(ustave)
1940- .... CLC 31
See also CA 116; 128; DLB 83

Leconte de Lisle, Charles-Marie-Rene
1818-1894 .... NCLC 29

Le Coq, Monsieur
See Simenon, Georges (Jacques Christian)

Leduc, Violette 1907-1972 .... CLC 22
See also CA 13-14; 33-36R; CAP 1

Ledwidge, Francis 1887(?)-1917 ... TCLC 23
See also CA 123; DLB 20

Lee, Andrea 1953- .... CLC 36; BLC
See also BW 1; CA 125

Lee, Andrew
See Auchincloss, Louis (Stanton)

Lee, Don L. .... CLC 2
See also Madhubuti, Haki R.

Lee, George W(ashington)
1894-1976 .... CLC 52; BLC
See also BW 1; CA 125; DLB 51

Lee, (Nelle) Harper
1926- .... CLC 12, 60; DA; WLC
See also AAYA 13; CA 13-16R;
CDALB 1941-1968; DLB 6; MTCW;
SATA 11

Lee, Helen Elaine 1959(?)- .... CLC 86

Lee, Julian
See Latham, Jean Lee

Lee, Larry
See Lee, Lawrence

Lee, Lawrence 1941-1990 .... CLC 34
See also CA 131; CANR 43

Lee, Manfred B(ennington)
1905-1971 .... CLC 11
See also Queen, Ellery
See also CA 1-4R; 29-32R; CANR 2;
DLB 137

Lee, Stan 1922- .... CLC 17
See also AAYA 5; CA 108; 111

Lee, Tanith 1947- .... CLC 46
See also CA 37-40R; SATA 8

Lee, Vernon .... TCLC 5
See also Paget, Violet
See also DLB 57, 153

Lee, William
See Burroughs, William S(eward)

Lee, Willy
See Burroughs, William S(eward)

Lee-Hamilton, Eugene (Jacob)
1845-1907 .... TCLC 22
See also CA 117

Leet, Judith 1935- .... CLC 11

Le Fanu, Joseph Sheridan
1814-1873 .... NCLC 9; SSC 14
See also DLB 21, 70

Leffland, Ella 1931- .... CLC 19
See also CA 29-32R; CANR 35; DLBY 84;
SATA 65

Leger, Alexis
See Leger, (Marie-Rene Auguste) Alexis
Saint-Leger

Leger, (Marie-Rene Auguste) Alexis
Saint-Leger 1887-1975 .... CLC 11
See also Perse, St.-John
See also CA 13-16R; 61-64; CANR 43;
MTCW

Leger, Saintleger
See Leger, (Marie-Rene Auguste) Alexis
Saint-Leger

Le Guin, Ursula K(roeber)
1929- .... CLC 8, 13, 22, 45, 71; SSC 12
See also AAYA 9; AITN 1; CA 21-24R;
CANR 9, 32; CDALB 1968-1988; CLR 3,
28; DLB 8, 52; JRDA; MAICYA;
MTCW; SATA 4, 52

Lehmann, Rosamond (Nina)
1901-1990 .... CLC 5
See also CA 77-80; 131; CANR 8; DLB 15

Leiber, Fritz (Reuter, Jr.)
1910-1992 .... CLC 25
See also CA 45-48; 139; CANR 2, 40;
DLB 8; MTCW; SATA 45;
SATA-Obit 73

Leimbach, Martha 1963-
See Leimbach, Marti
See also CA 130

Leimbach, Marti .... CLC 65
See also Leimbach, Martha

Leino, Eino .... TCLC 24
See also Loennbohm, Armas Eino Leopold

Leiris, Michel (Julien) 1901-1990 ... CLC 61
See also CA 119; 128; 132

Leithauser, Brad 1953- .... CLC 27
See also CA 107; CANR 27; DLB 120

Lelchuk, Alan 1938- .... CLC 5
See also CA 45-48; CAAS 20; CANR 1

Lem, Stanislaw 1921- .... CLC 8, 15, 40
See also CA 105; CAAS 1; CANR 32;
MTCW

Lemann, Nancy 1956- .... CLC 39
See also CA 118; 136

Lemonnier, (Antoine Louis) Camille
1844-1913 .... TCLC 22
See also CA 121

Lenau, Nikolaus 1802-1850 ...... NCLC 16

Lispector, Clarice 1925-1977 . . . . . . **CLC 43**
See also CA 139; 116; DLB 113

Littell, Robert 1935(?)- . . . . **CLC 42**
See also CA 109; 112

Little, Malcolm 1925-1965
See Malcolm X
See also BW 1; CA 125; 111; DA; MTCW

Littlewit, Humphrey Gent.
See Lovecraft, H(oward) P(hillips)

Litwos
See Sienkiewicz, Henryk (Adam Alexander Pius)

Liu E 1857-1909 . . . . **TCLC 15**
See also CA 115

Lively, Penelope (Margaret)
1933- . . . . **CLC 32, 50**
See also CA 41-44R; CANR 29; CLR 7; DLB 14; JRDA; MAICYA; MTCW; SATA 7, 60

Livesay, Dorothy (Kathleen)
1909- . . . . **CLC 4, 15, 79**
See also AITN 2; CA 25-28R; CAAS 8; CANR 36; DLB 68; MTCW

Livy c. 59B.C.-c. 17 . . . . **CMLC 11**

Lizardi, Jose Joaquin Fernandez de
1776-1827 . . . . **NCLC 30**

Llewellyn, Richard
See Llewellyn Lloyd, Richard Dafydd Vivian
See also DLB 15

Llewellyn Lloyd, Richard Dafydd Vivian
1906-1983 . . . . **CLC 7, 80**
See also Llewellyn, Richard
See also CA 53-56; 111; CANR 7; SATA 11; SATA-Obit 37

Llosa, (Jorge) Mario (Pedro) Vargas
See Vargas Llosa, (Jorge) Mario (Pedro)

Lloyd Webber, Andrew 1948-
See Webber, Andrew Lloyd
See also AAYA 1; CA 116; SATA 56

Llull, Ramon c. 1235-c. 1316 . . . . . **CMLC 12**

Locke, Alain (Le Roy)
1886-1954 . . . . **TCLC 43**
See also BW 1; CA 106; 124; DLB 51

Locke, John 1632-1704 . . . . **LC 7**
See also DLB 101

Locke-Elliott, Sumner
See Elliott, Sumner Locke

Lockhart, John Gibson
1794-1854 . . . . **NCLC 6**
See also DLB 110, 116, 144

Lodge, David (John) 1935- . . . . **CLC 36**
See also BEST 90:1; CA 17-20R; CANR 19; DLB 14; MTCW

Loennbohm, Armas Eino Leopold 1878-1926
See Leino, Eino
See also CA 123

Loewinsohn, Ron(ald William)
1937- . . . . **CLC 52**
See also CA 25-28R

Logan, Jake
See Smith, Martin Cruz

Logan, John (Burton) 1923-1987 . . . . . **CLC 5**
See also CA 77-80; 124; CANR 45; DLB 5

Lo Kuan-chung 1330(?)-1400(?) . . . . . **LC 12**

Lombard, Nap
See Johnson, Pamela Hansford

London, Jack . . **TCLC 9, 15, 39; SSC 4; WLC**
See also London, John Griffith
See also AAYA 13; AITN 2; CDALB 1865-1917; DLB 8, 12, 78; SATA 18

London, John Griffith 1876-1916
See London, Jack
See also CA 110; 119; DA; JRDA; MAICYA; MTCW

Long, Emmett
See Leonard, Elmore (John, Jr.)

Longbaugh, Harry
See Goldman, William (W.)

Longfellow, Henry Wadsworth
1807-1882 . . . . **NCLC 2, 45; DA**
See also CDALB 1640-1865; DLB 1, 59; SATA 19

Longley, Michael 1939- . . . . **CLC 29**
See also CA 102; DLB 40

Longus fl. c. 2nd cent. - . . . . **CMLC 7**

Longway, A. Hugh
See Lang, Andrew

Lopate, Phillip 1943- . . . . **CLC 29**
See also CA 97-100; DLBY 80

Lopez Portillo (y Pacheco), Jose
1920- . . . . **CLC 46**
See also CA 129; HW

Lopez y Fuentes, Gregorio
1897(?)-1966 . . . . **CLC 32**
See also CA 131; HW

Lorca, Federico Garcia
See Garcia Lorca, Federico

Lord, Bette Bao 1938- . . . . **CLC 23**
See also BEST 90:3; CA 107; CANR 41; SATA 58

Lord Auch
See Bataille, Georges

Lord Byron
See Byron, George Gordon (Noel)

Lorde, Audre (Geraldine)
1934-1992 . . . . **CLC 18, 71; BLC; PC 12**
See also BW 1; CA 25-28R; 142; CANR 16, 26, 46; DLB 41; MTCW

Lord Jeffrey
See Jeffrey, Francis

Lorenzo, Heberto Padilla
See Padilla (Lorenzo), Heberto

Loris
See Hofmannsthal, Hugo von

Loti, Pierre . . . . **TCLC 11**
See also Viaud, (Louis Marie) Julien
See also DLB 123

Louie, David Wong 1954- . . . . **CLC 70**
See also CA 139

Louis, Father M.
See Merton, Thomas

Lovecraft, H(oward) P(hillips)
1890-1937 . . . . **TCLC 4, 22; SSC 3**
See also AAYA 14; CA 104; 133; MTCW

Lovelace, Earl 1935- . . . . **CLC 51**
See also BW 2; CA 77-80; CANR 41; DLB 125; MTCW

Lovelace, Richard 1618-1657 . . . . **LC 24**
See also DLB 131

Lowell, Amy 1874-1925 . . **TCLC 1, 8; PC 12**
See also CA 104; DLB 54, 140

Lowell, James Russell 1819-1891 . . **NCLC 2**
See also CDALB 1640-1865; DLB 1, 11, 64, 79

Lowell, Robert (Traill Spence, Jr.)
1917-1977 . . . **CLC 1, 2, 3, 4, 5, 8, 9, 11, 15, 37; DA; PC 3; WLC**
See also CA 9-12R; 73-76; CABS 2; CANR 26; DLB 5; MTCW

Lowndes, Marie Adelaide (Belloc)
1868-1947 . . . . **TCLC 12**
See also CA 107; DLB 70

Lowry, (Clarence) Malcolm
1909-1957 . . . . **TCLC 6, 40**
See also CA 105; 131; CDBLB 1945-1960; DLB 15; MTCW

Lowry, Mina Gertrude 1882-1966
See Loy, Mina
See also CA 113

Loxsmith, John
See Brunner, John (Kilian Houston)

Loy, Mina . . . . **CLC 28**
See also Lowry, Mina Gertrude
See also DLB 4, 54

Loyson-Bridet
See Schwob, (Mayer Andre) Marcel

Lucas, Craig 1951- . . . . **CLC 64**
See also CA 137

Lucas, George 1944- . . . . **CLC 16**
See also AAYA 1; CA 77-80; CANR 30; SATA 56

Lucas, Hans
See Godard, Jean-Luc

Lucas, Victoria
See Plath, Sylvia

Ludlam, Charles 1943-1987 . . . . . **CLC 46, 50**
See also CA 85-88; 122

Ludlum, Robert 1927- . . . . **CLC 22, 43**
See also AAYA 10; BEST 89:1, 90:3; CA 33-36R; CANR 25, 41; DLBY 82; MTCW

Ludwig, Ken . . . . **CLC 60**

Ludwig, Otto 1813-1865 . . . . **NCLC 4**
See also DLB 129

Lugones, Leopoldo 1874-1938 . . . . . **TCLC 15**
See also CA 116; 131; HW

Lu Hsun 1881-1936 . . . . . . **TCLC 3; SSC 20**
See also Shu-Jen, Chou

Lukacs, George . . . . **CLC 24**
See also Lukacs, Gyorgy (Szegeny von)

Lukacs, Gyorgy (Szegeny von) 1885-1971
See Lukacs, George
See also CA 101; 29-32R

Luke, Peter (Ambrose Cyprian)
1919-1995 . . . . **CLC 38**
See also CA 81-84; 147; DLB 13

Lunar, Dennis
See Mungo, Raymond

Lurie, Alison 1926-........ **CLC 4, 5, 18, 39**
See also CA 1-4R; CANR 2, 17; DLB 2;
MTCW; SATA 46

Lustig, Arnost 1926-.............. **CLC 56**
See also AAYA 3; CA 69-72; CANR 47;
SATA 56

Luther, Martin 1483-1546.......... **LC 9**

Luzi, Mario 1914-................ **CLC 13**
See also CA 61-64; CANR 9; DLB 128

Lynch, B. Suarez
See Bioy Casares, Adolfo; Borges, Jorge
Luis

Lynch, David (K.) 1946-.......... **CLC 66**
See also CA 124; 129

Lynch, James
See Andreyev, Leonid (Nikolaevich)

Lynch Davis, B.
See Bioy Casares, Adolfo; Borges, Jorge
Luis

Lyndsay, Sir David 1490-1555 ...... **LC 20**

Lynn, Kenneth S(chuyler) 1923-.... **CLC 50**
See also CA 1-4R; CANR 3, 27

Lynx
See West, Rebecca

Lyons, Marcus
See Blish, James (Benjamin)

Lyre, Pinchbeck
See Sassoon, Siegfried (Lorraine)

Lytle, Andrew (Nelson) 1902-...... **CLC 22**
See also CA 9-12R; DLB 6

Lyttelton, George 1709-1773....... **LC 10**

Maas, Peter 1929- .... **CLC 29**
See also CA 93-96

Macaulay, Rose 1881-1958 ..... **TCLC 7, 44**
See also CA 104; DLB 36

Macaulay, Thomas Babington
1800-1859 .... **NCLC 42**
See also CDBLB 1832-1890; DLB 32, 55

MacBeth, George (Mann)
1932-1992 .... **CLC 2, 5, 9**
See also CA 25-28R; 136; DLB 40; MTCW;
SATA 4; SATA-Obit 70

MacCaig, Norman (Alexander)
1910- .... **CLC 36**
See also CA 9-12R; CANR 3, 34; DLB 27

MacCarthy, (Sir Charles Otto) Desmond
1877-1952 .... **TCLC 36**

MacDiarmid, Hugh
.... **CLC 2, 4, 11, 19, 63; PC 9**
See also Grieve, C(hristopher) M(urray)
See also CDBLB 1945-1960; DLB 20

MacDonald, Anson
See Heinlein, Robert A(nson)

Macdonald, Cynthia 1928-...... **CLC 13, 19**
See also CA 49-52; CANR 4, 44; DLB 105

MacDonald, George 1824-1905..... **TCLC 9**
See also CA 106; 137; DLB 18; MAICYA;
SATA 33

Macdonald, John
See Millar, Kenneth

MacDonald, John D(ann)
1916-1986 .... **CLC 3, 27, 44**
See also CA 1-4R; 121; CANR 1, 19;
DLB 8; DLBY 86; MTCW

Macdonald, John Ross
See Millar, Kenneth

Macdonald, Ross..... **CLC 1, 2, 3, 14, 34, 41**
See also Millar, Kenneth
See also DLBD 6

MacDougal, John
See Blish, James (Benjamin)

MacEwen, Gwendolyn (Margaret)
1941-1987 .... **CLC 13, 55**
See also CA 9-12R; 124; CANR 7, 22;
DLB 53; SATA 50; SATA-Obit 55

Macha, Karel Hynek 1810-1846.. **NCLC 46**

Machado (y Ruiz), Antonio
1875-1939 .... **TCLC 3**
See also CA 104; DLB 108

Machado de Assis, Joaquim Maria
1839-1908 .... **TCLC 10; BLC**
See also CA 107

Machen, Arthur.......... **TCLC 4; SSC 20**
See also Jones, Arthur Llewellyn
See also DLB 36

Machiavelli, Niccolo 1469-1527 .. **LC 8; DA**

MacInnes, Colin 1914-1976...... **CLC 4, 23**
See also CA 69-72; 65-68; CANR 21;
DLB 14; MTCW

MacInnes, Helen (Clark)
1907-1985 .... **CLC 27, 39**
See also CA 1-4R; 117; CANR 1, 28;
DLB 87; MTCW; SATA 22;
SATA-Obit 44

Mackay, Mary 1855-1924
See Corelli, Marie
See also CA 118

Mackenzie, Compton (Edward Montague)
1883-1972 .... **CLC 18**
See also CA 21-22; 37-40R; CAP 2;
DLB 34, 100

Mackenzie, Henry 1745-1831 .... **NCLC 41**
See also DLB 39

Mackintosh, Elizabeth 1896(?)-1952
See Tey, Josephine
See also CA 110

MacLaren, James
See Grieve, C(hristopher) M(urray)

Mac Laverty, Bernard 1942-....... **CLC 31**
See also CA 116; 118; CANR 43

MacLean, Alistair (Stuart)
1922-1987 .... **CLC 3, 13, 50, 63**
See also CA 57-60; 121; CANR 28; MTCW;
SATA 23; SATA-Obit 50

Maclean, Norman (Fitzroy)
1902-1990 .... **CLC 78; SSC 13**
See also CA 102; 132; CANR 49

MacLeish, Archibald
1892-1982 .... **CLC 3, 8, 14, 68**
See also CA 9-12R; 106; CANR 33; DLB 4,
7, 45; DLBY 82; MTCW

MacLennan, (John) Hugh
1907-1990 .... **CLC 2, 14**
See also CA 5-8R; 142; CANR 33; DLB 68;
MTCW

MacLeod, Alistair 1936- .... **CLC 56**
See also CA 123; DLB 60

MacNeice, (Frederick) Louis
1907-1963 .... **CLC 1, 4, 10, 53**
See also CA 85-88; DLB 10, 20; MTCW

MacNeill, Dand
See Fraser, George MacDonald

Macpherson, James 1736-1796 ...... **LC 29**
See also DLB 109

Macpherson, (Jean) Jay 1931-...... **CLC 14**
See also CA 5-8R; DLB 53

MacShane, Frank 1927-........... **CLC 39**
See also CA 9-12R; CANR 3, 33; DLB 111

Macumber, Mari
See Sandoz, Mari(e Susette)

Madach, Imre 1823-1864........ **NCLC 19**

Madden, (Jerry) David 1933- .... **CLC 5, 15**
See also CA 1-4R; CAAS 3; CANR 4, 45;
DLB 6; MTCW

Maddern, Al(an)
See Ellison, Harlan (Jay)

Madhubuti, Haki R.
1942- .... **CLC 6, 73; BLC; PC 5**
See also Lee, Don L.
See also BW 2; CA 73-76; CANR 24;
DLB 5, 41; DLBD 8

Maepenn, Hugh
See Kuttner, Henry

Maepenn, K. H.
See Kuttner, Henry

Maeterlinck, Maurice 1862-1949 ... **TCLC 3**
See also CA 104; 136; SATA 66

Maginn, William 1794-1842...... **NCLC 8**
See also DLB 110

Mahapatra, Jayanta 1928-......... **CLC 33**
See also CA 73-76; CAAS 9; CANR 15, 33

Mahfouz, Naguib (Abdel Aziz Al-Sabilgi)
1911(?)-
See Mahfuz, Najib
See also BEST 89:2; CA 128; MTCW

Mahfuz, Najib................. **CLC 52, 55**
See also Mahfouz, Naguib (Abdel Aziz
Al-Sabilgi)
See also DLBY 88

Mahon, Derek 1941-.............. **CLC 27**
See also CA 113; 128; DLB 40

Mailer, Norman
1923- ...... **CLC 1, 2, 3, 4, 5, 8, 11, 14,
28, 39, 74; DA**
See also AITN 2; CA 9-12R; CABS 1;
CANR 28; CDALB 1968-1988; DLB 2,
16, 28; DLBD 3; DLBY 80, 83; MTCW

Maillet, Antonine 1929-........... **CLC 54**
See also CA 115; 120; CANR 46; DLB 60

Mais, Roger 1905-1955 .... **TCLC 8**
See also BW 1; CA 105; 124; DLB 125;
MTCW

Maistre, Joseph de 1753-1821.... **NCLC 37**

Maitland, Sara (Louise) 1950-...... **CLC 49**
See also CA 69-72; CANR 13

Major, Clarence
1936- .... **CLC 3, 19, 48; BLC**
See also BW 2; CA 21-24R; CAAS 6;
CANR 13, 25; DLB 33

Martin, Webber
See Silverberg, Robert

Martindale, Patrick Victor
See White, Patrick (Victor Martindale)

Martin du Gard, Roger
1881-1958 .... **TCLC 24**
See also CA 118; DLB 65

Martineau, Harriet 1802-1876.... **NCLC 26**
See also DLB 21, 55; YABC 2

Martines, Julia
See O'Faolain, Julia

Martinez, Jacinto Benavente y
See Benavente (y Martinez), Jacinto

Martinez Ruiz, Jose 1873-1967
See Azorin; Ruiz, Jose Martinez
See also CA 93-96; HW

Martinez Sierra, Gregorio
1881-1947 .... **TCLC 6**
See also CA 115

Martinez Sierra, Maria (de la O'LeJarraga)
1874-1974 .... **TCLC 6**
See also CA 115

Martinsen, Martin
See Follett, Ken(neth Martin)

Martinson, Harry (Edmund)
1904-1978 .... **CLC 14**
See also CA 77-80; CANR 34

Marut, Ret
See Traven, B.

Marut, Robert
See Traven, B.

Marvell, Andrew
1621-1678 ..... **LC 4; DA; PC 10; WLC**
See also CDBLB 1660-1789; DLB 131

Marx, Karl (Heinrich)
1818-1883 .... **NCLC 17**
See also DLB 129

Masaoka Shiki................. **TCLC 18**
See also Masaoka Tsunenori

Masaoka Tsunenori 1867-1902
See Masaoka Shiki
See also CA 117

Masefield, John (Edward)
1878-1967 .... **CLC 11, 47**
See also CA 19-20; 25-28R; CANR 33;
CAP 2; CDBLB 1890-1914; DLB 10, 19,
153; MTCW; SATA 19

Maso, Carole 19(?)- .... **CLC 44**

Mason, Bobbie Ann
1940- .... **CLC 28, 43, 82; SSC 4**
See also AAYA 5; CA 53-56; CANR 11,
31; DLBY 87; MTCW

Mason, Ernst
See Pohl, Frederik

Mason, Lee W.
See Malzberg, Barry N(athaniel)

Mason, Nick 1945-............... **CLC 35**

Mason, Tally
See Derleth, August (William)

Mass, William
See Gibson, William

Masters, Edgar Lee
1868-1950 ...... **TCLC 2, 25; DA; PC 1**
See also CA 104; 133; CDALB 1865-1917;
DLB 54; MTCW

Masters, Hilary 1928- .... **CLC 48**
See also CA 25-28R; CANR 13, 47

Mastrosimone, William 19(?)-...... **CLC 36**

Mathe, Albert
See Camus, Albert

Matheson, Richard Burton 1926-... **CLC 37**
See also CA 97-100; DLB 8, 44

Mathews, Harry 1930-......... **CLC 6, 52**
See also CA 21-24R; CAAS 6; CANR 18,
40

Mathews, John Joseph 1894-1979... **CLC 84**
See also CA 19-20; 142; CANR 45; CAP 2;
NNAL

Mathias, Roland (Glyn) 1915-...... **CLC 45**
See also CA 97-100; CANR 19, 41; DLB 27

Matsuo Basho 1644-1694........... **PC 3**

Mattheson, Rodney
See Creasey, John

Matthews, Greg 1949- .... **CLC 45**
See also CA 135

Matthews, William 1942-......... **CLC 40**
See also CA 29-32R; CAAS 18; CANR 12;
DLB 5

Matthias, John (Edward) 1941-..... **CLC 9**
See also CA 33-36R

Matthiessen, Peter
1927- .... **CLC 5, 7, 11, 32, 64**
See also AAYA 6; BEST 90:4; CA 9-12R;
CANR 21; DLB 6; MTCW; SATA 27

Maturin, Charles Robert
1780(?)-1824 .... **NCLC 6**

Matute (Ausejo), Ana Maria
1925- .... **CLC 11**
See also CA 89-92; MTCW

Maugham, W. S.
See Maugham, W(illiam) Somerset

Maugham, W(illiam) Somerset
1874-1965 ...... **CLC 1, 11, 15, 67; DA;
SSC 8; WLC**
See also CA 5-8R; 25-28R; CANR 40;
CDBLB 1914-1945; DLB 10, 36, 77, 100;
MTCW; SATA 54

Maugham, William Somerset
See Maugham, W(illiam) Somerset

Maupassant, (Henri Rene Albert) Guy de
1850-1893 .... **NCLC 1, 42; DA; SSC 1;
WLC**
See also DLB 123

Maurhut, Richard
See Traven, B.

Mauriac, Claude 1914-............ **CLC 9**
See also CA 89-92; DLB 83

Mauriac, Francois (Charles)
1885-1970 .... **CLC 4, 9, 56**
See also CA 25-28; CAP 2; DLB 65;
MTCW

Mavor, Osborne Henry 1888-1951
See Bridie, James
See also CA 104

Maxwell, William (Keepers, Jr.)
1908- .... **CLC 19**
See also CA 93-96; DLBY 80

May, Elaine 1932- .... **CLC 16**
See also CA 124; 142; DLB 44

Mayakovski, Vladimir (Vladimirovich)
1893-1930 .... **TCLC 4, 18**
See also CA 104

Mayhew, Henry 1812-1887 ...... **NCLC 31**
See also DLB 18, 55

Mayle, Peter 1939(?)-............ **CLC 89**
See also CA 139

Maynard, Joyce 1953-............ **CLC 23**
See also CA 111; 129

Mayne, William (James Carter)
1928- .... **CLC 12**
See also CA 9-12R; CANR 37; CLR 25;
JRDA; MAICYA; SAAS 11; SATA 6, 68

Mayo, Jim
See L'Amour, Louis (Dearborn)

Maysles, Albert 1926- .... **CLC 16**
See also CA 29-32R

Maysles, David 1932-............. **CLC 16**

Mazer, Norma Fox 1931- .... **CLC 26**
See also AAYA 5; CA 69-72; CANR 12,
32; CLR 23; JRDA; MAICYA; SAAS 1;
SATA 24, 67

Mazzini, Guiseppe 1805-1872 .... **NCLC 34**

McAuley, James Phillip
1917-1976 .... **CLC 45**
See also CA 97-100

McBain, Ed
See Hunter, Evan

McBrien, William Augustine
1930- .... **CLC 44**
See also CA 107

McCaffrey, Anne (Inez) 1926-...... **CLC 17**
See also AAYA 6; AITN 2; BEST 89:2;
CA 25-28R; CANR 15, 35; DLB 8;
JRDA; MAICYA; MTCW; SAAS 11;
SATA 8, 70

McCall, Nathan 1955(?)-.......... **CLC 86**
See also CA 146

McCann, Arthur
See Campbell, John W(ood, Jr.)

McCann, Edson
See Pohl, Frederik

McCarthy, Charles, Jr. 1933-
See McCarthy, Cormac
See also CANR 42

McCarthy, Cormac 1933-..... **CLC 4, 57, 59**
See also McCarthy, Charles, Jr.
See also DLB 6, 143

McCarthy, Mary (Therese)
1912-1989 ... **CLC 1, 3, 5, 14, 24, 39, 59**
See also CA 5-8R; 129; CANR 16; DLB 2;
DLBY 81; MTCW

McCartney, (James) Paul
1942- .... **CLC 12, 35**
See also CA 146

McCauley, Stephen (D.) 1955- ..... **CLC 50**
See also CA 141

Metcalf, John 1938-. . . . . **CLC 37**
See also CA 113; DLB 60

Metcalf, Suzanne
See Baum, L(yman) Frank

Mew, Charlotte (Mary)
1870-1928 . . . . **TCLC 8**
See also CA 105; DLB 19, 135

Mewshaw, Michael 1943-. . . . . **CLC 9**
See also CA 53-56; CANR 7, 47; DLBY 80

Meyer, June
See Jordan, June

Meyer, Lynn
See Slavitt, David R(ytman)

Meyer-Meyrink, Gustav 1868-1932
See Meyrink, Gustav
See also CA 117

Meyers, Jeffrey 1939- . . . . **CLC 39**
See also CA 73-76; DLB 111

Meynell, Alice (Christina Gertrude Thompson)
1847-1922 . . . . **TCLC 6**
See also CA 104; DLB 19, 98

Meyrink, Gustav . . . . **TCLC 21**
See also Meyer-Meyrink, Gustav
See also DLB 81

Michaels, Leonard
1933- . . . . **CLC 6, 25; SSC 16**
See also CA 61-64; CANR 21; DLB 130;
MTCW

Michaux, Henri 1899-1984 . . . . . . **CLC 8, 19**
See also CA 85-88; 114

Michelangelo 1475-1564. . . . . **LC 12**

Michelet, Jules 1798-1874. . . . . . . **NCLC 31**

Michener, James A(lbert)
1907(?)- . . . . **CLC 1, 5, 11, 29, 60**
See also AITN 1; BEST 90:1; CA 5-8R;
CANR 21, 45; DLB 6; MTCW

Mickiewicz, Adam 1798-1855 . . . . . **NCLC 3**

Middleton, Christopher 1926- . . . . . . **CLC 13**
See also CA 13-16R; CANR 29; DLB 40

Middleton, Richard (Barham)
1882-1911 . . . . **TCLC 56**

Middleton, Stanley 1919-. . . . . . . **CLC 7, 38**
See also CA 25-28R; CANR 21, 46;
DLB 14

Middleton, Thomas 1580-1627. . . . . . . **DC 5**
See also DLB 58

Migueis, Jose Rodrigues 1901- . . . . . **CLC 10**

Mikszath, Kalman 1847-1910 . . . . . **TCLC 31**

Miles, Josephine
1911-1985 . . . . **CLC 1, 2, 14, 34, 39**
See also CA 1-4R; 116; CANR 2; DLB 48

Militant
See Sandburg, Carl (August)

Mill, John Stuart 1806-1873 . . . . . **NCLC 11**
See also CDBLB 1832-1890; DLB 55

Millar, Kenneth 1915-1983 . . . . **CLC 14**
See also Macdonald, Ross
See also CA 9-12R; 110; CANR 16; DLB 2;
DLBD 6; DLBY 83; MTCW

Millay, E. Vincent
See Millay, Edna St. Vincent

Millay, Edna St. Vincent
1892-1950 . . . . . **TCLC 4, 49; DA; PC 6**
See also CA 104; 130; CDALB 1917-1929;
DLB 45; MTCW

Miller, Arthur
1915- . . . . **CLC 1, 2, 6, 10, 15, 26, 47, 78;
DA; DC 1; WLC**
See also AITN 1; CA 1-4R; CABS 3;
CANR 2, 30; CDALB 1941-1968; DLB 7;
MTCW

Miller, Henry (Valentine)
1891-1980 . . . . **CLC 1, 2, 4, 9, 14, 43, 84;
DA; WLC**
See also CA 9-12R; 97-100; CANR 33;
CDALB 1929-1941; DLB 4, 9; DLBY 80;
MTCW

Miller, Jason 1939(?)- . . . . **CLC 2**
See also AITN 1; CA 73-76; DLB 7

Miller, Sue 1943- . . . . **CLC 44**
See also BEST 90:3; CA 139; DLB 143

Miller, Walter M(ichael, Jr.)
1923- . . . . **CLC 4, 30**
See also CA 85-88; DLB 8

Millett, Kate 1934-. . . . . **CLC 67**
See also AITN 1; CA 73-76; CANR 32;
MTCW

Millhauser, Steven 1943-. . . . . . **CLC 21, 54**
See also CA 110; 111; DLB 2

Millin, Sarah Gertrude 1889-1968 . . **CLC 49**
See also CA 102; 93-96

Milne, A(lan) A(lexander)
1882-1956 . . . . **TCLC 6**
See also CA 104; 133; CLR 1, 26; DLB 10,
77, 100; MAICYA; MTCW; YABC 1

Milner, Ron(ald) 1938-. . . . . . **CLC 56; BLC**
See also AITN 1; BW 1; CA 73-76;
CANR 24; DLB 38; MTCW

Milosz, Czeslaw
1911- . . . **CLC 5, 11, 22, 31, 56, 82; PC 8**
See also CA 81-84; CANR 23; MTCW

Milton, John 1608-1674. . . **LC 9; DA; WLC**
See also CDBLB 1660-1789; DLB 131, 151

Min, Anchee 1957-. . . . . **CLC 86**
See also CA 146

Minehaha, Cornelius
See Wedekind, (Benjamin) Frank(lin)

Miner, Valerie 1947- . . . . **CLC 40**
See also CA 97-100

Minimo, Duca
See D'Annunzio, Gabriele

Minot, Susan 1956- . . . . **CLC 44**
See also CA 134

Minus, Ed 1938-. . . . . **CLC 39**

Miranda, Javier
See Bioy Casares, Adolfo

Mirbeau, Octave 1848-1917. . . . . . . **TCLC 55**
See also DLB 123

Miro (Ferrer), Gabriel (Francisco Victor)
1879-1930 . . . . **TCLC 5**
See also CA 104

Mishima, Yukio
. . . . **CLC 2, 4, 6, 9, 27; DC 1; SSC 4**
See also Hiraoka, Kimitake

Mistral, Frederic 1830-1914 . . . . . . **TCLC 51**
See also CA 122

Mistral, Gabriela. . . . . **TCLC 2; HLC**
See also Godoy Alcayaga, Lucila

Mistry, Rohinton 1952-. . . . . **CLC 71**
See also CA 141

Mitchell, Clyde
See Ellison, Harlan (Jay); Silverberg, Robert

Mitchell, James Leslie 1901-1935
See Gibbon, Lewis Grassic
See also CA 104; DLB 15

Mitchell, Joni 1943-. . . . . **CLC 12**
See also CA 112

Mitchell, Margaret (Munnerlyn)
1900-1949 . . . . **TCLC 11**
See also CA 109; 125; DLB 9; MTCW

Mitchell, Peggy
See Mitchell, Margaret (Munnerlyn)

Mitchell, S(ilas) Weir 1829-1914 . . **TCLC 36**

Mitchell, W(illiam) O(rmond)
1914- . . . . **CLC 25**
See also CA 77-80; CANR 15, 43; DLB 88

Mitford, Mary Russell 1787-1855. . **NCLC 4**
See also DLB 110, 116

Mitford, Nancy 1904-1973. . . . . **CLC 44**
See also CA 9-12R

Miyamoto, Yuriko 1899-1951 . . . . . **TCLC 37**

Mo, Timothy (Peter) 1950(?)-. . . . . . **CLC 46**
See also CA 117; MTCW

Modarressi, Taghi (M.) 1931-. . . . . . **CLC 44**
See also CA 121; 134

Modiano, Patrick (Jean) 1945-. . . . . **CLC 18**
See also CA 85-88; CANR 17, 40; DLB 83

Moerck, Paal
See Roelvaag, O(le) E(dvart)

Mofolo, Thomas (Mokopu)
1875(?)-1948 . . . . **TCLC 22; BLC**
See also CA 121

Mohr, Nicholasa 1935-. . . . . . **CLC 12; HLC**
See also AAYA 8; CA 49-52; CANR 1, 32;
CLR 22; DLB 145; HW; JRDA; SAAS 8;
SATA 8

Mojtabai, A(nn) G(race)
1938-. . . . . **CLC 5, 9, 15, 29**
See also CA 85-88

Moliere 1622-1673 . . . . **LC 28; DA; WLC**

Molin, Charles
See Mayne, William (James Carter)

Molnar, Ferenc 1878-1952. . . . . **TCLC 20**
See also CA 109

Momaday, N(avarre) Scott
1934- . . . . **CLC 2, 19, 85; DA**
See also AAYA 11; CA 25-28R; CANR 14,
34; DLB 143; MTCW; NNAL; SATA 48;
SATA-Brief 30

Monette, Paul 1945-1995. . . . . **CLC 82**
See also CA 139; 147

Monroe, Harriet 1860-1936. . . . . . . **TCLC 12**
See also CA 109; DLB 54, 91

Monroe, Lyle
See Heinlein, Robert A(nson)

Montagu, Elizabeth 1917-. . . . . **NCLC 7**
See also CA 9-12R

Montagu, Mary (Pierrepont) Wortley
  1689-1762 .... **LC 9**
  See also DLB 95, 101

Montagu, W. H.
  See Coleridge, Samuel Taylor

Montague, John (Patrick)
  1929- .... **CLC 13, 46**
  See also CA 9-12R; CANR 9; DLB 40;
  MTCW

Montaigne, Michel (Eyquem) de
  1533-1592 .... **LC 8; DA; WLC**

Montale, Eugenio
  1896-1981 .... **CLC 7, 9, 18; PC 12**
  See also CA 17-20R; 104; CANR 30;
  DLB 114; MTCW

Montesquieu, Charles-Louis de Secondat
  1689-1755 .... **LC 7**

Montgomery, (Robert) Bruce 1921-1978
  See Crispin, Edmund
  See also CA 104

Montgomery, L(ucy) M(aud)
  1874-1942 .... **TCLC 51**
  See also AAYA 12; CA 108; 137; CLR 8;
  DLB 92; JRDA; MAICYA; YABC 1

Montgomery, Marion H., Jr. 1925- .. **CLC 7**
  See also AITN 1; CA 1-4R; CANR 3, 48;
  DLB 6

Montgomery, Max
  See Davenport, Guy (Mattison, Jr.)

Montherlant, Henry (Milon) de
  1896-1972 .... **CLC 8, 19**
  See also CA 85-88; 37-40R; DLB 72;
  MTCW

Monty Python
  See Chapman, Graham; Cleese, John
  (Marwood); Gilliam, Terry (Vance); Idle,
  Eric; Jones, Terence Graham Parry; Palin,
  Michael (Edward)
  See also AAYA 7

Moodie, Susanna (Strickland)
  1803-1885 .... **NCLC 14**
  See also DLB 99

Mooney, Edward 1951-
  See Mooney, Ted
  See also CA 130

Mooney, Ted .... **CLC 25**
  See also Mooney, Edward

Moorcock, Michael (John)
  1939- .... **CLC 5, 27, 58**
  See also CA 45-48; CAAS 5; CANR 2, 17,
  38; DLB 14; MTCW

Moore, Brian
  1921- .... **CLC 1, 3, 5, 7, 8, 19, 32**
  See also CA 1-4R; CANR 1, 25, 42; MTCW

Moore, Edward
  See Muir, Edwin

Moore, George Augustus
  1852-1933 .... **TCLC 7; SSC 19**
  See also CA 104; DLB 10, 18, 57, 135

Moore, Lorrie .... **CLC 39, 45, 68**
  See also Moore, Marie Lorena

Moore, Marianne (Craig)
  1887-1972 .... **CLC 1, 2, 4, 8, 10, 13, 19,
  47; DA; PC 4**
  See also CA 1-4R; 33-36R; CANR 3;
  CDALB 1929-1941; DLB 45; DLBD 7;
  MTCW; SATA 20

Moore, Marie Lorena 1957-
  See Moore, Lorrie
  See also CA 116; CANR 39

Moore, Thomas 1779-1852 .... **NCLC 6**
  See also DLB 96, 144

Morand, Paul 1888-1976 .... **CLC 41**
  See also CA 69-72; DLB 65

Morante, Elsa 1918-1985 .... **CLC 8, 47**
  See also CA 85-88; 117; CANR 35; MTCW

Moravia, Alberto ...... **CLC 2, 7, 11, 27, 46**
  See also Pincherle, Alberto

More, Hannah 1745-1833 .... **NCLC 27**
  See also DLB 107, 109, 116

More, Henry 1614-1687 .... **LC 9**
  See also DLB 126

More, Sir Thomas 1478-1535 .... **LC 10**

Moreas, Jean .... **TCLC 18**
  See also Papadiamantopoulos, Johannes

Morgan, Berry 1919- .... **CLC 6**
  See also CA 49-52; DLB 6

Morgan, Claire
  See Highsmith, (Mary) Patricia

Morgan, Edwin (George) 1920- ..... **CLC 31**
  See also CA 5-8R; CANR 3, 43; DLB 27

Morgan, (George) Frederick
  1922- .... **CLC 23**
  See also CA 17-20R; CANR 21

Morgan, Harriet
  See Mencken, H(enry) L(ouis)

Morgan, Jane
  See Cooper, James Fenimore

Morgan, Janet 1945- .... **CLC 39**
  See also CA 65-68

Morgan, Lady 1776(?)-1859 ...... **NCLC 29**
  See also DLB 116

Morgan, Robin 1941- .... **CLC 2**
  See also CA 69-72; CANR 29; MTCW;
  SATA 80

Morgan, Scott
  See Kuttner, Henry

Morgan, Seth 1949(?)-1990 .... **CLC 65**
  See also CA 132

Morgenstern, Christian
  1871-1914 .... **TCLC 8**
  See also CA 105

Morgenstern, S.
  See Goldman, William (W.)

Moricz, Zsigmond 1879-1942 ..... **TCLC 33**

Morike, Eduard (Friedrich)
  1804-1875 .... **NCLC 10**
  See also DLB 133

Mori Ogai .... **TCLC 14**
  See also Mori Rintaro

Mori Rintaro 1862-1922
  See Mori Ogai
  See also CA 110

Moritz, Karl Philipp 1756-1793 ...... **LC 2**
  See also DLB 94

Morland, Peter Henry
  See Faust, Frederick (Schiller)

Morren, Theophil
  See Hofmannsthal, Hugo von

Morris, Bill 1952- .... **CLC 76**

Morris, Julian
  See West, Morris L(anglo)

Morris, Steveland Judkins 1950(?)-
  See Wonder, Stevie
  See also CA 111

Morris, William 1834-1896 .... **NCLC 4**
  See also CDBLB 1832-1890; DLB 18, 35, 57

Morris, Wright 1910-... **CLC 1, 3, 7, 18, 37**
  See also CA 9-12R; CANR 21; DLB 2;
  DLBY 81; MTCW

Morrison, Chloe Anthony Wofford
  See Morrison, Toni

Morrison, James Douglas 1943-1971
  See Morrison, Jim
  See also CA 73-76; CANR 40

Morrison, Jim .... **CLC 17**
  See also Morrison, James Douglas

Morrison, Toni
  1931- .... **CLC 4, 10, 22, 55, 81, 87;
  BLC; DA**
  See also AAYA 1; BW 2; CA 29-32R;
  CANR 27, 42; CDALB 1968-1988;
  DLB 6, 33, 143; DLBY 81; MTCW;
  SATA 57

Morrison, Van 1945- .... **CLC 21**
  See also CA 116

Mortimer, John (Clifford)
  1923- .... **CLC 28, 43**
  See also CA 13-16R; CANR 21;
  CDBLB 1960 to Present; DLB 13;
  MTCW

Mortimer, Penelope (Ruth) 1918-.... **CLC 5**
  See also CA 57-60; CANR 45

Morton, Anthony
  See Creasey, John

Mosher, Howard Frank 1943-...... **CLC 62**
  See also CA 139

Mosley, Nicholas 1923-........ **CLC 43, 70**
  See also CA 69-72; CANR 41; DLB 14

Moss, Howard
  1922-1987 .... **CLC 7, 14, 45, 50**
  See also CA 1-4R; 123; CANR 1, 44;
  DLB 5

Mossgiel, Rab
  See Burns, Robert

Motion, Andrew (Peter) 1952-...... **CLC 47**
  See also CA 146; DLB 40

Motley, Willard (Francis)
  1909-1965 .... **CLC 18**
  See also BW 1; CA 117; 106; DLB 76, 143

Motoori, Norinaga 1730-1801 .... **NCLC 45**

Mott, Michael (Charles Alston)
  1930- .... **CLC 15, 34**
  See also CA 5-8R; CAAS 7; CANR 7, 29

Moure, Erin 1955- .... **CLC 88**
  See also CA 113; DLB 60

Mowat, Farley (McGill) 1921- . . . . . **CLC 26**
See also AAYA 1; CA 1-4R; CANR 4, 24,
42; CLR 20; DLB 68; JRDA; MAICYA;
MTCW; SATA 3, 55

Moyers, Bill 1934- . . . . **CLC 74**
See also AITN 2; CA 61-64; CANR 31

Mphahlele, Es'kia
See Mphahlele, Ezekiel
See also DLB 125

Mphahlele, Ezekiel 1919- . . . . . **CLC 25; BLC**
See also Mphahlele, Es'kia
See also BW 2; CA 81-84; CANR 26

Mqhayi, S(amuel) E(dward) K(rune Loliwe)
1875-1945 . . . . **TCLC 25; BLC**

Mr. Martin
See Burroughs, William S(eward)

Mrozek, Slawomir 1930- . . . . **CLC 3, 13**
See also CA 13-16R; CAAS 10; CANR 29;
MTCW

Mrs. Belloc-Lowndes
See Lowndes, Marie Adelaide (Belloc)

Mtwa, Percy (?)- . . . . **CLC 47**

Mueller, Lisel 1924- . . . . **CLC 13, 51**
See also CA 93-96; DLB 105

Muir, Edwin 1887-1959 . . . . **TCLC 2**
See also CA 104; DLB 20, 100

Muir, John 1838-1914 . . . . **TCLC 28**

Mujica Lainez, Manuel
1910-1984 . . . . **CLC 31**
See also Lainez, Manuel Mujica
See also CA 81-84; 112; CANR 32; HW

Mukherjee, Bharati 1940- . . . . **CLC 53**
See also BEST 89:2; CA 107; CANR 45;
DLB 60; MTCW

Muldoon, Paul 1951- . . . . **CLC 32, 72**
See also CA 113; 129; DLB 40

Mulisch, Harry 1927- . . . . **CLC 42**
See also CA 9-12R; CANR 6, 26

Mull, Martin 1943- . . . . **CLC 17**
See also CA 105

Mulock, Dinah Maria
See Craik, Dinah Maria (Mulock)

Munford, Robert 1737(?)-1783 . . . . **LC 5**
See also DLB 31

Mungo, Raymond 1946- . . . . **CLC 72**
See also CA 49-52; CANR 2

Munro, Alice
1931- . . . . **CLC 6, 10, 19, 50; SSC 3**
See also AITN 2; CA 33-36R; CANR 33;
DLB 53; MTCW; SATA 29

Munro, H(ector) H(ugh) 1870-1916
See Saki
See also CA 104; 130; CDBLB 1890-1914;
DA; DLB 34; MTCW; WLC

Murasaki, Lady . . . . **CMLC 1**

Murdoch, (Jean) Iris
1919- . . . . . . **CLC 1, 2, 3, 4, 6, 8, 11, 15,
22, 31, 51**
See also CA 13-16R; CANR 8, 43;
CDBLB 1960 to Present; DLB 14;
MTCW

Murnau, Friedrich Wilhelm
See Plumpe, Friedrich Wilhelm

Murphy, Richard 1927- . . . . **CLC 41**
See also CA 29-32R; DLB 40

Murphy, Sylvia 1937- . . . . **CLC 34**
See also CA 121

Murphy, Thomas (Bernard) 1935- . . . **CLC 51**
See also CA 101

Murray, Albert L. 1916- . . . . **CLC 73**
See also BW 2; CA 49-52; CANR 26;
DLB 38

Murray, Les(lie) A(llan) 1938- . . . . . **CLC 40**
See also CA 21-24R; CANR 11, 27

Murry, J. Middleton
See Murry, John Middleton

Murry, John Middleton
1889-1957 . . . . **TCLC 16**
See also CA 118; DLB 149

Musgrave, Susan 1951- . . . . **CLC 13, 54**
See also CA 69-72; CANR 45

Musil, Robert (Edler von)
1880-1942 . . . . **TCLC 12; SSC 18**
See also CA 109; DLB 81, 124

Musset, (Louis Charles) Alfred de
1810-1857 . . . . **NCLC 7**

My Brother's Brother
See Chekhov, Anton (Pavlovich)

Myers, L. H. 1881-1944 . . . . **TCLC 59**
See also DLB 15

Myers, Walter Dean 1937- . . . **CLC 35; BLC**
See also AAYA 4; BW 2; CA 33-36R;
CANR 20, 42; CLR 4, 16, 35; DLB 33;
JRDA; MAICYA; SAAS 2; SATA 41, 71;
SATA-Brief 27

Myers, Walter M.
See Myers, Walter Dean

Myles, Symon
See Follett, Ken(neth Martin)

Nabokov, Vladimir (Vladimirovich)
1899-1977 . . . . . **CLC 1, 2, 3, 6, 8, 11, 15,
23, 44, 46, 64; DA; SSC 11; WLC**
See also CA 5-8R; 69-72; CANR 20;
CDALB 1941-1968; DLB 2; DLBD 3;
DLBY 80, 91; MTCW

Nagai Kafu . . . . **TCLC 51**
See also Nagai Sokichi

Nagai Sokichi 1879-1959
See Nagai Kafu
See also CA 117

Nagy, Laszlo 1925-1978 . . . . **CLC 7**
See also CA 129; 112

Naipaul, Shiva(dhar Srinivasa)
1945-1985 . . . . **CLC 32, 39**
See also CA 110; 112; 116; CANR 33;
DLBY 85; MTCW

Naipaul, V(idiadhar) S(urajprasad)
1932- . . . . **CLC 4, 7, 9, 13, 18, 37**
See also CA 1-4R; CANR 1, 33;
CDBLB 1960 to Present; DLB 125;
DLBY 85; MTCW

Nakos, Lilika 1899(?)- . . . . **CLC 29**

Narayan, R(asipuram) K(rishnaswami)
1906- . . . . **CLC 7, 28, 47**
See also CA 81-84; CANR 33; MTCW;
SATA 62

Nash, (Frediric) Ogden 1902-1971 . . **CLC 23**
See also CA 13-14; 29-32R; CANR 34;
CAP 1; DLB 11; MAICYA; MTCW;
SATA 2, 46

Nathan, Daniel
See Dannay, Frederic

Nathan, George Jean 1882-1958 . . . **TCLC 18**
See also Hatteras, Owen
See also CA 114; DLB 137

Natsume, Kinnosuke 1867-1916
See Natsume, Soseki
See also CA 104

Natsume, Soseki . . . . **TCLC 2, 10**
See also Natsume, Kinnosuke

Natti, (Mary) Lee 1919-
See Kingman, Lee
See also CA 5-8R; CANR 2

Naylor, Gloria
1950- . . . . **CLC 28, 52; BLC; DA**
See also AAYA 6; BW 2; CA 107;
CANR 27; MTCW

Neihardt, John Gneisenau
1881-1973 . . . . **CLC 32**
See also CA 13-14; CAP 1; DLB 9, 54

Nekrasov, Nikolai Alekseevich
1821-1878 . . . . **NCLC 11**

Nelligan, Emile 1879-1941 . . . . **TCLC 14**
See also CA 114; DLB 92

Nelson, Willie 1933- . . . . **CLC 17**
See also CA 107

Nemerov, Howard (Stanley)
1920-1991 . . . . **CLC 2, 6, 9, 36**
See also CA 1-4R; 134; CABS 2; CANR 1,
27; DLB 6; DLBY 83; MTCW

Neruda, Pablo
1904-1973 . . . . . **CLC 1, 2, 5, 7, 9, 28, 62;
DA; HLC; PC 4; WLC**
See also CA 19-20; 45-48; CAP 2; HW;
MTCW

Nerval, Gerard de
1808-1855 . . . . . **NCLC 1; PC 12; SSC 18**

Nervo, (Jose) Amado (Ruiz de)
1870-1919 . . . . **TCLC 11**
See also CA 109; 131; HW

Nessi, Pio Baroja y
See Baroja (y Nessi), Pio

Nestroy, Johann 1801-1862 . . . . . . **NCLC 42**
See also DLB 133

Neufeld, John (Arthur) 1938- . . . . . . **CLC 17**
See also AAYA 11; CA 25-28R; CANR 11,
37; MAICYA; SAAS 3; SATA 6, 81

Neville, Emily Cheney 1919- . . . . **CLC 12**
See also CA 5-8R; CANR 3, 37; JRDA;
MAICYA; SAAS 2; SATA 1

Newbound, Bernard Slade 1930-
See Slade, Bernard
See also CA 81-84; CANR 49

Newby, P(ercy) H(oward)
1918- . . . . **CLC 2, 13**
See also CA 5-8R; CANR 32; DLB 15;
MTCW

Newlove, Donald 1928- . . . . **CLC 6**
See also CA 29-32R; CANR 25

Newlove, John (Herbert) 1938- . . . . . **CLC 14**
See also CA 21-24R; CANR 9, 25

Newman, Charles 1938- . . . . **CLC 2, 8**
See also CA 21-24R

Newman, Edwin (Harold) 1919- . . . . **CLC 14**
See also AITN 1; CA 69-72; CANR 5

Newman, John Henry
1801-1890 . . . . **NCLC 38**
See also DLB 18, 32, 55

Newton, Suzanne 1936- . . . . **CLC 35**
See also CA 41-44R; CANR 14; JRDA;
SATA 5, 77

Nexo, Martin Andersen
1869-1954 . . . . **TCLC 43**

Nezval, Vitezslav 1900-1958 . . . . . . **TCLC 44**
See also CA 123

Ng, Fae Myenne 1957(?)- . . . . **CLC 81**
See also CA 146

Ngema, Mbongeni 1955- . . . . **CLC 57**
See also BW 2; CA 143

Ngugi, James T(hiong'o) . . . . **CLC 3, 7, 13**
See also Ngugi wa Thiong'o

Ngugi wa Thiong'o 1938- . . . . . **CLC 36; BLC**
See also Ngugi, James T(hiong'o)
See also BW 2; CA 81-84; CANR 27;
DLB 125; MTCW

Nichol, B(arrie) P(hillip)
1944-1988 . . . . **CLC 18**
See also CA 53-56; DLB 53; SATA 66

Nichols, John (Treadwell) 1940- . . . . **CLC 38**
See also CA 9-12R; CAAS 2; CANR 6;
DLBY 82

Nichols, Leigh
See Koontz, Dean R(ay)

Nichols, Peter (Richard)
1927- . . . . **CLC 5, 36, 65**
See also CA 104; CANR 33; DLB 13;
MTCW

Nicolas, F. R. E.
See Freeling, Nicolas

Niedecker, Lorine 1903-1970 . . . . **CLC 10, 42**
See also CA 25-28; CAP 2; DLB 48

Nietzsche, Friedrich (Wilhelm)
1844-1900 . . . . **TCLC 10, 18, 55**
See also CA 107; 121; DLB 129

Nievo, Ippolito 1831-1861 . . . . **NCLC 22**

Nightingale, Anne Redmon 1943-
See Redmon, Anne
See also CA 103

Nik. T. O.
See Annensky, Innokenty Fyodorovich

Nin, Anais
1903-1977 . . . . . . **CLC 1, 4, 8, 11, 14, 60;
SSC 10**
See also AITN 2; CA 13-16R; 69-72;
CANR 22; DLB 2, 4, 152; MTCW

Nissenson, Hugh 1933- . . . . **CLC 4, 9**
See also CA 17-20R; CANR 27; DLB 28

Niven, Larry . . . . **CLC 8**
See also Niven, Laurence Van Cott
See also DLB 8

Niven, Laurence Van Cott 1938-
See Niven, Larry
See also CA 21-24R; CAAS 12; CANR 14,
44; MTCW

Nixon, Agnes Eckhardt 1927- . . . . . . **CLC 21**
See also CA 110

Nizan, Paul 1905-1940 . . . . **TCLC 40**
See also DLB 72

Nkosi, Lewis 1936- . . . . **CLC 45; BLC**
See also BW 1; CA 65-68; CANR 27

Nodier, (Jean) Charles (Emmanuel)
1780-1844 . . . . **NCLC 19**
See also DLB 119

Nolan, Christopher 1965- . . . . **CLC 58**
See also CA 111

Norden, Charles
See Durrell, Lawrence (George)

Nordhoff, Charles (Bernard)
1887-1947 . . . . **TCLC 23**
See also CA 108; DLB 9; SATA 23

Norfolk, Lawrence 1963- . . . . **CLC 76**
See also CA 144

Norman, Marsha 1947- . . . . **CLC 28**
See also CA 105; CABS 3; CANR 41;
DLBY 84

Norris, Benjamin Franklin, Jr.
1870-1902 . . . . **TCLC 24**
See also Norris, Frank
See also CA 110

Norris, Frank
See Norris, Benjamin Franklin, Jr.
See also CDALB 1865-1917; DLB 12, 71

Norris, Leslie 1921- . . . . **CLC 14**
See also CA 11-12; CANR 14; CAP 1;
DLB 27

North, Andrew
See Norton, Andre

North, Anthony
See Koontz, Dean R(ay)

North, Captain George
See Stevenson, Robert Louis (Balfour)

North, Milou
See Erdrich, Louise

Northrup, B. A.
See Hubbard, L(afayette) Ron(ald)

North Staffs
See Hulme, T(homas) E(rnest)

Norton, Alice Mary
See Norton, Andre
See also MAICYA; SATA 1, 43

Norton, Andre 1912- . . . . **CLC 12**
See also Norton, Alice Mary
See also AAYA 14; CA 1-4R; CANR 2, 31;
DLB 8, 52; JRDA; MTCW

Norton, Caroline 1808-1877 . . . . . . **NCLC 47**
See also DLB 21

Norway, Nevil Shute 1899-1960
See Shute, Nevil
See also CA 102; 93-96

Norwid, Cyprian Kamil
1821-1883 . . . . **NCLC 17**

Nosille, Nabrah
See Ellison, Harlan (Jay)

Nossack, Hans Erich 1901-1978 . . . . . **CLC 6**
See also CA 93-96; 85-88; DLB 69

Nostradamus 1503-1566 . . . . **LC 27**

Nosu, Chuji
See Ozu, Yasujiro

Notenburg, Eleanora (Genrikhovna) von
See Guro, Elena

Nova, Craig 1945- . . . . **CLC 7, 31**
See also CA 45-48; CANR 2

Novak, Joseph
See Kosinski, Jerzy (Nikodem)

Novalis 1772-1801 . . . . **NCLC 13**
See also DLB 90

Nowlan, Alden (Albert) 1933-1983 . . **CLC 15**
See also CA 9-12R; CANR 5; DLB 53

Noyes, Alfred 1880-1958 . . . . **TCLC 7**
See also CA 104; DLB 20

Nunn, Kem 19(?)- . . . . **CLC 34**

Nye, Robert 1939- . . . . **CLC 13, 42**
See also CA 33-36R; CANR 29; DLB 14;
MTCW; SATA 6

Nyro, Laura 1947- . . . . **CLC 17**

Oates, Joyce Carol
1938- . . . . . . **CLC 1, 2, 3, 6, 9, 11, 15, 19,
33, 52; DA; SSC 6; WLC**
See also AITN 1; BEST 89:2; CA 5-8R;
CANR 25, 45; CDALB 1968-1988;
DLB 2, 5, 130; DLBY 81; MTCW

O'Brien, Darcy 1939- . . . . **CLC 11**
See also CA 21-24R; CANR 8

O'Brien, E. G.
See Clarke, Arthur C(harles)

O'Brien, Edna
1936- . . . **CLC 3, 5, 8, 13, 36, 65; SSC 10**
See also CA 1-4R; CANR 6, 41;
CDBLB 1960 to Present; DLB 14;
MTCW

O'Brien, Fitz-James 1828-1862 . . . **NCLC 21**
See also DLB 74

O'Brien, Flann . . . . **CLC 1, 4, 5, 7, 10, 47**
See also O Nuallain, Brian

O'Brien, Richard 1942- . . . . **CLC 17**
See also CA 124

O'Brien, Tim 1946- . . . . **CLC 7, 19, 40**
See also CA 85-88; CANR 40; DLB 152;
DLBD 9; DLBY 80

Obstfelder, Sigbjoern 1866-1900 . . . **TCLC 23**
See also CA 123

O'Casey, Sean
1880-1964 . . . . . . **CLC 1, 5, 9, 11, 15, 88**
See also CA 89-92; CDBLB 1914-1945;
DLB 10; MTCW

O'Cathasaigh, Sean
See O'Casey, Sean

Ochs, Phil 1940-1976 . . . . **CLC 17**
See also CA 65-68

O'Connor, Edwin (Greene)
1918-1968 . . . . **CLC 14**
See also CA 93-96; 25-28R

O'Connor, (Mary) Flannery
1925-1964 . . . . **CLC 1, 2, 3, 6, 10, 13, 15,
21, 66; DA; SSC 1; WLC**
See also AAYA 7; CA 1-4R; CANR 3, 41;
CDALB 1941-1968; DLB 2, 152;
DLBD 12; DLBY 80; MTCW

O'Connor, Frank . . . . **CLC 23; SSC 5**
See also O'Donovan, Michael John

Page, P(atricia) K(athleen)
1916- .... **CLC 7, 18; PC 12**
See also CA 53-56; CANR 4, 22; DLB 68;
MTCW

Paget, Violet 1856-1935
See Lee, Vernon
See also CA 104

Paget-Lowe, Henry
See Lovecraft, H(oward) P(hillips)

Paglia, Camille (Anna) 1947-....... **CLC 68**
See also CA 140

Paige, Richard
See Koontz, Dean R(ay)

Pakenham, Antonia
See Fraser, (Lady) Antonia (Pakenham)

Palamas, Kostes 1859-1943 .... **TCLC 5**
See also CA 105

Palazzeschi, Aldo 1885-1974 ...... **CLC 11**
See also CA 89-92; 53-56; DLB 114

Paley, Grace 1922-.... **CLC 4, 6, 37; SSC 8**
See also CA 25-28R; CANR 13, 46;
DLB 28; MTCW

Palin, Michael (Edward) 1943-..... **CLC 21**
See also Monty Python
See also CA 107; CANR 35; SATA 67

Palliser, Charles 1947-............ **CLC 65**
See also CA 136

Palma, Ricardo 1833-1919........ **TCLC 29**

Pancake, Breece Dexter 1952-1979
See Pancake, Breece D'J
See also CA 123; 109

Pancake, Breece D'J............... **CLC 29**
See also Pancake, Breece Dexter
See also DLB 130

Panko, Rudy
See Gogol, Nikolai (Vasilyevich)

Papadiamantis, Alexandros
1851-1911 .... **TCLC 29**

Papadiamantopoulos, Johannes 1856-1910
See Moreas, Jean
See also CA 117

Papini, Giovanni 1881-1956....... **TCLC 22**
See also CA 121

Paracelsus 1493-1541............. **LC 14**

Parasol, Peter
See Stevens, Wallace

Parfenie, Maria
See Codrescu, Andrei

Parini, Jay (Lee) 1948-........... **CLC 54**
See also CA 97-100; CAAS 16; CANR 32

Park, Jordan
See Kornbluth, C(yril) M.; Pohl, Frederik

Parker, Bert
See Ellison, Harlan (Jay)

Parker, Dorothy (Rothschild)
1893-1967 .... **CLC 15, 68; SSC 2**
See also CA 19-20; 25-28R; CAP 2;
DLB 11, 45, 86; MTCW

Parker, Robert B(rown) 1932-...... **CLC 27**
See also BEST 89:4; CA 49-52; CANR 1,
26; MTCW

Parkin, Frank 1940-.............. **CLC 43**
See also CA 147

Parkman, Francis, Jr.
1823-1893 .... **NCLC 12**
See also DLB 1, 30

Parks, Gordon (Alexander Buchanan)
1912-................ **CLC 1, 16; BLC**
See also AITN 2; BW 2; CA 41-44R;
CANR 26; DLB 33; SATA 8

Parnell, Thomas 1679-1718......... **LC 3**
See also DLB 94

Parra, Nicanor 1914-........ **CLC 2; HLC**
See also CA 85-88; CANR 32; HW; MTCW

Parrish, Mary Frances
See Fisher, M(ary) F(rances) K(ennedy)

Parson
See Coleridge, Samuel Taylor

Parson Lot
See Kingsley, Charles

Partridge, Anthony
See Oppenheim, E(dward) Phillips

Pascoli, Giovanni 1855-1912 ...... **TCLC 45**

Pasolini, Pier Paolo
1922-1975 .... **CLC 20, 37**
See also CA 93-96; 61-64; DLB 128;
MTCW

Pasquini
See Silone, Ignazio

Pastan, Linda (Olenik) 1932- ...... **CLC 27**
See also CA 61-64; CANR 18, 40; DLB 5

Pasternak, Boris (Leonidovich)
1890-1960 ...... **CLC 7, 10, 18, 63; DA;
PC 6; WLC**
See also CA 127; 116; MTCW

Patchen, Kenneth 1911-1972 ... **CLC 1, 2, 18**
See also CA 1-4R; 33-36R; CANR 3, 35;
DLB 16, 48; MTCW

Pater, Walter (Horatio)
1839-1894 .... **NCLC 7**
See also CDBLB 1832-1890; DLB 57

Paterson, A(ndrew) B(arton)
1864-1941 .... **TCLC 32**

Paterson, Katherine (Womeldorf)
1932- .... **CLC 12, 30**
See also AAYA 1; CA 21-24R; CANR 28;
CLR 7; DLB 52; JRDA; MAICYA;
MTCW; SATA 13, 53

Patmore, Coventry Kersey Dighton
1823-1896 .... **NCLC 9**
See also DLB 35, 98

Paton, Alan (Stewart)
1903-1988 ...... **CLC 4, 10, 25, 55; DA;
WLC**
See also CA 13-16; 125; CANR 22;
MTCW; SATA 11; SATA-Obit 56

Paton Walsh, Gillian 1937-
See Walsh, Jill Paton
See also CANR 38; JRDA; MAICYA;
SAAS 3; SATA 4, 72

Paulding, James Kirke 1778-1860.. **NCLC 2**
See also DLB 3, 59, 74

Paulin, Thomas Neilson 1949-
See Paulin, Tom
See also CA 123; 128

Paulin, Tom.................... **CLC 37**
See also Paulin, Thomas Neilson
See also DLB 40

Paustovsky, Konstantin (Georgievich)
1892-1968 .... **CLC 40**
See also CA 93-96; 25-28R

Pavese, Cesare
1908-1950 ..... **TCLC 3; PC 12; SSC 19**
See also CA 104; DLB 128

Pavic, Milorad 1929-............ **CLC 60**
See also CA 136

Payne, Alan
See Jakes, John (William)

Paz, Gil
See Lugones, Leopoldo

Paz, Octavio
1914- .... **CLC 3, 4, 6, 10, 19, 51, 65;
DA; HLC; PC 1; WLC**
See also CA 73-76; CANR 32; DLBY 90;
HW; MTCW

Peacock, Molly 1947-............. **CLC 60**
See also CA 103; CAAS 21; DLB 120

Peacock, Thomas Love
1785-1866 .... **NCLC 22**
See also DLB 96, 116

Peake, Mervyn 1911-1968....... **CLC 7, 54**
See also CA 5-8R; 25-28R; CANR 3;
DLB 15; MTCW; SATA 23

Pearce, Philippa .... **CLC 21**
See also Christie, (Ann) Philippa
See also CLR 9; MAICYA; SATA 1, 67

Pearl, Eric
See Elman, Richard

Pearson, T(homas) R(eid) 1956- .... **CLC 39**
See also CA 120; 130

Peck, Dale 1968(?)- .... **CLC 81**

Peck, John 1941- .... **CLC 3**
See also CA 49-52; CANR 3

Peck, Richard (Wayne) 1934-...... **CLC 21**
See also AAYA 1; CA 85-88; CANR 19,
38; CLR 15; JRDA; MAICYA; SAAS 2;
SATA 18, 55

Peck, Robert Newton 1928-.... **CLC 17; DA**
See also AAYA 3; CA 81-84; CANR 31;
JRDA; MAICYA; SAAS 1; SATA 21, 62

Peckinpah, (David) Sam(uel)
1925-1984 .... **CLC 20**
See also CA 109; 114

Pedersen, Knut 1859-1952
See Hamsun, Knut
See also CA 104; 119; MTCW

Peeslake, Gaffer
See Durrell, Lawrence (George)

Peguy, Charles Pierre
1873-1914 .... **TCLC 10**
See also CA 107

Pena, Ramon del Valle y
See Valle-Inclan, Ramon (Maria) del

Pendennis, Arthur Esquir
See Thackeray, William Makepeace

Penn, William 1644-1718.......... **LC 25**
See also DLB 24

Pepys, Samuel
1633-1703 .... **LC 11; DA; WLC**
See also CDBLB 1660-1789; DLB 101

Poe, Edgar Allan
    1809-1849 ..... **NCLC 1, 16; DA; PC 1;**
                                    SSC 1; WLC
    See also AAYA 14; CDALB 1640-1865;
    DLB 3, 59, 73, 74; SATA 23

Poet of Titchfield Street, The
    See Pound, Ezra (Weston Loomis)

Pohl, Frederik 1919- .... **CLC 18**
    See also CA 61-64; CAAS 1; CANR 11, 37;
    DLB 8; MTCW; SATA 24

Poirier, Louis 1910-
    See Gracq, Julien
    See also CA 122; 126

Poitier, Sidney 1927- .... **CLC 26**
    See also BW 1; CA 117

Polanski, Roman 1933- .... **CLC 16**
    See also CA 77-80

Poliakoff, Stephen 1952- .... **CLC 38**
    See also CA 106; DLB 13

Police, The
    See Copeland, Stewart (Armstrong);
    Summers, Andrew James; Sumner,
    Gordon Matthew

Polidori, John William
    1795-1821 .... **NCLC 51**
    See also DLB 116

Pollitt, Katha 1949- .... **CLC 28**
    See also CA 120; 122; MTCW

Pollock, (Mary) Sharon 1936-...... **CLC 50**
    See also CA 141; DLB 60

Polo, Marco 1254-1324 .... **CMLC 15**

Pomerance, Bernard 1940-........ **CLC 13**
    See also CA 101; CANR 49

Ponge, Francis (Jean Gaston Alfred)
    1899-1988 .... **CLC 6, 18**
    See also CA 85-88; 126; CANR 40

Pontoppidan, Henrik 1857-1943 ... **TCLC 29**

Poole, Josephine .... **CLC 17**
    See also Helyar, Jane Penelope Josephine
    See also SAAS 2; SATA 5

Popa, Vasko 1922-................. **CLC 19**
    See also CA 112

Pope, Alexander
    1688-1744 .... **LC 3; DA; WLC**
    See also CDBLB 1660-1789; DLB 95, 101

Porter, Connie (Rose) 1959(?)- ..... **CLC 70**
    See also BW 2; CA 142; SATA 81

Porter, Gene(va Grace) Stratton
    1863(?)-1924 .... **TCLC 21**
    See also CA 112

Porter, Katherine Anne
    1890-1980 ...... **CLC 1, 3, 7, 10, 13, 15,**
                                    27; DA; SSC 4
    See also AITN 2; CA 1-4R; 101; CANR 1;
    DLB 4, 9, 102; DLBD 12; DLBY 80;
    MTCW; SATA 39; SATA-Obit 23

Porter, Peter (Neville Frederick)
    1929- ....**CLC 5, 13, 33**
    See also CA 85-88; DLB 40

Porter, William Sydney 1862-1910
    See Henry, O.
    See also CA 104; 131; CDALB 1865-1917;
    DA; DLB 12, 78, 79; MTCW; YABC 2

Portillo (y Pacheco), Jose Lopez
    See Lopez Portillo (y Pacheco), Jose

Post, Melville Davisson
    1869-1930 .... **TCLC 39**
    See also CA 110

Potok, Chaim 1929- .... **CLC 2, 7, 14, 26**
    See also AITN 1, 2; CA 17-20R; CANR 19,
    35; DLB 28, 152; MTCW; SATA 33

Potter, Beatrice
    See Webb, (Martha) Beatrice (Potter)
    See also MAICYA

Potter, Dennis (Christopher George)
    1935-1994 .... **CLC 58, 86**
    See also CA 107; 145; CANR 33; MTCW

Pound, Ezra (Weston Loomis)
    1885-1972 ...... **CLC 1, 2, 3, 4, 5, 7, 10,**
        13, 18, 34, 48, 50; DA; PC 4; WLC
    See also CA 5-8R; 37-40R; CANR 40;
    CDALB 1917-1929; DLB 4, 45, 63;
    MTCW

Povod, Reinaldo 1959-1994 .... **CLC 44**
    See also CA 136; 146

Powell, Adam Clayton, Jr.
    1908-1972 .... **CLC 89; BLC**
    See also BW 1; CA 102; 33-36R

Powell, Anthony (Dymoke)
    1905- .... **CLC 1, 3, 7, 9, 10, 31**
    See also CA 1-4R; CANR 1, 32;
    CDBLB 1945-1960; DLB 15; MTCW

Powell, Dawn 1897-1965 .... **CLC 66**
    See also CA 5-8R

Powell, Padgett 1952-............. **CLC 34**
    See also CA 126

Powers, J(ames) F(arl)
    1917- .... **CLC 1, 4, 8, 57; SSC 4**
    See also CA 1-4R; CANR 2; DLB 130;
    MTCW

Powers, John J(ames) 1945-
    See Powers, John R.
    See also CA 69-72

Powers, John R. .... **CLC 66**
    See also Powers, John J(ames)

Pownall, David 1938-............. **CLC 10**
    See also CA 89-92; CAAS 18; CANR 49;
    DLB 14

Powys, John Cowper
    1872-1963 .... **CLC 7, 9, 15, 46**
    See also CA 85-88; DLB 15; MTCW

Powys, T(heodore) F(rancis)
    1875-1953 .... **TCLC 9**
    See also CA 106; DLB 36

Prager, Emily 1952- .... **CLC 56**

Pratt, E(dwin) J(ohn)
    1883(?)-1964 .... **CLC 19**
    See also CA 141; 93-96; DLB 92

Premchand....................... **TCLC 21**
    See also Srivastava, Dhanpat Rai

Preussler, Otfried 1923-........... **CLC 17**
    See also CA 77-80; SATA 24

Prevert, Jacques (Henri Marie)
    1900-1977 .... **CLC 15**
    See also CA 77-80; 69-72; CANR 29;
    MTCW; SATA-Obit 30

Prevost, Abbe (Antoine Francois)
    1697-1763 .... **LC 1**

Price, (Edward) Reynolds
    1933- .... **CLC 3, 6, 13, 43, 50, 63**
    See also CA 1-4R; CANR 1, 37; DLB 2

Price, Richard 1949- .... **CLC 6, 12**
    See also CA 49-52; CANR 3; DLBY 81

Prichard, Katharine Susannah
    1883-1969 .... **CLC 46**
    See also CA 11-12; CANR 33; CAP 1;
    MTCW; SATA 66

Priestley, J(ohn) B(oynton)
    1894-1984 ....**CLC 2, 5, 9, 34**
    See also CA 9-12R; 113; CANR 33;
    CDBLB 1914-1945; DLB 10, 34, 77, 100,
    139; DLBY 84; MTCW

Prince 1958(?)- .... **CLC 35**

Prince, F(rank) T(empleton) 1912- .. **CLC 22**
    See also CA 101; CANR 43; DLB 20

Prince Kropotkin
    See Kropotkin, Peter (Aleksieevich)

Prior, Matthew 1664-1721.......... **LC 4**
    See also DLB 95

Pritchard, William H(arrison)
    1932-....................... **CLC 34**
    See also CA 65-68; CANR 23; DLB 111

Pritchett, V(ictor) S(awdon)
    1900- .... **CLC 5, 13, 15, 41; SSC 14**
    See also CA 61-64; CANR 31; DLB 15,
    139; MTCW

Private 19022
    See Manning, Frederic

Probst, Mark 1925- .... **CLC 59**
    See also CA 130

Prokosch, Frederic 1908-1989.... **CLC 4, 48**
    See also CA 73-76; 128; DLB 48

Prophet, The
    See Dreiser, Theodore (Herman Albert)

Prose, Francine 1947-............. **CLC 45**
    See also CA 109; 112; CANR 46

Proudhon
    See Cunha, Euclides (Rodrigues Pimenta) da

Proulx, E. Annie 1935- .... **CLC 81**

Proust, (Valentin-Louis-George-Eugene-)
    Marcel
    1871-1922 ... **TCLC 7, 13, 33; DA; WLC**
    See also CA 104; 120; DLB 65; MTCW

Prowler, Harley
    See Masters, Edgar Lee

Prus, Boleslaw 1845-1912 .... **TCLC 48**

Pryor, Richard (Franklin Lenox Thomas)
    1940-....................... **CLC 26**
    See also CA 122

Przybyszewski, Stanislaw
    1868-1927 .... **TCLC 36**
    See also DLB 66

Pteleon
    See Grieve, C(hristopher) M(urray)

Puckett, Lute
    See Masters, Edgar Lee

Puig, Manuel
    1932-1990 ... **CLC 3, 5, 10, 28, 65; HLC**
    See also CA 45-48; CANR 2, 32; DLB 113;
    HW; MTCW

Purdy, Al(fred Wellington)
1918- . . . . **CLC 3, 6, 14, 50**
See also CA 81-84; CAAS 17; CANR 42;
DLB 88

Purdy, James (Amos)
1923- . . . . **CLC 2, 4, 10, 28, 52**
See also CA 33-36R; CAAS 1; CANR 19;
DLB 2; MTCW

Pure, Simon
See Swinnerton, Frank Arthur

Pushkin, Alexander (Sergeyevich)
1799-1837 . . . . **NCLC 3, 27; DA; PC 10;**
WLC
See also SATA 61

P'u Sung-ling 1640-1715 . . . . **LC 3**

Putnam, Arthur Lee
See Alger, Horatio, Jr.

Puzo, Mario 1920- . . . . **CLC 1, 2, 6, 36**
See also CA 65-68; CANR 4, 42; DLB 6;
MTCW

Pym, Barbara (Mary Crampton)
1913-1980 . . . . **CLC 13, 19, 37**
See also CA 13-14; 97-100; CANR 13, 34;
CAP 1; DLB 14; DLBY 87; MTCW

Pynchon, Thomas (Ruggles, Jr.)
1937- . . . . . **CLC 2, 3, 6, 9, 11, 18, 33, 62,**
72; DA; SSC 14; WLC
See also BEST 90:2; CA 17-20R; CANR 22,
46; DLB 2; MTCW

Qian Zhongshu
See Ch'ien Chung-shu

Qroll
See Dagerman, Stig (Halvard)

Quarrington, Paul (Lewis) 1953- . . . . **CLC 65**
See also CA 129

Quasimodo, Salvatore 1901-1968 . . . **CLC 10**
See also CA 13-16; 25-28R; CAP 1;
DLB 114; MTCW

Queen, Ellery . . . . **CLC 3, 11**
See also Dannay, Frederic; Davidson,
Avram; Lee, Manfred B(ennington);
Sturgeon, Theodore (Hamilton); Vance,
John Holbrook

Queen, Ellery, Jr.
See Dannay, Frederic; Lee, Manfred
B(ennington)

Queneau, Raymond
1903-1976 . . . . **CLC 2, 5, 10, 42**
See also CA 77-80; 69-72; CANR 32;
DLB 72; MTCW

Quevedo, Francisco de 1580-1645 . . . . **LC 23**

Quiller-Couch, Arthur Thomas
1863-1944 . . . . **TCLC 53**
See also CA 118; DLB 135, 153

Quin, Ann (Marie) 1936-1973 . . . . . . **CLC 6**
See also CA 9-12R; 45-48; DLB 14

Quinn, Martin
See Smith, Martin Cruz

Quinn, Simon
See Smith, Martin Cruz

Quiroga, Horacio (Sylvestre)
1878-1937 . . . . **TCLC 20; HLC**
See also CA 117; 131; HW; MTCW

Quoirez, Francoise 1935- . . . . **CLC 9**
See also Sagan, Francoise
See also CA 49-52; CANR 6, 39; MTCW

Raabe, Wilhelm 1831-1910 . . . . **TCLC 45**
See also DLB 129

Rabe, David (William) 1940- . . . **CLC 4, 8, 33**
See also CA 85-88; CABS 3; DLB 7

Rabelais, Francois
1483-1553 . . . . **LC 5; DA; WLC**

Rabinovitch, Sholem 1859-1916
See Aleichem, Sholom
See also CA 104

Racine, Jean 1639-1699 . . . . **LC 28**

Radcliffe, Ann (Ward) 1764-1823 . . **NCLC 6**
See also DLB 39

Radiguet, Raymond 1903-1923 . . . . **TCLC 29**
See also DLB 65

Radnoti, Miklos 1909-1944 . . . . **TCLC 16**
See also CA 118

Rado, James 1939- . . . . **CLC 17**
See also CA 105

Radvanyi, Netty 1900-1983
See Seghers, Anna
See also CA 85-88; 110

Rae, Ben
See Griffiths, Trevor

Raeburn, John (Hay) 1941- . . . . **CLC 34**
See also CA 57-60

Ragni, Gerome 1942-1991 . . . . **CLC 17**
See also CA 105; 134

Rahv, Philip 1908-1973 . . . . **CLC 24**
See also Greenberg, Ivan
See also DLB 137

Raine, Craig 1944- . . . . **CLC 32**
See also CA 108; CANR 29; DLB 40

Raine, Kathleen (Jessie) 1908- . . . **CLC 7, 45**
See also CA 85-88; CANR 46; DLB 20;
MTCW

Rainis, Janis 1865-1929 . . . . **TCLC 29**

Rakosi, Carl . . . . **CLC 47**
See also Rawley, Callman
See also CAAS 5

Raleigh, Richard
See Lovecraft, H(oward) P(hillips)

Rallentando, H. P.
See Sayers, Dorothy L(eigh)

Ramal, Walter
See de la Mare, Walter (John)

Ramon, Juan
See Jimenez (Mantecon), Juan Ramon

Ramos, Graciliano 1892-1953 . . . . . **TCLC 32**

Rampersad, Arnold 1941- . . . . **CLC 44**
See also BW 2; CA 127; 133; DLB 111

Rampling, Anne
See Rice, Anne

Ramsay, Allan 1684(?)-1758 . . . . **LC 29**
See also DLB 95

Ramuz, Charles-Ferdinand
1878-1947 . . . . **TCLC 33**

Rand, Ayn
1905-1982 . . . . . . **CLC 3, 30, 44, 79; DA;**
WLC
See also AAYA 10; CA 13-16R; 105;
CANR 27; MTCW

Randall, Dudley (Felker)
1914- . . . . **CLC 1; BLC**
See also BW 1; CA 25-28R; CANR 23;
DLB 41

Randall, Robert
See Silverberg, Robert

Ranger, Ken
See Creasey, John

Ransom, John Crowe
1888-1974 . . . . **CLC 2, 4, 5, 11, 24**
See also CA 5-8R; 49-52; CANR 6, 34;
DLB 45, 63; MTCW

Rao, Raja 1909- . . . . **CLC 25, 56**
See also CA 73-76; MTCW

Raphael, Frederic (Michael)
1931- . . . . **CLC 2, 14**
See also CA 1-4R; CANR 1; DLB 14

Ratcliffe, James P.
See Mencken, H(enry) L(ouis)

Rathbone, Julian 1935- . . . . **CLC 41**
See also CA 101; CANR 34

Rattigan, Terence (Mervyn)
1911-1977 . . . . **CLC 7**
See also CA 85-88; 73-76;
CDBLB 1945-1960; DLB 13; MTCW

Ratushinskaya, Irina 1954- . . . . **CLC 54**
See also CA 129

Raven, Simon (Arthur Noel)
1927- . . . . **CLC 14**
See also CA 81-84

Rawley, Callman 1903-
See Rakosi, Carl
See also CA 21-24R; CANR 12, 32

Rawlings, Marjorie Kinnan
1896-1953 . . . . **TCLC 4**
See also CA 104; 137; DLB 9, 22, 102;
JRDA; MAICYA; YABC 1

Ray, Satyajit 1921-1992 . . . . **CLC 16, 76**
See also CA 114; 137

Read, Herbert Edward 1893-1968 . . . . **CLC 4**
See also CA 85-88; 25-28R; DLB 20, 149

Read, Piers Paul 1941- . . . . . . **CLC 4, 10, 25**
See also CA 21-24R; CANR 38; DLB 14;
SATA 21

Reade, Charles 1814-1884 . . . . **NCLC 2**
See also DLB 21

Reade, Hamish
See Gray, Simon (James Holliday)

Reading, Peter 1946- . . . . **CLC 47**
See also CA 103; CANR 46; DLB 40

Reaney, James 1926- . . . . **CLC 13**
See also CA 41-44R; CAAS 15; CANR 42;
DLB 68; SATA 43

Rebreanu, Liviu 1885-1944 . . . . **TCLC 28**

Rechy, John (Francisco)
1934- . . . . **CLC 1, 7, 14, 18; HLC**
See also CA 5-8R; CAAS 4; CANR 6, 32;
DLB 122; DLBY 82; HW

Redcam, Tom 1870-1933 . . . . **TCLC 25**

Roth, Joseph 1894-1939 . . . . **TCLC 33**
See also DLB 85

Roth, Philip (Milton)
1933- . . . . . . **CLC 1, 2, 3, 4, 6, 9, 15, 22,
31, 47, 66, 86; DA; WLC**
See also BEST 90:3; CA 1-4R; CANR 1, 22,
36; CDALB 1968-1988; DLB 2, 28;
DLBY 82; MTCW

Rothenberg, Jerome 1931- . . . . **CLC 6, 57**
See also CA 45-48; CANR 1; DLB 5

Roumain, Jacques (Jean Baptiste)
1907-1944 . . . . **TCLC 19; BLC**
See also BW 1; CA 117; 125

Rourke, Constance (Mayfield)
1885-1941 . . . . **TCLC 12**
See also CA 107; YABC 1

Rousseau, Jean-Baptiste 1671-1741 . . . **LC 9**

Rousseau, Jean-Jacques
1712-1778 . . . . **LC 14; DA; WLC**

Roussel, Raymond 1877-1933 . . . . . **TCLC 20**
See also CA 117

Rovit, Earl (Herbert) 1927- . . . . **CLC 7**
See also CA 5-8R; CANR 12

Rowe, Nicholas 1674-1718 . . . . **LC 8**
See also DLB 84

Rowley, Ames Dorrance
See Lovecraft, H(oward) P(hillips)

Rowson, Susanna Haswell
1762(?)-1824 . . . . **NCLC 5**
See also DLB 37

Roy, Gabrielle 1909-1983 . . . . . . **CLC 10, 14**
See also CA 53-56; 110; CANR 5; DLB 68;
MTCW

Rozewicz, Tadeusz 1921- . . . . **CLC 9, 23**
See also CA 108; CANR 36; MTCW

Ruark, Gibbons 1941- . . . . **CLC 3**
See also CA 33-36R; CANR 14, 31;
DLB 120

Rubens, Bernice (Ruth) 1923- . . . **CLC 19, 31**
See also CA 25-28R; CANR 33; DLB 14;
MTCW

Rudkin, (James) David 1936- . . . . . . **CLC 14**
See also CA 89-92; DLB 13

Rudnik, Raphael 1933- . . . . **CLC 7**
See also CA 29-32R

Ruffian, M.
See Hasek, Jaroslav (Matej Frantisek)

Ruiz, Jose Martinez . . . . **CLC 11**
See also Martinez Ruiz, Jose

Rukeyser, Muriel
1913-1980 . . . . **CLC 6, 10, 15, 27; PC 12**
See also CA 5-8R; 93-96; CANR 26;
DLB 48; MTCW; SATA-Obit 22

Rule, Jane (Vance) 1931- . . . . **CLC 27**
See also CA 25-28R; CAAS 18; CANR 12;
DLB 60

Rulfo, Juan 1918-1986 . . . . **CLC 8, 80; HLC**
See also CA 85-88; 118; CANR 26;
DLB 113; HW; MTCW

Runeberg, Johan 1804-1877 . . . . . . **NCLC 41**

Runyon, (Alfred) Damon
1884(?)-1946 . . . . **TCLC 10**
See also CA 107; DLB 11, 86

Rush, Norman 1933- . . . . **CLC 44**
See also CA 121; 126

Rushdie, (Ahmed) Salman
1947- . . . . **CLC 23, 31, 55**
See also BEST 89:3; CA 108; 111;
CANR 33; MTCW

Rushforth, Peter (Scott) 1945- . . . . . **CLC 19**
See also CA 101

Ruskin, John 1819-1900 . . . . **TCLC 20**
See also CA 114; 129; CDBLB 1832-1890;
DLB 55; SATA 24

Russ, Joanna 1937- . . . . **CLC 15**
See also CA 25-28R; CANR 11, 31; DLB 8;
MTCW

Russell, George William 1867-1935
See A. E.
See also CA 104; CDBLB 1890-1914

Russell, (Henry) Ken(neth Alfred)
1927- . . . . **CLC 16**
See also CA 105

Russell, Willy 1947- . . . . **CLC 60**

Rutherford, Mark . . . . **TCLC 25**
See also White, William Hale
See also DLB 18

Ruyslinck, Ward 1929- . . . . **CLC 14**
See also Belser, Reimond Karel Maria de

Ryan, Cornelius (John) 1920-1974 . . . **CLC 7**
See also CA 69-72; 53-56; CANR 38

Ryan, Michael 1946- . . . . **CLC 65**
See also CA 49-52; DLBY 82

Rybakov, Anatoli (Naumovich)
1911- . . . . **CLC 23, 53**
See also CA 126; 135; SATA 79

Ryder, Jonathan
See Ludlum, Robert

Ryga, George 1932-1987 . . . . **CLC 14**
See also CA 101; 124; CANR 43; DLB 60

S. S.
See Sassoon, Siegfried (Lorraine)

Saba, Umberto 1883-1957 . . . . **TCLC 33**
See also CA 144; DLB 114

Sabatini, Rafael 1875-1950 . . . . **TCLC 47**

Sabato, Ernesto (R.)
1911- . . . . **CLC 10, 23; HLC**
See also CA 97-100; CANR 32; DLB 145;
HW; MTCW

Sacastru, Martin
See Bioy Casares, Adolfo

Sacher-Masoch, Leopold von
1836(?)-1895 . . . . **NCLC 31**

Sachs, Marilyn (Stickle) 1927- . . . . . **CLC 35**
See also AAYA 2; CA 17-20R; CANR 13,
47; CLR 2; JRDA; MAICYA; SAAS 2;
SATA 3, 68

Sachs, Nelly 1891-1970 . . . . **CLC 14**
See also CA 17-18; 25-28R; CAP 2

Sackler, Howard (Oliver)
1929-1982 . . . . **CLC 14**
See also CA 61-64; 108; CANR 30; DLB 7

Sacks, Oliver (Wolf) 1933- . . . . **CLC 67**
See also CA 53-56; CANR 28; MTCW

Sade, Donatien Alphonse Francois Comte
1740-1814 . . . . **NCLC 47**

Sadoff, Ira 1945- . . . . **CLC 9**
See also CA 53-56; CANR 5, 21; DLB 120

Saetone
See Camus, Albert

Safire, William 1929- . . . . **CLC 10**
See also CA 17-20R; CANR 31

Sagan, Carl (Edward) 1934- . . . . **CLC 30**
See also AAYA 2; CA 25-28R; CANR 11,
36; MTCW; SATA 58

Sagan, Francoise . . . . **CLC 3, 6, 9, 17, 36**
See also Quoirez, Francoise
See also DLB 83

Sahgal, Nayantara (Pandit) 1927- . . . **CLC 41**
See also CA 9-12R; CANR 11

Saint, H(arry) F. 1941- . . . . **CLC 50**
See also CA 127

St. Aubin de Teran, Lisa 1953-
See Teran, Lisa St. Aubin de
See also CA 118; 126

Sainte-Beuve, Charles Augustin
1804-1869 . . . . **NCLC 5**

**Saint-Exupery, Antoine (Jean Baptiste Marie
Roger) de**
1900-1944 . . . . **TCLC 2, 56; WLC**
See also CA 108; 132; CLR 10; DLB 72;
MAICYA; MTCW; SATA 20

St. John, David
See Hunt, E(verette) Howard, (Jr.)

Saint-John Perse
See Leger, (Marie-Rene Auguste) Alexis
Saint-Leger

Saintsbury, George (Edward Bateman)
1845-1933 . . . . **TCLC 31**
See also DLB 57, 149

Sait Faik . . . . **TCLC 23**
See also Abasiyanik, Sait Faik

Saki . . . . **TCLC 3; SSC 12**
See also Munro, H(ector) H(ugh)

Sala, George Augustus . . . . **NCLC 46**

Salama, Hannu 1936- . . . . **CLC 18**

Salamanca, J(ack) R(ichard)
1922- . . . . **CLC 4, 15**
See also CA 25-28R

Sale, J. Kirkpatrick
See Sale, Kirkpatrick

Sale, Kirkpatrick 1937- . . . . **CLC 68**
See also CA 13-16R; CANR 10

Salinas (y Serrano), Pedro
1891(?)-1951 . . . . **TCLC 17**
See also CA 117; DLB 134

Salinger, J(erome) D(avid)
1919- . . . . . . **CLC 1, 3, 8, 12, 55, 56; DA;
SSC 2; WLC**
See also AAYA 2; CA 5-8R; CANR 39;
CDALB 1941-1968; CLR 18; DLB 2, 102;
MAICYA; MTCW; SATA 67

Salisbury, John
See Caute, David

Salter, James 1925- . . . . **CLC 7, 52, 59**
See also CA 73-76; DLB 130

Saltus, Edgar (Everton)
1855-1921 . . . . **TCLC 8**
See also CA 105

Schumacher, E(rnst) F(riedrich)
1911-1977 .... **CLC 80**
See also CA 81-84; 73-76; CANR 34

Schuyler, James Marcus
1923-1991 .... **CLC 5, 23**
See also CA 101; 134; DLB 5

Schwartz, Delmore (David)
1913-1966 ... **CLC 2, 4, 10, 45, 87; PC 8**
See also CA 17-18; 25-28R; CANR 35;
CAP 2; DLB 28, 48; MTCW

Schwartz, Ernst
See Ozu, Yasujiro

Schwartz, John Burnham 1965- .... **CLC 59**
See also CA 132

Schwartz, Lynne Sharon 1939- ..... **CLC 31**
See also CA 103; CANR 44

Schwartz, Muriel A.
See Eliot, T(homas) S(tearns)

Schwarz-Bart, Andre 1928- .... **CLC 2, 4**
See also CA 89-92

Schwarz-Bart, Simone 1938- .... **CLC 7**
See also BW 2; CA 97-100

Schwob, (Mayer Andre) Marcel
1867-1905 .... **TCLC 20**
See also CA 117; DLB 123

Sciascia, Leonardo
1921-1989 .... **CLC 8, 9, 41**
See also CA 85-88; 130; CANR 35; MTCW

Scoppettone, Sandra 1936- .... **CLC 26**
See also AAYA 11; CA 5-8R; CANR 41;
SATA 9

Scorsese, Martin 1942- .... **CLC 20, 89**
See also CA 110; 114; CANR 46

Scotland, Jay
See Jakes, John (William)

Scott, Duncan Campbell
1862-1947 .... **TCLC 6**
See also CA 104; DLB 92

Scott, Evelyn 1893-1963 .... **CLC 43**
See also CA 104; 112; DLB 9, 48

Scott, F(rancis) R(eginald)
1899-1985 .... **CLC 22**
See also CA 101; 114; DLB 88

Scott, Frank
See Scott, F(rancis) R(eginald)

Scott, Joanna 1960- .... **CLC 50**
See also CA 126

Scott, Paul (Mark) 1920-1978 .... **CLC 9, 60**
See also CA 81-84; 77-80; CANR 33;
DLB 14; MTCW

Scott, Walter
1771-1832 ...... **NCLC 15; DA; PC 12;
WLC**
See also CDBLB 1789-1832; DLB 93, 107,
116, 144; YABC 2

Scribe, (Augustin) Eugene
1791-1861 .... **NCLC 16; DC 5**

Scrum, R.
See Crumb, R(obert)

Scudery, Madeleine de 1607-1701 ..... **LC 2**

Scum
See Crumb, R(obert)

Scumbag, Little Bobby
See Crumb, R(obert)

Seabrook, John
See Hubbard, L(afayette) Ron(ald)

Sealy, I. Allan 1951- .... **CLC 55**

Search, Alexander
See Pessoa, Fernando (Antonio Nogueira)

Sebastian, Lee
See Silverberg, Robert

Sebastian Owl
See Thompson, Hunter S(tockton)

Sebestyen, Ouida 1924- .... **CLC 30**
See also AAYA 8; CA 107; CANR 40;
CLR 17; JRDA; MAICYA; SAAS 10;
SATA 39

Secundus, H. Scriblerus
See Fielding, Henry

Sedges, John
See Buck, Pearl S(ydenstricker)

Sedgwick, Catharine Maria
1789-1867 .... **NCLC 19**
See also DLB 1, 74

Seelye, John 1931- .... **CLC 7**

Seferiades, Giorgos Stylianou 1900-1971
See Seferis, George
See also CA 5-8R; 33-36R; CANR 5, 36;
MTCW

Seferis, George .... **CLC 5, 11**
See also Seferiades, Giorgos Stylianou

Segal, Erich (Wolf) 1937- .... **CLC 3, 10**
See also BEST 89:1; CA 25-28R; CANR 20,
36; DLBY 86; MTCW

Seger, Bob 1945- .... **CLC 35**

Seghers, Anna .... **CLC 7**
See also Radvanyi, Netty
See also DLB 69

Seidel, Frederick (Lewis) 1936- ..... **CLC 18**
See also CA 13-16R; CANR 8; DLBY 84

Seifert, Jaroslav 1901-1986 ..... **CLC 34, 44**
See also CA 127; MTCW

Sei Shonagon c. 966-1017(?) ...... **CMLC 6**

Selby, Hubert, Jr.
1928- .... **CLC 1, 2, 4, 8; SSC 20**
See also CA 13-16R; CANR 33; DLB 2

Selzer, Richard 1928- .... **CLC 74**
See also CA 65-68; CANR 14

Sembene, Ousmane
See Ousmane, Sembene

Senancour, Etienne Pivert de
1770-1846 .... **NCLC 16**
See also DLB 119

Sender, Ramon (Jose)
1902-1982 .... **CLC 8; HLC**
See also CA 5-8R; 105; CANR 8; HW;
MTCW

Seneca, Lucius Annaeus
4B.C.-65 .... **CMLC 6; DC 5**

Senghor, Leopold Sedar
1906- .... **CLC 54; BLC**
See also BW 2; CA 116; 125; CANR 47;
MTCW

Serling, (Edward) Rod(man)
1924-1975 .... **CLC 30**
See also AAYA 14; AITN 1; CA 65-68;
57-60; DLB 26

Serna, Ramon Gomez de la
See Gomez de la Serna, Ramon

Serpieres
See Guillevic, (Eugene)

Service, Robert
See Service, Robert W(illiam)
See also DLB 92

Service, Robert W(illiam)
1874(?)-1958 ...... **TCLC 15; DA; WLC**
See also Service, Robert
See also CA 115; 140; SATA 20

Seth, Vikram 1952- .... **CLC 43**
See also CA 121; 127; DLB 120

Seton, Cynthia Propper
1926-1982 .... **CLC 27**
See also CA 5-8R; 108; CANR 7

Seton, Ernest (Evan) Thompson
1860-1946 .... **TCLC 31**
See also CA 109; DLB 92; JRDA; SATA 18

Seton-Thompson, Ernest
See Seton, Ernest (Evan) Thompson

Settle, Mary Lee 1918- .... **CLC 19, 61**
See also CA 89-92; CAAS 1; CANR 44;
DLB 6

Seuphor, Michel
See Arp, Jean

**Sevigne, Marie (de Rabutin-Chantal) Marquise
de** 1626-1696 .... **LC 11**

Sexton, Anne (Harvey)
1928-1974 .... **CLC 2, 4, 6, 8, 10, 15, 53;
DA; PC 2; WLC**
See also CA 1-4R; 53-56; CABS 2;
CANR 3, 36; CDALB 1941-1968; DLB 5;
MTCW; SATA 10

Shaara, Michael (Joseph, Jr.)
1929-1988 .... **CLC 15**
See also AITN 1; CA 102; 125; DLBY 83

Shackleton, C. C.
See Aldiss, Brian W(ilson)

Shacochis, Bob .... **CLC 39**
See also Shacochis, Robert G.

Shacochis, Robert G. 1951-
See Shacochis, Bob
See also CA 119; 124

Shaffer, Anthony (Joshua) 1926- .... **CLC 19**
See also CA 110; 116; DLB 13

Shaffer, Peter (Levin)
1926- .... **CLC 5, 14, 18, 37, 60**
See also CA 25-28R; CANR 25, 47;
CDBLB 1960 to Present; DLB 13;
MTCW

Shakey, Bernard
See Young, Neil

Shalamov, Varlam (Tikhonovich)
1907(?)-1982 .... **CLC 18**
See also CA 129; 105

Shamlu, Ahmad 1925- .... **CLC 10**

Shammas, Anton 1951- .... **CLC 55**

Shange, Ntozake
1948- .... **CLC 8, 25, 38, 74; BLC; DC 3**
See also AAYA 9; BW 2; CA 85-88;
CABS 3; CANR 27, 48; DLB 38; MTCW

Shanley, John Patrick 1950- .... **CLC 75**
See also CA 128; 133

Snyder, Zilpha Keatley 1927- . . . . . . **CLC 17**
See also CA 9-12R; CANR 38; CLR 31;
JRDA; MAICYA; SAAS 2; SATA 1, 28,
75

Soares, Bernardo
See Pessoa, Fernando (Antonio Nogueira)

Sobh, A.
See Shamlu, Ahmad

Sobol, Joshua. . . . . **CLC 60**

Soderberg, Hjalmar 1869-1941 . . . . **TCLC 39**

Sodergran, Edith (Irene)
See Soedergran, Edith (Irene)

Soedergran, Edith (Irene)
1892-1923 . . . . **TCLC 31**

Softly, Edgar
See Lovecraft, H(oward) P(hillips)

Softly, Edward
See Lovecraft, H(oward) P(hillips)

Sokolov, Raymond 1941- . . . . **CLC 7**
See also CA 85-88

Solo, Jay
See Ellison, Harlan (Jay)

Sologub, Fyodor . . . . **TCLC 9**
See also Teternikov, Fyodor Kuzmich

Solomons, Ikey Esquir
See Thackeray, William Makepeace

Solomos, Dionysios 1798-1857 . . . **NCLC 15**

Solwoska, Mara
See French, Marilyn

Solzhenitsyn, Aleksandr I(sayevich)
1918- . . . . . . **CLC 1, 2, 4, 7, 9, 10, 18, 26,
34, 78; DA; WLC**
See also AITN 1; CA 69-72; CANR 40;
MTCW

Somers, Jane
See Lessing, Doris (May)

Somerville, Edith 1858-1949 . . . . . . **TCLC 51**
See also DLB 135

Somerville & Ross
See Martin, Violet Florence; Somerville,
Edith

Sommer, Scott 1951- . . . . **CLC 25**
See also CA 106

Sondheim, Stephen (Joshua)
1930- . . . . **CLC 30, 39**
See also AAYA 11; CA 103; CANR 47

Sontag, Susan 1933- . . . **CLC 1, 2, 10, 13, 31**
See also CA 17-20R; CANR 25; DLB 2, 67;
MTCW

Sophocles
496(?)B.C.-406(?)B.C. . . . . **CMLC 2; DA;
DC 1**

Sordello 1189-1269 . . . . **CMLC 15**

Sorel, Julia
See Drexler, Rosalyn

Sorrentino, Gilbert
1929- . . . . **CLC 3, 7, 14, 22, 40**
See also CA 77-80; CANR 14, 33; DLB 5;
DLBY 80

Soto, Gary 1952- . . . . **CLC 32, 80; HLC**
See also AAYA 10; CA 119; 125; CLR 38;
DLB 82; HW; JRDA; SATA 80

Soupault, Philippe 1897-1990 . . . . . . **CLC 68**
See also CA 116; 147; 131

Souster, (Holmes) Raymond
1921- . . . . **CLC 5, 14**
See also CA 13-16R; CAAS 14; CANR 13,
29; DLB 88; SATA 63

Southern, Terry 1926- . . . . **CLC 7**
See also CA 1-4R; CANR 1; DLB 2

Southey, Robert 1774-1843 . . . . **NCLC 8**
See also DLB 93, 107, 142; SATA 54

Southworth, Emma Dorothy Eliza Nevitte
1819-1899 . . . . **NCLC 26**

Souza, Ernest
See Scott, Evelyn

Soyinka, Wole
1934- . . . . . . **CLC 3, 5, 14, 36, 44; BLC;
DA; DC 2; WLC**
See also BW 2; CA 13-16R; CANR 27, 39;
DLB 125; MTCW

Spackman, W(illiam) M(ode)
1905-1990 . . . . **CLC 46**
See also CA 81-84; 132

Spacks, Barry 1931- . . . . **CLC 14**
See also CA 29-32R; CANR 33; DLB 105

Spanidou, Irini 1946- . . . . **CLC 44**

Spark, Muriel (Sarah)
1918- . . . . **CLC 2, 3, 5, 8, 13, 18, 40;
SSC 10**
See also CA 5-8R; CANR 12, 36;
CDBLB 1945-1960; DLB 15, 139; MTCW

Spaulding, Douglas
See Bradbury, Ray (Douglas)

Spaulding, Leonard
See Bradbury, Ray (Douglas)

Spence, J. A. D.
See Eliot, T(homas) S(tearns)

Spencer, Elizabeth 1921- . . . . **CLC 22**
See also CA 13-16R; CANR 32; DLB 6;
MTCW; SATA 14

Spencer, Leonard G.
See Silverberg, Robert

Spencer, Scott 1945- . . . . **CLC 30**
See also CA 113; DLBY 86

Spender, Stephen (Harold)
1909- . . . . **CLC 1, 2, 5, 10, 41**
See also CA 9-12R; CANR 31;
CDBLB 1945-1960; DLB 20; MTCW

Spengler, Oswald (Arnold Gottfried)
1880-1936 . . . . **TCLC 25**
See also CA 118

Spenser, Edmund
1552(?)-1599 . . . . **LC 5; DA; PC 8; WLC**
See also CDBLB Before 1660

Spicer, Jack 1925-1965 . . . . . . **CLC 8, 18, 72**
See also CA 85-88; DLB 5, 16

Spiegelman, Art 1948- . . . . **CLC 76**
See also AAYA 10; CA 125; CANR 41

Spielberg, Peter 1929- . . . . **CLC 6**
See also CA 5-8R; CANR 4, 48; DLBY 81

Spielberg, Steven 1947- . . . . **CLC 20**
See also AAYA 8; CA 77-80; CANR 32;
SATA 32

Spillane, Frank Morrison 1918-
See Spillane, Mickey
See also CA 25-28R; CANR 28; MTCW;
SATA 66

Spillane, Mickey . . . . **CLC 3, 13**
See also Spillane, Frank Morrison

Spinoza, Benedictus de 1632-1677 . . . . **LC 9**

Spinrad, Norman (Richard) 1940-. . . **CLC 46**
See also CA 37-40R; CAAS 19; CANR 20;
DLB 8

Spitteler, Carl (Friedrich Georg)
1845-1924 . . . . **TCLC 12**
See also CA 109; DLB 129

Spivack, Kathleen (Romola Drucker)
1938- . . . . **CLC 6**
See also CA 49-52

Spoto, Donald 1941- . . . . **CLC 39**
See also CA 65-68; CANR 11

Springsteen, Bruce (F.) 1949- . . . . . . **CLC 17**
See also CA 111

Spurling, Hilary 1940- . . . . **CLC 34**
See also CA 104; CANR 25

Spyker, John Howland
See Elman, Richard

Squires, (James) Radcliffe
1917-1993 . . . . **CLC 51**
See also CA 1-4R; 140; CANR 6, 21

Srivastava, Dhanpat Rai 1880(?)-1936
See Premchand
See also CA 118

Stacy, Donald
See Pohl, Frederik

Stael, Germaine de
See Stael-Holstein, Anne Louise Germaine
Necker Baronn
See also DLB 119

**Stael-Holstein, Anne Louise Germaine Necker
Baronn** 1766-1817 . . . . **NCLC 3**
See also Stael, Germaine de

Stafford, Jean 1915-1979 . . . **CLC 4, 7, 19, 68**
See also CA 1-4R; 85-88; CANR 3; DLB 2;
MTCW; SATA-Obit 22

Stafford, William (Edgar)
1914-1993 . . . . **CLC 4, 7, 29**
See also CA 5-8R; 142; CAAS 3; CANR 5,
22; DLB 5

Staines, Trevor
See Brunner, John (Kilian Houston)

Stairs, Gordon
See Austin, Mary (Hunter)

Stannard, Martin 1947- . . . . **CLC 44**
See also CA 142

Stanton, Maura 1946- . . . . **CLC 9**
See also CA 89-92; CANR 15; DLB 120

Stanton, Schuyler
See Baum, L(yman) Frank

Stapledon, (William) Olaf
1886-1950 . . . . **TCLC 22**
See also CA 111; DLB 15

Starbuck, George (Edwin) 1931- . . . . **CLC 53**
See also CA 21-24R; CANR 23

Stark, Richard
See Westlake, Donald E(dwin)

Stringer, David
See Roberts, Keith (John Kingston)

Strugatskii, Arkadii (Natanovich)
1925-1991 .... **CLC 27**
See also CA 106; 135

Strugatskii, Boris (Natanovich)
1933- .... **CLC 27**
See also CA 106

Strummer, Joe 1953(?)- .... **CLC 30**

Stuart, Don A.
See Campbell, John W(ood, Jr.)

Stuart, Ian
See MacLean, Alistair (Stuart)

Stuart, Jesse (Hilton)
1906-1984 .... **CLC 1, 8, 11, 14, 34**
See also CA 5-8R; 112; CANR 31; DLB 9,
48, 102; DLBY 84; SATA 2;
SATA-Obit 36

Sturgeon, Theodore (Hamilton)
1918-1985 .... **CLC 22, 39**
See also Queen, Ellery
See also CA 81-84; 116; CANR 32; DLB 8;
DLBY 85; MTCW

Sturges, Preston 1898-1959 ...... **TCLC 48**
See also CA 114; DLB 26

Styron, William
1925- .... **CLC 1, 3, 5, 11, 15, 60**
See also BEST 90:4; CA 5-8R; CANR 6, 33;
CDALB 1968-1988; DLB 2, 143;
DLBY 80; MTCW

Suarez Lynch, B.
See Bioy Casares, Adolfo; Borges, Jorge
Luis

Su Chien 1884-1918
See Su Man-shu
See also CA 123

Suckow, Ruth 1892-1960
See also CA 113; DLB 9, 102; SSC 18

Sudermann, Hermann 1857-1928 .. **TCLC 15**
See also CA 107; DLB 118

Sue, Eugene 1804-1857 .... **NCLC 1**
See also DLB 119

Sueskind, Patrick 1949- .... **CLC 44**
See also Suskind, Patrick

Sukenick, Ronald 1932- ..... **CLC 3, 4, 6, 48**
See also CA 25-28R; CAAS 8; CANR 32;
DLBY 81

Suknaski, Andrew 1942- .... **CLC 19**
See also CA 101; DLB 53

Sullivan, Vernon
See Vian, Boris

Sully Prudhomme 1839-1907 ...... **TCLC 31**

Su Man-shu .... **TCLC 24**
See also Su Chien

Summerforest, Ivy B.
See Kirkup, James

Summers, Andrew James 1942- ..... **CLC 26**

Summers, Andy
See Summers, Andrew James

Summers, Hollis (Spurgeon, Jr.)
1916- .... **CLC 10**
See also CA 5-8R; CANR 3; DLB 6

Summers, (Alphonsus Joseph-Mary Augustus)
Montague 1880-1948 .... **TCLC 16**
See also CA 118

Sumner, Gordon Matthew 1951- .... **CLC 26**

Surtees, Robert Smith
1803-1864 .... **NCLC 14**
See also DLB 21

Susann, Jacqueline 1921-1974...... **CLC 3**
See also AITN 1; CA 65-68; 53-56; MTCW

Suskind, Patrick
See Sueskind, Patrick
See also CA 145

Sutcliff, Rosemary 1920-1992 ...... **CLC 26**
See also AAYA 10; CA 5-8R; 139;
CANR 37; CLR 1, 37; JRDA; MAICYA;
SATA 6, 44, 78; SATA-Obit 73

Sutro, Alfred 1863-1933.......... **TCLC 6**
See also CA 105; DLB 10

Sutton, Henry
See Slavitt, David R(ytman)

Svevo, Italo .... **TCLC 2, 35**
See also Schmitz, Aron Hector

Swados, Elizabeth (A.) 1951-...... **CLC 12**
See also CA 97-100; CANR 49

Swados, Harvey 1920-1972 .... **CLC 5**
See also CA 5-8R; 37-40R; CANR 6;
DLB 2

Swan, Gladys 1934- .... **CLC 69**
See also CA 101; CANR 17, 39

Swarthout, Glendon (Fred)
1918-1992 .... **CLC 35**
See also CA 1-4R; 139; CANR 1, 47;
SATA 26

Sweet, Sarah C.
See Jewett, (Theodora) Sarah Orne

Swenson, May
1919-1989 .... **CLC 4, 14, 61; DA**
See also CA 5-8R; 130; CANR 36; DLB 5;
MTCW; SATA 15

Swift, Augustus
See Lovecraft, H(oward) P(hillips)

Swift, Graham (Colin) 1949- .... **CLC 41, 88**
See also CA 117; 122; CANR 46

Swift, Jonathan
1667-1745 ...... **LC 1; DA; PC 9; WLC**
See also CDBLB 1660-1789; DLB 39, 95,
101; SATA 19

Swinburne, Algernon Charles
1837-1909 ...... **TCLC 8, 36; DA; WLC**
See also CA 105; 140; CDBLB 1832-1890;
DLB 35, 57

Swinfen, Ann.................... **CLC 34**

Swinnerton, Frank Arthur
1884-1982 .... **CLC 31**
See also CA 108; DLB 34

Swithen, John
See King, Stephen (Edwin)

Sylvia
See Ashton-Warner, Sylvia (Constance)

Symmes, Robert Edward
See Duncan, Robert (Edward)

Symonds, John Addington
1840-1893 .... **NCLC 34**
See also DLB 57, 144

Symons, Arthur 1865-1945 .... **TCLC 11**
See also CA 107; DLB 19, 57, 149

Symons, Julian (Gustave)
1912-1994 .... **CLC 2, 14, 32**
See also CA 49-52; 147; CAAS 3; CANR 3,
33; DLB 87; DLBY 92; MTCW

Synge, (Edmund) J(ohn) M(illington)
1871-1909 .... **TCLC 6, 37; DC 2**
See also CA 104; 141; CDBLB 1890-1914;
DLB 10, 19

Syruc, J.
See Milosz, Czeslaw

Szirtes, George 1948-............. **CLC 46**
See also CA 109; CANR 27

Tabori, George 1914-............. **CLC 19**
See also CA 49-52; CANR 4

Tagore, Rabindranath
1861-1941 .... **TCLC 3, 53; PC 8**
See also CA 104; 120; MTCW

Taine, Hippolyte Adolphe
1828-1893 .... **NCLC 15**

Talese, Gay 1932-................. **CLC 37**
See also AITN 1; CA 1-4R; CANR 9;
MTCW

Tallent, Elizabeth (Ann) 1954- ..... **CLC 45**
See also CA 117; DLB 130

Tally, Ted 1952-................. **CLC 42**
See also CA 120; 124

Tamayo y Baus, Manuel
1829-1898 .... **NCLC 1**

Tammsaare, A(nton) H(ansen)
1878-1940 .... **TCLC 27**

Tan, Amy 1952- .... **CLC 59**
See also AAYA 9; BEST 89:3; CA 136;
SATA 75

Tandem, Felix
See Spitteler, Carl (Friedrich Georg)

Tanizaki, Jun'ichiro
1886-1965 .... **CLC 8, 14, 28**
See also CA 93-96; 25-28R

Tanner, William
See Amis, Kingsley (William)

Tao Lao
See Storni, Alfonsina

Tarassoff, Lev
See Troyat, Henri

Tarbell, Ida M(inerva)
1857-1944 .... **TCLC 40**
See also CA 122; DLB 47

Tarkington, (Newton) Booth
1869-1946 .... **TCLC 9**
See also CA 110; 143; DLB 9, 102;
SATA 17

Tarkovsky, Andrei (Arsenyevich)
1932-1986 .... **CLC 75**
See also CA 127

Tartt, Donna 1964(?)-............. **CLC 76**
See also CA 142

Tasso, Torquato 1544-1595 .... **LC 5**

Tate, (John Orley) Allen
1899-1979 .... **CLC 2, 4, 6, 9, 11, 14, 24**
See also CA 5-8R; 85-88; CANR 32;
DLB 4, 45, 63; MTCW

Tate, Ellalice
See Hibbert, Eleanor Alice Burford

Tate, James (Vincent) 1943- ... CLC 2, 6, 25
See also CA 21-24R; CANR 29; DLB 5

Tavel, Ronald 1940- .... CLC 6
See also CA 21-24R; CANR 33

Taylor, C(ecil) P(hilip) 1929-1981... CLC 27
See also CA 25-28R; 105; CANR 47

Taylor, Edward 1642(?)-1729.... LC 11; DA
See also DLB 24

Taylor, Eleanor Ross 1920- .... CLC 5
See also CA 81-84

Taylor, Elizabeth 1912-1975 ... CLC 2, 4, 29
See also CA 13-16R; CANR 9; DLB 139;
MTCW; SATA 13

Taylor, Henry (Splawn) 1942- ...... CLC 44
See also CA 33-36R; CAAS 7; CANR 31;
DLB 5

Taylor, Kamala (Purnaiya) 1924-
See Markandaya, Kamala
See also CA 77-80

Taylor, Mildred D. .... CLC 21
See also AAYA 10; BW 1; CA 85-88;
CANR 25; CLR 9; DLB 52; JRDA;
MAICYA; SAAS 5; SATA 15, 70

Taylor, Peter (Hillsman)
1917-1994 ..... CLC 1, 4, 18, 37, 44, 50,
71; SSC 10
See also CA 13-16R; 147; CANR 9;
DLBY 81, 94; MTCW

Taylor, Robert Lewis 1912- .... CLC 14
See also CA 1-4R; CANR 3; SATA 10

Tchekhov, Anton
See Chekhov, Anton (Pavlovich)

Teasdale, Sara 1884-1933......... TCLC 4
See also CA 104; DLB 45; SATA 32

Tegner, Esaias 1782-1846........ NCLC 2

Teilhard de Chardin, (Marie Joseph) Pierre
1881-1955 .... TCLC 9
See also CA 105

Temple, Ann
See Mortimer, Penelope (Ruth)

Tennant, Emma (Christina)
1937- .... CLC 13, 52
See also CA 65-68; CAAS 9; CANR 10, 38;
DLB 14

Tenneshaw, S. M.
See Silverberg, Robert

Tennyson, Alfred
1809-1892 .. NCLC 30; DA; PC 6; WLC
See also CDBLB 1832-1890; DLB 32

Teran, Lisa St. Aubin de .... CLC 36
See also St. Aubin de Teran, Lisa

Terence 195(?)B.C.-159B.C....... CMLC 14

Teresa de Jesus, St. 1515-1582...... LC 18

Terkel, Louis 1912-
See Terkel, Studs
See also CA 57-60; CANR 18, 45; MTCW

Terkel, Studs .... CLC 38
See also Terkel, Louis
See also AITN 1

Terry, C. V.
See Slaughter, Frank G(ill)

Terry, Megan 1932- .... CLC 19
See also CA 77-80; CABS 3; CANR 43;
DLB 7

Tertz, Abram
See Sinyavsky, Andrei (Donatevich)

Tesich, Steve 1943(?)-......... CLC 40, 69
See also CA 105; DLBY 83

Teternikov, Fyodor Kuzmich 1863-1927
See Sologub, Fyodor
See also CA 104

Tevis, Walter 1928-1984 .... CLC 42
See also CA 113

Tey, Josephine................... TCLC 14
See also Mackintosh, Elizabeth
See also DLB 77

Thackeray, William Makepeace
1811-1863 .... NCLC 5, 14, 22, 43; DA;
WLC
See also CDBLB 1832-1890; DLB 21, 55;
SATA 23

Thakura, Ravindranatha
See Tagore, Rabindranath

Tharoor, Shashi 1956- .... CLC 70
See also CA 141

Thelwell, Michael Miles 1939- ..... CLC 22
See also BW 2; CA 101

Theobald, Lewis, Jr.
See Lovecraft, H(oward) P(hillips)

Theodorescu, Ion N. 1880-1967
See Arghezi, Tudor
See also CA 116

Theriault, Yves 1915-1983........ CLC 79
See also CA 102; DLB 88

Theroux, Alexander (Louis)
1939- .... CLC 2, 25
See also CA 85-88; CANR 20

Theroux, Paul (Edward)
1941- ..... CLC 5, 8, 11, 15, 28, 46
See also BEST 89:4; CA 33-36R; CANR 20,
45; DLB 2; MTCW; SATA 44

Thesen, Sharon 1946-............ CLC 56

Thevenin, Denis
See Duhamel, Georges

Thibault, Jacques Anatole Francois
1844-1924
See France, Anatole
See also CA 106; 127; MTCW

Thiele, Colin (Milton) 1920- .... CLC 17
See also CA 29-32R; CANR 12, 28;
CLR 27; MAICYA; SAAS 2; SATA 14,
72

Thomas, Audrey (Callahan)
1935- .... CLC 7, 13, 37; SSC 20
See also AITN 2; CA 21-24R; CAAS 19;
CANR 36; DLB 60; MTCW

Thomas, D(onald) M(ichael)
1935- .... CLC 13, 22, 31
See also CA 61-64; CAAS 11; CANR 17,
45; CDBLB 1960 to Present; DLB 40;
MTCW

Thomas, Dylan (Marlais)
1914-1953 ... TCLC 1, 8, 45; DA; PC 2;
SSC 3; WLC
See also CA 104; 120; CDBLB 1945-1960;
DLB 13, 20, 139; MTCW; SATA 60

Thomas, (Philip) Edward
1878-1917 .... TCLC 10
See also CA 106; DLB 19

Thomas, Joyce Carol 1938-........ CLC 35
See also AAYA 12; BW 2; CA 113; 116;
CANR 48; CLR 19; DLB 33; JRDA;
MAICYA; MTCW; SAAS 7; SATA 40,
78

Thomas, Lewis 1913-1993 .... CLC 35
See also CA 85-88; 143; CANR 38; MTCW

Thomas, Paul
See Mann, (Paul) Thomas

Thomas, Piri 1928-.............. CLC 17
See also CA 73-76; HW

Thomas, R(onald) S(tuart)
1913- .... CLC 6, 13, 48
See also CA 89-92; CAAS 4; CANR 30;
CDBLB 1960 to Present; DLB 27;
MTCW

Thomas, Ross (Elmore) 1926- ...... CLC 39
See also CA 33-36R; CANR 22

Thompson, Francis Clegg
See Mencken, H(enry) L(ouis)

Thompson, Francis Joseph
1859-1907 .... TCLC 4
See also CA 104; CDBLB 1890-1914;
DLB 19

Thompson, Hunter S(tockton)
1939- .... CLC 9, 17, 40
See also BEST 89:1; CA 17-20R; CANR 23,
46; MTCW

Thompson, James Myers
See Thompson, Jim (Myers)

Thompson, Jim (Myers)
1906-1977(?) .... CLC 69
See also CA 140

Thompson, Judith .... CLC 39

Thomson, James 1700-1748...... LC 16, 29
See also DLB 95

Thomson, James 1834-1882...... NCLC 18
See also DLB 35

Thoreau, Henry David
1817-1862 ...... NCLC 7, 21; DA; WLC
See also CDALB 1640-1865; DLB 1

Thornton, Hall
See Silverberg, Robert

Thurber, James (Grover)
1894-1961 .... CLC 5, 11, 25; DA; SSC 1
See also CA 73-76; CANR 17, 39;
CDALB 1929-1941; DLB 4, 11, 22, 102;
MAICYA; MTCW; SATA 13

Thurman, Wallace (Henry)
1902-1934 .... TCLC 6; BLC
See also BW 1; CA 104; 124; DLB 51

Ticheburn, Cheviot
See Ainsworth, William Harrison

Tieck, (Johann) Ludwig
1773-1853 .... NCLC 5, 46
See also DLB 90

Tiger, Derry
See Ellison, Harlan (Jay)

Tilghman, Christopher 1948(?)-..... CLC 65

Tillinghast, Richard (Williford)
1940- .... CLC 29
See also CA 29-32R; CANR 26

Timrod, Henry   1828-1867 . . . . NCLC 25
See also DLB 3

Tindall, Gillian   1938- . . . . CLC 7
See also CA 21-24R; CANR 11

Tiptree, James, Jr. . . . . CLC 48, 50
See also Sheldon, Alice Hastings Bradley
See also DLB 8

Titmarsh, Michael Angelo
See Thackeray, William Makepeace

Tocqueville, Alexis (Charles Henri Maurice
Clerel Comte)   1805-1859 . . . . . NCLC 7

Tolkien, J(ohn) R(onald) R(euel)
1892-1973 . . . . . . CLC 1, 2, 3, 8, 12, 38;
DA; WLC
See also AAYA 10; AITN 1; CA 17-18;
45-48; CANR 36; CAP 2;
CDBLB 1914-1945; DLB 15; JRDA;
MAICYA; MTCW; SATA 2, 32;
SATA-Obit 24

Toller, Ernst   1893-1939 . . . . TCLC 10
See also CA 107; DLB 124

Tolson, M. B.
See Tolson, Melvin B(eaunorus)

Tolson, Melvin B(eaunorus)
1898(?)-1966 . . . . CLC 36; BLC
See also BW 1; CA 124; 89-92; DLB 48, 76

Tolstoi, Aleksei Nikolaevich
See Tolstoy, Alexey Nikolaevich

Tolstoy, Alexey Nikolaevich
1882-1945 . . . . TCLC 18
See also CA 107

Tolstoy, Count Leo
See Tolstoy, Leo (Nikolaevich)

Tolstoy, Leo (Nikolaevich)
1828-1910 . . . . . TCLC 4, 11, 17, 28, 44;
DA; SSC 9; WLC
See also CA 104; 123; SATA 26

Tomasi di Lampedusa, Giuseppe   1896-1957
See Lampedusa, Giuseppe (Tomasi) di
See also CA 111

Tomlin, Lily . . . . CLC 17
See also Tomlin, Mary Jean

Tomlin, Mary Jean   1939(?)-
See Tomlin, Lily
See also CA 117

Tomlinson, (Alfred) Charles
1927- . . . . CLC 2, 4, 6, 13, 45
See also CA 5-8R; CANR 33; DLB 40

Tonson, Jacob
See Bennett, (Enoch) Arnold

Toole, John Kennedy
1937-1969 . . . . CLC 19, 64
See also CA 104; DLBY 81

Toomer, Jean
1894-1967 . . . . . . CLC 1, 4, 13, 22; BLC;
PC 7; SSC 1
See also BW 1; CA 85-88;
CDALB 1917-1929; DLB 45, 51; MTCW

Torley, Luke
See Blish, James (Benjamin)

Tornimparte, Alessandra
See Ginzburg, Natalia

Torre, Raoul della
See Mencken, H(enry) L(ouis)

Torrey, E(dwin) Fuller   1937- . . . . CLC 34
See also CA 119

Torsvan, Ben Traven
See Traven, B.

Torsvan, Benno Traven
See Traven, B.

Torsvan, Berick Traven
See Traven, B.

Torsvan, Berwick Traven
See Traven, B.

Torsvan, Bruno Traven
See Traven, B.

Torsvan, Traven
See Traven, B.

Tournier, Michel (Edouard)
1924- . . . . CLC 6, 23, 36
See also CA 49-52; CANR 3, 36; DLB 83;
MTCW; SATA 23

Tournimparte, Alessandra
See Ginzburg, Natalia

Towers, Ivar
See Kornbluth, C(yril) M.

Towne, Robert (Burton)   1936(?)- . . . . CLC 87
See also CA 108; DLB 44

Townsend, Sue   1946- . . . . CLC 61
See also CA 119; 127; MTCW; SATA 55;
SATA-Brief 48

Townshend, Peter (Dennis Blandford)
1945- . . . . CLC 17, 42
See also CA 107

Tozzi, Federigo   1883-1920 . . . . TCLC 31

Traill, Catharine Parr
1802-1899 . . . . NCLC 31
See also DLB 99

Trakl, Georg   1887-1914 . . . . TCLC 5
See also CA 104

Transtroemer, Tomas (Goesta)
1931- . . . . CLC 52, 65
See also CA 117; 129; CAAS 17

Transtromer, Tomas Gosta
See Transtroemer, Tomas (Goesta)

Traven, B.   (?)-1969 . . . . CLC 8, 11
See also CA 19-20; 25-28R; CAP 2; DLB 9,
56; MTCW

Treitel, Jonathan   1959- . . . . CLC 70

Tremain, Rose   1943- . . . . CLC 42
See also CA 97-100; CANR 44; DLB 14

Tremblay, Michel   1942- . . . . CLC 29
See also CA 116; 128; DLB 60; MTCW

Trevanian . . . . CLC 29
See also Whitaker, Rod(ney)

Trevor, Glen
See Hilton, James

Trevor, William
1928- . . . . CLC 7, 9, 14, 25, 71
See also Cox, William Trevor
See also DLB 14, 139

Trifonov, Yuri (Valentinovich)
1925-1981 . . . . CLC 45
See also CA 126; 103; MTCW

Trilling, Lionel   1905-1975 . . . . CLC 9, 11, 24
See also CA 9-12R; 61-64; CANR 10;
DLB 28, 63; MTCW

Trimball, W. H.
See Mencken, H(enry) L(ouis)

Tristan
See Gomez de la Serna, Ramon

Tristram
See Housman, A(lfred) E(dward)

Trogdon, William (Lewis)   1939-
See Heat-Moon, William Least
See also CA 115; 119; CANR 47

Trollope, Anthony
1815-1882 . . . . . . NCLC 6, 33; DA; WLC
See also CDBLB 1832-1890; DLB 21, 57;
SATA 22

Trollope, Frances   1779-1863 . . . . . NCLC 30
See also DLB 21

Trotsky, Leon   1879-1940 . . . . TCLC 22
See also CA 118

Trotter (Cockburn), Catharine
1679-1749 . . . . LC 8
See also DLB 84

Trout, Kilgore
See Farmer, Philip Jose

Trow, George W. S.   1943- . . . . CLC 52
See also CA 126

Troyat, Henri   1911- . . . . CLC 23
See also CA 45-48; CANR 2, 33; MTCW

Trudeau, G(arretson) B(eekman)   1948-
See Trudeau, Garry B.
See also CA 81-84; CANR 31; SATA 35

Trudeau, Garry B. . . . . CLC 12
See also Trudeau, G(arretson) B(eekman)
See also AAYA 10; AITN 2

Truffaut, Francois   1932-1984 . . . . CLC 20
See also CA 81-84; 113; CANR 34

Trumbo, Dalton   1905-1976 . . . . CLC 19
See also CA 21-24R; 69-72; CANR 10;
DLB 26

Trumbull, John   1750-1831 . . . . NCLC 30
See also DLB 31

Trundlett, Helen B.
See Eliot, T(homas) S(tearns)

Tryon, Thomas   1926-1991 . . . . CLC 3, 11
See also AITN 1; CA 29-32R; 135;
CANR 32; MTCW

Tryon, Tom
See Tryon, Thomas

Ts'ao Hsueh-ch'in   1715(?)-1763 . . . . . . LC 1

Tsushima, Shuji   1909-1948
See Dazai, Osamu
See also CA 107

Tsvetaeva (Efron), Marina (Ivanovna)
1892-1941 . . . . TCLC 7, 35
See also CA 104; 128; MTCW

Tuck, Lily   1938- . . . . CLC 70
See also CA 139

Tu Fu   712-770 . . . . PC 9

Tunis, John R(oberts)   1889-1975 . . . CLC 12
See also CA 61-64; DLB 22; JRDA;
MAICYA; SATA 37; SATA-Brief 30

Tuohy, Frank . . . . CLC 37
See also Tuohy, John Francis
See also DLB 14, 139

Tuohy, John Francis 1925-
See Tuohy, Frank
See also CA 5-8R; CANR 3, 47

Turco, Lewis (Putnam) 1934- ... **CLC 11, 63**
See also CA 13-16R; CANR 24; DLBY 84

Turgenev, Ivan
1818-1883 ...... **NCLC 21; DA; SSC 7;**
WLC

Turgot, Anne-Robert-Jacques
1727-1781 .... **LC 26**

Turner, Frederick 1943-.......... **CLC 48**
See also CA 73-76; CAAS 10; CANR 12,
30; DLB 40

Tutu, Desmond M(pilo)
1931- .... **CLC 80; BLC**
See also BW 1; CA 125

Tutuola, Amos 1920- ... **CLC 5, 14, 29; BLC**
See also BW 2; CA 9-12R; CANR 27;
DLB 125; MTCW

Twain, Mark
..... **TCLC 6, 12, 19, 36, 48, 59; SSC 6;**
WLC
See also Clemens, Samuel Langhorne
See also DLB 11, 12, 23, 64, 74

Tyler, Anne
1941- .... **CLC 7, 11, 18, 28, 44, 59**
See also BEST 89:1; CA 9-12R; CANR 11,
33; DLB 6, 143; DLBY 82; MTCW;
SATA 7

Tyler, Royall 1757-1826.......... **NCLC 3**
See also DLB 37

Tynan, Katharine 1861-1931 .... **TCLC 3**
See also CA 104; DLB 153

Tyutchev, Fyodor 1803-1873 ..... **NCLC 34**

Tzara, Tristan .... **CLC 47**
See also Rosenfeld, Samuel

Uhry, Alfred 1936-.............. **CLC 55**
See also CA 127; 133

Ulf, Haerved
See Strindberg, (Johan) August

Ulf, Harved
See Strindberg, (Johan) August

Ulibarri, Sabine R(eyes) 1919- ..... **CLC 83**
See also CA 131; DLB 82; HW

Unamuno (y Jugo), Miguel de
1864-1936 .... **TCLC 2, 9; HLC; SSC 11**
See also CA 104; 131; DLB 108; HW;
MTCW

Undercliffe, Errol
See Campbell, (John) Ramsey

Underwood, Miles
See Glassco, John

Undset, Sigrid
1882-1949 .... **TCLC 3; DA; WLC**
See also CA 104; 129; MTCW

Ungaretti, Giuseppe
1888-1970 .... **CLC 7, 11, 15**
See also CA 19-20; 25-28R; CAP 2;
DLB 114

Unger, Douglas 1952-............. **CLC 34**
See also CA 130

Unsworth, Barry (Forster) 1930-.... **CLC 76**
See also CA 25-28R; CANR 30

Updike, John (Hoyer)
1932- ...... **CLC 1, 2, 3, 5, 7, 9, 13, 15,**
23, 34, 43, 70; DA; SSC 13; WLC
See also CA 1-4R; CABS 1; CANR 4, 33;
CDALB 1968-1988; DLB 2, 5, 143;
DLBD 3; DLBY 80, 82; MTCW

Upshaw, Margaret Mitchell
See Mitchell, Margaret (Munnerlyn)

Upton, Mark
See Sanders, Lawrence

Urdang, Constance (Henriette)
1922- .... **CLC 47**
See also CA 21-24R; CANR 9, 24

Uriel, Henry
See Faust, Frederick (Schiller)

Uris, Leon (Marcus) 1924-...... **CLC 7, 32**
See also AITN 1, 2; BEST 89:2; CA 1-4R;
CANR 1, 40; MTCW; SATA 49

Urmuz
See Codrescu, Andrei

Ustinov, Peter (Alexander) 1921-.... **CLC 1**
See also AITN 1; CA 13-16R; CANR 25;
DLB 13

Vaculik, Ludvik 1926-............. **CLC 7**
See also CA 53-56

Valdez, Luis (Miguel)
1940- .... **CLC 84; HLC**
See also CA 101; CANR 32; DLB 122; HW

Valenzuela, Luisa 1938-... **CLC 31; SSC 14**
See also CA 101; CANR 32; DLB 113; HW

Valera y Alcala-Galiano, Juan
1824-1905 .... **TCLC 10**
See also CA 106

Valery, (Ambroise) Paul (Toussaint Jules)
1871-1945 .... **TCLC 4, 15; PC 9**
See also CA 104; 122; MTCW

Valle-Inclan, Ramon (Maria) del
1866-1936 .... **TCLC 5; HLC**
See also CA 106; DLB 134

Vallejo, Antonio Buero
See Buero Vallejo, Antonio

Vallejo, Cesar (Abraham)
1892-1938 .... **TCLC 3, 56; HLC**
See also CA 105; HW

Valle Y Pena, Ramon del
See Valle-Inclan, Ramon (Maria) del

Van Ash, Cay 1918-............. **CLC 34**

Vanbrugh, Sir John 1664-1726 ...... **LC 21**
See also DLB 80

Van Campen, Karl
See Campbell, John W(ood, Jr.)

Vance, Gerald
See Silverberg, Robert

Vance, Jack .... **CLC 35**
See also Vance, John Holbrook
See also DLB 8

Vance, John Holbrook 1916-
See Queen, Ellery; Vance, Jack
See also CA 29-32R; CANR 17; MTCW

Van Den Bogarde, Derek Jules Gaspard Ulric
Niven 1921-
See Bogarde, Dirk
See also CA 77-80

Vandenburgh, Jane .... **CLC 59**

Vanderhaeghe, Guy 1951- .... **CLC 41**
See also CA 113

van der Post, Laurens (Jan) 1906- ... **CLC 5**
See also CA 5-8R; CANR 35

van de Wetering, Janwillem 1931- .. **CLC 47**
See also CA 49-52; CANR 4

Van Dine, S. S. .... **TCLC 23**
See also Wright, Willard Huntington

Van Doren, Carl (Clinton)
1885-1950 .... **TCLC 18**
See also CA 111

Van Doren, Mark 1894-1972..... **CLC 6, 10**
See also CA 1-4R; 37-40R; CANR 3;
DLB 45; MTCW

Van Druten, John (William)
1901-1957 .... **TCLC 2**
See also CA 104; DLB 10

Van Duyn, Mona (Jane)
1921- .... **CLC 3, 7, 63**
See also CA 9-12R; CANR 7, 38; DLB 5

Van Dyne, Edith
See Baum, L(yman) Frank

van Itallie, Jean-Claude 1936-....... **CLC 3**
See also CA 45-48; CAAS 2; CANR 1, 48;
DLB 7

van Ostaijen, Paul 1896-1928 ..... **TCLC 33**

Van Peebles, Melvin 1932- ...... **CLC 2, 20**
See also BW 2; CA 85-88; CANR 27

Vansittart, Peter 1920-............ **CLC 42**
See also CA 1-4R; CANR 3, 49

Van Vechten, Carl 1880-1964 ...... **CLC 33**
See also CA 89-92; DLB 4, 9, 51

Van Vogt, A(lfred) E(lton) 1912-..... **CLC 1**
See also CA 21-24R; CANR 28; DLB 8;
SATA 14

Varda, Agnes 1928-.............. **CLC 16**
See also CA 116; 122

Vargas Llosa, (Jorge) Mario (Pedro)
1936- .... **CLC 3, 6, 9, 10, 15, 31, 42, 85;**
DA; HLC
See also CA 73-76; CANR 18, 32, 42;
DLB 145; HW; MTCW

Vasiliu, Gheorghe 1881-1957
See Bacovia, George
See also CA 123

Vassa, Gustavus
See Equiano, Olaudah

Vassilikos, Vassilis 1933-......... **CLC 4, 8**
See also CA 81-84

Vaughan, Henry 1621-1695........ **LC 27**
See also DLB 131

Vaughn, Stephanie................ **CLC 62**

Vazov, Ivan (Minchov)
1850-1921 .... **TCLC 25**
See also CA 121; DLB 147

Veblen, Thorstein (Bunde)
1857-1929 .... **TCLC 31**
See also CA 115

Vega, Lope de 1562-1635.......... **LC 23**

Venison, Alfred
See Pound, Ezra (Weston Loomis)

Verdi, Marie de
See Mencken, H(enry) L(ouis)

Walker, Margaret (Abigail)
1915- .... **CLC 1, 6; BLC**
See also BW 2; CA 73-76; CANR 26;
DLB 76, 152; MTCW

Walker, Ted...................... **CLC 13**
See also Walker, Edward Joseph
See also DLB 40

Wallace, David Foster 1962-....... **CLC 50**
See also CA 132

Wallace, Dexter
See Masters, Edgar Lee

Wallace, (Richard Horatio) Edgar
1875-1932 .... **TCLC 57**
See also CA 115; DLB 70

Wallace, Irving 1916-1990...... **CLC 7, 13**
See also AITN 1; CA 1-4R; 132; CAAS 1;
CANR 1, 27; MTCW

Wallant, Edward Lewis
1926-1962 .... **CLC 5, 10**
See also CA 1-4R; CANR 22; DLB 2, 28,
143; MTCW

Walpole, Horace 1717-1797......... **LC 2**
See also DLB 39, 104

Walpole, Hugh (Seymour)
1884-1941 .... **TCLC 5**
See also CA 104; DLB 34

Walser, Martin 1927-............. **CLC 27**
See also CA 57-60; CANR 8, 46; DLB 75,
124

Walser, Robert
1878-1956 .... **TCLC 18; SSC 20**
See also CA 118; DLB 66

Walsh, Jill Paton.................. **CLC 35**
See also Paton Walsh, Gillian
See also AAYA 11; CLR 2; SAAS 3

Walter, William Christian
See Andersen, Hans Christian

Wambaugh, Joseph (Aloysius, Jr.)
1937-...................... **CLC 3, 18**
See also AITN 1; BEST 89:3; CA 33-36R;
CANR 42; DLB 6; DLBY 83; MTCW

Ward, Arthur Henry Sarsfield 1883-1959
See Rohmer, Sax
See also CA 108

Ward, Douglas Turner 1930-....... **CLC 19**
See also BW 1; CA 81-84; CANR 27;
DLB 7, 38

Ward, Mary Augusta
See Ward, Mrs. Humphry

Ward, Mrs. Humphry
1851-1920 .... **TCLC 55**
See also DLB 18

Ward, Peter
See Faust, Frederick (Schiller)

Warhol, Andy 1928(?)-1987........ **CLC 20**
See also AAYA 12; BEST 89:4; CA 89-92;
121; CANR 34

Warner, Francis (Robert le Plastrier)
1937-...................... **CLC 14**
See also CA 53-56; CANR 11

Warner, Marina 1946-............. **CLC 59**
See also CA 65-68; CANR 21

Warner, Rex (Ernest) 1905-1986.... **CLC 45**
See also CA 89-92; 119; DLB 15

Warner, Susan (Bogert)
1819-1885 .... **NCLC 31**
See also DLB 3, 42

Warner, Sylvia (Constance) Ashton
See Ashton-Warner, Sylvia (Constance)

Warner, Sylvia Townsend
1893-1978 .... **CLC 7, 19**
See also CA 61-64; 77-80; CANR 16;
DLB 34, 139; MTCW

Warren, Mercy Otis 1728-1814... **NCLC 13**
See also DLB 31

Warren, Robert Penn
1905-1989 .... **CLC 1, 4, 6, 8, 10, 13, 18,
39, 53, 59; DA; SSC 4; WLC**
See also AITN 1; CA 13-16R; 129;
CANR 10, 47; CDALB 1968-1988;
DLB 2, 48, 152; DLBY 80, 89; MTCW;
SATA 46; SATA-Obit 63

Warshofsky, Isaac
See Singer, Isaac Bashevis

Warton, Thomas 1728-1790........ **LC 15**
See also DLB 104, 109

Waruk, Kona
See Harris, (Theodore) Wilson

Warung, Price 1855-1911........ **TCLC 45**

Warwick, Jarvis
See Garner, Hugh

Washington, Alex
See Harris, Mark

Washington, Booker T(aliaferro)
1856-1915 .... **TCLC 10; BLC**
See also BW 1; CA 114; 125; SATA 28

Washington, George 1732-1799...... **LC 25**
See also DLB 31

Wassermann, (Karl) Jakob
1873-1934 .... **TCLC 6**
See also CA 104; DLB 66

Wasserstein, Wendy
1950- .... **CLC 32, 59; DC 4**
See also CA 121; 129; CABS 3

Waterhouse, Keith (Spencer)
1929-...................... **CLC 47**
See also CA 5-8R; CANR 38; DLB 13, 15;
MTCW

Waters, Frank (Joseph) 1902-...... **CLC 88**
See also CA 5-8R; CAAS 13; CANR 3, 18;
DLBY 86

Waters, Roger 1944-.............. **CLC 35**

Watkins, Frances Ellen
See Harper, Frances Ellen Watkins

Watkins, Gerrold
See Malzberg, Barry N(athaniel)

Watkins, Paul 1964-.............. **CLC 55**
See also CA 132

Watkins, Vernon Phillips
1906-1967 .... **CLC 43**
See also CA 9-10; 25-28R; CAP 1; DLB 20

Watson, Irving S.
See Mencken, H(enry) L(ouis)

Watson, John H.
See Farmer, Philip Jose

Watson, Richard F.
See Silverberg, Robert

Waugh, Auberon (Alexander) 1939-.. **CLC 7**
See also CA 45-48; CANR 6, 22; DLB 14

Waugh, Evelyn (Arthur St. John)
1903-1966 ...... **CLC 1, 3, 8, 13, 19, 27,
44; DA; WLC**
See also CA 85-88; 25-28R; CANR 22;
CDBLB 1914-1945; DLB 15; MTCW

Waugh, Harriet 1944- .... **CLC 6**
See also CA 85-88; CANR 22

Ways, C. R.
See Blount, Roy (Alton), Jr.

Waystaff, Simon
See Swift, Jonathan

Webb, (Martha) Beatrice (Potter)
1858-1943 .... **TCLC 22**
See also Potter, Beatrice
See also CA 117

Webb, Charles (Richard) 1939-...... **CLC 7**
See also CA 25-28R

Webb, James H(enry), Jr. 1946-.... **CLC 22**
See also CA 81-84

Webb, Mary (Gladys Meredith)
1881-1927 .... **TCLC 24**
See also CA 123; DLB 34

Webb, Mrs. Sidney
See Webb, (Martha) Beatrice (Potter)

Webb, Phyllis 1927-............... **CLC 18**
See also CA 104; CANR 23; DLB 53

Webb, Sidney (James)
1859-1947 .... **TCLC 22**
See also CA 117

Webber, Andrew Lloyd............. **CLC 21**
See also Lloyd Webber, Andrew

Weber, Lenora Mattingly
1895-1971 .... **CLC 12**
See also CA 19-20; 29-32R; CAP 1;
SATA 2; SATA-Obit 26

Webster, John 1579(?)-1634(?) .... **DC 2**
See also CDBLB Before 1660; DA; DLB 58;
WLC

Webster, Noah 1758-1843 .... **NCLC 30**

Wedekind, (Benjamin) Frank(lin)
1864-1918 .... **TCLC 7**
See also CA 104; DLB 118

Weidman, Jerome 1913-............ **CLC 7**
See also AITN 2; CA 1-4R; CANR 1;
DLB 28

Weil, Simone (Adolphine)
1909-1943 .... **TCLC 23**
See also CA 117

Weinstein, Nathan
See West, Nathanael

Weinstein, Nathan von Wallenstein
See West, Nathanael

Weir, Peter (Lindsay) 1944- .... **CLC 20**
See also CA 113; 123

Weiss, Peter (Ulrich)
1916-1982 .... **CLC 3, 15, 51**
See also CA 45-48; 106; CANR 3; DLB 69,
124

Weiss, Theodore (Russell)
1916- .... **CLC 3, 8, 14**
See also CA 9-12R; CAAS 2; CANR 46;
DLB 5

Welch, (Maurice) Denton
1915-1948 .... **TCLC 22**
See also CA 121

Welch, James 1940- .... **CLC 6, 14, 52**
See also CA 85-88; CANR 42; NNAL

Weldon, Fay
1933- .... **CLC 6, 9, 11, 19, 36, 59**
See also CA 21-24R; CANR 16, 46;
CDBLB 1960 to Present; DLB 14;
MTCW

Wellek, Rene 1903- .... **CLC 28**
See also CA 5-8R; CAAS 7; CANR 8;
DLB 63

Weller, Michael 1942- .... **CLC 10, 53**
See also CA 85-88

Weller, Paul 1958- .... **CLC 26**

Wellershoff, Dieter 1925-.......... **CLC 46**
See also CA 89-92; CANR 16, 37

Welles, (George) Orson
1915-1985 .... **CLC 20, 80**
See also CA 93-96; 117

Wellman, Mac 1945- .... **CLC 65**

Wellman, Manly Wade 1903-1986 .. **CLC 49**
See also CA 1-4R; 118; CANR 6, 16, 44;
SATA 6; SATA-Obit 47

Wells, Carolyn 1869(?)-1942 ...... **TCLC 35**
See also CA 113; DLB 11

Wells, H(erbert) G(eorge)
1866-1946 .... **TCLC 6, 12, 19; DA;
SSC 6; WLC**
See also CA 110; 121; CDBLB 1914-1945;
DLB 34, 70; MTCW; SATA 20

Wells, Rosemary 1943-............ **CLC 12**
See also AAYA 13; CA 85-88; CANR 48;
CLR 16; MAICYA; SAAS 1; SATA 18,
69

Welty, Eudora
1909- ...... **CLC 1, 2, 5, 14, 22, 33; DA;
SSC 1; WLC**
See also CA 9-12R; CABS 1; CANR 32;
CDALB 1941-1968; DLB 2, 102, 143;
DLBD 12; DLBY 87; MTCW

Wen I-to 1899-1946 .... **TCLC 28**

Wentworth, Robert
See Hamilton, Edmond

Werfel, Franz (V.) 1890-1945 ..... **TCLC 8**
See also CA 104; DLB 81, 124

Wergeland, Henrik Arnold
1808-1845 .... **NCLC 5**

Wersba, Barbara 1932-............ **CLC 30**
See also AAYA 2; CA 29-32R; CANR 16,
38; CLR 3; DLB 52; JRDA; MAICYA;
SAAS 2; SATA 1, 58

Wertmueller, Lina 1928- .... **CLC 16**
See also CA 97-100; CANR 39

Wescott, Glenway 1901-1987....... **CLC 13**
See also CA 13-16R; 121; CANR 23;
DLB 4, 9, 102

Wesker, Arnold 1932- .... **CLC 3, 5, 42**
See also CA 1-4R; CAAS 7; CANR 1, 33;
CDBLB 1960 to Present; DLB 13;
MTCW

Wesley, Richard (Errol) 1945-....... **CLC 7**
See also BW 1; CA 57-60; CANR 27;
DLB 38

Wessel, Johan Herman 1742-1785 .... **LC 7**

West, Anthony (Panther)
1914-1987 .... **CLC 50**
See also CA 45-48; 124; CANR 3, 19;
DLB 15

West, C. P.
See Wodehouse, P(elham) G(renville)

West, (Mary) Jessamyn
1902-1984 .... **CLC 7, 17**
See also CA 9-12R; 112; CANR 27; DLB 6;
DLBY 84; MTCW; SATA-Obit 37

West, Morris L(anglo) 1916-..... **CLC 6, 33**
See also CA 5-8R; CANR 24, 49; MTCW

West, Nathanael
1903-1940 ..... **TCLC 1, 14, 44; SSC 16**
See also CA 104; 125; CDALB 1929-1941;
DLB 4, 9, 28; MTCW

West, Owen
See Koontz, Dean R(ay)

West, Paul 1930- .... **CLC 7, 14**
See also CA 13-16R; CAAS 7; CANR 22;
DLB 14

West, Rebecca 1892-1983 .. **CLC 7, 9, 31, 50**
See also CA 5-8R; 109; CANR 19; DLB 36;
DLBY 83; MTCW

Westall, Robert (Atkinson)
1929-1993 .... **CLC 17**
See also AAYA 12; CA 69-72; 141;
CANR 18; CLR 13; JRDA; MAICYA;
SAAS 2; SATA 23, 69; SATA-Obit 75

Westlake, Donald E(dwin)
1933- .... **CLC 7, 33**
See also CA 17-20R; CAAS 13; CANR 16,
44

Westmacott, Mary
See Christie, Agatha (Mary Clarissa)

Weston, Allen
See Norton, Andre

Wetcheek, J. L.
See Feuchtwanger, Lion

Wetering, Janwillem van de
See van de Wetering, Janwillem

Wetherell, Elizabeth
See Warner, Susan (Bogert)

Whalen, Philip 1923- .... **CLC 6, 29**
See also CA 9-12R; CANR 5, 39; DLB 16

Wharton, Edith (Newbold Jones)
1862-1937 ...... **TCLC 3, 9, 27, 53; DA;
SSC 6; WLC**
See also CA 104; 132; CDALB 1865-1917;
DLB 4, 9, 12, 78; MTCW

Wharton, James
See Mencken, H(enry) L(ouis)

Wharton, William (a pseudonym)
.... **CLC 18, 37**
See also CA 93-96; DLBY 80

Wheatley (Peters), Phillis
1754(?)-1784 .... **LC 3; BLC; DA; PC 3;
WLC**
See also CDALB 1640-1865; DLB 31, 50

Wheelock, John Hall 1886-1978 .... **CLC 14**
See also CA 13-16R; 77-80; CANR 14;
DLB 45

White, E(lwyn) B(rooks)
1899-1985 .... **CLC 10, 34, 39**
See also AITN 2; CA 13-16R; 116;
CANR 16, 37; CLR 1, 21; DLB 11, 22;
MAICYA; MTCW; SATA 2, 29;
SATA-Obit 44

White, Edmund (Valentine III)
1940- .... **CLC 27**
See also AAYA 7; CA 45-48; CANR 3, 19,
36; MTCW

White, Patrick (Victor Martindale)
1912-1990 .. **CLC 3, 4, 5, 7, 9, 18, 65, 69**
See also CA 81-84; 132; CANR 43; MTCW

White, Phyllis Dorothy James 1920-
See James, P. D.
See also CA 21-24R; CANR 17, 43; MTCW

White, T(erence) H(anbury)
1906-1964 .... **CLC 30**
See also CA 73-76; CANR 37; JRDA;
MAICYA; SATA 12

White, Terence de Vere
1912-1994 .... **CLC 49**
See also CA 49-52; 145; CANR 3

White, Walter F(rancis)
1893-1955 .... **TCLC 15**
See also White, Walter
See also BW 1; CA 115; 124; DLB 51

White, William Hale 1831-1913
See Rutherford, Mark
See also CA 121

Whitehead, E(dward) A(nthony)
1933- .... **CLC 5**
See also CA 65-68

Whitemore, Hugh (John) 1936-..... **CLC 37**
See also CA 132

Whitman, Sarah Helen (Power)
1803-1878 .... **NCLC 19**
See also DLB 1

Whitman, Walt(er)
1819-1892 ..... **NCLC 4, 31; DA; PC 3;
WLC**
See also CDALB 1640-1865; DLB 3, 64;
SATA 20

Whitney, Phyllis A(yame) 1903-.... **CLC 42**
See also AITN 2; BEST 90:3; CA 1-4R;
CANR 3, 25, 38; JRDA; MAICYA;
SATA 1, 30

Whittemore, (Edward) Reed (Jr.)
1919- .... **CLC 4**
See also CA 9-12R; CAAS 8; CANR 4;
DLB 5

Whittier, John Greenleaf
1807-1892 .... **NCLC 8**
See also CDALB 1640-1865; DLB 1

Whittlebot, Hernia
See Coward, Noel (Peirce)

Wicker, Thomas Grey 1926-
See Wicker, Tom
See also CA 65-68; CANR 21, 46

Wicker, Tom .... **CLC 7**
See also Wicker, Thomas Grey

Wideman, John Edgar
1941- .... **CLC 5, 34, 36, 67; BLC**
See also BW 2; CA 85-88; CANR 14, 42;
DLB 33, 143

Wiebe, Rudy (Henry) 1934-... **CLC 6, 11, 14**
See also CA 37-40R; CANR 42; DLB 60

Wieland, Christoph Martin
1733-1813 .... **NCLC 17**
See also DLB 97

Wiene, Robert 1881-1938........ **TCLC 56**

Wieners, John 1934-.............. **CLC 7**
See also CA 13-16R; DLB 16

Wiesel, Elie(zer)
1928- .... **CLC 3, 5, 11, 37; DA**
See also AAYA 7; AITN 1; CA 5-8R;
CAAS 4; CANR 8, 40; DLB 83;
DLBY 87; MTCW; SATA 56

Wiggins, Marianne 1947-......... **CLC 57**
See also BEST 89:3; CA 130

Wight, James Alfred 1916-
See Herriot, James
See also CA 77-80; SATA 55;
SATA-Brief 44

Wilbur, Richard (Purdy)
1921- .... **CLC 3, 6, 9, 14, 53; DA**
See also CA 1-4R; CABS 2; CANR 2, 29;
DLB 5; MTCW; SATA 9

Wild, Peter 1940-................ **CLC 14**
See also CA 37-40R; DLB 5

Wilde, Oscar (Fingal O'Flahertie Wills)
1854(?)-1900 .... **TCLC 1, 8, 23, 41; DA;
SSC 11; WLC**
See also CA 104; 119; CDBLB 1890-1914;
DLB 10, 19, 34, 57, 141; SATA 24

Wilder, Billy .... **CLC 20**
See also Wilder, Samuel
See also DLB 26

Wilder, Samuel 1906-
See Wilder, Billy
See also CA 89-92

Wilder, Thornton (Niven)
1897-1975 ...... **CLC 1, 5, 6, 10, 15, 35,
82; DA; DC 1; WLC**
See also AITN 2; CA 13-16R; 61-64;
CANR 40; DLB 4, 7, 9; MTCW

Wilding, Michael 1942-.......... **CLC 73**
See also CA 104; CANR 24, 49

Wiley, Richard 1944-............. **CLC 44**
See also CA 121; 129

Wilhelm, Kate .... **CLC 7**
See also Wilhelm, Katie Gertrude
See also CAAS 5; DLB 8

Wilhelm, Katie Gertrude 1928-
See Wilhelm, Kate
See also CA 37-40R; CANR 17, 36; MTCW

Wilkins, Mary
See Freeman, Mary Eleanor Wilkins

Willard, Nancy 1936-........... **CLC 7, 37**
See also CA 89-92; CANR 10, 39; CLR 5;
DLB 5, 52; MAICYA; MTCW;
SATA 37, 71; SATA-Brief 30

Williams, C(harles) K(enneth)
1936- .... **CLC 33, 56**
See also CA 37-40R; DLB 5

Williams, Charles
See Collier, James L(incoln)

Williams, Charles (Walter Stansby)
1886-1945 .... **TCLC 1, 11**
See also CA 104; DLB 100, 153

Williams, (George) Emlyn
1905-1987 .... **CLC 15**
See also CA 104; 123; CANR 36; DLB 10,
77; MTCW

Williams, Hugo 1942-............ **CLC 42**
See also CA 17-20R; CANR 45; DLB 40

Williams, J. Walker
See Wodehouse, P(elham) G(renville)

Williams, John A(lfred)
1925- .... **CLC 5, 13; BLC**
See also BW 2; CA 53-56; CAAS 3;
CANR 6, 26; DLB 2, 33

Williams, Jonathan (Chamberlain)
1929- .... **CLC 13**
See also CA 9-12R; CAAS 12; CANR 8;
DLB 5

Williams, Joy 1944-............. **CLC 31**
See also CA 41-44R; CANR 22, 48

Williams, Norman 1952-.......... **CLC 39**
See also CA 118

Williams, Sherley Anne
1944- .... **CLC 89; BLC**
See also BW 2; CA 73-76; CANR 25;
DLB 41; SATA 78

Williams, Shirley
See Williams, Sherley Anne

Williams, Tennessee
1911-1983 ..... **CLC 1, 2, 5, 7, 8, 11, 15,
19, 30, 39, 45, 71; DA; DC 4; WLC**
See also AITN 1, 2; CA 5-8R; 108;
CABS 3; CANR 31; CDALB 1941-1968;
DLB 7; DLBD 4; DLBY 83; MTCW

Williams, Thomas (Alonzo)
1926-1990 .... **CLC 14**
See also CA 1-4R; 132; CANR 2

Williams, William C.
See Williams, William Carlos

Williams, William Carlos
1883-1963 .... **CLC 1, 2, 5, 9, 13, 22, 42,
67; DA; PC 7**
See also CA 89-92; CANR 34;
CDALB 1917-1929; DLB 4, 16, 54, 86;
MTCW

Williamson, David (Keith) 1942-.... **CLC 56**
See also CA 103; CANR 41

Williamson, Ellen Douglas 1905-1984
See Douglas, Ellen
See also CA 17-20R; 114; CANR 39

Williamson, Jack .... **CLC 29**
See also Williamson, John Stewart
See also CAAS 8; DLB 8

Williamson, John Stewart 1908-
See Williamson, Jack
See also CA 17-20R; CANR 23

Willie, Frederick
See Lovecraft, H(oward) P(hillips)

Willingham, Calder (Baynard, Jr.)
1922-1995 .... **CLC 5, 51**
See also CA 5-8R; 147; CANR 3; DLB 2,
44; MTCW

Willis, Charles
See Clarke, Arthur C(harles)

Willy
See Colette, (Sidonie-Gabrielle)

Willy, Colette
See Colette, (Sidonie-Gabrielle)

Wilson, A(ndrew) N(orman) 1950- .. **CLC 33**
See also CA 112; 122; DLB 14

Wilson, Angus (Frank Johnstone)
1913-1991 .... **CLC 2, 3, 5, 25, 34**
See also CA 5-8R; 134; CANR 21; DLB 15,
139; MTCW

Wilson, August
1945- .. **CLC 39, 50, 63; BLC; DA; DC 2**
See also BW 2; CA 115; 122; CANR 42;
MTCW

Wilson, Brian 1942-.............. **CLC 12**

Wilson, Colin 1931-............ **CLC 3, 14**
See also CA 1-4R; CAAS 5; CANR 1, 22,
33; DLB 14; MTCW

Wilson, Dirk
See Pohl, Frederik

Wilson, Edmund
1895-1972 .... **CLC 1, 2, 3, 8, 24**
See also CA 1-4R; 37-40R; CANR 1, 46;
DLB 63; MTCW

Wilson, Ethel Davis (Bryant)
1888(?)-1980 .... **CLC 13**
See also CA 102; DLB 68; MTCW

Wilson, John 1785-1854.......... **NCLC 5**

Wilson, John (Anthony) Burgess 1917-1993
See Burgess, Anthony
See also CA 1-4R; 143; CANR 2, 46;
MTCW

Wilson, Lanford 1937-....... **CLC 7, 14, 36**
See also CA 17-20R; CABS 3; CANR 45;
DLB 7

Wilson, Robert M. 1944-........ **CLC 7, 9**
See also CA 49-52; CANR 2, 41; MTCW

Wilson, Robert McLiam 1964- ..... **CLC 59**
See also CA 132

Wilson, Sloan 1920-.............. **CLC 32**
See also CA 1-4R; CANR 1, 44

Wilson, Snoo 1948-.............. **CLC 33**
See also CA 69-72

Wilson, William S(mith) 1932- ..... **CLC 49**
See also CA 81-84

Winchilsea, Anne (Kingsmill) Finch Counte
1661-1720 .... **LC 3**

Windham, Basil
See Wodehouse, P(elham) G(renville)

Wingrove, David (John) 1954-...... **CLC 68**
See also CA 133

Winters, Janet Lewis .... **CLC 41**
See also Lewis, Janet
See also DLBY 87

Winters, (Arthur) Yvor
1900-1968 .... **CLC 4, 8, 32**
See also CA 11-12; 25-28R; CAP 1;
DLB 48; MTCW

Winterson, Jeanette 1959-......... **CLC 64**
See also CA 136

Wiseman, Frederick 1930-......... **CLC 20**

Wister, Owen 1860-1938 .... **TCLC 21**
See also CA 108; DLB 9, 78; SATA 62

Witkacy
See Witkiewicz, Stanislaw Ignacy

Witkiewicz, Stanislaw Ignacy
    1885-1939 .... TCLC 8
    See also CA 105

Wittgenstein, Ludwig (Josef Johann)
    1889-1951 .... TCLC 59
    See also CA 113

Wittig, Monique 1935(?)-......... CLC 22
    See also CA 116; 135; DLB 83

Wittlin, Jozef 1896-1976 .... CLC 25
    See also CA 49-52; 65-68; CANR 3

Wodehouse, P(elham) G(renville)
    1881-1975 ... CLC 1, 2, 5, 10, 22; SSC 2
    See also AITN 2; CA 45-48; 57-60;
    CANR 3, 33; CDBLB 1914-1945;
    DLB 34; MTCW; SATA 22

Woiwode, L.
    See Woiwode, Larry (Alfred)

Woiwode, Larry (Alfred) 1941-... CLC 6, 10
    See also CA 73-76; CANR 16; DLB 6

Wojciechowska, Maia (Teresa)
    1927-...................... CLC 26
    See also AAYA 8; CA 9-12R; CANR 4, 41;
    CLR 1; JRDA; MAICYA; SAAS 1;
    SATA 1, 28

Wolf, Christa 1929- .... CLC 14, 29, 58
    See also CA 85-88; CANR 45; DLB 75;
    MTCW

Wolfe, Gene (Rodman) 1931-....... CLC 25
    See also CA 57-60; CAAS 9; CANR 6, 32;
    DLB 8

Wolfe, George C. 1954-........... CLC 49

Wolfe, Thomas (Clayton)
    1900-1938 ... TCLC 4, 13, 29; DA; WLC
    See also CA 104; 132; CDALB 1929-1941;
    DLB 9, 102; DLBD 2; DLBY 85; MTCW

Wolfe, Thomas Kennerly, Jr. 1931-
    See Wolfe, Tom
    See also CA 13-16R; CANR 9, 33; MTCW

Wolfe, Tom .... CLC 1, 2, 9, 15, 35, 51
    See also Wolfe, Thomas Kennerly, Jr.
    See also AAYA 8; AITN 2; BEST 89:1;
    DLB 152

Wolff, Geoffrey (Ansell) 1937- ..... CLC 41
    See also CA 29-32R; CANR 29, 43

Wolff, Sonia
    See Levitin, Sonia (Wolff)

Wolff, Tobias (Jonathan Ansell)
    1945-.................... CLC 39, 64
    See also BEST 90:2; CA 114; 117; DLB 130

Wolfram von Eschenbach
    c. 1170-c. 1220 .... CMLC 5
    See also DLB 138

Wolitzer, Hilma 1930-........... CLC 17
    See also CA 65-68; CANR 18, 40; SATA 31

Wollstonecraft, Mary 1759-1797..... LC 5
    See also CDBLB 1789-1832; DLB 39, 104

Wonder, Stevie .... CLC 12
    See also Morris, Steveland Judkins

Wong, Jade Snow 1922-.......... CLC 17
    See also CA 109

Woodcott, Keith
    See Brunner, John (Kilian Houston)

Woodruff, Robert W.
    See Mencken, H(enry) L(ouis)

Woolf, (Adeline) Virginia
    1882-1941 .... TCLC 1, 5, 20, 43, 56;
                            DA; SSC 7; WLC
    See also CA 104; 130; CDBLB 1914-1945;
    DLB 36, 100; DLBD 10; MTCW

Woollcott, Alexander (Humphreys)
    1887-1943 .... TCLC 5
    See also CA 105; DLB 29

Woolrich, Cornell 1903-1968....... CLC 77
    See also Hopley-Woolrich, Cornell George

Wordsworth, Dorothy
    1771-1855 .... NCLC 25
    See also DLB 107

Wordsworth, William
    1770-1850 .... NCLC 12, 38; DA; PC 4;
                                      WLC
    See also CDBLB 1789-1832; DLB 93, 107

Wouk, Herman 1915-......... CLC 1, 9, 38
    See also CA 5-8R; CANR 6, 33; DLBY 82;
    MTCW

Wright, Charles (Penzel, Jr.)
    1935-................... CLC 6, 13, 28
    See also CA 29-32R; CAAS 7; CANR 23,
    36; DLBY 82; MTCW

Wright, Charles Stevenson
    1932-................ CLC 49; BLC 3
    See also BW 1; CA 9-12R; CANR 26;
    DLB 33

Wright, Jack R.
    See Harris, Mark

Wright, James (Arlington)
    1927-1980 .... CLC 3, 5, 10, 28
    See also AITN 2; CA 49-52; 97-100;
    CANR 4, 34; DLB 5; MTCW

Wright, Judith (Arundell)
    1915-.................... CLC 11, 53
    See also CA 13-16R; CANR 31; MTCW;
    SATA 14

Wright, L(aurali) R. 1939-......... CLC 44
    See also CA 138

Wright, Richard (Nathaniel)
    1908-1960 .... CLC 1, 3, 4, 9, 14, 21, 48,
                        74; BLC; DA; SSC 2; WLC
    See also AAYA 5; BW 1; CA 108;
    CDALB 1929-1941; DLB 76, 102;
    DLBD 2; MTCW

Wright, Richard B(ruce) 1937- ...... CLC 6
    See also CA 85-88; DLB 53

Wright, Rick 1945-............... CLC 35

Wright, Rowland
    See Wells, Carolyn

Wright, Stephen Caldwell 1946- .... CLC 33
    See also BW 2

Wright, Willard Huntington 1888-1939
    See Van Dine, S. S.
    See also CA 115

Wright, William 1930-............ CLC 44
    See also CA 53-56; CANR 7, 23

Wroth, LadyMary 1587-1653(?) ..... LC 30
    See also DLB 121

Wu Ch'eng-en 1500(?)-1582(?)....... LC 7

Wu Ching-tzu 1701-1754 .... LC 2

Wurlitzer, Rudolph 1938(?)- ... CLC 2, 4, 15
    See also CA 85-88

Wycherley, William 1641-1715 .... LC 8, 21
    See also CDBLB 1660-1789; DLB 80

Wylie, Elinor (Morton Hoyt)
    1885-1928 .... TCLC 8
    See also CA 105; DLB 9, 45

Wylie, Philip (Gordon) 1902-1971... CLC 43
    See also CA 21-22; 33-36R; CAP 2; DLB 9

Wyndham, John................... CLC 19
    See also Harris, John (Wyndham Parkes
    Lucas) Beynon

Wyss, Johann David Von
    1743-1818 .... NCLC 10
    See also JRDA; MAICYA; SATA 29;
    SATA-Brief 27

Yakumo Koizumi
    See Hearn, (Patricio) Lafcadio (Tessima
    Carlos)

Yanez, Jose Donoso
    See Donoso (Yanez), Jose

Yanovsky, Basile S.
    See Yanovsky, V(assily) S(emenovich)

Yanovsky, V(assily) S(emenovich)
    1906-1989 .... CLC 2, 18
    See also CA 97-100; 129

Yates, Richard 1926-1992 ..... CLC 7, 8, 23
    See also CA 5-8R; 139; CANR 10, 43;
    DLB 2; DLBY 81, 92

Yeats, W. B.
    See Yeats, William Butler

Yeats, William Butler
    1865-1939 ..... TCLC 1, 11, 18, 31; DA;
                                      WLC
    See also CA 104; 127; CANR 45;
    CDBLB 1890-1914; DLB 10, 19, 98;
    MTCW

Yehoshua, A(braham) B.
    1936-.................... CLC 13, 31
    See also CA 33-36R; CANR 43

Yep, Laurence Michael 1948-...... CLC 35
    See also AAYA 5; CA 49-52; CANR 1, 46;
    CLR 3, 17; DLB 52; JRDA; MAICYA;
    SATA 7, 69

Yerby, Frank G(arvin)
    1916-1991 .... CLC 1, 7, 22; BLC
    See also BW 1; CA 9-12R; 136; CANR 16;
    DLB 76; MTCW

Yesenin, Sergei Alexandrovich
    See Esenin, Sergei (Alexandrovich)

Yevtushenko, Yevgeny (Alexandrovich)
    1933-............. CLC 1, 3, 13, 26, 51
    See also CA 81-84; CANR 33; MTCW

Yezierska, Anzia 1885(?)-1970 ..... CLC 46
    See also CA 126; 89-92; DLB 28; MTCW

Yglesias, Helen 1915-........... CLC 7, 22
    See also CA 37-40R; CAAS 20; CANR 15;
    MTCW

Yokomitsu Riichi 1898-1947 ...... TCLC 47

Yonge, Charlotte (Mary)
    1823-1901 .... TCLC 48
    See also CA 109; DLB 18; SATA 17

York, Jeremy
    See Creasey, John

York, Simon
    See Heinlein, Robert A(nson)

Literary Criticism Series
Cumulative Topic Index

This index lists all topic entries in Gale's *Classical and Medieval Literature Criticism, Contemporary Literary Criticism, Literature Criticism from 1400 to 1800, Nineteenth-Century Literature Criticism,* and *Twentieth-Century Literary Criticism.*

Topic Index

NCLC Cumulative Nationality Index

IRISH
- Allingham, William **25**
- Banim, John **13**
- Banim, Michael **13**
- Boucicault, Dion **41**
- Carleton, William **3**
- Croker, John Wilson **10**
- Darley, George **2**
- Edgeworth, Maria **1, 51**
- Ferguson, Samuel **33**
- Griffin, Gerald **7**
- Jameson, Anna **43**
- Le Fanu, Joseph Sheridan **9**
- Lever, Charles (James) **23**
- Maginn, William **8**
- Mangan, James Clarence **27**
- Maturin, Charles Robert **6**
- Moore, Thomas **6**
- Morgan, Lady **29**
- O'Brien, Fitz-James **21**

ITALIAN
- Da Ponte, Lorenzo **50**
- Foscolo, Ugo **8**
- Gozzi, (Conte) Carlo **23**
- Leopardi, (Conte) Giacomo **22**
- Manzoni, Alessandro **29**
- Mazzini, Guiseppe **34**
- Nievo, Ippolito **22**

JAPANESE
- Higuchi Ichiyo **49**
- Motoori, Norinaga **45**

LITHUANIAN
- Mapu, Abraham (ben Jekutiel) **18**

MEXICAN
- Lizardi, Jose Joaquin Fernandez de **30**

NORWEGIAN
- Collett, (Jacobine) Camilla (Wergeland) **22**
- Wergeland, Henrik Arnold **5**

POLISH
- Fredro, Aleksander **8**
- Krasicki, Ignacy **8**
- Krasinski, Zygmunt **4**
- Mickiewicz, Adam **3**
- Norwid, Cyprian Kamil **17**
- Slowacki, Juliusz **15**

ROMANIAN
- Eminescu, Mihail **33**

RUSSIAN
- Aksakov, Sergei Timofeyvich **2**
- Bakunin, Mikhail (Alexandrovich) **25**
- Bashkirtseff, Marie **27**
- Belinski, Vissarion Grigoryevich **5**
- Chernyshevsky, Nikolay Gavrilovich **1**
- Dobrolyubov, Nikolai Alexandrovich **5**
- Dostoevsky, Fedor Mikhailovich **2, 7, 21, 33, 43**
- Gogol, Nikolai (Vasilyevich) **5, 15, 31**
- Goncharov, Ivan Alexandrovich **1**
- Herzen, Aleksandr Ivanovich **10**
- Karamzin, Nikolai Mikhailovich **3**
- Krylov, Ivan Andreevich **1**
- Lermontov, Mikhail Yuryevich **5**
- Leskov, Nikolai (Semyonovich) **25**
- Nekrasov, Nikolai Alekseevich **11**
- Ostrovsky, Alexander **30**
- Pisarev, Dmitry Ivanovich **25**
- Pushkin, Alexander (Sergeyevich) **3, 27**
- Saltykov, Mikhail Evgrafovich **16**
- Smolenskin, Peretz **30**
- Turgenev, Ivan **21**
- Tyutchev, Fyodor **34**
- Zhukovsky, Vasily **35**

SCOTTISH
- Baillie, Joanna **2**
- Beattie, James **25**
- Campbell, Thomas **19**
- Ferrier, Susan (Edmonstone) **8**
- Galt, John **1**
- Hogg, James **4**
- Jeffrey, Francis **33**
- Lockhart, John Gibson **6**
- Mackenzie, Henry **41**
- Oliphant, Margaret (Oliphant Wilson) **11**
- Scott, Walter **15**
- Stevenson, Robert Louis (Balfour) **5, 14**
- Thomson, James, **18**
- Wilson, John **5**

SPANISH
- Alarcon, Pedro Antonio de **1**
- Caballero, Fernan **10**
- Castro, Rosalia de **3**
- Espronceda, Jose de **39**
- Larra (y Sanchez de Castro), Mariano Jose de **17**
- Tamayo y Baus, Manuel **1**
- Zorrilla y Moral, Jose **6**

SWEDISH
- Almqvist, Carl Jonas Love **42**
- Bremer, Fredrika **11**
- Tegner, Esaias **2**

SWISS
- Amiel, Henri Frederic **4**
- Burckhardt, Jacob **49**
- Keller, Gottfried **2**
- Wyss, Johann David Von **10**

Nationality Index

Title Index

ISBN 0-8103-9297-6